Contents

Figures, Tables & Photographs

Figures

Tables

Multi-Party Politics in Kenya

The Kenyatta & Moi States & the Triumph of the System in the 1992 Election

DAVID W. THROUP
&
CHARLES HORNSBY

James Currey
OXFORD

E.A.E.P
NAIROBI

Ohio University Press
ATHENS

James Currey Ltd
73 Botley Road
Oxford
OX2 0BS

East African Educational Publishers
Kijabe Street, PO Box 45314
Nairobi, Kenya

Ohio University Press
Scott Quadrangle
Athens, Ohio 45701, USA

First published 1998

1 2 3 4 5 01 02 00 99 98

British Library Cataloguing in Publication Data
Throup, David
Multi-party politics in Kenya : the Kenyatta & Moi states & the triumph of the system in the 1992 election
1. Democracy – Kenya 2. Elections – Kenya 3. Kenya – Politics and government – 1978–
I. Title II. Hornsby, Charles
324.9'6762'042

ISBN 0-85255-809-0 (James Currey Cloth)
ISBN 0-85255-804-X (James Currey Paper)

Library of Congress Cataloging-in-Publication Data is available

ISBN 0-8214-1206-X (Ohio University Press Cloth)
ISBN 0-8214-1207-8 (Ohio University Press Paper)

Typeset in 10/10½ pt Baskerville
by Long House Publishing Services, Cumbria, UK
Printed in Great Britain
by Villiers Publications, London N3

Photographs

Acknowledgements

This book began with an invitation from Tom Young to participate in a conference at London University's School of Oriental and African Studies in March 1992 on multi-party politics and elections in Africa. Meeting for the first time for several years, the authors were pleased to discover that our assessments of the prospects for political pluralism in Kenya and our predictions of the forthcoming election were very similar. Following the conference, we began to write the introductory chapter and by the end of 1994, the manuscript was virtually complete. Producing any book is a collective enterprise, especially one in which the two authors have lived over 3,000 miles apart in respectively London and Accra and the final task of preparing and checking end notes along with the production of tables, graphs and maps has proved to be a protracted process.

Our greatest debt lies with the Nuffield Foundation, which provided us with a generous grant to finance two visits to Kenya to observe the final stages of the party primaries and the whole election campaign from late November 1992 to January 1993. David Throup would also particularly like to thank Sir Brian Fender, then Vice-Chancellor of Keele University, and Professor Martin Harrison and his colleagues in the Politics Department for granting him special leave of absence in the middle of term to undertake this research. We also wish to acknowledge the help and assistance of the staff of the University Library at Cambridge, Rhodes House at Oxford, and the Institute of Commonwealth Studies and SOAS libraries in London over many years of study.

Amongst those in Kenya to whom we owe a debt of gratitude are Grace Githu, the director of NEMU, and her staff and the NEMU Council of Elders for their advice and assistance throughout the campaign. We would also like to acknowledge the assistance we received from the staff of The Daily Nation: while the journalists freely shared their knowledge and insights into Kenyan politics, and enabled us to gain access to their back archives, the newspaper's librarians provided us with invaluable information, press cuttings and photographs.

Charles Hornsby would particularly like to thank his godfather Isaac Omolo-Okero for his wisdom and guidance, while David Throup owes a great debt to George and Rose Waruhiu, and his former student Patricia, who provided him with introductions to key figures in the Democratic Party and to local activists in Githunguri, and for hosting his visits on Nomination and Election Days.

Judy Geist, as ever, proved invaluable as a source of hard psephological information, while Joel Barkan, USAID Governance Adviser, provided a host of introductions to members of the diplomatic corps and opposition politicians. Patrick Smith, the editor of *Africa Confidential,* provided us both with press accreditation and inspired us by his boundless energy, while Suzanne Mueller freely discussed recent political developments. Paul Muite, Robert Shaw, Raila Odinga and Njenga Mungai of FORD-Kenya took time from their hectic campaign schedule to brief us on events and their hopes for Kenya's future, while FORD-Asili's legal adviser, Gibson Kamau Kuria, discussed the development of the campaign for multi-party democracy and enabled David Throup to consult the legal affidavits prepared by those FORD-Asili candidates who were prevented from presenting their nomination papers. Frank Holmquist, Michael Ford and Nelson Kasfir provided us with a valuable link to the American observer missions, while Michael Holman and Julian Ozanne of *The Financial Times* shared information and travel expenses. As always, the people of Kenya were eager to explain the details of their country's politics to two interested foreigners.

Charles Hornsby would like to acknowledge the staff of Kenya Shell Ltd, for their insights into local political and economic issues; Wóuter de Vries and Hetty ter Haar for volunteering their house, their friendship and their time during 1992 and 1993, and for providing innumerable videos of Kenyan television campaign coverage. John Lonsdale, as ever, maintained a close interest in all stages of this work, inspiring by his example as well as providing continuous encouragement. Mike and Kathy Kirkwood have proved wonderfully efficient copy-editors, even if text and graphics have had to wend their way from London to Accra, back to London, on to St. Vincent and then back to Cumbria. We would like to acknowledge the invaluable role played by first, Gill Allen, and then, John Wright, in providing technical advice and support.

Many of the ideas and conclusions in this book have been presented at various academic meetings, including the SOAS Conference on Democracy in Africa in March 1992; the African Studies Association of the United Kingdom meeting at Stirling University in September 1992; the South-East Regional Seminar on African Studies at Charlottesville, Virginia, in October 1992; Keele University in February 1993; the African Studies Centre at Cambridge in February 1993; the three day meeting on the Kenyan Elections, organised at Hampshire College, Massachusetts, by Frank Holmquist and Michael Ford, in August 1993; and the African Studies Association meeting in Boston in November 1993. Much of the drafting of the first chapters was completed at the Carter G. Woodson Institute for Afro-American and African Studies at the University of Virginia. David Throup would like to thank the late Armstead Robinson and Joseph C. Miller and the staff of the Institute for their support and encouragement.

Finally, we owe a debt of gratitude to our families and friends. Charles would particularly like to thank his mother and father, Peter and Jennifer Hornsby, who as ever, provided security and practical advice; the management of Shell, for their understanding both in London and Kenya; Preeti Mehta, for her support and endurance through the long nights of writing this book; and Gifty Annang, for being who she is. For his part, David would like to thank the old Banda gang, who first introduced him to the wonders of Kenya in 1976–79; Shalini Sharma who was always willing to discuss the politics of her homeland; and Sabhita Raju, who attempted to persuade him to accept even more draconian manuscript cuts. The book would never have been finished without the support and love of Julia Anne McDonough. She took time off from finishing her PhD and Law degree to be our most severe editor while attempting to ensure that Wags, Scout and Buster, our dogs, did not distract me for too long from the task in hand.

Accra, Ghana
& Kill Devil Hills, North Carolina
August 1997

About the Authors

David W. Throup is the author of *The Economic and Social Origins of Mau Mau* (James Currey, 1987) and has published numerous articles on Kenyan politics. He teaches African Politics at Keele University in Staffordshire, England, and has been Visiting Assistant Professor at the University of Virginia, Research Associate at the Johns Hopkins School of Advanced International Studies, and twice Senior Research Fellow at the Carter G. Woodson Institute for Afro-American and African Studies at the University of Virginia. Although he is currently on a four year secondment as Senior Research Officer in the Africa Research Unit of the Foreign and Commonwealth Office in London, the opinions expressed in this book are those of the authors and do not represent the official views of the FCO or of Her Majesty's Government.

Charles Hornsby was educated at Oriel and St Antony's Colleges at Oxford, where he studied Politics, Philosophy and Economics and wrote a D.Phil thesis on 'The Kenyan Member of Parliament, 1969–83'. He subsequently studied Computer Science at University College, London, and was a Research Associate at the University of Surrey. He has published a number of articles on Kenyan Politics and is currently working in Ghana.

To the people of Kenya:
may they find the leaders they deserve.

Figure 1.1 An Ethnic and Linguistic Classification of Kenyans

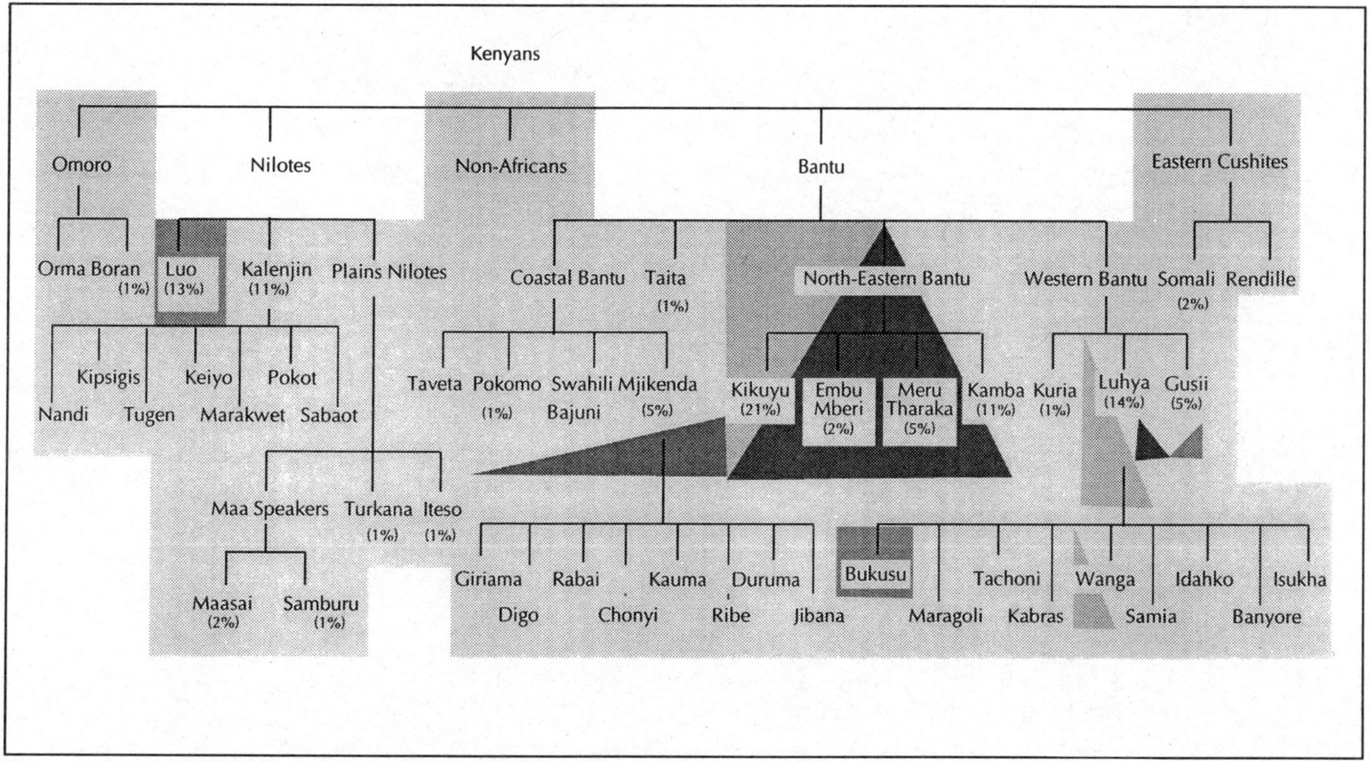

Kenyans

Omoro
Orma (1%)
Boran (1%)

Nilotes
Luo (13%)
Kalenjin (11%)
Nandi
Kipsigis
Tugen
Keiyo
Marakwet
Pokot
Sabaot
Plains Nilotes
Maa Speakers
Maasai (2%)
Samburu (1%)
Turkana (1%)
Iteso (1%)

Non-Africans

Bantu
Coastal Bantu
Taveta
Pokomo (1%)
Swahili
Bajuni
Mijikenda (5%)
Giriama
Digo
Rabai
Chonyi
Kauma
Ribe
Duruma
Jibana
Taita (1%)
North-Eastern Bantu
Kikuyu (21%)
Embu Mberi (2%)
Meru Tharaka (5%)
Kamba (11%)
Western Bantu
Kuria (1%)
Luhya (14%)
Bukusu
Maragoli
Tachoni
Kabras
Wanga
Samia
Idahko
Banyore
Isukha
Gusii (5%)

Eastern Cushites
Somali (2%)
Rendille

One

Introduction

The general election of 29 December 1992 was an event of vital importance to all Kenyans. Both opposition leaders and domestic and foreign commentators believed that the result would determine whether the country would evolve into a stable, competitive, multi-party state or return to repressive single-party rule. Would Kenya follow the example of Zambia, sweeping away after three decades of rule the party that had secured independence, or the Cameroons, entrenching in power the old regime through electoral malpractice?[1] All the political parties, as well as the numerous candidates for President, Parliament and local government, the press, observers, church leaders and diplomats, not to mention ordinary voters, invested tremendous physical and emotional energy in the contest and awaited the result with a mixture of eagerness, hope and trepidation. After 29 years of independence and one year of multi-party democracy, the government of President Daniel Toroitich arap Moi had to face the first electoral challenge to its rule. This book is about that challenge – about the evolution of the Kenyan state, the emergence of the opposition, the re-establishment of multi-party politics, the political contest of 1992 (culminating in the election), and the Moi regime's reconsolidation of power during 1993 and 1994.

There have been few detailed book-length studies of elections in Africa. Perhaps the most notable remains the study of *The Kenyatta Election* of 1960–1 by George Bennett and Carl G. Rosberg, Jnr.[2] Kenya, moreover, has attracted relatively little scholarly attention since President Moi came to power in the late 1970s, apart from historical studies of the colonial period. This paucity is especially noticeable in view of the considerable interest shown in the country by scholars in the 1960s and early 1970s, and the continuing high profile of Kenya in the Western media. Apart from Jennifer Widner's recent study of the rise of Moi's 'party state' (which already looks rather dated so rapid has been the pace of political events since 1990), Joel Barkan's revised comparative investigation of policy making in Kenya and Tanzania, and David Leonard's account of the careers of four senior civil servants, *African Successes (*which devotes most of its attention to the Kenyatta and early Moi years), little work has been done to analyse the rise, sudden decline, and seeming revival of the Moi state.[3]

This book attempts to explain both what happened in Kenya and why, during the vital six years from the fraudulent national and party elections of 1988 through to the summer of 1994, when the direction of events in the new 'democratic' era had become clear. For over twenty years, Moi and the Kenya African National Union (KANU) had staunchly defended the one-party system as quintessentially African. In December 1991, however, forced by a combination of internal and external events, Kenya embarked on a new road in which neither Moi nor his party believed. The immediate causes of this sudden conversion lay in the events of 1988–91: a combination of internal protest, external pressure for change and a series of mistakes by the governing élite which brought into serious question its ability to govern the country. In these years, President Moi's authority began to unravel and his always fairly feeble 'party state' disintegrated under pressure from radical intellectuals and politicians in Nairobi, criticism from bilateral aid donors (led by the United States), and economically based dissent from the country's largest and most developed community, the Kikuyu of Central Province. Some of the roots of these events lay in the inherent limitations of authoritarianism, but most were contingent, a combination of circumstances that propelled Moi into a sudden and ill-considered experiment in multi-party democracy.

The 'democratisation' process in Kenya was a relatively peaceful affair, providing both a classic study in civil protest and testimony to the power of the external world over the Kenyan economy and upon the attitudes of Kenyans. From 1990, at the peak of the government's authoritarian hold over all aspects of the country's life, it took only two years for the single-party system, with all it implied about the role of the state and the autonomy of the individual, to be humbled and abandoned in the last weeks of 1991. Despite this, after 12 months of political ferment and the emergence of four substantial opposition parties, KANU and its Presidential candidate Moi triumphed in the December 1992 general election. The opposition was divided, defeated and humbled, and during 1993–4 the ruling party gradually developed a strategy which ensured that it would dominate electoral politics until the millennium.

This book seeks to explain the evolution of the democracy movement, why the government decided to accede to its demands, the events that led to the government's electoral victory, and the reasons why the emergence of multi-party electoral competition was unlikely to lead to a peaceful transition between governing parties in 1992 (or the next election, due in 1997). Although heralded as a substantial change in political direction, the commitment of Kenya's leadership and its people to the realities of multi-party democracy was always ambiguous. From the beginning, the electoral process was manipulated and compromised by the ruling party to enhance its prospects of victory; although foreign groups sent observers to the polls, they were unable to prevent substantial electoral malpractice, which ensured the outright victory of KANU.[4]

Following independence in 1963, the Kenyan government under successive Presidents Jomo Kenyatta and Daniel arap Moi followed a strategy of capitalist economic development, pro-Western orientation and political incorporation, tempered by a growing authoritarianism and propensity to violence. Throughout the 1980s the government harassed the opposition, church leaders and lawyers who dared to criticise it. The dramatic changes occurring in the Soviet Union and Eastern Europe were a major influence on the Kenyan élite in the early 1990s. They seemed to presage not only the fall of one-party regimes around the world, creating a new Western commitment to democratisation in the less developed world, but to demonstrate the value of aid in effecting such changes.[5] Following the detention of ex-Ministers Kenneth Matiba and Charles Rubia and dissident Raila Odinga on 4 July 1990, the opposition rebuilt and organised a new, more effective coalition to challenge the regime. Its two key leaders during 1991, octogenarian radical Oginga Odinga (father of Raila) and prominent lawyer Paul Muite, took advantage of every opportunity to challenge KANU's legitimacy, dismissing President Moi's claim that multi-party politics would be divisive and exacerbate ethnic rivalries. But almost as soon as the new opposition movement, the Forum for the Restoration of Democracy (FORD) was registered, certainly once Oginga Odinga had declared in early February 1992 his ambition to become the party's Presidential candidate, the underlying ethnic cleavages of Kenyan political life became starkly evident. Despite the apparent early unity of Kikuyu and Luo leaders, the pre-election period revealed how entrenched the enmity between the two communities had become since independence, so that even mutual self-interest could not hold them together.[6]

The year-long campaign from the legalisation of the opposition to election day on 29 December 1992 witnessed a series of errors, accidents and miscalculations. In our opinion, however, this protracted campaign did not alter the result fundamentally. Although the precise course of events could not be predicted, the importance of ethnic cleavages in Kenyan political life always made it likely that the major opposition force would fragment into rival ethnic factions, weakening the opposition and ensuring the return of President Moi and KANU to power. The greatest surprise of the period was the manifest incompetence and unrealistic expectations of all the opposition parties which, despite every opportunity to unite to face the common foe, remained deeply divided. At times the opposition seemed so intent on self-destruction that it lost sight of KANU's inherent strength, which stemmed primarily from its continuing control of the governmental machine.[7]

The period confirmed the vital importance of the Provincial Administration which, as in colonial times, still provided the essential framework of central control over the rural areas. Provincial and District Commissioners, the government's regional officials, played a prominent role in KANU's campaign, harassing opposition candidates and supporters, controlling licences for meetings, and even distributing money and food on behalf of the ruling party, while employing the police and security forces to disrupt opposition meetings and to monitor their activities. Such harassment effectively prevented the opposition parties from conducting a viable campaign in at least one third of the country's 188 constituencies. Outside the major cities, the main ethnic strongholds of the opposition parties, and a few closely contested regions, the opposition parties found it impossible to function effectively. Even in the contested areas, lying along the physical borders between opposing political parties or in the ethnic homelands of non-aligned groups such as the Akamba and the Gusii, the Administration severely hampered the opposition. The conduct of the election in the so-called 'KANU zones' of the Rift Valley Province also graphically demonstrated the government's lack of commitment to democratic procedures. Administration police and the General Service Unit (GSU) harassed and assaulted opposition supporters, prevented opposition candidates from presenting their nomination papers, and on polling day virtually forced the entire population of the Kalenjin heartlands to vote for Moi. Nevertheless, despite the government's control of the electoral process through the Electoral Commission, and the use of state-sponsored intimidation and bribery, voters on polling day still failed to produce a clear majority for KANU and Moi, necessitating the implementation of emergency plans to tilt the balance of the election towards KANU in at least 10 per cent of the Parliamentary seats.

The role of Western governments in these events was critical. Not only did they force the election upon the Kenyan government, they also financed and monitored it. In the end, however, they were unable to control the underlying political processes. In a situation of uncertainty where abuses were limited in extent and severity, they had no option but to give the government the benefit of the doubt and to judge the election a qualified success, awarding what the Kenyan *Daily Nation* called a 'C-minus pass'.[8] Foreign observers lacked the resources, the time and the understanding of the Kenyan political system to spot skilful manipulation of the election results, whilst their masters at home had a deep predisposition towards 'stability' and a reluctance to 'rock the boat'. The West's accommodation of KANU since the election, culminating in the restoration of rapid disbursement aid in November 1993, has removed one of the main props of the opposition parties, which had relied on the United States, Germany and Scandinavia to safeguard them against repression by the state and rescue them from their own incompetence. The opposition's future is fraught with difficulties and the prognosis for multi-party politics in Kenya remains poor.

The 1992 election revealed both the deep commitment of ordinary Kenyans to the electoral process and their fundamental cynicism about the government's willingness to conduct free and fair elections. The sudden establishment of multi-party democracy had been a panic reaction by the regime to the abrupt cessation of rapid disbursement aid from the West; it was not based upon a fundamental desire for or understanding of multi-party politics on the part of either the government or the people. It most certainly was not a serious response by the government to the deep-seated anger and dissatisfaction among the masses with political events since the 1982 coup attempt. Neither the state nor many opposition supporters accepted the legitimacy of opposition. Many in the larger communities saw multi-party politics primarily as a means to seize control of the state and the funding it controlled, while President Moi and his Kalenjin ethnic group were determined to defend their gains. Although KANU exacerbated the situation, inciting ethnic rivalries and clashes in the Rift Valley, President Moi's jeremiads against the evils of multi-party politics had validity. The introduction of multi-party politics, as he had warned, divided Kenyans into rival, ethnically based political parties. As in the 1960s, during the country's brief first experiments with multi-party politics, ethnic factors, rather than class or ideology, determined the political loyalties of most Kenyans.[9]

It remains unclear to what extent multi-party democracy will endure in Kenya. While the population in the heartlands of the four main political parties enthusiastically participated in the process, elsewhere, in the cities and amongst the communities without a national contender, the turn-out was surprisingly low. Neo-patrimonialism – the politics of clientage – has developed its own logic, based on peasant rationality. All Kenyan political parties are patronage parties and have no independent existence or policy foundation in the absence of the all-powerful leader. Political preferences were based on calculations of personal or local advantage, determined by two key questions: who would secure election? And how much in the way of jobs and development schemes would they deliver if elected? In a stratified, heavily populated society, personal advantage has come to be a key determinant of political activity. The implication of this is that opposition can only be sustained in the long term on the basis of an independent bourgeoisie, which can provide sufficient financial incentives to their supporters to retain autonomy from government. Events since the election seem to suggest that only the Kikuyu possess the long-term determination and the financial strength to resist the blandishments and pressures wielded by those who control the state. To quote Philip Ochieng', 'Western democracy is conceivable and workable only in societies which have a long history of independent material and intellectual foundation.'[10] The key mistake of FORD's 'Young Turks' in 1992 was to believe that they could build a party on the basis of ideas, idealism and ideology.

The information and analysis presented in this book is based upon many years' work on Kenyan politics, and sprang out of the authors' mutual belief, in the early weeks of 1992, that structural factors would ensure the re-election of President Moi and KANU. Although the majority of the international and Kenyan press then believed that the new FORD party would win a landslide victory, the authors considered that the financial resources of the state, its control of the means of coercion (especially the Provincial Administration), the ruling party's under-estimated strength in the peripheral areas and the logic of Kenya's ethnic politics meant that KANU's chance of victory was always good. Even at the peak of FORD's popularity, immediately after the repeal of Section 2(A) of the constitution, which had outlawed the registration of opposition political parties, electoral victory for any party except KANU was always unlikely.[11] The atmosphere of euphoria, confusion and misinformation that existed in Kenya throughout 1991 and 1992 exaggerated the appeal and unity of the fledgling opposition parties and seriously underestimated KANU's popularity and political resilience. After several months monitoring events that culminated in the disintegration of FORD into two rival Kikuyu- and Luo-based parties (FORD-Asili and FORD-Kenya), the authors' opinions were confirmed, and they took the decision to visit Kenya in order to document the elections. It was our intention to produce not only an analytical study, but also an historical record of a key moment in the political life of the country. We hope this book will encourage other studies of electoral politics in Africa and reawaken interest in contemporary Kenyan politics.

Notes

1 Interesting accounts of the transition to multi-party democracy in Zambia can be found in Julius O. Ihonvbere, 'From Movement to Government: The Movement for Multi-party Democracy and the Crisis of Democratic Consolidation in Zambia', *Canadian Journal of African Studies,* vol. 29, no. 1 (1995), pp. 1–25; and Michael Bratton, 'Economic Crisis and Political Realignment in Zambia' in Jennifer A. Widner (ed.), *Economic Change and Political Liberalization in Sub-Saharan Africa,* The Johns Hopkins University Press, Baltimore, 1994, pp. 101–28. For Cameroon see Nicholas van de Walle, 'Neopatrimonialim and Democracy in Africa, with Illustration from Cameroon', pp. 129–57 in the same volume. Jennifer A. Widner's own article, 'Political Reform in Anglophone and Francophone African Countries', pp. 49–79 in the book, provides a useful comparison of the democratisation processes in Francophone and Anglophone Africa. See also Stephen Ellis, 'Rumour and Power in Togo', in *Africa,* vol. 4, no. 63 (1993), pp. 462–76, for a failed transition.

2 George Bennet and Carl G. Rosberg, Jr., *The Kenyatta Election, 1961,* Oxford University Press, London, 1961.

3 Jennifer A. Widner, *The Rise of a Party-State in Kenya: From Harambee to Nyayo,* University of California Press, Berkeley, 1992, pp. 130–97; Joel Barkan (ed.), *Politics and Public Policy in Kenya and Tanzania,* Praeger, New York, 1979 and 1984; and David Leonard, *African Successes: Four Public Managers of Kenyan Rural Development,* University of California Press, Berkeley, 1991. Widner's book has come in for considerable criticism but its general argument that Kenya became an increasingly authoritarian state during the 1980s and that the ruling party KANU developed into a key apparatus of political control is well founded. Leonard's book contains a fascinating account of the career of Simeon Nyachae.

4 The weaknesses of the various international observer groups can be discerned from their published reports of the December 1992 election. The most important ones were, *The Presidential, Parliamentary and Civic Elections in Kenya: 29 December, 1992: The Report of the Commonwealth Observer Group,* Commonwealth Secretariat, London, 1993; and the International Republican Institute's 'Preliminary Statement of Findings, Kenyan General Elections, December 29, 1992', 1 January 1993, 'January 4, 1993, Follow-Up Statement', and its final report, *Kenya: The December 29, 1992 Elections,* Washington D.C., 1993. For a more critical view, see B. A. Andreassen, G. Geisler and A. Tostensen, *A Hobbled Democracy: The Kenya General Election, 1992,* Bergen, 1993, prepared by the Norweigian observer team from the Chr. Michelsen Institute.

5 This was perhaps most explicitly articulated by Douglas Hurd, the British Secretary of State for Foreign and Commonwealth Affairs, in a speech to the Overseas Development Institute on 6 June 1990, when he drew a parallel between 'recent dramatic events in eastern Europe' and Africa, emphasising 'the need to move away from the inefficient and authoritarian models of the past...[as] centralised political, economic and social structures have failed to deliver the goods.' See Gordon Crawford, *Promoting Democracy, Human Rights and Good Governance Through Development Aid: A Comparative Study of the Policies of Four Northern Nations,* University of Leeds Centre for Democratization Studies Working Papers on Democratization, 1995.

6 The growth of Kikuyu–Luo rivalry in the 1960s is most easily traced in Cherry Gertzel, *The Politics of Independent Kenya, 1963–1968,* East African Publishing House, Nairobi, 1970.

7 David Throup, 'Elections and Political Legitimacy in Kenya', *Africa,* volume 63, no. 3 (1993), pp. 390–4.

8 *Sunday Nation,* leader article, 3 January 1993, p. 6.

9 David Throup, 'Elections and Political Legitimacy in Kenya', *Africa,* volume 63, no. 3 (1993), pp. 390–4.

10 P. Ochieng', *I Accuse the Press: An Insider's View of the Media and Politics in Kenya,* Initiatives Publishers, Acts Press, Nairobi, 1992, p. 15.

11 The authors successfully predicted both KANU's victory and the size of its margin in two articles presented at the Africa Studies Association of the United Kingdom at the University of Stirling in September 1992, 14 weeks before the General Election.

Two

The Independence Struggle

The Development of Political Consciousness

Kenya faced severe problems at independence in 1963. During the 1950s, its various racial and ethnic groups were divided both by economic differentiation, encouraged by the British colonial government, and by the consequences of Africa's first war of liberation, the 'Mau Mau' Emergency. This revolt, which became more serious after the detention of Kenyan African Union (KAU) leader Jomo Kenyatta and other nationalist leaders on 20 October 1952, was not simply a rebellion against British colonialism but also a civil war among the Kikuyu, Kenya's largest ethnic group.[1] It set poor Kikuyu, who were being dispossessed by ambitious commercial farmers, against the chiefs, successful entrepreneurs and local Christians. Many Luo, Abaluhya, Kalenjin and the people of the Rift Valley and Coast Provinces were reluctant to rally behind Kikuyu leadership, and most other Kenyans remained on the sidelines waiting to see whether the Kikuyu fighters or the colonialists would triumph. Even when Mau Mau was defeated militarily, and the Mau Mau leader in the Nyandarua forest, 'Field Marshall' Dedan Kimathi, was captured in October 1956, Kikuyu society remained deeply divided. Seven years later, at independence, the country's integrity was at best uncertain.[2]

The legacy of democratic institutions from the colonial era was mixed. Until the late 1950s, formal political institutions evolved as tools for the white settler community to influence colonial policy. These were adapted, however imperfectly, to represent the voice of the substantial Asian community, but the Legislative Council remained alien to African political interests. After the defeat of the Mau Mau insurrection in 1952–5, it was clear that whatever political democratisation took place would be on the terms of the British. The colonial government was far from happy about being forced into a 'premature' transfer of sovereignty but was able to influence the form it would take, ensuring that power would be handed over at independence to an African élite favouring the world view that the British felt appropriate. The first elections in which Africans were allowed to vote for their own representatives were held in 1957, less than seven years before independence.[3] Until then all the African Members of the Legislative Council had been appointed by the Governor. Following the banning in 1953 of KAU, the first true African political party, African political organisations had been restricted to the district level, a legacy which was to have long-term implications for the structure of independent Kenya's politics.[4] The only survivor of the old order of nominated African leaders was the recently appointed Member for the Rift Valley, Daniel arap Moi. A village school teacher from Baringo District, Moi won the new Rift Valley African seat with the votes of his Kalenjin ethnic group (Moi was a Tugen, one of the smaller Kalenjin sub-'tribes').[5] Even more than his predecessor, Jomo Kenyatta, who remained in detention until 1961, Moi was 'present at the creation' of electoral politics in Kenya. Another individual elected for the first time was the youthful firebrand nationalist from Nyanza Province, Oginga Odinga. These first competitive elections were also notable because no politician was elected from the Kikuyu community, one quarter of the Kenyan population. The veteran constitutionalist, Eliud Mathu, who had been the first African Legislative Councillor nominated in 1944, was defeated in the new Central Province constituency by a Meru school teacher. Since most Kikuyu had been implicated deeply in Mau Mau, few met the colonial government's 'loyalty' qualification.[6]

Between 1957 and 1960, two rival factions began to emerge from the network of district parties, trades union and other organisations. The two largest ethnic groups – the Kikuyu and the related Embu and Meru peoples of central Kenya, and the Luo from the shores of Lake Victoria – adopted a more confrontational stance against British colonial rule than the spokesmen from the smaller, less developed ethnic groups concentrated in the Rift Valley, Coast Province and in the semi-arid far north.[7] Meanwhile, Kenyatta, the founding father of Kenyan nationalism, continued to languish in confinement in remote Turkana, while thousands of Mau Mau detainees remained in prison camps. Both the white settlers and the British government remained determined that Kenya would remain a 'White Man's country' until the killing of prisoners at Hola Detention Camp in 1959 initiated a reassessment by the Conservative government of Harold Macmillan.[8]

The First Multi-Party Era, 1960–4

The first Lancaster House conference, held in London in January and February 1960, effectively sealed the Kenya settlers' fate, determining that the colony would advance swiftly towards African majority rule and shortly afterwards to full independence. Although the African delegation at the conference formed a united front, already cleavages were beginning to appear among the African Elected Members, which would lead to the formation of two rival political parties in the early months of 1960, KANU and the Kenya African Democratic Union (KADU). Their similarities in name reflected their underlying commonality of need – to weld together the independent, district-oriented local power grouping which had emerged over the previous 15 years into a national coalition which could triumph electorally. They were, however, fundamentally different in political orientation. From the beginning of multi-party politics in Kenya, ethnicity proved to be more powerful than ideology in determining political loyalties. KANU was the party of the majority tribes, the densely populated, more rapidly differentiating ethnic groups, particularly the Kikuyu (with approximately one-quarter of the population) and Luo (with a sixth). It campaigned for a strong central government in Nairobi, a prominent state role in the economy, the supremacy of Parliament and open competition for resources (in which their communities would perform relatively well). By contrast, KADU was the party of the smaller ethnic groups in the Rift Valley, in the semi-arid north, and at the Coast. KADU's leader, Ronald Ngala, came from Kilifi on the Coast. KADU's policy of *Majimboism* (federal government or regional autonomy) was accompanied by liberal economic policies more attractive to Western and settler interests. It favoured a division of powers and an American-style federal government, and was strongest amongst those peoples desiring the freedom to be left alone. President Moi's coalition three decades later reflected these same divisions. KADU in 1961, like KANU in 1992, secured the support of Moi's Kalenjin people in the central Rift Valley; neighbouring Nilotic groups, including the Turkana, Samburu and Maasai; sections of the Abaluhya; and the Mijikenda people at the Coast.[9]

In the early 1960s KANU had appeared to be more 'left-wing' than its rival, favouring the nationalisation of European-owned farms and businesses, while KADU leaders were willing to work with the more liberal settlers in the New Kenya Party. Besides being eager to attract continuing Western investment, KADU (like Kalenjin leaders 30 years later) wanted to devolve as much power as possible from Nairobi and pressed for a federal system under the *Majimbo* constitution, which would create eight Regional Assemblies, responsible for wide areas of policy such as housing, local government, social services, education and the police, leaving the National Assembly in Nairobi with control over defence, foreign affairs, macro-level economic policy and central finances. This arrangement promised to leave KADU in command of wide areas of policy in its political strongholds in the Rift Valley and Coast Provinces even if – as was inevitable, given the ethnic arithmetic – KANU was swept to power in Nairobi with the support of the Kikuyu and the Luo.[10] Ideology counted less than ethnicity and the appeal of Kenyatta in determining political loyalties. Both parties attempted to secure Kenyatta's endorsement before the crucial 1961 elections, but the already emerging ethnic logic of Kenyan politics ensured that the former KAU leader was identified with KANU, the party of his fellow Kikuyu, which emerged victorious at the 1961 elections, despite the complex electoral rules and over-representation of the European settler community and the sparsely populated hinterland.[11]

The colonial regime remained reluctant to come to terms with the need to rehabilitate Kenyatta, who continued to languish in gaol, despite the 'wind of change' blowing from Downing Street.[12] The Governor, Sir Patrick Renison, remained obdurate, even denouncing Kenyatta as 'the leader to darkness and death', who could not be politically rehabilitated.[13]

Most officials were still convinced that Kenyatta had master-minded the Mau Mau movement and believed that more moderate, pro-British leaders, such as KADU's Ronald Ngala and KANU's Tom Mboya, should be encouraged to emerge. The British government encountered stiff resistance from its local officials to the pace of African political advance after 1960, especially over Kenyatta's rehabilitation. Renison, advised by die-hards in the Provincial Administration, and under pressure from settler leaders, insisted that Kenyatta must remain under restriction at Maralal and would not be permitted to re-enter politics. As a result of KANU's refusal to take office as long as Kenyatta remained in restriction, a short-lived coalition between KADU and the more moderate European settlers, supporters of Michael Blundell's New Kenya Party, was formed but could do little to re-establish confidence. Mounting African discontent, coupled with pressure from the Colonial Office, forced Renison to back down. The Macmillan government was convinced that only Kenyatta could heal the colony's divisions and that to transfer power without incorporating the former KAU leader into the political process was futile.[14]

Released from restriction late in 1961, Kenyatta soon took over the leadership of KANU and entered the Legislative Council at a by-election.[15] Shortly afterwards, the KADU–New Kenya Party coalition was dissolved and replaced by a grand coalition between the two main African parties in which Kenyatta and KADU leader Ngala served as Ministers of State during the run-up to the crucial May 1963 elections. These polls saw a replay of 1961, minus the 'fancy franchises' and special status of European voters and candidates. In these pre-independence elections, KANU once again clearly defeated KADU, mobilising the support of voters in Embu and Meru, Kitui, Kisii and the Taita Hills, as well as in the party's strongholds in Central and Nyanza Provinces and Nairobi. The May 1963 elections produced an all-African Assembly, apart from the two European representatives whom Kenyatta subsequently nominated.[16] It was Kenya's last experience of national multi-party elections or true multi-party democracy, in which the defeat of the incumbent government in a free election could lead to the replacement of that government, until those on 29 December 1992, nearly 30 years later.

The new government, which led Kenya to full independence within the Commonwealth on 12 December 1963 – *Uhuru* Day – commanded the support of the main ethnic groups and of the most economically developed regions. The constitution was based on the Westminster model of Parliamentary sovereignty, with a formal division between opposing political blocs each intending to seize complete power over the state, with a major addition, a regional system of provincial assemblies with their own designated areas of authority. Kenyatta soon curtailed and eventually abolished the regional administrations, concentrating control once more in Nairobi. The country was divided into eight provinces – Central, Nairobi, Eastern, North-Eastern, Coast, Rift Valley, Western and Nyanza – which were sub-divided into 41 districts.[17] In December 1964, Kenyatta also converted his position from that of Prime Minister to that of President. Rather than ruling through his fledgling political party, Kenyatta chose to retain the Provincial Administration, which had so zealously repressed Kikuyu protest in the

1950s, making it directly accountable to his own Office.[18] Provincial and District Administrators continued to exert almost as much political power after independence as they had during the 75 years of British rule, when they provided the administrative framework of colonial authority, supervising appointed chiefs and headmen in every location, and directing communal labour, agricultural 'betterment' campaigns and tax collection.

Kenyatta's political career by the mid-1960s already dated back nearly 40 years, endowing him with a political legitimacy that was enjoyed by no other Kenyan politician. Jomo Kenyatta was a symbol of Kenya's independence and nationhood, a leader whom no one could criticise, the founding father of both nationalist politics and the nation.[19] One of Kenyatta's first tasks was to consolidate his position among his own Kikuyu community, healing the divisions created by social differentiation and the Mau Mau civil war. Kenyatta also needed to satisfy the demands of Kenya's other main ethnic groups, coopting their leaders into the ruling élite, while rewarding the masses with smallholder plots in the former White Highlands. As independence approached, thousands of settlers had fled the country, displaying a singular lack of confidence in Kenyatta and his government. The new government controlled 'cheap' loans for indigenous entrepreneurs and jobs for university graduates in the new civil service, providing a diverse array of patronage rewards. The rapid departure of many settlers from the White Highlands, moreover, created new opportunities for African commercial farmers, who took over European farms, while some of the landless – especially former Mau Mau fighters – were resettled in smallholder development schemes such as the Million Acres Scheme in Nyandarua District and elsewhere. These opportunities, coupled with the pre-independence social revolution of land titles and consolidation, which had been implemented by the British during the Emergency, helped to heal the divisions amongst the Kikuyu and guaranteed a period of political stability after 1963. The opening of the White Highlands to African settlement also enabled Kenyatta's government to divert the

Table 2.1 Six Political Periods During the Kenyatta Era

Phase	Period	Key Issues
(1)	1963–4	KANU's take-over of KADU and the consolidation of the first single-party era
(2)	1964–6	Conflict between the left and right in KANU, leading to the formation of the Kenya People's Union (KPU)
(3)	1966–9	Multi-party competition between KANU and the KPU; growing harassment of the opposition
(4)	1969–75	The mature Kenyatta system and the era of backbench radicalism
(5)	1975–6	The murder of Josiah Mwangi Kariuki and growing repression as the regime confronts left-wing Kikuyu opposition
(6)	1976–8	The twilight years: the 'Change the Constitution' Movement and the cash crop boom

commercial farming ambitions of Kikuyu and Abaluhya (proto-)capitalists from the overcrowded former Reserves, where they might have generated strong opposition from the landless, to former European farms in the Rift Valley.[20] Astute use of government patronage, civil service and parastatal appointments, low-interest loans, government contracts, and rural and urban land grants, meanwhile, ensured the loyalty of the vast majority of the educated élite and the political class. Even trades union leaders were incorporated into the spoils system as the Central Organisation of Trades Unions (COTU) was brought firmly under government control after independence and its leaders coopted into the ruling power structure.[21]

The Kenyatta era divides into six distinct political periods, each of which presented the regime with its own specific problems (see Table 2.1).

The Single-Party State Emerges, 1963–4

Following the attainment of independence, multi-party democracy lasted only one year. Jomo Kenyatta moved rapidly to consolidate his personal authority and to create a government of national unity. Facing a state determined to consolidate what authority it had, and without any intention of implementing the regional constitution imposed upon it, KADU quickly collapsed. Both winners and losers now agreed there was little to be gained for their communities from a Westminster-style process of confrontation leading to an electoral contest every five years. Assessments of the 'challenges to nationhood' viewed national identity and stability as key. National unity was believed to be threatened by the divisiveness which a confrontational electoral system entailed. More pragmatically, KADU was quickly worn down by defections. Under pressure from their constituents to secure more development funds and from the state to abandon their opposition, KADU Members of Parliament soon began to cross the floor of the National Assembly to join the ruling party in return for favours, preferment and a better deal for their communities in the allocation of national development budgets. Those who crossed early secured the most favourable terms. On the first anniversary of independence in December 1964, the opposition formally dissolved itself and its remaining members joined KANU, creating a *de facto* single-party state.[22]

Internal Conflicts and the Triumph of the Right, 1964–6

The incorporation of KADU into KANU speeded the process of internal division within the governing party. Kenyatta's ruling coalition was an uneasy combination of moderates and radicals, which had survived two years in power because the factions were evenly balanced. Despite Kenyatta's conservative, pro-Western, pro-business policy, his party contained a substantial number of radicals who wished to nationalise foreign-owned corporations, to seize settler farms without compensation, and for Kenya to follow a non-aligned foreign policy. The radicals were led by Vice-President Jaramogi Oginga Odinga from Nyanza Province and former

Mau Mau activist Bildad Kaggia, while Kenyatta and KANU Secretary-General Tom Mboya were the key figures in the moderate camp.[23] Mboya, Odinga's major rival from the Luo community, was a young, Western-backed, charismatic politician who had emerged from the trades union movement to be Kenyatta's political fixer. The infusion of KADU moderates into KANU, and their growing role in the state (in December 1964, Daniel arap Moi had entered the Cabinet as Minister of Home Affairs) strengthened Kenyatta's hand against the radicals. By mid-1965, radical dissatisfaction with the direction of political events had created open schisms within the élite. An increasingly exasperated Kenyatta demonstrated how he was to respond to such internal threats to the stability of the regime or challenges to his authority – by brute force. KANU backbenchers who were campaigning for the creation of the East African Community, for example, were silenced partly by the detention of their leader John Keen (the first detention without trial in independent Kenya). Another thorn in Kenyatta's side was Odinga's Asian ally, Pio da Gama Pinto, who was murdered in February 1965.[24]

After 17 months of increasingly bitter factional strife, in March 1966 Kenyatta's coalition fell apart. The crisis was precipitated by a series of rigged KANU elections, directed by Odinga's Luo rival Mboya, which eliminated supporters of the radical faction from party posts throughout the country.[25] This culminated in Odinga's demotion from his position as party Vice-President at the ruling party's Limuru Conference. Supported by Minister of Information and Broadcasting Achieng'Oneko – former Mau Mau leader Bildad Kaggia, the leading Kikuyu radical, had already been dismissed as Assistant Minister of Education for criticising the slow pace of Africanisation in the civil service – Odinga resigned from the Cabinet to launch a new political party in April 1966.[26]

Odinga and the Kenya People's Union 1966–9

Odinga immediately announced the creation of a new political force, an avowedly socialist party to be known as the Kenya People's Union [the KPU]. This was backed by roughly one fifth of the Parliamentary party, including many Kikuyu and Luo. The KPU's goal was to create a more left-wing party, to oppose the growing conservatism and Western orientation of the KANU leadership, and to try to replace the persistently ethnic basis of politics with a cleavage based on ideological, class or socio-economic grounds.[27]

KANU's response was harsh. The government rushed through the National Assembly in one day the fifth amendment to the constitution, which required MPs who defected to another party to resign and face a by-election. The Speaker then declared vacant the seats of the 29 Members of the National Assembly who had already defected. Many others were intimidated into withdrawing their support from the KPU. This legislation was to prove of vital importance 26 years later, enabling President Moi, like Kenyatta, to restrict the flow of defectors to the opposition, maintaining KANU's monopoly of the National Assembly until the dissolution in

October 1992. The resulting by-elections in 1966, known collectively as the 'Little General Election', reduced Odinga's KPU to a rump of nine, virtually all Luos from Nyanza Province. The state campaigned heavy-handedly, using ethnic pressure and extensive cheating in Kikuyu seats to ensure victory. Ethnicity and state power again proved more influential than class or ideology in determining political preferences.[28] Multi-party opposition from the Luo, however, forced Kenyatta to reconstruct his coalition, and to rely even more upon new allies from the old KADU. Former KADU leader Ronald Ngala entered the Cabinet after Odinga's departure, and Daniel arap Moi received the coveted Vice-Presidency in January 1967.[29]

During this brief phase of multi-party politics in 1966 to 1969, KANU exercised strict control over the political process, refusing to accept the legitimacy of the opposition. KPU officials were severely restricted in their ability to hold meetings, their branch registrations were delayed by the Registrar of Societies, and their officials were detained and harassed. In 1968, for example, the state refused 42.7 per cent of KPU applications for branch and sub-branch registration, a figure which rose to 57.9 per cent of applications in 1969. By contrast, only 1.8 per cent of KANU branch registrations were rejected.[30] The District Administration also refused to authorise opposition rallies or *Harambee* [self-help] meetings. The Provincial Administration, supported by the KANU youth wing, harassed KPU candidates and interrupted their few meetings. A new law in 1968 required all candidates for local and national office to be endorsed by a political party, preventing the KPU putting up candidates in those areas where their branches had not yet been registered. Other obstacles were placed in the way of KPU local government councillors and some councils even expelled all their KPU members, without the slightest legal basis.[31] The extent of the government's determination to block the opposition was demonstrated at the 1968 local government elections, when all 1,800 KPU candidates were disqualified on Kenyatta's personal instructions, because of supposedly incorrect nomination papers, so that the opposition lost all local representation. Susanne Mueller has argued that 'the KANU regime never allowed the KPU to compete freely with the dominant party in a general country-wide election, or to engage openly in organisational activities ... the regime's monopoly of sanctions and economic resources enabled it to buttress the dominant party, and to blunt opposition activity on a country-wide basis'.[32] This was to happen again in 1992–3.

In July 1969 the assassination of KANU Secretary-General Tom Mboya led to rioting by Luo youths in Nairobi and Kisumu and further ethnic polarisation. In defence, Kikuyu leaders initiated a massive oathing campaign in which almost every adult Kikuyu male was forced to swear in mass oath-taking ceremonies, on pain of death, to keep the Presidency in the 'House of Mumbi' (among the Kikuyu). Soon after, the state found the excuse for confrontation it was seeking. In October 1969, just before the first post-independence general election, Kenyatta's visit to open Kisumu hospital in Luoland led to angry confrontations with a stone-throwing crowd when demonstrators threatened Kenyatta's car, and the President's bodyguard opened fire on the crowd, leaving at least 100 dead. Immediately afterwards, the KPU was banned and its leaders detained.[33] These events demonstrated two fundamental features of Kenyan political culture – the refusal of government to accept challenges to its right to rule, and the rapid reversion of the constitutional opposition to its ethnic bastion.

The Mature Kenyatta State, 1969–75

After three years of confrontation, Kenya's brief experience of multi-party politics had ended and the country once again became a single-party state. This time, KANU was to remain the sole political party for over 20 years. Theoretically, dissident politicians could form parties to challenge KANU's monopoly of power but the Registrar of Societies, who had the right to deny a legal existence to any society or organisation, blocked all attempts to register.[34]

The Open Single-Party State

Although Kenyatta's Kenya was undoubtedly an authoritarian single-party state, political life remained remarkably open and its press comparatively free by African standards. In many respects, the years 1969 to 1975 marked the apogee of the Kenyatta state, when the ageing President was still sufficiently active to retain control of his subordinates and ruled with legitimacy because of his nearly four decades as leader of the nationalist movement. The single-party state under Kenyatta remained relatively willing to incorporate dissent, responsive to criticism and capable of dealing with local discontent and the rise of new leaders. Although challenges to Kenyatta personally, such as that of the KPU, were crushed, as long as politicians remained in the party and did not criticise the President himself, they retained considerable freedom. Academics at the University of Nairobi enjoyed a false freedom to criticise the regime in lectures and in the national press, so long as they expressed their doubts in English rather than in one of Kenya's vernacular languages.

General elections provided a mechanism by which the regime could incorporate new blood, remain informed of local grievances, and legitimate its power. This was demonstrated by the defeat of several senior Cabinet Ministers in 1969 and 1974. Only Kenyatta, whose position as President could not be questioned, and his closest ally, Minister of State in the Office of the President Mbiyu Koinange, were above opposition. The 1969 general election, which took place only weeks after the banning of the opposition, demonstrated the vitality of the electoral process. Although multi-party politics had been abandoned, critics of the Kenyatta regime and of Kikuyu hegemony, such as Martin Shikuku and Nandi leader J. M. Seroney, were re-elected. Josiah Mwangi Kariuki and former Nairobi Mayor Charles Rubia also criticised the regime from within, while the majority of Luo Members of Parliament elected in 1969, such as COTU Chairman Denis Akumu – who would be returned to Parliament on FORD-Kenya's ticket in 1992 – owed greater loyalty to Odinga than to Kenyatta. Turn-out was fairly low: only 1.7 million of the nearly 3.7 million registered voters (46.7 per cent) bothered to vote in 1969, compared with

83.6 per cent in 1961 and 71.6 per cent at the 1963 independence elections.[35]

Despite the low level of participation and the ban on the KPU opposition, the 1969 elections administered a severe shock to the government, and produced dramatic changes in the National Assembly. Five Cabinet Ministers and 14 out of 29 Assistant Ministers were rejected by the electorate. The change-over on the backbenches was even more dramatic. Only 27 of the 101 backbenchers in the 1963–9 Parliament were returned. Many had disappointed their constituents, spending little time in the rural areas, and had failed to secure funding for development projects or self-help *Harambee* schools. The introduction of primary elections to select KANU candidates in 1968 had transformed the political scene, undermining the position of ineffective backbenchers or even Ministers who had devoted too little time to their previously safe constituencies. Many MPs, who had been confident that they could control sub-branch selection committees, were repudiated by the electors. Old-guard politicians of limited education, who had been selected to stand as KANU candidates in 1961 and 1963 because of their prominence in the nationalist movement, proved particularly vulnerable. The 1969 results were not an aberration. Five years later, in 1974, in the last election of the Kenyatta era, the turn-over was almost as severe: four out of 20 Cabinet Ministers were defeated, while 18 out of 35 Assistant Ministers, and 61 out of 102 backbenchers lost their seats.[36]

Under the 1969 regulations, all Kenyans were permitted to participate in the ruling party's primary now that KANU was the country's only registered political organisation. In theory, formal Parliamentary elections took place two weeks after the KANU primary, but since victors of the primary were deemed to be returned unopposed, this was a pure formality. Although modelled on the competitive single-party elections in Tanzania, which restricted the number of candidates to two per constituency, in Kenya any number of candidates could contest the primary, provided they were cleared by KANU headquarters, which almost all were. In 1969, a rule requiring six months' membership of KANU was placed upon potential candidates to avoid the remaining KPU leadership taking over KANU in Nyanza. Prominent members of the KPU found it impossible to secure approval to stand in this or the next two elections. Oginga Odinga and former Cabinet Minister Achieng'Oneko were refused clearance in 1974 and again in 1979, after Kenyatta's death, despite the fact that both had been permitted to rejoin the ruling party on their release from detention.[37]

Although all candidates in the Kenyatta era polls ostensibly endorsed KANU's official manifesto, rival candidates drew support from different clans or sub-clans, from different religious denominations and – in ethnically mixed urban constituencies in Nairobi, Mombasa and Nakuru, and in the former White Highlands settlement areas – from particular ethnic groups. In the more ethnically homogeneous Central, Nyanza and Western Provinces, candidates appealed to rival sub-clan or clan interests. Most candidates campaigned on the basis of their past support for *Harambee* self-help development projects, outlining future schemes they would promote when elected. Local factors predominated and class consciousness and ideology played little part in determining voters' preferences.[38]

The freedom of backbench MPs was at its peak between 1969 and 1975. Josiah Mwangi Kariuki, Kenyatta's former private secretary and an ex-Mau Mau detainee, now an Assistant Minister, became the leader of a sizeable group of radicals in the National Assembly. His critique of the government's development policies and over-reliance on Western aid appealed to radical intellectuals and to landless Kikuyus. The 1969 and 1974 elections brought into the National Assembly a number of outspoken young radicals, several of whom sympathised with the ideological message of the banned KPU. In fact, the KANU front bench after 1969 encountered more focused criticism from its new backbench 'informal opposition' than it had ever endured from the few KPU MPs. Numbering more than 40 MPs, the backbenchers regularly condemned government policy throughout the 1969–74 Parliament, forcing the government to withdraw a number of proposed Bills. Although they operated within well-defined limits, Kenya's Parliamentarians were never more outspoken, nor more effective as a legislative check upon the executive than during the middle years of Kenyatta's Presidency. Immediately after the 1974 general election, in fact, KANU backbenchers almost captured control of the day-to-day working of the National Assembly. One of their leaders, Nandi MP Joseph Seroney, was even elected Deputy Speaker, enabling the radicals to control debates and to manipulate the Parliamentary timetable whenever he was in charge of the House. Kenyatta's irritation with the internal opposition was also shown by the fact that all four Assistant Ministers in the radical faction – including J. M. Kariuki, Charles Rubia and Burudi Nabwera – were dropped in the new 1974 government.[39]

The early 1970s were not, however, a period of complete calm. The regime had been shaken in 1971 by the discovery of a coup plot largely among Kamba politicians and military officers to kill Kenyatta and Vice-President Moi, thereby clearing the way to State House for recently appointed Kamba Chief Justice Kitili Mwendwa. Two MPs were detained and Mwendwa and the Chief of the General Staff, although they could not be tied directly to the plotters, were forced to resign. Nonetheless, several of the alleged participants in the foiled coup subsequently prospered, a characteristic of the Kenyan political system.[40]

Kenyatta and the Ruling Party

President Kenyatta determined the framework within which rival factions contended for power and within which different ethnic groups and districts fought for state patronage, especially new development schemes. This arrangement reduced the risk of ethnic rivalries endangering the state's stability. KANU throughout the Kenyatta years remained a weak organisation at the local level and lacked ideological coherence. Kenyatta operated a complex neo-patrimonial system rather than a party state, and did not attempt to mobilise or control the masses through the local party apparatus. Cabinet Ministers, of course, were better placed than Assistant Ministers or ordinary Members of Parliament to direct development schemes and government projects to their constituencies, to secure loans and contracts, or to gain positions on the boards of parastatals such as the Industrial and Commercial Development Corporation for their prominent supporters.

Kenyans continued to judge the performance of their Parliamentarians by their capacity to bring 'pork' back to their constituencies.[41] General elections every five years provided the population with a sense of participation and endowed the regime with a considerable degree of political legitimacy and popular support. Civil society, especially organisations such as the Law Society of Kenya, the Kenya Farmers' Association, the Kenya Coffee Planters' Cooperative Union, and the National Christian Council of Kenya, remained outspoken, continuing to criticise the government, while the National Assembly remained the focal point of Kenyan political life. Even the press survived relatively unscathed. The main newspapers, moreover, were identified with specific national political factions. The *Standard* was the mouthpiece of the Gikuyu, Embu and Meru Association (GEMA) and was identified with the anti-Moi 'Change the Constitution' Movement in 1976–8 (see below).[42]

As we have noted, after independence considerable power remained with the Provincial Administration. At independence the government had decided to retain the colonial legal framework which allowed the Administration to control political activity in the countryside through such legislation as the Public Order Act and the Chiefs Act. Provincial and District Commissioners were directly responsible to the Office of the President, rather than to the new political class, local authorities or KANU headquarters. Indeed, as Seroney and Shikuku pointed out in debate immediately before they were arrested in 1975, KANU had become a moribund organisation. Although the ruling party existed in name, in practice it did not meet, had no powers, and was subordinated entirely to the power of the executive branch of government.[43] In June 1965, for example, Kenyatta had disbanded the vocal KANU backbenchers group and as early as 1966 KANU Organising Secretary John Keen – in 1991 to become Secretary-General of the Democratic Party – described the organisational state of the ruling party as 'appalling' in an open letter to Kenyatta. He complained that a delegates' conference had not been held since 1962, the Secretariat had not met since February 1964, the party was £20,000 in debt, telephones had been cut off at party headquarters and party staff had not been paid for seven months.[44] After the March 1966 Limuru Conference, there were no formal party sub-branch, branch or national elections for more than a decade. When Secretary-General Tom Mboya was assassinated in 1969, for example, his assistant Robert Matano took over, serving as acting Secretary-General for the next nine years.

Kenyatta and his senior advisers had concluded that the party could not afford open elections in every sub-branch, splitting the party and exacerbating divisions between the pro- and anti-Moi coalitions, and highlighting opposition to Kikuyu hegemony. As a result, the President avoided calling nation-wide party elections for more than a decade. When finally elections were called in December 1976, they threatened to be even more divisive than feared, as the 'Change the Constitution' camp gathered to challenge Vice-President Moi and his allies. The fate of FORD in 1992 and the disputes which developed over the Democratic Party's elections in 1993 confirm the wisdom of Kenyatta's decision to avoid divisive party elections for as long as possible.

The 1970s saw the growth of Kikuyu dominance over the economic and political life of the country, associated with the state's pro-Western and nominally free-enterprise culture. This was combined with one of the most intrusive and all-embracing state presences on the continent.[45] Although Kenyatta himself remained relatively even-handed, Central Province became once more the most economically developed and successful area. As well as dominating the world of business, the Kikuyu and their related peoples also engaged in assertive purchasing of traditional Maasai and Coastal lands, moving extensively outside their original homelands.

The Murder of Josiah Mwangi Kariuki and the Crackdown on Dissent, 1975–6

Kenyatta in the 1960s had been able to reward the educated African élite with employment, parastatal sinecures, government loans and – most important of all – land. Then, during the last years of his rule in the mid-1970s, Kenya enjoyed a period of unprecedented economic prosperity as the international price for Kenyan coffee and tea soared, following the destruction by frost of the Brazilian coffee harvest, at the same time as the tourist industry boomed. This period of prosperity enabled the regime to weather the murder of Kikuyu dissident Josiah Mwangi Kariuki in 1975. Although a wealthy man himself, Kariuki was an ex-Mau Mau leader who spoke out for the poor man, and during the early 1970s he had posed a growing challenge to the Kenyatta regime's legitimacy among the Kikuyu masses. Whereas Oginga Odinga and the KPU, and even senior Cabinet Minister Tom Mboya had challenged the authority of the state from outside its Kikuyu stronghold, Kariuki spoke from within the Kikuyu community on behalf of those have-nots who had gained little from the first decade of independence. Always a significant political figure, in the late 1960s he had become the leader of a growing opposition to Kenyatta's policies amongst his own Kikuyu supporters and a senior figure in the informal opposition, attempting to mobilise the Kikuyu masses – the *masakini* (literally, the poor) – against the conspicuous wealth of the Kikuyu élite, especially Kenyatta's relatives and close allies. Many commentators had tipped Kariuki for the Ministry of Agriculture in 1969, but his appointment had been rescinded at the last minute.[46]

Members of Kenyatta's inner circle had become concerned that the Nyandarua MP was threatening the regime's popularity inside its own ethnic bastion. In 1975 he vanished, and after several days of confusion and contradictory reports his body was discovered in the Ngong' hills, south-west of Nairobi. He had been badly beaten and then shot dead. The discovery created a tremendous furore, provoking open attacks on the state apparatus from Kariuki's supporters and colleagues. Suspecting state collusion, the Assembly set up a Parliamentary Select Commission of Enquiry to identify how and why Kariuki had been killed. The resulting investigation revealed that the MP had last been seen alive leaving the Hilton hotel in central Nairobi in the company of GSU Commander Ben

Gethi. Numerous stories implicated senior politicians and Kenyatta's own personal bodyguards in the killing. Special Branch officers, who were at this time conducting their own power struggle with the élite GSU, leaked much of the information which formed the Select Committee's findings.[47] The report incriminated senior members of the regime, including the President's brother-in-law Mbiyu Koinange and Gethi. Defeating a 'three line' government whip, backbenchers in Parliament, supported by Cabinet Minister Masinde Muliro and two Assistant Ministers, voted to accept the report (but only after the final page, calling for the investigation of Mbiyu Koinange and the Nyeri Mayor in connection with the killing, had been torn out by Kenyatta himself). Embarrassed, Kenyatta immediately dismissed Muliro and his two colleagues, although Finance Minister Mwai Kibaki, who had abstained and was the only Government Minister to attend Kariuki's funeral, was judged too valuable a technocrat to be sacked.[48]

The murder shattered the relatively benign image that the government had fostered for the past six years. Nairobi University students rioted in the streets of the capital and the regime's reputation was severely damaged among the Kikuyu masses, especially in Nyandarua and Nyeri, Kariuki's birthplace. Kariuki's murder and the protests it provoked also brought about a dramatic change in the regime's treatment of its critics. The media, academics and dissident backbenchers suddenly found that they had much less freedom to manoeuvre as the regime clamped down on all forms of criticism, especially when the Kikuyu poor were the intended audience. Dissident backbench MPs now found that their freedom was curtailed drastically. In Kenyatta's own words, MPs would toe the line, or he would crush them 'like a hawk among the chickens'.[49] Within two years of Kariuki's death, dissidents Martin Shikuku, Seroney and George Anyona were detained without trial for criticising the ruling party and the probity of influential Attorney-General Charles Njonjo. Others, such as Mark Mwithaga and Seroney's Nandi protégé, Chelegat Mutai, were gaoled and lost their Parliamentary seats, charged with minor crimes. This judicious combination of rewards and intimidation broke up the backbench coalition; some members defected to the government, while others decided that it was wise to remain silent. The regime was no longer willing to tolerate criticism.[50]

The Twilight Years, the 'Change the Constitution' Movement and the Cash Crop Boom

Kenyatta, now in his late eighties, was deteriorating in health and no longer controlled his government colleagues with the same effectiveness. The aftermath of Kariuki's murder was the last time Kenyatta actively entered the political arena. From 1976, the regime began to drift as rival factions contended for power.

In October 1976 prominent Kikuyu politicians, who had long resented Moi's continued occupancy of the Vice-Presidency, attempted to block his automatic accession to the Presidency on Kenyatta's death. Leaders of the powerful Gikuyu, Embu and Meru Association, including several relatives of the ageing President led by Kenyatta's nephew Dr Njoroge Mungai, attempted to initiate a constitutional change to block Moi's automatic assumption of the Presidency for 90 days. Sensing Kenyatta's days were now numbered, these supporters of the 'Change the Constitution' Movement needed to alter the constitutional provision to give them a chance to keep the Presidency in Central Province, and preferably in Kiambu, the centre of the regime and Kenyatta's home. During Kenyatta's last years, the district had three members in the Cabinet, compared with a maximum of one in every other district. The Kiambu clique were backed by a substantial factional coalition from other ethnic groups, particularly amongst those outside the current centres of power. Other leaders, however, including some Kikuyu technocrats (most notably Minister of Finance Mwai Kibaki and Attorney-General Charles Njonjo) and probably President Kenyatta himself, considered that Kikuyu economic and political hegemony would in the long term be safer under a non-Kikuyu President, such as Moi, than if another member of the Kenyatta family occupied the Presidency, exacerbating discontent among Kenya's other ethnic groups. But although Njonjo, with Kenyatta's approval, blocked discussion of constitutional change in October 1976, bolstering Moi's position, KANU's impending sub-branch elections revealed that the party and country remained deeply divided over the succession.[51]

Moi had for some years been developing his relationship with Kikuyu outside the élite of Kiambu District, building up his own network of allies. The voters and leaders of northern Kikuyuland, from Nyeri, Kirinyaga and Nyandarua, were as resentful of the privileged position of Kiambu and associates of the Kenyatta family as people from other provinces. Moi knew his chances of succeeding Kenyatta depended upon the Kikuyu being divided. Initially, the inner circle of the Kiambaa-Gatundu clique underestimated Moi's skills. The Vice-President had been unable to prevent Kenyatta's long-time friend Mbiyu Koinange from encroaching upon the powers of the Ministry of Home Affairs, taking over responsibility for Internal Security, the Immigration Department and the Police, leaving the Vice-President in control of only the Prison Service. Moi, however, had proved his value to the regime on several occasions, most notably in his role as leader of government business in the unruly National Assembly during the Commission of Enquiry into the murder of J. M. Kariuki. Moi's hesitant but honest style had commanded respect where the blustering of several other senior Ministers merely intensified opposition. Moreover, the Vice-President had proved undeviatingly loyal during his long stint as Kenyatta's deputy.[52] Following the defeat of Foreign Minister Dr Njoroge Mungai at the 1974 election, moreover, the Kiambu Kikuyu inner circle did not have a viable candidate to replace Moi. Presidential candidates had to be elected Members of Parliament. With Mungai unable to stand, and Mbiyu Koinange, the regime's 70-year-old *éminence grise,* too old and too unpopular to challenge Moi, the Kiambaa-Gatundu faction found itself without a viable candidate just as Kenyatta's health began to deteriorate. Attorney-General Njonjo, supported by Kenyatta, consequently had little difficulty in stopping the 'Change the Constitution' Movement in its tracks, confirming Moi's position as the constitutional successor.[53]

The first KANU sub-branch, branch and national elections in over a decade, which commenced in December 1976 and January 1977, however, provided the anti-Moi forces with one last chance. After more than a decade of inactivity, local party members were asked to select new constituency (sub-branch) and District level (branch) officers as a prelude to the first National Delegates' Conference in twelve years. The elections divided the ruling party throughout the country into two rival camps. Two groups – 'KANU A' and 'KANU B' – fought to control the selection of delegates to the National Conference. As in 1964–6, both factions sought to establish nation-wide followings. Thus Taita Towett, a prominent Kipsigis Kalenjin Minister from Kericho District, was persuaded to challenge Tugen Kalenjin Vice-President Moi for KANU's National Vice-Presidency, while the leader of the 'Change the Constitution' Movement, Dr Mungai, stood for the position of National Chairman rather than directly challenging Moi. Although ethnicity remained the most important factor in Kenyan politics, with most Kikuyu and politicians from neighbouring Embu, Meru and Ukambani supporting the 'Change the Constitution' forces, 'KANU A' and 'KANU B' both managed to construct national coalitions, incorporating political leaders from far beyond their ethnic strongholds. With the last-minute cancellation of the Delegates' Conference because of the sudden deterioration in President Kenyatta's health, however, the two factions never openly contended for control of the ruling party or the succession. The constitution and party leadership remained unchanged. As a result, despite rumours of attempted coup plots, Vice-President Moi succeeded as President without open opposition on Kenyatta's death in August 1978.[54]

Despite the uncertainty during President Kenyatta's last years, following Kariuki's murder, as the political élite struggled among themselves over the succession, the regime remained surprisingly stable because of the economic windfall created by high commodity prices in the mid-1970s for Kenya's main export crops – coffee, tea and pyrethrum – and the booming tourist industry, which more than offset the quintupling of oil prices in 1973–4. The cash crop boom ensured that the last years of the Kenyatta era were peaceful and stable, even prosperous, for most Kenyans. It was clear even then, however, that Kenyatta's patronage system was living on borrowed time. The neo-patrimonial system he had created on the back of the colonial government's social engineering and land consolidation in Kikuyuland and the opening of the White Highlands was being rapidly undermined by Kenya's demographic explosion. The rewards of state patronage had extended far beyond the Kikuyu inner circle which surrounded the President. Leaders of virtually all of Kenya's ethnic sub-nationalist movements, with the exception of the Luo after 1966, had been incorporated into this system of government, controlling all facets of political and economic activity.[55] Political bosses were sustained in office as long as they provided benefits – jobs, loans and development schemes – to their followers, while electoral politics enabled constituencies to repudiate failed patrons in favour of more development-minded leaders. But as early as the 1970s the rapid expansion of Kenya's population, which had grown at a rate of 4.2 per cent per annum since independence, doubling every 17 years, was beginning to endanger the stability of the system and the regime. Demands for cooption were threatening to exceed the supply of patronage posts, land and financial rewards, as the disruptive effects of rapid population growth became evident. Kenyatta's successor would have to operate in a much more difficult political and economic world where patronage resources would be stretched. Could the system survive or would Kenya(tta)'s relatively benign single-party regime disintegrate under the strain of attempting to satisfy its clients?

Notes

1 As General Secretary of the Kikuyu Central Association and editor of the Gikuyu language newspaper, *Muigwithania*, (literally, 'The Reconciler'), which had sought to unite the new mission-educated élite with the Kikuyu rural masses in the 1920s, Jomo Kenyatta had played a key role in the development of Kikuyu political consciousness. In the 1930s, he had confirmed this reputation with the publication of *Facing Mount Kenya*, which had defended Kikuyu culture and traditions from missionary criticism. After his return to Kenya from Britain in 1946, moreover, Kenyatta had emerged as the founding-father of Kenyan nationalism, serving as leader of the Kenya African Union from June 1947 until his detention in October 1952. For two accounts of the background to the Mau Mau revolt, see David W. Throup, *Economic and Social Origins of Mau Mau*, James Currey, London, 1987 and John Lonsdale and Bruce Berman, *Unhappy Valley*, James Currey, London, 1991.

2 David Goldsworthy, *Tom Mboya: The Man Kenya Wanted to Forget*, Heinemann, London, pp. 166–94, provides the best modern account of the political divisions within the nationalist movement. See also George Bennet and Carl G. Rosberg, Jr, *The Kenyatta Election, 1961*, Oxford University Press, London, 1961, *passim.*

3 Wm. R. Louis and Ronald Robinson, *Journal of Imperial and Commonwealth History*, vol. 22, no. 3 (1994), pp. 462–511 and Frank Furedi, *The New Ideology of Imperialism: Renewing the Moral Imperative*, Pluto Press, London and Boulder, Colorado, 1994, *passim*, for differing views of the political economy of the end of Empire. A briefer statement of Furedi's interpretation can be found in his paper, 'Diagnosing Disorder: The Anglo-American Management of African Nationalism, 1948–1960', pp. 1-27, presented to the African Studies Association of the United Kingdom conference at Stirling University, 8–10 September 1992. There are detailed accounts of the 1957 election in G. F. Engholm, 'African Elections in Kenya, March 1957' in W. J. M. Mackenzie and Kenneth Robinson (eds), *Five Elections in Africa*, Oxford University Press, Oxford, 1960, pp. 391–461; David Goldsworthy, *Tom Mboya*, pp. 67–72; and Jack R. Roelker, *Mathu of Kenya: A Political Study*, Hoover Institution Press, Stanford, 1976, pp. 125–6.

4 David Goldsworthy, *Tom Mboya*, pp. 18–20.

5 David Throup, 'Daniel arap Moi', in Harvey Glickman (ed.), *Political Leaders of Contemporary Africa South of the Sahara: A Biographical Dictionary*, Greenwood Press, 1992, pp. 168–74.

6 Jack R. Roelker, *Mathu of Kenya*, pp. 134–42.

7 David Goldsworthy, *Tom Mboya*, pp. 111–16, 120–7 and 131–46.

8 Robert Shepherd, *Iain Macleod: A Biography*, Hutchinson, London, 1994, pp. 155–9. See also David Goldsworthy, *Colonial Issues in British Politics*, Oxford University Press, Oxford, 1971, pp. 362–5.

9 C. Sanger and J. Nottingham, 'The Kenya general election of 1963', *Journal of Modern African Studies*, vol. 2, no. 1 (1964), pp. 1–40. See also David Throup, 'The Construction and Destruction of the Kenyatta State' in M. G. Schatzberg (ed.), *The Political Economy of Kenya*, Praeger, New York, 1987. pp. 44–6.

10 *Ibid.* See also *The K.A.N.U. Manifesto*, Dar El-Hana Press, Cairo, 1960.

11 Carl G. Rosberg, Jr, and G. Bennett, *The Kenyatta Election, 1961, passim.*

12 The official Corfield Report on *The Origins and Growth of Mau Mau, published in 1960, Sessional Paper No. 5 of 1959–60,* Government Printer, Nairobi, 1960, had signalled the determination of certain elements of the Secretariat and Field Administration to prevent Kenyatta's political rehabilitation. For official discussion of the Corfield Report see PRO CO 822/1851 and CO 822/1897..

13 *Ibid.,* and J. Murray-Brown, *Kenyatta,* George Allen and Unwin Ltd. , London, 1972, pp. 300–1; and Robert Shepherd, *Iain Macleod: A Biography,* pp. 243–4. The discussions on Kenyatta's future can be found in PRO CO 822/1909–1913, especially CO 822/1909, draft statement by Sir Patrick Renison, 20 April 1960. See also the remarks by C. Sanger and J. Nottingham in 'The Kenya general election of 1963', *Journal of Modern African Studies,* vol. 2, no. 1 (1964), p. 3.

14 David Goldsworthy, *Tom Mboya,* pp. 183–5.

15 Kenyatta was finally released on 1 August 1961. Robert Shepherd, *Iain Macleod: A Biography,* p. 244, and PRO CO 1910–1913.

16 C. Sanger and J. Nottingham, 'The Kenya general election of 1963', *Journal of Moderan African Studies,* vol. 2, no. 1 (1964), pp. 1–40.

17 *Ibid.,* pp. 9–21.

18 C. Gertzel, 'The Political Administration in Kenya', *Journal of Commonwealth Political Studies,* vol. 4, no. 3 (1966), pp. 201–15. See also Gertzel's *The Politics of Independent Kenya,* East African Publishing House, Nairobi, 1970, pp. 23–31; John Okumu and Frank Holmquist, 'Party and Party-State Relations' in Joel Barkan (ed.), *Politics and Public Policy in Kenya and Tanzania,* Praeger, New York, 1979 and 1984, pp. 53–4, and Goran Hyden, 'Administration and Public Policy', in Joel Barkan (ed.), *Politics and Public Policy,* p. 115. Kenyatta's view can be found in 'Speech by His Excellency the President at the Kenya Institute of Administration, 15 December, 1965', Kenya News Agency, Handout No. 768.

19 David Throup, 'The Construction and Destruction of the Kenyatta State', pp. 37–43.

20 *Ibid.,* pp. 41–6. See also Christopher Leo, *Land and Class in Kenya,* University of Toronto Press, Toronto and London, 1984, pp. 97–170; Gary Wasserman, *Politics of Decolonization: Kenya Europeans and the Land Issue, 1960–65,* Cambridge University Press, London, 1976, *passim;* and Apollo Njonjo, 'The Africanization of the "White Highlands": A Study in Agrarian Class Struggles in Kenya, 1950–1974', unpublished PhD dissertation, Department of Politics, Princeton University, 1977.

21 R. Sandbrook, *Proletarians and African Capitalism: the Kenyan Case, 1960-72,* Cambridge University Press, London, 1975, pp. 40–2, 126, 136–7, 166–7 and 179. See also the *Presidential Ministerial Committee on Trade Unionism,* Government Printer, Nairobi, 1965.

22 C. Gertzel, *The Politics of Independent Kenya,* pp. 54–5 and p. 63.

23 *Ibid.,* pp. 42–72, and David Goldsworthy, *Tom Mboya,* pp. 232–47.

24 Oginga Odinga's account of these events can be found in his autobiography, *Not Yet Uhuru,* Heinemann, London, 1967, pp. 284–97.

25 David Goldsworthy, *Tom Mboya,* pp. 234–47; Cherry Gertzel, *The Politics of Independent Kenya,* pp. 54–72; and Oginga Odinga, *Not Yet Uhuru,* pp. 297–300.

26 *Ibid.*

27 David Goldsworthy, *Tom Mboya,* pp. 241–6. See also Susanne D. Mueller's unpublished PhD dissertation, 'Political Parties in Kenya: The Politics of Opposition and Dissent, 1919–1969', Department of Politics, Princeton University, 1972, which provides the most detailed account available of the KPU.

28 The best account of the 1966 'Little General Election' remains Cherry Gertzel, *The Politics of Independent Kenya,* pp. 73–124.

29 *Ibid.,* pp. 144–73; and David Throup, 'The Construction and Destruction of the Kenyatta State', pp. 41–8.

30 Susanne D. Mueller, 'Government and Opposition in Kenya, 1966–69', *Journal of Modern African Studies,* vol. 22, no. 3, pp. 408–12. Bildad Kaggia was gaoled for a year for holding an illegal meeting and several of his KPU colleagues were detained without trial for undisclosed reasons.

31 *Ibid.,* pp. 413–15. In June 1966, for example, the Rift Valley Provincial Advisory Council barred three KPU members from attending meetings.

32 *Ibid.,* p. 426. See also Republic of Kenya, Director of Local Government Elections, *The Local Government Elections Legislation: Extracts from the Local Government Regulations 1963 (L.N. 256/63) Concerning Local Government Elections,* pp. 1–87, Government Printer, Nairobi, July 1968.

33 D. Goldsworthy, *Tom Mboya*, pp. 285–6.
34 Susanne D. Mueller, 'Government and Opposition in Kenya, 1966–69', pp. 408–12. provides a detailed account of the law governing party registration, i.e. the Societies Ordinance of 1952. See also C. P. W. Hornsby, 'The Role of the Member of Parliament in Kenya, 1969–83', unpublished D.Phil dissertation, Oxford University, 1985, pp. 80–5.
35 David Throup, 'Elections and Political Legitimacy in Kenya', *Africa*, vol. 63, no. 3 (1993), p. 375.
36 *Ibid.*, pp. 375–9; and Charles Hornsby and David Throup, 'Elections and Political Change in Kenya', *Journal of Commonwealth and Comparative Politics*, vol. 30, no. 2 (July 1992), pp. 178 and 185–8.
37 *Weekly Review*, Nairobi, 19 October 1979, pp. 9–10.
38 Charles Hornsby and David Throup, 'Elections and Political Change in Kenya', *Journal of Commonwealth and Comparative Politics*, vol. 30, no. 2 (1992), p. 181; and Jennifer A. Widner, *The Rise of a Party-State in Kenya*, University of California Press, Berkeley, 1992, pp. 56–66.
39 David Throup, 'Elections and Political Change in Kenya', *Africa*, vol. 63, no. 3 (1993), pp. 377–89.
40 *Weekly Review*, Nairobi, 4 October 1985, pp. 3–4.
41 Joel D. Barkan. 'Bringing Home the Pork: Legislator Behavior and Political Change in East Africa', in Joel Smith and Lloyd Musolf (eds), *Legislatures in Development: Dynamics of Change in New and Old States*, Duke University Press, Durham, North Carolina, 1978, pp. 265–88. See also Barkan's 'Political Linkage in Kenya: Citizens, Local Élites, and Legislators', Occasional Paper, Center for Comparative Legislative Research, University of Iowa, September 1974.
42 David Throup, 'The Construction and Destruction of the Kenyatta State', in M.G. Schatzberg (ed.), *The Political Economy of Kenya*, pp. 49–50; and David Throup, 'Elections and Political Legitimacy in Kenya', *Africa*, vol. 63, no. 3, 1993, pp. 380–1.
43 Charles Hornsby and David Throup, 'Elections and Political Change in Kenya', pp. 183–4.
44 David Goldsworthy, *Tom Mboya*, pp. 238–9.
45 A legacy of the colonial era's agricultural development initiatives, efforts to preserve white dominance and the Mau Mau struggle. See Cherry Gertzel, *The Politics of Independent Kenya*, pp. 1–31.
46 David Throup, 'The Construction and Destruction of the Kenyatta State', in M.G. Schatzberg (ed.), *The Political Economy of Kenya*, pp. 51–2.
47 Information from a European diplomat who was close to opposition leaders in this period.
48 C. P. W. Hornsby, unpublished dissertation, 'The Member of Parliament in Kenya, 1969–83', Oxford University, 1983, pp. 299–300 and 314–15.
49 David Throup, 'The Construction and Destruction of the Kenyatta State', in M. G. Schatzberg (ed.), *The Political Economy of Kenya*, pp. 51–2.
50 David Throup, 'Elections and Political Legitimacy in Kenya', pp. 379–80.
51 David Throup, 'The Construction and Destruction of the Kenyatta State', in M.G. Schatzberg, (ed.), *The Political Economy of Kenya*, pp. 43–67; and J. Karimi and P. Ochieng', *The Kenyatta Succession*, Transafrica, Nairobi, 1980, pp. 8–51. See also Jennifer A. Widner, *The Rise of a Party-State*, pp. 110–18.
52 David Throup, 'The Construction and Destruction of the Kenyatta State', in M.G. Schatzberg (ed.), *The Political Economy of Kenya*, pp. 47–50 and 52–3.
53 *Ibid.*, pp. 48–53.
54 J. Karimi and P. Ochieng, *The Kenyatta Succession*, *passim*.
55 Kenyatta's refusal to incorporate the Luo fully into his coalition was symbolised by the fact that after the events of October 1969 he never visited Nyanza Province again.

Three

The Creation of the Moi State

By the time of President Jomo Kenyatta's death in August 1978 Kenya had acquired the reputation of being one of the most open polities in Africa. Intensely competitive and comparatively fair national and local elections had been held regularly, despite KANU's monopoly of political participation since 1969.[1] The press remained comparatively outspoken, and the churches, the trades union movement and the legal profession and judiciary were relatively free to defend civil society. After the accession of President Daniel arap Moi, however, Kenyans' freedoms diminished. The state became more authoritarian, dissent was stifled and political power became increasingly focused on specific ethnic groups.

During his first decade in office, the new President was to face far more difficult circumstances than his predecessor. First, Moi came to power just as the cash crop boom of the mid-1970s was ending and as Kenya's appeal as a tourist centre began to level off. The price for tea and coffee has plummeted and smallholder producers have received a diminishing proportion of the international price of their crops.[2] The easy economic benefits of land consolidation were nearly exhausted and the urban population was still expanding at more than 10 per cent per annum. Throughout the Moi era, state patronage has been in short supply and the President has had to make difficult decisions about which groups to coopt. Political patrons have found it increasingly difficult to satisfy the demands of their clients as resources have diminished, while Kenya's population has continued to grow at more than 4 per cent per annum. There are now nearly twice as many Kenyans as when President Moi took office.[3]

Secondly, Moi was a Kalenjin, not a Kikuyu. Under Kenyatta, the Kikuyu had come to dominate business and commerce, the civil service, many of the professions and, of course, politics. During the mid-1970s boom, Central Province had become one of Africa's few examples of self-sustaining, dynamic, peasant agriculture, based on the cultivation of coffee and tea for export and vegetables for Nairobi. With a comparatively elaborate communications and power infrastructure, Kikuyuland lay at the heart of the Kenyan economy in a way that the Kalenjin areas, the core of President Moi's new political coalition, did not. The new President's attempt to restructure Kenya's political economy, to broaden the development base, and to reward his allies in the Rift Valley and in Western and Coast Provinces undermined the regime's political stability by alienating Kikuyu businessmen and civil servants (the emerging state bourgeoisie), who found that their influence had declined and that they were losing contracts to Asians and their Kalenjin front-men. Admirable though Moi's attempt to broaden the patronage network was, by diverting resources away from Central Province he not only endangered Kenya's political stability but threatened to kill the entrepreneurial initiative of Kikuyu peasants who had created much of the country's prosperity.[4]

Thirdly, Moi was not Kenyatta. He had held on to the Vice-Presidency for 11 years because he was a compromise candidate who appeared not to pose a threat to the major power blocs behind the throne. Moi lacked his predecessor's political prestige and the legitimacy which Kenyatta had gained as the 'father of independence'. He also lacked the education and intellect required personally to master the civil service and politics to the extent that Kenyatta had. During the first years of his rule, consequently, the new President relied upon his close advisers, particularly Charles Njonjo and Mwai Kibaki. Moi's first task was to establish his position with the assistance of the two Kikuyu technocrats, who had controlled financial and legal affairs under Kenyatta. This task dominated the first 24 months of Moi's Presidency. The new President's room to manoeuvre was at first limited, but as the 1980s passed Moi became more entrenched and established his own political network, and Kikuyu leaders correspondingly became increasingly opposed to the regime. Unable any longer to rule through consensus, Moi had to adopt an increasingly authoritarian stance.

The decay of Kenya's civil society partly reflects the decline of the neo-patrimonial political structure created by Kenyatta, which depended on the flow of patronage from powerful local bosses to their constituents in return for political support. In the early 1980s, Kenya's second President began to abandon Kenyatta's system of ruling through district barons who had their own independent fiefdoms. Unlike Kenyatta, many of his fellow leaders considered that Moi had no particular right to rule and that the President, in return, did not fully trust them. The new President began to by-pass the established political structures in the districts in order to consolidate his position by a populist appeal to the rural masses, and by appointing his own nominees, who depended upon Moi's support for their authority and position.

Moi's Presidency can be divided into the eight distinct periods summarized in Table 3.1.

The Consolidation of the Moi Presidency, 1978–80

Moi came to power as the leader of a coalition which was openly opposed to the continuing dominance of the Kenyatta family and a coterie of Kikuyu business leaders, recruited mainly from Kiambu District. After his accession to the Presidency, Moi set about consolidating his position in alliance

Table 3.1 Eight Political Periods During Moi's Presidency

Phase	*Period*	*Key Issues*
(1)	1978–80	President Moi establishes himself in office; directed by Vice-President Kibaki and Attorney-General Njonjo
(2)	1980–2	Moi becomes increasingly independent, while Njonjo challenges Kibaki for the Vice-Presidency
(3)	1982–3	The attempted *coup d'état* and its aftermath
(4)	1983–5	Njonjo's disgrace, the 1983 general election and the Commission of Enquiry into Njonjo's affairs
(5)	1985–90	The mature Moi system and the attempt to create a party state
(6)	1990–Dec. 1991	Mounting internal and external pressure for political pluralism
(7)	Dec. 1991– Dec. 1992	The multi-party era and the December 1992 general election
(8)	1993–	KANU reconsolidates its control while the opposition proves ineffective

with Minister of Finance Mwai Kibaki and Attorney-General Charles Njonjo, creating a 'rainbow coalition' of ethnic interests which later would enable him to undermine Kikuyu hegemony.

During his first twelve months in office, the new President made few mistakes, drawing universal praise for the smoothness of the transfer of power. Political prisoners, including politicians Martin Shikuku and M. J. Seroney and prominent novelist Ngugi wa Thiong'o, were released from detention in December 1978. The political restraints of the Kenyatta era seemed to have been lifted. The tension which had pervaded the country during Kenyatta's last years vanished as the new President asserted his authority.[5] Kenyans praised themselves as the first black African state peacefully to transfer power under the constitution from one President to another. This political honeymoon only ended when KANU headquarters refused to clear former KPU leaders Oginga Odinga and Achieng' Oneko to contest the 1979 general election on the KANU ticket.[6]

Nonetheless, the 1979 elections were probably the most competitive and open of all those in the one-party state. Kenyatta's former associates found that they had to face their constituents without the backing of the District Administration, while their challengers were eager to identify themselves with Moi's new regime. Ex-Minister of State Mbiyu Koinange, for example, was easily defeated by GEMA head Njenga Karume in Kiambaa and the new broom also swept out many Kenyatta era figures in Western and Nyanza Provinces. Most of the Kikuyu élite survived, however, and adapted to the new order.

On the other hand, the elections also revealed authoritarian tendencies which the new President had concealed during his eleven years as Kenyatta's Vice-President. Unlike Kenyatta, who had always remained above the fray, Moi actively campaigned for a slate of candidates around the country, who appeared to offer a 'new deal', a populist alternative to the old élites of the Kenyatta era. Most of those who received his endorsement triumphed. The reality in Moi's Kalenjin heartland, however, was very different from the myth which the President's advisers were skilfully constructing in the media around the *Nyayo* ideology of 'love, peace and unity'. Moi had never been particularly popular or highly regarded by other Kalenjin politicians, and a widely held view was that he had sold out Kalenjin land interests in return for personal preferment during the 1960s and 1970s. As Treasurer of KADU in the first year of independence, Moi had compromised with Kenyatta over conflicting Kalenjin–Kikuyu interests in the Essageri salient and in the Lembus Forest, the borderland between the Kalenjin Reserves and the former White Highlands, which had been the scene of extensive Kikuyu land purchases. The open hostility of some Kipsigis and Nandi leaders to his preferment showed the insecurity of the new President's ethnic base.[7]

Once President, however, Moi moved swiftly to secure the enduring support of his home community. The 1979 general election in the central Rift Valley provided the worst example of electoral rigging since the 1968 local government elections. The District Commissioner in Nandi, acting on instructions from the Office of the President, ensured that Seroney, Moi's main political rival among the Kalenjin, was defeated in Tinderet. Taita Towett was also 'defeated' in Kericho and, in Kitale, ex-Minister Masinde Muliro was removed by the simple expedient of switching the results announced for himself and his opponent, an action which contributed to the resignation of the then Supervisor of Elections, Norman Montgomery. Throughout the Kalenjin heartlands of Baringo, Elgeyo-Marakwet, Nandi and Kericho, long-serving MPs were replaced by Moi's henchmen; in some seats, troops from the dreaded GSU were deployed to dragoon voters to the polls and to ensure that they voted the right way. Among the beneficiaries of the new era was Moi's personal secretary, Nicholas Kiprono arap Biwott, who was unopposed in his seat in Elgeyo-Marakwet (which borders on Moi's own). His opponent, who had defeated Biwott in 1974, was persuaded that to continue 'fighting' the President's choice was not in his best interests, and after withdrawing he was appointed Chairman of the Horticultural Crops Development Authority, Director of the Cooperative Bank and finally Chairman of the Kenya Tourist Development Authority as compensation.[8]

President Moi had refrained from undertaking a major Cabinet reshuffle in 1978, although Koinange had been sidelined immediately.[9] After the election, however, Moi brought his supporters into key positions: Nicholas Biwott and G. G. Kariuki, a former Kikuyu Assistant Minister from Laikipia who had backed Moi for the succession, became the key Ministers in the Office of the President, while Henry Kosgey, who had replaced Seroney in Tinderet, and Jonathan arap Ng'eno who 'beat' Taita Towett entered the Cabinet as Ministers of Transport and Water Development. Their appointments carried the message that cooperation with the new regime would be rewarded. The President's freedom of action, however, was still hedged in by Kibaki and Njonjo, who were respectively Vice-President and Minister of Finance, and Attorney-General. He was not yet master in his own house.[10]

The Struggle for the Vice-Presidency, 1980–2

The second phase of Moi's Presidency – the period 1980–2 – was dominated by increasingly open factional conflict amongst the new ruling team, as Njonjo quietly challenged Kibaki for the Vice-Presidency. Conflict had broken out almost as soon as Moi took office, and tensions between the Kibaki technocrats and the Moi/Njonjo team had even been evident in Central Province in the 1979 elections. Njonjo's supporters warned that Kibaki had too much power, combining the positions of Vice-President and Minister of Finance, and they blamed him for the deteriorating economic situation. Kibaki, whose interests lay more in economics than in the cut and thrust of politics, looked increasingly at risk. In 1980, Njonjo, having reached the retirement age of 60 for civil servants, took the plunge into electoral politics, after serving 17 years as Attorney-General.[11] Having secured the resignation of the incumbent MP for his Kikuyu constituency, in return for a substantial financial donation, he took up his Parliamentary seat unopposed soon after. His campaign was orchestrated by a young Kiambu lawyer from the area, Paul Muite. Following his election, Njonjo re-entered the Cabinet as Minister for Constitutional Affairs, a post which reflected his continuing control of all aspects of the legal judicial process, but one with rather less power than he had hoped to obtain.

The growing tensions between the two 'in' Kikuyu teams, with the third group, the Kenyatta-era leaders, on the sidelines, enabled Moi to make effective use of divide-and-rule tactics to enhance his own authority. As the two senior Kikuyu politicians skirmished, Moi began cautiously to reduce the power of his erstwhile 'controllers' and to recruit new allies, such as Abaluhya leaders Elijah Mwangale from Bungoma and Moses Mudavadi from Vihiga, who was also his brother-in-law. The President also promoted non-Kikuyu technocrats in the civil service and solidified his base in the Rift Valley. Moi also demonstrated considerable political finesse in 1980, when he banned 'tribal associations' for disrupting national unity, forcing the Kikuyu élite, identified with GEMA, to adopt a less conspicuous business role, and striking at the heart of their commercial empires built up during the Kenyatta era. Gradually, Kikuyu were retired from the civil service and were replaced as government appointees to parastatal boards.[12]

In February 1982, Moi felt strong enough to move against his former Kikuyu patrons. In a key reshuffle, Kibaki was demoted from the powerful Ministry of Finance to the Ministry of Home Affairs. At the same time, Moi also demoted Njonjo's close ally, G. G. Kariuki, removing him as Minister of State in the Office of the President with responsibility for National Security, where he had frequently clashed with Nicholas Biwott.[13] Biwott was also transferred to a less sensitive post, becoming Minister for Energy, where he was to stay for nearly a decade. The Ministry provided a lucrative source of income, both from bids for government contracts and through Biwott's partnership with President Moi in Kobil, which was granted a monopoly in the importation of refined petroleum products. Although Kibaki continued to serve as Vice-President, from this time he withdrew from the political limelight, and did little to protect himself against increasingly strident criticism from the growing Njonjo team. The President, however, realised that he needed to maintain Kikuyu confidence and sought to consolidate his relations with Njonjo by appointing Arthur Magugu, the son and grandson of prominent colonial chiefs from Kiambu and a close personal friend of Njonjo's, to the Ministry of Finance.[14]

1982 was the year in which tensions within the Kenyan élite over the future control of the state reached their height. It was also the year in which the constitution was changed to confirm that KANU was the only legal political party, following the failed attempt of Oginga Odinga and the Gusii dissident George Anyona to register a new political party, the Kenyan Socialist Alliance. They had attempted to take advantage of the fact that Kenya since the banning of the KPU in 1969 had been simply a *de facto* rather than *de jure* single-party state. In theory, other political parties were allowed to challenge KANU's monopoly of power, but all such attempts had been rejected by the Registrar of Societies. Confronted by permanent exclusion from political activity, following their failure to secure approval as KANU candidates, Odinga and Anyona had decided that they had nothing to lose by directly challenging the ruling party by seeking to register a new, radical party. Needless to say, the Registrar of Societies refused registration and shortly afterwards legislation (drafted by Njonjo's legal adviser Paul Muite) was rushed through the National Assembly by Vice-President Kibaki to make Kenya a *de jure* single-party state.[15]

The August 1982 *Coup d'État* and Its Consequences

On 1 August 1982, rank and file members of the Air Force staged an attempted *coup d'état*. Although the true motivations of those involved remain obscure, it is widely believed that there were two, if not three coups in preparation, by different military and political groups, with very different aims and objectives. The most serious appears to have involved senior Kikuyu politicians and officers in the army and police. The disbanding of GEMA, the promotion of non-Kikuyu in the military and civil service, and the withdrawal of government contracts and loans from Kikuyu businesses and finance houses had alienated many figures within the Kikuyu élite. Rumours abounded in Nairobi before the Air Force coup of a plot by Kikuyu officers to overthrow the President when he was attending the Organisation of African Unity (OAU) Conference in Tripoli over the second weekend in August. When Luo junior officers and other rank and file Air Force members struck first, all was confusion. Although the army put down the coup, the delayed response of the army and police revealed the High Command's lack of loyalty to the President. Major-General Kariuki of the Air Force and Police Commissioner Ben Gethi – two Kikuyu who had risen to high office under Moi – were discovered to be disloyal and for the first time Moi became seriously concerned about Njonjo's continued loyalty.[16]

The coup attempt transformed Kenya's political scene. Severely shaken, President Moi relied increasingly upon Army Chief of Staff Major-General Jackson Mulinge, who had remained loyal during the confused events of 1 and 2 August. For nearly a year, he and other senior Army officers exerted almost as much influence over government decisions as members of the Cabinet. Isolated even before the attempted 1982 coup from Kenya's largest ethnic group, Moi became even more unwilling to trust his remaining Kikuyu advisers. Luo leaders also suffered, since apparently the majority of the Air Force coup plotters had been Luo junior officers. Oginga Odinga was placed under house arrest, and his son Raila detained.[17]

In the two years following the attempted *coup d'état,* Moi systematically moved against the remaining senior Kikuyu in the officer corps, replacing them with Kalenjin. Prominent Kikuyu army commander Major-General Joe Musomba was removed and made Ambassador to Pakistan in order to facilitate the rise of Kalenjin officers such as Lieutenant-General John Sawe, who replaced Musomba as army commander and deputy chief of the General Staff. In 1985, however, senior Special Branch officers warned the President that his attempt to Kalenjinise the senior levels of the officer corps was creating grave discontent among senior and middle-level Kikuyu and Kamba officers, who believed that their promotions were being blocked. After this warning, President Moi became cautious. Lieutenant-General Sawe was retired in 1985 and appointed High Commissioner to Canada. Unable to advance his 'own team' too fast, Moi began instead to promote representatives of the small and politically marginal pastoralist ethnic groups. Lieutenant-General Mahmoud Mohammed, a Somali who was already commander of the reformed 'Air Force '82', succeeded Chief of Staff Mulinge, while Major-General Lengees, a Samburu, took command of the Army. Creations of the President without an independent political base, Mohammed and Lengees proved reliable surrogates for the complete Kalenjin take-over of the armed forces' command structure.[18] Despite this, in the mid-1980s Kikuyu and Kamba still formed the largest element in the officer corps. One third of lieutenant-colonels and colonels, and one-quarter of the highest ranks – brigadiers and above – were Kikuyu, and the Kamba component was even larger. By contrast, Kalenjin officers occupied only one fifth of the senior posts; the same proportion as the Luo in the middle ranks.[19] The purge of Kikuyu members of the officer corps continued throughout the 1980s, however, systematically reducing the threat of a coup attempt from their ranks. The most sophisticated sections of the armed forces, including the armoured brigades, were placed under the control of pro-Moi officers.

Similar changes occurred in the police and the élite GSU. Following the fall of Ben Gethi because of his failure to counter the August 1982 coup with sufficient zeal, both the police and the GSU came under the command of Meru officers – Bernard Njinu and Evaristus M'Mbijiwe – while Kalenjin were appointed to senior ranks. Although Njinu's deputy in the police was a Mkamba, three of the eight provincial heads of Special Branch, the new head of CID Noah arap Too, and the deputy commissioner of the GSU were now all Kalenjin.[20]

The Downfall of Charles Njonjo, 1983–4

In the meantime, political affairs had taken a new turn. The fourth phase of the Moi Presidency was dominated by the fall of Charles Njonjo and its ramifications, including the 1983 general election. Njonjo's 1980–2 bid for power had undermined Kibaki's influence within the government, but Njonjo's own influence also waned when his enemies – Kalenjin, Abaluhya and Kikuyu – united to prevent his rise to the Vice-Presidency and schemed to discredit him with the President. In 1981, his opponents had persuaded his successor as Attorney-General, Joseph Karugu, to prosecute the Minister's cousin, Andrew Muthemba, for illegally importing weapons into the country. The affair had cast doubt upon Njonjo's loyalty.[21] The Minister's enemies now hinted that he was not only attempting to replace Kibaki as Vice-President but also preparing to challenge President Moi, and was probably behind the coup plot that had been forestalled by the Air Force revolt. Such behaviour could not be tolerated.

Almost as soon as the coup was defeated, Moi began to isolate the former Attorney-General. Njonjo's ambition and arrogance during his 17 years as the government's chief law officer had alienated many. Police investigators had provided the former Attorney-General with damning evidence about a host of senior politicians and businessmen, which he had not hesitated to deploy to secure his political ends. Once the President withdrew his protection from Njonjo, they had the chance to take their revenge.

In 1983, the Minister's rivals struck. Njonjo's fall was as swift and complete as his rise had appeared inevitable. Denounced as the agent of a foreign power – supposedly Britain – which was allegedly grooming him to replace Moi, radical Members of Parliament, led by Lawrence Sifuna, and conservative supporters of the former 'Change the Constitution' Movement rushed to denounce him whilst Njonjo was overseas. Mwangale, who himself had Vice-Presidential ambitions, led the assault. President Moi finished off his old ally by refusing to repudiate the attacks.[22] In the frenzied atmosphere, more and more Members of Parliament and KANU branch officials hurried to disassociate themselves from the disgraced Minister and to declare their support for the President. Flight from the Njonjo camp became a stampede when Moi called a snap general election, and set up a Judicial Commission of Enquiry into Njonjo's behaviour.[23]

The 1983 Election

The 1983 election was intended to purge the system of Njonjo supporters and to provide a new breed of political leaders who would owe their loyalty more directly to Moi, rather than through intermediaries whose ambitions could not be trusted. It did not, however, achieve all that Moi required. With the lowest turnover of any general election, the 1983 contest shattered Njonjo's power base, excluding the former Attorney-General from Parliament, and eliminating other key allies such as G. G. Kariuki and Joseph Kamotho.[24] Not all Njonjo's closest allies, however, were defeated. Charles Rubia survived in Nairobi, Stanley ole Oloitipitip won in Maasai Kajiado, and Finance Minister Arthur Magugu was victorious in Kiambu District's Githunguri constituency. Moi's confidence in his ability to dominate electoral politics without rigging was damaged; henceforth, he was to rely more upon the central and District party machinery as the key agents of political control.

Moi's purge of the Kalenjin political establishment continued in these polls: six of the 17 'landslide' victories occurred in the President's Kalenjin heartland and two seats in Baringo, the President's home District, were unopposed. Once again the number of 'dissident' MPs returned to Parliament declined, although a few managed to survive by jumping on the anti-Njonjo bandwagon. Kikuyu resentment at the changing face of politics surfaced clearly, however, in the Central Province results. While Njonjo's power was weakened in his home areas, it was not entirely destroyed. More importantly, the Kikuyu leaders who won victories in 1983 were far from the pliant figures for whom Moi had hoped. The Kikuyu electorate returned an educated and outspoken cohort of MPs, who were more willing than their predecessors to defend Kikuyu interests. A number of second-level politicians, who had served without distinction for a number of years, were defeated by educated, wealthy, better-connected technocrats, who had risen to the forefront of the civil service and the business world during the Kenyatta years. Many had been closely connected to the Kenyatta 'family' and the disbanded GEMA in the 1970s. Chairman of Kenya Breweries Kenneth Matiba's 1979 victory in Mbiri in Murang'a District, when he had defeated senior Cabinet Minister Julius Kiano, and Njenga Karume's victory in Kiambaa had pointed the way. Four years later, they were joined by several other experienced Kikuyu business leaders, who had entered politics in order to defend the economic position of the Kikuyu community. In Murang'a, John Michuki, formerly the executive chairman of the Kenya Commercial Bank and close ally of Kenneth Matiba, defeated Joseph Kamotho in the Kangema constituency. John Mateere Keriri, the former managing director of the Development Finance Company of Kenya, won Kirinyaga West. George Muhoho, an ex-priest and brother-in-law of President Kenyatta, easily carried Juja in Kiambu District and Francis Thuo, the ex-Chairman of the Nairobi Stock Exchange, won Kigumo. These new Kikuyu MPs were effective debaters, especially on economic issues, and after 1983 they actively attempted to stem the flow of funds from Central Province. In the new government formed after the 1983 election, several received Assistant Ministerial posts, and Moi was forced to appoint one of their leaders – Kenneth Matiba – to the Cabinet.[25]

President Moi's Search for Kikuyu Allies in the Wake of the Njonjo Affair

Despite the election results in Central Province, Njonjo's political demise appeared to have strengthened the regime, consolidating Moi's alliance with Abaluhya leaders, the representatives of Kenya's second largest ethnic group, and enabling the President to improve relations with a series of influential leaders whom the powerful Minister had alienated. Moi appeared to have enhanced his position by disgracing an over-mighty subject. The next 18 months, however, were to see a serious erosion in the President's position as the protracted Commission of Enquiry into Njonjo's affairs created a surge of sympathy for the disgraced politician throughout Kikuyuland.[26]

The Commission of Appeal Court judges, chaired by the Guyanese Mr Justice Miller, heard evidence for nearly a year. The 'prosecution' was led by Lee Muthoga, who later would be active in the National Election Monitoring Unit, while the defence was led by William Deverell, the son of a former colonial administrator, and Njonjo's protégé Paul Muite. In the end, after a year of revelations and media speculation, few charges were substantiated although Njonjo was implicated in the misuse of *Harambee* development funds and in an attempt by mercenaries to overthrow the government of Albert Renee in the Seychelles. Attempts to tie Njonjo to the various 1982 coup plots, however, failed. The disgraced Minister was also alleged to have been building a network of alliances with key members of the National Assembly in order to challenge Moi for the Presidency in a constitutional *coup d'état* within the KANU Parliamentary group. The details of the plot were never fully proved, although several formerly prominent MPs were expelled from the ruling party and political life.

The purges, the Judicial Tribunal into Njonjo's affairs, and the 1985 KANU elections destroyed the remainder of the former Attorney-General's support. They also ushered in a more authoritarian era in Kenyan politics. In the 18 months after the election, many of Njonjo's most senior associates were stripped of their positions, expelled from the National Assembly and thrown out of KANU. Among those expelled were Kajiado political boss, Cabinet Minister Stanley ole Oloitipitip, and the ex-Minister of State, G. G. Kariuki, who had represented Laikipia West since 1969. Joseph Kamotho, who had been Murang'a's sole Cabinet member from 1979 to 1983, and Jackson Kalweo from Meru District were both suspended indefinitely. The cyclical nature of Kenyan politics is revealed when one realises that nine years later the three senior Njonjo supporters still alive (Oloitipitip was dead) would once again carry KANU's hopes in 1992. Kariuki would re-emerge as the ruling party's candidate in Laikipia; Kamotho would be KANU's Secretary-General and the party's leading defender in Central Province; whilst Kalweo would win Igembe constituency for KANU. Most of the Njonjo supporters who fell from power with the disgraced Minister in 1983–4 are now back, serving as loyal supporters of President Moi.

Njonjo had been far from popular. Most Kikuyu outside south-west Kiambu, where Njonjo's father Josiah had been a prominent colonial chief for more than four decades, had regarded the ousted Attorney-General with suspicion. The former chief's son in his pin-stripe suits was judged too élitist, aloof and pro-British. The events of 1983 and 1984, however, convinced many that he was being made a scapegoat by anti-Kikuyu interests. Suddenly, Njonjo became a martyr. If the coup attempt had first revealed the regime's precariousness, the rapid growth of Kikuyu support for Njonjo exposed alarming weaknesses in the regime's support in Central Province. Moi's response was to shift Kikuyu alliances once again, turning gradually to rely upon two groups whom he had had little time for in the past, the Kenyatta-era Kiambu élite who had opposed his succession to the Presidency and the ex-Mau Mau veterans of Nakuru and Nyeri, who for 20 years had been politically marginalised by the victors in the 1950s conflict.

Even before Njonjo's downfall, immediately after the attempted *coup d'état*, Moi had started to improve relations with Kikuyu leaders in Central Province and Nakuru. The President attempted to court former GEMA leaders in order to reduce his dependence upon Kibaki and Njonjo, and to restore the confidence of the Kikuyu business community and the morale of senior civil servants and army officers. More politically imaginative, however, was his decision in 1983–4 to turn to the network of ex-Mau Mau fighters in order to secure the support of poor Kikuyus, who had gained little from Kenyatta's rule. Moi brought into the fold populist ex-Mau Mau leaders such as Kariuki Chotara in Nakuru District and Waruru Kanja in Nyeri, who soon emerged as Vice-President Kibaki's main local opponent.[27] The President's long-term aim was to mobilise the Kikuyu rural masses against the élites, who had done so well under Kenyatta but were now being squeezed by Moi's redirection of state patronage. Njonjo's disgrace initially appeared to underwrite these new alliances, since none of the leaders of these Kikuyu factions had been close to the ex-Minister. The President seemed to have secured the support of three important Kikuyu groups: the technocrats around Kibaki who had clashed with the disgraced Minister for the past five years, the Kenyatta family and the ex-Mau Mau. The factions, moreover, were divided among themselves and could not unite against the President.[28]

Moi's use of the ex-Mau Mau groups, however, caused him problems. Central Province politics could no longer simply be analysed in terms of the legacy of Mau Mau or in terms of pro- and anti-Mau Mau factions. Some former Mau Mau fighters had prospered, but most remained poor and landless and had become politically disillusioned. They had gained little from Kenyatta's supposed concentration of development on Central Province. President Moi also found it difficult in the deteriorating economic climate to fulfil their expectations. The more he relied upon Kariuki Chotara in Nakuru and Waruru Kanja in Nyeri to bolster his regime, the more they became discredited with the Kikuyu masses once it became clear that few new resources would be directed towards Central Province and the Kikuyu diaspora in Nakuru, Laikipia and elsewhere.

In addition, relations between Rift Valley and Central Province Mau Mau leaders quickly deteriorated. Many ex-fighters resented Chotara's rapid rise to political prominence, and were soon denouncing Chotara and his Naivasha associates for not sharing the money they had secured from President Moi, and for his growing authoritarianism. Chotara, nevertheless, became ever more powerful. He served as a nominated Member of Parliament from 1983 and as KANU Chairman in Nakuru District from 1979 until 1988, and became a member of the party's national disciplinary committee. During the mid-1980s, development resources poured into Naivasha, Chotara's base, transforming the sleepy market town into a hive of business activity with a host of plush new government offices, banks and businesses. Waruru Kanja and the Mau Mau leadership in Central Province, by contrast, remained politically isolated and were unable to dent the control of the Kikuyu establishment, especially in Nyeri where Vice-President Kibaki remained firmly in control. Thus, even before Chotara died in January 1988, President Moi's alliance with former Mau Mau fighters was collapsing.[29]

The Kenyatta family faction was also divided and unable to offer firm support to the regime. Its most conspicuous leaders were Kenyatta's nephews, Dr Njoroge Mungai in Nairobi and Ngengi Muigai, who had succeeded Kenyatta as Member of Parliament for Gatundu. Moi's attention particularly focused on Ngengi Muigai and former GEMA leader Njenga Karume. A self-made businessman who had been detained during the Mau Mau Emergency, Karume had made a fortune by securing the contract to distribute beer throughout southern Kiambu. By the late 1970s, Karume was a director of more than 70 companies, the leader of GEMA, and one of the key figures in the business world. Moreover, although he had defeated Koinange in 1979, Karume remained close to the Kenyatta family. Karume and Ngengi Muigai emerged in the mid-1980s as key political interlocutors between Moi, the Kiambu élite and the wider Kikuyu community. Although Muigai became an influential Assistant Minister and wealthy oil speculator, his political base in Thika town, the main concentration of voters in his constituency, remained precarious. Meanwhile, Dr Mungai had been defeated at the 1983 general election. The family, of course, still exerted considerable influence, but even in Kiambu its influence was declining, as its control of patronage evaporated. Many considered that its members were sacrificing the interests of the Kikuyu community in order to protect their own extensive business interests. After the advent of multi-party politics, they would pay for their pusillanimous attitude.

'L'État c'est Moi':[30] The Attempted Construction of a Party State, 1985–90

The President's dominance was reflected in the revived importance of the ruling party – possibly the most significant political development of the 1980s – which now provided the main means by which the government controlled political debate. According to the 1982 constitutional amendment establishing a *de jure* single-party state, only members of KANU could serve in Parliament. Unlike Kenyatta, who had relied upon the Provincial Administration, directly controlled from the Office of the President, to maintain control in the localities, Moi used the ruling party to monitor public sentiment and to suppress opposition. Local activists, as well as prominent political leaders, used it to silence their rivals and to secure their expulsion from KANU. The potential cost of political activity became much higher as ex-Ministers were disgraced and financially squeezed, while less powerful critics were jailed. Members of Parliament, in their desperation to survive, traded allegations and counter-charges with little regard for the frailty of freedom of discourse in Kenya.

Political strife in the districts became focused on control of the local party branch, which provided rivals with an institutional base from which to challenge sitting MPs. Since the 1960s Kenyatta's reliance on the Provincial Administration to control grassroots political activity had so lowered the temperature of local politics that by the mid-1970s the party had become almost completely moribund. KANU had only stirred back to life for local sub-branch and branch elections early in 1977, in preparation for national party elections later that year, but these had been cancelled when Kenyatta fell ill. Sixteen months later, Moi had assumed the Presidency. The new President had immediately called the KANU Delegates' Conference into session in order to consolidate his position. Njonjo and G. G. Kariuki had constructed a regional slate, uniting powerful interests from all eight provinces behind the President and Vice-President Kibaki. The 1978 KANU elections had provided the first hint that the ruling party would play a more important political role under Moi than during the Kenyatta era.[31]

Now, with Njonjo disgraced and Kibaki almost powerless, the President began in earnest to reconstruct the party and state in his own image, promoting Kalenjin and Abaluhya interests at the expense of Central Province. KANU headquarters purged Njonjo's supporters from local branches and established a national disciplinary committee to facilitate strict control of local activists and MPs. The 1985 KANU elections marked the beginning of the fifth phase of the Moi Presidency. Even more than the 1983 and 1988 general elections for the National Assembly, the 1985 and 1988 KANU elections enabled President Moi to remove the last remaining independent district bosses from the Kenyatta era. Henceforth, power became increasingly centred on Moi. For the first time in Kenya's history, the party became the main focus of authority, relegating MPs to a subordinate position. Only the President's close associates were elected to key positions within KANU's National Executive. Although Kibaki narrowly held on to the party Vice-Presidency, many other survivors from the Kenyatta era were swept away, including Robert Matano who was ousted as Secretary-General after 16 years in office, and Isaac Omolo-Okero, the Luo leader and National Chairman. The selection of figures such as David Okiki Amayo and Burudi Nabwera – both clients of Moi's who had lost their seats in the 1983 election and were no longer popular in their own areas – for the two leading positions within the KANU apparatus marked the final consolidation of the Moi state.[32]

The 1985 KANU elections revitalised branches which had long been inactive. Party membership rocketed as, throughout the country, a KANU membership card became near-essential for advancement in the civil service or access to loans and other state services. These elections also presaged the destruction of Parliament as an institution with a role in the political system, as legitimacy was deliberately and consciously shifted elsewhere. The party now became the focus of political conflict. This new stress on the party had little ideological content, however, apart from obedience to the wishes of the President, a fact encapsulated in the *Nyayo* (footsteps) philosophy, which gradually altered from its original meaning of Moi's following in the footsteps of Kenyatta to that of everyone else following in Moi's footsteps.[33] Ideology is important, however, in building a self-sustaining, cohesive political party, and one of the key weaknesses of this new search for authority and legitimacy was that whilst Kenyans pragmatically bowed their heads to this new order, they had no particular commitment to what it represented. When the time for change came, they were equally happy to abandon the bogus ideology of *Nyayoism*. The rise of the party also created new tensions, since control of the party machine became vitally important. KANU's resurgence even briefly reduced the prestige of the Provincial Administration, creating problems as local party leaders and District Commissioners struggled for primacy.

The Paranoid Style of Kenyan Politics

After the fall of Njonjo, no politician could follow an independent line or build national-level coalitions which were not entirely subordinated to the Office of the President. After only five years in office, Moi had become all-powerful. Kibaki clung to the Vice-Presidency, but was treated with suspicion and played a subsidiary role in the endless factional conflicts, while Njonjo was utterly disgraced. Once-powerful adversaries such as Njoroge Mungai now sought the President's patronage and political approval. The President was raised above the political battle which went on around him as rival factions competed to proclaim their loyalty to the regime and to *Nyayo*. Opposition to the will of the government was denounced as subversion, and independently minded MPs found it increasingly difficult to secure a hearing. Fighting between the different factions continued as the President emerged as the final court of appeal from the rulings of KANU's Disciplinary Committee. The language of political debate became debased as rival groups denounced one another. Policy differences largely ceased to matter: the only criterion for political survival was to have the President's support. Even the most established district bosses or 'big men' became less secure, while the cost of political failure became more draconian and the sole test of survival became absolute loyalty to the President.[34]

This increasingly repressive atmosphere became evident in September 1986, when delegates attending the ruling party's annual conference clashed with clergymen from the National Christian Council of Kenya (NCCK), especially Bishops of the Anglican Church of the Province of Kenya such as Henry Okullu of Maseno South and Alexander Muge of Eldoret. The Bishops opposed the party's recent decision to introduce 'queuing' to elect KANU MPs to the National Assembly. The new regulations required voters to queue publicly behind the candidate of their choice or his nominee at a series of gathering points, clearly revealing their political preferences to their neighbours and local officials. The new electoral process ensured that those who controlled the count, the Provincial Administration, could be directed to return the government's choice with much greater ease. The Law Society of Kenya (LSK), led by its Chairman, also defended Kenya's secret ballot against this new pressure for 'African democracy', claiming that the decision infringed voters' constitutional rights. Although Vice-President Kibaki was lukewarm about the new proposals, only Masinde Muliro (the ageing Abaluhya politician who had been elected to the colonial Legislative Council in 1958 and had served as Treasurer of KADU from 1960 to 1964), Charles Rubia (the first African Mayor of Nairobi and a Cabinet Minister from 1979 to 1983) and Assistant Minister of Labour Kimani wa Nyoike (a former leader of the Kenya Teachers' Union) dared to defend publicly the secret ballot and the regime's clerical critics. The ruling party, however, had already employed 'queuing' in its 1985 KANU elections and asserted that the system's critics had been given ample opportunity to express their doubts.[35] Refusing to back down or to introduce exemptions for civil servants and clergymen, KANU stalwarts condemned defenders of the secret ballot as subversives in the pay of foreign governments who were unwilling to accept the primacy of the ruling party. Prominent members of the Presbyterian Church and the Chairman of the LSK were also denounced.[36]

The new policy was symptomatic of the growing authoritarianism of the Kenyan government, which can be characterised as a new 'paranoid style' of Kenyan politics. KANU leaders asserted the political primacy of the party over all other institutions in Kenya, including Parliament and the judiciary. As Jennifer Widner has pointed out, Kenya was becoming – in so far as its resources permitted – a party state.[37] In the same period, Parliament revised the constitution, abandoned the secret ballot, and curtailed the autonomy of the judiciary and of the Auditor-General. The freedom of the press was reduced and intellectuals harassed and gaoled for subversion. Political discourse was more constrained than ever before.

Whether cause or effect, the 1986–7 period was also one in which a subversive organisation, known as *Mwakenya,* surfaced for the first time, as the state engaged in a wave of detentions, arrests and imprisonment of alleged subversives involved in this movement. Whether this organisation ever had any real importance is questionable, since it did little to harass the state, but it provided a convenient excuse to crack down on independent political activity. The mid-1980s was also a period in which two new figures emerged as key players in the political game: Minister for Energy Nicholas Biwott, and Simeon Nyachae, Chief Secretary and Head of the Civil Service. Biwott, from Elgeyo-Marakwet, a quiet backroom assistant to the President for many years and MP for a constituency next to his own, emerged by the mid-1980s as probably the second most powerful man in the country. His political acumen was widely respected and he appeared to enjoy Moi's unquestioned trust in a way that only Koinange had with President Kenyatta.[38] His only real rival was a very different kind of man: Simeon Nyachae was a senior civil servant of renowned abilities from Kisii District, who had risen through merit to serve as the most powerful official in the land as Head of the Civil Service and Secretary to the Cabinet. He too was widely respected and at the height of his power in this period could treat Cabinet Ministers with scarcely veiled contempt.[39]

The Impact of Election 'Rigging' on the Political Process

For 15 years, general elections during the Kenyatta era had provided a real means by which ordinary voters could express their judgement on local MPs. In all the country's post-independence elections, many Cabinet Ministers and Assistant Ministers had lost their seats, as well as large numbers of backbenchers. Incumbents tended to do better than challengers because sitting Members could campaign on their development records, played an important role in local life and could secure support from national coalitions to assist them gain re-election. Despite these advantages, the proportion of votes received by incumbents fell after they were first elected, as their support eroded. Voters demonstrated considerable dissatisfaction with MPs who rarely visited their constituencies.[40] Ministers and Assistant Ministers, with greater access to state patronage, were far more successful at securing re-election than ordinary backbenchers. Three quarters of Cabinet Ministers were re-elected in 1969, and in 1983 the proportion rose to more than four fifths. On average, however, Kenyan Members of Parliament remained in office for only 7.2 years.[41]

This volatility highlights two characteristic features of Kenyan politics in the Kenyatta and early Moi years. The first is the lack of stable political factions, leading to a pattern of alternation and renewal of the élite. The second, far more important, is the substantial effect that ordinary voters had on the political process through their ability to judge harshly the performance of all but the President. Whether individual victories or defeats had much effect on policy issues is unclear (individual Ministers had particular views on particular issues facing the government, but they did not tend to campaign on them openly). The electoral process, however, tied the decision-making élite tightly to peasant expectations, and to winning and rewarding their loyalty by their ability to develop their constituencies. This process helped maintain the existing pattern of regional, and therefore ethnic, competition for resources. It favoured those who were already wealthy and powerful, since their greater financial strength, organisational acumen and personal authority were key in persuading voters that they would be more effective local patrons.[42] It also placed a check upon the excesses of the élite, forcing them to conceal more extreme corrupt practices for risk of being seen to be feathering their own nests, and required them to share their wealth with their constituents in numerous different ways. Neo-patrimonialism after independence represented in many ways a reconstruction of the principles of 'moral ethnicity'.

One of the most obvious results of the new authority of Moi, and of the Office of the President, over all aspects of political life, was the destruction of the National Assembly as an independent institution and therefore as a legitimising tool for the state. Elections throughout the 1960s and 1970s had helped to legitimise the regime, symbolising participation in a modern 'democratic' state. Kenyans believed that they could change their leaders through the political process, whilst elections sublimated hostility to the regime by enabling electors to throw out the President's allies. After President Moi came to power, however, elections became increasingly expensive and subject to rigging.[43]

Before Kenyatta's death, local administrators had sometimes intervened to prevent the election of a government critic, but systematic rigging of the result in a sizeable number of constituencies was unknown. The Provincial Administration, which oversaw elections and acted as Returning Officers at the count, had never been neutral, but it became more and more overtly partisan during the 1980s. KANU headquarters denied candidates unpopular with the regime clearance, as had happened on a small scale under Kenyatta, and declared others bankrupt by calling in government guaranteed loans. 'Anti-establishment' candidates who did manage to secure clearance and to present their nomination papers to the Returning Officer found it difficult to secure permission to hold political meetings, or found that the population had been called to compulsory locational *barazas* (assemblies) at exactly the time their meetings had been licensed, or that their meetings were cancelled at the last moment or broken up by Administration *askaris*. Government critics rarely enjoyed the financial resources of regime supporters or influential Ministers, who liberally handed out large sums of money and could transport voters wholesale from their home areas to register and vote. Local chiefs, the lowest rung of the Administrative hierarchy, frequently campaigned for their favoured candidate, as in the Kakamega constituency of influential Abaluhya Cabinet Minister Moses Mudavadi, President Moi's brother-in-law, in 1983 and 1988.

Moi's intervention in the politics of Nandi and Kericho Districts, the most developed Kalenjin areas, aroused considerable resentment. Politicians of long standing, such as Seroney and Taita Towett, were forced out as early as 1979 because they had failed to support Moi in the mid-1970s. Moi's victory was incomplete, however, as the new MPs retained some independence. Baton-wielding GSU troops had to be deployed once more in 1983 in Nandi District to ensure the victory of Moi's chosen slate, including his old school friend Stanley arap Metto in Mosop. This shocked Alexander Muge, the newly elected Bishop of Eldoret, whose condemnation of the malpractice incurred arap Metto's enmity, a feud which was to be of some importance in the events of 1990–1. Election rigging increased considerably as the Office of the President and members of the President's inner circle, most notably the then Energy Minister Nicholas Biwott and Chief Secretary Nyachae, targeted their rivals in the ruling party and opponents within the Cabinet.[44] Throughout Moi's first decade in power, however, the use of coercion remained rare. The President preferred to use cash to cement his alliances.

The 1988 General Election: Biwott's Parliament

The 1988 election introduced a new level of electoral malpractice into Kenyan politics, one which was to presage the demise of the ruling party. Key figures in the government were determined that they would control the new Assembly and silence their critics for good. The elections were fought under the new 1986 queue voting system, in which KANU party members voted in public for their candidate by lining up behind his or her representative. This 'primary' was to be followed by a run-off under the secret ballot system between the top two or three candidates only if no candidate won over 70 per cent of the vote. This system greatly facilitated voter intimidation and election malpractices. Queuing ensured that there were no embarrassing ballot papers left over after the poll and Returning Officers – the local District Commissioners – could merely declare a result, however fraudulent, while candidates who secured more than 70 per cent of the primary vote did not have to submit to the ignominy of a secret ballot. As Moi himself acknowledged later, 'the implementation of the queuing system of voting left a lot to be desired'.[45]

The result in 1988 was a rigged and shambolic contest in which at least one third of the electoral contests (over 60 seats) were rigged and manipulated blatantly to ensure that the 'right' candidate won.[46] Once more much of the malpractice was concentrated in the Kalenjin areas. In Nandi Henry Kosgey, who had been rigged in against Seroney in 1979, was rigged out nine years later. The Returning Officer (the District Commissioner) announced that the Minister's opponent, Kimunai arap Sego, had secured 70.1 per cent of the queue vote. Although Nandi voters had resented Seroney's removal in 1979, Kosgey had proved himself an effective Member of Parliament and by the mid-1980s had become quite popular, and correspondingly more independent. Now the President's henchmen determined to replace him with a more pliable representative. Several other first-round results in the Kalenjin areas and in the constituencies of known dissidents were equally dubious. In Mosop, Robert Tanui got 73.8 per cent against another Nandi problem politician, Stanley arap Metto, who, although close to the President, had now fallen out of favour with the new Kalenjin élites.[47]

In Kikuyuland, Kimani wa Nyoike and Charles Rubia – two of the two most independent-minded Members of Parliament – were 'defeated', despite the fact that both were extremely popular with their constituents. Rubia was rigged out at the primary stage in his city centre Nairobi constituency of Starehe, where Kiruhi Kimondo was announced to have secured 70.5 per cent on the first ballot. According to reports, the Returning Officer announced two different sets of results until Rubia intervened to point out that the officials had miscalculated and Kimondo's vote was still less than 70 per cent. Rubia then suggested that they change the result yet again in order to spare him the farce of having to contest an equally rigged secret ballot. The Returning Officer obliged.[48] In Kinangop constituency, Kimani Wa Nyoike lost the queuing primary when his opponent was announced as the winner with 72.9 per cent of the vote. Shortly afterwards the former Assistant Minister was arrested, charged with being in contact with the subversive National Liberation Movement and gaoled.[49] Joshua Angatia, from Elijah Mwangole's fiefdom of Kakamega, another backbench maverick, soon followed them out of the National Assembly when he was unseated in an election petition, having survived the election with a majority of seven. He lost the ensuing by-election, which was rigged. Kenneth Matiba, big businessman, trouble-shooting Minister and the most outspoken defender of Kikuyu interests within the Cabinet, even went so far as to employ a helicopter and video camera to take photographs of the queues of voters in his Kiharu constituency: the video was to be released to the international press if the District Commissioner declared his opponent the winner. The Rt. Rev. David Gitari, the Anglican Bishop of Mount Kenya East, whose diocese covers Kirinyaga District, also took video photographs of the lines of queuing voters.

Subsequent by-elections in Butere in 1988 and Kiharu in 1989 were no better. In the former, the approved candidate's vote was multiplied by ten, giving a near 100 per cent turn-out, in order to remove the enormously popular maverick politician Martin Shikuku, the 'people's watchman', whose independent political line had proved a constant irritation to the President's team.[50] The latter poll was of even more importance. It was occasioned by the September 1988 KANU elections, which followed soon after the general election. In this, the ruling party's inner core had consolidated their successes and organised equally extensive abuses, which struck new blows at the heart of the Kikuyu business establishment. Amongst other abuses, Kenneth Matiba was openly cheated out of his local party position. He protested and re-runs were held in December. When he was defeated again, in an unprecedented move he resigned from the government and was immediately drummed out of the party and Parliament. The resulting by-election saw a contest between the man Matiba had defeated in 1979, the well-respected ex-Minister Dr Julius Kiano, and a political neophyte. Unsurprisingly, the queue voting saw a massive victory for Kiano, the results of which were photographed by a local reporter before they were reversed by the Returning Officer (Kiano was seen as too experienced and independent a figure), converting a victory for Kiano of

Photo 3.1 The real results of the Kiharu by-election, showing Dr Kiano, the loser, with 92.46 per cent of the vote.
Courtesy of Nation Group Newspapers

9,566 to 780 into a defeat by 2,000 to 11,000 (see Photo 3.1).[51]

Although the 1988 polls were a triumph for the state over its imagined and real opponents, they also laid the groundwork for its downfall. The adoption of queue voting symbolised the end of the National Assembly as any form of watchdog on the executive. The abuses were so extensive that the legitimacy of the Assembly was almost destroyed in the minds of Kenyans, and the state was seen even more clearly as concerned only with its own interests, at the expense of those of the ordinary people. Henceforth, the Assembly served as little more than an impotent talking shop. MPs were seen as tools of the centre, not local representatives, because their success was due to state rigging, not popular support. As tools of the centre, their commitment to the patron–client system was severely weakened.[52] Queuing destroyed the confidence of ordinary people in the political process, and popular participation in politics plummeted. Many people refused to register in 1988, and turn-out in the KANU primary in many constituencies was extremely low. Many educated Kenyans referred to them as a 'sham' and a 'farce'. The number of registered voters fell by nearly 1.2 million compared with the 1983 general election. This anger at the destruction of their neo-democratic heritage – their right to choose their leaders, if not change what they did once in office – was an important inspiration behind the popular protests of 1990–1. The 1988 elections also unseated many senior politicians with considerable popular support, persuading them that single-party electoral politics in the new era was a dangerous profession. Many of the leaders of the opposition in the 1990s were KANU leaders who had been defeated in these 1988 polls.

The Breakdown of Neo-Patrimonialism

The result of Moi's accession, the increasing centralisation of political activity and the economic and demographic problems the country experienced was the destruction of the patronage networks and stable clientage structures which the Kenyatta era had built. Kenyatta had worked with and helped develop a bottom-up style of political activity, in which leaders had to secure local political legitimacy in order to win a place at the national table. He worked with, respected and thereby coopted the leaders of the country's ethnic sub-nationalist movements, bringing powerful individuals such as African People's Party leader Paul Ngei, Ronald Ngala and Masinde Muliro of KADU, and district bosses such as Jackson Angaine of Meru into the government. Kenyatta had only questioned his Ministers' local authority in exceptional circumstances. Factional strife throughout the Kenyatta era, consequently, had been focused largely upon Parliament. Most prominent politicians had controlled their constituencies and local party branches, and local factional rivalries had been fought out on County Councils and in agricultural cooperatives rather than within KANU. Thus the patronage system remained exceptionally stable throughout the Kenyatta era. Ministers appointed to the Cabinet remained in office for long periods, some for 15 years or more. Few resigned or were dropped. From 1966–9 and again after the first post-independence elections in 1969, the distribution of Cabinet portfolios was exceptionally stable. Masinde Muliro was the only Minister to be sacked in the entire 15 years, and only four resigned.[53]

In contrast, Moi tended to favour the reverse approach, in which politicians, and Ministers particularly, were centrally appointed representatives of the state, a transmission belt to ensure that the will of central government was enacted in the regions. Provincial 'big men' were no longer respected as powerful political bosses in their own right, whose support had to be maintained and rewarded by a flow of patronage to their clients.[54] As a result, under Moi, Ministers have been promoted, demoted and disgraced with increasing frequency. Fourteen Ministers were sacked between 1982 and 1990, and more 'not reappointed' after the elections (see Table 3.2). The much more rapid turnover of Ministers drastically reduced the office's prestige and power in relation to the Provincial Administration, and particularly in comparison with the rising prestige and power of KANU headquarters. Real power no longer necessarily corresponded with Ministerial position, as the continued prominence of Sharrif Nassir, Assistant Minister and Mombasa KANU Chairman, has long indicated. In the three years between the formation of the 'new look' 34-member Cabinet in 1988 and December 1991, nine Ministers were sacked or resigned. Four of these were expelled from KANU and, therefore, the Assembly, and one of the four – Matiba – was detained. Two more, including murdered Foreign Minister Robert Ouko, died, and one – long-time political survivor Paul Ngei – lost his Ministerial position and seat in

Table 3.2 Ministerial Dismissals 1963–91

Year	Sackings	Not reappointed after general election	Forced resignations	Voluntary resignations
1963				
1964				
1965				
1966				Achieng' Oneko Odinga, Murumbi
1967				
1968				
1969				
1970				McKenzie
1971				
1972				
1973				
1974				
1975	Muliro			
1976				
1977				
1978				
1979				
1980				Njonjo
1981			Karugu	
1982	Kamere, Oloo-Aringo			
1983		Oloitipitip, Onyonka, Rubia	Njonjo	
1984	Mango			
1985	M'Mbijiwe Matano			
1986				
1987	Omamo			
1988	Mwamunga	Nyakiamo, Omanga, Mwendwa		
1989	Kitele, Sego, Koech		Karanja	Matiba
1990	Kanja, Makau		Okondo	
1991			Muli	

the National Assembly because of bankruptcy. The governing structure was clearly in crisis, as the traditional role of the Minister as a long-term District boss, who secured rewards for his ethnic group in return for their support for the regime, collapsed.

Economic Troubles

The political sensitivity of Moi and KANU and the decline of stable district alliances was also a response to increasing economic pressure. Kenya's population by the late 1980s was four times larger than at independence and the time bought by land consolidation schemes and the development of smallholder cash crop cultivation had been exhausted. Kenya faced an acute demographic crisis with a population growth rate of 4.2 per cent, one of the highest in Africa. Pressure on the land in the rural areas was growing constantly, while thousands were flocking every year to Nairobi and, increasingly, to secondary towns such as Machakos, Eldoret and Kitale – all of which now had populations of over 100,000. Every year more than 300,000 children graduated from school, of whom less than 7 per cent could secure a job in the wage sector. For most of the 1980s, Kenya's GDP *per capita* remained static or declined as industrial production stagnated and foreign exchange earnings from coffee, tea and tourism fell. As a result, the government came under intense pressure from the World Bank and the International Monetary Fund to accept their structural adjustment prescriptions.

This demographic explosion intensified competition for state resources. The depleted supply of patronage reduced the power of local district bosses, who found it difficult to deliver the patronage needed to protect their positions, and undermined the stable hierarchies of the Kenyatta era. The state remained, as in most other African countries, the main employer for secondary school leavers and university graduates, and a key source of patronage for politicians and senior civil servants. The Directorate of Personnel Management, for example, revealed that the establishment of central government Ministries numbered 111,746, compared with the approved figure of 85,528. The total civil service workforce had grown from 65,932 in 1967–8 to 158,977 in 1979, and to 270,005 by 1990. The *Weekly Review* echoed the widely voiced complaint that:

> It is as a result of the recurrent costs financing crisis that has swept through government ministries that roads are poorly maintained, supplies of equipment in hospitals are short, and government offices lack basic requirements ... and health centres in rural areas are often closed because of the lack of medical supplies.[55]

The problem stemmed in part from the Moi government's tripartite agreement with the trades union and Kenyan employers in 1979–81, which had required both the public and private sectors to increase employment by 10 per cent. As a result, civil service numbers increased by 12 per cent in 1980 and 1981, and continued to rise rapidly throughout the 1980s. Despite pressure since the early 1980s from the IMF to reduce numbers, the Kenyan government had taken little action.[56]

Sessional Paper No. 1 of 1986 on Economic Management and Renewed Growth acknowledged that civil service employment could not continue to expand at the rate of 7.4 per cent as over the previous decade, but the expansion of the secondary school system and the dramatic growth of the universities – from 7,036 students in 1989 to 21,488 in 1990 – maintained the pressure upon the government to absorb school- and university-leavers in the civil service. The Kenyan government's agreement with international financial institutions in 1990 to reduce salaries and the number employed in the civil service, no longer guaranteeing employment to university graduates as civil servants or teachers, to stop recruitment and upgrading positions without the agreement of the Treasury, and to hold civil service and teachers' salary increases to 4 per cent (below the level of inflation which was running at 30 per cent), provoked outrage among students and teachers, and protests in the streets of Nairobi. These jobs in the lower levels of the civil service and the teaching profession enabled the government to pacify university graduates who could not be absorbed by the private sector, while positions in the parastatal hierarchy enabled the regime to satisfy more important clients.[57]

The logic of neo-patrimonialism precluded the government from tackling problems of overstaffing or the inefficiency and corruption of the parastatal sector without seriously damaging its own political base. Attempts to revive the country's main export crops – coffee and tea – and to pay a higher proportion of international commodity prices to rural producers, moreover, would have benefited primarily the Kikuyu populated areas, which were main centres of cash crop production, and rewarded those most hostile to the regime. Key figures in the government, including Nicholas Biwott and Elijah Mwangale, were determined that the influence of the Kikuyu should not be revived. Consequently, Kenya's balance of payments position declined as rural small-holders retreated to subsistence production or marketed food crops, which could be sold in Nairobi and other nearby urban centres rather than for export. With the gradual withdrawal of the Kikuyu peasantry from cash crop production, the foreign exchange earnings of the state also became more constrained.

Divide and Rule

Moi exacerbated this situation by pursuing a policy of divide-and-rule among the political élite. As soon as local leaders developed their own constituency, and became capable of speaking with an independent voice, they were sacked or otherwise humbled, and replaced by other, less independent persons. This process intensified after the 1988 election, when Moi picked ex-Vice Chancellor of the University of Nairobi Josephat Karanja, an élitist Kikuyu without extensive local support, as his new Vice-President. Karanja had been 'elected' in Nairobi's Mathare seat in 1988 on a 6 per cent turnout in the queue voting. After only one year, Karanja proved too independent or too arrogant, and he was brought down in a classic campaign of innuendo and attacks by minor political figures, with the sanction of Moi and Biwott. It ended with Karanja's resignation and his expulsion from the party, along with several colleagues.[58]

As the size of the Cabinet expanded from 23 under Kenyatta to 34 in 1988, its quality declined. Few old-style District bosses were represented. Indeed, apart from Biwott, Elijah Mwangale in Western Province and former Vice-President Mwai Kibaki, who was now demoted to Minister of Health, Moi seemed to favour relatively inexperienced individuals, whose political position depended on his patronage, and who had neither political nor administrative experience, financial wealth nor executive backgrounds. Most came from the Kalenjin and Abaluhya areas, the core of Moi's new order. The frequent movement of subordinates ensured that no one could build up sufficient support to challenge Moi's authority or to establish an independent patronage network. The one exception was Biwott, who remained as Energy Minister throughout the period 1982–91. From this position, he built a lucrative business empire in collaboration with the President, becoming a major petrol retailer through Kobil, and established his own protective network within the civil service and the Special Branch. Biwott's position in the regime was unique, a function of his ability, Kalenjin origins, loyalty to Moi and willingness to play the 'backroom boy' to Moi's front-man. Otherwise, Moi deliberately sought to divide responsibility and power between mere figureheads, retaining few relatively independent power brokers. Over time, some leaders, such as Dr Robert Ouko in Kisumu and Henry Kosgey in Nandi District developed an independent stature, but their new popularity reduced their influence with the President rather than enhanced it. Kosgey lost his Parliamentary seat in 1988, while Ouko's independence seems to have contributed to his subsequent death.

Moi's concern that his colleagues were tempted to supplant him may in fact have been justified, as was shown by the Njonjo affair in the early 1980s. This centrally organised divide-and-rule policy clearly contributed to a narrowing of the regime's political base during the 1980s, however, gradually alienating group after group without securing the stable support of replacements. This was compounded by the economic downturn which began almost as soon as Moi had taken office. Moi's rule had commenced with the doubling of the price of oil, which by the end of 1980 was absorbing 50 per cent of Kenya's foreign exchange earnings, and with falling cash crop prices and a decline in tourist revenue. The President also continued to encounter strong opposition from the Kikuyu-dominated business world and the main Churches to his policies. Even the civil service was less than enthusiastic.

Kenya's mounting economic problems and the resulting shortage of resources also increased factional strife, further undermining the authority of district bosses. The problem was most acute in Central Province, which was hardest hit by the collapse of international coffee prices following the 1976–8 boom, and by the new regime's direction of government and private investment to the Kalenjin and Abaluhya areas. The competition for resources was exacerbated by President Moi's determined attempt to restructure central government, reducing the claims of Central Province, while encouraging private capital, led by the Kenya Commercial Bank, to invest in areas neglected under Kenyatta, especially Moi's own Baringo District and the wider Kalenjin region. The construction of a new Kalenjin-centric state, based upon a precarious alliance between the President's Kalenjin and Elijah Mwangale's Abaluhya ethnic groups, plus some Gusii, Kamba and the geographically and economically marginal pastoral areas, intensified the competition for resources. These changes produced a kaleidoscopic competition or scramble among local political patrons for resources to confirm their popular authority, creating a merry-go-round struggle for office and patronage, which permeated the heart of the state.

Conclusion

As electoral rigging and malpractice increased during the 1980s, and as the centre's alliance with powerful district bosses collapsed, the President's position became more precarious and, in response, the regime became more autocratic. At the same time, the reconstruction of the country's political economy at the expense of the Kikuyu was continuing, arousing ever more opposition. It could not dislodge the Kikuyu from their economic pre-eminence, however. Rather, it overlaid the pyramid of economic power, dominated by the 'GEMA tribes', with a veneer of Kalenjin and Asian businessmen and parastatal leaders, becoming rich on government contracts and state positions. The result was a deep-seated and widespread dissatisfaction amongst Kenya's largest and most important communities. Despite this, in the main, they remained quiet. The Kikuyu knew too well the risks of overt opposition to the state. KANU provided the main mechanism with which to suppress dissent, but those who persisted in their criticism, ranging from powerless young intellectuals at the university and other recent graduates in the underground *Mwakenya* movement to influential politicians like Kimani wa Nyoike, were detained or imprisoned.[59]

The costs of political and business life rose, both in terms of the money needed to maintain an independent position when facing state-financed opponents, and the risks associated with political disgrace. For the inner circle, however, the financial rewards increased as corruption at the highest levels of government grew. Biwott was rumoured to be involved in various corrupt deals and dubious business activities, as were President Moi and his four sons. The regime increasingly seemed to depend upon popular apathy and fear of the security forces, with the active support only of Kalenjin and Abaluhya regions, who were profiting most visibly from the regime, and a selection of favoured military and political leaders, many of them unpopular in their home districts or from politically marginal regions. As the regime became more authoritarian after 1985, its popular base diminished among the country's three main ethnic groups. Its position was weakest in Central Province and Nairobi, where the direction of resources away from Kikuyu-controlled businesses and the effects of the difficult economic situation were most strongly felt. Kikuyu politicians found that they had less and less to offer as they became further removed from the inner circle of the Moi regime. President Moi actively encouraged the suspicion of Kenya's other communities towards the Kikuyu. The long years of Kikuyu hegemony in the 1960s and 1970s had sown seeds of suspicion and resentment among other Kenyans. Thus, however unpopular Moi became, he had one tremendous advantage – that he came from a minority community, not from the Kikuyu. By contrast, most of the regime's critics came from Central Province, reflecting a divide which was to dominate the struggle for change, and which also was to hold the seeds of the opposition's final defeat.

Notes

1 C. P. W. Hornsby, 'The Role of the Member of Parliament in Kenya, 1969–83', unpublished D.Phil. thesis, Oxford University, 1985, *passim.*

2 *Economist* Intelligence Unit, Quarterly Country Reports, Kenya, 1978 to 1982.

3 Republic of Kenya, *Kenya Population Census*, 1989, volume 1, Central Bureau of Statistics, Office of the Vice President, Ministry of Planning and National Development, March 1994, calculated that 21,544,329 Kenyans were counted in the August 1989 census. See also, World Bank, *Kenya: Population and Development*, Africa Regional Office, World Bank, Washington D.C., 1980, *passim;* and *Accelerated Development in Sub-Saharan Africa: An Agenda for Action,* Africa Regional Office, World Bank, Washington, D.C., 1981, pp. 112–14.

4 David Throup, 'The Construction and Destruction of the Kenyatta State' in M. G. Schatzberg (ed.), *The Political Economy of Kenya,* pp. 57–64. One informant pungently expressed the opinion that development resources were taken away from Central Province to build roads in Baringo 'for cows to sleep on'.

5 *Ibid.,* pp. 52–67. See also Jennifer A. Widner, *The Rise of a Party-State in Kenya,* pp. 130–61.

6 *Weekly Review,* Nairobi, 19 October 1979, pp. 3–4.

7 David Throup, 'The Construction and Destruction of the Kenyatta State', pp. 43–6. See also C. Sanger and J. Nottingham, 'The Kenya general election of 1963', *Journal of Modern African Studies,* vol. 2, no. 1 (1964), pp. 20–3.

8 David Throup, 'The Construction and Destruction of the Kenyatta State', pp. 35–6, 43–50 and 52–70; *Weekly Review,* Nairobi, 10 November 1979, pp. 9–10 and p. 19; and several informants from Nandi District.

9 *Weekly Review,* Nairobi, 15 September 1978, pp. 2–6; 6 October 1978, pp. 9–13; and 13 October 1978, pp. 10–17.

10 Jennifer A. Widner, *The Rise of a Party-State in Kenya,* pp. 133–7.

11 *Weekly Review,* Nairobi, 25 April 1980, p. 5. Njonjo had long wanted to enter politics, but Kenyatta had told him to wait when he had requested permission to contest a Kikuyu constituency in 1974.

12 Jennifer A. Widner, *The Rise of a Party-State in Kenya,* pp. 137–43.

13 *Weekly Review,* 5 March 1982, pp. 4–5. G. G. Kariuki was apparently so incensed at his transfer that he removed all the furniture, even the carpets, from his office in the Office of the President, when he was moved to Lands and Settlement.

14 *Ibid.* Magugu proved a failure as Finance Minister, demonstrating little understanding of the complex economic problems confronting the regime. He even failed to deliver the 1983 Budget on time, having to postpone its Parliamentary presentation until certain financial details were finalised.

15 Jennifer A. Widner, *The Rise of a Party-State in Kenya,* pp. 137–43; and Kiraitu Murungi, 'Forms and Illusions of Democracy in Africa's One-Party States', paper presented as the Seminar on Human Rights Research, Harvard Law School, Cambridge, Massachusetts, May 1991, quoted in Widner, p. 145.

16 David Throup, 'The Construction and Destruction of the Kenyatta State', pp. 64–5. See also the extensive coverage in the Kenyan media, especially, *Weekly Review,* 6 August 1982, pp. 3–17; 13 August,1982, pp. 8–16; 20 August 1982, pp. 4–10; 27 August 1982, pp. 3–7; 3 September 1982, pp. 3–4; and 14 January 1983, pp. 13–18; and *Viva Magazine,* August 1982, pp. 3–22. *Africa Confidential,* London, 25 August 1982, pp. 1–3 and *Race and Class,* vol. 24, no. 3 (1983), pp. 221–326 contain interesting analyses of the *coup d'état* and the political situation in Kenya. From this time on, Njonjo no longer had unrestricted access to the President.

17 *Weekly Review,* 20 August 1982, pp. 4–8; and 3 September 1982, pp. 3–7.

18 David Throup, 'The Construction and Destruction of the Kenyatta State', pp. 65–7; and *Africa Confidential,* London, 2 January 1985, p. 7; 14 August 1985, p. 8; and 9 April 1986, p. 2. Mohammed's brother Maalim Mohammed became MP for Dujis and Minister of State in the Office of the President in 1983. Lengees's brother also became MP for Samburu West, ensuring the army's political representation in the ruling circles.

19 *Ibid.*

20 *Africa Confidential,* London, 2 January 1985, p. 7.

21 David Throup, 'The Construction and Destruction of the Kenyatta State'. See also Kate

Currie and Larry Ray, 'State and Class in Kenya: Notes on the Cohesion of the Ruling Class', *Journal of Modern African Studies*, vol. 22, no. 4 (1984), pp. 559–93; and 'The Pambana of August: – Kenya's Abortive Coup', *Political Quarterly*, vol. 57, no. 1 (1986), pp. 47–59.

22 David Throup, 'The Construction and Destruction of the Kenyatta State' pp. 67–8; Jennifer A. Widner, *The Rise of a Party-State in Kenya*, pp. 147–9. See also *Weekly Review*, 22 April 1983, pp. 4–5; 6 May 1983, pp. 4–5; 20 May 1983, pp. 4–13; and 27 May 1983, pp. 4–7 and 12–15; and *Financial Times*, London, 14 May 1983, p. 2; 16 May 1983, p. 2; and 17 May 1983, p. 4.

23 David Throup, 'The Construction and Destruction of the Kenyatta State', pp. 68–70; Jennifer A. Widner, *The Rise of a Party-State in Kenya*, pp. 147–9.

24 *Weekly Review*, 23 September 1983, pp. 3–9; 30 September 1983, pp. 3–9; and 28 October 1983, pp. 3–6. Electoral malpractice was near certain in some cases, particularly in G. G. Kariuki's Laikipia West seat.

25 *Ibid.*

26 David Throup, 'The Construction and Destruction of the Kenyatta State', pp. 68–70.

27 *Ibid.*, pp. 69–70; and Jennifer A. Widner, *The Rise of a Party-State in Kenya*, pp. 148–9. Chotara, a Kikuyu from Murang'a District, was a Mau Mau fighter who had been detained for several years. He was the man who attempted to kill Kenyatta whilst in detention, and he only emerged as a significant political figure after Moi's accession.

28 *Ibid.* Kanja's ex-Mau Mau supporters in Nyeri, for example, were battling Kibaki's allies for control of the local KANU branch, and opposed the dominant position enjoyed by Kiambu under Kenyatta.

29 *Weekly Review*, 28 February 1986, pp. 3–4 and 6–7; 4 April 1986, pp. 4–7; 18 April 1987, pp. 8–9; 27 June 1986, pp. 3–4; and 25 July 1986, pp. 3–5; and *Africa Confidential*, London, 9 April 1986, pp. 1–3.

30 The phrase appears to have been first used by Sholto Cross in his article, 'L'État c'est Moi: Political Transition and the Kenya general election of 1979', Discussion Paper No. 66, University of East Anglia, April 1983.

31 David Throup, 'Elections and Political Legitimacy in Kenya', Africa, vol. 63, no. 3 (1993), pp. 383–4.

32 Jennifer A. Widner, *The Rise of a Party-State in Kenya*, pp. 150–97.

33 Daniel T. arap Moi, *Kenya African Nationalism: Nyayo Philosophy and Principles*, Macmillan, London, 1986, *passim*, ; and George I. Godia, *Understanding Nyayo: Principles and Policies in Contemporary Kenya*, Transafrica, Nairobi, 1984. See also Daniel arap Moi, *Transition and Continuity in Kenya*, selected speeches, East Africa Publishing House, Nairobi, 1979; and *Continuity and Consolidation in Kenya*, selected speeches, East Africa Publishing House, Nairobi, 1982; and G. P. Benson, 'Ideological Politics versus Biblical Hermeneutics: Kenya's Protestant Churches and the Nyayo State', in Holger Bernt Hansen and Michael Twaddle (eds), *Religion and Politics in East Africa*, James Currey, London, 1995, pp. 177–99.

34 It is notable that some of the most robust denunciations of Moi's critics were made by future opposition leaders, such as Josephat Karanja (later of FORD-Asili), John Keen (who became Secretary-General of the DP) and Peter Oloo-Aringo (who was the first Minister to defect to FORD-Kenya). Jennifer A. Widner, *The Rise of a Party-State in Kenya*, pp. 150–97; and David Throup, 'Elections and Political Legitimacy in Kenya', *Africa*, vol. 63, no. 3 (1993), pp. 383–9.

35 David Throup, 'Render unto Caesar the Things that are Caesar's: The Politics of Church–State Conflict in Kenya, 1978–1990', in Holger Bernt Hansen and Michael Twaddle (eds), *Religion and Politics in East Africa*, pp. 153–5. See also Michael Paul Maren, 'Kenya: The Dissolution of Democracy', *Current History*, vol. 86, no. 520 (May 1987), pp. 210–12.

36 David Throup, 'Render unto Caesar the Things that are Caesar's: The Politics of Church-State Conflict in Kenya, 1978–1990', pp. 154–5. For an account more sympathetic to the Moi regime, see G. P. Benson, 'Ideological Politics versus Biblical Hermeneutics: Kenya's Protestant Churches and the Nyayo State', in Holger Bernt Hansen and Michael Twaddle (eds), *Religion and Politics in East Africa*, pp. 177–99.

37 Jennifer A. Widner, *The Rise of a Party-State in Kenya, passim.* See, however, P. Anyang' Nyong'o, 'State and Society in Kenya: The Disintegration of the Nationalist Coalitions and the Rise of Presidential Authoritarianism, 1963–78', *African Affairs*, vol. 88, no. 351 (1989), pp. 229–51, which dates the rise of 'Presidential Authoritarianism' to the Kenyatta era.

38 It is noteworthy that the Kenyan press has never attempted a major survey of Biwott's

career. Details of his rise to power have been culled from a large number of sources and much of our information comes from private conversations with prominent Kenyans, who wish to remain anonymous. See, however, *Weekly Review*, 17 February 1989, p. 9 for one exception.

39 David K. Leonard, *African Successes: Four Public Managers of Kenyan Rural Development*, pp. 103–24.

40 Charles Hornsby, 'The Social Structure of the National Assembly in Kenya, 1963–83', *Journal of Modern African Studies*, vol. 27, no. 2 (1989), pp. 275–96; and Charles Hornsby and David Throup, 'Elections and Political Change in Kenya', *Journal of Commonwealth and Comparative Politics*, vol. 30, no. 2 (1992), pp. 185–90 and 195–7.

41 *Ibid.*

42 *Ibid.* See also Joel D. Barkan, 'Bringing Home the Pork: Legislator Behavior and Political Change in East Africa' in Joel Smith and Lloyd Musolf (eds), *Legislatures in Development: Dynamics of Change in New and Old States*, pp. 265–88. For background material on how the political élite has evolved from that characteristic of a newly emerging state into one in which the wealthy and successful economically and within the state apparatus use their successes to achieve political power, see C. P. W. Hornsby, 'The Role of the Member of Parliament in Kenya, 1969–83', unpublished D.Phil. dissertation, Oxford University, 1985.

43 David Throup, 'Elections and Political Legitimacy in Kenya', *Africa*, vol. 63, no. 3 (1993), pp. 383–9.

44 *Ibid.* In 1983, for example, Zachary Onyonka, who had been in the Cabinet for 14 years, faced considerable harassment from the Administration and Police, and was even charged with attempted murder when a youth was shot and killed by the Minister or one of his bodyguards. Onyonka's difficulties stemmed from the animosity of his long-time foe Simeon Nyachae, the newly appointed Secretary to the Cabinet and head of the Kenyan Civil Service, who came from a neighbouring seat in Kisii District. Nyachae ensured that Onyonka lost his cabinet post in 1983 and KANU chairmanship in the district in 1985.

45 For the text of President Moi's speech, see *Weekly Review*, 7 December 1990, p. 15.

46 Charles Hornsby and David Throup, 'Elections and Political Change in Kenya', Journal of Commonwealth and Comparative Politics, vol. 30, no. 2, 1992, pp. 193-95; and David Throup, 'Elections and Political Legitimacy in Kenya', Africa, vol. 63, no. 3, 1993, pp. 387-88.

47 *Ibid.*

48 *Ibid.*

49 *Ibid.*

50 One of the authors witnessed the queuing in this seat in the by-election.

51 *Weekly Review*, 3 February 1989, pp. 10–12; 17 February 1989, p. 12; and 24 February 1989, pp. 4–6.

52 Charles Hornsby and David Throup, 'Elections and Political Change in Kenya', *Journal of Commonwealth and Comparative Politics*, vol. 30, no. 2 (1992), pp. 195–6; and David Throup, 'Elections and Political Legitimacy in Kenya', pp. 383–7. The relationship between 'rigging' and the MP's ability to represent the seat is seen with the discovery that five of the seven Kisii MPs elected in 1988 were 'absentee', not even having houses in their constituencies. See *Daily Nation*, 14 November 1992, p. 11.

53 Charles Hornsby and David Throup, 'Elections and Political Change in Kenya', pp. 189–90; and David Throup, 'Elections and Political Legitimacy in Kenya', pp. 386–7. The voluntary resignations were Achieng' Oneko and Oginga Odinga, who left to form the KPU, Joe Murumbi as Vice-President in December 1966 and the sole European Cabinet Minister, Bruce McKenzie, who stood down as Minister of Agriculture after seven years in office in 1970.

54 *Ibid.*

55 *Weekly Review*, 3 September 1993, p. 18. See also R. Sandbrook, *Africa's Economic Revival*, Cambridge University Press, London, 1993, pp. 44–70 for a general analysis of the over-development of the African state, especially the state bureaucracy.

56 *Weekly Review*, 3 September 1993, pp. 17–23.

57 *Ibid.*

58 *Weekly Review*, 24 March 1989, pp. 3–5; 28 April 1989, pp. 3–9; and 5 May 1989, pp. 9–16.

59 Jennifer A. Widner, *The Rise of a Party-State in Kenya*, pp. 177–8 and 220–1.

Four

The Regime in Crisis, January 1990–December 1991

By the end of the 1980s, President Moi had established complete control over both party and government, and through his political and business associates ran an increasingly partisan, corrupt and feared administration. Following the end of the Cold War, Western donors were becoming increasingly concerned about the style and direction of the government, but had shown little sign of abandoning this 'legitimately elected', pro-Western ally. Opposition existed among 'radicals' and 'dissidents', but there seemed little prospect of change. Two years later, the situation had been transformed. Kenya was a multi-party state with a serious opposition party which appeared likely to sweep all before it, while the government and ruling party were discredited, demoralised and increasingly unable to govern. How did this happen?

Between 1985 and 1989, KANU had moved from strength to strength. The party had become increasingly autocratic, detaining critics of the regime and disciplining the few politicians who spoke out in the National Assembly.[1] In 1990, however, the government began to show signs of weakness. The reasons for this were a complex combination of economic difficulties, external pressures, state violence and corruption, accident, and a suppressed but always alert opposition, ready to seize the initiative when the chance emerged. Four critical events ushered in the new era, provoking popular discontent and encouraging the regime's critics to speak out. These were the fall of communism in Eastern Europe and the ending of the Cold War; the regime's blatant manipulation of the 1988 national and party elections; the murder of Foreign Minister Dr Robert Ouko in February 1990; and the withholding of Western aid in November 1991 by the Paris Group of bilateral donors, who were dissatisfied with the slow pace of economic and political liberalisation. The crucial figure in at least two of these was Nicholas Biwott, the Minister for Energy and the President's right-hand man. Biwott's greed by the end of the 1980s had exceeded permitted bounds. Had the country been stable and the economy booming, donors probably could have been placated, as in the 1970s, but by the end of the first decade of Moi's rule, Kenya was facing acute economic problems.

The government's resistance to economic liberalisation and the IMF's structural adjustment programme had exhausted the patience of the country's main donors, especially the United States, which was also disillusioned with the regime's continued authoritarianism. Outside the Kalenjin zones in the central Rift Valley, parts of Western Province and Asian and Arab businessmen, supporters of the regime were in the minority. After more than a decade in power, blaming problems on Kikuyu hegemony no longer silenced the discontented.

The Church and the Law Society of Kenya Take up the Challenge

As the state and ruling party became increasingly repressive, politicians had been silenced one by one. As a result, dissent was transferred into those national institutions which still retained an independent voice. With the trades unions muzzled and students harassed and suppressed, only the main Churches and professional bodies, such as the LSK, dared to speak out. The various Churches commanded tremendous respect at all levels of Kenyan society. Kenya is a deeply religious society, and many people saw the Church leadership as a bastion of moral propriety and principle, willing to criticise the regime and corrupt Ministers while the press and the political process had become tarnished. The NCCK's National Pastors' Conference in August 1986 had marked a turning point, when the Churches had finally responded to attacks by KANU and spoken out in defence of the secret ballot. Until then, only a few individuals had dared to criticise the government; henceforth, liberation theology began to play a larger role, and Church leaders recognised that the NCCK could sustain an anti-government movement.[2] As political freedoms declined, so the individuals who had led the 1986 assault, Bishop Okullu and John Gatu, were joined by a younger generation of Church leaders, most notably the CPK's Rt Rev. David Gitari, Bishop of Mount Kenya East, and the Rt Rev. Dr Alexander Muge, the Bishop of Eldoret, the Rev. Dr Timothy Njoya of the Presbyterian Church of East Africa (PCEA), and the Rt Rev. Mgr Mwana a'Nzeki, the Roman Catholic Bishop of Nakuru, who was also the secretary of the Kenya Catholic Bishops' Conference. In 1986 their protests had been muzzled, but under the surface discontent had simmered on.[3]

The beginnings of the opposition alliance were founded on a combination of common interests, principles, and personal ties. Following Kenneth Matiba's resignation from the Cabinet and his expulsion from the ruling party in January 1989, the ex-Minister had developed a strategy to challenge KANU's monopoly on political power. Despite his expulsion, Matiba and his allies continued to control the Murang'a KANU branch, harassing Secretary-General Kamotho, his long-time opponent. Having secured his own District, Matiba then began to prepare a broader assault on the regime. Supported by Charles Rubia and advised by two lawyers who had been radicalised by KANU's authoritarian behaviour, Paul Muite and Kamau Kuria, Matiba began to hold secret meetings with a number of prominent Kenyans who had become disillusioned with the regime.

These included the Rt Rev. Dr Henry Okullu, the Bishop of Maseno South, one of the CPK's most distinguished spokesmen on Church–state relations and political matters, and other Church leaders.[4] Henry Okullu had long been politically active, and had spent several years in the 1970s as editor and then columnist of the CPK newspapers *Target* and *Lengo,* before becoming Bishop of Maseno in 1974. Despite Okullu's regular clashes with the then powerful Charles Njonjo, Church–state affairs had remained reasonably amicable throughout the Kenyatta era. President Moi, by contrast, had failed to appreciate the influence of the major Churches, and had not recognised the strength of their opposition to his regime. By attempting to suppress criticism by Church leaders, Moi had encouraged the Churches to organise, starting a process of political self-education for a younger generation of clergymen who increasingly saw themselves as preaching the Gospel against state oppression.[5] During the 18 months from January 1989 to June 1990, Okullu met Matiba and Paul Muite five times, usually at secret evening meetings at various people's homes.[6]

Muite, aged 46, had not become involved in politics until the early 1980s. During the 1970s, he and George Waruhiu had built up one of Kenya's first and most distinguished African law firms – Waruhiu and Muite Advocates. Pin-striped examples of legal propriety, the two lawyers had modelled themselves on former Attorney-General Charles Njonjo and had prospered from lucrative briefs from the government and parastatals during the Kenyatta era. Both senior partners enjoyed close contacts with the Kikuyu political establishment and the business community. When Njonjo was elected as a Member of Parliament in 1980 for Kikuyu in south-west Kiambu, he had sought assistance from Muite, who came from the same constituency. When Njonjo fell from power in 1983, Muite had assisted Bill Deverell as junior counsel in his defence before the Miller Commission. Muite's close identification with Njonjo had aroused considerable resentment in those legal quarters who criticised the former Attorney-General for blocking the Africanisation of the Bar. This hostility had become apparent when Muite, who had served as Vice-Chairman of the Law Society of Kenya from 1981 to 1982, was defeated in his bid for the chairmanship, contrary to convention. For the first time, African lawyers, who were now in a majority, had out-voted British expatriate members of the Bar who had hitherto dominated the profession.

Muite's defeat in the Law Society's elections, the growing alienation of the Kikuyu élite from the Moi regime, and finally Njonjo's downfall and the Commission of Enquiry into his affairs had transformed Muite from an establishment lawyer into a radical dissident. After the 1982 coup, Muite defended former Air Force commander Major-General Peter Kariuki, who was sentenced to four years' imprisonment for failing to suppress a mutiny.[7] The Njonjo Commission kept him in the public eye throughout 1984 as a prominent critic of the regime. Then in 1986 he was one of the radical lawyers – along with Gibson Kamau Kuria, Kiraitu Murungi and Japheth Shamalla – who encouraged Law Society Chairman G. B. M. Kariuki to denounce the introduction of queue voting.[8] Supported by Gitobu Imanyara's recently established *Nairobi Law Monthly,* this small group of lawyers became increasingly outspoken in their denunciations of the Moi regime's human rights record. Two years later, in 1988, the same group led the legal community's opposition to the constitutional amendments that removed the security of tenure of High Court judges, the Attorney-General, and the Comptroller and Auditor-General. By 1989, some of them, impressed by the dramatic changes taking place in Eastern Europe, began to call for the restoration of multi-party politics.

By then, Muite had become the leader of the radical lawyers. He had established a close friendship with former Nairobi University law lecturer Gibson Kamau Kuria, a graduate of Dar es Salaam and Oxford, who provided the intellectual justification for the radicals' critique of the government and of the rulings of senior judges.[9] When the government refused to allow Kuria to leave the country to collect a human rights award from the Kennedy Foundation in the United States, Muite went to speak on his behalf. Muite's remarks ensured that his passport was also withdrawn on his return to Kenya.[10] In 1989, Muite represented three Kiharu sub-branch KANU officials who had claimed that a by-election, caused by Kenneth Matiba's resignation from the Cabinet over the rigging of the earlier party elections in the constituency, had been equally flawed (see pp. 43–4).[11] When the state decided not to proceed with the prosecutions, many believed that it had backed down because Muite and Matiba had threatened to publicise the widespread malpractice at the 1988 elections, undermining the government's legitimacy. Later that year, the radicals proposed Muite once again for the Chairmanship of the Law Society. When Muite lost, he and his backers protested that the election had been rigged 'KANU-style' and sought to overturn the result in the courts.[12] By the end of the 1980s, Muite had been transformed from a quiet, non-political defender of arch-conservative Attorney-General Njonjo into the leader of Kenya's radical lawyers, emerging as a vocal critic of the regime. He also began to speak out in support of greater political freedom, calling for the abolition of single-party rule.

The first public challenges to the government's authority began at the start of 1990. On 1 January 1990 the Rev. Timothy Njoya, the outspoken Presbyterian cleric who had emerged in the 1980s as one of the Kenyan government's most outspoken critics, delivered a sermon at St Andrew's Church, Nairobi. Reflecting upon the amazing changes which had occurred in Eastern Europe during the previous year, culminating in the violent overthrow of the Ceaucescu regime in Romania, Njoya speculated upon how long it would be before similar pressures would erupt in Kenya. Njoya's sermon demonstrated the comparative freedom still enjoyed by senior Church figures. Journalists, academics, trades unionists, even MPs would have been detained for making a similar attack. Njoya was soon joined by Bishop Okullu and by veteran dissident Oginga Odinga, Kenya's first Vice-President, who supported the call for the legalisation of opposition parties. They claimed that KANU was isolated from popular opinion, which could only be freely expressed with the registration of new parties and the establishment of a freer political climate.[13]

Despite the publicity it received and the uproar it created, Njoya's sermon had spoken in veiled terms and had failed openly to condemn the ruling party. Bishop Okullu, by contrast, decided that a clearer message was required and in late April 1990, emboldened by the recent release of Nelson Mandela and the legalisation of the ANC in South Africa, he publicly stated that only multi-party politics would guarantee full accountability and transparency.[14] The dramatic events in South Africa, following those in Eastern Europe the previous year, appeared to confirm the worldwide crisis of authoritarianism.

The Death of Robert Ouko

Matiba's opposition had been taken for granted since 1989, and despite their wide support and confrontational posture, the Churches had been cowed in 1986. What began to change in 1990 was a collapse of the government's own will to preserve its monopoly of power, a response to increasing Western concern and the death of two senior political figures. The first key moment was the murder of Foreign Minister Robert Ouko, a non-partisan administrator and recent anti-corruption investigator, in February 1990. A civil service technocrat, Ouko had served for more than a decade as the senior Kenyan official in the East African Community. When the Community had finally collapsed in 1977, President Kenyatta had brought him into the Cabinet as Minister for Community Affairs. Elected to Parliament in 1979 as the MP for Kisumu Rural, Ouko had emerged as the most powerful and securely ensconced Luo Minister. Although he was not particularly popular, he was widely acknowledged to be one of the government's most capable administrators and, therefore, a national political figure who might have emerged as a serious contender for the succession, free from the stigma attached to a Kikuyu candidate.

On 16 February 1990, however, Ouko was found shot dead and his body burned near his home at Koru in Kisumu district. His ankle was shattered, and his body so severely burned that experts had to work for a week to reconstruct the charred remains.[15] He had not been seen since the early hours of 13 February. Ouko's murder and the revelations and inconsistencies of the subsequent police and judicial inquiries were one of the crucial drivers behind the campaign for multi-party democracy, crystallising concerns about corruption and the power of those close to the President. Ouko's murder suggested that Moi, like Kenyatta, might be willing to kill those closest to him. Although the state had become increasingly authoritarian during the late 1980s, the Moi government had so far refrained from murdering its opponents, unlike Kenyatta's inner circle, who were widely believed to have removed Pio da Gama Pinto, Tom Mboya, Ronald Ngala, and J. M. Kariuki from the political scene.[16] Ouko's death suggested a new era of political violence was dawning. Wild rumours circulated in the streets of Nairobi and Kisumu about how the Foreign Minister had died, setting off riots in the capital.

Concerned by the apparent culpability of senior government and administration figures in his death, Moi immediately called in Britain's New Scotland Yard to investigate. Superintendent John Troon led an extensive investigation into the circumstances of Ouko's death, despite a significant lack of cooperation amongst segments of the administration, and initial pressure to declare the killing a suicide. Troon's report was never made public, most probably because it proved far too embarrassing to the government. As early as May 1991, *Africa Confidential* reported that 'the enquiry has already torn holes in the official version of events surrounding Ouko's murder, which all Kenya believes was politically motivated'.[17] There have been many theories as to why Ouko was killed, but most focus on three key figures: President Moi, Nicholas Biwott and the Permanent Secretary in charge of Internal Security, Hezekiah Oyugi. Moi, it is believed, was concerned that the United States might be grooming Ouko as a possible successor. When the President and Foreign Minister visited Washington in late January 1990, Moi had been irritated by the warm reception given Ouko and felt that he had been slighted. When the President requested increased American aid at an interview attended by Ouko at the State Department, senior State Department officials had not only refused but had criticised the high level of corruption in the Kenyan government, even suggesting that the President should use some of the funds he had invested out of the country to meet the country's foreign exchange difficulties.[18] It is widely rumoured that the President's dubious business deals and foreign exchange transactions had been enumerated in detail during the interview, leaving no doubt as to Moi's personal corruption. Humiliated in front of Ouko, Moi had been angered further when the Washington press addressed questions to the Foreign Minister rather than himself. Having left school to become a primary school teacher, Moi's English is halting and his speeches tend to ramble. By contrast, Ouko spoke with ability and sophistication on complex issues. He was popular and at ease with foreign journalists. Following his dressing down in Washington, Moi had returned to the Kenyan High Commission in London in a fury, refusing to have anything to do with Ouko, whom he blamed for the fiasco. Ouko was even forced to travel on a commercial airline, as Moi would not permit him on the same plane and, once home, his security protection was withdrawn.[19]

The Foreign Minister was no saint. He had been rigged into Parliament in 1988 against Job Omino, the popular Chairman of the Kenya Football Federation and founder of Gor Mahia, the top Luo football team. Delays to the completion of Kisumu Molasses Plant, however, were directly affecting his constituency. Construction had been frozen following revelations about the ruinous terms and conditions imposed by influential Kenyans involved in the deal.[20] As a result, Ouko had begun to prepare a memorandum on the subject of high-level corruption for the President. Among those whom the Foreign Minister's investigation had alarmed was Biwott. Superintendent Troon in his evidence to the subsequent Commission of Enquiry suggested that Ouko and Biwott had clashed over the latter's demand to BAK, an Italian-Swiss consulting firm, for a sizeable kickback during discussions over reviving the molasses factory. Ouko's sister subsequently claimed that Biwott had received a $4,000,000 commission from the international contractor Asea Brown-Boveri in return for securing the order to supply electrical equipment to the plant. She informed the Commission that her brother had declared that Biwott was 'a dangerous and corrupt man'.[21] Troon was convinced that during the last weekend before his murder Ouko had been preparing a report for the President about demands for bribes relating to the factory. This report would have implicated Biwott and several other senior Ministers, including Vice-President and Minister for Finance George Saitoti and Minister for Agriculture Elijah Mwangale. Troon observed, 'The BAK allegations of corruption and the dispute with Nicholas Biwott are key.'[22] Ouko, he suggested, had clashed with Biwott over the matter during their trip with President Moi to the United States. The Superintendent recommended a thorough investigation of the whole affair, even suggesting that the files Ouko had been working on at his Koru home had been removed by police investigators or the Special Branch.

Ouko may have been killed for entirely different reasons, however. The state subsequently prosecuted his close friend Jonas Anguka, the Nakuru District Commissioner, for the murder. He was acquitted in July 1994, after the prosecution had suggested that he might have been motivated by personal jealousy, believing that his wife, Ouko's personal assistant, was having an affair with the Foreign Minister. It is also possible that Ouko was murdered by his own farm labourers, the last people to see him alive, and that his Luo colleague Anguka was simply a sacrifice to appease the popular belief that the murder was a political killing.[23] The role of deceased Permanent Secretary Oyugi, whose presence at Ouko's house on the night of the murder was confirmed even by prosecution witnesses, remains unexplained.

The Politicians Enter the Fray

On 3 May 1990, three months after Ouko's death, the long-awaited 'second front' emerged among the Kikuyu. Addressing a stunned press conference, Kenneth Matiba and Charles Rubia openly denounced corruption within the ruling circle and blamed the government for the declining economy and the climate of oppression which had developed in recent years. At a second press conference, the following week, the former Ministers were even more outspoken as they launched a campaign for the restoration of multi-party democracy. Matiba and Rubia pointed out that the immediate spate of attacks on them had 'proved our point that a one-party system stifles criticism ruthlessly and hence eliminates the fundamental human freedom'.[24] Only the introduction of multi-party democracy, they argued, would ensure greater openness and accountability in the political system. Many of their specific complaints were familiar. Single-party rule, they asserted, had resulted in 'tribalism' and mediocre appointments to public office; growing interference in the affairs of organisations outside the political arena, such as the disbanded Kenya Farmers' Association; mismanagement of other bodies such as the Kenya Planters' Cooperative Union, the Coffee Board of Kenya and the Kenya Tea Development Authority; and widespread embezzlement, shady deals and the sidelining of experienced personnel in government agencies and parastatals.

The ex-Ministers also criticised the adoption of ill-considered policies, such as the 8–4–4 reorganisation of primary and secondary education, and

Photo 4.1 Kenneth Matiba and Charles Rubia launch their campaign for Multi-Party Democracy, May 1990.
Courtesy of Nation Group Newspapers

the over-rapid expansion of higher education. They argued that unemployment had risen because of the government's failure to support existing industries; and even blamed shortages of essential drugs and equipment in major hospitals on single-party rule. All these problems, Matiba and Rubia claimed, had been exacerbated by secret decisions and dubious deals. Future policies, they contended, needed to be considered carefully in open debate rather than being motivated by the vested financial interests of powerful politicians and civil servants.[25]

Both former Ministers came from Murang'a District. They had prospered during the Kenyatta years, although neither had been particularly close to the 'Family Circle', and had widespread business interests, ranging from manufacturing to agriculture and tourism. Murang'a, one of the poorest, least fertile parts of Central Province, like other Kikuyu areas had been 'squeezed' economically as President Moi diverted resources elsewhere. They had been driven from the Cabinet and Parliament, and disciplined by KANU; their businesses had lost government and parastatal contracts, loans had been foreclosed and foreign exchange denied. Neither man, however, had been willing to back down in order to reach an accommodation with the regime. Rubia enjoyed the reputation of being a truculent, none-too-scrupulous street fighter, while Matiba was known to be determined, arrogant and one to bear grudges. Motivated partly by self-interest, under attack they chose to fight back.[26] For the first time in a decade, the Moi regime was faced by a serious challenge from the two distinguished former Ministers, who as wealthy businessmen reflected the grievances of the influential Kikuyu business and professional communities.

Over a few weeks, Matiba and Rubia effectively transformed the long-repressed underground movement for multi-party democracy into a mass movement which for the first time threatened the government's control. Their wealth, importance and ability to articulate the grievances of both the urban poor and the Kikuyu business élite – indeed, of all who had lost out under the Moi government – made them a far greater risk than so-called 'radicals', such as Koigi wa Wamwere, George Anyona and even Oginga Odinga who, harassed and expelled from KANU, were excluded from the political process, and whose attempts to form opposition parties had been routinely rejected. Matiba and Rubia, by contrast, spoke for a large group of businessmen, bankers and other professionals, who were exasperated by the Moi government's continuing hostility to Kikuyu interests. United, they might in the early 1980s have been able to prevent the onslaught against Kikuyu capital, but by remaining silent and hoping that they could reach personal accommodations with the regime they had been humbled one by one. By 1990, however, the economy was in such straits that many Kikuyu business leaders were looking for someone openly to defend their interests. Former Vice-President Mwai Kibaki, Kiambu KANU Chairman George Muhoho, KANU Secretary-General Kamotho and the other remaining Kikuyu members of the government had been cautious for too long or were clients of Moi. Matiba and Rubia, by contrast, once they were expelled from the ruling party and found that their businesses were being squeezed, were sufficiently self-confident – or arrogant – to believe that they could challenge the regime and get away with it.

Matiba, the senior partner in the alliance, had prepared his challenge to the government with great care. Ever since his expulsion from KANU, he had met regularly with a small circle of advisers to plan his campaign. Among those present on a regular basis were lawyers Paul Muite and Gibson Kamau Kuria, Rubia, and Philip Gachoka (his business partner). Matiba and his colleagues also met secretly with a number of outspoken clergymen, including Bishop Okullu.[27] The Rev. Bernard Njeroge, who later became a key figure in FORD's and then FORD-Asili's Secretariat (and is now the controversial CPK Bishop of Kajiado), acted as an intermediary between Okullu and Matiba. Matiba was also in contact with Minister of Health Mwai Kibaki, who was invited to attend the secret gatherings but always failed to turn up, fearing that he might be found out.[28] Muite and Kamau Kuria played a crucial role in devising Matiba's and Rubia's key initial statement, and advised the two politicians on how far they could go in criticising the government without being arrested. Matiba's and Rubia's replies to the press at these May meetings were carefully rehearsed so as not to provide the government with a pretext to arrest them. The former Ministers were advised to focus the debate on the issue of freedom of assembly, on the basis that it was impossible to tell if Kenyans supported multi-party democracy or KANU's single-party state so long as they did not have the freedom to meet to discuss the question.[29]

The Matiba-Rubia campaign for political reform in 1990 and the Oginga Odinga Forum for the Restoration of Democracy campaign, the following year, were both part of a carefully considered strategy and followed a similar course. Both developed from a campaign directed by a small group of civil rights lawyers, dissident clergymen and ex-politicians, who were willing to challenge the government's legitimacy, enlisted more and more popular enthusiasm and support, and then successfully orchestrated a direct confrontation with the regime by attempting to organise a mass meeting, which they knew the authorities would refuse to license. By focusing popular attention on the meeting on both occasions, in July 1990 and again in November 1991, the opposition was able to mobilise the Nairobi masses – predominantly Kikuyu and experiencing many privations – against KANU and President Moi, successfully puncturing the ruling party's claim to have mass support.[30] In many respects, the lawyers and clergy in the opposition were more important than the ex-politicians. Rubia, Odinga, and later Martin Shikuku, Masinde Muliro and Josephat Karanja, were figureheads more than effective planners of the opposition's strategy. Only Matiba played an important role in the planning of the scheme and the focus on the issue of freedom of assembly, whereas Muite and his supporters in the Law Society played a vital behind-the-scenes role. This explains why the 'Young Turks' after FORD's registration so resented the prominence of old-style politicians like Shikuku, who had played no part in the campaign, and why Shikuku and his colleagues were so suspicious of Muite, Gitobu Imanyara and James Orengo.

President Moi's response to the new campaign for pluralism exemplified the low level to which political debate had sunk in Kenya. Besides denouncing the ex-Ministers for destabilising the country, the President informed a rally in Kirinyaga that Matiba and Rubia were plotting his assassination and the death of other senior government officials. Such claims were a traditional smear tactic in Kenyan politics.[31] As KANU leaders rushed to denounce their former colleagues, Matiba's home was ransacked and his wife, Edith, seriously injured by a 15-man armed gang, believed to be members of the GSU, in search of the ex-Minister. Mrs Matiba reported that her assailants addressed one another as 'Corporal' and 'Captain'.[32] Reinforcing the emerging ethnic dimensions of this political crisis, several MPs claimed that the ex-Ministers and their supporters in the Churches were 'tribalists'. They suggested that the campaign for multi-party politics was an attempt to destabilise the regime in order to re-establish Kikuyu hegemony, and pointed out that virtually all President Moi's critics were Kikuyu. KANU leaders claimed that most Kenyans had benefited from the Moi government's more equitable distribution of development funds and his broad coalition of diverse groups. There was enough truth in this to create concern about the impact of the restoration of Kikuyu leadership, a concern that was to be reinforced during the years to come.

The Detention of Matiba and Rubia

Three days before they were to hold an unauthorised meeting at Nairobi's Kamukunji Stadium, the government called Matiba and Rubia's bluff. On 4 July 1990, both were arrested and then detained under the Preservation of Public Security legislation, the colonial regulation frequently used to remove opponents of the state who had not committed a crime. Charles Rubia had just left the Fourth of July celebrations at the American Ambassador's residence and made his way to the Muthaiga Country Club in north Nairobi, when he was arrested and 'unceremoniously dragged out of a meeting' by ten policemen. Raila Odinga, the son of former KPU leader Oginga Odinga, was also detained.[33]

As former Cabinet Ministers with extensive business interests and contacts in all parts of Kenya's ruling élite, Matiba and Rubia had considered that they were immune from detention. Neither former Attorney-General Charles Njonjo nor ex-Vice President Josephat Karanja had been detained when they had fallen from power. Moreover, Matiba and Rubia had been carefully coached by Muite and Gibson Kamau Kuria on precisely how far they could go without overstepping the law. Both knew that their carefully devised confrontation with the government was reaching a crisis. If the planned meeting at Kamukunji Stadium took place on 7 July 1990, and attracted a vast crowd – as seemed almost certain – KANU would lose face and the opposition's claim that most Kenyans wanted to end KANU's autocracy and corruption would be strengthened. The government, however, had not reacted after their two press conferences. Although KANU and the Nairobi Provincial Administration were seriously embarrassed about the prospect of an opposition rally attracting vast crowds, going ahead with the Kamukunji meeting alone would probably not have merited detention. Muite and his colleagues were briefly held a year later after organising a similar illegal rally. President Moi and his inner circle of advisers were, in fact, much more alarmed by Matiba's and Rubia's private conversations with Raila and Oginga Odinga. The government panicked when Special Branch officers, who had tailed Matiba and Rubia, reported that the two Kikuyu ex-Ministers had spent a considerable time at a meeting in Agip House, Oginga Odinga's Nairobi business headquarters.[34]

Matiba and Rubia, advised by Muite and Kamau Kuria, had begun to recruit a team of prominent politicians who had fallen from grace under the Moi regime, to demonstrate the national appeal of their campaign. Among the seven individuals on their list were Abaluhya leaders Masinde Muliro from Rift Valley Province and Martin Shikuku from Western Province, and Oginga Odinga from the Luo community of Nyanza Province.[35] *Jaramogi* Oginga Odinga, however, was reluctant to re-enter the political fray because his propane gas company had recently secured a sizeable loan from the Industrial Development Bank, a government-controlled parastatal, and Odinga wished to secure the loan before risking antagonising the regime with new political ventures.[36] The Luo leader promised, however, that he would join the campaign in the not too distant future. In order to gain Odinga's support, Matiba and Rubia even proposed that the veteran Luo politician should be the opposition's leader, in order to rebuild the Kikuyu-Luo alliance of the early 1960s. When Odinga complained that 'the first marriage' had brought few rewards for the Luo and wondered what he would get for 'a second marriage', Matiba and Rubia had agreed that he should be the opposition's future presidential candidate, a key concession which was to have enormous repercussions two years later. The Kikuyu ex-Ministers also explained that they were considering the establishment of the post of Prime Minister, who would control the ordinary business of the government, leaving the position of President as a symbol of national unity above the political battle.

Photo 4.2 DP and FORD leaders hold a joint conference at Chester House. *Courtesy of Nation Group Newspapers*

Relations between the veteran Luo radical and the conservative Kikuyu businessmen were amicable. The voice of dissent in Kenya for nearly three decades, despite detention and other harassment, Odinga retained formidable political clout as the uncrowned leader of his people, and his allies had continued to dominate politics in northern and central Nyanza Province until the mid-1980s. With his attempts to return to the political mainstream continually frustrated by the government, during the 1980s Odinga had become more and more resentful and critical of President Moi. In 1987 he had issued a series of 'open letters' to President Moi, castigating the government and KANU leaders for seeking to identify him with the underground *Mwakenya* movement. He had demanded the right to participate in politics either through KANU, as an independent, or through the formation of an opposition party. Three years later, when Matiba and Rubia issued a similar demand, for the first time in nearly three decades, it seemed that Odinga had influential allies.[37]

Moi and his advisers had long feared that the ageing Luo leader might form a coalition with Kikuyu radicals and dissident intellectuals from the University of Nairobi. The danger of an alliance between Matiba and Odinga posed an even greater threat, frightening Moi into taking precipitate action. The President correctly feared that they were plotting to revive the old Kikuyu-Luo alliance which had brought Kenya to independence. Such a coalition would have posed a serious challenge to KANU, uniting two of the country's three largest, most educated and economically developed ethnic groups against the ruling party. In an attempt to head off this coalition, the government detained Matiba and Rubia and arrested Raila Odinga, a controversial activist who had been detained twice before, as a warning to his father not to become involved.

The result was open confrontation. As news of the detentions spread, the depth of Kikuyu hostility to Moi's regime became evident. Despite the state's ban and threats, three days later supporters of the multi-party movement attempted to gather on Saturday, 7 July 1990 – *Saba Saba*[38] – at the Kamukunji grounds where the illegal rally was to have taken place. Riot police dispersed the crowd with batons and tear gas, igniting three days of rioting in the poorer quarters of Nairobi.

The trouble quickly extended to smaller towns throughout Kikuyuland, leaving more than 20 dead and over 1,000 arrested before the police could restore order. Most of the violence occurred in areas that were to become FORD-Asili or DP strongholds, such as Kiambu, Nakuru and Nyeri town.[39] Opposition leaders fled into hiding or, like George Anyona, were arrested as the state's authority was quickly reasserted. Gibson Kamau Kuria, the civil rights lawyer, sought refuge in the American Embassy and Paul Muite also vanished from sight. Eventually Kuria was permitted to leave Kenya for the United States, while friends of Muite, with access to the President, negotiated the Nairobi lawyer's return from hiding. Muite was required to apologise to the President for his frequent criticisms of the regime.[40] By compromising and releasing the dissident lawyers, the Kenya government averted an immediate showdown with the United States, permitting its domestic critics to continue functioning under close supervision. Opposition had not been crushed, however, and internal and external supporters of multi-party democracy now had two powerful new symbols of the state's intolerance around which to mobilise further protests.

Bishop Muge's Death

KANU's confidence was further weakened a month later on 14 August 1990, when a second prominent individual, Bishop Alexander Muge of Eldoret, was killed in a car crash.[41] The controversial Bishop's death was another event that galvanised opinion, confirming the view of the KANU moderates that the government should not 'mess with the Churches'. Since his appointment in 1983 Muge had become the main focus of resistance to the Moi coalition in Nandi District. He had regularly criticised Moi's childhood friend, Stanley arap Metto, the MP for Mosop, as well as Metto's defender, Nicholas Biwott, and the Nandi County Council leaders. The Bishop had even suggested that the President himself was ill-advised. He had spoken out against corruption, suggesting that a prominent local politician – presumably Biwott – had stolen several farms which he had bought with money collected by the landless. In 1988 and again in 1990, Muge had referred to this issue and suggested that he would soon reveal the full extent of the theft and corruption in high places. But after clashing with President Moi over the extent of food shortages and famine in the arid West Pokot District of his diocese, Muge in the year before his death had sought to rebuild relations with the President, absolving him personally from the charges of corruption. He had disassociated himself from Bishop Okullu and the Rev. Dr Njoya's 1990 castigation of single-party rule, and had defended the ruling party, echoing President Moi's claim that multi-party politics would simply divide Kenyans into rival ethnic parties. Elements within the Church considered that he had been 'bought off'.[42]

Muge's death, following so soon after Ouko's murder, profoundly shook public confidence, awakening memories of the mysterious automobile accident and death of former KADU leader Ronald Ngala under Kenyatta. That the government would take the blame was made inevitable by the fact that Minister of Labour Peter Okondo had warned publicly that Muge should not visit Busia or he would not return alive. Muge had challenged the Minister to carry out his threat, leading a Church delegation to Busia town, which was part of his diocese, and holding several services and prayer meetings. On his way back to Eldoret, the Bishop's car was hit by a runaway milk truck, killing him instantly. The rumour quickly circulated that he had been murdered and that the crash had been orchestrated by the police. The turnboys on the truck were even reputed to have had walkie-talkie radio transmitters so that they could time the collision.[43]

Popular anger erupted in both Eldoret and Nairobi, where the Bishop's body was taken to lie in state, as Church leaders denounced the government, castigating the regime for all manner of evils. Ministers, especially KANU hardliners, such as Elijah Mwangale, were jostled by the angry crowd when they attempted to pay their respects or attend the memorial service at All Saints' Anglican Cathedral. Okondo was compelled to resign from the Cabinet for his remarks. It is impossible to determine the truth. It was probable that Muge's death was indeed accidental, but in Kenya, reality often follows the public image. Church leaders were carried away by the resulting emotional furore, some even denouncing the regime for being in league with the devil and alleging that Muge had been murdered by witchcraft. No government Ministers could attend the funeral, as Church leaders refused to shift the date from 22 August, the twelfth anniversary of Kenyatta's death.[44]

The Reform Process Begins, June–December 1990: The Saitoti Commission

The detention of Matiba, Rubia and Raila Odinga had demonstrated that the government would not tolerate the possible emergence of a Kikuyu-Luo coalition, and initially demoralised the human rights activists. From the perspective of President Moi and his Kalenjin advisers, however, the first signs were emerging of an alliance which had the potential to break their stranglehold on politics in the country. The Ouko murder remained a thorn in their side, the professions and the Churches remained hostile, growing questions were being asked in the West, and the *Saba Saba* riots had revealed the government's vulnerability to mass protest. It was time to compromise.[45]

The first break in the logjam came in June before the *Saba Saba* protests. 'Doves' in the ruling party pressed KANU into reform in an attempt to placate the country. On 21 June President Moi announced that a Commission would be appointed under the chairmanship of Vice-President Saitoti to investigate (and by implication reform) the party's electoral and disciplinary procedures, and thereby improve its image. From the original ten 'hawkish' members which included Sharrif Nassir, Biwott, Mwangale and Oloo-Aringo, it was quickly expanded to 19, including more moderate figures such as Kibaki, John Keen, trades unionists, and representatives of women's' organisations, the law and the Churches. From July until October 1990, to the surprise of many, the Commission provided an open forum for indictment of the regime and a source of demands for reform. As it travelled around the country, speakers even questioned the continuation of the single-party state, while others proposed a two-term limit for the Presidency. Witnesses throughout the country complained about corruption, government inefficiency, and the autocratic behaviour of KANU branch officials. The extent of popular frustration astounded the party leadership, and the resulting Report recommended numerous major changes to the existing system.[46]

The reform proposals that the committee finally formulated met stiff resistance from KANU hardliners, however, when the Special KANU Delegates' Conference assembled in Nairobi in December 1990. Speaker after speaker denounced the Report's recommendations, as Moi sat impassive, until at the last minute he rose and, to the shock of many of his Cabinet colleagues, demanded that the Report be accepted *in toto*. A sullen conference unanimously acceded, a pattern which was to be repeated a year later. Some of the reforms adopted could be implemented by KANU's National Executive, while others required legislation. The most important was the abandonment of the hated queue voting and the 70 per cent primary rule in parliamentary elections.[47] The establishment of a new national disciplinary committee was approved, expulsion from the party abolished and the post of KANU National Vice-Chairman created. The Conference also resolved to establish an anti-corruption tribunal in an attempt to meet public calls for the appointment of an independent ombudsman. It was also recommended that the 40,000 shilling ceiling on campaign expenditure be abandoned, since it could not be enforced. A few weeks before, President Moi had also instructed that the security of tenure of High Court judges, the Attorney-General, the Comptroller and Auditor-General, and members of the Public Service Commission would be restored, only three years after it had been removed. Moi and Secretary-General Kamotho assured delegates and the press that KANU would introduce further reforms in the near future in order to fulfil the recommendations of the KANU Review Committee, under the ruling party's new commitment to 'managed change'.[48] Personally endorsed by Moi, the reform process was now under way.

Less than a month after KANU's Conference, however, it became apparent that the ruling party had not really changed its ways. Although queue voting had been abolished, KANU headquarters was still insisting on vetting and approving candidates.[49] Moreover, although the Conference had decided to abandon expulsions of dissidents, the new rules adopted by the party's National Executive looked very similar to the old. The 31 members who had already been expelled were to have their sentences commuted to one-year suspensions but, if their local branch did not recommend their readmission, the suspension could be extended. The same meeting of the National Executive, in fact, announced the suspension for two years of ex-Minister Maina Wanjigi, Belgut MP Ayub Chepkwony and two local politicians in Trans-Nzoia and Kericho. The two MPs had been dismissed from the government shortly before the suspensions and Chepkwony had been ousted from his position as Kericho District KANU Chairman for 'causing disunity'. Although suspension enabled them to retain their seats in Parliament (unlike those Members who had been expelled earlier), they would not be able to contest the next general election if it occurred before they were fully rehabilitated. As the press pointed out, 'the new measures achieve all that the past expulsions managed, namely locking certain people out of active politics'.[50]

Unsurprisingly, the measures failed to satisfy the government's critics. Odinga insisted that the introduction of multi-party politics provided the only way to open up the political system. Former Nairobi Mayor Andrew Ngumba, who had been expelled from KANU in 1987, was equally dismissive. He challenged the ruling party to restore basic freedoms and to accept diverse political viewpoints, complaining that respect for human rights had declined since the Kenyatta era.[51]

The Attempt to Register the National Democratic Party

Although his son had been detained, Oginga Odinga refused to be silenced. In November 1990, he announced that he intended to form a new political party and in his New Year message to the people of Kenya he declared that '1991 must be the year for the repeal of Section 2(A) of the Kenyan constitution so as to establish multi-party democracy in our Republic'. KANU leaders treated the announcements with contempt, encouraging the view that Odinga's political influence was declining and few MPs bothered to comment. The three Trans-Nzoia Members of Parliament even suggested that Odinga 'should stop day-dreaming and enjoy his political pension'.[52]

Odinga was far from alone, however. Other critics were making similar demands and a groundswell of voices in support of multi-party politics developed. Early in January 1991, Masinde Muliro also called on President Moi to repeal section 2(A) of the constitution, observing that this would 'restore freedom of association and bring about political stability'.[53] He urged the President to release Matiba, Rubia and Raila Odinga from detention, warning that Kenyans should look for 'unity in diversity'. Gitobu Imanyara, the editor of the *Nairobi Law Monthly,* even filed an application in the High Court to have the 1982 legislation making Kenya a *de jure* single-party state declared invalid.[54] Martin Shikuku, the maverick former MP for Butere in Kakamega District, also demanded that the 1982 changes in the constitution be repealed.[55] More and more lawyers, clergymen and 'excommunicated' politicians seemed willing openly to challenge KANU's monopoly on political power.

On 13 February 1991 – the first anniversary of the murder of Dr Robert Ouko – Odinga summoned the Kenyan and international press to Chester House to announce that he was forming an opposition political party, the National Democratic Party (NDP). Odinga stressed that the NDP sought to secure the 'restoration of democracy and justice'. Odinga was undaunted by the insuperable obstacle to the NDP's registration presented by the *de jure* single-party state, relying instead on the guarantees of political freedom in Chapter V of the constitution and of freedom of association in Section 80. If Zambia, Cape Verde and Senegal could operate a multi-party system, why couldn't Kenya? The government, Odinga warned, was undermining Kenya's harmonious ethnic relations. The radio, for example, was being 'used to send messages of war and fear mongering'. As a result:

> a master–servant relationship has emerged between the government as the master and the people as the supplicant servants. As the master harasses its servants, even courts of justice have been unable to come to the defence of the humble and meek.[56]

The government was paralysed and had no moral courage, seeking merely 'to protect the narrow interests of the ruling class'. Only with the restoration of multi-party democracy would people be free to speak out against corruption and tyranny and to repudiate KANU.

But these aims, Odinga cautioned, could only be secured by 'an organised political force'. The NDP, therefore, sought to 'provide an opportunity for Kenyans to establish a system of conflict resolution which is open, non-violent, democratic and just'. The Luo leader invited 'all Kenyans, wherever they are, to join our Party, and to join in the campaign for establishing democracy and social justice in Kenya. . . . The people must have a voice against such bad government and a right to change such government. This is our stand. This is our challenge.'[57]

The government attempted to suppress all news of the party. The Kenyan press carried no accounts of Odinga's press conference for three days until on Friday, 15 February the *Weekly Review* reported the meeting. When the first extensive commentaries on the new party finally appeared in the *Nairobi Law Monthly* and *Society* two weeks later, issues of the two magazines were confiscated immediately and the former's editor, Imanyara, was arrested early in March, ostensibly for publishing a 'seditious attack' on the government.[58]

Odinga's efforts to register the NDP failed, of course. In mid-March 1991, the Registrar of Societies Joseph King'aru refused to accept the party's draft constitution. Discontented politicians, including Masinde Muliro and Martin Shikuku, refused to participate, suggesting that Odinga was out of touch with political realities, and had few close allies outside the Luo community.[59] In fact, the ex-KPU leader had been unable to attract a strong team of supporters. The *Kenya Times* denounced the NDP officials as 'Odinga's team of nonentities'. Only Ougo Ochieng', a former MP for Bondo, had even served in Parliament. The emerging coterie of younger dissident professionals, such as Paul Muite and Gitobu Imanyara, still remained outside the explicitly political arena. Following his watershed election as Chairman of the Law Society of Kenya on 9 March 1991, however, Muite, taking up an open opposition stance, urged the government to register the new party.[60] His election was an open challenge to KANU, which it refused to confront.

Odinga continued to harass the government with statements in favour of multi-party politics. He was an old man in a hurry. Nearly 80 years old, he still desperately wanted to serve as President and considered that with his son in detention and himself too old to be harassed (given Kenyan respect for old age) he had little to lose from a full-scale assault on the Moi regime. He also kept the NDP in the news by appealing the Registrar's decision. Both the *Nairobi Law Monthly* and *Finance* carried detailed interviews with Odinga in March, outlining the NDP's programme.[61] By manipulating the appeal's process, waiting for four weeks to register the party and then delaying lodging his appeal against the Registrar's decision for another three weeks, Odinga managed to secure considerable publicity and retained the right to continue organising and publicising his group. Even KANU spokesmen implicitly acknowledged the NDP's existence while castigating Odinga's attempt to establish an opposition party. Meanwhile, Odinga employed Muite's argument, first expounded in his inaugural address as Chairman of the Law Society of Kenya in February 1991, that Section 80 of the constitution, by guaranteeing freedom of association and debate, authorised the registration of a second political party, provided it merely concentrated on promoting public debate and did not attempt to put forward candidates for election to the National Assembly or local government bodies. Even if the High Court rejected the NDP's appeal, the debate could be continued before the Court of Appeal, enabling Odinga to maintain his campaign against KANU's monopoly of power well into July 1991.[62]

As the new party attracted more attention, it became clear that KANU had underestimated the appeal of the aged Luo leader. KANU leaders therefore began to denounce Odinga more aggressively. Politicians throughout Nyanza Province, led by the party's National Chairman Peter Oloo-Aringo, were compelled to join these attacks, as their loyalty was being questioned as long as they remained silent. Until this time, because of Odinga's age and the widespread impression that his authority had waned, the government had adopted a 'softly softly' approach towards his campaign. Now, however, politicians dismissed Odinga as a has-been from an earlier generation, out of touch with contemporary opinion, and they started to rake up discreditable charges from his past.[63] Vice-President Saitoti and Assistant Minister of State in the Office of the President John Keen (who had assisted Saitoti's election in 1988) claimed, for example, that Odinga had imported weapons from the Soviet Union in the mid-1960s to overthrow the Kenyatta government.[64]

Finally, the government arrested the Luo leader in Kisumu while on his way to Nairobi early in May 1991, for concealing illegal weapons in the compound of his Bondo home. Odinga protested that the night before he had set out for Nairobi, his night-watchman had disturbed some 'thugs' who had broken into his compound in order to plant weapons and thereby implicate him in subversive activities. The police dismissed Odinga's allegations, of course, but the suspicion remained that the regime was up to 'dirty tricks'. Odinga, moreover, refused to be silenced and maintained the pressure on the Moi regime by announcing in mid-May that he intended to sue Saitoti and Keen for injuring his character, by alleging that he had committed treasonable acts.[65]

The Fall of the Soviet Empire in Eastern Europe and the Arrival of the New American Ambassador

It had become clear by the end of 1990 that the Moi government faced a serious crisis. Members of Kenya's political class and the educated élite had been profoundly shaken by the blatant rigging of the 1988 General Election, by the murder of Foreign Minister Ouko and by the death in mysterious circumstances of Bishop Muge. Kenyans in general were facing mounting inflation, food shortages and all-too-evident growing corruption among senior government Ministers and the management of parastatals. The government was also coming under mounting pressure from the United States, other Western bilateral donors, the IMF and the World Bank, which were now beginning to press for political, as well as economic, reforms. The public hearings of the Saitoti Commission had revealed the depth of public dissatisfaction with the regime. It was clear that fundamental reforms were required if KANU was to recoup its position.

The collapse of the Soviet Empire in Eastern Europe in 1989 had a major impact on dissident leaders in Kenya and on the external support for the KANU government. The Civic Forum movement in East Germany and Vaclav Havel's 'Velvet Revolution' in Czechoslovakia demonstrated that a mass popular movement could topple even the most entrenched authoritarian regimes. Even in Africa, single-party states appeared to be collapsing around the continent in 1991. Military regimes were toppled in Mali and Niger, President Kaunda of Zambia agreed to hold multi-party elections in November – and lost by a large margin – while Mobutu Sese Seke of Zaire, Omar Bongo of Gabon and even Felix Houphouet-Boigny of the Côte d'Ivoire were confronting demands for multi-party democracy and free elections. The United Democratic Front (UDF) in South Africa, which brought together civic associations and trades union activists to challenge the apartheid regime from 1983 onwards, was another role model, following its successful campaign for the release of Mandela and the legalisation of the ANC and other African political organisations. President Moi appeared to be one of the most outspoken opponents of political pluralism, frequently reiterating his view that the formation of opposition parties would divide Kenyans along ethnic lines and hinder economic development.[66]

At the same time, the Bush Administration's new Ambassador to Kenya, Smith Hempstone, the former chief executive of the *Washington Times* newspaper, emerged in early 1989 as a forceful critic of corruption and single-party rule. Hempstone, a political appointee, dared to speak out against the regime where a career diplomat might have adopted a more cautious line. Relations between the Ministry of Foreign Affairs and the US Embassy rapidly deteriorated. Apart from a brief hiatus in late 1990, when the United States required Kenyan assistance during the Gulf War, relations between the United States and the Kenyan government cooled rapidly from late 1989. Hempstone expressed his views uninhibitedly to the opposition press and protected Gitobu Imanyara, the editor of the *Nairobi Law Monthly,* and Pius Nyamweya, the editor of *Society,* from the wrath of the regime. His non-conformist activism led KANU MPs to

Photo 4.3 American Ambassador Smith Hempstone
Courtesy of Nation Group Newspapers

denounce Hempstone for intervening in Kenya's internal affairs, and even to suggest that he should be deported or banned from moving around the country. The American Embassy became a centre of refuge for left-wing dissidents and, KANU MPs believed, a source of covert funding for the opposition.[67]

To the dismay of the Kenyan authorities, however, it became apparent that, despite his right-wing political background, Hempstone was merely enunciating opinions that were widely held in Congress. Although the Bush Administration might not have instructed him to intervene so actively in support of the campaign for greater democracy in Kenya, it would not repudiate him or order his recall. The international climate was changing. The end of the Cold War made Kenya's geopolitical position marginal, and Kenyan greed over the Mombasa Base agreement antagonised US policy makers. At the same time, the failure of the government to attack corruption and implement structural adjustment coincided with a growing lobby on Capitol Hill against Kenya's poor human rights record. Congressmen from both major parties demanded that US aid to regimes in Africa, including Kenya, be reduced and made conditional upon liberalisation and an improved human rights record.[68]

Similar sentiments (although more muted) were also beginning to be expressed within British policy-making circles, although the British High Commission in Nairobi, led by High Commissioner Sir Roger Tomkys, continued to defend the Moi regime. He insisted that more could be achieved by encouraging the government to reform behind closed doors. Pushed by the Americans and increasingly alarmed by the deteriorating political position in Kenya during 1990, especially by the deaths of Ouko and Muge and the detention of Matiba and Rubia, the Foreign Office (if not the High Commission in Nairobi) began to ponder the wisdom of being too closely identified with the Moi government. Opposition leaders in Britain, such as Dr David Owen of the Social Democratic Party and Sir David Steel, the Foreign Affairs spokesman of the Liberal Democrats, both took a close interest in Kenya. Kenneth Matiba had met David Owen in February 1990 and had discussed the launch of an opposition party. Mrs Thatcher had enjoyed a close personal relationship with President Moi, but following her downfall in November 1990 the British government's attitude began to change. During the summer of 1991, the Assistant Under-Secretary for Africa, Simon Hemans, who had served as Deputy High Commissioner in Kenya in the early 1980s, led a policy review in Whitehall. It is also rumoured that Foreign Secretary Douglas Hurd pressed Kenyan Ministers attending the Commonwealth Heads of Government meeting in Cyprus in September 1991 to introduce political reforms and to consider the legalisation of opposition political parties. Hurd had warned that aid to African governments might be made conditional upon liberalisation,but his private advice to senior Kenyan Ministers had been ignored.[69]

The writing had been on the wall for a long time. As early as November 1990, Western governments, meeting in Paris on 19 November, had considered reducing their aid to Kenya, which financed nearly 30 per cent of government expenditure. The five Scandinavian governments which contributed $60 million worth had expressed concern, like the Americans, at human rights violations. Kenya and Norway had broken diplomatic relations on 22 October 1990, when dissident politician Koigi wa Wamwere had been arrested. The international financial institutions, meanwhile, were also pressing the Kenya Government to reduce corruption, liberalise the economy and thin out the bloated civil service.

First Signs of Weakness, April–May 1991

Odinga's actions and the resulting furore had kept the issue of multi-party democracy alive. It was the issue of human rights and activism within non-governmental associations, however, which continued to provide the driving force for political change. Although Matiba, Rubia and Raila Odinga were still in detention, and Gibson Kamau Kuria was in exile in America, the remaining opposition leaders decided to base their strategy on the previous year's plan. As in 1990, they focused on organising public meetings, rather than forming a political party. After Matiba and Rubia had been detained, the secret meetings between Muite and Bishop Okullu had continued at Muite's home. Okullu had opposed as futile Odinga's attempt to form another political party and, like Muite and the Rev. Bernard Njeroge, considered that they should attempt to organise a human rights crusade.[70] This idea became known as the 'Peace and Justice' movement. Muite and other radical lawyers and clergy, however, had a broader plan, seeking to use the human rights crusade to secure wider political goals, leading eventually to the formation of a 'Civic Forum or UDF-style' protest movement. To this end, they needed to enlist the support of old-guard politicians, who were better known than Muite and his lawyer colleagues. This time, Odinga was involved from the start and acted as the figurehead leader for the movement.[71]

Paul Muite intensified his campaign against the government, securing in May 1991 the approval of the Council of the LSK for the appointment of a tribunal to enquire into decisions of Chief Justice Alan Hancox and Mr Justice Norbury Dugdale. Nine members of the Council signed the statement, protesting that the judges' decisions made it clear that 'in their efforts to suppress and even punish the advocates of fundamental rights, the authorities are readily assisted by a section of the judiciary'.[72] The statement especially criticised Dugdale, a British citizen. It was Dugdale, for example, who had dismissed the complaint of Professor Wangari Maathai, coordinator of the Green Belt Movement, against the construction of KANU's new headquarters in Nairobi's *Uhuru* Park; denied Bishop Muge's widow's application to have a public inquest into her husband's death; and refused to stand down in December 1990 from hearing Koigi wa Wamwere's attempt to secure dismissal of the treason charges against him. In May 1991 Dugdale was also hearing the case brought by Gitobu Imanyara to nullify Section 2(A) of the constitution. Muite and his colleagues also denounced Hancox, who had taken over as Chief Justice in late 1989. The lawyers complained that Hancox had retained Justice Dugdale 'as the permanent duty judge' and protested that recent decisions by the High Court were undermining confidence in the judicial system.[73] The protest brought the new Law Society Committee into further direct confrontation with senior members of the judiciary and the government.

May 1991 saw another opposition advance, when the incompetent Attorney-General Matthew Muli was dismissed, partly because of financial impropriety and legal errors, but also because he had been unable to control the furore surrounding Ouko's murder. Muli was replaced by a more liberal figure, Amos Wako, who enjoyed the reputation of being a human rights lawyer because of his previous work with the United Nations and Amnesty International, although he had remained aloof from the radical lawyers who had supported Paul Muite's election as Chairman of the LSK. In office, Wako was to prove less of a reformer than his admirers had hoped, compromising his principles to ensure the survival of the Moi regime, but he was a key figure in arguing for change within the government, and was quick to drop sedition charges against opposition figures.[74]

On 12 April 1991 Charles Rubia was released from detention, almost nine months after his arrest. The press speculated that he had been released because the Rubia family had rejected opportunities to challenge the government, in contrast to Odinga and Kenneth Matiba's wife and daughters, who had adopted a far more confrontational attitude. Matiba had even signed an affidavit, condemning his detention and asserting that he would not abandon his political beliefs.[75] In fact, the former Nairobi Mayor was freed from detention because of ill health and, shortly after returning home, entered Nairobi Hospital for a medical examination before going to Britain for major stomach surgery.[76] After his release Rubia appeared unwilling to speak to the press, perhaps because he was too ill after his operation, but he castigated *Society* magazine for suggesting that he had done a deal with the government to secure his freedom. In an interview with the *Daily Nation,* the ex-Minister declared that he would continue to speak out and campaign for political liberalisation and urged President Moi to release Matiba and Raila Odinga. Some opposition leaders feared that Rubia's forthright remarks would set back the release of the other two detainees.

Reports then began to circulate that Matiba had suffered one or more strokes and was near death. The government initially insisted that the ex-Minister was in good health, although it soon became clear that the reports were true. By June 1991 Matiba's health was so fragile that Police Commissioner Kilonzo informed President Moi that the former Cabinet Minister was likely to die in detention if he suffered another stroke. The President is reported to have observed that he did not want 'any martyrs', and Matiba was released the next day, 9 June 1991, in extremely frail health.[77] He was transferred immediately into hospital in England, where he was to remain for nearly a year, diagnosed as having suffered two major strokes. Raila Odinga was the last to be released two weeks later, shortly after his lawyer Dr John Khaminwa filed applications in the High Court challenging the constitutional validity of his detention.[78]

The Formation of FORD, May–November 1991

In May 1991, James Orengo, a 40-year-old lawyer and former dissident MP, and Gitobu Imanyara, the editor of the *Nairobi Law Monthly,* had dinner with British politician Sir David Steel. The former leader of the Liberal Party, Steel had been raised in Kenya where his father had been Moderator of the Church of Scotland Mission during the last decade of colonial rule, and had maintained a close interest in Kenyan politics. During dinner, the British politician suggested that as KANU was blocking attempts to register an opposition party, critics of the ruling party should emulate the Civic Forum movements in Czechoslovakia and East Germany. In 1989, these had brought down the Communist dictatorships by uniting civic associations, local activists, the Churches, intellectuals and other opponents of the regimes in a broad coalition. Since technically a similar coalition in Kenya would not be classified as a political party, it would not have to be registered under the Societies Ordinance. James Orengo invented the name FORD – the Forum for the Restoration of Democracy – with echoes of both the Civic Forum and American liberalism.[79]

Encouraged by Steel's suggestion and in close consultation with Paul Muite and Bishop Henry Okullu, the opposition leaders persuaded Oginga Odinga to abandon his futile attempt to register the NDP and to announce that he was launching FORD as an umbrella organisation for all interests and individuals committed to the repeal of Section 2(A) of the constitution and to the establishment of multi-party politics. Muite, Orengo, Peter Anyang-Nyong'o and the recently released Raila Odinga then met for dinner with former Cabinet Minister Dr Munyua Waiyaki in an attempt to persuade him to join the campaign, to serve as its most senior Kikuyu representative while Matiba and Rubia were still recuperating in London. Waiyaki was reluctant to become involved, however, and shied away, fearing detention.[80]

The strategy behind FORD was the same as in the 1990 campaign for multi-party democracy. The civil rights lawyers and radical clergy, soon to become known as the 'Young Turks', realised that to bring down a dictator his prestige must be punctured and the power of the regime demystified. The opposition leaders, thus, sought to provoke another crisis. To do this, they organised a major public rally under the guise of a prayer meeting for the new Peace and Justice Commission to be held at the CPK's All Saints' Cathedral in Nairobi in June 1991. Rubia was to be the keynote speaker. Meeting secretly at night with Bishop Okullu, the Chairman of the Commission, and the Rev. Bernard Njeroge, its organising secretary, the Young Turks prepared their plan. Muite and his colleagues considered that the government would not be able to intervene to prevent the rally, since it was being presented as a Church gathering. The authorities threatened Archbishop Kuria, however, and he backed out at the last moment, cabling from Canada that the meeting must be cancelled until he could discuss the matter further with them on his return.[81]

At this stage Oginga Odinga and Rubia were the only politicians involved, although Ambassador Hempstone had also agreed to attend. Bishop Okullu, who was from Odinga's Siaya district, had kept the Luo leader fully informed of his secret meetings with Matiba and Muite. Odinga had encouraged Okullu to continue the discussions and the two were agreed about the need to devise a strategy to undermine KANU and the single-party system. Now they and the Young Turks decided that the time had come to enlist the support of other prominent Kenyans. Thus, on his return from Canada, the Archbishop's resolve was bolstered and the prayer meeting rearranged for July, while other prominent figures were persuaded to participate.[82]

In the event, however, the prayer meeting was never held. Without consulting his colleagues, the Rev. Bernard Njeroge informed the press that the 'convention' would be preceded by a huge procession from the railway station to the Cathedral in an attempt to publicise the meeting and to encourage people to participate. The Nairobi Provincial Commissioner warned that no licence to process had been granted and implied that the march would not be permitted, and both Bishop Okullu and Archbishop Kuria became alarmed. Okullu even telephoned the Primate to say that he would not participate.[83] Then, the Friday before the prayers were scheduled, President Moi despatched Special Branch officers to warn the three main organisers – Muite, Imanyara and Japeth Shamalla – that there would be serious consequences if they went ahead. When they arrived at Muite's office at six o'clock on Friday evening, the Special Branch informed him in Gikuyu that they were instructed by 'the highest authority in the land' to kill him if he went ahead with the meeting. Muite was not convinced and was determined to call their bluff.[84] The Special Branch also threatened Archbishop Kuria, however, and fearful of the consequences he called off the meeting without consulting Muite or the other organisers.

This climb-down marked a turning point in the opposition's strategy. The decision antagonised the Young Turks, who considered that the Primate should have displayed greater courage. They calculated that the government would not be able to carry out its threats.[85] As a result, the lawyers and politicians decided to press ahead with their 'Civic Forum' plan without active Church support, weakening the alliance that had developed since January 1989. Instead, Muite and his colleagues decided to recruit eight prominent political elders – one from each Province – to serve as front-men for the opposition. Oginga Odinga from Nyanza was already committed, Dr Waiyaki from Nairobi had refused, while Rubia was also reluctant to antagonise the government again. His son was soon to be married and the wedding had already been delayed once while Rubia was in detention.[86] The Young Turks, however, were confident that Kenneth Matiba would participate, once he had recovered from his stroke. In the interim, Muite persuaded Matiba's friend and business partner Philip Gachoka to come in as the ex-Minister's representative from Central Province. Gachoka displayed considerable courage as he was already on bail pending trial for sedition. Then Muite persuaded the respected elder statesman of Abaluhya politics, Masinde Muliro, to join the group.[87]

Muite and Muliro had decided not to invite Martin Shikuku, the former MP for Butere, who was widely regarded as a political maverick, because he and Muliro did not get on. But while Muite and Muliro were agreeing to exclude Shikuku from the list of FORD elders, Raila Odinga, acting on his own, telephoned Shikuku and asked him to join.[88] Initially reluctant, Shikuku soon changed his mind and brought with him two associates, Ahmed Salim Bamahriz, a Councillor from Mombasa who had clashed with Mombasa KANU Chairman Sharrif Nassir, and former Machakos MP George Nthenge. The organisers also sought to recruit Ahmed Khalif Mohammed as the representative from North-Eastern Province, but he finally refused to join the list of elders because it might embarrass his colleagues on the Supreme Council of Kenya Moslems. Nonetheless, with Shikuku's assistance, Odinga and his advisers had almost managed to recruit one representative from each Province: Odinga represented Nyanza; Shikuku, Western; Muliro, the Rift Valley; Gachoka, Central; Nthenge, Eastern; and Bamahriz, the Coast. Only Nairobi and North-Eastern Province were unrepresented. But although Odinga and the Young Turks accepted Nthenge and Bamahriz as the representatives for Eastern and Coast Provinces, from the first they owed their loyalty more to Shikuku than to FORD's collective leadership.

On 4 July 1991, the anniversary of the Matiba and Rubia detentions, Oginga Odinga publicly announced the formation of FORD. Once again the government pressured the press not to report the story so that only the *Standard* had a tiny announcement of its formation. The new unofficial pressure group of six was small enough to avoid indictment under the restrictive laws banning unlicensed meetings of more than six persons (a useful coincidence). Soon, however, the announcement produced a government response. In August 1991 FORD was declared an illegal organisation; in September, President Moi said that its supporters would be 'crushed like rats'.[89] Emboldened by the government's paralysis, created by the damaging allegations about the Ouko murder, and the involvement of Biwott and other Ministers in various corruption scandals, and with the tacit support of the United States, FORD continued to harass KANU.

The first public declaration of the new movement's aims in August 1991 produced an entirely unanticipated popular response, convincing both the Young Turks and the old-guard politicians that they had mass support and might even be able to topple the Moi regime. As a result, Muite and his colleagues decided to press ahead, demanding a licence to hold a mass meeting at Nairobi's Kamukunji stadium in early November. This direct challenge to the regime, an obvious replay of the attempt by Matiba and Rubia to call a meeting in July 1990, aroused tremendous enthusiasm in the capital and nearby Kikuyu areas. FORD's figurehead leaders were transformed overnight into political heroes, although the strategy had actually been devised by the Young Turks, who remained behind the scenes.[90]

Even at this early stage, divisions were beginning to appear between the old guard and the Young Turks, particularly between Martin Shikuku and Paul Muite. The old politicians considered that once Muite and the other lawyers had set up the movement and brought the elder statesmen together, they should back out and leave politics to the professionals. Thus, although Muite, Orengo, Imanyara, Anyang-Nyong'o, Raila Odinga and Shamalla were the brains behind the new movement, and wanted to be recognised publicly, the politicians were determined to keep them in the background. These arguments became ever more intense as support for FORD continued to grow. While relations between the Young Turks and Shikuku rapidly deteriorated, however, Muite and his colleagues maintained an effective working relationship with Oginga Odinga.

The second Kamukunji rally, planned for 16 November 1991, posed a direct challenge to the government's authority. Many Kenyans, unaware of the two ex-Ministers' negotiations with Odinga, believed that Matiba and Rubia had been detained for summoning the first rally. FORD, consequently, seemed to be challenging the regime to detain its leaders, provoking a second round of rioting. On the day of the proposed rally, the police attempted to prevent people making their way to Kamukunji stadium and to arrest FORD's leaders. Muite spent the night before in hiding in the house of a foreign diplomat but he, Odinga and others were arrested before they could reach the rally.[91] Muliro, Shikuku, Orengo and Gachoka, however, managed to lead a procession through the city, joined by US, German and Swedish diplomats. Thus, although the rally did not go ahead, FORD had won another propaganda victory and had demonstrated publicly Western support for its challenge to the regime. In protest at the arrests, for example, the Germans recalled their Ambassador, Berndt Mutzelberg.[92]

The government attempted to defuse trouble in Nairobi by despatching the FORD leaders to be arraigned individually in their home Districts rather than prosecuting them in the city, where the political atmosphere remained volatile. To their surprise, however, they found popular dissent to be as wide and as vocal in these rural areas as in Nairobi. Each trial quickly turned into a focus for mass opposition demonstrations, and the government abandoned the prosecutions soon after.[93]

Biwott and the Rise of *Majimboism*

As KANU came under increasing attack in late 1991, prominent Kalenjin members close to President Moi were forced to defend their positions. As the leader of government business in the National Assembly, Nicholas Biwott was widely regarded as the 'real Vice-President', despite the fact that he did not hold national office in the ruling party, serving merely as the Rift Valley's representative on the National Executive. During his rise, Biwott had made enemies among senior Kalenjin leaders; he made even more during the 1983 and 1988 General Elections, when he pushed them aside to make way for his own protégés and supporters. It was alleged that the Minister had bought three farms in Uasin Gishu for 1,400 families dispossessed from the Kerio Valley by the mining operations of the Kenya Fluorspar Company in 1979, which he subsequently refused to hand over. Before his death, Bishop Muge had taken an interest in the complaints and had started to make veiled references to 'land grabbers' and to high-level corruption, which many linked to Biwott. As we noted earlier, several prominent figures in the CPK believed that Biwott had ordered Muge's death.[94]

With the downfall of Njonjo and G. G. Kariuki in 1983, Biwott had emerged as one of the most powerful figures in the government and the most important Kalenjin politician after the President. Biwott was one of KANU's 'hard men', a strong supporter of queuing and an opponent of dissident Church leaders and lawyers. When his business dealings and personal corruption were revealed to the public by the investigators into Ouko's murder, and as opposition to single-party rule continued to mount, Biwott attempted to unite Kalenjin politicians behind his leadership, identifying the community's interests with his own political survival, and to secure an ethnically pure Rift Valley state into which the government could retreat *in extremis*.

In October 1991, as the forces opposed to the government mounted, Biwott once more initiated the call for *Majimboism* or Provincial self-government. In the early 1960s, the *Majimbo* constitution had been designed to protect the interests of the smaller ethnic groups. At a series of public meetings, the Energy Minister and his allies encouraged the Kalenjin to take control of the Rift Valley and to silence criticism from 'immigrants' (Kikuyu and Luhya residents) who had moved into the former White Highlands with the post-independence small-holder settlement schemes. Beset by calls for multi-party democracy and for the disclosure of their land deals and business interests, Biwott and his colleagues deliberately began to incite Kalenjin fears about their future in a Kenya without Moi as President.

Many non-Kalenjin politicians in the Rift Valley saw the campaign as a threat to their survival, aimed at creating a Kalenjin-dominated province which would pay even less attention to their opinions and the interests of their constituents. The most outspoken critic of the proposal, however, was Assistant Minister in the Office of the President John Keen, who had represented Kajiado North in Parliament from 1969 to 1983. Keen had re-entered politics in 1988 as a close ally of Finance Minister George Saitoti who now represented his old constituency, replacing Saitoti as a nominated MP. By 1991, however, Keen had become a political ally within the government of the moderate Kikuyu, led by Minister of Health Mwai Kibaki. Keen feared that the Maasai and Kikuyu voters of his own area on the periphery of the Rift Valley would suffer neglect from a perpetually Kalenjin-controlled Rift Valley Provincial Administration. In October 1991, he was dismissed from the government.[95] Keen's attack on *Majimboism* was endorsed by another senior hardliner and Cabinet Minister, now turned reformer, Peter Oloo-Aringo. In a veiled reference in October 1991 to Biwott and other Kalenjin leaders, Oloo-Aringo had criticised 'political godfathers' who were usurping the President's position. The ensuing uproar raged for several days. After this, his days in the government and in KANU were numbered. The embattled Minister even had to deny rumours that he had resigned from the ruling party and fled the country, seeking political asylum.[96]

Biwott's attempt to defend his position was to have serious consequences. Beginning with scattered land clashes in Nandi, a new political phenomenon emerged, as Kalenjin 'warriors' attacked Kikuyu, Luhya, Luo, and Gusii residents around the borders of the Kalenjin area in order to create a pastoralist-only zone totally loyal to KANU and President Moi, following a speech by Minister of Local Government William ole Ntimama condemning Kikuyu settlement in Narok. Unemployed Maasai (and later Kalenjin) youths were offered land (seized from the other ethnic groups) as a powerful incentive to support the 'ethnic cleansing' campaign.[97]

Biwott, Oyugi and the Commission of Enquiry into Ouko's Death

Despite the fact that President Moi had emerged as one of Africa's most outspoken opponents of multi-party democracy, by November 1991 the pressures upon KANU had become so great that it was in serious difficulties and its grasp on power was under attack. Support for the opposition had continued to grow both within and outside Kenya. Considerable numbers of people in Central and Nyanza Provinces were dissatisfied with Moi and the continuing Kalenjinisation of the Kenyan state, and support for the illegal opposition continued to grow. Inflation and unemployment continued to rise and Kenya's balance of payments to deteriorate. Meanwhile, the regime came under ever increasing pressure, especially from the American, Canadian and German governments, to liberalise politically as well as economically, permitting the formation of opposition parties and free press comment. The bubble of state invincibility had been burst, as much by the Saitoti Commission as by the Matiba/Rubia protests and *Saba Saba* riots.

Internally the Ouko Enquiry continued to preoccupy the nation with unsavoury details implicating Biwott, Hezekiah Oyugi, Nyanza Provincial Commissioner Julius Kobia and Nakuru District Commissioner Jonah Anguka. Within the ranks of the élites outside the centre of power, open dissent was growing. Former Vice-President Dr Josephat Karanja, one-time Chief Secretary and Head of the Civil Service Simeon Nyachae, disgraced Cabinet Minister G. G. Kariuki, former Deputy Speaker Samuel arap Ng'eny, and other prominent former politicians such as James Nyamweya, James Osogo and Dr Munyua Waiyaki, all urged the ruling party to introduce reforms and permit more open discussion of political issues. The strict control of political discourse, which KANU hardliners had exercised since 1983, was beginning to disintegrate.[98]

Despite his reluctance, President Moi finally decided that to permit an investigation to continue in relative freedom would be less disastrous for the regime's credibility than to suppress further discussion. In May 1991 he set up a Commission of Enquiry into the death, which worked until 26 November 1991. At first, however, the Commission made little progress. It was only after months of confused, inconsistent and clearly false testimony that the Enquiry sprang to life when Superintendent John Troon of New Scotland Yard testified in November 1991, providing a unique window into the hidden world of Ministerial-level politics and corruption.[99]

Hezekiah Oyugi had aroused Troon's suspicion from the first by discouraging the Superintendent from announcing that he was treating Ouko's death as a suspected homicide rather than suicide. Troon informed the Commission of Enquiry that he suspected that Ouko might have met Oyugi in Nairobi on 7 February 1990 – the day before he left for his Koru farm – to discuss his corruption report. Details of this key day in Ouko's life remained unclear, arousing considerable speculation. The police also now believed that Oyugi had spent the night of 9 February at the Sunset Hotel in Kisumu, although Oyugi insisted that the booking had been cancelled and he had spent the night at his home in South Nyanza. Troon judged that Oyugi's 'answers in general were evasive.... In fact, all Oyugi's statements amount to denials, negative answers or answers that leave many doubts as to his knowledge surrounding Dr Ouko's death.' The Police Superintendent concluded: 'By virtue of the motives I have outlined, I suspect that Mr Oyugi and Mr Biwott have some knowledge or involvement in the death of Dr Ouko.... These two gentlemen are my principal suspects.'[100]

At the end of October 1991, Moi finally acted, retiring Oyugi from his post and transferring Biwott to the less influential Ministry of Industry. Then, three weeks later, a few days after Superintendent Troon presented his evidence, Moi suddenly dissolved the Enquiry, to the astonishment of the Commissioners. Its shutdown was gazetted on 25 November, the same day that the Commission members publicly protested at police harassment.[101] The last day of the Enquiry's transcript ends with the note that a new witness was due to be called the next day, 26 November. This witness was to have been Hezekiah Oyugi. The same day, Oyugi was arrested, along with Nakuru District Commissioner Anguka and Nicholas Biwott.

Six years later, Ouko's murder is as yet officially unsolved. Although former District Commissioner Jonah Anguka was tried and acquitted for the murder, he was widely believed to be a 'fall guy' for someone more senior. District Commissioners do not normally decide to murder government Ministers without instructions. A number of the protagonists in the case have died subsequently, including most importantly Hezekiah Oyugi himself, whose death in August 1992 aroused great suspicion. Oyugi fell ill shortly after his release from prison with an unusual neurological ailment. Many Kenyans suspected that he had been 'injected with the disease' while under arrest to stop him implicating not only Biwott but also President Moi. Despite his pivotal role in the late 1980s, the government sent no condolences to his family, and the only Minister who turned up for the funeral, Dalmas Otieno, was forced to leave by angry mourners who believed that Oyugi had been murdered.[102] Whatever the truth about the deaths of Ouko and then Oyugi, the Commission of Enquiry into Dr Ouko's murder created a tremendous political crisis which threatened the survival of Moi's regime. In order to survive, the President had to abandon both his closest ally, Nicholas Biwott, and Oyugi, the key figure in the state's security apparatus.[103]

Biwott's Businesses and the Banks

Biwott's downfall also had important repercussions in the business community and, especially, in Kenyan banking circles. Biwott's business interests covered a wide spectrum of activities, including two key petroleum distributing agencies – Kobil and Kenol (the Kenya National Oil Company) – Air Kenya Aviation Ltd, Wescon Ltd and ABC Foods Ltd, as well as several other concerns. So-called 'political banks' had lent the former Minister of Energy approximately £24 million, which had never been repaid. The Central Bank indicated that Biwott's HZ group of companies owed £9 million to Trade Bank and between £5 million and £8 million to Pan African Bank. The latter bank had built up a close relationship with Biwott during his nine years as Minister of Energy, handling the business of Kenol. Biwott had also borrowed from Citibank, the major American corporation, whose Kenyan subsidiary was owed £8 million. The *New York Times* reported that four fifths of the loan had been secured by letters of credit against Biwott's Swiss bank accounts. While he remained in power, the Energy Minister had blocked all attempts to secure repayment. It took the intervention of the American Embassy with 'higher authorities' and a threat from Citibank and other foreign-controlled banks to pull out of Kenya to secure repayment. Eventually, the Central Bank intervened, enabling Trade Bank to acquire control of the Yaya Centre, an exclusive suburban shopping mall that Biwott had developed, which provided the security for loans from the Deposit Protection Fund. The Pan African Bank also had to seek assistance from the Central Bank to cover its money from Biwott's business empire.[104]

Reports in the *Financial Times* speculated that several other banks might face similar difficulties, having lent money to powerful political figures who had fallen from grace. Several Kenyan banks had been 'created in the 1980s with the support of senior politicians, who had organised their funding through large deposits from parastatals'.[105] These banks had also extended unsecured credit to companies owned by prominent political figures. Biwott, Vice-President Saitoti, and President Moi and his sons had been prominent participants in these dubious enterprises. Inadequate attention had been paid to prudent financial monitoring of these loans, and the Central Bank had been reluctant to pry too deeply into the banks' affairs, given their powerful patrons. Such instability in the financial sector boded ill for Kenya's discussions with its already disillusioned donors. Further crises were clearly in store.

In the weeks before the next Paris Group meeting of Western donors in November, the Kenyan government faced yet another problem. 'Tiny' Rowland, the chairman of Lonrho, a major investor in Kenya, protested about Biwott's behaviour and the extent of corruption at high levels of the Kenyan government. Using his prestigious British newspaper, *The Observer,* in the autumn of 1991 Rowland encouraged the publication of stories highly critical of the Moi government. He particularly complained about Biwott's intervention to frustrate Lonrho's bid for the construction of the western Kenyan oil pipeline project, although Lonrho subsidiaries had initiated and surveyed the project. Rowland was quoted as saying that 'The trouble with Biwott is that everyone in Kenya knows that he has collected tens of millions in commissions, but not from us, which is why we didn't get the sugar or the pipeline, or any other contract for that matter....'[106] It was rumoured that several donor agencies had refused to have any dealings involving the Minister when millions of dollars had disappeared as kick-backs on the Turkwell hydro-electric project. The *Financial Times* reported, back in March 1986, that the project had cost 'more than double the amount the Kenya government would have to pay for it if it had been subjected to international competitive tendering'.[107]

The Paris Group Meeting and its Political Consequences, November 1991

The Kenyan government was becoming increasingly isolated. By September–October 1991 the donor community had decided that dramatic action was required. An international press campaign in early November 1991 attacking corruption, and specifically Kenyans' holdings overseas which the IMF estimated unofficially at US$2.62 billion, clearly presaged the donors' commitment to change. The Kenyan leadership, however, ignored this as American propaganda.[108] On 25–26 November 1991, however, Kenya's bilateral aid donors met in Paris to review their aid relationship with Kenya. Virtually all of Kenya's main Western trading partners and aid donors attended the meeting, which brought together representatives of Canada, Denmark, Finland, France, Germany, Italy, Japan, the Netherlands, Sweden, Switzerland, the United Kingdom, the United States, the African Development Bank, the European Union, the European Investment Bank, the IMF, and the United Nations' Development Programme, while Belgium, Saudi Arabia and the OECD sent observers.[109] To the government's utter surprise, on the second day of the meeting the donors decided to suspend balance of payments support and other rapid disbursement aid for six months. This decision, despite all the warning signs, deeply shocked the government, although the psychological effect of the decision was probably greater than its immediate economic impact. Kenya, the long-time favourite of the West, was being treated as one of Africa's pariah regimes. Beset by mounting domestic and international pressure for multi-party democracy, the revelations at the Commission of Enquiry into Ouko's death, reaction against the Kalenjin call for *Majimboism,* and the continuing opposition of the main Churches and the LSK, the Moi regime felt hopelessly beleaguered. The Paris Group's decision to suspend aid the same day as Biwott and Oyugi were arrested broke the regime's resolve.

Officials of the Ministry of Finance insisted that Kenya had attempted to meet the demands of the IMF and the World Bank, reducing its budget deficit from 9.5 per cent of the gross domestic product to 4.8 per cent during the last year. The prices of several agricultural products had been decontrolled since 1986. Payments to farmers, the Ministry claimed, had been improved for coffee, cotton, maize and pyrethrum, in an attempt to ensure that producers received a higher proportion of the international producer price. Kenyan officials considered that considerable progress had been made.[110] The President's speech on *Jamhuri* Day, 12 December 1991, pointed out that Kenya had always honoured its international debts and had reduced expenditure and attempted to attract local and foreign investment. During this period, he pointed out, manufacturing exports had increased by 70 per cent and the civil service wage bill had been cut. Inefficient parastatals were being advertised for sale and income tax collection improved.[111]

Representatives of the donors, the World Bank and the IMF, by contrast, made it clear that further support for Kenya, to be considered in six months' time, would be conditional upon decisive action to redress macro-economic imbalances, to improve the financial discipline of public enterprises, to begin a serious attempt to reduce the size of the civil service, and 'to provide an environment that is consistently supportive of private investment and initiative'.[112] The suspension of rapid disbursement aid and balance of payments support created immediate problems for the Kenyan government. The Ministry of Finance acknowledged that the country would require another Sh12,200 million in additional balance of payments support in the 1991–2 financial year.[113] *The Times* of London, in an editorial of 27 November 1991, spelled out starkly the choice before the regime. 'Good government,' the editorial observed, 'is now recognised as vital if aid is to be effective. President Moi continues to provide very bad government. Until he reforms, there should be no question of resuming foreign aid.'[114]

President Moi and his inner circle had to assess political as well as economic pressures, of course. With the Ouko crisis now striking at the heart of the government, it was becoming evident that they could not withstand the continuing domestic and external pressure for political liberalisation. But could KANU withstand a competitive election? How irreparably had the regime's support base been damaged? Above all, could it withstand, or perhaps prevent, a Kikuyu-Luo alliance? Following Ouko's death, and with Odinga in the forefront of opposition leadership, KANU ran the risk of a mass defection in the Luo Districts of Nyanza Province. The Kikuyu of Central Province and Nairobi remained bitterly hostile, while Gusii, Luo, Abaluhya and Kikuyu 'settlers' in the Rift Valley were also now alarmed by the demand for *Majimboism* by local Kalenjin leaders and by threats of 'ethnic cleansing' unless non-Kalenjin in the province declared their loyalty to President Moi and KANU. The ruling party's committed supporters in Rift Valley Province – the Kalenjin, Maasai, Samburu and Turkana – comprised only 15 per cent of Kenya's population and controlled only 34 or 35 seats in the National Assembly, only one third of the number required for an overall majority.

The party's moderates knew that KANU could not survive without the support of such 'swing' ethnic groups as the Gusii and Abaluhya, who between them returned another 30 MPs. Several prominent KANU leaders appeared to understand these problems, although most of them had fallen out of favour with the President's inner coterie and subsequently would defect to opposition parties. Even the *Weekly Review,* which by the late 1980s was much less critical of the ruling party than it had been during the last Kenyatta years, observed that:

> KANU cannot afford to be complacent. The ruling party should have realised by now that its ham-fisted politics have to a large extent been responsible for driving figures who would otherwise have been valuable assets into the hands of the opposition, the most obvious examples being Shikuku, Muliro, Matiba and Rubia. FORD has since thrived by attracting the support, if not the membership, of a large number of disaffected politicians across the country. The recent flood of support for FORD in the period leading up to and following the aborted Kamukunji rally could be taken as an indication that it has the capacity to recruit on a large-scale to its ranks, which should be seen soon enough, as the psychological barriers against participating in opposition politics are shattered.
>
> For one thing, KANU will have to realise that it will no longer be able to use an iron fist against its own members. It now has to cope with the task of wooing members, well aware that its strength in numbers came about at a time when there was no alternative and membership of the party was virtually mandatory for some people.[115]

Many KANU leaders did not appear to understand this basic fact, however.

The Legalisation of the Opposition, December 1991

On 26 November 1991 Nicholas Biwott was sacked and, along with Oyugi, arrested for complicity in the murder of Robert Ouko. Occurring on the same day as the West rejected continued bilateral aid, this 'double whammy' completely destroyed the government's will to resist. Many KANU hawks owed their election to the National Assembly to the ex-Minister. In fact, some Cabinet Ministers were little more than his nominees, possessing little political support on their own. Even outside the Kalenjin heartlands, Ministers such as Burudi Nabwera, Samson Ongeri and Joseph Kamotho – all conspicuous hardliners – stood little chance of re-election in unrigged, multi-party polls. For nearly two decades, Biwott had been President Moi's closest political and business associate. His downfall now threatened the regime's survival. His removal from Moi's side also briefly gave the moderates greater influence within the ruling circle.

Under intense domestic and foreign pressure, President Moi reluctantly decided that he had no option but to make a dramatic gesture. He therefore summoned a special KANU National Delegates' Conference at the Kasarani sports stadium in Nairobi to be held on 2 December. Many of the 3,600 delegates who arrived for the hastily summoned conference expected to hear the President announce that Kenya would prepare to withstand foreign intervention in its domestic affairs. It was only after a short break, two hours into the meeting, that National Organising Secretary Musyoka announced that the delegates had been summoned to decide whether KANU should remain the only legal party or if opposition parties should be permitted to register. It seemed likely that KANU's leaders had decided only at this late stage that they would go through with the decision, or else were attempting to present the party's hardliners with a *fait accompli*.[116]

The majority of speakers opposed the move to political pluralism. Samburu KANU Chairman Job Lalampaa, for example, declared, 'We in Samburu know only one party – KANU – and we are totally opposed to multi-parties.' Similar sentiments were expressed by delegates from Mombasa, North-Eastern Province and Nairobi. Even the KANU National Organising Secretary opposed the change, arguing that Kenya would be torn apart by ethnic rivalries if opposition parties were legalised. 'The choice', he observed, 'is between KANU and violence.'[117] The debate revealed a clear generational division in KANU ranks. Older officials and self-proclaimed former 'freedom fighters' almost universally opposed any change in the ruling party's political monopoly. A few younger delegates, such as Assistant Minister for Planning Noor Abdi Ogle, a hardliner from North-Eastern Province, concurred, even suggesting that Kenya should remain a single-party state 'forever'.[118] Several of these were members of the 'Biwott class of '88' and owed their political loyalties to him. At that moment, however, Biwott was still in gaol, having been arrested six days earlier, and unable to act to prevent any change to the *status quo*. Finally, after several hours of debate, Moi stood up and announced that he intended to repeal Section 2(A) of the constitution, which nine years earlier had made Kenya a *de jure* single-party state, and legalise political opposition to KANU. Despite their public opposition, a stunned conference unanimously concurred.[119]

As well as adopting the recommendation to repeal Section 2 of the constitution, the seventh resolution of the Delegates' Conference reflected the bitter internal struggles going on in the party. It asserted that 'discipline be emphasised through all levels of the KANU leadership, and that any leader who does not toe the party line of support for the government should resign his or her party and/or government post'. The final resolution to be approved also reflected the exasperation of President Moi and his close colleagues with foreign intervention in Kenya's domestic affairs, which they felt had forced them, against their will, into this ill-advised experiment. The resolution condemned:

> All foreign countries which are giving money to a few individuals and groups in Kenya in order to cause chaos by telling and encouraging some people not to obey the laws of the country and the constitution. Foreign countries should respect our sovereignty and take us as we are ... [while] any person or party that receives money from foreign countries should be dealt with severely according to the laws of the land.[120]

Two days later, a bill was introduced in the National Assembly, formalising this seismic change in political life. The proposal was rushed through parliament in six days (rather than the usual 14), coming into effect as Constitutional Amendment No. 2 (1991) on 10 December, so that President Moi could discuss the decision in his *Uhuru* Day speech on 12 December.

Whether President Moi's decision was an inspired tactic or an ill-considered response to pressure remains unclear. Also unclear is the exact reason why he made the decision that it was time to change. Certainly he had been pressured heavily by Western leaders in the previous three months that some form of change was required, and diplomatic sources suggest that he had made his decision in principle some time before but, concerned about the strength of hardline opposition to reform, had waited until the moment was ripe. Specifically, it appears that KANU moderates, including Saitoti, persuaded the President that resumption of Western aid was conditional on political reform, and that KANU could legalise opposition parties, win a snap election and keep the money rolling in. It is clear that Moi was under intense pressure in the period 25 November–2 December, as he lost his closest ally to gaol and found Western governments arrayed against him. Without Biwott, the hardliners were caught by surprise.

By deciding to accede to international pressure for greater political pluralism before it was inevitable, President Moi had seized the initiative back from FORD, enabling KANU to control the legislative process which would legalise opposition parties and to prepare the multi-party electoral process to KANU's advantage. Although FORD had won the legal right to compete, the government remained hostile to open debate, a free press, and the norms of Western-style pluralist democracy. Moi and KANU would fight hard to win the forthcoming election, and their methods would be rather different from those used by those leaders whose conversion to multi-party democracy was more deep-rooted.

Notes

1 Jennifer A. Widner, *The Rise of a Party-State in Kenya, passim.*

2 David Throup, 'Render Unto Caesar the Things that are Caesar's: The Politics of Church–State Conflict in Kenya, 1978–90', in Holger Bernt Hansen and Michael Twaddle (eds), *Religion and Politics in East Africa,* James Currey, London, 1995, pp. 143–76.

3 *Ibid.,* pp. 154–73.

4 Bishop Okullu's publications include *Church and Politics in East Africa,* Uzima Press, Nairobi, 1974; *Church and State in Nation Building and Human Development,* Uzima Press, Nairobi, 1984; and 'Church and Society in Africa', in B. Onimode *et al.* (eds), *Alternative Development Strategies for Africa: Coalition for Change,* Institute for African Alternatives, London, 1990, pp. 79–97.

5 David Throup, 'Render Unto Caesar the Things that are Caesar's: The Politics of Church-State Conflict in Kenya, 1978–90', pp. 147–73.

6 Interview with the Rt. Rev. Dr Henry Okullu, London, May 1994.

7 *Weekly Review,* Nairobi, 21 January 1983, pp. 4–5.

8 Interview with Paul Muite, Nairobi, November 1993.

9 Interview with Gibson Kamau Kuria, Nairobi, December 1992.

10 *Weekly Review,* 9 December 1988, p. 10. See also *Weekly Review,* 7 April 1989, pp. 13–16.

11 *Weekly Review,* 16 December 1988, pp. 4–9; and 23 December 1988, pp. 4–7. See also *Weekly Review,* 24 February 1989, pp. 4–6, and 21 April 1989, pp. 14–15.

12 *Weekly Review,* 23 September 1988, p. 17; 30 September 1988, p. 16; 7 October 1988, p. 12; 21 October 1988, pp. 4–7; 4 November 1988, pp. 14–15; 16 December 1988,

pp. 4–9; and 23 December 1988, pp. 4–7.
13 *Weekly Review*, 5 January 1990, pp. 5–6; and 12 January 1990, pp. 3–9.
14 *Weekly Review*, 4 May 1990, pp. 6–9 and 15–17. For the magazine's coverage of Mandela's release and the trend towards multi-party politics elsewhere in Africa, see the issues for 16 February 1990, pp. 43–46 and 50–51; and 4 May 1990, pp. 9–25.
15 *Weekly Review*, 23 February 1990, pp. 3–27; 2 March 1990, pp. 4–28; 9 March 1990, pp. 4–10; 16 March 1990, pp. 10–12; and 23 March 1990, pp. 4–10.
16 For details of earlier cases of political assassination see David Throup, 'The Construction and Destruction of the Kenyatta State', in M. G. Schatzberg (ed.), *The Political Economy of Kenya*, pp. 50–52; and *Weekly Review*, 23 March 1990, pp. 4–9.
17 *Africa Confidential*, 31 May 1991, vol. 32, no. 11, pp. 5–6.
18 Information from a senior Kenya Government official. See also *Weekly Review*, 16 August 1991, pp. 7–8.
19 *Ibid.*
20 *Economist* Intelligence Unit, Quarterly Country Report, Kenya, no.4 (1991), pp. 15–16. See also *Weekly Review*, 16 August 1991, pp. 8–12; and 23 August 1991, pp. 17–29.
21 *Economist* Intelligence Unit, Quarterly Country Report, Kenya, no.4 (1991), p. 9.
22 Troon's testimony as reported in *Weekly Review*, 29 November 1991, p. 7.
23 This conclusion was drawn by one of the authors based on reading press reports of the Anguka trial.
24 *Weekly Review*, 11 May 1990, pp. 6–12; and 18 May 1990, p. 8.
25 *Ibid.*, especially, 18 May 1990, p. 8.
26 Interviews with several Kikuyu businessmen, Nairobi, December 1992. See also the articles in *Weekly Review*, 11 May 1990, pp. 10–12. It should, however, be noted that in January 1990 Matiba had sought readmission to KANU; see *Weekly Review*, 26 January 1990, pp. 15–16; and 2 February 1990, pp. 4–6.
27 Interviews with Paul Muite, Nairobi, November 1993, and Rt. Rev. Dr Henry Okullu, London, May 1994.
28 Interview with Rt. Rev. Dr Henry Okullu, London, May 1994.
29 Interview with Paul Muite, Nairobi, November 1993.
30 *Weekly Review*, 6 July 1990, pp. 11–12; 13 July 1990, pp. 3–12 and 16–18; 15 November 1991, pp. 17–18; and 22 November 1991, pp. 10–15.
31 *Weekly Review*, May or June 1990. See also the remarks by President Moi when he announced the appointment of the Saitoti Commission into KANU's internal affairs as printed in *Weekly Review*, 6 July 1990, pp. 9–10 and his remarks during a visit to Nakuru, reported in the same issue, p. 12.
32 *The Economist*, 23 June 1990, p. 83. See *Weekly Review*, 4 January 1991, p. 17, for the trial of those subsequently arrested.
33 *Weekly Review*, 13 July 1990, pp. 16–19.
34 Interview with Paul Muite, Nairobi, November 1993. See also *Weekly Review*, 22 November 1991, pp. 11–13 for details of the second Kamukunji rally.
35 Interview with Paul Muite, Nairobi, November 1993.
36 *Ibid.*
37 *Weekly Review*, 15 June 1990, pp. 13–14.
38 *Weekly Review*, 13 July 1990, pp. 3–23. *Saba Saba* means literally 'the seventh of the seventh'.
39 *Ibid.* pp. 3–11.
40 *Weekly Review*, 27 July 1990, p. 9 for an account of Muite's meeting with President Moi. On the fate of other radicals see the issues for 13 July 1990, pp. 18–23; and 20 July, pp. 20–21 for the fate of Gibson Kamau Kuria.
41 *Weekly Review*, 10 August 1990, pp. 10–12; 17 August 1990, pp. 4–11; and 24 August 1990, pp. 4–21.
42 Muge had created difficulties for his episcopal colleague, the Rt. Rev. David Gitari, when he reported to the Special Branch that the two bishops had held a secret meeting with representatives of the Kenya National Liberation Front, while attending a World Council of Churches' gathering in Canada. See *Weekly Review*, 5 May 1989, p. 19 and interviews with senior officials of the Church of the Province of Kenya, September 1990.
43 *Weekly Review*, 17 August 1990, pp. 4–11; and 24 August 1990, pp. 4–21.
44 *Weekly Review*, 24 August 1990, p. 7 and p. 11; and 31 August 1990, pp. 15–18.
45 As *Africa Confidential* presciently observed, however, 'it was too late for Moi simply to bring in some new blood while keeping intact the one-party system. The logic of reform now is

that he must go further, and delegate power to a government which commands a Parliamentary majority which is the product of fair elections.' Such a step, in May 1991, remained too big for Moi to contemplate. *Africa Confidential,* 31 May 1991, vol. 32, no. 11, p. 5.

46 *Weekly Review,* 6 July 1990, pp. 9–10 for President Moi's statement, announcing the appointment of the Commission. For reports of the Commission's first meetings see the issues for 27 July 1990, pp. 3–8; 10 August 1990, pp. 4–12; 17 August 1990, pp. 13–17; and 31 August 1990, pp. 19–27.

47 *Weekly Review,* 7 December 1990, pp. 4–21; and 14 December 1990, pp. 3–10.

48 Kamotho, quoted in *Weekly Review,* 1 February 1991, pp. 10–11.

49 *Weekly Review,* 4 January 1991, pp. 11–12; and 25 January 1991, p. 4.

50 *Ibid.*

51 *Weekly Review,* 11 January 1991, pp. 6–7; and 1 February 1991, pp. 4–6 and p. 8.

52 *Weekly Review,* 11 January 1991, pp. 6–7.

53 *Ibid.*, p. 7.

54 *Ibid.*, p. 8. See also *Weekly Review,* 17 May 1991, p. 18; and 31 May 1991, pp. 19–21.

55 *Weekly Review,* 8 March 1991, pp. 4–5.

56 *Nairobi Law Monthly,* March–April 1991. See also *Weekly Review,* 15 February 1991, p. 8; 15 March 1991, p. 10; 22 March 1991, pp. 3–6; 29 March 1991, pp. 10–11; 26 April 1991, pp. 8–9; and 31 May 1991, pp. 21–23; 21 June 1991, pp. 21–22; and 28 June 1991, pp. 11–13 for Odinga's skilful manipulation of the registration process.

57 *Nairobi Law Monthly,* March–April 1991, p. 44.

58 *Weekly Review,* 8 March 1991, pp. 4–5 and 13–14; and *The Independent,* 20 March 1991, p. 21.

59 *Weekly Review,* 8 March 1991, pp. 4–5.

60 *Weekly Review,* 15 March 1991, pp. 3–10.

61 *Nairobi Law Monthly,* March–April 1991.

62 *Weekly Review,* 12 April 1991, pp. 15–17 and 26 April 1991, pp. 8–9. See also *Weekly Review,* 15 February 1991, p. 8; 15 March 1991, p. 10; 22 March 1991, pp. 3–6; 29 March 1991, pp. 10–11; 31 May 1991, pp. 21–23; 17 May 1991, p. 18; 21 June 1991, pp. 21–22; and 28 June 1991, pp. 11–13. The final rejection of the NDP's registration is recounted in *Weekly Review,* 26 July 1991, pp. 4–14. The case was heard before Mr Justice Norbury Dugdale, the chief target of the LSK's criticism of political judges.

63 *Weekly Review,* 3 May 1991, pp. 6–7; 10 May 1991, p. 15; and 17 May 1991, pp. 19–20.

64 *Weekly Review,* 26 April 1991, p. 9.

65 *Weekly Review,* 17 May 1991, pp. 19–20.

66 See the sermons by Rev. Dr Timothy Njoya and the Rt. Rev. Dr Henry Okullu early in 1990 and Odinga's comments in January 1991, quoted in *Weekly Review,* 5 January 1990, pp. 5–6; 12 January 1990, pp. 3–9; and 11 January 1991, pp. 6–7.

67 No proof has ever emerged of such American financial support, though it cannot be entirely ruled out.

68 *Weekly Review,* 11 January 1991, pp. 10–11; 22 February 1991, pp. 11–13; 22 March 1991, p. 16; 29 March 1991, pp. 8–10; and 5 April 1991, pp. 11–13 for some of Hempstone's clashes with Kenyan politicians. One of the authors attended a meeting of American policy makers in Washington D.C. in May 1990, where the tone was highly critical of the Kenyan government.

69 Interview with senior Kenyan government official. See also *Weekly Review,* 20 September 1991, pp. 6–7 for how British attitudes were interpreted by one part of the Kenyan press.

70 Interview with Rt. Rev. Dr Henry Okullu, London, May 1994.

71 Interview with Paul Muite, Nairobi, November 1993.

72 *Weekly Review,* 17 May 1991, p. 15. See also the issue for 6 September 1991, pp. 4–15 when the crisis came to a head.

73 *Ibid.*, and interview with Gibson Kamau Kuria, Nairobi, December 1992.

74 *Weekly Review,* 17 May 1991, pp. 6–10. Wako had enjoyed a distinguished legal career, serving as chairman of both the KLS and of the African Bar Association in the early 1980s. He had a high reputation as a human rights lawyer. In November 1982, he had been appointed by the United Nations Secretary-General to serve for three years on the board of trustees of the UN Voluntary Fund for Victims of Torture. See *Weekly Review,* 26 November 1982, p. 17.

75 *Weekly Review,* 17 May 1991, pp. 20–1.

76 *Weekly Review,* 19 April 1991, pp. 3–6.

77 *Weekly Review*, 14 June 1991, pp. 4–7.
78 *Weekly Review*, 21 June 1991, pp. 19–21 and 28 June 1991, pp. 9–11.
79 Interview with Paul Muite, Nairobi, November 1993.
80 *Ibid.*
81 Interviews with Paul Muite, Nairobi, November 1993, and Rt. Rev. Dr Henry Okullu, London, May 1994.
82 *Ibid.*
83 Interview with Rt. Rev. Dr Henry Okullu, London, May 1994.
84 Interview with Paul Muite, Nairobi, November 1993.
85 *Ibid.* See also *Weekly Review*, 26 July 1991, p. 20; and 2 August 1991, pp. 3–6.
86 Interview with Paul Muite, Nairobi, November 1993; and *Weekly Review*, 9 August 1991, pp. 20–22.
87 *Ibid.*
88 *Ibid.*
89 *Weekly Review*, 30 August 1991, pp. 4–7; and 4 October 1991, pp. 4–7.
90 *Weekly Review*, 22 November 1991, pp. 10–13.
91 *Ibid.*, and interview with Paul Muite, Nairobi, November 1993.
92 *Weekly Review*, 22 November 1991, pp. 13–15.
93 *Weekly Review*, 6 December 1991, p. 15.
94 *Weekly Review*, 29 November 1991, pp. 14–15; and David Throup, 'Render Unto Caesar the Things that are Caesar's: Church–State Conflict in Kenya, 1978–90', pp. 170–1.
95 *Weekly Review*, 4 October 1991, pp. 10–11; and 18 October 1991, pp. 10–13 for Keen's disagreement with Kalenjin and Maasai leaders' calls for *Majimboism*.
96 Oloo–Aringo's attempt to unite Luo Members of Parliament against the authoritarian attitudes of Rift Valley politicians can be traced in *Weekly Review*, 11 October 1991, pp. 3–4; 18 October 1991, pp. 3–10; 8 November 1991, pp. 3–4; and 29 November 1991, pp. 10–14. Clashes erupted along the Kisumu–Nandi border early in November: see *Weekly Review*, 15 November 1991, pp. 10–17 and 29 November 1991, pp. 17–18. By the end of the month, Oloo–Aringo was attempting to back track from his politically exposed position, which was being further undermined by South Nyanza leader and Cabinet Minister, Dalmas Otieno: see *Weekly Review*, 29 November 1991, pp. 13–14.
97 *Weekly Review*, 1 March 1991, pp. 4–12. The section is also based on interviews conducted in Nairobi, Central Province and the Rift Valley during December 1992.
98 *Weekly Review*, 11 October pp. 7–17; and 25 October 1991, pp. 3–10 (President Moi urges moderation); 8 November 1991, pp. 28–30 (the defeat of Kenneth Kaunda in Zambia); 15 November 1991, pp. 4–7 (Superintendent Troon gives his evidence to the Ouko Commission); 22 November 1991, pp. 3–9 (the fall of Biwott); and pp. 10–15 (the second Kamukunji rally); 29 November 1991, pp. 3–9 (Biwott's arrest); and p. 28 (the Paris Club meeting).
99 *Weekly Review*, 15 November 1991, pp. 4–10. See also *Sunday Nation*, 4 October 1991, p. 1.
100 *Ibid.*; and *Weekly Review*, 29 November 1991, pp. 3–9.
101 Kenya Government Gazette, 25 November 1991.
102 *Weekly Review*, 14 August 1992, pp. 16–17; 21 August 1992, pp. 14–15; and 28 August 1992, pp. 22–4.
103 *Weekly Review*, 22 November 1991, pp. 3–9; and 29 November 1991, pp. 3–9.
104 *Weekly Review*, 22 November 1991, pp. 7–8. See also *Financial Times*, London, 27 November 1991, p. 4.
105 *Ibid.*, and *Weekly Review*, 6 December 1991, p. 28.
106 *Weekly Review*, 15 November 1991, pp. 28–32. See also the issue for 22 November 1991, pp. 22–3.
107 Quoted in *Weekly Review*, 22 November 1991, p. 8.
108 *Weekly Review*, 15 November 1991, p. 27.
109 *Weekly Review*, 6 December 1991, pp. 25–6.
110 *Weekly Review*, 22 November 1991, pp. 21–2; 29 November 1991, p. 28; and 6 December 1991, pp. 25–6.
111 *Weekly Review*, 20 December 1991, pp. 11–12.
112 Quoted in *Weekly Review*, 6 December 1991, p. 26.
113 *Weekly Review*, 29 November 1991, p. 28.
114 *The Times*, London, 27 November 1991.
115 *Weekly Review*, 6 December 1991, p. 5.
116 *Ibid.*, pp. 7–8.
117 *Ibid.*, p. 7.
118 *Ibid.*, p. 8.
119 *Ibid.*, p. 9.
120 *Ibid.*

Five

The Rise and Fall of the Opposition, December 1991–October 1992

Following the introduction of political pluralism, the ruling party was divided into two main groups. Moderates, led by the then Minister of Health Mwai Kibaki, saw the decision as an opportunity for the party to reform itself and to pay greater attention to public opinion. Kibaki informed the press that he intended to remain in KANU in an attempt to end speculation that he was about to defect to the opposition. Political commentators anticipated that he would play a prominent role in KANU's attempt to hold on to Kikuyu votes as the ruling party's most credible standard-bearer in Central Province, returning to the political limelight after three and a half years on the sidelines.[1] John Keen also suggested that the ruling party needed to make fundamental reforms in order to present a credible alternative to FORD. The hardliners, reeling from Moi's decision, were slightly heartened by the release of Biwott after 10 days' confinement, just after the conference, for 'lack of evidence'.

'On the Crest of A Wave': The Emergence of FORD as a Political Party

When President Moi bowed to international pressure to repeal Section 2(A) of the constitution and permit the registration of opposition political parties, FORD was transformed swiftly into a government in waiting, seemingly certain of victory at the next general election, due within a year. Yet the new party faced major problems. Although committed on paper to pluralism, Kenya remained a centralised, authoritarian state in which the civil service acted as the direct organ of the ruling party, and traditions of peaceful legitimate dissent were weak. The transition to multi-party politics also brought to the surface divisions between different ethnic groups, and generational conflicts between old-guard politicians and the Young Turks (as they became universally known), the young professionals who had spearheaded change. Soon the rival groups were locked in a battle to control the new party.

With the restoration of multi-party politics after 22 years, in December 1991 and January 1992 new recruits flocked into FORD as disgruntled politicians abandoned KANU and Kenya's professionals considered that it was now safe to identify with the opposition. From 2 December onwards, Central Province and to a lesser extent Nyanza were swept by waves of resignations from KANU, as political leaders and tens of thousands of voters defected *en masse* to the new movement. They included many well-respected politicians outside the current leadership, and some senior figures within the existing government. Two of Moi's Ministers – the embattled Minister for Employment and Manpower Development Peter Oloo-Aringo from Nyanza and Njoroge Mungai from Nairobi – immediately defected to FORD. Other Kikuyu defectors included former Vice-President Josephat Karanja and former Chief Secretary and Head of the Civil Service Geoffrey Kariithi, who resigned as an Assistant Minister on 27 December.[2]

This influx of new recruits challenged the authority of FORD's six political founders. Martin Shikuku felt particularly threatened since his relations with the Young Turks were poor, and he resented the recruitment of former KANU politicians. Supported by Bamahriz and Nthenge, whose base in the party was even more insecure, in the days before FORD's registration in December 1991 Shikuku threatened to walk out and to launch a rival party. He was particularly alarmed by the growth of Kikuyu influence within FORD, identifying Paul Muite as a key opponent. Muite symbolised to his critics all that was wrong in FORD: the over-prominent role of politically inexperienced young professionals in the party's inner councils and the infiltration of members of the Kikuyu establishment who wished to restore the privileged position that the community had enjoyed under Kenyatta. Shikuku and his allies sought in these early days to prevent Muite, Gitobu Imanyara and Luo political scientist Peter Anyang-Nyong'o being coopted into FORD's leadership. He argued that FORD's interim steering committee should only include the movement's six formal founders.[3] Only when the party had been registered, new members recruited and local branches organised, should a duly constituted party convention select a new team of leaders. In response, Muite and his associates argued that former members of the government – like Shikuku – should themselves be excluded from FORD. Several were close friends of Raila Odinga and consequently had access to party Chairman Oginga Odinga.[4]

Even when a compromise was reached, Shikuku, advised by Abaluhya lawyers Japheth Shamalla (a former Permanent Secretary for Foreign Affairs) and Benna Lutta (a retired judge) secretly rewrote FORD's constitution over the weekend of 21 and 22 December 1991.[5] A few days later, the other five members of FORD's interim council gathered at Agip House, Oginga Odinga's business headquarters, surrounded by reporters and excited supporters waiting to accompany them to the Registrar's office to submit their registration papers for the new political party. Shikuku, however, had already presented revised registration papers, strengthening his own position in FORD's inner circle. These changes reduced the size of the party's National Executive (NEC) from 32 to 25 – cutting down the proposed number of national officers from 16 to eight, to be elected by FORD's Annual Delegates' Conference which would convene after grass-roots elections. Power should continue to lie with FORD's six founding fathers. To preserve FORD unity, Odinga and Masinde Muliro, backed by Philip Gachoka, accepted Shikuku's demands. Odinga became FORD's interim Chairman, with Muliro as his Vice-Chairman, while Shikuku served as the party's Secretary-General.[6] Presented with Shikuku's *fait accompli,* the Young Turks who dominated the interim NEC had no alternative but to acquiesce in order not to delay FORD's registration, which took place on 31 December 1991, ushering in the new era of multi-party democracy.

The new party faced great problems, however, in converting a successful protest movement into a political party with a coherent ideology and clear line of command. FORD leaders now modelled their new organisation on the only other political movement they had known – KANU – and reproduced the ruling party's structure of constituency level sub-branches, District-wide branches, an annual National Delegates' Conference and an all-powerful NEC. FORD leaders also had to decide whether the new party should admit anyone who wanted to join, regardless of their past statements, or should restrict membership to critics of KANU's authoritarian behaviour. Despite his own past, Shikuku favoured a much stricter admissions policy than Odinga and the Young Turks, who had criticised KANU's leadership throughout the 1980s, but on this issue he was outvoted. Almost from its registration, therefore, FORD suffered from an endemic factionalism. Its leaders were divided not only by their different views of party policy but by ethnicity and generation. These divisions quickly developed into a network of rival alliances, which soon became bickering factions, jostling for the party's Presidential nomination. Once these divisions became apparent to the general public, the great emotional response to multi-party democracy and the tremendous popular enthusiasm created by FORD's registration would be replaced by disillusionment with politicians and the political process amid the failed hopes that had been aroused.[7]

The Formation of the Democratic Party of Kenya

Following President Moi's announcement, moderates within the ruling party began to push for thorough-going reforms and fresh sub-branch elections. Senior Kikuyu politicians, such as former Vice-President Mwai Kibaki, seemed to have no intention of deserting KANU.[8] They hoped that the President's announcement would usher in a new age of party reform, ending the authoritarianism of the late 1980s and ensuring that the party and government would be more responsive to the views of ordinary Kenyans. The downfall of Nicholas Biwott appeared to have shattered the power of the party's hardliners, enabling Kibaki and his associates to press for radical reforms, going much further than those outlined by the Saitoti Commission, whose recommendations had been debated by the KANU Delegates' Conference precisely twelve months earlier. For the past year, the Commission's recommendations had been blocked. Kibaki and his colleagues, however, believed that in the new pluralist political climate, they would be able to persuade President Moi to reform his government and revitalise the ruling party in order to defeat FORD.[9]

Kibaki and the other KANU reformers, however, met opposition from the Kalenjin inner circle around the President and from party Secretary-General Kamotho, who resented Kibaki's prestige among Kikuyu MPs. For the last two years, Kamotho had sided with the Kalenjin hardliners to block reforms. Now he joined them to prevent Kibaki's political rehabilitation, encouraging President Moi's fears that his former Vice-President might be planning to defect to the opposition and suggesting that he was disrupting the ruling party by challenging the authority of District Chairmen elected in 1988. Instead of seizing the opportunity to reform, the members of Moi's inner circle were determined to entrench their position, driving their critics into the arms of the opposition. They distrusted Kibaki and his associates, drawn from the old élite of the Kenyatta era, and were more intent upon defending their positions in KANU's hierarchy than undermining FORD. Most had not yet realised that they would have to fight a real election against a real opposition under the supervision of Western observers, and would be forced to discard the authoritarian methods of single-party rule.[10]

As this struggle for power within the ruling party was fought out in December 1991, it was easy for Kamotho, the Kakamega political boss Elijah Mwangale and the Kalenjin inner circle to isolate Kibaki and the reformers, persuading President Moi that his former Vice-President and other Kikuyu politicians were plotting to disrupt the ruling party by purging many of Moi's closest supporters. As Christmas approached, Kibaki seized every opportunity to emphasise that KANU was about to launch a though-going clean-up with party elections from the grassroots to a new National Executive, urging Kenyans to continue supporting the ruling party which had presided over the nation's social and economic development since independence. As Kibaki's reform campaign gathered momentum, however, the Minister of Health became increasingly isolated from President Moi. Then on Christmas Day, informed that the President was about to dismiss him, Kibaki contacted friends at the Kenya Television Network (KTN), persuading them to interrupt their scheduled programmes to announce that he had resigned from the government. Kibaki attempted to justify his actions by explaining that he had resigned to protest the rigging of the 1988 KANU elections and the dissolution of the Commission of Enquiry into Ouko's death. Two days later, he announced that he intended to launch a new political party, the Democratic Party of Kenya (DP).[11]

Kibaki's resignation created a new crisis, effectively destroying KANU's position in Kikuyuland, including Nairobi. The onslaught against Kikuyu interests for the past 14 years meant that even long-serving Cabinet Ministers realised that with the legalisation of FORD they had little chance if they did not abandon KANU and distance themselves as far as possible from President Moi.[12] In the first two weeks after Christmas, many prominent figures in Nyeri and Kiambu followed Mwai Kibaki into opposition, including the Kiambu KANU Chairman and Minister George

Muhoho, Assistant Minister for Agriculture John Gachui and Assistant Minister for Cooperative Development Njenga Karume.[13] Apart from KANU Secretary-General Kamotho, few senior Kikuyu politicians remained loyal to Moi. The party organisation in Kiambu, Nyeri, Nyandarua and Kirinyaga was thrown into chaos by widespread resignations, and throughout January 1992 there was a continuous flow of present and former MPs, local KANU officials and other prominent Kenyans into the opposition parties.[14] Kibaki was joined by old-time allies and colleagues from the past, including ex-Ministers Eliud Mwamunga, MP for Voi in Taita-Taveta, and Kyala Mwendwa, MP for Kitui West/Matinyani in Kitui District, who had served briefly in the Cabinet before the 1988 general election, whilst FORD also benefited from a series of defections as numerous MPs and senior politicians, especially from Murang'a and Nairobi (the home areas of Matiba and Rubia) abandoned the ruling party.

By 1 January 1992 KANU had virtually no prospect of winning seats in either Central Province or Nairobi, where the élites had defected *en masse*. In the Luo Districts of Nyanza Province, although the existing KANU leadership had remained in office, almost the entire population – led by Odinga's old political allies such as James Orengo, Phoebe Asiyo, Achieng' Oneko and Denis Akumu – defected to follow their old messiah. Despite Secretary-General Kamotho's protestations on behalf of the ruling party, the only question that now remained was whether Kibaki or Matiba would be able to attract the most support.

The *Daily Nation* and the *Standard*, the country's two main newspapers, were also swept away by the euphoria which surrounded the return of multi-party politics.[15] Although the DP clearly had a less widespread political appeal than either FORD or, indeed, KANU, being too closely identified with big business and the Kikuyu power élite of the Kenyatta period, the party seemed likely to do well in Kibaki's home District of Nyeri and in Kiambu, where it was supported not only by the late President's nephew (Ngengi Muigai), brother-in-law (George Muhoho) and son (Uhuru Kenyatta) but also by Njenga Karume, the former Chairman of GEMA, which had exercised considerable political and business influence before President Moi had forced all 'tribal associations' to disband in 1980.

Another prominent figure to cast his lot with the DP was former Kajiado North MP John Keen, whom Moi had appointed a nominated MP. In 1988, Keen had campaigned for the election in his former constituency of George Saitoti, who for the last five years had held the key post of Minister of Finance. Following the downfall of Josephat Karanja in 1989, Saitoti had been elevated to the Vice-Presidency and had become a close business as well as political partner of President Moi. Keen had been rewarded for his work, becoming an Assistant Minister, but had soon fallen foul of the Kalenjin hardliners around the President. A former member of KADU, Keen in the early 1960s had supported the call for *Majimboism,* but as the voice of Kalenjin politicians became increasingly strident he became concerned that self-government for the Rift Valley Province would entrench Kalenjin hegemony at the expense of his fellow Maasai and the large numbers of Kikuyu who had settled in Kajiado North during the previous two decades.[16] By 1991 Keen had distanced himself from Saitoti, becoming a leading moderate. Shortly after criticising Kalenjin demands for *Majimbo* in September and October 1991, he was dismissed from his position as Assistant Minister in the Office of the President.[17]

Having resigned from the government, Democratic Party Chairman Mwai Kibaki also raised the *Majimbo* issue, warning that the President's inner circle seemed to be inciting violence in order to fulfil Moi's claims that political pluralism would exacerbate ethnic animosities. Several Church leaders in the troubled areas also criticised the behaviour of the police and Provincial Administration as bands of so-called Kalenjin 'warriors' attacked the homes and smallholdings of Kikuyu, Luhya and Luo settlers in the former White Highlands.[18] The resignation of senior Kikuyu MPs from KANU removed the final restraints on an all-out attack on Kikuyu settlers in the Rift Valley. Local Kalenjin officials now saw them as a 'fifth column' for the two opposition parties and pushed ahead with plans to create a KANU zone from which the opposition would be excluded. This programme drove the Kikuyu even more deeply into the arms of the opposition, both FORD and the DP, as the rival opposition parties struggled to gain Kikuyu votes. This division, reflecting as it did a real difference in political orientation as well as ethnic interests, created a serious rift in the opposition from the outset.

FORD leaders castigated Kibaki and his allies for having remained so long in the government. Why had they taken three years to condemn the rigging of the 1988 elections? Why had they not spoken out against corruption or in favour of multi-party politics like Matiba and Rubia in 1990? Why had they not protested when the government had detained the two Kikuyu leaders and dispersed those who had attempted to gather on 7 July 1990? Wilson Onyango, spokesman for the unregistered Transport Association of Kenya, an organisation of *matatu* owners who supported Kenneth Matiba, was among the sceptics:

> Where was Kibaki when Ouko was being murdered? *Wanachi* are now asking that. Does it take Mr Kibaki three years to know that elections were rigged? Where has he been all these years? Why had he surfaced? Why did not Kibaki resign at the time Ouko was murdered? It is an open case that Mr Kibaki has been bought by KANU to fight FORD under disguise.... Mr Kibaki has shown that he is the tribalist number one in this country.... It is better people vote for Moi than Kibaki.... We will vote for Moi, because Moi is not a charlatan like Kibaki.[19]

Onyango's questions, broadcast on the Kenya Television Network news, were difficult to answer. Kibaki and his colleagues had been too pusillanimous towards the Moi government for too long. They had hesitated to protest against the onslaught on Kikuyu business interests and the preferential development projects for the Rift Valley and Western Province, preferring to protect their own positions and businesses. Their restraint had long since been identified by many ordinary Kikuyu as cowardice, losing them credibility with the masses in Nairobi and Kiambu. By contrast, Kenneth Matiba and Charles Rubia had protested, endangering their health and wealth, and had suffered the penalty of being detained for nearly a year. No senior DP politician appeared to have risked anything, only abandoning KANU once opposition supporters had already won the right to challenge its monopoly on power. Many Kenyans wondered why Kibaki and his colleagues had not simply joined FORD, with whose aim of greater political freedom they professed to concur.[20]

Many FORD supporters suggested that the DP was no more than a device to divide the Kikuyu electorate, taking votes away from FORD. Nearly all the key figures in the Democratic Party had been senior members of President Moi's government and of KANU until the end of December. No fewer than 60 FORD politicians from Central Province accused Kibaki of being 'a spoiler aiming to divide the opposition in the interests of the KANU government'. Of the key figures in the new party only John Keen had dared to speak out against the Moi government's policies and to condemn the campaign for *Majimboism*. Others suggested that Kibaki had only abandoned KANU when he fully appreciated the depth of public hostility to the ruling party and had judged that the momentum of the opposition was irresistible, even in his own Othaya constituency.

It seemed that the DP leaders were motivated by two forces: personal ambition and class interest. The Kikuyu élite found it impossible to believe that Oginga Odinga, the former KPU leader and most prominent left-winger in independent Kenya's first government, could be relied upon to lead the nation. Many old-guard DP leaders behaved as if they had a natural right to govern. Moi had 'stolen' their power and endangered their personal wealth: they were determined that they should not lose out again, letting power slip out of Kalenjin hands only to be captured by the Luo who, after their experience under Kenyatta, had even less reason to favour the Kikuyu élite. Quite apart from their sense of 'Divine Right', exemplified by a belief in their own technocratic and entrepreneurial abilities, the DP leaders represented, far more than either KANU or FORD, the interests of Kenya's indigenous bourgeoisie. It was singularly appropriate that Njenga Karume, identified as Kenya's most successful entrepreneur and representative of indigenous capital by Nicola Swainson, should be one of the DP's leading members and its main financier. The DP, far more than the radical FORD or the clientalist KANU, was the party of big business, favouring economic liberalisation and the privatisation of inefficient parastatals.

Kikuyu small-holders in Central Province and Nakuru District were among the rural Kenyans most likely to benefit from market forces, receiving a higher price for their commodities on the free market than from the monopsonistic government-appointed boards, which controlled the marketing of coffee, tea, maize, milk and other agricultural produce. Local coffee and tea cultivators throughout Central Province complained that their money was being 'eaten' by the state and the National Federation of Cooperatives (the KNFC).[21] As Hans Hedlund observed in his 1990 study of the Kibirigwi Farmers' Coffee Cooperative, it was 'difficult for the committee members to openly question the current state order. Open criticism could be taken as an attack on the existing national political order.'[22] During 1991 and 1992 Kikuyu small-holders were to become even more dissatisfied with the government's pricing policy and its failure to remit payments on time. Although President Moi had addressed some of these problems with regard to milk back-payments in 1991, KANU's *ad hoc* measures had failed to get to the roots of the problem or to satisfy disgruntled producers. FORD, in theory, was committed to economic liberalisation, rolling back the economic interventionism of the state, but the DP appeared more credible in its commitment to market economics.[23]

Commentators recognised from the first that the DP might be too élitist to attract the support of many ordinary Kenyans. As the *Weekly Review* expressed it, 'the names of those who had resigned after Kibaki and those who attended his press conference read more like the roll call of a certain golf club than the register of a political party'.[24] Despite the party's attempt to publicise the roles of John Keen and Eliud Mwamunga, a Maasai and a Taita, the DP appeared to be a party of the Kikuyu élite, closely identified with the former Kenyatta regime. The press, for example, noted that Kibaki's press conference at the Jacaranda Hotel to announce the formation of the party had been attended by four members of the Kenyatta family, including the ex-President's brother-in-law, his nephew and two of his sons. In the past, such élite support had proved a tremendous asset to fledgling political factions within the ruling party, but in the new multi-party era, in a climate where many Kenyans were thoroughly disillusioned with the Moi regime and the old order, such support would prove an electoral liability.

By early January, the drift of senior politicians into the DP was slowing, and it was already clear that outside its ethnic base in Central Province and Nakuru District, the DP had little chance of winning many constituencies. Even in Central Province, it was stronger in Kiambu and Nyeri than in Murang'a, where Kenneth Matiba and FORD dominated the scene. The most significant non-Kikuyu backers were Mwamunga, Mwendwa, two former Machakos MPs, Jonesmus Kikuyu and Joseph Munyao; Julius Muthamia, a former Meru District MP; and Ismail Yunis, former Secretary-General of the Dock Workers' Union in Mombasa. The DP attracted few prominent personalities from either Embu or Nyandarua, while its local leaders from the Coast, North-Eastern Province and the Kalenjin areas of the Rift Valley were political nonentities. Unlike KANU and FORD, the DP initially appeared to be an almost exclusively Kikuyu organisation, based on the technocratic and business abilities of Mwai Kibaki, who had served continually in government since 1 June, 1963, and in the Cabinet since April 1966. Kibaki's leadership was unquestioned. Indeed, as the *Weekly Review* put it, 'the DP is Kibaki and Kibaki is the DP'.[25]

Despite its attempt to portray itself as a national political movement, the DP's electoral strength was concentrated in a few Districts. In vast areas of the country the party had virtually no organisation and even less popular appeal. Kibaki and his colleagues needed to recruit prominent figures from outside its immediate catchment area, especially in Western Province, Nyanza and the Rift Valley if the DP was to cease being 'a tight network of élitist, largely Central Province types'.[26] Constituencies where the Democratic Party seemed likely to be able to mount a serious political challenge are shown in Table 5.1.[27] Many of these 16 seats were far from

Table 5.1 Constituencies Dominated by the Democratic Party, January 1992

District	Constituency	Candidate
Kiambu	*Juja*	George Muhoho
Kiambu	*Kiambaa*	Njenga Karume
Kiambu	*Gatundu*	Ngengi Muigai
Murang'a	*Kieni*	Munene Kairu
Murang'a	*Gatanga*	John Gachui
Kitui	*Kitui West/Matinyani*	Kyale Mwendwa
Machakos	*Machakos Town*	Jonesmus Kikuyu
Machakos	*Mbooni*	Joseph Munyao
Meru	*Imenti Central*	Julius Muthamia
Nakuru	*Nakuru Town*	Mark Mwithaga
Kijiado	*Kijiado North*	John Keen
Wajir	*Wajir South*	Ahmed Safari Mumba
Kilifi	*Bahari*	John Safari Mumba
Taita-Taveta	*Voi*	Eliud Mwamunga

certain victories. Keen, for example, would face a very difficult contest against Vice-President George Saitoti. As the *Weekly Review* observed, 'the DP will have to work overtime in the coming months to project itself as a truly national political party.... With fewer than 20 identifiable candidates with a chance of capturing a parliamentary seat, the DP will find it difficult to proclaim itself an equal partner in what still remains a two-horse race between KANU and FORD.'[28]

FORD's Early Meetings

In January 1992, 20 months after Kenneth Matiba and Charles Rubia had held their first press conference, FORD finally was authorised by the state to hold a series of major meetings throughout Kenya. Its first authorised rally was at Kamukunji in Nairobi, the party's symbolic home, on 18 January. Estimates of the number attending the rally varied from a cautious 100,000 by the BBC to 500,000 by the *Daily Nation,* to more than one million by party organisers. By any standard, it was huge, and a clear signal that KANU had little chance of ever recovering the support of Nairobi and its neighbouring areas. The crowd's enthusiasm was clear as the throng chanted FORD's slogan, 'FORD, *haki na ukweli*' (literally, 'FORD, justice and truth'), while Odinga outlined the party's programme and denounced KANU for an hour.[29]

Odinga introduced the major themes that were to become the cornerstones of the opposition's political assault on KANU: repression, corruption, violence, unaccountability and incompetence. He emphasised that when in power FORD would protect freedom of assembly, property, the freedom to settle in any part of the country and Kenyans' right to speak openly and to criticise their government. Condemning KANU for the fact that Kenyans did not enjoy these basic rights after three decades of independence, Odinga denounced the regime for detaining or driving into exile its many critics. He called for further enquiries into the murders of Robert Ouko and Bishop Muge, suggesting that they had been killed because of their attempts to uncover corruption at the highest levels of the government. He castigated the Moi government and condemned its failure to stop the recent outbreaks of ethnic violence in the Rift Valley.[30]

Stressing FORD's commitment to 'accountability and transparency', the FORD Chairman demanded that the government should be more open and responsive to the people's wishes. Only with the removal of the Moi regime, he declared, could freedom be restored and a system of constitutional checks and balances introduced to prevent the accumulation of power by the executive. It was essential, he argued, that free discourse be permitted in the National Assembly, that the judiciary should be independent and the civil service professional and free from political control. Reflecting the recent political changes in Eastern Europe and in various Afro-Marxist states, Odinga, who as recently as 1982 had attempted to establish a Kenyan socialist party, assured his audience and the international community that FORD supported a competitive market economy and economic liberalisation, and would dismantle parastatals and reduce government intervention in economic affairs.[31] Warning that the government might call early elections in April 1992, before FORD's organisation was prepared, the opposition leader urged that intra-party talks should be held to sort out election rules. The Provincial Administration, he insisted, should play no part in the process, which should be organised by an independent electoral commission under the scrutiny of foreign observers. In fact, President Moi and KANU's leadership were in no hurry in January 1992 to call an election. Morale had been badly hit by the decision to legalise the opposition, and by the subsequent defection of so many members of the ruling party. KANU had little to gain by an imminent election and much to gain by waiting for FORD to self-destruct.

FORD had secured the support of most of the organisations and individuals that had campaigned against KANU's monopoly of political power in recent years. Its position, however, was far from secure. It was less well established than KANU in most parts of the country, was actively opposed by the Provincial Administration and the police, and had yet to select a presidential candidate, whereas KANU was united behind President Moi and was fully backed by the whole government machine. As events were to prove, the selection of a Presidential candidate was potentially a hazardous process.

Odinga's speech did not go into details about FORD's policies, but nonetheless it revealed looming problems for the opposition. The Luo veteran's lacklustre delivery highlighted his age and frailty. Other FORD leaders were equally unimpressive. Martin Shikuku's and Ahmed Bamahriz's remarks, for example, revived concern that they were anti-Asian. Shikuku had returned to his favourite theme, that after 29 years of independence Africans had not progressed far in the world of commerce. Such comments aroused fears that FORD might adopt radical measures to reduce Asian and European business influence. A tension also existed within the party between liberals and advocates of greater state intervention, which cross-cut ethnic and generational loyalties. In general, FORD's Kikuyu members and those from neighbouring Eastern Province tended to place greater emphasis upon the protection of individual rights, including those of personal freedom of expression and of property, while its Luo and Abaluhya members tended either to hark back to the statist ideology of the KPU or had belonged to neo-Marxist intellectual circles at the University of Nairobi.

Many ordinary Kenyans in the crowd at FORD's first meeting came away discouraged. FORD leaders had devoted too much time to attacking President Moi and KANU, rather than outlining the party's policies or explaining what people could do to help the party. Many were disappointed that FORD seemed to be simply a different clique of old-style political leaders, castigating their opponents, with apparently little vision of the future or understanding of people's frustration and eagerness to become involved in the political process.[32] The first FORD rally, nevertheless, was judged a tremendous success by party officials and the media.

The Nairobi rally was the first of a hectic series of FORD meetings over the next week, in Machakos, and in Mombasa and Voi on the Coast.[33] All the rallies attracted vast crowds. KANU's regime of intimidation disintegrated as, for the first time in more than a decade, Kenyans felt free to denounce President Moi's regime. In Mombasa, Odinga sought to downplay fears in the business community that FORD would follow an interventionist economic programme and attempted to reassure Asians and Europeans about their future. The FORD Chairman denounced corruption and mismanagement in major Coast industries, including the Kenya Ports Authority, the nearby Ramisi sugar refinery, and the Kilifi cashew nut processing plant, and announced that a FORD government would restore democratically elected local government in Mombasa and Nairobi, after more than a decade of administration by government-appointed city commissions.[34] Martin Shikuku and Kamba leader George Nthenge, by contrast, used the Mombasa gathering to denounce their critics in the party. Shikuku, for example, claimed that he was the only major leader who cared about the interests of 'the small man' and attacked recent recruits who had occupied prominent positions in KANU.[35]

The division between KANU's long-time critics and last-minute deserters was papered over successfully in these first few weeks. The rivalry between the Young Turks and Martin Shikuku, by contrast, grew stronger. Several Young Turks complained to journalists that Shikuku at Mombasa had launched into 'a lengthy ego trip of self-glorification at the expense of the party' and by his anti-Kikuyu stance was risking their ability to form an effective, national organisation.[36] They claimed that Shikuku did not understand that FORD was no longer a small pressure group but had become a major national political party, which needed to appeal to all sectors of the population. FORD could not afford to alienate Kikuyu voters or former KANU supporters, including the wealthy Asian community, for whom Shikuku was something of an 'Idi Amin' figure. Muite, indeed, had denounced Shikuku in an interview to *The Independent* of London on the eve of the first rally, warning even then that FORD might split after the general election.[37]

The Democratic Party's First Rally

The DP was much slower than FORD in organising rallies. Its first meeting at *Uhuru* Park in Nairobi took place on Saturday, 15 February before a crowd of between 50–200,000 people. The DP rally was much better organised than FORD's Kamukunji meeting three weeks earlier. Members of the youth wing, dressed in white and orange T-shirts emblazoned with the party's symbol in the national colours – black, green and red – were organised into task groups responsible for seating distinguished guests and the media, providing security, selling party badges, booklets, flags and T-shirts, and cheerleading. By the early afternoon, virtually every space in *Uhuru* Park had been filled as the crowd were entertained by the popular Kikuyu musician, Watailor, and a troupe of acrobatic dancers, dressed in the party's colours. The crowd cheered the arrival of every prominent figure, shouting, 'DP, *Umoja na Haki*' (literally, DP, unity and justice).[38]

DP leaders were anxious to downplay the party's image as an élitist, Kikuyu-dominated organisation. The rally organisers took great care to ensure that the speakers reflected a party with a nation-wide appeal. Several Kikuyu leaders were kept in the background, or were interspersed with party representatives from all over the country. Kibaki, the Democratic Party's unchallenged leader, was the main speaker. Other major speeches were made by Secretary-General John Keen; former Cabinet Minister Eliud Mwamunga, the ex-MP for Voi in Coast Province, who was the party's interim Treasurer; Mohammed Jahazi, ex-MP for Mvita in Mombasa, Sharrif Nassir's old rival; and the party's Assistant Organising Secretary Ahmed Ogle, the former MP for Wajir South in North-Eastern Province. By contrast, former Cabinet Minister George Muhoho, the MP for Juja in Kiambu, and Assistant Ministers Njenga Karume, John Gachui and Ngengi Muigai remained in the background. Although representatives from different branches were presented to the crowd, few prominent non-Kikuyu figures appeared. The absence of representatives from Nyanza and Western Province, the homes of the country's second- and third-largest ethnic groups, was most striking. Indeed, the party's provisional list of meetings did not include any rallies in the two Provinces.[39]

Kibaki gave a very effective speech at the *Uhuru* Park meeting. In contrast to FORD's leadership, the DP leader never once sank to attacking individuals. Indeed, Kibaki did not even mention FORD, but concentrated upon denouncing the government, and the rampant corruption and 'tribalism' in KANU. The bulk of the speech was devoted to a careful analysis of Kenya's economic problems: an issue on which Kibaki was universally acknowledged to be the country's most experienced and informed politician. The former Finance Minister noted the difficulties faced by the country's farmers, especially the low prices they received from government marketing boards; the drain on resources from inefficient parastatals, such as the Kenya Posts and Telecommunications Corporation, Kenya Power and Lighting, the Kenya Ports Authority and the Kenya Railways

Corporation; and the pervasive problem of corruption. Kibaki claimed that the Treasury had been required to provide the poorly managed state corporations with 28 billion shillings in the previous year. Funds, he alleged, were being withdrawn from the National Social Security Fund to finance the private businesses ventures of important people, leaving state pensions and social security unsecured.[40]

The DP leader demanded that farmers' associations should be allowed to operate without government interference and urged that local and foreign investors should be encouraged to invest in order to create more jobs. The operation of the new 8–4–4 education system also needed to be examined carefully. With regard to the coming election, Kibaki endorsed many of the demands made earlier at FORD rallies and by DP Secretary-General John Keen. Identity cards would have to be issued to 3,500,000 new voters, the 1987 electoral register would have to be updated, an independent electoral commission appointed, and foreign observers invited to oversee the election.[41]

Little in Kibaki's speech differed from FORD's demands. The two parties were divided more by personality and ethnicity than by ideology. The DP rally, however, produced a much more united image then FORD's tumultuous affair, where personal, ethnic and ideological differences were already reflected in the main speeches. If FORD was to fragment along ethnic lines, as already seemed possible, then the DP's image of competence and unity would appear increasingly attractive, especially to voters from Kikuyuland, Embu, Meru and Ukambani. One journalist, for example, observed:

> The DP's carefully crafted message seems to be getting across and, given time and the opportunity to exploit the in-built weaknesses in FORD, it is likely to grow. The DP's strength lies in the party's projecting itself as a responsible, well-organised group with a keen sense of the challenges of the future, and its performance so far has been up to par. Unlike FORD, whose image has been badly dented in the past two months by intermittent leadership wrangles and jostling for position, which presents the picture of an unwieldy convergence of contending factions united only by the common desire to capture power at the polls – if it does not destroy itself before then – the smaller and more manageable DP has succeeded in packaging itself as the 'party of issues'.[42]

The media predicted that in a direct election for the Presidency, moreover, Mwai Kibaki, who had served thirteen years as Minister of Finance and ten years as Vice-President, would do considerably better than the DP's Parliamentary candidates and if Odinga were FORD's nominee might well turn the Presidential contest into a three-way race. Many Kenyans now remembered the 1970s, when Kibaki had been Minister of Finance, as a time of comparative prosperity, when the international commodity prices for Kenya's main export crops had reached new heights. The DP's élitist image might be dismissed by the media as an electoral liability, but conversely it conveyed a message of technocratic competence and prosperity to many voters.[43]

KANU Raises the Stakes

December 1991–February 1992 was probably KANU's darkest hour. No one knew who was loyal or who was about to defect to the opposition and the government was still reeling from the Western freeze on aid. But even then, it retained control over the Provincial Administration and the security forces, and could rely upon the support of the political establishment in most of the country. The mass defections of these early months never threatened KANU's control over the Rift Valley (outside Nakuru and Laikipia Districts), the Coast or the North-East, whilst its opponents' penetration of Western, Eastern and Kisii in Nyanza was patchy. President Moi still possessed the resources for a formidable counter-attack.

The first major FORD rallies in the urban areas had passed without serious incident, but, as KANU's campaign to hold on to power gathered momentum, disruptions of FORD meetings became increasingly common. The first signs of a KANU fight-back emerged when FORD's attempt to open a branch at Ngong in Vice-President Saitoti's Kajiado North seat encountered determined opposition.[44] Raila Odinga and local activist Mrs Wambui Otieno were injured by pro-KANU Maasai *moran* or 'warriors': Otieno was admitted to Nairobi Hospital with head and rib injuries. FORD protested at the failure of police to intervene, contrasting the affray at Ngong with the resolute police response in Bungoma town when FORD supporters threatened to disrupt a KANU rally.[45] Efforts by FORD activists to organise in Gusii and Nandi in Nyanza Province also provoked violence. As KANU leaders sought to reassert control over the political scene, the Provincial Administration and the police disrupted opposition meetings, prevented FORD establishing local offices and simply refused to license opposition meetings. The authorities also ignored attacks on opposition activists by KANU supporters. In early March, baton-wielding riot police broke up a FORD demonstration in Nairobi in support of hunger strikers at 'Freedom Corner'. FORD's first main rally at Garissa in North-Eastern Province in early March was typical of the problems faced by the opposition in these early days. Trouble started when a large crowd of KANU supporters began to throw stones as Oginga Odinga's aeroplane tried to land at the town's airstrip. Chanting pro-KANU slogans and waving large portraits of President Moi, youth-wingers sat on the runway to try to prevent the aircraft from landing. When finally it managed to land, the crowd besieged it and had to be held back by the police, who were forced to fire teargas. Later a vehicle carrying FORD leaders to the rally was pelted with stones and its windscreen shattered. When Odinga and his colleagues reached the meeting site, more stones were thrown and FORD officials had to protect the aged party Chairman from the barrage with cushions.[46]

The MP for Lagdera constituency, Hussein Maalim Mohammed, a Minister of State in the Office of the President and brother of Chief of Staff General Mahmoud Mohammed, claimed that FORD members had staged the incidents in order to discredit the government. FORD members, he alleged, had also acquired arms from Somalis fleeing Kenya's war-stricken neighbour and were planning a campaign of violence to disrupt the District. Joseph Kamotho, KANU's hardline Secretary-General, concurred, alleging that terrorists and 'subversive elements' had joined the opposition. Odinga responded by denouncing KANU for 'political thuggery'. He urged foreign diplomats to intervene in order to 'prevent this great country from declining into a state of civil war'.[47]

The day after Odinga visited Garissa, FORD supporters clashed with police at several places in Kiambu District as they waited for local party branches to be officially opened. Police had warned the crowds of FORD supporters to disperse, contending that the gatherings had not been licensed, and fights had broken out when they moved in. Later they had followed FORD leaders from branch opening to branch opening, provoking further confrontations. Clashes continued in Nairobi a few days later.

The Emergence of Kikuyu–Luo Rivalries in FORD's Secretariat, January–March 1992

Harassed by the Provincial Administration, the police and KANU activists, FORD soon faced further internal problems. Despite the influx of new recruits, and the symbolic importance of the other five FORD leaders, Odinga remained the centre of political authority in the new movement. Within days of initiating FORD's campaign to depose Moi, Odinga had made a declaration which, whilst necessary in the context of demystifying the institution of the Presidency, was to prove his and his colleagues' undoing. At FORD's second rally at Machakos on 22 January 1992, as well as announcing that FORD's constitution and its methods of selecting candidates would soon be forwarded for consideration to party branches, Odinga declared that despite his age he was a candidate for the party's Presidential nomination. By declaring his wish to take the Presidency, Odinga, a symbol of Luo identity or 20 years, inevitably forced the Kikuyu to consider their alignment with FORD, so as to ensure that they too would be represented within the contenders for supreme authority.[48]

Odinga was determined to win political power, and for that he knew he must seek accommodations with the existing power structures in various regions of the country, He was also determined to retain the service of his talented and able advisers, despite Shikuku's opposition. The balance of power within the party remained uncertain, especially as the precise powers of FORD's six founding fathers had not been clearly spelled out and FORD's formal structure remained inchoate and unapproved by any legitimising body. Thus, Shikuku's revisions of the party's rules proved a Pyrrhic victory, since Odinga largely ignored them and found ways to bring the Young Turks and ex-KANU recruits into key positions within the party anyway. By the end of January 1992 Odinga had established a 108-member national steering committee and a 14-member interim executive council, even though they did not appear in the constitution. The steering committee included the 14 executive members, plus two members from each of the country's 46 Districts, and Kenneth Matiba and Charles Rubia.

The establishment of seven committees to devise policy and oversee FORD's affairs and the creation of a central party Secretariat under Peter Anyang-Nyong'o, who had been working for the UN Economic Commission for Africa, further strengthened the party's image and bolstered Odinga's position.[49]

FORD's well-balanced team brought together experienced politicians and the younger professionals who had played an important part in the campaign against KANU since 1986. Two of Matiba's close allies – Rubia and Gachoka – headed the finance committee and organisation and recruitment, while Shikuku was made responsible for devising party policy as head of the public policy committee. Young Turk Imanyara was placed in charge of publicity and information, while Anyang-Nyong'o as FORD's full time Executive Officer was given the most important job of all. The Chairman's willingness to listen to these younger men consolidated their support for the ageing Luo leader.[50] Only Odinga could have brought together such an impressive team in a genuinely cooperative effort. Several of the Young Turks, of course, were friends of Odinga's son, but others, like Muite, were supporters of Kenneth Matiba. By including representatives of several ethnic groups, various professions, and different ideological perspectives, FORD could tap a wide network of informed and well-connected advisers, as it began to prepare its manifesto.

The opposition party, however, was already becoming seriously divided by early February 1992. Shikuku, Nthenge and Bamahriz remained concerned that Odinga and his close advisers were willing to welcome virtually anyone into the party, and that the status of these new-found converts within FORD, especially the Kikuyu, would directly reflect their political significance in the old order, rather than their importance in the new era. Odinga's 'broad church' or 'rainbow coalition' strategy worked well while support for FORD continued to grow, but in adversity it exacerbated the party's divisions. There certainly appeared to be an element of opportunism in the behaviour of some defectors, either because their political prospects were weak under the single-party system or because they perceived the political strength of the opposition in their home areas. Peter Oloo-Aringo, for example, clearly had little hope of holding his Alego constituency in Odinga's Siaya heartland unless he defected to FORD.[51]

Meanwhile, without a powerful figure at the centre of the FORD leadership, the party's Kikuyu members felt that they did not exercise sufficient power. Apart from Muite, who appeared best-suited to an organisational role, their most prominent representative was Philip Gachoka, a little known figure whose sole purpose was to act as their representative until Matiba, their chosen leader, could return from exile. Kikuyu concern intensified after Odinga's announcement that he would seek the party's Presidential nomination.[52] Only a week later, on 29 January, Kikuyu leaders began to express their concerns publicly. A party delegates' conference had been summoned for this day, ostensibly to prepare FORD's strategy in the forthcoming general election. Instead debate centred on a proposal by Kimani wa Nyoike, the former MP for Kinangop, to broaden the party's leadership. In normal circumstances, wa Nyoike's scheme might well have been accepted with little debate. He merely suggested that various vacant positions in the party hierarchy be filled and the role of the various advisory committees, which had already been set up, be formally recognised. Non-Kikuyu leaders, however, saw wa Nyoike's proposal to reduce the authority of the six founders, transferring power to a 34-member steering committee, as an attempt by the Kikuyu to capture control of the party's secretariat. Wa Nyoike made the mistake of suggesting that two new Vice-Chairmen be appointed, along with two Deputy Secretaries-General and a host of other assistants, including the creation of a new post of Secretary for Legal and Constitutional Affairs which seemed to his opponents to have been designed for Paul Muite.[53]

Instead of considering this reorganisation on its merits, FORD's leadership divided into pro- and anti-Kikuyu factions. Shikuku and Muliro both sided with the anti-Kikuyu faction, which warned the Kikuyu that they could leave and form their own party if they were dissatisfied with FORD. Odinga ended the debate by transferring the matter for further consideration to the party's legal and constitutional policy committee. But as the *Weekly Review* observed, this compromise 'was clearly aimed at buying time while attempts were made to deal with the real issues at stake, but developments this week indicate that it is no longer going to be easy to sweep matters under the carpet'.[54]

Already by February 1992 FORD unity was being stretched by the personal ambitions of Odinga, Shikuku and Muite and by Matiba's looming presence in London. These rivalries were intensified, however, by the fact that Odinga, Shikuku and Matiba commanded the support of their fellow 'tribesmen' – the Luo, Abaluhya and Kikuyu, Kenya's three largest ethnic groups. It was already clear that none of them had made serious inroads into the ethnic base of their opponents. FORD was well placed to win an election as long as it remained united, drawing on Kenya's most developed and densely populated rural areas, as well as on the support of voters in Nairobi, Nakuru, Kisumu and to a lesser extent Mombasa. But none of its leaders, not even octogenarian Oginga Odinga, ever commanded a nation-wide following. The majority of FORD supporters owed their allegiance to an inchoate ideal, or to a group of individuals who had taken on the role of defender of their interests, and the importance of these regional self-defence associations made it extremely difficult to disregard ethnicity as a primary determinant of political allegiances. Factionalism stemmed from the leaders' jockeying for position and was intensified by ethnic rivalries. It was made worse at times by the political inexperience of key Young Turk leaders, who did not always find the transition from gadfly to statesman easy to make. Policy differences also had a genuine role in these early days, reflecting an underlying tension between the statists and the liberals in the party. Tactical differences provided the ammunition for day-to-day controversy as party leaders squabbled over whether FORD should become a broad church or only recruit those who had condemned the ruling party's growing authoritarianism, and over the new party's governing structure. These four causes of tension – personality, ethnicity, tactics, and policy – tended to reinforce one another.

The threat to party unity became public when FORD held its first rally in Paul Muite's stronghold, Kikuyu town, in Kiambu District, on Saturday,

1 February 1992, and the Kikuyu mantle was openly placed on Matiba. Speakers assured the crowd that Kikuyu interests would be protected in FORD and that Kikuyu members would play a prominent role in the party. As Matiba's daughters sat prominently on the platform, Muite and Philip Gachoka informed the rally that Matiba was totally committed to FORD and explained that party members would soon have the opportunity to elect their leader. Kimani wa Nyoike declared that the Kikuyu intended to play a key role in the party: 'You know that we, the Kikuyu people, are many and cannot afford to be sidelined in current politics,' he said. FORD provided, he argued, the only vehicle for the Kikuyu to influence the course of political debate and to get rid of President Moi.[55] Nonetheless, ethnic chauvinism was tempered with a dose of realism. Denouncing the DP as politically irrelevant, wa Nyoike warned that to support it was to be marginalised politically in an exclusively Kikuyu party which could never hope to capture power.[56] Kikuyu discontent was again revealed clearly at the party's first rally in Murang'a at Kiharu, Matiba's old constituency, early in February. The District was FORD's Central Province stronghold. Although Gachoka read a message from London in which Matiba urged the establishment of an independent Electoral Commission, other speakers were more concerned to promote Matiba's Presidential bid and to denounce his opponents in FORD, while castigating the DP for destroying Kikuyu unity. Matu Wamae, for example, told the crowd that when he had met Matiba in London recently, the Murang'a politician had been 'fit and healthy', as recently published photographs in the Kenyan press had demonstrated.[57] Kimani wa Nyoike condemned Kibaki and his colleagues as 'the Destruction Party', while others compared the DP to 'TB', whose spread might prove fatal to Kikuyu interests.[58] Paul Muite, Matiba's chief representative in FORD's inner circle, stressed the need for Kikuyu voters and the neighbouring people of Embu and Meru to stand together. Muite suggested that neighbouring Uganda had fallen into chaos because the Baganda, the largest and most developed ethnic group, had mistakenly preferred to support their own communal party, the Kebaka Yekka, instead of forming alliances with other communities. The Kikuyu, he warned, should not make the same mistake. Only FORD could create a multi-ethnic coalition, capable of winning seats in every Province and challenging KANU for control of the government.[59]

When Muite's speech was reported in the media, a storm erupted.[60] Although the thrust of Muite's speech clearly supported a broad ethnic movement, he was also reported as urging Kikuyu to 'remain united as GEMA so as to remove Moi and KANU'. Many non-Kikuyus denounced his remarks as an attempt to revive the disbanded Gikuyu, Embu and Meru Association (GEMA), which had been banned by President Moi in 1980. Muite was already emerging as a scapegoat for KANU's anger.[61] Non-Kikuyu KANU leaders, like Mombasa KANU Chairman Sharrif Nassir, did not hesitate to play on the widespread suspicion of a Kikuyu plot to take over the country or to recall the days of Kikuyu hegemony under Kenyatta. Nassir warned that Muite and his associates in FORD were 'all out to usurp the leadership of the country at the expense of other tribes'.[62] DP leader Mwai Kibaki also seized the opportunity to attack Muite. Kibaki was experienced at speaking the language of national unity and eager to dissociate himself and the DP from Muite's 'tribalism'. 'The time people talked of tribal politics', he claimed, 'is long gone and, in fact, anyone who talks about it is the real enemy of Kenya.'[63] Unfortunately, all too many Kenyans were beginning to envision 'a tribal' political future for the country.

Not all the speakers at Kiharu, however, had been Kikuyus. Luos Raila Odinga and veteran politicians Achieng' Oneko had attended, and had warned that the government would employ 'every method' to divide the Kikuyu and Luo communities. Nonetheless, the ethnic divisions were becoming evident. It was widely noted that only two of FORD's six founders – Gachoka, who came from Murang'a, and Bamahriz – had attended the first major opposition meeting in Kenneth Matiba's home District. Oginga Odinga, Masinde Muliro and Martin Shikuku – the party's three political heavyweights – and George Nthenge had been conspicuously absent.

The Feud Begins: Odinga and Matiba Enter the Race, February 1992

For the first two months of its life, despite its internal wrangling, FORD had presented the image of a generally united group. Its first rally in Nairobi had brought together most of the government's main critics including politicians, the legal profession, the media, the university and the Kikuyu business establishment. In those heady days, a FORD victory at the forthcoming general election seemed assured. Odinga's declaration for the Presidency threw the main opposition organisation into turmoil, confirming that his ambition to become President remained undimmed.[64] He was, however, 80 years old and in poor health. His stringent regimen of meetings in early 1992 severely taxed his strength, and after the party's third major rally in a week at Mombasa on Saturday, 25 January the FORD Chairman was forced to leave for his hotel before the rally ended. The next day, Odinga had been too weary to attend their rally at Voi.[65] Along with US Embassy officials, many party leaders, especially the lawyers and intellectuals in Nairobi – and many Kikuyu – had hoped that the Luo veteran would forego the contest and leave the post for Matiba, who had launched the campaign for multi-party democracy and then spent nearly a year in detention.[66] Odinga, however, remained adamant that he was capable of serving as the head of the executive, rather than merely as a figurehead President. He rejected all suggestions that Matiba might be offered the post of Prime Minister with effective control of the government's day-to-day affairs.

Matiba, although still recovering in London, was equally determined that the Presidency should be his.[67] Odinga, after all, was old, in frail health, and had played little part in mainstream politics for more than two decades. His record as an advocate of socialism, moreover, made him unattractive to the business community. Neither leader would give way to the other, and the Young Turks lacked the authority and popular prestige to repudiate their patrons. On Tuesday, 4 February 1992 Matiba announced from London that he would challenge Odinga for the Presidency. Although at the same time Matiba declared that 'tribalism is no longer a factor in Kenya's politics', his decision immediately revived FORD's appeal among Kikuyu voters, some of whom had shown signs of shifting to the Democratic Party.[68]

FORD soon began to fragment into rival ethnic factions, as political differences, personal self-interest and the tradition of ethnically and locally based political action converted technical arguments over procedures into fundamental cleavages between communities. The party's Luo leaders rallied behind Odinga, while apart from Waruru Kanja, the former MP for Nyeri Town, the Kikuyu began to coalesce behind Matiba. The long-time Abaluhya leaders Masinde Muliro and Martin Shikuku had not yet entered the contest, but both were biding their time in the hope that circumstances would require a more neutral candidate. In the meantime, both were more likely to support Odinga than the truculent Matiba.

The divisions at the top of FORD were mirrored by similar struggles at virtually every level of the party. Various groups had rushed to join the opposition when multi-party democracy had been restored. Frequently they had little in common. Some recruits had been harassed by local KANU officials for years, others had been part of the local KANU power structure and had castigated the civil rights defenders until they or their patrons had fallen from grace. Now both sets of recruits formed rival local FORD organisations. In the rush to establish FORD's presence, the party's national leaders simply recognised most of the various self-appointed local organisations in the expectation that anomalies could be rectified at a later date. In the meantime, however, the rival groups were struggling to consolidate their local positions and to secure financial support and equipment from party headquarters. By early February 1992 FORD constituencies and District branches throughout the country were riven by infighting. The struggles were most intense in Western Province, South Nyanza, Kiambu, Meru and Mombasa – areas where FORD was likely to do well in the election but where it lacked a dominant party leader. Rival groups nominated delegates to the interim steering committee, alleging that their opponents were impostors who had played little part in the struggle against KANU. Every District was supposed to send only two representatives to the committee but some faction-ridden areas sent as many as six members from different groups, who refused to accept their opponents' legitimacy or to be merged into a single District branch.[69]

Relations between Martin Shikuku and Paul Muite remained particularly poor. Shikuku considered that Muite was no more than a stalking horse for Kenneth Matiba. Another of Muite's most outspoken opponents was another Nairobi lawyer, Japheth Shamalla, a Luhya, who had helped Shikuku secretly revise FORD's constitution and who had been a rival of Muite's in the LSK. Shamalla had taken umbrage at Muite's remarks that sections of FORD's constitution dealing with the key issue of the method of nomination of local government, Parliamentary and Presidential candidates – Shamalla's handiwork – had been drawn up badly and that the opposition party would have to review these clauses. They stipulated that the party's Presidential candidate would be chosen by a secret ballot of rank and file members.[70]

Beginning a battle that would continue until FORD fell apart, late in February 1992 Shamalla protested in an open letter to Chairman Odinga that Section 13 of the party's constitution could not be amended by the present interim committee but only by the Annual Delegates' Congress. The provisions would have to remain unchanged until the Congress was called. They rejected the suggestion of Muite and other leaders that FORD might have to follow KANU's example and leave the nomination of its Presidential candidate to mandated delegates, because direct party elections would be too costly and difficult to organise. This issue was more than personal and procedural, however. Shamalla and Shikuku – ironically, given later developments – saw Muite's proposal as an attempt to promote Matiba's Presidential candidacy and to increase his own and Kikuyu influence. In a bitter letter to the Kikuyu lawyer, Shamalla observed:

> If your conscience no longer conforms to the aspirations that helped us bring the current FORD leaders together last August, it will be in the interest of the party and the country for those you represent to leave FORD altogether rather than continue manipulating the party in pursuit of your personal ambitions.[71]

Muite, of course, dismissed such claims. He reiterated that FORD's constitution had been drafted hastily in order to apply for registration and that it was becoming increasingly apparent that certain changes needed to be made. A new document was being devised for consideration by the party's first Annual Delegates' Congress. Shamalla dismissed Muite's response, insisting that no one was drafting a new constitution, although he acknowledged that certain provisions were being reconsidered.[72] Oginga Odinga attempted to downplay the dispute, but Shamalla was supported by Martin Shikuku and George Nthenge, who informed the press in two press conferences at the end of February that FORD's constitution should not be tampered with. In an attempt to reduce the momentum of Matiba's bid for the nomination, they insisted that FORD's constitution was not a temporary set of rules governing the party, but a finished document. FORD's Presidential candidate would be selected by all party members, not by a small clique behind closed doors.[73]

These divisions deepened during March and April 1992, as Muite won the support of other Young Turks for his proposed changes, although most were associated with Odinga, rather than with Matiba's camp. Attention focused on the repeal of Section 13, which governed the nomination of the party's Presidential candidate. Muite and his supporters contended that the new party could not afford to organise a poll of all party members which, they estimated, would cost at least Sh300 million. Such a large sum could be better spent organising FORD's campaign against President Moi. They proposed that constituency sub-branches elect delegates to District level meetings to select Parliamentary candidates and delegates to FORD's Annual Congress, who would choose the party's Presidential candidate. Martin Shikuku and other founders, however, continued to argue that the changes would reduce popular participation in the selection process.[74]

The General Strike, 2–3 April 1992

Prodded by political dissident George Anyona's criticism of FORD's failure to highlight the plight of political prisoners, the opposition party had first considered organising a General Strike to press the government to release all detainees and others awaiting trial on political charges in February.[75] The date suggested for strike action, in early March, had passed without incident but a clamp-down on the women hunger strikers at 'Freedom Corner' reactivated the threat. At the end of March, FORD leaders again began to consider organising a two-day General Strike to press their demands for change on the government and re-emphasise their control over the urban masses. Once the date was set, Vice-Chairman Muliro, who was responsible for planning the strike, flooded businesses and homes in Nairobi with leaflets warning people not to go to work on Thursday and Friday, 2–3 April, and not to travel around the city. The government responded by threatening to dismiss civil servants who failed to turn up and warned that the organisers of the strike would be prosecuted.[76]

The call for a strike had started with a single aim – securing the release of all political prisoners – but opposition leaders gradually added new demands, including the appointment of an independent Electoral Commission. As the initial rationale for the strike shrank into the background, the protest became a trial of strength between the government and FORD. The authorities insisted that they would crush any attempt to stop people going about their business, and President Moi denounced the strike organisers as anarchists. On Monday, 30 March, KANU National Chairman Ndolo Ayah added that FORD would be held responsible for any damages or deaths, indicating that the government might seek financial redress from the opposition. He claimed that FORD was seeking to seize power in a bloody coup under cover of the strike.[77]

The strike call also divided the opposition. Although FORD's call was supported by KENDA leader David Mukaru-Ng'ang'a, most of the other political, social and religious institutions associated with the anti-government protest were more critical. Mwai Kibaki distanced the DP from the protest. Although his party supported the aim of securing the release of all political prisoners, Kibaki publicly claimed that he did not believe that the strike would secure the desired result. In fact, DP leaders resented the fact that FORD had announced the strike without any consultation and they did not want to appear subordinate to the more widely based party.[78] The Roman Catholic Church and the Church of the Province of Kenya also condemned the confrontation. The Rt Rev. Ndingi Mwana'a Nzeki, the most outspoken of the Catholic Bishops, described the strike call as 'hasty and counter-productive'. The National Council of Churches of Kenya also warned that the strike would merely provide an excuse for hooligans to riot and loot.[79] Muliro wrote to the Central Organisation of Trades Union (COTU) seeking support, but the request was rejected by the COTU Secretary-General, Joseph Mugalla, who was to emerge as a KANU candidate in the general election. COTU had been closely controlled by the government for over twenty years, and most trades union leaders remained loyal to KANU even after FORD emerged. Mugalla explained to the press that the strike would lead to massive lay-offs and 'precipitate a national economic disaster'.[80] Two powerful unions, the Union of Posts and Telecommunications Employees and the Railway Workers' Union, also refused to support the strike. Even certain FORD leaders were uncertain about the merits of the scheme.

The confrontation between FORD and the government was a draw. FORD's strike call was successful in Nairobi and Kisumu, but in most of the country business continued as usual. Most of the disruption stemmed from the fact that *matatu* owners had refused to operate their vehicles, bringing transport in the city to a standstill. Shops in Nairobi's central business district were also closed in case of rioting and the threat of looting. Some factories in the business area attempted to operate as usual but many workers failed to appear, especially on the first day of the strike. Government workers, however, heeded the President's warning that they would be dismissed if they failed to attend. Government offices, hospitals, parastatal corporations and tourist hotels, continued to operate as usual. Essential services were also maintained.[81]

There were violent clashes between strike supporters and the authorities in the poorest parts of the city. Vehicles were set on fire, and along the Juja Road the GSU fought running battles with young rioters, most of whom were members of Nairobi's large number of permanently unemployed. By the end of the strike, 83 people had been arrested in Nairobi. Clashes between the police and strike supporters also occurred in Kiambu town, where the police fired on a crowd of 500 protesters. On the second day, the strike began to crumble. *Matatus* began to operate and workers were able to make their way into central Nairobi. Most businesses returned to normal. The situation remained tense, however, in some of the poorer parts of Nairobi and Nakuru. The government was able to claim that most Kenyans had ignored the protest. KANU Secretary-General Kamotho called it a 'flop' and declared that its failure demonstrated that FORD did not command the support of most Kenyans, while Minister for Employment and Manpower Development Archbishop Stephen Ondiek threateningly commented: 'I have a long list of job-seekers and I am waiting for employers to give me a report on those who did not go to work.' Government spokesmen also mocked the fact that businesses controlled by prominent FORD members, such as Oginga Odinga's East African Spectre Ltd, Matiba's Alliance Hotels and Paul Muite's law firm had continued to function as normal.[82]

FORD leaders, by contrast, insisted that the strike had been a tremendous success. Chairman Oginga Odinga, for example, said that 'the success of the strike clearly demonstrates that Kenyans have broken down the shackles of the culture of fear and silence ... [and that] no amount of intimidation, harassment or violence will ever again subjugate or compromise our people in the face of injustice, oppression and exploitation'.[83] The strike's organisation, however, had suffered from FORD's failure to develop a grassroots structure and KANU's hold on the loyalty of the trades union hierarchy. Party leaders had failed to give a clear lead and many workers had been intimidated by KANU's threats. Given Kenya's high level of unemployment, especially in the main cities (30 per cent of able-bodied males), many people had hesitated about not going to work. The most ardent enforcers of the strike had been unemployed youths in the shanty towns. Apart from the publicity which it gave the opposition and the fact that FORD had withstood all threats and pressed ahead with the strike, little was achieved. Political prisoners remained in gaol, the government had not established an independent Electoral Commission and FORD's other demands were still unmet.

Ethnic Clashes and the Meetings Ban, March–April 1992

In the wake of the strike, the opposition parties united on a different issue. The ethnic clashes, which had begun at the end of 1991, were continuing with increasing severity in many parts of the country, and the government, attempting to associate them with opposition political activity, placed a complete ban on all political meetings on 20 March, provoking immediate protests from all the opposition parties.[84] Oginga Odinga initially gave the government one week to rescind the ban before FORD proceeded with its planned rallies at Nyahuhuru, Busia and Kitui, while DP Secretary-General John Keen announced that the DP would go ahead with its planned meetings in Nyeri and Mombasa on 4 and 11 April, although the party cancelled a major rally at Nakuru which would have been its first major meeting outside Central and Eastern Provinces.[85]

The President's intervention rejuvenated the opposition parties, whose performance had become increasingly lacklustre, providing them with a vital complaint. Both FORD and the DP in recent weeks has proved unable to raise issues to capture the electorate's attention. FORD's General Strike had been only a partial success, and the euphoria of January had long since waned. The fate of political prisoners and the campaign to secure an independent Electoral Commission no longer aroused much enthusiasm. Now, however, the opposition's stance was supported by the NCCK and Archbishop Kuria, the head of the Anglican Church of the Province of Kenya. The opposition parties also agreed upon demanding an independent Electoral Commission and neutral officials to monitor the voter registration process and the election, instead of depending as in the past on the Provincial Administration. FORD leaders, however, continued to denounce the DP as spoilers who would divide the anti-KANU vote, portraying it as a party of the Kikuyu élite who had collaborated with KANU until the end of 1991.[86]

The opposition parties continued throughout April to complain about the ban on their meetings. FORD insisted that its supporters had a right freely to associate freely and to organise meetings. It pointed out that the District Commissioners had approved its rallies at Busia, Nyeri and Kitui immediately before the President's announcement. Odinga noted that these venues were nowhere near the ethnic clash zones and concluded that the ban was designed simply to muzzle the opposition as local chiefs, District Commissioners and the President himself remained free to hold meetings.[87] Promising 'to continue to mobilise our forces through non-violent and legitimate means', Odinga warned the government that it had ten days to lift the ban on political rallies before the main opposition party went ahead with its meetings. DP Secretary-General John Keen reiterated a similar ultimatum on 6 April, giving the authorities two weeks to reconsider.[88]

Early in May, President Moi yielded to external and internal pressures and lifted the ban. KANU leaders wanted to reduce the political temperature and were coming under growing pressure from Western governments and the Commonwealth Secretariat to permit opposition rallies. President Moi also announced on 21 April that the Commonwealth would despatch an observer team to monitor the elections. It seems likely that the President, eager to secure international recognition for his re-election, reluctantly bowed to pressure from senior Commonwealth officials. International legitimacy required a more 'level playing field' for the electoral contest. Free access to the media and freedom of assembly were minimum requirements.[89]

Matiba's Break With Muite

Speculation continued to rage about Matiba's health. Back in January his son, Raymond, had announced that the former Minister was in good health and would soon return to Kenya. Two days later, the KANU-controlled *Kenya Times* claimed that Matiba in a telephone interview had told them that he was too ill to become President and would not be seeking any leadership position in FORD.[90] A few days later, Matiba repudiated the story and announced that he was fully recovered and would return to Kenya at the end of January or in early February. Next, Wamae was photographed shaking hands with Matiba. Wamae insisted that the photographs disproved stories that the ex-Minister's right hand was paralysed.[91] A few days later, Matiba declared that he was fully recovered, intended to seek FORD's Presidential nomination and would return home at the end of March. Two months later, he was still in London, receiving an almost endless stream of FORD officials at his London flat.

Matiba maintained a high profile, issuing a series of press statements on the Kenyan political scene, demonstrating that he remained in close contact with developments at home. Like his colleagues in Nairobi, Matiba was calling for the appointment of an independent Electoral Commission, the release of all political prisoners, the suspension of all but humanitarian aid and money to finance the election, and the publication of a precise election timetable. The ex-Minister also welcomed a proposed Constitutional Amendment Bill gazetted on Tuesday, 3 March 1992 (see Chapter 7), which introduced the idea of a post of Prime Minister, who would chair the Cabinet. This created speculation that Matiba might be interested in the post himself, leaving Oginga Odinga to become a figurehead President, thereby solving the political impasse in FORD. Indeed, several KANU MPs opposed the proposed legislation precisely because they feared that it would end the crisis in the opposition party.[92]

Wealthy, self-confident and arrogant, Matiba believed that he was the only candidate fit to oppose President Moi. Matiba not only had vast financial resources, which he was willing to throw into the campaign, but considered that he was entitled to the Presidency because he had launched the campaign for multi-party democracy in May 1990. He had been detained and had suffered a serious stroke while in isolation at Hola on the Tana River. Other opposition leaders – like Shikuku, Muliro and Josephat Karanja – might have lost their seats in Parliament and faced financial problems when the banks foreclosed their loans, but few senior politicians had suffered from the wrath of the Moi regime as badly as Matiba.

Less than a week before the General Strike began, on 2 April, Dr Josephat Karanja, Paul Muite, George Nyanja (a Matiba supporter from Kiambu), Professor Peter Anyang-Nyong'o, Richard Kimani, Raila Odinga, Charles Rubia and Kimani wa Nyoike all flew to London. Although it appears that the leaders were *en route* to different cities for personal and business reasons, as they passed through London several of them held private meetings with Kenneth Matiba, who was still recuperating.[93] As one of Matiba's closest aides, who had represented the ex-Cabinet Minister before the detainees' review tribunal, it had been assumed by political commentators until March 1992 that Paul Muite was the ex-Minister's representative in FORD's inner circles. Accompanied by two other radical lawyers, Gitobu Imanyara and James Orengo, Muite now travelled to London with a very different message. He hoped to persuade Matiba to accept the Vice-Presidential nomination on an Odinga-led ticket, in order to preserve FORD's unity. Muite had become convinced that a struggle for the nomination between Odinga and Matiba would damage the opposition party's image and, perhaps even more importantly, that Matiba's poor health precluded him from being a viable Presidential candidate. Rumours were already circulating in Nairobi that the former Murang'a Cabinet Minister, nearly a year after his stroke, was still unable to read or write. His temper had become even more explosive, he refused to accept advice and his thoughts had become increasingly rambling. By contrast, Muite had been impressed by Oginga Odinga's shrewd balancing of the rival factions in FORD and by his openness to new ideas. As the most charismatic Kikuyu member of the party in Matiba's absence, and a highly respected lawyer with close ties to the Kikuyu-dominated business world, Muite had become an increasingly influential figure. By April 1992, he was no longer content to be merely Matiba's representative in FORD's inner circle, but had come to have substantial political ambitions of his own.[94]

Odinga and his son Raila encouraged Muite's belief that he might be an acceptable compromise candidate for the Vice-Presidency in order to enlist Kikuyu support for Odinga's Presidential bid. Given the Luo leader's age and faltering health, Muite, an ambitious man, saw this as the best prospect for his own rise to the Presidency. Odinga, he calculated, would defeat Matiba, Shikuku or Muliro for the FORD Chairmanship and become the nominee to challenge President Moi. With a Kikuyu, like Muite, as Odinga's running mate, FORD could launch a serious challenge to Moi and undermine Mwai Kibaki's appeal to Kikuyu voters. In all probability, Odinga would live for only a few years as President and then

Muite would succeed. He therefore decided to support the former KPU leader, rather than to serve as the campaign director of Matiba's challenge to FORD's established hierarchy.

Muite's attempt to convince Matiba to make way for Odinga and a younger generation of leaders was a disastrous failure. Matiba not only rejected the idea out of hand, but threw Muite out of his home in fury. He had swiftly followed this up by removing his companies' legal business from the Waruhiu and Muite law firm. Matiba's refusal was probably the most critical event in FORD's history, destroying the party's unity and leading to the future rupture and the formation of two rival parties, which effectively ensured President Moi's re-election. Accounts of the meeting soon leaked out. The *Standard* reported the affair as a generational revolt by younger FORD leaders against the old guard. On his return to Nairobi, Muite denied the press accounts of the conversation, while Matiba remained silent. As a result, the former Law Society Chairman was now exposed to the wrath not only of Shikuku, who saw this as another attempt by the Young Turks to challenge the authority of more established leaders, but also of Matiba's massive personal following among the Kikuyu.[95]

Matiba still commanded considerable support within FORD. His defence of the Kikuyu poor in 1990 was reinforced by his image as a decisive 'man on horseback' who would use his enormous business acumen to sort out the country's problems. Like Ross Perot in the USA, Matiba's strength lay in his enormous personal financial resources, and in the widespread belief that a man who could run a multi-million pound business was capable of running the country in the same way. His personal style, although abrasive, was also a strong asset. Unlike the DP, who were seen as collaborators with the hated government, Matiba was perceived as a man who would not compromise – someone who would take on Moi face to face. Crudely expressed, 'Matiba had guts, while the DP were cowards'. Even Muite's defection did little to reduce Matiba's popularity, instead creating trouble for Muite in his previously safe Kikuyu constituency in Kiambu. Several members of his local party, for example, condemned his break with Matiba, suggesting that Muite was being over-ambitious and should be censured. In fact, Kikuyu support for Matiba seemed to grow as the ethnic divisions within FORD became increasingly evident, threatening to divide the party into Kikuyu- and Luo-controlled factions.

FORD's Manifesto

Meanwhile, FORD's campaign to remove KANU continued. Never knowing when a snap election might be called, in mid-April FORD published its election manifesto. The 64-page document, subtitled 'Charter for the Second Liberation', provided an impressive analysis of Kenya's problems, a reflection of the policy orientation of FORD-Kenya's intellectual young leaders. It failed, however, to excite the public. The three major parties had few policy differences. All agreed in principle that corruption was bad, that state intervention in the economy had gone too far and that the parastatal sector needed to be privatised, that cash crop producers needed greater incentives, that education and health care needed improving, economic output should increase, and that political stability was needed to attract more international investment and to encourage tourism, a major foreign exchange earner. KANU, the DP and the rival FORD factions were also agreed upon the solutions to these problems. All the parties were committed to promoting the development of a mixed economy with greater economic liberalisation than had characterised Kenya's statist development strategy in the 1970s and 1980s. The differences arose over the operation of the neo-patrimonial system and over the various parties' willingness to curtail corruption and to actually implement radical – and socially divisive – reforms.[96]

Oginga Odinga's opening message in the Charter summarised the opposition's case against the Moi regime. The country was in decline, he contended, not simply because of the world-wide recession or the failure of Kenya's exports to compete on the international market, but because of widespread corruption among the ruling élite, who were robbing the country's assets to build up foreign bank accounts. There was nothing wrong with ordinary Kenyans, merely with the ruling élite and KANU. 'All the money that should have been spent on making the lives of our people better', he argued, 'has gone into the pockets of a few people close to the top leadership of our nation.' Moreover:

> as we approach the general election, we have seen the KANU government suddenly making all sorts of promises about the good things it is going to do. It is also trying to tempt Kenyans by giving out some of the wealth stolen from our public coffers. Why did it wait 14 years to show this concern for those who are suffering in poverty?
>
> The answer is obvious: the KANU government will do anything it can to keep itself in power, so that the same people can go on eating away at the riches of our nation, and so that those who have committed crimes against our people can be protected from exposure.[97]

By contrast, FORD's team consisted of professional people of great skill and talent, who would work for the nation's development. They had refused to be bribed by KANU and had supported the opposition in difficult times, proving their courage and commitment. 'Do not think only of what you are being offered today,' Odinga advised. 'Think how you have suffered for the past 14 years. And remember that you have no reason whatsoever to believe that, under a KANU government, anything will be any different in future.'[98]

The FORD manifesto provided a careful assessment of the tasks ahead. While President Moi's government was reluctant to implement fully the economic liberalisation demands of the IMF and the World Bank, fearing the protests that sharp increases in the cost of food and the dismissal of large numbers of civil servants would create, FORD also appreciated that economic restructuring would be a painful process. The manifesto, for example, outlined cutbacks in the civil service and parastatals, committing itself to reducing the government's direct and indirect involvement in the economy. Every encouragement would be given to local entrepreneurs, 'both small and big', to participate. The Kenya Posts and Telecommunications Corporation, Kenya Railways, Kenya Power and Lighting and the Ports Authority would be subjected 'to private sector management disciplines and possible eventual privatisation of some functions which are not easily amenable to be run as public concerns'.[99] Major cutbacks would also have to be made in the civil service. Salaries and wages absorbed over 70 per cent of the government's recurrent budget. 'Over-staffing and unjustified hiring practices have greatly damaged the operations of the civil service,' the Manifesto declared. 'It is increasingly accepted that the civil service could be halved and still carry out all the functions it currently performs.' A FORD government would also build on the Moi government's attempt to rationalise the import licensing system and would support a careful removal of all foreign exchange controls 'as the economy permits' and a policy of trade liberalisation. To support such a programme, the Central Bank of Kenya would be made a more independent and professional organisation, governed by economic not political priorities. Above all, the party intended to promote agricultural expansion, fully recognising the pivotal role of the agricultural sector in the economy. 'Kenya's agro-economic sectors [should be] given a stable and conducive environment with a set of market oriented policies and signals.' The opposition also promised to encourage more direct participation in development decisions.[100]

Critics of the opposition, such as the *Weekly Review,* suggested that FORD's manifesto contained little that was different from established government policy. The *Weekly Review* was particularly critical of FORD's proposals for controlling the financial sector, suggesting that FORD clearly 'begrudges the flourishing of financial institutions owned by interests aligned to the ruling party, KANU'.[101] In fact, FORD quite rightly identified the crucial importance of the government's investment decisions to the health of Kenyan financial institutions. The public sector provided approximately 80 per cent of deposits, the private sector only 20 per cent. Multinational corporations operating in Kenya invested their surplus funds with multinational banks, such as Barclays and the Standard Bank, rather than in more insecure local institutions.

Another major target for attack by FORD was the Provincial Administration, which was a relic from colonial days when the British had required such an administrative corps to govern 'the natives'.[102] From its beginnings as an agency of pacification and control, of taxation and labour recruitment, 'the offices have remained rural extensions of the executive. While emphasising law and order, these offices do not represent local interest in any way. Indeed they stand in the way of local participation in many cases.'[103]When Moi came to power, he had swiftly purged the senior levels of Kenyatta's Provincial Administration. Within two years, all eight Provincial Commissioners had retired. The last to go was Eliud Mahihu, who clung to his Coast Province fiefdom, which he had controlled for an unprecedented eleven years.[104] The FORD Manifesto rightly identified the Provincial Administration as one of the corner-stones of the regime, performing the same monitoring role as during the colonial period. The party, therefore, proposed to abolish the whole system. Its powers would be transferred to democratically elected District Councils with enhanced functions. People should control their own affairs and select their own officials, rather than being monitored by agents of the central government. The party intended to maximise participation in public affairs: 'A government for the people must be a government by the people.'[105] The identification of development schemes and the deployment of resources, FORD contended, needed to be returned to the people. Those in control of managing development should be responsive to local demands and ought to be liable to electoral defeat if they failed to deliver.

FORD identified three other areas where the government's performance was lamentable: education, health care and the provision of social services. The 8–4–4 education system, introduced in the mid-1980s, was agreed by all the opposition parties to be a disaster. The emphasis in primary schools had shifted from skill-based to content-based education, which teachers found hard to test and children frustrating. Secondary schools lacked vital facilities and teachers were over-stretched, while the university system had expanded five-fold in the last five years without any increased provision of lecture rooms or academic staff. Morale had collapsed in the university system. FORD, perhaps paradoxically, advocated the concentration of resources on a few élite institutions – at both the secondary and university levels – which could produce enough high-quality graduates to satisfy Kenya's immediate needs. Higher education policy, FORD declared, needed to take into account Kenya's 'sobering economic reality'.[106] Policy would have to be rationalised, re-emphasising the importance of non-university technical education and accepting that it was unrealistic to promise university education to everyone who aspired to it. Industry and business needed workers with appropriate skills rather than large numbers of unemployable graduates. Even the rapid *Harambee* system needed to be brought under control and 'very carefully re-evaluated and a dispassionate balance sheet established to determine to what extent Kenyans can continue with the *Harambee* initiative without over-taxing the contributors'.[107] This was a dramatic departure from popular thinking on education for the last 60 years, which ever since the development of the independent school system in the 1930s had accepted local education initiatives and attempted to underwrite them with limited state financial support.

FORD's manifesto was equally critical of the provision of health services. The whole medical infrastructure, it claimed, had been neglected by the Moi government. Morale among hospital medical and nursing staff was poor, corruption was widespread, the system was inefficient and decaying, weighed down by excessive bureaucracy and red tape. Once again, FORD advocated a more thoroughgoing version of the government's policies, accepting the principle of cost-sharing and recognising the problems of expanding the provision of services. The opposition also favoured more emphasis on preventive medicine and, like KANU, FORD gave a high priority to family planning and containing AIDS.[108]

The manifesto suggested that, in most areas, FORD would merely do what KANU was already committed to doing but, as the *Weekly Review* observed, 'in a better, more accountable and transparent manner'.[109] The key differences were: was the government going to go through with its promises? Which areas were to receive the investment and new development schemes? How far could the government go in reducing the central economic role of the state without undermining its neo-patrimonial foundations and the post-independence system of patron–client ties that held the state together politically? The opposition parties could advocate radical measures, limited only by the social problems and unemployment that wholesale economic liberalisation would engender. KANU, the beneficiary of the present patronage system, by contrast, was more constrained.

Throughout the 1980s, the government had pursued the chimera of satisfying the IMF, the World Bank and bilateral donors with modest economic reform while leaving intact its patronage network. Vital liberalisation schemes were touted and, indeed, approved and then largely ignored. Just enough was done to satisfy the donors and to keep the Kenyan economy afloat, while not disrupting the neo-patrimonial relationships that sustained the regime politically. By 1992, however, it was becoming evident, as Kenya's economic situation deteriorated, that more fundamental economic reforms were required. The World Bank and the IMF would no longer be satisfied with the partial promises and even more partial measures of the mid-1980s. But drastic action, such as the wholesale dismantling of the parastatal sector, especially the influential state marketing boards, would disrupt President Moi's coalition. As long as President Moi remained in power, economic factors were subordinated to political requirements: Kenya's economic development depended on increased production and, therefore, upon incentives for the main export crop-producing area – Kikuyuland – while the regime's political survival depended upon diverting resources away from Central Province to the coalition of interests which had prospered during the 1980s, most notably the Kalenjin, the Abaluhya and the Asian business community. It was virtually impossible, consequently, for the Moi government to tackle these problems. FORD and the DP, by contrast, had nothing to lose and Kikuyu and Luo voters much to gain from dismantling the statist regime.[110]

George Anyona Spurns FORD

FORD suffered another setback during April when George Anyona, who had been released on bail in February pending an appeal against his seven-year conviction for sedition, refused to endorse the opposition party. In the past, Anyona had been a close ally of Oginga Odinga in the formation of the Kenya Socialist Alliance. In June 1990, as the campaign for multi-party democracy led by Matiba and Rubia gathered momentum, Anyona had prepared a draft constitution for a new opposition party – the Kenya National Congress – and contributed articles to Imanyara's *Nairobi Law Monthly*.[111] In the aftermath of the *Saba Saba* riots of 1990, Anyona and two associates had been arrested and, after a year's delay, prosecuted for sedition. During his two years in confinement, the Gusii radical had attempted to establish contact, through his lawyer Paul Muite, with Odinga, Matiba and Rubia, among others, encouraging them to establish a movement for multi-party democracy and political reform. When FORD became a registered political party, local activists in his native Nyamira District had required little prompting to select Anyona *in absentia* as branch Chairman, expecting that on his release he would join other radicals in the new party.

Following his emancipation, however, Anyona renounced his nomination. Interviewed by the *Weekly Review* in April 1992, Anyona complained that 'FORD was in too much of a hurry to form a party and take power. The original basic concepts were sidelined and betrayed and then FORD took on board people who were not democratic, and who were known to have been responsible for the oppression and dictatorship suffered by Kenyans.'[112] The new opposition, Anyona said, had been compromised by admitting careerists who had little commitment to free debate and Kenyans' civil rights. He disagreed with Odinga's 'broad church' strategy, arguing instead that 'the priority now should be to raise consciousness among Kenyans that the same old oppressive system is intact.... That structure must first be changed before Kenyans can claim to enjoy genuine and true freedom with which to form political parties. That is what the struggle has been all about and I don't see why people are in such a hurry to be in government.'[113] Civil society, he argued, needed to be rebuilt and a pluralist political culture created in Kenya, whereas FORD seemed willing to play the old political game in a futile bid to capture state power on KANU's terms. Events were to prove that Anyona's analysis was correct. Instead, Anyona attempted to establish a local chapter of Amnesty International to campaign for the release of political prisoners. He also launched Alternative View, an organisation which sought to educate Kenyans about the conditions required to sustain multi-party democracy.[114]

The Gusii politician had been sceptical about the course of political developments even before he was detained after the *Saba Saba* riots in July 1990. He had warned Odinga in June 1990 not to trust Matiba and Rubia, whom he viewed as corrupted by the system. Anyona, like Muite and Bishop Okullu, believed that it was pointless to try to register an opposition political party, which would be blocked by the government. Instead, he urged Odinga to take the lead with Masinde Muliro, another political veteran whom Anyona respected, in launching a campaign for political pluralism. Only by strengthening the foundations of civil society could political freedom be secured.[115] In detention, Anyona continued to propagate his message, secretly drafting the constitution for such a movement in letters to Odinga which his lawyers smuggled out of Naivasha gaol. Transferred to Kamiti maximum security prison in southern Kiambu, Anyona again warned Odinga in December 1991 not to transform FORD into a political party but to campaign for fundamental changes in the political system. Elections were futile unless the political system was reformed fundamentally. Even before he was released in March 1992 Anyona believed that his worst fears had been confirmed. Already FORD's leaders were squabbling over the perquisites of power rather than working to enhance debate and acceptance of democratic norms. The new parties, he feared, would prove little different from KANU, having been created by unreconstructed members of the old political élite rather than being based on the wishes of the people. Riven by ethnic rivalries and the personal ambitions of Matiba and Odinga, Anyona judged that FORD was heading for disaster. In these circumstances, he reluctantly decided to have nothing to do with the new party. Democracy, he believed, could only be sustained by empowering the masses and encouraging the development of a democratic consciousness from the grassroots. While others squabbled for positions in FORD, Anyona decided to launch a long-term campaign to democratise Kenya's political life.[116]

Anyona's decision was a serious blow to FORD's aspirations in Kisii and Nyamira, especially as his ally at the 1988 elections, ex-Chief Secretary Simeon Nyachae, despite being courted by the DP, decided to support KANU (see Chapter Six). The two Gusii Districts – along with Embu, Meru and Ukambani in Eastern Province and Kakamega and Bungoma in Western Province – were marginal areas where the general election would be closely fought between KANU and the opposition. Anyona's leadership would have strengthened FORD greatly, enabling it to capitalise on Gusii dismay at the recent outbreak of ethnic violence along the border with Kericho District.

Matiba's Return

The Kenyan media had carried numerous reports of visits by prominent opposition figures to London and had speculated for months about the former Minister's influence, assessing the impact of his return to active politics on FORD and the DP.[117] Would the main opposition party split into rival Luo and Kikuyu factions if Matiba tried to secure its Presidential nomination? Would Kikuyu supporters desert the party in favour of Kibaki's DP if Odinga was selected, or would Luo members become alienated and turn back to KANU if they had to vote for a Kikuyu? Hilary Ng'weno in an editorial in the *Weekly Review* considered that:

> It is the ethnic factor that will determine the outcome of this contest and indeed the main contest of the general election. Typically of politicians in the country, everyone tried to play down the issue of ethnicity in politics. Now the reality is staring everyone in the face. To get anywhere in Kenya politics one has to garner the support of one's ethnic group. In the process, one tends to alienate members of other ethnic groups. The successful politician is the one who can build on the foundations of his or her ethnic affiliations whilst managing to build viable bridges across ethnic lines. The battle between Mr Matiba and Mr Odinga for the leadership of FORD is going to be an early test of whether or not ethnicity still matters in Kenya politics.[118]

Another major focus of interest was Matiba's health. How far had he been incapacitated by his stroke? Could he read or write? Would he be able to lead an active political life, campaigning throughout the country? Above all, when would he return home?

Matiba's family and spokesmen had initially encouraged the impression that the ex-Minister would return to Kenya at the end of January or in early February, but the months had passed and he had remained in London. Matiba, the shrewd politician, kept himself in the public gaze, however, encouraging speculation about his political ambitions, especially the likelihood that he would challenge the octogenarian Odinga for FORD's Presidential nomination. He also called for the publication of a general election timetable, proposed several changes in FORD's constitution, issued a joint call with Raila Odinga and Charles Rubia for the suspension of Western donor aid, and welcomed Attorney-General Wako's proposal for the creation of the post of Prime Minister.[119] During his exile, however, Matiba became increasingly isolated, falling out with Paul Muite. The former Cabinet Minister, moreover, held no formal position within FORD's hierarchy, although the press speculated that Gachoka might cede his position as National Organising Secretary. There would have to be lengthy negotiations on his return to satisfy the rival ethnic factions. Matiba's image as the champion of Kikuyu interests, heralded in various Kikuyu popular songs, could be sustained only if he were to challenge Oginga Odinga for FORD's Presidential nomination. Any other course would quickly see Kikuyu voters turning towards the DP.[120]

Then on Saturday, 2 May, Matiba returned after a ten-month absence. Speaking to the press a few days before his departure, the ex-Minister had acknowledged that he still had to take things easy and had not regained full use of his right hand. 'I am not going to tear around the country 24 hours a day,' he observed. 'I am still recuperating so I will play myself in slowly.'[121] The ethnic cleavage in the main opposition party was starkly demonstrated by the fact that only Kikuyu leaders, led by Charles Rubia, Maina Wanjigi and Kimani wa Nyoike, ventured to the airport to welcome him home. By contrast, Oginga Odinga was in Western Province, addressing a rally in Busia town, during which he reaffirmed his intention to seek the party's Presidential nomination and questioned Matiba's health, while Secretary-General Shikuku was preparing for a rally in Mumias on Monday, 4 May. Other prominent non-Kikuyu leaders claimed that they had been snubbed by the welcoming committee, which had discouraged their presence at the airport or at the ensuing festivities. Matiba's return highlighted the extent to which FORD had become two rival, Luo- and Kikuyu-led factions.[122]

Thousands, led by his mother, two daughters, sister and fellow detainee, Charles Rubia, crowded the airport terminal, while thousands more waited outside the building, to greet Matiba and his wife Edith. The throng was so great that a brief welcoming ceremony and prayers had to be cancelled and the returning hero was swiftly whisked away in a two-mile long motorcade to Nairobi's All Saints' Cathedral. Frenzied crowds lined the route into Nairobi from the airport, ensuring that the journey took two hours, blocking Uhuru and Kenyatta Avenues up to the Cathedral. At the Cathedral, the crowd, festooned with FORD stickers, hats and T-shirts, had started to gather before daybreak. The throng was so great that Archbishop Kuria was delayed for 20 minutes as he attempted to push his way through the crowd. Matiba was clearly overwhelmed by the massive welcome. But when he was invited to speak briefly from the pulpit, the congregation tensed as he slowly made his way from the front pew with a stiff right leg and arm, the surviving signs of his stroke and delicate brain surgery. Then cheers erupted when he began his 12-minute address in English and Swahili in a clear, deep voice.[123]

After the service, Matiba and his wife travelled to his Riara Ridge home in Limuru. Along the route, he stopped to greet excited crowds which had gathered at various small trading posts on the side of the road, and banana stems festooned the road for the last three and a half miles to his home. During the afternoon, limousines and overloaded lorries carried well-wishers to his house where a lunch had been arranged and three huge tents erected. Then, on Sunday, the Matibas held a more private luncheon for close friends and political allies, during which the former Cabinet Minister held a press conference.

Matiba's main asset was his popularity among the Kikuyu masses, who regarded him as a hero who had defended their community's interests against Kalenjin and Asian encroachment since Kenyatta's death, and acknowledged his courage in launching the campaign for multi-party democracy in May 1990. His great personal wealth, which far surpassed that which could be tapped by Odinga and his allies, and his ability to raise contributions from other prominent Kikuyu businessmen were additional advantages; as were his proven organisational skills. Indeed, the extraordinary scenes welcoming Matiba home, from the initial reception at the airport, through the vast crowds lining the route into Nairobi, the ceremony at the cathedral, to the two receptions at his Limuru home, had confirmed Matiba's popular appeal, demonstrating that he would give President Moi and the Provincial Administration which would orchestrate KANU's campaign a run for their money.[124]

The euphoria which Matiba aroused among the Kikuyu masses equalled the initial enthusiasm which FORD's first rally at Kamukunji had evoked, suggesting that the Kikuyu politician might be able to revive FORD's momentum, sweeping all before him in a barn-storming, populist campaign. The press immediately began to wonder if Matiba could undermine the DP's position in Central Province and in neighbouring Embu, Meru and Ukambani. His triumphal return surprised Odinga and his other critics in FORD and dumbfounded the DP leadership. Matiba's popularity in Nairobi and along the route to Limuru suggested that FORD's prospects in Kiambu might be much better than had been thought, especially if Matiba could enlist the support of established local FORD leaders such as businessman Lawrence Nginyo Kariuki in Kiambaa, architect George Nyanja in Limuru, and Paul Muite in Kikuyu, especially as he was judged invincible in his native Murang'a. The DP, however, had a strong presence in Kibaki's native Nyeri, where only Waruru Kanja and Matu Wamae had joined FORD, in Meru and Embu, and in Kitui where former Cabinet Minister Kyale Mwendwa appeared set to fight it out with FORD's Titus Mbathi and his own sister-in-law, KANU's Nyiva Mwendwa. The three major parties also appeared evenly balanced in Machakos, where Joseph Munyao was the local DP leader, George Nthenge was identified with FORD, and former Chief of Staff, Major-General Mulinge with KANU. If Matiba could enlist the support of the majority of Kikuyu, and attract backing from Eastern Province, he might be able to equal Odinga's bloc vote among the Luos, who still formed the bulk of FORD support.

Ideologically, little distinguished the candidates within FORD or, indeed, any of the parties. Kenyan politics is about personalities and ethnic loyalties rather than ideology or class. The manifestos differed but slightly in their commitment to political reform, improved human rights and economic liberalisation. FORD, however, was more diverse and divided than its two main rivals, reflecting the fact that originally it had been a United Democratic Front-style protest movement, established to secure democratic reforms. It consequently remained a disparate coalition of ethnic and ideological interests, bringing together rich Kikuyu businessmen and establishment politicians, like Matiba and Rubia, with more radical figures, like Odinga and Shikuku, and the new political generation of lawyers and other professionals among the party's Young Turks. By contrast, both KANU and the DP possessed a more settled (and in certain respects narrower) political base, with the DP representing the former Kikuyu élite and Kikuyu big business, while KANU was a coalition of the new beneficiaries of state patronage. Kibaki's leadership was unquestioned in the DP, just as President Moi's was in KANU, whereas strife-ridden FORD was divided into rival Odinga and Matiba blocs.

Matiba, as the *Saba Saba* riots had proved, could appeal to what the *Weekly Review* called 'the Kikuyu psyche', but could he establish a national image, appealing to other ethnic groups? Among the Kikuyu, he was seen as a fighter, whilst Kibaki was judged to have compromised for too long with the regime. But as a senior civil servant in the 1960s, and former chairman of Kenya's largest private corporation – Kenya Breweries – in the early 1970s, many non-Kikuyus believed that Matiba too was closely identified with the era of Kikuyu hegemony under Kenyatta. Indeed, his power base among FORD's Kikuyu activists, and his close association with other powerful Kikuyu politicians such as Charles Rubia, former Vice-President Josephat Karanja, and ex-Ministers Maina Wanjigi and Kimani wa Nyoike aroused suspicion and fear rather than confidence and trust among other ethnic groups. The ethnic polarisation of FORD, in large part fostered by Matiba's acolytes, not only weakened the party's challenge to KANU but also reduced Matiba's own prospects of ever securing the Presidency. Uncertain of his own health, he was in too much of a hurry to sweep Odinga aside. Even in May 1992, it was clear that FORD's only hope of victory was for Matiba to support Odinga, accept the party's Vice-Presidential nomination, and energetically campaign for the octogenarian's triumph in the hope that Odinga would be too frail to exercise effective power or would soon die, transferring power to the Kikuyu leader. Virtually all of FORD's leaders in April to October 1992, however, over-estimated the opposition party's prospects of defeating President Moi, underestimating the extent of popular support for KANU in the Rift Valley, the Coast, North-Eastern Province, and in parts of Western and Eastern Provinces. Only a united FORD, with Matiba and Odinga working in harness for victory, might have stood a chance of defeating KANU with its control over government patronage and the state machine, given that the DP would already split the opposition vote. Matiba's determination to secure FORD's nomination at any cost was to shatter the main opposition party, split the Kikuyu vote with the DP, and ensure President Moi's re-election.[125]

Martin Shikuku Eats *Ugali* at State House, May 1992

Shikuku further complicated the contest in mid-May when he announced that he too intended to contest FORD's Presidential nomination. Although his candidacy was dismissed as a joke, his entry made it even more difficult to assess the strength of the Odinga and Matiba factions and reduced both front-runners' hopes of winning a major share of the vital Luhya vote.[126] Shikuku and Matiba, however, found themselves drawn together. Both were populist politicians whose best hope of securing the nomination depended upon appealing to the mass of party members over the head of the Secretariat in a direct vote. Like Matiba, the veteran Shikuku presented himself as the defender of the 'ordinary Kenyan' against the state and the business and political élites. His appeal, however, was limited by the traditional sub-ethnic rivalries, which had bedevilled Luhya politics since the 1950s. Shikuku was a member of the small Marama 'sub-tribe', which formed the majority of the population in his Butere constituency but it was uncertain that he would be able to extend his appeal to the two largest 'sub-tribes', the Bukusu in Bungoma (whose political leader was Muliro) and the Maragoli of Kakamega (led by KANU's Musalia Mudavadi), let alone to the ten other groups in the four Luhya Districts.

Not surprisingly, when Matiba returned, he supported Shikuku, George Nthenge and Ahmed Salim Bamahriz against the Young Turks. He feared that the organisational reforms in FORD would consolidate the power of the pro-Odinga faction within the Secretariat. Thus, although Martin Shikuku had attacked Matiba at his Mumias rally, two days after the former Cabinet Minister's return, the two politicians had much in common. Both had become profoundly suspicious of Paul Muite's ambitions, disliked the influence of the Young Turks, doubted Oginga Odinga's ability to lead the FORD campaign and the country, and consequently favoured the direct selection of the party's Presidential candidate by ordinary members.[127] Many observers believed that the Luhya vote would be crucial in FORD's Presidential primary: the party's two most prominent Luhya, Masinde Muliro and Martin Shikuku, however, both harboured their own Presidential ambitions, although they were susceptible to courtship by the two front-runners. Although the press had suggested that Muliro might become Odinga's running mate, he had held secret meetings in London with Matiba in late April, shortly before the Murang'a politician's return to Kenya. Shikuku too was uncommitted. For a quarter of a century he had denounced Kikuyu political and business power, and had frequently clashed with the old-guard Kikuyu politicians around Matiba, but he had equally little in common with Young Turks like Raila Odinga, Gitobu Imanyara and Paul Muite, who had restricted his access to Odinga. Both major factions disliked and distrusted Shikuku but needed Luhya support to capture the nomination and to defeat President Moi and KANU.

Announcing his candidacy, Shikuku had launched immediately into an all-out attack on his rivals, claiming that some opposition leaders were as corrupt as KANU politicians. Under pressure from the Luhya veteran, FORD had appointed a special committee under the chairmanship of former

Wundanyi MP, Mashengu wa Mwachofi, to investigate the sources of its candidates' wealth.[128] Many believed that Shikuku's attacks on 'opportunists with questionable integrity' were directed at Matiba's Alliance Hotel group and Odinga's more modest fortune. The Luhya leader hoped that the campaign would enhance his populist image, embarrass his Kikuyu foes within FORD and raise his political profile. Since the legalisation of the party, Shikuku had come under severe criticism. His colleagues had denounced him for not being 'a team player', criticising him for revealing inter-party disputes to journalists. Odinga had condemned him for his attack on Muite, Orengo and Imanyara when they had gone to Western Province to open new FORD branches, trespassing on what Shikuku regarded as his own turf.[129] He had also exacerbated divisions within the party by his claims that *nyang'au* (literally, hyenas, but more colloquially Kikuyu 'fat cats') were infiltrating the party. Thus, isolated and with minimal financial resources, Shikuku stood little chance of winning many Luo or Kikuyu votes. His candidacy, however, meant that the Luhya could no longer be incorporated into either the Odinga or Matiba coalitions without his support, compelling the two front-runners to build more diverse trans-tribal coalitions from the smaller ethnic groups. Both contenders would find this task difficult. It required them to distance themselves from their more rabid fellow 'tribesmen' in order to appeal to a national constituency.

Shikuku threw the political scene into even greater uproar on 20 May when, accompanied by Luhya colleague Japheth Shamalla, he enjoyed a private dinner with President Moi at State House. The Luhya politician claimed that he had attempted to consult FORD leaders before accepting the invitation, but the notice had been so short that he had only been able to contact George Nthenge in advance, although he reported the discussion to Odinga, Muliro and Denis Akumu. When Muliro and Akumu revealed the meeting at FORD rallies in Nairobi on 23 and 24 May, Shikuku was shaken by the uproar and personal attacks. He had been a critic of the regime since his dismissal as an Assistant Minister in 1985 (and, indeed, for some time before) and had built his political reputation upon the claim to be incorruptible and by denouncing the dubiously gained wealth of his foes. Now they could get their own back. Rumours quickly circulated that Shikuku had received 30 million shillings (approximately $600,000) from Moi to finance his bid for FORD's Presidential nomination, ensuring that the opposition party would remain divided. When the news broke, FORD leaders, who had suffered attacks from Shikuku, rushed to denounce him as a traitor. Observers suggested that the President was attempting to exploit Shikuku's political isolation and shortage of money in order to destabilise FORD. Some argued that the meeting explained Shikuku's maverick behaviour during the past six months, suggesting that he might have supplied secret information about FORD's tactics to KANU.[130] DP Secretary-General John Keen even seized the opportunity to claim that it was FORD, not the Democratic Party, that was really 'KANU B'.[131]

Beset by his enemies, Shikuku desperately attempted to defend his reputation, releasing a press statement which claimed that Odinga had welcomed the dialogue with President Moi initially but had changed his mind when Muliro and Akumu had publicised the secret meeting. Shikuku went on the counter-attack, complaining that Odinga behaved like a dictator, controlling FORD like 'a family company' and excluding other leaders from key decisions.[132] On Tuesday, 26 May, Shikuku claimed in an interview with *Weekly Review* journalists that 'I am the cleanest and most transparent politician in Kenya.' He pointed out that he had been instrumental in the establishment of the wa Mwachofi committee to investigate the fortunes of FORD leaders.[133] He had also played a key role in the appointment of a 13-member committee to draw up a code for FORD officials and candidates in order to ensure that they were of impeccable character. Some of his opponents, he claimed, had feared that he would use the committee to undermine their positions. Now, they were attempting to pre-empt the enquiries by discrediting 'an honest man'.[134] Whatever the truth of the various allegations, Shikuku's reputation as the incorruptible defender of ordinary Kenyans was tarnished and his bid for FORD's Presidential nomination damaged, leaving the real contest to Odinga and Matiba, who continued the struggle to broaden their ethnic support.[135]

FORD's Divisions Intensify, June–July 1992

The contest between the Odinga and Matiba factions continued to dominate the affairs of FORD throughout May and June. Many FORD leaders suffered from a deep ambivalence in attitude: whilst most denied ethnicity as a key political variable, they as much as their more 'realistic' colleagues, by their growing roots in the local political organisations in their home areas, were helping to reinforce the same divisions. Gradually, over the summer, the parties and factions polarised around an alignment of personalities, ethnicity and policies which made an identification with ethnic interests easy. Hilary Ng'weno of the *Weekly Review* pointed out in an editorial that 'the confusion in the opposition party FORD is not just a matter of organisational ineptitude. It is first and foremost an ethnic struggle for the control of the party between Luo and Kikuyu leaders.'[136]

The crisis in FORD reached a climax in late July 1992, when Matiba announced that not only did he want to be the party's presidential nominee but that he would also attempt to oust Odinga as party Chairman when FORD elections began. Matiba also proposed that FORD's headquarters should be removed from the city centre Agip House, the site of Odinga's private business, to more neutral territory at Muthithi House in Westlands to the north of the city centre, which had been loaned to Matiba for the party's use by a Kikuyu supporter. Odinga and his supporters responded by taking Matiba to court for printing and distributing unauthorised party membership cards to bolster his support in the forthcoming elections.[137]

At the end of July, an attempt was made to heal the wounds when the party's four most prominent leaders – Odinga, Matiba, Muliro and Shikuku – held a joint press conference. The four veterans had assured the press that FORD would not fall apart and that they would rally behind the victorious candidate in the nominations. Shortly afterwards it was announced that the court case against Matiba was being abandoned. The press conference proved, however, to be the lull before the storm. The meeting of FORD's national steering committee on 23 July, which decided not to continue with the court case, refused to accept the Matiba faction's demand that the party elections should be postponed. Shikuku, who was still aligned with the Agip House faction, announced as the party's Secretary-General that the polls would go ahead and that FORD supporters would be permitted to vote by showing a voter's card, even if they did not possess a party membership card.[138] This decision ran the risk of permitting KANU supporters to participate in the election of FORD delegates and therefore of FORD's Presidential and Parliamentary candidates.

Odinga then went on the offensive, attempting to demonstrate that with Paul Muite's backing he could appeal to Kikuyu voters. In late July, he leaked news of a secret meeting with former Attorney-General Charles Njonjo, encouraging the press to believe that Njonjo was a FORD supporter and favoured Odinga for the Presidential nomination.[139] Other prominent Kikuyu, such as former Foreign Minister Dr Munyua Waiyaki also declared their support for the Luo leader. Waiyaki had been a supporter of Odinga's since 1960. In 1966, when the Luo leader had abandoned KANU to form the opposition KPU, Waiyaki had resigned his position in the government as Deputy Chief Whip but had not crossed the floor. Although he had served in the Cabinet from 1974 to 1983 under Kenyatta and Moi, Waiyaki had been regarded as one of its most left-wing members. He had clashed frequently with Attorney-General Njonjo, who represented the interests of the Kikuyu establishment. If Odinga could secure the support of both Charles Njonjo and Munyua Waiyaki at ideologically opposed ends of the political spectrum, it momentarily appeared that the aged Luo leader might be capable of making inroads into Matiba's Kikuyu support.[140]

The Ethnic Battle to Control FORD

Matiba and his supporters responded to the Odinga faction's enlistment of Charles Njonjo and the entry in mid-July of Masinde Muliro into the contest by enlisting Martin Shikuku to join them in opposing the pro-Odinga faction's timetable for the party's elections.[141] The real reasons for Shikuku's sudden switch of allegiance at this crucial moment remains unclear. It may have been the result of his continued frustration with the Young Turks, and Muite in particular. He may also have realised that his own leadership bid was doomed, seeing personal advantage in backing Matiba and the real possibility of securing the Vice-Presidential position on the ticket. In any case, Shikuku's decision was a key moment. Matiba was now backed by four of the six 'founder members' of the party: Secretary-General Shikuku, Organising Secretary Philip Gachoka, assistant secretary Ahmed Salim Bamahriz and Treasurer George Nthenge.

The five decided at a secret meeting on Monday, 27 July to call off the impending elections, due to start with sub-branch elections on Saturday, 1 August and to culminate in FORD's first Annual Delegates' Conference on 23 August. Announcing the decision at a press conference the next day, Shikuku contended that the four founding members of FORD constituted a majority of the registered officers of the party and, therefore, possessed the authority to postpone the nomination exercise.[142] The Muthithi House team proposed that the elections should be delayed until free and fair polls could be organised. The 'stop Odinga camp' also placed advertisements in the national press, announcing that the FORD elections had been postponed.

Odinga responded later in the day by announcing that the polls would go ahead as planned. He argued that Matiba and his backers had no authority to override the decision taken by the party's 108-member National Steering Committee. The Committee was the party's supreme governing body. This ambiguity surrounding the authorities of the relevant bodies remained a key point of weakness, helping to prevent the crisis being resolved. Odinga also announced that an emergency Steering Committee meeting had been called for Thursday, 30 July and hinted that disciplinary action might be taken against Matiba, Shikuku and the 'renegade element within the party'.[143] Shikuku countered, informing the press the next day, 29 July, that Odinga's attempt to summon an emergency meeting of the Steering Committee was illegal since the final power within the party lay with its six registered founders. In this war by press conference, the now united Young Turks also summoned journalists on the same day, the day before FORD's emergency Steering Committee met, to announce that the elections would go ahead as planned.[144] To outside observers, these moves typified FORD's descent into the worst kind of intra-party KANU factionalism.

The crisis escalated the next day, 30 July, when the meetings of the National Executive Committee in the morning and the emergency Steering Committee in the afternoon proved inconclusive. Press photographs of the morning NEC meeting showed Oginga Odinga sitting alone at a table prepared for the six founders. Sentiments were running high and it was proposed that the 'rebels' should be dismissed from the Executive. Moderates, however, managed to ensure that the absentees would be given a final chance to conform. It was announced once more that the polls would go ahead. Those branches which were prepared could hold elections as planned, while others were permitted to defer the elections for a week, provided all elections were finished and District delegates had been selected by the time the National Delegates' Conference met in Nairobi on 23 August 1992.[145]

The afternoon Steering Committee also authorised Odinga to open discussions with the rival DP about a possible merger or electoral pact. Now that the original Luo–Kikuyu alliance between Odinga and Matiba was nearing collapse, some FORD strategists were attempting to minimise the damage and to forge a new electoral agreement with Kibaki's forces. The main opposition party, they appreciated, could not afford simply to abandon Kikuyu votes in Central Province and Nairobi if it was to secure a majority of seats in the National Assembly and to get 25 per cent of the vote in five Provinces to oust President Moi. This vital tactical issue was to recur throughout the election period, although no lasting agreement was ever made.[146]

When it became apparent that the Odinga faction would press ahead with the FORD elections, even if they were boycotted by supporters of

Matiba and Shikuku, pro-Matiba activists attempted to secure a legal injunction to stop the elections. Ironically, the respondents in the case were Shikuku and Gachoka. The Agip House team's lawyer, indeed, pointed out that the two officials were 'party to manoeuvres aimed at blocking the polls'.[147] High Court Judge Akiwumi circumvented the problem by declaring that the court had no authority to intervene in FORD's internal affairs. This set an important precedent for the election period.[148] As a result, after nearly two weeks of confusion and recrimination, FORD's elections finally began on Saturday, 1 August, in those areas which supported the Odinga faction.

Muliro: The Compromise Candidate

Throughout this confusion, Masinde Muliro attempted to present himself as an honest broker, committed to neither side. In the 1960s, Muliro had been the main leader of the Abaluhya – Kenya's second largest ethnic group – and a powerful figure in the opposition Kenya African Democratic Union. His influence had subsequently waned, especially after his dismissal from the Cabinet in 1975. In the National Assembly between 1984 and 1989, he had emerged as one of the most outspoken defenders of civil liberties and as a forceful critic of the increasing authoritarianism of the ruling party. Although he had initially been reluctant to support the Matiba-Rubia campaign for multi-party politics or to endorse FORD, Muliro's decision to join the fledgling party enormously increased its influence in the Rift Valley's Trans-Nzoia District and in the neighbouring Bungoma District of Western Province, where members of Muliro's Bukusu community predominated. As the Kikuyu–Luo rift widened during the first half of 1992, Muliro began to see himself as a compromise candidate, an elder statesman who might heal the party's divisions. He announced his bid for FORD's Presidential nomination – the fourth declaration – in mid-July.[149]

On Thursday, 30 July – the day the Odinga faction summoned FORD's Steering Committee into emergency session – Muliro wrote to the party's five other founding fathers, expressing dismay at the crisis confronting the party and suggesting that a Steering Committee meeting should be convened for Wednesday, 5 August, under his neutral chairmanship. The Luhya political veteran urged his colleagues to sacrifice their personal ambitions for the good of the country. His chances of playing 'honest broker' or of becoming a compromise candidate were always slim, however, and it soon became clear that neither the Matiba-Shikuku faction nor Odinga's supporters were willing to attend.[150] The crisis had gone too far to be so easily patched up. By early August, therefore, Muliro's hopes of emerging as a compromise FORD Presidential candidate had collapsed. He was viewed as being too old and too frail to lead the party, following a heart attack in 1983. He was also on the verge of bankruptcy – ever since he had lost the 1989 by-election, his creditors, encouraged by the government, had called in their loans and refused additional credit. Neither Odinga nor Matiba, moreover, was willing to stand down for him. Realising that his bid to emerge as a compromise candidate had failed, Muliro now decided to participate in the Agip House polls and henceforth to align himself more clearly with Odinga's forces, to increase his chances of emerging as FORD's Vice-Presidential candidate.[151]

The Split in FORD Widens

The polls organised by the Agip House faction went ahead in the first week of August, despite the boycott by Matiba and Shikuku. Though Odinga's backers claimed that the polls progressed satisfactorily in all but three of Kenya's 46 Districts, this was incorrect. Over large swathes of the country, including many of the pastoral areas, Central Province and much of Nairobi, the elections were either not held at all or saw only a token participation. In Nairobi, where the Odinga and Matiba factions both had considerable support, there were outbreaks of violence, especially in Langata constituency, where Raila Odinga hoped to be selected as FORD's Parliamentary candidate against intense opposition from Kimani Rugendo, a Kikuyu aligned with Matiba. There were several serious clashes in Kibera, the constituency's largest shanty town.[152] One of the clashes left an Odinga supporter dead, and during the FORD primary, a supporter of Rugendo was stabbed to death when he attempted to run off with some ballot papers. Support for the Agip House faction was also strong in Embakasi in eastern Nairobi, where both Kikuyu and Luo workers had settled with their families in large numbers. The pro-Odinga slate, led by Munyua Waiyaki, swept to victory.[153] Matiba supporters, however, protested that most of the officials supervising the Langata and Embakasi polls on Saturday, 1 August, were Luos known to support Oginga Odinga in the party feuding, and that little interest had been shown in voting in the capital's six other constituencies, where the local FORD organisation was dominated by his supporters.

Not surprisingly, the FORD polls went ahead with the least trouble in Nyanza Province, Oginga Odinga's political bailiwick. Yet, even there, opposition was aroused when the Luo leader attempted to ensure that Peter Oloo-Aringo, KANU's former Chairman and ex-Minister of Education, was returned. Oloo-Aringo had lost the sub-branch vote but, to the fury of local residents, Odinga had insisted upon a recount and then declared that the ex-Minister had been elected. Oloo-Aringo had entered politics as a protégé of Odinga's, but had become increasingly critical of his mentor as Odinga's influence waned. By 1988, Oloo Aringo had become KANU National Chairman, and in that position was very hostile toward the Moi regime's critics. In December 1991, he had suddenly re-emerged as an advocate of political pluralism. In Oginga Odinga's eyes, Oloo Aringo's wide political experience made him indispensable to FORD. By contrast, the Young Turks – including Raila Odinga – viewed the ex-Minister with scarcely veiled contempt and were determined to prevent him from exercising any influence in FORD's inner councils.[154]

At a meeting of the pro-Odinga forces on Monday, 3 August, Gitobu Imanyara, the Chairman of FORD's publicity and information committee, announced to the press that those who had boycotted the first round of party elections could not participate in the party's first Annual Delegates' Conference at the end of the month. Those party branches which had held location and sub-branch meetings – that is, those that were pro-Odinga – would go ahead on their own and elect new national office holders.[155] This announcement meant that Matiba and Shikuku would be stripped of office and their main backers excluded from the party's inner circle, leaving Odinga and Muliro in complete control. Finally, Agip House had decided to crush their opponents.

Matiba and Shikuku, having boycotted FORD's elections, now had no alternative but to reject the whole process. By refusing to participate, their supporters had decisively lost out to the pro-Odinga forces if the party remained united. Matiba might have been able to salvage some delegates to the FORD convention, as most Central Province constituencies had not yet held elections, but Shikuku's base in Western Province had been lost and pro-Odinga forces had captured virtually all the delegates from contested areas. Unless new elections could be held, Matiba was now going to have to 'go it alone'.

Matiba and Shikuku faced severe problems as they attempted to establish a major national political party. Whilst four of the six founders supported Matiba, only four of 14 (the same four) NEC members were aligned with Muthithi House. Most branches, outside of Central Province and Nairobi, remained loyal to Odinga. Matiba and Shikuku were able to enlist the support of only four of Nairobi's ten representatives – former mayor Andrew Ngumba, Kihara Waithaka, Charles Rubia and Wanguhu Ng'ang'a – despite the fact that the Kikuyu formed the majority of the city's population. The faction's support in Kenya's other seven Provinces was even worse, as can be seen in Table 5.2.[156]

On a national level, Matiba's support was clearly weaker than Odinga's. The meeting at Muthithi House revealed that only six of Kenya's 46 District FORD branches backed Matiba's faction, compared with 27 that remained loyal to Odinga, while 13 others were divided. The Muthithi House group had failed to establish any presence in 13 Districts, including such densely populated areas as Kilifi and Taita-Taveta in Coast Province, Machakos in Eastern Province, Bungoma in Western Province, and in Nyamira and all four Luo Districts, whilst its presence in the 'KANU zones' was little more than token.

Many commentators questioned how long the Matiba-led alliance would survive. Many believed that Shikuku would eventually return to KANU's fold after 'eating *ugali* at State House'.[157] In the short term, however, it seemed that Shikuku was reconciled to serving as Matiba's Vice-Presidential running mate. Matiba controlled and financed the faction and the bulk of its support would come from Central Province and Nairobi, but Shikuku still exerted considerably more power than he had at Agip House. Thus Shikuku's decision to join the Matiba camp had endowed him with considerable influence. In return, Shikuku brought Matiba's faction a certain populist legitimacy and a wider ethnic appeal.

By mid-August, any hope that the two main factions might step back from destroying FORD had been shattered. Both Muthithi House and

Table 5.2 Officials of the Agip House and Muthithi House FORD Factions

	Agip House	**Muthithi House**
	NATIONAL EXECUTIVE COMMITTEE	NATIONAL EXECUTIVE COMMITTEE
	Oginga Odinga	
	Masinde Muliro	
	Martin Shikuku	*Martin Shikuku*
	George Nthenge	*George Nthenge*
	Philip Gachoka	*Philip Gachoka*
	Ahmed S. Bamahriz	*Ahmed S. Bamahriz*
	Paul Muite	
	Peter Anyang' Nyong'o	
	Japheth Shamalla	
	Joe Odinga	
	Raila Odinga	
	Mukhisa Kituyi	
	James Orengo	
	Gitobu Imanyara	
	NAIROBI	NAIROBI
	Andrew Ngumba	*Andrew Ngumba*
	Kihara Waithaka	*Kihara Waithaka*
	Charles Rubia	*Charles Rubia*
	Wanguhu Ng'ang'a	*Wanguhu Ng'ang'a*
	John Khaminwa	Maina Wanjigi
	Munyua Waiyaki	Kimani Rugendo
	Luke Obok	Pius Njogu
	Denis Akumu	Alala Sande
	Apudo Zolo	Maliyamungu Ambaisi
	Obare Asiko	Samuel Ondalo
	COAST PROVINCE	COAST PROVINCE
Mombasa	*Emmanuel Maitha*	*Emmanuel Maitha*
Mombasa	Sheikh Hussein Namoya	Luyai Liyai
Kwale	Mbwana Warrakah	Kassam Juma
Kwale	Roger Chemera	Kitauri Hassani
Kilifi	Morris Mboja	no representative
Kilifi	Simeon Alfred Mole	no representative
Tana	River Haji Omar	Maalim Haji
Tana	River Sheikh Ulaya	
Lamu	Mohammed Bunu	Mohammed Musoma
Lamu	Omar Mzamil	Kanja wa Muchiri
TaitaTaveta	Mashengu wa Mwachofi	no representative
Taita Taveta	Alsayo Aroko	no representative
	NORTH-EASTERN PROVINCE	NORTH-EASTERN PROVINCE
Garissa	Abdi Hassan	Kassim Shurei
Garissa	Morgan Abdi Noor	Ahmed Abdi Daud
Wajir	*Ahmed Khalif*	*Ahmed Khalif*
Wajir	Abdulahi Adan	Abdulahi Mohammed
Mandera	*Mohammed Maalim*	*Mohammed Maalim*
Mandera	Isaac Haji	Rashid Farra

Table 5.2 cont.

	Agip House	Muthithi House
	EASTERN PROVINCE	EASTERN PROVINCE
Marsabit	*Ahmed Osman Bachu*	*Ahmed Osman Bachu*
Marsabit	*Abdi Kalam*	*Abdi Kalam*
Isiolo	*Hassan Guyo*	*Hassan Guyo*
Isiolo	Nassir Mohammed	Ali Ndogu
Meru	*Erastus Mbaabu*	*Erastus Mbaabu*
Meru	Victor Gituma	Henry Kinyua
Tharaka-Nithi	Muriithi Muriithi	no representative
Tharaka-Nithi	Muthongo Muoo	no representative
Embu	Godfrey Nguru	Elkana Muriuki
Embu	Sammy Muriuki	Njeru Kathangu
Kitui	Julius Ngila	Julius Ngila
Kitui	Permenas Munyasia	Titus Mbathi
Machakos	Aaron Mutunga	no representative
Machakos	Joshua Kitonga	no representative
Makueni	Masoa Muindi	Masoa Muindi
Makueni	Joseph Kimau	Munyoki
	CENTRAL PROVINCE	CENTRAL PROVINCE
Nyandarua	*Kimani wa Nyoike*	*Kimani wa Nyoike*
Nyandarua	*Lavan Mucemi*	*Lavan Mucemi*
Nyeri	Waruru Kanja	Kabuya Muito
Nyeri	Makanga	John Mbau
Kirinyaga	*Matere Keriri*	*Matere Keriri*
Kirinyaga	Cyprus Mungai	Geoffrey Kariithi
Murang'a	*Muturi Kigano*	*Maturi Kigano*
Murang'a	*Patrick Njuguna*	*Patrick Njuguna*
Kiambu	*George Nyanja*	*George Nyanja*
Kiambu	Josephat Karanja*	Ngoima wa Mwaura
	RIFT VALLEY PROVINCE	RIFT VALLEY PROVINCE
Turkana	no representative	no representative
Turkana	no representative	no representative
West Pokot	*James Korellach*	*James Korellach*
West Pokot	*James Lukwo*	*James Lukwo*
Samburu	no representative	no representative
Samburu	no representative	no representative
Trans-Nzoia	Zachariah Shimechero	Salim Ndamwe
Trans-Nzoia	Ezekiel Okul	
Uasin	Gishu Kibor Talei	Amos Mbugua
Uasin	Gishu Edward Ojwang	Kimingi
Elgeyo-Marakwet	*John Chebii*	*John Chebii*
Elgeyo-Marakwet	*Kiptanui Cheptile*	*Kiptanui Cheptile*
Nandi	Simeon Chepsiror	Frederick Rono
Nandi	John Birgen	
Baringo	*Jeremiah Muchiri*	*Jeremiah Muchiri*
Baringo	Kipruto Kibor	Joseph Wakaba
Laikipia	Dickson Manyara	Stephen Njuguna
Laikipia	Patrick Macharia	Francis Wanyange

Table 5.2 cont.

	Agip House	Muthithi House
	RIFT VALLEY PROVINCE	RIFT VALLEY PROVINCE
Nakuru	John Kamanagara	Charles Liwali
Nakuru	Ben Odhako	
Narok	*Harun Lempaka*	*Harun Lempaka*
Narok	Joseph ole Kilusu	
Kajiado	*Oliver Seki*	*Oliver Seki*
Kajiado	Gerald Mahinda	Gerald Mahinda, Philip Odupoy, and J.K. Ng'ang'a
Kericho	Joshua Shijenga	
Kericho	Daniel Kamau	M.N. Kabugi
Bomet	no representative	no representative
Bomet	no representative	no representative
	WESTERN PROVINCE	WESTERN PROVINCE
Kakamega	*Francis Obongita*	*Francis Obongita*
Kakamega	Macanja Ligabo	Jacob Mukaramoja, Abraham Mulamba
Vihiga	Arthur Ligabe	Elijah Enane
Vihiga	Oyanji Mbaja	Herman Asava
Bungoma	Mohammed Noor	no representative
Bungoma	Saulo Busolo	no representative
Busia	Philip Wangalwa	Ogola Auma Osolo
Busia	James Osogo, Fred Oduke	John Omudanga
	NYANZA PROVINCE	NYANZA PROVINCE
Siaya	Jonah Ougo Ochieng	no representative
Siaya	Peter Oloo Aringo	no representative
Kisumu	Ogangoto Thim	no representative
Kisumu	Peter Anyumba	no representative
Homa Bay	Joseph Ouma Muga	no representative
Homa Bay	Otulla Fadhili	no representative
Migori	Charles Owino	no representative
Migori	John Linus Aluoch	no representative
Kisii	*Saul Nyareru Bosire*	*Saul Nyareru Bosire*
Kisii	Cosmas Obara	
Nyamira	Abuya Abuya	no representative
Nyamira	Henry Obwocha	no representative
WOMEN'S AND YOUTH REPRESENTATIVES		SECRETARIAT REPRESENTATIVES
Women	*Wambui Otieno*	*Kenneth Matiba*
Women	Jael Mbogo	Bernard Njeroge
Youth	Maina Wachira	Bedan Mbugua
Youth	Joshua Rajuai	Ngotho Kariuki
		Stephen Ndichu
		G.B.M. Kariuki

* Former Vice-President Karanja did in fact join Matiba's faction, eventually becoming its most prominent member in Kiambu and one of the few former Ministers to support FORD-Asili.

Names in italics show members of FORD's National Steering Committee who attended the break-away meeting at Muthithi House on Friday, 7 August, suggesting that they were sympathetic to the Matiba-Shikuku faction in the party, which eventually became FORD-Asili.

Agip House were intent upon controlling the FORD rump, whatever damage their public disputes might be doing to the party. On 7 August Martin Shikuku informed the press that the Registrar-General had registered Muthithi House as the new FORD headquarters, implying that the authorities had approved the Matiba-Shikuku faction as the official successor of the united party.[158] Four days later, on 11 August, he announced that Oginga Odinga had been replaced as party Chairman by George Nthenge. Accompanied to the press conference by three of the party's founder members – Nthenge, Gachoka and Bamahriz – as well as Matiba, Shikuku read out a letter to Odinga, notifying him that he had been suspended from office for refusing to explain his actions at a NEC meeting which had been held by the Muthithi House faction on Friday, 7 August.[159] Neither Odinga nor interim Vice-Chairman Masinde Muliro had attended. The following day, 12 August, Odinga responded by informing the press that Shikuku, Nthenge, Gachoka, Bamahriz and Shamalla were deemed to have abandoned their duties and had been dropped from an enlarged FORD interim Executive Committee. Matiba's name was not even mentioned.[160] Matiba reiterated that Muthithi House had become FORD Party headquarters, whilst Wanguhu Ng'ang'a, FORD's Vice-Chairman for publicity and information, claimed that Agip House was now merely 'Mr Odinga's private offices'.[161]

The situation was thrown into further confusion when the Registrar of Societies advised James Orengo that FORD's registered headquarters was still deemed to be at Agip House and that the registered office bearers were exactly as they had originally been. The Registrar acknowledged that he had received notification of a 'change of office and change of chairman' but observed that he had not registered these alterations because 'there is doubt as to whether the changes were made in accordance with the constitution of the society'.[162] Neither faction, consequently, seemed to be able to claim that they were legally recognised as FORD. As the *Weekly Review* pointed out, 'the only thing the two factions have left in common is the name FORD'.[163]

Masinde Muliro's Death

Kenyan politics – especially Western Kenyan politics – was turned upside down just before nine o'clock on the morning of Friday, 14 August 1992, when Masinde Muliro suffered a heart attack and died at Nairobi airport while waiting to clear passport control after an overnight flight from London. Muliro had flown to Britain on Monday evening and spent a hectic three days attempting to raise money for his bid for the FORD Presidency. He had met the Assistant Under-Secretary for Africa at the Foreign and Commonwealth Office, business leaders with large-scale investments in Kenya at the East Africa Association, officials at Conservative Central Office and members of FORD in Britain; he had held a press conference and been interviewed by the BBC.[164]

The trip to Britain had followed immediately a busy weekend of political activity in Trans-Nzoia during which Muliro had been elected a delegate to FORD's convention for Cherangani constituency. Indeed, for the last nine months, the senior Abaluhya politician had followed a heavy schedule as FORD Vice-Chairman. Many, including Muliro's physician Professor Arthur Obel, had wondered how long he could sustain the pace, given his history of heart disease. It was nearly ten years since Muliro had suffered his first major heart attack.

By the time that he departed for London, many commentators believed that Muliro, exasperated by the underhand methods of Matiba and Shikuku, had decided to support Odinga and Agip House. Commenting from London, Muliro had condemned the Muthithi house suspension of Odinga as illegal. Muliro had participated in FORD's elections and had encouraged local party officials in his own District and in Bungoma to go ahead with the election of delegates for the party's convention later in August. Muliro's death removed the last chance of reconciliation between the divided FORD factions. His death also highlighted the divisions within FORD's leadership and reawakened fears that the government might murder opposition leaders. Speculation was heightened by the announcement in London that former Permanent Secretary in the Office of the President Hezekiah Oyugi, who had been implicated in the murder of former Foreign Minister Dr Robert Ouko, had died of a mysterious neurological illness on 8 August, and by the fact that Nicholas Biwott had not only flown to London but had returned to Nairobi on the same plane as Muliro. Indeed, the press reported that the two men had chatted briefly, while waiting to clear immigration, a few minutes before Muliro suffered his fatal heart attack. These rumours were compounded by the haste with which Muliro's doctor summoned a press conference on Friday afternoon, with the help of the Deputy Commissioner of Police, to announce that he had signed the death certificate and that a post-mortem examination was not required.[165]

The rival FORD leaders met on Monday evening, when both visited the Muliro family. Odinga urged Matiba to participate in FORD's Delegates' Congress, which was scheduled for the next weekend. Sitting side by side, they listened while the chairman of the funeral committee and other senior Luhya FORD leaders appealed for party unity and prayed that 'in Muliro's death, FORD will come together in unity'.[166] Partly in order to give the Muthithi House faction time to reconsider and also to honour Muliro, the Agip House executive announced that the Delegates' Congress would be postponed for two weeks until after Muliro's funeral. Many opposition supporters hoped that Muliro might be able to achieve in death what he had failed to do in life.

The Kikuyu–Luo Divide and the Agip House Election

Meanwhile the party elections organised by the Agip House faction had been progressing. After a first week marred by violence, the two subsequent weeks of voting had progressed without serious incidents. The Muthithi House group still refused to participate and had announced that they would begin their own elections on 5 September. Kenya's main opposition party would then have two rival sets of officials in every District, two rival national executives and, indeed, two distinct party constitutions and Presidential candidates. Odinga, however, now had a decisive advantage. In most parts of the country, apart from Central Province and Shikuku's Kakamega District, the elections had continued and by the weekend of 21–23 August, most areas had selected District Branch officials. The National Delegates' Conference was now due to assemble in Nairobi on 4 September. Out of respect for Muliro, however, elections had been postponed in South Nyanza, the five Abaluhya-dominated Districts in Western Province and Muliro's own Trans-Nzoia District in Rift Valley Province. By contrast, the Matiba-Shikuku group at Muthithi House had not held even sub-branch elections.

Oginga Odinga's attempt to persuade Matiba and Shikuku to return to the fold after the death of Muliro had made little progress. The Agip House leader had nominated four powerful emissaries – James Osogo, Dr Munyua Waiyaki, Peter Kibisu and John Birgen, the former chairman of the Maize and Produce Board who as FORD chairman in Nandi District was one of the most prominent Kalenjin in the opposition party – to negotiate with the rival group.[167] Shikuku, acting on behalf of Muthithi House, had refused to accept the authority of Odinga's nominees, however, since the Luo leader and his allies had supposedly been suspended from office. The Matiba-Shikuku group continued to insist that they were the 'real' FORD. They also instituted legal action, seeking an injunction to prevent Odinga and his followers from holding elections and to nullify those that already been held.[168] The two groups were still locked in a propaganda war in the national press, blaming each other for the strife which was threatening to destroy FORD's credibility.[169] Raila Odinga and Akumu claimed that 'soldiers of fortune, hired by Muthithi House dissidents' had attempted to disrupt voting at Kiambaa, north of the capital, and in the Kariokor and Starehe working-class districts of Nairobi. By contrast, Mombasa FORD officials, led by Ahmed Salim Bamahriz, alleged that Oginga Odinga had met activists in Mombasa and encouraged them to seize control of FORD headquarters in the city.[170] While FORD leaders hurled abuse at one another, the opposition's public appeal was seriously tarnished.

Most members of the public had little doubt that FORD's troubles stemmed from the personal ambitions of its leaders – especially Odinga and Matiba – and from the refusal of Luo and Kikuyu politicians to work together. This élite rivalry reflected deeper social antagonisms. Ethnicity remained the most powerful force in Kenyan politics. Cultural stereotypes ran deep and the mutual antipathy between Kikuyus and Luos was intense. Many Kikuyu would have found it extremely difficult to vote for 'an uncircumcised Luo'. The situation among the Luo was even starker: while voters in Siaya, Kisumu and South Nyanza would vote overwhelmingly for FORD's Parliamentary candidates and for Oginga Odinga, a Kikuyu candidate for the Presidency might even secure fewer Luo votes than President Moi. However disgruntled many Luo were with KANU and Moi, there was an undercurrent of discontent with the Kikuyu, despite their apparent rejection of KANU. Many ordinary Luo considered that Nyanza Province had faired considerably better under Moi than during the 15 years of Kenyatta's rule. Thus, although Luo Young Turks like Raila Odinga might be willing to come to terms with a suitable Kikuyu leader, Luo voters and the older ex-KPU generation of politicians were more hostile to the Kikuyu than to the Kalenjin and KANU. Indeed, several well-educated Luo privately expressed the view that it was better to be dominated by a member of a small, comparatively under-developed ethnic group, like the Kalenjin, than by the Kikuyu. Ethnic enmity between Kikuyu and Luo members of FORD became increasingly evident during late August and early September 1992, as both rival groups became more and more concerned about the failure of the Registrar of Societies to approve their take-over of FORD. Matiba's supporters were particularly concerned that the upcoming Agip House National Delegates' Congress would supersede FORD's interim National Executive, sweeping away Muthithi House's main claim to legitimacy. Unless Odinga and his followers could be stopped, they would claim to the Registrar of Societies and to the Courts that they were FORD's newly elected leaders. Two Kiambu FORD leaders, George Nyanja and Stephen Ndichu – both later elected FORD-Asili Members of Parliament – were particularly outspoken in their attacks, asserting that the Kikuyu would never tolerate Luo leadership. Muthithi House seemed to be urging its followers to disrupt FORD's National Delegates' Conference in order to prevent the selection of a new National Executive and Oginga Odinga's nomination as the party's Presidential candidate.[171] Intemperate voices existed in the Agip House camp as well. Raila Odinga in an interview with the London-based *Guardian* newspaper was quoted as having declared that 'the country is not ready for another Kikuyu president so they won't vote for Matiba'.[172] Such remarks played into KANU's hands.

This growing ethnic cleavage suddenly made KANU appear a more respectable force. President Moi had warned consistently that multi-party politics would exacerbate ethnic rivalries, dividing Kenyans into hostile ethnically based parties, and would undermine development and nation-building. Only eight months after FORD had been registered as a political party to challenge KANU, his words appeared prescient. The main opposition party was in chaos. Meanwhile, government and opposition supporters were at each others' throats as 'Kalenjin warriors' attempted to create 'ethnically cleansed' enclaves. Kikuyu, Gusii and Abaluhya settlers were being driven out of Kalenjin-dominated areas in the Rift Valley, while Kalenjin residents in Nairobi were regularly being beaten up and now rarely travelled on *matatus*. The country was on the verge of splitting into four ethnically based political parties.[173]

In the end FORD's National Delegates' Congress went ahead without trouble. The Muthithi House faction's threat to disrupt the proceedings came to nothing. More than 2,500 delegates assembled at the City Stadium on Friday, 4 September to approve the key changes to FORD's constitution and to elect Odinga as FORD chairman and, under the new constitution, as its candidate for the Presidency. The processing of delegates took much longer than had been anticipated so that proceedings did not get under way until after noon. Agip House leaders attempted to emphasise their pan-tribal appeal and to repudiate suggestions that they represented a Luo-dominated organisation. After an opening speech by Odinga, the next two speakers had been prominent Kikuyu – Dr Munyua Waiyaki and Professor Wangari Maathai. Wangari Maathai acknowledged the progress that Kenyans had made since independence but cautioned that 'voting the government out of power is one thing.... Getting out of the prevalent culture of violence, injustice, corruption and greed [will require] a political, cultural and social revolution at the personal, family, community, institutional and national levels [and] as we all know, revolutions take a long time to mature.'[174] Maathai was followed by several other prominent speakers, drawn from the different provinces. Finally James Orengo explained the constitutional changes, steering the Congress to approve the party's new rules.

By the time the election of FORD's new National Executive Council began it was already mid-afternoon. Oginga Odinga was returned unopposed as the party's Chairman and, therefore, became its Presidential candidate. At 5.30 pm, the first contested election occurred when FORD's Kiambu District chairman Paul Muite was opposed by the party's Busia District Chairman, former Cabinet Minister James Osogo. Balloting took more than an hour and Muite's victory by 1,847 to 392 votes was not announced until 7 pm. The voting continued to go slowly. By 11.25 most delegates were tired, cold, and hungry and only too eager to accept Orengo's proposal that the remaining 25 members of the 37-member Executive Committee be selected by the party's General Council (which included all officials already elected by the Congress and District Branch chairmen and secretaries).[175] FORD's attempt at political openness had proved to be much more demanding and time-consuming than most participants had anticipated.

Agip House leaders attempted to stage-manage the Congress but had failed, partly because they were badly organised but also because the delegates were too enthusiastic to be regimented easily into voting for approved candidates. Whereas KANU elections lasted only a few minutes, 'with all the bargaining and balanced apportionment of seats having been concluded well in advance, the horse-trading at the FORD elections was taking place as the meeting was in progress'.[176] Some delegates, however, led by former Wundanyi Member of Parliament Mashengu wa Mwachofi, complained that the nomination process was too stage-managed, differing little from the process of ethnic and provincial balancing that KANU had employed throughout the Moi years. Mwachofi protested that the previous evening a list of candidates for various FORD executive positions, including his own name, had been circulated around the delegates' hotels. KANU had employed a similar device in 1978, when a new National Executive Committee had been elected to support the new President, Daniel arap Moi. Agip House was less well organised and its delegates less obedient than KANU's, and the faction leaders were unable to make their choices stick. Wa Mwachofi protested that FORD leaders seem as determined as KANU officials to secure the election of an approved list of names to positions in the party hierarchy, denouncing the elections as 'a KANU-type, stage-managed sham'.[177]

Nevertheless, it was vital that the Agip House faction preserve an ethnically balanced selection of leaders, drawn from all eight Provinces, in order to ensure that FORD could not be stigmatised, like the DP, as a mono-ethnic party. The infamous list of approved office holders had attempted to ensure some degree of ethnic balance. Kenya's three largest ethnic groups would share FORD's three most important posts, demonstrating that the new party was committed to national unity. Two prominent Abaluhya were proposed for the position of First Vice-Chairman – James Osogo, Busia Branch Chairman and ex-Cabinet Minister, and Kijana Wamalwa, Muliro's heir apparent and former Member of Parliament for Saboti – while the party's three leading Kikuyu – Paul Muite, Dr Munyua Waiyaki and Professor Wangari Maathai – were to contest the post of second Vice-Chairman.

FORD's leaders had decided to court the Abaluhya community after Muliro's death and intended to guarantee them the Vice-Presidential nomination. They realised that the Kikuyu, the country's largest ethnic group, had to be given a senior position in the party, but appreciated that the party was unlikely to secure many Kikuyu votes. The Abaluhya had been unable to agree upon a single nominee, however, dividing their support between Osogo, Wamalwa and Peter Kibisu. By contrast, Kikuyu delegates had united behind Muite. Dr Waiyaki had refused to be nominated and Professor Maathai had also withdrawn in favour of Muite. In the end, Wamalwa and Kibisu had also supported Muite, realising that his victory over Osogo was assured, so that contrary to planning the Kikuyu lawyer had emerged as the second most powerful figure in the party. While the balloting was progressing, intensive lobbying by party leaders had taken place to ensure that Wamalwa then secured the second Vice-Chairmanship.

Soon, intensive lobbying and trading of votes was taking place not only around the podium but throughout the stadium as the ethnic calculus of Kenyan politics asserted itself. For example, uproar greeted the nomination of Linus Aluoch, a Luo, from Homa Bay District for the post of second deputy national organising secretary. Delegates from the Coast, Eastern and Western Provinces protested, shouting, 'that's enough Luos', forcing him to withdraw. By contrast, the nomination of John Birgen, FORD chairman in Nandi District and the party's most prominent Kalenjin recruit, evoked applause and three other candidates from Laikipia, Kirinyaga and Tharaka-Nithi Districts withdrew in his favour.[178]

Although the Congress had run several hours behind schedule and the election of two thirds of the National Executive Committee had had to be abandoned, the Agip House faction's convention was a tremendous success. Supporters of the Muthithi House faction had failed to appear and the speeches and voting had gone without a hitch. Odinga and his colleagues secured favourable press coverage, undoing some of the damage which the party infighting of the previous six weeks had done to FORD's reputation. Far from appearing as a Luo-dominated clique, Odinga and his advisers had managed proceedings so that the party appeared to be a national political force, eager to incorporate all ethnic groups and committed to defeating KANU. Both the Kikuyu and Abaluhya, the ethnic groups most identified with the rival Muthithi House faction, had played a prominent role: their leaders, Paul Muite and Kijana Wamalwa, had secured the number two and three posts in the party. Agip House's ethnic and provincial representation, however, was still unbalanced. Whilst the Luo and Bukusu Luhya had two leaders each, Muite was the only Kikuyu, Nairobi had no representatives and both the Kamba and Coast Province were far from satisfied with their share of positions. Reconciling these conflicting claims would be difficult.

Table 5.3 The FORD (Agip) Executive[179]

Position	Name	District	Province	Ethnicity
Chairman	Oginga Odinga*	Siaya	Nyanza	Luo
1st Vice-Chairman	Paul Muite	Kiambu	Central	Kikuyu
2nd Vice- Chairman	Kijana Wamalwa*	Trans-Nzoia	Rift Valley	Luhya
Secretary-General	Gitobu Imanyara*	Meru	Eastern	Meru
Treasurer	Abdikadir Hassan	Garissa	North-Eastern	Somali
Organising Secretary	Abuya Abuya*	Nyamira	Nyanza	Kisii
1st Deputy Secretary-General	Joseph O. Muga*	Homa Bay	Nyanza	Luo
2nd Deputy Secretary-General	Joseph Khaoya	Bungoma	Western	Luhya
1st Deputy Treasurer	Dan Kitheka*	Kitui	Eastern	Kamba
2nd Deputy Treasurer	Patrick ole Seki*	Kajiado	Rift Valley	Maasai
1st Deputy Organising Secretary	Morris Mboja*	Kilifi	Coast	Mijikenda
2nd Deputy Organising Secretary	John Birgen*	Nandi	Rift Valley	Kalenjin

* These candidates were elected unopposed.

Divisions in Muthithi House and the Formation of the KNC[180]

The smooth progress of the pro-Agip House Delegates' Congress and Odinga's unopposed election as FORD Chairman and Presidential candidate had serious consequences at Muthithi House. Odinga and his allies now seemed to have absolute control over the party. Many senior officials expected that Matiba and Shikuku would find it impossible to maintain their claim to be FORD's legitimate leaders. But on Tuesday, 8 September, while dejected members of the Muthithi House Steering Committee were meeting, the Registrar of Societies announced that he could not register the newly elected officials since Shikuku as FORD's Secretary-General possessed essential documents which he refused to hand over to the new officials.[181] When the Committee meeting had started, former Cabinet Ministers Charles Rubia and Maina Wanjigi, and ex-Assistant Minister of Labour Kimani wa Nyoike from Nyandarua District had been close to persuading Shikuku and Matiba finally to agree that Muthithi House should abandon the conflict and seek legal recognition as a new political party. But when news reached them of the Registrar-General's refusal to register Odinga's new officials, Muthithi House decided to press ahead with their own elections and to continue the legal struggle to be registered as the official successors of the original FORD. The Steering Committee announced that location elections would begin on Saturday, 12 September, and culminate in a National Congress on 25 and 26 September.[182]

Several prominent members opposed this decision.[183] Although Matiba and Shikuku still harboured ambitions of capturing FORD's Presidential nomination, most of the Muthithi House Steering Committee merely wished to ensure that they would be able to stand for Parliament when the general election was finally called. They were much more interested in ensuring that the Muthithi House faction was registered as a political party and in taking on KANU than in embarking upon a protracted legal battle with Agip House, which could only damage further the opposition's credibility. Moreover, if President Moi called an early general election in the next few weeks, the opposition might be so bitterly divided as to be unable to field candidates.

Nonetheless, Matiba and Shikuku remained confident. The Registrar-General's refusal to register the FORD leaders convinced them that they might still be able to defeat Odinga in the courts. Muthithi House lawyers insisted that Odinga's claims to control FORD and to be party Chairman were constitutionally invalid. Section 20 of the Societies Act specifically stated that no registered society could change its name or amend its constitution without the prior consent of the Registrar-General, which Odinga and his colleagues had not secured. The Act also required that such applications had to be accompanied by minutes of a meeting of its registered officers approving the changes, signed by at least three officers of the society. With the death of Masinde Muliro, however, Oginga Odinga was the only one of FORD's six registered officers to be identified with the Agip House group. Thus the meeting at Nairobi Stadium had not been constituted legally and consequently could not amend FORD's constitution or change the procedure for electing the party's Presidential candidate. Shikuku informed the press that the Muthithi House faction was seeking 'no favours from the government, only strict adherence to the Societies Act', and warned that 'there could be a state of chaos if the government registered the Odinga group'.[184] Although it ran contrary to public perception, Matiba had an extremely strong case. By 18 September, two weeks after the Agip House elections, Imanyara still had made no progress in securing the registration of the pro-Odinga officials. Matiba was also confident that President Moi would not dare call an early general election without FORD's participation. The international community, he realised, would not approve such an election as a fair test of Kenyan public opinion. There could be no contest until the dispute between Muthithi House and Agip House for control of FORD had been settled.

These differences over Muthithi House's strategy created deep divisions within the Matiba-Shikuku camp. Rubia and other Kikuyu leaders had already begun to make contingency plans if Matiba's high-risk strategy failed. The idea of forming another party had been discussed, despite the fact that the proposal was anathema to both Matiba and Shikuku. President Moi and KANU, they argued, were the only ones who stood to gain from Muthithi House's failure to consolidate support and to establish a local organisation in those constituencies which it stood the best chance of winning. As soon as the Agip House Congress had taken place, the Muthithi House dissidents, led by Rubia, had also attempted to open negotiations with Odinga. Their terms for re-entry, however, had been too high. Rubia and his colleagues had demanded that they receive half the seats on the party's new National Executive Committee. In the immediate aftermath of the successful Agip House elections, this had been too much for Odinga and his colleagues to accept for the return of a few prominent Kikuyu ex-Ministers.[185] Once again, the leaders of FORD's rival factions seemed more interested in their own personal prestige than in the defeat of President Moi and KANU.

There was also great personal dissatisfaction with Matiba's autocratic and intolerant style. Since the break with Odinga in late July, frequently Matiba had behaved as though he considered Muthithi House to be his personal fiefdom and had been unwilling to listen to the concerns of his colleagues, who realised that their own political standing was being eroded. Matiba's and Shikuku's personal dispute with Odinga was now seen as endangering the campaign against President Moi and the ruling party. The formation of a new party, they considered, would free Muthithi House from futile legal battles and enable the opposition to get on with defeating KANU.[186]

Finally, early in September 1992, this division came to a head. After the meeting of the Muthithi House group's Steering Committee on Wednesday, 9 September, former Nairobi Mayor Andrew Ngumba and Kenneth Matiba had a furious row in front of journalists. Ngumba had confronted Matiba, asserting that he had made a serious error in opposing the plan to register as a new political party, while an angry, gesticulating Matiba had denounced Ngumba and his associates as 'self-seekers' who ignored the interests of ordinary Kenyans. Some party members, Matiba claimed, had attempted to 'mess things up' after he had left a party meeting the previous day. Ngumba had replied, 'Ken, I have been with you all along but since you are no longer listening, I have gone and I leave you with Gachoka to advise you,' before stalking out of the building.[187]

Matiba's position was now under serious threat. Most of the prominent Kikuyu politicians, who had welcomed him back to Kenya in May, were arrayed against him. The group, which included three former Cabinet Ministers (Charles Rubia, Maina Wanjigi and Titus Mbathi), a former Secretary to the Cabinet and Head of the Civil Service (Geoffrey Kariithi), two former Permanent Secretaries (Harun Lempaka and Matere Keriri), a former head of the Kenya Teachers' Union (Kimani wa Nyoike), a former Mayor of Nairobi (Andrew Ngumba) and the ex-Managing Director of the Kenya Cooperative Union (Henry Kinyua), represented a formidable array of talent and political experience. Andrew Ngumba had been a reforming Mayor of the city after ousting Margaret Kenyatta from office in the late 1970s, and in 1983 had defeated Dr Munyua Waiyaki in Nairobi's Mathare Valley seat. He had fled into exile in Sweden when the

Moi government withdrew state funds from his Rural and Urban Credit Finance Company in 1986, which had become over-extended by granting loans to small Kikuyu businesses in his constituency. Kimani wa Nyoike was a flambuoyant former teachers' union leader, Assistant Minister of Labour, outspoken government critic in the 1980s and arrested dissident. Titus Mbathi, when Minister of Labour in the early 1980s, had challenged Paul Ngei's control of Machakos District. Geoffrey Kariithi was one of the first Africans recruited to the colonial District Administration in the early 1950s and one of the first African Permanent Secretaries, just before independence, rising to be Permanent Secretary in the Office of the President, Secretary to the Cabinet and Head of the Civil Service for most of the 1970s. Elected to Parliament in 1988 for his native Kirinyaga, Kariithi had twice served as an Assistant Minister. Harun Lempaka, a Maasai, had been a long-serving civil servant and one of the few people willing to stand up to the autocratic William ole Ntimama in Narok District. They were the most experienced politicians and executive officials in the formerly united FORD, and had endowed the opposition party with administrative credibility to rival KANU and the DP.[188]

Initially, Wanjigi, Rubia and wa Nyoike had second thoughts about breaking with Matiba and Shikuku, partly because of the two men's popularity but also because Matiba seemed to have access to almost unlimited funds.[189] None of the dissidents possessed the personal wealth to finance a national election campaign. Matiba, by contrast, was so committed to capturing the Presidency that he was willing to risk his own personal fortune and to carry almost single-handedly the burden of financing Muthithi House and the forthcoming election. Indeed, Matiba's proprietal attitude to Muthithi House partly stemmed from the fact that he was bankrolling the enterprise. On the other hand, his willingness to underwrite the organisation, to finance the campaign and to risk his fortune reflected his almost maniacal belief that he was destined to become President. The vast sums of money that he was already pouring into politics reflected his sense of destiny, which had heightened his ordinary arrogance and authoritarian tendencies. Several people interviewed by the authors, who knew Matiba well, considered that he was potentially more dangerous than President Moi. One Kikuyu observed that 'Matiba is more intelligent than Moi, more arrogant than Moi, and more ruthless than Moi'.[190]

The disgruntled leaders decided to wait to see what would happen in the forthcoming Muthithi House elections. If they could secure the support of sufficient delegates at sub-branch and branch elections, they would be able to force Matiba and Shikuku to compromise. Moreover, by then the Registrar of Societies would probably have decided whether to register the new Agip House officials or to confirm the status of Shikuku and FORD's other founding fathers. Nothing was to be gained by precipitate action. Consequently, none of the prominent politicians in the anti-Matiba camp attended the press conference on Saturday, 12 September, which they had called 72 hours previously. Instead, they despatched their lawyer to address the meeting. He explained that several figures, whom he refused to name, were dissatisfied with Matiba's autocratic behaviour, that they had decided to participate in the elections for Muthithi House's National Congress, but that they were preparing to launch their own party if that became necessary.[191]

It seems that the rebel group at first merely wanted to force Matiba to pay greater attention to Kikuyu interests, and to their own political significance. Shikuku had emerged from the faction fighting in FORD as Matiba's chief ally, a fact which the Kikuyu resented, since many felt they were more important politicians than the Luhya maverick. Far from backing down, however, Matiba appeared determined to push ahead with his legal battle with Odinga for formal control over FORD. Matiba believed that he was so popular with ordinary voters, especially in southern Kikuyuland and the capital, that he could capture power with their votes. Anyone who stood in his way, be they President Moi or even former allies such as Rubia, would be swept aside in a pro-Matiba electoral avalanche. Although he appeared in danger of becoming politically isolated, Matiba dismissed his critics, observing, 'I will go to the people. I don't need politicians.' Most observers – including his opponents in Muthithi House – considered that Matiba was vastly overestimating his appeal to the masses, and that without his most senior supporters he would be isolated and doomed. They were to be proved wrong.[192]

As the conflict grew, Matiba and Shikuku pressed ahead with preparations for their own elections. Sub-branch or constituency level polls were held in several districts during the second weekend of September. Contrary to earlier boasts by the faction's leaders, the elections appeared to be no better organised than those of the rival Agip House. Newspaper reports indicated that there was considerable violence in some constituencies, the worst occurring in Narok, when armed Maasai *moran* favouring KANU killed one FORD supporter. In several areas, including Meru District and most of Coast, North-Eastern and Nyanza Provinces – Odinga's stronghold – the elections failed to take place. Reluctantly Shikuku was forced to postpone Muthithi House's National Delegates' Congress for a week so that late elections could be organised in several areas. Even where voting took place, defeated candidates sometimes complained. Ms Martha Njoka, a defeated candidate in Kirinyaga District, for example, protested to Church of the Province of Kenya Bishop David Gitari, the local returning officer, that former Secretary to the Cabinet Geoffrey Kariithi had rigged his election as Gichugu sub-branch chairman. Election agents, she claimed, had refused to permit her supporters to enter the polling stations to cast their votes. She defected to the DP. Complaints of malpractice, however, were rare by the standard of KANU elections. In most areas, the elections were judged fair by the press, although few results were reported.[193]

Shortly before the Muthithi House National Delegates' Congress convened, the dissident leaders realised that they were likely to lose the battle within Muthithi House FORD.[194] Matiba's popularity among Nairobi's Kikuyu masses had been so great that both Rubia and Wanjigi had been forced not even to contest their sub-branch elections. Andrew Ngumba sought election, but was defeated early in the process and eliminated from the contest for Nairobi District Chairman, which was won by Kimani Rugendo, a Matiba loyalist. Only Kimani wa Nyoike (Nyandarua) and Harun Lempaka (Narok) among the dissidents won election as branch chairmen. It was clear that Matiba and Shikuku would command a secure majority of delegates at Muthithi House's National Congress and that the strategy of continuing the legal fight to be recognised as the 'real' FORD would be endorsed overwhelmingly. [195]

In the end, instead of attempting to register as another new political party, Matiba's critics adopted an easier course. On 30 September, three days before the Muthithi House Congress was to meet, they gathered before the television cameras at Ufungamano House in Nairobi to announce that they had taken over a small existing party, the moribund Kenya National Congress which Nairobi businessman Onesmus Musyoka Mbali had registered earlier in the year. Mbali's transfer of the KNC's registration certificate to ex-Cabinet Minister Titus Mbathi was broadcast on national television. Such a take-over could not be blocked or held up by the Registrar of Societies, since only a change of office bearers was required.[196]

The new KNC leaders sought to portray themselves as a national political force, attempting to minimise the perception that they were primarily a group of dissident Kikuyus who had fallen out with Matiba, and who had little appeal outside Central Province and Nairobi. Titus Mbathi, the party's new Chairman, had been an able former Minister of Labour and this, plus his career as a prominent civil servant and community development official and the fact that he was not a Kikuyu, made him an ideal candidate to front the new KNC. Over the last decade, however, he had played little part in active politics. The Kikuyu 'big boys' took most of the remaining posts. Charles Rubia became the new party's first Vice-Chairman, Kimani wa Nyoike Secretary-General, and Maina Wanjigi second Deputy Secretary-General. Dr Chibule wa Tsuma from Coast Province became second Vice-Chairman, with original founder Onesmus Musyoka Mbali as first Deputy Secretary-General. At the last moment Harun Lempaka decided to remain with Matiba, while Andrew Ngumba defected to the DP.[197]

The new party's first problem was to overcome George Anyona's threat to take them to court for using the name 'Kenya National Congress'. Anyona had been preparing to launch a party of the same name when he was detained back in July 1990 and, while in prison, he had drafted the party's constitution and rules. When Mbali had registered another party with the same name in February 1992, Anyona was still in prison, and had since made several unsuccessful attempts to reclaim the name. He now again protested that the former Muthithi House leaders had no right to usurp the name of his party and to ignore the fact that he had a court suit pending. Moral principles apart, however, Anyona's position was weak, and the new team was soon firmly established with their 'third-hand' name.[198]

The new KNC leaders sought to present their party as an attempt to bring together FORD's feuding factions by downplaying personal rivalries. They insisted that the KNC would not nominate a Presidential candidate and that their candidates would only contest civic and Parliamentary elections. This strategic decision may well have been a mistake. Although it protected them somewhat from the bitter struggle between the Presidential leaders, they were simply swamped by the weight of ticket voting in the final poll. Mbathi and Rubia suggested a similar strategy should be adopted in the Parliamentary elections, where the factions should select the most popular local opposition leader to challenge KANU. But, as the *Weekly Review* observed, these were 'noble aims but probably pipe dreams'. Few local politicians were willing to stand down so that their rivals in the opposition could have a better chance of defeating the ruling party. FORD-Kenya leaders, for example, would have liked Mrs Wambui Otieno, their candidate in Kajiado North, to stand down in order to give DP Secretary-General John Keen a better chance against Vice-President Saitoti, but they could not prevail until the last minute. Ideological or policy differences were of little importance. The disintegration of FORD had been caused by the personal ambitions of Odinga and Matiba, rather than by policy differences. The three parties which had emerged from the original FORD would fight the elections on 29 December on the same political manifesto: neither Matiba nor the KNC ever devised a policy programme to supersede the one prepared by the united FORD earlier in the year.

Mbathi and Rubia suggested that the new party would soon see a wave of defections from the warring Agip House and Muthithi House factions when opposition leaders came to realise, as the general election drew closer, that unity was the only way to defeat KANU. In many respects, the KNC leaders preached the same message of opposition unity as Masinde Muliro had done before his death. Indeed, Muliro would have been an ideal Presidential candidate for the KNC. As it was, only one of Muliro's supporters, Dr Chibule wa Tsuma, defected from Agip House to the new party. Ironically, wa Tsuma soon became the focal point of deep divisions within the KNC as he began to protest about Kikuyu domination and secret deals with the DP and attempted to promote his own candidacy for the party's Presidential nomination, ignoring the leadership's strong support for Mwai Kibaki.

Despite appearing so late on an already crowded political scene and lacking a clear political image, the KNC had three strengths. It offered a middle path between the two unrecognised FORD factions and the DP. Its leaders were politicians of considerable stature who appeared able to deliver a considerable number of votes in Nairobi, Nyandarua and Machakos, and could win 5–10 seats in Parliament. The party also still hoped to attract recruits from the twin FORDs. Openings still existed in mid-October 1992, for defectors to play a prominent role in the new party as a majority of positions on the KNC's NEC remained unfilled. The KNC leaders, however, were primarily motivated by the desire to safeguard their own political careers by securing re-election to Parliament.

The formation of the KNC further confused the political scene. Would the new party actually survive to election day or was it simply a stalking-horse, portending yet another major realignment of political forces? Rumours circulated that the KNC leaders might ally with Professor Wangari Maathai's 'Middle Ground Group' among Agip House activists, which was also seeking to unite the rival FORD factions. The two groups were in close contact. Journalists also speculated that the KNC might simply be a ruse to safeguard Matiba's Presidential ambitions if he lost the legal battle for recognition as the rightful leader of FORD. Other accounts suggested that the KNC leaders were planning to join Mwai Kibaki's DP, as Andrew Ngumba had done.[199]

Similar rumours existed with regard to Odinga. If Agip House was refused registration, Odinga and his colleagues, it was suggested, would join David Mukaru-Ng'ang'a's Kenya National Democratic Alliance (KENDA). The Marxist former history lecturer at the University of Nairobi made little secret of his respect for Oginga Odinga. His refusal to join FORD may well have stemmed from the fact that in his native Murang'a FORD was dominated not by the populist radicals around Odinga but by Kenneth Matiba and his coterie of Kikuyu big businessmen such as John Michuki, former chairman of the Kenya Commercial Bank, whose political ideology had little in common with Mukaru-Ng'ang'a's Marxism. On several occasions, Mukaru-Ng'ang'a had proclaimed that only Odinga was a candidate of sufficient stature to unite the opposition. Now that FORD had split, KENDA might well offer Odinga and his colleagues a fall-back if their FORD faction was refused registration.[200]

The Democratic Party's Emergence as a Serious Force, May–June 1992

Until May, the DP made little attempt to break out of its Central Province stronghold and the neighbouring parts of Eastern Province. FORD controlled the Luo areas of Nyanza Province, whose loyalty to Oginga Odinga were unshakeable, while Masinde Muliro and Martin Shikuku controlled the loyalties of those Western Province voters who did not still back KANU. The Kalenjin, Maasai and Turkana Districts of the Rift Valley were KANU's stronghold, the personal bailiwicks of President Moi, Nicholas Biwott and William ole Ntimama. Only in Nakuru and Laikipia, the two Kikuyu Districts in the Rift Valley, did the DP have a major presence. The party had managed, however, to enlist two prominent non-Kikuyus: Secretary-General John Keen, who had long represented the Maasai constituency of Kajiado North in the National Assembly, and its interim Treasurer Eliud Mwamunga, a former Cabinet Minister, who came from Voi in Taita-Taveta District in Coast Province. The party had also given a prominent role at its rallies to Nandi District DP chairman, Kiptoo arap Koech, who although not a politician of the first rank was willing fearlessly to condemn the attacks by so-called 'Kalenjin warriors' on Kikuyu, Luhya, Luo and Gusii settlers in the Rift Valley. Indeed, arap Koech claimed during rallies at Ruring'u stadium in Nyeri on Saturday, 23 May and the following day at Karuri stadium in Kiambaa, Njenga Karume's base, that the 'Kalenjin warriors' had taken an oath to drive all non-Kalenjins out of the Rift Valley.[201] DP leaders were careful to exonerate the Kalenjin community as a whole, pointing out that they too had suffered in the violence. Karume, for example, had urged the assembled Kikuyu not to victimise the Kalenjin as a whole. The incidents were the responsibility of President Moi and a few irresponsible Kalenjin and Maasai politicians. The Kiambaa crowd, however, had been inflamed by rumours that 'Kalenjin warriors' had massacred 50 Kikuyu school children in Nyandarua and western Kiambu.[202] Party leaders were not always so free of ethnic bias. George Anyona, for example, had recently pointed out that the party had given money only to Kikuyu victims of the ethnic clashes and not to Luo, Luhya and Gusii.[203]

FORD, of course, continued to castigate the DP, suggesting that its leaders still secretly supported KANU. They pointed out that John Keen was the only DP leader to have risked his freedom in the campaign to secure multi-party democracy during 1990 and 1991. By contrast, they claimed, the DP was no more than a splinter group from the ruling party, or 'KANU B'. Martin Shikuku, for example, frequently sought to embarrass the rival party by demanding to know why President Moi so rarely attacked the DP. Most Kenyans were encouraged to see it as the party of rich Kikuyu, and both FORD and KANU derided it as 'an exclusive club that discusses politics at golf courses'.

The *Kenya Times,* KANU's mouthpiece, sought to discredit the party in April by suggesting that it was financed secretly by the former GEMA organisation. The paper alleged that former GEMA Chairman, Njenga Karume, now the DP's Kiambu Branch Chairman, was colluding with Kibaki to raise money for the party by selling assets of Agricultural and Industrial Holdings, the front company established by GEMA leaders to divest their vast land and share portfolio when President Moi had ordered the disbanding of 'tribal associations' in 1980. Karume had denied the charge, of course, dismissing the story as 'a malicious fabrication by an old KANU dis-information task-force'.[204] Allegations identifying the DP with GEMA and the era of Kikuyu dominance under Kenyatta proved a constant problem for the party, emphasising the continuing Kikuyu domination of Kenya's 'third force'. As Paul Muite had discovered earlier, GEMA was regarded by non-Kikuyu as a malevolent power. The DP sought to counteract such impressions by declaring that it was ready to field candidates in all 188 constituencies. Moreover, as FORD became ever more immersed in its own internal problems, the DP appeared to be much better organised than the larger opposition party. Its leaders claimed that they were quietly touring the country, opening branches and supervising the recruitment of new members, while FORD lapsed into civil war.[205]

Then, in late May and June, the DP attracted four prominent defectors: former Minister of Labour and ex-chairman of the Electoral Commission James Nyamweya, who had been MP for Nyaribari in Kisii from 1963 to 1979; Matu Wamae, the former MP for Mathira in Nyeri District (who defected from FORD); Charles Murgor, a former Kalenjin Assistant Minister and ex-Provincial Commissioner who had represented Eldoret South from 1969 to 1983;[206] and former Deputy Speaker, Samuel arap Ng'eny, the ex-MP for Aldai in Nandi District. Ng'eny's defection was a major coup as he was the most prominent Kalenjin politician to defect to the opposition. He had been forced out in 1988 and had played little role in local affairs since, but in May 1992 he had joined other radical Kalenjin leaders in criticising those involved in the ethnic clashes.[207] These recruits bolstered the DP's claim to be a serious national political force and suggested that there might be some discontent, especially among the Nandi, within President Moi's ethnic stronghold. Adherents of the Church of the Province of Kenya (CPK) in Nandi, who had suffered during the attacks on the late Bishop Muge, had increasingly come to resent the control of District politics by members of the African Inland Church, among whose adherents were President Moi and the leaders of the Nandi KANU branch and the County Council. Nonetheless, it was always unlikely that many Kalenjin voters would desert Moi.[208]

During the first four months of 1992, the DP had retained a moderate, highly conservative image, emphasising its leaders'– and especially Mwai Kibaki's – image as competent technocrats who could restore Kenya's economic prosperity and good government.[209] The campaign was not without success. *Finance,* a Nairobi magazine, in mid-March praised 'the re-birth of Mwai Kibaki', observing that 'Kibaki, by sheer guts and intellectual capability ... [had] swiftly emerged as a vital symbol of the emerging democratic society.'[210] He had caused panic within the government by denouncing the systematic looting of the economy through the mismanaged parastatals and the diversion of Sh28,000 million to private accounts. 'Rarely has anybody in competitive politics delivered such a scathing attacks on KANU and Moi with such oratorical mastery and fluency.'[211] Kibaki had thrown off his image as a man of expediency and had emerged as a forthright critic of the corrupt regime. If he could sustain this performance, the magazine judged that the DP might emerge as a powerful third force, providing a 'new liberal party' alternative to the corruption and brutality of KANU, and the radicalism of FORD.

The DP still had limited appeal, however, and would have to contend with the return of Kenneth Matiba. *Finance* warned:

> Already analysts are unanimous that the DP may not survive if Kenneth Matiba returns and captures the leadership of FORD. Without the Kikuyu constituency, the DP is merely a gathering of wealthy individuals that had it too good in Kenyatta's and, to some extent, Moi's years.[212]

Thus the DP's prospects still appeared limited. The party seemed unable to break out of its Kikuyu bastion or to appeal to younger, more radical voters who had become disillusioned by the factional divisions in FORD. Kibaki and his colleagues were also too cautious. They had disassociated themselves from FORD's call for a General Strike in early April, and had also refused to support the hunger strike at Freedom Corner in Nairobi's *Uhuru* Park, which the detainees' female relatives had launched on 28 February.[213] The DP had refused to participate in the first series of party meetings convened by FORD in February, merely despatching Secretary-General Keen to observe the proceedings. Then, in May, at the symposium organised by the National Council of Churches of Kenya , the DP had rejected the proposal by radicals in FORD and KENDA and Social Democratic Party (SDP) leader Johnstone Makau that the NCCK-sponsored meeting should declare itself a 'sovereign' national convention, and launch a national civil disobedience campaign.[214] Such caution had proved counter-productive, enabling FORD leaders to condemn the DP as a pro-KANU ploy, established to divide the opposition. The DP leadership could not support the Freedom Movement, FORD pointed out, because as senior KANU politicians until December 1991, they had endorsed KANU's authoritarian behaviour and had sought to obstruct the pro-democracy movement until the very last moment.[215]

KANU also maintained its pressure on the DP. In late May, President Moi announced that the two opposition parties were training 'secret armies' to overthrow the government and suggested that John Keen was in charge of the DP's assassination squad.[216] These allegations exasperated Kibaki, who demanded that President Moi substantiate these claims and called for a boycott of the *Madaraka* Day celebrations on 1 June, marking the twenty-ninth anniversary of Kenya's attainment of self-government.[217] The hostility of the *Weekly Review's* editor, Hilary Ng'weno, to the DP was revealed when he condemned Kibaki's change of tactics as 'embarrassing' and 'out of character'.[218] Ng'weno highlighted the fact that the main celebrations at Nairobi's Nyayo Stadium, addressed by President Moi, had been well attended, while down-playing the sparse attendance at local gatherings organised by the District Administration. Kibaki, he suggested, was attempting to present a new tough image to counteract Matiba's inroads into the Kikuyu vote.

Other DP leaders also adopted a more confrontational approach. The late President Kenyatta's nephew and successor as MP for Gatundu, Ngengi Muigai, one of Kenya's wealthiest men, attempted to lead a protest march through Thika when his licence to hold a meeting was withdrawn at the last moment by the Kiambu District Commissioner. Riot police fired tear gas canisters into the march, filling the Kenyatta family's compound at Gatundu, where DP supporters had gathered, with noxious fumes.[219] In another incident, the party's Nandi activist, Paul Kiptoo arap Koech, was arrested for a breach of the peace following his allegations at a rally in Nyeri that some Kalenjin had taken an oath to drive members of other 'tribes' out of the Rift Valley.[220] Kibaki also attempted to seize an advantage by announcing that the DP would hold grassroots elections during June and July before either FORD or KANU. He attempted to portray his party as an equal challenger, presenting it as a viable alternative to a divided FORD, appealing to non-Kikuyu voters while attempting to consolidate its position in Central Province.

As the DP became more active and a more serious force, KANU became increasingly concerned. At first, KANU chiefs had devoted little attention to the party, concentrating their attacks upon the more serious challenge from FORD. But as the threat from FORD receded and it became more and more preoccupied by its own internal power struggles, the DP solidified its base in Kikuyuland and in parts of Eastern Province, and began to establish a presence in the Gusii Districts and in some parts of KANU's own Rift Valley stronghold. The government-controlled Kenya Broadcasting Corporation now began to present the DP in a hostile light. The KBC had hardly reported FORD's first rally at Kamukunji in January 1992, but had given extensive coverage to the launching of the DP as part of a campaign to build up the third party; now the Corporation switched its attacks, portraying Kibaki's party as an élitist 'tribal movement' that wanted to turn the clock back to the Kenyatta era of Kikuyu control.

KANU also feared that Kibaki, a product of the Catholic Mangu High School, might be supported by the country's Catholic Hierarchy as the country's leading Roman Catholic politician. Since 1990, Kenya's Catholic Bishops' Conference had become increasingly critical of the government. During 1990 and 1991, the Bishops' Conference had issued two pastoral letters on political issues each year, but in the six months since the legalisation of multi-party politics in December 1991, the Bishops had issued five pastoral letters, all highly critical of KANU and the Moi regime.[221] On 8 May 1992, for example, a delegation of Bishops had bluntly accused Moi of complicity in the ethnic violence, later releasing, much to the President's fury, a report to the press of their State House meeting. They had also supported the NCCK's call for a boycott of voter registration until a neutral Electoral Commission was appointed.[222] Some KANU leaders feared that the Roman Catholic hierarchy might endorse the DP officially. Benjamin Kositany, the MP for Mosop in Nandi, a prominent member of the AIC, denounced the Bishops at a press conference on 1 June, claiming that they were campaigning for the DP.[223]

President Moi himself raised the issue during an address at Nakuru stadium on Sunday, 21 June. The President complained that the churches were being partisan and threatened the NCCK with deregistration.[224] The Council's chairman, Anglican Bishop Henry Okullu, who had played such a key role with Paul Muite in the launching of the Justice and Peace Convention in June 1991, warned KANU leaders that such a move would be counter-productive, alienating many church-going Kenyans as well as the international Christian community. The more belligerent Rev. Dr Timothy Njoya even urged the President to carry out his threat, warning of the civil resistance that would follow, while Martin Shikuku taunted the President, declaring at a rally in Kakamega on 22 June that 'President Moi should know that the NCCK, the Roman Catholic Church, the Church of the Province of Kenya and the opposition parties have now united to ensure that the ruling party loses during the forthcoming multi-party elections.'[225] The major churches stood united against the regime, supporting the opposition's call for the appointment of an impartial Electoral Commission and for reforms in the voter registration process. The DP's relationship with the Roman Catholic Church, however, aroused KANU's particular concern as the two organisations became increasingly outspoken. KANU leaders feared that the Roman Catholic Church might establish as close a relationship with the DP as the NCCK and the Church of the Province of Kenya enjoyed with FORD. The DP, however, was a secular political movement. Its leaders were drawn from a number of denominations and the party was never likely simply to articulate the views of the Catholic Church. Kibaki himself, as Minister of Health from 1988 to December 1991, for example, had fully endorsed Kenya's active birth control policy despite the hostility of the Catholic hierarchy.

As Kibaki toured the country during August and September, visiting Kisii, Nyamira, Lamu, Nandi, Makueni, Kiambu, Nyeri, Uasin Gishu, Kisii again, and then Tana River, he encountered constant hostility and harassment from KANU activists, the Provincial Administration and the police. His officials also experienced problems. At the end of August, Nakuru DP chairman and former MP, Mark Mwithaga, and two other branch officials were arrested after allegedly advising Kikuyu residents at Gilgil to fight back if they were attacked by 'Kalenjin warriors'. Secretary-General Keen and national official Joseph Munyao were also denounced: the first for failing to promote development schemes during his 20-year career as an MP and the latter for criticising the Asian community's continuing domination of the retail sector.[226] To make matters worse, Kenneth Matiba, realising that attack was the best way to confirm the loyalty of Kikuyu voters, continued to mock the DP, refusing to acknowledge that it was a serious challenger for power and dismissing rumours that the party might merge with FORD as 'a big joke'.[227] An angry John Keen counter-attacked, observing that Matiba's Presidential ambitions were 'a dream and a big joke'.[228]

Whenever the DP leader ventured into KANU's heartlands, he encountered carefully organised harassment. An important rally in Kapsabet, scheduled for 3 September, was cancelled with less than 24 hours notice by the District Commissioner. Kibaki was to have toured Aldai, Tinderet and Mosop with the party's new Nandi District chairman, Samuel arap Ng'eny, before addressing the meeting.[229] Then, in early September, after a successful tour of Uasin Gishu with local party chairman Charles Murgor, during which he had opened a DP office in Eldoret and been cheered in the streets, Kibaki had been stopped from entering Moi's Bridge by 100 pro-KANU youths, armed with pangas and arrows.[230] The most serious incident occurred on Sunday, 13 September, when the DP leader was ambushed at Sotik in Kericho District, where he had stopped to greet local residents. A crowd of youths had attacked, overturning one car and smashing two windscreens, forcing DP security men to shield Kibaki as stones rained down on the vehicles. John Keen, speaking after Kibaki had opened the new DP office, condemned the attack as 'an attack of desperation that will not stop the DP from launching the offensive in so-called KANU zones'. A shaken DP leader arrived in Kisii town only to discover that the District Commissioner had cancelled the rally at the last moment in order to hold a *Harambee* fund-raising meeting for university students, conducted by local KANU leader Simeon Nyachae.[231] Three of his convoy's Mercedes Benz cars were impounded for allegedly unpaid hotel bills, and there was a stand-off between armed police and DP security men when the DP team visited the home of local activist Simon Chacha, who ironically was a former District Commissioner.[232] The 'invective flowed fast and furious'[233] when Kibaki encountered a mob in Limuru, where he had gone to welcome the recruitment of the immediate former Member of Parliament. Kibaki charged that the incident had been organised by Youth for KANU '92, which was 'instilling a culture of violence'. He asserted that the whole KANU leadership suffered from 'primitive paranoia ... [and adopted] the tactics of stone-age man'. They were 'psychopaths and sycophants'.[234]

The *Kenya Times* also intensified its attacks. Issues of 'KANU Briefs' in the paper had derided the party for not holding its much-heralded local elections in June and July, and claimed that the party 'was owned by Njenga Karume' for whom Kibaki was merely a front-man.[235] The *Kenya Times* even asserted that the DP had hired gunmen to assassinate President Moi.[236] Refuting the allegations, Kibaki warned that 'violence is part of KANU's stock in trade'. Secretary-General Keen accused the government of 'using the Provincial Administration and Youth for KANU '92 to intimidate the opposition'.[237] DP and FORD leaders, whom the paper had alleged were training their own terrorist squad, dismissed the reports with Kibaki leading the way, filing a Kenya record Sh200 million suit for defamation against the KANU-controlled newspaper.[238]

The DP seems to have attracted closer attention from KANU for two reasons. First, since the crisis in FORD, it had emerged as a much more serious political force and was attempting to undermine KANU's control of Kisii and Nyamira and to establish a presence in the Kalenjin heartlands, establishing offices in Nandi and Uasin Gishu.[239] Secondly, Kibaki had threatened in several speeches to arrest KANU leaders for corruption when the DP came to power, directly attacking the President and other members of the inner circle. Wherever he went, the DP leader denounced high-level corruption, government inefficiency, the deteriorating economy, and raised contentious local issues. During his tour of Tana River, a backwater where KANU had expected little opposition, for example, Kibaki promised to revitalise the Bura irrigation scheme and to rescind the ban on using canoes, a cheap mode of transport.[240] He also denounced Moi's misuse of state resources to finance KANU activities, such as the President's tour of North-Eastern Province in late September.[241]

Yet, despite such whirlwind tours and the enlistment in September of prominent Luhya businessman Alfred Sambu, a friend of the late Masinde Muliro, who launched a DP branch in Bungoma, the party remained strongest in Central and Eastern Provinces. The party had gained few recruits as a result of FORD's troubles; the main beneficiary had been KANU. Peter Kibisu in Western Province, Emmanuel Maitha in Mombasa, and Ahmed Khalif from North-Eastern Province had all abandoned FORD to return to the ruling party.[242] The DP's greatest success was the enlistment of veteran Kamba leader Paul Ngei, the self-proclaimed 'King of Machakos', who had lost his seat in the Cabinet in November 1990 when he had been declared bankrupt after a protracted legal battle.[243] Ngei, however, was a controversial figure who for nearly three decades had been a member of KANU governments. Even in Machakos his popularity was uncertain. Nevertheless, in recent weeks, Kibaki had eclipsed Matiba, whose reputation had been tarnished by the disintegration of FORD, developing a new, more combative image to emerge revitalised as the front-runner for Kikuyu votes.[244] Kibaki's energetic campaigning at least ensured that the DP's opponents in KANU, as well as in FORD, had to take it as a serious challenger.

FORD Finally Splits, September–October 1992

Three days after the KNC was launched, Kenneth Matiba was elected Chairman of FORD by the Muthithi House National Delegates' Congress. After the split, Matiba was supported by only the four FORD founders, Shikuku, Nthenge, Bamahriz and Gachoka, plus former Vice-President Josephat Karanja of Kiambu District, now the only senior Kikuyu to remain loyal to Matiba. Nonetheless, the first signs now emerged that Matiba's contempt for his political colleagues might not be the disaster many expected. More than 4,800 delegates from 45 Districts attended the meeting at Hillcrest Secondary School, which was owned by Matiba, in Nairobi's wealthy Karen suburb. Only Siaya, Oginga Odinga's home, sent no representatives. Matiba and Shikuku were elected unopposed as Chairman and Secretary-General, while George Nthenge, the former Machakos MP, became Vice-Chairman in the new organisation. Salim Ahmed Bamahriz, FORD's other founding father, became the new Organising Secretary, and Harun Lempaka, who had considered defecting, was surprisingly elected National Treasurer. Abdullahi Maalim as Assistant Secretary-General, Wanguhu Ng'ang'a as Assistant Organising Secretary and political unknown Elijah Mamboleo as Assistant Treasurer completed the line-up of eight national officials.[245]

The delegates confirmed Odinga's suspension and endorsed FORD's original constitution, which Agip House had amended on 4 September. The party's Presidential, Parliamentary and Local Government candidates were to be chosen later through secret ballot elections among the party's mass membership. Although Shikuku did not oppose Matiba for the post of Chairman at the Congress, he made it clear that he still intended to contest the party's Presidential nomination.

Now that both factions had held sub-branch, branch and national elections, the battle to inherit FORD's name and stature as the originator of multi-party democracy in Kenya reached its climax. Registrar of Societies Omondi Mbago was faced with two rival slates of national officials. Both Chairman Matiba and Shikuku seemed willing to take the dispute to the courts.[246] Meanwhile, the Odinga camp was becoming increasingly alarmed by the failure of the Registrar of Societies to approve their FORD officials.[247]

Anticipating stalemate after the Muthithi house elections, in the first week of October Odinga abandoned the strategy of waiting patiently for the Registrar to make a decision, denounced the government for interfering in the process and led two angry marches through the streets to Sheria House, where he insisted upon seeing the Attorney-General. Accompanied by Vice-Chairmen Paul Muite and Kijana Wamalwa and Agip House's Secretary for Legal Affairs, James Orengo, Odinga protested that the government should stop interfering and urged that the Registrar make an early ruling.[248] The Registrar explained that the delay in registration had been caused by the fact that the pro-Matiba and pro-Shikuku forces had lodged a large number of objections to the constitutional changes and to the election of new officers. Paul Muite, however, dismissed this as an excuse and informed the press that 'the delay in effecting changes of particulars can only be seen as part of President Moi's design to stage-manage confusion so as to gain advantage in presidential elections'.[249] The Agip House Vice-Chairman warned that FORD's supporters were becoming restless and that it would soon be impossible to control their frustration or to stop them taking to the streets to protest the delay.

Oginga Odinga also wrote to President Moi, urging him to intervene to secure the registration of the Agip House officials. Unless he and his supporters could take part, he complained, the elections would not be free and fair. The President, Odinga cautioned, should 'think on this and ponder well its implications'.[250] President Moi responded publicly on Monday, 12 October, when he warned a rally in Kirinyaga District that the opposition had no one to blame but themselves if they were not ready to fight an election. He hinted that a general election was imminent and that he was confident that he would be returned to State House and that KANU would have a secure majority in Parliament. The *Weekly Review* judged that the President 'is raring to go'.[251] The government was well aware, however, that it had little to gain from an election if the rival FORD factions were so locked in battle that neither could participate effectively. Such an outcome would dissatisfy many Kenyans, would fail to reassure the international community, would not secure the resumption of international aid, and would not provide President Moi and KANU with the political legitimacy required to govern for the next five years.

Even before the President made his remarks in Kirinyaga, in fact, Attorney-General Wako had offered a solution to the impasse, suggesting that both the Agip House and Muthithi House factions preserve the name 'FORD' with unique additional elements, following which he would register both their National Executive Committees so that two separate parties could take part in the elections. Wako warned that the alternative was for the Registrar of Societies to give the two factions one month to reach a compromise, to seek arbitration or to take the problem to the courts. If no action was taken, the Registrar-General could then deregister the society, outlawing both factions.[252] He had intervened to offer a solution which he hoped would be acceptable to both factions. Now more confident of victory, it was in KANU's interests to confront two separate FORD parties and to re-establish its right to rule Kenya by securing an overwhelming majority in 'free and fair' elections.

Realising that the election was now imminent, Odinga, Matiba and Shikuku decided to accept the Attorney-General's proposal. The Agip House faction quickly decided to adopt the name FORD-Kenya, while the Muthithi House politicians finally decided to take the title FORD-Asili (literally, 'the original' FORD), thereby still claiming that they were the only legitimate successor to the party originally registered on 31 December 1991. Matiba informed the press that 'Ours is the original FORD. We have retained FORD's constitution and membership cards. It is not a new party. We have only changed the name to avoid confusion with a new party which was formed by the Agip faction.'[253] Odinga's FORD-Kenya, however, secured FORD's lion symbol, although the party's original colours and famous two finger 'V' salute were to be used by both parties.

The Failure of the Middle Ground, May–October 1992

The ending of the FORD dispute cut the ground from underneath the KNC. Now both FORDs were registered, there was little true purpose to their party, since their strategy of mediating between rival factions had vanished, and few leaders from either FORD would now defect. There was even less prospect that Oginga Odinga, Kenneth Matiba or Martin Shikuku would now abandon their campaigns for the Presidency, or that the DP's

Mwai Kibaki would stand down. Despite the personal prestige of its leaders, there appeared to be little support for the KNC. The result, over the next few weeks as the election approached, was a haemorrhage of support back to its now secure parents by its national officials.

KNC leaders, nevertheless, still tried to build some form of unity. In mid-October they approached the National Council of Churches of Kenya and the Kenya Catholic Bishops' Conference to organise a meeting of all opposition parties to consider establishing a common front against President Moi and KANU.[254] FORD, as we have seen, had first brought political leaders together in February, but both KANU and the DP had refused to participate.[255] Then, on 11 May, the NCCK had intervened, calling a meeting of all parties, including KANU, to discuss the ethnic clashes and the democratisation process. Once again, the government had refused to participate. Even then, only a week after Matiba's return to Kenya, Bishop Henry Okullu had expressed his frustration at the opposition's divisions, complaining that the rival parties and factions had let the people down: 'Our people are asking, what has gone wrong? Where shall our true liberators come from?' he declared. Despite KANU's refusal to participate, the symposium had issued an ultimatum, demanding that the government dismantle the Electoral Commission within two weeks or face widespread civil disobedience. Little, however, came of these threats. Then on Thursday and Friday, 11 and 12 June, the NCCK invited the parties to a symposium at its Limuru conference centre, where Okullu and former PCEA Moderator George Wanjau attempted to ensure closer collaboration between the opposition parties. The DP delegation had been led by Kibaki, George Muhoho and John Keen, while Muliro, Shikuku, Muite, Anyang-Nyong'o and Mukhisa Kituyi had led the FORD team. Minor party leaders Johnstone Makau of the SDP, Mohammed Akram Noor of the Labour Party Democracy, and Mukaru-Ng'ang'a of KENDA, and prominent figures from a host of NGOs, including the Law Society of Kenya, the International Commission of Jurists, the Professionals' Committee for Democratic Change, the Release Political Prisoners pressure group, the Kenya Chapter of the Federation of Women Lawyers, the League of Women Voters, the National Council of Women of Kenya, and the unregistered Green Party had also attended. Even the Kikuyu traditionalist Ngonya wa Gakonya of the Tent of the Living God had attended, representing the unregistered Democratic Movement (DEMO).[256]

The two-day meeting had discussed the problems encountered by opposition parties in registering local sub-branches and securing permission to hold meetings, as well as the failure to reform the Electoral Commission and the causes of the ethnic violence. Once again, FORD radicals and KENDA leaders had pressed for the establishment of a National Convention, uniting Muliro and other FORD moderates with the DP leaders. Indeed, Kibaki had threatened that the DP would walk out of the meeting if Muite's motion calling for a vote on the proposal was approved. The DP leader contended that the participants at the meeting were not all of equal importance and that, therefore, a vote would be meaningless. The gathering, however, approved the report of the Rev. George Wanjau's independent enquiry into the ethnic clashes,[257] and reiterated the opposition's rejection of the present Electoral Commission, calling for the suspension of voter registration and the delineation of new constituency boundaries, and for the release of all political prisoners. As a sop to the radicals, the delegates also appointed a task force to consider the establishment of a National Convention and decided to boycott voter registration.[258] The NCCK's intervention had failed, however, to bring the opposition parties closer together.

By early October, few moderates remained. KNC leaders Mbathi, Rubia and wa Nyoike still hoped, nevertheless, that the opposition leaders could be persuaded to name a single Presidential candidate acceptable to all ethnic and ideological interests. A similar initiative was launched the following week by Professor Wangari Maathai's Middle Ground Group. Now that the election appeared imminent, Maathai began to lobby more assertively for the nomination of a compromise Presidential candidate who would maximise the vote against President Moi, and enhance the opposition's chances of securing 25 per cent of the vote in five Provinces (see Chapter Seven). The response to the Middle Ground Group's initiative, however, was almost universally hostile. Matiba and Shikuku argued that the only solution was for the people directly to elect the opposition's Presidential nominee, rather than to have him selected 'through the dictates of tribal arithmetic'.[259] Even Mwai Kibaki, who praised Maathai's efforts to unite the opposition, refused to participate in the discussions. Given Wangari Maathai's prominent position in the party, FORD-Kenya despatched two leaders, Paul Muite and James Orengo, to the gathering, but the meeting was pointless without the presence of the other main opposition parties. Only the tiny KENDA, the Labour Democratic Party and the Social Democratic Party were willing to participate without reservations. Mbathi and Rubia, meanwhile, were attempting to reach agreement with the DP in the last week of October to 'prepare the ground for a common approach in the forthcoming general election'.[260] They hoped to maximise their own support by agreeing to back Kibaki as President, whilst the DP would not field candidates in the KNC leaders' own constituencies.

The complete failure of Maathai's meeting made it even clearer that 68-year-old President Moi would be opposed by three main rivals: the octogenarian Oginga Odinga for FORD-Kenya; Mwai Kibaki for the DP; and either Kenneth Matiba or Martin Shikuku for FORD-Asili. Kenya's opposition was more fragmented than it had been at the beginning of the year and President Moi's prospects of holding on to office appeared better than ever. Even before the first general election speech was made, let alone its first ballot cast, Kenya's opposition leaders had let the country down by their personal rivalries and conflicting ambitions.

By early August 1992, FORD was divided into two irreconcilable factions which seemed destined to become separate parties, fighting over the party's claim to be the original movement for multi-party democracy. A series of miscalculations, tensions based on personal positions and conflicts over the fundamental direction of change had forced what was always a fractious leadership coalition into open warfare. Not only were Odinga and Matiba both determined to be Kenya's first multi-party President, the parties and their supporters were unable to constrain their ambition in the collective interest. FORD was gifted and cursed with two individuals who felt they had a God-given right to State House, and the hierarchical structure of political authority, plus their own personal characteristics, made it impossible for the institutions and individuals within their respective factions to control them.[261] Both camps claimed that they were the 'original' FORD: Matiba had launched the campaign for multi-party democracy in May 1990 and had the support of four of the party's six founding fathers, while the pro-Odinga forces had a majority nationally and on both the interim Executive and Steering Committees. Both sides had made a major contribution to the party and helped to make it an effective political force in the first months of 1992. In much of the country, however, this factional divide was viewed with dismay, and local leaders resisted alignment with either faction until the end. An Odinga-Matiba team, with the aged Luo leader as FORD's figurehead leader and Presidential candidate and Matiba, the younger Kikuyu businessman, as his Vice-Presidential candidate, would have proved formidable opposition to President Moi and KANU. Such a ticket could have carried Central Province, Nairobi, Nyanza, parts of Eastern Province and much of Western Province. It might even have taken 25 per cent of the vote in KANU's Rift Valley heartland. The united FORD Steering Committee before the split had included representatives from 43 Districts: only Samburu, Turkana and Bomet had failed to nominate delegates.[262]

The power struggle and the gradual fragmentation of FORD which resulted, destroyed much of the moral advantage which they had originally possessed.[263] The ruling party and the DP were the main beneficiaries of the split. Both President Moi and Mwai Kibaki proved better than Odinga at controlling their parties, faced little opposition, and were supported by experienced politicians who had played a key role in running the country for nearly three decades. FORD, by contrast, had enlisted the support of fewer senior politicians with government experience. Those who did join the party – such as Oginga Odinga, Masinde Muliro and Munyua Waiyaki – had been out of the Cabinet for many years. Its Secretariat was dominated by Young Turks, most of whom had never even been elected to Parliament. The disputes, however, greatly diminished enthusiasm for the opposition party and led to a growth of support for the DP. FORD's support in Eastern Province particularly suffered, with local party leaders one by one moving towards the strongest opposition party in their District. As the personal rivalries within FORD's leadership became more and more vituperative, the party's factional struggles and its leaders came to resemble KANU's more and more, rather than exemplifying a new political order that could solve the nation's problems. FORD was ceasing to be a credible alternative government and becoming no more than a vehicle for protest votes.[264]

The conflict also made it likely that voting in most areas would be determined by ethnic rivalries and local issues and loyalties, rather than by national political issues and the parties' policy manifestos. Nevertheless, to describe it as ethnic politics is far too simplistic: it was factional politics with an ethnic basis. Both factions were national coalitions designed to seize power, consisting of a loose coalition of senior leaders with a more or less stable regional basis of support, around a single leader with a rock-solid base. Odinga was clearly going to take Northern and most of Southern Nyanza. Among the Bukusu, Muliro's legacy and the presence of Mukisa Kituyi and other Young Turks would ensure a solid turn-out amongst the Abaluhya. Elsewhere, all depended on how the parties split, and whether the resulting organisations could establish a solid base when competing against each other as well as the DP and KANU. Matiba had a clear dominance in Nairobi and Murang'a, but elsewhere his position was far from strong. Shikuku's support gave him some backing in Kakamega district in Western Province, but since Shikuku came from a small Luhya clan, his success elsewhere in the District was far from certain. Neither had really penetrated KANU's home areas.

It was also becoming clear that the young professionals were finding it difficult to convert mass protest support into effective machines for electoral mobilisation, and that some were losing out to more established machine politicians in their local areas, more experienced at giving the voters what they wanted. There was a clear tension, which was to become even more obvious after the election, between the 'intellectuals' who tended to view themselves as national figures, without particular loyalties to their local areas except in so far as was necessary to ensure their continued return to the national stage, and the populists, mainly old-time machine politicians, who saw their interests lying much closer to home in the traditional Kenyan manner.

Notes

1 *Weekly Review*, 3 January 1992, p. 3. See also, *Weekly Review*, 13 December 1991, p. 10.
2 *Weekly Review*, 3 January 1992, pp. 3–17, and 10 January 1992, pp. 3–8. See also *Nairobi Law Monthly*, no. 39, December 1991, p. 2 and pp. 12–17; and *Finance*, 16–31 December 1991, pp. 2–3 and 16–17. Geoffrey Kariithi, as a senior Kikuyu civil servant from the Kenyatta era, was initially expected to join Mwai Kibaki's DP, see *Weekly Review*, 3 January 1992, pp. 10–11. Kariithi, however, opted for FORD and was elected chairman of its pro-Matiba Kirinyaga branch, see *Standard*, 22 September 1992, p. 4.
3 *Weekly Review*, 14 August 1992, pp. 6–9; 13 December 1991, pp. 3–8; 3 January 1992, pp. 19–20; and 10 January 1992, pp. 8–10.
4 *Weekly Review*, 10 January 1992, pp. 8–10.
5 *Weekly Review*, 3 April 1992, p. 6; 14 August 1992, pp. 6–9; and 6 March 1992, pp. 11–12.
6 *Weekly Review*, 10 January 1992, p. 9; and 17 January 1992, pp. 11–12.
7 *Weekly Review*, 7 February 1992, pp. 3–9.
8 Kibaki had served as Minister of Health since his demotion from the Vice-Presidency in 1988.
9 *Weekly Review*, 3 January 1992, pp. 3–5.
10 *Ibid.*
11 *Ibid.*, p. 3. See also *The Times*, London, 3 January 1992, p. 7.
12 *Weekly Review*, 3 January 1992, pp. 14–15.
13 *Finance*, 15 March 1992, pp. 14–15 provides a detailed assessment of the DP's prospects under the headline, 'The Rebirth of Mwai Kibaki'.
14 *Weekly Review*, 3 January 1992, pp. 5–15; and 10 January 1992, pp. 3–7; and *Summary of World Broadcasts*, 4 January 1992 and 10 January 1992, p. 1.
15 See the issues of the two papers for this period.

16 *Ibid.*, pp. 12–13; and *Weekly Review*, 4 October 1991, pp. 8–10.
17 *Ibid.*
18 *Weekly Review*, 3 January 1992, pp. 22–3; 10 January 1992, pp. 17–18; 17 January 1992, p. 17; and 24 January 1992, pp. 18–19.
19 *Ibid.*
20 *Weekly Review*, 3 January 1992, p. 4. For a hostile attack on Kibaki for his career in the Moi regime see *Society*, no. 3, 9 March 1992, p. 3. Gitobu Imanyara's *Nairobi Law Monthly*, no. 40, January 1992, pp. 24–5 presented the DP as the party of the World Bank and as a revamped KANU.
21 *Society*, no. 5, 30 March 1992, pp. 41–2. See also Hans Hedlund, *Coffee, Cooperatives and Culture: an Anthropological Study of a Coffee Cooperative in Kenya*, Oxford University Press, 1992, p. 88.
22 *Ibid.*, p. 83.
23 *Society*, no. 5, 30 March 1992, pp. 41–2.
24 *Weekly Review*, 3 January 1992, p. 4; and *Nairobi Law Monthly*, no. 40, January 1992, pp. 24–5.
25 *Ibid.*
26 *Finance*, 15 March 1992, p. 15.
27 This table has been devised from information in *Weekly Review*, 3 January 1992, pp. 3–15; 10 January 1992, pp. 3–5; and 21 February 1992, pp. 4–5.
28 *Weekly Review*, 21 February 1992, p. 5.
29 *Weekly Review*, 24 January 1992, pp. 3–9; *Nairobi Law Monthly*, no. 40, January 1992, pp. 20–3; *Finance*, 15 February 1992, pp. 4–5; and *Summary of World Broadcasts*, 20 January 1992.
30 *Ibid.*
31 *Weekly Review*, 24 January 1992, p. 8; and *Nairobi Law Monthly*, no. 40, January 1990, pp. 21–3.
32 Interviews with various journalists, academics and rally participants, Nairobi, December 1992.
33 Subsequent rallies were announced during the first week in January for Machakos on 22 January; Mombasa, 25 January; Wundanyi and Voi, 27 January; Nakuru, 1 February; Kisumu, 7 February; Kakamega, 8 February; Embu, 14 February; Nyeri, 15 February; and Garissa on 16 February. For the details, see *Weekly Review*, 10 January 1992, p. 9.
34 *Weekly Review*, 31 January 1992, pp. 12–14.
35 *Ibid.*
36 *Weekly Review*, 7 February 1992, pp. 5–7.
37 Quoted in *Weekly Review*, 31 January 1992, p. 7 and p. 14
38 *Weekly Review*, 21 February 1992, pp. 3–7; *Finance*, 15 March 1992, pp. 14–15; and *Summary of World Broadcasts*, 18 February 1992.
39 *Weekly Review*, 21 February 1992, p. 4; and *Finance*, 15 March 1992, pp. 14–15.
40 *Weekly Review*, 21 February 1992, p. 5.
41 *Ibid.*, p. 6.
42 *Ibid.*, p. 5.
43 *Finance*, 15 March 1992, pp. 14–15.
44 *Weekly Review*, 28 February 1992, pp. 12–14. *Summary of World Broadcasts*, 12 February 1992, p. 3, reported an attack on FORD's interim National Organising Secretary Philip Gachoka when he attempted to return to Nairobi from a rally in Kakamega via Kabarnet in President Moi's home district of Baringo.
45 *Weekly Review*, 28 February 1992, pp. 12–13. See also *Society*, no. 3, 9 March 1992, pp. 6–9 for photographs of Wambui Otieno's injuries.
46 *Weekly Review*, 6 March 1992, pp. 9–10.
47 *Ibid.*, p. 10.
48 *Weekly Review*, 31 January 1992, pp. 4–11.
49 *Weekly Review*, 7 February 1992, pp. 5–7; and 6 March 1992, pp. 11–12.
50 *Ibid.*
51 *Weekly Review*, 14 February 1992, pp. 6–8; and 20 March 1992, pp. 18–19.
52 *Weekly Review*, 7 February 1992, pp. 3–4. See also the issue for 31 January 1992, pp. 4–6.
53 *Weekly Review*, 7 February 1992, pp. 5–7.
54 *Ibid.*, p. 7.
55 *Weekly Review*, 21 February 1992, pp. 8–9.

56 *Ibid.*, p. 8.
57 *Ibid.*, pp. 8–9.
58 *Ibid.*, p. 8.
59 *Ibid.*, pp. 8–9. See also *Summary of World Broadcasts*, 18 February 1992, p. 5.
60 The most detailed account of Muite's speech is to be found in *Society*, no. 3, 9 March 1992, pp. 20–2, which actually reproduced the controversial section of Muite's remarks in Gikuyu and English. Muite in the most important paragraph had warned, 'What I am saying is that we should be united. Permit me to speak openly. The most important thing for the GEMA tribes is to remove Moi and KANU. I hasten to say that there are things we should keep in mind and pray to God as GEMA people. We should keep in mind how Uganda became chaotic and many people have died in the process. We should remember that it was the Baganda tribe which brought about the chaos in Uganda. Do you know that? The Bagandas organised themselves and formed a tribal party, forgetting that even if they were the majority tribe, there were other tribes. They formed a small party called *Kabaka Yekka*, meaning Kabaka Only. Do you, GEMA tribes, want us to have a *Kabaka Yekka* of our own?' The crowd had roared back 'No'.
61 *Weekly Review*, 21 February 1992, p. 9; and *Finance*, 15 February 1992, pp. 14–15, 34–40 and 42–52.
62 *Weekly Review*, 21 February 1992, pp. 9–11.
63 *Ibid.*, pp. 10–11. See also Hilary Ng'weno's editorial comment about Muite's remarks on p. 1 of the same issue.
64 Daily Telegraph, London, 5 February 1992, p. 9.
65 *Weekly Review*, 31 January 1992, p. 6 and p. 14.
66 Interviews with senior officials at the American Embassy, Nairobi, December 1992.
67 The KANU-controlled *Kenya Times* had attempted to sow dissension among the opposition by suggesting on Sunday, 5 January 1992, that in an exclusive 'interview' Matiba had suggested that he might join Mwai Kibaki's newly launched Democratic Party of Kenya, rather than FORD. The following day's edition on 6 January 1992, had publicised the 'interview' with Matiba under the headline, 'I'm too ill to lead – Matiba'. Matiba quickly refuted the stories in a real interview, see *Daily Nation* and *Standard*, 8 January 1992.
68 *Weekly Review*, 7 February 1992, pp. 3–5. But see also the issue for 14 February 1992, pp. 8–9. See also *Finance*, 15 March 1992, pp. 14–15 for a very favourable assessment of Kibaki and the DP. The same issue contained brief biographies of Presidential hopefuls, Odinga, p. 25; Matiba, p. 26; Muite, p. 27; and Kibaki, p. 27 and p. 31.
69 *Weekly Review*, 7 February 1992, pp. 6–7.
70 *Weekly Review*, 6 March 1992, pp. 11–12.
71 *Ibid.*, p. 11.
72 *Ibid.*
73 *Ibid.*, pp. 11–12.
74 *Ibid.*
75 *Society*, no. 4, 23 March 1992, pp. 10–17 and pp. 19–21; *Finance*, 15 March 1992, pp. 4–7; and *Monthly News*, April 1992, pp. 17–18, contain reports of the women's protests and clashes with the riot police. See also *Society*, no. 15, 8 June 1992, pp. 40–2 for COTU's relations with KANU.
76 *Weekly Review*, 3 April 1992, p. 8.
77 *Ibid.* For a pro-opposition account of the incident, see *Finance*, 15 February 1992, p. 16 and pp. 28–33.
78 *Weekly Review*, 3 April 1992, p. 8.
79 *Ibid.*
80 *Ibid.* For an analysis of the close relationship between COTU and KANU see *Society*, no. 10, 4 May 1992, pp. 30–2; *Society*, no. 15, 8 June 1992, pp. 40–2; and *Society*, no. 7, 13 April 1992, p. 39. For a more detailed analysis, see Michael Chege, 'The State and Labour in Independent Kenya', in Peter Anyang' Nyong'o (ed.), *Popular Struggles for Democracy in Africa*, pp. 248–64, The United Nations University/Third World Forum, Zed Books, London and New Jersey, 1987.
81 *Weekly Review*, 10 April 1992, p. 1 and pp. 4–10.
82 *Ibid.*, p. 8; *Society*, no. 8, 20 April 1992, pp. 19–21 ; and *Monthly News*, May 1992, p. 14.
83 *Weekly Review*, 10 April 1992, p. 8.
84 *Weekly Review*, 27 March 1992, pp. 13–15.

85 *Weekly Review*, 3 April 1992, p. 9.

86 *Weekly Review*, 10 April 1992, pp. 9–10. See also *Society*, no. 9, 27 April 1992, pp. 31–3, for a lengthy interview with Denis Akumu, who denounced the Churches, the DP and the SDP for bending under government pressure.

87 *Weekly Review*, 3 April 1992, p. 9.

88 *Ibid.*

89 *Weekly Review*, 24 April 1992, pp. 16–17; and *Society*, no. 9, 27 April 1992, p. 21. See also, *Monthly News*, May 1992, p. 14.

90 *Weekly Review*, 7 February 1992, pp. 3–5; 31 January 1992, p. 6; and 3 April 1992, pp. 4–5.

91 Quoted in *Weekly Review*, 3 April 1992, pp. 4–5. See also *Finance*, 15 April 1992, pp. 18–30.

92 *Weekly Review*, 6 March 1992, pp. 14–16; and 13 March 1992, pp. 3–14.

93 *Weekly Review*, 3 April 1992, p. 4.

94 Interview with Paul Muite, Nairobi, November 1993; *Weekly Review*, 3 April 1992, pp. 4–5; 17 April 1992, pp. 3–10; and *Finance*, 15 April 1992, pp. 31–3.

95 *Weekly Review*, 17 April 1992, pp. 3–6; and *Finance*, 15 April 1992, pp. 31–3.

96 *FORD Manifesto: Charter for the Second Liberation*, 1992, Agip House, Nairobi, 1992, *passim*. See also *Weekly Review*, 17 April 1992, pp. 10–13. For comparison see the *KANU Manifesto: Charter for the Second Liberation*, Nairobi, 1992, and the *Democratic Party Manifesto*, Nairobi, 1992.

97 *FORD Manifesto: Charter for the Second Liberation*, 1992, p. 4.

98 *Ibid.*, p. 5.

99 *Ibid.*, pp. 17–25. See *Society*, no. 5, 30 March 1992, pp. 45–6; and *Monthly News*, April 1992, pp. 29–33, for press reports of IMF pressure to reduce the size of the civil service and to reform parastatals.

100 *FORD Manifesto: Charter for the Second Liberation*, 1992, p. 25.

101 *Weekly Review*, 17 April 1992, pp. 11–12.

102 *FORD Manifesto: Charter for the Second Liberation*, 1992, pp. 14–15.

103 *Ibid.*, p. 14.

104 The most detailed account of Kenyatta's death is provided by Joseph Karimi and Philip Ochieng', *The Kenyatta Succession*, pp. 165–70. Mahihu, who had attended the bedside, had immediately informed Moi, enabling the Vice-President to make his way to Nairobi to assume control of the government machine. He was one of the handful of senior Kikuyu officials who remained loyal to President Moi in the year of crisis in 1992.

105 *FORD Manifesto: Charter for the Second Liberation*, 1992, p. 13. See also *Society*, no. 9, 27 April 1992, pp. 18–19; and *Society*, no. 5, 30 March 1992, pp. 45–6. For an attack on the politicisation of the Provincial Administration, see *Monthly News*, May 1992, pp. 11–13.

106 *Ibid.*, pp. 41–3. For a wider critique of the 8–4–4 system see *Society*, no. 10, 4 May 1992, pp. 33–4.

107 *FORD Manifesto: Charter for the Second Liberation*, 1992, p. 41.

108 *Ibid.*, pp. 44–52.

109 *Weekly Review*, 17 April 1992, p. 13.

110 David Throup, 'The Construction and Destruction of the Kenyatta State', in M.G. Schatzberg (ed.), *The Political Economy of Kenya*, pp. 53–64 and 70–3.

111 *Weekly Review*, 24 April 1992, pp. 10–11. See also the issues for 14 February 1992, p. 13 for details of Anyona's treatment in prison and 21 February 1992, pp. 13–15 for his release. *Weekly Review*, 28 February 1992, pp. 10–12 carried reports of an interview with Anyona.

112 *Weekly Review*, 24 April 1992, pp. 3–9; *Society*, no. 3, 9 March 1992, pp. 33–9; and *Monthly News*, April 1992, pp. 21–2. These reports were confirmed in an interview with Anyona in London, February 1995. See also *Society*, no. 12, 18 May 1992, pp. 30–1 for Anyona's rather belated condemnation of the ethnic clashes.

113 *Weekly Review*, 24 April 1992, pp. 7–8.

114 *Ibid.*, p. 11. See also *Society*, no. 10, 4 May 1992, pp. 24–5; and *Society*, no. 12, 18 May 1992, pp. 30–1 for Anyona's condemnation of the ethnic clashes.

115 Interview with George Anyona, London, February 1995; and *Society*, no. 3, 9 March 1992, pp. 33–9.

116 *Ibid.*, and *Weekly Review*, 24 April 1992, pp. 7–9. On 9 June 1992, however, Anyona decided to launch his own political party – which became the Kenya Social Congress. See *Weekly Review*, 12 June 1992, p. 15; and 3 July 1992, pp. 21–2.

117 *Weekly Review*, 3 April 1992, pp. 4–5.
118 *Weekly Review*, 8 May 1992, p. 1.
119 *Weekly Review*, 3 April 1992, p. 4.
120 *Weekly Review*, 1 May 1992, pp. 4–6.
121 *Ibid.*
122 *Weekly Review*, 8 May 1992, pp. 4–6.
123 *Ibid.*, pp. 6–9.
124 *Society*, no. 12, 18 May 1992, pp. 24–5 and pp. 36–7 for a statement of Matiba's ambitions.
125 *Weekly Review*, 1 May 1992, pp. 4–6; and 8 May 1992, pp. 6–9. *Finance*, 15 April 1992, pp. 18–30, carried a strongly pro-Matiba story, contrasting the ex-Minister's health with that of his political rivals, Moi, Oginga and Kibaki. For British views of Matiba's return see, *Independent*, 4 May 1992, p. 10; and *Africa Confidential*, vol. 33, no. 9, 8 May 1992, pp. 1–3.
126 *Weekly Review*, 15 May 1992, p. 4 for John Keen's reaction.
127 *Ibid.*, pp. 4–6.
128 *Society*, no. 14, 1 June 1992, pp. 29–30.
129 *Weekly Review*, 15 May 1992, pp. 4–6; and *Society*, no. 15, 8 June 1992, pp. 13–14.
130 *Weekly Review*, 29 May 1992, pp. 4–7.
131 *Ibid.*, p. 7.
132 *Ibid.*; and *Society*, no. 15, 8 June 1992, pp. 8–12.
133 *Society*, no. 14, 1 June 1992, pp. 29–30.
134 *Weekly Review*, 29 May 1992, pp. 7–9.
135 *Weekly Review*, 29 May 1992, pp. 4–10; *Society*, no. 15, 8 June 1992, pp. 8–14; and *Monthly News*, July 1992, pp. 22–3.
136 *Weekly Review*, 7 August 1992, p. 1. See also *Weekly Review*, 8 May 1992, pp. 4–6 and pp. 10–12; 15 May 1992, pp. 4–12; and 12 June 1992, pp. 11–12, for details of Martin Shikuku's candidacy for FORD's Presidential nomination and the manipulation of the party's constitution by rival ethnic factions. Details of Masinde Muliro's candidacy can be found in the issue for 26 June 1992, pp. 4–8. Further information about FORD's disintegration can be found in *Society*, no. 9, 27 April 1992, pp. 6–9; no. 12, 18 May 1992, pp. 23–5; no. 13, 25 May 1992, pp. 36–7; no. 14, 1 June 1992, pp. 26–30; no 16, 15 June 1992, pp. 15–19; *New Era*, 26 May 1992, p. 23, which records the disillusionment of one member of FORD's National Steering Committee, F. J. M. W. Mukeka. For an analysis of the political consequences see *Weekly Review*, 8 May 1992, pp. 4–9; and *Africa Confidential*, vol. 33, no. 9 (8 May 1992), pp. 1–3.
137 *Weekly Review*, 17 July 1992, pp. 3–9; 24 July 1992, pp. 4–8; and 7 August 1992, pp. 4–12.
138 *Weekly Review*, 7 August 1992, pp. 4–9; and *Society*, no. 23, 3 August 1992, pp. 8–14.
139 *Weekly Review*, 31 July 1992, pp. 3–12.
140 *Ibid.*, pp. 10–12; and *Society*, no. 24, 10 August 1992, pp. 6–11.
141 *Weekly Review*, 7 August 1992, pp. 4–8. Shikuku had made clear his opposition to the Delegates' Conference selecting FORD's Presidential candidate from the beginning of the controversy. For one statement, see *Weekly Review*, 15 May 1992, pp. 11–12.
142 *Weekly Review*, 7 August 1992, pp. 4–5.
143 *Ibid.*, pp. 5–6.
144 *Ibid.*, pp. 6–8 and 11–12; *Society*, no. 24, 10 August 1992, pp. 26–7.
145 *Weekly Review*, 7 August 1992, p. 6.
146 *Ibid.*, p. 12.
147 *Ibid.*, p. 6.
148 *Ibid.*
149 *Weekly Review*, 24 July 1992, pp. 8–10. See also the issue for 14 August 1992, pp. 10–11.
150 *Weekly Review*, 7 August 1992, pp. 10–11.
151 *Weekly Review*, 14 August 1992, pp. 10–11. See also *Summary of World Broadcasts*, 7 August 1992, p. 17.
152 *Weekly Review*, 7 August 1992, pp. 8–10; and *Summary of World Broadcasts*, 4 August 1992, pp. 4–5.
153 *Weekly Review*, 7 August 1992, p. 8.
154 This view was perhaps most eloquently expressed by George Anyona in an interview with *Weekly Review*, 24 April 1992, p. 9, who observed that 'perhaps the only difference

between me and Odinga is the fact that he regards Mr Oloo-Aringo as a hero while I think Aringo is a villain.'

155 *Weekly Review*, 7 August 1992, p. 5 and pp. 11–12.
156 The table is adapted from the one in *Weekly Review*, 14 August 1982, p. 8.
157 *Weekly Review*, 29 May 1992, pp. 4–9.
158 *Weekly Review*, 14 August 1992, pp. 4–5 and 9–10.
159 *Ibid.*, pp. 3–6.
160 *Weekly Review*, 21 August 1992, pp. 3–5; and 14 August 1992, pp. 3–6.
161 *Ibid.*, pp. 3–4 and p. 5. For further analysis of FORD in disarray, see *Nairobi Law Monthly*, no. 45, August–September 1992, pp. 16–18.
162 *Weekly Review*, 21 August 1992, p. 11.
163 *Weekly Review*, 14 August 1992, pp. 3–6. See also *Society*, no. 25, 17 August, 1992, pp. 18–20; and no. 26, 24 August 1992, pp. 19–21, which judged that 'current events in FORD have graphically exposed some of the opposition old guard as an aggregate of self-seekers, only anxious to replace the KANU regime, and President Daniel arap Moi, with another dictatorship'.
164 *Weekly Review*, 21 August 1992, pp. 3–6; and *Society*, no. 26, 24 August 1992, p. 7 and pp. 21–2 and p. 29.
165 *Weekly Review*, 21 August 1992, pp. 6–7; and 28 August 1992, pp. 21–2; and *Society*, no. 27, 31 August 1992, p. 16. For further speculation, see *Nairobi Law Monthly*, no. 45, August–September 1992, pp. 28–9; *Society*, no. 26, 24 August 1992, p. 7 and pp. 21–2; and *Society*, no. 28, 7 September 1992, pp. 22–3.
166 *Ibid.*, p. 4.
167 *Weekly Review*, 28 August 1992, p. 18; and *Society*, no. 28, 7 September 1992, pp. 8–9.
168 *Ibid.*
169 *Society*, no. 26, 24 August 1992, p. 2, pp. 19–21 and p. 29.
170 *Weekly Review*, 28 August 1992, p. 18; and *Society*, no. 28, 7 September 1992, pp. 8–9.
171 *Weekly Review*, 28 August 1992, p. 19; and 4 September 1992, pp. 4–5.
172 *Weekly Review*, 28 August 1992, pp. 18–19.
173 *Weekly Review*, 4 September 1992, pp. 3–6; 11 September 1992, pp. 3–5; and 25 September 1992, pp. 3–15. See also *Standard*, 10 September 1992, p. 8; and *Standard on Sunday*, 13 September 1992, p. 8.
174 *Weekly Review*, 11 September 1992, p. 7.
175 *Ibid.*, p. 9; *Society*, no. 30, 21 September 1992, pp. 16–18 and pp. 22–3; and *Summary of World Broadcasts*, 7 September 1992. For details of FORD-Kenya's manifesto, see *Society*, no. 30, 21 September 1992, pp. 29–30.
176 *Weekly Review*, 11 September 1992, p. 14.
177 *Ibid.*, p. 10.
178 *Ibid.*, p. 12.
179 *Ibid.*, p. 14. See also *Society*, no. 30, 21 September 1992, pp. 22–23; and *Nairobi Law Monthly*, no. 45, August–September 1992, pp. 19–20.
180 The Kenya National Congress.
181 *Weekly Review*, 11 September 1992, p. 3; and *Standard*, 10 September 1992, p. 1.
182 *Weekly Review*, 11 September 1992, pp. 3–5; and *Society*, no. 30, 21 September 1992, pp. 18–20. See also *Standard*, 11 September 1992, p. 2. The Matiba faction's position was further strengthened when the popular Kikuyu Member of Parliament for Molo, John Njenga Mungai, announced at a press conference at the Foreign Press Centre at Chester House on Friday, 11 September that he was quitting the ruling party to join the Matiba-Shikuku faction of FORD. Mungai stated that he would travel to Nakuru to participate in the grassroots elections called by the Muthithi House group. In the end, the Muthithi faction's Congress had to be postponed until 3–4 October in order to allow the sub-branch and branch elections to be completed. See *Daily Nation*, 23 September 1992, p. 5.
183 *Society*, no. 29, 14 September 1992, *passim;* and *Society*, no. 30, 21 September 1992, pp. 18–20.
184 *Weekly Review*, 18 September 1992, p. 7. See also *Nairobi Law Monthly*, no. 45, August–September 1992, pp. 16–18 for a pro-Agip House interpretation of the registration law; and *Standard* on Sunday, 13 September 1992, pp. 1–2.
185 *Weekly Review*, 18 September 1992, pp. 3–5; and *Nairobi Law Monthly*, no. 45, August–September 1992, pp. 16–18. See also *Daily Nation*, 17 September 1992, p. 3.

186 *Weekly Review*, 18 September 1992, p. 3.
187 *Ibid.*
188 *Ibid.*, pp. 3–5; and *Weekly Review*, 2 October 1992, pp. 9–10.
189 *Standard*, 26 September 1992, p. 4, reported Kimani wa Nyoike's denial that the dissidents in the Muthithi House faction intended to launch a new political party. Wa Nyoike had just been elected chairman of the faction's Nyandarua District branch.
190 Interviews with Kikuyu businessmen and lawyers, Nairobi, December 1992.
191 *Weekly Review*, 18 September 1992, pp. 3–4.
192 *Standard on Sunday*, 13 September 1992, p. 8.
193 *Weekly Review*, 18 September 1992, pp. 5–6.
194 *Daily Nation*, 30 September 1992, p. 4.
195 *Weekly Review*, 18 September 1992, pp. 5–6; and *Standard*, 26 September 1992, p. 4.
196 *Weekly Review*, 2 October 1992, pp. 9–10. See also *Summary of World Broadcasts*, 20 October 1992, p. 6. Anyona was consequently compelled to relaunch his party under a new name – the Kenya Social Congress. See *Weekly Review*, 18 October 1992, pp. 13–14 and *Summary of World Broadcasts*, 14 October, 1992, p. 12.
197 *Weekly Review*, 2 October 1992, pp. 9–10; and 9 October 1992, pp. 3–6.
198 *Weekly Review*, 9 October 1992, p. 3.
199 *Ibid.*, pp. 3–6.
200 *Ibid.*, p. 6 and p. 8.
201 *Weekly Review*, 29 May 1992, pp. 37–38; and *Summary of World Broadcasts*, 26 May 1992, p. 2.
202 *Weekly Review*, 29 May 1992, pp. 37–8; *Society*, no. 14, 1 June 1992, p. 18 and pp. 23–5; and *New Era*, 26 May 1992, pp. 3–7. These rumours were incorrect.
203 *Ibid.*, pp. 12–13.
204 Reported in *Weekly Review*, 24 April 1992, pp. 18–19.
205 *Weekly Review*, 29 May 1992, pp. 37–8.
206 Murgor was the brother of William Murgor, the former MP for Kerio Central in Biwott's home district.
207 *Weekly Review*, 26 June 1992, pp. 14–16.
208 For evidence of growing Nandi dissatisfaction with KANU, see *Society*, no. 12, 18 May 1992, p. 23; no. 15, 8 June 1992, pp. 24–5, for an attack on Biwott; no. 20, 13 July 1992, pp. 44–5; no. 23, 3 August 1992, pp. 28–9; no. 24, 10 August, pp. 24–5; and no. 25, 17 August 1992, pp. 27–8; and *Monthly News*, September 1992, pp. 24–5.
209 *Monthly News*, April 1992, p. 11.
210 *Finance*, 15 March 1992, p. 14.
211 *Ibid.*, pp. 14–15.
212 *Ibid.*, p. 15.
213 *Society*, no. 4, 23 March 1992, pp. 10–17 and pp. 19–21.
214 *Weekly Review*, 5 June 1992, pp. 4–7; and *Society*, no. 13, 25 May 1992, pp. 26–7 and 30–5.
215 *Weekly Review*, 10 April 1992, pp. 9–10.
216 *Society*, no. 14, 1 June 1992, pp. 8–13. For Keen's resposne to the allegations, see *Society*, no. 28, 7 September 1992, pp. 18–19.
217 This was the date that Jomo Kenyatta had taken office as Kenya's first (and only) Prime Minister.
218 *Weekly Review*, 5 June 1992, p. 1. The previous month, Kibaki had called for Moi's resignation as President for failing to stop the ethnic clashes, see *Society*, no. 10, 4 May 1992, p. 13. In July, he denounced KANU and the Provincial Administration for making preparations to 'rig' the elections, see *Society*, no. 19, 6 July 1992, pp. 8–11; and joined with other opposition leaders in criticising the impartiality of the Electoral Commission, *ibid.*, pp. 12–14.
219 *Ibid.*, p. 12; and *Summary of World Broadcasts*, 26 June 1992.
220 *Weekly Review*, 5 June 1992, pp. 4–7. *New Era*, 26 May 1992, pp. 13–14 criticised the 'Kikuyu nationalism' of DP rallies. Many Kikuyu believed that 'Kalenjin warriors' had massacred 50 schoolchildren in raids into Nyandarua and western Kiambu, see *New Era*, 26 May 1992, pp. 3–7, which blamed FORD for instigating the rumours. For a more impartial assessment, see *Society*, no. 14, 1 June 1992, p. 18 and pp. 23–5.
221 See for example, *Weekly Review*, 14 February 1992, p. 11; and *Society*, no. 6, 6 April 1992, pp. 6–16. *Society*, no. 15, 8 May 1992, pp. 24–5 contains a report of the NCCK

symposium.

222 *Weekly Review*, 19 June 1992, pp. 3–7; and *Society*, no. 9, 27 April 1992, pp. 27–8 for criticism of the Electoral Commission. *Society*, no. 11, 11 May 1992, p. 2, and pp. 32–3; and *Society*, no. 12, 18 May 1992, pp. 19–20; and *Monthly News*, May 1992, pp. 6–7 contain the NCCK's condemnation of the ethnic clashes. See *Society*, no. 12, 18 May 1992, pp. 19–20 for an account of the Catholic Bishops' meeting with President Moi; and *Society*, no. 27, 31 August 1992, pp. 21–4 for a further attack by the Roman Catholic Church.

223 *Weekly Review*, 5 June 1992, pp. 11–12; and *Society*, no. 15, 8 June 1992, pp. 21–5.

224 *Society*, no. 19, 6 July 1992, pp. 18–19; and *Society*, no. 20, 13 July 1992, pp. 35–9.

225 *Weekly Review*, 26 June 1992, p. 10. See also *Society*, no. 18, 29 June 1992, pp. 22–4; and *Nairobi Law Monthly*, no. 43, June 1992, pp. 8 and 10.

226 *Weekly Review*, 21 August 1992, pp. 13–14; and 28 August 1992, p. 20; and *Society*, no. 25, 17 August 1992, pp. 16–17. For earlier anti-Asian remarks by Keen, see *Summary of World Broadcasts*, 10 March 1992, p. 2; and *Weekly Review*, 31 July 1992, pp. 19–20; and by Martin Shikuku, *Society*, no. 19, 6 July 1992, pp. 35–6. *Society*, no. 9, 27 April 1992, pp. 37–40 provides an overview of Kenyan Africans' attitudes towards the Asian community.

227 *Weekly Review*, 21 August 1992, p. 13. The pro-KANU *New Era* magazine also suggested that the DP was unlikely to win more than 20 seats, see *New Era*, 26 May 1992, pp. 16–17.

228 *Weekly Review*, 21 August 1992, p. 13. As FORD disintegrated there was increasing speculation that the DP might form an alliance with Odinga's Agip House faction, see *Summary of World Broadcasts*, 5 August 1992, p. 5; and *Society*, no. 25, 17 August 1992, pp. 8–13.

229 Former Deputy Speaker arap Ng'eny had been MP for Aldai from 1969 to 1983. *Standard*, 3 September 1992, p. 5. See also *Society*, no. 12, 18 May 1992, p. 23; no. 15, 8 June 1992, pp. 24–5, for an attack on Biwott; no. 20, 13 July 1992, pp. 44–45; no. 23, 3 August 1992, pp. 28–9; no. 24, 10 August, pp. 24–5; and no. 25, 17 August 1992, pp. 27–8; and *Monthly News*, September 1992, pp. 24–5.

230 *Weekly Review*, 11 September 1992, p. 17.

231 *Standard*, 14 September 1992, pp. 1–2; and Daily Nation, 14 September 1992, p. 4.

232 *Weekly Review*, 18 September 1992, p. 10.

233 This was the title of an article in *Weekly Review*, 9 October 1992, p. 11, reporting Kibaki's more combative style.

234 *Ibid.*

235 Quoted in *Weekly Review*, 18 September 1992, p. 10. For further reports on the DP's failure to hold grassroots elections, see *Weekly Review*, 2 October 1992, p. 8.

236 *Daily Nation*, 17 September 1992, p. 1 and p. 14.

237 *Weekly Review*, 18 September 1992, p. 10; and 2 October 1992, pp. 4–6. The DP secured an injunction barring The *Kenya Times* from publishing further defamatory articles, suggesting that DP leaders were plotting to assassinate President Moi, *Weekly Review*, 25 September 1992, p. 16; and Daily Nation, 29 September 1992, p. 2. See *Standard*, 24 September 1992, p. 4, for the *Kenya Times*' counter-suit. For early articles on YK '92 activities, see *Society*, no. 9, 27 April 1992, pp. 25–6; and *Monthly News*, May 1992, pp. 8–9.

238 *Weekly Review*, 2 October 1992, pp. 4–6.

239 The growing strength of the DP was first noted in July, see *Monthly News*, July 1992, pp. 13–15.

240 *Ibid.*

241 *Ibid.*, p. 5.

242 *Ibid.*, p. 6.

243 For an assessment of Ngei, see *Monthly News*, May 1992, pp. 20–2; and for details of his bankruptcy, *Society*, no. 21, 20 July 1992, pp. 32–3. See also *Society*, no. 24, 10 August 1992, pp. 44–5; and *Monthly News*, August 1992, pp. 22–3.

244 *Weekly Review*, 9 October 1992, p. 11.

245 *Ibid.*, pp. 6–8.

246 *Ibid.*, p. 8; and *Standard*, 18 September 1992, p. 5.

247 *Daily Nation*, 17 September 1992, p. 15; The *Standard on Sunday*, 15 September 1992, pp. 1–2; *Standard*, 16 September 1992, p. 3; *Standard on Sunday*, 27 September 1992, pp. 1–2; and *Sunday Nation*, 27 September 1992, pp. 1–2. David Mukaru-Ng'ang'a also became

concerned that the Registrar of Societies might ban KENDA (the Kenya National Democratic Alliance), see *Standard on Sunday*, 20 September 1992, p. 3; and *Sunday Nation*, 20 September 1992, p. 1.

248 *Weekly Review*, 9 October 1992, p. 8.

249 *Ibid.*

250 *Ibid.*

251 *Weekly Review*, 16 October 1992, pp. 4–9.

252 *Ibid.*, p. 5 and p. 11.

253 *Ibid.*, p. 11; and *Summary of World Broadcasts*, 14 October 1992, p. 12; and 16 October 1992.

254 *Weekly Review*, 16 October 1992, pp. 12–13.

255 DP Secretary-General John Keen had attended the first meeting as an observer. See *Weekly Review*, 19 June 1992, pp. 3–4.

256 *Weekly Review*, 19 June 1992, pp. 7–9.

257 *Ibid.* The enquiry had been appointed at the May meeting. It concluded that 'President Daniel arap Moi had lost control and/or authority over governance, with warlords promoting insecurity coming in to fill the vacuum', declared its total lack of confidence in the government, and resolved to take legal action against it over the clashes and against the Kenya Broadcasting Corporation for 'propagandising for KANU'.

258 *Ibid.*

259 *Weekly Review*, 23 October 1992, p. 14.

260 *Weekly Review*, 30 October 1992, p. 14.

261 *Weekly Review*, 14 August 1992, pp. 3–12; and *Society*, no. 25, 17 August 1992, pp. 18–20.

262 *Weekly Review*, 14 August 1992, p. 8.

263 *Monthly News*, September 1992, pp. 7–11.

264 Early in June 1992, according to the Kenya Broadcasting Corporation, 200 youths, including former top officials of the FORD Youth Congress, marched to State House to declare their loyalty to President Moi, denouncing opposition leaders for their 'self-aggrandisement'. See *Summary of World Broadcasts*, 5 June 1992.

Six

KANU Fights Back
December 1991–October 1992

KANU in Crisis

By the end of 1991 KANU was in serious difficulties. The fall-out from the Commission of Enquiry into the death of Foreign Minister Dr Robert Ouko, implicating Energy Minister Nicholas Biwott, Permanent Secretary Hezekiah Oyugi, Nyanza Provincial Commissioner Julius Kobia and Nakuru District Commissioner Jonah Anguka, posed serious problems for the Moi regime, further eroding support among Luos. Before Ouko's murder in February 1990 and the suspicious death of Bishop Alexander Muge of Eldoret in August that year, Moi's defenders had contrasted the regime's treatment of outspoken critics with the murders of Pio da Gama Pinto, Tom Mboya and Josiah Mwangi Kariuki during the Kenyatta era. Although KANU had become increasingly authoritarian and more people were held in detention, the Moi government in its first decade had refrained from murdering opponents. Ouko's death appeared to mark a new era of violent intimidation.

Although Ouko had been far less popular than Tom Mboya, the ruling party nevertheless risked mass defections in Luoland. In 1969, following Mboya's assassination, incumbent Luo MPs who had failed to disassociate themselves from the regime had been repudiated by the voters at the ensuing general election. The Moi government was in a desperate plight as Kikuyu voters had been completely alienated by the regime's deliberate shift of resources from Central Province and the Kikuyu regions of the Rift Valley. By early 1992 KANU's position was also under attack among the Gusii and Abaluhya. The non-Kalenjin 'settler' communities in the Rift Valley were alarmed by the Kalenjin demand for *Majimboism* and by threats of 'ethnic cleansing' unless they declared their loyalty to President Moi and KANU. The ruling party's supporters in Rift Valley Province – the Kalenjin, Maasai, Samburu and Turkana – comprised only 15 per cent of Kenya's population and controlled 34 or 35 seats in the National Assembly, only one third of the number required for an overall majority.

KANU moderates realised that the party could not afford to antagonise such vital ethnic groups as the Gusii and Abaluhya, who between them returned another 30 MPs. Several prominent non-Kalenjin KANU officials appeared to understand these problems, but the inner circle around the President was dominated by hardliners who were unwilling to make any concessions to the Kikuyu and Luo communities, which they rightly identified as the core of opposition support. Several of the KANU moderates later defected to the opposition. National Chairman Peter Oloo-Aringo joined FORD before the end of the year, as did the disgraced former Vice-President Josephat Karanja and former Foreign Minister Dr Munyua Waiyaki, while former deputy Speaker Samuel arap Ng'eny, a Nandi, would become the most prominent Kalenjin politician to defect to the DP. Others, such as sometime Chief Secretary Simeon Nyachae, who had emerged as a key figure in Gusii politics, and former Cabinet Minister G. G. Kariuki, would remain loyal to the ruling party, leading its campaigns in Kisii and Laikipia. All of them now favoured reform, however, and urged KANU to adopt a less autocratic attitude towards its critics.

By the end of November 1991, serious cracks were beginning to appear in KANU's façade of national legitimacy. Dissidents, such as Maasai politician John Keen and Peter Oloo-Aringo (still a Cabinet Minister and KANU National Chairman), outspoken Kikuyu MP for Molo Njenga Mungai, and Johnstone Makau, the MP for Mbooni in Makueni, criticised the ruling party's National Executive. Keen and Oloo-Aringo had already virtually defected. The Maasai leader, for example, observed that the process of reform was irreversible and urged the speedy establishment of a multi-party system.[1] The fact that they were willing to speak out indicated that KANU's strict control over political discourse was disintegrating. Discontent among Luo and Kikuyu KANU MPs quickly gathered momentum as Kalenjin and Maasai leaders in the Rift Valley openly campaigned for *Majimboism*. The weekend before KANU's Special Delegates' Conference assembled in Nairobi, Minister for Regional Development Onyango Midika, whose constituency had been seriously disrupted by clashes with the Gusii, asserted at a public rally that Kenya must join the pro-democracy movement.[2] Even the *Weekly Review* observed that:

> KANU cannot afford to be complacent. The ruling party should have realised by now that its ham-fisted politics have to a large extent been responsible for driving figures who would otherwise have been valuable assets into the hands of the opposition, the most obvious examples being Shikuku, Muliro, Matiba and Rubia. FORD has since thrived by attracting the support, if not the membership, of a large number of disaffected politicians across the country. The recent flood of support for FORD in the period leading up to and following the aborted Kamukunji rally could be taken as an indication that it has the capacity to recruit on a large-scale to its ranks, which should be seen soon enough, as the psychological barriers against participating in opposition politics are shattered.
>
> For one thing, KANU will have to realise that it will no longer be able to use an iron fist against its own members. It now has to cope with the task of wooing members, well aware that its strength in numbers came about at a time

when there was no alternative and membership of the party was virtually mandatory for some people.[3]

Most KANU leaders, however, did not understand the changing political environment. Leaders of the *Majimbo* campaign remained determined to push ahead, whatever the political cost, with their search for the chimera of Kalenjin self-rule.

The treble blow to the regime's morale caused by Biwott's arrest, the decision of the donors at the Paris Club meeting to suspend project aid, and mounting dissent within KANU, compelled President Moi to accede to his critics' demands to repeal Section 2(A) of the constitution. The desperate decision may have been taken primarily to minimise discontent with the proroguing of the Commission of Enquiry into Ouko's death, preventing embarrassing revelations about Biwott's involvement in the corruption surrounding the Kisumu molasses plant. The legalisation of opposition political parties also distracted attention from the release of Biwott and Oyugi after less than two weeks in gaol. It is possible that President Moi decided to sacrifice the single-party state in order to protect Biwott – and perhaps himself – by ending investigations into Ouko's murder. The Commission was instructed to stop its hearings and to complete a report on the evidence which had been presented, while the Kenyan Police investigated the charges against Biwott, Oyugi, Anguka and others. Then a notice appeared in the *Government Gazette* revoking its appointment. No report ever appeared. President Moi's gamble may have worked in the short term but the ramifications of Ouko's murder remained a serious problem for the regime.[4]

Biwott's sacking and subsequent arrest threw KANU's hawks into disarray. Although the ex-Minister announced in Parliament that he would overcome his enemies, declaring that he was 'a man, a total man', and Somali hardliner Noor Abdi Ogle assured Kenyans that Biwott would regain his old status after the elections – a prophecy that was to prove only too correct – his apparent downfall created a major crisis within the ruling party, especially among the disgraced Minister's protégés who had depended upon his support to make their way to Parliament in 1988. The decision by Kenya's bilateral aid donors in November 1991 to suspend balance of payments support for six months also rocked the regime, although the psychological effect of the decision, as we have noted, was probably greater than its immediate economic impact.[5] Under such pressures, President Moi concluded that he had no option but to inform KANU's National Delegates' Conference that he intended to repeal Section 2(A) and to legalise the registration of opposition parties.

The Immediate Reaction

Opposition supporters reacted with jubilation to the constitutional changes while most KANU activists were downcast. Incidents occurred at several *Jamhuri* Day rallies as jubilant FORD supporters taunted KANU leaders and District Commissioners. In Homa Bay, the chairman of the South

Nyanza County Council, Elisha Aketch Chieng, was shouted down and Minister for Transport and Communications Dalmas Otieno, the chairman of KANU's South Nyanza branch, was also barracked. The District Officer and KANU officials in Muhoroni in Central Nyanza were booed when they mentioned the ruling party and met with shouts of 'We want FORD'. Provincial Commissioner Lekolool reacted angrily in Kakamega when the crowd refused to give KANU's one-finger salute, warning, 'You have just eaten food provided by KANU. Why can't you respond?' In Busia town, the police attacked opposition supporters. Local KANU leaders blamed 'prominent traders' whom, they alleged, were 'destabilising the area' by bringing in outside agitators.[6] President Moi and Secretary-General Kamotho lambasted the *Daily Nation* and the *Standard* for devoting too much attention to the incidents, which went unreported in the KANU-controlled *Kenya Times*. Speaking at a KANU rally in Nakuru, the President claimed that the two papers clearly supported FORD and were attempting to create the impression that the party did not have mass support.[7]

KANU, Kenya's ruling party since independence, was in deep trouble. Throughout December, it appeared incapable of adapting to the new world of multi-party politics. Some elements within the party wanted it to reform and to compete in fair elections. Led by Minister of Health Kibaki, they were confident that KANU would sweep the Rift Valley and the Coast, do well in many parts of Eastern Province, and remain highly competitive in Western Province, Nairobi and Central Province. Only the Luo parts of Nyanza Province were acknowledged to be lost. Hardliners in the party, however, did not want to adjust to the political changes required by multi-party democracy and were unwilling to hold new grassroots elections.

The party's morale deteriorated further in the first two weeks after Christmas as prominent figures in Central Province followed Mwai Kibaki into opposition. Although most (especially in Nyeri and Kiambu) joined Kibaki's new Democratic Party, several, including Geoffrey Kariithi and Maina Wanjigi, opted for FORD. KANU's position in Kikuyuland and in the capital appeared extremely weak. Throughout January 1992 there was a continuous flow of present and former MPs, local KANU officials and other prominent Kenyans into the opposition parties.[8]

The *Daily Nation* and the *Standard,* the country's two main newspapers, were also swept away by the euphoria which surrounded the return of multi-party politics. Most journalists, apart from those on the *Kenya Times,* favoured FORD. As members of Kenya's intelligentsia, they looked for political guidance to FORD's Gitobu Imanyara, James Orengo and Peter Anyang-Nyong'o, and to radicals at the University of Nairobi and Kenyatta University who also supported Odinga and Matiba.

The ruling party experienced profound problems as it adjusted to multi-party politics. Not only did many old-guard leaders in Central and Nyanza Province defect to the new opposition parties but the ruling party's headquarters machine was also seriously disrupted by defections and continuing purges as Secretary-General Kamotho sought to secure absolute control. Most KANU hardliners adopted a low profile during the first weeks of multi-party politics. Only Kamotho remained highly visible. He seemed to have learnt little from the debacle in the party's fortunes. Many considered that he had been too incautious in his attacks on the opposition, while others held him responsible for driving Kibaki and other prominent Kikuyu out of the party, doing irreparable damage to KANU's prospects in Central Province and Nairobi. Rumours circulated that he was to be replaced as KANU's main spokesman by Minister for Planning and National Development Dr Zachary Onyonka, the long-serving Gusii politician. After three years in office, Kamotho had alienated a considerable number of his Cabinet colleagues and senior officials. He personified to many all that was wrong with KANU. Kikuyu MPs, who had remained loyal to KANU, were becoming especially concerned. KANU's organisation in Central Province had been completely disrupted by defections to FORD and the DP, yet more than a month later, no preparations had been made to select new officials who could lead the party into the coming election. As a result, KANU was ill-prepared to fight off the challenge from FORD and the DP in Central Province. Kikuyu MPs were becoming concerned that they stood little chance of holding their seats. At the end of January 1992 KANU dismissed David Pius Mugambi, who had been the party's full-time National Executive Officer for nearly three years. With Mugambi's departure, five of the seven officials recruited to head the newly established party directorates in 1989 had been dismissed, along with most of their assistants. In May 1991, acting on Kamotho's instructions, Mugambi had overseen a clear-out of the party machine. Only ex-MP Julia Ojiambo (the Director of Youth and Women's Affairs), the Director of Internal Audit and two Deputy Directors had survived. Now Mugambi himself had been dismissed for being 'ineffectual'. The purges had stemmed from Kamotho's battle with KANU National Chairman Oloo-Aringo for control of the party apparatus. Now that Oloo-Aringo had defected to FORD, Mugambi, who had been blamed for the May 1991 sackings, was sacrificed as Kamotho attempted to silence those who criticised KANU's repression of free debate. Several of those dismissed earlier had defected to FORD, including Tom Obondo, who had been KANU's director of Recruitment and Registration, and Carnisius Kirugara, formerly Deputy Director of Legal and International Affairs.[9]

In early February 1992 it looked as if Kamotho's position in the party hierarchy was slipping as further divisions in KANU's ranks appeared. Critics complained that the party machine was abysmally ill-equipped to cope with the electoral challenges of multi-party democracy, while the Secretary-General attracted further bad publicity by urging his Murang'a supporters to beat up FORD activists. The opposition press seized on the announcement by KANU's new National Chairman, Ndolo Ayah, that Kamotho and Luhya hardliner Elijah Mwangale had been reprimanded at a meeting of the party's National Executive on Tuesday, 4 February 1992. Kamotho, however, dismissed reports that he had been demoted and replaced as the party's chief spokesman by Minister for Planning and National Development Dr Zachary Onyonka.[10] In fact, Onyonka was merely given responsibility for explaining KANU's economic programme, while Kamotho remained in charge of the campaign against the opposition – though the 4 February special meeting of the National Executive did reprimand Kamotho and Minister of Agriculture Mwangale for bringing the party into disrepute by their ill-considered attacks on the opposition.

Mwangale, the Bungoma District KANU Chairman, had urged the Luhya to unite behind KANU, encouraging Masinde Muliro and Martin Shikuku to return to KANU so that the Luhya could exert greater influence within the ruling party. The Minister had also suggested that it was time that the Luhya, Kenya's second largest ethnic group, occupied one of the two key offices. Some of his enemies in KANU interpreted the remarks as a veiled bid to secure the Vice-Presidency, suggesting that Mwangale hoped to replace Vice-President Saitoti. Mwangale's hopes of the post had been dashed in 1988 and again in 1989, when Moi had appointed Josephat Karanja and then George Saitoti. The Luhya Minister's numerous enemies even suggested that he had attacked President Moi, proposing that he should give way as President after 14 years in office.[11]

KANU's Hidden Strength

Following FORD's successful rallies in Nairobi, Mombasa, Machakos and Murang'a, it seemed to many Kenyans that an opposition victory was inevitable. KANU appeared on the verge of collapse and President Moi's chances of holding on to power extremely slim. Under the joint leadership of Jaramogi Oginga Odinga and Kenneth Matiba, FORD seemed likely to sweep the country, apart from the Kalenjin heartlands and possibly Kibaki's home District of Nyeri. This hubris was to prove fatal. Even at the peak of euphoria for FORD, KANU's prospects were nowhere near as bad as opposition leaders believed. In Central Province, the party organization was severely disrupted, but in most other parts of Kenya, it remained intact and, overall, KANU was in a much better position to fight Presidential and Parliamentary elections than either of the new opposition parties, which had yet to form local branches in most parts of the country or, where they existed, were disorganized and divided between rival factions. The *Kenya Times* and the Kenya Broadcasting Corporation also remained loyal to the ruling party, presenting a one-sided view of the news.

KANU possessed a number of additional advantages. First, not all Parliamentary constituencies are the same size: the largest constituency, Molo, had nearly twenty times as many electors as the smallest. Urban areas, where FORD was strong – especially Nairobi – are under-represented. It is, in fact, possible to win more than half the seats in the National Assembly with only 39 per cent of the vote, provided the party's strength is concentrated in the sparsely populated, less developed parts of the country, such as the Rift Valley, Maralal, Isiolo and Moyale Districts in Eastern Province, and in North-Eastern Province. It was not perhaps entirely coincidental that KANU was strongest in precisely these areas. The Rift Valley, for example, contained 44 constituencies, nearly half the number required to secure an overall majority in Parliament, and KANU's hold on 35 of these was unshaken. Opposition leaders and commentators sympathetic to FORD and the DP underestimated the depth of popular support for the ruling party – and to a lesser extent for President Moi – in large parts of the country. They believed – and many would continue to think right up to the election – that support for KANU had withered, reduced to the President's Kalenjin ethnic enclave, with the formation of a registered opposition.

FORD, for example, consistently overestimated its popular support in Coast and North-Eastern Province after it established an electoral alliance with the Islamic Party of Kenya (the IPK), and considered that it had a good chance of securing the majority of MPs from both Provinces. In fact, the IPK's appeal was limited to unemployed youths in Mombasa and the tourist resort of Malindi, where the impact of semi-naked European tourists was felt most acutely. Elsewhere in Coast Province, even among the largely Moslem Digo population of Kwale District and in Lamu, and in North-Eastern Province's ten seats, support for KANU remained solid. The ruling party remained firmly in control of the vast, sparsely populated areas, such as Maasailand, Turkana and Samburu in Rift Valley Province, or Marsabit and Mandera in Eastern Province, and remained competitive not only in Taita-Taveta District at the Coast, but in Machakos, Makueni and Kitui Districts in Ukambani and in Meru and Tharaka-Nithi. Even in Western Province, KANU was stronger than the opposition in Vihiga and Busia Districts, while Kisii and Nyamira Districts in Nyanza Province also favoured the government and might return between six and ten KANU MPs. A few observers also questioned whether Odinga was as popular in South Nyanza as his advisers believed, since the area had supported Tom Mboya and KANU rather than the KPU in the late 1960s. Only in Kikuyuland was it clear that KANU had little chance of victory.[12]

Once President Moi began to fight back, launching an active campaign early in February 1992, it quickly became evident that KANU's hopes were far from forlorn. Outside of Central Province, Nakuru District, Nyanza and certain parts of Western Province and the Coast, it was becoming increasingly clear, the opposition's appeal was limited. A united opposition might have given KANU a stiff battle but a fragmented one stood little chance. KANU's candidates in Nairobi, for example, would be in grave difficulties if they faced a single opposition candidate, but if FORD and the DP both put up candidates in every constituency, KANU stood a good chance of winning two or three seats in the capital, despite its reputation as an opposition bastion.

The ruling party was in crisis throughout December 1991 and January 1992, but as 1992 progressed it became evident that support for KANU was both more resilient and more widespread than opposition leaders believed. KANU had an established organisation in every part of the country. It remained a credible political force even in Central Province and Nairobi. In the heartlands of KANU strength – the central Rift Valley and parts of Western Province – FORD and the DP hardly existed. The Provincial Administration and the police, moreover, remained loyal to President Moi and could be deployed to harass opposition activists.

KANU's Counter-Attack

As soon as the decision was taken to authorise the registration of opposition political parties, KANU headquarters launched a campaign to stress that only the ruling party was a national political force and represented all Kenyans rather than particular ethnic groups. On *Uhuru* Day, less than a week after the Special Delegates' Conference, full-page advertisements ran in the national press and political weeklies stressing that 'KANU has remained the vanguard and motive force for independence, freedom and progress. Through its unfaltering commitment to the *Nyayo* tenets of Love, Peace and Unity, it has welded the people of Kenya into one harmonious whole, thus ensuring development and the attainment of happiness for all.' This emphasis on KANU as the best guarantee of stability and development was to become a constant theme of party leaders throughout the year-long campaign, reaching a crescendo in December 1992 in the final run-up to the general election, despite the covert encouragement by certain party leaders of 'ethnic cleansing' in the Rift Valley.[13]

President Moi went on the offensive almost immediately, holding a major rally in Nakuru town on 14 December 1991. The site had been selected carefully, enabling the President to raise KANU morale in what would be a crucial 'swing' area. Nakuru is a primarily Kikuyu town and, therefore, natural opposition territory, but it is also home to many Kalenjin, including members of President Moi's own ethnic sub-group the Tugen. Luhya and Luo settlers had also migrated to the town in sizeable numbers. The District's KANU branch in the 1980s, under Kariuki Chotara and Wilson Leitich, had been one of the most hardline, adopting a ruthless attitude to dissidents. The town, as the headquarters of the Rift Valley, was also at the centre of the recent *Majimbo* debate, and would become a refuge for many Kikuyu families attacked in the forthcoming ethnic violence.

The President was accompanied by 24 Cabinet Ministers and a host of other prominent politicians, sending the clear message that KANU was determined to fight to retain control. He made much of the fact that opposition leaders had been calling for multi-party democracy for months, but now that it had been granted, they were urging the President not to call immediate elections, complaining that they were not ready to fight a national campaign. The President announced that the ruling party would begin an aggressive month-long recruitment campaign in January to demonstrate its popularity and that further rallies would be held in other towns, including Nairobi.[14]

Other KANU leaders had a cruder approach. Davidson Kuguru, the octogenarian Minister for Home Affairs and National Heritage, KANU's Assistant Treasurer and MP for Mathira in Nyeri District, declared at Karatina's *Jamhuri* Day celebrations that the Kikuyu would never agree to be governed by an uncircumcised Luo like Oginga Odinga. Kuguru had been appointed to the Cabinet, following Matiba's resignation, in an attempt by President Moi to maintain a Kikuyu presence at senior levels of the government. A man of limited education, Kuguru exercised little control over his Department and failed to adapt to the new multi-party environment. Njenga Mungai, still a KANU MP – later of FORD-Asili – remonstrated, declaring that such statements only contributed to KANU's unpopularity and that 'this is a moment when we need unity and not statements that will hurt other tribes'. Several other KANU leaders, however, made similar derogatory remarks, prompting Luke Obok, a long-time Oginga Odinga aide, to observe that Kaguru's remarks were 'a good reflection of the quality of thinking we can expect from the KANU Cabinet'.[15] Luo members of the ruling party were incensed. Foreign Minister Wilson Ndolo Ayah suggested that Kuguru should be punished and Minister for Regional Development Onyango Midika proposed that the errant Kikuyu Minister should be repudiated as KANU's candidate at the coming election.

The government's reputation among Luo voters had suffered an even more serious blow when Nicholas Biwott and Hezekiah Oyugi were released on Tuesday, 10 December 1991 because of insufficient evidence to convict them of murdering Dr Robert Ouko. Dr Oki Ooko Ombaka, who had represented Nairobi-based members of Ouko's Ominde clan before the Enquiry, complained of 'a total cover-up' by the authorities. The government, he alleged, had made every attempt to block the Enquiry's investigation. Former Cabinet Minister Ngala Mwendwa protested that the release of two 'principal suspects' would have 'very serious political repercussions'.[16] FORD Secretary-General Martin Shikuku also castigated the government, observing that the decision confirmed widespread suspicions that the police and security services in the early stages of the investigation had been attempting to destroy, rather than discover, evidence. Meanwhile, a jubilant delegation of students from South Nyanza, who had received help with their fees from Oyugi, marched through Nairobi to celebrate the former Permanent Secretary's release, while Ouko's family and neighbours in Central Nyanza were astounded and grief-stricken by the decision. Ouko's death would have major political consequences in Siaya and Central Nyanza, confirming the area's support for Oginga Odinga and FORD.[17]

Biwott's plight appeared desperate. His political career seemed finished and many believed that his vast business empire was about to founder. Some commentators suggested that he would soon be ousted as Elgeyo-Marakwet KANU chairman and forced to resign his Parliamentary seat as the ex-Minister's enemies in his Kerio South constituency gathered to test his power. Biwott's abrasive, even intimidating style had alienated many people in the District who alleged that he had become a virtual dictator whose decisions could not be questioned. Members of the Marakwet community protested that the Minister had concentrated development in the Elgeyo areas. Former MP Kurgat criticised the disgraced Minister, observing that Biwott's dismissal had strengthened KANU and persuaded various people who had been contemplating defection to remain loyal, while ex-Kerio Central MP, William Murgor, a long-time foe of the Minister, supported Kurgat. For the first time in nearly 13 years, Biwott's opponents felt free to challenge the ex-Minister in his own bailiwick. Tabitha Seii and Joseph Barsulai, executive secretary of the Uasin Gishu branch of the National Union of Teachers, even announced that they would oppose him in the forthcoming general election. Biwott's authority was dented but his political allies remained firmly in control of local affairs, stressing that he remained District chairman. Biwott, moreover, was popular in his constituency. Under his patronage, the road system had improved greatly and so had the quality of local schools, until St Patrick's at Iten was one of the best secondary schools in the country.[18]

Reports of Biwott's political demise underestimated the ex-Minister's close relations with President Moi and the extent of his influence within the state system. During the past 14 years, Biwott had created his own patronage network in the central bureaucracy, the Provincial Administration, the security services and the Special Branch. He even controlled the recruitment and rotation of the Presidential bodyguard and it was rumoured that some key officials were more loyal to Biwott than to Moi. President Moi's Cabinet reshuffle on 16 December 1991 indicated that reports of Biwott's total disgrace were perhaps exaggerated, for he appointed Paul Chepkok, MP for Kerio Central and one of the ex-Minister's closest allies, as Assistant Minister for Industry. Equally significant to close students of Kalenjin politics was the announcement that Dr Ben Kipkorir, the long-serving Executive Chairman of the Kenya Commercial Bank, was being removed and compenstated with the sinecure position of chairman of General Motors (Kenya). Biwott, a Keiyo, had long been suspicious of Kipkorir, a Marakwet and former lecturer at the University of Nairobi, perhaps fearing his intellectual ability and seeing a potential rival in his own District. Personally honest, Kipkorir was the antithesis of the corrupt, get-rich-quick circle connected with Biwott. Now that Biwott had fallen from power, he may well have forced the President to dismiss his rival to safeguard his own influence in Elgeyo-Marakwet. Events during 1992 demonstrated that President Moi was frequently unable to control his erstwhile protégé.[19]

Under arrest in early December 1991, Biwott had been unable to stop the repeal of Section 2(A) of the constitution, but on his release from prison, he became increasingly active as KANU began to devise its election strategy. President Moi's first task was to re-establish Kalenjin unity by appeasing powerful dissidents, such as Francis Lotodo among the Pokot and Henry Kosgey in Nandi, who had both fallen out with Biwott in the mid-1980s. Lotodo, who threatened to join the Democratic Party, was assured that he would be given a Cabinet post when KANU was re-elected, while Nandi leaders, who complained that the last three general elections in the District had been rigged and voters dragooned to the polls by the GSU, insisted upon KANU holding a free and open primary in order to select its parliamentary candidates. Unless Nandi people could freely express their views in the primary, choosing their preferred candidates, the ruling party would be faced with open revolt and defections to the DP in one of its most important bastions.

Nairobi was another problem. Early in January 1992, two of the city's most prominent politicians, Minister for the Environment and Natural Resources Dr Njoroge Mungai and former Minister of Agriculture Maina Wanjigi, announced that they were abandoning KANU for FORD. The two men had been locked in battle for control of the city's KANU branch. Mungai and his team had been suspended from office after 15 years, and Wanjigi and his associates had appeared to be on the verge of taking over. Then Wanjigi, whose suspension had only just been lifted, made the mistake of supporting the reform movement within the ruling party, alarming Moi and his advisers: however much they might distrust Mungai, Wanjigi would be even more difficult and rather more energetic in defending Kikuyu interests. Now, as Kikuyu leaders deserted the ruling party, the leaders of the two rival Nairobi factions decided that KANU was finished in the capital and that the future lay with FORD. Their defections threw KANU's Nairobi organisation into disarray as several contenders struggled to seize the post. David Mwenje, an Assistant Minister and MP for Embakasi, had been prepared to stand against Mungai and Wanjigi in November 1991, and clearly still wanted the job. KANU headquarters, however, moved quickly to minimise the potential fall-out by restricting the election to the 40-member Branch Executive Committee. In the end, only two candidates emerged: Vice-Chairman Fred Omido, the Luo MP for Makadara, and Mungai's old opponent in Dagoretti, Clement Gachanja, who like Kenneth Matiba had risen to public attention as chairman of the Kenya Football Federation. A shrewd but unscrupulous political operator, Gachanja was willing to sell himself to the highest bidder. President Moi knew that he would remain loyal and provide a Kikuyu front for KANU in Nairobi as long as supplies of money helped to solve the liquidity problems of his businesses.[20]

Gachanja, benefiting from the support of KANU headquarters, emerged victorious by appealing to Kikuyu voters and critics of the former branch officials, with 23 votes to Omido's 17. He warned that he would expose the 'misdeeds' of Mungai and his associates and reveal their plans to undermine the President and government. The new chairman, however, was faced immediately with a protest from KANU Youth organizers, who complained that Mungai and the branch executive had refused to hand out 210,000 shillings promised by President Moi. The trouble stemmed from the fact that recently *matatu* operators and country-bus companies had refused to pay the so-called 'KANU levy' which had provided the salaries of KANU Youth officials. *Matatu* operators had long resented the 'policing' role of these unemployed young men and during the next year were to emerge as a major financial support for Kenneth Matiba's faction within FORD and then later for FORD-Asili. Nairobi, of course, was an opposition stronghold and the new KANU chairman would have a most difficult task leading the campaign to hold the ruling party's eight seats in the city.[21]

By the end of January 1992, when FORD held its first mass rally at Nairobi's Kamukunji stadium, KANU had not yet devised a strategy to counteract the appeal of the opposition. Secretary-General Kamotho dismissed the vast gathering as a bunch of 'curious youth without voting legitimacy'.[22] Since the political transformation brought about by the abandonment of KANU's monopoly, Kamotho had been one of the few senior politicians, apart from President Moi and Vice-President Saitoti, still willing to take on the opposition at every opportunity. He had a well-merited reputation of being a hard, even unscrupulous political fighter. As one Nairobi journal noted, 'Never shy of facing the press, Kamotho will also break any rule in the book in order to defend KANU's image.'

By contrast, the KANU hawks – Sharrif Nassir of Mombasa, Elijah Mwangale of Kakamega, James Njiru of Kirinyaga, Kalonzo Musyoka,

Burudi Nabwera, William ole Ntimama of Narok, and Wilson Leitich of Nakuru – had remained unusually quiet. At the end of January 1992, however, they began to find their voices. Kuria Kanyingi, the outspoken director of motor vehicle inspection, who had become an influential figure in the Kiambu KANU branch – most of whose leaders had now defected to the DP – also began to speak out once more, though party leaders appeared to be devoting more time to discussing policy. Kamotho and KANU's new National Chairman, Foreign Minister Wilson Ndolo Ayah, challenged FORD and the DP to address specific policy issues, but the ruling party itself still lacked a coordinated national response to the new political situation. The much-heralded major recruitment drive, which was supposed to have started at the beginning of the year, had made little progress by the end of January. Party leaders were resisting holding grass-roots elections – a proposal first put forward by Mwai Kibaki and John Keen before they launched the DP. Even a journal as sympathetic to the ruling party as the *Weekly Review* judged at the end of January that 'despite the fact that the opposition looks set on making full use of its newly-founded freedom to hold public rallies, KANU leaders seem to be responding rather slowly and the party has yet to be seen to be exploiting to the full whatever talents and resources it has'.[23]

The ruling party did have one piece of good news when retired Chief of the General Staff General Jackson Mulinge announced that he would contest Kathiani constituency in Machakos District for KANU. Two prominent opposition leaders came from the constituency: George Nthenge, one of FORD's six founders, and Johnstone Makau, the leader of the Social Democratic Party. Mulinge had played the key role in holding the senior echelons of the military loyal to Moi in August 1982. The General's influence was obvious to all who visited the constituency, travelling along well-maintained tarmaced roads through the Machakos Hills to Kathiani town, where the paved road ended. Kathiani also boasted a new hospital, incongruously situated in this small settlement off the main routes to Nairobi and Machakos town. The ending of Paul Ngei's 30-year domination of Machakos politics, former Cabinet Minister Johnstone Makau's defection to form the SDP, and mounting dissatisfaction with KANU's illiterate branch chairman, Mulu Mutisya had left KANU's ranks in disarray: Mulinge's conspicuous presence in Kathiani would be a vital asset to the government in this key marginal District.[24]

Moi Makes His Move

Early in February 1992 President Moi began a vigorous drive to restore KANU's morale and to demonstrate that support for the regime was much stronger than the press and the opposition imagined. If the President had not acted then, it is possible that the drift away from KANU might have become a serious haemorrhage of support as politicians rushed to the opposition, especially FORD, in a desperate attempt to preserve their careers. President Moi's tours throughout the country demonstrated that the ruling party was far from finished. In mid-February, the President spent a week touring different parts of Coast Province, concluding with a rally at the Mvita grounds in Mombasa, where Odinga had spoken three weeks earlier.

Sharrif Nassir orchestrated a tremedous greeting for him, drawing an even larger crowd than Oginga Odinga and other FORD leaders had done, and proving that KANU had very considerable support in Mombasa and, indeed, throughout Coast Province.[25] The media reported that the crowd at the KANU rally was probably the largest gathering ever seen in Mombasa. Better attended than Odinga's, the KANU rally was also much better organised. Lines of placard-waving KANU members marched past the President, shouting pro-KANU slogans and singing patriotic songs. The President attracted large crowds throughout the visit. Smaller meetings were held in Kwale on Wednesday, 12 February; at Lamu on Thursday morning; at Hola in Tana River District, where Matiba and Rubia had been held in detention, that afternoon; and in Kilifi on Friday. After the giant Mombasa rally, the President continued to Taita-Taveta District in a direct challenge to the DP's Mwamunga and FORD's Mwashengu wa Mwachofi, the District's two main politicians. At almost every point, local leaders assured the President that they and the people were remaining loyal to KANU. FORD's support in Coast Province suddenly looked much less formidable than immediately after its Mombasa rally.[26] Clearly KANU would mount a strong campaign throughout the Province and, judging by the crowds, might well win most of the Coast's 20 Parliamentary seats. Only in wa Mwachofi's Wundanyi and Mwamunga's Voi did the opposition seem to be secure.[27]

In his speeches, the President stressed KANU's economic record. No government, he declared, could guarantee jobs, but KANU had a proven record of service, promoting economic diversification and bringing major new development projects to the Coast. In several places, he warmly endorsed local party leaders and called for the sitting MP to be returned. Throughout his tour of Kwale, the President was accompanied by the District's three MPs, Boy Juma Boy (Matuga), Kassim Mwamzandi (Msambweni) and Ali Bidu (Kinango). The President also used his control of the government 'pork barrel' to answer some of the opposition's criticisms, announcing that the government was attempting to re-open the Ramisi sugar factory and the cashew nut processing plant at Kilifi. He informed local officials and the crowds who gathered that new incentives would be provided to increase production and that the Kilifi plant might be privatised.[28]

On his visit to Lamu, the President addressed the long-run problem of land allocation and the failure of the Lake Kenyatta settlement scheme, which had brought hundreds of Kikuyu small-holders and their families from Kiambu to cultivate vegetables and fruit. Opening a new KANU office, the President also announced that he had instructed the Ministry of Lands and Housing to expedite the adjudication of title deeds. The President returned to this issue on his visit to Taita-Taveta where he attempted to outbid FORD interim Vice-Chairman Masinde Muliro's declaration that the opposition party would alienate land from the vast Tsavo National Park for landless local residents. The President informed the crowd, in response to a request from local Wundanyi MP Darius Mbela (who as it happened was the Minister for Lands and Housing), that the Ministry should develop a programme for settling landless squatters in the National Park. In Mombasa, the President had earlier instructed the Kenya Ports Authority to review workers' wages. One of KANU's main advantages over both FORD and the DP was to be its control of government patronage. By the end of his visit President Moi was confident that the Coast was '100 per cent KANU' and that the government would secure a landslide in the Province.[29]

All three main parties had scheduled a series of meetings in the major cities, and their spokesmen seemed equally adept at playing on local interests and problems. KANU had recovered its confidence, however, and as divisions within FORD became increasingly apparent was confident that it would win the general election. In an interview given to Britain's Independent Television News at the end of his Coast tour, President Moi declared this confidence and castigated foreign governments and humanitarian organisations for financing the opposition parties. The outbreaks of ethnic violence, the President argued, demonstrated that he had been right to warn that multi-party politics would create discord and revive 'tribal' rivalries.[30] The President did not mention the prominent role played by KANU leaders in Nandi, Kericho and the Uasin Gishu in encouraging the attacks, insisting that only KANU was the party of national unity. He was to repeat this claim throughout the remaining ten months before the election. Throughout this period, Moi maintained a hectic schedule, rebuilding the morale of KANU workers.

The government was also twisting the arms of senior politicians considering defection and attempted to make life as difficult as possible for those who had chosen to join the opposition. As a result, three Kikuyu politicians were forced to abandon their plans to join the opposition. Cabinet Minister Arthur Magugu of Kiambu and Murang'a KANU chairman and ex-Minister Dr Julius Kiano were both tempted to join Kibaki's DP, realising that they had little chance of re-election if they remained in KANU. Equally, KANU could not afford to lose the backing of two such prominent Kikuyu leaders. Both men were deeply in debt, however, having bought coffee farms at the height of the 1970s cash crop boom with large loans from the commercial banks, which they had been unable to pay back when cash crop prices fell. President Moi warned both men when they made speeches advocating political liberalisation, raising speculation that they were contemplating defection, that the government would withdraw its financial guarantees of their loans and encourage the banks to foreclose. Other creditors would become alarmed, creating even more serious problems for Magugu and Kiano. They would not be able to fight the fortcoming election if they were declared bankrupt. Their only hope was to remain in KANU and to accept financial support from Moi.[31]

The case of Dr Njoroge Mungai was similar. Mungai, however, had announced early in January that he was abandoning KANU and would join FORD. He had resigned his seat in the Cabinet, seemingly forfeiting his position as MP for Westlands and the chairmanship of Nairobi's KANU branch, castigating KANU as 'beyond repair'. The former Minister complained that 'corruption, which implies dishonesty and greed' had 'permeated the government apparatus to such an extent that the government was badly stigmatised'. KANU and the government, he asserted, had violated human rights and had rigged recent elections so blatantly as to destroy confidence in the political process.[32] Mungai rapidly discovered, however, that his defection to FORD was not universally welcomed. Martin Shikuku and other FORD founding fathers feared the inrush of former KANU politicians, especially prominent Kikuyu, and attempted to block their membership. Mungai also realised that with so many other Kikuyu recruits – including his Nairobi rivals Maina Wanjigi and Charles Rubia, not to mention the recuperating Kenneth Matiba and younger, less compromised figures such as Paul Muite – already ensconced in the opposition party's leadership, it was unlikely that he would be given a prominent role in FORD.

The former leader of the 'Change the Constitution' movement had waned in influence since President Moi came to power. His power base in Nairobi had never amounted to much, and his popular support appeared minimal. Several opposition leaders believed that he was simply a spy for KANU, and many found it difficult to forget Mungai's speech in Narok in October 1991, shortly before the aborted Kamukunji rally, when he had vowed 'to root out opposition elements from Nairobi even if he had to flush them out from under their beds without their trousers'.[33] Other KANU leaders had made similar speeches in recent years, including John Keen who was now the DP's Secretary-General, and Peter Oloo-Aringo, now once again a close confidante of FORD Chairman Oginga Odinga, but Mungai's had seemed especially gratuitous, being widely seen as an attempt to placate his Kalenjin critics and rivals in his own Nairobi base. Many considered that Mungai had simply been buying popularity at the opposition's expense. Now he was trying to join them. Had the man no political principles?

Mungai soon discovered that he had little to offer to the opposition. He and Wanjigi were not even permitted to speak to the crowd at FORD's Kamukunji rally. The two Nairobi politicians were virtually ignored at this major meeting in their supposed urban bailiwick. Under pressure from Shikuku, Odinga had refused to nominate Mungai to any key policy-making body and he had played virtually no role in FORD's recruitment campaign in his own Westlands constituency, which was headed by Wanguhu Ng'ang'a, an ally of Matiba's and a member of FORD's steering committee. KANU, for its part, moved rapidly after his defection to embarrass the ex-Minister financially, withdrawing backing for his loans and contracts that had been awarded to his businesses. Mungai realized that he faced bankruptcy and political oblivion if he remained in FORD, while President Moi was willing to welcome him back to KANU as a symbol of continuity with the Kenyatta era, demonstrating the support of an old rival and a member of the still-powerful Kenyatta family. As a result, only five weeks after he had abandoned KANU, Mungai returned to the ruling party and was even permitted to resume his seat in the National Assembly as his resignation had never been gazetted officially.[34]

Mungai, however, had lost his seat in the Cabinet to the sole European MP, Langata's Philip Leakey, and, as we have noted, had been replaced as KANU chairman in Nairobi by his old foe Clement Gachanja, who had lost no time in blaming Mungai for the low morale of KANU supporters in the city. Realising the error of his ways, Mungai now claimed that KANU was beginning to correct its weaknesses, pointing to the recent enactment of an anti-corruption bill and the arrest of former parastatal chiefs. President Moi warmly welcomed the ex-Minister back into KANU's ranks and the head of Nairobi's KANU women's movement and the Westlands sub-branch urged Gachanga to step down so that Mungai could take over again as branch chairman. Other KANU leaders were less happy to see him return. President Moi, in order to encourage further defectors to return to KANU, announced that Mungai was to be appointed to the specially created post of KANU National Vice-Chairman with a seat on the party's National Executive in order to assist Secretary-General Kamotho carry the party's message to the country. Mungai did not regain his seat in the Cabinet, however, and was to play little part in KANU's campaign even in Nairobi and Kikuyuland.[35]

Majimboism and the Origins of 'Ethnic Cleansing'

The September 1991 calls for *Majimboism* had excited ethnic rivalries. Kalenjin politicians warned that if multi-party democracy was established, 'non-natives' (non-Kalenjin) would be driven out of the Rift Valley. Relations between the ethnic groups consequently deteriorated rapidly, despite the fact that Luhya leaders Elijah Mwangale and the late Moses Mudavadi, the President's brother-in-law, had long been key figures in Moi's inner circle. The first ethnic violence erupted early in November 1991, six weeks after the first *Majimbo* rally, when clashes took place around Tinderet in Nandi District. The incidents were confined to Miteitei farm, a settlement site, and were similar to the 1984 confrontation at Kapkangani which the local Administration had quickly ended. This time, however, the conflict escalated, dividing the settlers on ethnic lines. Spreading along the Nandi-Luo border with Kisumu District, the fighting became increasingly serious. Then trouble commenced in Bungoma and the Trans-Nzoia. The clashes briefly died down at the end of the year, despite the fact that local KANU leaders attempted to enforce their claim that the Rift Valley was 'an exclusive KANU zone'.[36]

By mid-January 1992 ethnic clashes were so widespread that the Roman Catholic Bishops issued a pastoral letter, condemning the incidents and castigating the government's failure to take action. Certain officials, the Bishops suggested, were abusing their authority, and had issued inflammatory statements inciting violence. Minister of Local Government William ole Ntimama, for example, declared Narok District 'a KANU zone'. Attempts by the opposition parties to establish branches or enlist recruits, he warned, would be resisted by force. Oginga Odinga responded to the warnings from Kamotho and ole Ntimama by declaring that FORD would retaliate if its members were attacked.

In mid-January the violence began again in Kamasai in Nandi District, where about 20 people – mainly Luhya – were killed and more than 1,000 rendered homeless. The Kenya Television Network's evening news showed chilling pictures of charred houses and property. In a tour of the troubled area, President Moi implicitly blamed the new opposition parties, which he claimed had aroused 'tribal' animosities. He stressed once more that Kenya was not yet ready for multi-party democracy. Henry Kosgey, the Nandi District KANU Chairman, and other Nandi MPs claimed that the attacks had been launched by thugs, and urged the police and the GSU to restore order.[37]

As the ethnic clashes on the western borders of the Rift Valley grew in intensity, President Moi appealed for toleration. Speaking at a fund-raising meeting at the Redeemed Gospel Church in Nairobi's Huruma Estate, the President instructed KANU leaders not to encourage ethnic violence or attacks on opposition activists. He reiterated, however, his belief that political pluralism would inflame ethnic rivalries. Local Kamasai residents claimed that their homes had been attacked by armed gangs of Kalenjin youths, while the police had stood idle. The Rt Rev. Cornelius Korir, the Roman Catholic Bishop of Eldoret – himself a Kalenjin – claimed that government officials and local KANU leaders were fanning the violence.[38]

On Monday, 24 February 1992, the day after the President's appeal, Assistant Minister for Manpower Development and Employment Pancras Otwani ordered FORD activists in his Amagoro constituency in Western Province to close their office by 6 March or he would lead his fellow Teso in burning it down. 'If any problem occurs on that date and people are injured,' he cautioned, 'then they should not blame us because I have issued a warning early enough.' KANU leaders in Nandi District, led by nominated MP Ezekiel Bargetumy; the Mayor of Kabarnet Philemon Chelagat and Nandi County Council chairman Samuel Chelule also ignored the President's appeals for peace. They warned opposition leaders 'never to set foot or endeavour to recruit in Nandi District or they will live to regret it'.[39]

Many KANU MPs and local officials appeared to have great difficulty in adjusting to multi-party politics. They behaved as if KANU was the only party. Opposition activists, however, also freqently went too far, provoking a brutal response from local KANU activists. As the *Weekly Review* pointed out:

> The opposition has not been entirely blameless in the escalating spirit of fiery rhetoric and violence.... Many cases have been reported of members of opposition parties trying to force others to chant their slogans or flash their party symbols. The verbal attacks by some opposition leaders on KANU, the government and the president have drawn angry protests from KANU leaders, who have called for respect by the opposition parties for the institution of the presidency.[40]

Attorney-General Amos Wako, like the President, appealed for tolerance, urging all party leaders to refrain from violent talk, abusive remarks and unsubstantiated allegations, as well as 'belligerent behaviour, provocation and intolerance of supporters of opposing parties'. The Attorney-General observed that 'if multi-party democracy is to flourish and not degenerate into disorder, turmoil and chaos', the parties would have to accept each other's right to exist and organize.[41]

The Political Backround to the Ethnic Clashes

Following the decision to legalise opposition parties, Moi's Kalenjin associates had begun systematically to fulfil the President's prophecy of ethnic conflict, attempting to secure by violence the consolidation of a Kalenjin-dominated enclave which could defend Kalenjin interests and *Majimboism* if FORD captured power. Such short-sightedness did not bode well for KANU's electoral prospects. The ruling party could not be returned to power simply on the basis of Kalenjin votes, or even if it won every seat in the Rift Valley – nearly one quarter of the National Assembly. KANU could not afford to alienate Luhya and Gusii voters, who controlled another 35 seats. President Moi could only fight back against FORD by building his own 'rainbow coalition', solidifying support for KANU in Coast, North-Eastern, Eastern and Western Provinces, as well as in the Rift Valley. Biwott was a political liability in most of these areas.

Faced by the real possibility of losing power, the initial reaction of the Kalenjin inner circle was to secure their own power base. They were detemined to ensure that Kericho, Nandi, Trans-Nzoia, Uasin Gishu, West Pokot, Elgeyo-Marakwat and Baringo Districts returned a full slate of 26 KANU MPs. Kipkalya Kones, an Assistant Minister for Agriculture and MP from Kericho District, warned opposition activists to keep out of Kericho which, he claimed, was 'a KANU zone'.[42] Anyone who attempted to open a FORD or DP headquarters would 'live to regret it'. Kipsigis youth, the Assistant Minister warned, had declared war on Luo workers in the District in retaliation for the murder of Kipsigis traders at Sondu. Kones, who was the Kericho District KANU branch secretary, also declared that KANU would 'hit very hard' at those who attempted to campaign for the opposition parties. Opposition leaders rushed to denounce KANU, claiming that the communal violence stemmed from the ruling party's fear of losing power. Dennis Akumu, a former MP for Nyakach and now a FORD activist, urged Luos to defend themselves 'until the time Kenya gets a government which values human life'. The constituency was badly disrupted by the clashes as hundreds of people fled settlements in the Rift Valley.[43]

The ethnic violence caused serious divisions among MPs, all of whom were still theoretically KANU supporters, as the National Assembly split along ethnic lines. Luo MPs united against Biwott while Kalenjin Members defended the ex-Minister when the National Assembly reconvened for the first time since before Christmas on 11 March 1992. Angry Luo MPs denounced their Kalenjin colleagues and Biwott in particular for masterminding the ethnic clashes. KANU leaders from outside the troubled zone attempted to conciliate but those from the clash areas spoke out in forceful terms, threatening to destroy the party. The MPs for Siaya District, for example, issued a press statement on Thursday, 19 March, expressing the opinion that the clashes were 'a carefully planned and executed operation' by people from the Rift Valley. Even Minister for Manpower Development and Employment Archbishop Stephen Ondiek, head of the Legio Maria, a powerful Luo independent church, accused Kalenjin leaders of encouraging the violence. The MPs also castigated the police and Provincial Administration for failing to intervene to protect Luo lives and property.[44]

By contrast, Kikuyu MPs adopted a cautious approach, expressing their concern that national unity was being undermined by ethnic violence. Led by Kirinyaga KANU Chairman and Minister for Culture and Social Services James Njiru, and Minister of State in the Office of the President Nahashon Kanyi from Nyeri, the Kikuyu MPs condemned the attempt to creat a KANU zone in the Rift Valley. Luhya Members of Parliament, led by Minister for Information and Broadcasting Burudi Nabwera, also urged the government to explain how the clashes had started and condemned the idea of 'zoning'. Far from uniting KANU, the ethnic clashes were beginning to polarise Kenyans, seriously reducing support for the ruling party in Nyanza and Western Provinces among the Gusii and Abaluhya 'swing' communities.

Despite the deployment of detachments of the GSU, the conflicts soon spread far beyond the original site to engulf the whole border country of the Rift Valley, Nyanza and Western Provinces. In mid-March, a new round of ethnic violence in western Kenya erupted. The seriousness and frequency of the incidents grew and the number of people killed or forced to flee their homes dramatically rose. The clashes initially remained concentrated along the border between Kericho and Kisumu Districts. Incidents occurred at Koguta and Sondu in Kisumu District where Kalenjin fighters attacked the homes and shops of Luos and other ethnic groups, leaving 25 dead. Then riots erupted at Sondu when FORD and KANU supporters clashed at the trading post.[45]

Local Luo leaders, loyal to KANU, feared that the violence would drive the Luo community even further into the Odinga camp. Nyakach MP Ojwang K'Ombudo, the Assistant Minister for Environment and Natural Resources, was both alarmed and angry. He urged his constituents to defend themselves against Kalenjin attackers. The MP demanded to know why the police and District Administration had failed to intervene, denouncing the Rift Valley Administration for siding with the Kalenjin. The police must be impartial, he declared, and be true to their motto, *Utumishi Kwa Wote,* (literally, 'service to all').[46]

Other Luo MPs were equally critical of the Kalenjin-dominated Provincial Administration and the Rift Valley police. Cabinet Minister Onyango Midika, the MP for neighbouring Muhoroni, whose constituency had been hit by communal violence in November, protested that the police had failed to protect the Luo population and alleged that members of the Provincial Administration had known in advance about the attacks. Similar allegations were made by Luhya leaders in the border areas of Bungoma, Kakamega, Trans-Nzoia and the Uasin Gishu Districts. Angered by the attitude of Kalenjin MPs, Assistant Minister Ojwang K'Ombudo banged the debating table with his shoe and protested, 'You are killing my people.... I don't want murderers to interrupt me on a point of order.... My people are being killed by KANU ... and the police and Provincial Administration in the Rift Valley just watch when my people are being killed.'[47] He warned that if pushed too far the Luo would march into Kericho. Indeed, he warned in a veiled threat to carry the troubles to President Moi's Baringo District: 'If the Kalenjin go on behaving the way they are doing, then we will go beyond Kericho.' When the Speaker required K'Ombudo to apologise and suspended him from the House, three other Luo MPs – Robert Jalang'o (Rarieda), Raymond Ndong' (Rangwe) and Matthews Otieno Ogingo (Ndhiwa) – walked out in solidarity.[48]

Similar sentiments were expressed by virtually all Luo Members, ranging from senior Cabinet Ministers to dissident backbenchers. Assistant Minister of Health Ocholla Ogur, for example, blamed Biwott for the clashes, accusing the disgraced Minister of organising a secret army to drive all non-Kalenjin residents from the Rift Valley. Rejecting Biwott's behind-the-scenes efforts to organise meetings between MPs from the affected areas, on Wednesday, 18 March 1992 Ogur demanded in the newly reconvened National Assembly, 'Can the Honourable Biwott send word to his army to declare a ceasefire and withdraw from the battlefield before we can talk peace?'[49]

The extent of Luo alienation from the government became increasingly evident the longer the clashes continued. While their constituents were being attacked and killed, and their houses set on fire and ransacked, KANU's Luo MPs could not afford to remain silent. Well aware that FORD would probably sweep South Nyanza, Kisumu and Siaya, the Province's sitting MPs were anxious to distance themselves from the claims of the party's Kalenjin leaders. Even before the clashes, KANU was in deep trouble throughout Nyanza Province. Ndong', who had resigned from KANU only to return within a month, warned that if the attacks on Luo settlers and workers on the Kericho tea estates did not stop, he might rejoin the opposition. Most MPs, however, knew that they had left it too late to defect to FORD. In most constituencies, the opposition party had already enlisted their local rivals, foreclosing their cooption.

Even the *Weekly Review,* which generally favoured the government, observed that 'KANU is set to be the biggest loser as a consequence of the clashes and the government's inability to nip them in the bud.'[50] The ruling party gained little from the violence. Its position in Nandi and Kericho was secure, despite the defection of fomer Assistant Speaker Samuel arap Ng'eny to the DP. The ethnic violence merely harmed the party's appeal to Luo, Gusii and Luhya voters. Before the violence, for example, KANU would probably have won all ten constituencies in Kisii and Nyamira, but by the end of March 1992 many of these were at risk.

As the situation deteriorated, the press became increasingly concerned about Kenya's political stability. The *Weekly Review,* for example, noted that 'whatever its causes, the ethnic violence has poisoned the country's political atmosphere and made it difficult for the establishment of a workable pluralistic system in which ethnic and other interests are subordinated to national interests'.[51] The fate of neighbouring Somalia, it cautioned, could easily befall Kenyans. Thousands of Luo had fled from Kericho back to Nyanza Province, and tension in the border areas of South Nyanza and Kisumu Districts remained high. Buses travelling from Kisumu to Nairobi by-passed Kericho, taking a much longer route through Nandi District and Eldoret.

In an attempt to improve relations with their Luo colleagues, the six Kericho MPs called for a meeting with leaders from Kisumu, Nyamira and South Nyanza to discuss the violent clashes. Unfortunately, the six Kipsigis MPs downplayed the role of their own community in the violence, placing responsibility for the recent incidents on Luo who, they alleged, had attacked and robbed Kipsigis traders at Sondu on the Kericho-Kisumu District border.

KANU leaders attempted to divert the blame for the violence to the opposition. The Office of the President alleged that FORD had formed a terrorist wing recruited from former members of the Kenya Air Force who had been dismissed following the attempted 1982 coup. The government claimed that 300 men were already in place and another 500 were filtering back into Kenya, having undergone guerrilla training in Libya.[52] These units had been inciting the violence in western Kenya and were responsible for the riots in Nairobi earlier in March. The statement alleged that FORD and the DP had established full-scale military wings and claimed that FORD was planning 'to escalate violent activities [in order] to promote violence, create fear and despondency among Kenyans and eventually blame it on the government'. The regime also alleged that FORD leaders had provoked the communal violence along the Kericho-Kisumu border, suggesting that

> This is a desperate attempt to win the Luo community back to FORD after the community's resentment of the GEMA plot ... they intend to sabotage vital installations, such as power and telephone lines, water system and transport network while impersonating our regular police force by using stolen service uniforms.[53]

The government warned that the infiltrators were seeking to promote further violence and would shoot those involved in riots in order to enflame ethnic relations. 'The full escalation and execution of the violence', the statement asserted, 'is scheduled to coincide with the planned national strike on April 2, 1992.... The sole purpose of the violent operations during that period will be to create the impression that the government has lost control.'[54]

Opposition leaders, of course, dismissed the government's allegations. They laid the blame at KANU's door, suggesting that Kalenjin leaders had incited the violence as a pretext to ban the opposition or at least to drive members of other ethnic groups from the Rift Valley. Some even mirrored the government's claim, suggesting that Youth for KANU '92 was behind the clashes. Several FORD and DP leaders believed that the new KANU youth movement provided a cover for a paramilitary organisation,which was being trained to disrupt the opposition parties meetings and to create inter-communal violence so that the government could justify a ban on the political opposition and the restoration of single-party rule.

The crisis reached a new peak in late March, spreading throughout the west of Kenya. The worst affected areas were along the Kericho-Kisii, Kericho-Kisumu, Nandi-Kakamega and Kakamega-Uasin Gishu borders.

There were also serious incidents in parts of Trans-Nzoia and Mount Elgon bordering Bungoma District. Roman Catholic Bishop Ndingi Mwana a'Nzeki of Nakuru estimated that up to 100,000 people had been displaced in the past five months and at least 60 people had died in clashes since the beginning of February.[55]

Even the government and Provincial Administration, which had hitherto claimed that the situation was under control, acknowledged that the violence had spread to the border areas of Kericho and Nyamira Districts, to Molo in Nakuru District, to Bungoma and Trans-Nzoia where ten people died in ethnic clashes in Saboti and Kwanza divisions on Sunday, 15 March. The government claimed that Sebei and Sabaot cattle rustlers from Kimilili division had raided a Teso cattle *boma,* setting off panic and slaughter among the local Sabaot, Bukusu and Teso residents which resulted in more than 100 houses being burnt down.[56] On Tuesday, 17 March, the *Daily Nation* and the *Standard* reported 18 deaths in incidents in Molo, Muhoroni and along the Kericho-Kisii border. According to the newspapers, 300 armed men had killed six people and injured eight others when they attacked Kikuyu and Gusii residents of Laenda and Borono farms, destroying 200 houses. Sixty houses and numerous granaries had also been set on fire along the Kericho-Nyamira border in fighting between Kipsigis and Gusii. The same day, five people were killed in Muhoroni and there were widespread clashes in other parts of Trans-Nzoia. By the end of the week, Gusii, Kikuyu and Luhya residents were mounting retaliatory attacks against the Kalenjin. Vice-President Saitoti acknowledged that more than 700 people had been arrested following the recent incidents and that 42 people had been killed the previous weekend.[57]

Leaflets threatening Luo, Gusii and Kikuyu workers on Kericho District's tea plantations suggested that there was a deliberate plot to drive all non-Kalenjin from the area. Far from uniting the ruling party, the ethnic clashes seriously damaged support for KANU throughout western Kenya, especially among the Gusii and Abaluhya, and made membership of KANU untenable for several Luo MPs.

As it was clear that KANU stood little chance of winning many seats in either Nyanza or Central Provinces, the Provincial Administration sought to make life as difficult as possible in these opposition strongholds. This heavy-handed approach merely ensured that the government's popularity deteriorated even further. In mid-March, for example, the police and the GSU went on the rampage for two days in the lakeside towns of Kisumu and Homa Bay. In Homa Bay, trouble had started when the police attempted to arrest a lame cobbler, suspected of trying to organise an illegal demonstration. By the end of the riot, 11 people had been injured and a truck belonging to the chairman of the South Nyanza County Council set on fire.[58]

Opposition officials, clergymen and lawyers denounced the violence in western Kenya and police brutality in Kisumu and Homa Bay, pointing out that the police had failed to stop the ethnic clashes, simply looking on as Kalenjin gangs looted and then burned the homes of Luo, Gusii and Luhya residents. Speaking at a rally in Nakuru, Odinga accused the government of using the police and GSU to terrorise Kenyan citizens.

Democratic Party Chairman Mwai Kibaki made similar allegations, warning that the government seemed to be inciting violence deliberately in order to fulfil its claims that political pluralism would exacerbate ethnic animosities.

Church leaders in the troubled areas also criticised the behaviour of the police and Provincial Administration. The most outspoken were two Roman Catholic Bishops, the Rt Rev. Mwana-a' Nzeki of Nakuru and the Rt Rev. Cornelius Korir of Eldoret, who was himself a Kalenjin. The two Bishops demanded to know why the Attorney-General did not prosecute KANU leaders who incited their supporters to drive other communities out of the Rift Valley. The Roman Catholic Archbishop of Kisumu, the Most Rev. Zaccheus Okoth, even accused the police of shooting unarmed Luo members of the public while simply watching armed Kalenjin mobs attack Luo homes. On a visit to strife-torn Sondu, the scene of the recent inter-ethnic clashes, the Archbishop, who was the secretary of Kenya's Roman Catholic Bishops' Conference, protested that the problems did not stem from 'multi-partyism' but were part of 'a well-orchestrated campaign to destabilise certain ethnic communities in western Kenya'. He claimed that 'arsonists and murderers ... are ferried to the District border in a well-planned and well-funded programme by politicians'.[59]

The Rt Rev. Dr Henry Okullu, the outspoken Anglican Bishop of Maseno South, dismissed the sitting Luo MPs as mere clients of the government. He claimed that they feared to stand up to President Moi and the KANU leadership because they were heavily in debt, and feared that their loans would be foreclosed by the banks if government guarantees were withdrawn. They were 'cowards' who had remained silent despite 'the wanton shooting of innocent people'.[60]

The Chronology and Typology of the Ethnic Clashes and Their Political Consequences

The clashes went through four distinct phases. The first round, in the immediate aftermath of the Rift Valley meetings in favour of *Majimboism* at the end of 1991 and during the first three months of the new multi-party era, were designed to secure KANU domination of the whole Rift Valley. During this phase, which lasted until early April 1992, the worst-affected areas were along the Rift's western border with Nyanza and Western Provinces, and the victims were Gusii, Luo and Abaluhya settlers. This phase was extremely dangerous politically for the ruling party, seriously endangering KANU's electoral support in the 30 vital 'ethnic marginals' populated by the Gusii and Abaluhya. The Luo vote was already lost to FORD, of course, but the incidents did little to restore the morale of the small band of KANU loyalists or of the incumbent Luo MPs.

In April 1992 the clashes entered a new, even more violent phase. Although gangs of armed Kalenjin remained active in the Trans-Nzoia and the Uasin Gishu – and would continue their activities right up to the general election in December – the main focus of the attacks switched southwards into Nakuru District, the major enclave of Kikuyu voters in the Rift Valley. From mid-April, Kikuyu maverick Njenga Mungai's Molo constituency became the main centre of attention as Kalenjin leaders attempted to drive Kikuyu residents from their small-holdings on the Mau escarpment in order to transform it into a solid KANU seat. Molo was the most ethnically heterogeneous constituency in Nakuru District (with the possible exceptions of Rongai and Nakuru Town) and since independence had attracted many Kikuyu ex-squatters as well as Kipsigis and Nandi. Violence also erupted on the Maasai side of the escarpment in Narok North, where William ole Ntimama was determined to guarantee a KANU landslide. One of KANU's leading hardliners, Ntimama was a fierce opponent of the opposition parties and, consequently, of 'disloyal' Kikuyu settlers in Narok District.

This second wave of clashes had less serious electoral consequences for KANU as the attacks on Kikuyu residents in Molo, Narok North, and the three Eldoret constituencies bolstered the ruling party's prospects. The continuing violence in the Uasin Gishu and Trans-Nzoia did not only hit the Kikuyu, however: many Abaluhya settlers fled back to the Bukusu heartland and to Kakamega District. Although the clashes probably guaranteed KANU victories in Eldoret South and Cherangani, which many commentators had believed would be won by the opposition, the price was high not only in terms of human suffering but also for KANU's electoral strength in Bungoma and Kakamega, compounding the unpopularity of Minister of Agriculture Elijah Mwangale, whose arrogance had already alienated many. As we have noted, the government now faced a difficult task in restoring its credibility with Abaluhya and Gusii voters. It was to be most successful in the areas furthest removed from the clashes, particularly in Vihiga and Busia Districts in southern and western Luhyaland, although Simeon Nyachae performed a remarkable job in Kisii and Nyamira in rebuilding KANU's support.

The third wave of ethnic clashes took place in the immediate run-up to the general election in December 1992, as KANU leaders in the Rift Valley made a final attempt to maximise President Moi's vote and to win the remaining 'ethnic marginals' – Molo, Eldoret South and East, Cherangani and Rongai. It was to succeed everywhere but Molo, where Njenga Mungai was equally determined to win the seat for FORD-Asili. Kalenjin and Kikuyu settlers had long lived side by side in Nakuru District. Molo MP Njenga Mungai alleged that Kalenjin youths were being transported in government trucks to the Menengai forest in order to attack Kikuyu settlers. When he was picked up by the police for questioning, and denounced by the District Commissioner and other local politicians, Mungai refused to back down. Although the Nakuru District Commissioner denied that there were any youths in the forest, local Kalenjin politician William Lasoi acknowledged that some young men had moved into the Mau escarpment forests 'to prepare for circumcision rituals'. Leaflets, moreover, were circulating widely throughout Nakuru and Kericho Districts, warning non-Kalenjin to leave the area. In fact, several Kericho tea plantations had to cease production before the election when their Luo, Gusii and Kikuyu pickers fled.[61]

In retrospect the main point of the clashes and of the harassment of the opposition communities in these constituencies was to ensure that no opposition candidate would receive 25 per cent of the Presidential vote. Early in the year, FORD and the Luo had appeared to be the main threat, but the focus of anxiety in KANU soon switched to Kikuyu settlers. Given the large Kikuyu presence in Nakuru and Laikipia Districts, where they formed a majority of the total population, it was imperative to minimise the Kikuyu vote everywhere else to ensure that neither Matiba nor Kibaki would reach the 25 per cent barrier.

The final wave of ethnic clashes took place early in 1993, after the general election, when those Kikuyu communities that had refused to heed the warning not to vote for the opposition were punished. The Parliamentary Select Committee, which was appointed on 13 May 1992, to investigate the clashes, under the chairmanship of Joseph Kiliku, a Kamba MP from Mombasa, concluded that the violence had started at Meteitei farm in the Tinderet division of Nandi District on the night of 29 October, 1991. The Select Committee identified nine separate clash centres when it presented its report on 4 September. Initially concentrated on the Nandi-Luo border, the attacks spread first to Trans-Nzoia, then to the Mount Elgon-Bungoma border, and finally to the Mau escarpment, where they were concentrated in Molo and Olenguruone divisions. The conflict in Mount Elgon, Trans-Nzoia, Molo and Olenguruone was the most protracted and violent, leaving 14,000 displaced in Bungoma, 12,000 in Trans-Nzoia, and 13,000 in the two Nakuru divisions.[62]

Few Kenyans believed President Moi's claim in mid-March that Libyan-trained guerrillas, working for FORD, had infiltrated from Uganda, or accepted his view that the *Daily Nation* and the *Standard* were misreporting the clashes.[63] Neutral observers and church leaders insisted that tens of thousands of people had fled their homes and were being housed in schools, churches and police stations in the surrounding areas. Even official police figures acknowledged that 68 people had died, 142 had been injured, 1,495 homes and 11 farms had been burnt down, and 55 vehicles destroyed, while 408 people had been arrested – 300 fewer than the authorities had claimed a week earlier. Press reports, however, suggested that many more people had died and many more homes had been destroyed. Unable to deny the seriousness of the clashes and the large numbers of people rendered homeless, the President and other KANU leaders reiterated the claim in late May and June that FORD had infiltrated trained assassins across the border with Uganda. Odinga and his colleagues refuted these claims, insisting that Kalenjin warriors and Youth for KANU '92 were masterminding the troubles.[64]

Victims of the violence had little confidence in the government, the police or the Provincial Administration, protesting that senior Kalenjin leaders, prominent in KANU, had masterminded the violence, directing the attacks by KANU Youth members, while the police and Administration had stood idly by. Church leaders also considered that the Administration and pro-KANU figures were deeply implicated in the violence. Kenya's Roman Catholic Bishops, for example, who usually adopted great caution in dealing with the government, issued a Pastoral Letter on 22 March 1992 accusing the authorities of 'complicity' in the clashes.[65] Clergymen from the Church of the Province of Kenya and the National Council of

Churches of Kenya, and prominent members of the International Commission of Jurists were equally outspoken. Their views were endorsed by one Kalenjin leader, Councillor Kipkitar Chumo, the Mayor of Kapsabet in Nandi District, who urged President Moi to discipline those Kalenjin politicians who had called in October 1991 for the introduction of *Majimboism*. The mayor claimed that the KANU rallies at Kapsabet and Kericho, five months earlier, had set off the clashes and alleged that incumbent Kalenjin MPs were responsible for much of the violence as they desperately sought to bolster their popularity.[66]

In the worst-affected areas along the Kericho and Nandi borders with Kisumu District, conditions began to return to normal towards the end of March. Ethnic relations, however, remained fraught. Several areas had been so disrupted that they experienced serious food shortages. Starvation and disease also threatened those who had fled to makeshift shelters organised by Churches. Clashes continued, however, in Molo, Trans-Nzoia and on the slopes of Mount Elgon, and threatened to spread to Nakuru town where large numbers of Kikuyu from Uasin Gishu and Molo had sought refuge.

The Political Rationale of the Clashes – 'Ethnic Cleansing' and Divisions within the Kalenjin Community

Why did the ethnic clashes occur? Certain Kalenjin leaders apparently judged that the incidents would confirm President Moi's predictions that multi-party democracy would ignite ethnic animosities and discredit opposition leaders and the advocates of multi-party competition. The international NGOs *Human Rights Watch* and *Africa Watch* judged, however, in their careful study of the ethnic clashes that:

> President Daniel arap Moi of Kenya confidently predicted that the return of his country to a multi-party system would result in an outbreak of tribal violence that would destroy the nation. His prediction has been alarmingly fulfilled. One of the most disturbing developments in Kenya over the last two years has been the eruption of violent clashes between different ethnic groups. However, far from being the spontaneous result of a return to political pluralism, there is clear evidence that the government was involved in provoking this ethnic violence for political purposes and has taken no adequate steps to prevent it from spiralling out of control.[67]

Certainly, some Kalenjin leaders believed that violence would encourage neutral ethnic groups to rally behind KANU and guarantee a Kalenjin enclave in the Rift Valley if Moi lost power. But one of the motives of the 'ethnic cleansing' campaign was to silence the ruling élite's critics within the Kalenjin community, especially among the Nandi and Kipsigis, and to provoke a mass reaction in support of President Moi. The Kalenjin were to be reunited behind KANU. In several settlement areas the process of land registration was under way. Individual titles were being issued to local residents, replacing the earlier communal title deeds. If Kikuyu, Abaluhya, Gusii and Luo settlers could be driven out of the Rift Valley borderlands before the process was completed, small-holdings could be appropriated by their Kalenjin former neighbours and they would forfeit all claims to the land.[68] *Human Rights Watch* and *Africa Watch* concluded that 'a long-term effect of the violence is the fact that land ownership patterns in the Rift Valley Province are being permanently altered to reduce the numbers of non-Kalenjin land-holders in the Province.' This proved a powerful incentive to the ethnic violence in several areas, including the Burnt Forest. In this way poorer members of the Kalenjin community could be bribed to support the Kalenjin ruling élite, President Moi and Nicholas Biwott.

The President's Kalenjin power base was far from entirely solid. Certain Nandi and Kipsigis leaders, who had been politically active in the 1960s and 1970s, had never been reconciled fully to Moi's political rise and resented the leadership of the President's Tugen and Biwott's Keiyo coterie, drawn from two of the smallest and least-developed Kalenjin sub-groups. Internecine rivalries posed a serious threat to KANU's electoral performance in its ethnic heartland. Throughout the first six months of 1992 and again during the KANU primaries in November, President Moi had to devote a disproportionate amount of effort to shoring up KANU's position among the Kalenjin, attempting to minimise personal rivalries and Nandi and Kipsigis dissatisfaction with the primacy of the Tugen and Keiyo communities of himself and Nicholas Biwott. Biwott aroused particular resentment among many Kalenjin politicians. In 1988, the then all-powerful Minister of Energy had ruthlessly used his prestige and patronage to eliminate potential rivals in the Kalenjin Districts, employing the Administration and the paramilitary GSU to rig the election. In Nandi, Kericho, West Pokot, the Uasin Gishu and in his native Elgeyo-Marakwet, Biwott had as many enemies as friends. Now that he appeared to have fallen from power, his enemies sought to undo the political damage inflicted on KANU's support in its ethnic home. Those who had been imposed at the 1988 general election and later the same year at the KANU party elections would have to be replaced by more popular standard bearers, able to mobilise the pro-KANU vote. There was a real danger that if the ruling party refused to clean up its act then many Nandi and Kipsigis voters would defect to the DP and FORD, led by Samuel arap Ng'eny and John Birgen, two highly regarded local figures.

Nandi and Kericho Districts are much more densely populated and 'developed' than the other Kalenjin areas and by the 1970s were already witnessing the intense development of capitalist agriculture and increasing social differentiation. Many of the President's closest Nandi and Kipsigis allies had been in the vanguard of this process, expropriating poorer cultivators who were forced off their small-holdings by land-grabbing politicians like Nicholas Biwott, who has been involved in several land disputes in recent years. As a result, many landless or dispossessed Nandi had moved to the rapidly expanding urban centres of Eldoret and Kitale, which had grown from small towns of 15–20,000 people at independence to major urban settlements with 200–250,000 residents by 1990. This migration brought the Kalenjin into conflict with Abaluhya settlers.[69]

Eldoret, in particular, has become the centre of a three-way struggle for local political dominance and for control of the area's Parliamentary seats. Three factions have emerged, representing the local Kalenjin élite, led by the mayor, a Tugen friend of the President; dispossessed Nandi who moved into the town as they were forced out of their home District; and the town's non-Kalenjin, primarily Abaluhya, residents. A similar struggle for political control developed in Uasin Gishu District and in its major town, Kitale, where Masinde Muliro struggled to maintain Abaluhya primacy.

The deepest discontent within the President's own community was to be found in Nandi District, the most densely populated and fertile Kalenjin District. During the 1970s, this had been the political base of Joseph Marie Seroney, Moi's strongest critic among the Kalenjin MPs. Nandi society was becoming more and more stratified as the wealthy prospered, acquiring businesses in the main towns, such as Kapsabet, and in nearby Eldoret in the Uasin Gishu, while the poor were being forced off the land, becoming a landless rural proletariat or joining Eldoret's growing number of unemployed.

Religious divisions also played an important part in Nandi politics. Most of President Moi's staunchest support came from adherents of the African Inland Church, a fundamentalist American-sponsored mission, while members of the Eldoret Diocese of the Church of the Province of Kenya found it difficult to secure contracts from the Nandi County Council or support for development projects. These rivalries had been exacerbated after 1983 by the growing confrontation between Bishop Alexander Muge of Eldoret – himself a Nandi from Mosop – and Stanley arap Metto, the area's MP. The conflict had begun when Muge, who had just returned to Eldoret as Bishop from Nairobi, had been shocked by the deployment of GSU platoons to oversee the 1983 general election. The Bishop protested at the blatant way in which arap Metto had been rigged into office. Shortly afterwards, the Mosop MP, now Assistant Minister of Education, had used his contacts in the County Council to stop the funding of a water development project at a CPK school in Muge's home village and suggested that Muge was an ally of disgraced Attorney-General Charles Njonjo, who had been a prominent lay member of the CPK.[70]

The feuding had continued until arap Metto fell from favour and lost the 1988 election. By then, Muge had emerged as one of the regime's most outspoken critics along with Bishop Henry Okullu of Maseno South in Luoland and the Rev. Dr Timothy Njoya of the PCEA. The Bishop had frequently clashed with the AIC-dominated leaders of Nandi County Council, who had supported their co-religionist arap Metto. President Moi, inevitably, had been dragged into the squabble. As a young boy, he had lodged with arap Metto's family when he was attending school and was himself an adherent of the AIC. On several occasions, the President condemned Bishop Muge for becoming involved in politics, warning him to keep to his pulpit. Some Nandi leaders feared that the Bishop was contemplating a political career.

Muge had also fallen foul of Nicholas Biwott who was an ally of arap Metto and the County Council leaders. Before his death the Bishop, as we noted earlier, had begun to speak out increasingly against corruption, suggesting that a prominent local politician – presumably Biwott – had stolen several farms which he had bought with money collected by the landless. First in 1988, and then again in 1990, the Bishop had referred to this issue and suggested that he would soon reveal the full extent of the theft and corruption in high places. After clashing with President Moi over food shortages and famine in arid West Pokot District, Bishop Muge had sought in the last year of his life to rebuild relations with the President, absolving him from the charges of corruption. In January 1990 the Bishop had also disassociated himself from Bishop Okullu and the Rev. Dr Njoya when they had castigated single-party rule and pointed to the sweeping changes that had occurred in Eastern Europe. Muge had defended the ruling party, echoing President Moi's claim that multi-party politics would simply divide Kenyans into rival ethnic parties. But before Muge's rapprochement with the President was completed, he was killed in a car crash on his way back to Eldoret from Busia, where he had recently been locked in controversy with local MP Peter Okondo, the Minister of Labour, who had unwisely threatened to kill him if he set foot in the District. As a result of the uproar which broke out on Muge's death, Okondo was compelled to resign from the Cabinet. Little attention was given to Muge's real political enemy – Nicholas Biwott.[71]

At first, prominent members of the CPK such as former Deputy Speaker Samuel arap Ng'eny disassociated themselves from the Bishop's attacks. But as the campaign against Muge and the CPK continued, and as the AIC members on Nandi County Council became increasingly intemperate in their statements, local politicians who belonged to the CPK were forced to speak out in support of the Church and eventually of their spiritual leader, Bishop Muge. Sectarian divisions had long played an important part in Nandi politics as the AIC and the CPK fought for political control, while the Roman Catholics, the largest denomination, attempted to remain neutral. Samuel arap Ng'eny and his colleagues had been rigged out at the 1988 general election, where the GSU was once again active, and the power of the AIC clique became even more dominant on the County Council and among the District's MPs. Following the Bishop's death in August 1990, CPK adherents became even more disillusioned, and with the legalisation of multi-party politics in December 1991 several, led by arap Ng'eny, were tempted to join the DP.

Nandi's KANU leaders, however, were divided among themselves. In fact, they were divided into three factions, led by Ezekiel Bargetuny (the hardline supporters of 'ethnic cleansing'), Henry Kosgey (the defenders of the *status quo*), and Mark arap Too (the reformers). Henry Kosgey had emerged after 1979 as the most important politician from the District and had served with reasonable competence in various Cabinet positions. Kosgey, however, had become too powerful to be trusted by Nicholas Biwott, who feared challengers from within the Kalenjin community for power behind the throne. Nominated MP Ezekiel Bargetuny, a prominent lay member of the AIC, waited in the wings to take over as chairman of the local KANU branch as Biwott's main local ally. The powerful Cabinet Minister's authority was also challenged by businessman Mark arap Too, the Managing Director of Lonrho (Kenya) who managed to secure election to the post in 1988. Arap Too, however, was unpopular among followers of the AIC, who complained that he was a Tugen and not really a Nandi.

Biwott, moreover, seemed to fear the moderate arap Too even more than Bishop Muge or Henry Kosgey, despite the fact that he had never stood for Parliament, perhaps because he was widely believed to be President Moi's illegitimate son.[72]

Biwott had managed to remove arap Too from the Nandi KANU chairmanship early in 1990, only to see him replaced by Kosgey. The ex-Minister was believed to be in a strong financial position to assert control of Nandi politics, having spent two years in the political wilderness allegedly 'milking' the Kenya National Assurance Company, of which he had become executive chairman after 'losing' the 1988 election. The advent of multi-party politics and President Moi's promise that KANU would hold grassroots elections wherever there was discontent with officials of the party branch, coupled with the 'ethnic cleansing' campaign launched by Bargetuny on neighbouring Uasin Gishu and Central Nyanza, had aroused grave concern in Nandi, which Kosgey seemed unable to control. KANU Youth members owed allegiance to Biwott and his local backers rather than to the more cautious Kosgey, who had disassociated himself from the campaign, attempting to promote discussions between Nandi and Luo MPs from the affected areas. As the violence mounted, arap Too and his supporters became increasingly critical of the branch leadership. KANU members in Kosgey's Tinderet political base even complained in mid-February 1992 that arap Too was holding night meetings and attempting to undermine the authority of the party leadership in Nandi. Arap Too's supporters responded by claiming in the new political idiom that Kosgey and his associates were not 'transparent' and alleged that they were 'panicking' about the political situation.[73]

Arap Too had become increasingly critical as the ethnic violence gathered momentum. He had been one of the few Kalenjin politicians to welcome Biwott's dismissal from the government in November, and in December 1991 he had begun to speak out against the clashes in the Rift Valley and along the Nandi-Kakamega border. Although he argued that the violence had been exaggerated by the press and claimed that the Nandi community were not responsible, he had nevertheless complained that local party leaders had not done as much as they ought to reconcile the feuding groups and to moderate Nandi youths. President Moi, on a visit to the area in January, had praised arap Too, suggesting that he might have a prominent role to play in ending the violence as he knew the area well. James Onamu, the MP for Hamisi, a Luo constituency which borders Nandi District and which had been disrupted by the ethnic violence, shortly afterwards visited arap Too's office in Nairobi to announce that he was returning to KANU, seeing arap Too as a mediator between Kalenjin and Luo interests.

The former KANU chairman also maintained good relations with the CPK in the District and had been the only senior KANU leader in the District to attend Bishop Muge's funeral in August 1990. Before his sacking, he had also criticised the District Administration and the County Council for mismanagement and corruption, selling government vehicles to local civil servants for only Sh10,000. If Biwott was busy stirring up Kalenjin chauvinists to drive out Kikuyu, Abaluhya, Luo and Gusii residents from the Uasin Gishu and the ethnic borderlands, and Kosgey was merely intent upon retaining control of Nandi KANU branch and securing election to Parliament, arap Too was the one KANU leader from Nandi District who appeared to understand the problems that 'ethnic cleansing' had created in Nyanza and Western Provinces among the Gusii, Abaluhya and Luo. He also seemed to be the only senior figure trusted by alienated elements within the District and able to keep CPK adherents loyal to the ruling party. The only questions were: could the ethnic violence be stopped before it drove the Abaluhya and Gusii into the arms of the opposition, and would Biwott and Kosgey allow arap Too to re-emerge as a key political figure?[74] With such problems in his own backyard, President Moi was frequently distracted during March, April and May 1992 from KANU's wider problems, neglecting the national campaign to rebuild the party's national image.

KANU also faced difficulties in West Pokot. In early April, clashes erupted along the Pokot-Elgeyo Marakwet border. Two decades of political instability in neighbouring Uganda, especially in Karamoja along Kenya's western frontier, meant that well-armed bandits could easily infiltrate across the border. As cattle raiding escalated, gangs in Pokot acquired increasingly sophisticated weapons. Local political boss Francis Lotodo had equipped his own well-armed private army. The three Pokot MPs, who had been backed by Biwott in 1988, came under growing pressure from Lotodo and his allies, who threatened to abandon KANU for the DP, shattering Kalenjin unity. President Moi, however, managed to bring Lotodo back in line with various promises, sacrificing the three incumbents. With little to lose, Christopher Lomada, Peter Nang'ole and Emmanuel Lotim attempted to defend their position by denouncing Lotodo and his secret forces. President Moi could not afford to ignore these factional conflicts that threatened his ability to maximise the Kalenjin vote for KANU.[75]

The Politics of the 'Swing' Communities

It was apparent that the main battleground of the election would be in the three ethnic 'swing communities' of the Gusii, Kamba and Abaluhya. KANU's prospects in these three areas, which covered nine Districts (Kisii, Nyamira, Machakos, Kitui, Makueni, Bungoma, Kakamega, Vihiga and Busia) was far from hopeless, in contrast with the situation in the Kikuyu and Luo regions, the heartlands of the DP and FORD. It was vital that KANU reform itself and select its most effective standard bearers. KANU's leading Luhya figure, Minister of Agriculture Elijah Mwangale, for example, seemed likely to face stiff opposition within his local party organisation. His authoritarian behaviour and failure to bring major development schemes had alienated many Abaluhya voters, especially in the two northern Districts of Western Province, Bungoma and Kakamega. KANU's ranks in Bungoma were deeply divided and morale was low. Mwangale's enemies believed that they could take advantage of the new political climate to challenge his authority, manipulating fears among the President's inner circle that the outspoken Minister was scheming to become Vice-President or even to replace Moi as KANU's Presidential candidate.[76]

It was clear that FORD's veteran leaders, Masinde Muliro (Bungoma) and Martin Shikuku (Kakamega) would pose a serious challenge to the ruling party in the their Districts and in neighbouring Trans-Nzoia and the Uasin Gishu, where many Abaluhya had settled. With 20 Parliamentary seats – 26 including the two Rift Valley Districts – KANU could not hope to retain power nationally if it did badly among Abaluhya voters in western Kenya.

A further 25 seats were competitive: 15 in Ukambani and two in the Gusii-populated Districts of Kisii and Nyamira. Between them, Gusii, Kamba and Abaluhya voters would return between 45 and 50 MPs, about a quarter of the National Assembly. These three communities were the key battleground of multi-party politics. KANU's leaders realised in March and April that they could not afford to lose these seats. Unfortunately, the escalating ethnic clashes endangered the ruling party's prospects among the Gusii and Abaluhya. This was an unacceptable price to pay for greater Kalenjin solidarity. Even worse, the KANU apparatus in all three regions was moribund. Local KANU leaders were discredited, autocratic and unpopular. It was clear that more attractive standard bearers were required to infuse life into KANU's grassroots organisation. New spokesmen, untainted by the excesses of the 'mature Moi state' dictatorship over the last seven years, would be needed to mount an effective campaign against the opposition parties, and to minimise the potentially catastrophic electoral consequences of the ethnic clashes. Let us now examine in some detail the struggle for grassroots renewal in these three vital regions: Gusii, Ukamboni, Bungoma and in the Kikuyu Districts of Kirinyaga and Laikipia where KANU attempted to revitalise its leadership and improve its image before the general election.

Politics in Gusii

At the beginning of the year KANU's position in the two Gusii Districts – Kisii and Nyamira – had appeared to be strong, with the distinct possibility that the party would win all ten Parliamentary seats. Only two figures appeared to threaten this unity: Simeon Nyachae, the former Chief Secretary and Head of the Civil Service, and George Anyona, the former MP for Kitutu East, who had been gaoled for sedition. When local leaders assembled at the Gusii Institute of Technology at the end of January, Nyachae's absence had appeared ominous. The retired civil service chief had a considerable following in Gusiiland. Nyachae had been blocked by his opponents in the branch, led by Minister of Planning and National Development Dr Zachary Onyonka, from contesting the 1988 election in his home constituency of Nyaribari Chache.

Their rivalry went back a long way. Five years earlier, when Nyachae had been the all-powerful Head of the Civil Service, controlling the Provincial Administration from the Office of the President, Onyonka had endured a rough election and then been dropped from the Cabinet. Held in custody for six months for shooting one of his opponent's supporters, Onyonka's political career had been in serious trouble throughout Nyachae's period of power. He was reported to hold the former Chief Secretary responsible for his political and legal troubles, and complained that

Nyachae had made no effort to secure his release or even better treatment.

When the Chief Secretary retired in December 1986, Onyonka had quickly re-emerged as the political boss of Gusii. In 1987, he had re-entered the Cabinet as Minister for Foreign Affairs and had quickly secured the support of most Gusii MPs against Nyachae, who was rumoured to be recruiting a slate of candidates to challenge a number of incumbent MPs. By 1988, when Nyachae's bid for Parliament was blocked, Onyonka had even established a good working relationship with Nyachae's former ally, branch chairman Lawrence Sagini, whom Onyonka had defeated in the 1969 general election in Kitutu West. After more than two decades at the top of the political ladder, Onyonka had become a shrewd political operator who was known to deliver rewards to his clients. Other Gusii leaders had been much less effective at bringing development projects to the two Districts. As Onyonka's career revived, Nyachae fell from grace. His critics had been waiting for his retirement: now they moved against him.[77]

The son of Senior Chief Musa Nyandusi, a prominent figure in the colonial history of Kisii who had held office for 44 years, Simeon Nyachae had entered the colonial civil service on his return from a government scholarship at Torquay College and Exeter University in 1958. The young Nyachae soon left government service to work as a labour and welfare officer for the East African Breweries. After 30 months, he returned to the civil service, taking up appointment as a District Officer in Kangundo in Machakos District. With the Africanisation of the Field Administration as independence approached, Nyachae rose rapidly and in December 1964 became District Commissioner in Nairobi. His next appointment was as Provincial Commissioner in Rift Valley Province, and in 1971 he was transferred to Central Province where he remained for the next eight years. In 1979, President Moi promoted him to the position of Permanent Secretary in the Office of the President with responsibility for coordinating development and organising information for the Cabinet. In July 1984, consequently, Nyachae had been the logical successor to Jeremiah Kiereini as Chief Secretary and Head of the Civil Service.[78]

During his 30 months as Chief Secretary, Nyachae had been an influential figure in government and had frequently clashed with Biwott and Oyugi, who resented his power. His position empowered him to 'exercise supervision [over] the office of the president and general supervision and co-ordination of all departments of government'. Some of Nyachae's critics alleged that the civil servant had become even more powerful than his political masters. When the post was abolished in 1986 Peter Oloo-Aringo charged that Nyachae as Chief Secretary had attempted to 'usurp the powers of the presidency by creating an alternative centre of power'.[79]

Following the triumph of the campaign for multi-party politics, both Kibaki's DP and FORD had approached the former civil service chief. Both parties hoped that he might be recruited. Nyachae's son Charles was a prominent human rights activist, serving as the current chairman of the Kenya Chapter of the International Commission of Jurists. Many of Charles Nyachae's legal associates were playing a prominent role in FORD and it was thought that his father might be tempted to join the opposition. When the former Chief Secretary failed to appear at the meeting at the Gusii

Institute of Technology, speculation mounted that he was about to defect.[80]

On 8 February, however, Nyachae announced that despite his differences with the two Gusii Cabinet Ministers, Dr Zachary Onyonka and Professor Sam Ongeri, he was going to remain loyal to KANU. Early the next week, he bought advertising space in the *Standard,* the *Daily Nation* and the *Weekly Review* to publicise his decision. The full-page advertisements, which appeared under the headline 'Multi-Party Politics', declared:

> There have been numerous appraches from friends and members of the Gusii community regarding my stand in the current multi-party politics. I would like it to be known that I am still a life member of KANU, having been issued with two life membership certificates – one by the late President, H.E. the Hon. Mzee Jomo Kenyatta and another by our current President, H.E. the Hon. D.T. Moi.
>
> So far, I am not convinced in my own mind that there are any strong reasons for me to change this position....[81]

Nyachae outlined five reasons why he had decided to remain in the ruling party. He explained that it would be naïve to abandon KANU, which had more than five million members, 'just because a few KANU officials, (who obviously don't exceed twelve individuals), have not conducted the affairs of the party and the management of the nation in a credible manner'. These people should be disciplined and voted out of office. Such 'arrogance and dictatorship' could be eliminated easily. KANU as a whole was not to blame for the excesses of a few individuals. He could not bring himself 'to leave an institution which played such a major role in securing our independence on the grounds that a few enemies and those who were in authority after my retirement misused their positions in harassing and humiliating me'. Political leaders should separate their personal problems from their personal ones. Moreover, Nyachae observed:

> I do not believe that the best way of dealing with our current political and economic-social problems is by running away from KANU and forming a contingent of a 'fighting' force from across another camp instead of battling within.
>
> I do not believe that joining any other party would automatically mean getting answers to the numerous problems facing us in the country. There is no party with immediate answers to these problems. In any case, I have all along been convinced that KANU and the government have developed sound policies for our country, but we have often gone wrong at the stage of interpreting and implementing these policies.[82]

Generalised allegations, Nyachae argued, would serve little purpose. Those who had abused their authority could be punished only on the basis of specific allegations and proof. 'It is quite clear to some of us', he observed, 'that there is always room for improvement in managing our national affairs. However, such improvement cannot come about through exercising revenge, vengeance or forming an opposition.'[83] The former Chief Secretary nevertheless acknowledged that the repeal of section 2 (a) of the constitution, leading to the formation of other political parties, had been 'a mature way of managing our national affairs'. The Kenyan government, like other executives, required 'a very strong system of checks and balances'.[84]

In deciding to remain in KANU, Nyachae claimed that he had considered carefully the 'well-being of the Abagusii' who were now living in many parts of Kenya. Not only was KANU the best means to ensure that the Gusii community did not antagonise other Kenyans, but it was also the best course to prevent divisions among Gusii leaders which would impair their ability to serve the people. 'We need unity', Nyachae warned, 'because we must jointly tackle the nightmare of unemployment among the Kisii young people; we must jointly deal with [the] current weak economy in our two districts. In other words, it is absolutely necessary that we maintain unity.'[85] Nyachae attempted to address the issue of the ethnic clashes head-on. Only through unity could the community assist Gusii university and school leavers to find jobs and help those members of the community who had been attacked recently in neighbouring Narok, Kericho, Nandi and Kitale and needed help in rebuilding their homes and businesses.

Finally, Nyachae noted, 'through political unity among the Abagusii, we should be able to deal with the problem connected with the imprisonment of Anyona, whose case is a definite political factor in the current Abagusii politics'. As a result of these considerations, Nyachae concluded, 'I wish, therefore, to repeat and emphasise that I have given these matters of multi-party politics serious consideration, and I have definitely not found a convincing reason as to why I should not remain in the same party where I have belonged since 1963.'[86]

Some journalists, nevertheless, suspected that Nyachae remained determined to purge officials of the Kisii KANU branch, including Cabinet Ministers Onyonka and Ongeri, and branch chairman Lawrence Sagini. The retired Chief Secretary had long believed that Gusii leaders had sold out to Biwott and his other rivals. From his retirement in 1986 until Biwott and Oyugi had been forced out of the government in November 1991, Nyachae's Sansora company had encountered a series of administrative and financial troubles. His relations with KANU branch officers remained extremely strained and on many issues, such as Anyona's release, Nyachae clearly wished to disassociate himself from the Kisii KANU establishment.

While KANU headquarters expected Nyachae to play an active role in the campaign, many of his supporters expected him to end the ethnic violence and to bring development schemes and other rewards to the two Districts. With ten seats at stake – seven in Kisii and three in Nyamira – KANU could not afford to neglect its one stronghold in Nyanza Province. Swing communities such as the Gusii, Abaluhya and Kamba became of prime importance. If Nyachae and his former rival Dr Onyonka could hold most of the Gusii seats for KANU, then the ruling party stood an excellent chance of winning the election; but if FORD made a strong showing in the area, KANU was heading for defeat. The contest in Kisii and Nyamira would be one of the key battles. Nyachae's decision to remain with KANU immeasurably strengthened the party's chances of victory at the national level.

Politics in Ukambani

The contest was going less well for the government in the other key swing communities – the Kamba and the Abaluhya. FORD had made major inroads among Kamba voters, especially in Kitui, although Major-General Mulinge, the former Army Chief of Staff, had announced that he would be a candidate for the KANU nomination in Kathiani. As yet, Johnstone Makau's Social Democratic Party had not had much impact on KANU's position in Makueni District. The governing party, consequently, seemed to be coming out on top in the battle with FORD for support in Ukambani.

The three Ukambani Districts – Machakos, Kitui and Makueni – were key swing areas with a total of 15 Parliamentary seats. All three parties hoped to do well. KANU retained considerable support in Kitui where Nyiva Mwendwa supported the ruling party, while her brother-in-law, who had been dropped from the Cabinet after the 1988 general election, had declared for the DP. The ruling party's appeal in Machakos, the most populous District, was bolstered by the announcement that former Army Commander Major-General Mulinge, 'the General', would be its candidate in Kathiani. Meanwhile, the General's former rival Paul Ngei, who had been the key figure in Machakos politics for nearly four decades until he had lost his seat in the Cabinet and in Parliament when he was declared bankrupt in December 1990, hesitated to abandon KANU for the DP until his legal difficulties were ended. Machakos was likely to prove one of the most closely contested Districts. All three major parties were well established, while Johnstone Makau, the leader of the SDP, came from neighbouring Makueni, which had been carved out of the south-eastern parts of Machakos.[87]

In both Machakos and Makueni, KANU leaders had been locked in bitter internal wrangling for several years. There had been three main factions, whose leaders were Paul Ngei, Mulu Mutisya and Johnstone Makau, the MP for Mbooni. But with the formation of FORD and the DP, the political picture had become even more complex. Members of both the Ngei and Makau factions had defected to the opposition, while others had remained loyal to KANU. In fact, comparatively few of the Mbooni MP's supporters had abandoned the ruling party when he formed the SDP. Both FORD and the DP had considerable support throughout Ukambani, however, as FORD's 22 January rally had revealed.

Relations between Ngei, Mutisya and Mulinge, the three most important figures in KANU, remained strained, and it seemed likely that those who lost out in struggles within the governing party might defect to the opposition. Ngei's loyalty was particularly suspect. In 1988, Major General Mulinge had challenged Ngei, who had been a Cabinet Minister for nearly a quarter of a century and Machakos's most prominent politician since the early 1950s, in his Kangundo bailiwick. The General, one of President Moi's most loyal supporters, had suppressed the attempted coup in August 1982, holding the army loyal despite anti-Moi sentiments among middle-ranking officers. Finally retiring in 1988, after 44 years in the Army and 15 years as Chief of the General Staff, Mulinge's loyalty was unquestionable. He had played a prominent role in development schemes in Kathiani, some of which had also benefited neighbouring Kangundo, where Ngei's development record was rather lacklustre. Leaders of the anti-Ngei faction had seen Mulinge as the ideal opponent to break the jaded Minister's domination of Machakos politics.

In 1988 nominated MP Mulu Mutisya, who had captured the KANU branch chairmanship from Ngei in 1985, had persuaded the General not to stand in his home constituency where the sitting MP, Laban Kitele, the Minister of Labour and KANU's National Organising Secretary, was a member of the Mutisya faction, but to challenge Ngei. The General had done extremely well. First reports from Kangundo indicated that he had secured more than 70 per cent of the vote in the KANU primary, apparently eliminating Ngei in the first round. The Minister, however, had petitioned the President and secured the right – the only case in the country – to a second ballot. The second time around, Ngei did substantially better, securing 6,240 votes compared to Mulinge's 10,758 and forcing the General to a secret ballot The greatest surprise, however, was still to come when the long-time political boss won the secret ballot, securing 15,562 votes to Mulinge's 13,271 in the most dramatic about-turn of the election. Wisely, General Mulinge had accepted his defeat and had been rewarded with the chairmanships of Kenya Railways and the Kenya Meat Commission, the latter an important position for the pastoralists of Ukambani.[88]

Important changes had taken place in the politics of Machakos and Makueni between 1988 and 1992, most notably the bankruptcy of Paul Ngei in November 1990 when he could no longer stave off his creditors, Kenya's two most important banks. The Kangundo politician's nine lives had finally been exhausted.[89] Many judged that he had survived so long not because of his own political skills but because his senior wife – the first of four – controlled the women's movement in Kangundo, protecting her husband's local power base through the female vote and because of residual respect for his grandfather, the formidable colonial Paramount Chief Masakau. In November 1990, however, the inevitable had finally happened: the banks' political and financial power had overridden Ngei's influence in the government and he had been declared bankrupt by the courts and compelled to resign from the Cabinet and to relinquish his seat in Parliament.[90]

The fortunes of Ngei's rivals, most notably Laban Kitele and Mulu Mutisya, had also declined. From 1985 to 1988, Kitele had been KANU's National Organising Secretary, as well as the Minister for Supplies and Marketing. He had barely managed to win the 1988 general election in Kathiani, however, against a strong challenger who came within 1,000 votes. Although Kitele had been reappointed to the Cabinet, becoming a Minister of State in the Office of the President, his political fortunes had soon begun to slip. In October 1988 he had been replaced as National Organising Secretary and as Eastern Province's representative in the party hierarchy by Kalonzo Musyoka, the MP for Kitui North and new Deputy Speaker of the National Assembly. Eight months later, Kitele had been dropped from the Cabinet and replaced by Johnstone Makau.

As Kitele's national political career began to fall apart, his local political opponents challenged him in Kathiani and demanded that he should be ousted as MP. These attacks gathered momentum in July 1990, with the riots after the detention of multi-party advocates Matiba and Rubia, when Kitele's name appeared on the list of reputed 'shadow Cabinet' members. Since then, the former Organising Secretary had attempted to keep out of the political limelight and to attract as little attention as possible. Now that

General Mulinge had turned his political attention to Kathiani, Kitele stood little chance of securing the KANU nomination against the constituency's most active and popular fund-raiser. With Ngei bankrupt, Kitele disgraced, and Branch KANU Chairman Mulu Mutisya in trouble, Mulinge had become the ruling party's effective leader and most important standard bearer in Machakos.

KANU's position in Machakos, the most populous of the three Kamba Districts, was far from hopeless. Neither FORD nor the DP had a local leader approaching Mulinge's stature or wealth. George Nthenge, one of FORD's six founding fathers recruited by Shikuku, had twice been MP for Machakos town in 1969–74 and in the early 1980s, but he was far from a front-rank politician. Moreover, although he was a powerful orator, he was a poor organiser. But KANU could not afford to be over-confident, especially in neighbouring Makueni and Kitui. Agnes Ndetei, a powerful and popular figure in Makueni District, recently carved out of the arid eastern fringes of Machakos, had long clashed with KANU boss Mutisya and, despite her election as Makueni District's first KANU branch chairman, seemed likely to defect to the DP in exasperation with the hostility of the Machakos KANU establishment. Mbooni MP Johnstone Makau had now launched his SDP but might still join either FORD or the DP, bolstering the opposition's prospects. Meanwhile, the Mwendwa family were fighting over control of Kitui as standard bearers of KANU (Nyiva, the widow of former Chief Justice and Kitui KANU chairman, Kitili Mwendwa) and the DP (her brother-in-law, former Cabinet Minister Kyale). Although Kyale Mwendwa had only stepped into the political limelight in 1985, following his brother's death in a car crash, as a former Cabinet Minister he might prove to be an effective advocate for Kibaki's party. Descendants of yet another powerful colonial chief, the three Mwendwa brothers – Eliud Ngala (a Cabinet Minister, 1963–74), Kitili (Chief Justice, 1967–71), and Kyale (long-serving Chief Educational Officer and then Cabinet Minister, 1986–8) – had dominated Kitui politics since independence and clearly, whatever the outcome of the election, a Mwendwa would remain the political boss of this most arid area. Gradually it became apparent that the DP was likely to be the main threat to KANU in all three Kamba Districts. The ruling party would have to field strong, energetic candidates if it was to fend off this challenge.[91]

Elijah Mwangale and the Politics of Western Province

Similar tensions existed in Western Province where the President's main Abaluhya allies, Elijah Mwangale and Moses Mudavadi, had their political bases. Conditions in Western Province deteriorated throughout April 1992, although most of the violence was concentrated in the Bukusu area in Bungoma District. Members of the Sabaot, a Kalenjin sub-group who lived on the slopes of Mount Elgon, clashed with local Bukusu residents. Well armed with AK-47 rifles which they had acquired from remnants of Obote's Ugandan army, gangs operating from the Mount Elgon forest attacked Bukusu settlements in the vicinity of Sirisia, 35 miles from Bungoma town.

By mid-April, 2,000 Bukusu had fled, 120 houses had been destroyed and the fleeing population's cattle seized. Bungoma MPs denounced the attacks, holding a press conference, to urge 'the two long-time friendly tribes – the Sabaot and Bukusu – to exercise restraint and particularly call upon the elders to intervene and restore peace'. Many Sabaot wished to secede from Bungoma, where they were heavily out-numbered by the Bukusu, and to establish an autonomous Mount Elgon District.[92]

Church leaders were again in the vanguard of the government's critics. The Rt Rev. Longinus Atundo, the Roman Catholic Bishop of Bungoma, denounced the security forces for complicity in the attacks and warned that a national disaster was imminent unless the tribal clashes ended.[93] Opposition leaders criticised the five Bungoma MPs for remaining silent despite the attacks on their constituents. Local FORD officials also criticised the District Commissioner and local police chief, and announced they would organise a demonstration against the security forces if the clashes did not end within a week. In response, Provincial Commissioner Francis Lekolool toured Kopsiro and Sirisia with senior police and GSU officers. Similar criticisms in Trans-Nzoia had ensured the recent removal of District Commissioner Francis Baya and Police Commander Kiplagat arap Soi. The government could not afford to ignore too-blatant inaction. Throughout May and June, the ethnic clashes rumbled on in Western Province along the border between the Bukusu of Bungoma District and the small Kalenjin Sabaot community who lived on the slopes of Mount Elgon, and along the Mau escarpment in Molo constituency where Kikuyu communities at places like Olenguruone were interspersed with Kalenjin and Maasai.[94] As the conflict along the ethnic frontier became increasingly serious during March–May 1992, discontent with the regime grew among Abaluhya deeper inside Western Province. The Abaluhya–Kalenjin violence represented a serious threat to Moi's Abaluhya allies, undermining support for KANU in this vital swing Province.

Elijah Mwangale, KANU Chairman in Bungoma District and Minister of Agriculture, had been one of the Moi regime's key figures throughout the 1980s. First elected to Parliament at the age of 30 in 1969, the back-bench Mwangale had soon earned a reputation as one of the most active and critical of MPs in the 1969–74 Parliament. In 1975 he had attracted national attention as chairman of the Parliamentary select committee into the disappearence and subsequent murder of J. M. Kariuki, the outspoken radical MP for Nyandarua North. Several other Abaluhya MPs had played an important role on the committee, including FORD Secretary General Martin Shikuku, who was to be detained a few months later, and Moi's Minister for Information and Broadcasting, Burudi Nabwera. Mwangale had been praised widely for his skilful handling of the select committee's confrontation with the government, although Shikuku had taken a much more combative line.[95]

Following the confrontation, during which FORD Vice-Chairman Masinde Muliro was dismissed from the Cabinet, Mwangale attempted to attract little controversy and began to rebuild his relations with members of the government. In December 1976 he had been elected chairman of Bungoma KANU branch, and had come second to then Minister for Power and Telecommunications Isaac Omolo Okero when he stood for the party's National Chairmanship in 1978, in large part because of his prominent role in the Kariuki committee. The following year, when the new President reconstructed his government after the 1979 general election, Mwangale entered the Cabinet as Minister of Labour. Abandoning his radical past, soon Mwangale had become an establishment figure and KANU boss in Bungoma, if not the most important political figure in Western Province.

Well known as a political heavyweight in the inner circles of both government and party, Mwangale throughout the 1980s was one of KANU's most hardline leaders. It had been Mwangale's then ally, Lawrence Sifuna, who had led the attack on 'a powerful politician who was being groomed by a foreign power to become President' in 1983, while Mwangale himself had been the first to identify the 'traitor' as Minister for Constitutional and Home Affairs Charles Njonjo . The next day, Njonjo had been dismissed from the Cabinet and a judicial Commission of Enquiry appointed to investigate his influence. Joseph Kamotho, the Secretary-General, might be more outspoken, but his control over Murang'a District had always been in doubt.[96]

For more than a decade, Mwangale had formed one of a triumvirate with Moses Mudavadi, KANU chairman in Kakamega, and the much less influential Peter Okondo in Busia District. When Mudavadi died and Okondo was forced to resign from the government in August 1990, Mwangale's stature had appeared even greater. Outspoken, even boorish, he tolerated little opposition in Bungoma or, indeed, from backbench MPs. He was a man of inordinate ambition. Ever since Njonjo had fallen from power, Mwangale had ambitions of becoming Vice-President or even President. Before the KANU party elections in mid-1985, he had been denounced by Vice-President Kibaki as a 'political tourist' for making secret trips to Nyeri and Kirinyaga to consult with Kibaki's local opponents, led by Waruru Kanja and James Njiru. For nearly a decade, he had complained that the Abaluhya, Kenya's second most numerous ethnic group, had never 'possessed' the Presidency or the Vice-Presidency. The introduction of multi-party democracy and the more open political climate that resulted, however, emboldened Mwangale's political opponents within the Bungoma KANU branch to challenge his power. Since early December 1991 Mwangale had maintained a low political profile, appearing in newspapers much less frequently than in the past. He appeared to have recognised that his hardline political style was ill-suited to the new political climate. He had been extremely active in Western Province, however, especially in his Bungoma bailiwick. Along with Burudi Nabwera, his Cabinet colleague, who was the MP for Lugari in neighbouring Kakamega District, Mwangale had toured Western Province, rousing support for the government. The two Ministers planned to hold a series of rallies in order to counteract FORD, the first of which took place in Bungoma town on Friday, 21 February.[97]

The Bungoma rally brought the crisis within KANU to a head. The meeting had not been a success. It had been marred by violence between KANU and FORD supporters, and had been attended by only ten of Western Province's 22 MPs. As the *Weekly Review* subsequently observed, 'The boycott of the rally by half the province's MPs was one of the first signals to Mwangale.' The journal speculated that 'the absent MPs were merely reacting to a perceived reality that Mwangale was already on shaky ground'. Certainly, the poor turn-out from the Province's politicians encouraged Mwangale's local rivals to make their move.[98]

Ever since Njonjo's fall from power, Mwangale had schemed to become Vice-President or even President. At the rally, Mwangale had urged the Abaluhya to unite behind KANU in order to maximise their political influence as Kenya's second largest ethnic group, rather than turn to FORD where their influence would be ignored by feuding Kikuyu and Luo politicians. Returning to his favourite theme – the failure of the Abalauhya to capture either Presidency or Vice-Presidency – he pointed out that there had been a Kikuyu (Kenyatta) and a Kalenjin (Moi) President, and two Kikuyu Vice-Presidents (Mwai Kibaki and Josephat Karanja), two Maasai (Joseph Murumbi and George Saitoti), one Luo (Oginga Odinga) and a Kalenjin (Daniel arap Moi). The time had come, he hinted, when the number two position in the government should be held by the Abaluhya. As the most important politician from Western Province, his inference was obvious: Elijah Mwangale should be Kenya's next Vice-President.

His opponents believed that they could twist this statement into a challenge to President Moi. Certainly, his remarks appeared to confirm that the Minister wanted to become Vice-President. Mwangale's critics informed the media that his words were 'directed to KANU as much as to FORD, and that he was indirectly telling President Moi to consider a Luhya for the KANU Vice-Presidency if he wanted to win Luhya support'. They noted that Mwangale had suggested that the Presidency ought to rotate between Kenya's main ethnic communities, perhaps even implying that President Moi, after three terms in office, should make way for the Abaluhya leader – Mwangale. The Minister's local rivals recognised that this suggestion would arouse the concern of the Kalenjin coterie around the President. Assistant Minister for Tourism and Wildlife Moody Awori, a senior Luhya MP, consequently, had rushed to criticise Mwangale, warning him to curb his 'unbridled ambition to be the first Luhya President'.[99]

On Monday, 24 February 1992 Mwangale was back in the headlines. The previous day eight Bungoma politicians – led by Assistant Minister for Foreign Affairs Joseph Muliro, the MP for Kanduyi Maurice Makhanu and former football administrator Alfred Sambu – called upon Mwangale to resign as District KANU chairman. They announced that if he refused to go quietly, they would petition President Moi to dissolve the branch and to call new elections, as had been done recently in Kirinyaga where another KANU hawk, James Njiru, was in political trouble. Mwangale summoned a press conference in Nairobi to reject their demands. Using tried and tested tactics, he even alleged that his enemies were plotting to assassinate him. His opponents gathered at Bungoma Town Hall on Tuesday, however, and announced that he had indeed been replaced as KANU chairman by Alfred Sambu. The coup appeared to have succeeded. Joseph Muliro, Maurice Makhanu, Alfred Sambu and the other plotters explained that they had deposed Mwangale because his arrogance and corruption had made him a political liability, incapable of maximising the KANU vote. His identification with KANU, they argued, 'had caused many people in the District to defect to FORD'. Makhanu was particularly outspoken, suggesting that 'KANU's image has been seriously tarnished by dictatorial party stalwarts such as Mwangale who are responsible for the problems that the nation is facing today'.[100]

Makhanu had managed to defeat former KANU Chief Whip Lawrence Sifuna, Mwangale's ally, by a narrow margin in Kanduyi in 1988; Sambu had lost the neighbouring Webuye seat by 314 votes out of 24,362 cast at the election; Assistant Minister for Foreign Affairs Muliro was also MP for Sirisia. Among Mwangale's leading opponents a key figure was Wilberforce Kisiero, Assistant Minister for Livestock Development, who was MP for the Sabaot-Kalenjin Mount Elgon constituency and KANU branch secretary. As branch secretary, it was Kisiero who had convened the meeting on Monday, 24 February, to oust Mwangale.

Mwangale had opposed the elections of Makhanu, Muliro and Sambu in 1988, and had excluded them from positions in the party hierarchy. Although Makhanu and Muliro had managed to scrape into Parliament, they knew that the Minister had supported the incumbents, Lawrence Sifuna and Peter Kisuya, and the victorious Joash wa Mang'oli in Webuye over Sambu. Sambu had brought an election petition against wa Mang'oli and protested about election rigging by the Provincial Administration and interference by Mwangale. The three politicians had teamed up to challenge the powerful Minister in the ensuing KANU elections in October 1988. Joseph Muliro had stood against Mwangale for the chairmanship, while Makhanu contested the post of vice-chairman. Mwangale's faction had swept to victory, of course, with the Minister securing 331 out of the 500 delegates' votes. In a dramatic reversal of the recent general election result, Mwangale's allies Sifuna and Kisuya had been elected to the posts of branch treasurer and assistant secretary. Kiserio, then an ally of Mwangale's, had become branch secretary.

Muliro and Makhanu had not been silenced, however. Although they had lost at the District level, both had managed to retain control of their own constituency sub-branches in Sirisia and Kanduyi. On several occasions during the next three years they used their power at sub-branch level to embarrass Mwangale, repudiating decisions taken by the Bungoma branch. Relations between Makhanu and Mwangale were particularly bad as Makhanu demanded that the branch chairman should consult him before holding any branch meetings at party headquarters in Bungoma town, which was in Makhanu's Kanduyi constituency. Mwangale refused, however, even presiding at several *Harambee* fund-raising meetings in Kanduyi without informing Makhanu.[101]

Makhanu had carried his attacks into the chamber of the National Assembly, where he seized every opportunity to embarrass Mwangale, asking a series of questions about development problems in Bungoma, especially about the lack of progress on the Kibabii Teachers' Training College and the Nzoia Sugar Company. In 1989 Makhanu had led the attack on Mwangale for his business relationship with disgraced Vice-President Karanja, demanding that Mwangale resign from the Cabinet and as Bungoma branch chairman. Mwangale had been able to secure the support of the branch, however, securing a resolution of support that required Makhanu to write an apology for his attacks. Makhanu, backed by Muliro, had nevertheless resumed his attacks on Mwangale.

Sambu's conflict with the powerful Minister stemmed from the fact that both came from the former Bungoma East constituency, before it had been divided by the last Boundary Commission into Kimilili and Webuye. Mwangale, fearful of Sambu's popularity as chairman of AFC Leopards, the prestigious Abaluhya football team, had sought to block Sambu's political hopes. Sambu also held Mwangale responsible for his difficulties at the football club before the 1988 election, claiming that Mwangale had instigated his banning from football administration in 1987 for allegedly attempting to 'fix' an important game in order 'to weaken his image before the 1988 general election'. By 1991, AFC Leopards had become the scene of political infighting, which forced Sambu's resignation as club chairman when Mwangale's ally, Mafula wa Musamia, was elected club secretary. It was widely rumoured that Mwangale wanted to become patron of the club, following the death of Kakamega KANU chairman Moses Mudavadi, who had held the post.[102]

Branch secretary Wilberforce Kiserio, who played such a key role in the attempt to oust Mwangale, by contrast, had always been a close ally of the Minister. Indeed, he owed his position as KANU branch secretary to the victory of the Mwangale-led slate in October 1988. The recent outbreaks of violence between the Sabaot and Bukusu sub-tribes, however, had divided the two men. Both Mwangale's Kimilili and Kisiero's Mount Elgon constituencies had been hit by the wave of violence. Mwangale had condemned Sabaot raids into Bukusu territory, while Kisiero claimed that the Minister's anti-Sabaot remarks had exacerbated the troubles. Mwangale's speeches, he protested, had spread confusion and hatred between the two communities. As a result, Kisiero switched sides in the power struggle, leaving Mwangale isolated, supported only by wa Mang'oli, the MP for Webuye, Sambu's opponent.

The Minister's position was made even worse by the fact that one of his key backers, former branch treasurer and one-time MP for Kanduyi, Lawrence Sifuna, had defected to FORD and his main ally in Sirisia, Peter Kisuya, the former MP and branch assistant secretary, had been almost completely eclipsed by Joseph Muliro's energetic promotion of development schemes and self-help projects. Furthermore, as the *Weekly Review* observed, 'the advent of multi-party politics appears further to have eroded part of Mwangale's base and opened cracks in his support in KANU that his opponents promptly capitalised on'.[103]

The dissident faction apparently decided to act after the poor turn-out for Mwangale's rally at Bungoma town on Friday, 21 February. Only eleven MPs from Western Province, including Muliro and Makhanu, had bothered to attend. The next day, the two MPs joined Sambu for a *Harambee* meeting in Sirisia, where Joseph Muliro announced that he had brought a gift of 100,000 shillings from the President to pay fees for school and university students in the area. The three anti-Mwangale politicians had then demanded that the Minister resign as branch chairman, otherwise they would petition President Moi to hold new elections, as had happened in Kirinyaga.

On Tuesday, 25 February, however, President Moi moved to protect his old ally, announcing at a rally in nearby Kitale that Mwangale's ousting was illegal since the officials had failed to consult KANU headquarters in Nairobi. The President appeared to have been irritated by the fact that Sambu had announced that the new Bungoma KANU leadership would seek to bring Masinde Muliro, FORD's interim Vice-Chairman, back to the party. Masinde Muliro had announced that he would contest Kimilili, his birthplace, directly challenging Mwangale, who had represented the constituency for the last 23 years. The President demanded to know, 'Who sent them to look for Muliro?' Moi was reluctant to abandon his long-time ally and to admit that Mwangale was a spent force.[104]

Political commentators attributed the growth of opposition to the Minister to the new, more open political climate. Those who had resented his behaviour now felt free to speak out. Such attacks had encouraged the anti-Mwangale faction in Bungoma to prepare their coup. Mwangale's recent speeches, they believed, had damaged his influence at party headquarters and alienated key officials and other Ministers, including perhaps President Moi. For the first time in more than a decade – apart from the brief moment in 1989 when his business partner Karanja was dismissed as Vice-President – Mwangale seemed vulnerable. The dissidents attempted to convince headquarters that the Minister was undermining KANU's chances of holding Western Province's vital 22 seats. Headquarters and President Moi, however, decided that Mwangale's continued leadership of the ruling party in Bungoma and Western Province was likely to produce more MPs than the untested leadership of Sambu. However unpopular Mwangale might have become in certain quarters, it was unwise to disrupt the local power structure with Muliro and Shikuku leading FORD's challenge in the region. They were to change their minds later in the year.

The attempt to oust Mwangale did not bode well for KANU in Bungoma. It appeared possible against the background of continuing ethnic clashes in Trans-Nzoia that a number of prominent KANU officials might defect to FORD. It also seemed clear that if Mwangale lost the support of the locally dominant Bukusu community his days were numbered. Support for KANU was more stable in Vihiga and Kakamega Districts, despite Martin Shikuku's popularity in Butere. The young Musalia Mudavadi, who had succeeded his father as MP for Sabatia, and his fellow Cabinet Ministers Burudi Nabwera and Bahati Semo were much more popular than Mwangale. Even in Busia District, where the party hierarchy had been disrupted by the downfall of former Minister Peter Okondo, KANU's support appeared to be holding firm.

Relations between KANU leaders in Bungoma did not improve during March, April and May. None of KANU's key local dissidents appeared at a rally in Bungoma town which had been organised in order to raise money for the District's 5,000 secondary school and university students. The Minister's supporters, nevertheless, were confident that they would win fresh party elections, and were reported to favour the holding of new polls so that Mwangale could demonstrate the strength of his support. As the press pointed out, Mwangale could 'take comfort ... from the fact that those who issued statements hailing his removal were either known supporters of his political opponents or his critics from outside the District, who might not make a big impact on the political equation in the District'.[105] The opposing faction, however, boasted that they had attracted supporters from unexpected quarters, including John Okwara, the MP for Butere in Kakamega District, who had benefited in 1988 from Martin Shikuku being rigged out of Parliament. Okwara urged KANU headquarters to ratify Mwangale's ousting. He had been irritated, the previous month, by Mwangale's suggestion before the President at a rally in Kimilili that the Butere seat should be kept open for FORD Secretary-General Shikuku in case he decided to return to KANU when the Kikuyu and Luo took complete control of the opposition.

Publicly, the Minister remained confident. When he appeared at a series of KANU rallies in the Rift Valley in the company of the President, it seemed that his local enemies had miscalculated. President Moi was unwilling to alienate his most formidable Abaluhya ally, even if he had dared to suggest that he might make a suitable Vice-Presidential running mate or even an alterantive President. Western Province and its 20 MPs – more than one fifth of the number needed by KANU to hold on to power – was too important to endanger.[106] Secretary-General Kamotho, consequently, insisted firmly that the attempt to oust Mwangale from the Bungoma chairmanship had been in contravention of KANU's rules. Unfortunately, this failed to address KANU's fundamental problems in Bungoma and Kakamega, leaving the party seriously exposed to the popularity of Masinde Muliro and Martin Shikuku with the Abaluhya masses.[107]

KANU's Divisions in Kirinyaga

Even in opposition strongholds, such as Kikuyuland, KANU was unwilling to abandon the fight. Party leaders were determined to salvage what they could from the forthcoming debacle. As a result, former hardliners who had unquestioningly defended the excesses of the Moi state in the late 1980s found themselves in difficulties and likely to be dropped. The pressure for reform grew as the year progressed and local critics pressed KANU headquarters to consider the political consequences of failing to abandon its old allies. James Njiru, another Cabinet Minister, came under attack in Kirinyaga District. Defeated at the 1983 general election, Njiru had returned to the National Assembly and had been appointed to the Cabinet. He had consolidated his position a few months later when he was elected branch chairman. For a brief period Njiru appeared to have become a powerful Minister, a member of the inner circle around President Moi and, along with the new Vice-President Josephat Karanja and Secretary-General Kamotho, one of the key figures in Central Province. His position as Minister of National Guidance and Political Affairs, a newly created post with rather Orwellian implications, enabled Njiru to intervene in political clashes with the National Council of Churches and the Law Society, who were opposing the introduction of queueing and the Constitutional amendment to reduce the security of tenure of High Court judges, the Attorney-General, and the Comptroller and Auditor-General.

Njiru had proved even more vitriolic and vindictive towards critics of the regime than Kamotho. The Rt Rev. David Gitari, the Anglican Bishop of Mount Kenya East, alleged that Njiru was attempting to murder him and had employed KANU youth-wingers to attack him and disrupt church events. The newspapers had headlined the Bishop's banning of the Minister from all church meetings.[108] Shortly afterwards, Njiru had been moved to a less contentious and less public Cabinet post where he could do little damage.[109]

In the three and a half years since the October 1988 KANU elections, opposition to the Minister had grown throughout Kirinyaga. At the 1988 general election Njiru had led a slate of candidates which had triumphed in the District's three constituencies. Njiru himself had been elected MP for Ndia, while his allies Kibugi Kathigi and Geoffrey Kariithi had won in Mwea and Gichugu, defeating a rival coalition led by Njiru's main local rival, Nahashon Njuno, who lost the Gichugu seat to Kariithi.[110] The three defeated MPs had complained that they had been 'rigged' out of Parliament by Njiru and the local Administration.

By the party elections in October 1988, Njiru's coalition was already beginning to fall apart as the Minister turned against former Head of the Civil Service Kariithi and patched up an alliance with long-time foe Njuno, who defeated Kariithi for the Gichugu sub-branch KANU chairmanship. Seven months later Kariithi had been dismissed from his position as an Assistant Minister when he was accused by the Kirinyaga KANU branch and Burudi Nabwera, then Minister of State in the Office of the President responsible for security affairs, with having met Ugandan diplomats and made secret trips to the neighbouring country. It soon emerged, however, that the security forces had confused another Kariithi, a Nairobi businessman who made frequent business trips to Kampala, with the former Chief Secretary, while the rumours had been encouraged by political enemies in his constituency, led by Njiru. The malevolent origin of the story, however, had not prevented Kariithi's expulsion from the government and public humiliation. It was hardly surprising that he was one of the first MPs to defect to FORD at the end of December 1991.[111]

Njiru's position had seemed secure until the raid on the home of Bishop Gitari. When the official report ordered into the affair by President Moi was not published, it was even more widely rumoured that Njiru, who had clashed frequently with the Bishop, had been implicated in the affray. The attack on the Bishop was only one of a series of violent political incidents in the District. Late in 1989 Njiru was abandoned by his ally, Kibugi Kathigi, the MP for Mwea, who teamed up with Kariithi when it appeared that the President's inner circle were about to dump Njiru as a political liability. The Minister survived, however, but early in 1990 President Moi visited Kirinyaga and attempted to reconcile the factions, shortly afterwards reappointing Kariithi to the government. The President had criticised politicians who told lies about their enemies, which many saw as a veiled reprimand for Njiru. Fighting between the rival factions nevertheless continued throughout 1990 and 1991, gradually sapping Njiru's local strength and his credibility with the President and KANU headquarters.[112]

When opposition parties were legalised, Njiru's enemies defected *en masse,* severely disrupting KANU's organisation throughout the District. Kariithi led the way, resigning as an Assistant Minister to join FORD. Other anti-Njiru politicians who joined the opposition included former MPs Matere Keriri, who had lost his Ndia seat to Njiru in 1988, and Simon Kanai of Mwea, and ex-District KANU branch vice-chairman Stephen Kiragu who had represented the former Kirinyaga South constituency between 1974 and 1979. Kiragu had once been a close ally of Njiru's. Further down the political ladder, the defections were even more numerous. The *Weekly Review* reported that 'Kirinyaga District has been hit hard by near wholesale defection of KANU officials to FORD or the Democratic Party at the lower levels, with most of the defectors attributing their moves to dissatisfaction with Njiru's domineering ways.'[113]

By early February 1992 the situation had become so bad that Njiru's opponents successfully lobbied KANU headquarters and the President to announce new elections for all offices in the Kirinyaga branch, from the grassroots to the branch leadership, including the position of branch chairman. Njiru seemed to be on the way out. Speculation focused on who would replaced him, with most observers backing his old rival, Njuno. The beleaguered Minister fought back, however, complaining that his opponents were planning to rig the polls. He alleged that the 1985 and 1988 polls had been rigged not on his instructions but by the District Administration on orders from above. Contrary to expectations, Njiru easily won the sub-location, location and sub-branch elections, being confirmed as sub-branch (constituency) KANU chairman, before emerging victorious in the District branch elections. His only declared opponent, Simon Njogu Kanai, failed to appear for the branch elections, having been defeated at the sub-branch level by the sitting MP for Mwea, Kibugi Kathigi, one of Njiru's main allies.

In December 1991 Kanai had defected briefly to FORD but had returned to the ruling party when President Moi announced that fresh branch elections would be held in Kirinyaga. If Kanai had been promised the branch chairmanship, his poor performance in his own Mwea sub-branch effectively eneded his hopes. Two other foes of Njiru, however, had remained with the opposition. As we have already noted, former Secretary to the Cabinet Geoffrey Kariithi, who had ousted Njuno in Gichugu in 1988, had resigned as an Assistant Minister at Christmas, shortly before defecting to FORD, where he was joined by Njiru's old foe in Ndia, Matere Keriri, who was appointed to the opposition party's Steering Committee. These defections had weakened the anti-Njiru forces, enabling the Minister to reassert control with comparatively little opposition.[114]

In the long term, the willingness of KANU headquarters to abandon so prominent a hardliner as James Njiru eroded the Kirinyaga boss's commitment to the party and may have proved a costly mistake, underming the morale of party leaders in other contested Districts. Ironically, faced by the prospect of defeat and loss of his position as Kirinyaga KANU chairman, Njiru had threatened to lead his supporters into either FORD or the DP – a promise which he was to fulfil in November when he lost the KANU nomination for Ndia. He was to contest the 29 December general election as FORD-Kenya's Parliamentary candidate, demonstrating all too clearly that principle counts for little in Kenya's faction-torn politics.

G. G. Returns from the Dead: Politics in Laikipia

The establishment of multi-party democracy sent KANU, as well as the opposition, scrambling for support wherever it could be found. During its time as Kenya's only political party, local KANU organisations in many Districts had been neglected under President Kenyatta, while President Moi's attempt – since the attempted *coup d'état* in 1982 and the downfall of Charles Njonjo in 1983 – to use the party as the main mechanism of political control and mobilisation had created its own set of problems. Now it was vital for KANU to find the strongest candidates to carry its message to the electorate. The fall-out from Njonjo's disgrace had affected several other powerful politicians, who had been allies of the influential Minister for Constitutional and Home Affairs. Kalenjin and Abaluhya leaders close to the President – most notably Nicholas Biwott and Elijah Mwangale – had used Njonjo's fall from power as an opportunity to stigmatise their own political opponents as associates of the former Minister.

One of the most conspicuous victims of Njonjo's political demise had been G. G. Kariuki, the influential Cabinet Minister and KANU chairman from Laikipia District. Geoffrey Gitahi Kariuki had been especially vulnerable for three reasons: first, he was, like Njonjo, a Kikuyu and therefore was distrusted by the Kalenjin and Abaluhya clique around President Moi; secondly, as Minister of State in the Office of the President in charge of internal security, Kariuki had worked very closely with Njonjo; thirdly, and probably most importantly, when he had been Minister of State, Kariuki had clashed with one of his colleagues, Nicholas Biwott.

The rivalry between 'G. G.' and Biwott had become so intense that in 1982 President Moi was forced to move them both out of the Office of the President: Kariuki had become Minister of Lands, Settlement and Physical Planning, while Biwott had been moved to the Ministry of Regional Development, Science and Technology.[115] Defeated for Parliament in 1983 by Joseph Mathenge, a small-holder who had dared to stand against him in 1979 despite the fact that President Moi had urged that Kariuki should be returned unopposed, the former Cabinet Minister was expelled from KANU the following year.[116]

Since September 1984, Kariuki had maintained a low profile, while seeking to demonstrate his continued support for the government. In February 1986, when President Moi was courting former Mau Mau fighters through his new alliance with Kariuki Chotara and Waruru Kanja, G. G. Kariuki had attended a rally of ex-Mau Mau at the Ruringu stadium outside Nyeri town and had even been permitted briefly to address the crowd. The press speculated that Kariuki might be attempting to work his way back by signalling his support for the President's new Kikuyu allies. If that was the case, he made little progress as President Moi curtly intervened, warning him to stick to private life. Kariuki's enemies were too insecure to permit his rehabilitation, yet, at the same time, too powerful to permit his return to political life. In 1987, Kariuki tried again, attempting to persuade KANU headquarters to permit his readmission to the party.[117] Once again, his rehabilitation was blocked and he was instructed to seek clearance from the Laikipia branch.

Kariuki's local rivals, who had benefited from his fall, were far from eager to see the former Minister return to politics and they procrastinated. As a result, Kariuki had not been readmitted to the party by the time of the 1988 general election, unlike Joseph Kamotho, another Kikuyu Cabinet Minister who had been defeated in the 1983 election and subsequently expelled from KANU as an ally of Njonjo's. Then, after the KANU election, in December 1988 President Moi announced that Kariuki should be readmitted. By remaining quiet, he had displayed his loyalty to KANU. The President announced that he would request KANU's National Governing Council to reinstate Kariuki. In fact, Kariuki was readmitted to the party at the meeting which expelled Kenneth Matiba and Kimani wa Nyoike. On his return, Kariuki issued a public statement, which declared that 'my coming back to the party fold as a member will always be geared towards the utilisation of my ability and skill to strengthen the mass movement – KANU'.

Leaders of the Laikipia branch had been far from eager to welcome Kariuki's rehabilitation. Joseph Mathenge, who had unseated him in 1983 – probably because the election was rigged by the Provincial Administration – was defeated in the first round of the 1988 election in Laikipia West. Another Kikuyu, Danson Ndumia, had taken his place, securing more than 70 per cent of the vote in the KANU primary according to the official result. Ndumia's colleague, Francis ole Kaparo, who had first been elected in 1988 as MP for Laikipia East, soon emerged as the more important political figure. Both MPs had been exceedingly lukewarm towards suggestions that changes should be made in the Laikipia party leadership to incorporate Kariuki. Ole Kaparo had declared that neither he nor his colleague had been elected on Kariuki's platform and warned that branch officials were 'not anybody's youth-wingers'. It was clear that Kariuki would face strong opposition from the incumbent MPs and District KANU leaders.[118]

Ndumia protested a few months later that Kariuki was attempting to undermine his position in Laikipia West and was building up a network of local councillors to challenge him for his position as District KANU chairman. Following these two incidents, Kariuki appeared to abandon any immediate attempt to recapture office and bided his time. The development of the campaign for multi-party democracy provided him with an ideal opportunity to demonstrate once more his loyalty to President Moi and KANU. Immediately after the detention of Matiba and Rubia in July 1990, Kariuki issued a statement decrying the need for opposition parties but warning that KANU should allow more freedom of debate within the party. As the pressure for political pluralism grew, Kariuki became more and more outspoken in defence of KANU and single-party rule. The ex-Minister contended that the cause of popular dissent was not single-party rule in itself, but rather the absence of adequate freedom within the party and sufficient checks on the executive by the legislature and judiciary.

These errors could be corrected without dismantling KANU's monopoly of power. Like President Moi, Kariuki warned that multi-party democracy would exacerbate ethnic divisions in the country.

Despite his support for the President's argument, local politicians denounced Kariuki for being a closet supporter of the multi-party movement. Joash wa Mang'oli, a close ally of Elijah Mwangale, even suggested that Kariuki had had a secret meeting with members of the multi-party movement at the Mount Kenya Safari Club in Nairobi. Following this spate of criticism, Kariuki became more rather than less outspoken. In November 1991 he prepared a lengthy statement of his views on the failings of African governments. Although he did not specifically refer to Kenya, Kariuki argued that personal rule by unpopular leaders had alienated the populace. They had then used force to hold on to power. The *Weekly Review* observed that

> hitting out at a culture that encouraged emperor worship, the singing of praise songs and the mandatory display of a leader's portrait even in private places, Kariuki argued for a system that instituted rational distribution of power, enforceable checks and balances, free and fair elections, limited presidential tenure and powers of amendment of constitutional provisions legalising the one-party system in order 'to allow for responsible diversity of political opinion'.[119]

It seemed as though Kariuki was moving towards endorsing the multi-party movement.

Yet when President Moi announced that opposition parties would be permitted to register, Kariuki endorsed the decision and reaffirmed his support for KANU. He called, however, for new grassroots party elections so that KANU could strengthen its position by removing unpopular leaders. The days of the Laikipia KANU leaders were clearly numbered. In the short term, however, ole Kaparo's position was also strengthened when following the defection of Kikuyu Ministers in the wake of Mwai Kibaki's Christmas Day resignation, he was appointed Minister for Industry, becoming the first Cabinet Minister from the District since Kariuki's downfall in 1983.

Ole Kaparo's time as the senior politician from Laikipia lasted less than two months, however, for in mid-February President Moi announced that fresh party elections would be held in the recently created Vihiga and Makueni Districts (which had been created from the over-large Kakamega and Machakos Districts), in strife-ridden Kirinyaga, and in Laikipia. The moment for G. G.'s return had finally come: KANU was in such desperate straits throughout Kikuyuland that it could not afford to spurn the support of an influential and charismatic Kikuyu politician who was willing to carry the party's banner not only in Laikipia – widely regarded as fairly safe KANU territory – but throughout Central Province and the Kikuyu areas of the Rift Valley.

Both sitting MPs were damaged by G.G.'s rehabilitation. Attempting to defend their positions, they had encouraged rumours in January that Kariuki was about to join the DP in order to block his take-over in Laikipia. Worst hit was Danson Ndumia, whose political career ended with Kariuki's return. Not only did the new party elections mean that he would lose his position as KANU branch chairman, which he had held since 1985, but he was almost certain to be replaced as KANU candidate in Laikipia West by Kariuki. Francis ole Kaparo might hold the Laikipia East nomination and his position as branch secretary, despite the fact that he had been a member of the 'stop Kariuki's rehabilitation' faction, but if Kariuki were elected to Parliament, ole Kaparo would stand little chance of keeping his position as Minister for Industry. A small District with only two MPs, Laikipia was unlikely to merit two Cabinet positions.

Kariuki's decision to support KANU was to have much wider repercussions. With the defection of Kibaki and Muhoho to establish the DP, and of Waruru Kanja and Maina Wanjigi to FORD, Kariuki immediately became, along with Joseph Kamotho and Njeroge Mungai, one of the three most important Kikuyu politicians to support KANU. Indeed, with his untarnished record and known opposition to Biwott and the Kalenjin circle around the President, Kariuki could claim to have defended the Kikuyu community's interests staunchly, at considerable cost to himself. Kikuyu voters were much more likely to listen to Kariuki's claim that KANU provided the best means to ensure Kenya's stability and continuing development, than to Kamotho, who had made so many enemies among the opposition that he had no option but to remain loyal to President Moi, or Njeroge Mungai, whose latest escapade had confirmed his reputation as a political opportunist. Thus, as soon as Kariuki decided to throw his lot in with KANU rather than joining Kibaki's DP, President Moi and KANU headquarters welcomed his decision and pushed the local party branch into holding grassroots elections so that they could exploit this new asset.

When the elections were finally held on 7–8 March 1992, Kariuki, as expected, emerged victorious, taking over as Laikipia KANU chairman after nine years in the political wilderness. The sitting MP for Laikipia West was pushed aside and decided not even to contest the sub-branch elections. Ndumia questioned KANU's motive for calling fresh elections and complained about the preferential treatment accorded the former Minister. It was, indeed, ironic that the same individuals around President Moi who had engineered Kariuki's downfall in 1983 were now responsible for organising his political comeback. By contrast, the MP for Laikipia East, Minister for Industry Francis ole Kaparo, the leading figure among the area's Samburu population, accepted the party's decision with grace – realising that he could no longer block Kariuki's political resurrection – and accepted the position of branch secretary. Kariuki clearly believed that KANU would triumph at the election and that he had a better chance of being elected for Laikipia West on the KANU ticket than the DP's. For their part, President Moi and KANU needed an effective champion among Kikuyu voters, who could defend the ruling party in Mwai Kibaki's Nyeri stronghold and in the areas of the Rift Valley which had been populated by Kikuyu small-holders since independence. As a former victim of the regime, who had been in the political wilderness since 1983, it was hoped that Kariuki would prove a powerful advocate for the ruling party and moderate the debacle that KANU seemed to be facing throughout Kikuyuland.[120]

Attorney-General Wako's Proposed Government Reorganisation

Although proposals to create the post of Prime Minister had been rejected in 1967, 1970, and again in 1980, the issue returned to the fore in 1992 and was considered by both KANU and the opposition. By the end of January, the government had recognised that it was necessary to reform the whole electoral procedure. Certain alterations, of course, were inevitable following the return to multi-party democracy. But others were carefully considered to benefit President Moi and KANU. Led by the DP Secretary-General, John Keen, the opposition parties were united in demanding that the President should be directly elected. The two opposition parties also condemned the idea that sitting KANU MPs should have the authority to change the electoral law and constitution, demanding the creation of a Constitutional Convention of representatives from all the parties and other interested bodies, such as the Churches and the Law Society, to consider new electoral regulations.

Many believed that direct Presidential elections would favour the DP's leader Mwai Kibaki, who because of his quarter of a century in office was expected to perform considerably better than his party. Rather surprisingly, the 1982 amendment to the constitution, which had made Kenya a *de jure* single-party state, had already paved the way for direct Presidential elections. In previous elections, the President had been elected by the National Assembly rather than by the voters. The 1964 republican constitution had provided for Presidential elections to be staged at the same time as those for Parliament, on a single ballot paper. MPs were returned to Parliament pledged to support their party's Presidential candidate. If the President died before the end of his term, then the National Assembly would become an electoral college to select the new head of state. The system ensured that the chief executive commanded a majority in the National Assembly and would be able to get his legislation approved. Subsequent constitutional changes in 1969 and 1970, the eighth and ninth amendments, stipulated new rules concerning Presidential succession and election. First, Presidential candidates must be at least 35 years old. Second, candidates must be supported by a registered political party and be proposed in writing by at least 1,000 registered voters. Third, if the President fell ill or died, the Vice-President would assume office for a period of 90 days, at the end of which new elections would have to be held. The ninth amendment also required registered political parties that participated in the Parliamentary elections to nominate a Presidential candidate and in theory introduced direct Presidential elections with separate polls for Parliament and President. By then, of course, Kenya had become a single-party state with the banning of the KPU in 1969, and no one ever opposed President Kenyatta or later President Moi as KANU's candidate. The President had been returned unopposed in 1974, 1979, 1983 and 1988.

The majority of voters and MPs believed that the President would continue to be selected by members of the National Assembly, as Moi had been following Kenyatta's death in 1978. But according to the constitution, if another candidate were nominated then direct elections would be held. Even when Kenya legally banned all opposition parties in 1982, rather than merely refusing them registration as had been the case for the previous 13 years, the provision for direct elections was maintained. Theoretically, it had always been possible for someone to stand against Moi as a rival KANU candidate, forcing the decision to the ballot box. With the resumption of political pluralism after more than 22 years of single-party KANU rule, Kenya was clearly set for its first direct Presidential contest, much to the alarm of President Moi and KANU.

As a result, the KANU government drafted new regulations without consulting the opposition. These were designed to prevent any opposition candidate winning the Presidency while KANU had a majority in the National Assembly.[121] The government, however, was forced to meet some of the opposition's demands, transferring control of the election to an independent Electoral Commission instead of the office of the Supervisor of Elections, which had functioned as part of the Attorney-General's chambers. Although the office of Supervisor of Elections was to be retained, it would now be subordinate to the independent Electoral Commission under a retired High Court judge, Mr Justice Zacchaeus Chesoni, whom opposition leaders claimed had been rescued from near-bankruptcy by Moi to perform this task. Chesoni's financial problems had been so severe that he had been compelled to resign from the Bench. Throughout his first six months in office as chairman of the Electoral Commission, he was to be extremely secretive, attempting to avoid all contact with the opposition parties. Such behaviour did little to build confidence in his neutrality.

On 3 March 1992 these issues came to a head when the Kenya *Government Gazette* published the text of a Bill, to be presented to Parliament the following week, which proposed direct elections for the Presidency, the abolition of the position of Vice-President, and the creation of the office of Prime Minister – although the President retained the right to appoint the Prime Minister, Deputy Prime Minister, Cabinet Ministers and Assistant Ministers, as well as Permanent Secretaries in the civil service. The Constitution of Kenya (Amendment) Bill, 1992 nevertheless drastically reduced the powers of the Presidency, transferring much of the day-to-day running of the government to the proposed Prime Minister. Future Presidents would be limited to two five-year periods in office and constitutional checks and balances would be bolstered to curtail the misuse of power.[122] Attorney-General Wako, whose chambers had devised the Bill, also proposed national referenda on matters of vital interest, greater independence for the Electoral Commission (extending its remit to cover local government elections) and the removal of the requirement that the President be selected from among MPs.

If the legislation had gone ahead, the President would have become a figurehead, no longer attending Cabinet meetings or playing a key role in the making of his government's decisions. He would have had the responsibility of devolving Parliament on the advice of the Prime Minister, however, and the ability to authorise national referenda. The proposed constitution also required the Prime Minister to 'keep the president fully informed concerning the general conduct of the government of Kenya and ... furnish him with such information as he may require with respect to any particular matter relating to the government of Kenya'.[123]

Opposition quickly grew, both within KANU and in opposition circles, once the proposed Bill began to be publicised. In many respects its strongest critics proved to be KANU MPs, who gave the Bill short shrift. They protested that Wako had conceded too much to the opposition. Barely a week after it had been approved at a full Cabinet meeting on Monday, 2 March, the KANU Parliamentary group rejected the scheme outright at a meeting on 10 March. Opposition leaders at their first joint consultative session, the previous day, had also rejected Attorney-General Wako's proposals. Whereas KANU MPs thought the Attorney-General had gone much too far and now instructed him merely to prepare amendments to the Presidential and Parliamentary Elections Act required by the decision to legalise opposition parties, opposition chiefs considered that Wako and his chambers had not gone far enough. Representatives from the various opposition parties anounced that they would appoint a team of constitutional and legal experts to consider the draft and advise them about securing a High Court injunction to prevent Parliament from considering the Bill.

What killed the Bill was not so much opposition from FORD and DP leaders, however, as growing doubts among MPs who remained loyal to KANU. Many, especially those from the Rift Valley and Western Province, were alarmed by the reduced powers of the Presidency. Commentators speculated that KANU's hawks had not understood the Bill's implications fully when it had been considered in Cabinet. Only when the press published detailed extracts and analysed precisely what the constitutional amendments entailed on Wednesday, 4 March, and the *Weekly Review* carried a detailed discussion of the proposals on 6 March, did the hardliners in the ruling party really understand what was at stake. As the Nairobi political journal explained the following week, 'Then the KANU hawks, who had apparently not realised the full import of the Bill ... went into action with a vigorous counter-attack aimed at killing the Bill before it ever saw the light of day.' The hawks were determined to preserve President Moi's power and the right to serve an unspecified number of terms. 'In this regard, [they] were completely blind to the possibility that either President Moi or KANU could come out the loser in the next general election.'[124]

One of the Bill's constitutional changes particularly irritated the hardliners, who were determined that the President should not be elected by 'direct, universal and equal suffrage' as proposed. The exisiting constitution provided in Section 5 (3) (e) and 5 (3) (f) that:

> In every constituency in which a poll is required to be taken both for the election of a president and for the election of a member of the national assembly, separate polls shall be taken; and [Section 5 (3) (f)] the candidate for president who is elected as member of the national assembly and who receives a greater number of valid votes cast in the presidential election than any other candidate for president who is elected a member of the national assembly shall be declared to be elected president.[125]

As we have observed, most MPs did not appreciate that, ever since the constitution had been amended in 1970, in theory Kenya's Presidents had been directly elected at the ballot box. Before the procedure had been modified in 1982, Section 5 (3) (e) of the constitution had provided that a single poll would take place for both the Presidential and Parliamentary elections. Candidates for President would be nominated by a particular political party – in practice, of course, always by KANU – and they would be 'paired' with Parliamentary candidates nominated by the same party 'so as to permit the voter to cast one vote for one of the pairs (which shall be taken to be a vote for each member of the pair who is a candidate in a contested election)'.

The provision had ensured that the winning Presidential candidate – and there had always been only one – would command a majority in the National Assembly. Since Kenya was a single-party state, the constitutional provision had made little difference to the provision in 1963, based on British practice, that the party leader commanding a majority of votes in the legislature would assume the position of head of the executive branch without direct popular approval. Thus, Kenyatta had been returned unopposed as MP for Gatundu in 1969 and 1974, and Moi for Baringo Central in 1979, 1983 and 1988, and had been declared elected as President. Only members of KANU, approved by party headquarters, had been permitted to contest these Parliamentary elections, and technically the winning candidate in each constituency was 'paired' with KANU's candidate for the Presidency, who was therefore endorsed in every single constituency.

As the media pointed out, the Constitutional (Amendment) Bill, 1992, proposed a fundamental reconstruction of the whole machinery of government. The *Weekly Review*, for example, observed:

> The Constitutional (Amendment) Bill, 1992, may well be history, but in its scope and far-reaching changes evidently designed to ensure the supremacy of parliament over the executive in the multi-party era, it remains one of the most significant documents ever published.[126]

Even FORD Vice-Chairman Masinde Muliro had acknowledged at the opposition parties' consultative meeting – the session had been boycotted by KANU – that the amendments would help protect political pluralism. Mwai Kibaki had also informed a DP rally in Nakuru that the changes met many of his party's requirements but had warned that a constitutional crisis might develop because of the Bill's failure clearly to delineate the powers of the President and those of the Prime Minister. Other opposition leaders had been more critical. Oginga Odinga of FORD, Secretary-General Keen of the Democratic Party, Johnstone Makau of the Social Democratic Party, and KENDA's David Mukaru-Ngang'a had castigated the Bill for attempting to keep President Moi in State House even if KANU lost the general election. Oginga and the other opposition leaders pointed out that the President would retain the power to appoint the Prime Minister, the Deputy Prime Minister, all Cabinet and Assistant Ministers, senior civil servants, judges, the commanders of the army, air force and navy, and other senior officers. He was merely required to appoint a Prime Minister 'from a political party which, in his judgement, is best able to command the support of the majority of the members of the National Assembly'.[127]

Opposition leaders pointed out that although the Bill suggested, but did not require, that this should be the leader of the party with the largest number of MPs, theoretically the President was entitled to turn to the leader of another party either to form a minority government or to see if he could construct an alternative coalition; he could also attempt to fragment the largest party by asking someone other than the leader to attempt to form a government. Opposition leaders feared that the people's will, reflected in the strength of parties in the National Assembly, could be circumvented by a Machiavellian head of state: even if FORD and the DP secured a majority of seats in the new legislature, Moi might be able to retain the Presidency by manipulating the constitution.

KANU hardliners, by contrast, wanted to maintain the executive powers of the Presidency and to erect as many obstacles as possible to the new opposition parties. Thus, when the Bill re-emerged in July, new rules had been introduced, based on Nigeria's Second Republic, which required the President to secure 25 per cent of the vote in at least five of the country's eight provinces. This provision was designed to strengthen Moi's position. KANU advisers believed that Mwai Kibaki, for example, had little appeal outside of Central Province and Nairobi where he was bound to secure more than a quarter of the vote, in parts of Eastern Province where he might reach the target figure, and in the Kikuyu-populated areas of the Rift Valley where he was likely to fail narrowly. In Nyanza, Western, Coast and North-Eastern Provinces, however, Kibaki and his party had little support. Thus, even if support for the DP candidate exceeded expectations, Kibaki was most unlikely to poll more than a quarter of the vote in more than four provinces. Odinga was a bit stronger. The Luo leader could expect to sweep Nyanza, poll well in Western Province, and probably reach 25 per cent in Nairobi, Eastern Province and at the Coast. His propects were less good in Central Province (where Matiba would have polled well above 25 per cent), the Rift Valley (where the mainly Kikuyu opposition vote was likely to defect to Kibaki), and North-Eastern (where support for any of the opposition parties was negligible). Thus Odinga might just have met the new requirement – until Kenneth Matiba and his mainly Kikuyu followers broke away to form FORD-Asili.

In many respects, Matiba was the strongest opposition candidate. It was becoming increasingly clear, however, that his health had been devastated by his stroke in detention. In perfect health and with the whole-hearted backing of Odinga and FORD's Young Turks, the Murang'a politician might have raised the FORD vote in Central Province to over 25 per cent and improved the party's performance in Nairobi, Eastern Province and the Rift Valley, ensuring that the main opposition party would surmount the 25 per cent barrier in the first two provinces, if not in the Rift Valley. Nyanza, moreover, would have remained loyal to FORD, although there might have been a slight defection of voters to the government. Thus, whereas Odinga could carry five provinces – Nyanza and Western for sure, and Nairobi, Eastern and the Coast by a narrow margin – Matiba might have guaranteed Nairobi and Eastern, held the Coast, and added Central Province, making a total of six. KANU's encouragement of the divisions in FORD, fuelling Matiba's personal ambition and the ethnic rivalries between the party's Kikuyu and Luo leaders, made this increasingly unlikely.

By contrast, President Moi was safe in the Rift Valley, North-Eastern and at the Coast, was likely to reach the 25 per cent mark in Western and Eastern Provinces, and might achieve the target in Nairobi. He had little chance, however, of reaching the target in Kenya's most densely populated Provinces, Central and Nyanza, where the Kikuyu and Luo vote is concentrated.[128] This proposal initially aroused little comment but it became the focus of increasingly vocal opposition from both FORD and the DP when Attorney General Wako presented an amended bill to Parliament in mid-July. This time Wako had been careful to consult the KANU Parliamentary Group before presenting the new Bill to the National Assembly.[129]

The original Bill had reflected Attorney-General Amos Wako's desire to remain above the political fray. Technically, the Attorney-General was a civil servant with *ex-officio* membership of the National Assembly rather than a party politician. Wako explained that since Kenya had ceased to be a single-party state in December, he had considered it inappropriate to be too closely identified with the ruling party and consequently had ceased to attend meetings of the KANU Parliamentary group, which had rejected his proposals. At the end of January 1992, in a speech to British MPs at the House of Commons on 'The Rule of Law and the Independence of the Judiciary', Wako had assured his audience that the new legislation that was being drafted in his chambers would facilitate the introduction of multi-party politics. He had assured the MPs that future elections would be organised by an impartial Electoral Commission rather than by the Provincial Administration and that they would 'not only be free, fair and without any rigging, but will also be seen to be free, fair and without any rigging'.[130]

The opposition parties naturally remained sceptical of Wako and the Attorney-General's chambers, doubting KANU's willingness to devise a fair election process. The opposition groups insisted that a constitutional convention should be summoned to devise the new electoral rules rather than leaving the task to incumbent KANU MPs. The convention would include members of all the political parties and representatives of special interest groups, such as the Churches, the National Christian Council, the Law Society, the Central Organisation of Trades Union and the Federation of Kenya Employers. The Roman Catholic hierarchy had also come out in favour of the plan in a pastoral letter. The Bishops had gone much further than opposition leaders, calling for an immediate dissolution of Parliament. Hilary Ng'weno, editor of the *Weekly Review,* who was emerging as the most effective apologist for the government, condemned the idea, pointing out that the opposition parties were far from ready to fight an immediate general election. The voters' register, which had been devised in 1987, needed to be updated before an election took place, local branches would have to be formed, and it would take the opposition parties at least three months to select constituency candidates and to agree upon a Presidential choice. Ng'weno noted that by law the registration process had to be spread over a minimum of five months 'for the law provides that not only should everyone who is eligible and wants to be registered as a voter be registered, but that the voters' roll be open to scrutiny in case of omissions or unwarranted additions.' He noted that 'Parliament will most certainly be dissolved and elections held – probably sooner than most people think. But it has to be done within the framework of the constitution and the law, not at the whim of pressure groups, even if these include bishops.'[131]

Lee Muthoga also warned that 'a national disaster of monumental proportions' might result if the elections were badly organised. The opposition's proposal was dismissed by the prominent Nairobi lawyer, who in 1984 had led for the government at the Njonjo Tribunal. Muthoga not only rejected the suggestion that a government of national unity should be formed, but scorned the idea of a convention, pointing out there was no need to replace an elected Parliament with 'an amorphous body of doubtful legal and constitutional validity'. Instead, he favoured a small committee with representatives from the various political parties to draw up the new rules. These could then be presented to Parliament for legislative approval.

A number of countries in Francophone Africa had already established constitutional conventions. In Niger, Benin and Congo these creations had stripped the former governments of most of their power. In Zaire, too, President Mobutu Sese Seko had been forced to summon a convention, but he had attempted to pack the gathering with his supporters.[132] Although many prominent opposition figures favoured a constitutional convention, a few, including Raila Odinga, were sceptical. Raila argued that now that FORD had been registered as a political party it should abandon the idea of a convention, and simply concentrate upon winning the coming general election. Kenneth Matiba was even more firmly opposed to the idea of FORD participating with KANU leaders in an interim government. The former Cabinet Minister considered that FORD would be 'tainted' by such an arrangement, and should instead concentrate upon ensuring that it won free and fair elections. The fairness of the elections could be assured by changing the composition of the Electoral Commission, ensuring that it was independent of the government, the Attorney-General's chambers and the Provincial Administration, and by requesting the secondment of observers from the Commonwealth and the United States.

A number of Muthoga's suggestions were congenial to the opposition. He urged that the number of Presidential terms should be limited and the independence of Parliament from the executive strengthened; that the Speaker should prorogue Parliament; that the Electoral Commission should be entirely independent of the government; the promulgation of a new code of conduct for all leaders; and legislation to stem the flight of capital into overseas banks. Muthoga also proposed that the investigative role of Parliament should be strengthened, introducing an American-style system of powerful Parliamentary committees to oversee not only government expenditure but key areas of government policy such as foreign affairs, the judiciary and the armed forces. Muthoga's statement, addressed to the three main political parties, contained one other provision that was soon to arouse political controversy. He was the first person to propose that Kenya introduce the constitutional provision discussed above which required the victorious Presidential candidate to poll not only a plurality of votes cast but at least 25 per cent of the votes in at least five Provinces. This proposal was to prove fatal to the opposition's prospects and, as we have noted, was quickly seized upon by KANU's campaign managers.[133]

KANU Devises New Obstacles for the Opposition

By the end of March 1992, with the beginning of the new Parliamentary session, Ministers began to appreciate the damage that the ethnic clashes were inflicting on KANU. Vital votes were being lost in Gusii and Abaluhya constituencies, making it increasingly difficult for the ruling party to secure a majority in the election. The Office of the President, therefore, attempted to dampen political animosities by prohibiting all political rallies for a week. President Moi, on his return from Europe, was fed false information by the Kalenjin hardliners, who blamed the opposition for the clashes; Moi then decided to extended the ban indefinitely. He declared that the ban had been introduced to prevent opposition leaders taking advantage of the crisis by blaming 'Kalenjin warriors' for the attacks.[134] The decision provoked immediate protests from John Keen, Martin Shikuku, George Anyona and other opposition leaders who feared that the ban was merely the first stage in a government plot to declare a state of emergency, suppressing the opposition. Shikuku protested that the ban, however justified in the areas hit by ethnic violence, ought not to apply to the whole country; while Anyona, always a stickler for constitutional propriety, insisted that it was illegal since it had not been published in the *Gazette*.[135]

In practice the ban came at a convenient time for the opposition. Public enthusiasm for political meetings was already declining and it was becoming difficult for both FORD and the DP to sustain the momentum of their earlier meetings during the rainy season. The opposition's repeated calls for an independent Electoral Commission and the amendment of the election process had not proved riveting subjects. Popular excitement was waning. Now opposition leaders could unite in condemnation of the government's decision to ban their meetings, while President Moi, government Ministers, KANU MPs and the Provincial Administration remained free to organise regular meetings to promote the ruling party. If the ban suited the opposition in some ways, however, it still had the disruptive effect KANU intended. Before the suspension, FORD leaders had been touring the country, seeking recruits and promoting the party's message. The ban inevitably hampered recruitment campaigns and attempts to establish grassroots party structures.

The ruling party clearly found it difficult to adjust to the requirements of multi-party politics, such as freedom of assembly and open access to the media. The government's reluctance to tolerate criticism was clearly demonstrated first by the indefinite suspension of all political rallies and then by the arrest of Njenga Mungai, the MP for Molo, on 23 March. Mungai had alleged several times that the clashes had been organised with the passive support of the District Administration and that the attackers had been transported to isolated Kikuyu settlements in vehicles bearing

GK number plates. FORD Steering Committee member Harun Lempaka, a former District Commissioner, and a Reuters journalist were also arrested, and three senior editors from the *Daily Nation* and the *Standard* were interrogated at police headquarters about their stories on the violence in Nairobi, Kisumu and Homa Bay. Even the *Weekly Review* observed snidely that the 'police have now shifted their focus from arresting marauders, murderers and arsonists to arresting the so-called "rumour mongers"'.[136]

As we have seen, KANU leaders also sought to silence the press, preventing the media from reporting the failure of the police and Provincial Administration to stop the gangs of 'Kalenjin warriors' as they attempted to create a 'KANU zone' in Rift Valley Province. Former Minister Peter Okondo, for example, proposed the establishment of a Press Complaints Commission on the British model. The newspapers, he complained, were abusing their power 'with grave consequences and risks to national security'.[137] Assistant Minister for Information and Broadcasting Sharrif Nassir, KANU's hardline party boss in Mombasa, concurred, observing that the press 'are becoming a dangerous weapon that could plunge the country into bloodshed'. Burudi Nabwera, the responsible Minister, singled out the pro-opposition magazines *Society* and *Finance* for particular blame. Both journals had devoted considerable space in the last few months to reports of the incidents.[138] Nicholas Biwott also intervened, suggesting that the magazines and the two main English-language newspapers were motivated by deliberate bias. He even claimed that the violence along the Nandi-Luo border had been started by the Luo. One of the few KANU leaders to defend the press was former Provincial Commissioner and nominated Member of Parliament Eliud Mahihu, who argued that controls would contradict the government's commitment to political openness, proposing that KANU should try to build a better relationship with the media. He pointed out that a press clampdown would antagonise powerful media moguls 'Tiny' Rowland and the Aga Khan, who owned the *Standard* and the *Daily Nation* respectively and were major investors in Kenya.[139]

In early April Oginga Odinga and Martin Shikuku gave the government ten days to lift the ban on political meetings and John Keen, the DP's Secretary-General, warned on 6 April that the government must remove the ban within two weeks or face widespread defiance. He pointed out that KANU officials were still busy making political speeches throughout the country and that the opposition demanded equal treatment. FORD leaders warned that unless the government acted, they would go ahead with planned meetings in Busia, Nyahuhuru and Kitui which had already been authorised, defying the order. Oginga Odinga dismissed suggestions that the opposition would play into the hands of the government by breaking the ban, observing that 'it was the same form of playing into the hands of the government that brought about the current multi-party era we are now enjoying'.[140] The opposition had been warned not to go ahead with the banned Kamukunji rally in November 1991, which had been forbidden by the Nairobi Provincial Commissioner. The confrontation had highlighted the extent of popular frustration with the Moi regime, however, and perhaps encouraged the international financial community to withdraw rapid disbursement aid to the Moi government later in the month. FORD would not only challenge the government's decisions in the courts but after ten days would go ahead with its meetings. The ban, Odinga argued, was 'an ill-considered strategy to muzzle the opposition'.[141]

DP leaders were equally adamant. Keen insisted that the party would go ahead with its planned rallies in Nyeri and, the following week, in Mombasa, even if KANU refused to lift the ban. The DP demanded that the Provincial Administration in the two towns license the meetings, 'otherwise we shall take stern action which the KANU government will live to regret'. Branches in other areas were instructed to go ahead with the preparations for meetings. Archbishop Kuria, the head of the CPK, also condemned the prohibition, declaring that it gave KANU an advantage over the opposition. Both FORD and the DP were heading for a clash with the government.[142]

The opposition parties also pressed the government to exclude the Provincial Administration from any part in the election process. As we noted in Chapter 3, District officials during the Moi era had become deeply implicated in election rigging, especially at the last polls in 1988, when suspiciously large numbers of 'difficult' politicians had been defeated in the KANU primary. The DP also demanded that the votes should be counted at polling stations, or at least at a counting centre for each constituency, rather than at a District-wide centre as in the past. Transporting ballot boxes after nightfall had facilitated malpractices, enabling officials to switch boxes or to stuff ballot papers into legitimate boxes.[143]

Plans for Voter Registration

As the opposition castigated the government for its ban on political gatherings and FORD defended its two-day general strike on 2–3 April 1992, Wilfred Kimalat, the Permanent Secretary for the Provincial Administration and Internal Security in the Office of the President – Hezekiah Oyugi's successor – announced that once the new election legislation had passed the National Assembly, the process of updating the voters' register would begin. In previous elections, this process had taken three months. Before the last election, voter registration had started in April 1987 but after three months only 2.4 million voters had registered, requring the period to be extended for another ten weeks. As we have noted, disillusionment with the political process was so great in 1987–8, following the introduction of queue voting, that many people had not considered it worth their while to spend their time getting their names on the electoral register. Even after, five and a half months, only six million voters had bothered to register, compared with the 7.9 million who were to register in 1992. The Register was closed in September 1987, Parliament was prorogued in December but not formally dissolved until early February 1988, the KANU primary took place later that month, and the general election itself finally occurred on 21 March 1988, in those constituencies where no candidate in the primary had secured over 70 per cent of the vote.

Justice Chesoni finally announced on 7 May 1992 that voter registration would commence on 8 June.[144] He claimed that the elections would be conducted impartially and that 'the electoral college is truly an independent body'. The Commission proposed to establish a minimum of 5,631 registration centres around the country to facilitate the process. Opposition leaders rightly doubted the Commission's freedom, denouncing it as unrepresentative and dominated by KANU sympathisers.

By 13 July, the Electoral Commission claimed that 6,778,732 had registered to vote, following a ten-day extension of the process. FORD, the Democratic Party, the SDP and KENDA all insisted that the registration exercise needed to be extended for another 60 days to permit an estimated 3–4 million more Kenyans to register. The opposition parties complained that the authorities were issuing identity cards so slowly that many potential voters would be denied the right to vote. Opposition leaders claimed that there were at least 8–10 million potential voters. Perhaps even more significant was the large increase of registered voters in the Rift Valley, KANU's stronghold, where the number on the register had increased by approximately 500,000 since 1987 to 1,664,958.[145] Big increases, however, had also taken place in certain opposition strongholds. Registered voters in Nairobi more than doubled from 297,953 in 1988 to 629,594, while Kiambu rose from 257,548 to 385,707 and the hotly contested Nakuru District from 192,413 to 372,579. Ngenga Mungai's Molo was the largest single constituency, increasing from only 58,977 to 106,827 by the official close of registration.[146] The government and the Electoral Commission, however, refused to heed the opposition's demands, closing the registration exercise on Monday, 20 July, after 43 days, by which time over 7,500,000 had registered compared with 5,562,877 in the period before the 1988 elections.[147]

By late May 1992, even before the voter registration process began, KANU leaders were confident that they would win the coming general election. Their assessment was strengthened by the opposition parties' hostile response to the announcement that voter registration would soon begin, suggesting that both FORD and the DP were ill-equipped to contest the election. FORD, as we saw in Chapter 5, was deeply divided between the Kikuyu and Luo protagonists of the Matiba and Odinga camps, while neither party had access to the financial resources of the ruling party, which could draw on the coffers of the state. President Moi and other KANU leaders almost gleefully taunted the opposition, challenging their interim officials to seek the voters' mandate.[148]

One pointer to the likely timing of the election – it proved to be very accurate – was given by the Speaker, Professor Jonathan Ng'eno, who published a notice in the *Gazette* extending the four months that a seat could remain vacant to eight months. Assistant Minister Peter Ejore, the long-serving MP for Turkana Central, had died the week that KANU's Special Delegates' Conference voted to authorise the registration of rival political parties. When Parliament reassembled in March, the Speaker officially declared his seat vacant, which required a by-election to take place before the end of July. The recently approved National Assembly and Presidential Elections Act, however, had authorised the Speaker to extend this period, which Ng'eno did in the first week of April, postponing the required by-election until the end of November. Opposition leaders failed to recognise the implication of Speaker Ng'eno's action: that the general election would take place in late November or early December.[149]

There were other indications that the government was preparing to reduce the length of the period between the start of voter registration and the holding of the election. The Attorney-General, for example, announced minor changes in the voter registration regulations – the National Assembly Election (Registration of Voters Amendment) Regulations – seeking to reduce the time in which voters could protest once the voters' roll was published from three to two weeks. The notice also replaced the Supervisor of Elections with a Director who was responsible to an independent Electoral Commission, rather than to the Attorney-General. The Electoral Commission was, in fact, the former Boundary Review Commission, which had been appointed in 1991 under the chairmanship of former High Court Judge Zacchaeus Chesoni, to define the new Parliamentary constituency boundaries. The new regulations were designed to speed up the process, enabling President Moi to call an election before the end of the year.

Under mounting pressure from the opposition and the West, President Moi also announced that Kenya would welcome observers from the Commonwealth and other international organizations. Although the President had committed Kenya to accepting outside observers when he had attended the Commonwealth Heads of Government meeting in Harare in October 1991, two months before the advent of multi-party politics, in recent months KANU leaders had appeared to back-track on the agreement. In March 1992, however, Commonwealth Secretary-General Chief Emeka Anyaoku visited Nairobi and held extensive meetings with the government. He warned President Moi that Kenya would have to accept external observers if it was to remain in good standing in the Commonwealth. Chief Anyaoku also supported FORD's and the DP's demand that an independent Electoral Commission should be established to organize the poll. KANU leaders, however, were still finding it difficult to adjust to the new political climate, and most were extremely reluctant to allow in outside observers.[150] Kalonzo Musyoka's recation was typical. At a Youth for KANU '92 rally, Deputy Speaker of the National Assembly Musyoka, who was also KANU's National Organising Secretary, dismissed the idea of outside monitors, suggesting that the only aim of Commonwealth observers would be to rig the elections on behalf of the opposition. He even claimed that Kenneth Kaunda's United National Independence Party had actually won the November 1991 Zambian polls but had been rigged out of office by the Commonwealth monitors. Musyoka belatedly realised that he had gone rather too far when his speech was reported in the *Daily Nation* and he attempted to claim that he had been misreported. The newspaper printed his denial, but in bold print stood by its story, pointing out that tape recordings of the meeting existed. Other KANU politicians were willing to make similarly wild claims, revealing the total lack of commitment in the government to the principles of multi-party democracy.[151]

The changes in the electoral law requiring the winning Presidential candidate to secure at least 25 per cent of the vote in five of Kenya's eight provinces and the registration exercise were two key elements in KANU's fight-back against an increasingly divided FORD. As we have observed, KANU was the party with the widest national support, particularly in the semi-arid pastoralist areas of the country, which had always elected a disproportionate number of Members of Parliament. The new 25 per cent rule, as we have seen, also worked to the ruling party's advantage. President Moi's support was more evenly divided throughout the country, whilst support for Matiba, Odinga and Kibaki was concentrated in certain ethnic areas – especially in Kikuyuland and Luo Districts of Nyanza Province.

Voter registration was equally fundamental – if not more so – to KANU's election strategy. Voters were transported from KANU strongholds and registered to vote in more marginal seats. A close scrutiny of the final registration figures, for example, reveals that KANU supporters in its safe seats in southern Kilifi and northern Kwale Districts at the Coast were transported to Mvita constituency, Sharrif Nassir's extremely precarious seat in city-centre Mombasa. Meanwhile, the ethnic clashes and more subtle forms of intimidation in the Rift Valley were designed to deter Kikuyu registration in order to ensure that neither Matiba nor Kibaki were able to reach the 25 per cent threshold in the Rift Valley despite the large Kikuyu populations in Nakuru and Laikipia.[152]

From the beginning of the year, President Moi and his advisers in the Office of the President, rather than KANU headquarters, fought an extremely skilful campaign to undermine opposition morale and unity, designed to ensure the President's re-election and to secure a working majority for KANU in the National Assembly. As we have noted, in March and April 1992, the ethnic clashes threatened to get out of hand, doing considerable damage to the President's popularity with Gusii and Abaluhya, as well as Kikuyu, voters – but by astute distribution of patronage the President was able to enlist the support of Simeon Nyachae and to bolster KANU's position in Vihiga and Busia Districts. The ethnic cleansing campaign, however, undoubtedly benefited KANU's position in Uashin Gishu and Trans-Nzoia, and ensured that only Moi secured more than 25 per cent of the Presidential vote in the Rift Valley.[153] In the Kalenjin heartlands, moreover, the President conceded a relatively open vote for the selection of KANU's Parliamentary candidates, forestalling a potential revolt against the ruling party among Kipsigis, Nandi and Pokot voters. Biwott and the hardliners were reined back in the Kalenjin Districts and allowed a free hand – at least for the first six months of the year – in ethnically mixed constituencies in the former 'White Highlands', such as the Trans-Nzoia and Uashin Gishu seats, and Molo and Rongai in Nakuru District.

It is now clear that KANU devised a carefully considered strategy to maximise its support and to undermine the opposition parties. New electoral laws, voter registration, violence, state patronage and the authority of District Administrations were all skilfully deployed as part of a careful plan to secure victory. By contrast, buoyed up by the initial euphoria for multi-party politics in Nairobi and Mombasa, Central Province and Nyanza, the opposition parties made the fatal mistake of believing their own propaganda, underestimating the formidable resources of the state machine and the resilience of KANU's bedrock support. By June 1992,

KANU leaders had recovered their self-confidence, begun to disassociate themselves from the party's most autocratic and unpopular District bosses, and were utilising state finances to fund the party's campaign, awarding salary increases and higher commodity prices to key groups of voters to bolster electoral support for President Moi and KANU's Parliamentary candidates. The challenge from FORD, the main opposition party, was receding as it became mired in ethnic conflict between the Luo and the Kikuyu over its Presidential candidate. Skilful manipulation of the electoral rules and voter registration increased KANU's advantage, while YK '92 was already emerging as a useful tool, not only carrying the battle into opposition strongholds but even more importantly enabling the central party apparatus to intervene directly in branch and sub-branch (i.e. District and constituency) affairs to redress grievances and select the most popular local candidates in order to maximise the KANU vote. The President's advisers in State House, the Office of the President and party headquarters in the middle months of 1992 proved themselves to be astute political tacticians. KANU chiefs had a much more realistic grasp of the party's strengths and weaknesses than officials of either FORD or the DP, and demonstrated that they were well equipped to take the opposition on and to defeat them on the new multi-party political 'playing field' – especially as it could be tilted in the ruling party's favour. In terms of sheer competence, KANU by mid-1992 deserved to win the forthcoming election and the opposition to lose.

Notes

1 *Weekly Review*, 18 October 1991, p. 11. See also *Weekly Review*, 4 October 1991, p. 10. For Oloo-Aringo's remarks see *Weekly Review*, 15 November 1991, p. 17, and 29 November 1991, pp. 10–11.
2 *Weekly Review*, 29 November 1991, p. 12.
3 *Weekly Review*, 6 December 1991, p. 5.
4 *Weekly Review*, 29 November 1991, p. 1 and pp. 3–6.
5 The meeting was attended by Canada, Denmark, Finland, France, Germany, Italy, Japan, the Netherlands, Sweden, Switzerland, the United Kingdom, the USA, the African Development Bank, the European Commission, the European Investment Bank, the IMF and the United Nations Development Programme. Belgium, Saudi Arabia and the OECD attended as observers. Representatives of the donors, the World Bank and the IMF made it clear that further support for Kenya, which would be reviewed in six months, would be conditional upon decisive action to redress macro-economic imbalances, to improve the financial discipline of public enterprises, to begin a serious attempt to reduce the size of the civil service, and 'to provide an environment that is consistently supportive of private investment and initiative'. The suspension of financial support created immediate balance of payments problems. The Ministry of Finance acknowledged that the country would require another Sh12.2 billion in additional balance of payments support in the 1991–2 financial year. See *Weekly Review*, 29 November 1991, p. 28; and 6 December 1991, pp. 25–6.
6 *Weekly Review*, 20 December 1991, pp. 12–13.
7 *Ibid.*
8 *Weekly Review*, 3 January 1992, pp. 3–15 and 10 January 1992, pp. 3–6.
9 *Weekly Review*, 3 January 1992, pp. 16–17.
10 Onyonka, a Cabinet Minister since 1969, was a member of the Gusii community, whose

ten Parliamentary seats would be hotly contested by all the main parties. More of a technocrat than a 'street fighter', Onyonka's appointment might have been helpful to the ruling party's prospects in Kisii and Nyamira, and among educated middle-class voters, but he lacked Kamotho's skills as a blatant populist. See *Weekly Review*, 7 February 1992, p. 8.

11 *Weekly Review*, 28 February 1992, pp. 3–7.

12 These remarks are based on discussions with several political commentators on Kenya between January and May 1992. Opposition leaders, especially in FORD-Kenya, continued to overestimate their strength almost until election day. This misguided confidence was replicated in most accounts of the Kenyan political scene by foreign journalists. See *Weekly Review*, 3 January 1992, pp. 15–16, for a more realistic assessment.

13 For example, the advertisement in *Weekly Review*, 13 December 1991, p. 27.

14 *Weekly Review*, 20 December 1991, pp. 3–5.

15 *Ibid*., pp. 5–6. Obok, an employee of the Odinga kerosene and gas company, devoted so much time to political activities that Raila Odinga dismissed him in 1994. He subsequently rejoined KANU and was rewarded with a parastatal sinecure.

16 *Ibid*., pp. 6 and 9.

17 *Ibid.*

18 *Weekly Review*, 22 November 1991, pp. 6–7 and 27 March 1992, pp. 8–11.

19 See below, especially Chapter 8.

20 *Weekly Review*, 10 January 1992, pp. 5–6 and 17 January 1992, pp. 14–15. Clement Gachanja was also interviewed by one of the authors in Nairobi in December 1992. For Mungai's return to KANU, see *Weekly Review*, 14 February 1992, pp. 6–8.

21 *Weekly Review*, 17 January 1992, pp. 14–15.

22 *Weekly Review*, 24 January 1992, p. 12.

23 *Ibid.*

24 *Weekly Review*, 31 January 1992, p. 18.

25 *Weekly Review*, 21 February 1992, pp. 11–12.

26 *Ibid.*

27 Information from opposition activists in the two constituencies.

28 *Weekly Review*, 21 February 1992, pp. 11–12.

29 *Ibid*., p. 12.

30 *Ibid.*

31 Confidential information from Kikuyu business leaders, December 1992.

32 *Weekly Review*, 14 February 1992, p. 14. See also the issue of 10 January 1992, p. 5.

33 For the context of Mungai's remarks, see *Weekly Review*, 4 October 1991, pp. 6–10.

34 *Weekly Review*, 14 February 1992, pp. 6–8.

35 *Society*, 5 (30 March 1992), p. 22 and *Weekly Review*, 20 March 1992, pp. 18–19.

36 *Weekly Review*, 13 September 1991, pp. 5–15 and 27 September 1991, pp. 5–10. See also the issues for 8 November 1991, pp. 3–4 and 15 November 1991, pp. 10–17.

37 *Weekly Review*, 17 January 1992, p. 17 and 24 January 1992, pp. 18–19. Report of the Parliamentary Select Committee to investigate Ethnic Clashes in Western and Other Parts of Kenya, 1992 (Nairobi: 1992) provides a detailed investigation into the oringins and course of the clashes. Another valuable account is Africa Watch, *Ethnic Violence in Kenya* (London and New York: 1994).

38 *Weekly Review*, 24 January 1992, p. 19.

39 *Weekly Review*, 28 February 1992, pp. 13–14.

40 *Ibid*., p. 14.

41 *Ibid.*

42 *Weekly Review*, 13 March 1992, p. 18.

43 *Ibid*., p. 19.

44 *Weekly Review*, 20 March 1992, pp. 8–9 and 27 March 1992, pp. 15–16. For the Kalenjin view see the issue for 20 March 1992, pp. 4–6.

45 *Ibid*., pp. 3–6.

46 *Society*, 5 (30 March 1992), pp. 10–15 and *Weekly Review*, 20 March 1992, pp. 4–5.

47 *Weekly Review*, 27 March 1992, p. 15.

48 *Ibid*., pp. 15–16.

49 *Ibid*., p. 15.

50 *Weekly Review*, 20 March 1992, pp. 9 and 12. See also the issue for 27 March 1992, p. 14.

51 *Weekly Review*, 13 March 1992, pp. 18–19.

52 *Weekly Review*, 20 March 1992, p. 7.
53 *Weekly Review*, 13 March 1992, p. 19.
54 *Ibid.*
55 *Weekly Review*, 20 March 1992, p. 11.
56 *Daily Nation*, 17 March 1992, p. 1; and *Standard*, 17 March 1992, p. 1. See also *Weekly Review*, 20 March 1992, p. 5.
57 *Weekly Review*, 20 March 1992, p. 5.
58 *Ibid.*, pp. 13–15.
59 *Ibid.*, p. 14.
60 *Ibid.*
61 *Weekly Review*, 27 March 1992, p. 13.
62 Report of the Parliamentary Select Committee to Investigate Ethnic Clashes in Western and Other Parts of Kenya, 1992 (Nairobi: 1992), pp. 67, 78 and 85.
63 For Moi's remarks see *Weekly Review*, 27 March 1992, pp. 13–14. A useful assessment of press coverage of the clashes can be found in *Weekly Review*, 20 March 1992, pp. 21–2.
64 *Weekly Review*, 29 May 1992, pp. 12, 14, 16–18, 20–1 and 23–4. The view of the Roman Catholic hierarchy can be found in the same issue on pp. 32 and 34.
65 *Weekly Review*, 27 March 1992, pp. 20–1.
66 *Ibid.* For Mayor Chumo's view, see p. 13 in the same issue. He claimed that most of them had been 'rigged' into Parliament in 1988.
67 Human Rights Watch/Africa Watch, *Divide and Rule: State–Sponsored Ethnic Violence in Kenya* (New York, Washington, Los Angeles and London: 1993), p. 1. The booklet provides a most useful assessment of the origins and course of the ethnic clahes.
68 *Ibid.* p. 76–9.
69 Janet Seeley's unpublished PhD thesis, 'Praise, prestige and power: the organization of social welfare in a developing Kenya town', Cambridge University, 1985, provides an interesting social survey of Eldoret.
70 David W. Throup, "Render unto Caesar the things that are Caesar's': church–state relations in Kenya', in M. Twaddle and H. B. Hansen (eds), *Religion and Politics in Eastern Africa* (London: James Currey, 1994).
71 *Ibid.* See also *Weekly Review*, 27 March 1992, pp. 8–10.
72 *Weekly Review*, 21 February 1992, pp. 15–16. See also the issue for 24 January 1992, p.19.
73 *Ibid.*
74 *Weekly Review*, 21 February 1992, pp. 15–16.
75 See *Weekly Review*, 10 April 1992, pp. 13–14 for reports of growing tension between the Pokot and neighbouring Keiyo peoples.
76 *Weekly Review*, 28 February 1992, pp. 3–6.
77 *Weekly Review*, 7 February 1992, pp. 11–12 and 14 February 1992, pp. 3–6.
78 See David K. Leonard, *African Successes: Four Public Managers of Kenyan Rural Development* (Berkeley and Los Angeles: University of California Press, 1991), pp. 103–24 for an interesting account of Nyachae's rise to power. See also *Weekly Review*, 14 February 1992, pp. 5–6.
79 Quoted in *Weekly Review*, 14 February 1992, p. 5.
80 *Weekly Review*, 7 February 1992, pp. 11–12.
81 *Weekly Review*, 14 February 1992, p. 21.
82 *Ibid.*
83 *Ibid.*
84 *Ibid.*
85 *Ibid.*
86 *Ibid.*
87 *Weekly Review*, 31 January 1992, p. 18.
88 *Ibid.*
89 *Weekly Review*, 30 November 1990, pp. 13–15 and 19–21 for an account of Ngei's legal and financial problems.
90 *Ibid.*, pp. 15–19 provides an interesting survey of Ngei's career.
91 *Weekly Review*, 31 January 1992, p. 18. And any guide to Ukambani.
92 *Weekly Review*, 17 April 1992, pp. 15–16. After the election, President Moi created a new Mount Elgon District.
93 The Roman Catholic bishops became increasingly outspoken during the years 1990 to

1992, frequently castigating the Moi regime in their Pastoral Letters. See *Weekly Review*, 29 May 1992, pp. 32–3 and the issue for 19 June 1992, pp. 14–15 for examples later in the year.

94 *Weekly Review*, 24 April 1992, pp. 19–20; and the issues for 1 May 1992, pp. 8–16; 8 May 1992, pp. 15–24; 15 May 1992, pp. 19–21, 22 May 1992, pp. 11–12; 29 May 1992, pp. 12–24; and 5 June 1992, pp. 21–2.

95 A brief survey of Mwangale's career can be found in *Weekly Review*, 28 February 1992, p. 7.

96 David W. Throup, 'The construction and destruction of the Kenyatta state', in Michael G. Schatzberg (ed.), *The Political Economy of Kenya* (New York: Praeger, 1987), pp. 67–8.

97 *Weekly Review*, 28 February 1992, pp. 3–6.

98 *Ibid.*, p. 3.

99 *Ibid.*, p. 4.

100 *Ibid.*, p. 3. See also pp. 5–6 for a more detailed analysis of the rivalries within KANU in Bungoma..

101 *Ibid.*, pp. 5–6.

102 *Ibid.*

103 *Ibid.*, p. 6.

104 *Ibid.*, p. 3.

105 *Weekly Review*, 6 March 1992, p. 14.

106 Further details of the Abaluhya campaign to secure KANU's Vice-Presidential nomination can be found in *Weekly Review*, 29 May 1992, pp. 9–10 and the issue of 5 June 1992, pp. 14–15.

107 *Weekly Review*, pp. 12 and 14.

108 An interesting assessment of Bishop Gitari's theological views can be found in Graham Kings, 'Proverbial, intrinsic, and dynamic authorities: a case study on scripture and mission in the dioceses of Mount Kenya East and Kirinyaga', in *Missiology: An International Review*, 24, 4 (October 1996), pp. 493–501. I am grateful to Canon Kings for this reference.

109 *Weekly Review*, 21 April 1989, pp. 11–13. See also the issue for 14 April 1989, pp. 4–10 for a detailed account of Gitari's hostile relations with Njiru and for 7 February 1992, p. 11.

110 *Weekly Review*, 7 February 1992, pp. 10–11.

111 *Ibid.*

112 *Ibid.*, and the issue for 13 March 1992, p. 23.

113 *Ibid.*

114 *Ibid.*

115 *Weekly Review*, 25 June 1982, pp. 3–6.

116 *Weekly Review*, 28 February 1992, pp. 8–9.

117 *Ibid.*, p. 9.

118 *Ibid.*, p. 10 and the issue for 13 March 1992, p. 22.

119 *Weekly Review*, 28 February 1992, p. 10.

120 *Weekly Review*, 13 March 1992, p. 22.

121 *Weekly Review*, 6 March 1992, pp. 14–16, and the issue for 13 March 1992, pp. 6–9.

122 *Ibid.*

123 *Weekly Review*, 6 March 1992, p. 16.

124 *Weekly Review*, 13 March 1992, pp. 3–8.

125 *Ibid.*, pp. 3–4.

126 *Ibid.*, p. 4.

127 *Ibid.*

128 *Weekly Review*, 24 July 1992, pp. 12–14.

129 *Weekly Review*, 17 July 1992, p. 26.

130 *Weekly Review*, 13 March 1992, p. 5. See also the issue for 31 January 1992, pp. 15–16.

131 See Ng'weno's editorial in *Weekly Review*, 14 February 1992, p. 1. A detailed report on the Roman Catholic bishops' Pastoral Letter was carried on p. 11 of the same issue.

132 *Weekly Review*, 14 February 1992, pp. 9–10.

133 *Ibid.* See also the issue for 24 July 1992, pp. 12–14 for the opposition's comments on the proposal when Attorney General Wako presented his revised Constitutional (Amendment) Bill to the National Assembly in mid-July.

134 FORD and KANU held each other responsible for the clashes; see *Weekly Review*, 29 May

1992, pp. 12, 14 and 20–24.

135 *Weekly Review*, 27 March 1992, pp. 14–15.

136 *Weekly Review*, 20 March 1992, pp. 21–22. See also the issue for 27 March 1992, p. 16.

137 *Weekly Review*, 3 April 1992, pp. 11–12.

138 On 21 April 1992, five editorial members of *Society* appeared in court in Mombasa to answer eleven charges of sedition, following a police raid on its offices in Tumaini House in Nairobi. Charges were brought against proprietor Pius Nyamora, his wife and three senior staff relating to stories published in the issues of 16 and 23 December 1991; 24 February 1992; 9 March 1992; and 13 and 20 April 1992. See *Weekly Review*, 24 April 1992, p. 23. *Society* was in trouble again in mid-June: see *Weekly Review*, 19 June 1992, p.17.

139 *Weekly Review*, 3 April 1992, pp. 11–12.

140 *Ibid.*, p. 9.

141 *Ibid.*

142 *Ibid.*

143 The request by the DP for constituency counting centres was subsequently accepted although the opposition parties continued to urge that counts should be undertaken at each polling station as in neighbouring Ethiopia, Tanzania and Uganda.

144 *Weekly Review*, 15 May 1992, pp. 12–14.

145 *Weekly Review*, 17 July 1992, pp. 19–20.

146 *Weekly Review*, 24 July 1992, p. 15.

147 *Ibid.*

148 *Weekly Review*, 22 May 1992, pp. 3–6 for an article entitled, 'Is KANU Ready?'

149 *Weekly Review*, 10 April 1992, p. 11.

150 Interview with officials from the Commonwealth Secretariat, Nairobi, December 1992. See also *Weekly Review*, 24 April 1992, pp. 16–17 and 19 June 1992, pp. 13–14.

151 *Weekly Review*, 24 April 1992, p. 17.

152 It should be noted that KANU was not the only party to bus its supporters into key marginal constituencies. The voter registration figures from Starehe in central Nairobi would suggest that Matiba's organization bussed large numbers of potential voters into Nairobi from his stronghold in Murang'a.

153 *Weekly Review*, 29 May 1992, pp. 20–1 provides details of the government's view of the clashes, while FORD's response appears on pp. 23–4.

Seven

The Electoral Process

As the 1988 elections had showed, a new electoral system could alter the political process significantly. Queue voting for Parliamentary and local government elections had forced voters to reveal their preferences, and facilitated widespread abuses. A system which for 20 years had provided legitimation through open primary elections lost much of its popular support. Already the Saitoti Commission had inspired the abolition of queuing. Now the electoral system had to be revised and updated to permit fair competition between national parties, something not seen since Independence.

In the summer of 1992, however, although KANU had committed itself to a multi-party election, the procedures governing it were unclear and KANU's ability to decide them was an important political weapon. The fairness of the procedures, consequently, became a point of contention between the government and an unstable alliance of opposition politicians and Western diplomats. Under pressure, the government and the Electoral Commission were forced into a series of concessions which made the electoral process more evenly balanced than they would have wished, but which still could not guarantee the freedom of the subsequent polls.

The Kenyan Westminster-style electoral system, established in 1963, divided the country into single-member constituencies in which all adults could register to vote, while candidates could stand in any constituency. On top of this had been overlaid the Presidential system, in which candidates for the Presidency were also directly and independently elected. No Presidential ballot had ever been held, however, leaving many uncertain as to how the process would work in the multi-party era. The selection of Presidential, Parliamentary and local government candidates had at independence been left entirely to the parties, but the development of the single-party state in 1964 meant that party caucuses would select MPs, eliminating voters from the process. The emergence of the KPU in 1966 compounded the problem, since the choice of an unpopular KANU candidate might hand victory to the opposition. As a result, the 1969 National Assembly and Presidential Elections Act had required parties to hold primary elections to select their candidates. KANU's original Bill prescribed the same queue voting as was introduced in 1988, but MPs in 1969 rejected this system, opting instead for a secret ballot in the primaries.[1] After the banning of the KPU, the KANU primary became the only election.[2] As well as the primaries, KANU also imposed a prior vetting process for candidates which caused many problems, particularly in Nyanza where it was used to bar the ex-KPU leaders from participation during the 1970s.[3]

As in many African states, disregard for the rule of law was not uncommon in Kenya. The Kenyan legal system has long been criticised for its subservience to authority. There was particular suspicion about the conduct of certain judges in the High Court. In 1992, the independence of the judiciary became a vital issue, as the opposition used the courts to contest almost every aspect of the electoral process. Kenya had a long tradition of comparatively free elections and many years of near-democracy, so that Kenyans cherished the notion of 'right' to a fair election, the violation of which had been a major driver for the multi-party movement. The longevity of constitutional rule had encouraged the development of a 'constitutional norm', particularly in the Nairobi élite, in which the rule of law was seen as morally paramount (although this was not always put into practice). Respect for the law and human rights were important themes in the campaign for multi-party politics. The law was also the most powerful political weapon the opposition could employ against the government. Because KANU leaders had staked their long-term survival on their ability to win a constitutional victory, they had to maintain the image of a free and fair election. Without any constitutional convention or other recognition of their role, and without any opposition members in Parliament, executive decisions could only be challenged through the courts. Here, the opposition parties were far stronger. Lawyers had led and sustained the multi-party movement, and in 1992 they took a prominent role in defending it through a succession of lawsuits contesting virtually all aspects of the election. The vital question was how far the government would go to sustain their control of the judiciary in the new democratic multi-party state. Central to this debate was the new Attorney-General Amos Wako, a respected human rights lawyer, who was now targeted by the opposition for his apparent embrace of the Moi regime.

Although the repeal of section 2(a) of the constitution permitted the formation of opposition parties, political parties still had to be approved by the Registrar of Societies, a government official, under the Societies Act. In the past, this device had been used to prevent opposition groups registering,[4] and after December 1991 the government continued to vet opposition parties. A number were refused registration, including the Green African Party, the Kenya Nationalist People's Democratic Party and, most controversially, the Islamic Party of Kenya (the IPK). The IPK was launched on 15 January 1992, but registration was refused on 7 February on the grounds that its programme offended the 'secular principle' of Kenya's constitution. The continued ability of the government to veto political organisations and to control their selection of office bearers remained a real constraint on Kenyans' freedom to organise politically.

The Electoral Commission

A major issue running throughout 1992 was the composition and conduct of the Electoral Commission, which was responsible for supervising all aspects of the elections. Appointed by President Moi on 26 September 1991, during the last days of the single-party state, its legal responsibilities and powers remained vague and circumscribed.[5] Its Chairman was explicit, for example, that the Commission had no authority to ensure that the media were impartial, or to issue permits for election rallies, as these were the responsibility of the government.[6] This failure to define the scope of the Commission's authority allowed key decisions to take place in the vacuum of authority between state and Commission, enabling both to deny responsibility. The previous Commission had been restricted to delineating constituency boundaries, since its other tasks, including supervising the elections, maintaining the register and educating voters had been unconstitutionally transferred to the Provincial Administration and the Supervisor of Elections in the 1960s. District Commissioners, for example, acted as Returning Officers. This changed with the introduction of multi-party politics, when the government had to establish a seemingly autonomous body. Thus, the Election Laws Amendment Act No. 1 of 1992 abolished the position of Supervisor of Elections and reinvested all powers in the Commission.

The Chairman of the Commission was Justice Zakayo Richard Chesoni, a Luhya lawyer from Western Province. Accused by other Commissioners and the opposition of incompetence and malevolence, and of concentrating all the Commission's decision-making powers in himself, he was a highly controversial figure whose actions were critical to the fairness of the elections.

As the *Monthly News* of August 1992 and the *Commonwealth Report* on the elections subsequently revealed, Justice Chesoni, a judge in the High Court since 1974, had in 1990 been declared bankrupt and removed from the bench for 'conduct inconsistent with the position, dignity and judicial integrity of a Justice of these Honourable Courts'.[7] In 1984, proceedings had been started against Chesoni for bankruptcy by a Kenya Commercial Bank subsidiary for Sh21 million. He had resigned, and the Attorney-General had dropped proceedings. In February 1990 Chesoni was reinstated as an acting judge on the basis that his financial affairs were now in order, but he immediately faced a new application to be committed to prison. Chesoni refused to resign and was dismissed on the recommendation of the Judicial Service Commission on 15 May 1990. The Commonwealth observer team, which had excellent access to Chesoni, suggested that his appointment as Chairman of the Election Commission 'could reasonably be interpreted by the opposition parties as an unmistakable signal that the government would use its powers to secure an advantage for the ruling party'.[8]

Photo 7.1
Justice Chesoni, Chairman of the Electoral Commission
Courtesy of Nation Group Newspapers

Both the financial insecurity of the ex-judge and the circumstances of his appointment inevitably brought into question his impartiality, especially since it was widely rumoured that President Moi had paid or written off his debts. The judge's early reluctance to meet the opposition and his collaboration with the Attorney-General in setting the election date was to reinforce suspicions that he was under pressure to ensure KANU's re-election.

There were ten other members of the Commission during the election period. Seven were appointed at the same time as Chesoni, representing a wide variety of backgrounds and ethnic origins, including representatives from all Kenya's provinces. The Vice-Chairman Jasper Mwathani Mbaka was a lawyer. Individual Commissioners were responsible for the organisation and conduct of the election in each province. Thus Habel Nyamu, a Kikuyu from Kirinyaga District, a long-time civil servant and managing director of the *Kenya Times*, supervised the elections in Central Province. Isaya Chelegut – a Kalenjin ex-Provincial Commissioner for Nyanza Province, Chairman of Nyayo Tea Zones and close personal friend, relative by marriage and business partner of President Moi – was in charge of the Rift Valley. Ahmed Abdalla Maawy was the Coast Commissioner.[9] In June 1992 the original nine members were joined by a new appointee, Margaret Kenyatta, the veteran ex-Mayor of Nairobi and the daughter of ex-President Jomo Kenyatta, possibly as a sop to opposition demands for impartiality, although she was to remain silent throughout the election. On 13 October, former Permanent Secretary Harrison Mule, who represented Eastern Province, resigned because of 'pressure of work' and was replaced by Samuel Kivuitu, a Kamba lawyer and ex-MP for Nairobi.[10] At the same time, the Commission's size was expanded again to include Gabriel Mukelele, a Luhya lawyer from Kakamega who could serve as the Western Province Commissioner. As will be seen, the incidence of electoral fraud appears to have varied with the political sentiments of individual Commissioners.

The failure to replace the Electoral Commission with a more neutral body was a key opposition complaint. The Commission began its task in almost complete secrecy, and appeared disorganised and unwilling to cooperate with the opposition. Commissioner Habel Nyamu later claimed that it did not have full-time staff or keep proper records. It also encountered difficulties dealing with the powerful Provincial Administration, which controlled its budget and supplies. The opposition parties persistently complained that Chesoni refused to meet them or provide details about polling stations or the names of Returning Officers. Some Western diplomats who encountered him in the negotiations believed that Chesoni was deliberately attempting to derail attempts to organise a fair poll. The opposition consistently called for an impartial Electoral Commission to be appointed and complained that the present one was run by KANU. As a result, in July 1992 Odinga, Kibaki, Johnstone Makau and David Mukaru-Ng'ang'a jointly sued for Chesoni to be removed as Chairman of the Election Commission since he was 'unfit and unqualified'. Their plea was dismissed by the High Court, however, on the technical grounds that the applicants had failed to prove that they were acting on behalf of other voters and, therefore, did not have the legal right to bring the proceedings.[11]

Little is known about the internal operation of the Commission, since most members remained silent, leaving public statements to Chesoni. It is known, however, that there were bitter internal disagreements and protests by a minority of Commissioners, which Chesoni did not address.[12] Following the release of guidelines on the conduct of the election, these divisions became public. On 7 November, Kikuyu Commissioners Habel Nyamu and Francis Nganatha, an ex-ambassador, who had been defeated in 1988 in Ndaragwa constituency in Nyandarua District, broke their silence in a scathing indictment which accused the Commission of 'leadership completely lacking in the basic rudiments of management and administration. It has been the kind of leadership that can only be described as doctored to suit somebody's "special" mission'.[13]

This public protest served notice on the government that Chesoni and the hardliners on the Commission were being too blatant. The uproar surrounding the election date and a private warning to President Moi from the Secretary-General of the Commonwealth were other factors that forced the Commission to adopt a more open attitude. In mid-November Moi called upon Chesoni to educate voters on the electoral procedures. The Commission then organised the first of a series of meetings with the leaders of the eleven political parties on 19 November. At the same time, it finally appointed Reuben Ryanga, a senior diplomat from the Ministry of Foreign Affairs, as Director of Elections.[14] Henceforth, the situation improved dramatically, with several congenial meetings between officials and opposition parties.

Setting the Date

The 1992 electoral process followed the same pattern as previous contests. The first stage was the formal dissolution of Parliament, which in 1992 took place on 21 October. Civil servants, teachers and parastatal employees then had to resign their positions if they wished to contest the election. Once the Assembly was dissolved, the actual election date was announced. In the past this had been the prerogative of the President, but in 1992 it was officially Justice Chesoni's role. Then language boards determined the proficiency of new candidates in English and Swahili, the official languages of the Assembly. The parties' own nomination process followed, then the official nomination day on which all candidates had to present their papers to the Returning Officers. A three-week campaign period followed, ending with polling day itself. Parliament had to reconvene within three months of its dissolution, in this case by 28 January 1993.

President Moi referred on several occasions to his 'secret weapon', his power to choose the date of the poll. With Parliament's five-year term not due to end until February 1993, Moi in practice could choose when to 'go to the country', and from January 1992 onwards he kept his opponents guessing. The lure of a snap election was resisted, and the KANU leadership decided to rely on their staying power, although this gave the opposition more time to organise. In fact, Moi left the decision to call the general election to the last minute, waiting for FORD to collapse. The government, however, was not satisfied with its advantage, and sought to manipulate the process even further in a transparently illegal action which confirmed the doubts which many had over the autonomy of the Attorney-General and the Electoral Commission. In legal notice 276 of 23 October 1992 Attorney-General Wako secretly 'corrected' the legislation governing the number of days allowed for the party primaries from 'not less' to 'not more' than 21 days, using the Attorney-General's power to rectify a 'clerical or printing error' to a law. This was unreported in the press. Obviously in collusion, ten days later on 3 November Justice Chesoni then suddenly announced the election date as 7 December. Nomination day was set for 11 November, giving the opposition parties only eight days to select their candidates. KANU clearly hoped by this to catch the opposition unprepared for their primary nominations, preventing them finding candidates in many areas, and minimising defections within their party following the numerous defeats which would inevitably occur amongst the candidates in KANU's own primaries.

The decision, however, was to provide one of KANU's most serious legal defeats. Four days later, on 7 November, George Anyona's KSC and FORD-Kenya both took the Electoral Commission to court under a certificate of urgency. After hearing the evidence, Justice Mbaluto ruled on

12 November that no errors had been adduced in the law so no correction was required, and that the clause had been 'sneaked in mischievously'. The planned dates were declared void, and KANU's plan was in tatters. Precisely why this happened remains unclear. Rumours suggest that some elements in KANU did not object to the party's legal reversal. The state's defence in the law suit was a shambles. The Electoral Commission, which professed a neutral role, submitted no replying affidavit because it claimed it was unaware of what the Attorney-General was going to say on the issue.[15] Wako, however, refused to comment. The day after the verdict, Wako explained that he had not been a party to the proceedings, and that had he been named, he would have explained the complicated constitutional issues involved, described the powers of the Attorney-General to revise laws and given his own views on the legal notice being challenged.[16] His statement was an exercise in ambiguity. It could be interpreted as a defence of the government, but also suggested that Wako, if called, might have spoken publicly against the legality of an action he had allegedly performed himself. The state made no attempt to appeal.

On 16 November, Chesoni announced the new nomination and polling days would be 9 and 29 December. Many observers found this timing surprising, placing the closing stages of the campaign during the Christmas holiday. Although KANU put a brave face on their failure to get away with their ruse – Japeth Kiti contended that 'We in KANU are grateful for the opportunity so kindly organised by the opposition'[17] – it was a blow to their plans. As a result, the nomination period for the parties effectively lasted from 3 November to 8 December. The primary election process was opened up, and the collusion with Attorney-General Wako in this invalid action further undermined confidence in the Commission.

The Presidential Election Process

A victory in the Presidential elections was the true prize from the introduction of multi-party democracy, as the divisions in FORD had shown. While the candidates for the election had been clear for some time, the procedures under which it was to be held were not, since Kenyans had never voted for their President before.[18] There was also a real concern among KANU leaders in early 1992 that they could lose both Presidency and Parliament on an open national vote. Thus they were determined to change the laws governing the Presidential election. At the same time, however, the government felt compelled to make concessions to the West by reducing the nominal powers of the Presidency.

On 3 March, 1992, three months after the introduction of multi-party democracy, these issues came to a head when the *Government Gazette* published the Constitution of Kenya (Amendment) Bill, 1992. The fate of this Bill, and its proposals for altering the role of the President, was described in Chapter 6. Following the KANU MPs' veto, the Bill was reformulated, re-emerging on 10 June, and eventually became the Constitution of Kenya (Amendment) No. 7, which Parliament accepted on 5 August 1992. The final reading was passed with very little debate in a record two hours by a majority of 140–1, a high turn-out in the KANU-only National Assembly.[19] This new Bill was more limited, making only three changes to the existing electoral provisions. As before, it restricted the President to two terms, but all the previous proposals were abandoned. Instead, it prohibited the formation of coalition governments, and introduced the requirement that the victorious candidate must secure 25 per cent of the vote in at least five of Kenya's eight Provinces.[20]

The requirement that the President form a government entirely from his own party stemmed from concern that although Moi would probably win the Presidential election due to divisions in the opposition, KANU might not win overall control of the House. It was the KANU Parliamentary group, which unanimously supported the revised Constitutional Amendment Bill on 14 July, which requested that this clause be inserted. This permitted Moi to form a minority government, and made far more difficult attempts to create an opposition coalition, as Ministerial rewards could no longer be shared out by a victorious President fronting a coalition of parties.

There was a widespread misunderstanding of the Presidential election process. Up to election day, the British High Commission and many others erroneously believed that whoever met the 25 per cent rule would win, whether they received a majority of the popular vote or not.[21] It was perfectly possible, many thought, that President Moi would be the only candidate to secure 25 per cent of the vote in five Provinces, even if another candidate secured the most popular votes. Some speculated that in such circumstances Moi, the incumbent, would remain in office. The government may deliberately have kept the situation ambiguous in order to facilitate a last ditch attempt to keep Moi in office if the worst happened. In the event of no outright winner in the first round, section 5(4) of the new legislation required that a second round be held immediately between the two candidates with the highest numbers of votes. KANU's determination to ensure that this did not happen was evident from the fact that absolutely no preparations were made to organise such a run-off.

Both the West and the opposition parties criticised the 25 per cent requirement. Kibaki argued that the Provinces were administrative structures and not constitutional entities requiring representation, and that the amendment violated the principles of universal suffrage. There were protests to Moi from 100 American Congressmen, who claimed that the Bill was 'clearly designed to prolong your regime's hold on power'. KANU, however, had a strong hand to play and Wako's response was cutting. He wondered if Moi's opponents were 'admitting that the current President can fulfil that requirement and that any other Presidential candidate cannot? If so, let them come out openly.'[22]

The two-terms amendment was to cause KANU problems. Why it was introduced is unclear – possibly as a tactic at a time when KANU feared losing the Presidency, possibly as a sop to the Western donors. In any case, ambiguities in the drafting of the clause left Moi open to legal challenges since the law did not state whether this new rule was retroactive or not. On 24 November, two voters attempted to gain an injunction against the President contesting the election, on the grounds that he had already served three terms and the constitution specified that 'No person shall be elected to hold office as President for more than two terms.'[23] Justice Akiwumi dismissed the request on 11 December 1992, though not on the substance of the complaint, only ruling that the matter should be raised in an election petition after the election, not before.[24] Precedent would suggest that such changes to the law are seldom retroactive, even though, unlike in the United States, no exemption was explicitly included. Certainly, Wako, when he introduced the Bill, made it clear that it did not disqualify Moi.[25]

Parliament also decided that to maximise turn-out, accountability and transparency, voting would take place in all three elections – local government, Parliamentary and Presidential – at the same time and that the votes would be counted and announced at the constituency, rather than District, level in order to reduce opportunities for confusion, error and (implicitly) rigging.

The Parliamentary Constituency Boundaries

In 1992, Kenya's National Assembly had 188 elected seats, plus 12 members nominated by the President; the Speaker and the Attorney-General. The boundaries of the parliamentary constituencies were set by the Election Boundaries Review Commission (the Electoral Commission) according to criteria such as natural groupings, population, and geographical size. In the past constituencies had been delimited primarily on ethnic lines, and had never been equal in population, given the problems of representing large, arid constituencies. The last boundary review, carried out in 1986 for the 1988 election, increased the number of seats by 30 from 158. Prior to this, the seat allocation had been left untouched since 1966, as all attempts to update it had been shelved due to the political disputes they generated. After 25 years of population growth, the distribution of people had changed dramatically. In 1983, for example, densely populated seats such as Nyeri, Mathare and Kericho East all contained over 100,000 registered voters, while tiny Baringo East and Marsabit South had less than 10,000 each. The real determinants of the 1986 review were political, however, not demographic. It did not abolish a single underpopulated seat, and established no new constituencies in Nairobi – a Kikuyu-dominated area with a substantial protest vote, whose population had grown dramatically since the early 1960s – or in Kenya's other major cities, despite the continuing influx of people to the urban centres. If urban and rural constituencies were equal in population, the capital would have been entitled to 16 MPs, instead of eight. Mombasa would have had six instead of four seats, and both Kisumu and Nakuru would have been entitled to two seats rather than one. Since the mid-1960s, Kenyan politics had been structured around rural coalitions competing for power in the centre. Rural, not urban voters, were at the core of electoral and political coalitions, and successive governments have prioritised rural issues such as commodity prices, crop marketing, and land. The need to avoid giving Nairobi its demographic due in 1986–7 can only be explained by a desire to maintain the over-representation of rural areas and especially of the semi-arid rural regions, in order to ensure that Parliament provided a counterweight to the economic power of the capital.

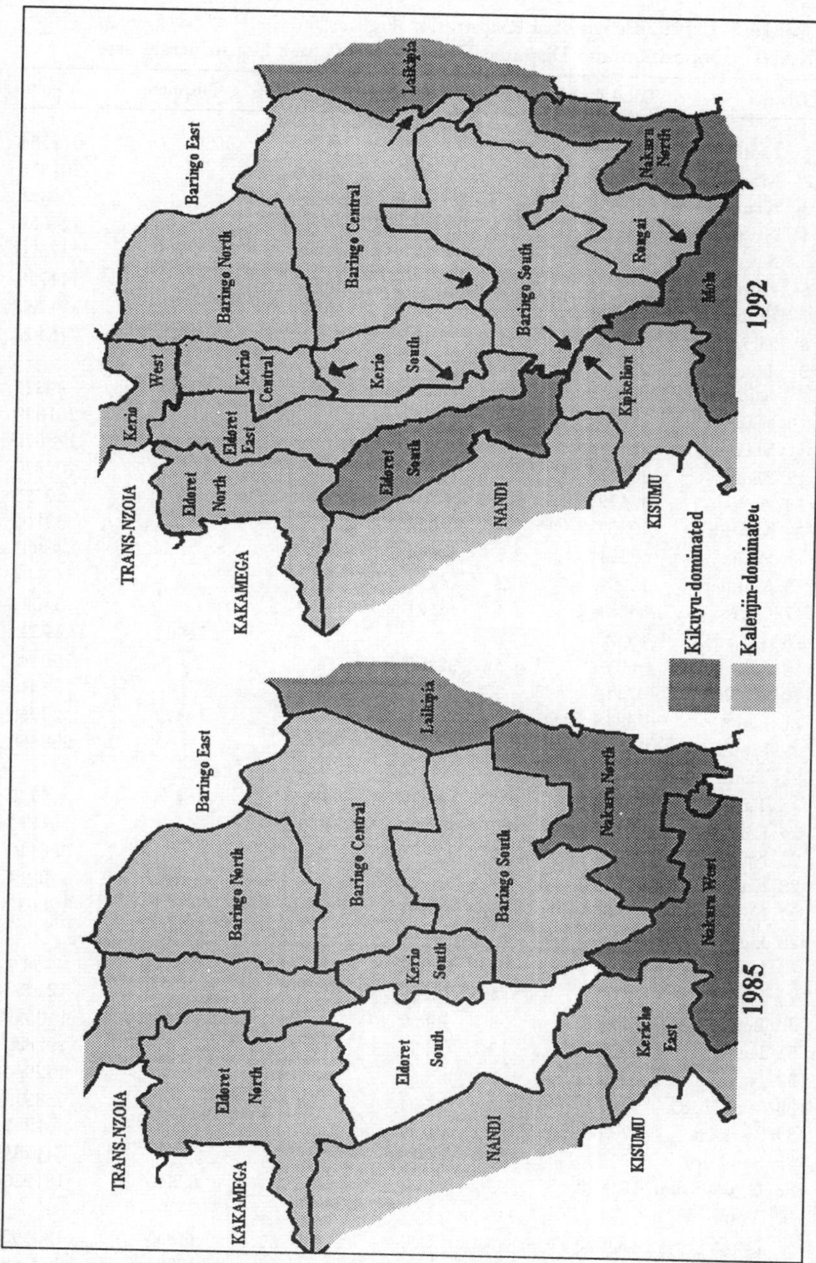

Figure 7.1 Changing Constituency Boundaries, 1985–92

Table 7.1 1992 Provisional Registration Figures:
KANU, Opposition and Disputed Districts by Average Constituency Size

District	Total Regd.	N.	KANU	Opposition	Disputed	Total
1 Nairobi	674564	8		84321		674564
2 Murang'a	301353	6		50226		301353
3 Kiambu	390823	7		55832		390823
4 Nyandarua	124637	3		41546		124637
5 Nyeri	247520	6		41253		247520
6 Kirinyaga	144729	3		48243		144729
7 Embu	139173	3		46391		1391733
8 Meru	278406	6			46401	278406
9 Tharaka-Nithi	90627	2			45314	90627
10 Machakos	251002	6			41834	251002
11 Makueni	178672	4			44668	178672
12 Kitui	207377	5			41475	207377
13 Isiolo	32522	2	16261			32522
14 Marsabit	52302	4	13076			52302
15 Wajir	43991	3	14664			43991
16 Mandera	42994	3	14331			42994
17 Garissa	54084	4	13521			54084
18 Tana River	49323	2			24662	49323
19 Kilifi	160499	5	32100			160499
20 Kwale	97348	3	32449			97348
21 Lamu	28943	2			14472	28943
22 Mombasa	258368	4		64592		258368
23 Taita-Taveta	65730	4			16433	65730
24 Laikipia	101772	2		50886		101772
25 Nakuru	386110	5		77222		386110
26 Kajiado	110314	3			36771	110314
27 Narok	128636	3	42879			128636
28 Elegeyo-Marakwet	87089	4	21772		87089	
29 Baringo	121032	4	30258			121032
30 Bomet	140555	3	46852			140555
31 Kericho	192880	3	64293			192880
32 Nandi	142960	3	47653			142960
33 West Pokot	68913	3	22971			68913
34 Turkana	57397	3	19132			57397
35 Samburu	42785	2	21393			42785
36 Uasin-Gishu	181920	3			60640	181920
37 Trans-Nzoia	133665	3			44555	133665
38 Bungoma	239156	5			47831	239156
39 Busia	253465	4			63366	253465
40 Vihiga	153024	4			38256	153024

Table 7.1 cont.

District	Total Regd.	N.	KANU	Opposition	Disputed	Total
41 Kakamega	301930	7			43133	301930
42 Siaya	208495	5		41699		208495
43 Kisumu	245970	5		49194		245970
44 Homa Bay	192700	5		38540		192700
45 Migori	161699	4		40425		161699
46 Kisii	266250	7			38036	266250
47 Nyamira	122658	3			40886	122658
Averages	169284		28350	52169	40654	7956362

The districts to benefit most were those where local Moi allies were particularly strong and could dictate the recommendations. Thus in Kakamega a new constituency was created for Bahati Semo, a long-term opponent of KANU strong-man Moses Mudavadi, and Lurambi South was split in two to separate KANU loyalist Burudi Nabwera from popular dissident Joshua Angatia. Machakos received three new seats, while neighbouring Kitui received none, because of KANU Chairman Mulu Mutisya's role as a power broker in the Moi coalition. Nyeri also received two new constituencies, strengthening its voice in an attempt to bolster the power of the anti-Kibaki faction in the District and to divert attention from Kibaki's impending demotion from the Vice-Presidency.

There were similar gerrymandering problems with specific seats. For example, Kisumu Town gained some large semi-rural areas 'largely due to the influence of Dr Ouko' who was attempting to counter his rival Job Omino's inroads in the urban areas.[26] There were also some little-reported alterations to District boundaries in the key area where the Kalenjin home districts of Baringo, Kericho and Elgeyo-Marakwet bordered on the settlement areas of Uasin Gishu and Nakuru. As well as creating new Kalenjin-dominated seats in Rongai and Eldoret East out of previously marginal constituencies, these changes dramatically enlarged Kerio South, Biwott's seat, to incorporate a substantial chunk of Eldoret (see Figure 7.1). President Moi's neighbouring constituency of Baringo Central also grew substantially. In the south, Baringo and Kericho Districts alienated substantial areas from Kikuyu-dominated Nakuru, and broke the division between eastern and western Kalenjin homelands by creating a narrow corridor which split off Uasin Gishu from Nakuru.

The government also failed to release the 1989 census figures, partly in order to avoid redrawing constituency boundaries. Although the Electoral Commission began a second review before the elections, intending to introduce 22 new constituencies, it abandoned these plans. As a result, reallocation did not correct the predominance of the rural population over the urban, or the dominance of the semi-arid and pastoral voters over the settled agricultural communities, a situation which favoured KANU and Moi.[27] Since 1963, as a result of the distribution of voters and seats, it has been possible for a party with a minority of the vote, concentrated in semi-arid seats, to win a majority of the Assembly. As Tables 7.1 and 7.2 show,

Table 7.2 KANU, Opposition and Disputed Districts by Average Constituency Size

District	Total registered voters	Number of constituencies	Dominant party (or none)	Average voters per seat
Nairobi	674,564	8	Opposition	84,321
Nakuru	386,110	5	Opposition	77,222
Mombasa	258,368	4	Opposition	64,592
Kericho	192,880	3	KANU	64,293
Busia	253,465	4	None	63,366
Uasin-Gishu	181,920	3	None	60,640
Kiambu	390,823	7	Opposition	55,832
Laikipia	101,772	2	Opposition	50,886
Murang'a	301,353	6	Opposition	50,226
Kisumu	245,970	5	Opposition	49,194
Kirinyaga	144,729	3	Opposition	48,243
Bungoma	239,156	5	Opposition	47,831
Nandi	142,960	3	KANU	47,653
Bomet	140,555	3	KANU	46,852
Meru	278,406	6	None	46,401
Embu	139,173	3	Opposition	46,391
Tharaka-Nithi	90,627	2	None	45,314
Makueni	178,672	4	None	44,668
Trans-Nzoia	133,665	3	None	44,555
Kakamega	301,930	7	None	43,133
Narok	128,636	3	KANU	42,879
Machakos	251,002	6	None	41,834
Siaya	208,495	5	Opposition	41,699
Nyandarua	124,637	3	Opposition	41,546
Kitui	207,377	5	None	41,475
Nyeri	247,520	6	Opposition	41,253
Nyamira	122,658	3	None	40,886
Migori	161,699	4	Opposition	40,425
Homa Bay	192,700	5	Opposition	38,540
Vihiga	153,024	4	None	38,256
Kisii	266,250	7	None	38,036
Kajiado	110,314	3	None	36,771
Kwale	97,348	3	KANU	32,449
Kilifi	160,499	5	KANU	32,100
Baringo	121,032	4	KANU	30,258
Tana River	49,323	2	None	24,662
West Pokot	68,913	3	KANU	22,971
Elgeyo-Marakwet	87,089	4	KANU	21,772
Samburu	42,785	2	KANU	21,393
Turkana	57,397	3	KANU	19,132
Taita-Taveta	65,730	4	None	16,433
Isiolo	32,522	2	KANU	16,261
Wajir	43,991	3	KANU	14,664
Lamu	28,943	2	None	14,472
Mandera	42,994	3	KANU	14,331
Garissa	54,084	4	KANU	13,521
Marsabit	52,302	4	KANU	13,076

Source: Based on 1992 provisional registration figures in *Weekly Review*.[28]

in 1992 KANU's strongholds tended to have far fewer voters than opposition constituencies.

This disparity became important with the advent of multi-party politics because the average size of a secure KANU constituency was only 28,350 voters, while seats in opposition areas were on average 84 per cent larger with 52,169 voters, and disputed areas lay in the middle. Thus, Nairobi (eight seats with an average 84,321 registered voters) had as many voters as Lamu, Tana River, Kwale, Kilifi, Taita-Taveta, Mandera, Wajir, Garissa, Isiolo, Marsabit and Turkana Districts combined (35 seats). Consequently, if KANU were to win its 'home areas', plus the smaller disputed Districts like Lamu, Tana River, Tharaka-Nithi and Kajiado, the ruling party could secure an overall majority of seats by winning seats containing less than 39 per cent of the registered vote (and of course, they would not need to win more than half the vote in the seats they won). Although it did not affect the Presidential election, the discrepancy in Parliamentary constituency size destroyed the opposition's chances of converting a numerical majority among the urban population and sedentary cultivators into a corresponding majority of Parliamentary seats.

Registration

The registration of voters is a key stage on the route to fair elections. If voters are prevented from registering, are assisted to evade the legal restrictions on multiple registration, or are transported from their home constituencies to register in politically marginal seats, then the fairness of the entire election is compromised. The registration process in Kenya is voluntary, as in the United States. Registration levels, however, have always been relatively high. Officially, voters have to demonstrate that they are aged 18, of sound mind, are Kenyan citizens, and own property or have lived in the constituency for at least five years (although this rule is unenforceable and rarely rigorously applied, giving many urban voters the legal choice to register where they work rather than where they live).

The 1992 election followed the pattern set in previous years. The announcement that voter registration would begin was taken to herald an election within six months. There has always been considerable paranoia about the registration process, which traditionally has been characterised by administrative incompetence and fraud, and 1992 was no exception. The registration exercise began on 8 June 1992, and finished on 20 July, having been twice extended to a total of 43 days. This was an extremely short period by the standard of previous elections, when registration had averaged three months. The available evidence suggests that register abuses and manipulations were widespread, and had national implications because of the need to maximise votes nationally and provincially in the Presidential elections. Unfortunately, at this vital stage there were no permanent Western observer groups in the country or accredited internal monitors to observe the process.

Registration rates were extremely low for the first month, because FORD and the DP boycotted the exercise. FORD interim Vice-Chairman

Table 7.3 Total Registration Figures for Kenyan Elections, 1992

Date	Registered
8 June	0
13 June	595,402
24 June	2,100,000
28 June	3,336,800
3 July	3,900,000
4 July	4,000,000
8 July	5,181,661
11 July	6,274,265
15 July	6,700,000
21 July	8,000,000

Source: NEMU Final Report and *Weekly Review*, 3 and 10 July 1992.

Masinde Muliro had called for a boycott in early June in an attempt to compel Attorney-General Wako to make concessions, contending that identity cards had not been distributed to large numbers of younger Kenyans, many of whom were believed to favour the opposition. Religious leaders also strongly criticised the registration process, demanding correction of these failings before registration continued. They also sought to pressure the government to dismiss the Electoral Commission and replace it with an 'impartial' body. The result was a coordinated boycott by the opposition parties and religious communities, and low registration in their urban strongholds.

The boycott backfired. Not only did the Western donor community look askance at politicians boycotting the first multi-party general election since independence, but the inability of opposition leaders to control their supporters soon became evident. Although party leaders could see the longer-term strategic advantage of pressing the government for further reforms, individual politicians knew that an election was imminent and that if their supporters were not registered they would lose. Thus there was persistent opposition within the FORD and DP ranks to the boycott call. When the Churches also abandoned the boycott, the opposition conceded on 2 July, claiming the government was 'responding positively' to their demand for an independent Electoral Commission and, just before the end of the registration period, calling for their supporters to register. Registration immediately picked up and, faced with thousands thronging the registration centres, the government granted the first ten-day extension. The period was then extended, at the last minute, by three more days. Figure 7.3 shows the major events of the registration period and their effects on overall registration.

The registration process closed before the opposition was happy, since there was no sign that the rate of registration was slackening. There was strong evidence from all over the country that large numbers of eligible voters had been unable to register and many claims by politicians and pro-opposition magazines that the issuing of identity cards, which was the duty of the government, not the Electoral Commission, was being delayed deliberately. This appeared to discriminate against younger voters, as many had to obtain national identity cards for the first time. Foreign observers and internal monitors reported extensive problems in areas as widely dispersed as Nairobi, Samburu and Kwale. A visiting United States Agency for International Development (USAID) team suggested that identity cards were much harder to obtain in opposition than government areas, where some people were issued with several.[29] On 14 July the leaders of the four main opposition parties sued the Attorney-General and Chesoni, seeking the nullification of the exercise on the grounds that the period was too short.[30] The Catholic Bishops and the NCCK urged that registration be extended until August, but the government refused.

In the end 7,956,354 voters had registered, a dramatic increase on 1988's 5.5 million, but little more than in the last free elections in 1983, when there were over 7.2 million voters.[31] The Electoral Commission insisted that according to the 1989 census, results of which were not published until 1994, only 9.6 million out of a total population of 24 million were eligible to register. Other estimates put Kenya's population and voting-age population much higher. The Commonwealth team, for example, believed that there were 26 million Kenyans and that the Electoral Commission had underestimated the number of unregistered adults by nearly one million.[32] The opposition claimed that 3.5 million young people had not been registered.

In some districts, there was evidence of partisan registration clerks deliberately making incorrect entries in the register. This was particularly prevalent in certain key marginal areas such as Trans-Nzoia, where *Society* reported that some Luhya names had been incorrectly entered in the register in June, and where Luhya youth also had problems in obtaining identity cards.[33] In many areas, there were reports that residence requirements were not properly checked; there were also rumours that in KANU zones under-age voters were being registered, and that no documentation was being demanded. In Wundanyi, for example, KANU was allowed to register voters living elsewhere simply by providing photocopies of their ID cards.[34] By contrast, the opposition claimed that in areas like Mwala in Machakos and Kajiado North chiefs and officials had made it difficult for people from opposition-supporting communities to register. There were claims in Mombasa that Somali refugees had secured identity cards and were registered. One of the ten volumes of names for the Makadara registration unit in Kisauni had allotted numbers with the names 'to be inserted when the time comes'.[35] The register, of course, was not computerised, and no means of cross-checking for duplication was possible.

There was also evidence of extensive, well-organised transportation of voters from safe seats into marginal areas. Transportation of voters *en masse* from other parts of the country had occurred many times before, generally from Central Province into the nearby urban areas. In urban areas it is particularly difficult to detect transportation, as many people register where they work and travel to and from their homes. The provision of free transport by candidates on polling day is also traditional, and is hard to distinguish from transporting voters from outside the constituency. Nonetheless, in 1992 the combination of deliberate register inflation, partisan officials, the limited time, delay in the issuing of identity cards and massive voter transportation proved a major influence on the fairness of the election.

Overall registration was not only far lower than expected but also extremely variable. An analysis carried out on behalf of the International Republic Institute (IRI), using unpublished data from the 1989 census, identified constituencies which experienced over- or under-registration on the basis of their estimated populations.[36] Adjustments were made for urban areas where the population increase was particularly rapid. These estimates were compared with the *Weekly Review's* list of registration figures on 31 July 1992 and cross-verified with other published sources of registration statistics. Although the calculations were necessarily fairly rough, as estimates had to be made of those who had reached 18 since 1989, these figures provide the best information available on national anomalies in registration. This analysis suggests a pattern of strategic over- or under-registration in key regions and constituencies (Table 7.2). There were a disproportionate number of marginals and government strongholds among these highly registered areas, headed by Lamu on the Coast where an implausible 98.8 per cent of the eligible population were registered. Eight of the 15 were from the Rift Valley, and the majority of the list were over-registered by the standards of previous elections and in comparison with adjacent districts. In some cases, such as Nakuru and Mombasa, the high figure was due to rapid immigration or the decision of voters to

Table 7.4 The Top 15 Districts by Percentage of the Eligible Population Registered

Province	District	Percentage registered	Type of area
Coast	Lamu	98.8	Marginal
Rift Valley	Laikipia	98.6	Opposition
Rift Valley	Nakuru	94.0	Marginal
Eastern	Isiolo	92.8	KANU
Rift Valley	Baringo	91.6	KANU
Coast	Mombasa	89.7	Marginal
Rift Valley	Kajiado	87.1	Marginal
North-Eastern	Garissa	87.0	KANU
Nyanza	Nyamira	84.9	Marginal
Rift Valley	Elgeyo-Marakwet	84.6	KANU
Rift Valley	Kericho	84.6	KANU
Rift Valley	Uasin-Gishu	84.5	Marginal
Rift Valley	Samburu	82.7	KANU
Coast	Tana River	82.0	Marginal
Central	Kiambu	80.5	Opposition

register in marginal constituencies. It is hard, however, to provide an explanation for the high registration rates in such semi-arid areas as Garissa, Samburu, Tana River, Baringo and Isiolo, other than by the inclusion of under-aged voters, transportation from outside the district, or multiple registration.

Examining the same data at the constituency level yields more interesting discoveries when compared with the political figures contesting the seats. Table 7.3 highlights the top 20 registration rates sorted by descending proportion of eligible voters registered. While the Nairobi seats were likely to be highly politicised, as they were marginal constituencies with residents from many different ethnic groups, the presence of other constituencies, such as both Laikipia seats, both Lamu seats, Simeon Nyachae's Nyaribari Chache, Vice-President Saitoti's Kajiado North, and the hotly contested Molo constituency indicates 'busing' or inflation. This was confirmed by reports that Simeon Nyachae endangered KANU victories in other Kisii seats because of the number of KANU supporters he had transported and registered in his own seat in order to secure a convincing victory. Many Maasai registered in Kajiado North were reported to have been brought in from elsewhere in Maasailand. The IPK alleged that in Mvita about 2,000 blank spaces were left in the register to enable people to vote twice.[37]

As confirmation of this statistical evidence, one of the authors counted the register at two particularly contentious polling stations in Molo, the seat with the highest registration in the country, where it was widely believed that huge numbers of KANU supporters were transported from Baringo and Kericho to register. In registration unit NKU/61/1 at Kipkewa Primary school registration centre in Kerisoi (which had been added to the original list of registration areas) in the Molo South ward, there were 13,172 names. This was an extraordinarily high number of voters for a single place. Moreover, almost all of them were Kalenjin (this can be determined from the first characters of their names and the use of arap) and 13,120 of them gave the same address – P.O. Box 290, Molo.[38] In the nearby registration centre NKU/64/1 at Chepkapirot, also in Kerisoi unit, between 3,000 and 4,000 people all gave the same address at Box 127, Molo. Indeed, this case was so blatant that it was visited by a member of the National Election Monitoring Unit team. The area proved to be a lightly populated forest station. The impression gained by the NEMU team and the authors was that these people had been transported to the area to register from elsewhere and had probably been double-registered. This view was borne out by the Molo result (see Chapter 12).

Figure 7.2 shows graphically the political nature of the registration battles. The country divided into three zones. The majority of seats lie in the 60–92 per cent range of eligible voters registered, while the outliers – greater than 93 per cent and less than 60 per cent – formed the other two groups.[39] The key area of high registration runs up the Rift Valley from Kajiado North, through Nakuru District and Kipkelion, the Keiyo seats of Elgeyo-Marakwet and most of Baringo, through to Laikipia. The figures for Uasin Gishu cannot be calculated, but it is suspected that Eldoret South, at least, would follow this pattern. Also standing out are the movement of

Table 7.5 Constituencies with the Highest Percentage Registration

Province	District	Constituency	Percentage of eligible voters registered	Significant figure
Nairobi	Nairobi	Starehe	171.2	Charles Rubia (KNC)
Nyanza	Kisii	Nyaribari Chache	142.5	Simeon Nyachae (KANU)
Rift Valley	Nakuru	Molo	133.4	Njenga Mungai (Asili)
Nyanza	Nyamira	Kitutu Masaba	119.2	George Anyona (KSC)
Rift Valley	Nakuru	Nakuru East	115.3	
Rift Valley	Kajiado	Kajiado North	114.2	Vice-President Saitoti (KANU)
Nyanza	Kisii	Nyaribari Masaba	110.3	James Nyamweya (DP)
Coast	Mombasa	Mvita	109.6	Sharrif Nassir (KANU)
Coast	Lamu	Lamu East	107.0	
Western	Busia	Bunyala	105.1	Peter Okondo (KANU)
Rift Valley	Baringo	Baringo Central	102.1	President Moi (KANU)
Rift Valley	Nakuru	Nakuru Town	99.2	Mark Mwithaga (DP)
Rift Valley	Laikipia	Laikipia West	98.7	G.G. Kariuki (KANU)
Rift Valley	Laikipia	Laikipia East	98.5	Minister Kaparo (KANU)
Eastern	Isiolo	Isiolo North	97.8	
Coast	Mombasa	Likoni	97.5	
North-East	Garissa	Dujis	97.4	Minister Maalim (KANU)
Coast	Lamu	Lamu West	95.7	
Rift Valley	Kericho	Kipkelion	94.5	
Rift Valley	Elgeyo-Marakwet	Kerio Central	94.1	

Source: Analysis of data produced for IRI by Judy Geist. The figures exclude Uasin Gishu District, where it was impossible to demarcate the constituency boundaries in the 1989 census figures.

peoples in Kisii, and from the south Coast into Mombasa. The implausibility of the Lamu, Dujis and Isiolo North figures is also reinforced.

We can control for traditional movements of people into the urban areas by combining these figures with those for registration in 1988 in the same seats, allowing us to focus on new movements. The figures since 1988 show massive new movements of voters into Nairobi and Mombasa, which can be explained by factors including rapid immigration to urban areas and their political marginality. Other areas showing rapid growth were Nakuru, Kajiado, President Moi's Baringo District, Bomet and Kericho – indeed, all KANU's Rift Valley heartlands. By contrast, the lowest figures were found in the rural Coast Province, especially in Kilifi, and there were very low increases in the Luhya and Luo areas, where FORD's boycott had had most effect. Where there was a large proportion of the eligible population registered, but a normal rate of increase, traditional registration preferences can be deduced, for example, among peri-urban voters opting to vote in the city constituencies where they work. Where there was a large proportion of the population registered to vote, and a large increase over the 1988 registration figures, the seat was either extremely marginal or urban; or the register was inflated; or supporters were bused into the constituency to register. Five key marginals stand out by this measure:

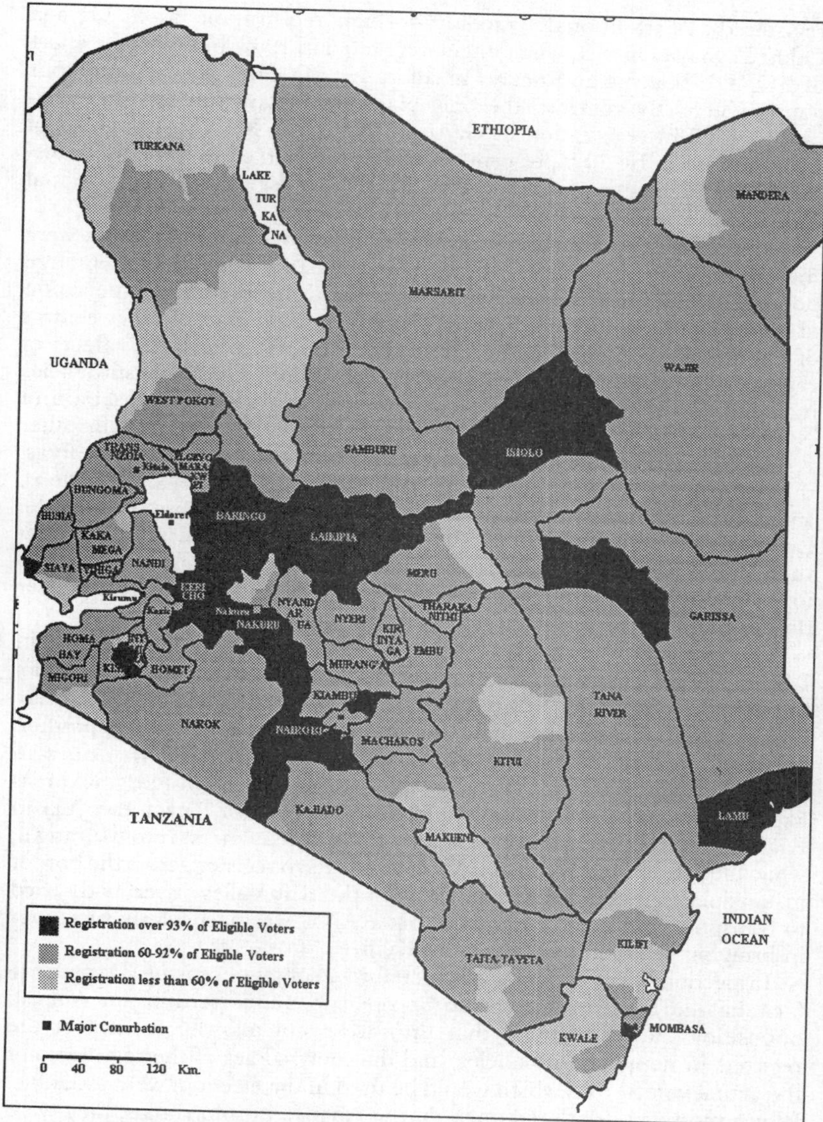

Figure 7.2 Registration by percentage of eligible voters

Starehe (262 per cent increase in the number of registered voters since 1988, and 171 per cent of estimated population registered), Mvita (155 per cent increase, 109 per cent registered), Kajiado North (103 per cent increase, 114 per cent registered), Molo (89 per cent increase, 133 per cent registered) and Nakuru Town (163 per cent increase, 99 per cent registered). A traditionally medium-to-high registration, as in Oginga Odinga's Siaya District, when under-registered in 1992, indicates the effect of FORD's boycott and delays in allocating ID cards to the numerous young voters. By contrast, the only plausible explanation for the extraordinary fall in registration in Ganze in Kilifi, the KANU stronghold of Minister Ngala, by 20.5 per cent from 1988, would seem to be the transporting of residents out of the constituency to register in the marginal Mombasa.

Thus there were four major problem areas in 1992. First, there were the urban areas of Nairobi, Mombasa and Nakuru, which had seen large population increases and were closely contested. In several, transportation of voters can be suspected. Second, there were a number of other centres of competition, mainly in the ethnic borderlands, where the effects of register manipulations and busing were evident. These constituencies included Kajiado North, Molo, Laikipia West, Nyaribari Masaba and Nyaribari Chache. Third, in Baringo Central and North, certain other KANU strongholds including Tinderet in Nandi, and a few marginal areas, the registration was unusually high by the standards of previous elections. Inflation of the register by KANU is believed to be the cause. Finally, the Luo Districts were particularly under-registered. Chesoni admitted that there could have been double registration in some areas and promised an investigation into these claims on 25 November, but no report was ever produced.[40]

The guilty party in most cases was KANU, as the polls later showed in Lamu, Kericho, Baringo, Elgeyo-Marakwet, Isiolo, Garissa and Kajiado, but KANU was not the only party to transport voters. The 25 per cent rule required all parties to focus their votes in the right areas. For the opposition parties there was little point in enhancing their massive majorities in Central Province or Nyanza, when votes were required in marginal areas like Nairobi and the Rift Valley. In Starehe, Nakuru Town and Juja in Kiambu, FORD-Asili almost certainly transported voters from Murang'a, while the DP assisted Nyeri and Meru residents to register across the border in Laikipia to maximise Kibaki's vote in the Rift Valley. Everybody tried to transport voters into Mombasa, but KANU was particularly successful in bringing people into Mvita from Kilifi.

Inspection of the registers was therefore a contentious issue. Despite the fact that they were supposed to be open to public scrutiny in August, opposition parties claimed that they were not allowed to inspect the registers in many constituencies, and that only copies of the registers, not the actual voters' rolls which would be used in the election, were available. Whilst most were declared open during August, in some areas, they were not made public. The Registration Officer even refused to let observers from the Federation of International Women Lawyers (FIDA) and the International Commission of Jurists (ICJ) inspect the Samburu register, for example.[41] The time to inspect the register was reduced from two months to one month, which made the rectification of anomalies harder.

There is also evidence of changes in registration figures after the close of the official exercise on 20 July. In Nakuru, Njenga Mungai protested that registration was continuing in Molo in August, although Justice

Chesoni explicitly denied this claim. *Society* similarly reported that registration officials in the Kerisoi area of Molo forest were still active well after the close of registration and that the Nakuru and Kericho District Commissioners had visited the area secretly. There were reports of a large exodus from Kericho District to the area, using at least 50 vehicles.[42] Similar allegations were made about Nairobi, Kisumu and Tana River.[43] As late as December, an Anglican Bishop claimed that registration was continuing and voting cards were still being issued in some parts of the country. These allegations can be confirmed by a careful study of the 'close of registration' figures, and a comparison with the election results and final statements of registration published at this time. Unusually, the *Weekly Review* did not mention the number of registered voters in its election coverage, but the *Daily Nation* did so on 31 December 1992 and the *Kenya Times* and *Standard* also provided official registration figures for various seats in their constituency profiles and elections results. The figures should not have differed significantly from each other, nor from the figures at the close of national registration, since only registration of Kenyans abroad (until 5 August) and voter protests at incorrect entries should have occurred.

Even allowing for transcription errors and late delivery of figures, resulting in older data being employed, there appears to have been a systematic process of registration continuing or significantly changing after the ending of the registration process in over 50 of the 188 seats. In certain constituencies, the registration figures differed in every report. Falls in registration by more than 800 voters, which should have been impossible, apparently occurred in 20 constituencies, some of them important marginals, including Narok North, Nyaribari Masaba, Imenti Central and Nakuru Town. More worrying, increases in registration occurred in roughly 35 seats, with some showing increases of more than 5,000 voters. These increased registrations revealed a regional bias. Coast Province, Nairobi and North-Eastern showed no major changes. In Western Province, two seats showed anomalous rises – Butere (Martin Shikuku's seat) and Lugari (Burudi Nabwera's seat, which was up by 3,870 voters). In Eastern Province, four seats showed large increases.[44] By contrast, in Central Province registration rose dramatically in nine seats, including five of the six Murang'a seats – Kangema, Kiharu (Matiba's seat, up 1,010), Makuyu (up 1,459), Gatanga (up 2,971), and Kigumo (up 3,228). Juja in Kiambu was up by 2,571. Kisii and Nyamira also saw continued rises in three of the ten seats, including Kitutu Masaba (George Anyona's seat, up 1,033), whilst five FORD-Kenya's South Nyanza seats continued to grow. Figure 7.3 provides a national picture of registration changes.

The worst increases were in the Rift Valley, where at least 12 seats grew significantly. Molo once more stands out, with 9,026 more voters by election day than when registration closed. Registration in two other Nakuru seats also increased dramatically: Nakuru East by 5,368 and Nakuru North by 2,021. Two of the four Elgeyo-Marakwet seats also grew (Kerio West by 6,913 and Kerio East by 4,810) as well as two of three Nandi seats, two of the three West Pokot constituencies, and three other KANU target seats in the Rift (Kipkelion, Saboti and Laikipia East).[45]

There appears to be a pattern whereby registration continued in

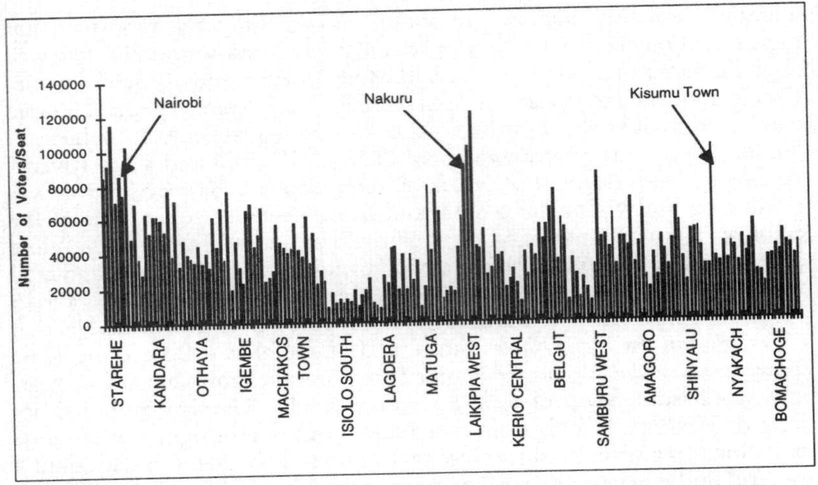

Figure 7.3 Total Registration (*Daily Nation*, 31 December 1992)
Source: Comparison of figures from close of registration 1992 with final reported registration figures.

Murang'a, Homa Bay, Elgeyo-Marakwet, Nandi, West Pokot and Nakuru Districts, and in a number of other individual constituencies after its official close. These seats were distributed among all the main parties, but it was KANU strongholds in the Rift Valley which formed the largest group, with FORD-Asili areas of Murang'a the other cluster. In Molo, we see confirmation of the claims of Njenga Mungai that KANU was importing voters. In four of five seats in Murang'a, however, the increases were larger than the total final KANU vote and the turn-outs were extremely high, suggesting late registration of FORD-Asili, not KANU, voters. Overall, about 100,000 voters 'appeared' after the close of formal registration, while another 60,000 vanished from other constituencies. To what extent this was a product of late information rather than late registration is unknown, but the pattern suggests the main beneficiaries were KANU and to a lesser extent FORD-Asili.

Presiding and Returning Officers

Another vexed question was the identity, background and political preferences of the officials who ran the election. The Returning Officers were appointed by the Electoral Commission and controlled the conduct of the election in their seats. They were assisted by their deputies and by district coordinators, who managed events in their districts.[46] Presiding Officers were each responsible for one particular polling station, and had a deputy for each stream of voters (there were several streams of voters in the larger stations). They were appointed by the Returning Officer in consultation with the Commission, which also appointed polling and counting clerks. Each Presiding Officer or deputy was assisted by six clerks, who marked the register and voters' cards, issued ballots and dipped voters' fingers into indelible ink.

For the first time since Independence, the Returning Officers for the seats and Presiding Officers for the polling stations were not officers of the Provincial Administration, a response to concerns over possible malpractice. This did not stop the choice of officials from proving contentious, however. The list of those nominated to organise the election was gazetted on 12 November. Despite Chesoni's promise that election officials would be non-partisan local notables and professionals, many were retired Provincial and District Commissioners or even serving government officials, unknown in the constituencies where they were to organise the elections.[47] The Nakuru East monitor from NEMU, for example, reported that 'Most of the [election officials] are civil servants, some of them are retired District Commissioners.... Further investigations should be done because they are not posted to the places they are known.'[48] In the important Embu constituency of Gachoka, the Deputy Returning Officer was a former District Officer sacked for inefficiency. In Mwatate, the Deputy Returning Officer was a retired Ministry of Information and Broadcasting official, and in the controversial Kitui West seat the same post was held by a senior civil servant from the NSSF, while the Returning Officer for Amagoro, who rejected the papers of all the opposition candidates, was a retired Brigadier.[49] Whilst the majority of officials acted with probity, it appears that preparations were made to ensure that staff sympathetic to KANU took up key positions in areas that the government and Electoral Commission expected to be vital to KANU's victory.

In the Rift Valley, a large proportion of the constituencies, even in predominantly Kikuyu areas such as Nakuru and Laikipia, had Kalenjin Returning Officers. Here, there seemed to be a policy of rotating officials so that the Returning Officers were civil servants not known in the area to which they were posted. In Turkana North, the Returning Officer was a Livestock Production Officer, his Deputy an Assistant Education Officer, while the Deputy Returning Officer for another Turkana constituency was a forester: all three came from Samburu. In Baringo, President Moi's home District, where it was necessary to ensure that Moi's victory was overwhelming, the officials were mainly Kipsigis (see Table 7.4). In Narok, the officials were allegedly all from Baringo, selected on instructions from KANU Minister ole Ntimama.[50] Similar claims were made about the Nakuru list, almost all of whom had Kalenjin names.

District Coordinators had a key role, since they had no operational responsibility and, therefore, could not be monitored as easily as Returning Officers. Some questionable appointments have also emerged here, including that of the Siaya District Coordinator Monye Ogol, who was the assistant secretary of KANU's Rarieda sub-branch.[51] Similar problems occurred at the Presiding Officer level. Generally, the Commission selected officials with the help of local chiefs who were of course KANU appointees. In Msambweni in Kwale District, a constituency later to prove contentious, one Presiding Officer and a deputy campaigned for the KANU candidate, and were arrested on polling day when they were discovered to be altering Presidential votes.[52] In Vihiga in Vihiga District, Presiding Officers and

Table 7.6 Some Baringo Election Officials

Position held	Constituency	Ethnic group	Post
Returning Officer	Baringo East	Kipsigis Kalenjin	Pastor of the Full Gospel Churches of Kenya
Deputy Returning Officer	Baringo East	Kipsigis Kalenjin	District Education Officer, Laikipia
Returning Officer	Baringo Central	Kipsigis Kalenjin	Retired District Officer
Deputy Returning Officer	Baringo Central	Kipsigis Kalenjin	Lecturer, Rift Valley Institute of Science and Technology

Source: NEMU Baringo DLO Report.

deputies were sacked for supporting KANU's parliamentary candidate.[53] Problems also appeared at the level of the clerks who would mark the register and pass out ballot papers, or count votes. They tended to be teachers, students or clerical officers, but in targeted seats their preferences for KANU were widely known. In Samia, the clerks were selected on 7 December, but local chiefs informed only known KANU supporters. During the selection, the chiefs and their assistants wore Kanu Youth T-shirts. Indeed, the Presiding Officers for eight polling stations were alleged to have been campaigners or agents of KANU candidate Moody Awori in 1988.[54] The clerks from Narok North were from KANU families; in Nakuru East they were reportedly from local banks and favoured KANU; in Embu they were mainly clerks from the District Commissioner's office and other ministries, vulnerable to state pressure.[55]

The opposition leaders publicised these problems on several occasions. The FORD-Asili candidates' seminar at the end of November, for example, protested at the 'ethnic bias in the selection of returning officers, particularly in the Rift Valley and North-Eastern Kenya provinces', while other opposition leaders, including Shikuku and Anyona, protested at the widespread use of retired civil servants and military personnel.[56] Local election monitors were aware of the danger and tried to obtain information about those involved, but in no case when poll monitors complained to their respective Returning Officers was any action taken.

The Western Governments and the Election

In the struggle to determine the electoral procedures and prepare for the campaign, there was a third player in the game: Western governments, embassies and non-governmental organisations. Western governments had been key players in the introduction of multi-party politics in Kenya. They also acted as referees, who had the power to deny funds to the government if they did not play fairly in the forthcoming election. They influenced electoral procedures, provided equipment, monitored the result and even funded the internal monitors. The two governments with the greatest impact in Kenyan politics in 1992 were the United States and Great Britain. The role of the United States and its Ambassador Smith Hempstone in the democratisation process has been mentioned. Hempstone elicited strong reactions from all who knew him. A journalist and managing editor of the right-wing *Washington Times* before being appointed Ambassador to Kenya in 1989, his main qualifications for the post seemed to be that he had written a book on Katanga 30 years before and that his wife was a friend of Barbara Bush. Nonetheless, he had played a pivotal role in the establishment of a democratic opposition. Despite his high public profile and active defence of the opposition, some Americans in Kenya were extremely critical, describing him privately as a drunkard who did virtually nothing. By December 1992 Hempstone's time in Kenya was limited, as he knew he would be replaced by the incoming Clinton Administration. Views have differed, even in the British High Commission, over whether he was a 'loose cannon' or was following State Department policy. Retired High Commissioner Johnstone, for example, took the view that Hempstone saw his appointment as a 'journalistic assignment' and implied that the US Ambassador had not realised fully what he was getting into. His successor, Sir Roger Tomkys, by contrast, believed that Hempstone's approach was in line with US policy.

American policy was certainly schizophrenic. The Bush Administration was committed to reducing aid to countries which refused to reform politically and to accept multi-party democracy. US bilateral aid to Kenya had been reduced from US$65 million in 1988–9 to US$60 million in 1990, and by 1992 was only US$19 million. No new commitments were being made, and Hempstone was active in supporting the rights of the opposition. At the same time, the United States continued to maintain the Mombasa base agreement, and to use Kenya as a supply centre and base for its Somalia operations. The Mombasa base agreement, signed in 1979, had given the United States access for its Rapid Deployment Force. The United States had lengthened the landing strip in Mombasa so that C-5s could land (also enabling commercial airline 747s to use the airport) and dredged Mombasa harbour so that US aircraft carriers could come into harbour. By 1989, however, the base was losing its appeal to the US military. The Gulf War demonstrated that aircraft carriers could replace permanent land bases, and Berbera in northern Somalia was more important than Mombasa as a base. The US Navy, however, wished to maintain Mombasa as a 'rest and recreation' base for the Seventh Fleet, as the nearest alternative was Perth in Western Australia.

The geo-political and strategic changes brought by the end of the Cold War meant that America was less dependent on Kenya and that the Bush Administration was more willing to respond to Congressmen who were castigating the Moi regime's human rights record. The Kenya government failed to recognise that its strategic bargaining position had deteriorated drastically and was demanding almost half of America's total planned military budget for Africa in exchange for continued use of Mombasa and other facilities: a price which the United States was unwilling to meet. Although American troop landings in Somalia, only two weeks before the Kenya election, strengthened the Kenyan government's bargaining position, as the country briefly became an important US supply-base – Smith Hempstone publicly called it 'an aircraft carrier' – the Bush Administration refused to supply anti-tank missiles to Kenya.

KANU hardliners profoundly distrusted the United States. They feared that the American landings in Somalia might be a launching base for a further attack on Kenya if Moi remained in power. They repeatedly claimed that the opposition parties and even the election monitoring bodies were funded clandestinely by the CIA. Accusations were made that FORD (and specifically the Odinga wing of FORD) had received funds from the USA and Germany. At a KANU rally in November, for example, FORD defector Emmanuel Maitha claimed that a Nairobi embassy had given each of the six FORD founders Sh3 million.[57] Foreign foundations interested in promoting democracy certainly provided funds. The German Friedrich Ebert foundation financed the printing of the *Charter for the Second Liberation.* Diplomatic circles suggested that the American and German governments had supplied technical advice, office equipment and other essential supplies to the parties, in an attempt to improve their organisation and ability to campaign. It was rumoured amongst the Luo community that Raila and the *Jaramogi* had both benefited substantially from foreign donations in the early multi-party era. FORD-Kenya officials strongly denied, however, that the party had received any financial assistance from the USA.

American Embassy officials suggested to the authors that at first Hempstone had favoured Matiba as the opposition's best Presidential candidate. The Embassy had expected Matiba on his return from London to unite the opposition and sweep Odinga aside. Matiba's intransigence, however, soon dispelled this illusion, and the United States looked increasingly to the Young Turks, who remained loyal to Odinga, and switched allegiances therefore to FORD-Kenya. The internal divisions within FORD reinforced KANU's belief in 'external interference'. Muthithi House leaders alleged at a National Executive Committee meeting on 31 August 1992, for example, that Odinga had received Sh128 million on his recent visit to Britain. This was immediately denied by Imanyara, who replied: 'They are probably the ones who might have received the money.'[58]

KANU also claimed that the opposition was in league with the Ugandans. President Moi himself alleged that Paul Muite had made a secret flight to Uganda between 22 and 26 December.[59] KANU leaders suggested that the Ugandan army would cross the border to support an attempt by FORD-Kenya to seize power when it lost the election. It seems more likely, however, that the Kenya government feared that Ugandan troops might intervene to protect the pro-opposition Luo and Luhya communities in western Kenya if the KANU regime attempted to take reprisals after the election. The Kenya-Uganda border had seen a number of military clashes, so far restricted to small-arms fire, especially in 1988. Several opposition leaders, such as Raila Odinga and Koigi wa Wamwere, had sought refuge in Uganda in the late 1980s, and relations between the Moi and Museveni governments had been strained ever since the National Resistance Movement (NRM) had seized power in January 1986, ending the lucrative business ties that Kenya's governing élite had enjoyed with the Obote and Okello regimes. Museveni, moreover, had reneged on the December 1985 Nairobi Accords between the NRM and the previous Tito

Okello regime, which Moi had spent a lot of time negotiating. As a result, Moi had never fully accepted the new government, and had been irritated further when he lost coffee transport contracts and failed to get the Ugandan government to cooperate with Lonhro to construct an oil pipeline from Kenya. The Kenya regime was also profoundly concerned about Uganda's close relations with Libya and Cuba. The Kenya government, consequently, deemed it prudent to move troops up to its western border, and attempted to deflect the blame onto FORD-Kenya and the Ugandans.

The British attitude to Kenya was also viewed as important, but aroused rather more suspicion among the opposition. British policy, which was strongly criticised by its Western allies and the opposition, was to support a free and democratic election, without favouring any party. Britain's major concern was with preserving stability and a managed transition to democracy, without any presumption about who should be in power. As well as being Kenya's largest trade partner and biggest aid donor – and training the army, police and Special Branch – the British government was also concerned by the large number of Asians eligible for entry into the UK as a result of holding British passports, in the event of a collapse of law and order. Implicitly, the British government's position was that economic reform was more important than political change, and that it simply wanted to see free and fair elections.[60] The British preferred a 'backroom style' of influence, and continued to meet President Moi and discuss issues, in contrast to Smith Hempstone, who towards the end of his tenure could no longer gain access to Moi.[61] There was, however, internal dissension about the British attitude, especially given the differences between the British and American approaches. The 'softly, softly' approach of former High Commissioner Tomkys, who retired in mid-1992, came in for strong criticism, some of it from within the Foreign and Commonwealth Office. Following the introduction of multi-party politics, the Foreign Office purged the Nairobi High Commission, appointing new officials who gradually began to establish relations with the opposition parties.

Despite these changes, there was a deep fear in FORD-Kenya of British support for Moi. The British helped to fund the election, and there was concern about the Conservative Party's links with KANU, including the business connections between Cecil Parkinson and Ketan Somaia, and their joint retention of Saatchi and Saatchi for their re-election campaigns. The opposition's concern was accentuated by an erroneous report by the Presidential Press Unit, widely broadcast by the KBC, that retiring British High Commissioner Sir Roger Tomkys 'wishes President Daniel arap Moi success in the forthcoming elections', which had to be swiftly denied. Lynda Chalker, Britain's Minster of Overseas Development, vehemently denied on numerous occasions that the British government was in any way supporting KANU, dismissing such reports as 'absolutely not true. These are stupid idiotic claims.'[62] Nonetheless, it is clear that the British government was dubious about the prospects of multi-party politics. At a post-election meeting at the Kenya Society in London, for example, ex-High Commissioner Tomkys queried whether the 'snake oil of multi-partyism' was necessarily the best thing for Kenya at the time and suggested it might not live up to its much touted claims.[63] Both he and Johnstone, his predecessor, argued that more pluralism within KANU would have been a better intermediate step.

The main influence on the election procedures was the long and painstaking efforts of the various embassies – particularly the Canadian, German and American – to pressure the Kenyan government to hold a reasonably fair election. Much of this was carried out through protracted negotiations with Chesoni over electoral procedures, trying to encourage the Electoral Commission to follow recognised standards. The USAID in Nairobi was particularly important in ensuring that larger ballot boxes were introduced with more effective seals. Their early statements, noting the media bias in favour of KANU, also had some impact. The USAID team liaised closely with the Governance group to support NEMU's monitoring activities (see below). The International Republican Institute and the Commonwealth were also influential in pressing the Commission to negotiate with the opposition.

Much of the 1992 election was paid for by the West. As sweeteners to ensure that the government played fair, and the facilities it provided were up to international standard, the British government particularly provided the Kenyans with election equipment and materials including Sh32 million for larger ballot boxes, office equipment and training of officials by British staff, totalling about £770,000. The United States provided 11,000 bottles of indelible ink, but otherwise gave mainly to the largest of the internal monitoring groups. There were many non-governmental donors willing to finance voter education and the monitoring groups. The result was a confusing competition as different NGOs funded numerous groups, many of whom were new, ill-organised and not always efficient in spending these funds.

USAID funded the International Foundation for Electoral Systems (IFES) to evaluate independently the government's budgeting requirements for the multi-party democracy transition. Since the donors were footing the bill for much of the election, they wished to ensure that it was properly managed and funded. In July 1992 several significant improvements to the electoral procedures were agreed upon, including the creation of an audit trail to trace the ballot papers through the electoral process, and the decision that ballots should be printed outside the country, to reduce concerns over fairness.[64] Eventually the ballot papers were printed in London at a cost of over Sh300 million (£6 million). Initially the Commission had suggested that all Presidential ballots be counted together in one place, a certain source of administrative chaos and a perfect opportunity to mislay boxes on the way to the count. The IFES objected and it was later agreed that the Presidential votes would be counted and announced at the constituency level. The IFES report specifically noted that the Commission budget did not include any allocation for a presidential run-off. This omission was never rectified and suggests that the government had no intention of losing the election on the first ballot. Although the constitution permitted a run-off and the balance of political forces made one likely, the Electoral Commission's coffers were empty and no preparations were made to hold one.

The International Human Rights Law Group, a non-partisan organisation to promote the rule of law in emerging democracies, also sent a group of three experts to examine the preparations for the elections and the institutional environment. They issued a critical report on 1 December, protesting amongst other things that 'the Electoral Commission has acted with extreme secretiveness and seems ill-prepared for the election'.[65] Reinforcing the opinions of the Western embassies and advance parties of observers, they accused the government of imposing a news blackout on the opposition and recommended that each major party 'be given a specified amount of free air time in the broadcast media'.[66] Little changed, although the opposition parties were permitted to broadcast a few television advertisements. More importantly, the group suggested that the 14-day notification for political meetings should be removed during the election campaign period. This became a source of conflict between government and opposition as the government waived the 14-day requirement during the campaigns proper, but insisted that District Officers had to be informed of and approve all meetings. The opposition parties insisted that they could hold as many meetings as they wanted and did not have to seek approval. The Group also recommended better training for election officials, clarification on how the ballot boxes would be transported from polling stations to the count, and more meetings between the Electoral Commission and the press and opposition parties. They also sought Chesoni's confirmation that no senior government officials would be involved in the polling or counting. Most of these requirements were met during the next few weeks as the government and the Electoral Commission realised that they had to meet minimum democratic requirements.

It was clear from the start of 1992 that Western governments wished to send monitors to ensure that the government and opposition both played fair when a general election was held. By international standards, the 1992 elections were therefore relatively well monitored.[67] Plans for the international monitoring effort were severely handicapped, however, by the change in the election date, which hampered deployment as many delegates were unwilling to miss Christmas at home. The majority of observers arrived in the days immediately preceding the poll, but all the important groups had advance teams on the ground prior to this, and numerous delegations visited the country in the run-up to the election. It was clear, however, that despite the presence of advance teams, the various observer groups were at a disadvantage compared with the government. Habel Nyamu, the dissident Commissioner responsible for liaison with the observers, suggested that the observers should have been in Kenya much earlier, but were delayed by the Electoral Commission.[68] Concerned at the potential authority of monitors to intervene in the election where they detected malpractice, the Commission stressed that the Kenyan constitution made no provision for monitors, who had the ability to intervene and demand the correction of abuses, but only for observers whose job, according to a booklet they produced, was only 'watching to see whether it is conducted in accordance with the electoral law … and that it is free and fair'.[69]

There were four types of external observers: the Americans; the team from the Commonwealth; those from other countries; and those who were not allowed to participate or withdrew before election day. The American observer group came from the International Republican Institute (affiliated to the Republican party). The IRI supplied 54 delegates from 13 countries, of a conservative disposition. They were supported by a team including a number of able and experienced Africanists. The IRI mounted two formal assessment missions in late October and early December 1992, and had representatives in Kenya from 29 October onwards. On 7 December, just before nomination day, the second IRI assessment team released *Kenya – Pre-Election Assessment Report,* a study of the electoral process and conduct of the campaigns so far.[70] This pinpointed the ethnic clashes and identified a number of other now familiar problems, including the composition of the Electoral Commission, the exclusion of the young from the voters' roll, and unequal access by parties to 'national resources' such as the media. The US team was well-informed, and amongst other activities, identified 30 key constituencies that should be monitored closely, using a series of criteria including registration anomalies and ethnic violence.

Original plans for 70 observers were scaled down following the changed election date, which created problems in finding volunteers. Embassy sources informed us that Ambassador Hempstone sent a telegram to the US State Department asking for replacements – 'Buddhists, Hindus or Moslems' – who were prepared to miss Christmas and come out before 28 December. Unfortunately, because of the change in date, at least one third of the IRI delegation did not arrive until the day before the election. The IRI was also accused privately of political bias in its selection of observers by USAID officials, as few Africanist academics were Republicans.[71] Hempstone asked for former President Jimmy Carter, who had undertaken similar missions in Latin America, South East Asia and Zambia, to be accredited as an observer for the IRI but his request was rejected by the White House. Following the defeat of the Bush Administration, several leaders of the IRI team appeared more interested in protecting their jobs in Washington than in monitoring the Kenyan election and spent much of December in the United States.

The second major monitoring group was the team from the Commonwealth. The 38 individuals, the largest Commonwealth contingent sent to an election, began assembling in early December, following technical visits by officials.[72] The team was led by Mr Justice Telford Georges, a judge from Trinidad and Tobago and former Chief Justice of Zimbabwe and Tanzania.[73] Its members included MPs and civil servants from various Commonwealth countries. Unfortunately, they and their advisers knew less about Kenya or its politics than might have been hoped. The main team arrived in Nairobi on 16 December, after being briefed by Commonwealth Secretary-General Anyaoku, and was on the ground for two weeks from 17 December 1992 to 2 January 1993. For the Commonwealth, the election was the first significant test of the heads of government summit in Harare in October 1991, which had confirmed the association's commitment to 'democracy, accountable administration and the rule of law'.[74] Like the IRI, the group was provided with detailed guidelines and checklists on what to look for when they made forays into the field to observe the campaigns, polling and the count.[75] Unfortunately, like the IRI, they

Photo 7.2 Arrival of the Commonwealth Monitoring Group
Courtesy of Nation Group Newspapers

arrived long after the serious nomination day problems of 9 December had occurred. Despite attempts to stress its impartiality, there was concern among the other monitoring bodies that the Commonwealth had been invited by President Moi to observe the election and to an extent viewed itself as reporting to the Kenya government. In previous elections, most notoriously in Uganda in 1980, but also in Zambia, the Seychelles and Ghana, the Commonwealth observers had made declarations about the fairness of the polls before full results were known. This did not happen in Kenya, though there were fears at some stages that they might do so, and talk among some of the other monitoring groups that the Commonwealth should be warned that they would be repudiated by the others if they did so.

The Commonwealth group were far from supine, however. They too protested at various stages during the campaign, particularly after nomination day, and issued several press releases expressing strong concern at the continued ethnic clashes and protesting at the unfair tactics used by the government. Patsy Robertson, the Commonwealth Secretary-General's Director of Information, arrived in Kenya on 9 December and played the leading role in handling the group's media contacts. When Secretary-General Anyaoku first visited in late October, Chesoni had as yet had no contact with the opposition parties, and was not even replying to their letters. The Secretary-General privately warned President Moi and Chesoni that the situation must improve. The IRI at this time was also pressurising Chesoni to consult with the opposition. On 13 December, after the nomination day fiasco, the Commonwealth advance team warned that this part of the election would be 'severely compromised ... if the end result was that a substantial number of prospective candidates would be unable to contest the elections'.[76] It was rumoured that the Commonwealth and IRI teams had expressed their willingness to abandon the election if the opposition wished, but that the rival parties considered it better to secure 50 or 60 seats in the National Assembly than no representation at all, even if they now belatedly realised that they were not going to win. Consequently, the offer was declined.

The third major group consisted of a number of small groups of observers from different countries and organizations, such as Sweden, Japan, the European Community, Egypt, and a two-man delegation from the American AFL-CIO who were guided carefully by representatives from COTU, Kenya's government-controlled labour organisation. The ICJ also sent a team (primarily from the United States), while the United Nations Electoral Assistance Unit sent four staff to coordinate the activities of the other observers.[77] Including diplomats, there were in all about 60 observers in this third group. The problems of coordination were severe, as each group of observers had its own objectives and agenda. Although several meetings were held, and areas allocated for observation before the election, there was to be significant overlap in the 'easy to reach' seats and little coverage of other areas.

Two groups who had played a crucial role in the Zambian elections were refused permission to attend the Kenyan polls by the Electoral Commission. The National Democratic Institute (NDI), the International Republican Institute's sister organisation, had been established in 1983 to work for democratic institutions in new and emerging democracies. They had conducted democratic development programmes in 40 countries and sent a five-man delegation to Kenya in February 1992, to assess the political environment and discuss preparations for the elections.[78] The NDI report emphasised the need for the Commission to be accountable and to be seen as such, that political parties should openly debate and present clear choices to the electorate, that the media should be non-partisan, and that there should be clear opportunity for new young voters to register. Partly as a consequence of its protest, it was refused permission to monitor the elections in July, ostensibly on the grounds that the NDI did not have a valid reason why its officials wanted to be in Kenya for 36 weeks. The NDI had played a vital role in monitoring the Zambian elections and had continued to operate in Zambia for one year afterwards. A last-ditch attempt to secure accreditation was rejected in August.

These events, plus the continued violence and bias in the preparations for the election, damaged the credibility of the electoral process severely in the eyes of the US Government. NDI's head Brian Attwood wrote to Commonwealth Secretary-General Anyaoku on 13 August claiming that 'credible elections will not be possible in Kenya'.[79] The Jimmy Carter Centre was also refused accreditation, according to Chesoni because it was 'interested in certain individuals and parties.'[80] On 13 August 103 US Congressmen vowed in a letter to President Moi to continue denying Kenya aid because no meaningful changes had occurred. They doubted Chesoni's impartiality and the government's commitment to multi-party democracy, and protested that the NDI had only been allowed into the country on condition that they did not meet the opposition at all. The Congressmen also accused the government of denying entry on 7 August to the delegation from the Robert F. Kennedy Memorial Center for Human Rights because Congressman Joseph P. Kennedy had criticised the regime's human rights record in June.[81] The Germans sent a 30-strong monitoring team, but withdrew in mid-December on the grounds that the election process was already fatally flawed and because its team had encountered government obstruction. It was widely rumoured in Nairobi that the Kenyan government had objected both to the size of the delegation and to the presence of several Social Democratic members of the Bundestag, who were known to have criticised the Moi regime's human rights record. Thus three of the most critical observer teams were denied entry or withdrew before the election.

The Domestic Monitors

Although the international monitors received by far the most attention, it was always recognised that internal observers would have to perform the bulk of the task of monitoring the election for simple reasons of numbers. Once the West had expressed interest in funding internal monitoring bodies, numerous Kenyan groups, particularly the Churches and the legal profession, made submissions to the donors to establish such independent monitoring bodies. The majority were fused together into one alliance just before the elections as a direct result of pressure from the West, for reasons of efficiency and to consolidate the confused funding situation. This alliance, known as the National Election Monitoring Unit (NEMU) was headed by a 'Council of Elders' which first met on 16 November in Nairobi. NEMU acted as a coordinating authority for four bodies interested in observation: the National Ecumenical Civic Education Programme (NECEP), itself an amalgam of religious groups; FIDA, the International Federation of Women Lawyers; The International Commission of Jurists (ICJ); and the Professional Committee for Democratic Change (PCDC). The NEMU group was well-educated and highly regarded in the Western embassies. It was also accused regularly of partisanship. NEMU openly focused most of its efforts on KANU, anticipating government rigging, and was viewed with some hostility by the ruling party. The fact that Grace Githu, the Chair of FIDA and elected administrative head, was the Githunguri DP candidate's sister did not help. The NEMU 'Council of Elders' was chaired by Duncan Ndegwa, a senior civil servant from the Kenyatta era, with the Rev. Lee Kobia as his deputy. The ICJ group was headed by Charles Nyachae, son of the KANU candidate for Nyaribari Chache, while prominent lawyer Lee Muthoga (from Kibaki's Othaya seat), who had acted for the state against Njonjo during the 1984 enquiry, led the PCDC. Githu had been chosen for the chief executive position over Muthoga, who was a far more experienced lawyer, because certain influential members of the Council of Elders did not fully trust him after his role in Njonjo's downfall and suspected that he might be a government plant. Inevitably, many NEMU elders, who approved the final report, had political histories, and some still had ties to the regime. Certainly, the organisation suffered from some internal disagreements, hardly surprising given its creation and its individual components. The Electoral Commission did not accredit the NEMU team as domestic observers until 6 November 1992.[82]

The NEMU group coordinated the recruitment, training and reporting of roughly 5,000 election observers throughout the country. As well as its election day monitoring, it had a number of individuals in the field covering the campaign well before election day (though the results of this were less valuable). The observers were divided into three groups: the poll monitors, who were the work-horses of the system; the count certifiers, who were allocated to attend the count in every constituency; and District and Provincial coordinators. The count certifiers' role was to observe the counting of the ballot papers after they were delivered from the polling stations to the central constituency counting hall and they were required, like the poll monitors, to be non-partisan and 'approved or accredited by the Commission' under National Assembly regulation 35(5).

The National Council of Women of Kenya, founded in 1964 as an umbrella for numerous women's groups, was the second major observer group to emerge from the confusion. It was accredited on 19 November 1992, after the party nominations. Its work was also funded by foreign development groups, in this case Sweden, the Danish International Development Agency (DANIDA) and Norwegian Church Aid. The NCWK was strongly oriented towards women, women candidates and women's issues, and focused on enhancing the role of women in Kenyan politics. They recruited and trained over 400 observers.[83] The third largest domestic monitoring group was the Catholic Secretariat, about whom less is known. Despite considerable pressure from USAID officials, NEMU remained reluctant to work closely with the Catholic Secretariat. On election day, however, it proved singularly effective, despatching priests to many polling stations and mounting a conspicuous presence at many counts. The priests were equipped with copies of NEMU's poll monitoring form and in areas where the Catholic Church had adherents were extremely effective.

The fourth and smallest domestic observer group was BEERAM, the Bureau of Election Education, Research and Monitoring, which was affiliated to the Peace Foundation Africa, a Christian Peace ministry. This group was led by Archbishop Manasses Kuria of the (Anglican) Church of the Province of Kenya. BEERAM also transferred some of its monitors to the larger NEMU effort, and in Central Province its representatives co-operated closely during both the poll and count with the Catholic Secretariat. BEERAM held a number of seminars for monitors, funded by the Swedish International Development Agency (SIDA) and others, which were attended by 628 future observers. Like the other observer groups, it was only accredited in November.

The origins of the international effort to finance the Kenyan observer groups were unusual, and highlighted divisions within the international community. The Canadian High Commission had for some time held meetings with diplomats from other countries on Wednesdays to discuss issues regarding women and development. In March–April 1992 a number of Kenyan organisations began to approach aid agencies and embassies for funds to develop programmes on 'civics and governance'. There was confusion over who was funding what, and some money was misappropriated. The Americans, therefore, became eager to establish a mechanism for mutual consultation, and the Canadians effectively became their frontmen, diverting some of the criticism which the American Embassy was receiving for playing so conspicuous a role in supporting political pluralism. The Canadian development group, consequently, evolved into a Democratic Development and Governance group, financed by international donors and led by Canadian diplomat Jack Titsworth. It was this group which coordinated disbursements to NEMU. The most 'hardline' countries, determined to press the Kenyan government and the Electoral Commission to meet some of the opposition's demands, were the United States, Canada, Germany and the Scandinavian countries, while the British remained reluctant to participate.[84]

Monitoring the election locally proved to be an extremely expensive process. Costs included buying voters' registers, advertising, secretariat expenses, and travel, training and subsistence for thousands of poll watchers (which was by far the most costly component). The funds to carry all this out simply did not exist in Kenya and Western governments and foundations paid the bill. The Democratic Development and Governance group contributed US$600,000 to NEMU's efforts to put a domestic monitor into virtually every polling station. NEMU specifically received financial and organisational help from the IRI and USAID, although privately the IRI was sceptical of NEMU's effectiveness. Overall, planned or actual disbursements for election monitoring constituted at least Sh32 million, or about US$850,000 (see Table 7.5), a very substantial figure.

It is questionable whether the internal monitoring groups would have emerged in the form that they did without Western financial support, especially as local politically aware élites were donating heavily to political parties rather than to monitoring organisations. Without external funds, only the three or four major Churches and the legal community would have organised domestic monitoring teams and these would not have been able to produce sophisticated reports or fully cover the country. Thus, to a great extent, the West actually built the internal monitoring effort.

The state tolerated the observer groups, not actively harassing them, though delaying as late as possible their accreditation and providing them with little documentation until the last minute. As a result, they were unable officially to monitor the primaries and, indeed, lacked documentation to witness the nomination day process.

The Technicalities of the Election

The mechanics of an electoral process can have a huge impact on its fairness. As the Western embassies and commentators had stressed throughout, different voting and counting methods can produce different results. Various methods favour the educated over the illiterate or make cheating easier or more difficult. There was a continuous struggle throughout 1992 between the Electoral Commission, supported by the Kenyan government,

Table 7.7 Contributions for Monitoring

From	Value of gift (in Sh)	To whom	For what
Canada/Canadian International Development Agency	700,000	FIDA/ICJ	Radio communication system to assist election monitoring
Canada/Canadian International Development Agency	2,800,000	FIDA/ICJ	To establish secretariat for domestic election monitoring and train monitors
DANIDA	619,000	FIDA	Equipping the secretariat
Norway/Norwegian Church Aid	2,000,000	NECEP/NCCK	Election monitoring activities
Netherlands	2,300,000	FIDA/ICJ/NEMU	Recruitment of 1,500 poll watchers, District Liaison Officers and extra secretariat personnel
Denmark	619,000	FIDA	Equipping secretariat
Denmark	2,500,000	YWCA	Seminars to train election monitors, especially to focus on women's issues
European Community	1,836,000	NEMU via FIDA/ICJ	To help disseminate voter education materials, equip the coordinators' office, and recruit and train 1,000 additional poll watchers and count certifiers
Netherlands	2,000,000	National Committee on the Status of Women	For workshop for 50 monitors and 8 coordinators, publicity, secretarial services, election day activities and a report
Denmark	1,100,000	NCWK	Monitor training and development
Germany	3,275,000	NEMU through FIDA/ICJ	For recruiting 1,000 poll watchers, 200 count certifiers, transport costs for secretariat staff and District Liaison Officers for three days, plus 20,000 copies of the NEMU handbook for election monitors in English and Kiswahili and establishment of a radio system for use in monitoring
Netherlands	1,200,000	NECEP/NEMU	Training workshop for 250 monitors and 50 District Liaison Officers, and for publicity and advertising
FORD Foundation	1,168,000	NEMU (FIDA/ICJ)	To produce a report on the election monitoring process

Table 7.7 cont.

From	Value of gift (in Sh)	To whom	For what
Sweden	1,030,000	NECEP	Election monitoring and civic education
Sweden	1,545,000	Peace Foundation Africa	Training election monitors
Sweden	1,545,000	National Committee on the Status of Women	Training election monitors
Sweden	1,000,000	NCWK	Training monitors and monitoring elections
Sweden	1,545,000	NEMU (through FIDA/ICJ)	Election monitoring
UK	140,000	PCDC	Monitoring new coverage
USA/USAID	3,500,000	FIDA/ICJ	Training domestic monitors
USAID	3,500,000	FIDA/ICJ	Workshops, training and election day expenses

Source: Confidential memo from one of the Embassies dated 15 December 1992, detailing all the pledges and spending they could identify by foreign governments and aid bodies towards the election. Disbursements have been converted to Sh at approximate prevailing exchange rates.

and the donors, who were funding much of the election, as to precisely how it should be conducted.

The ballot papers followed the standard British model, with the name of the candidate and his party, and space for a cross to be inserted in the correct box. They were similar to previous Kenyan ballot papers, with the addition of party names against the candidates. Since three elections (Presidential, Parliamentary and local government) were being held simultaneously, different coloured papers were used for each. The printing of the papers was a point of contention long before the election. There was real concern that the government would have additional ballots made, which could be marked and distributed early to officials to stuff into boxes. As FORD-Kenya's Imanyara explained, 'Our fear is that KANU might place a parallel order for ballot papers with the same serial numbers as the genuine papers.'[85]

The Electoral Commission rejected an offer by the European Community to finance the printing of papers, and instead delivered the contract to the British firm of De La Rue. There was no publicity as to which British firm had been chosen, and there was a widespread concern that Harrisons, a Lonrho subsidiary, was going to be used. This concern arose because of Tiny Rowland's close relations with the Moi regime, especially with former Nandi KANU Chairman Mark arap Too, who was Lonrho East Africa's Deputy Chairman.[86] Diplomatic sources suggested to the *Economic Review* that the commercial firms could be pressured more easily than the European Community.[87] The ballot papers were due to be sent from England on 10 December, accompanied by an Election Commissioner.

The party symbols were chosen by the parties themselves, rather than balloted for as under the one-party system. The order of the parties on the ballot papers, however, was determined by balloting. It was a great relief

Table 7.8 Party Position and Symbols on Ballot Papers

Position	Party	Party symbol
1	KSC	Dove
2	KNC	Key
3	KENDA	Leopard
4	FORD-Kenya	Lion
5	FORD-Asili	Two Raised fingers
6	KANU	Cockerel
7	DP	Lantern
8	SDP	Rhino
9	PICK	Child
10	LPD	Torch

Source: Daily Nation, 26 November 1992, p. 2.

to the opposition that KANU did not win the top position (see Table 7.8).

The ballot boxes, provided by Britain, were larger than those used in previous elections and were constructed of strong polyurethane rather than wood. The number of boxes delivered was an extremely contentious issue as the government was widely suspected of importing too many in order to rig the elections.[88] The British High Commission reported that 35,000 boxes would be delivered, and according to Chesoni, 31,347 were distributed to the districts. Three boxes were employed per polling stream for the separate Presidential, Parliamentary and local government elections, though only one box per stream was required in those constituencies where KANU's Parliamentary and civic candidates were returned unopposed. The whereabouts of these unneeded extra boxes was later to give rise to some concern. The remaining boxes were held in the Commission stores, and one unnumbered box was sent to each constituency for training purposes (itself an opportunity for abuse).

The boxes were designed to hold 800–850 ballots each. On average the Commission expected that only 600–700 people would actually vote (that is, 70 per cent to 87.5 per cent turn-outs).[89] The boxes were serialised: the Presidential with a serial number ending in P; the Parliamentary ending in PA; and the local government in L. Each number was unique. The numbers allocated to each box were published beforehand in the press, though this did not prevent the production of boxes with the same numbers if carefully planned.[90] Presiding Officers and the candidates' agents were to attach plastic seals (Presiding Officers green, agents yellow) to the lid. Seals were unique and designed to show that the box had not been opened. Unfortunately, the seals were easily put on the wrong way round, which made it possible to remove them without cutting. Chesoni himself made this mistake at a press conference called to demonstrate the security measures that were being taken. As in previous Kenyan elections, the index finger of each voter was to be marked in indelible purple ink, 11,000 bottles of which were donated by USAID at a cost of Sh2.8 million.

Over most of the country, the siting of the polling stations and the counting halls was uncontroversial. The 188 counting halls and nearly 5,700 polling stations, with 10,424 polling streams were gazetted by the Electoral

Commission on 6 December.[91] Chesoni reassured the opposition that there were no stations inside army barracks as had been feared.[92] Most were in primary schools and social halls. There was some cause for concern, nevertheless, in a few marginals. In battle-scarred Eldoret South the transfer of the counting hall from Eldoret Town to Kesses, an isolated area surrounded by angry and aggressive Kalenjin, was seen as putting more pressure on the Kikuyu opposition. Some polling stations were discovered to be sited in the same building as the local KANU headquarters and, in Mvita, a station was relocated, at the last minute, close to the Mombasa KANU Branch headquarters.[93]

The size of polling station varied greatly, depending on geography and population density, and the distribution of polling stations was far from even. We compared the distribution of polling stations and streams figures from the *Government Gazette* of 4 December 1992 with the total number of registered voters in each seat (using final figures for registered voters from the *Daily Nation's* election results and elsewhere). The actual number of voters per polling stream varied considerably, from 320 in Samburu East to 1,180 in Mount Elgon. In many cases, this could be explained by the need for geographical coverage, since people cannot be expected to trek too many miles to vote and in areas like Turkana fewer voters per station would be expected. Nonetheless, some results were still anomalous (see Figure 7.4). The predominantly KANU zones of Marsabit, Samburu, Lamu and Baringo were the four districts with the fewest voters per box, while two of the heavily clash-hit constituencies – Mount Elgon and Eldoret South – had the highest and seventh-highest number of voters per box in the country, perhaps indicating an expectation that very few people would actually vote after the ethnic cleansing campaign.

For the first time, votes were to be counted at constituency centres, rather than being transported long distances to district headquarters. This was generally welcomed because it reduced opportunities for confusion and tampering with ballot boxes. Proposals to count at each polling station, which might have minimised local rigging, were rejected as too complex an administrative task. Boxes, therefore, had to be transported from the polling stations to the counting centre for each constituency, accompanied by candidates' agents. Results were to be announced by the Returning Officer for each constituency and the state-controlled and independent media were permitted to watch and broadcast these results.

One final addition to the legal morass surrounding the election was the creation of a ten-point code of conduct to be followed by all parties, proposed by Attorney-General Wako on 12 November. It bound the parties to adhere to the laws, do their utmost to prevent election offences by their supporters, respect the rights of others, maintain peace, avoid abuse, condemn violence and abjure ethnically inflammatory speeches. The opposition parties, however, were lukewarm, since they felt KANU was not even following the constitution, let alone a 'mere gentlemen's agreement'. Nevertheless, the code was issued on 5 December by Chesoni, as an enlarged 20-point document.

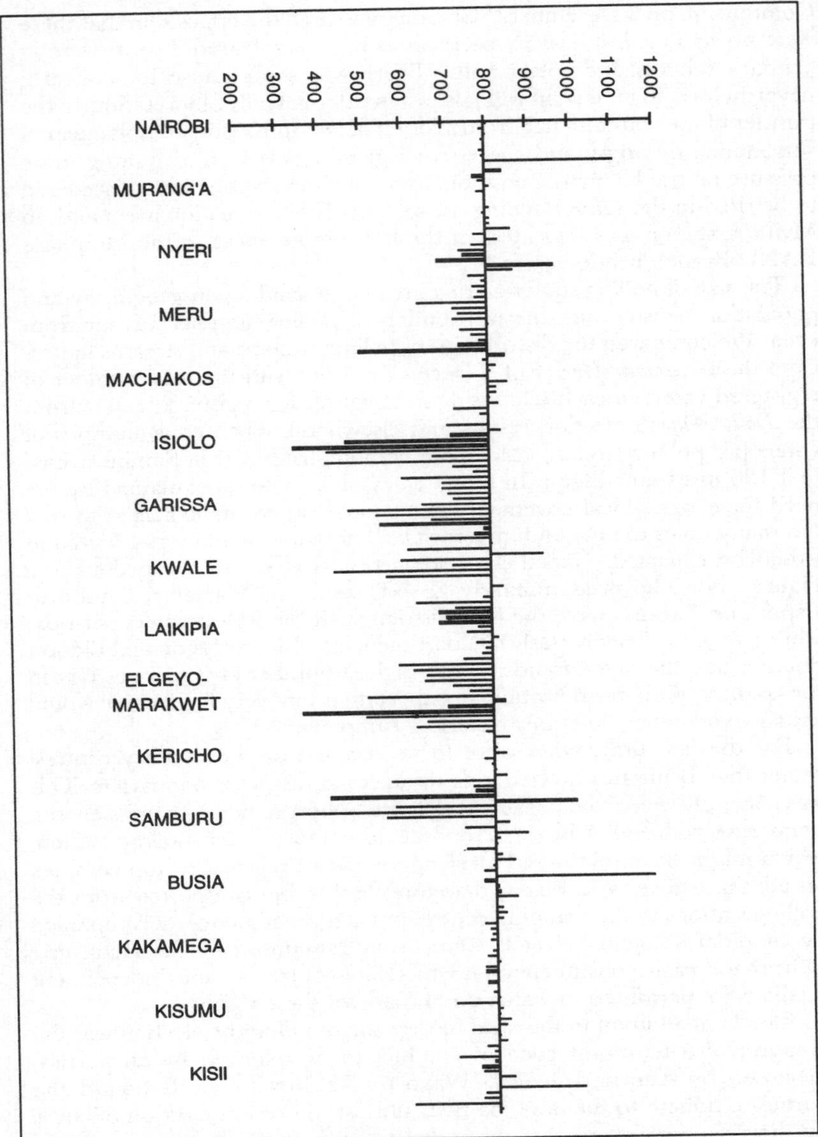

Figure 7.4 Comparison of Registered Voters with Gazetted Number of Ballot Boxes and Streams

Source: Government Gazette, 4 December 1992. Standard constituency sequence used.

Voter Education

A major issue in a country where access to information was difficult and literacy low was how to inform voters of their rights and responsibilities, and to educate the public about the mechanics of the election. Voter education programmes should have been the responsibility of the Electoral Commission. It was generally agreed that 'many Kenyans are ill-equiped [sic] with the requisite knowledge of what this election exercise entails'.[94] The Commission seemed reluctant, however, to carry out substantial voter education, perhaps fearing that it would reduce KANU's hold over the semi-arid periphery, where political consciousness was lowest. The Western aid donors offered the Commission direct funding for voter education on several occasions, but it was rejected. As Commissioner Nyamu said in 1993, 'Funding had been promised overwhelmingly ... the Commission's management alone can answer the question as to why no such funds were taken advantage of.'[95] The opposition and the NCWK criticised the Commission heavily for this laxity, though the Commission did publish a series of advertisements in the media, sponsored by the European Community and *Kituo Cha Sheria* (the Legal Advice Centre), and posters on 'How to vote on 29th December 1992'.[96]

As a result, much of the burden fell on the Kenyan monitoring groups and NGOs, funded directly by the West to the sum of at least Sh35 million (about US$700,000). NEMU held voter education seminars; FIDA and the YWCA sought to explain democratisation and its meaning; and *Kituo Cha Sheria* produced cassettes and videos advising on the voting process in English and Kiswahili.[97] BEERAM produced brochures on voting and elections, while the Legal Aid and Education Programme (LEAP) produced two leaflets. The United States Embassy also became directly involved, with the campaign 'Ink your finger for a clean election' explaining the reason for the indelible ink that they had provided. In addition, there were grants from Sweden, Denmark, and the FORD Foundation covering issues such as training programmes for leaders, developing legal aid, education and research projects, supporting the Law Society of Kenya and the *Nairobi Law Monthly,* funding constitutional policy papers and supporting human rights. These amounted to at least Sh12.4 million.

There were many problems during the second half of 1992 (as in previous elections) with voters selling their voting cards. Many viewed their cards as monetary assets, which could be sold to the highest bidder, either for destruction (if you were a supporter of another party) or re-use by an impostor. For example, the NECEP claimed that YK '92 was buying voters' cards in Muhoroni and Nyakach in Kisumu District, and two people were arrested with hundreds of spoilt voters' cards in Vihiga.[98] The NCCK issued instructions to voters not to 'sell their birthright'. There were other problems due to the anomalies in registration. The basic principle that only those voters registered in a seat could vote in that constituency was clear, but what happened in the numerous cases where a name appeared on the register, but the voter had no card, or they had a card but were not on the register? Would they be allowed to vote? What other documentation would suffice as identification? At the last minute, Chesoni changed the rules, announcing that voters who had lost (or indeed sold) their cards could still vote if they were on the register.

Table 7.9 Contributions for Voter Education

From	Value of gift (in Sh)	To whom	For what
Canada	700,000	NECEP	To establish a church-based national civic education programme
Canada	1,400,000	League of Kenyan Women Voters	Production of a voters' handbook directed towards women
Canada	750,000	PCDC	Civic education and research on KBC broadcasting
Norway/ Norwegian Church Aid	2,300,000	NECEP	Civic education
Norwegian Foreign Office	2,500,000	NCCK/NECEP	Civic education
DANIDA	2,000,000	NECEP	Civic education and election monitoring (4 million more not disbursed due to failure to account for first 2 million)
DANIDA	10,400,000	Legal Education and Aid Programme (LEAP)	To write and publish election booklets
Germany (Hanns Seidel Foundation)	12,100,000	NCCK and Protestant Church Organisation	Education for participatory democracy
Sweden	500,000	YWCA	Education of women in development
Sweden	500,000	League of Kenyan Women Voters	To create awareness of voting amongst women.
UK	270,000	PCDC	Fostering public awareness
USAID	1,365,000	*Kituo Cha Sheria*	Media education programmes

Source: Confidential memo from one of the Embassies dated 15 December 1992

Conclusions

By December 1992 the electoral process was distinctly biased in favour of the ruling party. The new 25 per cent rule, state control of registration, the choice of officials and the behaviour of the Electoral Commission in general, all benefited KANU. There were, moreover, concerns about key aspects of the electoral process, including the location of the ballot boxes and the uniqueness of the ballots. It was clear, however, that the Western governments were heavily committed to the election, and were willing to spend large amounts of financial and political capital in attempting to bring it about. By Kenyan standards, Sh80 million (US$2.1 million) for monitoring, voter education and related activities is a large sum. It is questionable, however, whether the Western donors always received value for money. There was considerable overlap of financial provision, and some of it appears to have been pledged for activities which did not take place. The West believed that the government intended to cheat, but hoped that they had made cheating so difficult that in most parts of the country the elections would be free and fair, and voters would be free to repudiate President Moi and KANU. They were to prove mistaken.

Notes

1 C. P. W. Hornsby's unpublished 1985 D.Phil. thesis, 'The Kenyan Member of Parliament, 1969–83', p. 38, observed three years earlier that queue voting 'would have caused chaos in a national election'.
2 *Ibid.*, for details on the electoral process in the 1970s and early 1980s.
3 *Ibid.*, pp. 85–90.
4 *Ibid.*, pp. 80–5.
5 *Government Gazette* Notice 4512, 4 October 1991. The previous commission, whose remit had expired, was chaired by James Nyamweya (who later joined the DP).
6 *Economic Review*, 16 November 1992, p. 5.
7 *Monthly News* and *The Presidential, Parliamentary and Civic Elections in Kenya: 29 December, 1992: The Report of the Commonwealth Observer Group* (Commonwealth Report), p. 64.
8 Commonwealth Report, p. 10.
9 *Standard*, 16 January 1993, p. 5.
10 *Daily Nation*, 14 October 1992, p. 4.
11 *Daily Nation*, 14 November 1992 p. 5.
12 Nyamu, speaking in Accra, quoted in *Sunday Nation*, 5 June 1993, p. 16.
13 Appendix 8, NEMU report.
14 *Government Gazette* Notice 5420, reported in *Standard* on Sunday, 22 November 1992.
15 Representative of the Commission Ramsay, reported in *Daily Nation*, 12 November 1992 p. 22.
16 Amos Wako, reported in *Daily Nation*, 13 November 1992, pp. 1–2.
17 Japeth Kiti, reported in *Weekly Review*, 20 November 1992, p. 4
18 Most MPs had no idea of the official procedure. See *Weekly Review*, 24 July 1992, pp. 12–14.
19 Waihenya Ndirangu (Nyeri Town) was the only MP who voted against. The bill was given presidential assent on 27 August 1992. See *Daily Nation*, 28 August 1992, p. 3.
20 Constitution of Kenya Amendment Act No. 6 of 1992 to section 9 of the constitution.
21 See for example Odinga's letter in *Society*, 21 November 1992.
22 Wako, reprinted in *Monthly News*, September 1992, p. 14.
23 Constitution of Kenya, II.1.9.(2), Rev. 1992, Government Printer, Nairobi.
24 *Nairobi Law Monthly*, No. 46 (October/November 1992), pp. 19–20 argued that it was retrospective. For the ruling, see *Kenya Times*, 12 December 1992, pp. 1 and 7. The issue was then raised by Matiba in his election petition.
25 Amos Wako, in the National Assembly, reprinted in *Society*, 24 August 1992, p. 33.
26 *Standard*, 16 December 1992, p. 14.
27 Nonetheless, minor alterations to the constituency boundaries continued in the build-up to registration.
28 A version of this information was presented at the ASA(UK) Conference in Stirling, September 1992.

29 Joel Barkan, 'Election Rigging in Kenya', 3 July 1992.
30 *Weekly Review*, 24 July 1992. This was unsuccessful.
31 C. P. W. Hornsby's thesis, p. 63, and *Weekly Review*, 31 July 1992.
32 See Commonwealth Report, pp. 3 and 11.
33 *Society*, 29 June 1992, p. 27.
34 Unpublished Mss. by Tom Wolf on the election in Taita–Taveta, p. 58.
35 Jahazi (DP), in *Daily Nation*, 14 November 1992, p. 2.
36 Judy Geist's Analysis on behalf of the IRI Constituency Registration Data, 1992 Elections.
37 *Kenya Times*, 8 December 1992, p. 4.
38 Personal inspection, Molo Register.
39 Source: Geist figures superimposed on Hornsby election maps. Figures for the Uasin Gishu were unavailable.
40 *Daily Nation*, 26 November 1992, p. 1.
41 NEMU DLO, Samburu.
42 *Society*, 10 August 1992, p. 31. See also the results of the study of those two registration units above.
43 *Daily Nation*, 8 December 1992, p. 2 and 14 November 1992, p. 2. Shikuku claimed in a letter to Chesoni that KANU's Gerishon Kirima was registering voters in his office in Starehe. He accompanied it with affidavits by voters saying they had been registered long after registration ended, see *Society*, 16 November 1992, p. 23.
44 Tharaka, Mwala, Runyenjes and Tigania.
45 Aldai (up 2215), Mosop (up 1989), Kapenguria (up 2277), Sigor (up 2164), Kipkelion (up 1945), Saboti (up 1868), Laikipia East (up 957).
46 They were responsible for supplying their returning officers with stationery, clerks and other needs.
47 Chesoni stated that the officials were selected from amongst lawyers and other professions by the Electoral Commission (Chesoni, in *Daily Nation*, 11 November 1992, p. 24) and that professionals, including lawyers, clergymen, management executives and university lecturers, were likely to form the bulk of the officers and their deputies (Interview with Chesoni, *Economic Review*, 16 December 1992, p. 5).
48 NEMU Nakuru East Election Monitor.
49 Kitui West, Amagoro, Gachoka Count Certifiers and DLO reports, NEMU, and personal observations.
50 This allegation was made by the NEMU Narok North Poll Monitor. That they were Kalenjin appears confirmed by a study of the names in the list of those nominated to the posts, which was published on 12 November in the *Government Gazette*, though it was incomplete. Rectifications and modifications were made just before the elections.
51 *Standard*, 28 November 1992, p. 5.
52 NEMU Msambweni Poll Monitor report, 31 December 1992.
53 *Kenya Times*, 26 December 1992.
54 Report from NEMU Samia Constituency Monitor, 5–14 December 1992.
55 NEMU Narok North Poll Monitor report, Nakuru East Count Certifiers Report and FIDA/ICJ Embu DLO Report.
56 The resolutions made at the First FORD–Asili Seminar for Presidential and Parliamentary nominees held on 20–22 November 1992 at the Limuru Conference Centre, p. 2. George Anyona claimed in a letter to the Electoral Commission that there was a preponderance of Kalenjin officials, and that the list included many civil servants, retired civil servants and military personnel (Anyona Press Conference, *Daily Nation*, 25 November 1992, p. 5). Shikuku also challenged Chesoni to explain why civil servants and members of the armed forces had been included, *Daily Nation* 15 November 1992, p. 3.
57 *Standard*, 2 November 1992, p. 3.
58 Gitobu Imanyara, *Daily Nation*, 1 September 1992, pp. 1–2.
59 *Kenya Times*, 28 December 1992, p. 4.
60 Interview with Dennis Keefe, First Secretary, British High Commission, Nairobi, December 1992.
61 Sir Roger Tomkys, meeting of the Kenya Society, Kenya High Commission, London, 27 January 1993.
62 Baroness Chalker, at Press Conference reported in *Society*, 28 September 1992, p. 18.
63 Sir Roger Tomkys, meeting of the Kenya Society, Kenya High Commission, London, 27 January 1993.

64 IFES Report, p. 20.
65 International Human Rights Law Group, *Facing the Pluralist Challenge, Human Rights and Democratization in Kenya's December 1992 Multi–Party Elections*, p. 4.
66 *Ibid.*, p. 6.
67 The European Community and the Commonwealth were officially invited by the Kenyan government. Moi on 22 October also asked the Americans, Japan, Finland and Norway to send observers, see *Daily Nation*, 23 October 1992.
68 *Economic Review*, 16 November 1992, p. 6.
69 The Role of Election Observers and the Code of Ethics, Nairobi , 1992, p. 1.
70 IRI, *Kenya: A Pre–Election Assessment.*
71 Discussions with USAID staff, 1992–3.
72 It had originally been planned to bring only 25.
73 He replaced the original choice, Michael Manley, who had retired for health reasons., *Standard*, 26 November 1992, p. 3.
74 See Julian Ozanne and Michael Holman in *Financial Times*, 29 December 1992.
75 See Commonwealth reproduction of Checklist for Polling Stations and Counting Centres, Annexe V, pp. 56–8.
76 Commonwealth statement, 13 December 1992.
77 *Electoral Assistance Activities Provided by the United Nations Since 1989*, EAU, 1993.
78 NDI Mission to the Republic of Kenya, February 3–7, 1992, International Delegation Report, NDI for International Affairs.
79 *Daily Nation*, 11 September 1992, p. 1.
80 Chesoni, quoted in *Economic Review*, 16 November 1992, p. 6.
81 *Daily Nation*, 14 August 1992, pp. 1–2.
82 Letter from Electoral Commission to Rev. Samuel Kobia, 6 November 1992.
83 NCWK Report.
84 Fairly hardline, but less so, were the Austrians, Swiss, Dutch and Belgians, whilst the French and Italians did not attend.
85 Imanyara, quoted in *Economic Review*, 12 October 1992, p. 5.
86 See for example letter from Mwai Kibaki to Jitegemea, November 1992, pp. 31–6.
87 *Economic Review*, 12 October 1992, p. 5.
88 See, for example, Jitegemea, November 1992, letter from Mwai Kibaki, pp. 31–5; and George Anyona's Press Conference, 1 November 1992, reported in *Standard*, 2 November 1992, p. 2.
89 Chesoni, quoted in *Kenya Times*, 26 December 1992, p. 21.
90 *Kenya Times*, 26 December 1992, p. 21.
91 This total was gained by manually counting all the figures reported in the *Government Gazette.*
92 *Daily Nation*, 7 December 1992, p. 1.
93 Commonwealth Report, p. 33.
94 *Advocate*, November 1992, p. 4.
95 Nyamu, speaking in Accra, *Daily Nation*, 5 June 1993, p. 16.
96 See, for example, Commonwealth Report, p. 67, Annexe XI.
97 See, for example, *Advocate*, November 1992, p. 4.
98 *Standard on Sunday*, 22 November 1992.

Eight

The Beginnings of the Campaign & the Party Primaries

Once the registration process had finished and the registers were opened in August, President Moi was free to go to the polls at any time. Parliament, supposedly composed entirely of KANU MPs, remained in session, but infiltrated by opposition sympathisers. Everyone knew that the elections were close, but no official announcement appeared. With FORD's formal division into two hostile parts in October 1992, however, KANU moved swiftly onto the offensive.

The campaign that followed was divided into two parts. From 21 October to 9 December, the parties marshalled their forces and nominated their candidates, while the campaign proper ran from 9 December to 29 December. This period was governed by a certain historical inevitability as politics returned to its traditional patterns of ethnic appeals, personal alliances and unprincipled calculations of self-interest. A combination of KANU's regional tactics and the opposition's inability to build stable, national factional coalitions meant that what had begun as a national movement for self-renewal, liberation and democracy gradually turned into bitter, ethnically oriented trench warfare. The opposition did keep some of its moral advantage, but it was severely weakened by internal conflict, and by its willingness to accept even the most compromised KANU die-hards. For KANU, the campaign and the election itself were a triumph. No political party that was so unpopular among such a large proportion of the population could have won an outright victory under such difficult circumstances without luck, planning and some electoral manipulation. The government walked a tightrope throughout. Facing Western pressure and widespread domestic discontent they had to hold an election, which they were unable blatantly to rig but could not afford to lose. They had to win, but with enough finesse for the West to give them the benefit of the doubt.

With the Provincial Administration and the police biased in favour of the ruling party, the opposition parties always faced a difficult contest.

Although the result of the election had already been influenced by the registration of voters and by the ethnic cleansing of non-Kalenjin from KANU's Rift Valley heartland, KANU officials and the Administration could not afford to relax political control. Nairobi, Central Province, the Kikuyu settlement areas in Nakuru and Laikipia Districts, and the Luo-populated districts of Nyanza had already been conceded to the opposition and KANU stood no chance of winning more than a handful of these seats. In 60 or so constituencies, it soon became clear that the election would be comparatively free and fair. Only massive intimidation, bribery and wholesale rigging could have secured a KANU victory here, and such brazen manipulation could not be concealed from outside observers. Away from opposition strongholds, the main urban areas and the foreign observers, the situation was different. This 'forgotten campaign' went largely unreported by the international press, but it was these 70 constituencies in the rural hinterland and semi-arid areas, outside the opposition ethnic enclaves and the KANU stronghold of the central Rift Valley, that determined the result. The contest in these seats was far from free and fair, with the Provincial Administration, local chiefs and the police intervening to ensure that opposition candidates found it extremely difficult to organise a campaign, to secure official approval for meetings, to move around their constituencies or to compete against the massive dispersal of money by KANU.

KANU's dominance was, however, threatened by one continuing wild card – the potential for mass defections to the opposition of KANU candidates not selected as the party's choice as MP or civic candidate. Once its plan to rush through the party primaries was defeated, KANU faced a tough seat-by-seat struggle to ensure that suitable candidates were selected, and that the loser remained loyal. In the main, it was to succeed.

Ethnic and Regional Patterns of Political Loyalty

Since their formation, the opposition parties had become significantly more regionally oriented. Ethnic divisions had triumphed over all attempts to restructure political cleavages on lines of have/have-not, pro-/anti-multi-partyism, economic liberals/statists or new blood/old guard. The reason was a combination of the opposition's fragmentation, the focus on traditional leaders, a historic trend towards communal solidarity, and 30 years of a political system which expected leaders to represent local interest. The events of 1992 demonstrated very clearly that, in Kenya at least, ethnic affiliations still remain the primary determinant of political allegiances. Thus the election campaign was fought in very different ways and between different parties in different regions of the country (see Figure 8.1). The great weakness of political commentators and the parties themselves was an inability to see that victory in one arena meant little in another, and that dominance in Nyanza, for example, would not translate into victory at the Coast. Although it appeared that the parties were competing at a national level, using national campaign techniques, this masked the reality of local differences.

The pattern of the division between communities was the result of a complex combination of historical alignments, tensions created during the Kenyatta era, the power of the state to reward participants in the state coalition, and above all, the impact of individual political leaders. Initially, the Kikuyu had defected wholesale to the opposition, a reflection of their status as the primary losers from the Moi era; their economic strength, which permitted them to fund an opposition movement; the greater urbanisation and radicalisation of the Kikuyu; and the role of their leadership in the events of 1991–2. Thus Central Province, Nairobi and the Kikuyu voters elsewhere (up to 30 per cent of the population) were clearly going to vote opposition. The Kikuyu, however, classically the community most affected by class differentiation and most likely to produce radical, socialist movements, found that both the élites and the masses were on the same side, and this became reflected in the division between the DP and FORD. The Luo, always the centre of opposition politics, remained solidly with FORD, and then FORD-Kenya, giving the opposition another 19 per cent or so of the population. But they were unlikely to vote with or remain stably allied with the Kikuyu élites, who many Luo still resented and feared as a consequence of their economic power and political strength during the Kenyatta era, when the Luo had suffered heavily as a result of their investment in the Kenya People's Union.

KANU had held onto its monolithic ethnic vote amongst the Kalenjin and other pastoral tribes. The Kalenjin had done very well by the Moi presidency and their aggressive stance, with the violence which continued around their borders against opposition-supporting communities, demonstrated a determination to resist any change. Despite the internal tensions and problems among the Nandi and Kipsigis, they were expected to rally round. The Turkana, Samburu and Pokot were always likely to stay with their pastoralist allies. The position of KANU amongst the Maasai was less secure, however, particularly given the huge immigration of Kikuyu into the Maasai areas south of Nairobi. The North-East and parts of Eastern Province were also likely to stay predominantly KANU. They were little developed areas, dependent on the government, where there was little support for the opposition, and likely to be few effective candidates willing to stand against KANU. On the Coast, it was generally felt that the Coastal Mijikenda and other peoples would also remain loyal, though views differed over whether the opposition might win a few seats, except that KANU was bound to lose much of Mombasa. Once the FORD-Kenya/IPK alliance was formalised, the Coast became even more open, although the loyalty of senior Coast leaders remained solidly with KANU.

This left a number of swing groups: the Gusii in Nyanza, the Embu, Meru and Kamba in the East and the Luhya of Western Province. These were the key marginal zones which both government and opposition had to win to clinch victory. In none of these communities was there an overwhelming preference for either government or opposition. In each case, few powerful KANU representatives had defected, and many people appeared to be waiting until the political situation clarified. By the late summer, it seemed that most of the Gusii (following Simeon Nyachae's

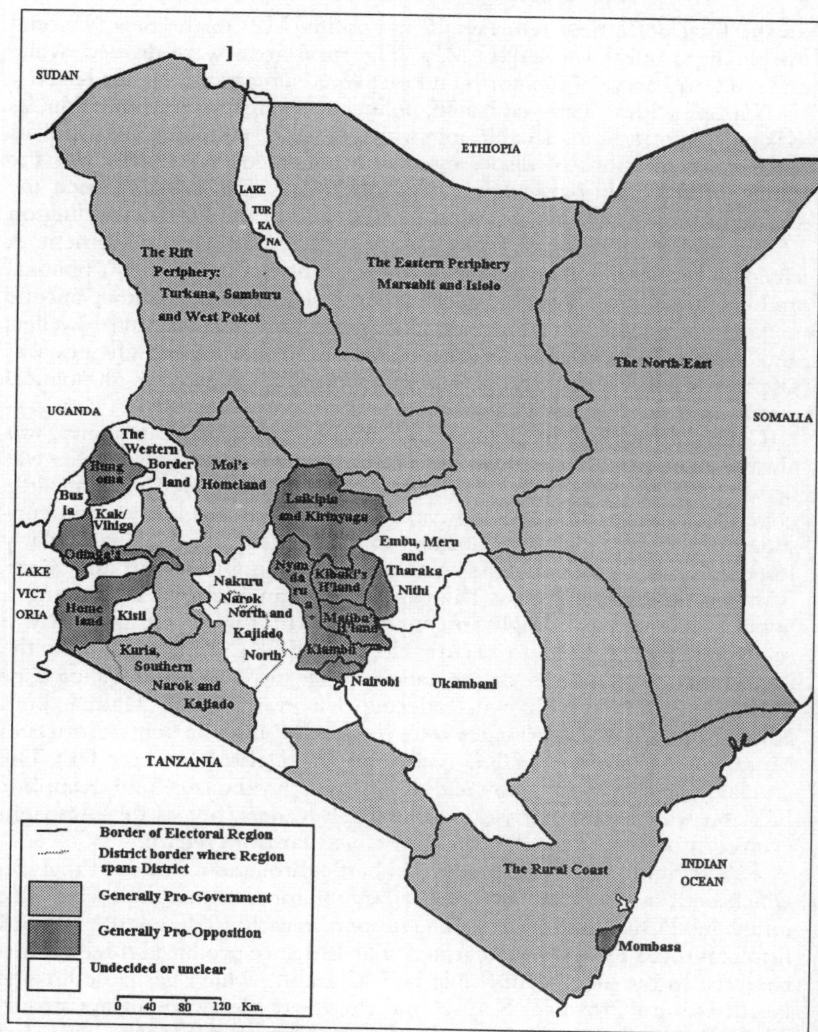

Figure 8.1 Kenya's Twenty Electoral Regions

lead) were likely to stay with KANU. The majority of the Luhya, Kenya's second largest ethnic group, were always likely to follow FORD, but with the split in the party, their position became less clear as the late Masinde Muliro's followers remained loyal to Odinga, while Martin Shikuku's joined FORD-Asili. The Embu would probably vote with the Kikuyu, whilst the Meru and Kamba, like the Luhya, would split.

A common thread was the division in political attitudes between urban areas, rural areas and the semi-arid regions of the north. The cities – Nairobi, Mombasa, Kisumu and Nakuru – were overwhelmingly pro-opposition.

In the final polls, they returned 12 opposition MPs to the new National Assembly to only two KANU MPs. The rural areas were divided, while the semi-arid areas of the north and east voted almost entirely for KANU.

Nairobi, with its large educated, politically sophisticated population, its Kikuyu majority and sizeable minorities of other ethnic groups, and its huge concentrations of dispossessed and alienated individuals, was the centre of the multi-party democracy movement. The city had been the centre of the 7 July *Saba Saba* riots in 1990 and of the FORD meeting on 16 November 1991 which had relaunched the multi-party movement. A city of at least two million people, it was the centre of the country's political and economic life.[1] Nairobi was clearly going to vote opposition, but the mélange of people, including wealthy Asians and Kikuyu, slum dwellers and workers (Kikuyu, Luo and Luhya), ensured that no constituency was safe territory for any party. A four-way fight in a winner-take-all political system gave no one any guarantees.

Central Province, the home of two of the Presidential candidates, was always an opposition stronghold. The main fight for Kikuyu votes was between Kibaki's DP and Matiba's new FORD-Asili. KANU had little hope of any seats, and although vast sums were poured into certain constituencies to assist Cabinet Ministers and Kikuyu loyal to Moi (particularly Joseph Kamotho in Kangema, Arthur Magugu in Githunguri and Kuria Kanyingi in Limuru), most Kikuyu KANU candidates were fighting a hopeless battle. Most sought to gain favour with the regime when it was re-elected rather than to secure election. FORD-Kenya, despite the importance of Paul Muite on the national stage, was always struggling once FORD split and the Kikuyu leadership left *en masse* with Matiba. Both Kikuyu Presidential candidates were 'rock solid' in their home districts of Murang'a (Matiba and FORD-Asili), and Nyeri (Kibaki and the DP). The crucial question was, who held Kirinyaga, Nyandarua and Kiambu? Kiambu was the home base of several DP leaders, but as the campaign evolved it became clear that the district was far from secure.

KANU and the DP were locked in battle throughout Eastern Province, which both saw as a key area with a large number of marginal seats. The undivided FORD had gained some support in early 1992, but the DP took firm control as FORD disintegrated. The Province produced three distinct contests. In the arid north (Isiolo and Marsabit), which has close links to North-Eastern Province, KANU and President Moi were always strong. The DP were the strongest party in Embu, Meru and Tharaka-Nithi, but KANU remained a serious contender and FORD had a presence in a few seats. There was a close 'house-to-house' battle in the three Kamba districts (known as Ukambani) where KANU's new leader General Jackson Mulinge opposed veteran Paul Ngei in Machakos and the Mwendwa family in Kitui for the DP.

North-Eastern Province, small, isolated and almost entirely pastoral, was a key area as a result of the 25 per cent rule. The arid, Somali-populated region, has been a land apart from most of Kenya since Independence. It was the scene of the *shifta* war of the 1960s and early 1970s, and has continued to be plagued by 'security problems' which were exacerbated by events in Somalia, where the ethnic Somalis of Kenya have close kinship and trade connections. The vast majority of the Somalis are Moslem, and are divided into several clans and sub-clans, of which the largest groupings are the Degodia, Ajuran and Mursale (all part of the Hawiye clan) and the Dawod who dominate the other Ogadeni groups. President Moi had relied upon Somalis far more than Kenyatta, and their increased importance was symbolised by the role of Major-General Mahmoud Mohammed as Chief of the General Staff, and his brother Maalim as Minister of State in the Office of the President.

Coast Province, outside the urban Mombasa, was an area where KANU had not been weakened by large-scale defections during 1992. The 16 seats of the rural Coast were a crucial area that the opposition had to penetrate to win. The main threat to the ruling party emerged from the unregistered Islamic Party of Kenya (IPK), which just before the election entered an alliance with FORD-Kenya whereby IPK candidates received the FORD-Kenya nominations in Mombasa and a couple of other Coast seats in return for Moslem support for the party elsewhere The IPK alliance gave FORD-Kenya much of Mombasa, but KANU still dominated the rural Coast, where the opposition was fragmented and under pressure from the government machine. In the two main rural districts, Kwale and most of Kilifi (the home of the powerful Ngala family), KANU was clearly going to win most seats. The situation was less clear in Tana River, Lamu, Taita-Taveta and in Kilifi's Malindi and Bahari, but the IPK in the rest of Coast Province was always weaker than FORD-Kenya activists claimed.

The Rift Valley had always been the most contentious province politically, for one reason – land. The 'White Highlands' were opened for settlement in the late 1950s and early 1960s on a 'willing buyer–willing seller' basis, irrespective of pre-colonial land-ownership. The result was a distribution of land in Nakuru, Uasin Gishu and Laikipia particularly that favoured the dominant financial and political community after Independence, the Kikuyu. The Rift Valley was Moi's and KANU's home, and their area of greatest strength, but contained the Kikuyu-dominated areas of Nakuru and Laikipia, and the Luhya areas of Trans-Nzoia, plus large minorities of other communities elsewhere, such as on the tea estates around Kericho Town. There were, therefore, four independent political regions in the Province, with very different electoral dynamics. The first was the Kalenjin 'homelands' of Baringo, Nandi, Elgeyo-Marakwet, Kericho and Bomet, where KANU was overwhelmingly dominant. The second region covered the Kalenjin periphery – the seats of Turkana, Samburu and Pokot (a Kalenjin sub-tribe, but with a distinct identity), plus the southern Maasai seats of Kajiado and Narok. Here KANU started well ahead, but without the same ethnic identification with Moi, they needed to contain defections to the opposition to ensure success. The third electoral zone was defined by a small regional conflict between KANU, FORD-Asili and FORD-Kenya for control of the strategic Uasin Gishu and Trans-Nzoia, ex-White Highland districts, in the west. The last region was centred on the bitter conflict in the borderlands between Kikuyu and Kalenjin residents for Nakuru District, and between Kikuyu and Maasai in Narok North and Kajiado North. Laikipia is better treated as part of Central Province. Although this analysis is expressed in terms of conflict and territorial gains, in a rather military metaphor, it is not entirely a metaphor. The ethnic clashes followed the Rift Valley boundaries, almost as if the Kalenjin were delimiting and securing their area.

The political situation in Western Province was the most complex and confused of all. In Bungoma, KANU's main opposition was the late Masinde Muliro's supporters in FORD-Kenya. The Bukusu sub-tribe in Bungoma had been alienated by clashes with the Sabaot population in the Mount Elgon constituency, who, like their fellow-Kalenjin, would vote overwhelmingly for KANU. Despite (or perhaps because of) Cabinet Minister Elijah Mwangale's backing KANU, the ruling party seemed likely to do badly throughout Bungoma. In Kakamega, KANU faced FORD-Asili's Martin Shikuku. Support for KANU, by contrast, had held up well in Vihiga and Busia districts in the south and west of the Province, where the opposition forces were much more divided. There, FORD-Asili and FORD-Kenya had some support, but not enough to guarantee seats in the new Parliament. KANU was likely to emerge as the largest parliamentary party, and no one doubted that Moi would secure 25 per cent in the Presidential poll.

Nyanza Province fell into two distinct areas. The four Luo districts were FORD-Kenya strongholds, totally committed to Oginga Odinga's 'last hurrah'. Although registration was comparatively low, it was clear that Odinga's candidates would secure overwhelming victories, sweeping away Archbishop Oluoch, Grace Ogot, and KANU's other remaining loyalists. Even in the southern Luo districts, FORD-Kenya was dominant, although some observers believed that President Moi might secure enough support, when combined with the Gusii vote, to give him 25 per cent from the Province in the Presidential election. The contest in Kisii and Nyamira, the two Gusii districts, was very different. Here, following former Cabinet Secretary Simeon Nyachae's decision to back the ruling party, KANU was clearly a powerful, though internally divided, force. Its main opponent differed from constituency to constituency, a reflection of the long-established importance of sub-clan voting in Gusii elections. Both FORD-Kenya and the DP had local pockets of support, and might emerge with two or three seats each, while maverick George Anyona of the Kenya Social Congress (KSC) was extremely popular in Kitutu Chache. The bulk of the Gusii Presidential vote and three or four Parliamentary seats, however, were likely to go to KANU, although at the height of the clashes in April and May this had seemed much less certain.

There were some intriguing parallels between events in 1992 and those in 1961–3, during the struggle for power before Independence (see Chapter 2). The KANU–KADU divide then had reflected different views on the economy, relationships with European settlers and other matters, but rested above all on perceptions of local interest. The minority groups of the Kalenjin, Coastal peoples and Luhya had favoured KADU as a bulwark against the dominance of the two largest ethnic groups, the Kikuyu and Luo and their allies. In 1992, the situation was disturbingly similar. As the election approached, it was becoming clear that KANU now represented the minority groups – the Kalenjin, the Coastal peoples, the Somalis, Maasai and others – led by Moi, one of KADU's original three leaders.

The two FORDs and the DP represented the old Kikuyu-Luo alliance of 1963, one faction of it led by Odinga, a leader of the KANU coalition at that time. Now, as then, Moi and his allies were asserting the need for *Majimboism,* or regional rights, against an alliance of the larger ethnic groups.

Defections Back to KANU

As the poll neared, KANU began to make use of one of its strongest weapons – the ability to tempt back defectors from the opposition parties, who were fearful of their electoral prospects, unlikely to win party nominations, or simply financially insecure. Both the DP and FORD élites proved vulnerable to defections, whilst FORD-Asili had few leaders of note in the party outside Central Province. Mass defections began as early as August, and by late September it was clear that the opposition's chances in pro-KANU areas were being weakened, following a series of defections by senior FORD and DP leaders encouraged and funded by senior KANU politicians. In part, this stemmed from the split in FORD. Indeed, the losers in the FORD-Kenya elections on 4 September provided a good illustration of the dictum that success is all-important in Kenyan politics. James Osogo, who lost FORD's First Vice-Chairmanship to Muite, for example, defected to KANU in October and was later nominated as a KANU candidate. Peter Kibisu lost the Second Vice-Chairmanship and defected back to the ruling party on 17 September. From Taita-Taveta, Mashengu wa Mwachofi attended the Congress but received no post and defected to the DP soon after, while Dr Chibule wa Tsuma from Kilifi went to the KNC. Pressure from KANU in areas where it was strong, and calculations of electoral and financial advantage further reinforced the shift between parties. KANU had considerable success in Coast Province. In Mombasa, Emmanuel Maitha defected back on 13 September 1992, while Kilifi DP Chairman John Mumba defected on 13 October, joining Maurice Mboja and Lesley Mwachiro who had returned earlier. Elsewhere, KANU's greatest successes were in re-enlisting SDP leader Johnstone Makau in Makueni – he rejoined the party at the last minute on 29 October – and in Wajir, with the re-enlistment of one of FORD's founders, Ahmed Khalif Mohammed, in the North-East.[2]

Whether politicians led their supporters in these defections or vice versa is a difficult issue to resolve. In late 1991 and early 1992, Odinga, Kibaki and Shikuku clearly led their communities into the unknown. Elsewhere, key machine politicians determined the allegiance of their local areas. After these early switches of political allegiance, however, the evidence suggests that politicians followed, rather than led, their local areas, concealing their true sympathies. The vast majority of defections occurred purely for personal advantage. The need to win the election was the overriding imperative. If candidates could not win the nomination in one party, because there was a stronger candidate, or if they thought they had a better chance with another party, then they changed allegiance. Being on the winning side was more important than political principle.

Voters and politicians, unused to a multi-party system, took time to adjust to the concept of parties with ideologies, institutions and objectives which transcended the individuals who composed them at local and national level. Indeed, since virtually all parties at the local level were still constructed on localist, clan and personal lines, the penalties imposed on candidates for lack of principle in switching parties were comparatively small. In the multi-party era, candidates still led their communities into and out of different parties. What many candidates, voters and commentators did not realise sufficiently clearly was that voting structures transcended local clan and clientage arrangements. As the election approached, the setting of political support into better defined boundaries overlaid stable patterns on previously fluid alignments. The 'trickle down' party identification from the Presidential election and from regional political identities and allegiances was so strong in most of the country that powerful individuals who had found new homes in minority parties, believing they could take their supporters with them, were to be very disappointed. Local politicians found that they could no longer hold on to their supporters in the face of the struggle between Presidential titans.

Defections to the Opposition

The voting down of the Kiliku report on 14 October was the last time that the unreformed Parliament truly assembled. Eight days later, President Moi adjourned Parliament indefinitely. Although the election date was still not known, this set a three-month limit on the period before Parliament had to reassemble. It was clear the election was imminent, and politicians finally were forced to decide which party they were going to support. On 28 October the President dissolved Parliament and the election battle began.

The dissolution marked the end of the 'phoney war'. Since the first round of defections in December 1991 and January 1992, the opposition had recruited no more incumbent MPs. This was both a political tactic and a response to the 1991 rule which had empowered the Speaker indefinitely to delay calling by-elections. Accordingly Ng'eno had refused to declare vacant any seats where the MP had defected, ensuring that the opposition had no voice in Parliament throughout 1992. As defectors could not immediately regain their seats, the flow of MPs to the opposition parties had halted. Yet this success had created certain problems for KANU. Opposition sympathisers had sat tight, to KANU's discomfort, making promises to both sides until the crunch came. Now, with nothing left to lose, defections revealed how weak KANU's control had been even of such a malleable Assembly as that elected in 1988. During the three weeks between the dissolution of Parliament and the start of the party primaries, nearly 10 per cent of KANU's Parliamentary force defected, along with numerous influential ex-MPs, mainly from Central Province. The defectors included one Minister (Onyango Midika from Nyanza), seven Assistant Ministers and the KANU Chief Whip. Many other ex-MPs and politicians defected at this time, correctly calculating that their last chance to jump ship had come. These defections were accompanied by, if they had not already been preceded by, the defection of local supporters, political factions and clans. Local councillors also shifted to the opposition throughout the same areas. KANU's attempt to organise a wave of defections was completely reversed, as politicians in opposition strongholds panicked, seeing their last chance of seats vanishing. Some had long been agents of the opposition in Parliament, whose preferences were well known. Others such as Amos Kimemia (Nakuru Town) saw the writing on the wall in their home areas and were effectively forced to defect.

Between the dissolution of Parliament and the primaries, 14 Kikuyu MPs and numerous former members of the Assembly defected: ten of the MPs joined the DP, two went to FORD-Asili and two to FORD-Kenya.[3] The defectors included three of the last four KANU MPs in Kiambu (the exception was Cabinet Minister Arthur Magugu, who was too deeply in debt to switch), and the virulent KANU hardliner, James Njiru, who had been sacked as Minister for Culture and Social Services on 14 October. Too unpopular to be permitted to carry KANU's banner in Kirinyaga District, Njiru eventually contested the election for FORD-Kenya! The defection of the incumbents from Central Province and the neighbouring areas of Nairobi, Laikipia and Nakuru destroyed KANU's remaining hopes amongst the Kikuyu, as they lost almost all their remaining MPs, mainly to the DP. KANU could merely respond by warning Kikuyu voters of the dangers of antagonising Kenya's present and future ruling party.[4] The success of the DP in recruiting prominent figures in Nakuru and even Murang'a was a reflection of the poor state of Asili at this time. Some Murang'a MPs, such as Francis Thuo (Assistant Minister and MP for Kigumo) and Nduati Kariuki (Assistant Minister and MP for Makuyu) undoubtedly would have won nominations (and later seats) if they had joined FORD-Asili. By contrast, Chris Kamunyu in Dagoretti read the political climate more accurately and later became FORD-Asili's MP for the constituency. The last-minute defections, however, included no prominent politicians from Nyeri, where the DP had things sewn up, confirming the widespread view that Nyeri's KANU leaders, who had defeated Kibaki's faction in 1988, commanded little credibility, whereas the ruling party's elections in Kiambu and Murang'a in 1988 had reflected the voters' wishes.

Outside Kikuyuland the drift to the opposition was far weaker, but still included several important catches in the closely fought areas of Ukambani, Western and the North-East: five MPs joined the DP, five went to FORD-Kenya, and three to FORD-Asili. The most notable defector outside of Kikuyuland was Onyango Midika, the MP for Muhoroni in Kisumu District, whom President Moi had dismissed as Minister for Regional Development on 3 October for secretly backing FORD-Kenya. The other two Luo defectors to FORD-Kenya, Job Omino (ex-Permanent Secretary, ex-chairman of the Kenya Football Federation and MP for Kisumu Town) and Assistant Minster Ochola Ogur (Assistant Minister and MP for Nyatike) were both significant figures in the local KANU hierarchy. There were also two significant defectors in Kakamega and Vihiga districts, Bahati Semo (MP for Vihiga) and Seth Lugonzo (Assistant Minister and

Photo 8.1 Ex-minister Paul Ngei joins the Democratic Party
Courtesy of Nation Group Newspapers

MP for Ikolomani) to FORD-Asili and the DP respectively.

There were also numerous defectors to the DP among the Akamba community. Ex-Cabinet Minister Paul Ngei, for example, finally switched to the DP on 26 October, abandoning hope of having his bankruptcy annulled. DP leaders realised that, although ineligible to stand, Ngei was still a potent force in Machakos. He was received into the party by Kibaki with due ceremony at Bruce House. The DP made two other important gains amongst the Akamba: Makueni District KANU chairman and MP for Kibwezi Agnes Ndetei; and Joseph Kiliku, Chairman of the Commission of Enquiry into the Ethnic Clashes and MP for Changamwe in Mombasa. Agnes Ndetei's defection demonstrated KANU's failure to keep local populist leaders in the fold. Ndetei had been allowed to win the KANU chairmanship of the new Makueni District because of her local popularity, despite her vocal stance on many issues and opposition to Machakos KANU chairman Mulu Mutisya. Her local opponents, led by Mutisya, were being edged out gradually by State House, but were themselves trying to drive Ndetei out of the party in a desperate attempt to force KANU's leadership to fall back on them. When she defected at the last minute, KANU was left in a weak position in the District.

The DP did very well from the post-dissolution defections, gaining substantially from the destruction of FORD as well as from KANU. At this time, it appeared the most coherent and well-organised opposition party. It recruited a number of popular KANU leaders who might earlier have defected to a united FORD, including Seth Lugonzo, Agnes Ndetei and Kiliku in Mombasa, without whom its national position would have been considerably weaker. It also picked up several defectors from FORD between September and mid-October. These included Martha Njoka in Kirinyaga, Andrew Ngumba in Nairobi, Kihika Kimani in Nakuru (who moved to contest Laikipia) and Alfred Sambu in Bungoma. Many of the last-minute recruits to the DP performed badly in the internal party nominations, however, or did not make their move public until the party nominations had actually started. Despite the problems stemming from the disintegration of FORD, FORD-Kenya at the same time recruited former Speaker of the National Assembly Moses arap Keino from KANU to stand in Kipkelion, as well as Ogur and Omino among the Luo. FORD-Asili, by contrast, enlisted only one significant figure from outside the Kikuyu – Bahati Semo – although it benefited from a late surge in North-Eastern Province where, in late October, 15 prominent North-Eastern leaders defected to FORD-Asili, including two ex-MPs in Wajir. In late October and early November, however, FORD-Asili's and Matiba's fortunes were at their nadir. Having split FORD, he had then split FORD-Asili, losing the support of most of the senior Kikuyu politicians, and retaining the backing of few well-known political figures apart from Martin Shikuku and former Vice-President Karanja.

The Campaign Opens

With registration completed, the 25 per cent rule in place, and a fragmented opposition, by early October 1992 KANU had decided that it could win. The ruling party launched its national campaign with a series of huge rallies on two successive weekends all over the country. On 17 and 18 October and again on 24 and 25 October, Ministers and MPs fanned out across the country to organise campaign meetings for KANU's candidates and President Moi, and to brief people on the election method for the primaries. The first series of 16 rallies extended from Kisumu to Wajir and revealed many of the elements of the KANU campaign, featuring personal attacks on opposition leaders, scarcely veiled threats and blatant promises to particular communities. On the positive side, they also stressed the party's national character and country-wide coverage, with the guests of honour carefully selected to demonstrate the ruling party's nation-wide support. Thus Mombasa KANU Chairman Sharrif Nassir, for example, led a rally in Mandera in the North-East, Secretary-General Kamotho, the party's leading Kikuyu from Murang'a, spoke in Nakuru, whilst Saitoti, Nyachae and eight other Ministers attended a large rally in Kisii. In FORD-Kenya's Nyanza stronghold there was anti-KANU violence following attempts to disrupt a rally led by Vice-President Saitoti in Minister Ayah's constituency of Kisumu Rural.[5] At this time, in his early campaign speeches, Moi was still trying to reach out to the opposition-supporting communities, emphasising that he was a 'clean leader' and a non-tribalist, who had done much for the Kikuyu and Luo. Moi even claimed on Kenyatta Day (20 October), that he would beat Odinga in

Luoland and win 80 per cent of the vote in Central Province.[6] With FORD split, the main focus of KANU's attacks was now the DP, who appeared their strongest opponent. A vicious battle of words had developed between the DP and KANU Kikuyu leaders at the end of September. Kibaki branded some KANU leaders 'psychopaths and sycophants', trying to shrug off the impression that he lacked the stomach for hand-to-hand political combat. In return, KANU's rallies focused on the weaknesses and failings of the DP.

Another feature of these first meetings was the principle they established that KANU would receive every assistance from the state in its campaign. Whilst KANU was campaigning, opposition leaders were protesting that they had not yet been authorised by the District Administration to hold any meetings. Secretary-General John Keen claimed the DP had been denied licences for a series of ten meetings round the country, while KANU was allowed to hold 15 rallies in the same period.[7] Intriguingly, the only opposition leader permitted to hold a meeting during these two weekends was Martin Shikuku, who spoke in Nakuru on 17 October with the Molo MP Njenga Mungai, who had just defected to FORD-Asili. In an attempt to enlist Luo support in this multi-ethnic seat, Njenga Mungai claimed that Foreign Minister Ouko had been assassinated by corrupt politicians and that Hezekiah Oyugi could have been killed in order to get rid of a key witness. Such allegations alarmed government leaders, and Mungai was arrested the next day.[8]

The FORD-Kenya–DP Alliance

One possibility, mooted several times before and during the election, was some form of alliance between the DP and FORD-Kenya (with the minor parties as bridesmaids). The Middle Ground Group of Professor Wangari Maathai, which was influential with American and European donors, had continued to preach cooperation and coordination between opposition parties in order to beat KANU. Whilst a full united front was extremely unlikely, since Matiba wholly rejected any cooperation with other parties, convinced that he would form the next government, there was still hope that the DP and FORD-Kenya could come to an agreement. Both recognised that, divided, they had little chance of victory, and both disliked FORD-Asili more than each other. In August, Raila Odinga had reported that FORD was having talks with the DP to draw up an electoral pact whereby the parties would fight the election with agreed Prime Ministerial, Presidential and Vice-Presidential candidates, and would not put up Parliamentary candidates against each other. Internal problems in FORD, however, put Kibaki off (at least publicly).

Nonetheless, efforts to rebuild some form of unity continued. On 16 October, leaders of FORD-Kenya and the minor parties KENDA, the Labour Party Democracy (LPD) and the SDP met at All Saints' Cathedral in Nairobi and asked the Middle Ground Group to work for a single presidential candidate. The other parties did not turn up.[9] On 21 October, however, facing marginalisation as the fifth party in the election and without a Presidential candidate of their own, the KNC agreed to support Kibaki.[10] On the same day, Mrs Maathai also declared that the opposition had agreed to field one candidate, though she did not say who it was.[11] It appeared that Matiba might be sidelined amongst the Kikuyu by a joint KNC-DP ticket, and had some arrangement been made with FORD-Kenya at this stage there was a real chance that a near-united front could have emerged. The next day, however, FORD-Kenya responded negatively to the DP-KNC statement by suggesting that the two parties should first hold grassroots elections.[12] FORD-Kenya's old guard remained reluctant to come to terms with the Kikuyu élites, as memories of the 1960s remained too strong. The more radical party was also over-confident at this stage.[13] It seemed that Matiba's new FORD-Asili party was in desperate trouble, suggesting that FORD-Kenya might inherit most of the remains of FORD. Consequently, two days later, Odinga ruled out a single opposition candidate for the Presidency.[14]

Nonetheless, secret meetings between DP and FORD-Kenya teams continued, and apparently outlined an agreement whereby Odinga would be the joint Presidential candidate. These were made public on 1 November, when Denis Akumu of FORD-Kenya revealed at a press conference that negotiations were well-advanced for a merger and that Odinga would be the candidate.[15] Paul Muite confirmed that discussions were taking place but regretted their premature disclosure. Akumu, a member of the Luo old guard, was probably attempting to derail the talks. Backing away the next day, Kibaki announced that he was also working with the IPK, and that the talks with FORD-Kenya were only in their preliminary stage.[16] The DP, like FORD-Kenya, was still reluctant to compromise, with some senior DP leaders considering that Kibaki had conceded too much whilst FORD-Kenya leaders felt the DP wished to run too much of the government. Thus the opposition's last chance to create some form of unity before the elections was lost. Further talks were held in the last few days before the poll, but led to nothing.

The Electoral Role of Interest Groups

The combination of patrimonialism and the one-party state in Kenya has ensured that interest groups have played a key part in Kenyan political life. With a weak party structure, some, such as GEMA in the 1970s and the Churches in the 1980s, served as vehicles for mass mobilisation when the party could not. The business community, of course, was intimately embedded in the political sphere, as was the civil service, and needed no explicit organisation or pressure group to represent its interests. A particular problem the government faced in 1992, however, was that the majority of the business community and significant parts of the civil service were sympathetic to the opposition. Consequently, Moi's opponents had access both to secret government papers and to substantial sources of income. The press, students and the professions were also generally hostile to KANU. The trades union movement, by contrast, played a limited role in 1992. COTU declared that it was neutral, but would sponsor labour leaders in any political party. Most major trades union officials sided with KANU, although a few local-level organisers stood for the opposition parties.

The Christian Churches were a key political influence. They had played a major role in nurturing the opposition and in monitoring the electoral process but were far from united. The majority of the major denominations provided tacit support to the opposition, while KANU was backed by some independent churches, including the Luo Legio Maria and President Moi's own African Inland Church. Different religious groups canvassed for different candidates and more than a dozen candidates in all political parties were clergymen or prominent members of the laity.

The largest religious community in Kenya, with probably 30 per cent of all Kenyans, was the Roman Catholic Church. It had a presence in almost every district, and was the largest denomination even in Nandi and Kericho districts. Its head, Maurice, Cardinal Otunga, had maintained a low political profile in the 1980s, leaving political controversy to the more forthright Mgr Mwana a'Nzeki, the Bishop of Nakuru and secretary of the Catholic Bishops' Conference. Since 1990, however, the Church had become more outspoken in its condemnation of authoritarian rule and had played an active role in the democratisation movement. Throughout 1992, the Catholic Church was in the vanguard of the movement for constitutional reform and among those holding the government responsible for the tribal clashes. In the weeks immediately before the election, the Catholic Bishops not only condemned the renewed ethnic violence in the Burnt Forest – from where many refugees fled to the sanctuary of the Catholic Cathedral in Nakuru – but also condemned the buying of votes and bribery of defectors, and the harassment and intimidation of opposition candidates.[17]

The Anglican Church (known as the Church of the Province of Kenya or CPK) was another active campaigner against the government. The CPK's adherents, clergy and Bishops are predominantly Kikuyu (eight of its 14 Bishops are from Kikuyuland), although it is also strongly established among the Luo and Luhya, and in Nandi and Trans-Nzoia. Politically, its most significant figures were: the Primate, Archbishop Manasses Kuria, a Kikuyu from Murang'a; the Rt Rev. David Gitari, the Bishop of Mount Kenya East, an outspoken Kirinyaga Kikuyu; the late Bishop Alexander Muge of Eldoret; and the Rt Rev. Dr Henry Okullo, the Bishop of Maseno South. Bishop Okullu, who had a strong following in Luo areas, had been one of the leaders of the democracy movement, and continually criticised the government's handling of the electoral process and the ethnic clashes, and its harassment of the opposition. The CPK also had a significant presence (20–25 per cent of the population) in the Kalenjin areas, where it was closely identified with the local DP: the DP candidate in Eldoret North, Daniel Tanui, was a CPK elder, as was the DP Chairman in Nandi. In the run-up to the General Election, however, KANU attempted to repair its relations with the CPK following the damage done by Muge's murder. If CPK members in Nandi voted for the DP, KANU not only feared that Kalenjin unity would be damaged irreparably but realised that it would be virtually impossible to rig the Presidential election in the area. The ruling party, consequently, had granted Nandi demands for a fair primary and had accepted the repudiation of Biwott's three allies, who had been rigged in four years earlier, and the selection of John Sambu, a CPK worker and close ally of the late Bishop Muge, as its candidate in Mosop.

The Presbyterian Church of East Africa (PCEA) played a mixed role. An overwhelmingly Kikuyu church, its most prominent political spokesman for over 20 years has been former Moderator the Rev Dr John Gatu, a Kiambu Kikuyu. Gatu had sought to preserve reasonable relations with the government and over the past decade had clashed frequently with his more outspoken colleague, Rev. Dr Timothy Njoya, former Minister of St Andrew's Church in Nairobi. It was Njoya, from Nyeri District, who had called in his New Year Sermon on 1 January 1990, for the abolition of KANU's single-party rule, drawing direct comparisons between authoritarian rule in Kenya and the Soviet bloc. Njoya was one of the first people to visit Matiba when he was recuperating in London and, with Okullu, had been a thorn in the regime's side.

The Methodist Church, led by Bishop Lawi Imathiu and concentrated in Meru, was more circumspect and was never identified with the opposition. The DP candidates in Meru, however, included several Methodist workers and officials, including Richard Maoka Maore in Ntonyiri and David Mwiraria in Imenti North. By contrast, the AIC, which developed from American Fundamentalist origins, was closely identified with the Moi regime. The AIC dominated the Kalenjin areas, particularly Baringo and Elgeyo-Marakwet, and was also strongly established in Nandi and Kericho. We have seen that President Moi himself was a member of the AIC, and the close links between the church and political establishments in Kalenjin areas, especially in Nandi, can be seen in the fact that the AIC head, Ezekiel Birech, was the father of former Cabinet Minister and Mosop MP John Cheruiyot.

The NCCK is an umbrella body of all the non-Catholic churches, including all Protestant churches and most of the Independents. Its Secretary-General, the Rev. Samuel Kobia, also acted as Vice-Chairman of NEMU's governing Council of Elders. Inside the NCCK, a rift had developed in the 1980s between the major international denominations (led by the CPK and the PCEA) which became increasingly critical of the government, and the Kenya-based Independent churches, which remained aloof from politics or supported the regime. In 1986, when the NCCK condemned queuing, the leaders of a number of Independent churches, including the African Orthodox Church, the small Kikuyu-based Pentecostal Church of Africa (PCA), the Legio Maria, and certain African Independent Pentecostal Church Assemblies (AIPCA) congregations, had condemned the NCCK's attitude and threatened to withdraw from the Council. The AIPCA was a Kikuyu-dominated Church, centred in Murang'a, Kiambu and Nakuru: in 1992 many AIPCA congregations favoured FORD-Asili, while adherents of the Nyeri-based African Orthodox Church generally supported the DP. The Legio Maria, which has substantial numbers of adherents in Siaya and Kisumu, by contrast, remained loyal to KANU, as did the PCA. The Legio Maria was the only denomination to be led by a prominent politician (and Cabinet Minister), Archbishop Oluoch, who was KANU's defending candidate in Ugenya. Nonetheless, Legio Maria voters were to reject their own leader unambiguously at the polls.

If the Christian Churches generally were aligned with the opposition, Kenya's Moslem community was hardly supportive of the state. Roughly 15 per cent of the population was Moslem, concentrated in the Coast Province districts of Kwale, Mombasa, Kilifi and Lamu, in Nairobi, and in North-Eastern Province among the Somalis. The Islamic movement has played a substantial role in political life for several years, although its political influence has not equalled its role in Tanzania. Recently, Moslem 'extremists' had aroused security concerns, in line with the growth in Islamic fundamentalism throughout the world. In 1990–2, the Moslem community made common cause with Christians in opposition to the KANU government, identifying restrictions on its freedoms and discriminatory treatment of Moslems. Radical preachers, such as Sheikh Balala in Mombasa, used the mosques to criticise KANU and to call for change. The IPK was formed in February 1992, chaired by Omar Mwinyi, but was refused registration on the grounds that it was discriminatory, requiring specific religious beliefs of its members. The party, however, did not disappear. With youth unemployment running at nearly 70 per cent, and the tourist industry in depression, many Mijikenda young men had turned in despair to radical Islam, which condemned the established order of society and its values. The arrest of Sheikh Balala for treason and the protracted court cases which ensued aroused widespread discontent not only among Mombasa's Arab population but also among local Mijikenda and other Moslem Africans. Balala had successfully built a resilient coalition between Mombasa's Arab spiritual élite and the mainly African faithful, drawing on their rejection of Western values and resentment at the local economy's economic difficulties. By contrast, the country's Moslem leadership had attempted to maintain good relations with the government.

The result was a bitter conflict in Mombasa between the militant IPK and hardline KANU boss Sharrif Nassir, which led to widespread violence, the destruction of KANU property and vehicles, mass arrests and regular street fighting. The situation deteriorated until it was out of control in August 1992, when Nassir, himself an Arab, attempted to remove all IPK symbols and banners from Mombasa prior to President Moi's visit. This prompted vicious street battles between KANU youth-wingers and IPK militants, and a massive demonstration of 10,000 IPK supporters on 24 August. Unable to put up its own Parliamentary and local government candidates, at the last minute IPK leaders formed a marriage of convenience with FORD-Kenya, which agreed to nominate five IPK members as its Parliamentary candidates in the four Mombasa constituencies and in Malindi. The IPK considered that FORD-Kenya best represented the original 'civic forum' ideology of the movement for political reform, although Moslem activists in Lamu preferred the DP. The alliance provoked some anger among FORD-Kenya members at the Coast, who lost their chance of the party's nomination. Nonetheless, the alliance survived the campaign with little difficulty, apart from one successfully papered-over incident in Lamu at the end of November, when Odinga made some unguarded utterances about the Koran having been written rather than given by Allah.[18]

The military played a crucial and little-examined role throughout the year, as much by their passivity as by their action. Not enough is known about the ethnic composition of the military, except at the most general level,[19] and almost nothing is known about the extent of support for KANU among the rank and file. Loyalty to KANU amongst the top echelons was strong, as the presence of Chief of Staff Mohammed's brother and ex-Chief of Staff Mulinge in the Cabinet after the election confirms. The *Watchman* made the interesting allegation in December that Mahmoud Mohammed had been given 20,000,000 shillings to hand out to 4,000 soldiers (5,000 shillings each) for voting KANU, and claimed that several soldiers had confirmed that this money did exist but that Mohammed had used it to build real estate instead.[20] The army was split, however – ethnically and politically – and could not be relied upon to provide unquestioning support. The view among those with contacts in the military was that army officers were unwilling to become involved in political repression. Back in February 1992, there had been widespread rumours that KANU wished to stage some form of military coup. Several FORD leaders, including Karanja (FORD-Asili, Githunguri) had been interrogated briefly by the Special Branch. There were also fears in April and May 1992 that the ethnic clashes were being used to fuel insecurity, which would enable the government to justify the declaration of a State of Emergency. Perhaps because Moi feared the external reaction, as well as the prospect of widespread rioting, no such events had occurred. Opposition leaders, nevertheless, wondered why the army had been left on the sidelines during the first serious bout of clashes, although troops were later deployed to stop violence in Trans-Nzoia. Whether they would have obeyed orders to seize power in the event of KANU losing power in the election is unknown.

Paranoia about the military was strong, particularly in FORD-Kenya. The army was placed on standby to maintain order during the election period. There were reports of military movements of heavy arms and equipment into the Rift Valley and North-Eastern Provinces, particularly Kericho, in the last few days of the campaign, and genuine fears that KANU was preparing a military secession in the event of losing the election, with most of the army's heavy equipment in areas outside opposition control. If the North had seceded, however, KANU's areas would have been heavily outnumbered (though with the majority of the weapons) and economically isolated, and would not have been able to sustain the revolt for long. It was far more likely that pastoralist officers would have attempted to launch a pre-emptive *coup d'état* if the opposition seemed likely to win, to keep Moi in power.

The Asian community was another important interest group, mainly because of its economic importance. Although restricted since 1968 in its business activities in the rural areas, Asian dominance of business in the urban areas had continued. Politically, Asians have been passive, preferring to secure their economic status through financial arrangements with powerful African partners such as Charles Njonjo and Moi. The Asian community remained loyal to KANU following the introduction of multi-party politics. Many were deeply concerned that their political protectors in KANU might lose power, leaving them exposed as obvious targets for pro-African anti-corruption leaders such as Martin Shikuku. In addition, like all businessmen, the Asian community was concerned about Kenya's future, and believed that if the Kikuyu returned to power, Asian economic interests would suffer. The only countervailing tendencies were a widespread belief that democracy would in the long term preserve political stability better than oppression, and the view that a DP government would restore the economy and generate growth, which would aid all businesses.

The Party Primaries and the Selection of Presidential Candidates

With the campaign now under way, the next step was to choose the candidates who would represent the parties in the Presidential elections, and in every civic and Parliamentary seat in the country. This struggle to find suitable candidates, and for candidates to find suitable parties, dominated November 1992. In previous elections, there had been no real selection process for the Presidential candidate. The incumbent – Kenyatta and then Moi – had always been elected unopposed. Things changed little in 1992. In three of the four main parties, the party leader was nominated unopposed as the Presidential candidate, a reflection of the dominance individuals held in political allegiances over fledgling party institutions. Despite pressure early in 1992 from Luhya leader Elijah Mwangale, Moi faced no real opposition in KANU.[21] He was nominated unopposed at Kasarani on 9 October 1992. Oginga Odinga was chosen automatically, as FORD-Kenya's constitution specified that the Party Chairman would be the Presidential candidate, provided he was suitably qualified.[22] Odinga had been unopposed at the September party elections. Kibaki was also unopposed as the DP's Presidential candidate, though no public DP elections for national officers took place.[23]

The sole exception was FORD-Asili. The Presidential nomination process in the original FORD was one of the core points of disagreement between the two factions. The Muthithi House (Matiba) faction had demanded an open primary among all party members, while the Agip House (Odinga) faction had determined on a Delegates' Conference system. It was essential, therefore, that Asili demonstrate their commitment to what they had preached by holding an open primary. The two main candidates were Matiba and Shikuku, with a third candidate, Dr Patrick Chege Njuguna, as a minor irrelevance. The election was held by a secret ballot of all party members, carried out at the same time as the local government and Parliamentary primaries on 10–12 November 1992, at approximately 9,000 'polling stations'. Some were properly managed

Table 8.1 FORD-Asili Presidential Primary Results

Province	Matiba	Shikuku	Njuguna	Total
Nairobi	33,167	13,450	n/a	47,000
Coast	49,148	12,581	n/a	62,000
Central	324,491	1,929	n/a	327,000
Rift Valley	142,403	52,483	n/a	195,000
Nyanza	60,920	7,454	949	70,000
Eastern	204,456	19,641	1820	226,000
North-Eastern	20,806	1,532	n/a	22,000
Western	13,393	333,076	n/a	346,000
Total	848,784	442,146	4,328	1,295,000

Source: Daily Nation, 18 November 1992, p. 1 and *Nairobi Weekly Observer,* 20 November 1992, p. 3. The n/a figures indicate that results for the third candidate were not reported.

stations with ballot boxes, others were merely open-air meetings. The process was little documented and attracted little attention from the media.

The result, announced a week later, was a convincing win for Matiba (see Table 8.1). The voting was ethnically polarised, with Matiba sweeping Kikuyuland and neighbouring areas such as Embu, where he secured 17,265 votes to Shikuku's 1,228. Western Province was equally emphatically for Shikuku. In Vihiga District, for example, Shikuku secured 30,866 votes, compared to Matiba's 1,963. Only a few districts were closely contested, including Mombasa which Matiba narrowly won by 4,893 to Shikuku's 4,336.[24] To the surprise of many who had predicted his return to KANU on his defeat, Shikuku accepted defeat graciously and promised to work with Matiba.[25]

If this primary turn-out was legitimate, it explains FORD-Asili's subsequent confidence during the campaign, since over 1.2 million party members (20 per cent of the electorate) participated in the primary. It is near certain, however, that these figures overstated the true level of FORD-Asili support, and were substantially inflated to support Asili's resurgence. At the time of the primaries in early November, FORD-Asili had almost vanished from the national stage, without FORD-Kenya and without the KNC leaders, who had defected only weeks before. It is known that some members of other parties voted in the Asili elections to help select candidates who would be easier to beat. KANU supporters may even have voted for Matiba to ensure his victory, in order to split the Kikuyu vote. Certainly, as Kwendo Opanga observed in the *Sunday Nation,* 'KANU strategists heaved a sigh of relief' that the Kikuyu vote would remain split and that Western Province, with no Presidential candidate of its own, was open for competition. If Shikuku had won, 'the prospect of a Luhya capturing the highest office in the land would have galvanised the Luhya voters behind Mr Shikuku'.[26]

In any case, the huge turn-out in Western Province (and to a lesser extent elsewhere) was quite implausible. There were approximately 850,000 registered voters in the Province, of which FORD-Asili secured only 185,000 in the General Election, compared with an alleged primary vote of double this. Few details of the votes in individual districts, let alone seats, were given, and documentary testimony concerning inflation of the vote has been found. In Samia, for example, Shikuku allegedly obtained 13,000 votes in the Presidential primary, while only 7,000 were cast to choose Asili's Parliamentary candidate at the same time. In the re-run, caused by protests at the previous election, several Presidential ballot papers were given to each voter.[27] In Trans-Nzoia, another Luhya area, Asili Rift Valley provincial representative Salim Ndamwe claimed that officials had made false poll reports in favour of Shikuku.[28] The fact that the primaries were held on a normal weekday reinforces their implausibility. FORD-Kenya leaders even claimed privately that Shikuku had manufactured his own defeat. Knowing he could not win against Matiba, they alleged, he inflated the Western figures even more than the others, in order to make it look like a contest, but without any intention of claiming victory. It certainly did not reinforce impressions of the probity of FORD-Asili. Nonetheless, aided by positive press coverage, the primary results gave Asili a shot in the arm.

There were no open primaries among the minor parties. There were several other minor potential Presidential candidates, however, including George Anyona for the KSC and David Mukaru-Ng'ang'a for KENDA. The most interesting Presidential declaration was that of Chibule wa Tsuma, the KNC Second Vice-Chairman, who after declaring for the Presidency at his first rally in November, was disowned by his own party.[29] KNC Chairman Titus Mbathi immediately re-emphasised that the KNC was committed to convincing the opposition parties to unite and did not intend to nominate a candidate for the Presidency. Nonetheless, wa Tsuma persisted. Quite why he did so is unclear, but it certainly caused some disturbance in the KNC, and contributed to the prevailing problems in agreeing a common front against KANU.

The Parliamentary Primaries

While the candidates for the Presidency had been reasonably clear since the summer, this was far from true at the local level. Factionalism centred around potential Parliamentary candidates had been endemic throughout the year. The 1992 Parliamentary primary elections in the major parties were far closer to previous Kenyan elections than the final contest. Like some previous elections, they were thoroughly rigged and dominated by factional alignments. These, combined with the variety of local contests, produced a picture of hideous complexity, in which even the broadest themes are hard to discern. Nonetheless, there was no doubt of the importance of the primaries to the average Kenyan. Because MPs influence local development decisions and the distribution of local resources, it is vitally important for the average Kenyan to have access to the local MP, who in turn needs to be sympathetic to the needs of constituents. Previous elections had been dominated by compacts between candidates and their supporters, providing a perfect example of clientelist politics. Candidates bought votes either openly or with development promises, at the expense of other areas of the constituency and the country. Since in many constituencies the primary effectively determined who would become the local MP, as one party was clearly dominant, the primaries provided the opportunity for local peasantry to decide what sort of candidate would represent them, and to where the resulting 'fruits of *uhuru*' would flow.

In 1992, however, the primaries took on a new role. With several competing national coalitions, there was strong pressure within each to build plausible, effective teams who could win a local victory, and boost the party's and its Presidential candidate's fortunes nationally. KANU's problem was to ensure that their losers stayed loyal. The main opposition parties did not have a strong local candidate in nearly one quarter of the country's seats. Their need was therefore to seize local political notables from KANU. Finding the right Parliamentary candidate was particularly important in 'swing' areas, since the endorsement of a figure with strong local support might bring the seat with it.

All candidates had to be nominated by a political party, as independents had not been permitted to stand since 1968. With ten parties fielding candidates, most politicians were able to find a party to represent. The LPD had never taken off, however, and its Presidential candidate, Mohammed Noor Akram, stood down for Odinga, while the SDP became an empty shell after Johnstone Makau's return to KANU. Thus, there were eight real parties. Of these, however, PICK (Party of Independent Candidates of Kenya) and the KNC (outside their core leadership) were little more than collections of independents, creating the illusion of a significant ticket by enlisting defeated contenders from the major parties at the last minute.

KANU had intended to call a *blitzkrieg* election, with a surprise announcement of the nomination date for 14 November, using the reduction in the period required to eight days to catch the opposition by surprise and to prevent KANU losers defecting and capturing the nomination for other parties. All the parties were therefore involved in a frenzied six-day round of nominations between 7 and 12 November, when the successful legal challenge from the opposition transformed the situation. None of the parties had been ready to meet the original deadline, but the opposition's successful legal challenge on 12 November posed the greatest threat to KANU. The delay enabled the mass defection of defeated or dropped candidates to the opposition and allowed the opposition parties to find candidates in many seats which would have remained uncontested if the government's original election timetable had remained intact. The result was a drawn-out, violent, and complex process as all the parties nominated, renominated and dropped Parliamentary candidates, and candidates swapped between parties, seeking adoption elsewhere after failing to secure nomination in their own party. Contests continued until the last possible minute, with primaries still being re-run on 7 December, only two days before the revised nomination deadline. The primaries clearly highlighted the problem of trying to develop a concept of electoral fair play, since the nominations in most parties were either uncontested, badly managed or blatantly rigged. This was a poor start to Kenya's first democratic election in nearly three decades.

The KANU Primaries

Compared with those of the other parties, KANU's Parliamentary and local government primaries were by far the best organised, best reported and most manipulated. Candidates had to be KANU life members, to have national identity and voter's cards, and to have satisfied national language proficiency requirements. As before, only the wealthy could apply, since on submitting their forms, civic candidates had to pay 5,000 shillings and Parliamentary ones 10,000 shillings.[30] On 9 October, KANU's leadership had proposed to the ruling party's Annual Delegates' Conference a new selection system whereby delegates from party sub-branches would nominate candidates. Such a procedure would have strongly favoured incumbent office-holders, but was overturned by the Delegates' Conference, which voted to have party members directly elect the nominees, although no method was actually prescribed. Moi then gave each branch the choice of a secret ballot or the discredited queue voting system *(mlolongo)*. The result was confusion, with nominations held by different methods in different areas. The official procedure stated that:

> At 10.00 a.m. on the respective polling days the presiding Officer shall call upon the eligible Party members assembled at the Polling Station to decide on the method of voting.... In the absence of agreement by the members assembled, voting shall be by secret ballot.[31]

This extraordinary confusion theoretically permitted each polling station to vote differently, meaning that thousands of ballot papers would be printed for seats that opted for queue voting and did not need them. In practice, the election method was decided in most seats by the KANU District branch. Thus, for example, Nandi, Vihiga and Mombasa destricts decided on queueing, whilst Migori's elections were held by secret ballot.[32]

The first round of nominations was held on 9–10 November 1992. Roughly two thirds of the primaries were held by queue voting, with the rest conducted by secret ballot. In each case, the result was near chaos, leading to a classic series of fraudulent elections. KANU had no up-to-date registers of members, the issuing of membership cards was barely controlled, and partisanship ran high. Many officials did not follow the electoral procedures, and many of the polls were heavily rigged. Returns from polling stations, for example, were altered in several constituencies before they were forwarded to the counting centre. This was easier to achieve in the primaries than in the General Election, since there was no clearly outlined election process, no independent scrutiny, and hence far more opportunities for abuse. Sale of KANU membership cards, transport of voters, and control of the count were crucial to electoral success. In several seats, disagreements over which system to use led to fighting, as in Eldoret. Candidates went round the more closely contested seats threatening and bribing voters, and buying membership cards from supporters of their opponents and the apathetic.[33] The *mlolongo* elections, such as those in fiercely-fought Eldoret North, were particularly suspect. Most results

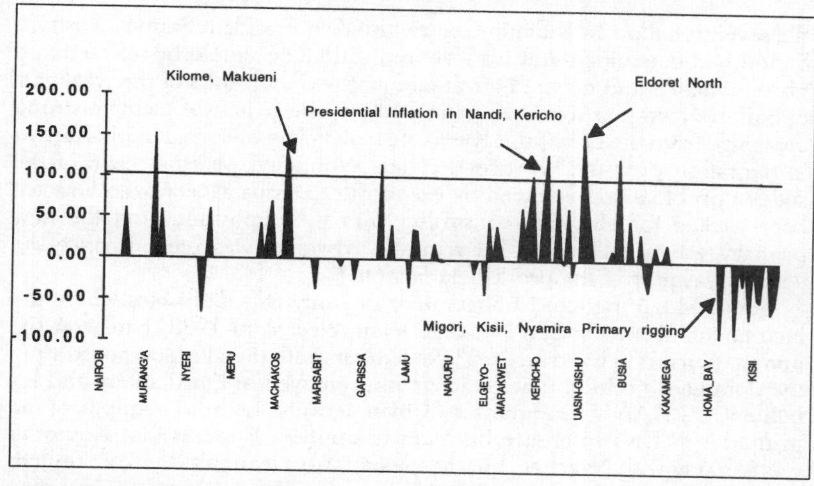

Figure 8.2 Percentage Increase of Votes in Final Election for KANU

were never publicly reported (for those that were, see Figure 8.2).

Once the first round was completed, around 12 November, the real battles started – to reverse those results which did not satisfy the dominant local faction, or had resulted in candidates whose chances of winning the seats were considered minimal. Japeth Kiti at KANU headquarters immediately ordered re-runs of the nominations in five seats: Nyaribari Masaba, Kajiado Central, Eldoret North, Kiambaa and Juja,[34] and also demanded a re-run in Malindi. Numerous protests, claiming rigging, flooded in from other seats, while some elections had been delayed. Thus, with the general election date still in doubt, the decision was taken to re-open the party nominations. On 13 November, therefore, KANU set up a Nominations Appeals Tribunal, chaired by lawyer Mutula Kilonzo, with representatives from each province.[35] Its task was to hear complaints about the Parliamentary nominations, whilst civic problems were delegated to local KANU branches. KANU officials, however, pre-empted the Tribunal before it had even started. Kiti annulled the elections in Likoni in Mombasa on 15 November, and on 18 November Secretary-General Kamotho himself ordered repeat nominations in six more seats: Wundanyi, Mwatate, Malindi, Makueni, South Mugirango and Bobasi. Thus, eleven elections were apparently annulled before the Appeals Tribunal even began hearing evidence.

Why were these results deemed unsatisfactory? Evidence of rigging was irrelevant, since most of KANU's nominations were rigged in some way. A better approach is to look at the areas and the candidates involved. Eldoret North was the centre of a bitter nomination battle between Tugen Assistant Minister Reuben Chesire (backed by YK '92 leader Cyrus Jirongo and possibly Moi) and Nandi ex-Assistant Minister William Saina (supported by the Biwott team and Uasin Gishu KANU Chairman Jackson Kibor). The election was re-run unsuccessfully six times, each poll degenerating into violence and rigging, until finally Saina triumphed on the seventh ballot. In Kajiado Central, in Vice-President Saitoti's District, Saitoti had demanded that his favoured candidate should be selected and his opponent stand down. This annulment was indicative of the weakness of Saitoti's own position in Kajiado District, where he was facing a strong challenge from the DP's John Keen, the beneficiary of considerable Kikuyu in-migration over the last two decades. Wundanyi was the scene of the sudden problems experienced by ex-Minister Darius Mbela, who had just been sacked for allegedly consorting with the opposition, and the new primary was a prelude to his removal. Mwatate was related, since the winner was part of the pro-Mbela faction.[36]

South Mugirango and Bobasi were the only two Kisii seats where the incumbents from the anti-Nyachae team, elected in 1988, had won the nominations. When re-run on 23 November, both then lost, demonstrating the dominant position that Nyachae now enjoyed in Gusii affairs and his influence at KANU headquarters, which permitted him to manipulate the primaries in Kisii to ensure his team triumphed. It seems that Kamotho was working with Nyachae, but the headquarters team was far from united: Japeth Kiti was a close ally of Jared Kangwana, Kisii opponent of Nyachae and ally of Saitoti. Things did not go entirely Nyachae's way, as revealed by the third annulment, of the primary in Nyaribari Masaba, where Minister Samuel Ongeri had lost to Nyachae's cousin Hezron Manduku. This bitter and violent struggle saw active campaigning by government officials for and against Professor Ongeri. Several people were injured during the repeats, which Ongeri again lost after widespread rigging.[37]

These early problems were nothing, however, compared to the torrent of protests which emerged during the hearings of the Appeals Tribunal, which sat in KANU headquarters at the Kenyatta International Conference Centre from 19 to 22 November and heard 187 complaints from 104 of Kenya's 188 seats.[38] Protests were particularly widespread and detailed in two areas: the marginal and near-marginal zones of Kisii and Nyamira (where nine out of ten seats were protested), Western Province, North-Eastern and Eastern Provinces; and in the KANU zones of the central Rift, where the result in every seat in Baringo and Elgeyo-Marakwet, apart from President Moi's and Biwott's, was appealed by the losers. Few defeated candidates, by contrast, bothered to protest in the opposition areas of Siaya, Kisumu, or Central Province, which the opposition parties were almost certain to win. Overall the Appeals Tribunal proceedings were a disaster for KANU. The protests indicated both the widespread extent of the rigging and the real risk of mass defections by losers to the opposition, while the bad publicity it generated reinforced people's belief that KANU could not be trusted to accept the results of its own elections, let alone the national ones.

On 25 November, the Tribunal rejected appeals from 61 seats and ordered repeat nominations in 43, nearly one quarter of the country.[39] The basis of its reasoning appears to have been a combination of official pressure and the desire to repudiate the most blatant rigging. The Tribunal seems actually to have listened to the evidence, although some specific verdicts may have been dictated by instructions from above, and its decisions caused immediate consternation in some government quarters.

Internal fighting immediately erupted, leading Secretary-General Kamotho to 'decide' that the Tribunal was not a legal body and that its decisions were not binding. He, consequently, unilaterally cancelled the renominations in twelve of the 43 seats, and put back in two others he had ordered to be re-held the week before in Taita-Taveta (particularly his Cabinet colleague's Darius Mbela's Wundanyi seat). He also wound up the Appeals Tribunal. .

Why this about-face took place is not known. Possibly the Tribunal had been less malleable than expected, or had followed its own agenda. The legal basis for Kamotho's annulments was questionable, and he was bitterly attacked by those who lost out, with some losers suggesting the Secretary-General was working for an opposition party.[40] It was clear, moreover, that Kamotho and National Executive Officer Kiti were not on the same side (several times overruling each other's announcements) in the feuding which threatened to disrupt KANU headquarters. The choice of seats where Kamotho intervened to cancel new elections was interesting, since at least five (Baringo East, Baringo North, Narok South, Kerio East and Konoin) were in KANU's Rift Valley stronghold, where the opposition challenge was non-existent. Kamotho accepted re-runs for Belgut, Bomet and Kerio West, however, in all of which hardline candidates, aligned with Biwott, had been selected in disputed circumstances.[41]

The chaotic factionalism and confusion at KANU headquarters

Table 8.2 A Provincial Summary of the Protests and Results

Province	Constituencies where complaints received by the Tribunal		Re-run ordered*	Kamotho reduced to
North-Eastern	8/10	(80%)	3	2
Western	15/20	(75%)	7	7
Nairobi	6/8	(75%)	0	1
Eastern	21/33	(64%)	8	6
Rift Valley	23/44	(52%)	11	6
Nyanza	14/28	(50%)	4	4
Coast	8/20	(40%)	3	2
Central	7/25	(28%)	5	4

* Including a few who were recommended to reconcile and, if that failed, to be re-run.

continued for another ten days. On 18 November, Japeth Kiti cancelled the Tribunal's re-run in Embakasi and in Zachary Onyonka's Kitutu Chache.[42] On 28 November a third figure entered the fray when KANU Deputy Executive Officer Mwandawiro, a business partner of Biwott's, declared the primaries in Othaya and Bomachoge had been called in error, and called new polls for Ndhiwa.[43] Kamotho, however, was clearly on the other side, since the next day party headquarters restated that elections were planned for Bomachoge, and Kamotho denied elections would be required in Ndhiwa at all.[44] This messy feuding continued for another week, involving 16 more constituencies, and even dragged President Moi into the battle.

Photo 8.2 Walji supporters protest outside KANU headquarters over Dr Mungai's attempt to secure the party's nominations in Westlands
Courtesy of Charles Hornsby

Most KANU candidates finally collected their nomination certificates from Kenyatta International Conference Centre on 7 December. Even then, the proceedings attracted demonstrators in support of Amin Walji, KANU's Asian candidate in Nairobi's Westlands constituency, who feared that former Cabinet Minister and ex-Nairobi KANU Chairman Njoroge Mungai, the incumbent, might successfully seek a last-minute reversal of his deposition. Overall, 54 of the 188 seats were ordered re-run at some point by national officials or the Tribunal. New elections were then cancelled at least once in 19 seats, concentrated in Nyeri (where KANU may have faced difficulties in preventing DP plants being selected); Taita-Taveta, where the Mbela issue was being fought out; Nairobi; Kisii and Baringo.[45]

By the end of this process, which did not finish until nomination day, KANU had created huge problems for itself in some areas and escaped them in others. The arbitrary nature of the internal conflicts led losers to denounce Kamotho bitterly and this, plus the rigging of the primaries themselves, led many to threaten defection or actually to join the opposition. Yet all was not as chaotic as it seemed. KANU used (and abused) its nomination procedures for two parallel purposes: to ensure that in marginal areas the most popular or best organised candidate in the constituency was nominated on the party ticket (whatever local party members thought) and to fight out political disagreements between 'ins' and 'outs', which usually corresponded with the division between hardliners, who had been swept into office in 1988, and reformers.

KANU headquarters, pushed by President Moi who had explicitly stated that he intended to do away with unpopular leaders, seems to have been anxious to repudiate hardliners with little popular support, who had been rigged into Parliament in 1988 when the ruling party had brutally and blatantly overruled local leaders and public opinion. In several KANU zones, four years later, party leaders recognised that they would have to pay much closer attention to popular demands if they were to maximise KANU's support. Nandi leaders, for example, warned President Moi that he must permit a free and fair primary in the District's three constituencies, if voters were not to defect *en masse* to the Democratic Party. As a result, for the first time since 1974 there appears to have been a reasonably fair election in the District. All three incumbent MPs and 45 local councillors were defeated in a massive purge of the dominant coalition, which had been fronted by former KANU District Chairman Mark arap Too. Too, paradoxically, represented the more moderate wing of the dominant faction in Nandi, and after his defeat urged compromise and cooperation with non-Kalenjin, in contrast to the warlike statements made by some other Nandi leaders.[46] Biwott's associates, the Branch's hardliners who had dominated the local County Council, also had little chance of winning endorsement in the new political climate. Thus the victors were the non-aligned group. The new KANU chairman Henry Kosgey, who had been rigged out in 1988, was unopposed in Tinderet, as the incumbent Kimunai arap Sego stood down at the last minute, later defecting to the DP. There were free ballots in the other two seats, which saw huge turn-outs. In Aldai, Minister John Cheruiyot, an ally of arap Too's, went down to defeat, protesting rigging, while arap Too, himself, lost Mosop to John Sambu, a CPK social worker and associate of Bishop Muge before his sudden death in August 1990.[47] In Bomet District, the 'out team' was also successful, revealing again the merry-go-round character of Kenyan politics, as two of the victorious KANU nominees had both been expelled from KANU in 1989, for reasons that were never made public, after falling foul of Biwott.

Within Nicholas Biwott's domain in Elgeyo-Marakwet and neighbouring Uasin Gishu, in parts of Kericho and in Moi's own Baringo District, hardliners won solid victories in a series of questionable elections. Biwott himself in Kerio South massively defeated his sole opponent Tabitha Seii, after which Seii defected to the DP, claiming that people had been forced to queue for Biwott. Biwott's ally, Paul Chepkok, won Kerio Central after the former Minister persuaded Chepkok's main opponent to stand down.[48] Biwott also engineered the defeat of his local opponent Francis Mutwol, the Marakwet spokesman in Kerio West. The Administration campaigned against Mutwol, Biwott's main local critic, and threatened non-Kalenjin residents with arson if they voted for him.[49] Party headquarters nullified the result, however, forcing the poll to be re-run. Biwott and his allies then ferried voters to the repeat nominations from Kerio Central, which were again won by Biwott's preferred candidate.[50] Biwott loyalists also won all of Uasin Gishu and most of Kericho and Bomet districts. Indeed, the elections showed just how dependent Moi was on his old ally in Moi's own home territories.

In marginal areas, however, the ruling party had to select the most popular candidate it could find in order to fight off the challenge from the opposition parties. Headquarters and YK '92 intervened to influence or

Table 8.3 Opposition Defectors, September–October 1992, Nominated by KANU

District	Seat	Candidate	Defected from	Date
Nakuru	Rongai	Willy Komen	DP	September 1992
Wajir	Wajir West	A. Khalif Mohammed	FORD Chairman Wajir Branch	10 September 1992
Mombasa	Kisauni	Emmanuel Maitha	FORD	13 September 199
Busia	Bunyala	James Osogo	FORD Chairman Busia Branch	October 1992
Kilifi	Bahari	John Safari Mumba	DP Chairman Kilifi Branch	13 October 1992
Makueni	Mbooni	Johnstone Makau	SDP Leader	29 October 1992
Meru	Imenti North	Silas Muriuki	not known	end October 1992

even blatantly to rig primaries, and to order some re-run and others not, in order to ensure that the ruling party had a full complement of strong candidates across the country. Thus unreformed local party officials such as Biwott loyalist Noor Abdi Ogle in Wajir South lost the primary after national KANU figures campaigned for his defeat. Ogle claimed that 1,100 Somali refugees were issued with KANU tickets and allowed to vote, and publicly accused Minister Maalim Mohammed and Provincial Commissioner Amos Bore of organising his removal.[51] The class of 1988 were frequently victims; many were unceremoniously dumped in favour of independent, more electable figures.[52]

As part of the process of 're-imaging', KANU also continued its policy of poaching popular local members of the opposition back into the fold. There appears to have been a secret policy of offering popular opposition figures who had a reasonable chance of success the KANU nomination if they defected. There were widespread rumours of financial incentives for defectors during the run-up to the nominations, but even more important than money was the right to contest the seat for KANU, especially as some opposition politicians, such as Emmanuel Maitha in Kisauni, feared that they were likely to lose their existing party's nomination. At least seven KANU candidates in marginal districts were last-minute defectors from the opposition. Five of them – Komen, Khalif Mohammed, Osogo, Makau and Mumba – were later to win their seats.

Since these deals with defectors were negotiated at the national level, it was frequently necessary to impose headquarters' choice on the local party. Moi's new right hand, the pressure group YK '92, was active on his behalf or that of KANU headquarters in ensuring that the deals were consummated (see Chapter 9). Ex-FORD member Emmanuel Maitha, for example, was imposed against incumbent MP Said Hemed, Sharrif Nassir's old ally, in Kisauni. The result was delayed for days as YK' 92 operatives destroyed ballot papers to ensure that Said Hemed lost, since Nairobi headquarters believed that he was unlikely to beat FORD-Kenya. Hemed alleged that 3,000 votes were stolen, and blamed YK' 92 and special aides of Moi for rigging him out.[53] Two days later, 900 ballot papers from the primary were found in a dustbin at the Mombasa Hotel, 843 of which had been for Hemed. Over 1,000 Hemed supporters burnt their KANU membership cards in protest and Hemed vowed not to support KANU.[54] Locked in a close contest with IPK leader Sheikh Balala in his own Mvita constituency, Nassir could not afford to permit YK '92 to antagonise the influential Arab community in Mombasa's Old Town, who supported Hemed. Overruled by Nairobi, the Mombasa KANU chairman's anger was clear, as he evicted YK '92's Mombasa branch from the KANU offices.[55] Nonetheless, the result stood.

There is also evidence that James Osogo, who had lost the national First Vice-Chairmanship of FORD-Kenya to Paul Muite, was rigged in against disgraced ex-Minister Peter Okondo in Bunyala. The seat saw a violent three-sided battle between Okondo, former Nairobi City Commissioner and ex-Kitale MP Frederick Gumo, and the newly rehabilitated Osogo. The Returning Officer declared Osogo the winner but refused to announce the result, and both losers swore that Osogo had 'imported people from a neighbouring country [i.e. Uganda] to vote for him and had rigged the whole exercise'.[56] In Bahari, incumbent Mtana Lewa was removed by YK '92 in favour of John Safari Mumba, a defector from the DP, while in North Imenti, Cabinet Minister Ntimama as Returning Officer ensured that his octogenarian colleague, Jackson Angaine, lost to Muriuki, a younger, more dynamic candidate.

What effect did the re-runs have? In the 54 constituencies where the primaries were at some point cancelled, they were actually re-run in at least 33 seats.[57] In only twelve constituencies, however, was the candidate altered. Only four were in KANU-dominated areas – Sigor in West Pokot, Kajiado Central, Mwatate in Taita-Taveta, and Kuria in Migori District – and in each case defections might have weakened KANU significantly. None were in KANU's Kalenjin heartland. Two were in opposition areas where KANU considered that it stood a chance (Butere in Kakamega and Gachoka in Embu) while the other six were key marginals (Makueni in Makueni District, Emuhaya and Shinyalu in Western, Likoni in Mombasa, and Bobasi and South Mugirango in Kisii). Whether it was worth all the trouble is doubtful. In the end, KANU won eight of the twelve, but would only have lost one or two more if the candidate had been different. In many areas, the rival factions in the ruling party simply fought themselves to a standstill and changed nothing in the end. Re-runs did help appease some losers, but not many. The subsequent defections of defeated contenders were probably made worse by the extent of the rigging, and KANU supporters were confused and disturbed. Huge amounts of time, money and effort were wasted. In three of the12 constituencies, the final losers in the KANU primaries defected anyway and only narrowly lost the General Election for their new parties. In these seats – South Mugirango, where the former KANU nominee secured 40 per cent for PICK; Sigor, where he polled 32 per cent for PICK; and Mwatate, where he polled 28 per cent for FORD-Asili – KANU's prospects may actually have been damaged by the imposition of approved candidates.

The result was that nearly half of KANU's incumbents were removed

Table 8.4 Party Posts Held by KANU Winners in Kericho and Bomet Districts

District	Constituency	KANU candidate	Local party post
Kericho	Buret	Jonathan Ng'eno	–
Kericho	Belgut	Kiptarus arap Kirior	Kericho Branch Chairman
Kericho	Kipkelion	Daniel Tanui	Kericho Branch Vice-Chairman
Bomet	Bomet	Kipkalya Kones	Bomet Branch Chairman
Bomet	Chepalungu	John arap Koech	Sub-branch Chairman
Bomet	Konoin	Nathaniel Chebelyon	–

Table 8.5 Party Posts Held by KANU Winners in Vihiga District

District	Constituency	KANU candidate	Local party post
Vihiga	Sabatia	Musalia Mudavadi	Vihiga Branch Chairman
Vihiga	Vihiga	Andrew Ligale	Vihiga Branch Vice-Chairman
Vihiga	Hamisi	Vincent M'Maitse	Vihiga Branch Secretary
Vihiga	Emuhaya	Sheldon Muchilwa	–

through the nomination process. Their performance was directly related to KANU's perception of their chances of victory. In safe KANU constituencies, hardliners and reformers were permitted to fight it out. In Biwott-controlled areas, the hardliners emerged victorious. In the 'soft' KANU zones and the marginal areas, President Moi and Kamotho were anxious to select popular candidates, who would maximise KANU's vote in the Presidential as well as Parliamentary elections. Unpopular sitting MPs, who had been rigged in four years earlier, had to be dropped in order to maximise the ruling party's chances. Thus incumbents did worst in the KANU zones of the Rift Valley (both in the Kalenjin core and the Rift periphery), the rural Coast and North-Eastern Province, where incumbents won only 20 out of 49 seats (41 per cent). In such areas, ex-politicians of standing, long *persona non grata* to KANU, such as G. G. Kariuki in Laikipia and Francis Lotodo in Pokot, were rehabilitated during the summer and appointed District leaders in the belief that they were well placed to bring in the local vote. Finally, in the hopeless seats, where KANU stood little chance of holding on, the incumbents who had remained loyal were re-adopted regardless of their alignment: 24 out of 31 (77 per cent) of KANU's remaining MPs in Central Province, Nairobi and Luoland were selected.

There were other reasons why some KANU candidates won and others lost. The first key determinant of the KANU nomination process was the electoral procedure adopted, which was decided by the local party. Party position was therefore important, as can be seen by taking a sample from two areas: Kericho and Bomet in the Rift Valley, and Vihiga in Western Province (Tables 8.4 and 8.5). This had also been true of the 'closed door' selection processes of the early 1960s, but it had almost died out in the 1970s with open competitive elections and the decline of KANU. Running the branch was a strong indicator of local influence, and only three branch

Table 8.6 Ministers' Performance in the KANU Primaries

Won unopposed	Won opposed	Lost or stood down	Unclear
Kamotho, Magugu, Kabingu-Muregi, Kyalo, Ndotto, Maalim, Kaparo, Moi, Ntimama, Saitoti, Mudavadi, Mwangale, Onyonka	Leakey, Ngutu, Ngala, Nabwera	Angaine, Nyagah*, Mibei, Cheruiyot, Ongeri	Kanyi, Kuguru, M'Mukindia, Masinde, Ayah, Oluoch, Otieno, K'Ombudo

* Nyagah was the only one not to attempt to defend his seat.

chairmen (Bidu in Kwale, Angaine in Meru and Lalampaa in Samburu) are known to have lost, though five others did not contest.

Government Ministers also did well, as they could use the resources of the state even more extensively than branch officials. Most were unopposed and, where they did lose, it tended to be to even better-connected candidates, rather than to populist newcomers. Ministers only fell when they had already lost the President's protection and were therefore fair game (see Table 8.6). The 'strong men' from the KANU districts tended to be unopposed, even when they were not Ministers, as with Nassir in Mvita, Stephen Musyoka in Kitui North, and ex-SDP defector Johnstone Makau in Mbooni.[58] Dr Ng'eno, the Speaker, in Buret, for example, faced only token opponents. The only Cabinet Minister who commanded President Moi's approval to face strong opposition was Katana Ngala of Kilifi District. He won only a narrow victory in Ganze, possibly because so many of his supporters had been transported to register in Mombasa to assist Shariff Nassir and KANU's other candidates.

The fourth conclusion is that most KANU primaries were fraudulent. It is almost impossible to enumerate the number of allegations of substantial rigging in the KANU primaries. They covered well over two thirds of the constituencies in the country, ranging from violence through to gross electoral fraud. In Central Province, Siaya and Kisumu, and those areas where KANU had little chance, the elections were reasonably fair. Elsewhere, fair contests were the exception rather than the rule. The use of *mlolongo* queue voting provided an easy means of fixing the result. The victory of 'approved' candidates can be ensured far more easily through cash payments to queuing voters than by threats or by stuffing ballot boxes. As Kisauni and Bahari showed, the returns from secret ballots could also be altered.

In most seats in Nairobi, for example, there were allegations of open bribery, importation of voters and favouritism by Returning Officers from headquarters.[59] No proper results were reported from most seats, probably because of the rigging and extremely low turn-outs. The elections were run by Nairobi KANU Chairman Clement Gachanja, who was unopposed in his own constituency as he arranged to have nominations in Dagoretti held on 9 November, one day earlier than all the others, without informing his opponents. Gachanja's agents were photographed handing out money to voters and there was violence as hundreds of supporters fought for their payments of 20 to 50 shillings each.[60] A case where KANU needed to select a plausible figure with a good chance for a marginal seat was in Westlands, where Dr Njoroge Mungai allegedly won the original nominations against Asian perennial candidate Amin Walji. The voting was marred by irregularities, forcing the poll to be repeated three times.[61] A third candidate stood down, citing mass importation of voters, open corruption of Presiding Officers and Returning Officers, and suggested that over 60 per cent of the voters were not valid residents of the seat. Mungai claimed he had actually secured the nomination with 3,262 votes to Walji's 2,633, but Kiti announced that Walji had won the election, although he refused to state how many votes each received. Mungai's defection to FORD at the beginning of the year and his re-defection later had sealed his fate. Headquarters considered that he had no chance of winning Westlands without the Kikuyu vote. Walji, who had performed strongly before, was judged a stronger standard-bearer who would be able to enlist the support of the constituency's large Asian community.

On the Coast, rigging was seen in numerous seats, including both Lamu seats, Likoni and Kisauni in Mombasa, and Bahari and Malindi, where the IPK were strong.[62] In some seats, this caused conflict. In Taveta, for example, Mwacharo Kubo defected to the DP after losing the nominations to European sisal plantation owner Basil Criticos, citing 'money dished out to voters'.[63] KANU headquarters apparently believed that Criticos would be able to finance a more lavish campaign and to enlist the support of his employees more effectively than Kubo in the General Election.

The Kisii and Nyamira KANU primaries were some of the most bitterly fought – and as heavily rigged as the 1988 elections, to remove those who had been rigged *in* on that occasion – as Simeon Nyachae sought to assert his authority. In the first polls, the two most powerful politicians, Onyonka and Nyachae, were unopposed. Andrew Omanga had stood down for Nyachae. In Kitutu Chache, Onyonka appeared to be facing Nicholas Siro, but Siro's papers 'went missing' when presented to KANU headquarters and he was barred from standing.[64] He protested to the Appeals Tribunal, claiming that systematic efforts were made to prevent his candidacy, including bribery offers from YK '92 leader Sam Nyamweya.[65] Elsewhere, all the other incumbents, the class of 1988 who had been put in to ensure the Nyachae team's defeat, lost disputed polls. In the two Kisii elections where the anti-Nyachae ticket won the first polls (Bobasi and South Mugirango), they were annulled and re-run, and both incumbents then lost. In Bobasi, incumbent Obure claimed he had won the nominations, polling 13,272 against Stephen Manoti's 6,464 votes, but was recorded as having lost. The true result was 'unclear' and new elections were held which Obure then boycotted.[66] In Nyaribari Masaba, the most severe of the pro- and anti-Nyachae struggles, Minister Samuel Ongeri lost in the first round, but managed to have the result overturned by the Appeals Tribunal. There were claims that the Nyandarua District Commissioner, who came from the area, was telling *wananchi* that the President had sent him to campaign for Ongeri. Ongeri, however, claimed the second election results were falsified and showed reporters figures suggesting he won the second election 12,245 to 11,533.[67] The elections were clearly rigged by someone, since all these figures were massively inflated.

Although incomplete, figures have been obtained for enough of the KANU primary elections – 68 results from 55 seats scattered round the country – to relate the total primary vote for KANU to its vote in the general election. The results allow us to confirm those seats where the primaries were clearly rigged. Most seats showed a roughly 20 to 50 per cent increase in the vote from KANU primary to the general election, for example from 7,127 to 10,172 in Masinga (up 43 per cent) and from 6,245 to 8,801 in Gachoka (up 41 per cent). In 20 seats, however, the number of votes cast in the primary exceeded the final vote for the KANU candidate in the General Election, a clear sign of malpractice.The Kisii, Nyamira, Turkana, Vihiga and Migori primaries are particularly suspect. In Migori itself, for example, Minister John Okwanyo massively rigged his nomination, recording a huge 29,217 votes in the primary, but polling a more

Table 8.7 Strong Evidence of Malpractice in KANU Primaries

Province	District	Seat	Fall in KANU vote from primary to final election
Eastern	Isiolo	Isiolo North	35%
North-Eastern	Mandera	Mandera East	23%
	Wajir	Wajir South	8%
Coast	Lamu	Lamu East	33%
Rift Valley	Kajiado	Kajiado Central	14%
	Narok	Narok West	40%
	Turkana	Turkana South	17%
		Turkana North	3%
Western	Vihiga	Hamisi	36%
		Emuhaya (1)	17%
Nyanza	Homa Bay	Ndhiwa (1)	90%
	Migori	Migori	86%
		Kuria (1)	27%
	Kisii	South Mugirango	67%
		Nyaribari Masaba (1)	47%
		Bobasi	43%
		Bonchari	1%
	Nyamira	Kitutu Masaba (1)	60%
		West Mugirango	50%
		Kitutu Masaba (2)	31%
		North Mugirango	11%

Source: Analysis of primary results. (1) Indicates first primary when re-run, (2) indicates second.

plausible 4,660 in the real election. With rigging on such a scale, little confidence should be placed in the accuracy of the results.

Another worrying pointer for the real election was the active involvement of Provincial and District Commissioners, the key Provincial Administration figures in the rural areas, in the KANU elections. The press or defeated KANU contenders reported that District and Provincial Commissioners were actively campaigning for particular candidates or participating in electoral abuses in Murang'a, Isiolo, Wajir, Kericho, Uasin Gishu, Turkana, Trans-Nzoia, Bungoma, Kakamega, Siaya and Kisii. Normally, their approved candidate emerged victorious, although occasionally the Administration's choice was unsuccessful. Some were particularly blatant, such as the chaos in the normally quiet Isiolo District. For two days running, the first KANU parliamentary and civic elections in Isiolo North were the scene of violence and widespread rigging, in which the Isiolo District Commissioner campaigned actively against the incumbent Charfare Mokku. Re-runs were forced by national headquarters, and again chaos resulted as Mokku 'lost', with the police beating up voters and personally counting the votes. The District Commissioner even ordered Mokku's arrest on 5 December, but the MP led a delegation to KANU headquarters in Nairobi and persuaded them that he was the best candidate to hold the seat.[68]

FORD-Kenya's Electoral College

The nomination procedures for the opposition parties were also confused, and it is hard to determine what really happened in many areas. Where primaries were actually held, they were less rigged but even more chaotic than KANU's. Unsurprisingly, the parties followed KANU's tradition of nominating locally known candidates from the same ethnic group as the local population. Many had been politically active in the past.

The FORD-Kenya nomination process began between 7 and 9 November 1992. Waruru Kanja as Director of Elections was responsible for the conduct of the polling. The elections were also overseen by a National Nominations Committee of five persons, none of whom were themselves standing as candidates. These had responsibility for timetabling and organising the polls, and for overseeing appeals, which had to be submitted within three days of the nominations. Unlike those of all the other parties, FORD-Kenya's primaries were held by the electoral college method, whereby sub-branch representatives and location and ward officials and delegates voted in a secret ballot to select the candidate, with a simple majority required.[69] The party elections in August had elected delegates to an electoral college. Each sub-location was supposed to hold its own party election to elect 25 people. These would then elect a committee and 25 delegates to represent the location, while a total of another 25 delegates would be elected 'at large' to represent the whole sub-branch. Thus, approximately 100 people would choose the Parliamentary candidate in each constituency. The aim was to avoid the cost of an open primary, the ostensible source of disagreement over the direction of FORD.

Although this had partly been a pretext, masking competing claims for power and personality differences within the party, the FORD-Kenya leaders-to-be had genuinely believed that it was logistically impossible to organise nation-wide primaries without government support. It was not just a question of money but of finding and hiring venues, when schools could not be used; of transporting people; appointing Returning Officers; and printing and distributing ballot papers.

Uniquely, the party required that, 'No member of Parliament or Councillor shall be, or continue to be an office-bearer at the branch, sub-branch and locational/ward or sub-locational levels.'[70] This was a major change to precedent, symbolising a near-unique attempt to create an independent party structure from the Parliamentary party. Parliamentary candidates had to be party members and qualified to be an MP, submit a pledge of commitment to human rights issues and give their background and reasons for joining the party. They were also required to pay a 'non-refundable' nomination fee of 5,000 shillings and to have a proposer, seconder and the support of at least ten registered local party members.[71]

FORD-Kenya quickly realised, however, that they could not stick to their procedure everywhere. Their party secretariat at Agip House was very weak, had no idea what was going on over much of the country, and continually found itself following rather than leading events. Outside Nyanza, and to some extent the Coast, FORD-Kenya was not well-established at the grassroots. The party had no candidates over much of the country and was desperate to get whomever they could. For example, as late as 22 November, Odinga said at a Voi rally: 'We do not have a candidate in Wundanyi' – and suggested that sacked KANU Minister Darius Mbela might like to take up the post.[72] Primaries, consequently, did not happen in many seats. Thus towards the end of the nomination period there was a frantic effort to find anyone who would stand, and the party relied upon defectors from other parties, with certificates being issued from central party headquarters regardless of official nomination processes. Without an efficient secretariat, they did not even know many people they were nominating, and in some cases were taken for a ride by candidates. There were also disagreements between factions as to who should be the candidate in certain areas. Certain party officials, particularly the Odinga family, selected candidates without reference to local opinion, as in Ndia, where FORD-Kenya already had a local, little known standard bearer. At the last minute James Njiru defected from KANU and visited the *Jaramogi*, who agreed Njiru would be the candidate and gave him 100,000/– to campaign.[73] FORD-Kenya recognised the weakness of this 'rainbow coalition' approach, but felt they had no alternative.

In Nairobi the FORD-Kenya candidates were a mixed bunch: three Luo, led by Raila Odinga in Langata; three Kikuyu; and two Luhya. Three were 'no hopers', but the others, particularly Odinga and the two Luhya candidates in Mathare and Makadara, were strong contenders. Embakasi caused particular problems. A deal had been made in the summer of 1992 to allocate different constituencies to different ethnic groups. It was claimed by the Luo old guard, however, that Raila Odinga broke this agreement, and persuaded Dr Munyua Waiyaki to move to Embakasi, ousting the original popular local candidate, Jael Mbogo, who was eventually persuaded to stand down by Oginga Odinga. National officials ignored the protests and simply declared Waiyaki the candidate at a meeting on 30 November. Another contestant obtained a court injunction to prevent Waiyaki being nominated until formal elections were held, but he too was eventually persuaded to stand down in the interests of party unity.[74] Waiyaki had moved across town partly to give a clear run at Mathare to former Nairobi Mayor Andrew Ngumba, who was then in FORD.

FORD-Kenya was always in trouble in Central Province after the split with Matiba, with two Kikuyu presidential candidates from the area. In Kikuyu constituency, Paul Muite faced no opposition. Elsewhere, the former Law Society Chairman put together the strongest ticket of ex-MPs and long-time contestants he could, but all FORD-Kenya's candidates in Kiambu were going to lose, so Muite had to take anyone foolish enough to stand. The party was only able to find four candidates in the 13 Nyeri and Murang'a seats, with the only serious contenders being ex-MP David Ng'ethe in Kandara and Waruru Kanja himself. In Eastern Province, FORD-Kenya was weak in Embu, being forced to take a defector at the last minute in Siakago and Gachoka, but slightly stronger in Meru, where Imanyara was contesting Imenti Central and Kiraitu Murungi Imenti South. They had few candidates of any substance amongst the Kamba or in Isiolo or Marsabit. In the North-East, they had a few plausible candidates, but most had little prospect.

The situation was different on the Coast. FORD-Kenya had kept the majority of Coast activists after the split, and the last-minute alliance with the unregistered IPK further strengthened the party, though it did mean that some FORD-Kenya candidates had to be dropped.[75] In Mombasa itself, IPK activists were nominated for twelve civil and three Parliamentary seats.

In the Rift Valley, there were few elections outside Nakuru, Uasin Gishu and Trans-Nzoia, the three areas where the party had a reasonable chance. In Nakuru, John Kamanagara the Nakuru Town chairman was their best bet, but they suffered a blow in Molo, where nominations were held but no one eventually stood.[76] There was trouble with the primaries in all three districts, much of it associated with Operation Moi Out activists. Elsewhere, FORD-Kenya had few plausible candidates apart from Moses arap Keino in Kipkelion. In Western Province, the elections were particularly well-reported in Bungoma, where FORD-Kenya was strong. A powerful team of Bukusu professionals was chosen, led by Musifari Kombo and Mukisa Kituyi, but in Kakamega (Shikuku's power-base) and Vihiga, the party was weak.

Not surprisingly, it was in the FORD-Kenya zone of Nyanza that the most heavily contested nominations took place. There was no shortage of candidates, or of infighting to obtain the nominations. *Jaramogi* attempted to obtain a slate of candidates that he could work with, endorsing several candidates before or during the nominations, including Phoebe Asiyo in Karachuonyo, Oloo-Aringo in Alego, Oki Ombaka in Gem, Job Omino in Kisumu Town, Ramogi Achieng' Oneko in Bondo and Peter Anyang' Nyong'o in Kisumu Rural.[77] This did not go down well, however, with democratic purists among the Young Turks, and several of the 'old-timer' national political figures were defeated by popular local candidates. Odinga's subsequent attempts to reinstate these losers earned him considerable hostility from the less pragmatic wing of FORD-Kenya. There was also an internal power struggle, with the old guard and Odinga competing with the Young Turks' candidates (led amongst the Luo by Raila).

In Siaya District, Odinga's home ground, former KANU National Chairman, veteran politician Peter Oloo-Aringo, was defeated in Alego in a shock result by a local journalist and ex-detainee prison-mate of Raila's, Otieno Mak'Anyango. There were six recounts, in which an ICJ observer was beaten up. The conflict pitted a compromised senior politician against a young martyr. It represented a generational conflict between Odinga's supporters, who were generally older people, and those whose loyalty was more with the Young Turks. It was also a conflict between the pragmatists, led by the *Jaramogi,* and the more 'ideologically sound'. Despite Oloo-Aringo's grudging acceptance of defeat on 12 November, Odinga then decreed fresh elections under a new electoral system, claiming 'massive malpractices had been detected' and saying he could not do without 'seasoned fighters' like Oloo-Aringo, although no formal appeal had been made.[78] In the end, however, Oloo-Aringo had to be dropped. Odinga's inability to reverse this decision marked out the limits of the old man's power. The reluctance of the Complaints Committee to intervene also suggested that they were unwilling to become involved in such a personalised contest. In Ugenya, 'Young Turk' James Orengo, Director of Legal and Constitutional Affairs, had no problems capturing the nomination to fight his brother-in-law, KANU's Archbishop Oluoch. In Gem, Dr Oki Ombaka (another Young Turk) spent about two million shillings on the nominations and defeated or deterred all rivals, including former Cabinet Minister Isaac Omolo Okero. In Bondo and Rarieda, Odinga and his long-time ally Ramogi Achieng' Oneko received the nominations.

The situation in Kisumu was even more tense with serious problems in three of five seats. In Kisumu Town, Job Omino, who had been defeated in rigged elections by Robert Ouko in 1988, only to replace the murdered Foreign Minister in another controversial by-election, had defected at the dissolution to FORD-Kenya and had then lost the party caucus nomination to a local man, Jim Adero Ageng'o. As a national figure, however, Omino was too important an ally to lose. Ageng'o was therefore 'prevailed upon' by Odinga to stand down, but was so dissatisfied that he defected to KANU and was nominated by the ruling party to contest the seat.[79] Thus, over three weeks, the KANU MP and the FORD-Kenya organiser swapped parties. In Muhoroni the situation was little better, as KANU Minister Onyango Midika, who had been sacked and then defected to FORD-Kenya, lost the nomination to a local activist, Onyango K'Oyoo. Kanja ordered new nominations, which the Appeals Committee rejected, but they were eventually held anyway on instructions from *Jaramogi.* After four failed attempts at nomination, the FORD-Kenya National Executive Council finally quashed K'Oyoo's nomination (believing him to be a KANU plant) and announced that the candidate who had come second would stand. K'Oyoo immediately rejoined KANU and campaigned for Moi.[80]

In Homa Bay, there was also trouble in two of four constituencies. The first Kasipul-Kabondo and Rangwe elections were annulled, but new elections were cancelled by the Tribunal.[81] In Migori District there was violence and some losers defected back to KANU, including ex-MP Oluoch Kanindo in Rongo. In Nyatike, Ochola Ogur defected from KANU two days before the FORD-Kenya nominations, and lost. New elections were immediately ordered, which Ogur controversially won on 3 December. By contrast, the Kisii and Nyamira nominations were quiet and little reported. FORD-Kenya did not have candidates in all the seats, as the case of Kitutu Chache showed, where Nicholas Siro defected from KANU after being prevented from standing and was immediately declared the FORD-Kenya candidate.[82]

There were several official or semi-official bodies involved in monitoring and organising the nominations. FORD-Kenya's National Nomination Committee was supposed to rule on nomination issues but the procedures and bodies became confused. The initial decisions were made by Waruru Kanja as Director of Elections, who nullified five Nyanza elections on 17 November.[83] There was also a Nominations Complaints Committee, chaired by Kijana Wamalwa, which reported on 24 November after a week-long hearing, reversing Kanja's decision on three of these contests. The institutional structures were clearly not up to the task, as was evidenced by their refusal to comment on the case of the controversial Alego elections, but the Council did serve to flush out KANU sympathisers who had successfully obtained the party nominations in Luo seats.

The lessons from the FORD-Kenya nominations were little different from those in KANU. Their electoral procedures were inadequate, some of their candidates were not above cheating, the party was riven by factionalism and could not organise itself properly. FORD-Kenya had also shown it did not have sufficient national coverage at the grassroots.

The Democratic Party of Kenya's Nomination Process

Like KANU, the DP held its elections mainly by secret ballot of party members, though their constitution permitted that 'any other acceptable method(s)' could also be used.[84] A number, including Githunguri, were held by queue voting or by show of hands. Candidates had to pay a 500 shillings application fee, plus fees of 2,000 shillings to contest the civic and 5,000 shillings to contest the parliamentary nominations.[85] Most of the DP nominations were held over the weekend of 7–8 November. Party membership cards and national identity cards were required to vote. The initial elections were chaotic in many areas, with long delays in polling. As with FORD-Kenya, a number of the last-minute defectors in Parliament lost their seats to better established local newcomers.

Outside Central Province, the primaries were not well attended. Turnout was poor in much of Nairobi, a guide to the future, although several candidates were unopposed. In Central Province, Kiambu was the home of many of the DP's most senior men – including Karume, George Muhoho and Ngengi Muigai – and most appear to have been nominated unopposed. Githunguri saw protests after the 7 November elections were disrupted by supporters of loser Karuga Njuguna, who grabbed the ballot boxes, forcing the Returning Officer, Professor Kimani of the University of Nairobi, to do a head-count by sending supporters of different candidates into different parts of the field. The other candidates both protested and later defected to PICK and the KNC. In the end, Rose Waruhiu, the favoured choice of the DP Secretariat, only obtained the nomination after submitting an affidavit from an American visitor who had photographed the queues of voters.[86] In Murang'a, the two most senior DP MPs from the area, ex-Assistant Ministers Nduati Kariuki (Makuyu) and Francis Thuo (Kigumo), both lost despite frantic last-minute efforts to get them nominated, since they would have polled far more votes than the eventual nominees. In Nyeri, Kibaki, of course, was unopposed in Othaya, but elsewhere the elections were extremely tense and heavily contested, since the DP were clearly going to win all the seats. Turn-outs were high and there were claims of rigging in Mukurueini, Nyeri Town and Kieni.[87] The Nyandarua elections were also heavily contested.

Eastern Province was the DP's other stronghold. Candidates in areas like Machakos were unopposed, but in Embu, the local Organising Secretary resigned in protest at rigging.[88] The Siakago elections were repeated twice, as Jeremiah Nyagah's son Norman unsuccessfully attempted to appease the loser, who then defected to the KNC and won the seat! In Meru and Tharaka-Nithi districts, several elections were disputed. In Imenti South, the primary had to be held three times, ending with a victory for the ex-KANU National Executive Officer, David Pius Mugambi. The loser defected to FORD-Asili, claiming rigging and alleging that Mugambi had himself selected all the Returning Officers and personally paid them 8,000 shillings each.[89]

On the Coast, the primaries suggested that the DP was very weak. In Changamwe, the party faced a crisis when their popular local candidate, recent defector Kiliku, failed to turn up for nominations. The unopposed victor, however, was persuaded to stand down in his favour. The loser in KANU's repeat nominations in Likoni, Suleiman Shakombo, defected to the DP at the last minute, and turned up on 9 December with DP nomination papers as well as the party's original candidate Grace Mwea. The rival candidates eventually agreed that Shakombo should stand.

The Rift Valley split into Kikuyu and non-Kikuyu areas, with little activity outside the former. The Nakuru District DP primaries were all heavily contested as the party expected to do well. The DP experienced problems with ballot box stuffing and other abuses in both Laikipia constituencies, where they expected to win. The eventual winner in Laikipia West was Kihika Kimani, the old-time 'Change the Constitution' movement leader from 1976.[90] John Keen sprang a surprise on George Saitoti by switching from Kajiado South, where he was registered as a voter, to Kajiado North on 10 November. The three other DP contenders all stood down in his favour.[91] In the central Rift, candidates were selected rather than elected, since it was too dangerous to hold an open contest, but the DP now became KANU's main opponent, as several defeated KANU leaders joined their team. The DP now had candidates in all four Baringo seats, whose names were kept secret to prevent KANU attacks. These included Henry Cheboiwo (Moi's old business partner) who became the DP candidate for Baringo North after losing the KANU nomination.

The DP was weak in Western Province, outside a few strongholds such as Webuye, and most candidates were unopposed. There were few elections in Luo Nyanza, but contested primaries were held in Kisii, where James Nyamweya led the party. Due to defections back to KANU by nominated candidates, they were forced into some last-minute substitutions in the area.

As with the other parties, some DP elections had to be re-run after allegations of rigging. The party had its own Electoral Commission, headed by Justice Benna Lutta, a retired Appeal Court judge. This faced a number of problems, including the claimed nullification of the entire DP nominations in Nyamira, called by James Nyamweya on 16 November and denied in a front-page statement in the *Daily Nation* two days later.[92] New elections were held in at least ten seats where the party had a chance of victory, including four Gusii constituencies on 3 December.[93] In some cases, as with Nakuru North and Ndia, this followed claims of ballot box stuffing, blank membership cards being used to vote and polling stations failing to open.[94] In Makuyu new elections intended to secure Nduati Kariuki's victory were cancelled at the last minute after the previous winner obtained a court injunction.

The FORD-Asili Nomination Process

FORD-Asili's Parliamentary and civic nominations were held at the same time as its Presidential polls, on 10 November 1992. Asili's nominations were the quietest of the parties, reflecting their 'underdog' position in many areas. An extremely high proportion of them appear to have been unopposed, as Matiba had acute problems in recruiting candidates. The only real contests were in Central and Western Provinces and the Luhya areas of the Rift, where the party was strongest. Over much of the country, no primaries were held, and candidates were selected rather than elected. It was reported by insiders, for example, that the FORD-Asili candidate for Mathare, Geoffrey Macharia, visited Matiba to request his endorsement to contest a civic seat in the area, but once Matiba realised they had no parliamentary candidate, he was nominated instead for the senior post.[95]

Officially, Asili's elections were conducted by a secret ballot of all members, on production of membership cards and national ID cards. Where elections were held, they used three ballot boxes at each polling station, with different coloured ballot papers for Presidential, parliamentary and civic elections. Martin Shikuku claimed the polls cost party coffers Sh22 million. The results were supposed to be announced at the sub-location or ward level and passed on to be aggregated.[96] As with KANU, there are serious questions surrounding the veracity of the reported results, and little hard information. Few contested election results were announced, and most seats reported no more than a list of the winners. Interestingly, the *Weekly Review* played up the FORD-Asili nominations, calling them 'successful', a reflection of KANU's desire to ensure that the two factions remained evenly balanced.

Little was reported on the Nairobi elections, and most candidates are believed to have been 'unopposed'. In Central Province, many candidates, including the party's main Kikuyu leaders such as Matiba himself in Kiharu, Josephat Karanja in Githunguri and Geoffrey Kariithi in Gichugu, were also unopposed. There were claims of rigging, however, by losers in Juja, and from Kandara, Kigumo and Kangema in Murang'a.[97] In Eastern Province, the primaries were little reported, and many were unopposed. In North-Eastern, the Coast and Nyanza it is not clear whether the party managed to hold serious contests at all.

The Rift Valley primaries were far more open, but were also marked by problems. There was KANU-inspired violence in the key Narok North seat (Minister ole Ntimama's seat), in which ballot boxes were destroyed. A loser in the other Maasai marginal, Kajiado North, claimed the elections were rigged by Matiba for the victor, Philip Odupoy, on the basis that a Maasai candidate would win Maasai votes, while the Kikuyu would vote for the party anyway.[98] In the KANU zones, no elections seem to have been held. As with the DP, candidates appear to have been selected, and their names kept secret for security reasons. In Baringo Central Dr Chege Njuguna (from Murang'a) declared that he had been nominated to stand against Moi at a meeting in Marigat on 10 November, although Shikuku denied this.[99] Nakuru's FORD-Asili primary campaign centred around Njenga Mungai, the maverick ex-KANU MP who had defended the rights of his Kikuyu settler community during the ethnic clashes. Mungai himself was unopposed, but the elections elsewhere were heavily contested. The first Nakuru Town elections, won by Shikuku's brother Charles Liwali, were nullified after the loser claimed that the ballot boxes had been stuffed. He obtained a high court injunction forcing a new election, which saw a low turn-out and more protests when Liwali won again.[100] The Nakuru East winner accused the local election commission of being a 'kangaroo court', chosen by Njenga Mungai to ensure that his supporters won seats, and he too filed an injunction preventing any new nominations.[101]

In Trans-Nzoia, where FORD-Asili had some hopes due to the high Luhya population (though as Bukusu, they were mainly with FORD-Kenya), the primaries were marred by several incidents. Problems were most severe in Kwanza, where the party's local leader Salim Ndamwe was a bitter opponent of Shikuku's. Shikuku visited Trans-Nzoia and 'nullified' Ndamwe's election in early December, but he was reinstated by the High Court the day before nominations.[102] In Uasin Gishu, all three FORD-Asili candidates were unopposed in an election which was described as having a huge Presidential turn-out, an interesting point given the final result.[103]

Western Province was Shikuku's territory and saw some lively elections in which it appeared Shikuku was nominating candidates as much as managing elections. Again, the most intense contests were in those seats where Asili had a good chance, but where there was no outstanding leader. In Kakamega, Shikuku's home turf, his slate was relatively uncontroversial and most candidates were nominated unopposed. Similarly, in Bungoma, a FORD-Kenya area, FORD-Asili's' nominations were trouble-free, but in Vihiga they were bitterly contested. The results indicate substantial rigging. The Sabatia nominations, for example, allegedly resulted in 15,386 votes being cast, although the party's candidate only polled 4,149 votes in the General Election. The loser's vote appears to have been inflated, in traditional KANU fashion, until it exceeded the winner's.[104] In Hamisi, the results were also suspect, whilst in Emuhaya, Shikuku was accused of rigging in his preferred candidate by the loser, Nehemiah Ayub Ochiel, who then defected to KANU.[105] In Nambale in Busia District, where Asili had a strong candidate, the local sub-branch chairman also defected to KANU after the nominations, alleging that ballot papers were tampered with and that 10,000 had gone missing.[106] In the FORD-Asili nominations in neighbouring Samia, the winning candidate incorrectly informed his opponents' supporters that their candidate had stood down. Multiple voting was common, while FORD youths were 'busy recruiting new members and issuing party cards to all those who were willing to vote irrespective of their political conviction'.[107]

The Minor Parties

None of the minor parties – the KNC, KSC, KENDA and PICK – appear to have held contested primary elections. KNC and PICK candidates were almost entirely defeated contenders from other parties. The KNC's constitution empowered its National Executive to nominate its candidates, and the only KNC election reported was leader Mbathi's unopposed nomination in Kitui Central, while the only KENDA nomination noted by the media was in Juja. No PICK or KSC primaries were reported in the press at all.

The Results

Gathering together these disparate reports, several themes become apparent. First, almost every living politician of note appears to have taken part for some party or other (and often for several). Many came out of retirement for one last try. Over one third of the country, the party primary for the dominant party effectively was the General Election, and was therefore contested vigorously. In the FORD-Kenya areas, for example, almost every ex-politician of note stood in the FORD-Kenya nominations, while KANU's nominations throughout Luoland were poorly contested. In many cases, there were more candidates for the dominant party primary than there were in the final election, and the quality of competition was often higher. The severity of the contest was primarily a function of the type of seat. The stronger the party was in the area, the harder fought the nominations were. In many areas where the opposition was clearly going to win, the KANU incumbent was left to face the music. The most heavily fought primaries, and some of the most rigged, were where the General Election was expected to be a walkover, as with FORD-Kenya's polls in Luoland, and KANU's in the central Rift (where the incumbent was removed in 12 of 17 seats). Key marginals, such as Kisii, which lost nine of its ten MPs (the exception being Minister Onyonka) were also fiercely contested.

Secondly, the party nominations for all parties were badly organised and saw extensive fraud. The rigging was particularly severe in the case of KANU, but occurred in all the parties. All of them proved willing to annul results, call new elections, and abandon their own procedures in order to select particular candidates. The parties also interfered in each others' primaries. There were persistent claims, for example, that some FORD-Kenya candidates in Nyanza were closet KANU supporters, planted subsequently to defect or stand down. Activists participated in other parties' primaries to help select weaker opponents. In Juja there were allegations that KANU supporters voted in the DP primary, whilst in Langata, FORD-Kenya supporters, still with KANU membership cards, voted for Dr Perez Olindo to try to remove Cabinet Minister Philip Leakey.[108] In Makueni, where KANU and the DP both re-ran their primaries on the same day, one KANU candidate withdrew, and 'his supporters boycotted the exercise and instead streamed [to] the local DP office to take part in a similar exercise that was going on'.[109] Three KANU losers in Taita-Taveta all claimed that DP supporters had voted for their victorious opponents.[110]

All the parties had many of their most senior men defeated and, for the first time, there was the genuine feeling of a 'new generation' of politicians emerging, not just in the opposition but also in KANU. This was a major change in the political system, a direct result of multi-party competition. If KANU had failed to improve its image in this way, the result of the election might have been different. We have already noted the carnage amongst the KANU incumbents, and this was replicated amongst the DP's ex-MPs who defected at the prorogation of Parliament, with nearly half (nine of 19) losing. Of the 186 MPs who were either incumbents at the dissolution or who had defected to the opposition at the beginning of the year, 71 (38 per cent) did not make it into the final election. Most were KANU members who lost their nominations, though four stood down.

The nomination process was sordid as much for the reaction of the losers as the technicalities of the process. It was rare for losers in marginal territories to continue to support their own party after defeat, and in many cases they simply joined another. The press was full of stories of defections and some re-defections. Some people moved through three parties in as many weeks. Their attitude was summed up by the eventual loser of the KANU nomination in Malindi, backbencher Francis Bobi Tuva,who said, 'If the Electoral Commission had informed me earlier that Mr Badawy would be the KANU parliamentary nominee for Malindi constituency, then I would have defected to any other party.'[111] Of the 115 MPs in the former Parliament who actually fought the December 1992 General Election, 16 did so on a different ticket to the one they had represented eight weeks earlier. KANU was fully aware of the risks it faced in holding its nominations first: losers might defect *en masse* to the opposition. It therefore made strenuous and relatively successful efforts to control the situation, including offers of parastatal positions to defeated candidates to remain loyal. Losers such as Reuben Chesire and William Kikwai in Eldoret,

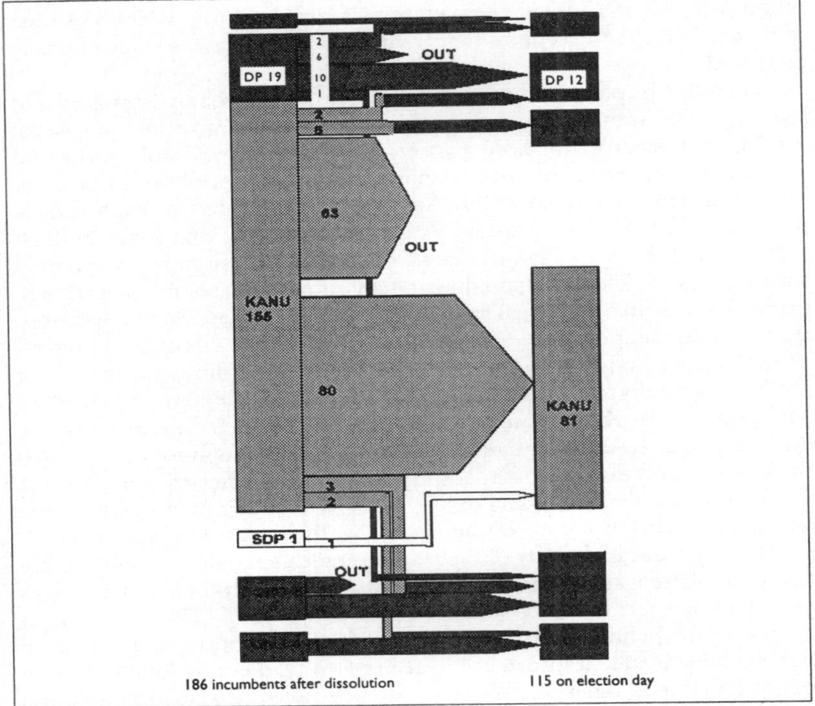

Figure 8.3 Political realignments of KANU MPs (Oct.–Dec.1992).

although the victims of rigging, were thereby persuaded to continue supporting KANU. As Figure 8.3 shows, KANU lost only 12 of 75 Parliamentary incumbents who did not secure renomination to opposition parties (17 per cent), mostly minor figures. Two were in Meru and three in Kisii, the scene of particular carnage amongst the incumbents. Five KANU MPs went to PICK, none to KNC, while a few joined FORD-Kenya, FORD-Asili and the DP.

KANU was less successful at holding on to losers who were not incumbents. Defections from the ruling party were concentrated where the opposition was weak and did not already have a candidate. Thus six of FORD-Asili's successfully nominated candidates came from KANU, but no one defected to them from any other opposition party, a comment on Matiba's unpopularity. Its gains were in the marginals – the Kamba areas, Meru, Taita-Taveta, Nyamira and Samburu – where candidates felt they stood a chance in a new party. Similarly, six DP candidates were losers from KANU seats like Wajir West and Likoni, but only one opposition loser from FORD-Kenya switched at the last minute to Kibaki's party. The DP was also the party of preference for KANU defectors from the central Rift, such as Kimunai arap Sego, Henry Cheboiwo and others, who were not to appear on the ballot papers.

FORD-Kenya's gains came in the peripheral KANU zones. They took nine candidates from KANU – ten if you include James Njiru in Kirinyaga who did not contest the KANU nominations – including six in the 'soft' KANU zones of Mandera, Garissa, Kericho, Turkana and Samburu. They also took one from Asili and three from the DP. Ten per cent of FORD-Kenya's successfully nominated candidates had made a last ditch jump having lost elsewhere, including some with a national profile. FORD-Kenya's national weakness paradoxically proved to be an asset.

By contrast, all but one of KANU's candidates had chosen KANU as their first choice. Since the ruling party's nominations were generally held first, this was hardly surprising, but the absence of defectors back to the ruling party during the nomination exercise is also interesting. Only one candidate, from Kisumu Town, returned to KANU after losing elsewhere and won the party nomination, the other exception being Johnstone Makau, who defected from his own party – the SDP – just before the nomination season.

The DP was particularly severely plagued by defections among the losers in its nominations: more so proportionately than any other party. Losers defected to the KNC in Siakago, Embakasi, Githunguri, Nyeri Town, Nakuru North and Nakuru East; to PICK in Githunguri, Kieni and Ndaragwa; to FORD-Asili in Imenti South; and to FORD-Kenya in Makueni and Ikolomani. Most ended up nominated as candidates. Others, in pique, campaigned for KANU.[112]

The choice of which party to join was mainly a pragmatic response to their local strength and the availability of 'slots', but certain types of defectors had their preferences. Thus, defeated DP candidates went to the KNC – seven of the nine identified defectors that the KNC nominated came from the DP, with one from each FORD. All but two were from Kikuyu areas. The 'pseudo-party' PICK was the opposite. At least 13 of their candidates came from KANU, five from the DP, two from FORD-Kenya and only one from FORD-Asili. PICK seems to have been the 'acceptable alternative to KANU', most of whose candidates campaigned for Moi. At least five were major contenders who were unlucky to lose, including KANU defectors Peter Okondo in Busia, Kombo in Kisii and Christopher Lomada in Pokot.

Conclusions

In the end, what difference did all the primaries, defections and re-runs make? The KANU re-runs made little difference to the results. Although the choice of candidate in 1992 influenced the distribution of votes between parties, it rarely changed the result. For the first time, party loyalty was the key factor in determining who won. KANU's appeals procedure was hugely wasteful, frustrating and contributed little in the end to its performance. There was no benefit in holding a new election under the same rigged conditions as the original. The spate of defections helped the Presidential candidacies of Matiba and Odinga, creating the impression of nation-wide support. All three opposition parties improved their national image, and may thereby have won more votes, but no more than three seats changed party as a result of defections during the nominations. The winning parties' majorities were so large that although defectors took votes from their original choices, the latter remained clearly ahead. Moreover, because of the ticket voting seen on polling day, candidates found it difficult to bring their traditional supporters over to their new party. Ethnicity proved more powerful than personal allegiances. The sole exceptions were Bonchari in Kisii, where Dr Protas Momanyi defected and, as a result, gave the DP its only Kisii MP, drawing upon the support of his own dominant clan in the constituency; Mbooni, where the SDP leader changed sides at the last minute; and Siakago, where the KNC won its sole seat after its candidate had lost the DP nomination. In addition, Abdi Ali Baricha in Mandera would probably have won (he polled 39 per cent of the vote), but for some KANU machinations.

Kenya's law and constitutional framework governing party primaries was far too weak. Because of the interdependence of state and party, it was difficult to contest rigging in the courts. During November, at least a dozen KANU candidates, including those in Embakasi, Westlands, Yatta, Kajiado Central, Bomet, Hamisi and Lugari in Western, and Kitutu Chache, Bobasi, and South Mugirango in Kisii, used the courts to challenge the KANU nominations. This also occurred in the DP and FORD-Asili. Losing candidates obtained injunctions demanding new elections, whilst some winning candidates also obtained injunctions preventing new elections. As the law governing party elections was weak and confused, Justice Akiwumi ruled at the end of November that the courts could only interfere in internal party matters where there had been a breach of natural justice or administrative or disciplinary powers had been exceeded.[113] Kamotho, at the same time, claimed the primaries were an internal matter and ordered KANU candidates to withdraw all such suits.[114] Chesoni then made it clear that Returning Officers should not accept the papers of candidates whose nominations were open to question. Concerned about KANU losing seats as a consequence, President Moi intervened at the last minute (with several suits still outstanding), demanding on 7 December that the courts should not rule on internal party matters. This led some to withdraw their suits. Nonetheless, some refused to be cowed, and the courts were pressured to rule on these issues swiftly. In Yatta, the defeated KANU candidate in the primaries was still trying to obtain an injunction, preventing Gideon Mutiso's nomination on 9 December, nomination day. Heard by the ubiquitous Mr. Justice Dugdale, the injunction was swiftly dismissed to ensure that Mutiso could be nominated.[115] In Westlands, Dr Njoroge Mungai won a High Court injunction restraining KANU from putting forward Walji's name until Mungai's suit had been heard. The case, however, was suddenly brought forward and Mungai lost the injunction on the eve of nomination, the judge leaving the reasons to be explained later.[116] It was those refusing to accept calls for second polls, such as the DP winner in Makuyu in Murang'a and KANU's David Mwenje in Embakasi, who did best. Some elections were reheld to meet legal challenges, but they were very few in number.

The primaries confirmed the need for the nominations to be governed by law, and for them to all take place on the same day, in order to minimise multiple voting and defections. There is no point in holding free elections if the primaries that select the candidates are rigged, especially when many constituencies are dominated by one particular party. The abuse of the party primary process provided a warning sign for the final elections on 29 December.

Notes

1 Since 1974, the city's economic importance, and the concentration of élites in the area, had ensured that many of its seats have been represented by political heavyweights, despite the urban electorate's volatility. Nairobi's political influence was greatest during the immediate post-independence period, reaching a peak in 1966 when four of the city's eight MPs were in the Cabinet. Matiba's former close ally Charles Rubia served as the city's first African Mayor from 1963 to 1969, as Minister for Local Government, Urban Development and Housing from 1979 to 1983 and for 19 years as the MP for the city centre Starehe constituency, until he was rigged out of Parliament in 1988. The other Nairobi MPs who have served in the Cabinet are Tom Mboya (1963–9), former Vice–President Joe Murumbi (1963–6), Dr Njoroge Mungai (1963–74 and 1990–January 1992), Mwai Kibaki (1966–74), Munyua Waiyaki (1974–83), Maina Wanjigi (1983–90), Vice–President Josephat Karanja (1988–9) and Philip Leakey (1992). In recent years, however, the capital's political influence has declined, and for most of the period since 1983, the city has had only one Cabinet Minister.

2 See *Daily Nation*, 3 November 1992, p. 1 for Makau's defections and reasons.

3 Sources: *Standard* and *Daily Nation*, October–November 1992.

4 General Gachui, Nominated MP, *Standard*, 2 November 1992, p. 1.

5 *Daily Nation*, 18 October 1992, p. 1.

6 *Daily Nation*, 21 October 1992, p. 1.

7 *Daily Nation*, 18 October 1992, p. 4.

8 *Daily Nation*, 19 October 1992, p. 28.

9 *Daily Nation*, 17 October 1992, p. 28.

10 Despite this, the KNC could not avoid local candidates standing against the DP in Nairobi, nor prevent Dr Chibule wa Tsuma from appointing himself the party's Presidential candidate, as their lawyer failed to serve the court order on him personally to prevent his nomination.

11 Since she probably did not know. See *Daily Nation*, 22 October 1992, p. 1.

12 *Daily Nation*, 23 October 1992.

13 They assured the editor of *Africa Confidential* that they would secure an overall majority in the National Assembly, for example.

14 *Daily Nation*, 25 October 1992, p. 1.

15 *Daily Nation*, 2 November 1992, p. 2.

16 *Daily Nation*, 3 November 1992, p. 24.

17 Newsletter of the Archdiocese of Nairobi, Vol. VI, Nos 9–12 (September–December 1992). Also see *Kenya Times*, 23 December 1992, p. 4.

18 *Sunday Nation*, 29 November 1992, p. 11.

19 See D. W. Throup, 'The Construction and Destruction of the Kenyatta State', in M. G. Schatzberg (ed.), *The Political Economy of Kenya*, p. 66.

20 *Watchman*, January 1993, p. 13.

21 There had been attempts in the late summer to challenge him internally, but none of the major figures in the party participated. Only a minor 35-year-old businessman, Charles Onyambu, and Paul Ngei (ineligible) openly challenged Moi. Ngei foolishly challenged Moi on 14 July 1992. See Ngei's interview in *Society*, 10 August, 1992, pp. 44–5. His bankruptcy was not annulled, however, leading him eventually to defect to the DP.

22 FORD-Kenya Constitution Part IV, article 12.

23 According to John Keen, the elections occurred at a secret DP Delegates' Conference. The DP announced its election rules in September, but stated that the regulations were confidential and that the election date was also secret, trying to avoid the problems experienced by other parties.(*Daily Nation*, 9 September 1992, p. 4) This probably meant

there was a closed door agreement by the leadership that Kibaki would be the candidate.

24 For these few Ford-Asili results, see the *Daily Nation*, 13 November 1992, p. 3 and p. 10; and *Sunday Nation*, 15 November, 1992, p. 3.

25 These included Nassir, who on 15 October had claimed that Shikuku would soon defect to KANU – 'He will definitely come to eat with us when the food is ready.' Nassir at KICC, *Daily Nation*, 16 October 1992, p. 3.

26 Opanga, *Sunday Nation*, 22 November 1992, Lifestyle section, p. 6.

27 NEMU Poll Monitor's report, Samia.

28 *Daily Nation*, 23 November 1992, p. 4.

29 *Standard*, 29 November 1992, p. 3.

30 Kamotho, in *Daily Nation*, 15 October 1992, p. 2.

31 Kamotho, KANU Nominations Advertisement, *Sunday Nation*, 8 November 1992, p. 14.

32 *Daily Nation*, 3 and 4 November 1992, and Nandi NEMU District Liaison Officer's report on the primaries.

33 As Moody Awori did in Samia, according to the NEMU Constituency Monitor for the area.

34 National Executive Officer Kiti, *Daily Nation*, 12 November 1992, pp. 5–6.

35 The tribunal's members were: Kassim Owango (ex-Chairman, Agricultural Society of Kenya), John Etemesei (ex-Provincial Commissioner), Julius Kobia (another ex-Provincial Commissioner), Julius Kiano (ex-Minister and Kenya Broadcasting Corporation Chairman), Bishop Arthur Gitonga (who had served on the Saitoti Commission), Mrs J. J. Kirui, Ibrahim Haji Mohammed and Simeon Mancho. *Daily Nation*, 20 November 1992, p. 4.

36 *Daily Nation*, 19 November 1992, p. 2.

37 *Daily Nation*, 30 November 1992, p. 1; *Weekly Review*, 4 December 1992, p. 15; and *Kenya Times*, 5 December 1992.

38 *Daily Nation*, 19 November 1992, p. 2.

39 *Daily Nation*, 26 November 1992, p. 1.

40 See for example the comments of Ndhiwa loser Akech Chieng in *Daily Nation*, 3 December 1992, p. 5.

41 The remaining seven, Kamukunji, Mutito, Kilome, Galole, Fafi, Taveta and Mukurueini were a mixed bag. *Daily Nation*, 27 November 1992, p. 1

42 *Daily Nation*, 28 November 1992, p. 5.

43 *Sunday Nation*, 29 November 1992, p. 20.

44 *Daily Nation*, 1 December 1992, pp. 4 and 5.

45 In the civic elections, the local committees were equally zealous in their organisation and reorganisation of elections, with a number of nominations cancelled and re–run.

46 *Kenya Times*, 14 December 1992, pp. 16–17. One reason for the resentment at arap Too was that he was widely believed to have a Tugen father at the highest levels of the government, and was therefore seen, as was Reuben Chesire in Eldoret, as representing a Tugen imposition on the Nandi.

47 Interestingly, the NEMU observer still reported violence and malpractice at several Mosop polling stations, and that in the areas he visited, the turn-out was low, at only 29 per cent.

48 Yusuf Keitany stood down at a meeting chaired by Biwott. *Daily Nation*, 27 October 1992, p. 4.

49 *Daily Nation*, 16 November 1992, p. 4 and *Standard*, 7 December 1992, p. 13.

50 *Kenya Times*, 1 December 1992, p. 19. The exception was Kerio East, where an independent candidate was elected.

51 Interview with Ogle in *Society*, 14 December 1992, p. 21; *Daily Nation*, 22 November 1992, p. 5; and *Nairobi Weekly Observer*, 20 November 1992, p. 4. He had also fallen out with the Mohammed clan.

52 In Siaya, Gilbert Oluoch was persuaded to call it a day, while Bob Jalang'o in Rarieda claimed he was rigged out by the Siaya District Commissioner and Rarieda District Officer. *Daily Nation*, 17 November 1992, p. 14. Other Class of '88 losers included John Cheruiyot, Kimunai arap Sego, Ngumba Njururi, Timothy Mibei, Minister Sam Ongeri and David Onyancha.

53 *Daily Nation*, 14 November 1992, p. 3.

54 *Daily Nation*, 19 November 1992, p. 2. It appears he was enticed back by the promise of a parastatal post.

55 *Standard*, 16 November 1992, p. 10.

56 Gumo, reported in *Daily Nation*, 12 December 1992, p. 2. See also *Daily Nation*, 13 November 1992, p. 5.
57 In another ten seats it is unclear what happened in the end.
58 In Mbooni, one potential candidate was later claimed to have been found dead. *Daily Nation*, 13 November 1992, p. 3.
59 Starehe, *Daily Nation*, 13 November 1992, p. 4; Langata, *Daily Nation*, 12 November 1992, p. 5; Westlands, *Daily Nation*, 11 November 1992, p. 4; and Kamukunji, *Daily Nation*, 14 November 1992, p. 4.
60 The KANU primaries in Nairobi were described in some detail in the *Daily Nation*, 10 November 1992, p. 5; and the *Weekly Review*, 11 December 1992, p. 18.
61 *Daily Nation*, 11 November 1992, p. 4.
62 *Kenya Times*, 8 December 1992, p. 23; and *Daily Nation*, 7 December 1992, p. 4.
63 Kubo, in *Sunday Nation*, 29 November 1992, p. 20.
64 *Daily Nation*, 14 November 1992, p. 12.
65 No election was ordered, despite a high court injunction ordering a new election. Siro reappeared as the PICK candidate.
66 *Daily Nation*, 14 November 1992, p. 3.
67 *Daily Nation* and *Kenya Times*, 5 December 1992.
68 *Daily Nation*, 6 December 1992, p. 2. Mokku secretly obtained a letter of nomination from Kamotho which enabled both candidates to present valid nomination certificates on nomination day. See *Kenya Times*, 16 December 1992, p. 25, and 18 December 1992, p. 36. Both candidates' papers were accepted, but headquarters ruled that Mokku was the official candidate.
69 Ford-Kenya Constitution, pp. 24–8.
70 Ford-Kenya Constitution, Article 14(g).
71 Despite this, the advertisement for the nominations specified that civic candidates should pay 4,000 shillings and Parliamentary candidates 7,000 shillings. See *Daily Nation*, 16 October 1992, p. 18.
72 *Standard*, 23 November 1992, p. 2.
73 Interview with Ford-Kenya leader, 1993.
74 This was Otieno Ombajo. See the *Daily Nation*, 7 December 1992, p. 24 and *Standard*, 8 December 1992, p. 2.
75 See for example the protest by a civic councillor candidate for Kisauni that he had been barred from standing by Odinga. *Daily Nation*, 14 November 1992, p. 3.
76 *Daily Nation*, 18 November 1992, p. 4.
77 For example, Odinga campaigned for Asiyo actively at Kendu Bay. *Daily Nation*, 2 November 1992, p. 32.
78 *Economic Review*, 23 November 1992, pp. 4–5, and Odinga in *Daily Nation*, 16 November 1992, p. 2.
79 *Daily Nation*, 14 November 1992, p. 4.
80 *Kenya Times*, 9 December 1992, p. 24 and 10 December 1992, p. 16; and *Daily Nation*, 9 December 1992, p. 5.
81 *Daily Nation*, 24 November 1992, p. 4.
82 *Daily Nation*, 7 December 1992, p. 32.
83 Alego, Nyando, Muhoroni, Rangwe and Kasipul–Kabondo. *Daily Nation*, 18 November 1992, p. 10.
84 DP Constitution (n.d.) p. 28.
85 *Daily Nation*, 27 October 1992, p. 24. These were lower than KANU's.
86 Personal conversations, 1992 and 1993. See also Karuga, *Daily Nation*, 20 November 1992, p. 15.
87 *Daily Nation*, 25 November 1992, p. 4, and *Kenya Times*, 8 December 1992, p. 4.
88 *Daily Nation*, 13 November 1992, p. 10.
89 *Daily Nation*, 10 November 1992, p. 2; 4 December 1992, p. 5; and 7 December 1992, p. 4.
90 Laikipia West elections were ordered re–run by DP headquarters but Kimani again won. See the *Daily Nation*, 13 November 1992, p. 3 and 20 November 1992, p. 5.
91 *Daily Nation*, 11 November 1992, p. 2.
92 See Nyamweya's call for annulment in *Standard*, 17 November p 5, and then *Daily Nation*, 19 November 1992, p. 1.
93 These were Bobasi, Kitutu Chache, Kitutu Masaba and North Mugirango. See *Daily Nation*, 4 December 1992, p. 5.

94 On Nakuru North, see *Daily Nation*, 19 November, 1992 p. 4, and *Daily Nation*, 24 November, 1992 p. 4.
95 Interview with *Daily Nation* journalist, November 1993.
96 Ford-Asili press advertisements, 7 November 1992.
97 They were generally rejected. *Daily Nation*, 16 November 1992, p. 5, and *Standard*, 20 November 1992, p. 5.
98 *Daily Nation*, 2 December 1992, p. 4.
99 *Sunday Nation*, 15 November 1992, p. 4.
100 *Daily Nation*, 15 November 1992, p. 5; *Daily Nation*, 5 December 1992, p. 4; and *Kenya Times*, 9 December 1992, p. 3.
101 *Sunday Nation*, 15 November 1992, p. 5; and *Daily Nation*, 9 December 1992, p. 4.
102 *Daily Nation*, 23 November 1992, p. 4; and *Kenya Times*, 9 December 1992, p. 3.
103 *Daily Nation*, 11 November 1992, p. 6.
104 *Daily Nation*, 2 December 1992, p. 5, and *Kenya Times*, 11 December 92 p. 4.
105 *Kenya Times*, 22 December 1992, p. 4.
106 *Daily Nation*, 14 November 1992, p. 4.
107 Samia NEMU Poll monitor.
108 *Weekly Review* 11 December 1992, p. 24.
109 *Standard*, 30 November 1992, p. 10.
110 Mlamba, Mcharo and Kachila. *Standard*, 17 November 1992, p. 3.
111 Tuva, *Kenya Times*, 25 December 1992, p. 19.
112 In Imenti North, the DP loser Mbogori campaigned for the KANU candidate. *Daily Nation*, 9 December 1992, p. 4.
113 Justice Akiwumi, *Daily Nation*, 1 December 1992, p. 1.
114 *Daily Nation*, 1 December 1992, p. 5.
115 *Kenya Times*, 10 December 1992, p. 17.
116 *Daily Nation*, 9 December 1992, p. 4.

Nine

The Election Campaign

1992 saw the first nation-wide campaign on national issues since Independence. In previous elections, in the one-party state, the main electoral factors had been clanism and localism, the personality and oratorical ability of the candidates, and their education, participation in self-help *Harambee* projects, personal wealth and ability to bring development and government jobs. Many observers and candidates expected that the 1992 general election would be fought on the same basis, and that the individual's prestige would be more important than their party ticket. This was not to be. The 1992 election campaign was fought between national tickets, although powerful local leaders funded their own campaigns and appealed to local factions. In the end however, regional and ethnic blocs were to prove the key to the outcome.

The election campaign was fought at three different levels, each with its own agenda. Local government candidates fought as individuals, allied to parties, to Parliamentary candidates and their party's Presidential nominee. Parliamentary candidates did the same, although they stressed national issues more strongly in their speeches, while Presidential candidates competed at the national level through large set-piece rallies, press statements and advertising, relying on their local candidates and supporters to campaign for them at the constituency level.

KANU emerged from the primary season as by far the strongest party, with a full ticket covering every constituency. Although weaker, the three main opposition parties had acquired numerous candidates in KANU's strongholds. In turn, they and KANU had lost candidates in their own areas to the KNC and PICK. KANU now needed to dig deeper into the opposition's support in the marginal areas and to ensure that the opposition did not make any significant inroads into KANU zones in the pastoral areas. December 1992 began well for the opposition, but by mid-month the opposition leaders had been prevented from campaigning in KANU's home areas, and Kibaki and Matiba were locked in a bitter battle of words for the Kikuyu vote. As the polls approached, the opposition's hopes began to wane.

KANU's Campaign Strategy

KANU's campaign slogan was that it was the party of 'Stability and Progress'. This message was an effective tactic in a conservative society, highly respectful of authority. This claim to guarantee stability was stressed repeatedly in the party's press advertisements and on television. While KANU had governed the country since Independence, the opposition parties were unknown quantities. KANU also claimed that multi-party politics had aroused ethnic rivalries and violence, carrying the implicit warning that Kenyans must be careful to ensure that the country did not become another Somalia. KANU's 64-page glossy manifesto, printed in English and Swahili, was released on 5 November 1992. It stressed the ruling party's economic achievements, nation-wide support, and its ability to lead the country safely into the future. Responding to pressure from the opposition, KANU promised 'accountability and transparency in the management of public affairs'. In line with IMF and World Bank requirements and with the programmes of the other parties, it supported the 'privatisation of all non-strategic parastatals', 'complete removal of foreign exchange controls' and 'the elimination of all unnecessary controls, licences and regulations'.[1] The party also promised to develop the *Jua Kali* (informal manufacturing) sector and emphasised its plans for increased employment and better services, stressing its development record since independence. The manifesto made a number of commitments on human rights, but was far from specific on how KANU would alter its existing policies. The party also funded a series of briefing notes in the *Kenya Times* on economic developments since 1963, stressing the continuity with Kenyatta's government. Its publicity campaign was well-organised, extravagantly funded and directed by Saatchi and Saatchi staff from South Africa.[2]

KANU's campaign in the field was based on rather different tactics, pithily described as 'bribe and tribe'. KANU had employed both the 'carrot' and the 'stick' very effectively against the opposition in the 1960s.[3] In 1992, this approach was to prove just as successful. In their Kalenjin homeland of Baringo, Elgeyo-Marakwet, Nandi, Bomet and Kericho, which the opposition had failed to penetrate, few voters understood 'multi-partyism'. There, KANU stressed that the Presidency would be taken away unless they voted for Moi. In the periphery of the Rift Valley – Turkana, Samburu, Pokot, Narok and southern Kajiado – and in North-Eastern Province, Isiolo and Marsabit, KANU maintained heavy administrative pressure to minimise the losses experienced during the primary elections, and to ensure that the non-indigenous residents (Kikuyu, Luo, and Luhya settlers and traders) were sufficiently intimidated either to vote for KANU or not to vote at all. The ruling party abandoned Central Province and Luo Nyanza to the opposition, bar a few key Ministerial seats where they hoped to salvage some parliamentary victories. KANU identified Kisii, and Eastern and Western Provinces, which together returned over a quarter of the Assembly, as crucial swing areas into which it poured money to improve its position. A similar situation existed on the Coast, although there the aim was to ensure that KANU's lead was maintained against a growing Islamic challenge.

KANU leaders condemned the opposition parties as 'tribalists', pointing out that only the ruling party had support throughout the country and candidates in all 188 constituencies. Darius Mbela, for example, warned that they were 'tribal clubs' who would consign the smaller tribes to the 'political dustbins'. During the President's tour of Mount Elgon, Assistant Minister Kisiero told the crowds that the bigger tribes had formed opposition parties 'to swallow the small ones like the Kalenjin and Sabaot'.[4] KANU leaders accused the DP of being GEMA in disguise, suggesting in the *Kenya Times* that Njenga Karume, Kenya's most successful capitalist and GEMA's former chief executive, was the real DP leader and that Kibaki would be dropped after the election.[5] KANU also exacerbated fears among the Maasai, Kalenjin and other pastoral 'tribes' that a Kikuyu victory would mean that their land would be expropriated for Kikuyu settlers. These tribal claims had some truth, as the opposition parties' support was ethnically narrower than KANU's. This exclusiveness, however, had been encouraged by KANU, which had made great efforts to neutralise opposition in its own strongholds. KANU was also ethnically based, remaining extremely weak among the Kikuyu and Luo, and far from strong among the Luhya, but its retention of many incumbents from the key marginal communities helped to buttress its image as a national party.

KANU also relied heavily on 'negative campaigning'. The ruling party constantly attacked its opponents, suggesting that they would endanger the country's stability for short-term political gain. It also made considerable efforts to divide the opposition during October–December 1992, when party leaders tried to exacerbate Kikuyu–Luo rivalries to ensure that the opposition parties did not negotiate an electoral pact. The KANU Briefs supplement in the *Kenya Times* highlighted conflicts between the Kikuyu and Luo, resurrecting Wambui Otieno's critical remarks about Luos during the 1987 S. M. Otieno burial case and stories of Kikuyu oathing in 1969. The newspaper reported that Paul Muite was no longer actively campaigning for Odinga in Kikuyu, and attempted to arouse fears of a Kikuyu victory among other ethnic groups.[6] KANU also highlighted other weaknesses in the opposition. It used to good effect the fact that the DP, unlike KANU, had never held elections to select its key officials. Boy Juma Boy, for example, told a KANU rally in Wundanyi, 'If the DP is a democratic party, how come they have not elected their leader as Mr Kibaki is just an interim chairman?'[7] Party leaders also made great play of the attempts by Odinga to impose his candidates in Nyanza, and the pro-KANU media provided detailed coverage of the bitter battle of words that developed between Kibaki and Matiba as the campaign neared its end.

The ruling party had one other advantage. Each of the opposition leaders had obvious personal weaknesses. Odinga was criticised for being old, infirm and for having done nothing for the Luo people in development terms in all his years as leader.[8] His supporters, according to the *Weekend Mail*, although a 'bright energetic lot', were inexperienced and 'could be vengeful and vindictive should they obtain power'.[9] Mwai Kibaki, of course, could not be faulted for age, or lack of experience, but he was denounced in October, when the DP looked the strongest challenger, as a 'fence sitter' and an opportunist for having resigned so late from the government. On 3 October, Joseph Kamotho called Kibaki a 'perpetual drunkard', and Clement Gachanja dismissed him as 'the alcoholic from Nyeri'.[10] On 18 October, Vice-President Saitoti claimed that Kibaki was involved in a plot to discredit Moi, involving a maize-selling conspiracy, and claimed that the DP leadership were the same 'Change the Constitution' team who had tried to topple Moi in 1976.[11] The government also sought to blame the DP leader for the country's economic difficulties, claiming he had mismanaged the economy when Finance Minister from 1969 to 1982. The criticisms of Matiba were obvious. The FORD-Asili leader was 'crippled and mad', and had resigned from KANU only when his own position was threatened. KANU also attacked Kibaki and Matiba for grabbing land at the coast when Ministers, and for being tribalists in their appointments when in power.[12]

In contrast, KANU promoted the image of President Moi as a God-fearing, temperate and caring leader, who was in good physical and mental health. Local Government Minister Ntimama, at a rally in Voi, called Odinga a 'ghost, with his red mouth', while Moi was a smart and 'handsome boy'.[13] The issue of religious affiliation was problematic given the schisms within Christian churches and the importance of the Moslem vote in the Coast and North-East. Nevertheless, Moi used the religious issue against his opponents, stressing his personal beliefs and frequently appearing on television at church services.

In an attempt to tarnish the opposition's human rights record, KANU also sought to emphasise the hypocrisy of some opposition leaders now professing belief in democratic government. The ruling party publicised declarations in support of President Moi and of single-party rule made by Kibaki and Keen when they were government Ministers. Local candidates employed similar tactics against other former KANU leaders, such as former Vice-President Karanja in Githunguri, who in the mid-1980s had been an intemperate hardliner. Voters were reminded that Paul Muite had helped draft the one-party state bill, and that Kibaki had seconded the motion to close debate on it in 1982.

KANU was vulnerable on another key issue – the ethnic clashes – which they had failed to control and which they were widely believed to have caused in the first place. Its response was classically authoritarian – to try to blame the opposition for the violence. KANU leaders made a series of attacks on outspoken opposition politicians, particularly those in FORD-Kenya. Raila Odinga was vilified as a guerrilla leader and Paul Muite's unguarded comment that a rigged victory for Moi would lead inexorably to violent conflict was frequently repeated by KANU under the headline 'Muite calls for Civil War'.[14] Throughout 1992, Moi had attempted to deflect blame for the clashes through a series of implausible allegations of opposition military preparations. In August alone he made five claims suggesting that the security forces had intercepted guns from Somalia, that Libyan terrorists were infiltrating the country or that the opposition were 'tribal parties interested only in provoking civil war'.[15] The *Kenya Times* in

September alleged the DP had paid Sh19 million to have Moi assassinated. No one, however, was arrested. Moi then accused Keen of having plotted to overthrow the government when he was an Assistant Minister. In October, the President declared that, 'These tribal clashes ... were introduced by FORD' and KANU even tried to blame the clashes on the Americans and the CIA.[16] On 30 October, Moi claimed that the opposition was planning to launch a guerrilla war in the Rift Valley if they lost.[17] On 20 November, he declared that 150 saboteurs, trained by the opposition, had entered Kenya from Uganda and were poised to create chaos during the elections.[18] This was followed by a YK '92 publicity parade of 45 'DP soldiers', who claimed that the DP had recruited them to destabilise the country.[19] When the government shut the Kenyan-Ugandan border in early December, Moi again claimed that foreigners were sneaking into the country and that the ethnic clashes were caused by Ugandan- and Libyan-trained terrorists.[20] While these allegations were widely dismissed as a futile campaign stunt, some viewed them with more concern as presaging another bout of ethnic violence, possibly designed to disrupt the elections. No one appears to have been charged concerning any of these alleged incidents, and it is very doubtful whether any of them had any basis in fact.

Opposition Campaign Issues

The opposition's campaign was fought on very different lines from KANU's, but many of the issues they raised were similar. Like KANU, the opposition parties targeted specific regions of the country, and mixed discussion of national issues with local promises and ethnic appeals. Despite their divisions, some unity of purpose remained amongst the non-FORD-Asili opposition, and the most complete manifesto produced was the *Post-Election Action Plan,* which had been drafted jointly by FORD and the DP in May 1992 and was launched on 4 November 1992, the day before KANU's, as a joint programme for FORD-Kenya, the DP, KENDA and the SDP. Sponsored by the left-wing German Friedrich Neumann foundation, the plan of action provided a detailed analysis of Kenya's economic and social problems, and offered a strategy for common action.[21] The document was too unfocused and not prioritised, but was effectively the only full economic statement of objectives produced by any party.[22] Kenya's political parties, however, were less divided over policy than by ethnicity and control of patronage. Even KANU ostensibly accepted many of the economic liberalisation policies suggested in the action plan. The document, however worthy, was ignored throughout the campaign.

FORD, before its split, also produced a manifesto, almost entirely written by the Young Turks, led by Professor Peter Anyang-Nyong'o, Dr Mukhisa Kituyi and Robert Shaw. FORD-Kenya took this over with minor changes, releasing it as the 82-page *FORD-Kenya Manifesto – Charter for the Second Liberation,* on 27 November. This promised the restoration of constitutionalism, a guarantee on human rights and, more radically, the abolition of the Provincial Administration, a massive scaling-down of the civil service, an ending to the 8–4–4 system of education, and the privatisation of parastatals. The abolition of the Provincial Administration, almost unchanged in power and function since the colonial era, was the most controversial proposal. FORD-Kenya proposed instead to transfer more limited powers to local government mayors and councillors. The party's proposed civil service cutbacks may have alienated some civil servants, who were under intense pressure to vote for KANU.

After the FORD split, with most of the intellectuals remaining with Odinga, FORD-Asili found itself with little time or talent to prepare manifestos, and published none. The party did not even have printed copies of its constitution, although in August it financed the publication of a 28-page booklet, *Ken Matiba, Man of the People,* which outlined Matiba's distinguished career and stressed his commitment to greater accountability in public affairs and his determination to 'build Kenya, not tribes'.[23] The DP published its own 51-page manifesto on 30 November, outlining liberal economic policies little different to those propounded by the other parties, but with slightly more emphasis on private enterprise, as befitted the party's big business roots. Nearly half the manifesto was taken up with economic matters. It also promised the end of corruption and detention, and reform of the 8–4–4 education system.

All the opposition parties were committed to repealing the detention laws and to liberalising the economy. In many respects, the manifestos were targeted as much at Western donors as the Kenyan élite, in an attempt to show that their money and efforts had not been wasted and that multi-party politics would produce reform. None of them really offered a plausible and coherent programme. In the words of Lee Muthoga, on election eve, 'No single party has set out what its policies are … what they [the opposition parties] say is what their leaders think the people would like to hear.'[24] FORD-Asili, particularly, made no attempt to define a national programme of action or principles, relying entirely on eulogies of Matiba as a natural leader.

The opposition's national press and hustings campaign focused upon five issues: the economy, corruption, violence and the ethnic clashes, human rights and election rigging, and the leadership qualities of their leaders – with a sixth, ethnic solidarity, always lurking in the background.

The Economy

KANU's major problem was the poor state of the economy. Since the early 1980s, Kenya had experienced serious structural problems which, combined with political repression, growing corruption and the state's refusal to liberalise, had led to the ending of Western quick-disbursement aid. Throughout 1992, the government, led by Saitoti, attempted to persuade Western governments that Kenya had liberalised, and deserved to be rewarded. There was no response. Concerned by the risk of instability, many companies scaled down their investment plans as businessmen awaited the outcome of the elections. This uncertainty caused further economic instability, adding to the economic problems caused by the government's policies and the cuts in foreign aid. Tourism, Kenya's largest export earner, plummeted as talk of 'tribal warfare' and election violence dramatically reduced holiday bookings and cut foreign exchange inflows.

At the same time, coffee and tea, Kenya's main export earners, were also experiencing problems, while the cost of funding the election bled the Central Bank dry of foreign exchange and inflation continued to soar.

With a former Finance Minister and internationally respected economist as its leader, the DP campaign particularly stressed economic issues, and its strong support amongst the business community reflected its pro-business orientation. Kibaki continually criticised the government's economic management. The DP's claims that the economy had collapsed and the health system was in tatters, however, conflicted to a certain extent with the fact that Kibaki had been Finance Minister (1969–82) and Health Minister (1988–91), and had served for ten years as Moi's Vice-President. FORD-Asili, in contrast, particularly stressed unemployment, whilst all the parties made vague promises to improve schools, and address poverty. It is clear that a DP government would have maintained a 'steady as she goes' style of economic management, which would have benefited the developed regions, particularly Central Province. It is less clear that a FORD-Kenya or Asili government would have followed stable economic policies. Whilst FORD-Kenya had clear economic views, some policies, such as the abolition of the Provincial Administration, would have created enormous problems. Effectively, FORD-Asili had no economic policies apart from 'do what Matiba says because he got very rich' and 'give money to the poor'. It is doubtful, given the lack of political and administrative experience in the party following the exodus of the KNC leaders, whether Asili could have formed an effective government.

Corruption

The second theme of the opposition campaign was state corruption. During the 1970s, when the coffee boom had vastly increased resources, corruption had become endemic in Kenya. The fact that there had been little danger of exposure, since everyone else had their hands in the till, led to an explosion of corruption in almost every sphere. Famous cases, such as the ivory-poaching scandals, Mama Ngina Kenyatta's ruby mines, Moi's and Biwott's charcoal racket, and coffee smuggling among the Kikuyu élite were only the tip of the iceberg. Moi's accession to the Presidency marked a change, as the leadership shifted from a Kikuyu-dominated bourgeoisie to a Kalenjin (and to a lesser extent Kamba and Luhya) leadership, backed by Asian capital. Major parastatals and key Ministries contained a thin veneer of Kalenjin leaders, over what remained a predominantly Kikuyu bourgeoisie. Less secure in their positions, which depended on political patronage, the 'looting' of Moi's place-men became even more open and aggressive.[25] Another major source of funds was land ownership, and particularly the allocation of government land to individuals (especially valuable plots in Nairobi and the Coast) and the grabbing of land set aside for landless settlers in Machakos, Embu, Kirinyaga, Kajiado, Narok and elsewhere.[26]

Corruption had been one of the driving forces behind the move to multi-partyism, and was a major issue in the election campaign. FORD-Kenya took the lead in a series of allegations, followed up by press statements, letters to Western embassies and advertisements. In an advertisement in the *Daily Nation* of 1 December 1992, it castigated Kenya Posts and Telecommunications (KP&T), chaired by a Kalenjin, as a 'den of looting'. Inventory calculations had revealed that the parastatal had only Sh1.2 billion worth of inventory, whilst Sh7.5 billion was on the books.[27] At the same time, FORD-Kenya also attacked the Kenya Meat Commission (KMC) – of which Biwott's brother was a director, and which previously had been chaired by KANU's candidate for Kathiani, General Mulinge – for involvement in a questionable deal for canning lines and rendering plants. According to FORD-Kenya, a French company, Hema Technologies, had won the contract, despite having submitted only the second highest bid, funded by a 'questionable' financial arrangement with Mitsubishi.

The next day the party was on the offensive over the Turkwell Gorge hydro-electric project. This huge hydro-electric power scheme in the Kerio Valley had been built by French companies. The project had been heavily criticised since its inception in 1986, and had been the subject of revelations during the Ouko enquiry. Robert Shaw described it as a 'stinking scandal'.[28] FORD-Kenya claimed that the water levels were simply too low for the project to be profitable (denying suggestions that it was contributing almost a third of the country's electricity requirements) and that the project had cost almost four times what it should, with kickbacks from the French company Spie Battignoles reaching $US400 million, according to allegations in the *Weekly Mail*.[29] The government and the companies involved responded, suggesting that the project was better value than a comparable World Bank development, but the questions remained.

By contrast, FORD-Asili made little reference to the issue, although Shikuku, whose anti-corruption stance was well known, demanded that Moi declare his personal wealth, whilst Matiba stressed his personal 'cleanliness' in speeches, such as that in Embu on 18 December, in which he rhetorically asked: 'Moi is the third richest man in the world. How did he get Sh88 billion banked abroad?'[30]

Another centre of corruption was the sugar industry, most of whose products are grown in the sugar cane belt of Western Province and Nyanza, and processed by five major factories, then transported to the KNTC for distribution. Despite being a major local crop, in which the country was self-sufficient as recently as 1979, shortages had grown and prices risen. Sugar distribution was regulated by the Ministry of Commerce, which had permitted cheap sugar imports in 1987–89, undercutting KNTC sugar: this had led to stockpiling and problems in paying farmers. It was alleged in 1991 that further sugar shortages had been artificially created, requiring 75,000 tonnes to be imported and sold above world prices. To ensure questions were not asked, Sh3 million allegedly had been placed in one Minister's account, Sh500,000 into another official's, and Sh1 million had been delivered by briefcase to the Office of the President.[31] Sugar cane growing dropped: combined with under-investment in machinery in the mills, this led to huge shortfalls and yet more imports. These had been arranged with particular importers and sometimes were sold privately, at prices more than double the official state-controlled price for local sugar. The worst problems with the mills appeared at exactly the time – April–June – that huge sugar imports were coming into the country. In

1992, Robert Shaw of FORD-Kenya accused the government of allowing a few favoured importers to capitalise on shortages by charging abnormally high prices.

One problem with FORD-Kenya's attack on corruption was its implications for the Asian community, some of whose members were deeply involved in government scandals. Ketan Somaia, only 29 when he began his meteoric rise to prominence in 1988 by buying Marshalls East Africa, was one of the President's close business associates. Another was Kamlesh Pattni, who owned Goldenberg and then established Exchange Bank. Asian businessmen were also involved with sugar imports, overpriced steam boilers for the Prisons Department and loans from the NSSF to 'political' banks. Somaia had founded Trust Bank, with two other Asians and Gideon Moi, the President's son. He also acquired Madhupaper International under duress, just after it was released from receivership, and took over BCCI in Kenya, renamed Delphius Bank. Earlier, he had acquired the International Casino in Nairobi for his backers. When the owners had refused to sell, Moi had decreed that gambling could only take place with foreign currency. With Kenyans needing a licence to hold foreign exchange, takings plummeted, forcing the owner to sell, whereupon the law was scrapped.[32] The Asian community was also frequently accused of failing to remit export earnings and many considered that the government favoured Asian-owned businesses at the cost of indigenous (particularly Kikuyu-controlled) companies.

State Violence

The opposition also denounced the government's use of extreme violence against its own citizens for political purposes. The murder of Robert Ouko in 1990, followed by the death of Bishop Muge, had been one of the major catalysts for change, and Ouko remained a symbol of the ills of the regime. The ethnic clashes and the rejection of the Kiliku report by Parliament also provided major campaign issues for opposition candidates throughout the country. Kibaki constantly denounced government violence, and Kennedy Kiliku (DP, Changamwe), the Chairman of the Commission into Ethnic Violence, who spoke with him on the platform in many DP rallies, was applauded widely for his report. The DP press campaign highlighted photographs of a murdered man, with an arrow in his back, reminding voters of KANU's responsibility for the clashes. The clashes created a groundswell of anti-government feeling, as Kikuyu settlers from the Rift Valley returned home to Nyeri and Kiambu with tales of violence and state disinterest. Rose Waruhiu, the DP candidate in Githunguri, introduced to a vast crowd at of one her final meetings a local woman who had been forced to flee from Burnt Forest, leaving her family to die.

The Rift Valley violence certainly backfired electorally, since KANU's losses in the rest of the country far outweighed their gains in the Kalenjin borderlands. The clashes, however, also gave KANU a new opportunity in certain marginal constituencies. Not only were people horrified by the violence, they were genuinely scared of the consequences to themselves and their communities of not voting for the ruling party, and in the ethnic borderland seats where KANU's threats of retribution could be carried out (such as Rongai, Eldoret South and Narok North), opposition supporters may have hesitated to vote against the government out of fear.

Human Rights, Democracy and Political Pluralism

The importance of human rights, democracy and pluralism to the opposition's rationale for existence cannot be overstated. The three major opposition parties differentiated themselves from KANU most clearly by their emphasis on the need to improve human rights, promising to repeal the Public Security Act (ending detention without trial), the Public Order Act, the Chiefs Act, and special identity card requirements for Somali Kenyans, and to restore the separation of powers and the independence of the judiciary. These promises were linked closely to a commitment to representative democracy. The parties stressed the need to entrench political pluralism and end election rigging in order to reintroduce true democracy. The opposition parties in their campaign rallies warned that the government would try to rig its way back into office. Martin Shikuku, for example, 'criticised the KANU government for rigging elections repeatedly contrary to the country's constitution'.[33] Prominent figures in the movement saw this as the key process, by which other social and economic ills would be righted later. Only when the population could choose its leaders and the state's policies without manipulation would true reforms take place.

There were, however, major internal divisions between (and within) the opposition parties over the modalities of change. While politicians like Matiba tended to argue for a fair fight under the existing rules in order to seize absolute power, others, including the FORD-Asili lawyer Gibson Kamau Kuria, denied that simply having new elections under the existing system, replacing 'bad' with 'good' leaders, would solve the problem. This view was also favoured by many of the clergy, the Law Society of Kenya, and the Professionals' Committee for Democratic Change (PCDC). They disagreed with the view that democracy and fair elections were synonymous, and argued throughout for a constitutional convention, to devise a new constitution, and the formation of a government of national unity to oversee the elections in the manner of the Lancaster House agreements of 1960 and 1962. But these groups lacked any real capacity to bring about such changes. Although the opposition had demanded a new constitution throughout 1992, KANU had no intention of abandoning its control of the state. The elections, consequently, were bound to be less than 'free and fair', although how far KANU would go to hold on to power was still unclear.

Personality

Like KANU, the opposition parties used their Presidential candidates' popularity and achievements as key parts of their campaigns. Indeed, personality overshadowed policy discussions by a long way. Odinga's supporters stressed the *Jaramogi's* long tradition of dissent, his sacrifices for political liberty, and his ability to work with a team of skilled young professionals. Kibaki's supporters, faced with their candidate's lack of charisma, stressed his 25 years' experience as a government Minister, his record of good economic management, and his proven ability to create prosperity. FORD-Asili stressed Matiba's success as a businessman, his leading role in the campaign for multi-party politics, and his willingness to stand up to President Moi in 1988 and 1990. Matiba, his supporters argued, had defended Kikuyu interests and the interests of ordinary Kenyans while the DP leaders had stayed in Moi's government until the single-party system had collapsed. Matiba, by contrast, had spent a year in detention and his health had suffered severely. He was a man of courage, principle and action, whereas Kibaki had been cowardly and timid.

Little love was lost between Matiba and the other opposition leaders. FORD-Kenya blamed Matiba for breaking up the party to advance his own selfish ambition, while the DP saw him as standing in the way of Kikuyu unity. Both believed that the FORD-Asili leader was too ill and too great a megalomaniac to hold the reins of power. Indeed, one prominent Kikuyu businessman, who detested the Moi regime, observed that 'Matiba is even more dangerous than Moi. Matiba is cleverer than Moi, more arrogant, and more ruthless.' The exodus of experienced politicians like Rubia, wa Nyoike, and Maina Wanjigi from Matiba's inner coterie suggested that the FORD-Asili leader was a difficult man to work with. Matiba's emphasis on his personal wealth as a guarantee of success, and on his suffering while in detention, angered many in the other opposition parties, who pointed out how others had spent longer in detention. As Pius Nyamora's editorial in *Society* stated, 'Detention ... is no qualification for the presidency.'[34] FORD-Asili in turn castigated Odinga as 'senile', Moi as corrupt and Kibaki as a coward who had also messed up the economy. His opponents made less of Matiba's illness than might have been expected. The true severity of his problems was recognised only after the election. Partly, this was because it was KANU leaders who made most of the suggestions, and people simply did not trust them. Matiba also managed to conceal his problems well, despite huge media attention. If people had realised the true extent of his incapacitation, his personal vote would undoubtedly have been smaller.

Ethnic Solidarity

At the grassroots level in Central Province, Luoland and parts of Western Province opposition candidates, like KANU, made open use of tribal solidarity arguments. Such tactics could only be employed in small-scale local meetings, as all the parties needed to present themselves as nationwide organisations. In a neo-patrimonial political system, like Kenya's, ethnicity, development and economic prosperity were closely linked. As a result, the economic importance of political victory cannot be overstressed. Many educated Kikuyu, for example, believed that their long-term survival as the dominant business community depended on either Matiba or Kibaki winning the election. Thus, in Molo, an ethnically tense seat following the clashes, FORD-Asili's Njenga Mungai campaigned on a strongly ethnic ticket, arguing that the Kikuyu needed to recapture the Presidency and the government for their tribe. He claimed, for example, that if the GEMA people did not vote for Matiba, the Presidency would never return to Kikuyuland.[35] FORD-Asili's Luhya candidates similarly called for Luhya ethnic solidarity behind Shikuku.

Local Issues

Like the government, local opposition leaders campaigned on constituency as well as national issues, though the core of their speeches usually addressed national problems. Government and opposition parliamentary candidates alike stressed what their party would do for the country, and what they would do for the local area if elected. This ranged from promises to upgrade local roads if elected, and to finish development projects already started, through to personal attacks on their parliamentary and civic opponents as opportunists or corrupt, and promises that land allocated to national parks would be de-gazetted and returned for settlement.[36] Candidates also promised development – although if they were in the opposition, their ability to influence the allocation of development aid would be reduced dramatically. In constituencies with pressing agricultural problems, opposition candidates emphasised their determination to address such issues. The speeches of George Mwicigi (KNC, Kandara) on the problems of the Kenya Tea Development Authority and its inability to process enough tea production in Murang'a, and Rose Waruhiu's criticism of the coffee and tea boards, and the closure of the East African Bag and Cordage factory in Githunguri, highlighted important local economic issues. Women candidates tended to stress the fact that women were in a majority in many rural seats, and that they needed a woman MP. Traditional personal and clan (or sub-clan) rivalries were also used in the campaign.

The Cash Dispensers

KANU's strategy depended less upon policy arguments than upon more material considerations. The ruling party employed the government's financial resources to tilt the playing field in its favour. KANU spent extraordinary sums of money on its campaign, very little of which could be accounted for. The poverty of ordinary Kenyans ensured that they were susceptible to financial inducements. Moreover, incurring the enmity of the state was extremely unwise in a society where the government dominated the economy. It was therefore essential for the government to create the impression that there was no chance of an opposition victory, and that only by voting for KANU would patronage continue to flow. With state control over the economy almost complete outside Nairobi and Central Province, and development dependent on state investment, the government could easily retard economic progress in those areas which voted against it and use the money to reward those zones which remained loyal. Such threats were made in several districts, but were most strongly directed at Luoland, where KANU leaders warned that if the Luo voted for FORD-Kenya, as they had for the KPU in 1966–9, development funds to Nyanza would be cut drastically. Even in Central Province, District Commissioners and KANU leaders warned voters that they would lose government jobs and development aid if they failed to vote for KANU, as it would form the next government anyway. On 17 and 18 October, in Nyeri and Kiambu, for example, Ministers Dalmas Otieno and Zachary Onyonka cautioned the Kikuyu that if they failed to elect KANU, they would suffer the same fate as the Luo under Kenyatta.[37]

The government targeted groups of voters with benefits designed to lure them back. In July, KANU had wooed voters with revisions to the 8–4–4 education system, and had substantially raised teachers', civil servants' and lecturers' salaries. Some political prisoners were also released.[38] On 10 October, the President promised that tea and coffee auctions would henceforth be held in foreign exchange, to ensure that farmers were protected against devaluation of the shilling.[39] The government also authorised the coffee board's third annual payment to farmers of Sh533 million on 4 December, just three and a half weeks before the election, in an attempt to bolster KANU's support in Kikuyu coffee-growing areas. On *Jamhuri* Day, 12 December 1992, President Moi rewarded four major groups: workers, women, civil servants and Moslems. He raised the minimum wage by 12 per cent, announced that women civil servants would receive house allowances, directed that Moslems be allowed time off work between eleven and one o'clock on Fridays to attend prayers, and raised the amount of foreign currency they could take abroad on the Haj.[40] The President also assured civil servants that under KANU their jobs were secure, in contrast to the cutbacks planned by the DP and FORD-Kenya.

Moi also intervened with incentives in important marginal constituencies. In August, the President had issued a Sh14 million cheque to compensate sugar cane farmers, who had not been paid after the collapse of Kwale's Ramisi sugar factory.[41] During the campaign proper, he focused his attention on Western Province. On 18 October, he ordered Minister Ngala to provide sugar cane farmers, who had not been paid for over a year, Sh20 million for deliveries to the Nzoia Sugar Company. Two weeks, later he was in Bungoma with another Sh20 million cheque as a personal gift to sugar farmers in Bungoma District. He also paid out Sh10 million in Kanduyi in Bungoma for a teachers' training college.[42] In December, Moi promised the establishment of a third district for the Meru.[43] In Siaya, Odinga's stronghold, he promised that Ukwala would be upgraded to a sub-district, and announced that the Yala sugar factory would be rehabilitated and some roads resurfaced.[44] On 10 December, the government also ended its ten-year-old ban on Mnazi (palm wine), in an attempt to appeal to voters at the Coast.[45]

These are traditional electoral tactics for incumbent governments. More serious was the use of vast sums of cash to fund KANU's campaign. KANU candidates received large sums from the centre, and no expense was spared in election advertisements and publicity, local organisation, transportation and rallies. KANU sub-offices were repainted throughout the country and dozens of new ones opened. The most successful tactic, however, was the distribution of food, cash and loans to voters in virtually every constituency to induce them to back the government. The sums spent will never be known, but certainly exceeded anything KANU, or even Moi and his business partners could afford.

Until October 1992, election spending by individual candidates in their constituencies had been limited to Sh40,000. This law had long been considered irrelevant by voters and candidates alike, since the practice of rewarding voters for their support lay at the heart of the selection of MPs. Candidates donated to local *Harambee* meetings and handed out gifts of salt, bread, sugar, beer, building materials and cash to voters, buying votes in exchange for goods and services. The most effective patron, who provided the most money and demonstrated that he could continue to provide *Harambee* contributions after the election, could buy the voters' support for some years.[46] The Statute Law (Miscellaneous Amendments) Bill of 1992 finally removed any upper limit on election spending. As a result, the 1992 election revolved around money. What the opposition and commentators missed when the Bill was approved was that future elections would not be fought on the basis of individuals versus individuals, but by the state versus the opposition. KANU ran a campaign in which money was nearly unlimited, and without access to state funding, the opposition was at a huge disadvantage.

Precisely where the billions of shillings came from is unclear, since KANU has never published accounts or revealed its sources of income. Clearly, however, the money was not provided by the party. It is believed to have come from a combination of President Moi's and his Ministers' and clients' vast personal wealth, from the state itself, and from a series of clever schemes which released so much cash into the money supply that they threatened Kenya's economic stability, creating serious inflation in the aftermath of the election.

One of the cleverest scams was the Goldenberg scandal, which operated throughout 1991–2, whereby the company 'exported' gold and diamond jewellery to fictitious companies in Switzerland and Dubai, and then claimed back money from the government as export compensation. These items either did not exist (Kenya does not produce much gold) or were grossly overvalued (according to Central Bank officials who tried to prevent the compensation being paid, by 15,000 per cent). The Vice-President also authorised compensation on diamonds, which were not eligible for such payments, and approved compensation for the spurious exports which was far higher (35 per cent) than authorised under the Local Manufactures (Export Compensation) Act (20 per cent until January 1992, then reduced to 18 per cent). All these payments went to one company, the sole authorised exporter, Goldenberg International Limited, chaired by Asian businessman Kamlesh Pattni, whose other director was James Kanyotu, former head of the Special Branch. The company also benefited from pre-export shipment finance, whereby the government would make payments in advance of export to assist local exporters, which should then have been repaid once the items had been shipped and sold. This money could in the meantime be used for other purposes. By January 1992, the company had been paid Sh580 million (US$11 million) in 'compensation'.[47]

The National Social Security Fund (NSSF) was another source of funds for KANU's campaign. The NSSF is the statutory authority to which private workers pay social security contributions in return for retirement benefits. Its new 24-storey headquarters building under construction in Nairobi, however, was a massively expensive white elephant. Construction cost had increased six times, rising from Sh468 million to over Sh3,000 million, and the building was still unfinished.[48] It was being built by Mugoya Construction, a company with close ties to President Moi. The NSSF also invested workers' money in buying expensive properties, previously owned by or allocated to senior politicians and their retainers, then sold to the NSSF at inflated prices, transferring massive volumes of money from the NSSF to these individuals, some of which is believed to have reached YK '92. The best-known scandal was broken by the *Daily Nation* in November, when it documented how the NSSF had purchased two properties belonging to Sololo Outlets, a company part-owned by YK '92 leader Cyrus Jirongo, for Sh1.2 billion, vastly in excess of their estimated value of 66 million shillings. This was not unique. The Fund had also made low interest deposits to ailing finance houses known to be 'suspect', including the National Bank of Kenya and its subsidiaries (which accounted for 39 per cent of the NSSF's short-term deposits). These finance houses, which included Exchange Bank, City Finance, Pan-African Bank, Consolidated Bank of Kenya, Transnational Bank and Trade Bank, were all experiencing serious bad debt and liquidity problems partly as a result of 'non-performing' loans to senior politicians. An internal audit report recommended that the NSSF finance manager P. L. B. Kubebea be suspended, but this was overturned by the Minister of Labour.[49]

To get this money into the economic system in a usable form, the government purchased bank notes. Paul Muite and Robert Shaw of FORD-Kenya claimed, as a result of a tip-off from informants in the Central Bank, that KANU was importing vast sums of notes from its British currency suppliers, De La Rue, in order to fund its campaign. They possessed documents from the Central Bank suggesting that KANU was importing approximately $200 million or Sh11,000 million in notes, producing a 76 per cent growth in the money supply, which was normally approximately Sh15,000 million. The Central Bank denied this. The evidence of inflation after the election, however, suggests that the money supply was indeed vastly inflated (see Figure 9.1). The opposition also alleged that a large proportion of the money in circulation had not been officially gazetted, and

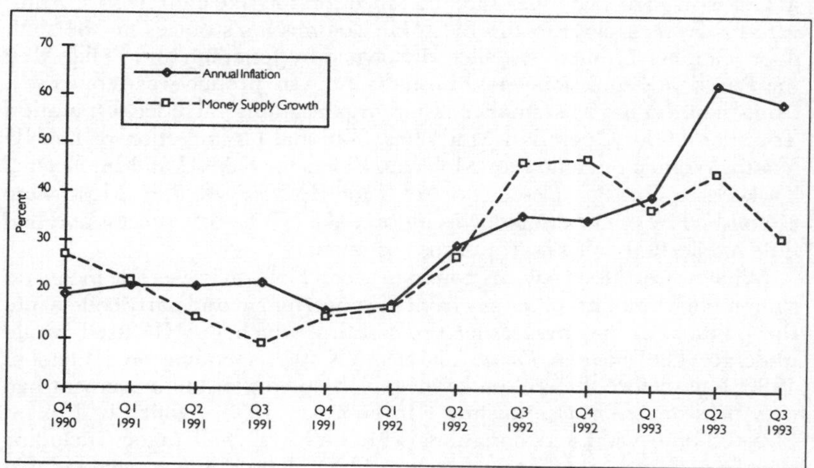

Figure 9.1 Money Supply and Inflation

was technically, therefore, not legal tender. These notes were dated 14 October 1991 and 2 January 1992 – the dubious 500 shilling notes were known by some in Nairobi as 'Jirongos' in honour of their prime beneficiary.

YK '92 and the Moi Fan Clubs

One of the most extraordinary aspects of the election campaign was the vital role played by pressure groups for KANU, in influencing candidate selection, organising the campaign and distributing the campaign funds. The strongest of these organisations, Youth for KANU '92 (YK '92), became one of the crucial campaigning organs for the ruling party, and was imitated by numerous less important groups. YK '92 was launched officially by Vice-President Saitoti on 7 March 1992 as a campaign organisation of young professionals eager to ensure that KANU won the coming general election. It was treated with great suspicion, however, by the opposition. Masinde Muliro, for example, denounced it as a KANU hit squad, trained to murder opposition leaders.

Its Chairman, Cyrus Shakhalaga Jirongo, a Luhya from Tiriki in Vihiga District, was a little known figure prior to his sudden emergence as YK '92 head. He was educated at Mangu High School and is believed thereafter to have served in the Ministry of Lands and Settlement. According to Nairobi gossip, he provided Biwott with information about the release of lucrative plots of land. Later, he had set up in business, without great success, until entering into business deals with the Moi family in the late 1980s. Henceforth, his fortunes prospered.[50] According to sources, Jirongo and an associate (possibly Ben Wakhungu, the founder secretary of YK '92) came up with the idea of establishing a youth campaign organisation for KANU. President Moi agreed to finance it directly, in order to serve the interests of KANU headquarters and the President. YK '92 had its offices in Cyrus Jirongo's Cippher Limited offices on the sixteenth floor of Anniversary Towers, close to the Electoral Commission's offices on the sixth floor. Cippher Limited was allegedly owned by Jonathan and Philip Moi, the President's sons, for whose business interests Jirongo was reputedly a front-man.[51] YK '92's smaller sister organisations included Operation Toroitich 2000, Operation Moi Wins, National Organisation of KANU Youth, Women in Action for Moi, Luo Elders for KANU and Intellectual Task-Force for the Re-election of Moi (INTAFORM).[52] Most were established by political unknowns in the wake of YK '92's success and had little intellectual coherence, purpose or impact.

What were these new organisations for? First, they were a means to siphon huge amounts of money from the government and party coffers into the political arena, by-passing the scrutiny which KANU itself would undergo. The *Economic Review* analysed YK '92's spending on 5 October 1992, long before the real outlay began. It noted that the movement had only held one *Harambee* meeting – in February 1992 – which had raised Sh2,400,000, yet listed donations which YK '92 had made, including specific donations amounting to at least Sh5 million.[53] Some suggested that large sums had been secretly contributed by wealthy politicians and power

Photo 9.1 YK'92 leader, Cyrus Jirongo
Courtesy Nation Group Newspapers

brokers. Njenga Mungai, for example, alleged that exiled businessman Ketan Somaia was secretly funding the group. As the spending grew, however, it became clear that only the government could be providing the funds. The *Weekly Express* claimed that YK '92 had a budget of Sh3 billion, 'mainly looted from parastatals such as the NSSF and Kenya National Assurance Company'.[54]

Second, YK '92 provided an alternative device by which Moi and a few influential KANU leaders could influence events in constituencies where they distrusted the local KANU machine. YK '92 was used during the primaries to clear out the old guard and create a new KANU, more acceptable to the masses. Its campaign was personalised around Moi, far more so than KANU's, and the organisation was distrusted by many District KANU bosses, whose power it threatened. Public attacks by party leaders on the group occurred during the campaign in Nakuru, Nandi, Bomet, Busia, Mombasa, Embu and West Pokot. KANU Branch Chairman Geoffrey Asanyo in Nakuru, for example, called for the dissolution of the YK '92 District branch, while KANU's Busia branch shut down the YK '92 District office in September because 'they would not allow the Youth for KANU '92 to open offices there unless KANU leaders were involved'.[55]

Third, YK '92 was an effective public relations exercise. It maintained a high profile in Nairobi, at a time when many politicians were absent campaigning. Supporters regularly held small, well-organised demonstrations around KANU headquarters and television coverage focused on these new young 'KANU leaders', who were highly articulate and less discredited than the hardliners such as Nassir, Mwangale and Ntimama. YK '92 also organised a number of supposedly politically neutral organisations and polling agencies, which claimed that President Moi and KANU would triumph.

YK '92 set up local campaigning groups in most Districts in the country, and by the end of September 1992 claimed to have nearly 1,000,000 members.[56] Some were alleged by the opposition to be strong-arm youth groups, organising behind-the-scenes violence, rather like the KANU youth wing in the 1960s. This claim was even made by retiring Minister for Health Jeremiah Nyagah, whose house was attacked several times by 'unknown persons'. Nyagah publicly expressed fear for his own safety and for the life of his son, the DP candidate for Gachoka.[57] He instructed the press to 'Go and tell the people that, if anything happens to Norman, myself, my family and close friends, then Operation Moi Wins and YK '92, who are politically causing confusion here, will be to blame.'[58] Many of the new organisations were also money-making ventures for those who had established them. The Embu YK '92 branch chairman, for example, complained that the national officials were 'squandering money and driving sleek cars, while deceiving President Moi that they were campaigning for him'.[59] Personal sources suggested that Joe Kimkung, a post-office clerk until he became National Chief Coordinator of YK '92, boasted of having purchased three houses at a cost of Sh3–4 million out of the proceeds of the organisation. During 1993, once they had outlived their use, and the organisation had been discredited, several key officials were to die suddenly, well before their time.

Many of the YK '92 national officials were Luhya (including the Chairman, founder secretary and national organising secretary) or Kalenjin (the vice-chairman, chief coordinator and director of operations, plus four or five executive committee members), though they had representatives from every major community. Whilst not political actors in their own right before the emergence of YK '92, they tended to have good links with senior KANU figures. Thus several of the Luhya had links to Elijah Mwangale. Founder secretary Ben Wakhungu was an advertising executive from Sirisia in Bungoma, who had also served on the committee of AFC Leopards, the football club favoured by Mwangale and other Luhya politicians. National organising secretary Rajab Walaula was also involved with Mwangale, and served as organising secretary of AFC Leopards. One of the founders, Joseph Murumba, was Elijah Mwangale's brother. National treasurer Sam Nyamweya, was a Kisii from Kitutu Chache and a supporter of Onyonka. Others were the actually relatives of prominent politicians. The national secretary, Munyua Waiyaki, was the nephew of FORD-Kenya's Dr Munyua Waiyaki. He was a close friend of Gideon Moi. The executive committee included Mweli Ngei, Paul Ngei's daughter, and there were several other committee members with names suspiciously similar to those of KANU politicians.

The enormous wealth and political importance of Jirongo and his team led to bitter internal bickering. This culminated in the firing of the vice-chairman and national treasurer on 12 November for involvement in the Baringo and Kisii KANU primaries. The reasons are unclear, but clearly they had run foul of powerful established politicians. One reason was that

YK '92 was involved in some form of conspiracy to groom 'a Luhya politician' to replace Vice-President Saitoti. The Vice-President fought back, attempting to oust Jirongo by an internal coup. He was backed by other prominent politicians, who feared that YK '92 leaders might use their money to destabilise their local parties. Whilst the majority of national officials supported Jirongo, many of the local branch leaders, particularly in the Kalenjin areas, were more hostile.

In certain districts, other bodies acted as the main campaign conduit for cash. The second most important group, 'Operation Moi Wins' was chaired by a Luo, Evans Ondieki. It was designed to stem the collapse of support for KANU in the Luo community, but in fact played a more prominent role in Eastern Province. Like YK '92, OMW had vast funds. Ondieki claimed that 'We are going to pour an amount of money you have never seen here before to ensure that President Moi is voted in again.'[60] He claimed that the group would spend Sh500,000 a week to ensure that the DP did not win Gachoka in Embu. The problems that KANU and President Moi faced in attempting to monitor the money allocated were highlighted when Ondieki and his travelling companions were robbed of Sh600,000 on 24 November.[61] The organisation distributed free food to hungry areas in Kitui, handed out money and made campaign promises on behalf of KANU, declaring, for example, that the ruling party would offer 20,000–30,000 jobs at the Coast to KANU supporters.[62]

The role of some KANU leaders was little different. Most KANU candidates received money either directly from President Moi, from party headquarters, or through YK '92. When Clement Gachanja replaced Njoroge Mungai as Nairobi KANU chairman, for example, he soon after purchased a Mercedes-Benz for cash, whilst KANU Secretary-General Kamotho was reported to be milking the system as much as possible, 'so that he does not have to go back to a kiosk after losing the elections'.[63] Arthur Magugu, the only Kiambu MP to remain loyal to the ruling party, was rumoured in Githunguri to have received Sh30 million to finance his campaign.

How KANU Spent the Money

Election campaigns cost huge amounts of money, even in developing countries. The expenditure required to produce election materials such as posters, flags, badges and handbills remains considerable. The cost of agents is high, and a major expense is the hire of vehicles to criss-cross the constituency campaigning, and to transport voters to rallies and to the polls, given the poor state of the roads and the large distances to be covered. KANU's Ministerial candidates were particularly well provided for in terms of vehicles. Many drove around in newly imported Mitsubishi Pajeros, which cost Sh3 million each. President Moi and Vice-President Saitoti also employed helicopters to move from rally to rally.[64] For ordinary Parliamentary candidates, campaign posters were generally provided by the parties. Estimates of the number of presidential posters printed range from 3,700,000 to 8,000,000, and the number of Parliamentary posters was roughly the same. T-shirts were another major campaign expenditure.

KANU and the DP both bought tens of thousands of T-shirts with the candidates' face and party colours on the front. Although advertising in the mass media is less costly than in the West, KANU purchased a plethora of advertisements in the press and produced sophisticated party political broadcasts on the two television networks, as well as financing an extensive poster campaign and distributing other goodies such as paper visors emblazoned with 'Stability and Progress', the ruling party's election slogan.

Even more money was used to bribe voters, opposition candidates and their supporters. Although bribery had become widespread since the 1974 election, for the first time the entire resources of the state were devoted to financing a campaign. Mombasa KANU chairman Sharrif Nassir admitted to one IRI election observer that KANU would spend Sh3,000 million on the election, and was planning to dispense half of it on polling day.[65] The *Nairobi Weekly Observer* estimated that President Moi directly and through proxies had given over Sh2,000 million (approximately £40 million) in donations to various causes between January and November 1992.[66] In Western Province, for example, Moi donated Sh800,000 for development projects in Vihiga District on 2 November, and Sh1 million to teachers' representatives from Kakamega on 26 November.[67] Ministers and Moi's men in the districts were used as conduits of money, much of it coming from the centre, some from their own pockets. Noah Wekesa in Trans-Nzoia, for example, gave Sh700,000 to teachers for Christmas, promising that they would be paid 'active allowances' if KANU won.[68]

In most constituencies candidates also directly 'bought' votes. KANU activists went house-to-house in Githunguri, for example, handing out up to 1,000 shillings. In Malava in Kakamega District they gave 20 shillings to every person with a voting card if they promised to vote for *Jogoo*.[69] At Saitoti's Ngong rally on nomination day, a witness to the 'money van' claimed that up to 1000 shillings was being given to each KANU supporter; and Amin Walji was seen several times dispensing bundles of 50 shilling notes from a large cash box in his vehicle to house servants in Westlands constituency.[70] In Mbooni up to election eve, KANU's candidate Johnstone Makau, who became a Minister in the new government, was handing out 20–50 shilling notes to voters. President Moi personally 'treated' the Presiding Officers from the Nyakach and Kisumu Town seats at State House when he visited Kisumu.[71]

Allegedly parastatal loans were also used for political purposes. The *Nairobi Weekly Observer* claimed that the government's Rural Enterprise Programme provided loans to voters on condition that they voted for KANU. The Agricultural Finance Corporation, a parastatal bank specialising in easy credit loans to farmers, also held huge unsecured loans in the build-up to the election, with the expectation amongst some that the loans would afterwards be written off.[72]

KANU also abused the distribution of relief food to persuade voters to support the ruling party, either by reporting that the food was donated by KANU, by distributing food at party meetings, or by only giving relief food to KANU members. In June 1992, the state had relaxed restrictions on maize movements, allowing the movement of up to 88 bags without a permit. Once the election date had been decided upon, however, President

Moi on 30 October banned all unlicensed movements of maize, to widespread protests.[73] It was reported that in Machakos, Kitui, Embu, Makuyu in Murang'a, Turkana and North-Eastern Province, local KANU officials only distributed food to KANU supporters.[74] Turkana DP activists protested that chiefs were under instruction not to feed DP supporters.[75] On 15 September KANU's Machakos branch organising secretary Francis Wambua reportedly declared that only KANU members would benefit from food relief to the area, and told chiefs to ensure that the distribution of relief food was done according to KANU membership registers,[76] while in Samburu, 'Government officials, for example, chiefs and assistant chiefs, used famine relief foodstuffs to influence people to vote for KANU candidates only....'[77] In Machakos Town donor relief aid was distributed by KANU with the statement that it was provided by the party, while in Embu District, 'KANU ... used the provincial administration to distribute finger millet (*wimbi*) and maize, not to mention money in all three constituencies.'[78] On 28 December, 500 bags of maize were brought to Kibwezi by the KANU Parliamentary candidate as a Christmas gift from Moi.[79] This appears to have been an effective tactic in some marginal areas.

The Opposition's Finances

None of the opposition parties could match KANU's financial resources. The DP was KANU's wealthiest competitor, funded by large contributions from Kikuyu big business, including such people as the chairman of East African Industries, Joe Wanjui. Wealthy businessmen gave sums of up to Sh50,000 to the party. Most DP candidates, however, were expected to finance their own campaigns, while DP headquarters expended its resources on Kibaki's Presidential campaign and a lavish press and television campaign. As a result, DP advertisements in the *Daily Nation* and *Standard* almost equalled KANU's in number, size and quality. It is possible that the party could have spent its resources more effectively by supporting local candidates rather than focusing so much on Kibaki's Presidential bid. On the other hand, the Presidential contest attracted widespread attention, and wealthy candidates who funded their own campaigns, such as Karume, Muigai and Muhoho, all lost to less well-known and poorer FORD-Asili opponents.

FORD-Asili was founded on Kenneth Matiba's own vast personal wealth. Asili also solicited and received contributions from the Kikuyu business community, which although primarily pro-DP, hedged its bets by also giving money to FORD-Asili. One of Matiba's inner circle was the wealthy BAT (Kenya) Chairman B. M. Gecaga, with close ties to the Kenyatta family. Wealthy candidates, such as John Michuki and Dr Josephat Karanja, financed much of their own campaigns, but even they had resort to the Asili coffers for loans. Matiba personally funded FORD-Asili's grassroots local government, Parliamentary and Presidential nominations at a cost of Sh22 million.[80] Party headquarters (i.e. Matiba) also met the cost of posters for all Parliamentary and local government candidates, estimated at Sh50 million. In these posters Matiba's face appeared prominently, with that of his candidate smaller alongside. Kwendo Opanga of the *Daily Nation* reported that one Presidential candidate (believed to be Matiba) had hired 200 vehicles in December. Matiba also promised money, vehicles, and support to his favoured candidates, and in certain areas (such as Central Province) delivered it. FORD-Asili provided four-wheeled drive vehicles (Pajeros) to its 30 main candidates at a cost of Sh54 million (US$1,800,000). In some cases, however, such as Githunguri, where FORD-Asili's candidate was a wealthy man, the money appears to have been a loan rather than a gift. After the election, Matiba pressed Dr Karanja to refund him large sums, forcing the former Vice-President to sell two large farms to pay his debt in March–April 1993.

FORD-Kenya was financially the weakest of the main parties. Odinga, although a millionaire, was far poorer than the three other major party leaders, while his main associates were middle-class professionals who, although well-off by Kenyan standards, did not command vast resources. The party received much unpaid support from well-wishers, and fervent support from the smaller weekly and monthly political magazines, but nationally its campaign was severely hampered by its relative poverty. A few individual benefactors gave large contributions to the central party, but in the main candidates funded their own campaigns. According to FORD-Kenya's Secretariat, most of its candidates personally received nothing from the central funds, which were concentrated on key marginal seats. Minor candidates such as those in Kwale received little more than 1,000 shillings to hire a car for a short time. All the production of posters was handled centrally, but Parliamentary and local government candidates had to reimburse party headquarters for the cost of the printing. Given its meagre resources, FORD-Kenya could afford little in the way of television or press advertising, and it was appealing for money to fund its campaign right up until election day.[81]

The confidential FORD-Kenya 1992 election accounts, made available by ex-party officials, provide insights into the way in which the money for the elections was raised and spent. They cover only the money raised centrally, not the sums handled directly by local branches. Although it is known that some additional money was raised and disbursed directly by party leaders without passing through the accounts, they clearly demonstrate that the central party had little money to spend. Its funds were obtained from two sources. The first was deposits for nominations from candidates wishing to contest seats on the party ticket. Local government aspirants had to pay 4,000 shillings, and Parliamentary contenders 7,000 shillings. But as the accounts noted, 'However, the party was not able to enforce this requirement uniformly as candidates from poorer parts of the country could not raise the cash and had to be exempted.'[82] Only Sh3.1 million was raised in this way. The other 80 per cent, over Sh14 million, came from a few large donations from anonymous well-wishers. Of the approximately Sh17 million (US$600,000) available for the election, FORD-Kenya spent Sh5,500,000 on publicity, and Sh4,500,000 on rallies and the party nominations. It disbursed directly to individuals for campaigning and organisation costs under Sh7,500,000 – less than KANU spent in some individual constituencies. The greater part was disbursed in numerous small donations to parliamentary candidates and coordinators of between Sh1,000 and Sh30,000. The party targeted its central party spending in ways that bore little relationship to its chances of victory (see Table 9.1). The largest spending was in North-Eastern Province and the Rift Valley, where FORD-Kenya won only one and two seats respectively; compared with Nyanza, which had the third lowest regional expenditure, where they won 20. The reason for this strange distribution was that the major part of the funds went to those candidates and seats where FORD-Kenya were not well-established and, therefore, did not have party branches with established memberships and incomes. The Nyanza figures show that almost every shilling spent there went not to the areas which the party would win – the Luo areas – but to the Gusii marginals. The Luo areas had sufficient members to provide their own financial support. Furthermore, FORD-Kenya needed little money in Luo constituencies since it was clearly going to win them. As with KANU, a large proportion of the money was spent on election eve, to hire vehicles to transport voters to the polls. In Western Province, Sh490,000 out of Sh760,000 disbursed (64 per cent) was spent this way.

Table 9.1 Direct FORD-Kenya Campaign Expenditure, 1992

Province	Direct contributions to candidates (Sh)	Number of seats	Spending/ seat (Sh)
Nairobi	436,040	8	54,505
Central	483,300	25	19,332
Eastern	1,266,305	32	39,572
North-Eastern	1,409,985	10	140,998
Coast	1,038,761	20	51,938
Rift Valley	1,507,930	44	34,271
Western	763,060	20	38,153
Nyanza	500,188	29	17,248
Total	7,405,569	188	39,391

Source: FORD-Kenya accounts

Nationally, FORD-Kenya spent least for most benefit in the Bukusu areas of Bungoma and the Luo constituencies of Nyanza Province. There were a few seats where party headquarters, according to its accounts, did not spent a single shilling. In some seats, the 'return on investment' could have been improved by better support. An example was Francis Nyukuri in Lugari, who secured 1,121 votes for only 5,000 shillings spent. FORD-Kenya, however, sometimes wasted the limited resources it had. Money was given to candidates like Andrew Mulamba in Malava who received Sh20,000 on 19 November but defected to KANU two weeks later, and Abdi Mahat in Ijara who received Sh102,000 before defecting to KANU during the campaign. There were also some seats where individuals received large sums of money but secured almost no votes. Party headquarters wasted over Sh100,000 each on donations to Dr Hezron Induko in Shikuku's Butere and Oyangi Mbaja in Vihiga, 'prestige' competitions where FORD-Kenya never had a chance of victory. Candidates like Dr Sirat Osman Warfa, who polled only 320 voters in Wajir South despite receiving Sh336,000 from FORD-Kenya headquarters, were clearly misleading party officials about their prospects.

Considerable money was spent on travelling to North-Eastern Province, because of the need to hire aircraft. Four air charters to Garissa during December cost Sh161,000. The production of posters, caps, flags and other paraphernalia was also paid for in part by central party funds. The party centrally distributed 2,000 posters for 126 Parliamentary candidates; half a million posters of the *Jaramogi*; posters for 1,000 local government candidates; 10,000 flags; and 50,000 posters which showed FORD-Kenya's *simba* (lion) victorious over KANU's *jogoo* (cockerel). The total cost was Sh1,514,500, but Agip House also paid separately for visors, banners, more flags, T-shirts and, of course, poster distribution.

KANU was not the only party to hand out money in direct bribes. Matiba donated large sums to support his candidates and as bribes to voters. Even in Machakos Town, for example, an area where Asili stood little chance of winning, its Parliamentary candidate gave 20 shilling notes to people at Kaloleni market on election eve.[83] Matiba also went to great expense to 'treat' the voters during his travels, especially in the Kikuyu areas. For example, in his tour through Nakuru District at the end of November, which doomed the DP in the district, his supporters handed out money and bought beer for everyone in the area. The DP and Asili also handed out money on election day, with reports of election day bribery by the DP coming from Kisumu Town and Mutito, and by FORD-Asili in Githunguri, Malava and Kuria.[84]

The Media

In any national election, the news media are a key source of information for voters and, therefore, a key electoral weapon for those who control them. For many years, the Kenyan print and broadcast media had been controlled by the government.[85] In the 1980s, press freedom to criticise the government had vanished, but flourished again with far greater independence than ever before after the introduction of multi-party politics. In 1992 a number of magazines emerged which were relatively unconstrained, and reflected a variety of political lines, generally hostile to the government. Coverage of the elections in the print media was extensive, although uneven in quality.[86] In contrast, the broadcast media remained state-controlled and partisan.

The most important medium for communicating electoral issues and events was the daily newspapers. Kenya has three national daily English-language newspapers: the *Standard* (owned by Lonrho), the *Daily Nation* (owned by a consortium in which the Aga Khan is the major shareholder) and the *Kenya Times* (owned by the Kenya Times Media Trust, a consortium originally including Robert Maxwell and KANU). The *Kenya Times* was the mouthpiece of the ruling party. The smallest of the three in sales, its coverage was unashamedly partisan. While the *Standard* and the

Daily Nation provided detailed reports of opposition rallies and were critical of the failure of the police and Provincial Administration to prevent the ethnic clashes, the *Kenya Times* and its Swahili sister devoted virtually no space to opposition activities, except to emphasise ethnic rivalries among the FORD leadership, and blamed multi-party democracy for the clashes.

The *Daily* and *Sunday Nation*, produced by the Nation Group, were by far the most successful and profitable papers, with a circulation of approximately 188,000 and a readership many times that figure.[87] In 1992, the Nation Group became the voice of the anti-government forces. Widely attacked by the government for being dominated by Kikuyu, the *Daily Nation* was the closest paper to being 'impartial', reporting evenly on government and opposition activities, but also trying to unearth scandals involving government members. Its most famous coup was its revelations concerning the sales of land by Jirongo's companies to the NSSF. This exposé was treated as an open declaration of war by the government, and henceforth relations became extremely strained. KANU organised paper vendors to burn copies of the paper in alleged protests at low commission rates.[88] *Daily Nation* reporters were assaulted several times during the election campaign in KANU zones. On 22 November, for example, three Nation Group employees were attacked at Kabarnet Hotel by YK '92 supporters, who stole their money and beat them, and on 5 December 'Kanu warriors' issued death threats against the paper's Nandi correspondent.[89] The *Kenya Times* took up the KANU cause and led a vicious press battle against the *Daily Nation,* accusing it of Kikuyu chauvinism, to which the paper responded in kind.

Even the *Daily Nation,* however, had its limits. Senior staff revealed that the Managing Editor's family had been threatened and his home invaded by YK '92 after the NSSF revelations, and that he had been warned that 'he would suffer' if there were any more reports about Jirongo. It was also reported that on 3 or 4 December 1992, a booklet was distributed in Nairobi by KANU representatives making a number of allegations about the Managing Editor's personal life in another effort to force the *Daily Nation* to toe the line. It is also known that certain stories went to the top of the paper for approval, but were never authorised for release. One particularly interesting example concerned President Moi's personal life. Although legal, there was a general consensus that it was extremely unwise to raise the issue of the churchgoing Moi's private behaviour. On Friday, 11 December, however, Matiba made a speech in Nyandarua District in which he directly attacked President Moi's treatment of his wife Lena, emphasising the contradiction between the president's public espousal of family values and his alleged affairs with the wives of the political élite, television personalities and others.[90] All references in the *Daily Nation* to Matiba's attack were explicitly deleted on instructions from the Chief Executive against the protests of the Managing Editor.[91]

The *Standard,* with approximately 75,000 daily sales, generally favoured KANU. Its editorials defended Moi against allegations of corruption and mismanagement, and the NCWK's election report quoted *Standard* journalists who complained that critiques of KANU were not printed.[92] The *Standard's* coverage of the election fluctuated as journalists, editors and the proprietor Tiny Rowland struggled to control the newspaper's political line. Journalists reported that Rowland periodically reined in the editorial board, requiring them to adopt a less critical attitude towards KANU, while they wanted the paper to follow the *Daily Nation's* example. Although the *Standard* did not produce any big exposés, it maintained a reasonably fair coverage of the opposition.

The most vibrant news sector was the weekly news magazines. The oldest, and once the pride of East Africa's press, was the *Weekly Review.* Long Kenya's only political weekly, its editorial independence had come under suspicion long before the election. Hilary Ng'weno, the Managing Editor, had very good relations with a number of KANU figures. The resignation of Sarah Elderkin, the co-founder of the magazine and senior editor since 1975, to become a party worker for Ford-Kenya during 1992, reinforced this shift in direction. Whilst the *Weekly Review* still provided well-written and timely news reports, it clearly supported KANU.

On the other side of the spectrum lay several rabidly anti-government magazines, which sprang up in or had been liberated by the multi-party era. Almost all were associated with Ford-Kenya's Young Turks. The main ones had been important gadflies in 1991 – the *Nairobi Law Monthly,* Gitobu Imanyara's magazine, which had led the fight for multi-party democracy in 1990; Njehu Gatabaki's *Finance* and Pius Nyamora's *Society.* There was also the *Nairobi Weekly Observer,* which was founded in late 1992 by the Managing Editor of *Society,* Blamwel Njururi. These fringe weeklies were extremely popular in Nairobi among the educated élite, but had little circulation in the rest of the country. They were expensive by Kenyan standards, costing roughly 40 shillings per copy.

These publications pushed the state's tolerance to the limit, constrained less by libel laws that by the threat of retribution. KANU leaders, unused to criticism, reacted aggressively, and the journals experienced serious police harassment. The Office of the President directed that no public or private institutions should advertise in *Finance, Society* or the *Nairobi Law Monthly,* as they were anti-government. Within two weeks of the registration of the first opposition parties, the police impounded 30,000 copies of *Society's* 13 January 1992 issue and obtained a court injunction restraining the publishers from selling it. Two months later, another 10,000 copies of the magazine were seized.[93] Then, on 16 April, the police raided *Society's,* offices, arrested Pius Nyamora and other editors and senior writers, and eventually charged five of them with sedition.[94] In May 1992, 19,000 copies of *Finance's* 31 May 1992 issue, headlined 'The Molo massacre: Moi is the Villain', were seized. In July, 10,000 copies of *Society* were again impounded. Police Chief Kilonzo claimed that the issue contained articles aimed at creating disaffection between the governments of Kenya and Somalia.[95] At the end of the month *Finance* editor Njehu Gatabaki was arrested in Nairobi: he and his wife were charged with failing to supply annual returns to the Registrar of Societies, and held in custody despite being granted bail. On 3 August, Gatabaki was also charged with sedition.[96] Ten days later, police arrested *Jitegemea's* editor Jamlick Miano and the magazine's treasurer for the July cover story, headlined, 'Moi killed democracy', and charged them with sedition.[97] There followed a brief lull, until the seizure of copies of the 5 November issue of *Finance* from its publishers.[98] The next day, the police seized another 50,500 copies of its 15 November 1992, issue, with the headline 'Impeach Moi', plus artwork and plates from the printers.[99] On 4 December, just before nomination day, the editor of the *Nairobi Weekly Observer* was arrested and charged with sedition for articles in the 20 November 1992 issue titled 'Moi's Blood Money',[100] and on nomination day itself 30,000 copies of *Finance's* 9 December issue, with the cover story 'Chaos', were seized from publishers Fotoform, although the CID and police subsequently denied they had done so.[101]

This sustained harassment led to several protests by the American government and prominent individuals from Britain, the United States, and elsewhere, although they had little effect.[102] At the same time, there were claims that some of these magazines were funded by the Americans, although no evidence was ever produced. Certainly, the magazines did not survive on their advertising revenue, since in fear of the government almost no one risked advertising in *Society* or *Finance.* Paradoxically, the one major advertiser to break the ban was KANU, which placed large advertisements in *Society* on the eve of the election.[103]

Thus 1992 was a period of flowering for the independent media, and both newspapers and magazines profited greatly from extensive advertising by the political parties during the campaign. The independent press was harassed severely, however, and the two national newspapers clearly practised self-censorship. The legacy of many years of state control and repression was not lifted overnight and, as the Commonwealth observers later pointed out, the print media sensationalised the election, always stressing violence and conflict.[104] Less attention was paid to the causes of violence and especially the clashes, discussion of which was effectively forbidden.[105]

Political coverage was far less satisfactory in the broadcast media. The opposition protested that throughout the year it was denied the right to advertise on radio and television, and complained that the broadcast media's reporting was biased and opposition activities ignored. There was considerable truth in all these allegations. The state-owned Kenya Broadcasting Corporation was the sole broadcaster on television or radio until 1991, when the Kenya Television Network was permitted to set up a second, independent (though partly government-owned) television channel. The KBC was a statutory corporation, whose purpose was to provide 'independent and impartial broadcasts' funded from public coffers. In the words of the Commonwealth report, the KBC had always 'devoted its news coverage to chronicling the comings and going of the President, his Ministers and various government functionaries'.[106] In 1992 this bias continued. The KBC devoted little time to FORD and the DP, while covering the President's journeys and speeches in considerable detail. The most blatant example of the KBC's partisanship took place in January, when the parastatal's radio and television channels totally ignored FORD's first historic rally in Nairobi. During the campaign, the KBC reported only defections to, not from, KANU, and gave prominence to YK '92. The KBC Chairman Julius Kiano, formerly a long-serving Cabinet Minister, was also the Murang'a KANU chairman. The KBC's partisan support of KANU did less damage than might be expected, however, since its television programmes were of such low quality that most viewers preferred to watch the rival commercial Kenya Television Network. KTN, by contrast, gave full coverage to opposition meetings and speeches – but was only available in the Nairobi area and reached only a tiny minority of the electorate.

Television had a limited impact on voters. With only about 0.5 per cent of Kenyans owning a set (mainly in Nairobi), few people were influenced in this way. The state-controlled radio, broadcasting in English, Swahili and several vernacular languages, was more influential and even more biased. Most homes had a radio, even in the rural areas, and this, along with the major newspapers, was the main means by which information was conveyed to isolated rural areas. KBC radio was consistently pro-KANU, with interminable songs in praise of Moi and a virtual blackout on opposition activities. The opposition parties had difficulty even securing paid radio advertising. On 21 October, FORD-Asili leaders publicly protested that the KBC had turned down their radio advertisements to announce the collection of nomination forms,[107] and the DP submitted eight alternative transcripts for radio advertisements, all of which were rejected by KBC 'as they do not meet KBC editorial standards'.[108] The NCWK produced several television commercials and radio scripts, attacking vote-buying and corruption in elections. The KBC refused to accept any of them.[109]

It was only in the campaign proper that any effort was made to redress the imbalance. On 14 October, Odinga initiated a lawsuit seeking to compel KBC to give equal air time to all parties. This suit was rejected as technically defective, but the issue was taken up by Commonwealth Secretary-General Anyaoku on his mid-November visit. As a result, Minister for Information and Broadcasting Burudi Nabwera announced on 24 November that equal coverage would be given on both radio and television. He promised that the KBC would allow all presidential candidates 90 seconds per day 'paid up' advertising on television and radio, plus live coverage, where possible, of their rallies.[110] Nevertheless, little changed. The DP did manage to advertise extensively on television in the last few weeks of the campaign, but even then, its commercial on KTN, shown on 10 December, was removed by the independent channel without explanation and never broadcast again.[111]

Professionals' Committee for Democratic Change (PCDC) established a monitoring unit to analyse the news broadcasts by the KBC in order to investigate their partiality. Their initial verdict was negative, and in October they too threatened to take the KBC to court, stating that KANU received far too much time, and that the KBC only reported favourable stories about KANU and unfavourable news about the opposition, and did not discriminate between Moi as head of state and party leader.[112] Throughout October 1992, the KBC carried no reports of any kind on either radio or television about the activities of any opposition party.[113] The final PCDC report covered the period from late October to just before the election. On KBC television, KANU received half the allotted news time, while the three opposition parties got only 1.5 to 5 per cent each. On radio, KANU received six times the airtime of the opposition parties combined. President Moi was invariably portrayed as a 'great leader', and KANU as 'the party of national unity', while the opposition leaders were tribal and trivial.[114] On KTN, by contrast, KANU received only slightly more than the others combined. Both news media were biased, but the KBC was far more so.

KANU's domination of the broadcast media, particularly the radio, was crucial. There was a vast difference between the extent to which urban and isolated rural voters were informed about political events, and KANU's victory depended upon the government being able to maintain its strict control in the less developed districts. The Electoral Commission and government never issued media guidelines, as any form of equality in radio coverage would have harmed KANU's campaign.

Party Advertising in the Media

For the first time in Kenyan history, political parties advertised extensively in the press and on television in the run-up to the elections. Unlike many other countries, Kenya did not provide free airtime for political parties, nor, indeed, was there any form of state funding or limits on donations by individuals. Thus, money played a key role. The cost of these advertisements was enormous. Full-page advertisements in the *Daily Nation* – KANU and DP advertisements sometimes ran to three pages – cost Sh40,000 on normal days and Sh60,000 on Friday. Kwendo Opanga of the *Daily Nation* provided a summary of party expenditure on advertising during December in the *Daily/Sunday Nation* and its Swahili counterpart, *Taifa Leo* (see Table 9.2). KANU had roughly a 2:1 advantage over the DP, which itself had a similar advantage over FORD-Asili, whilst FORD-Kenya was the poorest party, with an advertising outlay only one tenth that of KANU's. The true figures were probably even more diverse, since the *Daily/Sunday Nation* was the opposition's closest friend in the news media. KANU made full use of its financial advantage, festooning all three major papers, the radio and television with advertisements. Opanga calculated that overall KANU must have spent Sh10 million on press advertising in December, excluding statements by pro-KANU groups of 'concerned parents', University Lecturers for Moi, YK '92 and others.

KANU's advertisements were extremely professional and reinforced their verbal campaign – warning of the risks of coups and instability, extolling the developments in Kenya since Independence, and endorsing

Table 9.2 Political Advertising Spending in the *Daily/Sunday Nation* During December 1992

Party	*D/S Nation* (Sh)	Taifa (Sh)
KANU	2,120,678	1,504,184
DP	1,103,191	367,868
FORD-Asili	511,140	25,920
FORD-Kenya	221,070	88,465

Source: Sunday Nation, 10 January 1993, 'Lifestyle', p. 4.
These figures excluded VAT and commission charges.

Moi the leader. The ruling party's full-scale press campaign began on 8 December with the 'Stability' series. Each followed a standard layout, beginning with 'Stability is Kenya's most precious possession'. The second, beginning on 12 December, stated that 'Stability means our mothers can provide good homes.' The third emphasised Moi's personal qualities, while the fourth gave various education statistics. KANU also ran a series of 'Progress Reports', advertisements containing economic statistics on development since Independence, covering industry, agriculture and living standards. These statistics made impressive reading, suggesting that as KANU had governed the country since Independence, it could take full credit for the country's development. The figures would have looked rather different, however, if they had been based on 1978, when Moi acceded to power, instead of 1963. Coverage built up to a crescendo on 28 December, when nearly six pages of the *Kenya Times* were devoted to KANU advertising, including a two-page appeal that 'On December 29th ... you have only one choice'; a half page on 'Landslide victory predicted for KANU'; a full page on 'Why Kenyans should vote for KANU' by 'parents'; a full-page 'Call to all religious communities to vote for Moi by Narok Maasai politicians'; a small advertisement to 'vote for *Jogoo*'; and a full-page 'Spot the Difference'. This last advertisement, which began on 22 December 1992, was particularly interesting as it attempted to make a virtue out of KANU's rigging of the Parliamentary nominations, emphasising that KANU was the only party with candidates in every constituency.

The opposition's advertisements challenged KANU directly on both economics and social stability. The DP used excerpts from its manifesto, flanked by full page photos of declining infrastructure and the dead bodies of people murdered during the ethnic clashes, to make its point that 'The country has been misgoverned and taken to the very edge of collapse.' Its advertisements claimed that 'Our economy is in ruins, our public service demoralised, our faith in politicians largely destroyed, our institutions have been vandalised and our people divided.' The DP's slogan was *Kura kwa DP ni kura kwa Kenya* ('A vote for the DP is a vote for Kenya'). The party produced a number of high-quality television advertisements, the most effective of which started in absolute darkness, gradually turned into a lamp – the DP's symbol – which illuminated the screen, and then changed into Mwai Kibaki's smiling face, while an authoritative voice outlined the reasons for supporting the DP.

FORD-Kenya's press, radio and television advertising was limited by its lack of funds. The DP as the party of Kikuyu big business and the old Kenyatta establishment, and FORD-Asili with access to Kenneth Matiba's personal fortune as well as to some funds from the Kikuyu business world, were both much better financed. As a result, FORD-Kenya was compelled to focus its expenditure on the immediate pre-election period, when KANU and the DP had already spent vast sums. In total, FORD-Kenya spent Sh660,419 (US$22,000) on the national media in the Christmas period. Roughly half of this was devoted to the press. Of the remainder, more was spent on television than radio, a rather surprising allocation.[115] FORD-Kenya funded 14 television advertising spots in the period 25–28 December, advertising twice a day on both KBC and KTN, culminating with four KBC advertisements on election eve. They began with a segment from Odinga's famous 1958 interview in which he praised Jomo Kenyatta as an 'honourable man' and acknowledged his leadership of the nationalist movement. Having thus courted the Kikuyu vote, the film then cut to the present, pointing out that Odinga had stood by his principles and defended the interests of the 'ordinary man for over thirty years'. The advertisement finished with close-ups of FORD-Kenya's younger leaders, emphasising that they were a team of well-educated young professionals from many ethnic groups who would work with Odinga to help him lead the country. Concluding with Robert Shaw, the European Kenyan businessman who played a prominent backroom role in FORD-Kenya's campaign, and a picture of a roaring lion, viewers were urged to 'vote FORD-Kenya, vote *Simba*'. Many commentators judged it the most effective television spot of the campaign. But although the spot may have worked for FORD-Kenya in Nairobi, it used up funds which might have been better spent elsewhere. By contrast, Matiba ran no television advertisements for FORD-Asili, spending the money more effectively on supporting constituency-level campaigns. FORD-Kenya's radio advertising was also concentrated on 25–28 December, with the KBC's National Service sending out five spots per day, and the General Service three. These cost less, but reached a much wider audience.

FORD-Kenya's press advertisements started on 19 December, twelve days after KANU and the DP. Most appeared in the two Nation Group newspapers. Like the other parties, FORD-Kenya placed two or three advertisements a day, culminating with a full-page advertisement on election eve which alone cost Sh82,000. It also funded an advert for the IPK, to bolster support amongst Moslem voters at the Coast. In all, FORD-Kenya's spent over Sh300,000, half its advertising budget, on newspaper advertising.

Overall, the press, radio and television campaigns of the various parties were both expensive and professional. Television was of little significance, and radio strictly controlled, so much of the conflict was fought out in the print media, where KANU's financial advantage was still clear but the opposition far stronger. How much of this money was well-spent remains moot, since the DP, which ran second in spending, was to perform far less well than expected, and the pattern of support amongst the different parties remained wholly regional, despite the national press advertising.

Opinion Polls and Predictions

1992 saw the first serious attempts to poll Kenyans on their political preferences since 1966.[116] In 1979, the *Weekly Review* had attempted a serious write-in poll, but its publication had so angered the government that it had temporarily cancelled all advertising in the magazine.[117] In the one-party state, KANU leaders had no desire for statistics on their popularity to be published by an objective outside body. Opinion polling, therefore, only really began once more when multi-party politics returned and has not yet managed to free itself in the public eye from the politicisation that affects every aspect of life in Kenya: most pollsters were believed to be partisan. This view was reinforced by the extremely biased write-in polls running throughout the year in news magazines, particularly *Society* and *Finance,* which respectively predicted massive wins for their favoured candidates, Odinga and Matiba.

There were six significant polls published during the election, two conducted by NEMU and four by KANU. The first serious poll was produced by NEMU and published in the *Daily Nation* on 7 December, 1992. This outraged all the parties by suggesting that Moi was the front-runner, and would receive 28.3 per cent of the vote, Kibaki 27.1 per cent, Matiba 15 per cent, and Odinga only 10.8 per cent.[118] A slightly higher percentage of people would have voted for KANU, the DP and FORD-Kenya as parties than for their Presidential candidates, while Matiba was more popular than his party – a suggestion which was to prove correct. The NEMU polls were bitterly criticised by almost everyone for showing a narrow lead for Moi. J. W. Onyango for example, in *Society,* dismissed the poll as statistically 'null and void.' He pointed out that the polls could not be, as had been claimed, statistically random, since to do this required access to the Registers, which were not yet available; that the sample size was unclear; that NEMU had not stated when the interviews had been conducted; and that the survey had to be biased because those who conducted it were politically partisan, favouring the DP.[119] In fact, most of these criticisms were unjustified. The study was carried out in secrecy, for fear of the staff involved being sacked, on the basis of the Rural Household Survey which had just been completed. In all, 812 households in 50 constituencies, drawn from 36 of the country's 47 Districts, had been questioned on political issues. The legitimate concerns were the small size of the sample; its ethnic unrepresentativeness (a key issue because of the ethnic pattern of voting); its neglect of North-Eastern Province; its rural bias; and the likelihood that the survey included a number of unregistered people. Nonetheless, the polls suggested that at this stage Moi and Kibaki were the two main contenders, with the others running slightly behind.[120] NEMU's second poll gave similar results.

KANU also served as the source of four polls. Constituency by constituency predictions were published by the *Weekly Review* of 25 December, which gave Moi 33 per cent of the Presidential vote, Kibaki 24 per cent, Matiba 21 per cent and Odinga 20 per cent. These figures were extraordinarily accurate, within 200,000 votes for the final figure for three of the candidates. They were accompanied by Parliamentary predictions which gave KANU only 77 certain victories, with 38 too close to call. They too predicted that the DP was running KANU second, with FORD-Asili well fourth in parliamentary seats. Its results are believed to have been based on an official KANU study (hence its reasonable accuracy). The Executive Club for Moi also carried out a poll on Christmas Eve, which accurately revealed the minority nature of KANU's support and yet its good chance of victory. On the basis of the polls, which are believed to have been officially commissioned by KANU, this group predicted a KANU victory by 103 seats, to 33 for Asili, 23 for FORD-Kenya and 19 for the DP, a distinctly different result, reflecting the last-minute swing in support away from the DP to Asili, but also KANU's interest in supporting

Table 9.3 Executive Club for Moi Polls[121]

Candidate	ECM poll (1)	ECM poll (2)	ECM poll (3)	*Weekly Review*	Actual figure
Moi	4,257,940	4.302,653	4,322,399	1,955,100	1,831,592
Matiba	1,141,097	1,171,966	1,175,498	1,242,900	1,439,076
Odinga	983,478	932,806	917,703	1,196,700	927,133
Kibaki	693,982	567,889	559,972	1,417,600	1,032,676

Note: Other figures negligible.

Matiba's bid for the Kikuyu vote.[122] The polls' Presidential predictions were far less accurate, accurately estimating the results for Matiba and Odinga, but grotesquely inflating Moi's result (more than doubling the final poll) and halving Kibaki's, again possibly with the intention of reinforcing the weakness of the DP and therefore the pointlessness of voting for Kibaki.

These attempts to poll the voting public revealed both the difficulties in Kenya of obtaining valid samples and the prevailing suspicion towards such polling amongst the political classes, who viewed them as either divination or party propaganda or both. Because all the parties had to be seen to be winning to have a chance of winning, there were no truly accurate non-political polls, and the sole attempt from NEMU was rejected out of hand by all participants.

Violence, Intimidation and Administrative Bias in the Campaign

Independent Kenya has never accepted the Westminster idea of administrative neutrality. Whatever the rhetoric, the Provincial Administration has been the arm of the government of the day. Civil servants work with and for politicians, and senior ones often become politicians. As Electoral Commissioner Habel Nyamu observed:

> Appointments, promotions, transfers, disciplinary actions and retirements often emanate from some powerful politicians whose concern for merit and/or professional qualification is as lacking as is their interference in civil service management and administration uncalled for.[123]

This partiality always threatened the introduction of true multi-party politics, with the state, as elsewhere in Africa, 'pretending that it can serve as both a referee of the game and as a player'.[124] Towards the end of the campaign, under pressure from the West, there was a loosening of restrictions, with statements by Moi and Permanent Secretary Kimalat, the head of the Provincial Administration, that the opposition should be treated fairly. Over much of the country, however, the playing field was far from level.

KANU supporters, aided by the Provincial Administration and the police, sustained a low-level campaign of violence against the opposition throughout the country. Although many incidents were minor affairs in which supporters of the opposition parties or members of minority ethnic groups were harassed in the traditional Kenyan manner, they formed a consistent pattern. Trouble was concentrated in marginal districts in the Rift Valley, such as Narok, Kajiado and Uasin Gishu. In KANU zones such as Baringo and Elgeyo-Marakwet, there were few reports of violence or intimidation because it was so pervasive that it was unwise even for the press to inquire too far into what was happening. The evidence suggests that much of the harassment of non-Kalenjin communities in KANU areas was organised centrally, a continuation of the threats made against them during the 1991 *Majimbo* rallies and the ethnic clashes of early 1992. In the opposition strongholds and the main urban areas, in contrast, KANU and the Administration could do little but slow their opponents' momentum. Elsewhere, harassment was more common. Chiefs called location *barazas* at the same time that opposition meetings were to take place; police cars trailed opposition candidates and recorded whom they met; and District Commissioners cancelled opposition meetings at the last moment or severely restricted the number of gatherings that they were permitted to hold. Opposition party members were also arrested and beaten up after clashes with KANU supporters. Local activists and candidates were stopped at roadblocks, summoned before security committees, and arrested or questioned for their remarks during campaign speeches. By contrast, the Administration and the police assisted KANU candidates, and KANU leaders and youth-wingers were given effective immunity from prosecution.

The Provincial Administration, in fact, played a key role in KANU's campaign, one far more important than those of YK '92 or the local party apparatus. Throughout the country, government officials, including most Provincial or District Commissioners and District Officers, consistently and publicly campaigned for the ruling party and harassed the opposition. Although President Moi publicly asked the Administration to be impartial, civil servants (a huge voting group of just under 300,000) were pressurised to support KANU. The President, himself, warned on 5 October that civil servants who sided with the opposition would be dismissed instantly.[125] Eastern Provincial Commissioner Antony Oyier stated in Embu that 'We are going to screen all the civil servants and those found to be anti-government will go.'[126] Western Provincial Commissioner Francis Lekolool and his Nyanza colleague Peter Kiilu warned local officials that civil servants must be 100 per cent loyal to the government of the day and that administrators sympathising with the opposition would be dismissed.[127] Laikipia District Commissioner Mohammoud Saleh informed civil servants in the district that 'You have to support KANU openly without hiding.'[128] The Baringo District Commissioner (a Kikuyu from Nyeri) was sacked in September when local KANU officials alleged that he had informed residents that famine relief had been provided by the DP. Several chiefs and other minor officials were also sacked for their opposition sympathies.

Although a few administrators appear to have remained neutral, the vast majority were pressed into service. As Tables 9.4 and 9.5 show, the PCs and DCs who were responsible for all aspects of the campaign process (bar the actual polling and count) were consistently biased, and many had in fact been involved in the rigged elections of 1988. Even the head of the

Table 9.4 Kenya's Provincial Commissioners, September–December 1992

Province	Provincial Commissioner	Background and pronouncements
Nairobi	Fred Waiganjo	Kikuyu. In 1988, he was responsible for the rigged Nairobi elections. Relatively neutral in 1992.
Central	Victor Musoga	He was Kiambu DC 1988, when the parliamentary and KANU elections were rigged to remove Ngengi Muigai and others. In 1992, he cancelled DP rallies.
Eastern	Antony Oyier	A Luo from South Nyanza. He was DC Kirinyaga 1988, and was accused of involvement in rigged elections. A bitter opponent of the Nyagahs in Embu during 1992. Threatened civil service on Moi day.
North-Eastern	Amos Bore	Nyanza PC in 1988 during rigged elections. In December 1992, he accused an opposition party of banditry.[129]
Coast	Mbuo Waganagwa	Siaya DC in 1988, during rigged election. Directed KANU's 1992 campaign on the Coast.
Rift Valley	Mohammed Yusuf Haji	Somali from Garissa. He was pro-KANU and critical of the opposition.
Western	Francis Lekolool	A Samburu. He was photographed with Ntimama wearing a KANU cap. He urged civil servants to support KANU on Kenyatta Day.[130]
Nyanza	Peter Kiilu	Demanded civil servants be 100 per cent loyal to the government of the day.

Source: Analysis of speeches and reports in press during 1992 and previous years. All the PCs remained in their posts throughout the election.

civil service, Cabinet Secretary Philip Mbithi, campaigned for KANU in his native Machakos, appearing with President Moi at rallies as evidence of the regime's good faith towards the Kamba. District Commissioners had fewer powers but greater operational responsibility than Provincial Commissioners and were even more vital to KANU's victory. Under the Public Order Act Cap. 56 of 1950, the police and Administration had wide powers of control over public gatherings, including some private gatherings. The District Commissioner could 'refuse permission if he is satisfied that the meeting is likely to prejudice the maintenance of public order, or to be used for any unlawful or immoral purposes'.[131] District Commissioners and the police, in practice, could delay meetings as long as they liked, cancel them without notice, and interrupt or end them if they deemed that the conditions of licence had been breached. This Act was widely employed to limit the opposition's freedom to campaign. Some DCs seem to have had instructions not to allow opposition parties to hold rallies on the same day

Table 9.5 Kenya's District Commissioners, September–December 1992

Province (District)	District Commissioner	Ethnic background and other information
Central		
Murang'a	David Mutemi throughout.	Kikuyu or Kisii (unclear). Participated in Murang'a KANU elections.[132]
Kiambu	Samuel Oreta throughout.	Luo. Refused licenses to DP and FORD-Kenya. Regularly cancelled meetings at last minute. Said the opposition leaders had nothing new to offer.[133]
Nyandarua	Ezekiel Machogu throughout.	Kisii. Instructed chiefs to support KANU on 11 November.[134] Denied opposition parties permits.
Nyeri	Charles Wa Nyoike (Nov. '92).	Kikuyu.
Kirinyaga	Francis Kibii Tiliteei throughout.	Kalenjin. DC Kakamega during invalid 1989 Malava by-election.
Eastern		
Embu	Mate (to early Dec. '92).	Embu. Continued to refuse clearance for opposition meetings.
	Muli Malombe (Dec. '92)	Malombe in office by 8 December.
Meru	Peter Saisi throughout.	Luhya. Machakos DC 1988, accused of rigging Kangundo elections, and replaced as Returning Officer.[135] In 1992, accused of campaigning for KANU on nomination day.[136]
Tharaka-Nithi	Joseph Mang'ira throughout.	Kuria.
Kitui	Peter Kipyegon Lagat (Oct. '92).	Kalenjin. Nephew of President Moi.[137]
Machakos	Wycliffe O. Ogallo. (Oct. '92)	Luo, replaced by Ogongo.
	Zachary Ogongo (Oct. '92).	Kisii.
Makueni	Peter Alubale (Nov. '92 onwards).	Luhya. Helped KANU candidate raise money. Attended a meeting of KANU aspirants at Tsavo Inn, Mtito Andei.[138]
Isiolo	Suleiman Toyya (Nov. '92 to mid-Dec. '92). Officially transferred. In practice never moved and returned to post in 1993.	Mijikenda. Accused of being involved in KANU nominations rigging.
Marsabit	Paul Olando (Nov. '92).	Luhya. According to the FORD-Asili district Coordinator, the DC called a meeting of the Burji community on the day before the election and instructed them to vote for Moi and KANU.[139]

Table 9.5 cont.

Province (District)	District Commissioner	Ethnic background and other information
North-Eastern		
Garissa	Francis Sigei (Dec. '92-'93).	Kalenjin.
Mandera	Eliud Parsankul until Dec. '92. Vacant onwards.	Maasai. Then vacant.
Wajir	Peter Raburu (Aug. '92).	Luo.
Coast		
Mombasa	John arap Ng'eno throughout.	Kalenjin. Mandera DC 1988.
Kilifi	Joseph B. Meng'ich throughout.	Kalenjin. Severely hindered opposition election campaign.[140]
Kwale	Ali Korane (Dec. '92).	Somali.
Taita-Taveta	Ng'ethe Mbugua (Oct. '92).	Kikuyu.
	Ndegwa (Dec. '92).	Kikuyu.
	Samuel Kipchumba arap Limo (Dec. '92).	Kalenjin. Limo was DC Trans-Nzoia 1988, during rigged election.
Lamu	John Sala (Dec. '92).	Luo. Narok DC 1988, when he favoured Ntimama.
Tana River	Peter Ndemo throughout.	Kisii. Accused by Odinga of being 'the most arrogant and notorious administrator' he had met. Barred all opposition meetings.
Rift Valley		
Nakuru	Ishmael Chelang'a throughout.	Kalenjin. Responsible for Nakuru during ethnic clashes.
Laikipia	Mohammoud Swaleh (Oct. '92).	Somali. 10 October, ordered civil servants to campaign openly for KANU.
Kajiado	Mutemi.	Kamba.
Narok	Calistus Akello throughout.	Luo. Attacked opposition leaders for spreading rumours.[141]
Baringo	Cyrus Kibera Maina. (Sept. '92)	Maina, a Nyeri Kikuyu, was denounced by Robert Kipkorir (Kerio) as a DP man and sacked soon after. Both *Kenya Times* reports incorrectly had Maina still in office. [142]
	Ibrahim Maalim Mahamud (Oct.-Dec. '92).	
Elgeyo-Marakwet	Wilson Chepkwony throughout.	Kalenjin. A long-time ally of Biwott.[143] Quiet.
Nandi	Francis Baya throughout.	Mijikenda. Quiet.

Table 9.5 cont.

Province (District)	District Commissioner	Ethnic background and other information
Kericho	Timothy Sirma until 15 December '92. Then Suleiman Toyya (did not take up post).	Sirma, a Kalenjin was the 1988 Kericho DC during rigged elections. He was accused of involvement in the ethnic clashes and instructed police to arrest anyone spreading malicious rumours against the government.[144] Demanded that those who opposed KANU sing the song of Jogoo or leave the area immediately, both in October and again on 11 December.[145] Transferred soon after. Toyya, a Mijikenda, was transferred from Isiolo.[146]
Bomet	John Abduba throughout.	Borana. Reassured non-Kalenjin of their security. Looked fair.
Samburu	John Gakuo (Aug. '92). Muli Ndambu (Nov. '92).	Gakuo, a Kikuyu, was replaced in late 1992 by Ndambu (Kamba).
Turkana	John ole Mositany throughout.	Maasai. Accused of refusing relief food to DP supporters. Supposedly transferred to Kakamega Nov. '92, but returned. Involved in KANU Turkana nominations.
West Pokot	Solomon Boit throughout.	Kalenjin. Warned bar owners who allowed their premises to be used by opposition party officials that their licences would be withdrawn.[147] Participated in mass rally of Pokot for KANU on election eve.
Uasin-Gishu	Paul Lang'at (Nov. '92 to 15 December '92). Eliud Parsankul thereafter.	Kalenjin. Mombasa DC 1988. Langat refused opposition parties licences. Paid tributes to Moi on *Jamhuri* Day.[148] Worked with Biwott to manage the Uasin Gishu KANU primaries.[149] Officially replaced by Parsankul (a Maasai), but was still in office on 19 December 1992.[150]
Trans-Nzoia	Wilfred Ndolo throughout.	Kamba.
Western		
Bungoma	Kibiti Ritari throughout.	Meru.
Kakamega	Andrew Mondoh throughout.	Luhya. Barred Odinga's meeting in Shinyalu at the end of November. Distributed money raised by Moi, involving YK '92 in December.[151]
Vihiga	David Mwangi throughout.	Kikuyu. Organised administration police to maintain order only at KANU primaries.

Table 9.5 cont.

Province (District)	District Commissioner	Ethnic background and other information
Busia	Benjamin Rotich (Dec. '92 onwards).	Kalenjin.
Nyanza		
Siaya	Kiritu Wamae (Dec. '92 onwards).	Kikuyu. Accused of openly campaigning for KANU, though he denied such reports.[152]
Kisumu	Godfrey Mate throughout.	Meru. Lamu DC 1988.
Homa Bay	Johnson Kibera (Oct. '92). Suleiman Muyika. (Dec. '92).	Kikuyu. Kibera was DC in December according to KANU briefs. Muyika's origin is unknown.
Migori	Hassan Haji throughout.	Somali.
Kisii	Harry Wamubeyi throughout.	Luhya. 1988 Kisumu DC during rigged elections. Accused by Nyamweya of denying opposition candidates permits. Ordered police to arrest any opposition candidate maligning the name of the President.[153]
Nyamira	William Kerario (Nov. '92 onwards).	Kuria. Said, 'All civil servants must support the government of the day.' Urged them to vote for Moi and KANU. Later denied that he had said civil servants supporting opposition parties would be sacked.[154]

Source: Collated from various press reports, August–December 1992.

as KANU. Others prevented the opposition from holding any meetings at all, as happened for example in Tana River District. The Administration insisted on licensing meetings, even when the official campaign period began, despite the protests of the opposition parties' legal experts who insisted that no licences were required under the new election rules, although the Administration did waive the requirement of 14 days' notice. In many areas, the police arrested opposition candidates and supporters for attempting to hold unlicensed meetings.

FORD-Kenya suffered particularly severely. The state attempted to restrict the party's activities in order to prevent incursions into KANU territory in the North-East, the Rift Valley, and Isiolo. In early October FORD-Kenya requested permission to organise a series of rallies, but received no reply until party officials announced that they would go ahead with meetings with or without licences. According to the FORD-Kenya Secretariat, the party was then refused rallies in Isiolo, Mandera and Garba Tulla on 30–31 October, and in Lodwar, Samburu, Kajiado and Elgeyo-Marakwet for 7 November. Other minor harassment included the cancellation of rallies at the last minute, such as Paul Muite's licence for a rally in Kikuyu on 15 November, the permit for which had been issued on 10 November, and was cancelled at the last minute by the District Commissioner, by which time the branch had spent money on posters and transport.[155]

DP leader Kibaki also castigated the Kiambu District Commissioner for refusing the party's applications to hold rallies in Kiambu several times without reason.[156] In retribution, Provincial Commissioner Musoga cancelled the DP's licence for a meeting in Kangema on the very day that it was to have taken place, with the result that 25 DP supporters, including the candidate's mother, were therefore arrested for holding an illegal meeting.[157] The DP had even more trouble campaigning inside KANU's home areas and in marginals. On 3 December a DP rally in Eldoret in Uasin Gishu scheduled for two days later was cancelled by the District Commissioner.[158] District Commissioners arranged for chiefs' meetings to coincide with opposition rallies, while chiefs in seats like Masinga distributed relief food at the same time as a DP rally.[159] The government, of course, insisted that all parties were being treated equally, but no KANU meetings are known to have been cancelled. Table 9.5 shows how deeply emeshed the DCs were in KANU's campaign machine .

This table confirms that the majority of DCs actively supported the KANU campaign; it also demonstrates a distinct ethnic bias in their appointment.[160] During October and November, 11 of 44 DCs in office were Kalenjin (about 11 per cent of the population), and only four Kikuyu (over 20 per cent of the population). The transfers of the two most controversial Kalenjin DCs in December were cosmetic, as they both quietly returned to their posts as soon as the pressure had died down. During the crucial pre-election period, nearly half the DCs (at least 21) came from the 'KANU tribes' (the Kalenjin, Somali, Mijikenda, Maasai, Samburu, Turkana or Kuria), while only nine were from the generally pro-opposition Kikuyu, Luo or Embu communities (who formed 40 per cent of the population). Several of the most politically marginal Districts had Kalenjin DCs, including Uasin-Gishu, Mombasa, Kitui and Nakuru. It is also interesting to note that most of the Kikuyu and Luo DCs served in opposition strongholds. It seems – however simplistic this may sound – that the government trusted DCs born within opposition-supporting communities less than others, and therefore placed them in areas where they could do little harm.

The KANU heartlands of Nandi, Elgeyo-Marakwet, Baringo, Kericho and Bomet were entirely closed to opposition leaders. Opposition in Moi's home District of Baringo simply was not permitted. The authorities did everything they could to prevent any resentment against Moi and his allies from being translated into support for the opposition. Henry Cheboiwo, ex-Assistant Minister and one of Moi's closest associates until 1986/7, had been MP for Baringo North until 1988. Having fallen out of favour, Cheboiwo had not defended his seat in 1988, but attempted to secure the KANU nomination in 1992, standing in the rigged nominations in Baringo. He had lost, and then declared his candidacy for the DP in the same seat. After this reckless act, he never returned home, fearing for his life. Retribution was swift. At the end of November, his son revealed that

Photo 9.2 Henry Cheboiwo's house burnt down in Eldama Ravine after he defected to the DP. *Courtesy of Nation Group Newspapers*

KANU supporters had threatened to burn down Cheboiwo's four-bedroomed house in Eldama Ravine in Baringo South.[161] The following day, the house was destroyed by unknown arsonists and his cattle killed.[162] Cheboiwo tearfully protested, 'If they can do this to me and I am a Tugen like Moi himself, how is any other Kenyan from another tribe safe in this country?'[163] The other DP and FORD-Asili candidates kept their intentions secret or were forced into hiding.

In other Kalenjin districts, the situation was equally difficult. In Nandi, for example, the DP Chairman, Samuel arap Ng'eny, a former Speaker of the National Assembly, received death threats, and left the country to undertake research in Great Britain even before clergyman Elijah Yego in early December gave non-Kalenjin residents a 26-day ultimatum to vote for Moi or get out of the area. 'If you are in Rome,' he warned, 'do as the Romans do, and if you are in Nandi, do likewise. The Nandi are for KANU and President Moi.'[164] Although Yego's remarks were widely denounced, the same threats were being made in most other KANU-dominated areas. No Kalenjin could avoid the message – 'Vote for KANU, or else'. President Moi himself told Luo workers in Kericho on 16 October 'to sing and dance to the tune of the Kipsigis'.[165] Non-Kalenjin in Elgeyo-Marakwet were also threatened with expulsion if they did not support KANU.

The situation was similar in parts of the Rift periphery. In Turkana, where the DP were now the main opposition to KANU, DP supporters were beaten up by KANU youths, but the police refused to record their complaints, whilst DP leaders themselves were beaten up and arrested for refusing to rejoin the ruling party.[166] On 7 December, KANU candidates called non-Turkana inhabitants of the area 'squatters' and openly threatened them to vote for KANU or to leave the district. If they failed to support KANU, one candidate declared, 'we shall snatch from you all these businesses and you will have nobody but yourselves to blame'.[167] On 24 November, the DC in neighbouring West Pokot warned that bar owners who allowed their premises to be used by opposition party officials, would have their licences withdrawn.[168] In Kapenguria the DP Parliamentary candidate abandoned his home and fled after KANU leaders resolved at a mass rally, attended by DC Solomon Boit, that everybody in West Pokot must support the party or leave the District.[169]

Ethnic borderlands with a pro-KANU indigenous population but with a substantial Kikuyu vote saw sustained violence designed to intimidate immigrant opposition supporters. The three Eldoret (Uasin Gishu) seats were the scene of some of the worst ethnic clashes. KANU was determined to win these seats – on the cusp of Kalenjin, Luhya and Kikuyu landholdings – by fair means or foul. As well as the continuing ethnic clashes in Eldoret South, there were numerous attacks on opposition leaders and their vehicles, and threats to the non-Kalenjin community. Dr Misoi, hardline KANU candidate for Eldoret South, warned that non-residents of the District should identify with its lifestyles and political culture. 'Our political culture is KANU,' he declared, warning that the party would do everything it could to prevent opposition candidates contesting elections in the District.[170] KANU Chairman Jackson Kibor also demanded that 'non-indigenous residents of Uasin Gishu District should leave politics to the indigenous people'.[171]

In Kajiado, similarly, trouble was concentrated in marginal Kajiado North, the seat of George Saitoti, and escalated when DP Secretary-General John Keen was adopted as candidate. The local DO, Reuben Rotich, was a well-known supporter of Saitoti, and was accused as early as June of beating up DP supporters.[172] Following a spate of incidents, on 10 October ten armed Saitoti supporters assaulted and seriously injured a DP official and a police officer.[173] John Keen was himself beaten up on 11 November.[174] In Narok, the flashpoint was Narok North, the home of Minister William ole Ntimama, who was facing a serious challenge from two opponents. During the registration exercise, three people had been killed by Maasai *moran* at Enoosupukea registration centre when warriors tried to prevent local Kikuyu registering, after Ntimama had warned non-Maasai to vote KANU or quit the area.[175] In November, both Asili's Harun Lempaka and a senior DP activist alleged that YK '92 and Ntimama were trying to kill them.[176] Two opposition supporters were killed in Narok town on 23–24 November.[177] Then, on 19 December, KANU youth-wingers terrorised the town just before Matiba arrived for a rally, and destroyed the FORD-Asili branch office shortly after it had been opened. Three days later, Ntimama threatened non-Maasai residents with eviction if they failed to vote for KANU. The same day, ethnic violence erupted at Enoosupukea (an area which was to experience even worse trouble after the election), when people in KANU Youth uniforms fired arrows at non-Maasai, while in Nairagie Nkare, a centre of Kikuyu settlement for nearly seven decades, 400 Kikuyu residents were summoned to a meeting and warned by a KANU civic councillor that they would face 'an impending reign of terror if they did not vote KANU in'. On 28 December, vehicles with loud-speakers moved round the Kikuyu areas, warning them they would be evicted if they did not vote for KANU. The DP candidate also alleged that the ruling party had undertaken mass oathing in parts of the seat.[178]

The state followed a sustained campaign of threats against settlers, particularly Kikuyu, in other seats which KANU viewed as its territory. Other communities were told to stay out of politics or defer to the political views of the local inhabitants, or they would be expelled or lose their business licences. In Kitui, for example, Minister Ndotto in September 1992 warned people from other ethnic groups to toe the line or be forced out of the region.[179] Assistant Minister Kimemia told non-Taitas, residing in Taita-Taveta District, to vacate the area as it was a KANU zone.[180]

Marginal constituencies also had problems, though they were less severe. In Western Province, more than 30 people were arrested and two seriously injured immediately before President Moi arrived at Shamakhokho centre in Vihiga on 22 October during his tour of the area. Fighting had started when KANU youth-wingers tried to uproot opposition signs, and escalated when opposition supporters started to throw stones at the President.[181] Opposition branch offices were frequent targets for KANU harassment, particularly in marginal Western Province, Kisii and Trans-Nzoia. The DP's Trans-Nzoia branch offices were shut down in September 'on instruction from higher authorities' and the party's colours were whitewashed and its signboard removed by KANU youths.[182] In Western Province, FORD's offices in Samia were painted over on 5 October;[183] its Bungoma branch, and Kimilili and Kanduyi sub-branches were all burnt down during September.[184] Minister Elijah Mwangale, on 3 October, warned the DP not to open an office in Bungoma, saying that: 'The DP is a tribal party which is not needed in Bungoma. If Mr Mwai Kibaki tries to venture in the district, the indigenous people, who are staunch KANU supporters, will burn down his party's offices.'[185] The DP Bungoma offices were looted four days later, and on 8 November the DP branch office in Kakamega District was also burnt down.[186] In Vihiga constituency, KANU supporters threatened to loot shops belonging to Kikuyu businessmen unless they stopped supporting FORD-Asili.[187] The DP Bonchari office in Kisii was also destroyed during fighting in November.

In North-Eastern Province, a key area for KANU, the Administration was also heavy-handed. On 30 October, for example, 60 FORD-Kenya officials, led by Raila Odinga, and hundreds of supporters had arrived for an unlicensed seminar in Mandera town. Police action then led to the injuring of several FORD-Kenya supporters. Odinga protested that his delegation had been harassed from their arrival. The Special Branch had 'followed them from the airstrip, cancelled their hotel bookings and arrested the hotel proprietor'.[188] He informed the press the Mandera police chief had told him that he had received instructions from Garissa to stop the seminar.[189] Elsewhere, in Mombasa, there were numerous battles between IPK and KANU supporters. Two people were also seriously injured when DP and KANU supporters fought during an attack on the DP headquarters in Mombasa on 19 November.[190]

At the local level, chiefs in areas such as Wajir instructed voters to back KANU. Some lower level DOs also became notorious for their partisan attitudes, particularly Kalenjin DOs in Mumias, Kajiado North and the Burnt Forest. As early as August, one DO in Nandi was already warning that 'any opposition leaders found selling opposition cards in my area will be crushed because this is a pure KANU zone'.[191] Throughout the country, state vehicles were used to campaign for KANU, with reports from areas as diverse as Nyeri, Tana River and Samburu Districts. In the latter, locals reported that Major-General Lengees used a military helicopter to campaign for his brother, the KANU candidate in Samburu West.[192]

'Meet the people' tours (walkabouts by politicians greeting their supporters), did not require licences, which enabled the opposition to circumvent the restrictions, but led to trouble when politicians attempted to address their supporters. On 27 November, for example, Paul Ngei and other DP leaders were barred from addressing the public on a tour of Kangundo in Machakos.[193] The opposition Presidential candidates encountered severe problems on their walkabouts (see Chapter 10). Trouble also occurred at the opening of opposition sub-branch offices. All the opposition parties refused to apply for licences for the openings, and tried to turn the gatherings into unlicensed meetings. Trouble erupted, for example, when the police intervened at the opening of FORD-Asili offices in Kiambaa.[194] Chiefs often took the opening of opposition party branches in their areas as personal slights, and demanded their closure. Opposition candidates were specifically instructed on numerous occasions not to criticise President Moi. Thus an Embu DO temporarily stopped a DP rally in September after speakers 'dragged in the name of the President'.[195] The Makueni police chief even threw a teargas canister into a crowd listening to Paul Ngei, who had disobeyed instructions not to attack the President.[196]

Bankruptcy proceedings were also a powerful weapon as they rendered persons ineligible to vote and to become MPs. During October and November, bankruptcy petitions or civil suits for the recovery of debts of varying sizes were launched against Job Omino (FORD-Kenya, Kisumu Town), Henry Cheboiwo (DP, Baringo North), Peter Oloo-Aringo (FORD-Kenya leader), the son of Maina Wanjigi (KNC, Kamukunji). Even Mwai Kibaki himself was sued twice, one a bankruptcy notice for Sh500,000.[197] Paul Ngei's bankruptcy was near annulment, save for the final paperwork, which mysteriously was delayed. Consequently, although Ngei played a prominent part in the DP's campaign in Ukambani, he could not fight the election himself. The government, however, discovered that it was impossible to break the core of DP or FORD-Asili support this way, as the Kikuyu élite who supported the two parties remained extremely wealthy despite Moi's 14 years in power.

The Provincial Administration also ignored illegal night meetings by KANU at which oathing, a traditional Kenyan method of vote rigging, was used to ensure ethnic unity or bind those at a ceremony to support particular candidates. Kikuyu leaders in 1969 had oathed almost the entire adult male population of Central Province to ensure that the Presidency never left the house of Mumbi (Kikuyuland). After the 1974, 1979 and 1983 elections, oathing was proved in several election petitions. By the late 1980s, however, it had declined as a political tactic with the advance of education and the growth of Christianity, but in 1992 oathing ceremonies were reported in several KANU areas. In Samburu, NEMU's District Liaison Officer alleged that KANU had oathed its supporters, and similar charges were made by the DP candidate in Narok North against Minister Ntimama. Arthur Magugu in Githunguri was also reported to have transported voters in the early hours of the morning to his home at Komothai to be oathed with the connivance of the District Administration.

In opposition strongholds, the government approach was different. Unable to assert overwhelming force in the face of organised anti-KANU violence, much of the conflict was verbal. In these areas, violence was small-scale, and focused on individual leaders and constituencies, such as Raila Odinga's campaign in Langata in Nairobi. In Central Province, the major problem was caused by FORD-Asili leaders clashing with KANU strongmen in a few constituencies, including Limuru in Kiambu and Kangema in Murang'a District. In Kangema, for example, there was also fierce fighting following an attack on Kamotho's 16-vehicle motorcade in November, which required the Minister's security men to fire into the air to disperse the hostile crowd. Seven people were seriously injured.[198] On 3 December, John Michuki (FORD-Asili) was attacked by Kamotho's security men after their convoys intersected, and the police had to fire to disperse their fighting supporters.[199] In opposition strongholds, it was the scattered KANU supporters who experienced the brunt of intimidation.

KANU's sole surviving MP in Kiambu District, Cabinet Minister Arthur Magugu in Githunguri, employed the local Administration and the police to harass FORD-Asili's Dr Josephat Karanja and the DP's Rose Waruhiu. In one incident, on 29 November, Waruhiu, her husband, the DP County Council candidate for Ikinu Ward, and several of their friends were arrested and held in gaol overnight for holding an illegal meeting, after attending a private lunch party. The incident, however, illustrated some of the problems that KANU faced in the new era of multi-party politics. An irate George Waruhiu had berated the officer-in-charge of Githunguri police station when he was released on bail, warning him that if the opposition won the election – which did not seem impossible – he would find himself immediately retired, without pension, from the police force for a glaring misuse of power. The very fact that Waruhiu could make such a threat, and that it was credible, indicated that Kenyan politics had entered a new era.

Luo Nyanza was the area where the ruling party was weakest and had the greatest difficulty campaigning. On 31 October, for example, FORD-Kenya supporters attacked a KANU rally at Ahero in Kisumu, and in December, KANU rallies were attacked and broken up by mobs in Karachuonyo, Nyakach and Kisumu Rural. Police had to fire in the air to save a mob from 'necklacing' former MP James Miruka Owuor in Nyando on 24 December.[200] As with opposition supporters in Baringo or Elgeyo-Marakwet, it was hard to find a non-civil servant in Siaya or Kisumu who would risk wearing a KANU badge. Rivalries between the opposition parties also produced intense violence in a few seats, especially in Nairobi, where FORD-Asili and FORD-Kenya contended for supremacy, and in Kiambu and Kirinyaga Districts where Asili and the DP supporters fought.[201] This violence continued to polling day, reflecting the deep roots that casual election violence has in Kenya, reflecting growing disrespect for the police and the legal system, and the high stakes that all parties knew they were playing for.

Some opposition leaders saw Kenya's closure of the Kenya-Uganda border on 7 December, announced as 'a measure meant to curb lawlessness', as another step in KANU's preparations to keep power.[202] Uganda is Kenya's largest trading partner in Africa, and third-largest export market (Sh2 billion in 1991). There were suggestions that the event was connected with Moi's claims that guerrillas were sneaking into the country to launch a 'terror campaign' during the election. More interesting were the Nairobi rumours that the real reason behind the closure was that Gideon Moi and/or Biwott had been caught buying arms by the Ugandan government, and were being held by Museveni in exchange for the release of political prisoners. The story varied somewhat over the several days it did the rounds, but was supported by Biwott's almost complete absence during nomination day when his nomination in Kerio South might have been expected to attract extensive press and television coverage. Other stories suggested that the ex-Minister had fallen from favour when the courts awarded a Sh60 million ruling against him on 14 December, Presidential nomination day. Most commentators, however, believed that the regime was either preparing to disrupt the polls in Nyanza and Western Provinces, where FORD-Kenya and FORD-Asili were likely to do well, or attempting to pre-empt possible Ugandan intervention in favour of the opposition.

President Moi's Campaign Trail

During the campaign, all the Presidential candidates and their entourages criss-crossed the country, attending major rallies and walkabouts. These American-style Presidential tours were an important tool for influencing local voters and communicating many issues via press reports to the public. The Presidential candidates were accompanied by their most senior supporters, and by candidates sufficiently confident of victory to afford the time away from their own campaigns. These rallies started long before the official Presidential campaign period opened on 14 December. All the candidates focused on the marginal areas, particularly Western and Eastern Provinces, the Coast and hotly-contested Nakuru District. They also occasionally ventured into their rivals' strongholds in order to show that they had a national following.

Moi began his campaign earlier than the other candidates. This was only the second time the President had faced a contested election, as he had been elected unopposed at every election since 1961. By February 1992, he had already begun moving around the country attempting to counter the influence of FORD and the DP. When the true campaign began, he became even more active, using two helicopters to move swiftly round the country. He commanded large crowds of supporters, some of whom were transported to meetings by the Provincial Administration, to ensure that his rallies always appeared well attended. He appeared as the main item in virtually every television new bulletin. KANU and Moi also used national days, such as the Kenyatta Day celebrations of 20 October and the *Jamhuri* Day celebrations on 12 December, to campaign. The Kenyatta Day celebrations saw YK '92, the KANU women's league and many other KANU groups play an active part in the televised celebrations from Nyayo stadium, which were little more than a KANU party rally.[203] A repeat performance on *Jamhuri* Day, when at least 17 KANU campaign groups were present, led to the walk-out of the American, German, Danish, Canadian and Swedish ambassadors. The time Moi could spend campaigning was limited, however, by his Presidential duties, whilst his speeches attracted significantly more critical attention than those of the opposition leaders.

President Moi devoted considerable attention to campaigning among the Kamba in Eastern Province, where there was a strong DP challenge. He also went on a tour of Meru District on 21–22 December during which he paraded senior Merus in the government and parastatals as evidence of his commitment to the area. His greatest concentration of effort, however, was on Western Province. He spent four days in Busia and Butere in early October, and on 22 October he inaugurated the new Vihiga District. In early November Moi visited Bungoma; on 27 November and 6 December he visited Kakamega and Vihiga Districts. The President also made a series of forays into opposition territory. He visited Siaya and Kisumu, Odinga's home territory, on 7 and again on 19 December; Nyeri, Kibaki's home, on 16 December; and Nakuru on numerous occasions; although he avoided Murang'a, Matiba's base. His efforts in these areas, however, were not successful. His first visit to Kisumu and Siaya was a disaster, with jeering crowds lining his route, breaking into FORD-Kenya's two-finger salute, and shouting '*Simba!*' as he passed. Some even threw stones at the GSU.[204] His visit to Nakuru was no joyride, either: his cavalcade was stoned by Asili supporters. The President's 'meet the people' tours were, of course, unaffected by government restrictions.

The Opposition Parties' Presidential Campaigns

Like President Moi, the opposition candidates criss-crossed the country on tours, with setpiece rallies in local stadia, and 'meet the people' tours as they passed through. They had a rather harder time, however, in obtaining licences for these meetings. In November, Wako had stated that the Administration should not meddle in 'meet the people' tours, but the Provincial Administration prevented the opposition leaders holding rallies on several occasions. Most opposition leaders were denied access to the KANU zones, and entry to the North-Eastern Province, Tana River, Marsabit and Isiolo was made very difficult, leaving their local candidates isolated and vulnerable. By the end of October, no opposition party had been able to organise a major rally in either Marsabit or Isiolo. On 21 November Kibaki and his entourage were prevented from flying to Mandera for a huge rally after a sudden change of government regulations required them to apply for clearance 72 hours in advance. Matiba and Odinga also claimed to have been stopped from flying to North-Eastern Province. The opposition parties' Presidential cavalcades were also routinely stopped and searched. Although 14 days' notice was not required, Presidential meetings had to be licensed, and permits were frequently withdrawn at the last minute on security grounds. FORD-Kenya and the DP faced particular problems in campaigning in areas which KANU considered marginal, such as Western Province. Matiba, by contrast, attracted little attention outside the key seat of Narok North.

Odinga's strategy was based on attaining a wide national coverage. He avoided much of Central Province, and hardly bothered to campaign in Luo Nyanza (where he was impregnable) but focused on the more marginal Western Province, the Coast, Kisii and Nyamira, and the North-East. Odinga's speeches focused on the need for change and on the development of neglected Districts. He also denounced the clashes, visiting affected areas in Kisii and Nyamira. Throughout his tours, he was heavily supported by Young Turk speakers, especially his son Raila, who effectively ran the Presidential campaign.

Odinga was the opposition Presidential candidate who ventured furthest into KANU territory, and consequently experienced the greatest problems in organising his campaign. On 22 November, during his three-day tour of Coast Province, Odinga's van was stoned at Hola in Tana River by a mob of 100.[205] Two days later, his rally in Kilifi was dispersed by riot police with teargas on orders of the DO, who claimed that it was unlicensed.[206] Then, on 28 November, he was prevented from addressing a huge crowd in Kakamega, as the meeting was unlicensed (President Moi had visited the town the previous day).[207] When Odinga insisted on 'greeting' the people, ten people were arrested for holding an illegal meeting. The same day, Odinga's Shinyalu rally was cancelled at the last minute by the DC for 'unavoidable reasons'. Following these incidents, Odinga abandoned his tour of Western Province on the second day. The FORD-Kenya leader fared little better, however, on his next campaign stop in Makueni in Eastern Province. His 'meet the people' tour was harassed by the police at various trading centres and he was prevented from using a loudspeaker to address the crowd which had assembled to see him open the local party headquarters, as the police contended that the meeting was unlicensed. Eventually, the police fired teargas to disperse the gathering. His attempt to visit Wajir, Garissa and Mandera was also 'foiled' in mid-December when his plane charter was cancelled at the last minute, although he reached the North-East briefly on Christmas Eve.

A sense of the problems faced by the FORD-Kenya may be gained from an account of Oginga Odinga's visit to Kwale District in Coast Province on 23 December. Clearly showing his age, wearing an incongruous mixture of FORD-Kenya *Simba* T-shirt, denim jacket, and pin-striped trousers, the aged Presidential candidate was near-abandoned on his arrival, fed pills, washed down by warm Coca-Cola. Raila Odinga took control of the meeting, haranguing the crowd with FORD-Kenya's slogan, *Uhuru, Haki na Ukweli* (literally, freedom, peace and prosperity) and exhorting them to vote for *Simba* – the lion. When the Presidential candidate finally began to speak, his soft voice failed to hold the crowd's attention for more than a few minutes. It was clear that the former KPU leader and 'grand old man of Kenyan politics' was now little more than a figurehead and that the party's Presidential campaign was really being waged by the Young Turks, especially Raila Odinga, who, while protecting his father, was also manipulating him. Rural Kenya is a profoundly gerontocratic society: old age is highly respected. Without Odinga's figurehead leadership, despite their abilities and courage, the Young Turks of FORD-Kenya would have been unable to stand as a national political force. Odinga was their key to power. Odinga's 30-year advocacy of the interests of 'the ordinary man' and his stature as the permanent critic of Kenya's political establishment endowed FORD-Kenya's campaign with vital credibility. FORD-Kenya's appeal extended far beyond the ethnic confines of the old KPU. Few of the local worthies who gathered at Tiwi, for example, had supported him against Kenyatta in the 1960s. Nonetheless, Odinga was too old, whilst the party was acutely short of funds and it was now clearly the underdog outside its Luo ethnic base and the Bukusu region of Western Province. The crowds who came to hear FORD-Kenya's Presidential candidate were motivated more by nostalgia than by any real sense that Odinga would be victorious: such hopes had faded as the campaign reached its final stage and few believed that they were seeing Kenya's future President.

Mwai Kibaki's tactics were similar to Odinga's, though his strategy was undermined by his growing insecurity in his home region. Like Odinga, in early December Kibaki made a six-day tour of Western Province. It was his first tour of the area and was harassed by the Provincial Administration, which was under instructions, as it had been with Odinga, to hinder the DP leader and to minimise the political damage in this crucial marginal area. On the first day, 3 December, the DO for Webuye in Bungoma ordered soldiers to open fire on a crowd of DP supporters whom Kibaki was addressing without a licence. Fortunately, the soldiers disobeyed the order, although they stopped and searched all 40 vehicles in Kibaki's convoy when they left town. The following day, Kibaki's vehicles were again searched by police, who armed and cocked their rifles, while Kibaki shouted in fury, 'Shoot me if you want ! Shoot us all ! You cannot continue harassing us like this.'[208] Later that day, the DO for Mumias tried to whip Kibaki as he continued to address impromptu gatherings on his tour, and threatened to use teargas on the Kibaki group. When the press questioned his actions, he replied, 'If you continue asking me silly questions, I will beat and lock you up, you foolish reporters. I will even shoot you!'[209] Kibaki's meetings in marginal Kitale and Eldoret in the Rift Valley on 5 December went little better. The Kitale rally was broken up by riot police, while 200 KANU supporters attacked the crowd at Eldoret. Throughout the rest of December, Kibaki spent most of his time defending his strongholds in the Kikuyu areas and Eastern Province, but by mid-December, it became evident that his support was gradually trickling away to Matiba in the key areas of Nairobi and Kiambu. Numerous voters reported that they would support a DP Parliamentary candidate, but vote for Matiba for President.

Matiba's campaign strategy was straightforward. He left Shikuku to handle Western Province, and abandoned Nyanza entirely to Odinga.

Instead, Matiba concentrated his energies on Central Province, Nairobi and the Kikuyu areas of the Rift Valley, attacking Kibaki head on. He used 'meet the people' tours and illegal night meetings as much as formal rallies, and there were large gaps in his publicly reported programme of visits and speeches. He hardly ventured into the KANU zones, and he did much less long-distance travel than the others, perhaps because of his precarious health, although he toured Coast Province just before Christmas. Where he did exert himself, Matiba proved the best campaigner of the election, with his campaign slogan 'Let the People Decide'. One of his strengths was his use of *matatus* to advertise FORD-Asili. It is not clear how far this was a deliberate strategy, or grew out of support for him among *matatu* owners, but throughout the urban areas, Central Province, and on the major roads in the Rift Valley as far as the borders of Kericho and Baringo, *matatus* were covered with Matiba posters, and sometimes transported voters free to his rallies.

As the campaign reached its peak, Matiba realised that he was far more popular than his Parliamentary and civic candidates, and that many people were considering ticket-splitting. He therefore began a series of speeches focusing on the need to elect a team that he could work with in Parliament. He began increasingly to urge crowds to vote for the 'three piece suit' of Presidential, Parliamentary and local government candidates, reminding them that when he became President, he would need 'at least 95, at least 95' FORD-Asili MPs. At some night rallies in areas like Githunguri in mid-December, his exhortations had a major impact on voters' intentions. Matiba's huge rally in Nairobi on Boxing Day confirmed his dominance in the capital, causing Kibaki to cancel his final meeting in Nairobi at the same venue the next day.

Kibaki's fight with Matiba, encouraged by KANU, provided some of the bitterest exchanges of the campaign. The conflict between the two leaders sharpened as FORD-Asili ate into the DP's support among the Kikuyu. Matiba launched the first assault on Kibaki on 9 December, claiming at a rally in Murang'a that Kibaki had betrayed him to Moi when he had attempted to organise a mass exodus from the Cabinet, following Kibaki's demotion from the Vice-Presidency in 1988.[210] Kibaki, of course, denied these allegations and responded by calling Matiba petty.[211] On 20 December, FORD-Asili's Chris Kamunyu claimed that Kibaki had betrayed the Kikuyu as Vice-President, and had 'observed helplessly' as the tribe was slowly weakened by Moi's government. He also criticised Kibaki for failing to fight to repeal section 2(a) of the constitution, observing that 'Mr Kibaki remained mute when Mr Kenneth Matiba was detained.'[212] Matiba also placed newspaper advertisements reprinting various statements by DP leaders from before the advent of multi-party politics, when they had been 'loyal' members of the KANU government.[213] The battle became increasingly fraught as politicians sensed that Kikuyu voters in Nairobi, Kiambu and Nakuru were moving *en masse* towards Matiba, repudiating not only Kibaki but the DP's Parliamentary candidates, many of whom had risen to power during the Kenyatta era. The FORD-Asili leader's populist campaign appealed to the Kikuyu masses, offering simple solutions to complex problems, while Kibaki was too cautious, too much of a technocrat after 25 years in power, and, like the DP as a whole, too closely identified with the old ruling élite of the Kenyatta era. The spectacle of the two leaders and their parties trading insults reinforced the feeling of disaster among opposition supporters in the last few days of the campaign. It was one of the tragi-comedies of the election that this internal struggle consumed so much effort and invective, leaving the election to go by default to KANU.

Parliamentary Nomination Day

Once the legal dispute over the validity of the original election date was resolved, nomination day for Parliamentary and civic candidates was set for Wednesday, 9 December 1992. Between eight o'clock in the morning and one o'clock in the afternoon (for Parliamentary candidates) and eight and noon (for local government candidates), candidates or their agents had to deposit their papers with the Returning Officer for the constituency, and have those papers vetted and accepted. There were to be contests in 188 parliamentary and 1,879 local government seats. The 36 hours leading up to nominations were extremely tense. It was still unclear in many constituencies who would actually stand and for which parties. There were nomination disputes running on: losers were still defecting at the last minute to other parties; and the opposition parties were trying to keep secret who they had lined up to oppose KANU in the KANU zones. Chesoni had directed Returning Officers not to accept forms from any candidate whose nomination was being challenged in court, though in the event no one was rejected for this reason (see Chapter 8).

Previous nomination days had always seen trouble, including physical efforts to prevent candidates presenting their papers and nominations that were refused by DCs for questionable reasons. In 1969, Mbiyu Koinange, Kenyatta's right-hand man, had had his prospective opponent in Kiambaa, Gideon Were Gathunguri, detained by the state just before nomination day. Five years later, Koinange had Gathunguri locked up for the night in the police cells to prevent him from submitting his papers so that Koinange could be returned unopposed. The same year, Minister Paul Ngei had prevailed upon his only opponent in Kangundo to stand down, after threatening his life and warning, 'If I am opposed we as a tribe will have a very bad position in the government.'[214] In 1979 in Baringo North, a candidate standing against Henry Cheboiwo, then one of Moi's right-hand men, had to disguise himself as a woman to reach the DC's office.[215] In 1983, when Mrs Tabitha Seii had first tried to stand against Nicholas Biwott in Kerio South, the Returning Officer had decided that a dark line on her form indicated her Kiswahili proficiency certificate had been cancelled, and refused her nomination.[216]

Trouble, therefore, was widely expected. DP headquarters by six o'clock on Tuesday evening had approved just over 180 candidates: the handful of uncontested seats were all in Siaya and Kisumu Districts, where FORD-Kenya was overwhelmingly popular. The DP had candidates in every Kalenjin constituency, including President Moi's Baringo Central. Candidates who might encounter opposition from defeated aspirants for the nomination were presented with a sworn affidavit, signed by Keen, declaring that they were the approved DP candidate for the constituency. DP candidates in six particularly difficult contests – John Keen in Kajiado North, where he was challenging Vice-President Saitoti; Norman Nyagah in Gachoka in Embu; Henry Cheboiwo in Baringo North and his colleague in Baringo South; Tabitha Seii in Kerio South, who was challenging Biwott; and the candidate in Runyenjes – left Nairobi on 8 December, with an armed security escort and an entourage of journalists in order to ensure that they would be able to get through to the Returning Officer or, if prevented, to make sure that the full story would appear in the media. FORD-Kenya had announced that it intended to field candidates in every constituency and published a list of 167 candidates the day before nomination day. Its candidates in Baringo, Laikipia, Bomet, parts of Murang'a and Nandi, were not published 'for security reasons' (fear of KANU or FORD-Asili reprisals).[217] FORD-Asili intended to cover rather fewer, roughly 146 seats, according to the *Weekly Review*.[218]

The 1992 nominations were the most compromised in Kenyan history. Despite requests from Chesoni for security for candidates, none was provided by the police. There were numerous violent incidents, assaults, kidnappings and attacks on candidates. At least 54 Parliamentary and more local government candidates were prevented from presenting their papers by KANU supporters or had their nominations refused by officials. These covered 37 different constituencies, mainly in the Rift Valley KANU zones of Baringo, Elgeyo-Marakwet, Nandi, Kericho and Bomet; in Wajir in North-Eastern Province; and in Kilifi and Busia (see Table 9.6).[219] Of these 54, only three were refused nomination by the returning officers for their respective constituencies for reasons which appear valid, such as not having a vital document with them. These included Titus Mbathi, the KNC Chairman, who was refused nomination for apparently having too few seconders.[220] Fifteen had their papers refused without good reason, for example being declared 'time barred' by officials long before 1 p.m., when nominations were still open, as happened to FORD-Kenya candidates in Makuyu, Wajir West and Turkana South, or having their papers rejected without reason, as happened to all three opposition candidates in KANU-dominated Amagoro in Busia. Five vanished without trace at some point on the way to be nominated, including FORD-Kenya candidates in Wajir East, Belgut, Kajiado South and Narok South. At least 30 were physically prevented by KANU activists or the police from ever reaching the offices where the Returning Officers waited.[221] From seat after seat, the story was the same, of police and/or KANU youth-wingers arresting, kidnapping, or detaining opposition candidates until after 1 p.m. In the eight 'home seats' of Moi and Biwott in Baringo and Elgeyo-Marakwet, 15 of the 16 opposition candidates were kidnapped or physically prevented from presenting their papers. The sole survivor was DP candidate Tabitha Seii in Kerio South, where three KANU youths grabbed her papers as her lawyer-agent tried to hand them over, but the police and her husband, an ex-soldier, managed to recover them. In only two more of the 17 Kalenjin homeland seats did any opposition candidates successfully run the gauntlet of KANU intimidation – Buret, where Dr Ng'eno was opposed by two no-

Table 9.6 Parliamentary Candidates Refused or Unable to Reach Nomination centres

	Party						
Province	FORD-Kenya	DP	Asili	KNC	PICK	KSC	TOTAL
Nairobi					1		1
Central	1						1
Eastern	3			1	1		5
North-Eastern	2	1	1	1			5
Coast	2	1	1				4
Rift	13	8	9				30
Western	2	2	1		1		6
Nyanza						2	2
Total	23	12	12	2	3	2	54

hopers and Kipkelion in Kericho District, the central Rift Valley constituency with the largest non-Kalenjin population. There, all the opposition candidates were nominated successfully, but the DP candidate was beaten up and robbed of his identity and voter's cards minutes after submitting his nomination papers, and the brother of Moses arap Keino (FORD-Kenya's candidate) was stabbed.

All three main opposition parties suffered, FORD-Kenya most. The DP and FORD-Asili losses were concentrated in the central Rift Valley, while FORD-Kenya's were more widely dispersed: the party lost two candidates in the key district of Kilifi on the Coast, for example. The result was that KANU was declared unopposed in all four Baringo constituencies, all three Nandi seats, three of the four Elgeyo-Marakwet seats, four of six Kericho and Bomet seats, one Narok seat, one Samburu seat, and in Samia and Wajir East. A few of the candidates who claimed that they were kidnapped were undoubtedly telling a pragmatic lie, as they knew that they would lose and then be unable to get loans or government jobs if they persisted in their unwise attempts to stand against government candidates. This was not true in most cases, however, where the opposition parties had enlisted senior figures who had fought hard to reach the ballots against KANU.

Evidence given by obstructed FORD-Asili candidates to the party's lawyer, Kamau Kuria, provides a graphic description of what happened in the central Rift Valley constituencies. FORD-Asili party officials in Kerio East, for example, claimed that President Moi himself had held a secret meeting of Kalenjin MPs, local chiefs, County Councillors, and District Administrators at his Kabarnet home to warn them that the Presidency would remain with the Kalenjin only if they organised to prevent opposition candidates presenting their papers. According to the FORD-Asili leaders, President Moi instructed his supporters to obstruct the opposition, to burn down their houses, and to drive non-Kalenjin out of the area. NEMU's District Liaison Officer for Baringo separately confirmed these claims, reporting that 'the Police, Provincial Administration and the Youth for KANU'92 were requested by the authority [i.e.

President Moi] to ensure that no candidates from other opposition parties are allowed to oppose a KANU candidate....'[222]

Samuel Mwaura, who was to have been the party's candidate in Kerio Central, had left home at 5.30 on the morning of nomination day, accompanied by two FORD-Asili local government candidates, to join their supporters who were assembling at a nearby primary school. Before they could do so, however, two *matatus*, transporting 20 KANU activists, kidnapped them and took them to the Chemunda forest where they were held, along with some FORD-Kenya Parliamentary and local government candidates, until 6 p.m. The FORD-Asili candidates asserted that their kidnappers had claimed 'to be enforcing a KANU zone from which candidates of opposition parties were to be excluded'.[223]

Francis Cheptile, FORD-Asili's nominee in Kerio East, submitted that on 8 December 1992 his Landrover was attacked about a mile from his home by a group of KANU supporters under the leadership of KANU's local County Council candidate. Local people had turned out in force to support him, however, and soon a crowd of between 400 and 600 people had gathered to guard his home and to ensure that he would be able to present his nomination papers the next day. Although appeals to Kalenjin loyalty had ensured that KANU was the dominant party in the constituency, there was widespread discontent over food shortages and the deteriorating security situation.[224] FORD-Asili's candidate, who had begun to organise in the constituency immediately after the legalisation of the opposition in December 1991, had attracted a considerable following in his own hard-hit location, causing concern to local officials. KANU leaders, therefore, were determined to prevent his name appearing on the ballot. Even while the 8 December fracas was going on, KANU's Parliamentary nominee Kisang' Cheserek was meeting with the DO and local chief to map out how to prevent the opposition candidates presenting their papers. At 7.30 on nomination day morning Cheptile set off for the Returning Officer's headquarters, accompanied by two FORD-Asili officials. At Kapkokil, however, they encountered a roadblock manned by KANU supporters armed with *rungus* and *simis* [traditional weapons], who informed them that Kerio East was a KANU zone. The FORD-Asili team returned to Cheptile's home, where they collected a group of 300 supporters and returned, putting KANU's supporters at the blockade to flight, as they moved towards Tot, the divisional headquarters. The advancing escort, however, encountered an even bigger group of KANU supporters, backed up by 20 armed GSU troops and police under the command of the local police inspector, when they were within 30 yards of the Returning Officer's headquarters. These kept the FORD-Asili candidate and his supporters at bay, within sight of the Returning Officer, from 9.50 in the morning until 2.30 in the afternoon, 90 minutes after the nomination process ended. When they attempted to push their way through the hostile crowd of KANU supporters, the GSU cocked their guns as if they were preparing to shoot.

The fate of FORD-Asili's candidates in Baringo District was more terrifying. Abbas Kipruto Mawboob (Baringo South), John Gakuo (Baringo East), and Joseph Theuri (Baringo North) had assembled on 8 December at the Riverside Hotel in Eldama Ravine, the main town in Baringo South.

When they attempted to leave at about 8.30 p.m., however, they discovered that the hotel had been surrounded by more than 100 KANU supporters, armed with stones, clubs and old tyres to 'necklace' the FORD-Asili candidates. Led by local KANU leaders, the crowd had threatened to burn Theuri's car and to kill the three men 'because they could not allow opposition parties to operate in the District'. As a result, the three candidates were trapped overnight at the hotel. When the wife of the Baringo South candidate tried to drive through the crowd to get them out of the hotel at 8 a.m. the next morning, she was assaulted. The three FORD-Asili candidates were forced to remain in the hotel, 'prisoners of the hostile KANU crowd', until 4 p.m. when the mob finally dispersed, 'loudly congratulating themselves for keeping the opposition parties from the District'.[225]

Dr Patrick Chege Njuguna, a Kikuyu from Murang'a who had stood against Matiba and Shikuku in the party's Presidential primary, announced his intention to contest President Moi's Baringo Central constituency for FORD-Asili on 14 November.[226] No incumbent President had been opposed at any general election, for reasons of prestige, and Njuguna's announcement greatly irritated Lawi Kiplagat, KANU's Executive Officer for Baringo District, who threatened that he would be beaten up if he ever set foot in the District. From 16 November, Njuguna's business offices in Westlands in Nairobi were monitored continuously by two plain-clothes policemen. He faxed NEMU before the nominations pleading for assistance and for observers to ensure that he was nominated. On Tuesday, 8 December, Njuguna left his office and had a drink at the Impala Club in Westlands, followed as usual by the police. At the club, he had proclaimed loudly that his agent would present his nomination papers and that he would remain in Nairobi. One of the plain-clothes policemen had even attempted to dissuade him from contesting the election, suggesting that President Moi should be elected unopposed. Njuguna had agreed to meet the policeman to discuss the matter further the next morning at the Hotel Intercontinental but, in fact, set out in a taxi for Nakuru at 1 a.m. on 9 December, nomination day, arriving three hours later.[227]

From Nakuru, he had caught a *matatu* to Kabarnet but, just as it set out, a security officer climbed into the vehicle. At the first stop, three uniformed traffic policemen had entered. When they reached Marigat at nearly 10.30 a.m., the security officer got out, leaving Njuguna to be watched over by the three traffic policemen. Then, as the vehicle started to leave for Kabarnet, he returned, accompanied by 'about 1,000' people, many dressed in KANU red shirts and berets, who surrounded the *matatu*, shouting that they knew that 'Dr Patrick Njuguna was inside' and demanding that all the passengers should identify themselves and produce their identity cards, voter registration and party membership cards. Njuguna was dragged from the *matatu* and his nomination papers destroyed, while the crowd clamoured that Baringo was a KANU zone. He was then taken to the health centre at Marigat and held there until 3 p.m., before being released by plain-clothes policemen about six miles outside Marigat town. Njuguna claimed that he had been informed by an Administration policeman that the DC, Baringo, knew that he was being detained and would protect him.[228]

The DP's Baringo Central candidate, Amos Kandie, also failed to make it to the nominations, leaving President Moi unopposed. According to a press release from the DP secretariat, his papers were rejected by the Returning Officer without reason. Kandie claimed several days later, however, at a rally in Kabarnet town, that he had simply been unable to find a proposer and seconder for his forms.[229] In Baringo North, DP candidate Henry Cheboiwo did not present his papers in person, being an obvious target for attack. Instead, his election agent attempted to present them on his behalf at Kabartonjo but was abducted in a vehicle allegedly driven by a nephew of the President and dumped in the forest. On his unwise return he was 'severely beaten' and the nomination papers taken by armed men.[230]

Michael Namudiero, FORD-Asili's candidate in Samia in Western Province, suffered a similar fate. He had left Nairobi, accompanied by his wife and three bodyguards, at about 7 p.m. on 8 December. They had arrived at Nakuru, where they stopped for refreshments, at about 9 p.m., intending to make their way to Samia via Marigat, Kabarnet and Eldoret – that is, through KANU's Baringo stronghold. When they reached Marigat at 10.30 p.m., they were stopped by a roadblock of logs and stones manned by 200 KANU supporters in the ruling party's red shirts and berets. The Asili candidate was forced out of his car, his nomination papers torn to pieces and 73,000 shillings stolen. Their attackers claimed that 'they had instructions from high authority not to allow the opposition parties' candidates to pass through Marigat'. The five were then held at Marigat overnight, before the candidate and his wife were taken at 7 a.m. to Kabarnet District hospital, where they remained captive until 2 p.m., by which time the nomination process had closed.[231]

Another particularly well-publicised incident occurred in the Rift Valley periphery constituency of Turkana South. There, the nomination papers for Eliud Kerio Long'acha (DP) were taken by an Administration police corporal, who snatched the briefcase containing the forms in the presence of other regular police. The DP candidate's lawyer was struck from behind by a plain-clothes policeman wearing dark glasses, who threw the briefcase containing Long'acha's papers to the driver of a government landrover, which sped off while the police cocked their guns and pointed them at the DP agent. No action was taken against these individuals, and the police officer was promoted a few weeks later.[232]

As a result of the events of 9 December, KANU candidates were unopposed in 18 Parliamentary seats, in only three or four of which was there genuinely no opposition. This catalogue of assaults and abuses of state power alone brings into question the fairness of the entire electoral process. No amount of hand-wringing by the Commission could conceal the fact that KANU and the state had organised a massive abuse of the electoral process. KANU would have won almost all the seats in a fair fight, but this was not its aim. It was a matter of pride to President Moi and Kalenjin leaders that the ruling party should demonstrate overwhelming popularity in its ethnic bailiwick. Party strategists wanted to save money and personnel to deploy elsewhere, and to transport Kalenjin voters to neighbouring marginal seats, such as Molo and Uasin Gishu. In a couple of cases, the nomination day events removed candidates who might indeed have won the seat (such as FORD-Asili's Samia candidate). In addition, by ensuring that there would be no Parliamentary elections in the Kalenjin areas, KANU ensured a far lower vote here for the opposition Presidential candidates and reinforced the popular impression that there was no alternative to Moi. NEMU noted that 'No one was reported arrested or charged before a court of law for this perpetration of violence.'[233]

There were a few cases, by contrast, where Returning Officers seem to have favoured the opposition. In Kieni in Nyeri, for example, the DP candidate and certain victor, David Munene Kairu, had arrived without his original language proficiency certificates and was sent back to collect them. Although he returned after the one o'clock deadline, his papers were accepted.[234] There were no attempts, however, to prevent the nomination of any of the Presidential candidates, who had to be nominated for a Parliamentary seat to be eligible for the Presidency. Nor were attempts made to refuse the papers of opposition candidates in opposition strongholds like Central Province. Equally, no KANU candidate was refused nomination, so that the ruling party was the only one to field candidates in all 188 constituencies.

Nomination day also witnessed election violence by supporters of all the main parties in at least 20 other seats where the opposition was strong, but KANU had a prominent candidate, such as Imenti Central in Meru, Mathira in Nyeri, Limuru in Kiambu, and Kangema in Murang'a, where KANU Secretary-General Joseph Kamotho narrowly escaped being lynched when presenting his papers. In at least four Luo seats, only intervention by the security forces permitted KANU's candidate to be nominated. In Odinga's Bondo, for example, William Odongo Omamo was prevented from presenting his papers until rescued by police.[235] In Migori, police shot and wounded three people when a mob attacked Minister John Okwanyo's car. The violence was no worse in 1992 then in previous elections, however, or in comparison with other Third World democracies such as India or Columbia. No one was killed, although nationally many dozens were hurt in stone-throwing and fighting.

Elsewhere, the 1992 nominations were peaceful. Candidates organised competing crowds and parades, mostly good-natured, demonstrating their support and encouraging waverers to join them. In the Nairobi area, nomination day demonstrated that Chris Kamunyu in Dagoretti, Raila Odinga in Langata and Paul Muite in Kikuyu were all likely winners. Candidates normally arranged not to arrive at the same time, to avoid scuffles between opposing convoys. In Dagoretti, for example, Mrs Mugo (DP) arrived at the hall first, at 8.45. Her clearance was delayed until 11.10 by the fact that details of her name in the register did not precisely match her voters' and identity cards precisely. Chris Kamunyu, consequently, arrived at 10.58 to find Mugo still there, and some slight scuffles broke out between the rival crowds of supporters. FORD-Asili's followers, chanting, 'KK number one', were clearly the strongest. In general, however, opposition supporters were tolerant of one another. Their common dislike of KANU was revealed when Clement Gachanga's parade arrived at 11.25, just as Kamunyu was about to leave. Opposition supporters rushed to meet them, calling Gachanga a thief and shouting 'We will kill the cockerel.'

The primary and nomination exercises stretched party secretariats to their limit. As a result, four constituencies saw two candidates from the same party turn up for nomination. In Mbita, two DP candidates turned up. In Taveta, KANU actually nominated two candidates, but only Basil Criticos's name appeared on the ballot; in Mombasa's Likoni seat, the DP experienced the same problem. In Malindi, Francis Bobi Tuva was barred at the last minute by KANU and replaced, ending his 29-year career as a backbencher. Chesoni refused to intervene, suggesting that the parties 'sort it out'.[236] NEMU and other poll monitors were allowed to watch the nomination process, although they were not yet officially accredited. Unfortunately, their coverage was incomplete and they did not have the authority to intervene in any way.

The opposition was shocked and furious at the events of nomination day. All three main parties called press conferences to protest the rigging and FORD-Kenya threatened to boycott the election if the Election Commission did not nullify the central Rift nominations, while the DP announced that they would contest ten cases in the courts. The foreign observer teams were also profoundly disturbed. Even British Foreign Secretary Douglas Hurd expressed concern. The Commonwealth observer group issued a press statement on 13 December, calling for speedy action to redress the 'alleged irregularities'. Spokesperson Robertson said, 'We are deeply concerned by the extent of the reports we have been receiving about allegations of violence, misconduct, and intimidation apart from general impropriety on the part of officials.'[237] The Commonwealth advance team stated that it would consider the election to be 'severely compromised' if a number of candidates were unable to contest.[238] Both the IRI and Commonwealth teams were disillusioned with the Electoral Commission and the government, and doubted if it was worthwhile going on if the election was to be rigged so blatantly. In private, however, opposition leaders argued that it was better to fight the election and to secure some presence in Parliament. All had invested far too much money and effort to withdraw without any return and central party control was probably too weak to prevent local candidates contesting the election in any case. Once again, the ambitions of local candidates conflicted with the wider interests of party headquarters. Behind the scenes Commonwealth pressure on Moi also produced little change.

Chesoni initially refused to confirm whether the 18 unopposed nominations were legal, but insisted that the Commission could do nothing to help those who had been abducted, suggesting that they seek redress in the courts.[239] It was rumoured in Nairobi that on the night of 10 December, the day after nominations, he had been willing to concede new nominations, but pressure from on high had dissuaded him. Instead, on Friday, 11 December, Chesoni established an elections complaints committee, chaired by himself, but restated that where Returning Officers had declared the candidate unopposed, the Commission had no power to overturn their decision.[240] Despite its overall responsibility for the conduct of the elections, Chesoni insisted the Commission could only address problems involving the incorrect rejection of papers by Returning Officers.[241] Complaints by five candidates in Turkana South, Amagoro, Wajir East,

Kangundo and Mumias, who had had their papers invalidly rejected by Returning Officers, were therefore accepted, reducing the number of unopposed seats to 16. Seventeen Parliamentary and seven local government candidates' complaints of kidnapping were referred to the police and the Attorney-General, but their only means of redress was to present an election petition after 29 December.[242]

Meanwhile, a furious opposition took a host of cases to court. Although attempts to create a joint legal case foundered, all the parties issued injunctions against elections taking place where their candidates had been barred. This briefly created problems for the government, since these seats in its ethnic homeland were vital to its hopes of securing an effective Parliamentary majority. To have left them unfilled, pending legal cases, would have threatened the government's survival. Victory in the courts was, therefore, essential. The first suit heard in the High Court was that of the DP's Henry Cheboiwo in Baringo North. Justice Joyce Aluoch accepted Cheboiwo's argument that his papers should be accepted, and issued an injunction restraining the Commission from publishing the name of his opponent Willy Kamuren as the MP. Cheboiwo's lawyers were unable, however, to prevent Kamuren obtaining more time to contest the lawsuit, making it pointless for Cheboiwo to continue to protest, as he would not appear on the ballot papers anyway.[243] KANU appealed, but the injunction was upheld by the Appeal Court just before Christmas. Patrick Chege Njuguna of FORD-Asili requested an identical injunction against President Moi's election as MP for Baringo Central. This was a crucial case, since it would render Moi ineligible for the Presidency if he was not officially an MP. The Baringo Central case, however, was delayed and heard separately from the others by the controversial Judge Dugdale, who dismissed it on the grounds that it was 'wrongfully brought to court, was misconceived and premature'.[244] Earlier the same day, the Appeal Court had upheld the injunction in Baringo North. Dugdale, nevertheless, reserved his ruling on whether Njuguna was able to appeal until well after the elections, and flatly refused to accept in court the Appeal Court's Cheboiwo ruling, which he was bound by law to follow, refusing to accept the document from Kamau Kuria.[245]

Legal cases were also filed by at least 11 other FORD-Kenya, DP and FORD-Asili candidates, to force the Electoral Commission to declare them nominated. Six were dismissed before polling day and the matter referred to the petition courts,[246] but the High Court did issue four more injunctions on behalf of FORD-Asili candidates in Samia, Baringo East and Kerio Central and the DP candidates in Baringo East and Kerio West. As a result, in these five constituencies, KANU's candidates were not gazetted, and the High Court ruled that parliamentary elections should not take place.[247] How these cases differed from President Moi's in Baringo Central was never explained. On 24 December, Chesoni officially gazetted the other 12 KANU MPs as having been returned unopposed.

The result of the parties' regional weaknesses, plus the abuses of nomination day, was that whilst KANU had candidates in all 188 parliamentary and most local government contests, the other parties were now far weaker. FORD-Asili had the fewest nominated candidates, with big gaps in the

Table 9.7 Nominated Candidates

Province	Seats	Nominated candidates		
		FORD-Asili	FORD-Kenya	DP
Nairobi	8	8	8	8
Central	25	24	15	24
Eastern	32	29	27	32
North-Eastern	10	9	8	9
Coast	20	17	17	19
Rift Valley	44	22	18	27
Western	20	18	17	18
Nyanza	29	15	29	16
Total	188	142	139	153

KANU zones and in Nyanza. FORD-Kenya failed to field candidates in much of the Rift Valley and was unrepresented in four of the six Murang'a seats and four of Nyeri's six seats. The DP emerged as KANU's strongest opponent (see Table 9.7). Among the smaller parties, the KNC were now fielding 52 candidates, mostly from the Kikuyu areas of Central Province, Nairobi and Nakuru. PICK's 32 candidates were concentrated in Nairobi, with a scattering of defectors elsewhere. The other parties – the KSC (ten candidates), SDP (one candidate) and KENDA (four candidates) – had proved to be of no importance at all.

The Remaining Candidates in the Parliamentary Elections

There were either 719 or 720 candidates nominated to contest the parliamentary elections, including the few who were reinstated.[248] This was an average of nearly four per seat – still lower than had contested in the open single-party state, when the average had been more than 4.5 candidates per seat in 1974, 1979 and 1983.[249] The single-party system had provided a mechanism by which new élites could enter the political arena at a comparatively high rate. In 1969, the first single-party election, two thirds of the candidates were new to national politics. Since then, the proportion had fallen, indicating that the system had become more stable and the élite more closed, but every constituency still on average had two new candidates at every election. The proportion of new candidates fell to 56 per cent in 1974, 38 per cent in 1979 and 40 per cent in 1983.[250] The 1992 election saw a major change. Although many of the most senior figures were old-timers, the majority of the candidates in every party bar KANU – in whose team 70 per cent were previous contenders – had never fought a parliamentary campaign before. The least experienced group were not the Young Turks of FORD-Kenya but the Asili candidates, of whom only 50 were previous contestants (35 per cent), whereas 57 of FORD-Kenya's 139 contenders were old hands (41 per cent). Amongst the DP candidates, 45 per cent had previous experience of a parliamentary campaign. Despite the increased proportion of new candidates, over 170 of the 530 opposition nominations had stood for parliament under KANU's colours in either 1983 or 1988.[251]

In most constituencies, the parties selected candidates from the majority community in that area, and usually from those who had been born in and had families in that seat. There was one minor exception: the DP relied on the Kikuyu diaspora in multi-ethnic areas. Thus the DP adopted Kikuyu candidates in Cherangani and Kwanza in Trans-Nzoia (a primarily Luhya area) and in Kinango in Kwale District, while all seven DP candidates in Nakuru and Laikipia Districts, and six of eight in Nairobi were Kikuyu. FORD-Kenya, KANU and FORD-Asili, in contrast, appear to have found it easier to recruit candidates from the majority communities, and were less reliant on settlers.

'The great and the good' from the civil service and earlier governments loomed large in the ranks of all the opposition parties, but particularly in the DP. The DP's candidates included four ex-Permanent Secretaries (colleagues of Kibaki's during his tenure as Vice-President) and four ex-Ministers: Mwai Kibaki, Eliud Mwamunga, George Muhoho and James Nyamweya. Many other DP candidates had held other senior government positions in the 1970s and early 1980s, including High Court Judge Benna Lutta; Isaiah Mathenge, the ex-PC for Rift Valley; Kyale Mwendwa, the Director of Education in 1968–77; three ex-Ambassadors and a former Chairman of the Kenya Ports Authority. The DP team also included ex-Assistant Ministers, old-time politicians of the second rank from the 1960s, and the normal selection of lawyers, churchmen, teachers and lecturers, plus small businessmen and industrial managers and engineers. The party attracted a few big businessmen (most of whom were former politicians), most notably Njenga Karume, Ngengi Muigai, Ben Ndubai, Alfred Sambu and Eliud Wamae.

Lawyers, by contrast, played a far greater role in FORD-Kenya. They had led the campaign for multi-party democracy in 1991, and throughout 1992 continued to harass the regime in the courts. Its legal officials included Paul Muite (Chairman of the Law Society in 1990–2 and First Vice-Chairman of FORD-Kenya), James Orengo (Secretary for Constitutional and Legal Affairs), Gitobu Imanyara (Secretary-General), Gervaise Akhaabi (Steering Committee) and Kijana Wamalwa (Second Vice-Chairman). Practising or ex-lawyers stood as FORD-Kenya candidates in at least eleven constituencies (in Makadara, Kikuyu, the three Imenti seats in Meru, Kwanza and Saboti in Trans-Nzoia, Alego/Usonga and Gem in Siaya District, Nambale and Samia). In contrast, Japeth Shamalla was the most prominent lawyer in FORD-Asili, which had only four lawyers or ex-lawyers among its candidates. Asili was the party of the self-made men, the meritocrats and small businessmen: they were populist, grassroots, 'hard men' rather than intellectuals. FORD-Asili's most surprising recruit in the profession was the party's lawyer, Gibson Kamau Kuria, who in the mid-1980s had been one of the few members of the legal community willing to defend detainees and political dissidents. Kuria had briefly considered standing for the united FORD against Mwai Kibaki in his native Othaya, but had reconsidered following the split. He re-emerged as FORD-Asili's legal adviser and a key figure in the party, although his law partner Kiraitu

Murungi was FORD-Kenya's candidate in Imenti Central. The presence of this quiet academic in FORD-Asili was always slightly incongruous.

KANU's team consisted mainly, of course, of incumbent MPs, with a sprinkling of third-rank previously defeated figures from the opposition areas. Its newcomers consisted of civil servants (including ex-DCs), businessmen, teachers, farmers and local councillors. KANU's candidates also included several soldiers or individuals with close ties to the military. Minister of State Maalim Mohammed was the brother of Major-General Mohammed, Chief of the General Staff; Peter Steve Lengees, MP for Samburu West, was the brother of Army Commander Major-General Lengees; while Jackson Mulinge, the party's candidate for Kathiani in Machakos District, had been Chief of the General Staff for most of the 1970s and 1980s, and still had close ties to the military élites, and at least one other Machakos MP was a retired colonel. Over one third of KANU's candidates were party branch officials who had seized party posts in September 1988, after the last general election.

Since the 1960s, the headstart which the new élites at Independence gained in the economic and political sphere has created a pseudo-medieval political system in Kenya. The huge socio-economic divisions between the peasant majority and the minority élites have continued or even grown with the allocation of land, contracts and jobs on the basis of family and political alliances. As with the baronial alliances of medieval Europe, strategic marriages between political families have been common, especially among the Kikuyu. The élites all know each other, were educated together, and are in business together. A good example of this can be seen in Githunguri, where the KANU and DP candidates came from the area's two most prominent 'gentry' families, the descendants of prominent colonial chiefs. The DP candidate Mrs Rose Waruhiu was married to local landowner George Waruhiu, whose aunt, brother Ben, and sister-in-law had all married into KANU Minister Arthur Magugu's family. George Waruhiu, moreover, had acted as best man at Magugu's wedding.

As a result of the entrenched power of certain families in particular localities, the desire to honour departed leaders, and KANU's recognition of the influence of local figureheads, the sons and other relatives of Cabinet Ministers and other prominent politicians have frequently been recruited to fill their positions. The dynastic element, therefore, has become extraordinarily strong in Kenya, and has been reinforced by President Moi, according to some, in the long-term expectation that he could obtain the Presidency for the man alleged to be his illegitimate son, Mark arap Too.[252] Thus several candidates in the 1992 election were the sons or brothers of prominent deceased politicians. Vihiga District was a particularly good example, since three of the four MPs when Parliament was dissolved were the sons of the previous MP for the seat, including Minister Musalia Mudavadi, the son of Moi's closest Luhya ally for many years, Moses Mudavadi, who was married to Moi's sister. There were three relatives of ex-KADU leader Ronald Ngala involved in the elections in Kilifi District (including his son, KANU Minister Noah Katana Ngala) and four relatives of Jomo Kenyatta: Dr Mungai (his nephew), who lost the Westlands KANU primaries; his brother-in-law George Muhoho (DP Juja); his nephew Ngengi Muigai (DP, Gatundu); and his niece Betty Tett (DP, Westlands). As we have seen, Kenyatta's daughter Margaret sat on the Electoral Commission.

There were also a few family battles. DP leader and former Minister Kyale Mwendwa, the brother of the former Cabinet Minister Eliud Ngala Mwendwa, was opposed in Kitui West by his sister-in-law, Winifred Nyiva Mwendwa, the widow of former Kitui KANU Chairman and local MP, the late Kitili Mwendwa. KANU Minister Archbishop Oluoch's brother-in-law, the prominent FORD-Kenya leader James Orengo, was the opposition party's candidate in his Ugenya seat. Another case of cross-party loyalty was provided by the Omido family, where father, Fred, was KANU's candidate in Nairobi's Makadara constituency, while son, David, was FORD-Kenya's standard bearer in Eldoret North. The brother of KANU's Burudi Nabwera stood for the DP in Malava. Norman Nyagah's position as DP candidate for Gachoka was slightly different – although his father was the KANU MP, Cabinet Minister and incumbent party chairman, it was far from clear where Mzee Jeremiah Nyagah's loyalties lay. By contrast, FORD-Kenya leader Oginga Odinga's son, Raila Odinga, played a prominent role in his father's Presidential campaign, as well as standing as the party's candidate in Langata; and deputy FORD-Asili leader Martin Shikuku's brother was the FORD-Asili candidate in Nakuru Town.

Presidential Nomination Day

The next stage was the nomination of candidates for the Presidency. This took place five days after Parliamentary nominations, between 8 a.m. and 1 p.m. on 14 December 1992, two weeks before election day. Eight candidates were expected by the Electoral Commission: those of the four main parties, plus the KNC, KSC, Labour Party Democracy (LPD), and KENDA. The Commission arranged that each candidate would present his nomination papers at Parliament buildings at a specified time in order to minimise confrontation between rival supporters. In addition, the parties were given nominated assembly sites for mass meetings afterwards. In contrast to the Parliamentary nominations, the Presidential nominations proceeded smoothly, fairly, and with maximum publicity, including live television coverage. No candidate was refused nomination, and efforts were made to ensure that those who arrived with incorrect documentation were offered the opportunity to correct it.

KANU supporters of Minister Ntimama, staying at the 680 Hotel, sprayed shops, walls and windows in the central business district during the night of 13–14 December with pro-KANU slogans to greet President Moi as he made his way to the Parliament building where the Electoral Commission waited to receive the Presidential candidates' nomination papers. Moi was the first candidate to arrive, at 8.30 a.m. His nomination was delayed when it was discovered that the President had arrived without an official letter from KANU nominating him as its Presidential candidate. This had to be produced hastily and rushed to Parliament from the party's headquarters. The President also threw Commission Chairman Chesoni into confusion when he handed over, in full view of the television cameras, a large sum of money. A flustered Chesoni eventually managed to stammer that the President did not have to hand over his deposit at that time.

KENDA's nominee David Mukaru-Ng'ang'a came second, and also experienced a problem since his sponsors' names did not match the Commission's list of registered office bearers. Assistants were despatched to obtain a paper from the Registrar of Societies confirming that the party's office bearers had changed. Meanwhile, the crowd in the city centre was swelling, with the two FORDs, especially Asili, drawing the most support. DP candidate Mwai Kibaki, in fact, faced barracking when he arrived. Kibaki presented the Commission with a vast pile of paper, informing Chesoni that he had 2,000,000 signatories for his nomination. By contrast, the KNC's Dr wa Tsuma was in hiding, fearing that the KNC leaders would attempt to serve him with the Court injunction preventing his nomination. He had to be proposed by the party's Assistant Treasurer and represented by his wife. John Harun Mwau, the 'boss' of PICK, was a surprise candidate, who turned up at the last minute. Contrary to popular belief, PICK had always intended to present a Presidential candidate, but were initially prevented from doing so by the Electoral Commission.[253] The LPD's candidate pulled out at the last minute and announced his support for FORD-Kenya.

FORD-Asili leader Kenneth Matiba received the biggest welcome from the Nairobi crowd. Accompanied by bodyguards and prominent FORD-Asili politicians, Matiba made his way to the Committee Room where the Commission was waiting. As he greeted the Commissioners, television viewers could see that the Asili leader was unable to use his right hand and was exerting tremendous will-power to appear physically normal. KTN television treated Matiba with considerable deference, recalling his distinguished career as a senior civil servant, successful businessman and as a Cabinet Minister before he launched his campaign for multi-party democracy. Oginga Odinga (FORD-Kenya) and George Anyona (KSC) were also nominated without incident.

The parties' supporters then dispersed to venues across the city for party rallies. President Moi's was at Nyayo National stadium; Odinga was exiled to *Jamhuri* Park in Nairobi's southern outskirts; Kibaki's rally was at Kasarani International Sports Centre in the northern suburbs; while Matiba addressed his supporters in *Uhuru* Park, just across the road from Parliament. Confrontational as usual, he led his supporters across the city to the symbolic Kamukunji grounds, where the initial rally for multi-party democracy was to have taken place on 7 July 1990. Anyona attracted a small crowd at City Stadium, while the other two scheduled speakers – Mukaru-Ng'ang'a and wa Tsuma – drew no one at all. Matiba's crowd was the largest, demonstrating that he was winning the battle with Kibaki for the Kikuyu vote in Nairobi and neighbouring Kiambu. At distant Kasarani, by contrast, Kibaki's' crowd was dwarfed by the huge stadium. FORD-Kenya's rally in *Jamhuri* Park was cheerful and optimistic, and probably marked the high point for FORD-Kenya in Nairobi. It was clear, however, that a high proportion of the supporters who wended their way into the suburbs, singing and chanting, carrying green branches and

Photo 9.3 Party leaders at Ford-Kenya's Rally in Jamhuri Park. *Seated right to left:* Abuya Abuya, Abdikadir Hassan, Gitobu Imanyara, Paul Muite, Oginga Odinga, Odinga's wife, Kijana Wamalwa, Waruru Kanja

Courtesy Charles Hornsby

pictures of Odinga, were Luo. The organisation of the rally was characteristic, with party leaders and an IPK representative sitting on a dais, while the major speakers were the party's Nairobi candidates, party officials, and the Odingas. Raila Odinga was clearly the 'anointed son', speaking in his father's traditional Luo beaded cap.

Campaign Rallies and Styles

In most of the country, Parliamentary candidates held their own rallies, joined by local government candidates, local notables, and guests from outside the constituency. In some districts, such as Busia, the candidates from the same party held joint rallies, as for example did the KANU candidates for Nambale and Bunyala.[254] In a few exceptional cases, different parties shared the same platform, in the traditional Kenyan style. In Wundanyi in Taita-Taveta, the DP and FORD-Asili shared the platform, while in Lamu East, all three opposition parties campaigned together.[255] In Lari in Kiambu, FORD-Kenya, KANU and the KNC held at least one joint rally, a reflection of the underdog status of these three parties in the area.[256] Candidates generally campaigned as a team with their party's local government candidates. Vehicles mounted with speakers toured the area beforehand, announcing the venue and time of the

Photo 9.4 Ford-Kenya's Rally at Jamhuri Park.
Courtesy Charles Hornsby

meeting. Most rallies were held in the afternoon between two and six o'clock. The speakers and agenda had to be precisely stated in advance in the application for a licence. Traditional dancers and party choirs were heavily used by all candidates to entertain the crowd.

A few urban and peri-urban candidates such as George Saitoti in Kajiado North and Wanguhu Ng'ang'a (FORD-Asili) in Westlands produced booklets on their policies and achievements. In general, however, the main method of communication was word of mouth, plus occasional rallies. The number of rallies held varied enormously between areas of the country. Some constituencies were hotbeds of activism with dozens of rallies. Others, such as Amagoro and Mount Elgon, were extremely quiet, with only one or two rallies in total.

Not all Parliamentary or local government candidates, however, campaigned for their own party's Presidential nominee. It was well known that some KANU leaders, recognising the slim chances of a KANU victory in their area, were campaigning for themselves, but not urging voters to support President Moi. These included G. G. Kariuki (Laikipia West), Arthur Magugu (Githunguri), Grace Ogot (Gem) and Elijah Mwangale (Kimilili).[257] This was an extremely sensitive matter, since candidates could never admit to party headquarters that they had failed to campaign for the President. Similarly, opposition candidates whose Presidential candidate was unpopular in their area also suggested that people vote for them, but 'make up their own minds' for the Presidency. Lawrence Nginyo Kariuki (FORD-Kenya, Kiambaa), for example refused to endorse Odinga and instead campaigned for Matiba, whilst Peter Lotitiyo (FORD-Kenya, Samburu West) actually campaigned for President Moi.[258] Many PICK candidates also campaigned for Moi. It was hard for central parties to impose discipline, since most were not even funding their campaigns. Nonetheless, such attempts to disassociate a candidate from his Presidential 'parent' had little effect.

The 'Forgotten Campaign' in Coast Province

The election in the rural Coast Province constituencies of Kilifi and Kwale Districts was typical of the contest outside the opposition parties' strongholds. FORD-Kenya's Jembe Mwakalu, for example, experienced a difficult time in Bahari, just north of Mombasa, despite the fact that as FORD-Kenya's Deputy Secretary for Human Rights and Democratisation, he was able to attract the attention of foreign correspondents. Mwakulu provided a good example of FORD-Kenya's candidates in the rural areas. Born in the constituency in 1950, a well-educated intellectual with several American degrees, he had joined the civil service and served as a DO in Kisumu and as personal assistant to the Nyanza PC. Resigning from the Provincial Administration when the Moi regime purged suspected radicals following the 1982 attempted coup, Mwakalu had fled to Uganda, where he taught, and then to Sweden, home of Kenyan dissidents at the time. Following the restoration of multi-party politics, Mwakalu had returned to Kenya in January 1992, and became an active member of FORD-Kenya's executive.

Mwakalu was one of FORD-Kenya's leading figures in Coast Province. The District Administration and local KANU leaders consequently seem to have overreacted, fearing that he would mobilise the discontent of the many landless Mijikenda squatting on the vast sisal estates with his slogan, 'land to the tiller'.[259] Between January and December 1992, Mwakalu had been arrested seven times, beaten and even tortured. Amnesty International had made him one of its 'prisoners of conscience' and urged its members to protest to the Commissioner of Police and Attorney-General Wako when Mwakalu was stabbed 16 times and had to be rushed to hospital.[260] Assaulted four times in April and May, Mwakalu had been attacked roughly once a week for the past six months. According to Mwakulu, the government had also tried to bribe him, offering him a Mercedes, a new house, payment of his salary for his nine years in exile, and even the party's nomination in Bahari if he would join KANU. When he started campaigning in the constituency, Mwakalu encountered a host of difficulties. Construction workers who were building a house for him were harassed by the police, then arrested and held in custody for two weeks. Shots were fired at other workers on the site and at the house where Mwakalu was staying. Then, on 19 October, 40 armed police, transported in government Landrovers, had stormed the building site, arrested all the workers, and hunted for Mwakalu for two weeks. Exasperated by the harassment and fearful that he would be arrested, Mwakalu had appeared before the Nairobi Principal Magistrate on 3 November 1992 and applied for a 100,000 shillings bond for all bailable offences, which technically barred the police from arresting him and putting him in remand custody until after election day.[261]

The Administration took no chances: a second DO was posted to the constituency, and the DC, the DOs, and the chiefs all actively campaigned for KANU. Mwakalu originally had sought permission to hold 33 rallies, but the DC approved only ten, with strict time limits. With less than a week to voting day, only five rallies had been held and FORD-Kenya's County Council candidates had been refused permission to hold any meetings. Some of Mwakulu meetings were cancelled at the last moment or villagers were called away to attend a state *baraza,* organised to clash with FORD-Kenya's meeting. KANU, by contrast, had organised 26 meetings and no time limit had been placed on its gatherings. The police attempted to trail Mwakulu wherever he went, putting up roadblocks to disrupt his schedule. As a result, Mwakalu was forced to use a different car each day and to sleep in a different house each night. With less than a week to election day, he still had not been able to campaign in half the constituency. Village elders, prominent figures in women's groups, and church leaders who supported FORD-Kenya were also targeted for intimidation.

Cost was no obstacle. The PC, who directed KANU's campaign at the Coast, had allocated 3,000,000 shillings to its Bahari campaign. KANU had 20 local offices in the constituency, whilst FORD-Kenya had only three. Government vehicles were also used to support the ruling party, transporting voters to rallies and to the polls. As in some other constituencies, KANU was buying voters' cards at 200 shillings each, and handing out payments of between 50 and 200 shillings, plus free *khangas* and T-shirts to local women. Its candidate, like others in Coast Province, made frequent trips to Mombasa to receive 'envelopes' of money from KANU headquarters. President Moi's brother-in-law Eric Bomett, the former MP for Nakuru North, acted as courier. He arrived in Mombasa on one of his journeys on Tuesday, 22 December with money to finance the campaign and to reward opposition defectors who were to be presented at the President's last major rally in Mombasa on Christmas Eve, two days later. KANU candidates from throughout the Province travelled to attend the rally and to receive suitcases of money to pay for the party's last drive.[262]

Candidates from FORD-Asili and the DP also encountered problems throughout the rural parts of Coast Province, although FORD-Kenya's were the most harassed. In Kaloleni, neither the DP nor FORD-Asili were permitted to open local headquarters, so that the campaign had to be fought out of the candidates' modest farm houses, which were situated on dirt roads, some miles from the main population centres. The constituency, by contrast, was festooned with KANU posters and sub-branch offices. KANU's candidate in Kaloleni, Mathias Keah, a young Price-Waterhouse accountant, had probably been rigged in against Chibule wa Tsuma in 1988, but nonetheless had proved an energetic and popular MP, and more effective than wa Tsuma, the KNC's Presidential and local Parliamentary candidate. The local issues were similar to those in Bahari: rural poverty, growing landlessness among the Mijikenda, and the poor quality of roads and services. The local agricultural economy was dominated by the coconut palm and its by-products – copra and *mnazi,* the local brew, which Dr wa Tsuma had campaigned to legalise. As in Bahari, much of the best land was owned by Asians and by up-country people with good political connections. Keah, who had been appointed an Assistant Minister, had secured money from his political patrons to improve educational facilities and had started to roof every school with corrugated iron. The constituency had also benefited from the patronage of Cabinet Minister Noah Katana Ngala, the MP for neighbouring Ganze, who actually lived in Kaloleni. As in Bahari, the PC had allocated Sh3 million to the Kaloleni campaign, which was spending about Sh100,000 per day.

By contrast, few opposition candidates, outside Mombasa, received much money from the party headquarters, and most had very limited personal financial resources. Mwakalu in Bahari had to borrow vehicles from friends and had gone into debt to raise Sh10,000 to fight the campaign. Unlike their counterparts in Kiambu and Nyeri, who were frequently extremely wealthy, the DP's standard bearers at the Coast, for example, were educated individuals of modest means. Matuga DP candidate Mudzo Nzili, for example, was a teacher at Kwale Secondary School and area secretary of the Kenya Union of Teachers; Mashengu wa Mwachofi in Wundanyi was a radical ex-MP, who could barely afford to run an old van to tour his mountainous constituency. Gabriel Ngala in Kaloleni was a (comparatively wealthy) local farmer, but with little backing from DP headquarters, harassed by the District Commissioner and the local chief, and supported by only a handful of even poorer local elders, he could provide little opposition to Keah. Even the 2,000 posters for the DP's Parliamentary candidate and the 1,000 posters for each County Council candidate had to be bought from DP headquarters at a cost of 35,000 shillings, virtually exhausting the constituency party's funds.

Defections

The election campaign confirmed the fragility of some politicians' allegiance to the opposition. Using cash and threats, KANU managed to lure back numerous opposition supporters, including many nominated candidates. Kenyans have become used over the years to backroom agreements that see politicians stand down for their opponents, in return for money and favours. In the past, the most noteworthy candidate withdrawals had been candidates standing against favoured associates of the inner leadership.[263] In 1992, the role of money and favours was stronger than ever before. FORD-Kenya leaders were convinced that Sh5 million was paid to their National Treasurer and Dujis candidate Abdikadir Hassan, who to their horror defected to KANU only four days after endorsing Odinga at the *Jamhuri* Park FORD-Kenya rally. Some candidates also succumbed to threats or pressure from the government. Violence had been employed in previous elections to deter candidates. In 1992, however, there were two sources of threats which had to be balanced – the government and local voters. In opposition areas, such as Murang'a, no matter how much the government could offer, the personal risks associated with defection to KANU remained greater. There were, therefore, few defections to KANU in the opposition heartlands. In North-Eastern Province, by contrast, the calculations were very different. There, the power of the state was far greater, with little private business or wealth. Opposition candidates and supporters were poorer, and their chances of victory uncertain, so they were far more vulnerable to both intimidation and bribery. Opposition candidates and party officials had started to drift back to KANU in September, but this process peaked in November and early December, when numerous candidates defected back and large groups of youths and poor people were paraded by KANU as defectors. Local opposition parties also played the defections game, parading alleged defectors from KANU and other parties at their rallies, attempting to give the impression that their party was likely to win victory nationally (and locally).

Defecting prospective opposition Parliamentary candidates were valuable trophies in the run-up to nomination day. If a candidate could be persuaded to stand down, the party would have to find a replacement, less well known, at extremely short notice. At least a dozen selected candidates from all parties defected back to KANU in these critical weeks. FORD-Asili lost all three of its Nandi candidates at the end of November.[264] On 4 December, only five days before nomination day, the DP candidate in West Mugirango also rejoined the ruling party, throwing the local DP into confusion, although it was able to nominate another candidate. A last-minute defection also left FORD-Kenya without a candidate in Malava in Kakamega District, but the party was able to find a replacement in Mandera West.[265]

From 9 December onwards, KANU aggressively targeted nominated opposition candidates, and over the next three weeks more than 50 parliamentary candidates decided to rejoin the ruling party. Most announced their decision at KANU press conferences or sent letters to the Chairman of the Electoral Commission, resolving to campaign for KANU. The reasons they gave followed a standard script and included alleged tribalism in the opposition parties; the opposition's lies, false promises and power-hungry leaders (especially Matiba); the lack of internal party democracy (especially in the DP); the need for local unity; and the failure of the opposition parties to provide any organisational or financial support. A good example of the latter was provided by Daniel Moracha Nyareru's defection letter in the *Kenya Times,* which stated, 'I had pressure from some agents. They wanted money every day when I couldn't move an inch. I couldn't afford it.'[266]

The ruling party emphasised persuading candidates to defect, firstly, because of the resulting publicity. Large-scale defections, especially of household names, indicated that opposition in an area was weakening and, since people wished to support the winner in order to ensure the flow of patronage and development projects, such reports reinforced KANU's dominance. The well-organised 'defection ceremonies', where politicians handed over their party documents and party registers, and led their supporters back into KANU, were therefore heavily reported in the *Kenya Times.* Such 'PR' events also suggested that there was little to choose between KANU and the opposition, since opposition leaders clearly could be bought. Less attractive but still useful were defectors who had failed to win the nomination. Having lost their chance of getting into Parliament, these ex-candidates needed to recover their election costs, so were vulnerable. At least a dozen such losers defected between the end of November and mid-December, from all the major parties.

Only about half the reports of Parliamentary defections in the *Kenya Times* were true. The newspaper's announcements of defections often proved to be about individuals who had lost, not won, the opposition party's nomination.[267] The paper also reported the same stories in a slightly different guise on different days, creating the impression that the number of defectors was greater than it actually was. Sometimes, they simply announced false information.[268] The paper claimed, for example, that all the DP candidates in Kisumu and Nyamira had defected when, in fact, only isolated individuals had done so. One of KANU's biggest triumphs came on 19 December, when the *Kenya Times* headlined the news that '400 Nominees Defect to KANU', suggesting that 400 local government and Parliamentary candidates had defected. In fact, almost all were local council candidates. KANU also encouraged rumours that other opposition candidates were standing down, weakening their support, since people were no longer sure whether they were in the race. The *Kenya Times* described, for example, how Abdi Ali Baricha (FORD-Kenya, Mandera Central) had been abducted from a Nairobi restaurant on 23 December and instructed to stand down, which he had now done.[269] In fact, he had done no such thing. These articles were effective in disheartening the opposition and making them suspicious of their own candidates' long-term commitment.

KANU's main purpose, however, was more straightforward. According to Section 19 of the National Assembly and Presidential Elections Act, once party candidates had been nominated, they could not be withdrawn from the ballot papers or replaced.[270] Thus, if a candidate who had been nominated officially could be induced to withdraw, their name remained on the ballot paper. Few people, however, would vote for a candidate who had already defected and was no longer campaigning. KANU's final haul was over 50 Parliamentary defectors (there were more which went unreported), and many more local government candidates (at least 10 per cent of the opposition's remaining candidates, following on from the 50 they had lost on nomination day). The defections peaked in the week of 18–25 December, just before the election. Some opposition candidates may even have been plants, closet KANU sympathizers who had been backed by KANU supporters in the opposition primaries in order to win the nomination, and then to defect to KANU, leaving their opponents without a candidate. No single KANU candidate defected, though the KANU candidate against Kibaki in Othaya may have stood down just before the election, while its Kiharu candidate (in Matiba's seat) never campaigned. The two FORDs suffered most, particularly in the Rift Valley and North-Eastern Province (see Table 9.8). As a result, KANU was unopposed in nine more seats in which all their opponents had defected, in addition to the 16 seats which they had secured on nomination day. Thus whilst KANU faced opposition in every Nairobi, Central, Eastern, Coastal,

Table 9.8 Nominated Candidates Defecting by Province and Party

Province	FORD-Asili	DP	FORD-KENYA	KNC	PICK	Total
Nairobi						0
Central						0
Eastern	3		3	2		8
North-East	6	5	7	2		20
Coast	2					2
Rift Valley	2	4	6	0	1	13
Western	1				3	4
Nyanza	3	3				6
Total	17	12	16	4	4	52

Western and Nyanza seat, four of ten North-Eastern Province and 21 of 44 Rift Valley seats were theirs without contest. By election day, FORD-Kenya and FORD-Asili had candidates in only two thirds of the seats, while the DP's coverage had fallen to three quarters of the total (see Table 9.9). Amongst the smaller parties, the KNC was reduced to 47 candidates, whilst PICK was cut to less than 28 active contenders. Nonetheless, the situation could have been worse. The defectors represented the least important sector of the opposition leadership. KANU won no more than one or two Parliamentary seats that it might otherwise have lost, as few candidates with any expectation of winning could be persuaded to stand down, dissuaded by the prospect of Parliament and access to power. The most serious blow was probably the loss of Abdikadir Hassan, and even he was unlikely to win. Some defections may even have been counter-productive, concentrating the opposition vote on the remaining candidates.

Table 9.9 Party Coverage by Polling Day

Province	Seats	FORD-Asili	FORD-Kenya	DP
Nairobi	8	8	8	8
Central	25	24	15	24
Eastern	32	27	24	32
North-Eastern	10	4	3	4
Coast	20	15	17	19
Rift Valley	44	19	13	23
Western	20	17	17	18
Nyanza	29	12	29	13
Total	188	126	126	141

The Vice-Presidency

One intriguing issue for the parties to resolve was the Vice-Presidential nominations. Since there had never been a Presidential election in Kenya before, no one really knew what role should be given to Vice-Presidential candidates, or, indeed, whether it was politically wise to nominate a Vice-President at all. All the parties eventually left the issue undecided. Saitoti confidently continued to play the part of Vice-President throughout the election, but his position was never secure, as a number of others (including Elijah Mwangale, Dalmas Otieno and Simeon Nyachae) had also been promised the position if they won.[271] It was also far from clear whether Saitoti would even win his seat, as his constituency of Kajiado North included large-scale peri-urban Kikuyu settlement spreading south from Nairobi, and he was facing two serious opponents, John Keen for the DP and Philip Odupoy for FORD-Asili. Saitoti ran probably the most expensive campaign of the election, with mass distributions of colour posters, money, caps, clothing for women and the production of a 16-page colour booklet extolling his virtues as a development-conscious leader. His nomination day parade was a PR extravaganza, managed by a professional public relations team, in which thousands of Maasai were imported from far afield.

Saitoti was never formally endorsed as the next Vice-President by Moi. As long as several communities (particularly the Luhya and Kisii) believed they had the Vice-Presidency in their grasp, they would fight even harder for a KANU victory. Moreover, while a Vice-Presidential candidate selected before 29 December might have been chosen in order to maximise the party's vote at the election, it would have gone against Kenyan tradition to appoint a powerful, potentially independent Vice-President. Since Odinga's resignation in 1966, Vice-Presidents had either had no effective power in the government (Murumbi, Moi and Kibaki in later years) or no national constituency from which to threaten the President (Karanja and Saitoti). Only in 1978, when he first came to power (like Kenyatta in 1963), had Moi been forced to appoint a politically significant figure, Kibaki, to the post.

Of the opposition parties, FORD-Asili came closest to selecting an official Vice-President, since Shikuku was Matiba's only possible choice and performed the role, although it was never formally bestowed. Indeed, meetings in Bungoma endorsed him as the next Vice-President.[272] FORD-Asili leaders, including Njenga Mungai, had argued strongly that Shikuku should be declared the party's official Vice-Presidential candidate at the Limuru conference of Asili candidates, in order to maximise the party's appeal among Luhya voters. In his usual style, however, Matiba had slammed his fist and declared that the choice of a Vice-President was a decision for him alone.[273] If FORD-Asili had explicitly endorsed Shikuku, it might have secured even more votes in Western Province as the only party to nominate a Luhya to one of its top two positions. As it was, Shikuku openly organised a regional party ticket within Kakamega District, and campaigned actively for his team. On 6 December, for example, he addressed a major rally in Lurambi accompanied by the FORD-Asili Shinyalu, Ikolomani and Lurambi candidates; on 13 December he spoke at a joint rally in Ikolomani, with candidates for Ikolomani, Mumias, Lugari and Malava; and on 17 December, he campaigned jointly with the Emuhaya candidate in Vihiga District.[274] According to FORD-Kenya's constitution, the Vice-President could only come from the party's First or

Second National Vice-Chairmen, Paul Muite and Kijana Wamalwa. Muite effectively eclipsed the quieter Luhya leader, but Wamalwa controlled a larger ethnic constituency, an issue which remained unresolved. The DP never chose a second-in-command, though John Keen played this role in public. He suggested in November that Kibaki would soon name a running mate, but a choice never occurred, partly because Keen, like Muite, had too small an ethnic constituency.

Did KANU Finance Another Party to Divide the Opposition?

Throughout 1992 it was widely believed that KANU was assisting and possibly even funding some opposition leaders in order to split the opposition. No one suggested that FORD-Kenya were tools of the regime, but at different times, both the DP and Asili fell under suspicion. In early 1992, the focus was on Kibaki and the DP, who were accused of being 'KANU-B,' little more than a device to divide the opposition and likely to rejoin KANU if they lost. By the end of the election period, however, the pressure was on Matiba and FORD-Asili. Many DP supporters believed that KANU was funding FORD-Asili in order to split both FORD and the opposition vote in Kikuyuland, and that Moi and Matiba would form a coalition government if KANU failed to secure an overall majority. Indeed, it was believed by some that the Vice-Presidency was reserved for Matiba. Martin Shikuku was particularly vilified for 'being used by KANU to destabilise the opposition'.[275]

The truth is difficult to ascertain. Evidence exists that FORD-Asili was compromised, but most is circumstantial. One concern was Asili's apparent wealth, which was able to match the DP's financial resources in the Kikuyu areas. Few DP supporters believed that Matiba had funded everything personally, although like Ross Perot he was certainly willing to spend his own fortune lavishly to become President. Matiba was also harassed far less than the other opposition leaders during his campaign. KANU tended to avoid direct criticism of him, concentrating its invective on the other leaders. Kamotho, for example, welcomed Matiba's declaration that he would vie for the FORD presidency, whilst *KANU Briefs* described Matiba as a 'capable administrator' and 'successful and very wealthy businessman', who was likely to fare better than Kibaki.[276] To KANU's benefit, Matiba's campaign tactics focused primarily on the DP, and he initiated the anti-Kibaki 'smear' campaign in the last days before the poll.

There were two more substantial issues. The first was the never-explained visit of Shikuku and Japeth Shamalla to State House for 'midnight *ugali*' with President Moi in June 1992. It was alleged after Shikuku's visit that he had received Sh30 million from Moi, and that his wife had admitted that 'we don't have to worry about money any more', although Shikuku had used the money against KANU. The second was the strange case of the Moi cheque. In the last days of the campaign, the DP xeroxed and distributed in Nairobi and Kiambu thousands of copies of a cheque purporting to be from President Moi to FORD-Asili. A Kenya Commercial

Bank cheque for Sh65 million, apparently issued on 8 December 1992, it was reported by the bank to be a fake. At least three errors were identified: numbers were written outside the box, and the branch name and account number were missing. Shikuku correctly claimed that the DP was behind the forgery, as a last desperate attempt to discredit Matiba.[277] The DP tried to conceal its origin by circulating stories that a number of people in the KCB's River Road branch had been sacked as a result.

The most likely explanation is that KANU did assist Matiba's ambitions covertly and may even have provided financial assistance to FORD-Asili, correctly calculating that Matiba could split both FORD and the Kikuyu vote. This would ensure that the opposition was split three ways, guaranteeing that no single leader could gain 25 per cent in five provinces or an overall majority. In Central Province, the collapse of either the DP or Matiba's FORD faction would have been a disaster for KANU, so they supported the weaker of the two parties.

The Opposition Cry Foul

Each opposition party, whilst it did not poll directly, had its own internal estimates of likely performance. All three reported the same thing – that by polling day, they could not win Parliament. Nonetheless, they still hoped to win the Presidency, and collectively to deny Moi a majority of the Assembly. The unofficial line from FORD-Kenya officials on 14 December was that the new Parliament would be divided almost equally between the four main parties, with KANU and the DP both winning 50 seats, while FORD-Kenya itself would gain only 40, and 48 seats would be divided between FORD-Asili, the KNC, KSC and PICK. They hoped for the Presidency, but knew they could not win a Parliamentary majority. FORD-Asili officials also admitted that they could not win Parliament well before election day: their bet was on Matiba in the Presidential contest. DP officials knew that they were heading for defeat and that Kibaki would gain fewer votes than Matiba in Nairobi and perhaps even in Central Province. By polling day, 29 December, most opposition leaders were too tired, dispirited, and disillusioned to care: most expected that KANU would rig the result massively anyway.

As the realisation began to strike home that the opposition parties were probably going to lose the election they had fought so strongly to hold, there was a short-lived attempt to appeal to the West to call off the poll at the last minute. Senior politicians from the three main opposition leaders met at Chester House in Nairobi on 21 December, 8 days before polling day, and threatened a boycott. This was generally viewed as a belated recognition of defeat, made far too late to have much credibility, in the country or outside. It was swiftly abandoned when church leaders, led by Archbishop Manasses Kuria of the CPK, opposed the idea.[278] The foreign observers were also unhappy. Ambassador Hempstone spoke for many when he observed, 'Even in an unfair situation, I think the opposition should contest it if only to get an opposition voice in parliament.' This again revealed the different attitudes of the participants among both the Kenyan opposition and Western observers: there were those who believed that the election could be won, or lost, on the basis of a 'free' election; and those who recognised that it was extremely unlikely that KANU would give way under any circumstances, and were merely using the election as part of a long-term campaign to remove the government, not as an end in itself. This last was the logic of those, such as Hempstone, Muite and others, who suggested that it was better to have 80 opposition MPs to criticise the regime in the new Parliament than none.

Conclusions

The 1992 election campaign showed the fertile and dynamic nature of Kenyan politics. Despite widespread pressure, for the first time entire communities 'declared autonomy' from the state-run political machine, and for the first time voters were faced with a real choice. Nonetheless, KANU's campaign, based on a clever combination of threats, bribery, state authority and popular deference, was a triumphant success. Despite its primary losses, they had been able to secure a decisive advantage in the Parliamentary election by polling day. Kenyans were no more able than other peoples to resist intimidation and bribery, and, despite their professed commitment to democracy, many key players were motivated primarily by money and a determination to hang on to power.

The campaign also had serious negative consequences on Kenya's political and economic life. It intensified ethnic divisions between communities; it almost bankrupted the economy; it created huge expectations of change which could not be fulfilled, whoever won; and it reinforced the view among the government leadership that the Kikuyu were its key opponents, who had to be driven out of politically marginal areas. The regional focus of opposition support was intensified by state repression, ensuring that political preferences were reinforced. As a result, ethnicity was to be the single most effective predictor of political preference.

The narrow base and limited abilities and authority of Moi's opponents had also emerged clearly by polling day. FORD-Kenya was clearly the most intellectual and national in orientation of the parties, but this disposed it to concentrate too much on national issues, fighting a Western-style campaign in an electoral situation where on-the-ground organisation and mobilisation remained the most successful approach. The hardline populism and organisational and leadership skills of Matiba had undermined Kibaki's 'safe pair of hands' strategy without providing a plausible alternative national government, whilst the other smaller parties had been eclipsed entirely.

Electoral fairness is a complex and ill-defined phenomenon. No election is absolutely fair, but the differences of degree are enormous. In Kenya's case, much depended on whether outside observers judged the election to have been reasonably 'free and fair'. The issue has two basic components: First, all the parties must be free to campaign on 'a level playing field', without bribery or threats. If this fairness criterion is violated, then, whilst the election is unfair, as long as people are determined enough to actually vote the way they wish, their opinions can still triumph. The second component is 'what you vote is what you get' – how people actually wish to vote must determine the result. If the votes reported are not those which were actually cast, or voters are forced at gunpoint to vote for a particular candidate, then the entire process is a charade.

By 28 December 1992 it was clear that the campaign, and the electoral law and administrative process which surrounded it, had been manipulated by the government in favour of KANU. Ambassador Hempstone summarised this view when he observed:

> President Daniel arap Moi had publicly committed himself to 'free and fair' elections.... Perhaps we can be forgiven for being just a little bit sceptical when virtually nothing has been done to allow for an effective domestic monitoring system, when the opposition has been hampered in its efforts to hold meetings or even open branch offices in many parts of the country, when the registration process has been terminated before 1 million young [voters] without Identity Cards have had a chance to register, when we read in the press that teachers, civil servants, the army and police have been admonished to vote for KANU...or else, when opposition access to the media has been limited, when KANU and the government has not been delinked, when dialogue among the political parties has been honoured in the breach rather than in the observance. The spirit of fair play and tolerance that is at the heart of the democratic process seems largely – if not entirely – absent.[279]

Even recognising the obstacles hindering democratic processes in developing countries and the administrative problems which must be solved, there were at least five minimum criteria on which the 1992 election campaign clearly failed the 'free and fair' test. First, the government abused the registration process, under-registering opposition supporters, over-registering pro-KANU voters and continuing to register names long after the official close of the process. Secondly, the regime failed to sever the connection between party and state, using chiefs and administration officials to campaign for KANU and to frustrate the opposition. The climate of authoritarianism and fear that this created, intensified by the ethnic clashes, significantly reduced opposition support in semi-arid areas, and prevented the opposition parties functioning at all in KANU's heartlands. Thirdly, the state used its funds to buy support and to bribe opposition politicians to defect. Fourthly, government control of the media, especially the KBC, distorted news coverage in favour of KANU. Fifthly, pro-KANU thugs were free to intimidate opposition supporters and to use violence not only to disrupt the opposition parties' campaigns, but also to prevent over a tenth of their candidates even presenting their nomination papers.

The impact of the Presidential election law, with its 25 per cent rule, and of the over-representation of KANU's strongholds was also to favour Moi and the ruling party, but the principle of regional representation has strong antecedents in other states such as the USA, and deviations in constituency size are common in Westminster-style countries such as Britain. Overall, the bribes, threats, interceptions of candidates and other anomalies were probably sufficient to invalidate the election in roughly one third of the country. In these areas, where the opposition parties were unable to organise, voters did not have a free or a fair choice on election day. This area included the whole central Rift Valley, much of North-Eastern Province, Isiolo, Marsabit, West Pokot, Turkana and Samburu Districts. The fact that KANU would probably have won most of these seats in a fair fight does not alter the fact that there was no fair fight. Over the rest of the country, whilst the campaign was clearly unfair, local solidarity and strong opposition leaders allowed voters still to cast their ballots on election day in a reasonable expectation that they had a genuine choice. As Lee Muthoga said just before the election, 'There is no chance of having a fair election. The situation is tilted in favour of the present administration. We can however have a free election.'[280]

One of the core questions surrounding the election was how far KANU would abide by the voters' wishes. It seems clear now that Moi, Biwott, Ntimama, Saitoti and other KANU leaders had no intention of relinquishing power under any circumstances. Their lives and property would have been forfeit. Whether they would win fairly or unfairly was an open question, but win they would, in both elections, and on the first Presidential ballot (see Chapter 7). As long as they thought they could win – without cheating too much – and secure Western aid once more, they were willing to 'walk the tightrope' of an election. If they had thought that they would still lose, despite the campaign, election day would probably have been disrupted. If Moi had failed to win the Presidential election decisively, there would have been no second-round run-off and the Parliamentary results would have been annulled (due to massive irregularities). Opposition supporters also feared military action if KANU lost. American citizens received detailed instructions of evacuation procedures in case of a breakdown of law and order, and the British High Commission updated its emergency evacuation plans.

The West, meanwhile, proved unable to influence the outcome at this late stage. They were well aware that KANU had the upper hand, and, though sceptical, could not reject the result on the campaign alone; nor could they declare the democratic practice of one of their closest African allies fraudulent without decisive evidence. Inured to electoral fraud by the experience of elections in other developing countries, they were as heartened by the willingness of KANU to hold a relatively free poll as they were discomfited by the evidence that it was far less fair than would be acceptable in any Western state.

On 28 December electioneering finished, with the nation tense for the huge logistical and political events to take place the next day. Despite the bias of the previous months, it was still unclear what the final result would be. Although Moi was likely to win, and KANU would be the largest party in the Assembly, it was far from certain that KANU would win a decisive victory in either election; if KANU fared badly, massive rigging was still on the cards.

Notes

1 KANU Manifesto, p.13.
2 Personal interviews, 1992 and 1993.
3 J. Barkan, 'Kenya: Lessons from a Flawed Election' *Journal of Democracy*, Vol. 4, No. 3 (July 1993) p.86.
4 *Sunday Nation*, 1 November 1992, p.2.
5 Kanu Briefs, *Kenya Times*, 23 December 1992, p.13.
6 Kanu Briefs, *Kenya Times*, 23 December 1992, p.16.
7 Boy, in *Standard*, 2 November 1992, p.11.
8 This message was disingenuous since Odinga had held no government or parliamentary position for 20 years and had been prevented from becoming involved in any major government development projects.
9 *Weekend Mail*, 31 December 1992, p. 5.
10 *Standard*, 4 October 1992, p. 2.
11 *Daily Nation*, 19 October 1992, pp. 1–2.
12 Nassir at KANU rally, 6 December; *Kenya Times*, 8 December 1992, p. 23.
13 Ntimama, reported in *Daily Nation*, 18 October 1992, p. 2.
14 *Standard*, 14 December 1992, p. 1.
15 *Economic Review*, 30 November 1992, p. 8.
16 Moi in *Daily Nation*, 17 October 1992, p. 2.
17 *Daily Nation*, 31 October 1992, p. 1.
18 Moi, Kiganjo Police Training College, *Daily Nation*, 21 November 1992, p. 1.
19 *Daily Nation*, 25 November 1992, p. 1.
20 Moi in Siaya District, *Daily Nation*, 8 December 1992, p. 1.
21 'Blueprint for a New Kenya', PEAP, Friedrich Naumann Stiftung, Nairobi, 1992.
22 Published with money from the Friedrich Neumann Institute, a German foundation.
23 Matiba, *Man of the People*, Nairobi, 1992.
24 *Weekend Mail*, 31 December 1992, Interview with Lee Muthoga, p. 4.
25 Henry Kosgey, for example, was renowned for looting the Kenya National Trading Corporation as Executive Chairman between 1989 and 1992. It is even possible to suggest that a new model of corruption emerged – a pastoralist model – based on 'grazing' over different businesses, rather than settled 'cultivation' or exploitation of one, which might have seen funds 'ploughed back' into the enterprise.
26 See for example *Wajibu*, Vol. 7, No. 1 1992 for a detailed list of land scandals.
27 FORD-Kenya advertisement, *Daily Nation*, 1 December 1992, p. 5.
28 *Daily Nation*, 2 December 1992, p. 11.
29 *Weekly Mail*, 7 January 1993, p. 23.
30 Matiba, quoted in *Daily Nation*, 19 December 1992, p. 4. The origin of the Sh88 billion claim is unknown.
31 *Sunday Times*, 24 November 1991.
32 *Sunday Times*, 24 November 1991.
33 *Standard*, 30 November 1992, p. 1.
34 *Society*, 28 December 1992, p. 4.
35 Njenga Mungai, *Sunday Nation*, 15 November 1992, p. 16.
36 For example, see claims by the DP candidate for Lamu East that a victorious DP would revoke the Dodori National Park gazettement. *Daily Nation*, 23 December 1992, p. 6.
37 Onyonka, in *Daily Nation*, 19 October 1992, pp. 1–2.
38 *Society*, 10 August 1992, p. 35.
39 *Daily Nation*, 11 October 1992, p. 1.
40 *Weekly Review*, 18 December 1992, p. 15, and *Kenya Times*, 13 December 1992, pp. 1–2.
41 *Standard*, 27 August 1992, p. 2.
42 *Sunday Nation*, 1 November 1992, p. 2.
43 *Kenya Times*, 23 December 1992, p. 4.
44 Moi, reported in *Daily Nation*, 8 December 1992, p. 2.
45 *Standard*, 11 December 1992, p. 3.
46 C. P. W. Hornsby, 'The Kenyan Member of Parliament, 1969–1983', D.Phil thesis, Oxford, 1986, pp. 123–7.
47 No customs duties were paid at the receiving countries, no documentation supplied to

prove the value of the items, no export documentation supplied, since the objects were all being carried out 'by hand', yet aircraft passenger reports showed no record of Goldenberg staff travelling on the specified days. See the *Kenya Gazette*, notice No. 6, *Gazette Supplement* No. 3, 10 January 1992; letters from the Kenyan government, Exports Division, to the Registrar of Companies, the Swiss Embassy and Office for Trade Promotion in Switzerland. Internal government documents querying the payment of compensation. All contained in the Goldenberg File, a collection of documents relating to the Goldenberg affair, shown to the authors by FORD-Kenya leaders in May 1993.

48 *Economic Review*, 7 December 1992, p. 4.
49 *Economic Review*, 7 December 1992, p. 6.
50 *Nairobi Law Monthly*, October/November 1992, p. 26.
51 *Weekly Express*, 23 December 1992, p. 2.
52 Others included 'Wazee for Moi Only (WAFOMO)', 'Moi Campaign Storm Organisation', 'Vote for Moi Team' (VENT)', 'Youth for Jogoo', 'Operation Jogoo Fagia (OJF)', 'KANU Women Action Group 92', 'Mzungus for Moi', 'Coast Thunder Campaign for Moi', 'Moi for Kenya', Rural Operation Campaign for Kanu and Moi', 'Toroitich Kanu Enter Again (TOKEA)', 'Executive Club for Moi', 'KANU Committee for Recruitment and Campaign (KCRC)', 'KANU Youth Patriots', 'Agents for the Return of KANU (ARK)', 'Operation KANU Wins (OKW)', 'Operation Ganze All Votes for Moi (OGAVOM)', 'Operation Saitoti Bunge', 'KANU Youth National Democratic Front', 'Retain Moi Elect KANU', 'Congress for the Propagation of KANU Policies', 'Kisii Youths for KANU Victory', 'KANU and Moi Alone (KAMA)', 'Support Moi Retain KANU', 'Luhya Pressure Front for Moi Wins (LPFFMW)', 'Central Youth Organisation for Jogoo', 'Save Kenya Elect Moi (SKEM)', 'Rural Operation Campaign for Kanu and Moi', 'Moi Re-election Victory (MRV)', and 'Democratic KANU Campaigners Alliance'.
53 *Economic Review*, 5 October 1992, p. 22.
54 *Weekly Express*, Vol. 1, No. 5, p. 1.
55 *Daily Nation*, 19 October 1992, and *Standard*, 28 September 1992, p. 12.
56 See Sammy Boit arap Kigen, *Daily Nation*, 1 October 1992, p. 14 and K. Opanga, Lifestyle, p. 4 *Sunday Nation*, 10 January 1993.
57 E.g. *Standard on Sunday*, 30 August 1992, p. 1
58 Nyagah, reported in *Nation*, 21 November 1992, p. 1.
59 George Kinyua, in *Daily Nation*, 28 November 1992, p. 4.
60 Ondieki, *Daily Nation*, 16 November 1992, p. 15.
61 *Daily Nation*, 26 November 1992, p. 12
62 *Daily Nation*, 30 November 1992, p. 5. They also gave out 25,000 shillings in Kitui town on 24 November. See the *Daily Nation*, 25 November 1992, p. 4.
63 *Nairobi Weekly Observer*, 20 November 1992, p. 7. Kamotho ran a kiosk in Nairobi after losing the 1983 election.
64 Kibaki, reported by Opanga in *Sunday Nation*, 10 January 1993, Lifestyle, p. 4.
65 Interview with IRI Election Observer, December 1992.
66 *Nairobi Weekly Observer*, 20 November 1992, p. 7.
67 *Standard*, 3 November 1992, p. 3.
68 *Weekly Express*, 14 December 1992, p. 5.
69 Malava Constituency election monitor's report.
70 *Society*, 16 November 1992, p. 23.
71 NEMU Kisumu DLO report.
72 *Nairobi Weekly Observer*, 20 November 1992, p. 9.
73 Moi at ASK, 30 October, *Daily Nation*, 31 October 1992, p. 1.
74 See for example, *Daily Nation*, 23 November 1992, p. 3, 30 November 1992, p. 2 and 2 December 1992, p. 5.
75 *Sunday Nation*, 29 November 1992, p. 5.
76 *Daily Nation*, 16 September 1992, p. 4.
77 NEMU election monitor's report, Samburu DLO, p. 4.
78 NEMU, Embu DLO report.
79 NEMU constituency officer, Kibwezi.
80 George Nthenge, reported in *Nairobi Weekly Observer*, 4 December 1992, p. 9.
81 Odinga, *Kenya Times*, 18 December 1992, p. 5.
82 FORD-Kenya's confidential 1992 election accounts, p. 2.

83 NEMU election monitor's report, Machakos Town.
84 NEMU Kisumu DLO report.
85 See for example, P. Ochieng', *I Accuse the Press: An Insider's View of the Media and Politics in Kenya*, Initiatives Publishers, Acts Press, Nairobi, 1992.
86 NEMU Report, p. 60.
87 Commonwealth Report, p. 28. The *Nation*, also produced *Taifa Leo*, a Swahili–language version of the daily.
88 This occurred in Kakamega on 18 October. The *Nation* claimed they were paid by YK '92. See *Daily Nation*, 19 and 20 October 1992.
89 *Daily Nation*, 24 November 1992, p. 3 and 6 December 1992, p. 5.
90 *Daily Nation*, 12 December 1992, p. 4.
91 Personal conversation, 1992.
92 NCWK Report, p. 7.
93 *Finance*, 9 December 1992.
94 *Society*, 3 August 1992, p. 22. *Daily Nation*, 17 October 1992, p. 3.
95 *Society*, 3 August 1992, p. 22.
96 Gatabaki was held in jail until 11 August. *Society*, 24 August 1992, p. 36. He was recharged with sedition on 6 October over the 31 May issue. See *Daily Nation*, 7 October 1992, p. 6.
97 *Daily Nation*, 13 August 1992, p. 2 and *Standard*, 21 August 1992, p. 4.
98 *Finance* claimed damages. *Daily Nation*, 12 November 1992, p. 32.
99 *Standard*, 6 November 1992, p. 12.
100 *Kenya Times*, 8 December 1992, p. 17.
101 *Daily Nation*, 2 December 1992, p. 1 and 3 December 1992, p. 32.
102 *Society*, 23 November 1992, p. 9.
103 *Society*, inside cover, 28 December 1992.
104 Commonwealth Report, p. 26.
105 According to a *Nation* reporter, a colleague and her driver, who had spent several weeks collecting detailed testimony on the clashes in Nakuru, were attacked, badly beaten and had all their notebooks taken by unidentified persons on their way back to Nairobi. Interview, November, 1993.
106 Commonwealth Report, p. 27.
107 *Daily Nation*, 22 October 1992.
108 Letter from KBC, 11 December 1992.
109 The scripts were reprinted in detail in the NCWK Report.
110 *Daily Nation*, 25 November 1992, p. 12.
111 Letter from Kibaki to Chesoni, 14 December 1992.
112 *Daily Nation*, 16 October 1992, advertisers announcement, PCDC, p. 25.
113 NEMU Report, p. 59.
114 NEMU Report, pp. 57–60.
115 The source for this information is confidential accounts for the FORD-Kenya campaign period.
116 Marco Surveys ceased publication in 1966, around the same time as the KPU was founded.
117 P. Ochieng', *I Accuse The Press*, p. 168. Polls made it rather harder for the government to then manipulate the results.
118 *Daily Nation*, 7 December 1992, p. 1.
119 J. W. Onyango, in *Society*, 21 December 1992, p. 5.
120 NEMU poll results, *Daily Nation*, 7 December 1992, p. 3.
121 *Kenya Times*, 28 December 1992, p. 22; 29 December 1992, p. 5; and NEMU, *The Multi-Party General Elections in Kenya*, pp. 216–17.
122 *Kenya Times*, 27 December 1992, p. 3, and advertisement in *Kenya Times*, 28 December 1992, p. 20.
123 Habel Nyamu in Accra, *Daily Nation*, 5 June 1993, p. 16.
124 Gibson Kamau Kuria, 'Human Rights and Democracy in Kenya: A Case for a New Approach', 23 October 1992. Seminar sponsored by Friedrich Ebert Institute, p. 21.
125 *Daily Nation*, 6 October 1992, p. 2
126 Oyier, *Daily Nation*, 11 October 1992, p. 5.
127 *Daily Nation*, 22 November 1992, p. 13.
128 Saleh, in *Daily Nation*, 11 October 1992.
129 *Kenya Times*, 14 December 1992, p. 5.

130 *Daily Nation*, 10 October 1992, p. 2 and 21 October 1992, p. 4.
131 Gathenji M., 'Use of Criminal Offences in Restraint of Freedom of Assembly', *The Advocate*, Vol. 2, No. 1, August 1992, p. 10.
132 *Daily Nation*, 4 December 1992, p. 5.
133 Oreta, Kenyatta Day speech, *Daily Nation*, 21 October 1992.
134 *Daily Nation*, 14 November 1992, p. 3.
135 *Weekly Review*, 4 March 1988 pp. 7–8.
136 *Kenya Times*, 12 December 1992, p. 6.
137 *Nairobi Law Monthly*, Oct./Nov. 1992.
138 Makueni District, NEMU DLO.
139 A. O. Bachu, in fax from Matiba, 28 December 1992.
140 Interview with candidate and personal observations, 1992.
141 *Standard*, 4 December 1992, p. 3.
142 See for example *Kenya Times*, 22 December 1992, p. 20.
143 *Weekly Review*, 14 May 1993, p. 13.
144 *Society*, 21 October 1992, p. 3.
145 Sirma, *Daily Nation*, 21 October 1992, p. 3.
146 *Kenya Times*, 24 December 1992, p. 3.
147 *Standard*, 25 November 1992, p. 4.
148 *Sunday Times*, 13 December 1992, p. 5.
149 According to KANU's incumbent loser arap Tarar. *Standard*, 23 November 1992, p. 1.
150 *Kenya Times*, 20 December 1992, p. 3.
151 *Standard*, 16 December 1992, p. 13.
152 According to Oloo-Aringo and the CPK election monitoring committee, *Standard*, 23 November 1992, p. 4. Denied these reports in *Kenya Times*, 25 December 1992, p. 4.
153 *Standard*, 13 December 1992, p. 3.
154 *Standard*, 16 December 1992, p. 13.
155 *Standard*, 15 November 1992.
156 Kibaki Press Conference, *Daily Nation*, 14 November 1992, p. 28.
157 *Daily Nation*, 15 November 1992, p. 4 and 17 November 1992, p. 14.
158 *Daily Nation*, 4 December 1992, p. 24.
159 *Daily Nation*, 28 September 1992, p. 3.
160 Some of this material is sourced (with corrections) from the *Kenya Times*, which produced a briefing document claiming (correctly) that Moi was less ethnically partisan than Kenyatta in his selection of DCs. *Kenya Times*, 24 December 1992, p. 14.
161 *Standard*, 30 November 1992, p. 11.
162 *Kenya Times*, 2 December 1992, p. 3.
163 Henry Cheboiwo, in *Daily Nation*, 2 December 1992, p. 1.
164 Yego, in Kapsabet, *Daily Nation*, 3 December 1992, p. 32.
165 Moi, reprinted in *Daily Nation*, 17 October 1992, p. 2.
166 *Sunday Nation*, 29 January 1992, p. 5, and *Sunday Nation*, 1 November 1992, p. 11
167 Francis Ewoton, reported in *Daily Nation*, 8 December 1992, p. 4.
168 *Standard*, 25 November 1992, p. 4.
169 *Kenya Times*, 28 December 1992, p. 22.
170 Dr Misoi, quoted in *Daily Nation*, 4 December 1992, p. 4.
171 Kibor, quoted in *Daily Nation*, 26 November 1992, p. 5.
172 DO Rotich later closed five shops where people went to sing opposition songs, following 'orders from above'.
173 Arrested at gunpoint, they were quickly freed on bail. *Daily Nation*, 21 October 1992, p. 24.
174 *Daily Nation*, 14 November 1992, p. 2.
175 A Kikuyu man was also speared to death at Ereteti registration centre in Narok South constituency.
176 *Daily Nation*, 21 November 1992, p. 4 and 26 November 1992, p. 5.
177 *Standard*, 27 November 1992, p. 3.
178 NEMU Monitor, Narok North pre-election report.
179 Ndotto, in *Daily Nation*, 28 September 1992, p. 4.
180 *Daily Nation*, 2 November 1992, p. 4.
181 *Daily Nation*, 26 October 1992, p. 1.
182 *Standard*, 30 September 1992, p. 4.

183 NEMU poll monitor, Samia.
184 *Standard*, 23 September 1992, p. 2.
185 *Daily Nation*, 4 October 1992, p. 29.
186 *Daily Nation*, 15 October 1992, p. 4 and 10 November 1992, p. 5.
187 *Daily Nation*, 25 November 1992, p. 5.
188 The Mandera DC denied this. See *Daily Nation*, 31 October 1992 and *Sunday Nation*, 1 November 1992, p. 1.
189 *Sunday Nation*, 1 November 1992, p. 2.
190 *Daily Nation*, 20 November 1992, p. 12.
191 Korir, in *Society*, 14 September 1992, p. 20.
192 NEMU, Tana River DLO report, Nyeri DLO report, Samburu DLO report.
193 *Sunday Nation*, 29 November 1992, p. 4.
194 *Daily Nation*, 25 November 1992, p. 5.
195 J. L. Makokha, reported in *Daily Nation*, 28 September 1992, p. 3.
196 *Daily Nation*, 23 November 1992, p. 4.
197 *Daily Nation*, 31 October 1992, p. 5, 19 November 1992, p. 2. *Kenya Times*, 7 December 1992, p. 3, 12 December 1992, p. 3. *Daily Nation*, 3 October 1992, p. 1. *Standard*, 21 November 1992, p. 12.
198 *Daily Nation*, 15 November 1992, p. 1.
199 *Daily Nation*, 4 December 1992, p. 2.
200 *Standard*, 27 December 1992, p. 21.
201 See for example the front page photos of fighting in Kiambu in *Sunday Nation*, 29 November 1992, p. 1 and *Standard*, 9 December 1992, p. 33.
202 *Daily Nation*, 8 December 1992, p. 1.
203 *Daily Nation*, 21 October 1992, p. 2.
204 *Daily Nation*, 7 December 1992, p. 32.
205 *Daily Nation*, 24 November 1992, p. 1.
206 *Daily Nation*, 25 November 1992, p. 24.
207 Richard Sirei, in *Sunday Nation*, 29 November 1992, p. 1.
208 Mwai Kibaki, *Daily Nation*, 5 December 1992, pp. 1 and 22.
209 Police official Mac'Ogwangi, quoted in *Daily Nation*, 5 December 1992, p. 22.
210 *Standard*, 10 December 1992, p. 3.
211 Kibaki, *Kenya Times* 21 Decenber 1992, p. 5.
212 Kamunyu, *Kenya Times* 21 December 1992, p. 2.
213 For example, the full-page advertisment of 22 December with headlines such as "KANU is my 'Home' – Kibaki', *Daily Nation*, 22 December 1992, p. 11.
214 Testimony of R. Mbondo, *Weekly Review*, 24 November 1975, p. 5.
215 Charles Hornsby, unpublished D.Phil. thesis, Oxford University, p. 97.
216 Seii, in *Wajibu*, Vol. 7, No. 3, 1992, p. 7. See also Hornsby Thesis, p. 100.
217 *Kenya Times*, 9 December 1992, p. p. 2 and 24.
218 *Weekly Review*, 27 November 1992, p. 4.
219 The Commonwealth Report suggests there were 43 official protests at Parliamentary and local government candidates being forcibly prevented from nomination, and 62 in total concerning nomination day. According to KANU's own lawyer, Shah, the problems affected 35 seats. *Kenya Times*, 25 December 1992, p. 3. Robertson from the IRI suggested that 45 seats might have been affected. Commonwealth Press Statement, 13 December 1992. Justice Chesoni suggested the Complaints Committee had examined 43 cases – Chesoni, in *Kenya Times*, 14 December 1992, p. 3.
220 *Kenya Times*, 11 December 1992, p. 4.
221 This material has been collated from several sources, including two letters from Raila Odinga (FORD-Kenya) to Justice Chesoni, dated 10 and 11 December 1992; the *Kenya Times*, 10 December 1992, p. 16, 11 December 1992, p. 4 and 12 December 1992, p. 5; Kibaki's protest reports, in the *Kenya Times*, 11 December 1992, p. 17; NEMU report pp. 46 and 53; *Standard* 11 December 1992, p. 13; petition testimony, *Standard*, 29 October 1993, p. 5; *Kenya Times*, 3 November 1993, p. 4; and NEMU, Baringo DLO report.
222 NEMU, Baringo DLO report, 15 December 1993.
223 Affidavits by Samuel Mwaura and John Kosgei Chebii, 14 December 1992. Civil Suits 6651 and 6652, heard by Justice Akiwumi, 17 December 1992.
224 Eastern Elgeyo-Marakwet had been badly hit by the failure of the rains and by cattle raids from neighbouring Pokot, which had reduced many people to abject poverty. The

disintegration of civil order in Karamoja, just over the Uganda border, meant that sophisticated weapons could be purchased cheaply by Pokot cattle rustlers.

225 Affidavits by Joseph Theuri, Abbas Kipruto Mawboob, and John Gakuo, 14 December 1992. Civil suits 6649 and 6653, heard by Justice Akiwumi, 17 December 1992.

226 *Sunday Nation*, 15 November 1992.

227 Affidavit by Dr Patrick Njuguna, 14 December 1992. Civil suit 6648.

228 *Ibid.*

229 *Society*, 21 December 1992, p. 31. The NEMU DLO, Baringo, reported his papers were rejected. See, however, Kandie, in *Kenya Times*, 14 December 1992, p. 1.

230 *Society*, 21 December 1992, p. 30 and NEMU Report, p. 46.

231 Affidavit by Michael Namudiero, 14 December 1992. Civil suit 6650, heard by Justice Akiwumi, 17 December 1992.

232 Police headquarters denied any of their staff were involved – see *Kenya Times*, 11 December 1992, p. 3. The promotion was reported in the *Daily Nation*, 13 January 1993, p. 4.

233 NEMU Report, p. 46.

234 The other candidates petitioned the Electoral Commission to have him disqualified, without success. *Kenya Times* 11 December 1992, p. 17.

235 *Weekly Review*, 18 December 1992, p. 10.

236 *Kenya Times*, 11 December 1992, p. 16.

237 Robertson, Commonwealth Press Statement, 13 December 1992.

238 Which is exactly what occurred. Commonwealth Press Statement, 13 December 1992.

239 *Kenya Times*, 11 December 1992, pp. 2 and 16. See also Commonwealth Report, p. 18.

240 *Kenya Times*, 12 December 1992, p. 2.

241 Chesoni, in *Kenya Times*, 14 December 1992, p. 3, and letter to Raila Odinga, 15 December 1992.

242 Commonwealth Report, pp. 18–19.

243 *Kenya Times*, 17 December 1992, p. 2 and 22 December 1992, p. 3.

244 *Kenya Times*, 25 December 1992, p. 1.

245 *Kenya Times*, 29 December 1992, p. 2.

246 *Standard*, 23 December 1992, p. 1 and *Kenya Times*, 23 December 1992, p. 3.

247 *Kenya Times*, 29 December 1992, p. 3.

248 The exact figure is subject to dispute – see for example Electoral Commission, reprinted in *Standard*, 19 December 1992, p. 1. KANU's *Kenya Times* advertisement, 22 December 1992, p. 13; *Society*, 28 December 1992, p. 29 – but the correct figure was either 719 (Electoral Commission final records) or 720 (our records).

249 Source: Hornsby thesis and subsequent analyses.

250 See Hornsby thesis, p. 69, for statistics 1969–83.

251 Analysis of news reports, previous historical biographical records, etc. It is possible that the figures for re-participation may be slight underestimates due to the lack of information in some pastoral areas.

252 K. wa Wamwere, *The People's Republic and the Tyrant.*

253 PICK produced a 'Legal Memorandum' arguing for their right to submit a presidential candidate, n.d..

254 *Standard*, 24 December 1992, p. 5.

255 *Standard*, 16 December 1992, p. 12 and *Kenya Times*, 17 December 1992, p. 23.

256 *Standard*, 24 December 1992, p. 3.

257 See for example, the *Kenya Times*, 22 December 1992, p. 19.

258 See the *Kenya Times*, 17 December 1992, p. 4 and 22 December 1992, p. 5.

259 Local residents had long complained that 'big men' – including DP Secretary-General John Keen, who was a large landowner in the area – had thrown the Mijikenda off land which they had cultivated for years, destroyed their homes, burnt or confiscated their crops, and evicted them in order to sell the land to the foreign-owned Vipinga sisal estate. KANU politicians had ignored their protests because the Mijikenda could not match the financial support provided by the plantation owners to the ruling party.

260 Interview with candidate, Kilifi, 23 December 1992.

261 *Ibid.*

262 Tom Wolf, in his study of the campaign in *Voi*, similarly reports that KANU candidate Douglas Mbela went to Mombasa early on 24 December to collect his money for the final stage of the campaign.

263 Major candidates such as Henry Kosgey in Kerio South (1979), Kibe in Kandara (1983) and Towett in Buret (1983) stood down before nomination day to allow their rivals to be elected, and were immediately recompensed by being appointed to the chairmanships of parastatals.

264 *Kenya Times*, 30 November 1992, p. 1 and 1 December 1992, p. 1.

265 *Kenya Times*, 5 December 1992, pp. 1–2.

266 Daniel Nyareru, *Kenya Times*, 25 December 1992, p. 7.

267 In at least three cases the candidate the *Kenya Times* reported as defecting had lost, not won, the opposition party's nomination (FORD-Kenya's Kaloleni and Wajir West candidates, and Nehemiah Ochiel for Asili in Emuhaya).

268 KANU and the *Kenya Times* named candidates for civic seats as Parliamentary seats or named candidates as standing down who weren't the candidate at all (for example, the defecting DP candidate for Mbita was reported as David Philip Omolo Lego, when the actual candidate was Thomas Nyambega).

269 *Kenya Times*, 26 December 1992, p. 3.

270 FORD-Kenya went to court to try to prevent its candidate in Dujis, Abdikadir Hassan, being struck off the election ballot papers because he had stood down.

271 Saitoti was so angered by Elijah Mwangale's pressure to dump him earlier in 1992 that he is believed to have secretly assisted FORD-Kenya's campaign against Mwangale.

272 *Sunday Nation*, 29 November 1992, p. 5.

273 Interview with FORD-Asili MP, 3 November 1993.

274 *Standard*, 7 December 1992, p. 5, 14 December 1992, p. 5 and 18 December 1992, p. 5.

275 John Keen, Kangema, in *Daily Nation*, 30 November 1992, p. 2.

276 'KANU Briefs', *Kenya Times*, 23 December 1992, pp. 14–15.

277 Shikuku, *Kenya Times*, 27 December 1992, pp. 1–2.

278 Manasses Kuria, press conference on 23 December 1992, reported in the *Kenya Times*, 24 December 1992, p. 2.

279 Ambassador Smith Hempstone, at American Business Associates of Kenya meeting, 15 October 1992.

280 Lee Muthoga, in *Weekend Mail*, 31 December 1992, p. 27.

Ten

Election Day & the Results

Election day, 29 December 1992, was a national holiday. Queues began to form while it was still dark, and by the official opening of the polls at six o'clock in the morning, nearly a million people were outside the polling stations. Over most of the country, election day was calm and peaceful, and the weather dry. There were serious administrative problems in some areas, however, leading to late starts and slow progress. Some presiding officers and their deputies were late to arrive and set up, or in a few cases did not turn up at all. Materials were delivered late to some stations, due to transport problems. Vehicles had no petrol or authorisation to buy it, or were simply inadequate to transport the materials. In Nambale, in Busia, the ballot boxes were delivered by public transport.[1] In Amagoro, the last materials were not delivered until 5.10 p.m., while in Tigania in Meru the materials never arrived at eight polling stations.[2] A few polling stations were shifted at the last minute, with no prior public announcement, and voters did not know where to go.[3] Others were far too small and poorly laid out. Once the ballot boxes had been inspected and confirmed to be empty by the officials and party agents, they were closed and sealed by Commission and party agents. There were problems in properly sealing the boxes. In many areas, due to poor training, the lid was forced onto the box rather than slid into place. At the East African Bag and Cordage station in Juja, for example, four of 21 boxes were improperly closed, and could have been opened without breaking the seals. In Mombasa, Bunyala and Kisii, poll clerks initially boycotted the election, as they had not been paid their allowances in advance. Rainfall caused heavy delays in the distribution of materials and voting in Isiolo, Marsabit, Tana River, Turkana and the whole of North-Eastern Province. In Garissa, appalling weather was a major contributor to the low turn-out and 20 polling stations in Fafi and Ijara were inaccessible until election day, while at Garsen in Tana River elections at eight polling stations did not take place until 31 December because they were inaccessible due to heavy rain.[4]

Photo 10.1 An improperly sealed ballot box in Nairobi's Langata constituency.

Courtesy of Nation Group Newspapers

As a result, most polling stations opened late.[5] Opening times of eight or nine o'clock were common, with exceptional problems leading to delays until the mid-afternoon. In some stations, due to heavy rain or late arrival of materials, voting continued into the next day.[6] With a few exceptions, these problems were not caused deliberately. Even in areas where administrative problems were unintended, however, the delays were not explained to *wananchi,* causing anger and frustration among the huge queues, especially before the stations opened.

Once voting started, new problems emerged. In many areas, only one Presiding Officer's stamp (required to validate the papers) was provided, so polling stations with many streams had a major problem. This forced delays while decisions were made on what to do, and then further delays when stamps were shifted from stream to stream or other stamps pressed into service. At the same Juja polling station, for example, they eventually solved the problem by stamping 50–100 ballots at a time and then rushing the stamp onto the next stream. These stamps wore out very fast.

There were also several serious errors in the ballot papers. Most concerned local government candidates, but there were problems with Parliamentary papers in Msambweni, Kanduyi and Makuyu, where candidates' names and party symbols had been mixed up or omitted.[7] In three Nyeri seats, Kieni, Tetu and Nyeri Town, and in Kwanza in Trans-Nzoia, some ballot papers were sent to other parts of the country, forcing long delays while they were returned. In Kisauni in Mombasa the wrong DP candidate was on the Parliamentary ballot papers, while supplies of ballot papers ran out in Nakuru East and Makueni, delaying voting.[8] In Amagoro, due to problems with local government papers, voting continued until 3.30 p.m. on 30 December. The party symbols were unclear in some seats, while in others it was found that the Electoral Commission's representative at the printer in Britain had failed somehow to notice that KANU's symbol appeared first on the list of parties, and not fourth as determined by the draw.[9]

The polling was also delayed by the vast number of voters. The voting population was far larger than in the last 'true' election in 1983 (nearly 5,500,000 compared with 3,300,000). Furthermore, no one had ever voted three times in a polling station before, since there had never been a contested Presidential election. The procedure used was new, and there had been few real attempts to educate voters. The entire process took roughly five minutes per person, longer than expected, creating long delays in opposition areas, especially Central Province, where there was a very high early turn-out. Many Kikuyu had feared that KANU supporters would vote early and then disrupt the poll. The opposition parties thus encouraged their supporters to vote early. In Baringo, Nandi and elsewhere in the Rift Valley officials also reported high early turn-outs, estimating that 75 per cent of the electorate had voted by 3 p.m. The election appears to have gone very smoothly, however, with virtually no one left to vote by mid-afternoon. Everyone had voted in most Samburu polling stations by 2 p.m, for example.[10]

Over most of the country, the queues were immense and lasted all day, and in some cases long into the night. Voters were good-natured and determined to vote, many remaining in the queues for five to six hours. Justice Chesoni ordered that late starting stations should remain open after the official closing time in compensation, and this happened almost everywhere. Once darkness fell, people continued to vote, using pressure lamps, though the late closing deterred women voters with children, who were reluctant to travel in darkness, reducing the overall turn-out.[11] In the worst-hit clash areas in Eldoret, the promised mobile polling stations did not turn up (and, according to the Returning Officer in Eldoret South, had never even been requested, despite Chesoni's assurances). Many waited for them: others trekked elsewhere to vote.

Where several streams were provided, voters were organised into queues, usually alphabetically, but occasionally (as in Kirinyaga) into one stream for men and one for women. KANU and opposition agents were present in most but not all seats, though not always with enough personnel to monitor multi-stream stations. Agents at most stations were extremely active in checking and challenging any potential problem, causing yet more delays. Where opposition agents were absent or few in number, there was significantly greater cause for concern about the fairness of the process. In Nyeri Town, fearing rigging, the DP were permitted to mark the boxes using their own highlighter pens.

Once a voter entered the station, an identity card and voter's card had to be presented to the clerks and checked against the register. The voter's card and the ballot paper were then stamped, the voter's electoral number was marked on the counterfoil and a 'voted' mark entered in the register. The voter's finger was dipped in indelible ink, and he was issued with stamped Presidential, Parliamentary and local government papers in that order. Voters marked and deposited these in turn in the relevant box. In most stations, there were no serious problems with voters arriving without proper documentation. 'Police Abstracts', certificates of lost identity cards, were generally accepted as proof of identity. Some stations permitted voters whose names were on the register but who had no card to vote, as Chesoni had specified. Others did not. In KANU's strongholds and rural stations within bitterly fought seats like Narok North, some voters were allowed to vote without any authorisation.[12] The American indelible ink proved to be easily washed off with water and *Omo* or lemon peel. By the evening, only the cuticle of the nail retained any stain, even when no effort had been made to remove it. There were suspicions in some seats that the ink used was not that which the Americans had delivered anyway, and ordinary ink was certainly used in areas, such as Tana River, where supplies of the official ink had been delayed. There were a few cases of faked and stolen voters' cards and even ballot papers, but the number of double voting attempts detected was minimal.

The three ballot papers were different colours, and were supposed to be obtained, marked and cast one by one into the respective Presidential, Parliamentary and local government boxes, but in many polling stations, voters were given all three simultaneously. It was thus quite easy to spoil votes by placing them in the wrong box, especially since many were only labelled, not colour-coded to match the ballot papers. In the unopposed KANU seats, voters were given only one ballot paper, for the Presidency.

There were deficiencies in the registers in several seats, where consecutive blocks of names were missing, despite voters having been issued with cards. The NCWK Report suggested 'anomalies' in the register in 51 of the 80 seats it assessed, and that in some areas, such as Nairobi, this was intentional.[13] The IRI also noted that in Starehe over 1,000 names were missing from the register in one station.[14] NEMU reports from around the country, however, suggest only 3–20 persons per station had register problems, and personal observation suggested that the Central Province registers were satisfactory.

There were serious problems with lack of secrecy in the balloting, due to the large number of illiterate voters and the pressure of space. Nationally, adult literacy was 53 per cent in 1992, an increase of only 10 per cent since Independence, and illiteracy rates remained extremely high in many areas. A Kajiado Central Presiding Officer near Magadi, for example, reported having to mark ballots for 90 per cent of voters.[15] The procedure adopted for dealing with illiterate voters was considered satisfactory by all parties over most of the country. The Presiding Officer had to mark the paper for the voter in the presence of the candidates' agents, who would witness and even in some cases assist. Announcing to all the agents the voter's preference was not ideal, however, and even where the voter could write, poor arrangements meant that agents could sometimes see their preference.

This effectively created a public rather than private vote. In some areas, this system was seriously abused. The illiteracy rate in some constituencies became implausibly high, as KANU had demanded in advance that all voters declare themselves illiterate, so that KANU agents could confirm they had voted *Jogoo* – all those who voted for themselves were noted down by agents as pro-opposition. The NCWK stated that:

> The illiterate game was played to perfection in places like Kajiado where observers suspected that voters had been intimidated to say they were illiterate so that while being assisted there would be no question as to their acquiescence to certain candidates.[16]

Similar reports were received from NCWK and NEMU observers in Baringo, Kajiado, Marsabit, Isiolo, Garissa and elsewhere. This was a serious infringement of the electoral process. Concerns about presiding officers over much of the country proved unjustified, and most, though harassed and confused, did a creditable job. Nonetheless, some showed partiality on the day. In marginal Msambweni, for example, a Deputy Presiding Officer was arrested after the discovery that he was a KANU campaigner and was caught erasing voters' marks.[17]

Many marginal constituencies saw bribery and campaigning by KANU and other political parties in the vicinity of polling stations. Posters were put up nearby, generally for KANU, and chiefs and others wore YK' 92 or KANU T-shirts while mobilising people to vote. Some isolated incidents were caused by over-enthusiastic local government candidates, and protests by observers usually led to the cessation of such activities. In at least ten per cent of seats (over 20 seats), however, it was more sustained, particularly in key marginal constituencies in Western and Eastern Provinces. Well-documented reports from the press, the opposition, NEMU monitors and foreign observers, revealed the massive distribution of cash to KANU voters by candidates, chiefs, agents and officials. In Sabatia in Vihiga, KANU supporters and candidates campaigned at several polling stations. In Emuhaya in the same district, poll monitors everywhere reported large numbers queuing for cash from the KANU Parliamentary candidate's agents.[18] In Malava in Kakamega and Nyakach in Kisumu they got only 10 shillings per person. In Machakos Town, Minister Kyalo's staff handed out 30 shillings to each voter on polling day and KANU was also bribing in Kilome in Makueni District. The NCWK reported that in Kajiado North an ex-chief handed out 10 shilling notes to queueing voters, and that in Murang'a, Kitui and Kirinyaga voters were bribed to vote *Jogoo*.[19] The Commonwealth noted that in Gachoka and Siakago in Embu, bags of millet from donor agencies were handed out, and that in Thika agents of an opposition party were seen handing out cash to voters.[20] Prices were higher in Nairobi, where in Starehe a promise of support cost KANU's Kirima 100 shillings on polling day.[21] The Tetu District Officer also campaigned for the ruling party, issuing KANU badges. In Kuria, both FORD-Asili and KANU bribed voters, as did the DP in Mutito.[22]

Everywhere, candidates transported voters to the polls in pick-ups and *matatus*. In most cases, it was a legitimate assistance for the old, or those living far away from a station. President Moi had banned the movement of lorries of people between districts on election eve, but this did not prevent the 'busing' of large numbers of voters both within and between constituencies. In a few cases, there is evidence that voters were brought in larger numbers from further afield. Some of the most serious allegations concerned Nakuru, where foreign observers witnessed large numbers camped on election eve at the Rift Valley Institute of Science and Technology, allegedly for a church service, who were all gone in the morning.[23] In some cases, such as Tetu, local voters physically prevented entry to 'foreigners' and, in Mombasa and Kajiado, 'imported' Somali voters were attacked by opposition activists.[24]

There was some poll violence, particularly in Kisumu and Migori Districts, where FORD-Kenya crowds appear to have carried out a show of force against KANU supporters. Constituencies where people were hurt on polling day or during the count included Kisumu Town, Alego and Kitutu Chache in Nyanza, and Kieni, Ntonyiri, Kibwezi and Lagdera. KANU's Kisumu office was burnt down.[25] Mercifully, however, violence was absent from election day and the count almost everywhere. Indeed, it was probably one of the least violent polls Kenya has held. The police acted with care and discretion throughout the country, and there were almost no incidents of violence or excessive force by Administration Police or GSU.

Once the poll closed, the counterfoils were checked, the boxes sealed, and everything reconciled in the polling stations. The sealing of the boxes took far too long in many areas, for unexplained reasons. There is the suspicion that some Presiding Officers had been encouraged to delay the process. The sealed ballot boxes and counterfoils then had to wait for transport to counting halls, one hall for each constituency. Here more problems emerged. Too few vehicles were provided for the monitors and party agents to accompany the boxes in some stations, although most officials allowed monitors and agents to travel with the boxes. The aim of the voters and most officials was to ensure that all boxes were accompanied to the count and remained visible at all times. A few officials, KANU agents, District Officers and the Special Branch had opposite instructions. In the event, popular vigilance prevented major introduction of papers at this stage, though boxes did turn up unaccompanied in a number of key seats.[26] Many agents' seals had been put on the wrong way round and, therefore, could be removed easily, permitting 'stuffing' during these trips.

The counting process was a significant point of contention, with far more complaints about the count than the voting itself. Most constituencies only started counting when all boxes were in (as was legally required), to reduce the risk of the introduction of late boxes or confusion over the numbers.[27] In Langata, where the counting hall was at the Bomas of Kenya, the boxes were lined up on the stage under spotlights, guarded by armed police, while the usual audience area was filled with a huge square counting table, with clerks on the inside, and agents, candidates, press and police outside (see Photo 10.2). No one had foreseen the delays that occurred, and although a few government seats began counting as early as 7 or 8 p.m., in most areas counting did not start until the small hours of the morning of 30 December. The process did not even begin in Garsen in Tana River until 1 January at 8 a.m., long after the national result was

Photo 10.2 Police guard ballot boxes waiting to be counted in Langata
Courtesy of Nation Group Newspapers

clear. By the morning of 30 December, when the newspapers finally went to press, not a single Presidential or Parliamentary result had been declared. The first results started to trickle in by mid-morning on 30 December, and built up to a flood on the night of 30–31 December, 1992. The count was carried out in most cases in the presence of the candidates, their agents and foreign and domestic observers, though most international observers spent only a few hours watching before retiring exhausted. In a few seats, local monitors were refused permission to observe the count, a ground for serious concern. Many counting centres were too small for the number of people involved. Officials also failed to pay full attention to the letter of the law. The agents' seals were often ignored and simply cut open without checking whether they were the originals or not. Officials also refused to let domestic monitors check and match up the seals in many areas.

Most seats counted Presidential ballots first, then Parliamentary and finally the local government votes. Some split the clerks into three groups and gave each group one set of election ballots, or counted the civic or parliamentary votes first. Githunguri and one or two other constituencies opted to count the Presidential, then the Parliamentary and then the local government results for each polling station before moving onto the next set of boxes, further delaying the declaration of the first result. The choice made little difference, as there were far too few clerks almost everywhere. Counting proceeded agonisingly slowly, partly because of the sheer volume of paper to be counted, while the clerks became increasingly tired as the night wore on and they were not relieved. In a few constituencies, clerks refused to count anything until they were paid, and there were riots and protests, during and after counting, over non-payment. Finally, the vigilance and care of the agents and concern for probity by officials led to numerous halts, inspections of papers, and minor recounts of disputed ballots. Many halls were chaotic, with tired, angry and tense crowds being held back by equally exhausted clerks and security personnel. Results were delayed longest in seats such as Nakuru East and Githunguri, where they counted polling station by polling station for all elections at once. Counting in Garissa District was also delayed due to problems with transport. Helicopters were used to shift the ballot boxes in Fafi constituency, and boxes were stranded due to breakdowns in Ijara, Lagdera and Dujis.[28] In Lagdera, most boxes had not even reached the count by mid-day on 30 December.

By the end of the second day of counting, there was a growing concern that the counts were being delayed deliberately to facilitate rigging, as agents and counting clerks tired, and opportunities to insert ballots grew.'[29] There is evidence that announcements of certain results were delayed after the counting had finished, while the Office of the President analysed and 'confirmed' them. The NEMU count monitors sometimes reported results hours before the press announcement (though in some cases it was the other way round). In some seats, the Returning Officers communicated the results by telephone (allegedly to *Jogoo* House or the Office of the President) before they were announced, or under-declared opposition votes, or delayed the announcement until they had consulted with the Office of the President. In Runyenjes, the result was released at three o'clock in the morning on 2 January, despite the fact that the count itself had ended at 6 p.m. on 31 December.[30] There is a suspicion that KANU had an emergency strategy in place should the first crucial results suggest that Moi would lose, to try to abort, cancel or rig the elections. In certain cases, such as Kitutu Chache and Vice-President Saitoti's Kajiado North, after initial results indicated a KANU defeat, new boxes were brought in just before the count finished which altered the result (see Chapter 11).

The results were announced by the Returning Officers on completion of each count. Some permitted cross-checking and verification by observers. Others, significantly, did not. A few even refused to report the result in an official declaration at all. There was no evidence that results reported by the press differed from those announced by Returning Officers – though occasionally, as in Mvita, the Returning Officer announced provisional results to the press as final. The majority of Returning Officers did their best in difficult conditions: one was described by a NEMU count certifier as 'a man of unbent integrity and very transparent'.[31] In a few seats, however, the District Administration simply took over the count, ignoring the Returning Officer. In seven out of the 80 seats it monitored, the NCWK reported that the results were announced by someone other than the Returning Officer.[32] Thus, for example, it was the District Officer in Samia who released the results.[33] The last count ended on the morning of 4 January 1993, six days after the election.

How to deal with spoilt papers was a major point of contention. In some constituencies, those found in the wrong box at the count (Parliamentary ballots found in the Presidential box, for example) were disallowed, as in

Kiharu: in others, such as Githunguri and Kimilili, they were collected up and reallocated at the end (known as 'astray' votes). There were problems with people marking votes incorrectly: ticking the symbol rather than placing a cross in the box, for example. These were generally declared spoilt. Some of these errors were caused by Presiding Officers deliberately marking the ballots incorrectly. The use of pencils rather than pens to mark ballots in polling stations also led to concern that voters' marks could later be erased, since clerks had pens and could erase pencilled votes.

Foreign Observers

The small foreign observer groups, the diplomats and the press concentrated their attention on the most convenient seats – Nairobi, Paul Muite's Kikuyu constituency and Vice-President Saitoti's Kajiado North. The IRI and Commonwealth teams travelled further afield. Both split into small teams, generally of two or three observers, and attempted to cover as much of the country as possible. In some cases, the observers only checked polling stations and passed on. In more significant constituencies, they stayed for long periods, although few lasted the entire count. The Commonwealth's 17 teams visited 283 polling stations and 35 counts, the IRI visited 229 stations, covering 46 constituencies.[34] Their 35 or so teams managed to cover the majority of the country, but inevitably could spend little time in most stations and could not reach most counts. Notably, the teams concentrated on the marginals rather than the KANU zones in the Rift Valley, and on Meru and Embu, not the Kamba Districts in Eastern Province. Both the Commonwealth and the IRI had targeted specific constituencies, with the IRI's preparation probably better, since they had identified not only contemporary hot-spots, but also areas with registration anomalies, past rigging histories, current evidence of rigging, and those that were key areas for the 25 per cent rule.[35] Both organisations also had checklists of likely problems: the IRI's including time of arrival of papers, serialising of boxes, times of opening and closing, placement of the boxes, assistance to illiterates, use of the indelible ink, correct sealing and transport, turning away of people, police activities and transporting of voters. It also emphasised some issues which were to become crucial in the counting process, including the disposal of unused ballots, the recording of serialised box information, disposal of unused boxes, maintaining an audit trail of which votes had come from what boxes, and watching out for the hiding of ballots for one candidate amid the piles of votes for another.[36]

Unfortunately, many of the IRI observers were still jet-lagged, and the commitment of some was in doubt.[37] Most of them knew little about Kenyan politics or past rigging methods, having been briefed on election law by a telephone conference call by the US Federal Election Commission's Craig Engle while they were waiting for a connecting flight to Nairobi at London's Heathrow airport on Sunday, 27 December. Most had declined to leave their families over Christmas when the election timetable was changed, and, consequently, had only left the United States on 26 December, reaching Nairobi the day before the election. After less than 24 hours' rest, they had then been transported before daybreak on 29 December, or the evening before, to the areas where they were to monitor the election. After another 18 hours of intense activity, most were not prepared to spend a further 24–48 hours observing the count.

The observation process was complicated by the numerous small delegations and Embassy groups, despatched by the Swiss, the Japanese, the Dutch, the Swedes, the Canadians, the American AFL-CIO and the European Parliament. These semi-official minor groups covered some additional areas, but duplicated the major teams in others, such as Nairobi, Taita-Taveta and Trans-Nzoia as they were loosely coordinated with, but not subject to, any of the other bodies.[38] Despite these efforts, there were no foreign observers in roughly half the counts. Too little attention was paid to the government areas, particularly the North-East, parts of Coast Province, and the central Rift Valley, while some Kamba seats would also have benefited from visits. Almost no one risked visiting the KANU heartlands to check that box stuffing and open voting was not going on. The observers stayed away from Baringo entirely, deterred by 'security concerns', and although individual Commonwealth dignitaries visited Nandi, Bomet and Eldoret South, it was not with the numbers or the expertise to detect problems.

NEMU and Other Local Observers

The four main domestic poll observer groups – NEMU, the NCWK, the Catholic Secretariat, and BEERAM – had no problems entering the polling stations or in monitoring on polling day. Most polling stations were manned by internal monitors, though again there was insufficient coordination between the different groups, so that some stations were covered by three or more teams while others were ignored. Roughly 90 per cent of constituencies and 75 per cent of polling stations were covered by one or other group, with the most obvious weakness being in North-Eastern Province, where everyone visited Dujis (where Minister Maalim Mohammed was standing) and ignored the other nine seats.

On polling day, NEMU fielded over 7,500 poll monitors and count certifiers, a huge administrative effort. NEMU provided the most widescale and effective national monitoring effort and, despite some inefficiencies and failures, its final verdict was based upon better information than any other study.[39] Transcript reports and personal observations suggests that most NEMU monitors were fully prepared and monitored events extremely well. Each NEMU poll monitor had a standard form to fill in, describing all the things seen, including times of opening and closing, observers attending and box numbers. BEERAM and the NCWK also produced election monitoring forms, while the Catholic Secretariat used NEMU's.

NEMU received useful returns from 1,722 polling stations (15 per cent of the total) and from 107 counts (57 per cent).[40] The coverage in Nairobi was complete, and of Central, Western and Nyanza Provinces very good. It received no reports, however, from Marsabit District in Eastern Province, Wajir, Mandera or most of Garissa in the North-East, and very little from Kilifi on the Coast, or from Samburu and West Pokot in the Rift Valley.[41] The majority of its officials had been organised and trained by FIDA/ICJ. Its aim was to have one monitor for every stream in each polling station, at least one and usually two count certifiers, a constituency monitor responsible for the whole constituency, and a District Liaison Officer (DLO) with responsibility for the whole District. The DLOs were a key group and included senior ex-DCs and prominent lawyers. Despite fears of intimidation, the vast majority of its nominated observers turned up, and showed enormous dedication.

The NEMU count certifiers also had a standard form, but their problems were far more acute, due to the length of time they had to remain at their posts, and the greater state pressure upon them. As it emerged, the count was the key period within which electoral abuses occurred, and NEMU and the other groups were all under-resourced for monitoring the count in comparison with the poll. The NEMU count certifiers also had problems with their reporting-in. One telephone number in headquarters in Bruce House was allocated to each Province, to be used by the certifiers when the result was released. Unfortunately, their attempts to call in the results were hampered by lack of public telephones, requiring some to walk many miles, and in some cases by lack of understanding. No preparations had been made for on-line checking of consistency between the results reported by the poll watchers and those announced. Moreover, NEMU had not prepared any standard forms for recording results, which led to extreme confusion as the night wore on.

The reports presented by the count certifiers and District Liaison Officers were thorough and trustworthy in most cases. Exceptions were unfortunately found. Some NEMU staff believed with hindsight that several poll monitors and count certifiers in the central Rift Valley had been bribed or were partial to KANU.[42] This was substantiated by the extremely terse, uninformative and uncritical reports submitted by monitors in areas like Nandi. It is suspected that similar problems were experienced by the other groups.

The NCWK sampled 80 constituencies, using 454 observers. Its coverage of Nairobi, Central and Eastern Provinces was good but it had fewer observers on the Coast, in Nyanza and Western, and its coverage was poor in the Rift Valley and North-East. Apart from Kerio South, Buret and Tinderet, the NCWK did not venture into KANU zones. The NCWK report judged 70 of the 80 constituencies they visited as having poor general arrangements, reflecting the gross inefficiency of the Electoral Commission. BEERAM fielded far fewer observers, visiting only 46 constituencies, with 370 monitors.[43]

There was considerable official hostility towards domestic monitors in some areas, particularly in the Rift Valley, and in key marginals. NEMU and the NCWK reported that their people had experienced harassment, particularly during the count, in some key problem areas, including Makadara, Starehe, Langata, Dagoretti and Mathare in Nairobi; Kiharu, Juja and Kikuyu in Central Province; Imenti North, Runyenjes, Machakos Town and Mwala in Eastern; Changamwe, Garsen and Galole on the Coast; Kajiado North and Buret in the Rift; Sabatia in Western; and Kitutu Chache, Nyaribari Chache and West Mugirango in Nyanza. This pressure proved to be a good indicator of malpractice.

Table 10.1 Presidential Election Results by Province and Candidate

Province	Moi		Matiba		Kibaki		Odinga		Total Vote
Nairobi	62,402	(16.6%)	165,533	(44.1%)	69,715	(18.6%)	75,898	(20.2%)	375,574
Central	21,882	(2.1%)	621,368	(60.1%)	372,937	(36.1%)	10,765	(1.0%)	1,034,016
Eastern	290,494	(36.8%)	80,515	(10.2%)	398,727	(50.5%)	13,064	(1.7%)	789,232
North-East	57,400	(78.1%)	7,440	(10.1%)	3,297	(4.5%)	5,237	(7.1%)	73,460
Coast	200,596	(64.1%)	35,598	(11.4%)	23,766	(7.6%)	50,516	(16.1%)	312,993
Rift Valley	994,844	(67.8%)	274,011	(18.7%)	111,098	(7.6%)	83,945	(5.7%)	1,467,503
Western	217,375	(40.9%)	192,859	(36.3%)	19,115	(3.6%)	94,851	(17.9%)	531,159
Nyanza	111,873	(14.4%)	26,922	(3.3%)	51,962	(6.4%)	609,921	(74.7%)	816,387
Total	1,962,866		1,404,266		1,050,617		944,197		5,400,324

Source: *Daily Nation*, 5 January 1993, p. 1.[44]

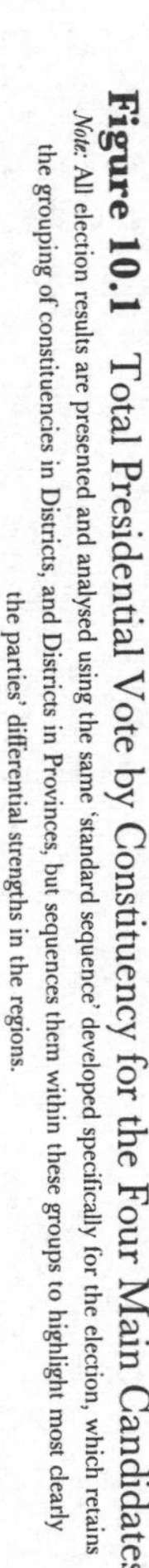

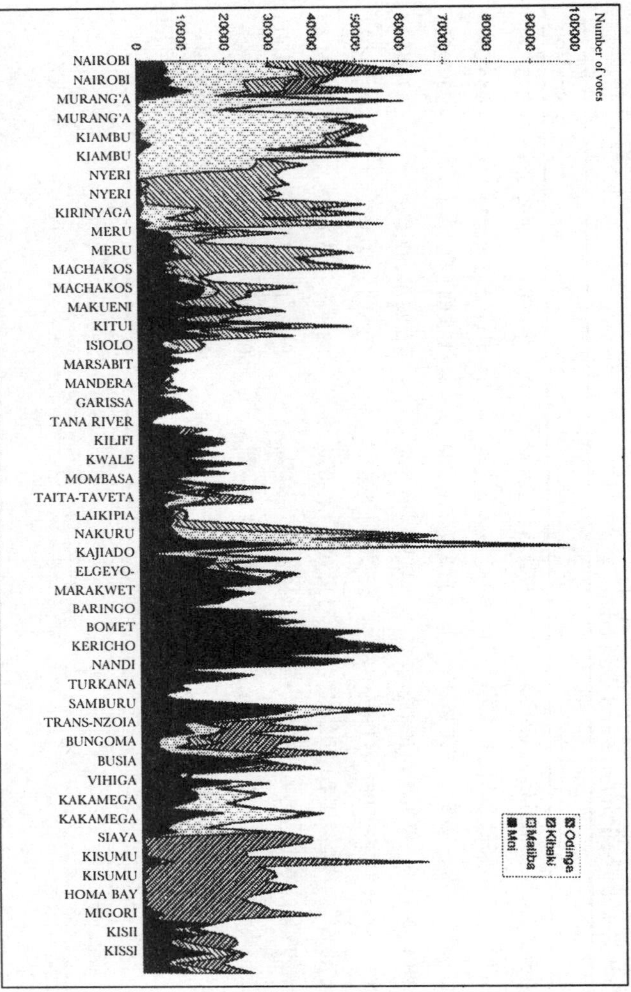

Figure 10.1 Total Presidential Vote by Constituency for the Four Main Candidates

Note: All election results are presented and analysed using the same 'standard sequence' developed specifically for the election, which retains the grouping of constituencies in Districts, and Districts in Provinces, but sequences them within these groups to highlight most clearly the parties' differential strengths in the regions.

The Presidential and Parliamentary Election Results

After more than three days of counting, the final result of the 1992 general election became known on 2 January 1993. The Presidential, Parliamentary and most civic elections were won by KANU. Incumbent President Daniel Toroitich arap Moi was re-elected with 37 per cent of the vote, while KANU won a narrow overall majority of 100 Parliamentary seats to the opposition parties' combined total of 88 MPs. This result was predictable, given the divisions in the opposition, ethnic arithmetic, and the authority of government. Electoral malpractice in the pre-election period, and during the vote and count nevertheless assisted this victory.

The Presidential Election Result

The Presidential election produced a decisive victory for Moi over his seven opponents. He polled 1,962,866 votes, half a million more than his nearest rival Kenneth Matiba, who secured 1,404,266. President Moi received 25 per cent of the vote in five provinces, as required by the revised Constitution, winning the largest number of votes in North-Eastern Province (78 per cent, the largest percentage score in a Province of any candidate), Rift Valley (68 per cent), Coast (60 per cent) and Western Province (40 per cent), and passing the 25 per cent barrier in Eastern, where the DP was extremely successful. Moi almost certainly won legitimately, in that he polled a larger number of genuine votes, cast by real voters, on polling day than any other single candidate.

In contrast, none of his opponents crossed the 25 per cent hurdle in more than three provinces. Kenneth Matiba came closest, winning Central (61 per cent) and Nairobi (44 per cent), and exceeding 25 per cent in Western. Mwai Kibaki won Eastern (49 per cent) and exceeded 25 per cent in Central (35 per cent), but failed to qualify in Nairobi where he scored only 18 per cent. Oginga Odinga won an overwhelming 76 per cent of the vote in Nyanza, but this was the only province in which he achieved 25 per cent. He missed qualifying in Nairobi and Western. The official Electoral Commission totals, announced on 4 January 1993, are presented in Table 10.1.

Less than an hour after the result was announced, Daniel arap Moi was sworn in as Kenya's first elected multi-party President. Although Moi won only just over one third of the vote, by polling day there had been little chance of any other candidate winning. Each challenger had a single regional centre of strength, but was so weak elsewhere that there was little chance that overall they could topple the incumbent. Their only hope was to deny Moi outright victory and force him into a run-off, either by preventing him winning 25 per cent in five provinces, or by one candidate winning more votes overall. Divided, they failed to achieve either. Nevertheless, nearly two thirds of the voters had voted against Moi, and his survival had depended upon the division in the opposition. Were it possible, the transfer of votes from any one of the major opposition candidates to any of the others would have given the opposition victory.

Despite being written off early in the campaign, Matiba emerged as the strongest challenger to Moi, timing perfectly his campaign and his apparent recovery from illness. His populist championing of the 'common man' achieved spectacular results in the Kikuyu Districts. His strength was entirely regional, however, concentrated in only six Districts. The most disappointed candidate was Mwai Kibaki, widely viewed as everybody's second choice, who came third. Despite a strong showing in many areas, his support in his own home bastion was so weakened by Matiba's late run that he ended up stronger in Eastern Province than in Nairobi or Central Province. Odinga's fourth place was poor, a response to the widespread aversion to a Luo President among some ethnic groups, and to an aged leader with a radical anti-establishment past. As with Matiba, Odinga's vote was regional – focused almost entirely on the Luo community in Nyanza and elsewhere. The other four candidates all performed miserably. George Anyona (KSC) polled only 12,273 votes; Chibule wa Tsuma (KNC) 10,221;

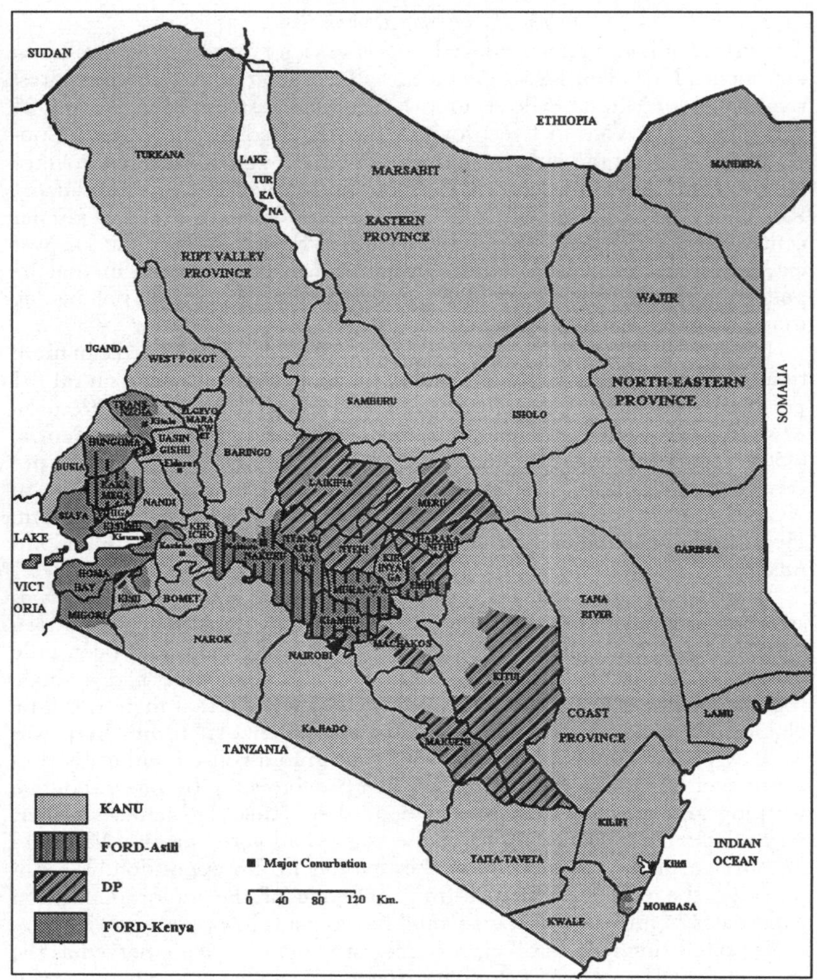

Figure 10.2 1992 Presidential Election Results

John Harun Mwau (PICK) 8,118; and David Mukaru-Ng'ang'a (KENDA) 5,766. Apart from exceptional seats (their home constituencies respectively), their tallies are counted under a category of 'others' henceforth where it is necessary to record them at all.

Presidential voting was predominantly regional and ethnic, as shown by Figure 10.1 which gives the Presidential election results by the candidate with the largest number of votes in each constituency. The extraordinary situation in Nakuru Town and Molo, where huge voter importation was used to try and wrest the seat away from Kikuyu representatives, shows up clearly. Few seats were marginal, and over at least half the country, excluding Nairobi, the Gusii constituencies, parts of the Coast, Eastern

Province and small parts of Western Province, there was effectively only one candidate. Nairobi, as expected, was an opposition victory, with KANU winning only one seat in Parliament and none of the Presidential polls in the city. The Central Province results provided an overwhelming triumph for the opposition: President Moi was reduced to a mere two per cent of the provincial vote, and in no constituency did he or KANU achieve a respectable total. Odinga's vote was even lower that Moi's. Ethnic solidarity ruled, and with one exception (Paul Muite in Kikuyu), the Central Province contest was entirely between the two Kikuyu heavyweights and their candidates. Northern Kikuyuland – the whole of Kibaki's home in Nyeri, the northern-most constituency of Nyandarua, Kirinyaga and the neighbouring Kikuyu District of Laikipia – was Kibaki's. Matiba won the entire south of Kikuyuland, including his home area of Murang'a, Kiambu and most of Nairobi. The great surprise was Matiba's victory in Kiambu, from where many DP leaders came.

Eastern Province saw three separate contests. In the arid north, covering Isiolo and Marsabit Districts, KANU and President Moi won massive, slightly suspect, majorities. Among the Embu and Meru, the DP took most seats, though KANU scraped through in a few places. In Ukambani, many seats were closely contested between KANU and the DP, and reported different victors in the Presidential and Parliamentary elections. The six Districts of Coast Province gave a clear but slightly questionable endorsement to KANU, outside the urban hotbed of Mombasa, which voted IPK/FORD-Kenya. Neither KANU's control of the Coast, however, nor the IPK's of Mombasa, was secure.

The Rift Valley split into four electoral zones. The first, the Moi heartlands of the central Rift, saw KANU candidates unopposed and huge Presidential victories for Moi, while Matiba, Kibaki and Odinga received virtually no votes. In the Rift periphery, KANU had 'persuaded' many opposition candidates to defect, and won every seat, some in controversial circumstances. In the western borderlands of Uasin Gishu and Trans-Nzoia, honours were split, with Ford-Kenya taking the west and KANU the east. In Nakuru, Kajiado North and Narok North, the spoils were also divided. FORD-Asili won four out of five Nakuru seats. KANU took Rongai in Nakuru and the Kajiado and Narok seats, but all seven were tainted by rigging. In Laikipia, which followed Central Province politically, the DP walked home despite KANU's hopes.

Western Province, the home of the Luhya people, was another key swing area. The Luhya were the most fragmented politically and socially of Kenya's major communities, with big differences in attitudes and allegiances between the relatively independent sub-groups and no Presidential candidate of their own. The election was decided almost as much by personal, clan and local issues as national divisions, and the result was unclear until the last minute. The Province split three ways, with only the DP playing little role. As expected, KANU dominated Busia and Vihiga Districts. Ford-Kenya took most of Bungoma, and FORD-Asili dominated Shikuku's Kakamega District.

Nyanza Province also split on ethnic lines. The Luo majority in the 18 seats of Siaya, Kisumu, Migori and Homa Bay districts gave Odinga and FORD-Kenya an overwhelming majority in every constituency. No other

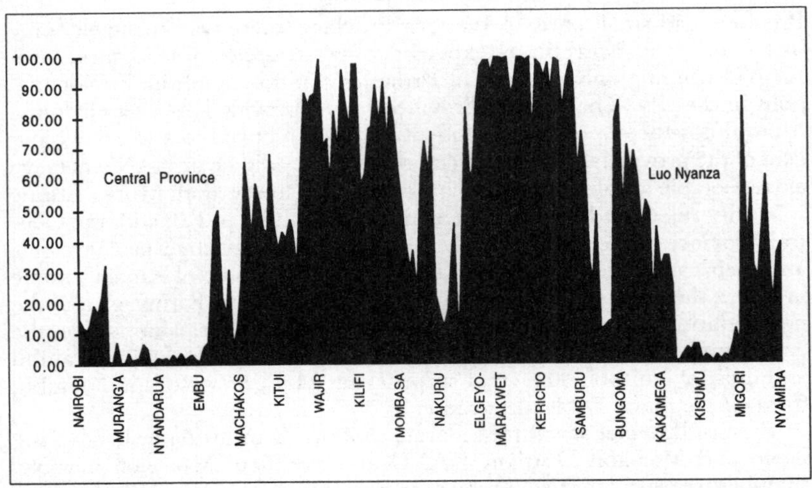

Figure 10.3 Moi's Percentage of the Presidential Vote, 1992

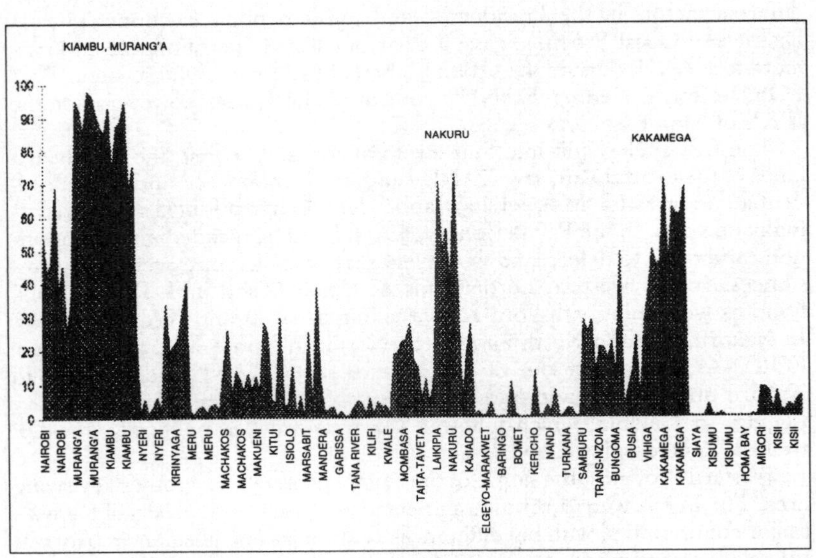

Figure 10.4 Matiba's Percentage of the Presidential Vote, 1992

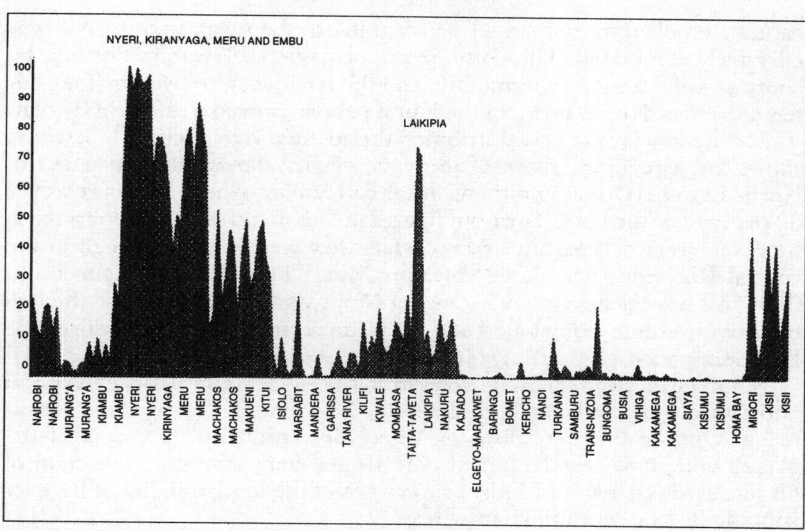

Figure 10.5 Kibaki's Percentage of the Presidential Vote, 1992

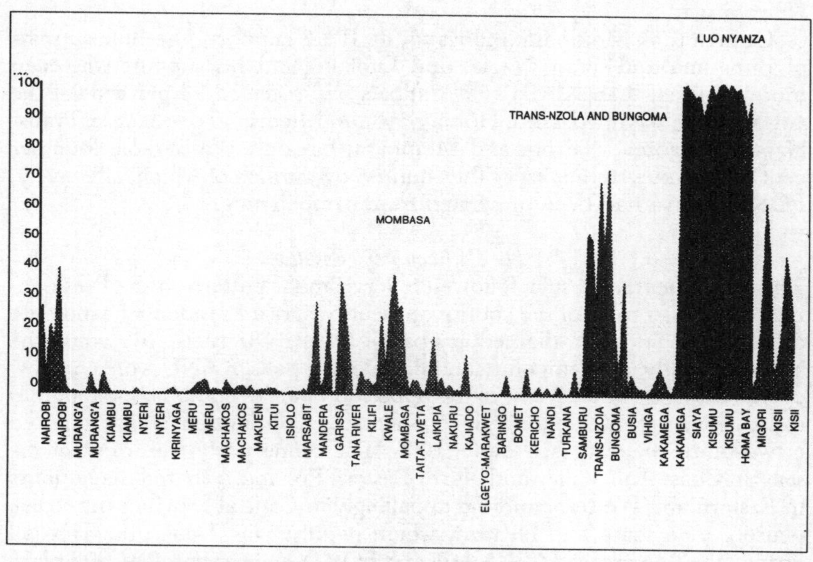

Figure 10.6 Odinga's Percentage of the Presidential Vote, 1992

candidate polled more than 11 per cent in any Luo seat, and KANU was effectively eliminated. The Gusii people of Kisii and Nyamira districts, by contrast, were a swing community, and the ten seats were won by four different parties. Kuria, home of the Kuria people, proved a safe KANU seat.

Moi had by far the best-distributed Presidential vote. Figure 10.3, which shows his percentage share of the vote, clearly shows the twin peaks of North-Eastern/Coast, and the Central Rift Valley, where he secured over 80 per cent of the vote. Turn-out figures in Coast and North-Eastern seats, however, were comparatively low, while they were extremely high in the central Rift seats, with huge votes for Moi. The percentage figures also show just how clear and wide-ranging Moi's victory was. Outside the two opposition ethnic homelands of Luo Nyanza and Central Province, the President polled very strongly indeed.

Matiba won overwhelming votes in southern Central Province (Kiambu and Murang'a), and also took Nairobi, Nyandarua, Nakuru and Kakamega. Outside these six districts, where he received 67 per cent of the overall vote, however, he polled only 10 per cent, a graphic reflection of his localised Kikuyu and Luhya support, and the implausibility of his ever winning 25 per cent in five provinces.

Kibaki's support was only slightly wider spread. He won northern Kikuyuland and most of Meru and Embu, plus Laikipia, but nowhere else. His vote in Ukambani and Kisii was strong but variable, partly as a consequence of state pressure and rigging. The DP was unlucky to win no Nairobi seat.

Odinga took Mombasa (thanks to the IPK's support), the Bukusu seats of Bungoma and Trans-Nzoia, and Luoland, but his support was even more localised than Kibaki's or Matiba's. He received 93 per cent of the votes cast in Siaya, Kisumu, Homa Bay, and Migori; 30 per cent in Trans-Nzoia, Bungoma, Nairobi and Mombasa; but only a miserable four per cent of the votes in the rest of the country, over much of which, effectively, FORD-Kenya had been prevented from campaigning.

The Parliamentary Results

The Parliamentary results followed a very similar pattern to the Presidential results over most of the country: in seats where a Presidential candidate did well, so did his Parliamentary party. Of the 188 seats, 168 voted the same way in the Parliamentary and Presidential polls. KANU won a narrow overall majority of twelve over the opposition parties combined, enough to form a government, but too little to amend the Constitution, which required a two-thirds majority (see Table 10.2). The ruling party won most of the seats in Coast, Rift Valley and North-Eastern Provinces, shared the honours in Eastern and Western, and did appallingly in Central Province (no seats), Nairobi (one seat), and Nyanza, where it only won 7 constituencies (all outside the Luo areas). FORD-Asili and FORD-Kenya shared second place with 31 MPs each, and the DP came in fourth with 23. FORD-Kenya did rather better than Odinga as Presidential candidate, as a result of its regional concentration of strength in Nyanza. Numerous KANU Ministers were defeated, in a pattern unprecedented since Independence. Among the well-known losers were all the Kikuyu and Luo Ministers, including Kamotho

Table 10.2 Distribution of Parliamentary Seats by Province, 1992

Province	KANU	FORD (K)	FORD (A)	DP	KNC	KSC	PICK	TOTAL
Nairobi	1	1	6					8
Central		1	14	10				25
Eastern	21	1		9	1			32
North-East	8	1					1	10
Coast	17	2		1				20
Rift Valley	36	2	4	2				44
Western	10	3	7					20
Nyanza	7	20		1		1		29
TOTAL	100	31	31	23	1	1	1	188

in Murang'a, Magugu in Kiambu, Otieno and Okwanyo in Migori, and Oluoch in Siaya. In Western Province, among the Luhya, both Mwangale in Bungoma and Nabwera in Kakamega were easily defeated.

KANU's 53 per cent of the Parliamentary seats was won with only 29.7 per cent of the vote, due to the multiplicative effect of the first past-the-post system and the national distribuition of constituencies (though KANU's vote would have been far higher if parliamentary polls had been held in the 16 seats they won unopposed). FORD-Asili won 24.3 per cent of the parliamentary vote and FORD-Kenya 20.7 per cent, for which both received 16 per cent of the seats. The DP was worst-hit, winning 22 per cent of the vote and only 12 per cent of the Assembly, reflecting its more evenly spread support.

The proportion of marginal seats the election produced reflects the extent to which it was a national contest, or a series of regional one-party victories. Given the lack of commitment of voters to specific parties when the parties themselves are in flux, and the level of electoral abuses seen, a victor's majority of ten per cent or less over the next candidate was chosen to define a marginal seat. Using this figure, only 29 seats (15 per cent) were marginal, concentrated in Nairobi, Mombasa, Eastern and North-Eastern Provinces, in certain parts of Western Province, and the two Gusii Districts, Kisii and Nyamira. Kisauni in Mombasa was the most marginal seat in the country. KANU won 15 of these marginals, a reasonable proportion, although several of the most questionable results are also among this group.

Turn-out Variation

Turn-out has always varied from constituency to constituency. Turn-out in the 1992 elections again varied considerably, in ways which affected the final result. President Moi's victory was underpinned by a huge nominal turn-out in the Kalenjin Districts. Although this turn-out was matched by that in the home Districts of the Kikuyu opposition leaders, it was implausibly large, both historically (given past turn-outs) and in the light of other information about what was happening in the region. Figure 10.7

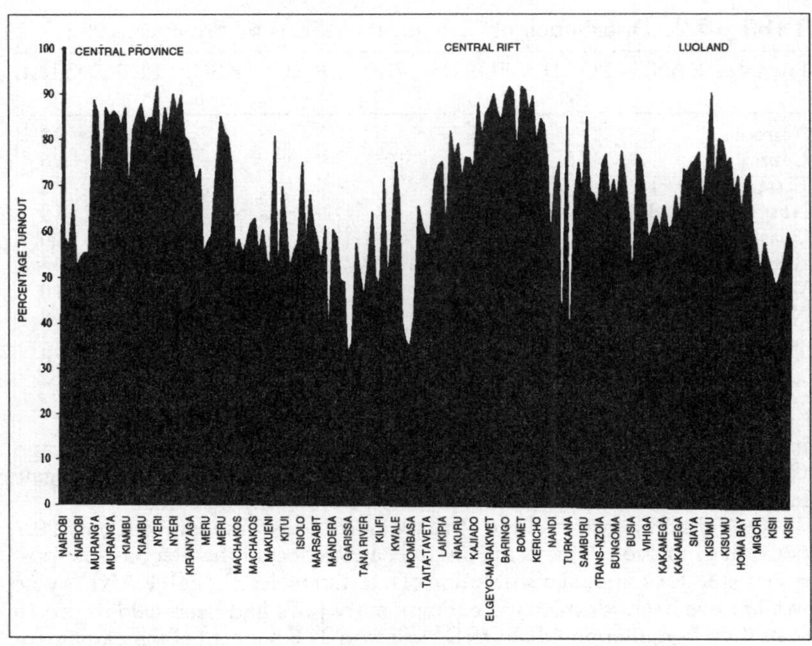

Figure 10.7 Presidential Turn-out, 1992 (percentages)

shows the turn-out variation, seat by seat, in 1992. It was higher than in many previous elections, but still surprisingly low (less than 65 per cent) over half the country, given that registration was optional and this was the first multi-party general election since independence.[45] Nairobi, most of Coast Province, North-Eastern, Isiolo, Marsabit, the Kamba areas and the Gusii Districts of Nyanza all showed low turn-outs, while almost every able-bodied individual turned out in Luo Nyanza, Central Province and the Kalenjin Districts, a consequence of local support for Presidential candidates in their ethnic bailiwicks. Lower turn-outs were seen in seats where late opening and closing led voters to return home.

Owing to the queue voting system of 1988 (which meant most primary figures were meaningless) and the boundary changes in 1987, there are no reliable figures by which to compare turn-out by seat with that of previous elections. We can, however, analyse the results at the regional level with the 1983 polls (Table 10.3). Turn-out was extremely high in Central Province, in some cases over 90 per cent. While this is an area with traditionally high voter participation, as one of the most politicised and best-developed regions of the country, these figures were, nevertheless, 27 per cent above the 1983 figures. In the core Matiba zone of Murang'a more than 85 per cent of eligible voters voted, and in Kibaki's Nyeri, there was an 86 per cent turn-out, due to the politicisation of the area around the two Kikuyu Presidential candidates. Turn-out was also high in the central Rift Valley in Elgeyo-Marakwet, Baringo, Kericho, Bomet and Nandi Districts,

Table 10.3 Turn-out in 1992 and 1983[46]

Province Region	1983 turn-out	1992 Presidential turn-out	Increase from 1983
Nairobi	30%	56%	26%
Central	58%	85%	27%
Western	47%	66%	19%
Nyanza	45%	66%	21%
Luo Nyanza	44%	72%	28%
Gusii Nyanza	48%	54%	6%
Coast	39%	49%	10%
Rural Coast	40%	54%	14%
Mombasa	35%	38%	3%
Eastern	52%	66%	14%
North-east	37%	52%	15%
Rift valley	49%	76%	27%
Central Rift	52%	85%	33%
Semi-arid Rift	44%	63%	19%
'White Highlands'	47%	70%	23%

Note: Figures exclude seats where a candidate was unopposed.

where it was 33 per cent higher than in 1983, the largest growth of any region of the country. Turn-out was comparatively low in Luoland, but was up by 28 per cent, roughly the same as in the other Presidential candidates' areas. Urban constituencies have always recorded lower turn-outs and this continued in 1992. The extremely low poll in Mombasa, the lowest in the country despite its marginality and politicisation, and only 3 per cent higher than in 1983, compared with the high registration rates there, may indicate unsuccessful plans for malpractice or transporting voters.

Presidential Candidates and Party Tickets

For twenty years, party and policy had been irrelevant in Kenyan elections. Elections had been determined by the personality and oratorical ability of candidates; their 'development' record; their role in government; alliances with other more senior politicians and business figures; clan allegiances and localism; the electorate's desire for an educated representative; candidates' organisational abilities; and by outright cheating.[47] In 1992, however, multi-party politics brought party-ticket voting back to Kenya, to a far greater extent than had been expected by anyone. Local issues and candidates were submerged over much of the country by a pattern of geographical and ethnic voting. The election was determined by party ties and the popularity of the rival Presidential candidates.

Most people voted a party ticket, with a very close relationship between a party's Presidential, Parliamentary and local government votes. Over at least half the country, this 'three piece suit' (to use Matiba's phrase) was driven by regional party and Presidential alignments, not the party membership of a favoured local candidate. The percentage of the vote received by different candidates for a party in the same region followed a regular pattern, so that all the Ford-Asili candidates in Murang'a, for example, received between 66 and 99 per cent of the vote, all the KANU candidates between 1 and 14 per cent. Similarly, all the FORD-Kenya Luo Nyanza candidates polled between 84 and 99 per cent, and all KANU's between 1 and 16 per cent. In Kakamega, all the KANU candidates polled between 23 and 50 per cent, and all the FORD-Asili candidates between 40 and 71 per cent. As a result, good candidates performed very badly if they were in the wrong party, and little-known first-timers triumphed over established politicians. Over most of the country, an individual strong candidate could only buck the trend by 10–20 per cent, and there was no relationship between candidates' votes in 1983 or 1988 and their 1992 performances. It was party and the Presidential candidates' 'coat-tails' that determined the results. Only in marginal areas, such as Kitui, Kisii and Mombasa, did local issues, organisation, and the candidates' abilities alter the result.

Nonetheless, although the Presidential candidates organised and led the election campaigns and were the rallying symbols for the parties, all of them, except Matiba, polled worse on average than did their party's Parliamentary candidates, as the polls had predicted. Nationally, Matiba benefited from a slight tendency to 'split ticket' in his favour. Figures 10.8 to 10.11 show, for each major party, the relationship between the percentage of the vote obtained by their Presidential and Parliamentary candidates. Where the point is below the line, the Parliamentary candidate out-polled his President; where the point is above, the Presidential candidate did better than his Parliamentary colleague. Most of the anomalous seats indicate unusual cross-voting, associated with a particularly strong local candidate. A few are indicative of electoral abuses.

Comparing Moi's performance with that of KANU's candidates, it is clear that KANU supporters ticket-voted over most of the country. In the areas where KANU was popular, Moi narrowly led his candidates, mainly because more pressure was placed on voters to cast their ballots for Moi in the Presidential election than was placed on them to elect local KANU MPs, but also because of local dissatisfaction with the ruling party following the primaries. Where KANU was less popular, he trailed them. Moi did better than his candidates in the Coast, worse in Eastern Province and Kisii, and overall came out slightly behind. He was more popular than his candidate (by two per cent or more of the vote) in 45 seats, and less so in 60. Unusual results include Mandera East and Sigor where voters backed Moi and PICK candidates who had lost the KANU primaries; and Bobasi in Kisii and Tharaka in Tharaka-Nithi where KANU's Parliamentary candidates did conspicuously better than President Moi. At the bottom left of the graph were several seats where Moi both did very poorly, but strong Parliamentary candidates managed to poll approximately 10 per cent more votes than Moi. These included Cabinet Ministers Arthur Magugu in

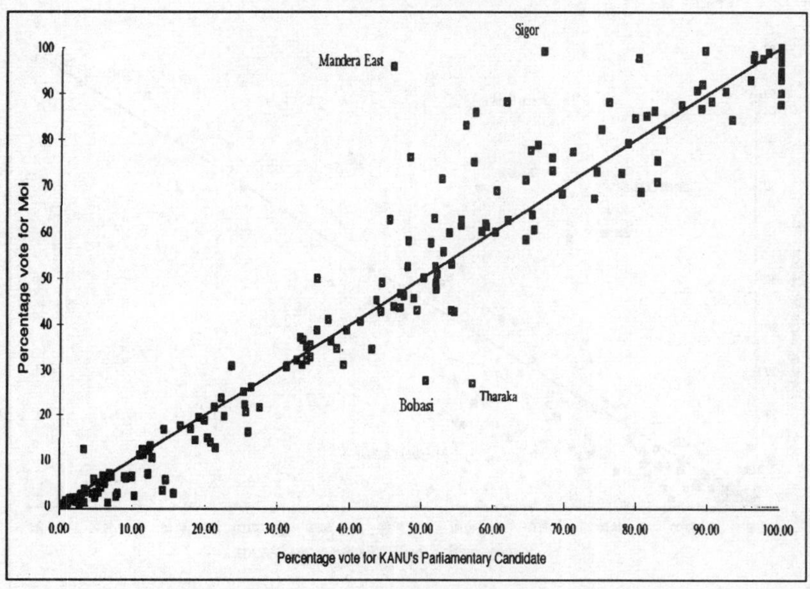

Figure 10.8 Moi and His Candidates' Votes

Note: The cluster on the far right of the KANU graph is the unopposed seats, in which the KANU candidate polled 100 per cent by definition.

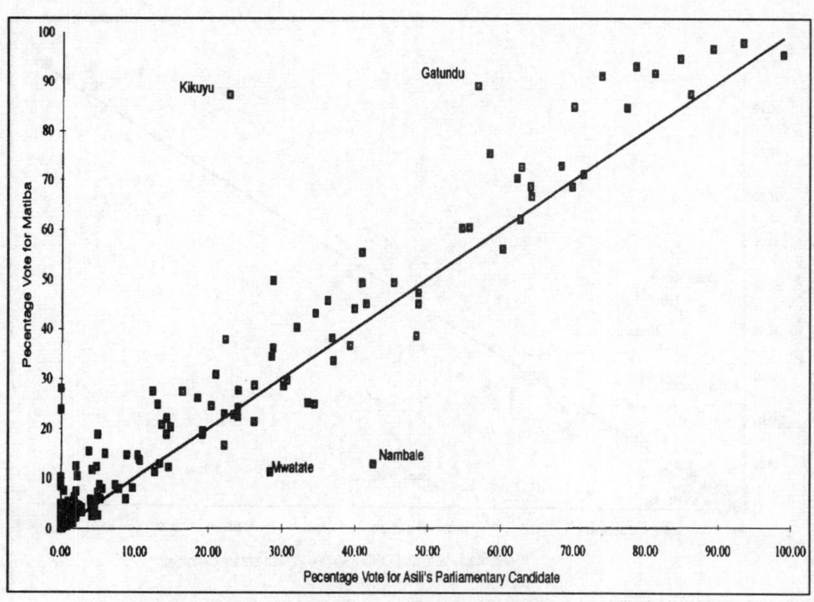

Figure 10.9 Matiba and His Candidates' Votes

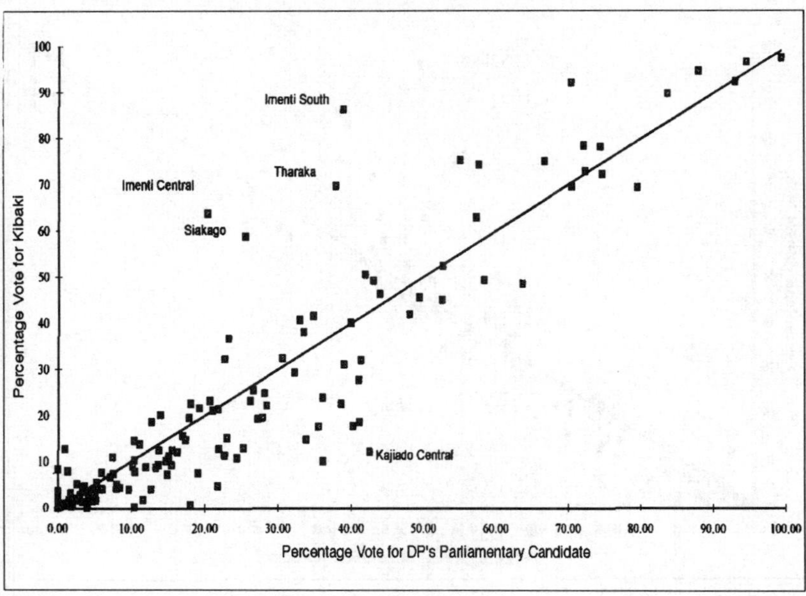

Figure 10.10 Kibaki and His Candidates' Votes

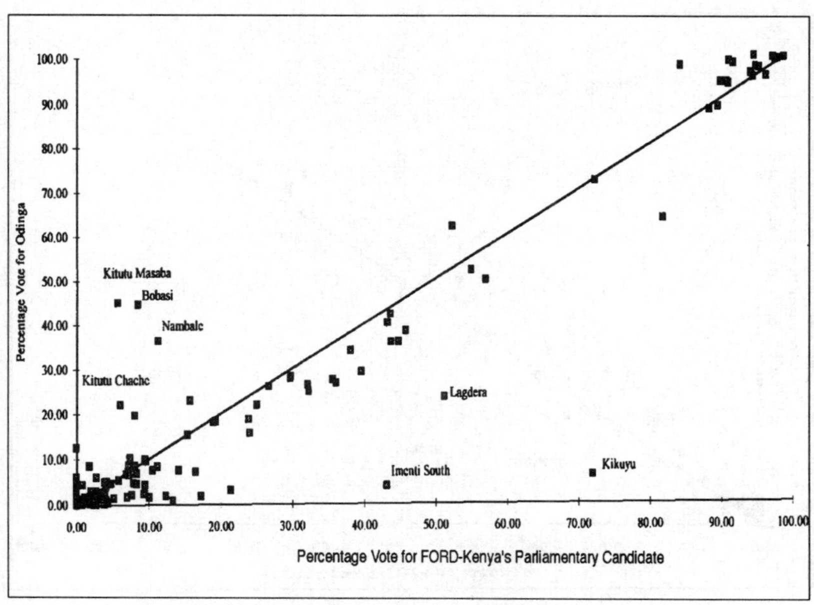

Figure 10.11 Odinga and His Candidates' Votes

Githunguri, Joseph Kamotho in Kangema, Lazarus Amayo in Karachuonyo, and Kabeere M'Mbijjwe in Imenti South.

By contrast, although FORD-Asili supporters also voted strongly for a party ticket, Matiba outshone the party's candidates over much of the country, particularly in Kiambu, Nairobi and Western Province. He polled worse than his candidate (by 2 per cent or more) in only 17 seats, and better in 81. Two exceptional constituencies in Figure 10.9 were Kikuyu and Gatundu, where individual candidates for other opposition parties (FORD-Kenya's Paul Muite and the DP's Ngengi Muigai) received a strong personal vote. By contrast, in Nambale, a strong personal vote for an Asili candidate was not transferred to Matiba.

The DP seems to have attracted the least party-ticket voting of the main parties (see Figure 10.10). As with Moi, a Presidential 'S-curve' emerges – where the DP did badly, its Parliamentary candidates led; where it did well, Kibaki out-polled his supporters. The DP was clearly a more locally based alliance than FORD-Kenya, KANU or FORD-Asili. The perception that Kibaki was not a strong electoral asset is confirmed by the fact that DP candidates outperformed him in 59 seats, compared with the 36 where he outperformed them. In Kajiado, for example, John Keen and his allies all polled between 10 and 30 per cent more votes than their Presidential candidate. There is a strong cluster towards the middle of the graph of seats where DP candidates secured 20–40 per cent of the vote, while Kibaki only received 5–30 per cent. By contrast, Kibaki massively out-polled his candidates in three Meru seats (Imenti South, Imenti Central and Tharaka), two of which are questionable for other reasons. The Siakago seat in Embu was also anomalous, because the loser of the DP primary defected to the KNC and won the seat, while his supporters voted for Kibaki.

Oginga Odinga was slightly less popular than his FORD-Kenya Parliamentary candidates, outpolling his candidates by two per cent or more in 26 seats, and worse in 42. His age and ethnicity seem to have created a 'lag' of 1,000 votes or more everywhere, with the exception of Kisii, where he did comparatively well (thanks to Parliamentary election rigging). Ticket voting was particularly clear in the Luo areas, where FORD-Kenya secured nearly 100 per cent (the cluster near the top of the graph). Exceptions included Kikuyu, Imenti South and Lagdera, where strong FORD-Kenya candidates overcame anti-Odinga feeling. These were precisely the three Young Turk MPs – Paul Muite, Kiraitu Murungi, and Farah M. Mohammed – who were to break with the Odinga line in 1993. On the other side, four seats stand out in which voters supported Odinga, but voted for another parliamentary candidate – Nambale, where people voted for Chrisantus Okemo (FORD-Asili) and Odinga; Kitutu Masaba, where they voted for George Anyona (KSC); and Kitutu Chache and Bobasi, where the results are believed to have been rigged. It is also clear that there were very few additional seats where FORD-Kenya came close to winning. The party won 20 seats overwhelmingly and polled well in a few isolated constituencies; but the vast majority of its candidates took less than 20 per cent of the vote. Despite its detailed policies and the prominent role its leaders had played in the movement for multi-party democracy, FORD-Kenya did not have the local-level organisation to support its national image.

The Local Government Elections

Little was reported in the press about the local government elections, which were held at the same time. In general, they followed party lines very closely, though popular local KNC, PICK or KSC candidates tended to perform better than their parties. KANU councillors won overwhelmingly in KANU areas in the North-East, the Rift Valley, and the Coast outside Mombasa. FORD-Kenya's victory in Luoland was almost total. Every single elected local government member there, county, urban and municipal, was a FORD-Kenya candidate, bar one PICK councillor.[48] As with the Presidency and Parliament, FORD-Asili won Nairobi's first civic elections in ten years, capturing 35 Council seats, compared with FORD-Kenya's nine, KANU's seven and the DP's four, and swept to victory in Kiambu and Murang'a. The DP won Kirinyaga, Laikipia and Nyeri; while Nyandarua was shared with Asili. In Eastern Province, KANU won majorities in the three Ukambani Districts, while the DP took Embu, Meru and Tharaka-Nithi. The urban areas were generally more pro-opposition, though KANU managed to win Mombasa (winning 13 seats, to FORD-Kenya's seven, FORD-Asili's two, and one for the DP), a major upset for the FORD-Kenya-IPK alliance which had carried two of the city's four Parliamentary constituencies.

There were, however, a few interesting anomalies. Somehow, KANU won the majority of seats in Nakuru Country Council, though it lost the municipal council (with 12 FORD-Asili seats to KANU's four) and won only one of five Parliamentary seats. KANU also won the majority of seats in Kisii and Nyamira, although the area split evenly in the Parliamentary elections. FORD-Asili won Eldoret (with eight seats to KANU's six, and one for FORD-Kenya), which was anomalous given that it lost all three Parliamentary seats in disputed circumstances to KANU. The ethnic background of the elected councillors reflected the tense nature of ethnic rivalries in that area: six of the eight Asili councillors were Kikuyu and two Luhya, while all KANU's were Kalenjin, and FORD-Kenya's one councillor was Luo.[49]

An Overall Assessment of the Electoral Process

Election day 1992 was poorly run, but successful nonetheless because of the goodwill and commitment of many Kenyans. The election monitoring process contributed substantially to the fairness of the election, acting as a deterrent and a detection mechanism in many marginal areas. The concept of election monitoring in Kenya, in the words of the NEMU report, 'seemed to have taken root',[50] though rigging flourished in the areas where it was organised by the state. The observers were simply not allowed into the count in these constituencies. Nonetheless, there was a fundamental weakness in the monitoring effort, reflected in the lack of information exchanged between bodies, and the lack of coordination from the summer onwards between international and national monitors, and between the different national groups, leading to wasted resources and duplication. As their final reports were to show, it also led to numerous mixed messages, weakening the impact of each. A single coordinated and integrated monitoring body, staffed by both internal and external monitors, is clearly essential in a future Kenyan or similar case.

There were serious question marks over the fairness of polling in the central Rift Valley, where voters were dragooned to the polls and had little choice but to vote for President Moi. Elsewhere, there appeared to be little blatant rigging on polling day itself. Certainly, the election was badly organised outside the KANU zones, but the vigilance and commitment of the population minimised rigging. Administratively, numerous minor improvements were required, some of which were addressed in the observer bodies' reports. The agents' seals did not always work properly and there was little that the agents could do if officials refused to let them accompany the boxes. The ballot papers and boxes should have been colour coded consistently. In an atmosphere of concern over fairness, steps need to be taken to reassure voters and agents, such as ensuring that voters mark with a pen, not a pencil, and that agents' seals are rather harder to cut through or replace. Poll clerks should be better trained, better facilities should be provided and better advance planning carried out. The need for civic education was also clear. Counting clerks should be more numerous and better trained, and election officials should be more openly recruited. All these recommendations will cost money and require careful organisation. Moreover, if Western countries continue to bankroll Kenya's elections, there is no reason why Western officials should not participate actively in the Electoral Commission.

In the event, despite all early predictions, KANU won a decisive victory in all three elections. The central question is, given the opposition's huge popularity, and the majority vote it received, why and how did this happen?

Notes

1 Commonwealth Report, p.32.
2 *Ibid.*, p. 31.
3 A classic example was a Mvita polling station, where the original site was changed to one just across the street from KANU Chairman Sharrif Nassir's office. IRI Final Report, p. 46.
4 *Kenya Times*, 31 December 1992, p. 13.
5 NEMU reported over 10 per cent of stations opening after 10 a.m. NEMU Report, p. 231.
6 Saku in Marsabit, *Kenya Times*, 31 December 1992, p. 19.
7 There is no evidence that this was intentional. It was simply a problem of time and resources.
8 These included Kirinyaga (stations /60 and /61), Meru, Molo constituency (NKU /98 and /79), Laikipia, Nyahuhuru, Kiambu and Busia. Sources included Matiba, faxed copies of letters to Electoral Commission, 29 December 1992.
9 See the *Report of the Election Monitoring Exercise. A Project of the National Council of Women of Kenya*, NCWK, 1993 (NCWK Report).
10 *Kenya Times*, 31 December 1992, p. 19.
11 NCWK Report.
12 Personal Conversation with a journalist who visited Narok North on polling day, 1993. Also NCWK Report.
13 NCWK Report, p. 18.
14 IRI Final Report, pp. 47–9.
15 *Kenya Times*, 1 January 1993, p. 4.
16 NCWK Report, p. 26.
17 Msambweni NEMU Poll Report, 31 December 1992.

18 Numerous NEMU poll monitors' reports, Emuhaya.
19 NCWK Report.
20 Commonwealth Report, pp. 36-7.
21 Interview with local residents, 30 December 1992.
22 Various NEMU Monitors and DLO reports.
23 IRI Observer. The BEERAM Report also confirmed major voter transportation in Nakuru.
24 The IRI discussed the Mombasa case. IRI Final Report, p. 47.
25 See for example, the Nyeri problems of Minister Nahashon Kanyi, *Kenya Times*, 31 December 1992 p. 18.
26 NEMU's summary reported that in 68 of 1722 stations agents were left behind, and there were problems in transporting the boxes in nearly 10 per cent of stations.
27 NEMU's sample reported 25 of 107 started before all were in.
28 *Kenya Times*, 31 December 1992, p. 3.
29 The Commonwealth expressed 'concern at the slow pace of counting of the ballots and the consequential delay in the release of the results'. *Commonwealth Report*, Summary, p. xi.
30 NEMU DLO report, Embu.
31 NEMU Poll Report, Limuru.
32 NCWK Report.
33 NEMU FIDA/ICJ Poll Report, Samia.
34 *Commonwealth Report* p. 59, and *Preliminary Statement of Findings, Kenya General Election, December 29 1992.*
35 Interviews with IRI advisers, 1992.
36 *IRI Election Day Checklist for Observers*, n.d.
37 A US official suggested that the visit was a 'holiday for Republican worthies from the mid-West'.
38 A small Nordic team visited 12 constituencies, including Taita-Taveta, Nairobi and Kitui. The Swedes visited Saboti and Kibwezi polling stations, but not the count. The Japanese Embassy visited 23 stations in Kajiado North, Trans-Nzoia and Nairobi. The Egyptian Ambassador himself toured 10 stations in Nairobi. There were also representatives from the American labour group AFL-CIO in Nakuru and a Dutch Embassy group who covered nine districts, including Laikipia, Elgeyo-Marakwet, Taita, Embu, Nairobi and Kitale. There was a group from the European Parliament, which visited rural Eldoret South, Nakuru, Naivasha and Uasin-Gishu. A Swiss Group visited Nairobi, Laikipia, Limuru and Mombasa.
39 See *The Multi-Party General Elections in Kenya, 29 December 1992. The Report of the National Election Monitoring Unit (NEMU)* (NEMU Report).
40 *NEMU Report*, pp. 231–2.
41 Analysis of NEMU Draft Report spreadsheets, Appendix 16, excluded from final report.
42 Informal conversation with NEMU official, November 1993.
43 *BEERAM Report*, p. 1.
44 A parallel count was carried out for the election and validated afterwards on the basis of published reports. This is used in the percentages given above and the results presented henceforth, due to errors in the presentation of results for individual seats in the national media and the Electoral Commission results. However, the aggregated results for the Presidential candidates were all within 20,000 votes nationally, so it is not necessary to present them here. Note, however, that the official election commission results understated Kibaki's support on the Coast and Odinga's in Western.
45 A similar result was seen in Zambia.
46 Definitions: Central Rift: Elgeyo-Marakwet, Nandi, Baringo, Kericho and Bomet. Peripheral Rift: West Pokot, Turkana, Samburu. White Highlands: Nakuru, Laikipia, Trans-Nzoia, Uasin Gishu (Narok and Kajiado excluded from sub-categories). Rural coast is rest of Coast minus Mombasa. Luo Nyanza is all Luo-occupied Nyanza seats (excluding therefore Kuria). Gusii Nyanza is Nyamira and Kisii districts. The 1992 registration figures are the final *Daily Nation* figures as announced by returning officers, not the original June 1992 *Weekly Review* figures.
47 See J. Barkan, *Politics and Public Policy in Kenya and Tanzania*, and Hornsby, unpublished Oxford 1985 D. Phil. thesis, 'The Kenyan Member of Parliament, 1969–83', *op. cit.*
48 *Weekly Review*, 5 March 1993, p. 11.
49 *Weekly Review*, 19 February 1993, p. 10.
50 *NEMU Report*, p. 117.

Eleven

Why KANU Won

KANU's decisive victory in the 1992 elections was a product of three independent factors. First, the opposition failed to present a united front; second, the election was fought regionally, and KANU had the edge in a sufficient number of regions, especially the less-populated but over-represented ones; and third, the state's bias and electoral malpractice were sufficient to swing the balance in crucial contested areas.

The most frequent explanation given for the opposition's defeat was that it was divided and had 'shot itself in the foot'.[1] The splits between the DP and FORD, then within FORD, and finally within FORD-Asili divided their strength, allowing KANU to win on a minority of both the Presidential and the Parliamentary polls. Too much effort was expended on internal in-fighting which could have been put to use against the common enemy; by promoting an image of disunity and weakness, the opposition's endemic factionalism also persuaded doubters to return to KANU. Simple arithmetic suggests that a united opposition or an electoral pact between any two parties would have out-polled President Moi and probably won the Presidential election. The opposition collectively received 63 per cent of the Presidential votes, which appears to suggest that either a DP/FORD-Asili alliance or a united FORD would have won an overall majority and 25 per cent in five Provinces, and therefore triumphed completely. In the Parliamentary election, if the opposition had fielded only a single candidate against KANU, assuming that 25 per cent of the voters who voted for the party running third would have returned to KANU, the government would have won only 87 seats, the opposition 101.

The reality, however, is somewhat different. FORD's disunity damaged its chances, but unity might not have been enough to alter the overall result. Whoever the Presidential candidate had been, once bitterness had begun to build up after May 1992, it would have reduced dramatically the turn-out from the ethnic homelands of the other. If Odinga had been the candidate of a united FORD, many Kikuyu would have voted for the DP in Central Province, Nakuru and Nairobi. Equally, if Matiba had been FORD's Presidential candidate, the commitment of the Luo to vote for him would have been in doubt, and a significant proportion would have opted for the 'devil they knew'. In each case, the result would have been very close. Thus the original formation of the DP as a second opposition party, centred in the most fervently pro-opposition region, itself was a major contributor to the opposition's defeat. Similarly a FORD-Kenya/DP alliance, as was close to agreement several times, would have increased their chances of winning, but by far less than the sum of Odinga's and Kibaki's votes. Odinga would still have had difficulty delivering Luo votes to a Kikuyu, while Kibaki would have been incapable of delivering Kikuyu votes to Odinga.[2] Only in the Parliamentary marginals would it have benefited them.

Once Matiba refused to accept the FORD Vice-Presidency, and all three opposition leaders were in the race, KANU's chances were good. The prospect of any of them standing down was small. Matiba's withdrawal would have made most difference, since the majority of his votes would have gone to FORD-Kenya or the DP, but he was too arrogant to accept his own fallibility and was the main obstacle to opposition unity. Odinga was determined to become President before he died. Kibaki showed the most willingness to deal, but Matiba's inroads into his support came too late for a counter-alliance with FORD-Kenya. Even if Kibaki himself had agreed to stand down for the good of the country, enough of his backers and the party's candidates would have rebelled to have aborted the deal. In any case, the better the opposition's chances of winning, the more KANU would have manipulated the election.

Another reason for KANU's victory was that they rigged the election. We have already seen the impact of KANU's electoral tactics on the fairness of the campaign. We now consider how 'free' the election was. Did the number of votes recorded for each candidate in each constituency actually match the voting intentions of those who queued to cast their ballots? Were they forced against their will to vote a particular way, and was there evidence that votes were destroyed, deliberately miscounted or inserted into the ballot boxes? This issue is complicated by the absence of detailed polling station reports in Kenyan elections. No official results at this level have been made public (although sanitised constituency records are available), and there is no national tradition of impartial analysis of voting patterns. Nonetheless, in the manner of a detective novel, it is still possible to discover roughly what happened, and why. On the basis of a detailed study of the results, and the reports of observers, the press and participants, it is our view that KANU cleverly manipulated the polls, and then rigged the count to ensure that they won an overall victory in both Presidential and Parliamentary elections. Over much of the country, the voting did not produce results that were grossly anomalous. Moi did not win Murang'a, nor did Kibaki win Nyanza. The government, however, tipped the balance by piling up as many votes as possible in its strongholds by 'open voting' in the Presidential election, and winning 10–20 key Parliamentary constituencies through ballot box stuffing and other malpractices at the count. The evidence for electoral abuses comes from two different sources:

statistical evidence for anomalies and procedural failures, and eye-witness reports from candidates, foreign and domestic observers and from the press. Whilst the statistical material alone proves nothing, if it can be linked to reports of malpractice, then a far more coherent and plausible picture of the scope and level of abuse is liable to emerge.

The Statistical Evidence for Electoral Abuse

The statistical evidence for malpractice on polling day and in the count comes from five different sources: discrepancies between Presidential and Parliamentary vote totals; performance imbalances between Presidential and Parliamentary candidates for the same party; turn-out variations; the number of spoilt ballots; and how long it took to announce the results.

Since the Presidential and Parliamentary polls were held on the same day, and most voters are likely to have cast their ballot for both elections at the same time, the total number of votes cast should have been roughly similar. There were some legitimate reasons for discrepancies. A few people genuinely voted in the Presidential poll, and returned or destroyed their ballot papers for the other two elections, but these were exceptional cases, widely noted and recorded by observers.[3] Voters sometimes placed their ballot papers into the wrong box, which in some seats were counted as spoilt ballots for one election, when they would have been valid in the other. There were also inaccuracies introduced by clerical errors during counting and the publication of the results. As all the results were tabulated by hand, on paper, errors were rife, and most of the reported results did not even match the station-by-station totals recorded by some NEMU observers. However, where such counting errors were accidental, they should have averaged out.

In fact, the total number of ballots counted in the 1992 Presidential and Parliamentary elections was significantly different in nearly 50 constituencies (30 per cent of the seats where both polls took place). If there were 20 or 30 more discarded, lost, or mis-voted papers at each polling stream for one election than the other, the total number of votes should have varied by at most roughly 800 ballot papers (one box). Any variation beyond this is considered to be significant. Many of these 50 significant discrepancies can only be explained by ballot box stuffing or destruction of votes, as had been common in previous Kenyan elections. With only two numbers to compare, it is impossible to tell whether votes were destroyed or added in. It would, however, be rational in marginal constituencies for rigging (if it occurred) to take place primarily in the Parliamentary election, in order to tip the balance and win the seat. In safe seats, the Presidential election would be more likely to be manipulated, since additional Parliamentary votes would not benefit the winner, while every Presidential vote counted.

In 28 seats, over half those where significant discrepancies appear, there were too many Presidential ballots and the seat was not marginal (see Table 11.1). Either the reported results were consistently wrong, counting was biased or someone had been inserting Presidential ballots in up to 15 per cent of constituencies. Kitui North was the most extreme case, with 11,271 too many Presidential votes, a result which surely was reported incorrectly. The excess Presidential ballots were concentrated in particular regions. This was most obvious in Murang'a District, where FORD-Asili won extraordinary victories in both Presidential and Parliamentary elections. It apparently polled too many Presidential votes in four of six Murang'a seats, with a difference of over 5,000 in Gatanga. Kenneth Matiba in Mbiri managed to poll over 3,000 more votes in the Presidential election than he did for himself in the Parliamentary contest. Imbalances were also seen in three Nakuru District seats. Among KANU's 'safe' seats on the Coast and the Rift Valley periphery there were also anomalies.

Table 11.1 'Safe' Seats with Too Many Presidential Ballots

Province	No of discrepancies	Seats and Presidential winner
Nairobi	0	
North-East	0	
Coast	3	Ganze, Malindi, Voi - KANU
Central	8	Githunguri, Kipipiri, Kiharu, Kandara, Makuyu, Gatanga – FORD-Asili
		Ndia, Gichugu – DP
Western	4	Kimilili – FORD-Kenya
		Nambale and Sabatia – KANU
		Shinyalu – FORD-Asili
Nyanza	3	Nyando, Kasipul-Kabondo, Alego – FORD-Kenya
Rift Valley	7	Kipkelion, Eldoret East, Samburu West, Narok West – KANU
		Molo, Nakuru North, Nakuru East – FORD-Asili
Eastern	3	Machakos Town, Moyale, Kitui North – KANU

Source: Cross-calculation of poll totals for each seat in both elections.

There were too few Presidential ballots in at least 13 more safe seats, where logic suggests Presidential papers were destroyed or under-counted (or unsuccessful attempts were made to stuff the Parliamentary boxes). Eleven of these were opposition seats, including Nyeri Town and Mathira (won by the DP), Rongo and Ugenya (FORD-Kenya), Nakuru Town (FORD-Asili), and Runyenjes (DP). In the latter case, there appear to have been over 5,000 ballots too few announced for Kibaki.

Marginal seats also reveal some anomalies. Four key marginal constituencies had far too few Parliamentary ballots. These were Kisauni, where FORD-Kenya won narrowly (a result later annulled); Rongai and Kajiado North which KANU won extremely contentiously; and Kitui Central, which was narrowly won by the DP. Destruction of ballots is a possibility in each case. Several more marginals had too many Parliamentary ballots, suggesting stuffing in the Parliamentary elections after the Presidential results were known. These included three important Eastern Province seats: Imenti Central (KANU win; 1,559 too many votes), Kitui

West (KANU win; 1,550 too many), and Gachoka (DP win; 2,114 too many).

Because ticket voting was so strong nationally, performance imbalances between the vote for the Presidential and Parliamentary candidates for the same party also provide some pointers to potential malpractice, although there are many other good reasons for local variations in support for a party (such as particularly strong or weak local candidates). Twenty Parliamentary seats were won by a party which lost the Presidential elections in that seat (see Table 11.2). Some of these victories were narrow, and were also associated with imbalances in the number of votes recorded. Overall, FORD-Kenya came out even, whilst Asili came out with one fewer Parliamentary seats than it had won in the Presidency. The real concern is with the DP and KANU. The DP lost seven Parliamentary seats to KANU which they won in the Presidency, six of them in Eastern Province, and gained only two from KANU, both in the same area.

Table 11.2 Split Results in 1992

Province	District	Seat	Party winning Parliament	Party winning Presidency
Nairobi	Nairobi	Westlands	KANU	FORD-Asili
Central	Kiambu	Kikuyu	FORD-Kenya	FORD-Asili
Coast	Mombasa	Kisauni	FORD-Kenya	KANU
	Mombasa	Changamwe	DP	FORD-Kenya
	Embu	Siakago	KNC	DP
	Meru	Igembe	KANU	DP
	Meru	Ntonyiri	DP	KANU
	Meru	Imenti Central	KANU	DP
Eastern	Tharaka-Nithi	Tharaka	KANU	DP
	Machakos	Mwala	KANU	DP
	Kitui	Mutito	KANU	DP
	Kitui	Mutomo	KANU	DP
	Kitui	Kitui Central	DP	KANU
North-Eastern	Garissa	Lagdera	FORD-Kenya	KANU
	Mandera	Mandera East	PICK	KANU
Western	Vihiga	Emuhaya	KANU	FORD-Asili
	Vihiga	Hamisi	FORD-Asili	KANU
	Kisii	Bobasi	KANU	FORD-Kenya
Nyanza	Kisii	Kitutu Chache	KANU	DP
	Nyamira	Kitutu Masaba	KSC	FORD-Kenya

We can focus attention separately on those seats where KANU candidates performed far better than President Moi. These included three constituencies in Nandi, Baringo and Bomet, where KANU's Parliamentary candidates were unopposed, but opposition Presidential candidates polled well, reflecting dissatisfaction with their status as KANU zones.

Table 11.3 Marginals Where KANU's Candidate Outperformed President Moi, 1992

District	Constituency	KANU's Parliamentary percentage	Moi's percentage	Extra KANU Parliamentary votes	KANU's margin of Parliamentary victory
Tharaka-Nithi	Tharaka	**57.09**	27.12	5,192	3,140
Kitui	Kitui North	**54.29**	42.74	−434	5,126
Kitui	Mutito	**54.13**	43.10	1,442	1,530
Kisii	Bobasi	**49.29**	27.70	4,953	3,370
Kakamega	Shinyalu	**42.61**	34.53	1,330	−2,425
Kitui	Mutomo	**39.11**	31.12	1,485	1,336

Note: Constituencies in bold were won by KANU.

There were also six marginals where the KANU candidate polled many more votes than Moi, five of which KANU won as a result (see Table 11.3). Three of these were in Kitui, a focus for concern over electoral malpractice.

The third statistical indicator is the large regional variations in turn-out. Because the parties were so regionally focused, the turn-out had a significant effect on the Presidential results. Of particular concern were the large turn-outs in the five Districts of Baringo, Elgeyo-Marakwet, Nandi, Kericho and Bomet, which recorded 90 per cent turn-outs and near 100 per cent votes for Moi. Calculating the percentage of the adult population which voted for the four Presidential candidates in their core heartlands, 68 per cent of eligible voters actually cast their ballots for Moi in these five Districts, 65 per cent of Nyeri adults voted for Kibaki, 61 per cent of Murang'a voters for Matiba, while only 49 per cent of Luo adults in Nyanza voted for Odinga. Despite his heartland being much larger and more sparsely populated, Moi managed to record the votes of the largest proportion of the adult population. Indeed, over half of Moi's Presidential vote came from the Rift Valley, and 30 per cent of it from the 17 constituencies from which KANU excluded opposition candidates. Areas like Baringo had a disproportionately large number of polling stations, given their population and size, and the threat to Moi's position undoubtedly galvanised Kalenjin voters to an extent never seen before. Nonetheless, on the basis of the past, and of likely turn-outs in such sparsely populated areas, these figures seem implausible.

The turn-out was statistically implausible in another way. In a few seats the rigging appears to have been so crude that turn-out levels over 100 per cent were seen. In most seats, officials failed to provide proper breakdowns of the registered voters and turn-out in each station to the poll monitors, making these calculations impossible. In a few cases, however, enough evidence was released, station by station, to permit the detection of such obvious rigging. These seats included the sensational Molo contest, where

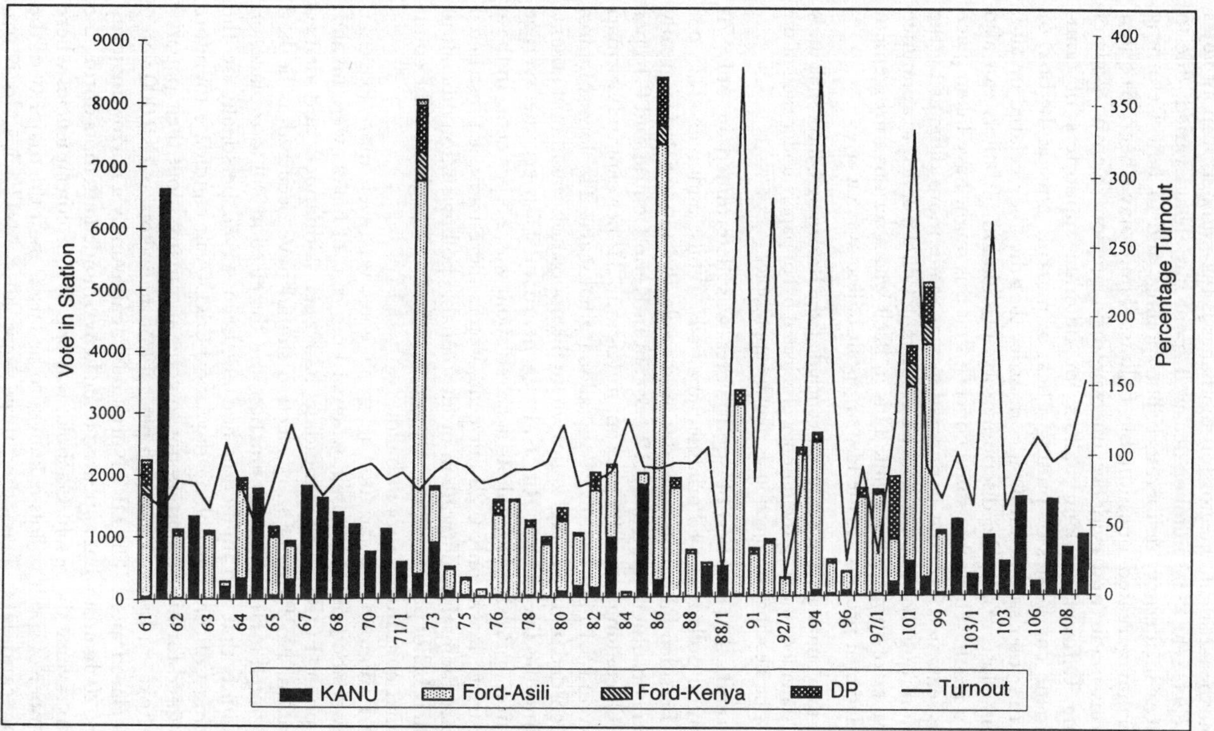

Figure 11.1 Malpractice In Molo

Source: Presidential results reports from poll monitors. Presidential results from five polling station were missing, so the results from the Parliamentary elections have been used instead.

rigging by both FORD-Asili and KANU is clear, even taking into account the ethnic concentration of support for both parties. Turn-out exceeded 100 per cent in sixteen polling stations, rising to 400 per cent at its highest (see Figure 11.1).

A fourth statistical detector for anomalies is the number of spoilt votes cast in each seat. The number declared spoilt has always varied, due to differences in literacy, deliberate ballot spoiling, and in how Returning Officers have treated questionable ballots. There have been frequent allegations made (and evidence uncovered) in previous Kenyan polls of Presiding Officers marking ballots for illiterate supporters of 'anti-government' candidates by putting a tick, or marking outside the box, or writing the voter's name alongside, in order that they be declared invalid. In a very close result, the discriminatory invalidation of ballots can also change a result. There was some concern that this might have taken place in some seats in 1992, but confirmation was made more difficult by the fact that in roughly 80 constituencies Returning Officers failed to announce the number of spoilt votes at all. This in itself was a serious infringement of the electoral process, as the law on spoilt ballots was clear:

> After the counting of votes is finally concluded, the Returning Officer shall draw up a statement showing the number of rejected ballot papers under such of the following headings of rejection as may be applicable.[4]

In the end, the number of spoilt votes was determined in only 70 Presidential polls and 84 Parliamentary polls. Whilst nationally 1.25 per cent of Presidential ballots were declared spoilt, the number varied greatly between constituencies, from 0.12 per cent in Kerio Central and 0.13 per cent in Chepalungu, to 4.33 per cent in Kisauni, 3.2 per cent in Nyaribari Masaba and 3.19 per cent in Mvita (all marginal seats). The lowest figures were recorded in the KANU zones where the opposition was almost absent. Excluding the five central Rift Kalenjin heartland Districts, the average proportion of Presidential ballots declared spoilt was 1.5 per cent. In these five Districts, it was only 0.29 per cent. Voters there had been instructed to declare themselves illiterate in order to enable polling station officials to fill in their ballot papers, while very generous leeway was given at the count as to what constituted a spoilt ballot.

The Parliamentary variation in spoilt votes was even more extreme. Two seats stood out. In Samia, where 10 per cent of ballots were invalid, the popular FORD-Asili candidate had been kidnapped and denied nomination. No Parliamentary election should have occurred as he had been granted a High Court injunction, but the election still took place, on the grounds that the injunction had not been served personally on the Returning Officer. On polling day, the FORD-Asili candidate therefore campaigned for his supporters not to vote, and many spoilt their papers.[5] In Gachoka, in Embu District, 6 per cent of the ballots, over 2,000 votes, were declared spoilt. The DP's Norman Nyagah won by a narrow majority of only 520 against what appeared to be heavy-handed attempts during the count to reverse the result. Gachoka was one of four constituencies where the number of spoilt ballots is known to be larger than the majority of the winning candidate. The other three were all KANU wins. In North

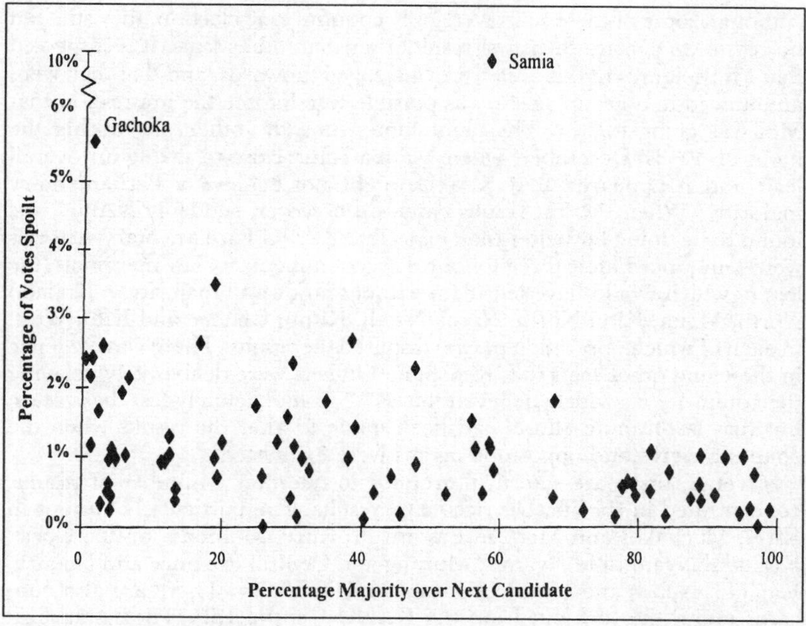

Figure 11.2 Spoilt Votes and Parliamentary Majorities: An Anomaly

Mugirango in Kisii, there were 632 spoilt votes with a KANU majority of only 137; in nearby Nyaribari Masaba, 428 spoilt votes with a 241 majority for KANU; and in Malava, 487 spoilt ballots with a majority of 300. In two more seats – Mvita in Mombasa (303 spoilt, 352 KANU majority), and Kitutu Chache in Kisii (562 spoilt, 652 KANU majority) – the winner's majority was similar to the number of spoilt ballots.

Indeed, a clear relationship emerges between the number of spoilt votes and the marginality of the Parliamentary seat. Closely fought seats had high numbers of spoilt votes, easy victories had few. Figure 11.2 shows the size of the candidate's majority against the number of spoilt ballots for the 84 known Parliamentary spoilt ballot results. There is no legitimate reason to expect any correlation between these two results. Nonetheless, it appears that the Returning Officers in safe seats were favouring the majority party (not just KANU), and in marginals were being extremely strict.

Our final circumstantial clue lies in the odd timing of the announcement of the election results. After a few small seats declared before noon on 30 December, Presidential results arrived in mid-afternoon from a large number of Rift Valley KANU seats in Baringo, Nandi and elsewhere, all of which gave huge majorities to President Moi. When 51 results had been declared in the Presidential election, Moi had won 600,377 (48 per cent) of 1,200,000 votes counted, compared with his final tally of 36 per cent.[6]

Although some of these seats were only counting one election, they still had no reason to declare their first result faster than other seats. It is suspected that Moi's figures in this area were 'massaged' upwards, and that they were announced in a group as early as possible to reinforce the impression that Moi was going to win. The pendulum swung the other way during the night of 30–31 December, when Matiba came close to taking an overall lead and it appeared that KANU might not achieve a Parliamentary majority.[7] When the last results came in, however, suddenly KANU was found to be doing far better than expected. KANU Parliamentary victories were announced after three to four days counting in six key marginals (the loss of which would have left them without an overall majority) – Kajiado North, Mvita, Kitui North, Narok North, Kitutu Chache and Kitui West, in each of which opposition parties disputed the results. There was evidence in these and other seats that Returning Officers were deliberately delaying the count. It was widely believed that KANU had actually lost these seats, but that last-minute efforts had been made to alter the results when the counting clerks and opposition agents were exhausted.

Overall, there are statistical grounds to question a number of results, concentrated in specific Districts. The results were particularly curious in Kitui, Machakos and Meru in Eastern Province, Mombasa on the Coast, Kisii and Nyamira in Nyanza, Murang'a in Central Province and Nakuru, Kajiado, Narok and Uasin Gishu in the Rift Valley. There are also concerns about the turn-out from the KANU Central Rift. These statistical indicators can be matched with the reports from poll monitors, the press and participants to provide a quite detailed picture of the abuses which occurred in the voting and counting. Information has been acquired from constituency reports, from the press, from the foreign observers, from FORD-Asili's protest faxes to NEMU during the election, from the petitions made by the parties after the election, but above all from several hundred NEMU observers' and count certifiers' own detailed, handwritten reports, filed during and immediately after the election. Credence cannot be given to all such complaints, since all Kenyan politicians are liable to call foul at the slightest excuse, and protests have been rife after every election.[8] Nonetheless, having cross-checked the reported malpractices with the statistical results, there are grounds to question both certain Presidential results and whether KANU indeed won an overall majority in the Parliamentary election.

The next section looks at the election from a regional perspective. We look at the real differences between the political allegiances and contests in different parts of the country and at the same time focus on the indicators of possible malpractice in these areas in order to explain both why KANU won, and how they cheated to do so. Because the contest was so different in different regions, with different factors driving the election, it is impossible to understand the result without recourse to regional studies. Some areas saw relatively fair contests, others were extensively rigged. Some areas saw massive government victories, some equally clear opposition triumphs, whilst key regions remained marginal. Only by cataloguing and analysing these apparent malpractices District by District is it possible to understand fully what was happening.

The Regional Election: Electoral Fairness and the Basis of KANU's Victory

We have seen that one reason why KANU won was that it retained a powerful hold over the majority of the country's regions. The 1992 election was not a consistent electoral contest between the same parties throughout the country. As with other African states, regional polarities dominated. Every District had its unique problems, ethnic affinities and short- and long-term political and economic interests which tended to favour government or specific opposition parties. The 'big picture' was the result of a combination of numerous smaller campaigns and conflicts. As discussed in Chapters 7 and 8, there were at least 19 different electoral regions, quite different in style, issues and competitors. The 1992 elections showed that despite 30 years of Independence and substantial economic development, Kenya remained a mosaic of communities with very different interests and attitudes. The 1992 contest for power revealed and indeed accentuated the division between the groups seeking regional autonomy, mainly pastoralists controlling large areas of lightly settled land, or with a distinct regional culture they wished to preserve, and the better-educated, often richer centralists, the majority of the population, densely populated and seeking new opportunities elsewhere. There was a real concern amongst minority groups that a Kikuyu victory would mean a return to the mid-1970s, when Kenyatta's Kikuyu dominated the government to an extent not seen under President Moi. Moi's strength was that he was seen (whatever the reality) as redressing the Kikuyu's long dominance to the benefit of others. Even Luo politicians privately suggested that they would rather be ruled by a dictator from a small 'tribe' than one from a larger 'tribe'. Reinforced by KANU's campaign strategy, to abandon the centre in order to consolidate the periphery, by polling day many in the semi-arid and less developed areas had come to see both FORDs and the DP as the vehicles of the 'majority tribes' – the early 1960s KANU alliance of the Luo and Kikuyu – pitted against the Coastal, Rift and other peripheral peoples. Thus KANU lost most of the large population centres, but won the less developed, arid and semi-arid areas, where fears of 'majority rule' and the desire for 'regionalism' had been reawoken in 1991.

The country divided into five major types of electoral region, characterised by the nature of the contest. The ethnic homelands of the Presidential candidates, comprising 25 per cent of the seats, were entirely 'safe'. The allied territories, covering 35 per cent of the seats in the country (but a far lower proportion of the population), were the largest single region, in which significant local leaders, in KANU's case allied with state power, ensured that the overall result in the District was clear, though turnouts and majorities were not, and there was the opportunity for the occasional local upset. Ten per cent of seats were contested primarily between two or more opposition parties, with KANU running third or worse. The ethnic borderlands between Kalenjin and opposition communities formed another smaller but distinct group, covering about 8 per cent of the country. Finally, 42 seats (22 per cent of the total) lay in the marginal communities, where even by polling day it was far from clear who was going to win. It was here and in the ethnic borderlands that the election was truly decided. Within these five archetypes, there were then various local contests with differing results. Over roughly half the country, election rigging was either not seen, or was detected and corrected before it could alter the result. The opposition homelands of Central Province and Luoland, particularly, seem to have been free of pro-KANU electoral abuses (such as ballot box stuffing, multiple voting, biased counting or incorrect results announcements), though there was intimidation by pro-opposition supporters in many seats.[9] Despite this, and some unsuccessful attempts made by KANU to stuff ballot boxes, there was little doubt that the votes cast correctly reflected voters' intentions. Western Province and the southern Coast also saw relatively few problems. The Rift Valley, however, was a mess, with few areas in which the process was completed satisfactorily, whilst Eastern Province, Nairobi, Mombasa the northern Coast, and Kisii and Nyamira all saw severe malpractices.

The Ethnic Homelands of the Presidential Candidates

Over a quarter of the country – 47 seats – the election was never seriously contested. Where the Presidential candidate was local, and had no local competition, ethnic allegiance to the party was the only determinant of success. In these areas (Moi was born in Baringo, Odinga in Siaya, Matiba in Murang'a, and Kibaki in Nyeri) the Presidential vote for the local man was overwhelming. In Murang'a, Matiba scored 94 per cent of the Presidential vote. In Nyeri, Kibaki did the same. In Luoland, Odinga reaped 95 per cent of the vote, and Moi received a 95 per cent vote in his five-District core. Every homeland Parliamentary seat was won by equally huge majorities for the relevant party. In all these areas feelings were intense and it is unlikely that other parties had a fair chance to express their views. Turn-outs were also extremely high, near 90 per cent. Had the Kikuyu vote not been split between Kibaki and Matiba, the 'ethnic homelands' of the two Kikuyu leaders would have been much larger. As it was, they competed for much of this territory. These regions saw little rigging in the Parliamentary contests, since there was little point. The main emphasis in voting was to maximise the Presidential vote, and these areas are the ones where Presidential ballot irregularities were most plausible.

Moi's Homeland. The five Kalenjin Districts of the central Rift – Baringo, Nandi, Elgeyo-Marakwet, Kericho and Bomet – were the core of KANU's national support. These were the KANU zones, from which the opposition was ruthlessly excluded throughout the campaign, and where opposition candidates were prevented from standing in all but three seats. KANU was strongest in the two eastern Districts of Baringo and Elgeyo-Marakwet, the homes respectively of Moi and Nicholas Biwott (see Figure 11.3). Both Districts were pastoralist or small-scale subsistence farming regions, lightly populated, with no real industry, and almost entirely Kalenjin, with the Tugen dominating Baringo and Elgeyo-Marakwet divided between the Keiyo in the south and the Marakwet in the north and west. Both Districts were little developed until the 1980s. Moi and

Biwott were genuinely popular here, and the opposition parties had little support. As Tabitha Seii, the sole opposition candidate to make it to the Parliamentary elections (in Kerio South) said before defecting to the DP: 'The other parties ... have no support in the area, because they did not even solicit support when they were newly formed.'[10] The only areas where the opposition had a chance was amongst the Kikuyu settlers in Baringo South and Kerio West, the latter having more than 4,000 Kikuyu and Luhya registered voters, nearly 25 per cent of the electorate.[11]

The nine south-western seats of Nandi, Kericho and Bomet Districts were the weaker part of Moi's homeland, but seven of the nine KANU candidates were unopposed, and KANU again achieved huge majorities in the Presidential elections. Bomet and Kericho Districts, the home of the Kipsigis Kalenjin, had many Kisii, Luo and Luhya migrant workers on the large tea estates, especially in the urban Kipkelion and Konoin. The ethnic clashes, however, had led many Luo workers to return to their homes across the border, and the threat of violence against the opposition was clear during the campaign. KANU managed to maintain its stranglehold on the District's politics, and the only prominent Kalenjin opposition leader, Moses arap Keino of FORD-Kenya in Kipkelion, performed creditably but was never likely to disturb KANU's dominance.[12] President Moi won massive majorities everywhere and all the KANU candidates were returned unopposed in Parliament and local government elections, with the exception of Kipkelion and Kerio South, where Biwott trounced Seii by a huge majority. In Baringo South, which borders onto Nakuru, Matiba polled well amongst the settlers.

The elections in Baringo North, East and Central were almost certainly fraudulent. Foreign observers were too frightened to enter this area, and there were few local monitors. Nonetheless, NEMU managed to find able count certifiers and District Liaison Officers, and they were caustic about the conduct of the polls. In Baringo Central, Moi's own constituency, most stations finished voting very early, reinforcing the suspicion that many voters had been transported south to Nakuru. There were few opposition agents, and turn-out was very high. The KANU vote is suspected to have been inflated, though it is unclear how.[13] In Baringo North, in contrast, the government did a very poor cover-up job. NEMU observers reported chiefs in uniform directing voters arriving by *Nyayo* bus and lorry. All voters claimed to be illiterate and when asked how they wanted to vote, just said '*Jogoo*.' Presiding Officers were marking papers for everyone, even the literate. There were death threats against opposition voters. There was no documentation or audit trail, no checking, and all votes were counted together. The turn-out was impossibly high, over 100 per cent in some stations, and 92 per cent overall.[14] An analysis of NEMU observers' returns also suggests there were simply too many boxes in several stations. The six stations shown in Table 11.5 were all recorded by the Electoral Commission in the gazetted figures as having one box only. In fact, they appear according to NEMU reports from six different individuals to have each had three boxes and far too many voters for the size of the seat. The number of votes cast in them (1,608 per box) was physically impossible, due to the size of the boxes, which should have been able to contain only around 900

Figure 11.3 The Rift Valley – KANU Heartlands and Ethnic Borderlands

Table 11.4 The Central Rift Results: Baringo, Elgeyo-Marakwet, Nandi, Kericho, Bomet

Constituency	KANU		FORD-ASILI		DP		FORD-Kenya		Others	
	Parl.	Pres.	Parl.	Pres.	Parl.	Pres.	Parl.	Pres.	Parl.	Pres.
Baringo East	100%	99%	–	0%	–	0%	–	0%	–	0%
Baringo North	100%	99%	–	0%	–	0%	–	0%	–	0%
Baringo Central	100%	100%	–	0%	–	0%	–	0%	–	0%
Baringo South	100%	88%	–	10%	–	1%	–	1%	–	0%
Kerio East	100%	100%	–	0%	–	0%	–	0%	–	0%
Kerio West	100%	95%	–	5%	–	0%	–	1%	–	0%
Kerio Central	100%	99%	–	1%	–	0%	–	0%	–	0%
Kerio South	98%	99%	–	1%	2%	0%	–	0%	–	0%
Mosop	100%	99%	–	0%	–	0%	–	0%	–	0%
Aldai	100%	98%	–	1%	–	1%	–	1%	–	0%
Tinderet	100%	94%	–	3%	–	1%	–	2%	–	0%
Konoin	100%	90%	–	1%	–	2%	–	6%	–	0%
Chepalungu	100%	100%	–	0%	–	0%	–	0%	–	0%
Bomet	100%	100%	–	0%	–	0%	–	0%	–	0%
Buret	100%	99%	?	0%	?	0%	?	0%	?	0%
Belgut	100%	100%	–	0%	–	0%	–	0%	–	0%
Kipkelion	78%	72%	11%	14%	??	5%	11%	8%	0%	0%

? = result misrecorded.

votes. In Baringo East NEMU reported that minors and people without voters' cards had been permitted to vote. Local chiefs and headmen had warned electors that official loans would be withdrawn if they failed to vote for Moi. The NEMU reporter even saw Presiding Officers and other election staff marking ballot papers for KANU for voters who had not turned out.[15] NEMU also reported that government and parastatal vehicles were used to transport voters, opposition agents were expelled, and everyone was instructed to pretend to be illiterate. Individuals wearing KANU T-shirts had been allowed into the count. There was an extremely high turn-out and no spoilt votes.[16]

In the remainder of the central Rift seats, it was rather harder to determine what had happened. In Elgeyo-Marakwet, little is known about what happened in Kerio East, West or Central, as observers' attention focused on Kerio South. There Nicholas Biwott's massive victory was enhanced by similar abuses. Voters were told to pretend to be illiterate so that the Presiding Officers could vote for them. One Presiding Officer was reported to have refused to permit anyone to vote anything except KANU. There were posters of Biwott and Moi displayed in some stations, and turn-out exceeded 100 per cent in some areas. Observers were confident that the clerks and Presiding Officers together had rigged the poll, though the count itself appeared fair.[17]

The three Nandi seats saw no Parliamentary elections. Nonetheless, turn-out in the Presidential and local government elections was again high.

Table 11.5 Baringo North Presidential Polling

Polling station	Registered	Used	Gazetted boxes	Actual boxes	Average per actual box	Turn-out %
BAR/47	5,050	5,490	1	3	1,830	108.71
BAR/48	4,065		1	3		
BAR/50	4,671		1	3		
BAR/51	3,230	3,680	1	3	1,227	113.93
BAR/53	5,050		1	3		
BAR/54	6,925	5,299	1	3	1,766	76.52
Total			6	18	1,608	95.16

Source: Kenya Gazette, and NEMU Poll Monitor Reports

NEMU observers in the three seats recorded perfect documentation of the elections, with box by box records of voting, and one Commonwealth observer reached two counts. Concerns remain: the records were too perfect and, most curiously, every box had a small number of opposition votes, scattered evenly amongst all the parties, large and small (for example, George Anyona out-polled Odinga in Mosop). There were no opposition agents over much of the area, and subsequent anecdotal reports suggested that turn-outs had in fact been low, rather than the 82 per cent claimed.[18] In contrast, the NEMU reports were confused and scanty in Kericho and Bomet. What they did provide suggests that the polls were generally fair. Nonetheless, there were again very high turn-outs, huge one-party votes and a very low number of spoilt votes. It is also known that in Konoin only KANU agents were present at the count, and the NEMU count certifier was immediately evicted.[19] What happened in the Buret Parliamentary contest is unclear. Although the two opponents of KANU's Jonathan Ng'eno had stood down, because their names were already on the ballots, there should have been a Parliamentary election. None appears to have been held.[20]

Luoland: Odinga's Homeland. The largest homeland was that of *Jaramogi* Oginga Odinga. From late 1991, it had been clear that he could count on the support of the vast majority of his Luo community in Nyanza Province. The result in the 18 seats of Siaya, Kisumu, Homa Bay and Migori (outside Kuria), circling Lake Victoria, was thus certain (see Figure 11.4). KANU put up candidates against FORD-Kenya, but most were sacrificial lambs, and the other opposition parties were unable to even find candidates in most Luo seats. Almost all these seats were entirely populated by ethnic Luo, with the sole exception of Kisumu Town, the urban centre, which had a substantial Asian business presence and various small immigrant communities, and Rongo and Migori in Migori District, which had some Luhya, Kuria, Somali and Gusii voters. Most of the Luo lands were intensive subsistence agricultural areas, little-developed, with some fishing and cotton cash-cropping. Odinga was completely unassailable in Siaya District, his birthplace and home, and the centre of Luo culture and

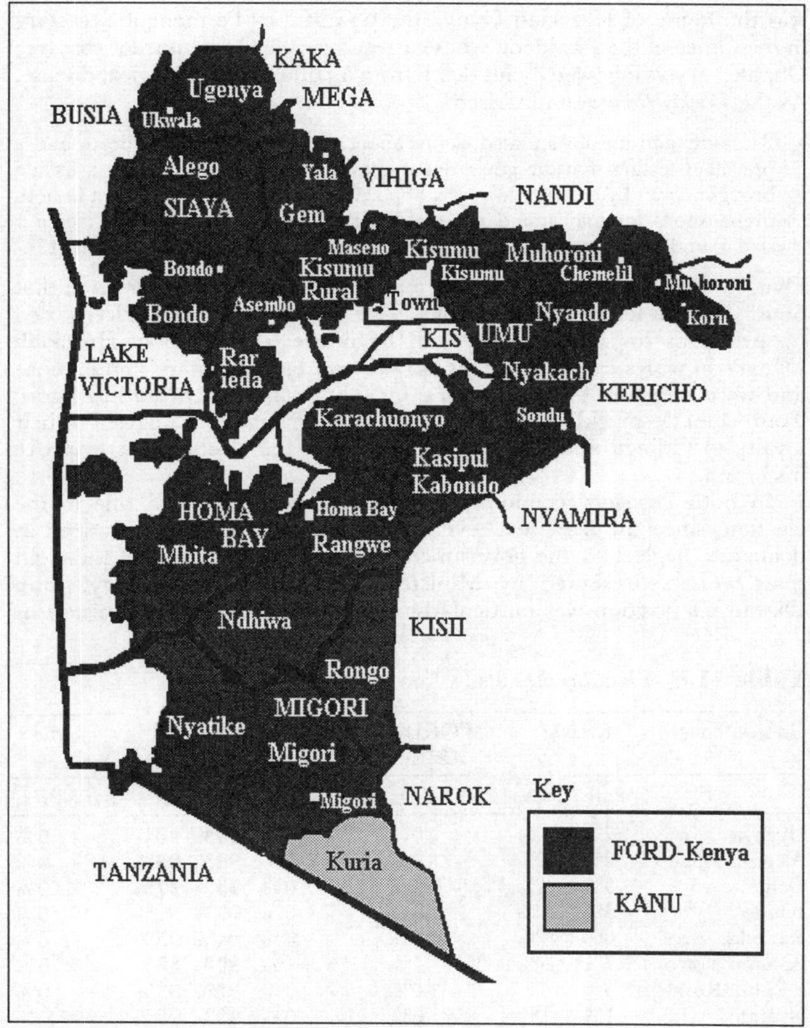

Figure 11.4 Odinga's Homeland – Luo Nyanza

of opposition to KANU since 1966. The situation was little different in neighbouring Kisumu District, the home of Robert Ouko. The District saw tribal clashes in Nyakach and Muhoroni, which reinforced the alienation from KANU. A major issue in Kisumu was the fate of the infamous Kisumu molasses plant, which had been abandoned in 1981 when 90 per cent complete.[21]

The situation was a little different in South Nyanza, split into Homa Bay and Migori Districts in 1992. Initially, it was far from certain that the south would follow Odinga to the same degree. South Nyanza, however, was the home of Hezekiah Oyugi, the powerful ex-Permanent Secretary in the Office of the President, whose arrest over the Ouko murder case (see Chapter 4) was followed by his death from an unusual neurological disease. As the *Weekly Review* summarised:

> Rumours and unsubstantiated claims about the cause of Oyugi's death and a prevalent feeling that the government abandoned Oyugi in death – a feeling brought about by the very low level of participation by the government in both preparations for and attendance at Oyugi's funeral – combined to create a strong undercurrent of anti-government resentment throughout the district.[22]

Oyugi's death, and transformation into another Luo martyr, ensured that South Nyanza fell to FORD-Kenya. The 'Oyugi factor', however, stored up problems for FORD-Kenya in the future, as several of Hezekiah Oyugi's protégés captured the FORD-Kenya Parliamentary nominations and were therefore elected as MPs, including Charles Owino in Migori, Tom Obondo in Ndhiwa, and Joseph Ouma Muga in Rangwe.[23] Their loyalty to Odinga and to the opposition after the election was to prove uncertain.

In both Districts, economic development also played a role in the election, since the area was severely underdeveloped. This was seen as deliberate neglect by the government, particularly since two of the eight seats were represented by Ministers. In Migori constituency, John Okwanyo's position was particularly weak, given his role as Minister for

Table 11.6 Election Results in Luo Nyanza

Constituency	KANU		FORD-ASILI		DP		FORD-KENYA		Others	
	Parl.	Pres.	Parl.	Pres.	Parl.	Pres.	Parl.	Pres.	Parl.	Pres.
Ugenya	7%	1%	0%	0%	2%	1%	**91%**	**98%**	-	0%
Alego-Usonga	2%	1%	-	0%	-	0%	**98%**	**99%**	0%	0%
Gem	5%	3%	-	0%	-	0%	**95%**	**97%**	-	0%
Bondo	5%	5%	-	0%	-	0%	**95%**	**95%**	-	0%
Rarieda	6%	4%	-	0%	-	0%	**94%**	**95%**	-	0%
Kisumu Town	7%	6%	3%	4%	1%	1%	**90%**	**88%**	-	0%
Kisumu Rural	9%	6%	-	0%	-	0%	**91%**	**93%**	-	0%
Nyando	1%	1%	-	0%	0%	0%	**99%**	**99%**	-	0%
Muhoroni	3%	3%	-	1%	1%	1%	**96%**	**95%**	-	0%
Nyakach	2%	1%	-	0%	-	0%	**98%**	**98%**	0%	0%
Kasipul-Kabondo	1%	0%	?	0%	-	0%	**96%**	**99%**	4%	0%
Karachuonyo	16%	3%	-	0%	-	0%	**84%**	**97%**	-	0%
Ndhiwa	3%	1%	-	0%	0%	0%	**97%**	**99%**	-	0%
Rangwe	5%	4%	-	0%	-	0%	**95%**	**95%**	-	0%
Mbita	8%	2%	0%	0%	0%	0%	**92%**	**98%**	-	0%
Rongo	10%	6%	-	0%	-	0%	**90%**	**94%**	-	0%
Migori	12%	11%	-	1%	-	0%	**88%**	**88%**	-	0%
Nyatike	9%	6%	-	0%	-	0%	**91%**	**94%**	-	0%
Kuria	**82%**	**86%**	5%	9%	5%	3%	8%	2%	-	0%

Water Development and the poor state of water supplies in his own constituency. One of KANU's best chances was in Rongo, where powerful Minister Dalmas Otieno, Oyugi's protégé, had a very good development record – although locals believed that he, too, had abandoned Oyugi in his hour of need.[24]

FORD-Kenya took all 18 Luo seats with massive majorities. The sole KANU leader to win a strong personal vote was Lazarus Amayo in Karachuonyo. Elsewhere, the FORD-Kenya team swept the board so completely that there was little concern over rigging. These Luo seats saw no major polling or counting problems. Anti-KANU feeling was very strong, however, and mobs burnt KANU branch offices and beat up KANU supporters in several seats including Nyatike and Muhoroni.[25] In several areas FORD-Kenya youth protested Moi's lead and fought battles with the GSU, who opened fire on hostile crowds.[26] Although one policeman was arrested after forcing people to vote for Odinga, KANU later petitioned the results of only three of these seats in the courts (see Chapter 12).'

Kibaki's and Matiba's Kikuyu Homelands. The other two homeland areas were far smaller. The six constituencies of Kenneth Matiba's home District of Murang'a were mainly agricultural, with large coffee and tea cash-crops and dairy farming (see Figure 11.5).[27] Murang'a was totally loyal to Matiba, and it was clear by election day that Asili would sweep both Parliament and Presidency. As befitted a one-party area, Murang'a also saw several significant KNC candidates (defectors from FORD-Asili), but they were eclipsed by the 'three piece suit'. The result, as expected, was a triumph for Matiba and FORD-Asili, though his victory was a little less complete than that of Odinga or Moi, as the DP performed creditably. The KNC and KANU also polled small but significant votes in Parliament, though almost everyone backed Matiba for President. KANU Secretary-General Joseph Kamotho did comparatively well in Kangema, polling a

Table 11.7 Murang'a Constituency Results

Constituency	KANU		FORD-Asili		DP		FORD-Kenya		Others	
	Parl.	Pres.	Parl.	Pres.	Parl.	Pres.	Parl.	Pres.	Parl.	Pres.
Kangema	14%	3%	74%	91%	10%	4%	2%	0%	-	1%
Kiharu	1%	1%	99%	95%	-	1%	-	2%	-	1%
Kigumo	1%	0%	94%	98%	5%	2%	-	0%	-	0%
Makuyu	6%	7%	66%	84%	12%	4%	8%	1%	8%	1%
Kandara	1%	1%	89%	96%	5%	2%	3%	0%	3%	1%
Gatanga	1%	1%	81%	92%	8%	5%	-	0%	10%	1%

creditable 14 per cent of the vote. KANU's second best performance was in Makuyu, where many Kamba were registered. Although there was little obvious evidence of malpractice, the turn-outs for FORD-Asili were very high, registration appeared to have continued after the official period, there

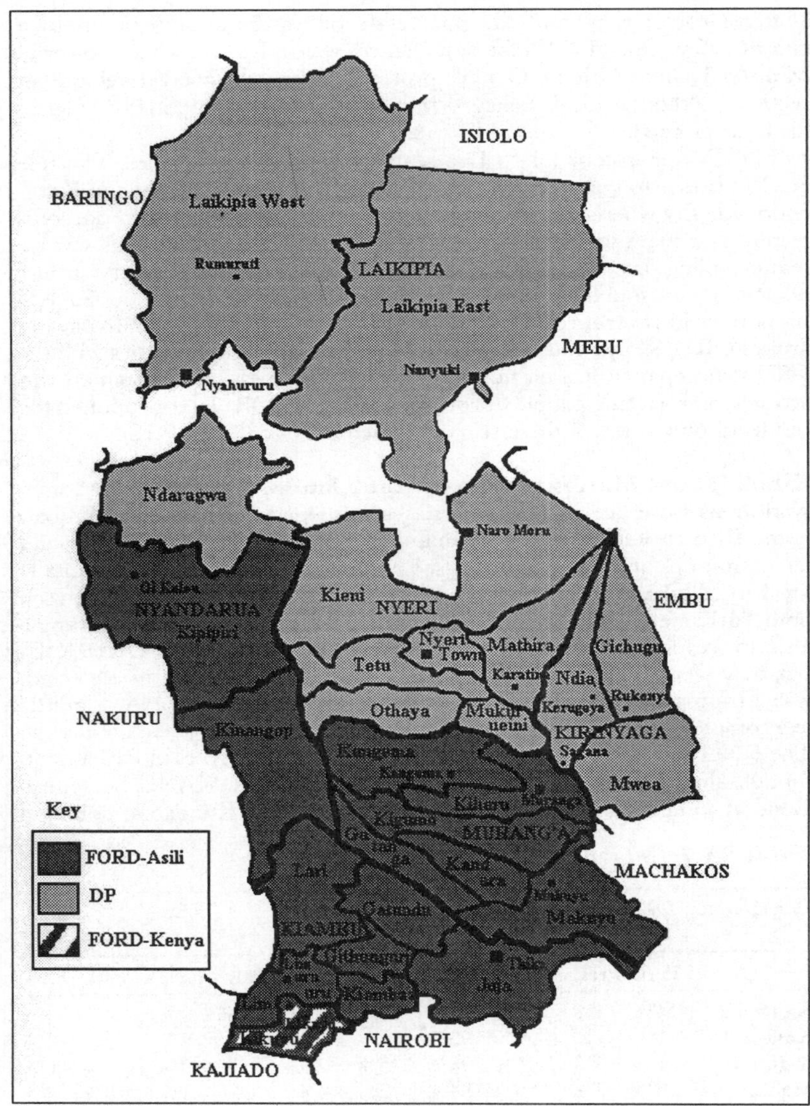

Figure 11.5 Central Province and Laikipia

were discrepancies between Presidential and Parliamentary totals, and the number of spoilt votes was very low indeed (only 5 out of 60,000 in Matiba's home of Kiharu, apparently). In Makuyu some Returning Officers did not allow agents to check seals or accompany boxes; in Kandara, count certifiers were barred from the counting hall. In Kangema, there were some discrepancies in reported results and some disorder at polling stations.[28]

The last homeland, Nyeri, the home of Mwai Kibaki, also provided few surprises. KANU was entirely eliminated, with their best vote in Mathira, where octogenarian Minister Kuguru polled 8 per cent. The decline of coffee farming in the area was a major campaign plank of protest against the government, but policy was always secondary to issues of ethnic solidarity. The KANU candidate in Kibaki's Othaya seat polled the lowest figure of any KANU candidate in the country, receiving only 276 votes. The KNC proved the only real opposition, most being defectors from the DP.

Table 11.8 Nyeri Election Results

Constituency	KANU		FORD-ASILI		DP		FORD-KENYA		Others	
	Parl.	Pres.	Parl.	Pres.	Parl.	Pres.	Parl.	Pres.	Parl.	Pres.
Othaya	1%	1%	–	1%	99%	98%	–	0%	–	0%
Nyeri Town	4%	3%	5%	5%	83%	90%	–	1%	8%	0%
Tetu	5%	2%	1%	1%	94%	97%	–	0%	–	0%
Kieni	4%	4%	3%	3%	93%	92%	1%	0%	–	1%
Mukurueini	2%	1%	9%	6%	70%	92%	1%	0%	18%	1%
Mathira	8%	3%	1%	2%	88%	95%	–	0%	3%	1%

The Allied Territories, Minority Tribes and State Power

The ethnic coalitions which the parties had become meant that individual powerful leaders could also deliver some more narrowly circumscribed areas. These 'allied territories' were predominantly KANU, run by second-rank KANU leaders such as Mohammed Maalim in Garissa and Noah Ngala in Kilifi. KANU also gained some of these seats as a result of the power of the state on the margins of the country, and of the anti-centralist votes of the smaller tribes. Where there was substantial opposition in these areas, it was from KANU candidates defecting at the last minute, thus putting a party gloss on local and personal issues which could no longer be resolved within KANU. As with the homelands, most of these seats were not closely contested, but turn-outs were lower, generally in the 50–70 per cent range, and votes for other parties were substantial. Most were clearly going to vote for their favoured party; the questions were how large the majority they would have, whether individuals could buck the trend and whether last-minute defections could weaken their dominance. Several of these constituencies experienced rigging.

Southern Coast Province. Three of the six Districts of the Coast – Kilifi, Kwale and Taita-Taveta – were KANU-dominated zones which the opposition had to penetrate in order to win (see Figure 11.6). Local leaders, state pressure and traditional alliances (this was an old KADU area) meant

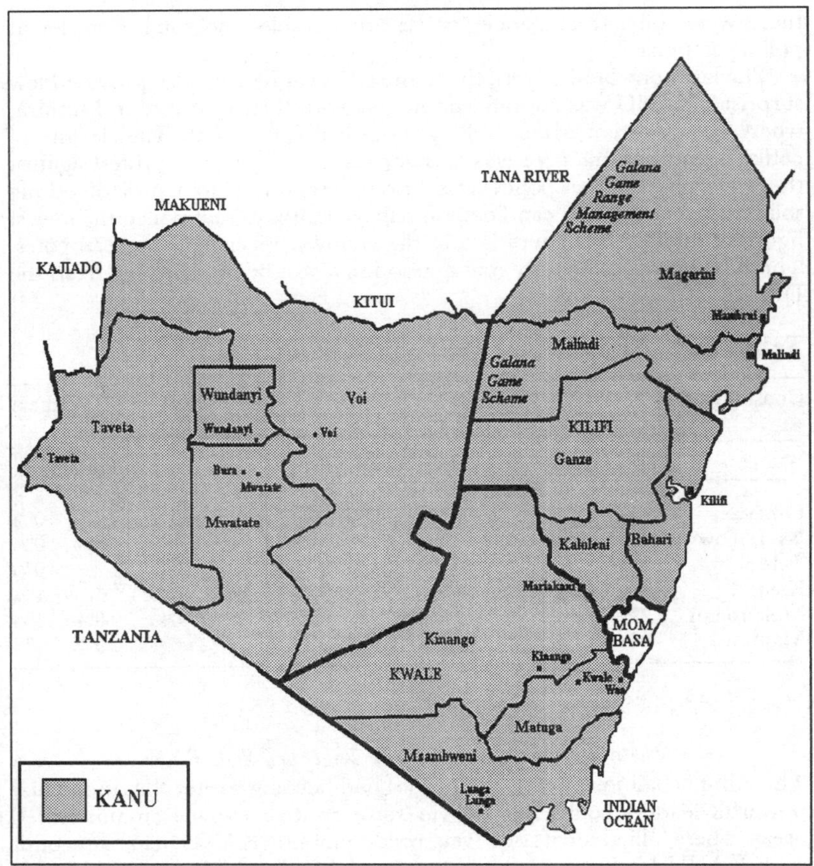

Figure 11.6 The South Coast – Kilifi, Kwale and Taita-Taveta Districts

that the ruling party's advantage was decisive, though it was forced to compromise in its candidate selection in the primaries to win some seats. The polling and the count appear to have been relatively free in nine of these 12 seats, those that KANU was confident of winning. Several polls saw small-scale bias in KANU's favour, such as YK '92 campaigning on polling day and polling stations moved to KANU offices (as in Kaloleni) but KANU's victories were decisive in most seats, so such anomalies probably did not change any results. It was less satisfactory in Mombasa, Tana River and Lamu Districts and the remaining three seats.

Kilifi and Kwale are the home Districts of the Mijikenda people, although both have substantial immigrant communities, especially Kamba settlers and migrant workers in the hotels along the coast. Kilifi, the home of Minister Noah Katana Ngala, was a pro-KANU District, with the only doubts before the election being over the extent of IPK influences in Bahari and Malindi. The campaign was fought heavy-handedly by KANU through the Provincial Administration, and the opposition had effectively lost the rural areas of Magarini, Ganze and Kaloleni by polling day, either because its candidates were unable to stand, or because they had been intimidated into passivity. Kwale, in contrast, was a forgotten District which raised little political interest outside Mombasa. Since the sacking of ex-Minister Robert Matano just before the 1988 elections, no prominent figures had emerged from the area, and national politics appeared to pass it by. The District has not developed greatly since Independence, and was dominated by the tourism industry (mainly in Matuga constituency), run largely by outsiders. It was, thus, natural KANU territory. KANU faced one specific problem, the closure of the Ramisi sugar factory in Msambweni, but this was partly addressed by Moi's pre-election offer of Sh12 million in compensation, accompanied by a directive that 10,000 acres of the sugar belt be subdivided among squatters.

Taita-Taveta District was less instinctive KANU territory. This District, which stretches from near the coast up into the fertile Taita Hills and over to the plains of Kajiado, was closer in character to an up-country area. The original inhabitants, the Taita and Taveta peoples, had been supplemented by Kamba settlers around Taveta, Kikuyu in Mwatate, and Luo and Luhya working on the huge sisal estates which dominated the flat lands. Land (or its lack) was a major issue, and the national conflict had a limited impact.[29] The major competitors were the DP and KANU. The two FORDs never really penetrated the area, partly as a result of the leading role played in the DP by Eliud Mwamunga, ex-Minister and the District's elder statesman, who was expected to do well in his partly-urban seat of Voi.[30] FORD-Asili played little public role, but was strengthened by last-minute defections from KANU. The DP candidate in Taveta and the FORD-Asili candidate in Mwatate were both significant KANU politicians, whose defeat in the nominations led to their defection. KANU's victory was far from certain, but their careful playing of the primary contest, and rehabilitation of local leader and (until the last minute) Minister Darius Mbela was enough to secure the District. There was a fair campaign and election, though KANU had the financial advantage. Mbela, or 'the Minister' as he was known (despite his sacking) was also well regarded and relatively popular.

Moi and KANU won all 13 seats in both Presidential and Parliamentary polls. Most were reasonably fair on polling day. Almost everywhere, President Moi out-polled his candidates, indicating split-ticket voting in favour of individual opposition politicians. In Kilifi, the only real competition came from the remaining FORD-Kenya candidates, though the IPK did not bring them anything like the hoped-for vote. Presidential candidate Chibule wa Tsuma performed creditably in Kaloleni for the KNC. In Ganze, there was little chance that KANU would lose, but Minister Ngala was determined that his victory would be decisive. One Presiding Officer was sacked for campaigning for him. The DP petitioned, claiming the Returning Officer and his agents influenced illiterates to mark papers for Ngala, refused to admit the opposition to the counting hall and denied them a recount; that boxes arrived unsealed; that DP agents were locked

Table 11.9 Kilifi, Kwale and Taita-Taveta Results

Constituency	KANU		FORD-ASILI		DP		FORD-KENYA		Others	
	Parl.	Pres.	Parl.	Pres.	Parl.	Pres.	Parl.	Pres.	Parl.	Pres.
Bahari	68%	76%	4%	5%	4%	4%	24%	16%	–	0%
Kaloleni	71%	77%	4%	4%	4%	2%	–	0%	20%	16%
Ganze	88%	91%	1%**	1%	11%	8%	–	0%	–	1%
Malindi	65%	78%	4%	6%	8%	7%	16%	7%	7%	2%
Magarini	89%	92%	0%	6%	1%	2%	9%	4%	–	1%
Kinango	89%	86%	–	3%	7%	7%	4%	3%	0%**	1%
Msambweni	*53%*	*71%*	*3%*	*5%*	*40%*	*18%*	*4%*	*5%*	*0%*	*1%*
Matuga	66%	79%	5%	3%	25%	13%	4%	4%	0%	1%
Taveta	60%	60%	22%	17%	10%	14%	7%	9%	–	0%
Wundanyi	74%	72%	10%	15%	15%	11%	–	1%	–	1%
Mwatate	57%	75%	28%	11%	10%	9%	4%	4%	–	1%
Voi	54%	61%	–	5%	35%	26%	8%	5%	–	1%

** Candidate stood down. Italics = questionable result.

out of four polling stations; and that Ngala bribed voters.[31] Turn-outs were reasonable in most seats, though surprisingly low (45 per cent) in Bahari.

The closest KANU came to defeat was in Msambweni in Kwale, where the DP candidate Mrs Marere Wamatai came near to victory, using her secondary school teacher position, Kikuyu immigrant support and gender (in a constituency with a 70 per cent female population). On polling day, a chief was ejected from one station for campaigning for KANU, illiterates' ballots were being marked preferentially for KANU and a Deputy Presiding officer was arrested for erasing DP symbols on ballot papers, so that they would be marked spoilt.[32] The Presidential count was fine, but the Parliamentary count saw protests and five clerks expelled for adding in votes from somewhere for the KANU Parliamentary candidate. Another Presiding Officer was expelled for marking ballots for KANU. Additional boxes were added in according to both NEMU and the NCWK, and a recount was refused.[33] KANU won with a narrow 3,000 vote margin on a turn-out which was 20 per cent higher than the average for the rest of Kilifi and Kwale.

In Taita-Taveta, the DP performed far worse than expected. The Taita, without a strong preference for any one candidate, voted conservatively.[34] The opposition's failure to win over this key group was a barometer of their national defeat. FORD-Asili emerged as the second party over half the District, mainly thanks to Kikuyu and Kamba immigrant votes and their popular local candidates. Darius Mbela, rehabilitated though not reappointed yet to his Ministerial post, received a strong personal endorsement in Wundanyi, an expression of anger at his sacking which ironically also boosted KANU.[35] Basil Criticos, the only European victor in the elections, the owner of the huge Taveta Sisal Estate, won a solid victory in

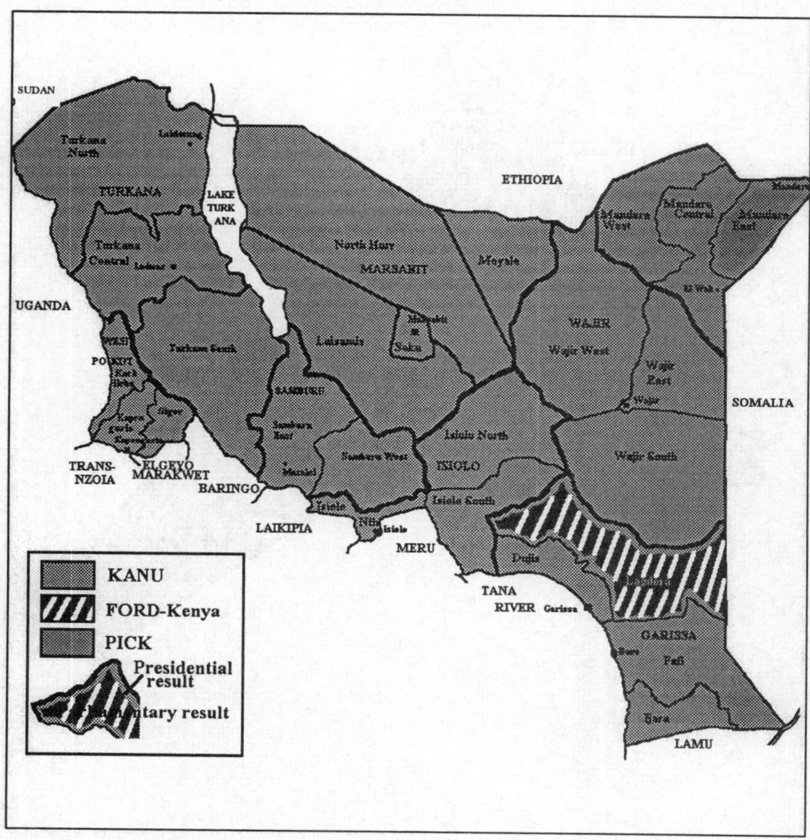

Figure 11.7 The Arid North – North-Eastern Province, the Northern Rift and Isiolo/Marsabit

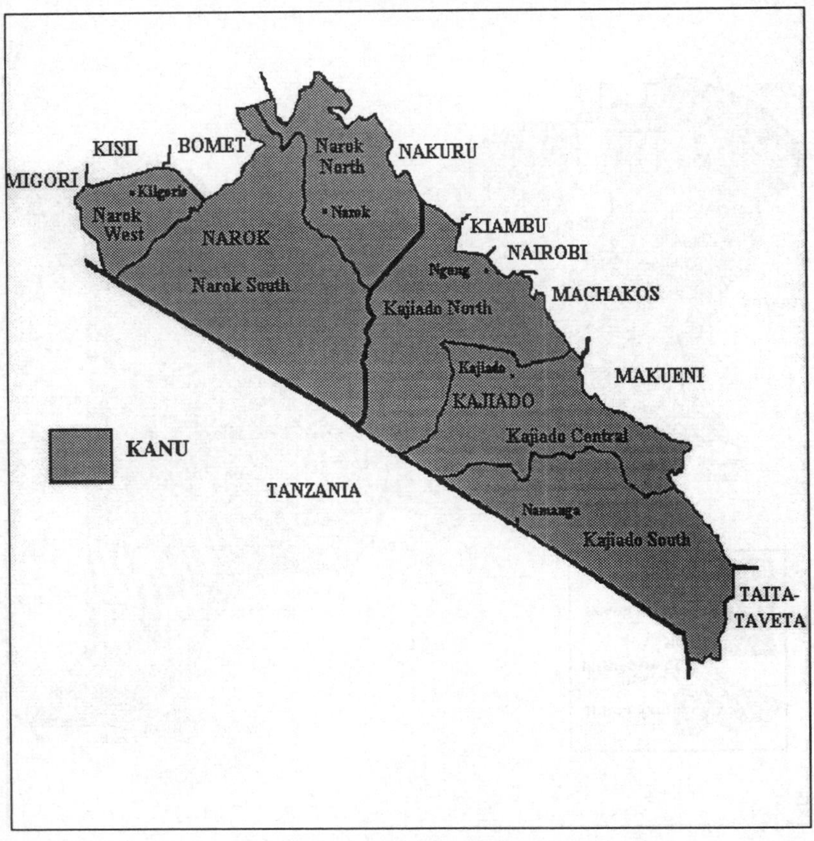

Figure 11.8 The Southern Rift Periphery –Kajiado and Narok

Taveta, partly reflecting the fact that the majority of the employed electorate worked for him, and that he had donated 3,000 acres of land to squatters in 1991.

The Rift Periphery. In both southern Narok and Kajiado (the southern Rift periphery), and West Pokot, Samburu and Turkana (the northern periphery), KANU was overwhelmingly dominant, but defections gave the opposition, particularly the DP, grounds for hope in certain seats, which were dashed by the events of nomination day and the heavy-handed government campaign. West Pokot, Samburu and Turkana are sparsely populated, semi-arid areas, experiencing serious security problems and food shortages, with a strong Provincial Administration. All three Districts were declared KANU zones, and the opposition had great difficulty penetrating the area (see Figure 11.7). The opposition parties were not permitted to hold any rallies in West Pokot or Turkana at all and, as elsewhere, the state controlled the immigrant communities by threats to their land-holdings. The eight seats had never been of political importance, and were under-registered in 1992, with a combined voting population of only 170,000. In all three Districts, the supporters of the opposition were mainly migrants, predominantly from the mercantile and widespread Kikuyu, concentrated in the 'urban' areas. Out in the pastoral camps, traditional loyalties, political naïveté, control of the key opinion-formers and government stress on its defence of minorities meant that the local population always remained predominantly KANU. In Samburu West, the

Table 11.10 Rift Periphery Election Results

Constituency	KANU		FORD-ASILI		DP		FORD-KENYA		Others	
	Parl.	Pres.	Parl.	Pres.	Parl.	Pres.	Parl.	Pres.	Parl.	Pres.
Kachileba	90%	98%	3%**	1%	6%**	1%	0%**	0%	-	0%
Kapenguria	90%	88%	10%	8%	1%	1%	-	2%	-	0%
Sigor	67%	99%	0%	0%	0%	0%	0%**	0%	32%	0%
Turkana North	96%	98%	-	0%	2%**	0%	2%**	1%	-	0%
Turkana Central	75%	82%	-	3%	22%**	3%	3%**	13%		0%
Turkana South	96%	93%	4%**	2%	0%**	2%	-	3%	-	0%
Samburu East	100%	98%	-	0%	-	0%	-	1%	-	0%
Samburu West	92%	90%	1%	5%	3%	5%	4%	4%	-	0%
Kajiado North	*52%*	*48%*	*22%*	*38%*	*23%*	*11%*	*3%*	*3%*	*0%*	*0%*
Kajiado Central	56%	83%	-	3%	43%	12%	1%	1%	-	0%
Kajiado South	53%	60%	5%	19%	41%	18%	-	2%	-	0%
Narok North	*62%*	*62%*	*24%*	*28%*	*13%*	*9%*	*1%*	*1%*	-	*0%*
Narok South	100%	97%	-	2%	-	1%	-	0%	-	0%
Narok West	57%	86%	-	1%	4%	1%	-	13%	39%	0%

** Stood down. Italics = questionable result.

KANU candidate had an added advantage – his brother was Major-General Lengees, Head of the Army, who campaigned for him and met influential non-Samburu businessmen to persuade them to vote KANU, in order to safeguard their businesses. Non-Samburu residents were warned they must vote KANU or face eviction from the area.[36] In West Pokot, north of Kitale, the majority of the population was Pokot, but nearly a quarter of the voters were Kikuyu, Luhya, Kisii, Luo and Turkana. Francis Lotodo, champion of Pokot rights against immigrant communities, was KANU's key asset in the District, and he provided the residual support on which the state built to seize victory in the area (see Chapter 6). KANU was not secure however, with the DP strong in Kachileba and an internal threat from a defector to PICK in Sigor. The huge and empty Turkana District, populated primarily by the nomadic Turkana people, had suffered heavily from famine and many voters had fled from bandit raids. The other parties had few followers, and most people feared to join the opposition in case KANU won. Nearly 70 per cent of voters were illiterate, and had little understanding of political parties. For example, a woman was overheard on polling day saying it was better to vote for a child (PICK) than a lion (FORD-Kenya) which ate their goats and animals.[37] The opposition mounted a late surge after the primaries as many of the losers defected to the DP. By election day, however, KANU had persuaded every single one to stand down.

Kajiado and Narok Districts were divided. The two northernmost seats were ethnic borderlands, in which the Kikuyu immigrant communities faced well-established Ministerial opponents George Saitoti in Kajiado North and hardline William ole Ntimama in Narok North. The remaining four seats, populated mainly by Maasai, were KANU zones, in which the DP was KANU's only plausible opponent. All four mainly Maasai seats saw easy victories for Moi (see Figure 11.8), but also revealed serious internal cleavages within the Maasai, as only one of the KANU Parliamentary candidates was safely elected (see Table 11.10). In Kajiado Central and South, KANU secured narrow majorities over popular local DP candidates in contests which were reasonably fair, taking into account that both KANU and the DP transported Maasai voters, and under-age people had identity cards and were allowed to vote in two stations. KANU also took all three Narok seats, including Ntimama's Narok North. Narok South was a genuine KANU zone, with no opposition candidates.[38] In Narok West, however, the large Kipsigis minority put up their own candidate, who had lost narrowly in the KANU nominations and then defected to PICK, polling 39 per cent and nearly beating KANU. Nonetheless, this was not opposition territory, and these were dissident KANU rather than opposition votes.[39] While voting in Narok West was fine apart from an unusually high 88 per cent turn-out, in Narok South, voters were again instructed to declare themselves illiterate. There were no opposition agents in some stations, and stuffing is suspected in at least one.

In the northern Rift, KANU was effectively unopposed in five of the eight Parliamentary seats by polling day. They won the remainder easily, save for Sigor, where the incumbent Christopher Lomada, who defected to PICK after losing the KANU nomination, retained his ethnic bloc vote.

Table 11.11 North-Eastern Province Results

Constituency	KANU		FORD-ASILI		DP		FORD-KENYA		Others	
	Parl.	Pres.	Parl.	Pres.	Parl.	Pres.	Parl.	Pres.	Parl.	Pres.
Wajir East	65%	71%	34%	25%	2%	3%	-	1%	0%	0%
Wajir South	*68%*	*73%*	*0%***	*0%*	*27%*	*25%*	*5%*	*1%*	*0%***	*0%*
Wajir West	*51%*	*58%*	*48%*	*38%*	-	*4%*	-	*0%*	*0%*	*0%*
Mandera West	83%	82%	2%	10%	0%	0%	15%	8%	-	0%
Mandera Central	60%	69%	-	2%	0%	0%	40%	29%	-	0%
Mandera East	46%	96%	0%	2%	0%	1%	0%	1%	54%	0%
Dujis	80%	84%	1%**	3%	15%	7%	4%**	5%	0%	0%
Lagdera	48%	76%	0%	0%	0%	0%	51%	23%	-	0%
Fafi	97%	97%	1%**	2%	1%**	0%	1%**	0%	-	0%
Ijara	96%	98%	1%**	0%	0%**	1%	3%	1%	-	0%

** Stood down. Italics = Questionable Parliamentary result.

In Samburu East, the KANU candidate was genuinely unopposed. FIDA/ICJ, however, were still refused entry to the count.[40] Samburu West was even more contentious. The Returning Officer 'refused to allow FIDA/ICJ Election Monitors into the counting hall alleging that FIDA/ICJ identification letters were not recognised by the Election Commission'.[41] It took three days to count. KANU's majority was massive and there were too many Presidential ballots. Turn-outs were very high. Although KANU would have won anyway, vote inflation in both Parliamentary and Presidential elections is suspected. In Turkana, NEMU reports on polling day and the count were positive, though most opposition parties had few agents in the stations. In Turkana North, only KANU agents were allowed into the count.[42] Turn-outs were low in Turkana North and South (32 and 26 per cent respectively) but wholly implausible in Turkana Central (85 per cent). There were no reports of events in West Pokot.

North-Eastern Province. Most of North-Eastern Province fell into a similar category, but as a Province in its own right, this sparsely populated area of Somali nomads, with ten constituencies (more than Nairobi), was of far greater importance, because of the 'five Province' strategy. Controlled by the Kenyan military, it was always likely to be KANU territory, but the importance of clanism, Islam, and the lack of information about what was happening in the area made predictions difficult. Most Somalis were Moslem, and were ripe for an Islamic party of dissent. The IPK and FORD-Kenya, therefore, worked hard to build support here. Indeed, FORD-Kenya was the only party to make serious and coherent attempts to contest KANU's hold on the Province.

Somalis had many reasons to be bitter about their treatment by the government, including the 1990 decision that they must all carry special identity cards to show they were not refugees from Somalia.[43] The area suffered severely from insecurity, with regular open clan warfare over the years and famine a constant threat. Other problems included the huge numbers of Somalis living in refugee camps in Kenya, two massacres by the security forces in 1980 and 1984, and the government's tacit support for ex-Somali premier Siad Barre and 'General Morgan' in southern Somalia, which led to military incursions by Somalis into Kenya and Kenya into Somalia. There was also widespread discontent with the dominance of General Mahmoud Mohammed, Chief of the General Staff, and his brother Minister of State in the Office of the President Hussein Maalim Mohammed, from Garissa, who were seen as doing little for ordinary Somalis.

Nonetheless, KANU always had the upper hand. The government controlled access into and out of this inhospitable region. Opposition leaders found it extremely difficult to enter the area. Meeting licences were hard to obtain and there was violence and intimidation against opposition candidates. The state also controlled the distribution of identity cards and famine relief. The relative poverty and lack of non-governmental sources of income also made Somali opposition candidates particularly vulnerable to inducements to stand down (see Chapter 9). KANU also had the loyalty of the Ogaden clans – which were doing well out of the Mohammed brothers' ascendancy – and was thus particularly strong in Garissa, the most densely populated District.[44] In some areas, KANU also had the better candidates. Strong local candidates were likely to be influential in any decision to defect *en masse* to another party, particularly in this clan-oriented and isolated area. KANU could woo the most popular and effective candidates in Mandera and Wajir, partly because of what they could promise them. KANU was determined to hold the Province, to obtain 25 per cent for Moi, and to deny it to any opposition party, particularly FORD-Kenya. As a result, Moi was always likely to win the Presidential vote, by fair means or foul. What was less certain was the impact of personality, split voting and clanism in the Parliamentary seats. The opposition fielded a strong set of candidates initially, but were whittled down by defections, while FORD-Kenya failed to get candidates nominated at all in two seats, and the DP lost their popular local candidate in Wajir West. Thus, by polling day, there was no more than one opposition candidate still standing in any Somali seat, and none at all in Fafi or Ijara.

As expected, KANU and Moi won the Presidential election in all ten seats by massive majorities, polling over 75 per cent of the overall vote. In five seats he received more than 80 per cent of the vote, and split voting was irrelevant. Turn-outs were reasonable. Parliamentary votes for the opposition Presidential candidates were directly derived from clan and local support for the remaining Parliamentary candidates in the area, not the other way round. Thus, Lagdera in Garissa saw a strong vote for Odinga, mainly a spin-off from a victorious local FORD-Kenya candidate, and FORD-Kenya was similarly the main opposition party in Mandera Central. In Wajir South, however, it was Kibaki who led the opposition pack, while in Wajir West and East it was FORD-Asili. (see Figure 11.9) Overall, KANU lost two Parliamentary seats. FORD-Kenya narrowly won Lagdera, and to everyone's amazement PICK won its sole seat in Mandera

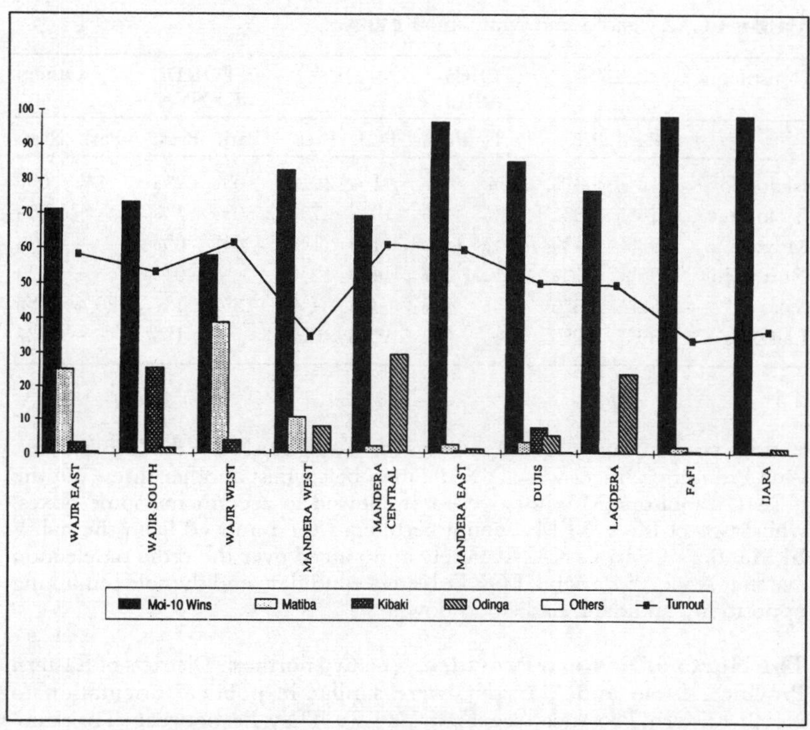

Figure 11.9 North-Eastern Province: Presidential Percentages of the Vote by Seat

East. In Wajir South, dominated by the Ogaden grouping of clans, the neophyte KANU candidate of the smaller clan beat two ex-MPs, including the DP National Organising Secretary A. A. Ogle, in a very odd result, which may have been rigged. In Wajir West, KANU's Parliamentary candidate, the FORD defector, also won narrowly, and slightly curiously given the ethnic arithmetic.[45]

Monitoring was sparse, as was press coverage, so the fairness of the election is unknown. What is known is that because of heavy rain the state transported boxes in helicopters, into which agents from opposition parties were not allowed. Kibaki later alleged pre-marking of ballot papers, but no other evidence of this has been found, and turn-outs were low, which would be unlikely if the boxes had been stuffed.[46] In the whole province, Dujis in Garissa was the only seat in which foreign or domestic observers reached the count. Even here, there was some campaigning for KANU. At large

Table 11.12 Isiolo and Marsabit Results

Constituency	KANU		FORD-ASILI		DP		FORD-KENYA		Others	
	Parl.	Pres.	Parl.	Pres.	Parl.	Pres.	Parl.	Pres.	Parl.	Pres.
Isiolo North	45%	63%	2%	4%	41%	32%	10%	2%	1%	0%
Isiolo South	76%	88%	5%	4%	19%	7%	0%	1%	–	0%
Moyale	93%	84%	6%	15%	1%	1%	0%	0%	–	0%
North Horr	86%	87%	0%	0%	14%	12%	–	0%	–	0%
Saku	62%	88%	2%	6%	3%	4%	13%	1%	20%	1%
Laisamis	89%	99%	0%	0%	10%	0%	–	1%	–	0%

stations voters were paid 100 shillings for voting KANU – the 'three *kukus*'. One Presiding Officer was a YK' 92 member, whilst another threw out the NEMU monitors. Monitors were not allowed to accompany some boxes, whilst two of three NEMU count certifiers were removed from the hall.[47] In Mandera Central, KANU falsely announced over the radio on election eve that Abdi Ali Baricha, FORD-Kenya candidate and the sole remaining opposition candidate, had stood down.[48]

The North of Eastern Province. The two northern Districts of Eastern Province, Isiolo and Marsabit, were similar in political orientation to North-Eastern Province (see Figure 11.7). They lie between Turkana/Samburu and North-Eastern Province, but are populated by Borana and Rendille nomads as well as Somalis.[49] The lightly populated area remained a political backwater and, as in the northern Rift, food shortages and banditry were major issues, with the spill-over of the Somali and Ethiopian wars leading to many deaths. In Isiolo, the DP was the main opponent, reflecting traditional close links with Meru, although recent Somali migration had changed the character of the area. In Marsabit, FORD-Asili was the dominant opposition party, having won the allegiance of both ex-MPs and council officials, but KANU was always ahead. The opposition parties were unable to organise major rallies and KANU's victory was overwhelming outside Isiolo North, where the DP came very close to winning Parliament and malpractice is suspected. The seat saw high increases in registration and high rates of registration. Three boxes were smuggled in from a station where there was no polling.[50] An agent of the KANU Parliamentary candidate was alleged by NEMU to be the Presiding Officer in one station and boxes from that station arrived unaccompanied. The DP and FORD-Asili both petitioned.

Second-Rank Opposition Regions. There were a few regions where the second-rank opposition leaders – Martin Shikuku for FORD-Asili, Paul Muite and Kijana Wamalwa for Ford-Kenya, Norman Nyagah, Eliud Mwamunga and James Nyamweya for the DP – proved able to guarantee more than their own seats. Most of these regional sub-leaders, particularly the DP in Kisii and Taita-Taveta, proved unable to deliver a decisive lead. The most successful sub-leader was Kijana Wamalwa among the Bukusu of Bungoma and Western Kitale, where Muliro's legacy won FORD-Kenya a solid victory in six seats. Although Shikuku won seven of the eleven seats in Kakamega and Vihiga for FORD-Asili, many were won by very narrow margins indeed. The area where the DP second-rank leaders did perform well (and would have performed better, were it not for electoral malpractice) was the area around Mount Kenya, a ring of seats covering Central Province, Eastern Province and Laikipia District. Though turn-outs were lower than Nyeri, and votes for the other parties substantial, this was the DP's second bastion.

Table 11.13 Kirinyaga and Laikipia Results

Constituency	KANU		FORD-ASILI		DP		FORD-KENYA		Others	
	Parl.	Pres.	Parl.	Pres.	Parl.	Pres.	Parl.	Pres.	Parl.	Pres.
Gichugu	5%	3%	37%	33%	57%	63%	0%	0%	–	1%
Ndia	2%	1%	19%	16%	55%	80%	1%	0%	23%	2%
Mwea	2%	1%	26%	21%	67%	75%	–	0%	5%	2%
Laikipia East	26%	22%	2%**	4%	72%	72%	–	2%	–	0%
Laikipia West	17%	17%	8%	12%	74%	69%	–	1%	1%	0%

** Stood down

Kirinyaga and Laikipia. In the three densely populated agricultural constituencies of Kirinyaga District, on the north-eastern border area of Kikuyuland (see Figure 11.5), the DP was always the dominant party, though Matiba's FORD-Asili made inroads towards the end of the campaign. Kirinyaga has always been the scene of intense political controversy, due to the powerful and strong-willed individuals competing for Parliamentary posts. It was also one of KANU's few hopes for a seat amongst the Kikuyu, which explains the decision to sack hardline Minister James Njiru just before the nominations (see Chapter 8), since he was the 'unacceptable' face of KANU in the area.[51] The tactic failed: public attempts by President Moi to bring Geoffrey Kariithi, FORD-Asili's local leader and ex-Head of the Civil Service, back into KANU to lead the government forces (now that his old enemy Njiru was ousted) were rebuffed.[52]

Laikipia, a wide expanse of open plains settled mainly by Kikuyu in the east but with Samburu and Maasai in the west, was also natural territory for the DP. Bordering Nyeri, Laikipia was mainly a settlement area for Nyeri Kikuyu, and they stayed true to their roots. Because it lies inside the Rift Valley rather than in Central Province, and contains a small but significant pastoralist population, KANU had hopes of an upset result. KANU had played its master stroke in early 1992, by rehabilitating the disgraced ex-Minister G. G. Kariuki (see Chapter 6). He and the new Maasai Minister for Industry Francis ole Kaparo were KANU's candidates. The DP team was led, in Laikipia West, by Dixon Kihika Kimani, ex-leader of the 'Change the Constitution' movement and one-time wealthy head of the Ngwataniro land-buying company. FORD-Asili played little role, and FORD-Kenya was unable even to find candidates.

In Kirinyaga, KANU was wiped out, with the only opposition to the DP coming from Asili. The DP won half to two thirds of the vote, despite having candidates with little political experience. James Njiru did appallingly in Ndia for his new party, FORD-Kenya (see Chapter 8) while his long-time opponent Nahashon Njuno was easily defeated as KANU's candidate in Gichugu. To the surprise of many, Geoffrey Kariithi lost Gichugu to the political neophyte lawyer and civil rights campaigner Martha Njoka (née Karua) of the DP. The KNC's John Matere Keriri was a notable loser to the DP in Ndia. Laikipia saw even easier DP victories, showing the dominance of ethnic solidarity over state pressure, although KANU polled better here than in any other Kikuyu-dominated areas. The results appear to have been accurate overall, but there were signs of small-scale stuffing in specific polling stations in both constituencies.

Embu, Meru and Tharaka-Nithi. To the east and south of Kirinyaga, the Eastern Province area of Embu, Meru and Tharaka-Nithi was also pro-DP, though its strength varied from seat to seat depending on the candidates and other local factors. Embu, populated by the Embu and Mbere peoples, with close ties to each other and more distant ties with Central Province, was the strongest DP territory. That Minister Jeremiah Nyagah effectively stood down in favour of his son Norman Nyagah, who was the DP candidate in his father's old seat, reinforced KANU's weakness in the area, although KANU poured enormous sums of money into Gachoka (see Chapter 9). The six constituencies of Meru District (and their new annexe, the two seats of Tharaka-Nithi District) were the home of the Meru and Tharaka peoples. Although few Meru KANU leaders had defected to the opposition during 1991–2, the DP was again dominant. Initially, the Meru had been predominantly FORD supporters, with Gitobu Imanyara their most prominent leader. With the problems in FORD, however, there was a steady drift of voters and leaders across to the DP. Kibaki visited the area regularly during the late summer, and by election day the DP was tipped to win most of the seats in a two-way fight with KANU. FORD-Asili was of no significance and FORD-Kenya's support was concentrated in only two seats. Embu and Meru, like Kirinyaga and northern Nyeri, were settled agricultural areas. Development issues, including coffee prices and land adjudication, were electorally important, as was clanism in some areas. Religion was another important issue, with the role of the Methodist Church, the dominant religious grouping, a primary factor in the opposition triumph in Imenti North. There, Minister Jackson Angaine's controversial defeat in the KANU primaries by a candidate supported by KANU's other Minister, Kirugi M'Mukindia, saw Angaine's supporters defect *en masse* to the opposition.[53] Imenti Central saw an unusual four-way race, between the nationally known but locally weak

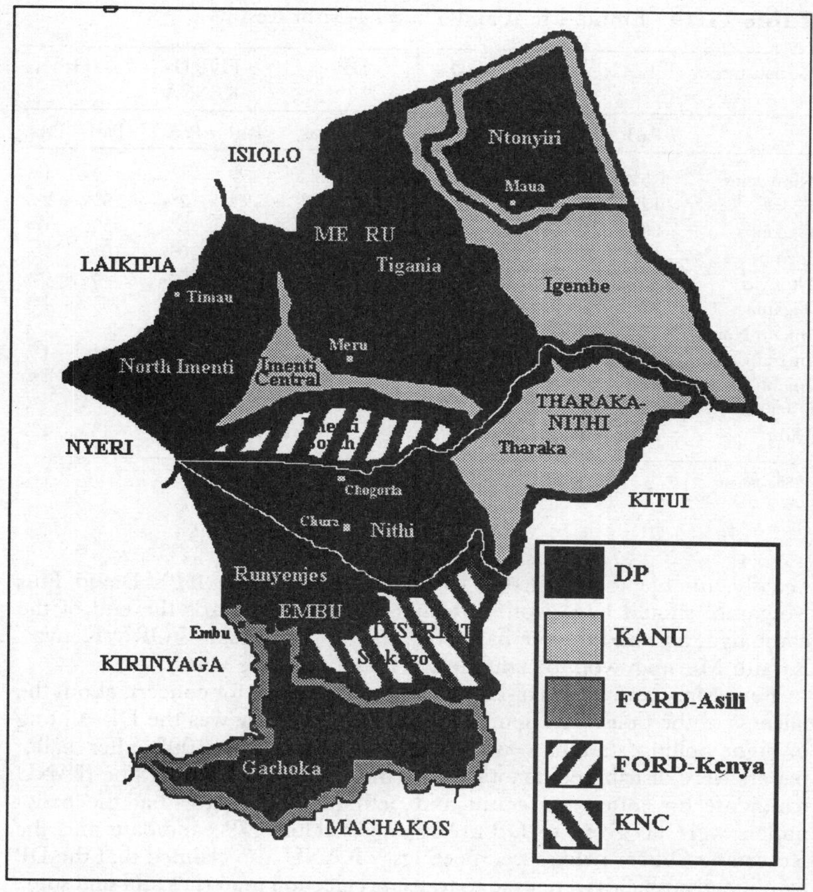

Figure 11.10 Embu, Meru and Tharaka-Nithi – The DP's Allied Territory

Imanyara (FORD-Kenya), ex-Kenya Planters' Cooperative Union Managing Director Henry Kinyua (KNC), Cabinet Minister Kirugi M'Mukindia (KANU), and Julius Muthamia (ex-Assistant Minister and DP chairman for Meru). FORD-Asili did not field a candidate against Kinyua, who had been a former Matiba ally before defecting to the KNC.

In all three Districts, the DP won the majority of seats and votes, although the results were closer than had been expected (see Table 11.14). The DP won nine of the 11 Presidential elections but, almost uniquely, seven seats split their Presidential and Parliamentary votes, with the DP somehow denied victory in five Parliamentary seats, three to KANU and one each to FORD-Kenya and the KNC (see Figure 11.10). In contrast, the DP's youthful Richard Maore won Ntonyiri (though KANU won the Presidency) on a personal vote. In Imenti South, KANU's M'Mbijjewe lost

Table 11.14 Embu, Meru and Tharaka-Nithi Results

Constituency	KANU		FORD-ASILI		DP		FORD-KENYA		Others	
	Parl.	Pres.	Parl.	Pres.	Parl.	Pres.	Parl.	Pres.	Parl.	Pres.
Runyenjes	5%	6%	22%	23%	70%	69%	3%	1%	-	1%
Siakago	12%	7%	21%	31%	25%	59%	12%	2%	29%	2%
Gachoka	26%	21%	32%	40%	33%	38%	4%	0%	5%	1%
Igembe	47%	46%	1%	2%	42%	50%	-	0%	10%	1%
Ntonyiri	35%	50%	0%**	1%	64%	48%	0% **	0%	1%	0%
Tigania	27%	22%	0%	3%	58%	74%	2%	1%	13%	1%
Imenti North	26%	16%	1%	3%	72%	78%	1%	2%	-	1%
Imenti Central	31%	31%	-	1%	20%	64%	21%	3%	27%	1%
Imenti South	15%	6%	1%	4%	39%	86%	43%	4%	2%	1%
Tharaka	57%	27%	2%	2%	38%	70%	3%	4%	-	1%
Nithi	21%	13%	3%	4%	74%	78%	1%	0%	1%	1%

** Stood down.

heavily, unable to speak due to throat cancer. The DP's David Pius Mugambi should have won, but injured himself towards the end of the campaign, and had to vote in a wheelchair.[54] As a result, FORD-Kenya's Kiraitu Murungi won, picking up the majority of the youth vote.

Four Meru and Tharaka-Nithi seats gave grounds for concern about the fairness of the polls. In Tigania, the main beneficiary was the DP. Voting in eight polling stations was delayed until 1 January 1993, after ballot papers were distributed chaotically by the Returning Officer. The KANU candidate boycotted the count and petitioned, claiming that the ballot papers were all given to DP areas, and that the DP candidate and the Returning Officer held secret meetings.[55] KANU also claimed that the DP candidate's vehicles were used to transport election materials and that some Presiding Officers were favouring the DP.[56] The Returning Officer was arrested and charged with neglecting his duties.[57] In Tharaka, the Presiding Officer in one station was asking illiterates, 'Who is your President?' When opposition agents objected, they were threatened.[58] Another station was allegedly manned by relatives of the KANU local council candidate. KANU won the Parliamentary seat and the DP the Presidency. There were anomalies in the vote count figures, and the DP petitioned. In Igembe, KANU candidate Jackson Kalweo was popular locally, having developed the area effectively, and had gained sympathy after being rigged out in 1988. His decision to remain with KANU (as it turned out in return for a Ministry if he won) gave KANU the seat. NEMU found the result generally satisfactory. Nonetheless, over 660 unstamped (and therefore possibly stuffed) ballots were found in two boxes, both Presidential and Parliamentary, which were then declared spoilt.[59] There was substitution of returns and miscommunication of results. Again, KANU won Parliament but the DP the Presidency. In the closely fought Imenti Central, the KNC performed well and the split opposition vote gave KANU Minister Kirugi M'Mukindia victory on a four-way split. FORD-Kenya's Secretary-General Gitobu Imanyara petitioned, claiming that 3,000 votes were somehow altered.

FORD-Asili performed well in Embu. They won the Presidential vote in the key seat of Gachoka, where the DP's Norman Nyagah narrowly won a Parliamentary victory. The veracity of the reported result is extremely doubtful. With the highest number of spoilt votes in the country, and a very close contest, poll reports suggest complete confusion, ballots under the tables and misreporting of count totals. NEMU staff claimed that the Returning Officer announced too small a total Presidential vote for the DP (there were 2,000 votes too few in total). The candidates boycotted the count after the Returning Officer refused to permit a recount, and KANU and Asili both petitioned. Two of the Embu results were suspicious, though no Parliamentary winner seems to have been changed by the events of the count. In Runyenjes, at least one Presiding Officer on polling day was asking illiterate voters, 'Do you want President Moi or whom do you want?'[60] There were major errors made during counting. The total announced by the Returning Officer was too low, and there were 5,000 fewer Presidential than Parliamentary votes.[61] FORD-Asili, KANU and FORD-Kenya all boycotted the count and KANU petitioned, claiming that the Returning Officer worked for the DP.[62] Siakago in Embu was the KNC's only Parliamentary victory, in a personal vote for a little-known candidate who had defected from the DP, in a seat that split five ways.

Bungoma. Bungoma District, the home of the Bukusu Luhya, was FORD-Kenya's only true 'allied territory'. Bungoma was a FORD hotbed of support from late 1991, with FORD leader Masinde Muliro bringing most Luhya over to the opposition. Although KANU's fortunes improved with Muliro's death and the split in FORD, the majority of the District stayed with FORD-Kenya and their local leaders Mukisa Kituyi (Kimilili) and Musifari Kombo (Webuye), in alliance with Muliro's 'heir' Kijana Wamalwa in neighbouring Trans-Nzoia. The District contained a large Kalenjin minority, however, the Sabaot people around Mount Elgon, a safe seat for KANU (see above). The ethnic clashes between Sabaot and Bukusu were a trump card for the opposition in seats like Kimilili, the seat of Minister Elijah Mwangale, whose star had been waning since the emergence of the multi-party movement. Among the economic issues were the problems of the sugar cane farmers, providing cane for the Nzoia Sugar Company whose payments and harvesting had been long delayed due to mismanagement.[63]

FORD-Kenya won a solid victory in three of the five seats, as in neighbouring Trans-Nzoia, with a huge personal endorsement of the newcomer Mukisa Kituyi against Mwangale in Kimilili (see Table 11.15). Kituyi was secretly backed by George Saitoti, as a result of Mwangale's earlier demands for the Vice-Presidency.[64] KANU did poorly elsewhere amongst the Bukusu, with the main opposition to FORD-Kenya coming from two popular local figures who had ended up in other parties. FORD-Asili's radical Lawrence Sifuna narrowly won Kanduyi, in an election in

Table 11.15 Bungoma Election Results

Constituency	KANU		FORD-ASILI		DP		FORD-KENYA		Others	
	Parl.	Pres.	Parl.	Pres.	Parl.	Pres.	Parl.	Pres.	Parl.	Pres.
Kimilili	13%	10%	4%	15%	1%	8%	82%	63%	0%	1%
Webuye	3%	12%	14%	22%	39%	22%	44%	42%	-	1%
Sirisia	21%	14%	4%	12%	3%	2%	72%	72%	-	1%
Kanduyi	19%	14%	41%	49%	2%	2%	38%	34%	-	1%
Mount Elgon	79%	79%	2%	3%	0%	0%	19%	18%	-	0%

which FORD-Kenya's defeated candidate petitioned, claiming that at some polling stations only the Asili and KANU names were offered to illiterates, that a sub-chief was bribing voters to vote for Asili and that KANU had assisted Asili. He also alleged that four campaign managers of Sifuna's were involved in the count and that there were fake ballots in two polling stations.[65] The DP's Alfred Sambu lost narrowly to FORD-Kenya in Webuye. Elsewhere in the District, FORD-Asili and the DP were of no importance.

The Internecine Battleground

While KANU had strong homelands and allied territories, the opposition parties, particularly FORD-Asili and the DP, fought for dominance over the capital and two Kikuyu Districts of Kiambu and Nyandarua. In most of these constituencies, KANU came third or even fourth. In the event, Matiba and FORD-Asili were the clear victors, winning 14 of these 18 seats; FORD-Kenya had two and KANU one, while the DP was humiliated, winning only one seat.

Nairobi: A Free-for-all. Nairobi saw one of the most complex and open sets of contests in the country. Its eight seats were all multi-ethnic constituencies, creating a multi-party competition for votes. Over half the voters, however, were from neighbouring Central Province, and it was the Kikuyu parties (FORD-Asili, the DP and to a lesser extent the KNC) who expected to do well. KANU was always on the defensive and had expectations of winning no more than one seat (either Minister Philip Leakey's Langata or the affluent suburb of Westlands). FORD-Asili was the dominant party, because of the predominance of Murang'a Kikuyu (from Matiba's home District) in the city. FORD-Kenya's best hope was in the southern suburbs of Langata, where Odinga's son Raila was engaged in a heavily contested three-way fight with Leakey and FORD-Asili. This election was a violent one, with strong Kikuyu-Luo animosity and at least one killed. FORD-Kenya also had hopes in Embakasi. Elsewhere, FORD-Kenya's candidates were deemed weak even by their own campaign team. FORD-Asili's candidates were also little known, and apart from Christopher Kamunyu ('K. K.') in Dagoretti, they had little in the way of a power base beyond their endorsement by Matiba.

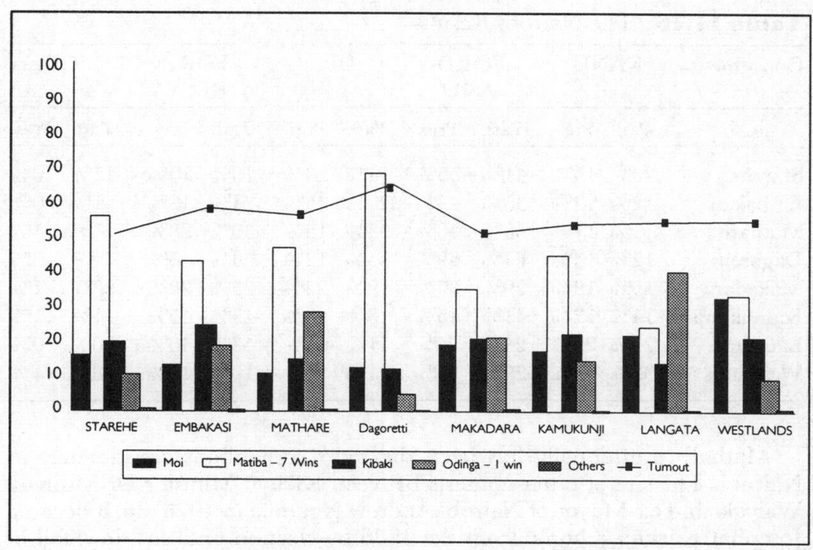

Figure 11.11 Nairobi Presidential Results

The Nairobi results were a triumph for FORD-Asili and Matiba personally, and a disaster for the DP and KNC, both of whom won nothing. Asili won the Presidential elections by a massive majority, with no other party gaining the necessary 25 per cent. In six of the eight seats, Matiba's victory was overwhelming (see Figure 11.11). He also won Westlands narrowly in the Presidency, where KANU took the Parliamentary seat due to PICK 'Boss' and local candidate, John Harun Mwau, who polled a creditable 8 percent and gave victory to KANU as a result. Some KNC, DP and KANU candidates had far greater electoral and personal stature, but were submerged under a wave of ticket voting in a Matiba 'landslide'. Matiba's only Presidential defeat was in Langata, where the Luo had registered in great numbers to elect Raila Odinga and his father. There was concern about possible malpractice by FORD-Asili in several seats.

In Langata, Raila Odinga won a solid personal endorsement. The Kikuyu vote was split between KANU, Asili and the DP, whilst Leakey did well to achieve 21 per cent of the vote. In Murang'a-dominated Starehe, a surprising result was the defeat of Charles Rubia (KNC). A national political figure, who would have won an overwhelming majority if he had remained in FORD-Asili, Rubia's campaign was lacklustre, and such was the irrelevance of the KNC that posters did not even have his party's name on them. He lost heavily to Kiruhi Kimondo (FORD-Asili), the same person who had been rigged in against him by KANU in 1988. In Dagoretti, the almost entirely Kikuyu peri-urban constituency which borders Kiambu, Chris Kamunyu won an overwhelming endorsement against KANU Chairman Clement Gachanja and Beth Mugo of the DP, Kenyatta's niece.

Table 11.16 The Nairobi Results

Constituency	KANU		FORD-ASILI		DP		FORD-KENYA		Others	
	Parl.	Pres.	Parl.	Pres.	Parl.	Pres.	Parl.	Pres.	Parl.	Pres.
Starehe	20%	15%	41%	55%	14%	20%	10%	10%	15%	0%
Embakasi	12%	12%	35%	43%	28%	25%	24%	19%	1%	0%
Mathare	11%	11%	36%	46%	23%	15%	30%	28%	–	1%
Dagoretti	12%	13%	64%	69%	15%	12%	8%	5%	–	0%
Makadara	19%	19%	29%	36%	19%	22%	25%	22%	8%	1%
Kamukunji	14%	17%	41%	45%	18%	23%	15%	15%	11%	1%
Langata	21%	22%	24%	24%	11%	14%	43%	40%	0%	0%
Westlands	33%	33%	29%	35%	21%	21%	10%	10%	8%	1%

Mathare traditionally has been the most contentious constituency in Nairobi. The site of bitter contests between Kikuyu Minister Dr Munyua Waiyaki and ex-Mayor of Nairobi Andrew Ngumba in 1978–86, it became Josephat Karanja's home from the 1986 by-election until his downfall in 1989. In 1992, Andrew Ngumba for the DP was overwhelmed by the FORD-Asili bandwagon, though again there were concerns about the fairness of the election and eventually the result was annulled. In Embakasi, FORD-Kenya's Waiyaki also lost to FORD-Asili's little known Henry Ruhiu, partly as a consequence of Luo anger at his imposition by Raila Odinga in place of Jael Mbogo. The DP came second. In Makadara, where the Luhya vote was largest, KANU, Asili and FORD-Kenya all fielded Luhya candidates and the vote split four ways. Again, the seat went to a little-known Asili candidate. Kamukunji was expected to go easily to the KNC candidate, former Cabinet Minister Maina Wanjigi. In fact, Asili's George Nthenge, the old Kamba ex-MP and FORD founder, won a massive victory as a spin-off from Matiba's success, despite his lack of money and an ethnic base in the seat. KANU's Amin Walji won Westlands, retaining the support of the Asian community, and campaigning 'financially' amongst the servants of the wealthy in the suburbs.

It appears that the groundwork was laid for some form of rigging in several seats. The perpetrators seem to have included both KANU and FORD-Asili. DP and FORD-Kenya both alleged collusion throughout the city by election officials, mainly in favour of FORD-Asili. At least five of the eight seats saw curious events and planned or actual abuses, mainly during the count, despite the huge media and observer presence.

In Starehe, in one polling station there were major register problems, with at least 1,000 voters disenfranchised as a result.[66] During the count, Charles Rubia and the NCWK both reported that a plainclothes policeman tried to smuggle bundles of ballot papers into the hall.[67] The NCWK also reported that substituted boxes were spotted and removed.[68] Gunshots were heard at one point. Everyone was thrown out of the count twice by the Returning Officer, including a KTN TV crew.[69] There was also a well-publicised incident in which thousands of unstamped ballot papers were taken by angry crowds from the car of a Presiding Officer, who was driving with them into the count. The Officer was badly beaten and Parliamentary ballot papers were circulating around the city later than day. The registration for the seat was extremely high and the turn-out low. In the end, it was unclear whether rigging was prevented or not. FORD-Kenya petitioned, claiming ballots for them were bundled with others found in a toilet, and that fake ballots were introduced and counted for FORD-Asili.[70] Dagoretti also saw evidence of rigging for FORD-Asili. According to NEMU testimony, the Returning Officer, some Presiding Officers and some clerks favoured FORD-Asili. Asili gave out money and campaigned on poll day, and bought drinks for clerks, who were reported to be counting FORD-Kenya, DP and KANU votes for Asili. Ballot boxes were also stuffed for FORD-Asili and Asili agents ran out with papers.[71] Since the Asili candidate was extremely popular, and the margin of victory huge, it is not believed that the Parliamentary result was changed, but Matiba's Presidential total may have benefited. In a curious twist, the DP Dagoretti and FORD-Kenya Starehe candidates both alleged that YK' 92 had rigged in FORD-Asili candidates in these two seats.[72]

In Mathare, FORD-Kenya successfully petitioned the result, claiming bribery by FORD-Asili, supporters missing from the register, and that FORD-Kenya's votes were mixed up with and counted for Asili.[73] In Embakasi, FORD-Kenya again appear to have suffered at the hands of FORD-Asili. The FORD-Kenya candidate claimed he was kept away from the counting tables, and that his votes were mixed and counted with those for Asili.[74] The DP candidate also claimed the Returning Officer refused recounts after errors were spotted, and even the KANU candidate alleged many of his votes were sorted into bundles for FORD-Asili, and that some ballot papers were unstamped.[75]

Langata was tense and violent on election day. FORD-Kenya imported numerous Luo voters and there were allegations of intimidation of voters to support Raila Odinga. In the end, the result appears to have been acceptable. There were, however, allegations here too that KANU had attempted to smuggle in ballots, and foreign observers reported that Minister Leakey had been found in possession of two ballot boxes.[76] Quite how Leakey had obtained these boxes was never made clear. Victoria Brittain reported in the London *Guardian* that local people had found 24,000 ballots pre-marked for Leakey, according to affidavits given to the Commonwealth team, though this was not mentioned in their report.[77]

FORD-Asili vs the DP: Kiambu and Nyandarua. Kiambu and Nyandarua in Central Province were also 'up for grabs'. Kiambu District was the centre of the Kenyatta regime and the most well-developed region of the country outside Nairobi. From the beginning of 1992 the area was one of the central zones of opposition to the government. Access to land remained a crucial issue, but the divide was less between KANU and the opposition than between the DP and FORD-Asili. The DP was overwhelmingly dominant among the élite when the campaign began, with five of the seven MPs in the party. However, anger and bitterness about their late exit from KANU, their involvement in unpopular state decisions and

Table 11.17 Kiambu and Nyandarua Election Results

Constituency	KANU		FORD-ASILI		DP		FORD-KENYA		Others	
	Parl.	Pres.	Parl.	Pres.	Parl.	Pres.	Parl.	Pres.	Parl.	Pres.
Limuru	6%	5%	86%	88%	5%	4%	2%	2%	1%	0%
Lari	4%	1%	84%	95%	5%	4%	1%	0%	6%	0%
Kikuyu	1%	2%	23%	87%	4%	5%	72%	6%	0%	0%
Kiambaa	2%	2%	70%	85%	24%	11%	4%	1%	-	0%
Githunguri	10%	2%	78%	93%	8%	4%	0%	0%	3%	1%
Gatundu	3%	0%	57%	89%	36%	10%	4%	0%	-	0%
Juja	6%	7%	68%	74%	16%	12%	8%	7%	2%	1%
Kinangop	3%	2%	58%	75%	28%	22%	-	0%	11%	1%
Kipipiri	3%	2%	63%	67%	32%	30%	1%	1%	-	1%
Ndaragwa	3%	2%	20%	24%	72%	73%	-	0%	4%	0%

corrupt land allocations, and their rejection of the FORD umbrella meant that they faced a strong challenge from youthful FORD 'outsiders'.[78] KANU was marginalised before the campaign began. Its only weapons were money and the threat that Central Province would lose out on development by opposing KANU, the party the region had founded.[79]

The other marginal District was the settlement area of Nyandarua to the west, far larger and less developed, and closer in orientation to Nakuru than the rest of Central Province. Previously part of the 'White Highlands', land ownership in it was transferred after Independence to Kikuyu squatters, immigrants from other Districts, and external land-holders. Milk production, pyrethrum (the natural insecticide), maize and horticulture were the main cash income generators. District politics had consistently been messy, factionalist and violent, characterised by the absence of national figures since J. M. Kariuki's death in 1975, apart from the charismatic ex-Assistant Minister Kimani wa Nyoike. In 1992, Nyandarua was the only Kikuyu-populated District which proved to be remotely marginal, between the DP and Asili. KANU was not a serious contender.

The election results in Kiambu were extraordinary. The DP (and KANU) leaders were comprehensively defeated by political unknowns from FORD-Asili, who were seldom even seen as contenders in news reports from the area. All the FORD-Asili candidates trailed Matiba, indicating a ticket vote and the importance of the 'coat-tails' effect in this area. Although it had only seven seats, Kiambu contained the greatest concentration of the Kenya business élite outside Nairobi, and the defeat of Karume and the DP leaders here was a real shock. The reasons for the DP's defeat included the perception of the DP as a golf-playing élite, but above all it was the consequence of a collective last-minute preference emerging to vote for Matiba for President, as the fighter willing to take on Moi, and his demand to be given a team he could work with in Parliament. Most voters believed that the FORD-Asili leader had stood up to defend the interests of ordinary Kikuyu, while the old Kenyatta élite had been more concerned to protect their own interests and had remained in Moi's Cabinet for too long.

The sole exception to the FORD-Asili bandwagon was the victory of Paul Muite for FORD-Kenya in Kikuyu constituency. This was a huge personal endorsement, unique in the country. Muite was in the 'wrong' party, but rather than abandoning him, as happened elsewhere, voters split their tickets. The likelihood of such vote-splitting was clear on nomination day, when the authors saw Matiba posters with Muite's face (torn from his own posters) pasted in to replace the unfortunate Asili candidate, creating a Muite-Matiba ticket. In Githunguri, Minister Arthur Magugu, who had dominated the seat since first winning it in 1969, lost easily to his old enemy Josephat Karanja, while the DP's Rose Waruhiu, who had had hopes of victory, was also trounced.[80] Kenyatta's brother-in-law George Muhoho, who the *Standard* had suggested 'does not appear seriously threatened',[81] lost massively to an Asili newcomer in Juja, which included parts of Thika town. There was evidence of voter importation here, probably from Murang'a. Only Ngengi Muigai (Kenyatta's nephew) in his old Gatundu seat, and founder member and DP financier Njenga Karume in Kiambaa even put up a fight.

Nyandarua was far closer. As expected, the DP dominated Ndaragwa, which bordered Nyeri and had been settled by Nyeri immigrants. Kipipiri and Kinangop, however, where most residents had originally migrated from Murang'a and Kiambu, followed Nakuru and voted Asili (see Figure 11.5). A surprise was the defeat of Kimani wa Nyoike (KNC, Kinangop), earlier described as 'clearly the front-runner in the constituency'.[82] Despite his prominent anti-KANU stance, wa Nyoike polled only 11 per cent of the vote.

The Regions of Ethnic and Party Competition

The fourth type of election covered four Districts and two additional constituencies, the ethnic borderlands of Nakuru, Uasin Gishu, Trans-Nzoia, Narok North and Kajiado North constituencies, and Mombasa on the Coast.[83] In these 17 seats, ethnic groups supporting KANU and opposition parties intermingled, and the competition for votes was influenced heavily by ethnic factors. These seats also saw much of the serious electoral violence, and were the focus of many of the ethnic clashes. In each case, KANU was strongest amongst the pastoralist and coastal peoples – the Maasai, Kalenjin and Mijikenda – while the dominant opposition party had strong Kikuyu or Luhya support.

Nakuru. Nakuru District was one of the most contested, controversial and violent Districts in 1992. As the major settlement area for the Kikuyu as they established land title up the Rift Valley in the early years of Independence, Nakuru and southern Uasin Gishu were the only Districts where the Kikuyu met the Kalenjin communities in large numbers. About 60 per cent of Nakuru was Kikuyu, with the Kalenjin second, but many Kisii, Luo and Luhya, especially in the urban areas. State House Nakuru and Moi's home in Kabarak (in Rongai constituency) were both in the

Table 11.18 The Nakuru Results

Constituency	KANU		FORD-ASILI		DP		FORD-KENYA		Others	
	Parl.	Pres.	Parl.	Pres.	Parl.	Pres.	Parl.	Pres.	Parl.	Pres.
Nakuru East	11%	12%	62%	70%	15%	10%	8%	7%	3%	1%
Nakuru Town	17%	18%	45%	49%	17%	15%	19%	18%	2%	0%
Molo	34%	36%	60%	56%	5%	5%	–	2%	–	0%
Nakuru North	7%	4%	63%	77%	28%	18%	2%	1%	0%?	0%
Rongai	47%	46%	35%	39%	12%	9%	6%	5%	–	1%

District. Nakuru was the centre of the most violent political events of the Independence period, and was also the site of some of the most serious ethnic clashes, in Molo, Nakuru East and Rongai, which left hundreds dead and tens of thousands displaced. The clashes caused intense ethnic polarisation in the District. The Kalenjin were entirely pro-KANU and the Kikuyu either FORD-Asili or DP, while among the smaller communities, the Luo supported FORD-Kenya and the Luhya Asili. All four incumbent Kikuyu MPs had defected to the opposition by polling day, leaving only the Kalenjin Rongai MP, Moi's brother-in-law Eric Bomett, in KANU. The Catholic Church was extremely active politically, supporting those dispossessed during the clashes, and campaigning against KANU. The majority of Kenya's 'political prisoners' came from Nakuru District, most notably Koigi wa Wamwere and Mirugi Kariuki who were from Nakuru North, and Rumba Kinuthia from Nakuru East. The key figure in the District was the sole defector to FORD-Asili, Molo MP Njenga Mungai. FORD-Kenya had some support after the FORD split, but Njenga Mungai's defection to Asili left them in a minority everywhere. The DP was fronted by another old-timer, radical Nakuru Town politician Mark Mwithaga, but it was Asili who had the advantage, in this District of populist radicalism. Matiba's visit during the campaign to Nakuru was particularly important in swinging the District behind Asili.

FORD-Asili won four of the five seats, with ethnicity the single most important factor as the Kikuyu voted solidly for Asili and DP candidates, and the Kalenjin supported KANU. The election and the results were severely affected, however, by rigging by both FORD-Asili and KANU in four of the five seats. Nakuru East (Naivasha), an 85 per cent Kikuyu constituency, was dominated by FORD-Asili. The urban Nakuru Town was a four-way race, with FORD-Asili coming in first. KANU performed creditably, partly due to the personal vote for new KANU Chairman Geoffrey Asanyo. The DP's Mark Mwithaga was expected to win, but the shift in Kikuyu support towards Matiba had an effect here also, although FORD-Asili's candidate was a Luhya, Martin Shikuku's brother. The Luo vote went to FORD-Kenya. The seat saw clear rigging. There was pre-voting for KANU in one area. FORD-Asili ballot papers were also found premarked, and Asili supporters pretending to be clerks were incorrectly counting ballots.[84] A KANU agent was arrested for taking part in the count. In Shabab station a KANU candidate was found marking ballot papers in a private car.[85] At Kaptembwa station, the registers were deliberately hidden to prevent people voting.[86] Some polling stations reported a turn-out of over 100 per cent. Many unstamped papers were declared spoilt. The hall was in chaos, and there were 3,600 too many Parliamentary ballots. There were attempts by YK' 92 to storm the hall.[87] KANU boycotted the count, claiming that FORD-Asili had rigged the election with the Presiding Officer, who admitted that clerks were counting the same votes for Asili twice.[88] FORD-Kenya petitioned Asili's victory, also claiming pre-election oathing amongst the Kikuyu. KANU and FORD-Asili votes were inflated, but whether the result was changed overall is less clear.

The election in Molo was also rigged blatantly by both FORD-Asili and KANU in an unparallelled competition of abuse. Voting in the seat was almost entirely ethnic. The constituency had had the highest and most controversial registration in the country, and the election result was equally extraordinary. Of the 16 polling stations which returned turn-outs in excess of 100 per cent, in eight almost every vote was for Asili, and in the others they were all for KANU. The impact of the new registration units apparently created after registration had officially finished (see Chapter 7) can also be seen in the results for units 61/1, 62/1, 63/1 and 64/1, each originally with FORD-Asili majorities and with new entirely KANU stations inserted. Polling station 61/1 (the infamous Kipkewa) produced 6,127 votes for KANU, and none for Asili; station 62/1 contributed 1,333 for KANU, and one for Asili; while 64/1 polled 1,776 votes for KANU and one for Asili. The last nine stations returned 8,198 votes for KANU and six votes for FORD-Asili. FORD-Asili agents reported mass voter importation and stamping and marking of ballots from midnight the night before, and agents barred from polling stations.[89] In one south Molo station, IRI observers reported that all the clerks and Presiding Officers had been substituted by new people masquerading as them, and party agents were marking ballots for voters without even bothering to ask people whom they supported. FORD-Asili were also rigging. Station 86, for example, returned 272 votes for KANU and 7,044 for Asili. A NEMU observer was arrested for photographing piles of consecutive ballots, folded in bundles of 30, from two stations.[90] People from Baringo and Kericho were transported in government buses to Nakuru in order to vote there, particularly to Technology Farm and Kiboron High School, from 26 December onwards.[91] IRI observers visited the forest station where so many had apparently been registered and found numerous people carrying suitcases. The day before, they had visited the Rift Valley Institute of Science and Technology, where at least 1,000 people had been camped. They were told that the crowd were there for a 'church seminar', but reported that they found the atmosphere frightening. When they returned on polling day all the people had vanished.[92] NEMU described the election as 'wholly fraudulent'.[93] It was widely believed that KANU brought roughly 15,000 people into the constituency to vote and had stuffed many other ballots, but that FORD-Asili also inflated by 5–10,000, so that the result was probably unaltered.

Nakuru East saw similar problems. The count was extremely slow, finishing on 3 January 1993, with the impression amongst observers that KANU was desperately trying to realise its last hope of a seat in a Kikuyu area. Boxes arrived without seals or serial numbers, and stuffed with KANU votes, but counting clerks were partisan for FORD-Asili and counted votes for other parties as Asili ballots.[94] At least one stuffed ballot box was introduced.

In the fifth seat of Rongai, Moi's home, which bordered Baringo, and was created in 1986–7 specifically to establish a more Kalenjin seat, KANU won a somewhat suspect victory. Voting was generally valid, though in some stations KANU agents took over, speaking in Kalenjin and wearing KANU badges.[95] Eleven clerks were seen deliberately bundling Asili, FORD-Kenya and DP ballots into the KANU piles.[96] One full box from NKU/132 contained only KANU ballot papers. There were reports that voters had been chased away from this station by YK '92 before polling started. The results were not announced when counting finished, and no candidate (not even KANU's) was willing to sign the Parliamentary results.[97] One certifier reported that Moi's total was announced as over 3,000 votes higher than the number actually counted. A Parliamentary recount was refused.

Kajiado and Narok North. The two northern Maasai seats of Kajiado North and Narok North were closer in orientation to Nakuru than the rest of Maasailand. Kajiado North saw the epic battle between the Vice-President George Saitoti and the DP Secretary-General John Keen, ex-MP for the seat, who had moved at the last minute from Kajiado Central (which he might well have won) to take on Saitoti. Ngong Town, no more than a few miles from Nairobi, was the centre of a major belt of Kikuyu settlement, and the numerous settlers preferred non-KANU parties, whilst the Maasai generally supported Saitoti. Other electoral influences included Saitoti's Vice-Presidential position and enormous wealth. Saitoti's development record was unmatched, but Keen had the ethnic advantage: as well as Kikuyu support, he could actually speak Maa (unlike Saitoti). FORD-Asili's

Table 11.19 Kajiado North Ballot Box Manipulation

Polling station	Registered	Original streams	Final streams	Average original voters per box
KAJ/2	2700	3	2	900
KAJ/3	n/a	8	6	n/a
KAJ/5	3505	4	3	876
KAJ/6	545	2	1	273
KAJ/7	6315	9	7	702
KAJ/8	1555	3	2	518
KAJ/13	n/a	3	2	n/a
KAJ/37	1375	3	2	458

Source: Individual NEMU poll monitors' questionnaire and written reports, compared with the gazetted number of boxes. There may have been more which were unrecorded.

Philip Odupoy, although he was running well behind on nomination day, benefited from the Asili wave amongst young Kikuyu towards election day, and in the end ran second to Saitoti. Mrs Wambui Otieno (FORD-Kenya) was politically irrelevant and backed Keen in the last few days, whilst the KNC's Oliver Seki actually campaigned throughout for Saitoti.

The count was seriously compromised. As Table 11.19 shows, there had been a consistent pattern of apparent over-ordering of boxes, given the number of registered voters in the station. Then, according to poll monitors and foreign journalists, at least 10 of these unnecessary polling streams were removed from voting at the last minute, freeing up at least 30 legally allocated ballot boxes. Where these additional boxes were by the end of the count is unclear. In addition, some rural stations had only KANU agents, and the vote there tended to be nearly 100 per cent for KANU. Some Somalis were also imported to vote. Keen protested at stuffing in two areas.[98] It was widely rumoured that Saitoti had nonetheless lost the election, probably to FORD-Asili's Odupoy rather than John Keen. Counting, however, took four days and it is suspected that KANU eventually reintroduced the now stuffed over-ordered boxes, thus leaving the correct official number of boxes at the end.

Narok also saw an epic battle in the northernmost constituency, Narok North. As with Kajiado, the issue of land-holding was crucial. The seat bordered Molo, and KANU fought the election on the basis of preventing the Kikuyu registering or voting. Local leadership was seen by many Maasai as the province of the 'indigenous people' (themselves), whilst settlers should concentrate on farming and 'leave the area's politics to the Maasai'.[99] This was a conflict of irreconcilable differences between a large immigrant community, who had bought land fairly, and a slightly larger, less-wealthy and less-educated group fearful of losing their traditional rights, and incited to fever pitch by claims that defeat would mean they would be driven from their homes. The constituency was a three-way struggle between the DP, Asili and KANU's William ole Ntimama, the hardline Minister for Local Government. Both Asili candidate Harun Lempaka and the DP's ole Tiampatti were powerful Maasai ex-DCs and businessmen. Lempaka, FORD-Asili National Treasurer, had the clan advantage,[100] while Ntimama might have been expected to lose, since the Maasai vote was split, whilst the 15,000 Kikuyu in the seat would vote for anyone except him.[101] Nonetheless, KANU won both Presidency and Parliament. Whilst there is no decisive evidence of malpractice, it is known that on polling day, the register was not being checked when people voted.[102] Some stations saw Presiding Officers favouring KANU, and everyone being marked for Moi. Here as in Baringo, 'polling stations used illiteracy to cover rigging'.[103] There was harassment of non-Maasai, while security personnel looked on.

Uasin Gishu and Trans-Nzoia. Further north and west, the two Districts of Uasin Gishu and Trans-Nzoia were also key battlegrounds, mainly between the two FORDs and KANU (see Figure 11.3). Trans-Nzoia was a settlement area, populated mainly by Bukusu Luhya from Bungoma District to the west, but with a substantial Kalenjin minority,

Table 11.20 Trans-Nzoia and Uasin Gishu Election Results

Constituency	KANU		FORD-ASILI		DP		FORD-KENYA		Others	
	Parl.	Pres.	Parl.	Pres.	Parl.	Pres.	Parl.	Pres.	Parl.	Pres.
Kwanza	34%	33%	5%	12%	5%	2%	55%	52%	1%	1%
Saboti	26%	26%	14%	21%	3%	3%	57%	50%	-	1%
Cherangani	52%	49%	15%	20%	6%	4%	27%	26%	0%	1%
Eldoret North	59%	61%	26%	29%	4%	3%	11%	8%	-	0%
Eldoret East	83%	75%	15%	25%	4%	0%	-	0%	-	0%
Eldoret South	65%	64%	30%	29%	4%	2%	-	4%	-	0%

mainly Nandi, concentrated in Cherangani. The area has always been closely bound into Bungoma politics, especially through Kitale East and then Cherangani MP Masinde Muliro. After Muliro's death, his mantle passed to his long-time supporter Michael 'Kijana' Wamalwa, ex-MP for Kitale West until 1989, who soon after became Second Vice-Chairman of FORD-Kenya. The ethnic clashes in Saboti and Kwanza, which killed at least 200 people, cemented opposition to KANU and polarised Luhya opinion behind Wamalwa. The result was another election based on ethnic solidarity. The DP and FORD-Asili played little role.

Things were very different in the three southern border seats of Uasin Gishu, divided between a majority Kalenjin population and a minority of Luhya in the west and Kikuyu in the south. Contesting their seats within the Biwott sphere of influence, KANU's candidates were a hardline, wholly Kalenjin team. The District was the scene of the worst ethnic violence in the election period, centred on Burnt Forest and the surrounding areas of Eldoret South. The area was seen as strategically crucial for KANU. As a result of the confluence of Kikuyu voters from the south and Luhya votes from the west, FORD-Asili dominated the opposition. Eldoret North, an area which had seen bitter internal battles in KANU, had almost 20,000 non-Kalenjin votes and was a key marginal seat. Eldoret South, with a Kikuyu majority and substantial Luhya minority, was expected to fall to Asili's Julius Chomba, as many Kikuyu in Eldoret town had registered in the southern seat. Dr Joseph Misoi, the Kalenjin incumbent, and the Administration used threats and renewed ethnic clashes during the campaign to intimidate opposition supporters, however, weakening the opposition parties substantially by polling day. Eldoret East was a safe KANU seat.

To the surprise of many, KANU won a solid victory in all three Uasin Gishu seats, with Asili running second and the other parties irrelevant. There were concerns about all three seats. In Kalenjin-dominated Eldoret East, a low initial turn-out seemed to have become extremely high (over 85 percent) by the close of the poll. In Eldoret North, the start of the count was delayed for 21 hours after formal close of poll, and FORD-Asili claimed that after completion the Returning Officer refused to release the result for a long period. The opposition withdrew after the discovery of piles of ballot papers marked for Saina in three stations, and FORD-Asili petitioned.[104] In the controversial Eldoret South, despite promises and a letter to the Returning Officer from Chesoni to ensure that mobile polling stations were provided, nothing was done, and many of the Kikuyu displaced did not vote.[105] NEMU reported no problems in polling or the count but KANU's victory was surprising, as it was expected to lose this predominantly Kikuyu seat.

In contrast, the elections in Trans-Nzoia were quite fairly conducted. FORD-Kenya easily won the two western seats of Kwanza and Saboti, but Muliro's old constituency Cherangani was lost by his son Mukasa Muliro to the incumbent KANU MP, a Nandi. Nearly half the 32,000 registered voters were Kalenjin and turned out strongly for KANU. The constituency did not suffer from the clashes, and arap Kirwa was less extreme than many of his colleagues. FORD-Kenya's candidate, Masinde Muliro's son, stormed out of the counting hall claiming rigging, and FORD-Kenya continued to allege malpractice.[106] Nonetheless, the results are on balance believed to be accurate.

Mombasa. The election issues and competition in the last ethnic borderland, Mombasa, were very different. A small, densely populated urban District, Mombasa had a population of well over half a million. Coastal Mijikenda, the largest group, formed only about 30 per cent of the population, and with a variety of communities living there, the election in all four seats was confused and closely contested. The forces of KANU at its most authoritarian faced the power of Islam in the IPK, a divide which overlapped the up-country/coastal divide which had played such a large part in politics in the past.

Table 11.21 The Mombasa Results

Constituency	KANU		FORD-ASILI		DP		FORD-KENYA		Others	
	Parl.	Pres.	Parl.	Pres.	Parl.	Pres.	Parl.	Pres.	Parl.	Pres.
Changamwe	22%	24%	12%	28%	36%	18%	30%	28%	-	1%
Kisauni	35%	37%	14%	23%	14%	10%	36%	26%	1%	1%
Likoni	24%	24%	24%	27%	6%	18%	46%	28%	1%	1%
Mvita	33%	39%	23%	19%	10%	9%	32%	27%	1%	1%

Both KANU and FORD-Kenya had formidable, well-organised networks of local activists in all four constituencies. While the DP and FORD-Asili were also well established in Changamwe and Mvita, FORD-Kenya was the main opposition party once its alliance with the IPK had been cemented, and the IPK provided their candidates in three of the four constituencies. Local FORD-Kenya officials expected an easy win in Likoni, the shanty settlement on the mainland south of Mombasa island. Salim Mwavumo, the FORD-Kenya candidate, could rely upon the support of his own Digo community and also the port's 10,000 Luo, who had registered here in large numbers. The contest in Kisauni to the north of the island would clearly be close, as one of FORD's original Mombasa leaders, Emmanuel Maitha, had defected back to KANU and been given KANU's nomination. He faced the FORD-Kenya/IPK candidate, Rashid Mzee, the principal of the Moslem Khalifa Secondary School. Changamwe, most of which lies on the mainland to the west of Mombasa island, was FORD-Kenya's weakest seat because of the popularity of Joseph Kennedy Kiliku, its incumbent MP, who had chaired the Commission of Enquiry into the ethnic clashes before defecting to the DP. Kiliku's Kamba community and Kikuyu workers were concentrated here, near the oil refinery.[107]

Mombasa's most intense battle took place in Mvita, the city centre constituency, which included part of the island's Arab and Swahili Old Town. One of the few four-way marginal seats in the country, it was the seat of Mombasa KANU Chairman and Assistant Minister Sharrif Nassir, who had been a staunch Moi loyalist since the 1970s. A shrewd, colourful populist, who had been one of the strongest opponents of the change to multi-party politics, Nassir had been one of the ruling party's most outspoken hardliners since the mid-1980s. Nassir had even spoken out at KANU's Special Delegates' Congress in December 1991 against repealing Section 2(a) of the constitution and permitting the registration of opposition political parties. Facing him for the IPK (under the banner of FORD-Kenya) was Omar Mwinyi, an outspoken *maalim* with a strong following among the city's unemployed youths and disgruntled Moslems. The IPK appealed mainly to young Arabs and Swahili, but the jailed Sheikh Balala and Mwinyi transcended the city's historical racial divide and enlisted Africans also to the Islamic cause. FORD-Asili's standard bearer was its National Organising Secretary Ahmed Salim Bamahriz, who had been one of FORD's six founding fathers. Well supplied with funds by Matiba, Bamahriz ran a strong, highly visible campaign, but was marginalised by the IPK-KANU conflict. The DP's candidate, Ismail Yunis, the Secretary General of the Dock Workers' Union, was also a well-known and powerful local figure. All four candidates were Moslems. All had money, though none could match Nassir's millions of shillings.

The Mvita campaign was colourful, violent and corrupt. Earlier in the year, IPK supporters had burnt down the local KANU headquarters and attacked Nassir's home, burning two of his motor-cars in speedy retaliation for the KANU chairman's verbal attacks on Sheikh Balala and the IPK. The fundamentalist IPK appealed to large sections of the community in Old Town, both young and old, and especially to Mombasa's numerous unemployed young males, a volatile political force with a high potential for violence. Nassir had countered by forming UMA – United Moslems of Africa – which drew most of its support from Mijikenda workers, and a fire-bomb campaign had started between the two sides. Since Balala's arrest, tension in the city was high, and IPK youths had clashed with the police and KANU supporters on several occasions as they demonstrated outside the Law Courts and marched through the central business district. Six days before the general election, when Balala was yet again remanded in custody by the Chief Magistrate, two demonstrators were killed in clashes as the IPK marched through the city centre.

In the event, KANU won Mvita, FORD-Kenya won Likoni and Kisauni, and the DP Changamwe, whilst Asili won nothing. There was substantial split-ticketing everywhere. Turn-outs were suprisingly low, between 34 and 41 per cent. At least two of the four results were of questionable accuracy, and the results in all four were petitioned. The worst problems were in Mvita, where some polling stations were moved at the last minute, poll observers were threatened by KANU supporters and Nassir himself campaigned on polling day.[108] Nassir's victory was a result of his mastery of political patronage, strong government support and financial resources, and the split in the opposition vote. There were less than 3,000 votes between KANU, FORD-Kenya and FORD-Asili, and the abstention of any one candidate would have won victory for another. The Returning Officer was rumoured to have favoured KANU in deciding which votes were declared spoilt. IRI observers reported that three stuffed boxes had been spotted, whilst the Returning Officer leaked Nassir's 'victory' to KBC before the count was completed. FORD-Kenya demanded a recount and petitioned.[109] In Kisauni, KANU were unlucky to lose the Parliamentary elections, as Moi won the Presidential vote and the large spoilt vote exceeded the FORD-Kenya candidate's majority. NEMU reported FORD-Kenya's narrow victory acceptable, but the Returning Officer refused a recount and ejected KANU's candidate Maitha from the hall. KANU petitioned, demanding a recount, which annulled the result.[110] In Likoni, the DP nominee somehow had his name replaced by that of the loser in the DP nominations due to an Electoral Commission error, leading DP supporters to vote FORD-Kenya for Parliament.[111]

The Swing Communities

The fifth type of election covers 42 seats inhabited by 'swing' ethnic communities. Over this quarter of the country, in all of which there was no significant Presidential candidate, either KANU and the opposition were too close to call, the community's allegiance was not wholly clear until election day, or adjacent seats were moving in different directions, a response to individual powerful leaders and specific local issues. These areas included the Kisii, Kamba, Bajuni, Orma and Pokomo of the north Coast, and the Luhya of Vihiga, Kakamega and Busia. Here, sub-clan, personality and local factors dominated. There was still party voting, but communities voted for different parties from constituency to constituency, and more votes ended up going different ways in the Parliamentary and Presidential elections.

The Akamba of Machakos, Makueni and Kitui. The 15 seats of Machakos, Makueni and Kitui, the home of the Kamba people, were a crucial swing region. The election was contested almost entirely between the DP and KANU, but they were running neck and neck in many seats. FORD-Asili was only of relevance in Kitui, and FORD-Kenya was irrelevant everywhere.

Machakos District is a densely populated area of rolling hills adjoining

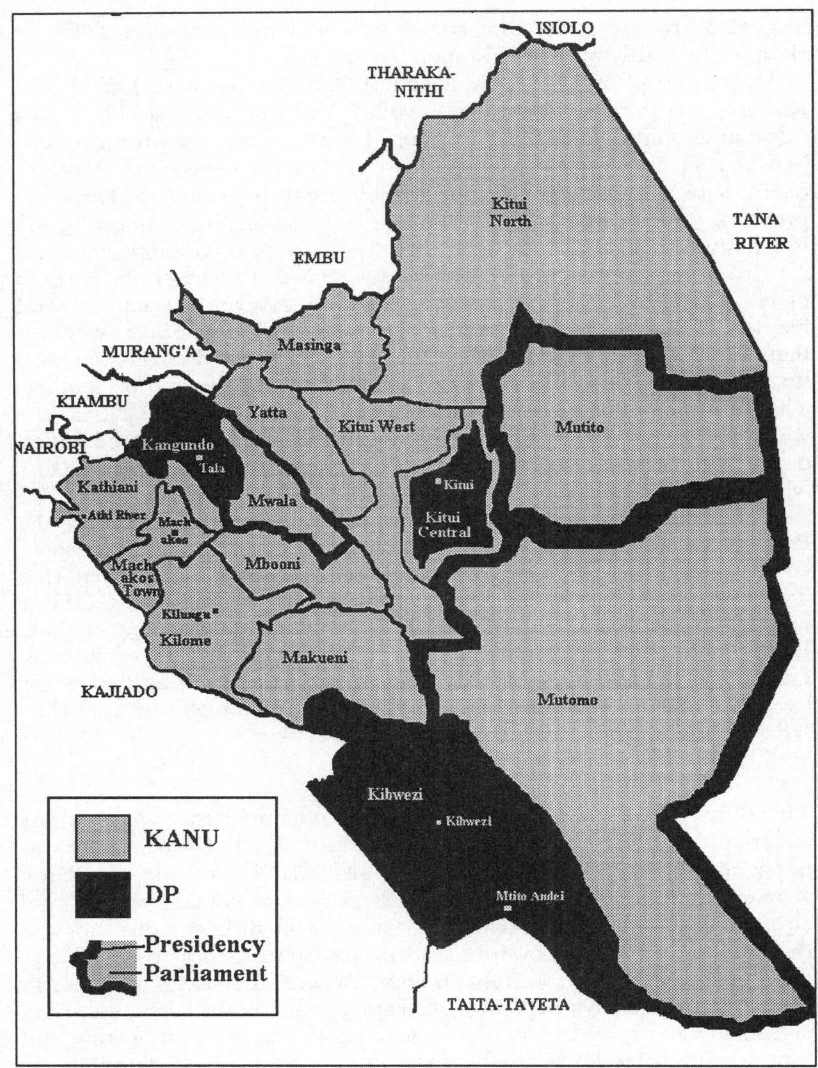

Figure 11.12 Ukambani, Machakos, Makueni and Kitui Districts

the huge Yatta plateau. Parts are very fertile but the area also suffers from rainfall problems. Coffee was the main cash crop, but problems with the coffee industry had led to substantial dissatisfaction. The DP fielded a strong ticket against a weak KANU group, with the exception of General Jackson Mulinge in Kathiani, who had initiated major developments in the constituency since retiring as the Chief of General Staff in 1986. Kathiani

Table 11.22 Machakos, Makueni and Kitui Election Results

Constituency	KANU		FORD-ASILI		DP		FORD-KENYA		Others	
	Parl.	Pres.	Parl.	Pres.	Parl.	Pres.	Parl.	Pres.	Parl.	Pres.
Masinga	74%	67%	9%	15%	17%	16%	-	2%	-	1%
Yatta	52%	52%	18%	26%	27%	19%	2%	1%	-	1%
Kangundo	41%	41%	5%	6%	53%	52%	-	1%	1%	1%
Kathiani	64%	58%	11%	14%	21%	23%	4%	4%	-	1%
Machakos Town	54%	53%	13%	11%	31%	32%	3%	2%	-	1%
Mwala	46%	33%	8%	9%	44%	55%	1%	1%	1%	1%
Mbooni	44%	43%	13%	13%	33%	41%	9%	2%	-	1%
Kilome	70%	68%	6%	8%	13%	19%	9%	2%	3%	1%
Makueni	44%	45%	15%	12%	40%	40%	2%	1%	-	2%
Kibwezi	33%	37%	5%	7%	58%	49%	4%	3%	-	2%
Kitui North	55%	43%	-	28%	41%	28%	1%	1%	3%	1%
Kitui West	37%	41%	34%	25%	23%	32%	1%	1%	5%	1%
Kitui Central	47%	47%	1%	5%	49%	45%	3%	1%	-	1%
Mutito	53%	44%	4%	4%	42%	50%	2%	1%	0%**	1%
Mutomo	39%	31%	31%	29%	23%	37%	7%	2%	-	1%

** Stood down.

boasted a new hospital, the Kathiani General Hospital, incongruously situated in this small settlement. KANU was confident of Masinga, Kathiani and Yatta, whilst the DP expected to take Mwala, Machakos Town and Paul Ngei's Kangundo. Unusually, neither of the standard bearers for the two main parties were standing for election. Paul Ngei, veteran nationalist, detained with Kenyatta, had been made bankrupt in 1990, preventing him from standing.[112] The KANU chairman and political boss of the District for many years, Mulu Mutisya, also declined to stand.[113] In Makueni District, part of Machakos until February 1992 when it was hived off as an independent District, the DP was led by last-minute defector Agnes Ndetei in the newly settled area of Kibwezi, stretching along the Nairobi-Mombasa road. She was expected to win. KANU was led by another last-minute defector, ex-leader of the SDP Johnstone Makau in Mbooni (where he too was expected to win) and Kasanga Mulwa in Ndetei's seat. Kilome and Makueni were too close to call. Several constituencies had been suffering from food shortages recently, which KANU played to their advantage.

The much larger and semi-arid Kitui District to the east was more subject to state pressure, outside the smaller population centres of Kitui West and Kitui Central. Here, the DP leader was MP and ex-Minister Kyale Mwendwa, whilst KANU was represented by Minister George Ndotto and Minister-to-be Stephen Musyoka in Kitui North.

KANU ended up winning 12 of the 15 Parliamentary seats, and ten of them in the Presidency. There were extensive electoral abuses in at least ten of these seats. In Machakos, the home of Paul Ngei, KANU won a series of easy victories, most of which look from NEMU and other records to have been relatively fair.[114] In Kangundo, the DP's sole victory, Paul Ngei's power overwhelmed Minister Joseph Ngutu. Ngei had survived so long partly because his senior wife controlled the local women's movement, which once again was turned out to support Ngei's favoured candidate. In the closely fought urban seat of Machakos Town, which the incumbent Minister Kyalo was defending against the popular ex-MP J. M. Kikuyu (DP), who was rigged out in 1988, NEMU reported KANU agents paying voters on polling day. At one station people voted without identity or voters' cards. Several Presiding Officers were uncooperative, and the NCWK reported that ballot boxes had arrived with 'marking anomalies'. The count was well monitored by American observers, however, and NEMU monitor and count reports were positive. Mwala, the home of Mulu Mutisya, was another decisive and questionable KANU victory. The opposition parties stormed out of the count claiming a ballot box had arrived open.[115] The DP petitioned their narrow Parliamentary defeat, after their clear 11 per cent victory in the Presidential election. Elsewhere in the District, a FORD-Asili agent was arrested in Yatta after complaining of irregularities, while the DP alleged KANU agents were counting votes, other agents were thrown out, some boxes were only accompanied by KANU agents, and there was oathing for KANU's Gideon Mutiso.[116] In Masinga, observers were not permitted to observe the count properly and the Returning Officer was uncooperative and threatened the NEMU monitors.

In Makueni, KANU won three of the four seats, two of them very narrowly, and the DP petitioned all three defeats. Everywhere, NEMU poll monitors reported cash distribution by KANU agents on polling day, and widespread treating of voters with food on the eve of poll or polling day itself. The scale of the Kilome victory was surprising, whilst in Mbooni KANU's Johnstone Makau was the victor in a contest which saw fraudulent counting, with KANU agents acting as counting clerks.[117] In Makueni constituency, although the Presidential result was plausible, the Parliamentary figures were more questionable. There was favouritism in handling spoilt ballots for KANU, the boxes were slow to arrive and there was some minor miscounting of votes from DP to KANU, but it probably did not change the result.[118] In Kibwezi, there were long delays in the delivery of boxes, and a NEMU observer reported that:

> suspicions mounted when for example ballot boxes from Kibwezi Primary School (MNI/113) were transported to the counting centre (St Joseph's Secondary School) at about 1.30 a.m. when polling had actually been completed by 7.30 p.m. Kibwezi Primary School is about 300 metres from St. Joseph's School. Six ballot papers [boxes] out of nine in this polling stations (MNI/113) had no glass compartments neither the name and number of the polling station.[119]

According to both NEMU and the NCWK, at least three boxes were swapped for the originals, but this was spotted and they were not counted. The DP won, with the suspicion that rigging had been prevented.

The Kitui Akamba split their vote in three of the five seats. KANU won two Parliamentary seats it lost in the Presidential elections (Mutito and

Mutomo), and won the Presidential vote in Kitui Central, which it narrowly lost for Parliament. The results in all five seats were affected by rigging. In three seats, there is sufficient evidence to suggest that the results were altered in KANU's favour. In Kitui West, a key seat, there were high increases in and rates of registration. Polling went well, but opposition agents were apparently bribed to disappear at some stations. The count was extremely slow, and the seat was one of the last to declare. Some boxes arrived 15 hours after the close of polling. The local DO helped count the ballots, boxes were unaccompanied, and NEMU and others reported substitution of returns, misreading of votes, fraudulence, miscommunication and counting of invalid votes. One box was full of bundles of papers stacked like bank notes.[120] The FORD-Kenya candidate claimed two pre-filled boxes were found under the counting hall table.[121] There were 1,200 too many Parliamentary votes, with a 500 KANU Parliamentary majority over FORD-Asili. The DP candidate Kyale Mwendwa, the favourite, walked out of the count and petitioned.

In Mutito, there was election day campaigning for both DP and KANU, including distribution by one KANU chief of 500 shilling notes. An NCCK observer was bribed to abandon his duties.[122] Presidential counting went well, and the DP won by 800 votes. KANU then won Parliament by 1,200 votes and the local government elections. Only KANU agents were allowed to accompany some boxes and one box arrived unsealed. The Returning Officer was uncooperative and local recounts were refused.[123] The number of spoilt votes was kept secret. There were protests at the Returning Officer's attitude, and all the opposition walked out. In Mutomo, the count was again doubtful, with many rejected papers and some DP ballots being counted as KANU's. One box arrived with a KANU agent only. Again, KANU won Parliament and lost the Presidency, and again there were too many Parliamentary ballots.

In Kitui North, which KANU's future Minister for Foreign Affairs won, the FORD-Kenya candidate was expelled from the hall after complaining that the Presiding Officer for one station had been altering the election return forms and marking ballot papers.[124] The turn-out was uniquely high, at over 80 per cent, with an excess of Parliamentary over Presidential votes. Counting took four days, finishing at 6.30 a.m. on 2 January 1993.[125] The DP petitioned, but it is unlikely that the result was altered by malpractices. In Kitui Central, the Asili agent reported that plainclothes policemen intercepted ballot boxes from one station, which were returned to the counting hall three and a half hours later.[126] The DP nevertheless won narrowly.

The Gusii. The second large swing community was the Gusii, in Kisii and its new sister District of Nyamira. The area was tiny and densely populated, almost entirely by Gusii. Agriculture was the mainstay of the economy. Crucial to KANU's hopes here was Simeon Nyachae, ex-Chief Secretary, whose endorsement and campaigning for KANU was the key to defeating the strong DP and FORD-Kenya challenge (see Chapter 6). The most important opposition leaders here were George Anyona, ex-detainee and KSC Presidential candidate, and James Nyamweya, DP local leader, an old government Minister from Kenyatta's days, who had lost his

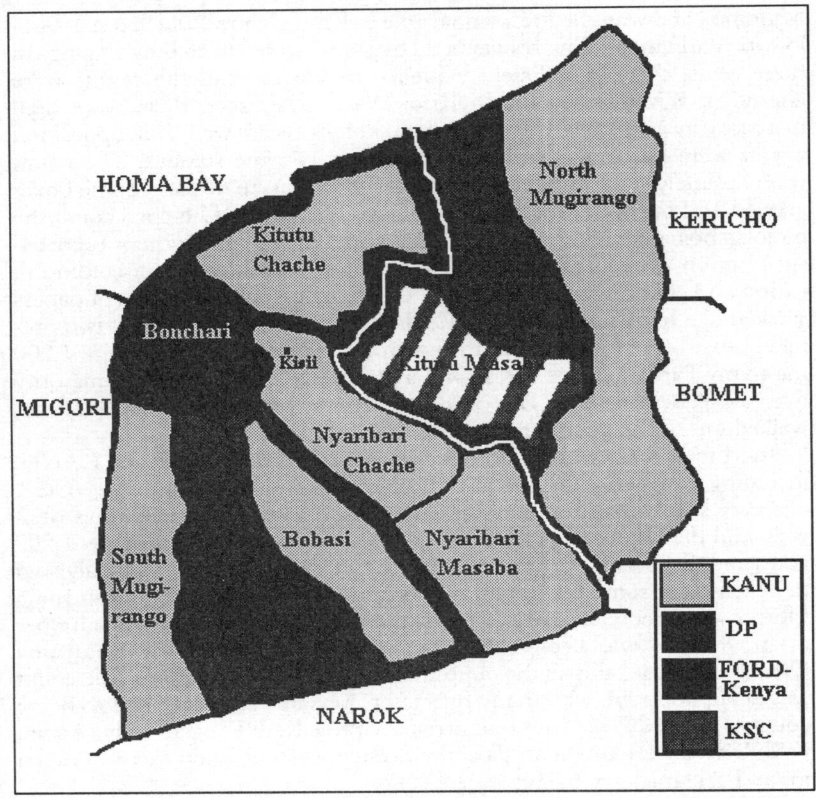

Figure 11.13 Kisii and Nyamira

seat in 1979. Registration was very uneven in Kisii District, as Nyachae in Nyaribari Chache bused large numbers of KANU supporters from adjacent seats. While this clinched his victory, it weakened KANU in the neighbouring constituencies.[127]

The area saw two separate elections and election campaigns: one internal to KANU and the other the multi-party 'official' one. The first was the battle by Nyachae's opponents in the local KANU branch to prevent the 'Nyachae steamroller' rolling over them. In 1988, they had managed to have the retired Head of the Civil Service and his supporters rigged out or barred from contesting the election: now he was intent on revenge. They failed, and the result was an exodus of incumbents (see Chapter 8).

Once the Nyachae team had won, they then faced a strong but fragmented opposition led by FORD-Kenya and the DP, and invigorated by extensive defections from the losing KANU faction. Most seats in the final election were three-way contests. FORD-Asili was irrelevant, and the KSC strong only in George Anyona's Kitutu Masaba. With no Presidential

Table 11.23 Election Results in Kisii and Nyamira

Constituency	KANU		FORD-ASILI		DP		FORD-KENYA		Others	
	Parl.	Pres.	Parl.	Pres.	Parl.	Pres.	Parl.	Pres.	Parl.	Pres.
Bonchari	37%	37%	7%	9%	53%	46%	3%	6%	–	2%
South Mugirango	53%	56%	0%	7%	1%	13%	6%	22%	*40%*	2%
Bomachoge	33%	31%	2%	1%	8%	4%	52%	62%	4%	2%
Bobasi	51%	29%	2%	8%	34%	15%	9%	46%	5%	2%
Nyaribari Masaba	49%	43%	1%	2%	48%	42%	2%	9%	–	1%
Nyaribari Chache	66%	62%	1%	2%	26%	24%	7%	11%	–	1%
Kitutu Chache	38%	32%	0%	4%	35%	42%	0%	20%	*27%*	3%
Kitutu Masaba	20%	19%	2%	2%	7%	11%	6%	45%	65%	23%
West Mugirango	34%	35%	2%	5%	18%	19%	45%	36%	1%	3%
North Mugirango	40%	39%	5%	6%	39%	31%	16%	23%	0%	1%

Italics = Post-primary defector from KANU.

candidate from the area, the elections were closer to a traditional Kenyan contest: less about party than about personality, organisation, development, money and clanism. The District saw a number of powerful fringe candidates, in keeping with the non-party nature of the contests in many areas. Clan loyalty was especially obvious in South Mugirango, where the incumbent MP, David Ondimu Kombo, won the first KANU nomination, lost the re-run and defected to PICK at the last minute, taking his clan supporters with him. In Kisii, KANU was always likely to win Nyaribari Chache, but were in trouble elsewhere. The DP expected victory in Nyaribari Masaba and Bonchari, while FORD-Kenya expected to take Bomachoge and South Mugirango. Marginal Bobasi had been the scene of violence back in December 1991, when the GSU put down protests in the town, which was followed by several ethnic clashes along the border with the Maasai of Narok. In Nyamira District, KANU was the underdog everywhere, and the DP, the KSC and FORD-Kenya all expected to win one seat.

In the event, the honours were shared. In the Presidential election, Odinga won four seats, Kibaki two and Moi four, with no one winning overwhelming majorities anywhere (see Figure 11.13). In the Parliamentary elections KANU won six of ten seats, taking two seats they lost in the Presidential elections (see Table 11.23).

The voting and count were severely rigged in KANU's favour in at least six of these ten seats, and seven produced election petitions. KANU's 25 per cent strategy for Nyanza depended on a good showing here, while Nyachae's hopes of the Vice-Presidency rested upon a decisive KANU victory. The Nyaribari Masaba result is particularly suspect. KANU's

Hezron Manduku, a close ally of Simeon Nyachae, won on an extraordinarily narrow margin over DP ex-Minister James Nyamweya, who had been expected to win, whilst more ballots were declared spoilt than KANU's majority.[128] Polling was fine in Bobasi, but the results were either incorrectly reported or blatantly manipulated. In Minister Onyonka's Kitutu Chache, one of the last to declare, KANU smuggled in ballot boxes and destroyed votes *en masse.* According to the NEMU count certifier, who was refused entry to the count, there were 29,901 votes cast. The total number of votes obtained according to the official Parliamentary result was only 21,024, a discrepancy (excluding 562 spoilt ballots) of 7,315 destroyed or removed votes, and in the Presidency 22,299, a discrepancy of 7,040. He found this out by watching through the windows, and talking to officials. His NEMU questionnaire was stolen. YK' 92 officials were allowed to enter the hall, and were caught bribing a clerk to tamper with votes. Most of the counting clerks were from the DC's office, and a senior official allegedly informed Onyonka about the progress of the rigging by telephone.[129] Simeon Nyachae won an overwhelming victory in Nyaribari Chache. The DP candidate petitioned, alleging that his name had been left off some ballot papers and many of his supporters' names were missing from the register. His agents were also denied the right to inspect ballots, seal the boxes or accompany them to the counting halls.[130] KANU, however, would probably have won this seat anyway. Bonchari, once described as 'the only constituency free of opposition in Kisii District', was won by the DP, specifically because of Protas Kebati Momanyi's last-minute defection after being rigged out of the KANU primary nomination. In South Mugirango, the incumbent MP (now in PICK) only just lost the seat to the KANU candidate.

In Nyamira District, George Anyona (KSC) won Kitutu Masaba securely, though voters backed Odinga for the Presidency. KANU took North Mugirango from the DP, to the surprise of many. There were violent scenes as all the opposition candidates alleged that five additional ballot boxes, one tied with string, were smuggled into the count using a government vehicle.[131] Again, KANU won the Parliamentary seat by only 137 votes, with 632 spoilt ballots. The DP and KSC petitioned. In West Mugirango in Nyamira, in contrast, FORD-Kenya won but both KANU and the DP alleged intimidation, campaigning, bribery and lost ballot boxes.[132]

Kakamega, Vihiga and Busia. The third large undecided community were the non-Bukusu Luhya, inhabiting Kakamega, Vihiga and Busia Districts. FORD-Asili had the upper hand in Kakamega, whilst Vihiga was more pro-KANU. In Busia, two seats, Amagoro and Samia, were strongly KANU, but the other two were undecided. Kakamega was the home of Martin Shikuku and his was the dominant presence in the District throughout the election. KANU's flag was flown mainly by Burudi Nabwera, hard-line Minister for Information and Broadcasting, who campaigned on the basis of dividing Luhya and Kikuyu, demanding that all Kikuyu leave rural Western Province and live in the towns, to leave businesses for the Luhya.[133] The DP and FORD-Kenya were irrelevant over most of these seats.

In contrast, KANU was the stronger in Vihiga District, due to the

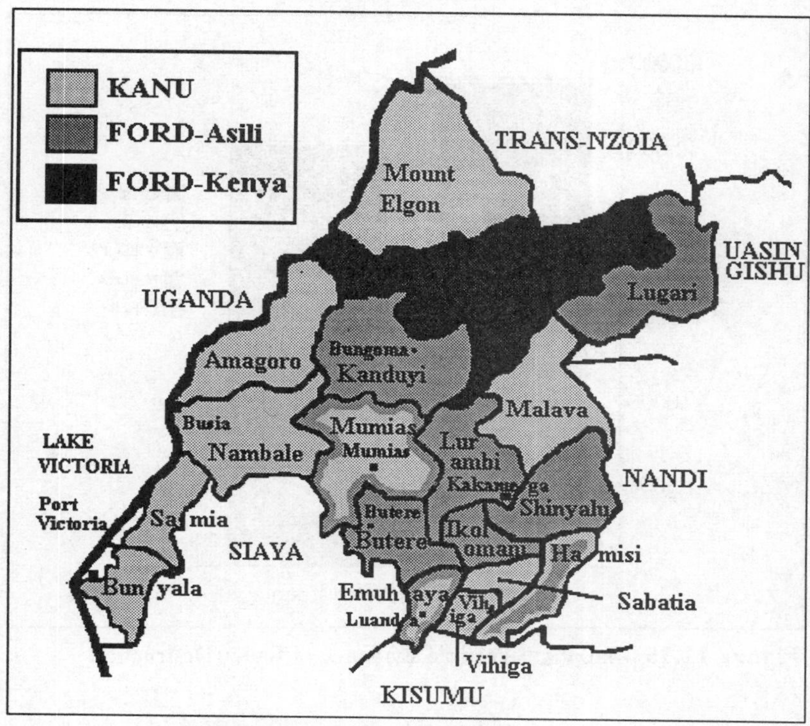

Figure 11.14 Western Province

Table 11.24 Election Results in Kakamega and Vihiga Districts

Constituency	KANU		FORD-ASILI		DP		FORD-KENYA		Others	
	Parl.	Pres.	Parl.	Pres.	Parl.	Pres.	Parl.	Pres.	Parl.	Pres.
Malava	50%	50%	49%	47%	1%	1%	-	2%	-	0%
Lugari	23%	20%	71%	71%	4%	1%	2%	5%	0%	1%
Mumias	47%	45%	40%	45%	5%	1%	8%	9%	1%	0%
Lurambi	31%	31%	63%	62%	1%	1%	5%	5%	-	2%
Shinyalu	43%	35%	55%	60%	1%	1%	2%	2%	-	1%
Ikolomani	38%	35%	56%	60%	1%	2%	5%	1%	0%	1%
Butere	25%	25%	70%	68%	1%	1%	4%	5%	-	1%
Sabatia	81%	69%	16%	27%	1%	1%	2%	3%	-	0%
Vihiga	58%	60%	39%	37%	-	1%	2%	2%	-	1%
Emuhaya	47%	44%	29%	50%	*22%*	5%	3%	2%	-	0%
Hamisi	48%	53%	49%	45%	3%	1%	0%	1%	-	0%

Italics = Last-minute defector from KANU.

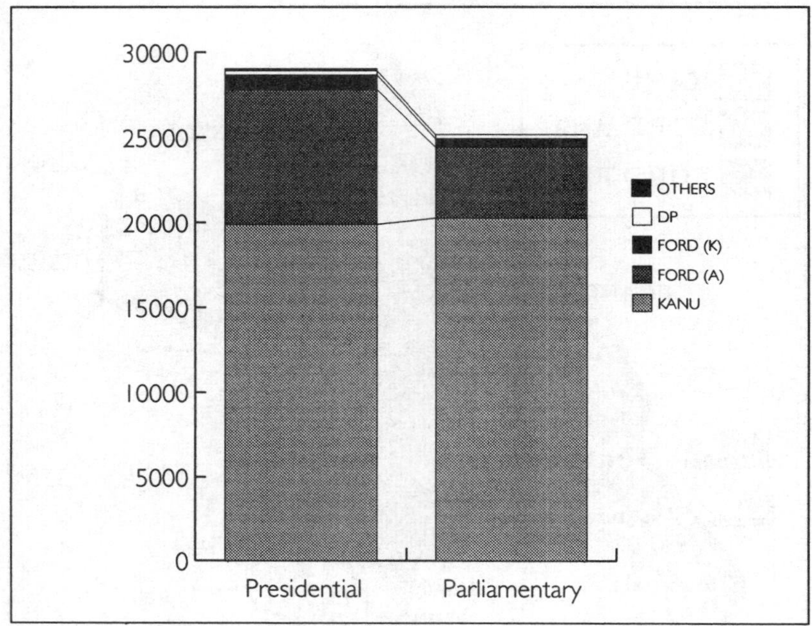

Figure 11.15 Sabatia – Possible Evidence of Ballot Destruction

influence of the late Moses Mudavadi (who died in 1989) and his son in obtaining massive development for the area. It was Moses Mudavadi's initiative that led to the creation of the new District, Vihiga, for his Maragoli people.[134] The opposition had few senior individuals here, since both Peter Kibisu (FORD-Kenya Chairman and ex-Vihiga MP), and James Onamu (ex-MP for Hamisi and FORD Branch chairman) had returned to KANU. Significant pressure was placed on the opposition. KANU youth-wingers threatened on 23 November to loot and burn down all Kikuyu-owned businesses in Mbale and Chavakali townships. Plans to set up a FORD-Asili office were quickly cancelled.[135] In Sabatia, Musalia Mudavadi was always safe. KANU was weak in Hamisi, as a result of the poor performance of Assistant Minister Vincent M'Maitse.[136] KANU's position in Emuhaya and Hamisi was worsened by the primaries, which were severely compromised.[137] The most interesting conflict was in Vihiga, where ex-incumbent MP Bahati Semo, now in Asili, faced ex-Permanent Secretary and long-time power broker Andrew Ligale for KANU.

The results were close but, particularly in Kakamega, satisfactory for FORD-Asili. Shikuku won a strong personal endorsement in Butere, while Cabinet Minister Nabwera was rejected decisively in Lugari with the worst vote of any KANU candidate. FORD-Asili won six of seven seats in the Presidential elections, and five in Parliament. In Mumias, a comparatively popular KANU MP Elon Wameyo managed to defeat the Asili candidate,

Table 11.25 Busia Election Results

Constituency	KANU		FORD-ASILI		DP		FORD-KENYA		Others	
	Parl.	Pres.	Parl.	Pres.	Parl.	Pres.	Parl.	Pres.	Parl.	Pres.
Amagoro	81%	85%	-	8%	12%	2%	-	4%	8%	1%
Nambale	44%	49%	42%	13%	2%	1%	11%	36%	-	1%
Samia	83%	72%	-	24%	-	1%	17%	2%	-	1%
Bunyala	56%	61%	0%	4%	1%	1%	7%	7%	*36%*	27%

Italics = Defector from KANU.

although Matiba won the Presidency. There was heavy bribery by KANU on the eve of the poll and KANU campaigning on polling day, and there were mixed-up papers in the count. The other KANU victory was a narrow squeeze for Minister-to-be Joshua Angatia in Malava. Angatia had been a dissident in the 1980s, who decided to stay with KANU, and was rewarded for his close and apparently legitimate victory.

The election was fought relatively fairly in Kakamega, but less so in Vihiga, where KANU performed rather better and the results in three of four seats were questionable. In Sabatia, there was a very high personal vote for Mudavadi, but watchers suggested up to 20 ballot boxes had been tampered with.[138] Minister Mudavadi's personal vote was 13 per cent above Moi's own vote, and comparison of Presidential and Parliamentary results suggests that about 4,000 Asili Parliamentary ballots were removed. In both Sabatia and Vihiga constituencies, FORD-Asili headquarters claimed that in some polling stations the Presiding Officers and poll clerks were marking all ballots for people, and no one was permitted to vote for themselves.[139] KANU's candidate narrowly lost Hamisi, though Moi won the Presidency. The sole creditable DP performance was in Emuhaya in Vihiga District, where a KANU primary loser defected to the DP, split the opposition vote and thereby allowed KANU victory. The count saw some theft of ballot papers and fraudulent counting. Again, KANU won the Parliamentary seat, and FORD-Asili the Presidency. In Vihiga constituency, the race was expected to be close, but in the event KANU won clearly. There was some counting for KANU of Asili votes. Bahati Semo boycotted the count, claiming that certain boxes had been stuffed.[140]

In neighbouring Busia District the fates of two seats, Bunyala and Nambale (the urban seat), were undecided right up to election day. Again, the major FORD-figure from the District, James Osogo, had defected back to KANU, and was given the KANU nomination in Bunyala, after which his opponent Peter Okondo defected to PICK. The result was that the ex-FORD chairman in the District stood on the KANU ticket and the KANU sub-branch chairman on an opposition (PICK) ticket. The party labels changed with bewildering speed, but the personal, locational and factional conflicts remained the same. In Nambale, new Minister Philip Masinde had contributed notably to development. Clanism was an issue, however, with Asili's Chrisantus Okemo, his major opponent, hailing from a larger clan of the Bakhayo.[141]

Busia was a very successful result for KANU, who won all four seats (see Figure 11.14). Both FORD-Kenya and DP had expected to win seats, but the DP did appallingly.[142] Samia and Amagoro were compromised by the inability of DP, Asili and FORD-Kenya candidates to make it to nominations. In Nambale, however, the Parliamentary and Presidential results were extremely close. There was large-scale ticket switching between Asili and FORD-Kenya, with voters backing Odinga for President and the FORD-Asili Parliamentary candidate. Peter Okondo performed credibly for PICK in Bunyala.

The Overall Situation

Barring last-minute defections and accidents, KANU was always likely to hold 63 seats in its ethnic homelands and allied territories – just over one third – and the opposition likely to take approximately the same. The election was therefore decided in the remaining 60 seats: the swing communities and, to a lesser extent, the ethnic borderlands, the areas where electoral malpractice was most obvious. KANU's victory was cemented in these areas (see Table 11.26).

The evidence suggests that the vote and the count in roughly two thirds of the 188 seats were relatively free and fair. The results were biased beforehand by the campaign and electoral procedures, but in over 120 seats, including the opposition strongholds, only low-level attempts at manipulation were seen. The situation was rather different elsewhere. There is strong evidence of counting anomalies and favouritism to KANU by Returning Officers in many areas, caused by the biased official recruitment procedure and by a hidden agenda amongst some officials. KANU was not the sole beneficiary, since FORD-Asili is known to have cheated too. As late as August 1993, Oginga Odinga claimed that Matiba had printed three million ballot papers himself in order to rig the elections.[143] Over-registration allowed multiple voting, under-age voting and other abuses. The massed transportation of voters on polling day was another important

Table 11.26 Seats in Each Group, by Category and Winner

Category	KANU	Opposition	Total
Ethnic homelands	17	30	47
Allied territories	45	19	64
Opposition conflicts	1	17	18
Ethnic battlegrounds	8	9	17
Swing communities	29	13	42
Total	100	88	188

Table 11.27 The 'True' Parliamentary Results

Party	Official total	Proposed 'real' total
KANU	100	85
FORD-Kenya	31	36
FORD-Asili	31	33
DP	23	31
KNC	1	1
PICK	1	1
KSC	1	1

tactic, the result of a liberal law governing registration. Biased or intimidated election officials allowed party managers to 'fill in' missing votes in party strongholds either by letting unqualified voters vote or, on a larger scale, by filling in ballots for non-voters after the close of the poll.

There is also evidence of extensive stuffing of boxes and destruction of ballots. The destruction of opposition ballots was carried out in two ways: at the count, on a small scale, by partisan counting clerks hiding other parties' ballots; and during the transportation of boxes to the count. Over much of the country, the transportation of boxes was so well-known a problem that the population and agents were enormously careful to ensure no tampering occurred. In a number of seats, however, boxes still arrived unaccompanied, some only for realistic, practical reasons, others because of fraud. Insertion of ballots into existing boxes and the introduction of entire new stuffed boxes into the count are particularly interesting, however, because they cannot be carried out without access to the ballot papers and the boxes. Both should have been impossible. There is no evidence of the multiple production of ballot papers (that is, producing more than one identical set), but over-ordering of papers in key areas is suspected. For example, a seat with 20,000 voters may have 25,000 ballots ordered for it; 22,000 would be distributed and 15,000 used. Then, during the count or while being transported to the counting centre, the additional 3,000 ballots would be added, legally marked and pre-stamped. These votes would be almost indistinguishable in the chaos of the counting hall from the genuine ones, leading to an easy victory for one candidate and a surprisingly high turn-out. These constituencies could be identified with detective work, because where good records were kept one could identify all the serialised books which went out, but it appears that the records are most incomplete or inaccurate where abuses occurred.

The most remarkable abuse, however, must be the insertion of entirely new properly stamped and marked boxes of papers into the counting halls. Although officially impossible, there was evidence from more than a dozen seats that it had occurred or been attempted. A clue as to how this was done was provided in June 1993, in a press report of a workshop in Ghana at which Electoral Commissioner Habel Nyamu, one of the two dissident Commissioners and the man responsible for Central Province, gave a paper on how to improve the functioning and role of Electoral Commissions. In his opening remarks, Nyamu made an extraordinary allegation, recorded by Kwendo Opanga in the *Daily Nation,* that 'to date, nobody in the world is prepared to tell the Commission (Kenya's) the whereabouts of 150 ballot boxes which were not received at the airport by the Commission's security force from the police'.[144] If this is true, it finally tells us how some boxes got out from Commission stores into the election – they were never placed there in the first place. To make it plausible, these boxes had to be prepared beforehand, transported to the seats where they would be inserted, serialised as copies of real boxes or with similar numbers, stuffed with ballots and then stored ready to slip in at a suitable moment. We have already enumerated stuffing and/or box insertions in Lamu West, Mvita, Nakuru Town, Molo, Kitui West, Sabatia, Kajiado North, Kitutu Chache, Baringo East, Msambweni, Garsen and Galole. In addition, in Nairobi, observers reported unsuccessful attempts to bring stuffed boxes into the count in Starehe and Langata. In Kirinyaga, a NEMU count certifier spotted an attempt to add eight boxes into the counting hall in one seat, though they were not counted.[145] In Laikipia West unsuccessful attempts were made to delay the count and introduce stuffed boxes.[146] In Kisumu Town, one of KANU's few targeted seats in the area, the NEMU DLO reported without comment that on polling day 'a businesswoman was beaten after being found with ballot boxes in her premises'.[147] In Elijah Mwangale's Kimilili seat in Bungoma, there was an attempt to sneak in one extra ballot-box, 25477-P, part-way through the count. It was spotted and the NEMU monitor threatened with eviction by the Returning Officer if he protested publicly. The box was not counted and it later vanished.[148]

In the Presidency, it is quite clear that Daniel arap Moi won the election legitimately. In comparison with each individual opposition candidate, Moi genuinely had greater and more broadly based support, particularly in the apolitical, less densely populated and government-controlled areas. Whether this would still have been the case had the competition for votes in the previous months been fairer is, of course, more questionable. On the other hand, it is equally clear that no other candidate would have won outright victory. Moi's total was inflated by double registration, importation of votes, and mass open voting in Nakuru, Narok, Uasin Gishu, Baringo, Elgeyo-Marakwet, Nandi, Kericho, Bomet, Pokot and Samburu. An educated estimate suggests that between 100,000 and 130,000 votes were manufactured in these Districts. Adding a number of other dubious results, perhaps 150,000–200,000 of Moi's 1.9 million votes were fabricated. Some opposition votes were probably destroyed to ensure that no opponent achieved 25 per cent in the Rift Valley and the North-Eastern Province. Matiba, who ran second with 1.4 million votes, was the candidate with the greatest apparent chance of defeating Moi. This figure is probably a reasonably accurate estimate of his true vote, however, as FORD-Asili was the beneficiary of malpractices in Nakuru, Nairobi and possibly Murang'a. FORD-Asili was less likely to have experienced vote destruction in the North-East, Central Rift Valley or Coast Province, as Asili was not the main challenger here. The vote for Odinga appears a slight under-count overall, influenced by events in Kisii, the Coast and the North-East. An estimate of misplaced ballots for Odinga would exceed 50,000. Kibaki's figure is also probably too low, by 50,000–100,000 votes, particularly in the central Rift, where the DP were the main opposition, Kisii, and Eastern Province.

Nonetheless, given the huge size of Moi's victory, rigging at this level could not alter the result. Moi still appears to be 300,000 votes clear of his nearest rival. Whether Moi received 25 per cent of the vote in five provinces is less clear, but the evidence suggests that he did. He certainly legitimately polled 25 per cent in the Rift Valley, North-East, Coast and Western Provinces. The major question is whether KANU's Eastern Province results were inflated to bring the President over the 25 per cent hurdle. In any case, there were no plans at all for a Presidential run-off between the two main candidates, no matter what the result had been. Despite the fact that a run-off between Moi and a second candidate was a likely scenario, the state had no intention of permitting the opposition to unite behind a single candidate and threaten Moi's survival: no funds were allocated and no organisation undertaken to prepare for such an eventuality.

In the Parliamentary elections, however, KANU did not receive the largest number of votes cast in an overall majority of the Parliamentary seats. Although it must remain circumstantial, our view is that KANU genuinely won only about 85 Parliamentary seats to the opposition's approximately 100, rather than the 100 seats KANU was declared to have won. In more seats than the KANU majority of 12, not only was there definite malpractice, but the outcome would have been different had the malpractice not taken place. Our analysis suggests that KANU probably lost 15–20 of the 100 seats it was declared to have won. The Nairobi and Central Province results were unaffected by KANU rigging, though FORD-Asili may have gained two seats illegitimately from FORD-Kenya in Nairobi. In Eastern Province, KANU should have lost Kitui West, Mutito and Mutomo, and possibly Tharaka, Machakos Town and Mwala. Nothing can be proved in the North-East. On the Coast KANU should have lost Garsen, Galole, Lamu West, Msambweni and probably Mvita; in the Rift Valley, Kajiado North and Rongai; in Western Province, Emuhaya (and possibly Vihiga and Mumias); and in Nyanza, Kitutu Chache, North Mugirango, Nyaribari Masaba and Bobasi. Substantial malpractice did not change the result in at least 20 other constituencies. Had all this not occurred, KANU would clearly have been the largest party with 85–90 seats, but the combined opposition would have won 100 constituencies (see Table 11.27).

Why was this scale of malpractice not detected by the observers ? There are several answers. The first is that, over roughly half the country, the vote and count were reasonably fair. Even in the seats listed here, many abuses were confined to a few ballot boxes, or unfair counting. Such issues could not change a result entirely – only if KANU was a serious contender could they tip the balance. Second, where KANU appears to have inflated the Presidential totals, it was done in a manner which is almost impossible to prove in law, and very difficult to prevent. Third, the manner in which the election was manipulated was different from District to District. If the Nandi votes were inflated, they were certainly rigged far more cleverly than those in Baringo or Tana River. Finally, electoral malpractice was reported in certain areas by numerous observers from many different groups – the problem was the inability to process these reports in time, and thus to gain a clear picture of the effects.

Enduring Interests and Ethnic Voting ?

The 1992 general election showed how polarised ethnically three of the five main communities in the country had become. The Kikuyu-dominated Districts of Central Province, Laikipia and Nakuru (the Kikuyu comprised over 95 per cent of the voting population in this area), cast 90 per cent of their votes for Kibaki and Matiba, 8 per cent for Moi (almost all in Nakuru, where the Kalenjin minority was substantial), and 2 per cent for Odinga (half in Nakuru). The unanimity of ethnic identification amongst the Kikuyu in the Presidential poll was near complete. The Luo (in the majority only in the 18 Luo seats of Nyanza) also voted entirely ethnically, polling 95 per cent of their votes for Odinga, 4 per cent for Moi and 1 per cent for Kibaki and Matiba combined. The Kalenjin majority in the five home Districts plus West Pokot and Eldoret voted 90 per cent for Moi, 8 per cent for Kibaki and Matiba combined (almost all in Eldoret) and 2 per cent for Odinga. Such polarisation bodes ill for any attempt to build an electoral system on lines other than 'alliances of communities'.

The parallels between the results of the 1963 and 1992 elections are striking, a reflection of the enduring nature of the differences in perceived self-interest between the 'majority' tribes and the less-developed communities. The struggle was now for control of an African state, not to wrest Independence from the British. The population had quadrupled, and the economic and social situation had changed immensely. Nonetheless, so many senior figures fought the election on such connected lines that on occasion the conflict reverberated back to the pre-Independence elections. The campaign saw talk of *Majimboism* and the unitary state, of land ownership and settlement; the use of detention without trial; and the need for a 'second liberation' from the legacy of colonialism so obviously shown by the persistent paranoia about the intentions of the British.

Comparing KANU's performance with that of the original KADU coalition of 1963, and the combined opposition parties with KANU in the same year, in two thirds of the Districts 1992 produced the same result as that seen nearly 30 years before. In 1963, KANU won Nairobi Province, the whole of Central Province and the Luo of Nyanza, just as the opposition did in 1992. They also carried Laikipia and Nakuru in the Rift Valley, just as the Kikuyu parties did 30 years later. KADU in 1963 won the whole Coast (minus the Taita) plus the Kalenjin, Maasai and Samburu areas of the Rift Valley, as KANU did in 1992. In 1963, as in 1992, the Luhya split three ways, some voting with the Kalenjin, some with the Kikuyu, others remaining independent. In 1963, the Kamba were divided between KANU and the African People's Party (APP); in 1992, between the DP and KANU, while the Embu and Meru voted in both elections predominantly with the Kikuyu. Overall, in 1992, the two FORDs and the DP together won 62 per cent of the vote, whilst in 1963 KANU and allied independents took roughly 65 per cent. The differences, however, are also illustrative. FORD's coalition was fundamentally more narrowly based than was KANU's in 1963. Although KANU in 1992 was weaker amongst the Bukusu of Bungoma and in the urban area of Mombasa than KADU had been in 1963, it proved stronger than Moi's old party had been amongst the Kisii, Kamba, Meru, Busia Luhya and Taita, and among some 'smaller tribes' – the Turkana, Teso and Kuria. In 1963, minor parties had acted as a 'third force' in the Kamba areas, Marsabit and Isiolo, whilst no elections were held in any of the Somali areas because of the *shifta* war. Such areas were vulnerable to state direction, and accordingly in 1992 KANU dominated these seats. Another change was that political competition was more open. In 1963, 33 of 37 Districts had voted overwhelmingly for one party or other. Only Narok, Kericho and Kakamega were split between the two major parties, while Kitui split KANU–APP. In 1992, by contrast, 14 of the same 37 areas (now divided into more Districts) split their vote; the main differences being the more open polling in Eastern and Western Provinces.

The Observers' Conclusions

The reaction to the election of the observer groups, both internal and external, was a critical issue. In each case, the audience for their reports was more external than internal, since the key issue, access to Western funds, remained unresolved.

The Foreign Observers

While the foreign observers, especially the IRI and Commonwealth teams, had played an important role during the election preparations, election monitoring had been their primary purpose. On election day, they had spread widely across the country. Now, they had to decide on two things: the fairness of the voting and counting process, and the overall validity and fairness of the whole election. Neither assessment was to be easy.

The IRI's preliminary statement of findings was released on Friday, 1 January 1993, and contained their key conclusions on the entire electoral process.[149] It revisited some of their earlier complaints about the conduct of the campaign. State manipulation of the administrative and security structure had 'damaged the electoral environment', the media had been repressed, candidates and supporters had been harassed, and significant numbers prevented from registering. There were administrative irregularities throughout the country, including improperly sealed boxes, and frequently security in boxes was compromised. The secrecy of ballots was also compromised because of high illiteracy rates and placement of booths. Registration problems were evident on polling day, with errors in the roll, double voting and purchase of voters' cards. The IRI also observed that, 'We discovered evidence to support complaints that registration lists were manufactured to allow for the importation of voters in Molo constituency,'[150] and expressed concern about the major fluctuations in voter turn-out. There had been delays in counting and reporting the results, partly as a result of administrative difficulties, but the IRI felt that there may also have been deliberate efforts to manipulate the process. Nonetheless, the IRI considered that Kenyans had displayed enormous commitment to the electoral process and 'heroic patience in the face of monumental delays'.[151] The police demonstrated in general 'restraint and professionalism', and the government and Electoral Commission had greatly improved in their attitude in the last few days.

The IRI was equivocal as to whether the election had been free or not. The elections constituted 'a significant and early step on Kenya's road back to democracy'.[152] Although there was evidence of cheating, it was not sustained or coordinated enough to invalidate the result. In the end, they failed to express a clear view either way, lamely concluding that 'the people of Kenya will be the final arbiters of whether this process has produced a free and fair result'.[153] A second follow-up statement was released on 4 January, when the counting was almost completed. This was slightly stronger in expression, recording grave concern about continued counting irregularities, and concluding that 'the electoral environment was unfair and the electoral process seriously flawed'.[154]

The IRI also acted as coordinators for the exchange of information between observers from the many different smaller groups, who at their meeting on 31 December in the Intercontinental Hotel's ballroom gave a similar picture to that presented by the Americans and Commonwealth. The Swedes were representative when they claimed that the problems had only been minor, and that 'this poll ... has been free and fair'.[155] Most were clearly inexperienced in African election monitoring or were poorly informed, in contrast to the IRI and Commonwealth teams.

The IRI's final 50-page report was published much later.[156] Its verdict, based on a longer period of analysis, was harsher, stressing the 'seriously flawed' nature of the election, and judging that 'most of the generally accepted standards for fair elections were not met', although they also argued that opposition disunity was a major contributing factor to their defeat. The IRI paid substantial attention to the problems already discussed in the voting arrangements, but insufficient attention to the count, and underestimated amongst other things the impact of the '100 per cent illiterates' approach in the KANU heartlands.[157]

The Commonwealth team was less critical throughout. Their first post-poll statement on 31 December 1992 was the strongest, expressing concern about the delays in issuing the results. It suggested that, in the area they visited, polling had been satisfactory despite 'the lack of real commitment on the part of the Government to the process of multi-party democracy'. They reaffirmed that 'there appears to be a reluctance to permit any real challenge in Districts which the ruling party considered to be its strongholds'.[158] Over the next three days, the team reassembled in Nairobi and drafted the official conclusion to the final report. This was published on 1 January 1993, just before the team left, whilst the final results were still trickling in. It was significantly weaker in tone, concluding that :

> Despite the fact that the whole electoral process cannot be given an unqualified rating as free and fair, the evolution of the process to polling day and the subse-

> quent count was increasingly positive to a degree that we believe that the results in many instances directly reflect, however imperfectly, the expression of the will of the people. It constitutes a giant step on the road to multi-party democracy.[159]

Their use of the phrase 'giant step' was questioned even by Great Britain's Baroness Chalker, who noted that the final report summary, written with more time, replaced 'giant' with 'first'. As with the IRI, these weasel words neither endorsed the elections not condemned them, reinforcing the impression of ambivalence surrounding Western interpretations of the result. When Commonwealth Secretary-General Anyaoku arrived in Kenya in January 1993, he received the draft report, and personally stressed that the election had 'broadly reflected the broad will of the Kenyan people'.[160] The final report issued on 25 January reaffirmed the original heavily qualified endorsement. Although listing many of the irregularities mentioned by the Americans and in this book, it refused to condemn the electoral process. The fact that the divisions in the opposition was a primary reason for their defeat, and their team's inability to prove that the irregularities seen were sufficient to invalidate the result, left the Commonwealth with little alternative but to give the election a qualified endorsement. Although the report was apparently one of the hardest-hitting Commonwealth reports ever, it failed to conclude whether the election was free and fair. The report skirted round irregularities, stating, for example, in contrast to the evidence presented here from NEMU, that they 'neither saw nor heard of substantiated evidence' of stuffing or substituted boxes.[161]

The issue of Justice Chesoni's bankruptcy, known to the opposition and published in the Kenyan press in the summer, raised a storm when publicised in the West by the British *Independent* on 11 January 1993. Although some Commonwealth officials had known of the bankruptcy for some time, the observer group was shown the documents after the election, not before, and there was a fierce debate over whether they should be published. Although it was agreed that the key documents detailing Chesoni's bankruptcy proceedings and financial problems would be included, they were in fact removed from the final report. Lord Tordoff stated, 'When the final document was signed, it was agreed that the documents would be part of the appendix. I am surprised they are not.'[162]

The Commonwealth report was particularly important outside the United States, as its verdict influenced whether the Kenyan government would soon become eligible once more for IMF, World Bank and multilateral donor aid. As a result, the Western press responded to the report with heavy criticism, and there was bitter debate in the British press as to whether the West had abandoned its commitment to democracy by legitimising the results of the election. A strong lobby argued that the Commonwealth group had failed in its fundamental duty, by refusing judgement on the issue for which it had been composed – whether the election was 'free and fair'. The *Guardian* questioned the validity of the election, whilst an *Independent* leader suggested the Commonwealth would regret its 'deeply ambiguous verdict'.[163] The *Independent* also asked the question, 'One wonders what, in the eyes of the Commonwealth, would constitute an unfree and unfair election.'[164] As *Africa Confidential* also argued on 8 January 1993, 'The West's "democracy police" have lost much of their credibility by their performance during the elections.' Although they knew the election had been unfair, they 'wanted to avoid being blamed for provoking civil unrest or for cutting off one of Africa's most potentially viable economies'.[165] The *Independent* suggested that Western governments had believed the presence of eminent persons would deter KANU from rigging: 'They were wrong and their bluff was called. They were not prepared to cry foul.'[166] The events of the election, plus the experiences of other observer groups in other countries, gave grounds for concern in several Western capitals, and inspired further thoughts on the role, purpose and approach of future Western electoral interventions.

The smaller observer groups also prepared their own internal or public reports. The European Community Mission submitted a report which did not differ substantially from that of the Commonwealth. The Norwegian component of the joint Scandinavian-Canadian delegation also prepared their own report, entitled *A Hobbled Democracy; The Kenya General Elections 1992*. This suggested that the irregularities and problems encountered in the run-up to the election 'cast very serious doubts indeed on the freeness and fairness' of the elections.[167] This report criticised the same issues as had the Americans and the Commonwealth team, but again concluded that, 'Despite countless irregularities observed, the authors of this report are not prepared to pass a judgement, in unequivocal terms, that the Kenyan general elections of 1992 were free and fair, or that they were not free and fair.'[168] They openly criticised the professionalism of the observers in general, and suggested that the rules governing monitoring were inadequate. They also raised publicly one of the major strategic mistakes made by the monitoring bodies, pointing out that 'Many of the international election observers had left the counting centres and the even the country long before counting was completed.'[169]

Most foreign governments quickly congratulated Moi on winning the election. In Britain, for example, the Commonwealth report and the election were debated in the House of Lords on 15 February 1993. During exchanges which included severe criticism of the regime, Baroness Chalker, despite her critical views in the past, was drawn into a robust defence of the KANU government, stating that:

> The return of President Moi was not the result of systematic rigging, or even of the malpractices described in the Commonwealth report, but of the division within the ranks of the opposition. Critics should bear in mind that no other country within a thousand miles of Kenya has given its electorate a similar opportunity to express its views.[170]

Kenyans, however, were profoundly dissatisfied with the performance of the foreign observer groups. There was a widely held perception that the Commonwealth particularly was unwilling to reject the election when their leaders would still have to meet with Moi around the table. The observers were also criticised heavily for being 'tourists', turning up just before the election, going to bed before the count was completed and leaving as soon as the election was over. The *Daily Nation* was particularly bitter. An editorial highlighted 'These blind observers and their slanted views', criticising those who were saying that the opposition leaders should accept Moi's victory. It angrily accused the foreign observers of having skewed the debate without enough real information, being too few to monitor activities properly, and spending too little time to detect sophisticated rigging. The *Nation* also suggested that:

> The observers might have come to Kenya with preconceived notions of how 'African' elections are usually conducted. When the observers failed to see blatant examples of bribery, police harassment, intimidation and other forms of gross violence, they concluded the process was being conducted in a free and fair manner.[171]

It is now reasonably clear that the foreign observers failed the crucial test – to report the outcome of the 1992 election correctly. Why they did this seems to stem from several interconnected things. The first problem was practical and logistical. None of the observer groups alone had the knowledge, statistical support or manpower to carry out a shadow count or evaluation of what was happening in the national context, and all were forced to rely on impressionistic evidence and the government, the press and the opposition for views.[172] They arrived late, some without extensive African and most without Kenyan experience. They were not organised to face a clever and determined campaign of resistance to their attempted scrutiny. Secondly, the experiences of the different observers were wildly different, some witnessing rigging, others not. The election was genuinely fair across enough of the country to prevent them from establishing – without the type of analyses carried out in this book – the likely extent and impact of malpractices, whilst the need to build a hasty consensus resulted in reports which failed to reach firm conclusions. From their personal observations, the situation in most of the seats the observers inspected was acceptable. They did not visit some of the areas where the problems were most acute, in the central Rift Valley, and most did not sit through the long, tense counts in which many of the problems emerged.

The third reason was the failure of the numerous independent groups to coordinate their activities and cooperate with each other as fully as possible. Though they worked together to an extent, each group had its own responsibilities and made many of its own arrangements. While the election day coverage was adequate, it could have been better. Equally important, the production of numerous different reports weakened the impact of each. Western governments did not succeed in binding together the internal and external observers into a single group. NEMU, particularly, had far better coverage, information and understanding of events than the foreigners, yet their slightly partisan report was effectively ignored, while the fair, but probably wrong reports from the Commonwealth and IRI teams received most attention.

Fourth, the foreign observers had no objective and impartial yardstick against which to measure the election. There was no clear understanding or agreement on what was the minimum acceptable level of malpractice permitted in an election that would still pass the undefined test the Kenyans had been set. Even if all the information had been available, it is hard to see the observers producing unambiguous conclusions, since they had set themselves ambiguous questions to answer. Finally, there may have been some 'bias' which predisposed the observer groups towards the government in a state of uncertainty.

The Kenyan Press, Local Observers, and the People

The internal monitors were more critical than the international monitors. NEMU released an initial statement on the elections on 2 January, expressing grave concern and calling the electoral process 'severely compromised'. Its subsequent report, *The Multi-Party General Elections in Kenya, 29 December 1992, The Report of the National Election Monitoring Unit (NEMU),* released on 3 March 1993, was by far the most complete and professional of the internal monitors. It collated the thousands of individual constituency reports and analysed them to draw overall conclusions about the election.[173] NEMU's conclusion was that 'the December 1992 elections were not free and fair', as the manner in which they were conducted even before polling day 'fell far short' of meeting the requirements, though on the positive side, the polls were by Kenyan standards competitive, and 'an important step in the development of multi-party democracy'.[174] NEMU criticised the opposition as exhausting their energies in self-destruction, but reserved their main anger for the government, which was accused of systematic bias in the preparations and holding of the election. As well as the actual events on polling day and the count, the report tried to tackle the identity card issue, criticised the preparation of the registers, and claimed that public inspection of the registers never took place 'due to the limited publicity given to it by the commission'.[175] Other issues NEMU criticised were (as with the Western observers) use of the media, administrative harassment, the tribal clashes, and the conduct of Chesoni. In NEMU's words, 'The charges of unpreparedness, partiality and inefficiency levelled against the Chairman and his Commission are, in our view, justified.'[176] In the final version of the report, published in June, the major change was the removal of all constituency-specific information, partly out of concern at being embroiled in election petitions. KANU, of course, rejected the report, calling it 'self-appointed, loaded with unproven and provocative anti-KANU allegations'.[177]

BEERAM issued an interim statement, on 31 December 1992, which noted some of the above problems and suggested that if they were not addressed by the Commission, then the election would not have been free and fair.[178] Their second press statement, on 3 January, remained ambivalent, noting anomalies but implying that Moi was legitimately elected as President and imploring all MPs and councillors to take their seats. Their report (issued in draft form), under the authorship of Manasses Kuria, the Anglican Primate and the Secretary/Executive Director of BEERAM, was the weakest of the three. Titled *The Road to Democracy,* it expressed concern at the various irregularities, including a few specific accusations about the areas they had visited. BEERAM claimed that the commission had 'deliberately caused the delays' in the count though they did not suggest why. It also specifically criticised the international observers for failing to monitor the count.[179] Their conclusion was that 'it is difficult for us at this stage to give a premium that the just concluded general elections were free and fair or NOT'.[180]

The NCWK's report fell mid-way between the two. It covered a wider area with better organisation and methodology than BEERAM's and provided a good picture of problems and issues of concern, particularly to women. The NCWK's conclusion was that 'we can safely conclude that the elections were not free, fair and peaceful',[181] though its analysis could have been improved. It conflated less relevant issues, such as late opening and the proportion of women in the electorate, with blatant rigging of the count, weakening the strength of its conclusions as an analysis of the fairness of the elections *per se*. The result was a set of figures which suggested that Nairobi and Central Province's elections were amongst the worst, when, in fact, the Central Province poll had been one of the best and most open.

Unsurprisingly, the opposition felt that it had been robbed of the election. On 1 January 1993, Matiba, Kibaki and Odinga called a joint press conference to reject the results, on the grounds that the election had been massively rigged. The response to their complaints from their supporters and the churches was critical, however, and their defeat was seen as a just punishment for their failure to unite. Under pressure both internally and from Western governments, the losers quickly agreed to take up their seats in Parliament. Matiba and his Kikuyu supporters, however, felt particularly bitter and refused from the beginning to accept the legitimacy of the election. In time, the DP and FORD-Kenya came to 'accept' the result, as a fitting punishment upon their failure to agree. They resolved to challenge the government through Parliament, and the polls through the courts.

The press were in open disagreement. Some took the view of *Mwananchi* that 'though riddled with uncountable irregularities, they were a crucial step down the road to multi-party democracy'.[182] Among the dailies, the *Kenya Times* heralded the result, as 'free and fair', calling the opposition leaders bad losers and accused them of 'schoolboy politics' in complaining.[183] The *Standard* knew where its bread was buttered, with a leader the day after Moi was sworn in headlined, 'Congratulations Daniel arap Moi', as it joined 'the rest of Kenyans in congratulating him and his party KANU for the overwhelming victory in the elections'.[184] The *Daily Nation* was more guarded, claiming rigging was extensive and that although KANU had won, the majority of voters had rejected them.[185] Even they, however, were prepared to headline (5 January 1993): 'Moi's in the seat, let's all back him.'[186] The hardline opposition magazines such as *Finance* and *Society* cried foul, of course, with *Finance* calling the elections 'shamelessly stolen'.[187]

When the result became clear, there was some anger against the Kamba amongst Kikuyu in Nairobi, and against the Luhya in some Luo-Luhya borderlands. There was also bitterness amongst many Luo that the Kikuyu had voted so overwhelmingly for one of their own, but in general the mood was quiet. Predictions of revolt by the Kikuyu in the event of defeat did not materialise, their spirits dampened by a combination of their total local victories, exhaustion and depression, and a simultaneous satisfaction that so many Ministers and KANU stalwarts had been defeated. There was a belief that KANU would be unable to govern effectively or to create a viable Cabinet from the rump of politicians with which Moi had been left. Some opposition leaders were not unhappy with the result, having secretly feared the triumph of one of the other opposition leaders almost as much as a weakened Moi's re-election. The internal observer groups also took their time reporting, thereby assisting the government in consolidating its authority at a time of uncertainty.

Overall, the verdict of the West was based on the logic that KANU was 'innocent until proven guilty', that its guilt was 'not proven', so the government was 'innocent'. That of Kenyans was in the main 'guilty until proven innocent', reflecting a significant difference in underlying perspective between the internal and external groups.

Conclusion

The 1992 election was over. The greatest test of the Kenyan political system since 1969, it had dominated political events and both the economy and social affairs since late 1991. KANU had won a decisive victory, based on the vote of less than one third of the country, partly as a result of the incompetence of the opposition, partly because of their willingness to bribe, threaten and cheat their way to victory, and partly because the government continued to represent the interests of key less-developed communities in the country, whose loyalties they were able to retain. Now, the political élite faced new challenges – to build a stable, Parliamentary democracy on the basis of a flawed election, an alienated and polarised population, and a government following a very different agenda.

Numerous technical recommendations on the electoral process can be made, many of which have already been described in the IRI report. Among the changes observers felt appropriate were, as expected, a multi-party Electoral Commission, more Parliamentary oversight of the civil service, a substantially improved and on-going voter registration process, more campaign time, new counting procedures, new campaign finance arrangements and better handling of electoral offences. All these are clearly needed, as was better organisation and preparation, and improved recruitment of polling clerks and officials. The IRI also called for further separation between KANU and the state, new rally procedures, open access to the media, and an end to civil service harassment. The problem is that either they cost money, or more importantly, they tend to weaken state control over the political process. As 1992 showed, administrative control of the political playing field was extremely important to a minority government's strategy. It is unlikely that many (if any) of the changes requested will be made before the next election, unless at that stage KANU feels sufficiently secure of victory to permit them. Better voter education is another issue which requires addressing. The abuse of the illiteracy process is a peculiarly Kenyan phenomenon which must also be addressed in future if elections are to be fairer. The NCWK therefore recommended that anyone able to sign their identity card should be required to vote secretly.[188]

Numerous improvements are also required in election monitoring. The Kenyan experience was in many ways a salutary one. Although the election was held and did not result in bloodshed, it seems that the objectives of the monitoring groups were either unclear, unlikely to be followed up in practice, or confused by their own multiplicity. A previously published standard for electoral contests certainly would have clarified the numerous different interpretations of 'free and fair'. Beyond this, it was a waste of resources and a source of great confusion to have so many independent monitoring groups and bodies, producing at least eight reports on the basis of different experiences. The West was determined that there be a multi-party election, and that was what it got. What they could not do was to enforce fairness in a situation where the government was determined to win. As Joel Barkan (a USAID official and key figure in the transmission of aid to the observer groups) also argued, the Kenyan elections exposed the limits of the donor community's ability to promote democratic reform. He noted that election monitoring can only be meaningful if it covers basic administrative issues, such as constituency boundaries and electoral law.[189] The observer groups' expectations were simultaneously too high and too low. They were too high in that they had not properly prepared or been funded to monitor cleverly organised, focused electoral manipulation. They were too low in that they were willing to accept the appearance of fairness without inquiring too far into the reality.

While the majority of the observer groups, both internal and external, viewed the election as a first key step on the road to greater openness, the evidence suggests, rather, that it was the high-point: 1992 is the closest that the opposition will get to defeating KANU in its current form.

Notes

1 See, for example, the views of foreign newsmen and observers at election time, as in the *EIU Kenya Quarterly Review*, No. 1, 1993, Julian Ozanne in the *Financial Times*, 31 December 1992, and the Norwegian report, B-A Andreassen, G. Geisler and A. Tostensen, *A Hobbled Democracy: The Kenya General Elections 1992*, p. 31.

2 When DP ex-Ministers continued in private to insist that they would never be led by an uncircumcised man, it suggests a real ill will, not just a disagreement over tactics. Private conversation, December 1992.

3 In the two Lamu seats, for example, such cases were running at a rate of only one to three per polling station. Observer reports, NEMU, Lamu constituencies.

4 *National Assembly and Presidential Elections Act*, Cap.7, p. 35. The NEMU Report draft identified that in 35 of the 107 seats where they observed the count, no such statement was made. NEMU Report draft, p. 233.

5 *Kenya Times*, 30 December 1992, p. 3.

6 Julian Ozanne, *Financial Times*, 31 December 1992.

7 The *Daily Nation* headlined on New Year's Day, 'Kenya Set for Minority Government', *Daily Nation*, 1 January 1993, p. 1.

8 See Charles Hornsby, 'The Member of Parliament in Kenya, 1969–83', unpublished D.Phil. thesis, Oxford, 1986, Chapter 5.

9 In Nyeri, there was concern about pro-DP intimidation and campaigning, and KANU petitioned five of the six seats after the poll.

10 Tabitha Seii, in *Society*, 28 September 1992, p. 38.

11 The constituency borders Cherangani in Trans-Nzoia.
12 Kericho town was festooned in posters for KANU's Bishop Tanui, and no hint of opposition presence could be found. Personal observation, December 1992. The opposition split their Presidential votes, and gave arap Keino and the FORD-Asili candidate 10 per cent of the vote each.
13 NEMU poll report, Baringo Central.
14 NEMU poll report, Baringo North.
15 NEMU election monitor, Baringo DLO report.
16 NEMU Baringo East DLO poll report. The certifier recorded nothing at all.
17 Several NEMU poll monitors and count certifiers in Kerio South.
18 Nandi contacts informally reported after the election that they believed the true turn-out had been no more than 30 per cent, and that Moi was extremely displeased with the result.
19 NEMU count certifier, Konoin.
20 For example, see the *Weekly Review*, 1 January 1993. Some NEMU reports suggest a poll was carried out, but no result were reported.
21 The rehabilitation of the plant became a crucial public issue during the Ouko enquiry when it emerged that Ouko had been working to open it against the opposition of a powerful clique of politicians, who according to the testimony had business interests in the rival Muhoroni plant.
22 *Weekly Review*, 4 September 1992, p. 10.
23 Charles Owino was manager of the Kisumu branch of the National Bank of Kenya, where Oyugi banked. Oyugi was widely believed to be the source of Owino's enormous funds, which he distributed around the constituency.
24 *Daily Nation*, 4 December 1992, p. 9.
25 *Kenya Times*, 31 December 1992, pp. 13 and 20.
26 *Kenya Times*, 1 January 1993, p. 14.
27 With less fertile soils and a drier climate, the area was the poorest of the Kikuyu core Districts, and many of its male inhabitants had moved to Nairobi to work.
28 All information taken from count certifiers' reports and poll monitors' reports, NEMU.
29 Wolf's forthcoming work on Voi and Wundanyi, *Multi-Party Politics in Taita, 1963 vs. 1992: From KANU to KADU*, deals in detail with the economics and social structure of the area, and draft sections from this work have been used several times in this section.
30 He lost his Ministerial seat in 1988 when he supported Kibaki during the attacks on him as Vice-President. Mwamunga also owned substantial land in Voi town, plus local ranches, and his alleged banking of sums raised by Moi for a hospital had also raised the political temperature. FORD-Asili gave him a clear run.
31 *Daily Nation*, 1 January 1993, p. 2. Also petition in *Weekly Review*, 19 February 1993, p. 14.
32 *Kenya Times*, 31 December 1992, p. 5.
33 NEMU, Kwale DLO report. The NCWK reported problems with ballot box identification.
34 See Wolf, MS forthcoming, *Multi-Party Politics*.
35 *Ibid.*, p. 4.
36 This background information was contained in a briefing on the political situation in the District from the NEMU DLO for Samburu.
37 NEMU, Turkana DLO report.
38 *Standard*, 28 November 1992, p. 12.
39 PICK's Arap Birir backed Moi for the presidency, though some Kipsigis votes did go to Odinga.
40 NEMU, Samburu DLO report.
41 NEMU, Samburu DLO report.
42 NEMU, Turkana DLO report.
43 See the reports in *Kenya Taking Liberties*, July 1991, An Africa Watch Report, Chapters 15 and 16.
44 The area has provided the vast majority of senior Somali politicians and administrators.
45 KANU's candidate was Degodia, and the majority of the constituency Ajuran.
46 *Standard*, 5 January 1993, p. 1.
47 Various Dujis NEMU reports. NEMU reported that, despite the facts above, the count otherwise appeared acceptable.

48 FORD-Kenya petitioned, without success.
49 The original border between North-East and Eastern Provinces defined the limits of Somali migration.
50 This was reported by both NEMU and the BEERAM observer. BEERAM Report, p. 21.
51 Njiru was forced to go to Odinga for the FORD-Kenya nomination, a poisoned chalice, as he was unable to defect to the DP or FORD-Asili owing to his personal unpopularity amongst the opposition and the fact that they already had candidates.
52 *Daily Nation*, 14 October 1992, p. 4.
53 Angaine himself was teetering between supporting the KANU candidate and the DP. *Kenya Times*, 20 December 1992 Focus p. 8.
54 Personal conversation with local residents, 1993.
55 Kiti, *Kenya Times*, 31 December 1992, p. 18. It was also claimed that the DP candidate distributed some boxes and ballots himself. *Daily Nation*, 3 January 1992, p. 3.
56 *Standard*, 13 October 1993, p. 4.
57 *Kenya Times*, 31 December 1992, p. 2.
58 FORD-Asili press statement, 29 December 1992 (timed 11.30).
59 *Kenya Times*, 2 January 1993, p. 3.
60 EBU/44 official, NEMU poll monitor report.
61 NEMU, Embu DLO report. Corroborated in principle though not in detail by the figures here.
62 Japeth Kiti, KANU NEO, in *Kenya Times*, 1 January 1993, p. 5
63 It was here that Moi made his Sh20 million 'personal donation', interpretable as an attempt to save KANU and Mwangale in Bungoma.
64 Personal conversation with a FORD-Kenya leader 1993.
65 *Daily Nation*, 4 January 1993, p. 4 and 22 June 1993, p. 3. KANU petitioned two Bungoma losses, once of which was later to result in a nullification of a FORD-Kenya leader's victory on the grounds that oathing had taken place, a curious result.
66 Whole blocks of names beginning with A, M, O and W appeared to have been deleted in Moi Avenue station, tending to under-count the Luhya and Luo vote particularly (and to a lesser extent the Kikuyu). Elsewhere, the voting was mainly satisfactory.
67 *Kenya Times*, 31 December 1992, p. 5.
68 NCWK Report, p. 19.
69 NEMU, also *Kenya Times*, 31 December 1992, p. 19.
70 *Weekly Review*, 5 February 1993, p. 17. Foreign observers informally corroborated this report.
71 NEMU count certifier's report, Dagoretti.
72 *Daily Nation*, 3 January 1993, p. 4. Again the foreign observers corroborated.
73 They demanded a re-scrutiny and recount of the votes. *Weekly Review*, 5 February 1993, p. 12.
74 See *Weekly Review*, 5 February 1993, p. 15. His petition failed on technical grounds.
75 *Daily Nation*, 13 January 1993, p. 6
76 They were filled with KANU T-shirts. *Weekend Mail*, 7 January 1993, p. 30. See also NCWK Report, p. 19.
77 V. Brittain, in the *Guardian*, 25 January 1993.
78 For example, Steffan Ndichu, editor of a monthly news magazine, *Thika Times*, had been gunning for the DP and George Muhoho in Juja since the establishment of multi-partyism. See, for example, *Thika Times*, January 1992.
79 In Limuru, for example, KANU's candidate and Moi's District proxy, Kuria Kanyingi, used to distribute money from his house to the local area on a regular basis, which people happily accepted, without the slightest intention of voting for him.
80 Details on the Githunguri election will be given in a forthcoming paper by one of the authors. Magugu's solid 10 per cent again gives a good estimate of the kind of margin (5 per cent+) a Ministerial position gave a candidate in an opposition area.
81 *Standard*, 23 November 1992, p. 13.
82 *Standard*, 3 December 1992, p. 14.
83 Despite its cosmopolitan nature and heavy ethnic competition, Nairobi is better seen as a 'spill-over' area from competition between opposition parties, since KANU was of little relevance in most seats.
84 NEMU poll report, Nakuru town.
85 BEERAM Report, p. 21.

86 BEERAM Report, p. 21.
87 IRI observer, 2 January 1993.
88 *Kenya Times*, 1 January 1993, p. 14.
89 Faxed Asili letter, 29 December 1992 (timed 17.09).
90 *Daily Nation*, 1 January 1993, p. 2. Njenga Mungai complained of anomalies in the ballot papers being counted from Chebara PS, Kipkewa PS (61/1), Baringo PS (63/1) and Ndoinet. *Kenya Times*, 1 January 1993, p. 3.
91 Matiba press statement, 27 December 1992. Also personal conversations with Molo Parliamentary candidate, November 1993.
92 IRI observer, 2 January 1993.
93 NEMU poll monitors' report, Molo.
94 NEMU count certifiers' report, Nakuru East.
95 NEMU poll monitors' report, Rongai.
96 NEMU count certifier, Rongai. This was also spotted also by FORD-Kenya agents, and protests were ignored by the Returning Officer.
97 NEMU poll monitor in Rongai, and IRI observer, 2 January 1993.
98 *Kenya Times*, 2 January 1993, p. 22.
99 MP Samson ole Tuya, in *Daily Nation*, 8 November 1992, p. 5.
100 He was the sole contender from the Ildamat clan, whilst Ntimama and Tiampati were both from the Purko clan.
101 *Standard*, 28 November 1992, p. 12.
102 Local journalist, personal conversation 1993.
103 BEERAM Report, p. 20.
104 FORD-Asili fax letter, 30 December 1992 (timed 10.05), and *Kenya Times*, 2 January 1993, p. 4.
105 Letter of 28 December 1992 from Chesoni.
106 *Kenya Times*, 1 January 1993, pp. 4–5, and conversations with FORD-Kenya leader December 1993.
107 This was where the secondary processing and import substitution plants erected in the 1970s were concentrated. Kiliku was also bolstered by his solid Akamba vote from the 10,000 voters of the Akamba Handicrafts Cooperative Society.
108 Mvita NEMU poll monitor report.
109 *Weekly Review*, 5 February 1993, p. 15.
110 The recount found that KANU had actually won. *Standard*, 13 October 1993, p. 1.
111 FORD-Kenya won, and the DP petitioned.
112 Despite allegedly paying off all the debts, he remained bankrupt, and once his advances to KANU were shunned, he turned to the DP and took much of Machakos and Makueni with him. Many of the DP offices opened in the Districts were opened by him, rather than Kibaki, and he was extremely active in their support.
113 The reasons behind this decision are unclear, since Mutisya had made preparatory moves to contest. He was, however, according to the *Kenya Times*, 'long regarded as one of the liabilities in the ruling party and should have been jettisoned earlier'. *Kenya Times*, 20 December 1992, p. 7.
114 Nonetheless, the DP petitioned four of their five defeats.
115 *Kenya Times*, 2 January 1993, p. 4.
116 *Daily Nation*, 4 January 1993, p. 4. *Daily Nation*, 6 January 1993, p. 14. Oathing is a traditional practice of mass swearing on pain of suffering or death to achieve a common goal, converted since the 1950s into a political instrument, and widely used in the 1963, 1969 and 1974 elections.
117 Although the Mbooni NEMU observers were happy, slightly surprisingly. Reports from the NEMU DLO and count certifier for Mbooni.
118 NEMU Makueni poll monitor report, Makueni District.DLO report
119 NEMU count certifier, Kibwezi.
120 This was seen on a video recording made by the DP candidate.
121 *Daily Nation*, 6 January 1993, p. 14
122 NEMU Mutito poll monitor report.
123 NEMU Mutito poll monitor report and count certifier report.
124 *Kenya Times*, 1 January 1993, p. 14 and also NEMU poll monitor, Kitui North.
125 NEMU Kitui North poll monitor reports. Although the administration and the count was generally felt to be acceptable, the Returning Officer refused to give his name.

126 FORD-Asili fax, 29 December 1992 (timed 11.30).
127 KANU were also allegedly buying opposition voting cards and destroying them. Robert Shaw, Chris Bichage, personal conversation, 14 December 1992.
128 NEMU reported that the count was satisfactory, but the DP petitioned.
129 NEMU count certifier's report, Kitutu Chache.
130 *Weekly Review*, 19 February 1993, p. 15.
131 *Kenya Times*, 2 January 1993, p. 3.
132 *Sunday Nation*, 3 January 1993, p. 16.
133 Burudi Nabwera, *Daily Nation*, 2 December 1992, p. 4.
134 Vihiga District was carved out of Kakamega soon before the election for the Maragoli, Tiriki and Banyore sub-tribes of the Luhya.
135 *Daily Nation*, 3 December 1992.
136 The Vihiga tycoon Abraham Ambwere supported the other KANU candidates, but refused to support M'Maitse. *Daily Nation*, 3 December 1992, p. 15.
137 There was talk of the losers in the KANU nominations in Emuhaya throwing their weight behind FORD-Asili because of the rigging.
138 NEMU Poll Monitor, Sabatia.
139 FORD-Asili press release, 29 December 1992 (timed 23.07).
140 *Kenya Times*, 31 December 1992, p. 18.
141 The result was believed to be determined by the votes of the Marachi sub-group of the Luhya, without a major candidate of their own. The seat was a comparatively high profile one, as Attorney-General Wako came from Nambale and so did the NSSF boss Martin Kunguru.
142 Despite the *Daily Nation's* impression that Kibaki was running Moi almost level in the area. *Daily Nation*, 7 November 1992, p. 11.
143 Oginga Odinga in *Daily Nation*, 30 August 1993, p. 4.
144 Habel Nyamu, speaking in Accra end May/early June 1993. Reported in *Daily Nation*, 5 June 1993, p. 16.
145 Reported by the NEMU DLO, Kirinyaga.
146 NEMU count certifiers' report, Laikipia West.
147 NEMU, Kisumu DLO report.
148 NEMU count certifier, Kimilili.
149 IRI, *Preliminary Statement of Findings Kenyan General Elections December 29, 1992,* 1 January 1993.
150 *Ibid.*, p. 2.
151 *Ibid.*, p. 1.
152 *Ibid.*, p. 2.
153 IRI, *Preliminary Statement,* 1 January 1993.
154 IRI, *January 4, 1993 Follow-Up Statement*, 29 December 1992.
155 Personal observation, 31 December 1992.
156 IRI, *Kenya: The December 29, 1992 Elections*, 1993.
157 They said, 'Whilst this may have occurred in isolated polling stations, the IRI did not hear reports that it was a widespread occurrence.' *Ibid.*, p. 47.
158 Commonwealth News Release, 31 December 1992.
159 Commonwealth Report, p. 40.
160 *Daily Nation*, 7 January 1993, p. 1, quote from Commonwealth Press Statement, 5 January 1993.
161 Commonwealth Report, p. 37.
162 Lord Tordoff, in the *Independent*, 25 January 1993.
163 *Independent* leader, 25 January 1993, p. 18.
164 *Independent,* 25 January 1993, p. 18.
165 *Africa Confidential,* Vol. 34, No.1, 8 January 1993.
166 *Independent,* 25 January 1993, p. 18. Commonwealth Secretary-General Anyaoku responded to these serious criticisms in 1 February's *Independent,* stressing the group's technical contributions and backroom dealings to secure fairer polls.
167 B-A. Andreassen, G. Geisler and A. Tostensen, *A Hobbled Democracy; The Kenya General Elections 1992,* p. v.
168 *Ibid.*, p. ix.
169 *Ibid.*, p. 30. The AFL-CIO representative in the contentious Nakuru count, for example, had left at 6.15 a.m., before the first polling station had been counted. Of the groups

attending the workshop on 31 December 1992, only the IRI appeared to have the majority of its staff still in the field.

170 Baroness Chalker, Hansard, Vol. 542, No. 95, 15 February 1993.
171 *Daily Nation*, commentary by Cathy Majtenyi, 13 January 1993, p. 6.
172 No parallel count was done apart from that at NEMU.
173 Their raw constituency and polling station reports have been extensively used in this book.
174 NEMU Final Report, p. 91.
175 The *Weekly Review* claimed in contrast that the EC did invite the public to inspect the registers soon after the end of registration. *Weekly Review*, 12 March 1993, p. 10.
176 NEMU Final Report, p. 88.
177 Kamotho, reported in *Standard*, 1 May 1993, p. 13.
178 Manasses Kuria and Benjamin K. Mwangi, *The Road to Democracy*, Peace Foundation Africa, 1993, p. 24.
179 *Ibid.*, pp. 19–21.
180 *Ibid.*, p. 29.
181 NCWK Report, p. 27.
182 *Mwananchi*, January/February, 1993, p. 1.
183 *Kenya Times*, 2 January 1993, p. 6.
184 *Standard*, 5 January 1993, p. 8.
185 *Sunday Nation*, leader, 3 January 1993, p. 6.
186 *Daily Nation*, 5 January 1993, p. 6.
187 *Finance*, 31 January 1993, editorial.
188 NCWK Report, p. 31.
189 J. Barkan, 'Kenya: Lessons from a Flawed Election', in *Journal of Democracy*, Vol. 4, No. 3 July 1993.

Twelve

KANU Rules the Nation

For Kenya, and for all the political parties, 1993 was a year of retrenchment and consolidation. KANU continued to strengthen its grip, while the opposition fragmented and realigned itself in the wake of defeat. As few people had experienced multi-party democracy, the first few months saw guarded sparring as all sides assessed their relative strengths and the limits of legal and practical authority. The election was quickly set aside, save for the election petitions, and the various groups now began for the first time to come to grips with the concepts of government and opposition, both in the new multi-party Parliament and outside in the country.

The themes which had dominated 1991–2 – state power, ethnic solidarity, the primacy of self-interest and of economics – continued to dominate political discourse. For KANU the worst was over as the opposition had been faced and defeated at its time of maximum support and unity. Nonetheless, care was required. With new, unstable political parties, and ethnicity a driving force, there was no guarantee that some event or individual might not initiate a new alliance or drive 'KANU tribes' into the hands of the enemy. It was essential to demonstrate that there was no alternative to KANU. KANU's strategy was therefore one of containment and attrition, not consensus, focusing on bringing marginal Districts back into the fold, isolating the core opposition-supporting communities (the Kikuyu, Luo and Bukusu Luhya), and on gradually weakening and further dividing the opposition parties, in the expectation that – isolated, without authority or money – they could be undermined gradually and picked off one by one. The key tasks were to rebuild a stable national political hierarchy, to contain the opposition, and to try to deal with the critical problem of the economic near-collapse they had instigated and the refusal of the West to resume direct balance of payment support.

The New Government

Within one hour of Zacchaeus Chesoni's declaring Moi the victor in the

Photo 12.1 Daniel arap Moi is sworn in as Kenya's first multi-party elected President

Courtesy of Nation Group Newspapers

1992 elections, at 10.57 a.m. on 4 January 1993, Daniel arap Moi was sworn in as Kenya's first multi-party elected President. It took ten days, the longest period in Kenyan history, to come up with his new administration, testimony to the difficulty of building a stable government from the remnants of the KANU Parliamentary party, and to the negotiations going on with other groups to incorporate them into the government.

The new government reflected the need both to woo the West and to assert KANU's authority. With the need to incorporate all communities gone, the number of Ministries was reduced from 32 to 23, and the number of Ministers from 33 to 25. Various Agriculture Ministries were consolidated into one super-Ministry; Labour and Manpower Development were combined; and other departments were streamlined. The Cabinet also symbolised the way in which policy would be conducted and rewards allocated in the new multi-party state. KANU's greatest weakness, having no representatives from the Kikuyu or Luo, was ignored. Rather than bringing into the government ex-politicians, businessmen or technocrats from these communities, Moi chose to nominate to Parliament and bring into the Cabinet two of his most loyal defeated Ministers, Dalmas Otieno and KANU Secretary-General Joseph Kamotho. This was a major break with precedent.[1] Kamotho and Otieno were the only Kikuyu and Luo nominated and given government positions, while the third nominated Minister, Kamwithi Munyi from Embu, was also a hardliner. No Kenyan government had ever had more than one nominated Minister, and the choice of Kamotho and Otieno, both decisively rejected by the electorate, was a snub to the voters. Their appointment was intended to ensure that influential Ministers, backed by the wealth of government patronage, could still act as the government's emissaries to the opposition-voting communities. Because of the near-exclusion of the Kikuyu and Luo, the ethnic composition of the new government was very unbalanced.

Moi's appointments rewarded loyalty in the key swing communities. Thus, although Simeon Nyachae did not get the Vice-Presidency, he was compensated with the number three position on the Cabinet list, taking control of the new Agriculture super-Ministry. General Mulinge's work in Machakos was similarly rewarded. Indeed, the Kamba were represented particularly strongly, being the second-largest Parliamentary group in KANU after the Kalenjin, with four Ministers.[2] The marginal Luhya also did very well, with four Ministries: Amos Wako continued to hold the Attorney-General's post; Musalia Mudavadi was promoted to be the new Finance Minister, replacing George Saitoti, in return for holding Vihiga District; Philip Masinde from Busia was reappointed; and, as a reward for his loyalty and as the government's only representative in the important Kakamega District, ex-dissident Joshua Angatia entered the Cabinet for the first time. The two Meru victors, Minister M'Mukindia and Jackson Kalweo, both received posts, as did Kamwithi Munyi for the Embu. Eastern Province, therefore, ended up with seven of the 25 member Cabinet (28 per cent). This approach ensured strong KANU and government representation in the marginal communities, who had to be brought across to KANU *en masse* to ensure victory in the future.

The 'safe' government areas profited little. Noah Ngala and Darius Mbela were the sole Coast Minsters, despite KANU's truimph in the region, and Maalim Mohammed remained the sole Somali. There were five Kalenjin Ministers, but they were kept away from the limelight: Moi represented Baringo; Francis Lotodo was rewarded for his loyalty in West Pokot; Jonathan Ng'eno, the ex-Speaker, received his reward in Kericho for his work in the previous Parliament; and, in a surprise appointment, newcomer John Sambu, a little-known figure and former ally of the late Bishop Muge, entered the Cabinet from Nandi, in preference to the far better-known Henry Kosgey. The Maasai retained their two key leaders, George Saitoti and William ole Ntimama.

The decision to keep George Saitoti as Vice-President, despite his appalling profile, reflected Moi's need to ensure that someone without independent political authority held the Vice-Presidency. Saitoti was also believed to be heavily supported by *éminence grise* Nicholas Biwott, who remained on the backbenches.[3] Although he lost his Finance portfolio, taking Planning and National Development instead, Saitoti officially remained number two, and other indicators suggested the new Cabinet would be as hardline as its predecessor. Moi also followed a clever new strategy of placing young, urbane professionals in the two key posts to deal with the West. The 32-year-old Luhya Musalia Mudavadi became Minister of Finance and Stephen Musyoka, also from a neutral ethnic group (the Kamba), took the Foreign Ministry. Western reactions to the new government were varied. Although his power had been trimmed, the donor community was extremely concerned about the continued presence of Saitoti. There was also concern about the appointment of Mudavadi, because of his youth and family relationship to Moi.

The Assistant Ministers, who made up the remainder of the government, were overwhelmingly 'backwoodsmen' from the minority tribes, though their numbers were cut dramatically. As usual, despite high expectations, no women Ministers were appointed, and only one Assistant Minister, who was allocated the traditional women's Ministry of Culture and Social Services.[4] Loyalty remained a key criterion in the associated reshuffle of the top ranks of the civil service. Nine permanent secretaries were removed, several of them Kikuyu from Murang'a. At the same time, some of the more controversial civil servants were reappointed, such as Wilfred Koinange as Permanent Secretary to the Treasury and Eric Kotut at the Central Bank. Moi's choice of his twelve nominated Members was another important signal. In the end, five defeated Ministers were appointed back to Parliament by the President, adding Francis ole Kaparo, the defeated Minister for Industry in Laikipia, Luo Wilson Ndolo Ayah and George Ndotto from Kitui to Otieno, Munyi and Kamotho. In contravention of KANU's manifesto commitment that 'Women must be given a higher proportion of the nominated seats in Parliament',[5] no woman was nominated. Following ole Kaparo's election as Speaker (see below), he was replaced by G. G. Kariuki, the other KANU candidate in Laikipia, in March 1993.

The New National Assembly

The new National Assembly, the first multi-party Parliament since 1969, was a dramatic contrast to its toothless predecessor. The vast majority of the 1988 team, many of them rigged into their positions, were rejected as soon as multi-party competition required plausible candidates. Even

Table 12.1 How the Incumbents Fared

Date of election	Number not in election	Lost	Won	% Re-elected (of new house)
1969	7	86	56	35%
1974	4	79	74	47%
1979	6	73	77	49%
1983	3	59	93	59%
1988	10	69	79	42%*
1992	72	65	49	26%

* 1988 saw a new house of 188 elected members, rather than 158.

Source: Elections and Political Change in Kenya 1969–88 and updated analysis for 1992.

counting as 'incumbents' the elected MPs who defected to the opposition in January 1993, and lost their seats as a result, only a quarter of the house had sat there four months before. This was the most drastic change in the Kenyan Parliament since 1963. Several of the so-called 'newcomers', however, were far from new to Parliament, and were recapturing seats they had held previously. These included Odinga, barred from standing since 1969, Shikuku, rigged out in 1988, and Matiba, expelled from KANU in 1989. Members of the previous KANU government did as badly as everyone else. Unlike previous elections, incumbent Ministers were slaughtered, with a re-election rate little different from that of Assistant Ministers and backbenchers.

Nevertheless, the new electoral system did bring into the political arena a new leadership, younger and less compromised by association with the old regime; combined with party selection procedures and the success of less-experienced underdog candidates in some areas, this led to the largest change in the composition of the house since 1963. No less than 54 per cent of the new Assembly had never been elected before. KANU had, unsurprisingly, the highest proportion of ex-MPs (59 per cent). Even in KANU, however, many new faces emerged, particularly on the Coast, which saw a real change in leadership, and in Kisii in Nyanza. Ford-Kenya came second, with 20 old-timers among 31 MPs, many of them in the large group of 'Odinga' Luo MPs from Nyanza. The rest of the FORD-Kenya Members were the Young Turks, few of whom had even stood before. FORD-Asili had the fewest ex-Members proportionately (29 per cent), only 9 of 31. Because the DP represented the establishment over much of Central Province, the Asili candidates had been chosen from lesser-known people, who had not stood before, and mainly came through on the Matiba bandwagon. The FORD-Asili new boys from Central Province were known as *manyangas,* a type of new *matatu.*[6] The DP, originally seen as the old guard party *par excellence,* had only seven previously elected MPs.

In socio-economic terms, the new Parliament was, as always, a middle-aged, predominantly male, well-educated, high-status group, part of the small élite which had always run Kenya. The oldest MP was now *Jaramogi* himself, at 81. The youngest was probably the 28-year-old Patrick Mzee (KANU), born in 1964, who inherited his father's seat in Turkana. Daniel arap Moi remained the father of the house, as the only man continuously in Parliament since Independence (indeed, since 1956), although a number of opposition MPs had played important roles in the Independence and pre-Independence political debates, including Odinga and Shikuku. There were some differences, however, from previous Parliaments. Kenyan women made a greater political impact in 1992 than ever before: 19 candidates stood, compared with 9 in 1983 and 1988, and six were elected as MPs, compared with a previous high of four in 1979. For the first time a significant female business and economic élite were contesting. Over half (ten) of the candidates came from the DP, but only three of their women won, two of these in Ukambani. KANU had one victory from three, FORD-Kenya one from five, and Asili's sole female candidate was a winner. FORD-Asili, the most aggressive and populist party, was also the most male-dominated.[7] Gender issues were stressed more widely both during the campaign and through, for example, the work of the NCWK in monitoring the elections from the viewpoint of women.

In ethnic background, Kenyan MPs remained closely representative of their communities. The ethnic breakdown of candidates and of MPs has remained essentially constant, due to the localist nature of the political system. Candidates from outside groups (for example, a Kikuyu in Luoland) and from small minorities inside a constituency seldom stand. A candidate is only considered qualified to represent an area if he is local, and his support will tend to be concentrated in the communities with which he has closest links, that is from where his family originate. Competing political parties tend to break down the direct relationship between ethnicity of population and candidates. Thus in 1963 a few MPs were elected in areas where they did not come from the majority group. This was seen to only a limited extent in 1992, however, a reflection of the enduring nature of ethnic differentiation and the ethnicity of the parties, and all bar three or four MPs represented minority communities in an area. George Nthenge was an exception in Nairobi, where he won a victory for FORD-Asili in a setting where his Kamba compatriots were in a minority. KANU was the most ethnically diverse of the parties, with by far the widest national coalition and at least twenty different ethnic groups amongst their elected MPs. FORD-Kenya was the most diverse opposition party, with members from seven different ethnic groups, whilst the DP and FORD-Asili were much more narrowly based (five and three groups respectively). All three opposition parties had more than 50 per cent of their Parliamentary party from one ethnic group: the Kikuyu in Asili (67 per cent) and the DP (52 per cent), the Luo (61 per cent) in FORD-Kenya. By contrast, Moi's Kalenjin ethnic group constituted only 26 per cent of the KANU Parliamentary group, a reflection of KANU's wider national base.

Kenyan MPs have always been well-educated, both by the standard of their compatriots and internationally, and education levels continued to improve in the House in 1992. Opposition MPs were significantly better educated than KANU's, a reflection of the lesser access of the pastoral areas to education. KANU had the only six MPs who had never received secondary education, although they had received primary education and then teacher training. Four of them were Ministers – Moi, Mulinge, Kalweo and Ntimama. A feature of the 101 new Members was the large number of practising lawyers, radical opponents of the state in 1991–2. They included Paul Muite, Gervaise Akhaabi and Kiraitu Murungi (FORD-Kenya), Japeth Shamalla (Asili) and Martha Njoka (DP). The law had proved one of the opposition's strongest weapons in the election period, and they now reaped their reward. In line with the growing importance of political families in Kenya, despite its rapid development and meritocratic, money-oriented society (see Chapter 9), there were numerous family links in the new Assembly. As well as clearing out some of the more ineffectual children of the élites, in Turkana Central Patrick Ejore, and in Gachoka Norman Nyagah replaced their fathers in their 'family seats'. Winifred Mwendwa replaced her brother-in-law Kyale in Kitui West, and James Orengo his cousin Archbishop Oluoch in Ugenya. Martin Shikuku and his brother were both elected to Parliament for

FORD-Asili (in Butere and Nakuru Town), whilst the first simultaneous father and son duo, *Jaramogi* Oginga Odinga and his son Raila, took their seats together for FORD-Kenya.

As in the 1960s, party officials did very well in obtaining their party nominations, but officials did less well in winning their seats. National officials did particularly badly since they tended to include representatives from all regions. The DP suffered particularly heavily, and most of its national and well-known District party leaders lost. Whilst Chairman Kibaki won, the Secretary General (Keen), Treasurer (Mwamunga), and Organising Secretary (Ogle) were all defeated. In KANU, the leadership also performed poorly. President Moi won, of course, as did Saitoti, but Secretary-General Kamotho, National Chairman Ayah and the Assistant National Treasurer all lost. FORD-Kenya lost its Secretary-General, Second Assistant Secretary-General and National Organising Secretary, whilst its Deputy National Organising Secretary and Treasurer had both defected back to KANU before election day.

KANU's Strategy: The Carrot and the Stick

The first theme of 1993–4 was the government's use of all means at its disposal to disorganise, distress and occasionally repress the opposition, whilst rewarding its own supporters, in order to make it clear that failure to be reincorporated within KANU would have strongly negative effects on the economic health of opposition communities and the personal security of their leaders. KANU continued to blame political violence in Kenya and outside on the opposition and 'the evils of multi-partyism'.[8] Unable to overwhelm the opposition by sheer force, and aware of the government's huge and continuing unpopularity in Nyanza, Central Province and Nairobi, KANU's tactics were directed at the long haul. The Kikuyu were abandoned to the opposition entirely, while the Luo were wooed through KANU's closet allies among FORD-Kenya's MPs in South Nyanza. Effort focused once more on the marginal Eastern and Western Provinces, where numerous development meetings and KANU rallies were held.

KANU followed a policy of non-cooperation with the opposition, not only in Parliament but in the country. No KANU members were permitted to attend or contribute at *Harambee* fund-raising meetings organised by opposition members. Opposition members in Districts like Meru were excluded from District development committees in order to curtail their influence over development and, therefore, limit their ability to reward their constituents. On several occasions senior KANU figures threatened that areas which had voted for the opposition would receive no development aid or assistance. In January 1994, for example, hardliner Kipkalya arap Kones threatened that, as Minister responsible for famine relief, he would ensure that only those areas which had voted KANU would receive relief.[9] Although it is not clear to what extent such warnings were actually carried out, the threat was important in cowing the undecided.

Opposition MPs were continually harassed, beaten up and threatened by the security forces, and at least 21 were arrested and charged during 1993, mainly with crimes such as addressing their constituents without the permission of the authorities. None of these arrests and threats resulted in custodial sentences, but the process was a major drain on the opposition's resources. Younger Luo and Bukusu FORD-Kenya MPs and the FORD-Asili Members from Central Province took a particularly confrontational line, and Young Turks like Raila Odinga, for example, were in court on numerous occasions. Njenga Mungai, FORD-Asili MP for the troubled Molo constituency, was another centre of attention for the security forces. His opposition to the 1991 *Majimbo* rallies had angered KANU hardliners then, and before the election he had been expelled from the House and threatened with arrest for tabling a list of 220 Kalenjin parastatal executives. Mungai's active defence of the Kikuyu during the ethnic clashes of 1992 and his victory in the elections were infuriating to the KANU leadership. In May 1993, Mungai and other FORD-Asili leaders were arrested and charged with incitement to violence and damage to property, following riots in Nakuru after the demolition of 600 kiosks in the town at the dead of night.[10] In June, he openly called for the establishment of an Asili army of 10,000 youth-wingers to help 'keep order' in Nakuru in the face of continuing ethnic clashes. Police even tried to arrest Mungai inside Parliament on 9 June 1993, despite his Parliamentary immunity.[11] As the centre of Kikuyu opposition to the clashes and the public face of Kikuyu defence against Kalenjin warriors, he was at great personal risk and was arrested repeatedly during 1993–4. Although there were no political murders during the period, a welcome absence, state harassment sometimes exceeded normal bounds. One Kisii FORD-Kenya MP was so severely beaten during the Bonchari by-election that he had to be carried into court on a stretcher, while rowdy Kikuyu and Luo youths around the Parliament building, who had barracked KANU leaders on the first day of Parliament, were attacked on the opening of the second session in March by armed Maasai *moran,* while the police looked on passively.[12]

At the same time as the stick was being wielded, there were numerous rewards on offer to tempt the vulnerable into defecting back to KANU. Loyalist areas were rewarded at the same time as the opposition was punished. Five new Districts were created during 1993–4, two of which, Mount Elgon and Kuria, were tiny one-seat Districts containing ethnic subgroups (the Sabaot Kalenjin and Kuria respectively) who had voted KANU in areas otherwise dominated by FORD-Kenya.

Meanwhile, dozens of KANU's defeated MPs and Ministers moved swiftly into well-paid posts in statutory boards and parastatal industries, as they had after every previous election. These included Clement Gachanja, the loser for KANU in Dagoretti in Nairobi, who became Chairman of the Kenya Bureau of Standards; Josiah Kimemia, the loser in Kinangop, who became Chairman of the National Irrigation Board, and Kuria Kanyingi, KANU's defeated candidate in Limuru, who became Chairman of the Kenya National Trading Corporation. Lawi Kiplagat, who had been removed in the controversial KANU nominations in Baringo South, was rewarded by being made Chairman of the parastatal reform programme's Executive Secretariat and Technical Unit. Reuben Chesire, who had lost the KANU nomination in Eldoret North, was made Chairman of the huge ICDC (Industrial and Commercial Development Corporation); ex-Minister Sam Ongeri, who was ousted from Nyaribari Masaba by the Nyachae team in Kisii, became Kenya's permanent representative to the UNEP; and Andrew Omanga, who had stood down for Nyachae in the primaries, became Executive Chairman of the Kenya National Assurance Corporation in January 1993. Said Hemed, rigged out in KANU's Kisauni nominations, was made Ambassador to Saudi Arabia. These positions provide them not only with incomes, but also with political springboards for recapturing their positions; they were also another means of ensuring that the state system remained partisan in its distribution of resources. One problem for the government, however, was that its opportunities for parastatal patronage were declining. The pressure to liberalise the economy, reduce corruption and waste, and eliminate state interference tended to cut the number and importance of posts Moi and his allies could offer, and restricted their ability to influence policy and to direct the allocation of rewards towards individuals and specific communities for political ends. This was one reason why the parastatal reform programme continued so slowly.

Opposition MPs were also offered financial inducements to return to the fold. The FORD-Kenya MP Ferdinand Obure (Bomachoge) claimed in a press conference that he had been promised Sh5 million (about $100,000), plus all campaign expenses for the by-election.[13] Other MPs experienced similar offers, and associated financial pressures in the calling back of government loans and pressure from creditors. This was explicit government policy. In the words of Moi in Kisii, 'I have given you the mandate to use all the resources at your disposal to get these people [opposition MPs] back to Kanu.'[14] The result of these tactics was similar to what had occurred in earlier periods of opposition, under both Kenyatta and Moi. The majority held firm, particularly in their homelands, where ethnic solidarity proved more powerful than state pressure, but the vulnerable in the marginal communities slipped away one by one. Only the Kikuyu and to a lesser extent the Luhya had the self-sustaining economic base which provided sufficient surplus to permit the financing of a stable opposition party. By the end of 1994, eight of the elected opposition MPs (nearly 10 per cent of the total) had defected: one from the DP, four from FORD-Asili and three from FORD-Kenya (although the opposition won back half these seats in the ensuing by-elections). KANU's position steadily improved in opposition territories, and by early 1994 it was already becoming clear that the opposition were unlikely to survive in a coherent form able to challenge KANU at the next election.

The Clashes Continue

The belief that the ethnic clashes were a political weapon relating to the elections proved false, and Kalenjin-Kikuyu conflicts in the Rift Valley continued throughout 1993–4. The state proved unable to control the situation in Nakuru, particularly in Molo, and in Eldoret South. Many dozens more were killed and thousands driven from their homes during these two years, despite the declaration of security zones and massive military deployments. Killings in Molo, mainly by Kalenjin warriors, peaked during June–August 1993. President Moi continued to blame the killings on the opposition, declaring, 'Personally, I know that these opposition leaders were the ones inciting the people and are behind the tribal clashes.'[15] Visits by Matiba with British Peer David Ennals, and by Kerry Kennedy, executive director of the Robert Kennedy Memorial Center for Human Rights, at the end of August both resulted in strong statements criticising and embarrassing the government for their incompetence or complicity. As a result, in September 1993, in both Nakuru and south Uasin Gishu, Moi declared 'security zones' in which security forces had complete freedom to act and journalists and even MPs were banned. Nonetheless, the violence continued, and more and more Kikuyu gave up the struggle and abandoned or sold their land. A Roman Catholic priest in Molo estimated that 90 per cent of the Kikuyu inhabitants of south Molo had been forced out by late 1993. As the ever-vocal Sharrif Nassir threatened: 'If you insult Moi, you are looking for clashes.'[16] KANU had warned on numerous occasions during the campaign that those who did not vote for Moi would suffer the consequences, and these warnings now came true. As a poll monitor for Nakuru town had observed presciently at the end of his report: 'The other information is that there is a plan to remove non-Kalenjins who are residing in Rift Valley Province for failing to vote for KANU Government.'[17] Behind the scenes, Nicholas Biwott remained a key figure, who was allegedly ferrying warriors from Kerio South into Uasin Gishu.

The clashes were both an important political weapon for the Rift Valley élite, and the greatest single danger to KANU's hegemony over the rest of the country. As long as the Kenyan government had not extensively murdered its own citizens, KANU's argument – that single-party rule provided an island of stability in an ocean of chaos (Uganda, Somalia, Ethiopia, Tanzania) – remained plausible. The clashes, however, provided strong evidence that the state was either actively killing its own citizens or conniving in their deaths. This severely harmed KANU's support in many affected and adjacent areas, undermining Western confidence and the party's legitimacy.

As killings continued in these contentious settled areas, mainly between Kikuyu and Kalenjin, the fighting spread to northern Narok, bordering Molo, in the Kikuyu-dominated area of Enoosupukia. The target here was again land. The Maasai, major losers from the British conquest in the early twentieth century, had controlled and grazed large areas of the Rift Valley. This land had been taken from them and they had been moved gradually into Kajiado and Narok. After Independence, in the land reallocations which then took place, the 'willing buyer willing seller' policy had meant that the Kikuyu, the wealthiest and one of the most densely populated communities, expanded greatly beyond their original borders, into areas such as Kajiado, Narok, and the northern Rift, buying land at low prices from the pastoralist herders. Now the twin objectives of securing resources for KANU-supporting communities and of punishing opposition voters combined, and from mid-1993 Maasai Minister for Local Government William ole Ntimama led a state-backed campaign to drive out Kikuyu settlers from parts of his constituency. Ntimama led a propaganda war on behalf of the 'indigenous' peoples of the Rift Valley (the pastoralist Maasai and Kalenjin) aimed at the settlers (the Kikuyu). Ethnic killings of Kikuyu began in April 1993 and were followed by regular threats that opposition-supporting communites should flee the area. In July 1993 Ntimama claimed that family planning was a ploy of the larger tribes to suppress the smaller ones, such as the Maasai, and told the Maasai not to be duped into family planning any more. After inflammatory speeches by Ntimama and a tour of areas which had voted for the opposition, during which the inhabitants of Enoosupukia were told they were living in a water catchment area (declared in August 1993) and had to leave, the killings started. In October 1993, Kikuyu settlers were attacked at night by security forces, Maasai *moran* and county council game rangers. At least 30 were killed and thirty thousand made refugees, fleeing to nearby towns where they were accommodated by local churches.[18]

To secure their long-term power, and protect their communities against Kikuyu influences, local KANU officials, particularly in the Rift Valley and the Coast, began to talk once more of *Majimbo* and regional governments. There were attacks on outsiders, mainly Kikuyu, in Elgeyo-Marakwet, in Laikipia, Kericho, Mount Elgon, Trans-Nzoia, Mandera, Garissa and Kericho. KANU hardliners openly acknowledged that their objective was ethnic purity. In many parts of the country, the state informally supported actions by its allies to threaten or undermine the role of Kikuyu businesses. In West Pokot in November 1993, for exanple, local people attacked and drove out 'foreigners' after the Pokot Minister Francis Lotodo (charged in 1984 with 'promoting warlike activities' against non-Pokot) demanded that all Kikuyu leave the area and instructed his fellow-Pokot to deal with the Kikuyu 'mercilessly'.[19] A few days before, Biwott had announced in another West Pokot rally that District development committees in the Rift Valley would soon meet to cancel all trading licences belonging to non-Kalenjin businessmen in the Province. There was also concern over the 1989 census which had been long delayed, officially because it was of inadequate quality, but according to many Kikuyu because it showed just how high a proportion of the population they really were.[20] At the end of 1994, it became clear that these events were part of a general strategy to press once more for a form of regional government in which KANU's minority communities would be able to seize enough land and resources to secure permanent control of the state.

Despite angry protests and ultimatums from Matiba and others, the Kikuyu did little but complain. Their leaders remained too well-educated, wealthy and with too much to lose to support 'direct action' or open conflict. The history of the 1950s Mau Mau rebellion and the efficiency of the security forces in stifling dissent in the past suggested that they would not challenge the authority of the state directly. The real danger for reciprocal violence lay in the younger post-Independence generation and the dispossessed Kikuyu peasants of the Rift, who began to arm themselves for self-defence.

Meanwhile, at least 100,000 of those displaced by the clashes of 1992 remained homeless. The government was receiving funds from the UNDP under a Sh1.4 billion agreement to fund the resettlement of all victims of tribal clashes throughout the country. While in some areas this resettlement process was working satisfactorily, observers suggested that in Molo and Narok North Kalenjin and Maasai, who had sold their land to Kikuyu settlers, were now returning, claiming to be the owners, and being 'resettled' there with UN money.

The Media

Attacks on the press and restrictions on the media also intensified after the election. With the contest over, numerous opposition publications were impounded, their editors arrested and charged with sedition, their copies destroyed by police and their vendors charged.[21] The main targets as before were *Society, Finance* and the *Nairobi Weekly Observer,* plus the radical Kikuyu Christian publications *Jitegemea* and *The Watchman.* Issues were also impounded of the new weekly newspaper *The People,* financially backed by Matiba. In April 1993, the government spotted the Achilles heel of the radical press: its printers. Fotoform Limited, the Westlands-based company which printed *Finance, Society, Mwananchi* and the *Economic Review* was raided on 30 April, when police seized 30,000 copies of *Finance,* plus plates and artwork. Two days later, six police officers returned and dismantled key components of the printing processes, and threatened staff not to try to repair it.[22] FotoForm's owner was charged with sedition.[23] For ten weeks, the radical magazines were unable to produce issues. Some were severely damaged, with *Society* having to cease paying journalists for two months, and appealing publicly to readers for donations to remain afloat. No sooner had they found a new printer, Colourprint Limited, which started printing *Society, Finance, Economic Review* and *The People,* than police raided Colourprint and impounded 20,000 copies of *Finance,* 100 of *Society* and two covers of the *Economic Review.* The police also threatened to dismantle their equipment. *Finance,* which never hit the streets again, gave up the unequal battle.[24] Kenneth Matiba, meanwhile, had been preparing a book about the Moi regime, *Kenya: Return to Reason,* which dealt with the corruption and abuses of the government. On 13 January 1994 200 police descended on the printers and seized all 15,000 copies. The next day, the book was banned.[25]

During 1994, the government's attention shifted to the journalists themselves, following their continued interest in ethnic clashes in the security zones. Reporters investigating the killings were tailed, beaten and their notebooks taken. After *Standard* journalists exposed killings in Molo, the managing editor and the journalists were arrested and charged with subversion. The news editor of the *Daily Nation* was also charged following a story alleging that a military helicopter had been used to transport attackers into Burnt Forest.[26] Despite this, the independent and anti-government press survived. The Nation group went from strength to strength, becoming even more actively pro-opposition and publishing a series of popular exposés in mid-1993 on the Goldenberg scandal, though they remained under tight surveillance.

The situation was little better in the television world. On 1 March 1993, KTN ceased to cover local news, leaving a national monopoly to the government KBC. This followed intense pressure on the network concerning their continued coverage of news about opposition politicians, particularly Matiba's ultimatum in Kiambu over the Rift Valley clashes the day before.

The Opposition

Shocked at their defeat, financially near ruin, and facing a new struggle to establish themselves in opposition, the aftermath of the election saw the opposition exhausted and depressed. Their persistent failure to build unity, and their continued adherence to a set of leaders most of whom had failed to transcend their limitations or achieve their goals gave the initiative throughout 1993–4 to KANU. The opposition leaders proved unable to take a truly 'Presidential' attitude in defeat, and each in turn revealed flaws which brought into question their suitability to lead the country. The pressure of defeat, personal self-interest, state harassment and the exposure of internal divisions on crucial matters of policy within the opposition parties therefore began the almost inevitable process of reconstruction and fragmentation.

All over the country, but particularly in government-dominated and marginal areas, middle-ranking opposition leaders defected back to KANU. Amongst the Kalenjin, KANU managed to mop up almost all the stragglers to produce a near-united front, including the long-suffering Baringo DP supporter Henry Cheboiwo who rejoined KANU in early March 1993. Among the Kamba, Paul Ngei, the eternal survivor, defected in June 1993, denying he had ever joined the DP. Amongst the Luhya, DP loser Alfred Sambu defected in May 1993. The first cracks came in Nyanza, with the defections of Charles Owino (FORD-Kenya, Migori) and Protas Momanyi Kebati (DP, Bonchari in Kisii) in early March 1993. In June 1993, FORD-Asili lost its Makuyu MP, Julius Njuguna Njoroge, who was nearly bankrupt. The Hamisi MP Khaneri defected in July, and in December 1993 he was followed by the Lugari MP from Kakamega. In May 1994, in a stunning blow, Matiba's FORD-Asili lost three of its remaining Luhya MPs (for Lurambi, Ikolomani and Shinyalu), leaving Martin Shikuku as one of only two Asili Western Province MPs. The MPs automatically lost their seats and a by-election was held, under the constitutional provisions established in 1966 to control defections from KANU. FORD-Kenya also suffered, as at least three more of their South Nyanza MPs – Tom Obondo, Professor Ouma Muga and Ochola Ogur – were 'closet KANU'. They openly called on several occasions for reconciliation with KANU, and even held public meetings declaring they were going to return to the ruling party. Obondo finally defected in May 1994.

The opposition parties, as with parties everywhere, were alliances of convenience to obtain power, and had even less intellectual commonalty than Western parties. These alliances were unstable, and riven by age, ethnic and other factions, which defeat exposed. Some opposition candidates had lost KANU nominations and defected at the last minute, and had no particular loyalty to their new parties. The large sums of money available to early defectors also provided an attractive incentive, reinforcing the importance of an independent financial base from which to challenge the state. Unsuccessful politicians were the most vulnerable, as they had no jobs, no prestige and no posts to compensate them for the risks they had undertaken. The opposition leaders also faced an example of the 'prisoners' dilemma', whereby the best course for them individually was to defect as soon as possible, even though they might have gained if all had held out together.

All three major opposition parties also experienced severe internal stresses, particularly tensions between the younger more radical élites and the old guard, stemming both from differences in strategy and a widespread perception amongst the disillusioned younger members that the older élites had thrown victory away by their failure to unite, and ought now to step aside for a new generation of leaders. In the face of defeat, and given their past history of attempts at cooperation, the 'natural' alliance between the DP and FORD-Kenya gradually expanded (though it was still damaged by tactical infighting, leading to their both putting up candidates in certain by-elections). Matiba and Asili remained aloof, however, and the conflict between the two wings of FORD, and the personal bitterness between Odinga and Matiba, continued to undermine all attempts at unity.

In the face of near-certain diminution and defeat, the opposition leaders continued to expend more energy combating each other than KANU. Matiba was the main stumbling block, remaining convinced of his destiny to rule the country. A particular problem was the status of the official leader of the opposition. As an inheritance from the Westminster model, the Kenyan constitution provided for an official opposition, bestowing priviieges upon the second-largest party in the House, if it held over 30 seats. Unfortunately, the 1992 election produced a tie in the number of seats between the joint-second largest parties. Although FORD-Kenya and the DP entered an informal electoral pact, from the moment Parliament opened there were squabbles between the two FORDs as to who should sit in the chair reserved for the leader of the opposition. The Speaker delayed making a decision until FORD-Kenya's Migori MP defected back in April 1993, when he gave the opposition leadership to the nationally weaker group – Asili. After the defections of two Asili MPs, Matiba was replaced in July 1993 by Odinga, who named his own shadow Cabinet, with Paul Muite as Deputy Leader. Odinga had tried to form a unified shadow Cabinet with the DP, but the DP yet again pulled out at the last minute. *Society* reported that Kibaki's Kikuyu supporters had threatened to defect to Asili if he became too closely aligned with Odinga. FORD-Kenya held on to the official opposition role thereafter.

Despite its success in 1992, FORD-Asili collapsed completely, a consequence of its narrow national base and its focus around Matiba's personal fortune and charisma. Matiba became increasingly ill and unbalanced, and in late 1993 it was revealed that as well as being unable to read, he had granted his wife power of attorney to sign documents for him, as he was also unable to write. The result was a leadership vacuum which led a small but influential Asili group headed by Njenga Mungai to call openly for Matiba's retirement. Although condenmed to defeat with Matiba as leader, FORD-Asili were unable to ditch their sponsor and founder in time to survive as a significant independent force. Asili's supporters outside Central Province and Nakuru melted away, with their support decimated amongst the Luhya of Kakamega and Vihiga Districts, Shikuku's home area, leaving them by late 1994 with only two of 11 MPs in the province (from an original total of seven). The only positive development for FORD-Asili was their reacquisition of the rump of the KNC leadership in February 1994, including Rubia, Wa Nyoike, Mwicigi, Keriri and KNC Chairman Mbathi, who had parted company with Matiba in 1992 just before Asili was registered.

With the fewest young Turks, the DP's main problems were its wider national spread, and the nature of its leadership. Although Kibaki endured, he remained passive, and failed to provide the inspirational leadership needed to mobilise the opposition. As a result, the DP gradually moved into the background, eclipsed by FORD-Kenya as the main opposition party. Younger DP members from Eastern Province, such as Norman Nyagah and Richard Maore, increasingly made common cause with a cross-party 'ginger group' of opposition backbenchers, including Asili and many FORD-Kenya MPs, which during 1993 became the main opposition grouping within the house.[27]

The major development within the Kikuyu in fact transcended party boundaries. Divided, marginalised, and under attack in the Rift Valley, the Kikuyu began to reconstitute the tribal alliance which had been so successful in dominating Kenyan politics in the 1970s: GEMA. The Gikuyu, Embu and Meru Association had been forcibly deregistered by the Moi government in 1980, because of its role in attempts to prevent his succession. In mid-1993, however, self-styled 'GEMA leaders' once more began to work together informally to represent their interests. In May, these GEMA elders publicly visited Moi in Kabarak to try to negotiate some form of deal over the ethnic clashes. Although refused registration, throughout 1993 and early 1994, GEMA politicians issued a series of statements on behalf of their community, and many politicians worked together informally to represent their interests. Paul Muite and the other GEMA Young Turks from the opposition parties were amongst those most committed, Muite particularly seeking a more secure political base than his lone status in FORD-Kenya. The GEMA group targeted the existing leadership of Kibaki and Matiba, arguing that both should give way to younger men (though Kibaki himself flirted with the GEMA revival, probably in the hope of strengthening his own Presidential candidacy).

The biggest changes, however, occurred within FORD-Kenya. Tensions were caused by the dominance of the Luo community, by Odinga's enormous personal authority and stature, and by his age and infirmity. Factional conflicts also swirled around the position of first Vice-Chairman Paul Muite, a Kikuyu in a party with almost no Kikuyu support, who was in line to inherit the Chairmanship when Odinga finally departed. The real problem, however, was that in May 1993 Odinga introduced a policy of cooperation with KANU, and led the radical opposition party into alliance with their most hated enemy. Although committed to defeating KANU, the FORD-Kenya leader believed that the only constitutional way to ensure that the Luo community was not entirely cut out of decision making and its share of the resources of the state was to cooperate with Moi. The government in turn promised to develop Nyanza, leaving Central Province temporarily isolated as the sole opposition centre. FORD-Kenya was the poorest of the political parties, and few of its leaders were big businessmen, able to fund the area's development. More fundamentally, the Luo had spent twenty years outside the centre of political and economic life and were vulnerable to KANU's (probably cynical) lure of a 'Nilotic alliance'. Odinga was led into this strategy and supported in it by a large number of older Luo MPs, plus the 'closet KANU' team from South Nyanza, many of whom had openly sympathised with KANU since their election.

There may also have been more mundane motives behind Odinga's sudden conversion. On 22 July 1993, Odinga admitted that in May he had received a gift of Sh2 million in cash (stuffed into a shoe-box) from the Chairman of Goldenberg International and Exchange Bank, Kamlesh Pattni, towards the costs of fighting the first by-elections.[28] Although he claimed that he did not know who the 'patriotic Kenyan' who had donated so large a sum was, it was widely believed that he had been quite aware of his visitor's provenance and of the gift he was bringing (FORD-Kenya were at this time in the middle of a powerful campaign to bring down Pattni and Saitoti over the Goldenberg scandal). Odinga was unrepentant, and the result was the inevitable disintegration of FORD-Kenya. The younger, more radical, elements in the party were furious at FORD-Kenya's association with KANU, and fearful of Odinga's intentions. The dozen or so Luo MPs who disagreed with this strategy (including Raila Odinga and James Orengo) could do little, however, because of *Jaramogi* Odinga's grip on the Luo vote. His hold over the non-Luo, such as Muite and Imanyara, was weaker, but this group was divided and weakened by the internal bickering over the succession. Wamalwa and the other Bukusu leaders suffered excruciating contortions in order to justify this policy, knowing that if Muite was driven out of the party, they would stand to inherit the Chairmanship.

The crisis came in September 1993. After the discovery that Odinga had received what in any other leader would unquestionably have been deemed a bribe, Gitobu Imanyara publicly alleged that the gift was intended to shut Odinga up over Goldenberg. He was narrowly voted out of office as party Secretary-General by the party's National Executive Committee on 17 September, and resigned from the party two days later. He was followed by First Vice-Chairman Paul Muite, Kiraitu Murungi (Imenti South) and Mohammed Farrah (Lagdera), plus Assistant Secretary for Economic Affairs Robert Shaw, all of whom resigned their party posts but did not leave the party itself.[29] The vast majority of FORD-Kenya's leadership and supporters remained in the 'Odinga faction', despite their private support and sympathy for Muite and his colleagues, forced into acquiescence by the practicalities of politics. Muite's resignation left the quiet Luhya leader Kijana Wamalwa as Odinga's sole legal heir.

With many of the non-Luo Young Turks out of the party, Odinga moved closer still to KANU, jointly presiding with Moi over the opening of the notorious Turkwell Gorge hydro-electric power scheme and *Harambee* meetings in Siaya, and embarking on an official visit in November to the United Kingdom in which he held talks with the British government about the possibility of entering into a coalition with KANU. The Luo young Turks remained restive, but the extraordinary political flexibility of the Kenyan poeple was shown by the enthusiasm with which the Luo populace welcomed KANU Ministers to Bondo. In November 1993, Minister Jonathan Ng'eno claimed at a Bondo KANU rally that Odinga would take over from Moi when the President finally retired.[30] Meanwhile, the small Muite faction of FORD-Kenya, working together with elements from the DP and Asili, attempted behind the scenes to build a trans-party alliance based on a more grassroots style of political activism, centred around the GEMA revival. A society was registered quietly in late 1993 to act as a 'front' for a new party, to be known as *Mwangaza* (the light).[31] Muite's group remained ethnically far too pure, however, to provide a national opposition force – like so many opposition moves, it was a defensive action to protect their existing holdings, rather than an attempt to take the battle to KANU.

KANU's Internal Stresses

By January 1994, one year after the election, KANU was the sole coherent political party in the country but it, too, experienced internal stresses during this period. These were the result of promises made and not fulfilled in 1992, of the normal factional jockeying for power, the elimination of the remaining 'old guard' KANU District leaders, and the emboldening of the middle-rank political bosses who for the first time saw that they had leverage over the state. The governing party still had weaknesses, particularly the fragile nature of its popular support (most people had voted for the opposition), and the internal divides which had been papered over for the election, most notably between the Rift Valley hardliners and the more 'moderate' Western, Eastern and Kisii leaders.

Held together by the personal authority of Moi, and by control of the state patronage network, without either KANU would also have split. Even then, there were bitter disputes, the most serious being that between the moderate reformers and the hardliners which led to the downfall, amongst others, of YK '92's powerful Cyrus Jirongo. While the moderate reformers argued for rapprochement with the West, opening the country up, and a more cooperative approach to Kenya's economic problems, the hardliners viewed this strategy as likely to preserve rather than eliminate the opposition. There were other schisms within the Cabinet, as Ministers and officials formed factional alliances. Simeon Nyachae was a particular victim of whispering campaigns, as the most ambitious and poweful government Minister outside the Biwott team. These conflicts were only kept in check by KANU's clear ascendancy and the need amongst all factions to maintain a united front. The ruling party's greatest fear was the defection of major representatives from swing communities, who for the first time since 1966 could hold the government to ransom.

KANU experienced particular problems in maintaining the loyalty of two key groups – Moslems and the Luhya. The security situation for the Somalis in North-Eastern Province remained appalling, and in April 1993 Minister of State Maalim Mohammed publicly attacked the North-Eastern Province PC, Amos Bore, for failing to combat the problem. He suggested that Moslems should vote for some party other than KANU, which would be more sensitive to their needs.[32] He was demoted to the irrelevant Ministry of Culture and Social Services. Although the situation later stabilised, KANU remained extremely sensitive to Moslem dissent, which also continued to simmer in the Mombasa area, where there were regular violent confrontations between IPK members and KANU supporters.

There were also internal schisms within the Kalenjin, with growing restlessness amongst the southern, traditionally better educated and developed Kipsigis and Nandi, about the dominance of the Tugen and Keiyo. Incidents included the near-defection of Kipruto arap Kirwa, the Nandi KANU MP for Cherangani in Trans-Nzoia and long a maverick opponent of Biwott's, in April 1994.[33] Nandi discontent with Tugen 'impositions' such as arap Too in Mosop and Chesire in Eldoret North was open, and the state even broke up meetings to be attended by the Nandi KANU chairman in Uasin Gishu, Jackson Kibor.

The ruling party initiated a new campaign to replace older, unsuccessful District Chairmen with new figures, particularly in marginal and opposition Districts, and where new Ministers had been appointed, changing the 'pecking order'. Seven chairmen were removed within a year of the poll, including old-timers such as Julius Kiano in Murang'a (too soft on FORD-Asili), Mulu Mutisya in Machakos (a political embarrassment), Kabingu-Muregi in Nyandarua (too weak), Nahashon Njuno in Kirinyaga (no longer a plausible leader), Jackson Angaine in Meru (too old), Burudi Nabwera in Kakamega (unsuccessful), and most notably the previously powerful Elijah Mwangale in Bungoma, who was ousted in a centrally organised coup led by Kamotho in July 1993. This reinvigorated the party in areas such as Kirinyaga, where Moi persuaded the Chairman of Kenya Airways, Philip Ndegwa to take on the task. Although this drove some, such as Mwangale and Nabwera, into the arms of FORD-Kenya, the combination of threats and rewards, plus the visible lack of a plausible alternative in the opposition, kept KANU in the main united.

Saitoti, Jirongo and the Luhya

This conflict was closely intertwined with another, concerning the roles of Cyrus Jirongo, George Saitoti and the Luhya community. The election was no sooner over than YK '92 moved to centre-stage. National Chairman Cyrus Jirongo had become too powerful for his own good, and had outlived his usefulness. Now, powerful groups close to Moi aimed to dispose of him and of YK '92, where many financial skeletons were buried. Almost as soon as the election was over, Jirongo's team were forced to defend their role in a series of advertising supplements lauding their achievements in the election and reinforcing their direct loyalty to Moi. In the next few weeks, however, the Jirongo group was beset by growing criticism from within YK '92 and from senior KANU politicians, claiming that millions of shillings had been siphoned off into their own pockets. Jirongo was a leading moderate, aligned with those who believed that KANU required reform, and who argued for 'national unity' rather than revenge against opposition-voting communities.[34] Indeed, Jirongo was now bitterly opposed personally to Saitoti and Biwott, and there were even rumours that Moi, who had long backed Jirongo personally, was using him to initiate the process of destroying Saitoti.

The hardliners, however, proved stronger. From January 1993 onwards, Saitoti's defenders, the Biwott group, and discontented factions in YK '92 – mainly District-level officials from the hardline areas such as Kericho, West Pokot and Baringo – actively demanded Jirongo's ouster, criticising KANU's poor performance in areas where large sums of money had supposedly been spent during the campaign.[35] With continuing revelations about the misappropriated funds, District branches began to be replaced and in early February the Busia YK' 92 Chairman and a bank manager were charged with the theft of more than Sh59 million from the National Bank of Kenya.[36] That Nicholas Biwott was behind this is likely. Ex-YK' 92 official Micah Kigen, who had been a personal aide to Nicholas Biwott, claimed to have been dismissed and threatened after refusing to follow Biwott's instructions to denounce Jirongo at this time.[37] Moi continued to defend 'his team', however, arguing that YK '92 required 'strengthening' not dissolution.

In early April 1993, in the wake of Moi's rejection of aid conditions and the beginning of the brief period in which Kenya decided to 'go it alone' economically, the hardliners raised the stakes. At a function in Kerio South, the hardline KANU 'warlords' of the Rift – Biwott and Ministers Saitoti, Ntimama, Ng'eno and Kones – warned 'true' residents of the Rift to be on guard against attacks from the opposition, while Kones threatened that the Rift would have only Kalenjin, Maasai and Turkana MPs after the next election.[38] Immediately afterwards, the clashes began once again in Narok. Attempts to discuss the clashes and banditry were prevented by the Speaker, in contravention of standing orders, initiating another walk-out of most of the opposition.[39] This Kerio rally was followed by the 'Kitengela Declaration', in which the Maasai (in the persons of Saitoti and Ntimama) and the Kamba (led by Ministers General Mulinge and Makau) pledged to cooperate. This was to be the breaking point, rousing memories of the alliances made in the build-up to the ethnic clashes of 1992.

Moderates, including senior Somali and Luhya politicians, now openly attacked Saitoti (and by association also Biwott) and protested at these 'irresponsible utterances'.[40] Jirongo led the attack, with a merciless indictment of the Vice-President, observing that 'Some of our national leaders have deteriorated in their vision to an extent where their own survival supersedes national interest'.[41] The underlying theme was the Luhya community's claim that the Vice-Presidency was rightfully theirs, as the country's second largest ethnic group, with Saitoti the sacrifice. Something, however, seems to have gone wrong. In the absence of clear direction from the top, the reaction of the Rift Valley hawks was rapid, and Jirongo himself, rather than Saitoti, became the victim. Jirongo's businesses and financial operations came under intense attack from the state, and he was placed under police surveillance and then interrogated.[42] Luhya allies and associates in the various scandals by which money had been removed from the NSSF for use in YK'92 began to be removed or arrested.[43] On 23 April 1993, Moi suspended YK '92, condemned Jirongo and robustly defended Saitoti. Once more, the KANU hawks were in the ascendancy.

The main thrust of the hardline attack concerned the notorious deal between Sololo Outlets and the NSSF to develop the Nairobi South 'B' housing project, under which Jirongo's firm was constructing some 500 housing units. This had not gone through normal tendering procedures. Indeed, all payments to Sololo were made with written approval from the Permanent Secretary to the Treasury, Koinange. Postbank Credit served as the conduit for the transfers of Sh2 billion in advances between the two. In the aftermath of the deal with the West, Postbank went into liquidation in mid-May and, at the same time, the press was given licence to attack Jirongo. Thus the *Weekly Review* now printed an attack on Jirongo's complex as a 'totally misplaced investment'.[44] On 26 May the NSSF unilaterally revoked the contract, claiming that the original figure of Sh1.2 billion was 'manifestly exorbitant', and that Sololo was now demanding Sh 2.65 billion for the development.[45] The result was a complex series of lawsuits originated by both Jirongo and the NSSF.[46] In this morass the only clear thing to emerge was that the government was out for Jirongo. His companies were seized by the receivers, his housing project cancelled and reallocated to another 'political' construction company, Mugoya, controlled by President Moi, and he then faced a massive Sh272 million income tax bill. Having risen so quickly, he now fell as fast. Yet he remained out of prison, and out of opposition politics, despite FORD-Asili's attempts to enlist his support.

The problem for KANU was that the fall of Jirongo and his allies was interpreted as a severe weakening of both the moderates' position and the status of the Luhya community within KANU. The result was several months of chaotic infighting within KANU and elements of the Luhya opposition, centred around Saitoti and his replacement in the Finance Ministry, Musalia Mudavadi. Problems between Mudavadi and Saitoti had emerged soon after the government was reformed, with a series of disputes relating to Saitoti's ability to continue controlling the economy.[47] The Luhya had split three ways in the general election (KANU had eight elected Luhya MPs, FORD-Kenya six, and FORD-Asili nine), and there were rumours of secret negotiations between Luhya MPs from government and opposition parties, which might even have involved a realignment of the Luhya Asili MPs with KANU, in return for a Luhya Vice-President.

At the same time, Saitoti was under continued pressure over his involvement in the Goldenberg scandal. A collection of papers leaked from within the government was tabled in Parliament by Anyang-Nyong'o of FORD-Kenya, which contained detailed correspondence on the scandal, involving protests and complaints from CBK and other government officials, evidence that the companies to whom the goods were exported were fraudulent, and correspondence indicating how the Treasury manipulated the law to ensure that Goldenberg received its huge payments (over US$45 million), including the payment of 35 per cent rather than the legal 20 per cent export compensation. At the same time, the *Daily Nation* ran a series of articles exposing the scam. The Law Society, in the absence of government action, began work to institute a private prosecution against those involved, including Saitoti himself.

Linking opposition pressure and the role of the Luhya was the COTU general strike against the government on 3 May 1993, for a 100 per cent wage increase and for the sacking of the increasingly compromised Saitoti. Although Kenyan law makes labour protests extremely difficult, and the government pressure to prevent it was intense, the strike went ahead with some success.[48] It represented the first real workers' reaction to the massive inflation and economic collapse facing the country. Since the peasantry and nomadic herders constituted the basis of government support, while they had been decimated in the towns, the workers had little expectation of support from KANU. As Moi correctly said, the strike was 'not for the welfare of the workers but to advance political interests'.[49] The strike was led by a Luhya, Joseph Mugalla, COTU Chairman and defeated KANU candidate for Ikolomani, who now aligned himself with the protest. He and COTU paid the price. Although the government announced a 17 per cent increase in the minimum wage a few days later, Mugalla was arrested on 1 May at the Labour Day celebrations, and the next year brought bitter conflicts within COTU as the government attempted to remove the existing trades union leadership.

At the same time, several other KANU Luhya politicians found themselves the objects of suspicion, reinforcing the Luhya's feeling of alienation from the government.[50] The battle for Luhya support also became linked with struggles to remove old-guard KANU Luhya leaders in Kakamega and Bungoma, particularly ex-Minister and KANU Chairman Elijah Mwangale. Mwangale, so long a stalwart hardliner, now found himself in open confrontation with the government, accusing KANU of using the Luhya community as scapegoats for the failings of other KANU leaders. He was questioned by police over his connections with Jirongo and faced debt claims from Pan-African Bank, who tried to auction his farm in Trans-Nzoia, while another of his farms was invaded by Sabaot 'tribesmen'.[51] Incensed by the destruction of his authority, Mwangale openly accused Nicholas Biwott of having 'fallen into disgrace in the eyes of many Kenyans', claiming that the 'total man' was 'total evil'.[52] Indeed, despite the fact that Mwangale was heading for oblivion, he even declared that he would stand against Saitoti for KANU's Vice-Presidency.[53]

By late 1993, Mudavadi's successes, Biwott's endurance and Moi's robust defence of Saitoti had dampened down this potential revolt, but for some time it was the most serious challenge the government faced internally, as the loss of the Luhya, a marginal community, would have been a critical failure in the regime's strategy.

Political Competition in Parliament, the Courts and By-Elections

The new multi-party Parliament proved less successful than many had hoped. Predictions that the opposition's able, intelligent and experienced members would be able to face down, out-debate and occasionally even outvote the government's narrow majority of only 24 seats were inaccurate. Despite some verbal victories, the opposition were unable to convert the existing structure into a significant additional legislative function or a substantive watchdog on the executive. The new speaker, ex-KANU Minister Francis ole Kaparo, who was selected in tight party voting, on several occasions failed to act in the impartial manner required by his post, particularly, once more, on opposition motions relating to the ethnic clashes. At the same time, the opposition's internal divisions were so extreme that its effective strength was no more than 70, particularly as several MPs were closet KANU supporters. Matiba's policy of extra-Parliamentary action, though it made him more dangerous from the government's perspective, also weakened Asili's role in Parliament. Matiba was openly contemptuous of Parliament throughout, walking out on several occasions and referring to it as 'a useless talking shop', and from June 1993 he boycotted Parliamentary sessions for all but technical appearances as 'a waste of time'.[54] The Assembly was also marred by open violent confrontation, alternating with periods of cooperation, characteristic of an institution which had failed to find a clearly defined function.

The government brought little controversial legislation before the House, and few situations resulted in a division. Although opposition and KANU backbench MPs could and did bring local matters before the House, as they had done in the single-party era, Parliament remained a talking shop, though one which certainly had the power to embarrass the government. The new MPs did on several occasions attempt to control government excesses by Parliamentary protest, but 'whipping' and other factors combined to reduce the impact of such actions. There were some efforts by the opposition to act together to change the legal framework governing politics. Ford-Kenya unsuccessfully pressured the government to repeal detention legislation, which remained on the statute book although there were officially no political detainees. All parties raised corruption issues, security problems, the ethnic clashes, the problems in Somalia, and continued government control over political activity through the Public Order Act, their control of the KBC and the use of the Provincial Administration. Nonetheless, little emerged in practice, partly because of the establishment of a new Law Reform Commission to examine alterations to existing legislation in many areas, which was also a useful excuse for delay. Similarly, the Parliamentary committees overseeing government activities such as the Public Accounts Committee, chaired by Odinga, seemed to be unable to perform effectively. There were quorum problems in Parliament for the first time on 8 June 1993, and these continued, a reflection of the difficulty the multi-party Parliament and MPs had in reconciling their long-term status as local activists and development administrators with their role as 'cannon fodder' and Parliamentary debaters, when the government had a clear majority and formal divisions were discouraged.

The sole occasion when the opposition seriously challenged KANU for control of Parliament came in late 1993. Following William Ntimama's speech in the Assembly defending the killing of Kikuyu by Maasai in his constituency – saying he had 'no apologies' for his actions, which had incited the violence – they persistently disrupted proceedings.[55] For a week, over 60 opposition MPs united to disrupt the operation of Parliament, barracking and refusing to be seated, determined to see Ntimama sacked or otherwise punished.[56] There were open exchanges of blows between KANU and opposition MPs and Ntimama's final arrival in the House to face his challengers led to his speech being entirely drowned out by shouts of 'murderer'. Moi and Ntimama stood firm, however, despite serious rumblings of dissent amongst up to 20 KANU moderates. As so often in the past, the crisis blew over, with little having been achieved.

The first serious discussion of constitutional amendments did not come until 1994. Then, continuing opposition demands to rewrite the constitution, including the limiting of Presidential powers and removing the Public Order Act, were supported by the clergy, including the Catholic Bishops. Having failed to make its mark in Parliament, the opposition and the clergy had been looking since late 1993 to build some form of national convention of experienced citizens from all parts of society, to rewrite the constitution. The precedents, membership and indeed the value of such a convention remained questionable. KANU's response was surprising. Rather than rejecting constitutional change outright, they seized upon the opportunity once more to reawaken the call for *Majimboism*. As in 1962, Rift Valley KANU politicians, led by William ole Ntimama and Nicholas Biwott, called for a regional system of government. The key goal seemed to be to ensure that the Kalenjin and Maasai could rule the Rift and expel the Kikuyu, since land ownership remained at the core of the argument. Indeed, there were rumours that Nicholas Biwott wished to be made Premier of the Rift Valley region, and even that he intended to take over when Moi finally died or retired. No one had a clear concept of what this would entail, however, or whether such a system of government would be remotely practical.

This issue stirred once more at the end of the year when, in response to a draft new Law Society of Kenya constitution, Moi publicly committed himself for the first time to such a regional system and invited experts from the United States to visit Kenya and help draw up a model. This was a clever trick, as the federally governed Americans were likely to favour KANU's federal system over the opposition's preferred unitary arrangement.

Majimboism had been one of the key planks of the 1963 election, following the 1962 concession to KADU's demand for a federal state, which had led to nearly 50 per cent of the state's revenue being allocated to the eight new regions. Once KANU had decisively won the election, however, the regional provisions were watered down, and although Kenya became independent within a formally federal state, with the majority party committed to its removal, it took only two years to eliminate all vestiges of *Majimboism* (including the regional Assemblies and the Senate) from the institutions of the state. The objections of KANU's leaders to federalism were prophetic. They viewed it as accentuating tribalism and corruption. In the words of the late Joe Murumbi, regionalism was 'a ghastly charter for inefficiency, corruption and ultimately poverty and suppression of our national aspirations' in which 'a few people want to carve out little kingdoms for themselves under the guise of protecting tribal interests'.[57]

The Conflict Continues: Election Petitions and By-Elections

Petitions by voters or defeated candidates against an election result are a fundamental part of the Kenyan electoral system, given the flawed nature of the electoral process, and have regularly revealed electoral malpractice.[58] In 1992, electoral petitions were even more numerous than before. For the first time in Kenyan history, there were six petitions against the Presidential poll, claiming that President Moi's election was void. There were two petitions from Matiba, one each from Imanyara and Orengo for FORD-Kenya, one by two voters represented by the DP's lawyer, and one from John Harun Mwau. All were eventually disposed of on procedural grounds, demonstrating the limitations of the law when in conflict with the executive, in a state where the judiciary's authority is incomplete.

The process of petitioning is enormously expensive. As well as their own costs and the legal fees of the losers, there is also the huge cost of transporting and 'treating' witnesses, collecting evidence and bribing everyone available to ensure your petition is not struck out or accidentally mislaid. Chesoni estimated that each individual case would cost between Sh1–1.5 million in legal fees. The rules governing petitions were changed just after Parliamentary nominations in 1992, to try to control their number.[59] Then, in 1993, the decision was taken to consolidate into one case all petitions concerning the same election. Thus all the petitions against Moi's election were heard as one.[60] The responsibility for allocating staff to hear the petitions was the unenviable responsibility of the Chief Justice. Two election petition courts were set up in March 1993 by the new Chief Justice, Justice Apaloo, a widely respected Ghanaian, who replaced Hancox, the controversial British (and ODA-funded) Chief Justice, whose contract had expired.[61] They were each presided over by three justices, who were generally viewed as people of some probity.[62] They now had a key role to play, with the theoretical ability to declare Moi's election invalid, and to destroy KANU's Parliamentary majority. As such a key group, they inevitably came under pressure, and their performance during 1993–4, though not necessarily their personal responsibility, still left much to be desired.

If 1993 taught one other lesson, it was that the opposition could not afford to rely upon the law courts to undo its defeats. The official petition process proved far too slow to address their grievances. Attention focused on legal arguments surrounding the various Presidential petitions, which were dismissed one by one, mainly on technicalities, whilst the Parliamentary petitions proceeded with agonising slowness.

Kenneth Matiba filed two petitions against Moi's election. The first was based on the grounds that had been raised before the election, namely that Moi had already served two terms and was therefore ineligible. The court struck this petition out on 25 May on the grounds that he was already pursuing another one.[63] His second covered the more serious issue of election irregularities, including violence and intimidation by KANU supporters and ethnic clashes in the Rift designed to reduce his vote. This petition and those of FORD-Kenya and Mwau were consolidated and heard jointly. The petition judges were Edward Torgbor, Shaikh Amin and J. A. Couldrey, generally reputed to be an independent and reasonably impartial group.

Almost as soon as Matiba's main petition hearing started, a problem emerged as his petition was signed not by himself, but by his wife, who had power of attorney for him.[64] Moi's lawyers urged it be struck out as inadmissible, but the court initially accepted its validity.[65] The petition hearing continued in October, but a series of delaying tactics by KANU lawyers on procedural issues delayed the hearing of the substantive issues until the end of the year.[66] In February 1994 the Court of Appeal ruled in favour of a submission by Moi's lawyers and struck Matiba's petition out, as the rules required it to be signed in person or thumbprinted, not signed by someone else. Meanwhile, Imanyara had withdrawn his petition against Moi, relating to the two terms rule, leaving only Orengo's protest. Thus, despite extensive malpractice and six petitions against his election, Moi was secured in office.

Petitions were also launched by KANU and opposition losers against the victors in 84 Parliamentary constituencies – nearly half the country's seats, and more than double those in any previous election. Only half of these were petitions against malpractice by KANU, as KANU petitioned opposition victors in some areas and the opposition fought it out internally. The major petition battle was between KANU and the DP, with KANU originating all but one of the cases against the DP, and the DP challenging a quarter of KANU's MPs. The DP focused on areas where it felt it had been robbed, especially Eastern Province and Kisii. KANU also hit FORD-Kenya hard, with eight of their 31 seats petitioned, but treated Asili lightly. FORD-Kenya focused proportionately more of its attention on FORD-Asili than KANU, with particular anger over the Nairobi results.

Table 12.2 Election Petitions

Petitions against		Petitioners				
PARTY	Number	KANU	FORD-Asili	DP	FORD-Kenya	Unclear
KANU	44	-	9.5*	24.5*‡	8	2
FORD-Asili	12	4	-	1	5	2
DP	15	14	1	-	-	
FORD-Kenya	11	8	2	1	-	
KNC	1	1				
PICK	1	1				
Total	84	28	12.5	26.5	13	4

Source: Press reports, 1993 and early 1994.
* Includes one joint petition between the DP and ASILI.
‡ Includes one joint petition between the DP and the KNC.

They would have filed even more petitions were it not for financial constraints. FORD-Kenya and the DP agreed in general not to petition each other's seats. Only three seats where candidates had been prevented from being nominated were petitioned by those barred or beaten: Samia, Amagoro and Tinderet. All the others were conceded without contest.

The result was a long, expensive and slow series of hearings that identified a number of malpractices, but seemed more adept at nullifying opposition victories than government ones. In 1993–4, four opposition victories were annulled, but none of KANU's. The majority were dismissed on procedural grounds, usually relating to filing out of time or failure to provide adequate details. These included Kajiado North, where the petition against George Saitoti by Narok lawyer and DP supporter Livingstone Simel ole Sane was struck out on 5 May 1993, after the petitioner denied he had even signed it, and claimed it was a forgery. This is extremely implausible, and suggests that pressure had been applied.[67] Many more, including the most serious anti-KANU petitions in Kisii and Ukambani, dragged on for year after year without even being heard, despite the Chief Justice's promise that they would be heard quickly.

Combining the ten Parliamentary vacancies due to defections, four due to election petitions and three deaths, 17 by-elections were held between May 1993 and December 1994. Of these, KANU won only seven – Bonchari in Kisii District, Hamisi in Vihiga, Lugari, Shinyalu, Lurambi and Ikolomani in Kakamega, and Mandera East in the North-East, all marginal seats. All 17 had been opposition constituencies, however, increasing the government's majority overall from 24 seats to 38, though they easily lost the five by-elections held in opposition strongholds in Nyanza and Central Province. The effect of their decisive defeats there, despite state pressure, threats and promises, was to discourage other defectors from the opposition heartlands from making the move. Thus, while successive KANU victories increased the pressure on the waverers in the marginals, the by-elections reinforced opposition Luo and Kikuyu solidarity.[68] The Makuyu MP's defection so incensed the local population that they attempted to murder him on several occasions.[69]

The first key feature of these results was that KANU's percentage of the vote rose in every contest, on average by 22.7 per cent. There were serious suspicions of outright electoral abuses in at least four by-elections. In most polls KANU sent high level delegations, most headed by Moi himself, and used traditional 'bully and bribe' tactics.[70] The marginal Bonchari saw severe violence, with KANU and FORD-Kenya groups engaged in a physical trial of strength which injured scores of people.[71] KANU won, with a very low turn-out and widespread complaints of massive election rigging which were confirmed by Western embassies and NEMU. In some seats, the Provincial Administration prevented the opposition campaigning publicly at all. In Makuyu in 1993, KANU was (unsuccesfully) committed to winning back one Kikuyu seat, and pulled out all the stops. Minister John Kyalo promised Makuyu residents electricity and Joseph Kamotho personally promised to pay the school fees of poor children and directed the Teachers Service Commission to put Makuyu teachers on its payroll if the people voted KANU. In Lugari in early 1994, police threatened to

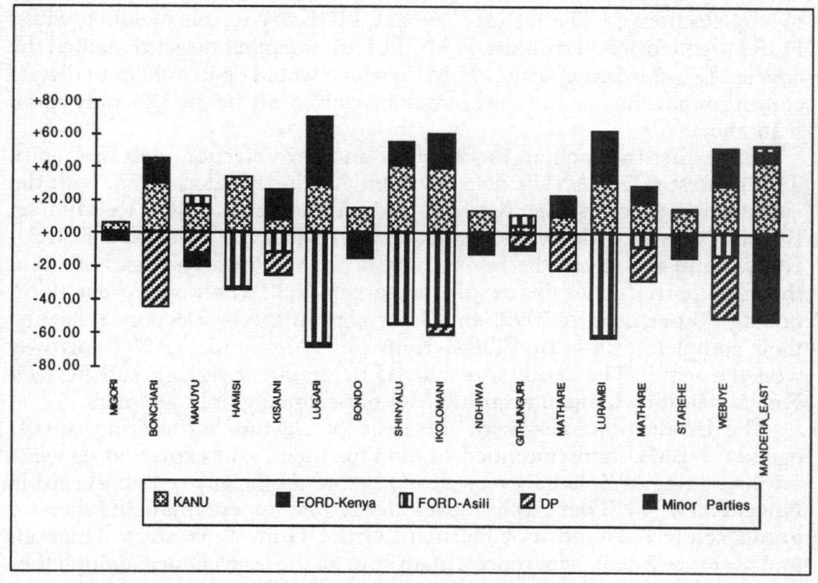

Figure 12.1 Changes in Percentage of the Vote in By-Elections, 1993–4

shoot dead the new Chairman of FORD-Kenya, Kijana Wamalwa, during his campaigning. Following this election, which was a key test for KANU against a resurgent FORD-Kenya, a FORD-Kenya election petition accused Moi of personally bribing voters on election day in the company of the wife of the Chairman of the Electoral Commission, Mrs Mary Chesoni. The petition also named the usual respondents, such as the DC and PC, who along with government Ministers were accused of bribery, the creation of three new polling stations in KANU areas (which saw high turn-outs), dishing out voters' cards and harassment of voters.[72] KANU's candidate was always the defecting MP, nominated using closed-door procedures, overriding KANU's official nomination process and sacrificing KANU's original candidates, since it was essential that the deals made with opposition MPs be seen to hold.[73]

Amongst the opposition parties, following an abject failure to agree candidates in Bonchari in May 1993, the DP decided not to contest ten of the polls, reflecting its willingness to defer where it was not the major opposition party. Where it did stand, it still lost 10 per cent of the vote. FORD-Asili were the worst losers, declining on average by 14.4 per cent, but they also failed to contest by-elections in two seats they had previously held in Kakamega District. FORD-Kenya emerged as the sole national opposition party, contesting 14 of the seats and increasing their vote on average by 11 per cent (see Figure 12.1).

Overall, therefore, FORD-Kenya's tally of seats rose by one, holding all five seats previously held and gaining Mathare from FORD-Asili (over two by-elections).[74] The DP lost one seat, PICK lost its sole member, whilst FORD-Asili forfeited six seats. KANU's Parliamentary target remained the coveted two-thirds majority (134 MPs) which would enable them to dictate constitutional change, but they remained stubbornly below 120, only seven seats short.

1994's first by-election, the result of another defection, was in Lugari. This contest saw KANU's defector from Asili nominated again, with the extraordinary result that KANU's old candidate, hardline ex-Minister Burudi Nabwera, defected to the newly revitalised Luhya-led FORD-Kenya, and was given the nomination (a case of the wrong candidate in the right party). Asili, the massive victors in 1992, ran a very poor third, polling 70 per cent in 1992, and 3 per cent in the by-election, reflecting their complete eclipse by FORD-Kenya in Luhyaland. KANU narrowly won the seat.[75] The result was marred by apparent rigging and FORD-Kenya petitioned, again accusing Moi of personally bribing voters.

The by-elections also kept the issue of election monitoring on the agenda. NEMU had continued to monitor them, and expressed its views on the rigging of Bonchari very clearly before it officially ceased to exist in November 1993. There were moves afoot to set up a permanent successor group centred around its Chairman, Grace Githu.[76] Western diplomats and observer groups sent representatives to all the by-elections, though they seemed able to do little to prevent abuses.

Aid, The West and the Economy

The third key issue the KANU team had to address was economic. Still without foreign financial support, and dogged by economic problems and massive corruption, the government needed finally to get the aid taps turned on again and to 'reward' key groups with economic benefits from their victory. For Kenyans, 1993 was a year of pain and retrenchment. The inflationary pressure introduced by the collapse of the shilling due to foreign currency exports, plus the printing of paper money, had ratcheted inflation up hugely, and the ordinary voters now had to pay the price. Year-on-year inflation was running at nearly 60 per cent in the last quarter of the year.[77] Crops continued to be affected by problems associated with lack of fertilisers, difficulties in receiving payment for produce deposited with processing factories, and the aftermath of the clashes. At the same time, foreign currency crises continued, brought on by capital flight and exacerbated by massive fraud; in turn, that damaged manufacturing imports. Although the situation began to stabilise by the end of the year, GDP growth for 1992–3 was, at 0.4 per cent, the lowest in the country's history. Facing a rapidly increasing and unserviceable debt, Kenya defaulted for the first time in its history on its foreign debt repayments.

1993 was also a year of continued stand-off and tense negotiation between the West and the Kenya government. The Kenyans remained confused and angry at their treatment by the donors, accusing the West of 'shifting the goal posts every time we are about to score by coming up with new aid conditions'.[78] Although aid conditionality remained, the West was far from united. Although the Western governments broadly endorsed the general elections, they (especially the Americans and Germans) remained concerned by the government's use of state violence and corruption, and, in private, by the abuses of the election period. The opposition continued to press them for a hold on quick-disbursing aid. The Kenyan government's primary target was the IMF and the World Bank, whose enthusiasm for political conditionality had never been great. On the eve of the IMF team's two week visit to Nairobi, on 19 February 1993, the government pre-emptively floated the exchange rate for the first time, relaxed price controls on fuel, maize and sugar, and allowed businessmen to keep 50 per cent of their foreign exchange earnings in retention accounts. The government apparently assumed that the IMF would report positively, that aid would be resumed and that this would prop up the shilling.[79]

Despite this, the IMF team reported negatively, saying that economic reform had not gone far enough to justify aid, particularly citing the rapid expansion of the money supply, the government deficit and the failure to take forward privatisation effectively.[80] An informal donors' meeting on 15 March 1993 in London also remained unconvinced.[81] Partly as a result, the economy's downward spiral continued. The shilling rapidly depreciated, further cutting the country's ability to import. Inflation rocketed. A week later, on 19 March 1993, Moi announced that the government was abandoning 'economically suicidal' IMF policies, and condemned the conditions for the resumption of aid as 'cruel, dictatorial and unrealistic'. On 22 March, controls on foreign exchange and prices were reimposed. Saitoti and Mudavadi are both believed to have argued strongly against this move, but to have been overridden by the Kalenjin clique around Moi.[82]

Evidence suggests that the President was willing to go it alone if the West did not resume financial support unconditionally, gambling on the West not being willing to see Kenya collapse.[83] Within days, however, the Kenyans began to back-pedal, denying reports and the claims of the hardliners that they had abandoned negotiations with the IMF – 'We are still negotiating with the Bank and the Fund as I speak to you'[84] – and refusing to concede that the government had reneged on reforms.

Combined with the political problems experienced, April 1993 was one of the darkest months for Kenya. Facing imminent economic collapse, the government was forced into a compromise with the financial institutions, who were themselves terrified that they would be held responsible for the collapse of the most dynamic and powerful economy in East Africa. On 20 April 1993, apparently backing off from confrontation, Moi increased interest rates from 25 to 45 per cent and shut down the Trade Bank and 12 other smaller 'political' banks, which were used to launder funds for the election. In return, the World Bank released US$85 million of frozen aid.[85] Although the economic situation remained poor, the crisis was past. Despite KANU's unpopularity in donor circles, political conditionality was seen as having failed, and the attention of the West focused on corruption and economic change. Having taken it to the brink, both sides were sufficiently relieved that a final break could be averted to reach an accommodation that both could tolerate, increasing the long-term likelihood of the resumption of aid. Nonetheless, the economy continued to suffer the consequences of 1992, with inflation peaking at 57 per cent in October 1993, and shortages of essential commodities.

Loans to 'political' banks such as the Trade Bank, (particularly the pre-export shipment financing system) were one of the major problems for the economy. These banks borrowed large sums from the government under various guises, and then passed on the money to political leaders. The closing down of the Trade Bank (declared technically insolvent back in 1992) and the issuing of arrest warrants for its owner were linked to attempts to obtain US$27 million in pre-shipment export finance using fraudulent documents. It was also a response to Western pressure, however, and to attempts by the then Chairman, Kassam, to recover some of the Sh450 million owed by Nicholas Biwott's companies in 'non-performing' loans. Meanwhile, parastatals such as the NSSF were being compelled to loan their money at below market rates to such institutions to fund their indebtedness. As long as the interest rates on these loans were kept low, inflation could not be controlled. The donors were resolute in demanding action on these banks, and the government was forced eventually to go further. On 20 May 1993 PostBank Credit (the go-between in the NSSF developments) was also liquidated. Nonetheless, concern continued, especially in the IMF, about the activities of the remaining institutions, especially the new Exchange Bank, which only began operation in late 1992 and continued to handle massive transactions and to receive huge advances with the CBK, at the same time as the Goldenberg scandal was emerging.

Foreign exchange retention accounts were reintroduced at a rate of 50 per cent for all exporters on 14 May, and further liberalisation followed. In late May 1993, the government attended an informal gathering with the donors in Paris, preparatory to the official Consultative Group meeting in November. This had no immediate impact, with political conditionality on good governance still high on the agenda. Attention was also focused on the budget, however, a key event which followed in June, in which the new Finance Minister established his authority. Mudavadi's main efforts were devoted to bringing inflation under control by substantial cuts in government spending.[86] In line with the new 'nice guy' image, Mudavadi's budget followed closely the prescriptions of the IMF and World Bank – sound monetary policy, liberalised trade (including an end to price control on all commodities by the end of 1993), lower taxes and tariffs, efficient tax administration, export incentives, parastatal reform and improved infrastructure. This included the final abolition of the notorious export compensation scheme. He also announced a civil service reform programme, aiming to reduce numbers by encouraging early retirement, with a final goal of a 45 per cent cut in manpower agreed with the World Bank and IMF. The actual application of this agreement remained slow because of its political impact, but nearly 16,000 jobs were due to go in 1993–6.[87] Reactions to the budget were positive everywhere, even among the opposition.[88]

The issue of the financial scandals which had dominated 1992 was never absent during 1993–4, as the government was forced by practical necessity and Western pressure gradually to close down the various loopholes which had been used to pump cash into the political arena during 1991–3. Despite the acres of prose written about the numerous unauthorised transactions and political banks, there was little attempt to link these transactions to the political élite, apart from Saitoti. The government simply ignored pressure from the media and the West to investigate Saitoti. Nonetheless, a series of financiers who had acted as middle men were arrested. The first to go had been Jirongo. He was followed by the Chairman of the Trade Bank, Kassam, and the Executive Chairman of Transnational Bank, Jared Kangwana, who was also Chairman of *Kenya Times* Media Trust (the holding company for KANU's press and media operations), a senior KANU supporter and close political ally of Saitoti's. Kangwana had been accused in a CBK audit (called by the World Bank) in mid-1993 of irregularly lending hundreds of millions of shillings to companies he owned. Lawyers then demanded the return of Sh400 million, following which Kangwana fled the country.[89]

The scandals being cleaned up were not only those of 1992. In April 1993, Kamlesh Pattni, the head of the Goldenberg organisation, sold to the CBK US$210 million in foreign currency, in return for a payment of Sh9,930 million to the Exchange Bank. This was a huge sum, equivalent to about 10 per cent of the government budget. Whilst the details remain obscure, what is clear is that the US currency was never paid, and that senior bank officials falsified documents to suggest that it had been, with fake accounts opened in Europe. The money was withdrawn, and almost certainly used to buy Forex-C certificates and transfer the money overseas.[90] It was universally believed that this scandal went beyond the middle-level staff who were eventually sacked to the top of the bank.[91] Other scandals involving Forex-C certificates, seen throughout 1993, were part of the reason why use of these certificates was discontinued. The CBK admitted that its internal accounting figures did not add up and that almost certainly it had paid out foreign exchange for more Forex-Cs than actually existed, with some certificates being 'recycled'.[92] The Exchange Bank and the other political banks abusing export facilities were alleged in April 1993 to have held over a third of the money then in circulation. The Exchange Bank was shut down finally in mid-1993. Pattni was arrested in March 1994 and again in June, when he was finally charged with the theft of Sh13,000 million. The chance of his not having had top-level political backers for these activities is nil.

The keenness of the government as well as the opposition press to follow up these scandals was a consequence of three things. The first was that tracks needed to be covered. All the scandals would eventually emerge, it was clear. The important thing was to set up appropriate fall guys, and close off the various conduits without fully exposing the destination of the funds. The second was that the government was under enormous pressure from the IMF and the World Bank, whose auditors were active in discovering several of the scams, and therefore were forcing the state to act. The third was that the government was genuinely keen to improve the economic situation, and the control of the currency was a key element in this.

On 23 July 1993 the heavily compromised Eric Kotut finally resigned and was replaced by a fellow-Kalenjin, Micah Cheserem, as CBK Governor.

This change, though a source of some concern initially, was symbolic of the government's willingness to deal with the West and internally with its economic liberalisation problems. It also provided a useful 'fall guy' for the abuses of the past, which began to decline under the new Governor. The combination of Mudavadi and Cheserem proved far more successful in liberalising the economy and in dealing plausibly with the West than Saitoti and Kotut.[93]

The key event was the first full Consultative Group meeting of donors in November 1993, two years on from the crisis which inspired the move to multi-party democracy. The IMF returned to Kenya in October to assess progress and, under heavy internal pressure to ensure that the report was positive, suggested that the economic changes made were sufficient for the resumption of aid. In the build-up to the meeting, it seemed that there were attempts to sabotage the resumption of aid by hardliners.[94] Nonetheless, on 22 November 1993, the bilateral and multilateral donors met in Paris and agreed the resumption of aid to Kenya. The meeting was a victory for KANU, for Moi and for Mudavadi, who many Westerners saw as the best chance they had of a decent Finance Minister. About US$850 million was pledged, including US$170 million in quick-disbursing aid from the IMF/World Bank and more from Japan, though there were disputes over the degree of conditionality which was to be applied. Some Western officials, particularly the Americans, suggested that aid would remain a 'drip feed', conditional on progress on the ethnic clashes and pluralism.

The parastatal reform programme continued to creep on throughout 1993–4, as part of the agreement with the World Bank. The need for change imposed by the West and the cost to the treasury associated with government ownership contrasted with the government's desire to retain control over the economic and therefore the political sphere. By mid-1994, it had sold off shares in 27 parastatal bodies, including most notably the Housing Finance Company of Kenya, Uchumi supermarkets and East African Oxygen. Most, however, were small industries in which the IDB (Industrial Development Bank) held shares, and many were in financial trouble. Dissatisfaction with its inability to address the core state bodies so central to the state's control continued, and there was also some disquiet over some of the state's disinvestment methods, under the direction of a committee chaired by a KANU MP from Baringo. Nonetheless, it appeared that 1994 would see a continued small-scale disinvestment programme, bringing money into the treasury and widening the ownership of the industrial infrastructure to bring in foreign and indigenous business communities. Further restrictions on the banking system were also introduced, to reduce the risk of fraud and the exposure of banks to liquidity crises due to unsecured lending.

The food shortage which had begun during 1993 with the price rises, which put staple crops beyond the means of many of the poor, were worsened by near-famine conditions in many parts of the country following poor rains and the planting problems caused by political violence. Agriculturally therefore, 1993 and 1994 continued to be difficult. Matters were made worse by the influx of up to 500,000 refugees from Somalia, Sudan and Ethiopia, and in mid-1993 the government was forced to appeal to the international community for food aid, since it had insufficient foreign exchange to buy supplies.[95] The impact of AIDS on the economic and social situation in the country also continued to widen.

Once agreement with the West had been reached, liberalisation of the economy continued, particularly deregulation of the exchange rate, with the gradual removal of controls and fees on foreign exchange transactions. In December 1993, the government relaxed company remittance restrictions. In February 1994 limits on remittances of earnings were raised further and companies were allowed to hold 100 per cent of export earnings in retention accounts, though their use was restricted. Further limits were removed in April 1994. At the same time, the financial position improved. With the floating of the exchange rate, the CBK's reserves improved rather than deteriorated, more than doubling to US$ 650 million in early April, and the exchange rate stabilised at 65 Kenya shillings to the dollar, despite continued high inflation. Effectively, therefore, the Kenyan government had won an economic victory through following the prescriptions of the moderates. Although their day-to-day control over the economy was slightly weakened, and their ability to 'play the system' to personal and factional advantage was reduced by the closure of the various loopholes permitting fraud, on the whole the recovery in the economy benefited the government politically.

Despite the recovery of the economy in early 1994, inflation and the budget deficit remained high, and the Kenyan external debt of US$500 million, now being serviced after rescheduling arrangements were made with the Paris Club in January, constituted over 25 per cent of GNP, still a heavy drain on the exchequer.[96] Although major improvements had been made economically since 1992, it was far from clear that Kenya was safe.

The Attitudes of Western Governments

Despite the gradual rapprochement with the West, friction continued between the state and Western governments, especially the Americans and the Germans. US Ambassador Smith Hempstone had finally left Kenya on 26 February 1993, to the public relief of the government, to be replaced by Ms Aurelia Brazeal, a career diplomat. Brazeal was believed to be less radical in her approach than Smith Hempstone, though likely to follow similar policies.[97] Smith Hempstone's views and forthright approach continued to be articulated by the German Ambassador, Bernd Mutzelberg, a persistent thorn in the side of the Kenyan government, criticising its behaviour on numerous occasions. Although in August 1993 Moi warned diplomats accredited to the country against associating with 'subversive elements' (he meant opposition politicians), Mutzelberg remained unabashed. Thus, he opened the ICJ-sponsored National Conference on Good Governance and Accountability with the claim that 'Nothing it seems has really changed.... Some people seem eager to turn the clock backwards and to return to the familiar methods of intimidation, threats and bribery', and restated the commitment of donors to ensure that the government honoured its promise to prosecute all those involved in the Goldenberg scandal.[98]

In March 1994, Moi accused the three main aid donors of 'persistent interference in the Kenya's internal affairs' and of partiality and subversion following their pressure to be able to monitor the Lugari by-election, where extensive rigging was expected.[99] Mutzelberg, however, was not alone, with Brazeal also openly calling on Kenyans to reject corruption, while the ever-garrulous Sharrif Nassir even suggested diplomatic relations be broken off with Britain because Britain was hosting numerous IPK militants. Such problems could not hide the continuing gradual rapprochement. Relations with Norway were resumed in April 1994, three years after they were severed, another step towards reintegration with the West and one which opened up the possibility of resumed Norwegian development aid.

The End of An Era

An era ended in Kenya politics on 20 January 1994, when the 82-year-old *Jaramogi* Oginga Odinga died in Kisumu. The result was a national outpouring of grief on a scale not seen since the 1970s, particularly amongst the Luo, but more widely amongst the millions of Kenyans who appreciated Odinga's enormous lifetime struggle for Kenya's Independence. In death, his cooperation with KANU was downplayed, and he became once more briefly a symbol of opposition resistance.[100] His funeral brought the DP and FORD-Kenya closer together than ever before, with Kibaki speaking emotionally and calling for unity.[101] Moi's courageous decision to attend the funeral with his Ministers, on FORD-Kenya's home turf in Bondo, almost led to a repetition of the Kisumu incident of 1969, with the real danger that the huge, simmering crowd of 300,000 mourners, completely out of control, would attempt to storm the Presidential guard. In the event, Moi and his Ministers escaped unscathed but shaken – and infuriated by the open personal attacks on him, particularly by James Orengo, who publicly called Moi a hypocrite, one of those 'who tortured and detained this great man, and now come here in false praise of his greatness'.[102]

Odinga's death was the first break in the log-jam of opposition politics. His death was almost certain, in the end, to break FORD-Kenya's mesmeric hold on the Luo community. In the meantime, however, it provided a heaven-sent opportunity. With the only man who could hold the party in alliance with KANU gone, Moi quickly recognised that there was little chance of continuing his accommodation, and ended the joint alliance. 'I will not accept to be abused, and, therefore, I will not cooperate with them,' he announced, calling on people in neighbouring Districts to ostracise the Luo.[103] FORD-Kenya and KANU were again at war. At the same time, the sole surviving member of the triumvirate elected in September 1992, Second Vice-Chairman Kijana Wamalwa, automatically became the first Luhya to head a major political party since 1964. Although Wamalwa remained a somewhat undistinguished figure, who had long lived in the shadow of others, he now had a brief opportunity in which to discomfit KANU seriously, by bringing a Luo-Luhya alliance into the field, alongside an emerging GEMA alliance (beneath the official opposition parties). Despite widespread speculation that the Luo would never let the leadership move from their community, Wamalwa was elected unopposed as the new party Chairman on 19 March 1994. His deputy, the First Vice-Chairman – a Luo to placate the majority supporters of the party – was lawyer and Ugenya MP James Orengo. He won a narrow 62–59 vote against Raila Odinga, who had expected to win the post easily but was now abandoned by the bulk of the Luo delegates in Orengo's favour. The Moslem representation in the party was also reinforced by the choice of Omar Mzee, FORD-Kenya/IPK MP for Kisauni in Mombasa, as Second Vice-Chairman.[104] Neither Wamalwa nor Orengo were charismatic politicians with national constituencies, but both were plausible, clever and committed to the need for change. All three leaders, for the first time in a Kenyan political party, were Young Turks.

For the next few months, the new party leadership managed to keep hold of both the rebel South Nyanza MPs, determined to defect, and to make deep inroads into KANU's and especially FORD-Asili's' hold on Western Province.[105] Despite many fears of Luo splits, and even the planned entry of CPK Bishop of Maseno South Henry Okullu into the political fray, the Luo community appeared to accept the justice of Wamalwa's inheritance. Asili showed even more obvious evidence of internal disintegration, with rumours abounding that Matiba would stand down and Shikuku's position as Luhya spokesman irretrievably weakened.[106] Matiba remained the sole unifying factor amongst his client MPs in Central Province, but elsewhere Asili supporters were up in arms and ready to quit. The death in February of Josephat Karanja, Asili's informal third in command, capped an appalling early 1994 for the party. The weakening of Asili could only be good news for the DP, and also for the Muite faction and the GEMA team. Thus, although KANU was itself in high spirits, with the improvements in the economy, the opposition also appeared to be moving slowly towards a sustainable future.

Increasingly, it appeared that Moi would face some form of two-pronged opposition if he waited until December 1997 for the next General Election: FORD-Kenya, with a Luo-Luhya support base, in some form of alliance with a GEMA-based party. The key questions were whether a Wamalwa/Orengo, Luo/Luhya party could hold the Luo vote whilst uniting the anti-government Luhya, and whether the Kikuyu and their allies could finally remove their existing leadership in time to fight a General Election in some form of loose but united federation of parties, combining FORD-Asili, DP and Muite-faction FORD-Kenya politicians. Would the old guard go down lightly, or would they (in some fashion) bring down the temple?

Nonetheless, KANU remained the clear favourite to win in 1997.[107] Its weaknesses at the periphery had been addressed one by one. Somehow, despite an inability to address many serious issues facing the country, a high level of incompetence in economic and social terms, and internal divisions, the KANU élites remained consummate political operators, though given a huge advantage by the system they controlled. More Asili MPs were likely to defect, perhaps accompanied by some FORD-Kenya members, leaving the opposition eventually with less than 80 MPs, probably with all the parties below the 30 mark and therefore unable to provide an official Parliamentary opposition. In the 1997 General Election, KANU is likely, bar a catastrophe, to win almost all the seats they took in 1992. Given a similar pattern of electoral abuses, and continued divisions in the opposition, they are likely to increase their lead. In fact, electoral malpractice is likely to become worse, since Western interest in democratic governance is bound to have waned by then, and since KANU has so spectacularly won its battle for aid.

The major risks for KANU after 1997 are further ethnic clashes, radicalising the Kikuyu to the point of insurrection, weakening the economy and destroying the remaining legitimacy of the government, and the death of Moi. As with all paranoid autocrats, Daniel arap Moi knows that the greatest risk to his survival will come from inside the party, not outside. Thus he has always been careful to ensure that although his right-hand men have risen to equal him in authority, because of his reluctance and personal unsuitability to manage the government machine directly, they have always, in time, been cut down to size. This is why Saitoti has survived so long – only when his hold on a major community is threatened will Moi move the Vice-Presidency elsewhere, to someone with independent authority (although Nyachae and Musalia Mudavadi remain contenders). There is no real challenger to Moi, with the authority to unite the Kalenjin and hold on to all the other communities. If the rumours of Moi's throat cancer prove true, and he does resign or die in the next few years, KANU's prospects are bleak. The squabble for the leadership that would follow would be bound to destroy the governing coalition, whoever seized the throne. A victory for Biwott would probably result in national revolt, a victory for any non-Kalenjin would destroy the Kalenjin alliance. In the present confused and chaotic state of the opposition, despite his having cheated himself into the position, and maintained it by fear, Moi's continued survival remains Kenya's best hope, until a new generation of leaders and a new constellation of parties emerges.

Postscript: The Political Scene, 1994–7

The last three years have witnessed continuing factional divisions within the opposition. KANU has made steady progress, winning by-elections and eroding support for the opposition in contested areas such as Kisii, Ukambani and Meru. The ruling party has maintained the pressure on opposition MPs, employing the District Administration to obstruct their rallies and recalling loans from state financial institutions, whilst offering monetary inducements to those who can be persuaded to defect. As a result, during the life of this Parliament there have been 30 by-elections, a surprisingly large number. Eleven MPs have died and five by-elections have been precipitated by the courts.[108] Meanwhile, no fewer than 15 MPs have switched parties (14 to KANU and one, Raila Odinga, from FORD-Kenya to the National Development Party).

KANU's performance in by-elections has far surpassed that of the opposition. The ruling party has held all six by-elections caused by the death of sitting KANU MPs.[109] Whilst gaining Mandera East from PICK as the result of an election petition and Nairobi-Starehe, following the resignation of former Nairobi Mayor Stephen Mwangi from the National Assembly, KANU's greatest success has been to hold eight of the 13 by-elections precipitated by the defection of opposition MPs. With a total of ten gains from the opposition, KANU had a total of 122 MPs by the time of the dissolution of Parliament.

By contrast, the total number of opposition Members has fallen from 88 in January 1993 to 76 by June 1997.[110] Defections cost the DP two seats in Bonchari and Kibwezi, where Dr Protas Momanyi and Agnes Ndetei, who had defected to the opposition just before the December 1992 poll, have returned to KANU.[111] It held one seat (Kennedy Kiliku's in Mombasa-Changamwe after a successful election petition) and picked up Kipipiri from FORD-Asili when Kimani wa Nyoike was time-barred from presenting his nomination papers. FORD-Asili, as we noted earlier in this chapter, was hit even more severely, following the mass defection of all but two of its Kakamega MPs, while both the KNC and PICK lost their only MPs, with one defecting to KANU and the other unseated on an election petition.[112] In all, Matiba's party has defended only three seats successfully, whilst losing eight (six to KANU, one to the DP and one to FORD-Kenya). FORD-Kenya, by contrast, has enjoyed a much better record, successfully defending the three seats where Luo MPs have crossed the floor to KANU.[113] It not only held Mombasa-Kisauni and Webuye after successful election petitions against it, but even gained Mathare in Nairobi from FORD-Asili.[114] In all, the main opposition party defended seven seats, gained one (Mathare) and lost one seat, following Raila Odinga's defection to the National Development Party.[115] Figure 12.2 provides details of the 30 by-elections since the present Parliament first sat in January 1993.

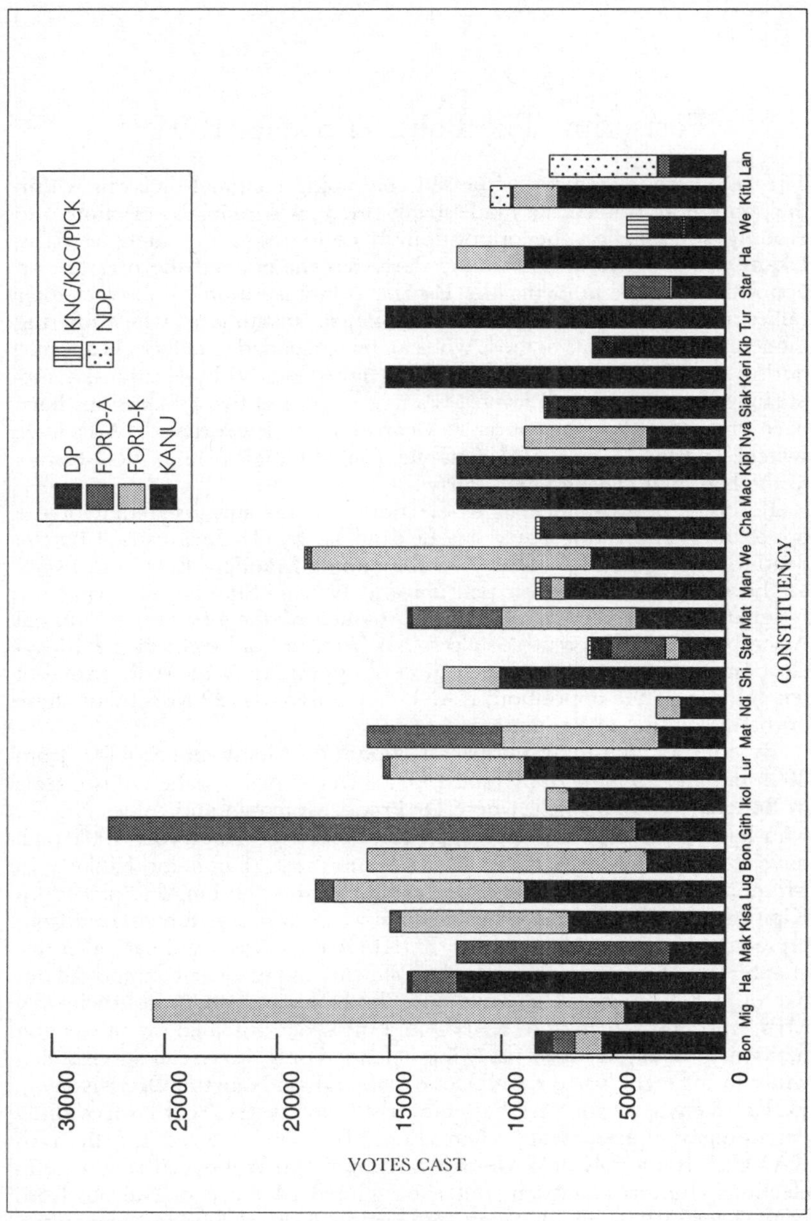

Figure 12.2 By-elections in Kenya, 1993–7

Matiba's support should not be underestimated, nor FORD-Kenya's position as the official opposition taken for granted. Despite the poor performance of his party in by-elections and the shrinking of FORD-Asili's base to its roots in southern Kikuyuland and Nairobi, following the break with Martin Shikuku, Kenneth Matiba remains a formidable political force. He is still much respected among ordinary Kikuyu voters, who disregard his poor health and erratic behaviour, whilst remembering his outspokenness, his courage, and particularly his willingness to court detention to defend their grievances. As a result, he is still able to mobilise the support of the capital's poorer residents and, if he were to stand for the Presidency in 1997, might well once again emerge as Moi's main opponent with between 15–20 per cent of the vote. By contrast, FORD-Kenya's showing in by-elections exaggerates its prospects at the next election. Michael Kijana Wamalwa, who succeeded Oginga Odinga as leader in early 1994, has failed to consolidate the party's strength in Western Province and its appeal to Luo voters is now being challenged by Raila Odinga's revitalised National Development Party.[116]

The opposition, faced with the widespread popular disillusionment with its performance and the likelihood of victory for President Moi and KANU at the next elections in 1997, has become even more divided. Personal animosities and factional rivalries over tactics have further reduced its effectiveness. FORD-Kenya has been divided particularly sharply by such disputes, spawning two new political movements: Paul Muite's Safina – Swahili for 'The Ark' – and Raila Odinga's take-over of the moribund National Development Party (the NDP) at the end of December 1996. Safina was officially launched on 13 May 1995, and sought registration under the Societies Act on 20 June. It was backed by a small but influential group of MPs, including human rights lawyer Kiraitu Murungi, FORD-Kenya's sole victor in Eastern Province, and former Director of the Kenya Wildlife Service, the famous palaeontologist, Richard Leakey. Antagonized by Muite's confrontational style and alarmed by exaggerated reports of Leakey's ability to raise money in Britain and North America, the government blocked the new party's registration, preventing it developing into a multi-ethnic radical coalition, appealing particularly to younger voters and the urban poor.

Raila Odinga's revitalisation of the NDP was the almost inevitable outcome of the tensions with Kijana Wamalwa since the Luhya leader had succeeded Oginga Odinga as the party leader in 1994. Dissatisfied with Wamalwa's lacklustre performance as official leader of the opposition in the National Assembly, since mid-1995 Raila Odinga has repeatedly challenged Wamalwa and James Orengo, his main Luo backer, mobilising the support of unemployed youths in Kisumu and other Luo towns to intimidate his opponents in FORD-Kenya as much as KANU. Unable to gain significant support in party branches beyond the Luo heartlands, Nairobi and Mombasa, Raila Odinga was unable to oust Wamalwa from the FORD-Kenya leadership. Even in Nyanza Province, Odinga encountered strong opposition from many Luo MPs who resented his confrontational tactics and unpredictable behaviour, while older people, business leaders and well-educated professionals deplored his reliance on hired ruffians and intimidation to enforce his views. Many Luo leaders rejected the notion that Raila had inherited his father's mantle. While the softly spoken *Jaramogi* Oginga Odinga had been widely revered, his son has become almost as widely feared. As a result, most Luo MPs have remained loyal to Wamalwa despite the younger Odinga's appeal to the rural masses.

The divisions within FORD-Asili have been just as intense and personalised. The marriage of convenience between Kenneth Matiba and Martin Shikuku fell apart soon after the December 1992 election. Matiba has refused to participate in the work of the National Assembly or to collaborate on a regular basis with Wamalwa and DP leader Mwai Kibaki, becoming even more erratic and dogmatic. In contrast, Shikuku has attempted to cooperate with other opposition leaders. Frustrated by Matiba's vitriolic temper and hostility to parliamentary work, many FORD-Asili MPs initially disassociated themselves from their party leader whilst others were bought off by KANU and defected. Most FORD-Asili MPs, however, have limited financial resources and as the 1997 elections drew nearer they began to restore relations with Matiba, who remains the party's paymaster. Without his financial backing and political endorsement, few sitting MPs are likely to defend their seats successfully, having ridden into office on the tails of Matiba's 'three-piece suit'.[117] Matiba's popularity among poorer residents of southern Kikuyuland and Nairobi, although not as great as it was in December 1992, is still strong. He remains the most powerful political figure among the shanty-town residents of the capital and is likely to emerge – if FORD-Asili participates in the next election – as official leader of the opposition.

Shikuku, however, insists that he is the party's legally elected secretary-general and that Matiba's attempts to replace FORD-Asili's National Executive Committee by holding new elections are unlawful and therefore, void, as only Shikuku and his supporters, who control this key forum, can authorise new polls.[118] Faced by the prospect of losing control of his own party in a protracted legal struggle, Matiba announced in late June 1997 that he had not registered to vote. Under the law, consequently, he can neither defend his Parliamentary constituency nor be a candidate for President. This decision indicates that Matiba himself – though this does not necessarily imply that all FORD-Asili MPs have been consulted or will accept their leader's decision – judges that the political 'playing field' is so tilted in KANU's favour that it is futile to participate in the elections. By boycotting (and possibly attempting to disrupt) the elections, Matiba hopes that so few voters will turn out to vote as to undermine the legitimacy of the Moi government with the international community by demonstrating to the international media the brutality of the state.

Mwai Kibaki's position as leader of the Democratic Party has also been challenged. Defeated DP candidate Ngengi Muigai, President Kenyatta's nephew and successor as MP for Gatundu, supported by a few Kamba MPs, including Kennedy Kiliku and Charity Ngilu, attempted during 1994, 1995 and 1996 to persuade the party to adopt a more confrontational strategy. But even with the support of his father-in-law Isaiah Mathenge, the MP for Nyeri Town, Muigai was unable to shake Kibaki's authority among the northern Kikuyu or to mount much of a challenge for the DP leadership. By June1997, Charity Ngilu, the MP for Kitui Central, who has emerged as an attractive new voice in national politics and a challenger to KANU's control of Ukambani, also concluded that she would be unable to defeat Kibaki if he decided to seek the party's Presidential nomination once again and, like Ngengi Muigai, decided to seek an alternative standard, joining Peter Anyang'-Nyong'o in the Social Democratic Party as its likely Presidential contender. By contrast, after carefully considering the balance of political forces in Kiambu District, Muigai and his sister (the DP's ex-candidate in Dagoretti) joined Matiba's FORD-Asili, the dominant political force in southern Kikuyuland and Nairobi. As candidate for the newly created Gatundu South constituency, Muigai will be locked in a battle royal with Uhuru Kenyatta, the late President's son, who is to fight the seat on behalf of KANU in what will probably be the most expensive contest of the 1997 campaign as both attempt to buy voters' support.[119] Muigai's departure reduces the DP's prospects of putting up a better performance in Kiambu and Nairobi than in 1992.

Although Kibaki has played an active role in the deliberations of the various pressure groups for political reform, his support, even in Nyeri District, has declined. In the three Kamba Districts, in Laikipia, and the former Embu and Meru Districts, where the DP had been politically competitive against the ruling party, its influence has diminished and it seems likely to win few seats outside of Kibaki's bailiwick.[120] The defection of Agnes Ndetei back to KANU was a serious blow to the party in Makueni, while Charity Ngilu's mounting dissatisfaction with Kibaki's lacklustre leadership, culminating in her defection to the SDP, undermines the party's prospects throughout Ukambani. Ngilu may be able to appeal to a wider constituency, mobilising women voters throughout central Kenya against the male domination of politics.[121] G. G. Kariuki also seems likely to mobilise KANU supporters in Laikipia to challenge the two sitting DP MPs.

For the past three years the opposition has been divided over what strategy to adopt to enable it to defeat President Moi and KANU in 1997. In 1995 and 1996 the more moderate elements sought to identify a single candidate to carry the opposition's standard against Moi; others sought to mobilise support behind a campaign for constitutional and administrative reforms which would create a more level political playing field, including demands for the appointment of a neutral Electoral Commission, the repeal of the licensing of meetings provisions in the Public Order Act, reducing the political role of chiefs, the immediate registration of all political parties and freedom of access to the media (especially the vernacular channels of the KBC). Although various names were mentioned – including that of Monsignor Ndingi Mwana a'Nzeki, Co-Adjutator of the Archdiocese of Nairobi, and those of various former Permanent Secretaries and other respected senior civil servants – as possible unifiers of the opposition, no one to date has emerged. The main obstacle has been that none of the party leaders seemed willing to stand down; Matiba, for one, refused to countenance any course but his own; Wamalwa believed that as official leader of the opposition, a moderate and a Luhya, he was best placed to lead the united opposition; while Kibaki, a Cabinet Minister for

26 years and Vice-President for ten, believed that the mantle should automatically fall on him. Given these ambitions, it was always unlikely that the campaign to select a single opposition Presidential candidate would make much progress.

Even the small Safina party was divided over the strategy to adopt. Richard Leakey, for example, considered that it would be impossible to extract any major constitutional or administrative concessions from the government and that it was futile to attempt to secure a more level political playing field. The only way forward, he argued, was to agree on a common Presidential candidate; Moi would then immediately face serious problems, having secured only 37 per cent of the Presidential vote in 1992. By contrast, his colleague Paul Muite believed that the opposition parties would be unable to agree on a single standard bearer and judged that the only way forward was pressure to secure the appointment of an independent Election Commission, freedom of assembly, and equal access to the electronic media and the press.

Similar minded individuals, drawn from the legal community, the churches, and human rights NGOs formed the 'Four Cs' – the Citizens Committee for Constitutional Change, led by Willy Mutunga, to press for legislative and constitutional reforms to create a level 'playing field' before the next election. This, however, made little progress and prospects of fairer and more open elections in 1997 seemed slight, especially after the Cabinet reshuffle of January 1997 which brought Nicholas Biwott back into office as Minister of State in the Office of the President. Biwott's political resurrection was widely interpreted as indicating that KANU was 'battening down the hatches' for the election. The impression was strengthened when tentative proposals for reforming the Public Order Act and the Chiefs' Act were rejected by the Cabinet. Biwott's return to office and the increasing imminence of fresh elections brought about a reassessment of opposition thinking. While the moderates pressed ahead with the campaign to secure political reforms in alliance with the NCCK, launching a National Convention at a conference in Limuru in April 1997, other more militant figures in the opposition, led by Matiba, Muite and Raila Odinga, began seriously to consider boycotting the 1997 election and launching a campaign of civil disobedience to undermine the legitimacy of the Moi government.

The more radical opposition leaders realised that they had little to lose. A careful and dispassionate assessment of developments over the past four and a half years suggests that KANU has made major inroads in the 'ethnic marginals' where it faced serious electoral competition in 1992: Kisii, Nyamira, Embu, Mbere, Meru, Nyambene, Machakos, Kitui and Makueni Districts. Although the party faces serious internal divisions in a number of these areas (as well as in its central Rift Kalenjin core, where many ordinary Kipsigis, Nandi and Marakwet are dissatisfied with KANU's failure to deliver on its election promises of development) its basic position is much stronger than at a similar stage before the 1992 election. If the parties were to compete on the same terms as then, KANU seems likely to win between 130–150 of the 210 seats, leaving the opposition with only 60–80 between them. FORD-Asili looks set to emerge as the main opposition party with about 20 MPs in southern Kikuyuland (including Nakuru District) and Nairobi; Raila Odinga's NDP will probably defeat FORD-Kenya and capture most of the seats in the Luo Districts of Nyanza Province and the IPK-controlled constituencies in Mombasa, giving the National Development Party between 15–20 MPs; while Kibaki's DP will probably be restricted to its Nyeri bastion with a few seats in neighbouring Districts, making a total of 10–12 MPs. The present official opposition, FORD-Kenya, may well be badly hit, losing many of its Luo seats to the NDP (and perhaps a few to KANU in three-way contests), seeing the return of less than a dozen MPs, drawn mainly from the Bukusu sub-tribe of the Abaluhya in Bungoma District and neighbouring constituencies in Trans-Nzoia.

Faced by the real prospect of a comparatively easy victory for President Moi and KANU in 1997, Matiba (who may be ousted by the courts as leader of FORD-Asili) and Muite (whose Safina party remains unregistered) have little to lose from calling for a boycott of the election. Raila Odinga's response has been more cautious. On the one hand he wants to present himself as the radical man of Kenyan politics but, at the same time, Odinga realises that it is vital that he defeats Wamalwa and the sitting Luo MPs who have remained loyal to FORD-Kenya in order clearly to demonstrate that he is the political 'boss' of the Luo and a worthy successor to his father, the *Jaramogi*. Thus, he is drawn between supporting the boycott and disrupting the poll in Nyanza Province, and taking part in the election, possibly emerging as the official leader of the opposition if (as now seems certain) Matiba refuses to participate.

In any case, the final few months of 1997 are likely to be extremely turbulent with the churches and the National Convention Executive Council – led by its three co-convenors Willy Mutunga of the Citizens' Committee for Constitutional Change, Davinder Lamba of the Mazingira Institute, and Bishop Zablon Nthamburi of the Methodist Church – pressing for consultations with the government on constitutional and administrative reforms; while Matiba, Muite, Raila Odinga and the recently returned Sheikh Balala organise popular protests in Nairobi, Mombasa and Kisumu. President Moi and his advisers will react with considerable brutality, unleashing the GSU as on 31 May and on 7 July 1997 ('Saba Saba' day), the seventh anniversary of the riots following the Matiba, Charles Rubia and Raila Odinga detentions in 1990. Then, under pressure from the international community and domestic public opinion, the government will seek to continue its discussions with the moderates in the opposition – the NCCK and the Roman Catholic Church, the National Convention Executive Committee, Wamalwa, Kibaki and Charity Ngilu – in an attempt to isolate and discredit the advocates of the boycott and disrupting the elections.

It is difficult to predict what will happen. Kenya may relapse into civil disorder but we do not consider that the country is in an immediate pre-revolutionary period or that President Moi will follow Mobutu Sese-Seko into exile – whatever the provocative chants of 'Moi-butu' by rioting Nairobi students. It seems more likely that the opposition boycott will disintegrate with FORD-Kenya, the DP, Charity Ngilu and the SDP – and probably Raila Odinga and the NDP – deciding to take part, accepting the modest reforms offered by the government in early August. In such circumstances, it is difficult to see KANU or President Moi being defeated. The opposition's scheme to maximise the advantages of its ethnic divisions by putting up 'favourite son' candidates in the main Provinces in order to prevent Moi securing 25 per cent of the vote in five Provinces looks almost certain to fail, despite the fact that the President secured only 39 per cent in Western and 37 per cent in Eastern Province five years ago.[122] Wamalwa has little support in either Vihiga or Busia, where voter registration in May and June was high, so that Moi will almost certainly gain 35–40 per cent in Western Province; and however popular Charity Ngilu is and however divided KANU's ranks may be in Ukambani, it seems equally certain that Moi will gain over 30 per cent in Eastern Province. Indeed, given a serious boycott by FORD-Asili, Safina and the NDP, it is even conceivable that the President might secure more than a quarter of the vote in both Nyanza Province and Nairobi. The lower the turn-out by opposition supporters, the better KANU's chances of victory are, as recent by-elections in the Westlands and Starehe constituencies in Nairobi have proved with KANU emerging victorious in polls with less than 5 per cent of registered voters participating.[123]

The opposition boycotts of the Ghanaian Parliamentary elections in 1992 and Zambia's in 1996 should provide a warning to the opposition. Kenya, in contrast to many other African countries, has a vibrant and resilient civil society, a powerful opposition political voice, and a relatively open print media: although it may not be a fully democratic society – as this book shows, the 1992 elections were undoubtedly rigged to ensure KANU's victory – and although the regime may be corrupt, nevertheless, Kenya has come a long way from the dark, autocratic days of 1982–1991 when Moi attempted to create a party state. President Moi will retire in 2002 (if not before), his successor will have to be selected, and a new constitution will have to be devised; the changes within KANU are likely to be as dramatic as those within the opposition parties. The next five years are likely to prove as interesting and important as the years since May 1990 when Kenneth Matiba and Charles Rubia launched their campaign for multi-party democracy.

Notes

1 In the past, defeated Ministers had not immediately been nominated to Parliament and reappointed to the Cabinet. As the Office of the President said after the 1969 election, 'His Excellency the President wishes it to be known that he will abide by the verdict of *wananchi* and there will be no consideration for these seats of anybody who has been defeated in the election', Office of the President, *Daily Nation* 11 December 1969, p. 1. Although after an interval of over a year, President Kenyatta had appointed his nephew, Njoroge Mungai, who had been defeated in Dagoretti at the 1974 election, as a nominated MP, Mungai was not readmitted to the Cabinet and lost his place in the political hierarchy.

2 Defector Johnstone Makau received his reward in Makueni District, John Kyalo was reappointed in Machakos, and the acceptable face of KANU was represented in the new choice of Foreign Minister, Stephen Kilonzo Musyoka, from Kitui District.

3 Of the five Kalenjin Districts, only Biwott's Elgeyo-Marakwet received no Cabinet post, a very significant omission, symbolising the continued strong support Moi had for Biwott, as it ensured Biwott faced no rival on his home turf.

4 Grace Ogot from the previous government was replaced by Winifred Nyiva Mwendwa.

5 *KANU Manifesto,* p. 56.

6 This was also the nickname of Steffan Ndichu, new Juja MP, *Daily Nation*, Weekender, p. 2.

7 Women candidates were: KANU – Ogot (Gem); Kimani (Runyenjes), Mwendwa (Kitui West); FORD-Kenya – Asiyo (Karachuonyo), Orie (Starehe); Otieno (Kajiado North); Nyaga (Gachoka); Mugeni (Runyenjes); DP – Njoka (Ndia), Mwendwa (Kitui Central), Ndetei (Kibwezi), Mugo(Dagoretti), Tett (Westlands), Waruhiu (Githunguri), Mwai (Lari); Mwea (Likoni), Wamatai (Msambweni), Seii (Kerio South); ASILI – Wanjiru (Kinangop).

8 Moi blamed the tribal carnage in Rwanda on this. See *Weekly Review*, 15 April 1994, p. 7. Assistant Minister Sharrif Nassir even called for a return to single-party rule in 1994.

9 *Weekly Review*, 8 April 1994, p. 12

10 He was held in the cells for two weeks. The case was moved to Kericho (in KANU territory) to be heard. *Daily Nation*, 13 May 1993, p. 5.

11 *Daily Nation*, 10 June 1993, p. 1

12 Bomachoge MP Ferdinand Obure was severely beaten by police whilst at a police station on May 19. He was arrested, had his valuables stolen and was brought to court unconscious on a stretcher. When he later recovered he was charged again, with disorderly behaviour, see *Standard*, 30 June 1993, p. 14. He recovered. According to Kamotho, who should know, the 'warriors' were KANU youth-wingers dressed for the occasion, 'to deal with opposition supporters'. Kamotho, Machakos Boys High School, in *Weekly Review*, 9 April 1993, p. 11.

13 *Weekly Review*, 12 March, 1993, p. 4. The same figure was mentioned in connection with the Makuyu MP's defection back to KANU.

14 Moi in Kisii in February, quoted in *Society*, 22 March 1993, p. 8.

15 EIU quoting Moi, *Economist* Intelligence Unit, *Country Report*, 4th Quarter 1993.

16 Nassir, at fund-raising meeting, *Weekly Review*, 19 February 1993, p. 11.

17 NEMU count certifier report, Nakuru Town.

18 See for example the *Economic Review*, 25–31 October, 1993, pp. 4–15.

19 See *Weekly Review*, 5 November 1993, p. 16–18.

20 When the census was published in its raw unanalysed form in March 1994, there was continuing dispute about its quality, and real concern that the figures had somehow been massaged to reduce the numbers of opposition tribes and increase those of KANU-voting groups. Indeed, the Kamba community apparently recorded the world's only case of zero population growth in a developing country. See *African Business*, May 1994, p. 7.

21 The editors of the *Watchman* (February), *Society* (February), *Finance* (February) and the *Nairobi Weekly Observer* were arrested and charged with sedition. Copies of the *Economic Review* were also seized. In June 1993, the editor of *Jitegemea* was charged with a second case of sedition, see *Standard*, 12 June 1993, p. 5. Most of the sedition cases were eventually dropped.

22 The cover story was a review of Moi's first 100 days in office since the General Election, *Weekly Review*, 7 May 1993, p. 19. Fotoform and the magazines lost a legal case to have the components returned, on the grounds that they were evidence.

23 *Daily Nation*, 12 May 1993, p. 5.

24 *Weekly Review*, 6 August 1993, p. 16.

25 *Weekly Review*, 21 January 1993, p. 18. It was banned in the *Kenya Gazette*.

26 See *Weekly Review*, 25 March 1994, p. 18 and 22 April 1994, p. 18.

27 Indeed, Norman Nyagah called openly for all three leaders to stand down. See for example *Daily Nation*, 5 June 1993, p. 5.

28 According to foreign diplomats in Nairobi, Odinga may have received more than he declared – perhaps even a total of Sh28 million.

29 See *Weekly Review*, 24 September 1993. The law appeared to provide that MPs lost their seats it they resigned from their party, but not if they were expelled, and the three

dissidents had no interest in resigning to fight by-elections at this time.

30 A risible notion. See *Weekly Review*, 5 November 1993, p. 23 and the *Economic Review*, 8–14 November 1993, pp. 4–7.

31 The full extent of Muite's behind the scenes alliances remained unclear, but according to the government's *Kenya Times*, his allies included numerous DP legislators and wealthy Kikuyu businessmen, even (allegedly) Njenga Karume, and some prominent Asili figures, such as John Michuki, Harun Lempaka and Njenga Mungai.

32 *Weekly Review*, 26 February 1993, p. 8.

33 *Weekly Review*, 1 April 1994, pp. 4–6; 8 April 1994, pp. 5–12; and 22 April 1994, p. 14.

34 See for example the advertising supplement in the *Standard*, 11 January 1993, p. 16

35 Thus undercutting claims that YK' 92 had played a pivotal role in KANU's victory. This group was led by Sammy Boit arap Kogo, a Biwott man, and included District officials from the more remote areas.

36 *Daily Nation* 11 February 1993, p. 1. The implication was than much more had been taken, presumably used in the campaign.

37 *Weekly Review*, 8 October 1993, pp. 13–14.

38 *Weekly Review*, 9 April 1993, pp. 3–7.

39 During the walkout, KANU passed the amended motion 'appreciating the efforts by the government'. *Weekly Review*, 16 April 1993, pp. 6–8.

40 The demoted Minister for Culture and Social Service Mohammed, Luhya assistant Minister Osogo MP Kirwa (a Nandi) and YK' 92 Chairman Cyrus Jirongo (Luhya) all bitterly criticised the Kitengela Declaration. See *Weekly Review*, 16 April 1993, p. 18.

41 Jirongo, quoted in *Weekly Review*, 23 April 1993, p. 5.

42 See the *Weekly Review*, 21 May 1993, pp. 8–9, and *Daily Nation*, 24 May 1993.

43 Key Luhya figures Martin Kunguru and Peter Kubebea were removed from the NSSF and Martin Chahonyo from the Postbank Credit Limited. After pressure from KANU Luhya politicians that KANU was 'blowing' their chances in Western Province, the three were quickly given alternative positions. Kunguru was made Managing Director of the Investment Promotions Centre and Kububea Deputy Managing Director of the Export Processing Zones. Chahonyo was appointed finance and administration manager of the KCB, but sent on immediate compulsory leave. See *Weekly Review*, 14 May 1993.

44 This claimed the huge investment was a waste of money and unlikely to reap a return, and irrelevant to the needs of Kenyans for adequate quality low cost housing. J. S. Isenye, in *Weekly Review*, 28 May 1993, p. 25.

45 *Weekly Review*, 4 June 1993 p. 17; and *Daily Nation*, 27 May 1993, p. 1, though how they had not discovered this until this time was unclear, since they had vehemently denied the same when the deal was discovered by the *Daily Nation* in 1992.

46 This was made even more complex by the fact that it only officially became a contractual agreement in February 1993, when work was already under way.

47 Mudavadi was forced to remain on the fourth floor of the Ministry of Finance, rather than taking the Minister's office. Saitoti also took away the parastatal reform programme from finance to his ministry. See *Weekly Review*, 12 February 1993, pp. 28–9.

48 Matters must first be considered by the FKE, the unions and the government, and then referred to the Industrial Court.

49 KBC Commentary, 30 April 1993.

50 Joash Wa Mang'oli and Fred Gumo were under financial scrutiny in early May, see *Weekly Review*, 21 May 1993, pp. 8–9. Meanwhile, Luhya opposition MPs protested vigorously at actions against their community, claiming the Luhya were 'used and discarded like toilet paper', and were supported privately by many KANU Luhya MPs.

51 *Weekly Review*, 3 September 1993, p. 16.

52 *Weekly Review*, 23 July 1993, p. 17.

53 *Ibid.*, p. 16.

54 Matiba, in *Daily Nation*, 12 June 1993, p. 1.

55 Ntimama, reported in *Weekly Review*, 29 October 1993, p. 12.

56 About 65 opposition MPs participated in these activities, the closest to unity yet seen, but even then excluding the seven-strong pro-KANU *duol* team from south Nyanza and a number of other absentees including Odinga, Matiba and Shikuku. See the *Weekly Review*, 29 October 1993 pp. 4–19, and 5 November 1993, pp. 4–15; and *Economic Review*, 1–7 November 1993, pp. 4–7. There were even allegations made in the house by Njenga Mungai that Ntimama personally participated in the killings. See *Economic Review*, 25–31

October 1993, p. 13.

57 Joe Murumbi, quoted in C. Sanger and J. Nottingham, 'The Kenya General Election of 1963', *Journal of Modern African Studies,* Vol. 2, No. 1 (1964), p. 16.

58 Petitions may be made by any person affected by the result, including candidates and voters, and need not be made by a political party. In practice, even when made by a voter, they have always been associated with a defeated candidate.

59 This limited the time a petition could be heard and tightened the rules for presentation of affidavits, and came into effect on 29 January 1993. *Kenya Gazette* notice dated 13 November, released on 10 December 1992.

60 *Weekly Review,* 19 February 1993, p. 15.

61 Although he was believed to have opposed for example the appointment of Chesoni, he was generally viewed as defending the one-party state, and in 1991 107 opposition leaders signed a petition requesting his removal. He was publicly accused by the new LSK chairman of being the 'root cause' of problems between judges and lawyers.

62 The first, the most important, was manned by judges Edward Torgbor, R. S. C. Omolo (with Alternate Shaikh Amin) and Jack A. Couldrey. The second bench was manned by Justices Emmanuel O'Kubasu, John Mwera and Gideon Mbito.

63 *Standard,* 26 May 1993, pp. 1–2. Matiba appealed to the High Court.

64 *Weekly Review,* 28 May 1993, p. 14.

65 *Daily Nation,* 2 July 1993, p. 1.

66 Matiba applied in July to recruit a UK QC, Tony Scrivener, and Larry Watt as foreign advocates, permission for which was denied by the Attorney-General. Matiba filed a certificate of urgency appeal which claimed that Moi himself had hired a QC who lives and practises in England (though also an advocate of the Kenyan High Court) without success. See *Daily Nation,* 10 November 1993, p. 28. In early October Moi applied to have 20 grounds struck out (these alleged intimidation by Moi supporters against voters and ethnic violence) on the grounds that adequate particulars had not been supplied. KANU also sought time to file replying affidavits. Hearing was deferred again to 14 December 1993, *Daily Nation,* 26 October 1993, p. 4.

67 Sane, a Keen activist, had declared as the DP candidate against Saitoti in August 1992, before Keen had switched at the last moment from Kajiado South. *Standard,* 6 May 1993, p. 13; *Weekly Review* 28 May 1993, p. 14; *Society,* 26 July 1993, p. 14; and *Sunday Nation,* 30 August 1992, p. 4, and 21 September 1992, pp. 34–5.

68 The Makuyu MP's defection so incensed the local population that they attempted to murder him on several occasions, see *Standard,* 24 June 1993, p. 1.

69 *Ibid.* Others were hit by local 'whispering campaigns', including Stephen Ndichu (Asili, Juja) himself, who claimed that KANU Ministers had been trying to entice him for Sh6 million. See *Weekly Review,* 23 July 1993, p. 24.

70 Minister John Kyalo promised Makuyu residents electricity if they voted KANU and Joseph Kamotho personally promised to pay the school fees of poor children, and directed the Teachers Service Commission to put Makuyu teachers being paid by schools on its payroll.

71 Odinga visited several times. Kibaki visited the weekend before, as did Moi (using an official visit). *Weekly Review,* 21 May 1993, p. 4. Even before nomination day, 50 KANU supporters seriously injured four FORD-Kenya supporters. On 28 April, nomination day, FORD-Kenya supporters attacked KANU supporters dishing out money. FORD-Kenya MP Ferdinand Obure was beaten unconscious by police and hospitalised for a long period when he went to the police station to demand the release of his arrested supporters.

72 *Weekly Review,* 15 April 1994, pp. 11–12.

73 Thus, for example, Kamotho simply announced that Protas Kebati was the Bonchari candidate, whilst in Migori Charles Owino was nominated in a closed door meeting of the KANU branch. See *Weekly Review,* 23 April 1993, pp. 7–8.

74 The second by-election was caused by the death in a car accident of the FORD-Kenya victor on polling day.

75 *Weekly Review,* 11 March 1994, pp. 4–10.

76 Interview with Grace Githu, November 1993. This became the Institute for Education in Democracy.

77 *Economist* Intelligence Unit, *Country Report Kenya* 1st Quarter 1994, p. 10.

78 Musyoka, during meeting with British High Commissioner, reported in *Society,* 22 February 1993, p. 5.

79 *Economist* Intelligence Unit, *Country Report Kenya*, 2nd quarter 1993.
80 The team also witnessed violence by the Special Branch against a chemist, working on killings in the Rift Valley, and were in the country during a severe crackdown on the radical press.
81 *Africa Confidential*, Vol. 34, No. 6, 19 March 1993.
82 *Economist* Intelligence Unit, *Country Report*, 2nd Quarter 1993.
83 *Independent*, 24 March 1993, p. 12.
84 Mudavadi, quoted in *Weekly Review*, 2 April 1993, p. 18.
85 The World Bank had in fact been allowing funds to move into the country for some time: according to the *Weekly Review*, US$116 million came in between December 1992 and April 1993.
86 Total development expenditure falling in 1992–3 from Sh3.5 billion. to 2.6 billion. This however was less than the Sh1 billion cut suggested by the IMF and World Bank in 1991.
87 *Standard*, 11 June 1993. Thus in *Society* in October 1993 we still see demands of senior politicians like Nyachae that 'all the unemployed graduates in the constituency should be absorbed into his Ministry and parastatals'. See *Society*, 18 October 1993, letter, p. 4.
88 Kibaki suggested the budget was 'good, as it contained no major increases in public expenditure', quoted in *Standard*, 11 June 1992, p. 3. Other DP MPs and businessmen cautiously welcomed the changes. FORD-Kenya's Anyang-Nyong'o dismissed it as a disappointment, but FORD-Kenya was generally muted. Asili was more critical, and most Asili MPs boycotted the budget speech. See *Daily Nation*, 12 June 1993, p. 1.
89 See *Weekly Review*, 5 November 1993, pp. 40–1. He was also removed as Chairman of KTN and Alico (Kenya) Ltd and questioned by police after his return.
90 *Weekly Review*, 1 April 1994, pp. 20–4.
91 There were numerous reshuffles of personnel, affecting both those compromised by abuses and those revealing them, during 1993–4.
92 The government began to implement its understanding with the IMF to mop up excess liquidity generated during October–December 1992, mainly through the political banks.
93 In May 1994, Mudavadi and Cheserem were feted openly by Western donors and investors.
94 They believed, possibly correctly, that it was impossible to keep control over the country in a situation where the government was forced to dismantle parts of its apparatus of state licensing and control. Thus the ethnic clashes in Narok were seen as a deliberate internal attempt to sabotage the efforts of the reformists.
95 *Weekly Review*, 21 May 1993, p. 32.
96 Kenya had not fallen into arrears until 1991, but had accumulated a Sh48 billion debt by June 1993.
97 She indeed proved relatively uncontroversial.
98 *Weekly Review*, 20 August 1993, p. 15.
99 *Weekly Review*, 11 March 1994, pp. 11–12.
100 The government did not accord him a state funeral, to much bitterness, though flags were flown at half-mast.
101 The funeral was extensively reported in the *Weekly Review* on 11 February 1994. Numerous foreign dignitaries attended. Matiba, as ever, bucked the trend to reconciliation, saying he saw no reason to attend Odinga's funeral since there had been no love lost between them.
102 Orengo, at the funeral, *Weekly Review*, 11 February 1994, p. 7.
103 Moi in Kericho, February 1994. See *Weekly Review*, 18 February 1994.
104 Details of the election can be found in the *Weekly Review*, 25 March 1994, pp. 4–11.
105 The depth of the Asili collapse in the West can be judged by the fact that in the Lugari by-election, which FORD-Kenya narrowly lost, they polled 45 per cent and Asili 3 per cent, when, in 1992, Asili had polled 69 per cent and FORD-Kenya 3 per cent.
106 Several senior Luhya politicians from outside Parliament defected to FORD-Kenya at this time, including Bahati Semo (from Asili), Peter Okondo (from PICK) and Burudi Nabwera (from KANU).
107 Their confidence in their political tactics was reflected in their willingness to provide advice and support secretly to the Malawi Congress Party in their similar struggle for survival.
108 The five by-elections resulting from election petitions have been in the Kisauni and Changamwe divisions of Mombasa, Mathare in Nairobi, Mandera East and Webuye.

109 In Machakos town, Kerio Central, Turkana Central, Hamisi, Nairobi-Westlands and Kitutu Chache.

110 Two seats were vacant at the dissolution; one FORD-Asili seat in Murang'a, where the incumbent defected to KANU, and the DP seat of Tetu in Nyeri, where the Member died in June 1997.

111 The sole KNC MP also successfully held his Siakago seat when he joined KANU in 1995.

112 As a result of these defections, KANU gained Lugari, Hamisi, Ikolomani, Lurambi and Shinyalu in March and June 1994. A detailed assessment of these by-elections can be found in *By-Election Report*, 27 June 1994, the Institute for Education in Democracy, Nairobi, 1994.

113 FORD-Kenya held Migori, Ndhiwa and Nyatike after defections to KANU, but lost Nairobi-Langata to the revitalised National Development Party in March 1997, following Raila Odinga's announcement of his resignation from FORD-Kenya on 31 December 1996. A detailed report of the Langata by-election can be found in *By-Election Observation Report, Kitutu Chache and Lang'ata Constituency, January 21 and March 11, 1997*, the Institute for Education in Democracy, Nairobi, March 1997.

114 FORD-Kenya successfully defended its gain at a second by-election on 2 November 1994, required by the death of Frederick Masinde, its original by-election victor, in a motor-car accident on election day in June 1994.

115 *Weekly Review*, 14 March 1997, pp. 4–6 and *By-Election Observation Report, Kitutu Chache and Lang'ata Constituency, January 21 and March 11, 1997*, the Institute for Education in Democracy, Nairobi, March 1997.

116 Professor Peter Anyang'-Nyong'o in Kisumu Rural, however, sought to distance himself from both camps by joining the moribund Social Democratic Party, whose Secretary-General is the Kikuyu intellectual Apollo Njonjo, another prominent political scientist. For criticisms of the decision see, *Weekly Review*, 21 March 1997, pp. 6–7.

117 *Weekly Review*, 7 March 1997, 4–6.

118 *Ibid.*, 30 May 1997, pp. 4–6.

119 *Ibid.*, 7 March 1997, pp. 6–7 and 16 May, 1997, pp. 5–9.

120 *Ibid.*, 14 March 1997, pp. 7–8.

121 *Ibid.*, 28 March 1997, pp. 4–8.

122 For an interesting but brief survey of thinking on the 1997 election see Okech Kendo, 'Kenya Presidency '97', *East African Standard*, Nairobi, June 1997.

123 For accounts of these by-elections, see the reports by the Institute for Education in Democracy, *Kibwezi and Starehe Constituency By-Elections, March 14 and April 10, 1996*, Nairobi, May 1996; and *Westlands and Hamisi By-Elections Report, June 10, 1996*, Nairobi, June 1996; and *Kitutu Chache and Lang'ata Constituency, January 21 and March 11, 1997*, Nairobi, March 1997.

Thirteen

Conclusions

The Emergence of Multi-Party Competition

The late 1980s had seen the concentration of power in the hands of the executive, especially the Provincial Administration, controlled from the Office of the President, and in the ruling party's revitalised central, disciplinary institutions. Jennifer Widner has suggested that this amounted to the creation of a 'party-state'.[1] Although this probably goes too far, KANU undoubtedly became increasingly authoritarian, overriding public opinion, rigging elections, silencing the independent media, and harassing autonomous institutions, such as the Churches and the Law Society. This creeping authoritarianism provoked a backlash beginning in 1989, especially amongst the once all-powerful Kikuyu élite, who increasingly became a focus of opposition to the Moi regime. The changing international environment, highlighted by the collapse of Communist rule in Eastern Europe in the last months of 1989, which coincided with the release of Nelson Mandela in South Africa and the mysterious death of Foreign Minister Ouko (both in February 1990), encouraged a number of prominent Kenyans to criticise single-party rule and to campaign for the introduction of multi-party politics.

The opposition emerged from a confluence of crises. Some fuses, such as the growing abuses of state power, the 1988 election rigging and the Ouko murder, were slow-burning. Others, such as the 1990 rebellion of Kenneth Matiba and Charles Rubia, Oginga Odinga's continuing determination to press for the legalisation of an opposition party, the Saitoti Commission, Western protests and the cancellation of aid by the Paris Group, were specific events – the products of personalities or political decisions which might easily have taken a different form. Church leaders, especially Bishops Okullu and Muge of the CPK and Reverend Dr Timothy Njoya of the PCEA, led the way, closely followed by radical lawyers Paul Muite and Gibson Kamau Kuria. The main Christian

Churches and the Law Society of Kenya had proved themselves to be the sole organisations with the institutional independence to stand up to the Kenyan regime during its most authoritarian phase, and they had nurtured the opposition in the dark days of the late 1980s. Still, the collapse of single-party rule in 1990 was far from certain. As the events of *Saba Saba* showed, the regime could still silence its critics physically. As with so many other autocratic regimes, it was when the chinks began to appear in its armour that previously cowed dissenters began to raise their heads. Indeed, the self-doubt and internal divisions demonstrated by the Saitoti Commission and the abandonment of queuing were almost as important as the opposition campaign in undermining the ruling party's credibility. As de Tocqueville pointed out, it is when reform begins that the control of the *ancien régime* starts to wither.

It still remains far from clear, however, whether KANU and Moi truly had no choice but to acquiesce in the institution of multi-party democracy, or indeed that the transition so far has been of much benefit to Kenyans themselves. Why, in that case, did President Moi and his colleagues in KANU's inner circle accept their most bitter opponents' demands, when they so publicly abhorred both the concept and the practice? Did they simply miscalculate, vastly overrating KANU's popularity? Or did they feel that, following the Paris Group meeting, they had no alternative if they were to avoid a financial crisis and civil unrest or a coup? We believe that Moi and his colleagues panicked when informed of the Paris Group's decision. Facing an already dangerous situation, with the Kikuyu and Luo overwhelmingly opposed to the regime and seeking (albeit mainly passively) its downfall, they overestimated the immediate impact of the cessation of balance of payments support, coinciding as this did with Biwott's arrest and the Ouko crisis. Moi appears to have cracked: against his own judgement, and under conditions of extreme secrecy, he personally reversed thirty years of state policy. Whether the motive was quick access to money or the possibility of relegitimising his leadership, is unknown. Certainly, the state initially appeared desperate for the aid, but technocrats in the Central Bank and the Ministry of Finance adapted and found ways to finance the election, regardless of the cost to the country's economic health. The Kenyan economy – and, therefore, ordinary Kenyans – had to finance President Moi's re-election and KANU's return to power.

The 1992 Election Campaign

Throughout the country, especially in their ethnic strongholds, the constituency headquarters of the opposition parties were hives of activity. The election was fought and directed for FORD-Kenya, FORD-Asili, the DP and the KNC, by local party members of modest social backgrounds. KANU, by contrast, was the party of government. Its campaign was orchestrated and directed by District Commissioners, chiefs and YK '92 officials, rather than local party activists. Although KANU boasted a host of bright, newly painted location and sub-location offices in virtually every constituency, these remained virtually empty. The KANU campaign was fought from the local District Office under the supervision of the Provincial Administration and the Office of the President. YK '92 served as the President's hit team, moving into constituencies to organise an effective campaign, frequently over the objections of the local party leadership. It was employed to ensure the defeat of ineffective or compromised incumbents and the maximisation of the pro-KANU – and especially the pro-Moi – vote on election day. In several areas, this meant repudiating the pro-Biwott men, who had been rigged in four years before, when popularity had not been an important criterion in candidate selection. Although it aroused considerable enmity, which was paid back after the election, YK '92 played a vital role in KANU's victory – as well as proving financially remunerative for its leaders – enabling the President to intervene directly in the factional feuds of local KANU sub-branches.

The tactics employed by KANU were predictable. As Widner said of Zaïre in 1990,

> Mobutu probably believed he could win an election. Caught by surprise when people first expressed discontent, Mobutu nonetheless controlled critical electoral resources and knew that the collapse of the country's road network and telecommunications system would make it very hard for parties to gain broad followings. He encouraged fragmentation among the opposition parties, in some instances providing the means to initiate groups that would absorb votes from the more powerful, better-organised parties.[2]

Substituting the use of security laws and the Provincial Administration for the collapse of the road network, this provides a good characterisation of the KANU strategy in the 1992 election.

Multi-party competition brought the KANU leadership closer to the grassroots. In those marginal areas where people did matter, KANU worked hard to ensure that it had the best candidates it could field. Old alliances and interests were swiftly discarded when the realities of national politics intruded. If KANU's hardliners had won and the ruling party had insisted upon putting forward the same candidates that had been rigged into Parliament in 1988, it is very likely that KANU would have lost far more seats on the Coast, in Eastern Province and, perhaps, even in Nandi and West Pokot. Darius Mbela in Taita-Taveta was sacked and re-appointed only weeks afterwards, when it became clear that he was far too popular to allow him to defect. Francis Lotodo in West Pokot had to be promised a Cabinet seat after the election to remain loyal. In Nandi there was widespread dissatisfaction, especially in Anglican circles, with the 1980s leadership. Only by coopting a prominent Anglican leader in Mosop, by cajoling and threatening other dissidents, but above all by dumping the three sitting MPs, did KANU stabilise the situation in the District. Multi-partyism in a context of patron–client relationships forces even the incumbent leadership to rebuild its mass support.

FORD-Kenya and especially the DP depended on central party officials, local leaders and a network of local activists to run the election. For both parties money was in short supply even in their ethnic strongholds. A considerable number of DP candidates were men of considerable wealth – as befitted the party of the old Kikuyu establishment – but most, as in

FORD-Kenya, came from the established middle class. Money was available but not in vast quantities. Indeed, the DP proved singularly inept in providing financial support to its candidates, devoting rather too much of its resources to running extensive advertisements in the press and on television. By contrast, FORD-Kenya made its more modest resources go a long way. Its television commercial was particularly effective, and though FORD-Kenya had insufficient money to run major advertisements, several magazines, such as *Finance* and *Society,* were sympathetic to the party, especially its Young Turks. The secretariat, however, was ineffective in targeting the party's most winnable seats. Considerable sums, as we have seen, were wasted in hopeless contests. Elsewhere strong candidates, such as Jembe Mwakalu in Bahari, were starved of funds.

The FORD-Asili campaign was rather different, although it too had a large number of enthusiastic activists in its strongholds. First, the party and the campaign were dominated by Matiba, who supplied much of the money for candidates throughout the country, fighting a brilliant and highly effective populist campaign. While candidates of the other three main parties in many areas disassociated themselves from their party's Presidential candidate, FORD-Asili's Parliamentary candidates clung to Matiba's coat-tails, understanding his immense popular following. Secondly, FORD-Asili's money was wisely spent at constituency level, targeted at specific groups of voters, rather than exhausted on expensive press and television advertisements. Until the last few days of the campaign, no FORD-Asili or Matiba advertisements appeared in the *Daily Nation* or the *Standard,* nor in any of the plethora of political magazines. FORD-Asili was the only party not to commission a television 'spot': It realised that most of its potential voters did not have access to television and preferred to finance constituency-level activities – especially, 'treating' voters – where money spent had the biggest return. Despite all the invective, the bitter press campaign of 1992 appears to have had little effect, serving primarily as a test of financial muscle to demonstrate that you and your party were important, rich, powerful, serious, and were bidding for national power. The DP, which was the only opposition party to attempt to compete with KANU in the press and to a lesser extent on television, did no better than its opposition rivals and it is doubtful that it received value for money in terms of the votes its media blitz cost. Political advertising, however, did provide a valuable financial subsidy to several of the fledgling news magazines and in that way contributed to the political debate and to the widening of civic freedoms.[3]

Most of FORD-Asili's victorious new MPs in Murang'a, Kiambu, Nakuru and Nairobi were men of comparatively modest means. FORD-Asili was fundamentally a one-man band (despite Martin Shikuku's contribution in Kakamega), retaining only a few experienced politicians – former Vice-President Karanja, ex-Kenya Commercial Bank Chairman John Michuki, former Chief Secretary and Secretary to the Cabinet Geoffrey Kariithi, and former Permanent Secretary and prominent lawyer Japeth Shamalla were the only men of conspicuous wealth – after the breakaway of the KNC. Most established politicians had been unable to tolerate Matiba's paranoia and arrogance.[4] Many observers, including members of the Kikuyu élite, wondered whether Matiba, if elected, might prove to be even more dictatorial than Moi.

Matiba's well-financed and charismatic campaign proved highly effective throughout southern Kikuyuland and Nairobi. In November, as he battled to regain his health for the campaign, FORD-Asili's prospects looked bleak and officials at Muthithi House, party headquarters, were despondent. But Matiba fought a brilliant campaign, articulating the grievances of the Kikuyu masses and drawing support from the poorest sections of society. Emphasising that, unlike the leaders of the DP, he had been willing to speak out against election rigging and corruption, standing up for freedom of speech and political pluralism in the dark days of 1990, and that he had suffered a year in detention, Matiba offered a simple but attractive message: 'Trust me and I'll fix things.' Moreover, many voters believed that he would be able to deliver and, if necessary, pay for it from his own pocket. By mid-December, he had clearly overtaken Kibaki in Nairobi, and by the last week of the campaign it was becoming clear that he would probably defeat the DP leader in Central Province, though the sheer extent of the pro-Matiba landslide, especially in Kiambu District, the former bastion of the Kenyatta family and the old Kikuyu order, was totally unexpected. In a very real sense, the Kenyatta era in southern Kikuyuland ended not in August 1978, but on 29 December 1992, when the mystique and residual power of the Kenyatta family in southern Kikuyuland was finally shattered by the vote for Matiba and the DP debacle.

The result confirmed not only the importance of patronage and ethnicity in contrast to class and ideology, but above all the appeal of populism and money. Throughout the country, Kenyans voted overwhelmingly for populists, not intellectuals. Both President Moi and FORD-Asili's Kenneth Matiba fought as populist candidates, attempting to identify themselves with ordinary voters, despite their vast wealth. There remains considerable support in Kenya for the eighteenth-century Western notion that political power should be the preserve of the extremely rich, since they are the only ones who do not need to abuse their positions to amass personal wealth. Throughout most of Kikuyuland, the FORD-Asili leader more than matched expenditure by KANU and, although the party received considerable donations from Kikuyu businessmen (just in case Matiba outpolled Kibaki), it was clear that much of the money was coming from his own pocket.

DP leaders and sections of the press, aware of the move towards FORD-Asili in the last two weeks of the campaign, promoted the idea that Matiba was no more than a stooge of the ruling party and probably in receipt of funds from Moi and KANU. Certainly, he spent lavishly: Matiba's portrait was festooned everywhere in Nairobi and southern Kikuyuland, appearing on virtually every *matatu* between Nakuru and Murang'a town, while FORD-Asili candidates were well-provided with vehicles, equipment and money to 'treat' voters. Equally clearly, FORD-Asili 'spoiled' the prospects of both FORD-Kenya and then the DP, as Matiba's arrogance first created havoc in the main opposition party and then prevented Kikuyu voters from uniting behind Kibaki. It was noticeable that Matiba made few attacks on the President, devoting far more time to denouncing opposition leaders

Odinga and Kibaki, and that the FORD-Asili leader's campaign was much less harassed by the Provincial Administration and the police than those of the other opposition parties. But if President Moi did provide covert funds to FORD-Asili to keep the opposition fragmented, it almost backfired, as Matiba's populist rhetoric generated more and more support, until by the last few days of the campaign, Matiba was in danger of outpolling Moi in the popular vote and, thereby, forcing a run-off. Although the accusations of financial support from Moi cannot be substantiated, considerable circumstantial evidence exists, and doubts will remain.

The dramatic changes of October–December 1991 were undermined not only by the ruling party but by opposition leaders as well. The popular euphoria and enthusiasm generated by the prospect of a new political future was swiftly hijacked by old-guard politicians who had fallen out with the regime during the 1980s. Although public opinion enthusiastically rallied behind the new opposition parties (especially FORD) when they were registered at the end of December 1991, when the parties sought to establish a credible grassroots organisation, they quickly became transformed into smaller versions of KANU in the 1970s. Veteran politicians like Shikuku, Matiba, Oloo-Aring'o and many other more minor figures from the past edged aside the Nairobi-based Young Turks and remoulded the parties in the image of the old system in order both to win the election and to provide themselves with new avenues for personal advancement. In so doing, they sowed the seeds of their own downfall.

The opposition parties all fell into the trap of emulating KANU in their political organisation. The DP, despite its name, did not pay much attention to democracy, preferring a self-perpetuating oligarchy of Kikuyu and related 'fat cats' over the danger of contested party elections, leaving themselves exposed to Matiba's invective; FORD-Asili was a one man show; while FORD-Kenya increasingly seemed a reincarnation of the KPU. President Moi, in fact, seemed at times a more attractive candidate than the octogenarian Odinga, the ailing and megalomaniacal Matiba, or the ineffectual Kibaki. At least, he was decisive, of sound mind and in good health. The opposition old guard failed to mobilise the huge commitment for change amongst Kenyans, which was so hopeful a sign in 1990–1, and by their eventual failure to overthrow the regime, they also failed to advance the campaign to improve human rights and basic liberties.

FORD's collapse into rival ethnic camps during 1992 highlighted the tendency towards endemic factionalism within this neo-patrimonial society. Wealthy individuals – or even those in alliance with wealthy individuals through the new party system – were expected to buy votes and to 'treat' their supporters. As before, the election was a vast mechanism to transfer resources from the privileged élite to the urban and rural masses in a three-week carnival during which social relations were turned upside down and power briefly passed into the hands of the illiterate artisan, the unemployed youth, or the grizzled peasant. All elections in Kenya have been closely tied to the patron–client system. This does not compromise their legitimacy; the legitimacy of the Kenyatta and early Moi years actually derived from the system. The fundamental problem with the widespread rigging of the 1988 elections was that it disrupted long-established patron–client structures. If politicians could no longer trade goods and preferment for support, the fundamental basis of the political system was undermined. District bosses and leaders, who had built a local base in order to bolster their position at the centre, suddenly found themselves disadvantaged against upstart administrators and 'lackeys' who could arrange to have themselves imposed. The attempt to create a party state after 1985 and to deny critics of President Moi any access to the political process wrought severe damage to the system, seriously damaging the political legitimacy of the regime among members of the political élite as well as among ordinary voters.

The failure of the opposition to unite before, during or after the election was a severe indictment of the leaderships' personalities, competence to govern, and, indeed, simple foresight, since it was obvious as soon as FORD began to split that, in the context of state rigging and pressure, this was likely to be the end of the opposition's chances of outright victory. As many suggested, the opposition shot themselves in the foot by failing to unite but, as we have shown, it probably would not have changed the result if they had agreed a joint ticket between any two of the three factions. Their best chance was the Odinga-Matiba ticket which had existed at the start. If Matiba had accepted the offered Vice-Presidency and actively campaigned for Odinga, the opposition might have stood a chance of defeating Moi. If they had, the death of Odinga on 20 January 1994 might have made Kenneth Matiba President of Kenya. But even then, Kibaki would probably have taken a large portion of the Kikuyu vote away from a united FORD. In any case, KANU would have responded by cheating more. A united FORD, therefore, might not have changed the result, but it would have made it harder to conceal the abuses.

The Results

There is evidence of widespread falsification of the 1992 election results, affecting at least 50 of the seats, in addition to the administrative incompetence highlighted on election day and the four days of counting that followed. Whilst over half the country the election was relatively fair, in the other half, particularly the government strongholds (Presidential) and marginal constituencies (Parliamentary), many problems were experienced. Both foreign and domestic observers reported serious irregularities in areas such as Nakuru and Eldoret, and evidence from defeated candidates and party agents suggests direct rigging of Parliamentary results for KANU stalwarts such as George Saitoti and Zachary Onyonka, particularly once the Presidential result was known. The turn-out in the pastoral and semi-arid Kalenjin heartlands of Baringo, Elgeyo-Marakwet, Kericho, Bomet and Nandi was an astonishing 87 per cent, compared with an average for the rest of the country of 67 per cent, and a turn-out in 1983, the last unrigged election, of only 52 per cent for the same area. In over 40 constituencies, the number of Presidential and Parliamentary ballots failed to match by more than 800 papers, a characteristic signal of ballot box stuffing. KANU also rigged the Parliamentary nominations in the 18

Kalenjin-core seats because of pride. It was determined to show that Moi and the ruling party commanded the loyalty of Kalenjin voters and wanted a clean sweep to establish momentum for the wider campaign.

Despite enormous and patient queues across the country, outside the Kalenjin home areas, and the opposition strongholds of Central Province and Luo Nyanza, the turn-out for the first multi-party general elections since independence was only 61 per cent, especially strange given the low registration levels achieved in June. Ethnic groups without parliamentary candidates in particular constituencies and the urban areas apparently did not vote in anything like the numbers expected.

The consensus opinion is that Moi would have won a narrow Presidential majority over Matiba even discounting rigging, but might well have lost control of Parliament. The government arranged that the Presidential results would be counted first, because Moi would almost certainly win. These results enabled the Office of the President and the Provincial Administration to work out which Parliamentary seats KANU was likely to win and how many they needed to fix to ensure that the party had a working majority in the new National Assembly.

If the December 1992 General Election demonstrated anything, it was the importance of party and ethnicity in Kenyan politics. In many respects this is a surprising conclusion. Every previous General Election in independent Kenya had pointed to the vital role of the individual politician. Now, with the reimposition of a more fundamental set of divisions, most communities rejected the politics of 'development' and clanism. Once the single-party state was swept away and ethnically based opposition parties emerged, individual candidates counted for much less than their party and the identity of its Presidential candidate. What began as an apparently national contest based on ideals ended as little more than an ethnic slanging match. Neo-patrimonialism shifted from the micro- to the macro-level. Thus, the Kalenjin and other pastoral communities of the Rift Valley voted overwhelmingly for their 'favourite son' Daniel arap Moi; northern Kikuyuland and neighbouring Embu similarly voted almost as one in support of Mwai Kibaki; the southern Kikuyu gave Matiba 90 per cent of their support; while Oginga Odinga carried Luoland by an even larger margin. Paul Muite's lonely outpost in Kikuyu was the sole exception, but even there Matiba secured 87 per cent of the Presidential vote, compared with Odinga's six per cent. True, in Kisii, Nyamira, Western Province and parts of Eastern and North-Eastern Provinces, the victorious candidate still had to have the 'right' clan or sub-clan connections, but this was because the élite and to an extent the masses had failed to reach a consensus on their own best interests.

The Prospects for Multi-Party Democracy

In many ways, Kenya was well run by Kenyatta's single-party state. Indeed, John Lonsdale, in his article 'States and Social Processes in Africa', went almost so far as to suggest that the Kenyatta regime in the 1970s provided just about the best that subjects (if not, quite, citizens) of African states can expect.[5] Kenyatta's relatively benign – and it needs to be acknowledged that in particular circumstances and for certain groups it was frequently far from benign – single-party rule, however, proved impossible to sustain in the deteriorating economic conditions of the 1980s and early 1990s. Any such concentration of power can only be maintained over the long term if an enlightened despot (or, even better, a saint) is in charge. Kenyatta approximated to this in several ways. He was a benevolent dictator; had no real fear of being deposed; and was happy to leave the day-to-day running of the state to technocrats in the civil service and Provincial Administration. Such conditions of benign neglect enabled the advantaged majority to gain at the expense of the disadvantaged minority. Thus, the Kikuyu benefited, while the Luo were neglected. The rich grew richer, while the poor continued to live in shanty towns. But the state facilitated the development of economic initiatives among the Kikuyu peasantry, enabling the more prosperous rural areas to take off into self-sustained growth.

Today, the Kikuyu are effectively disenfranchised. Despite the fact that President Moi secured only 2 per cent of the vote in Central Province, he remains in power and the Kikuyu areas continue to be excluded from state patronage. Indeed, Kikuyuland is in an even more invidious position than it was before the advent of multi-party politics. Although the community's interests were squeezed throughout the 1980s, Kikuyu leaders could exert some influence on government decisions, as long as Mwai Kibaki, Kenneth Matiba, Arthur Magugu and George Muhoho, among others, sat in the Cabinet. With the failure of KANU to win a single seat in Central Province, the Kikuyu presence is reduced to Joseph Kamotho, who had to be nominated to Parliament after losing his Murang'a constituency to the Matiba tidal wave. Not only are the Kikuyu disenfranchised because they lost the election, but the indirect influence they had on policy through Provincial Commissioners, Ministers, and key civil servants has disappeared as well.[6]

Throughout 1993 and 1994, Local Government Minister William ole Ntimama seemed intent upon fulfilling his campaign promise to reduce Kikuyu influence by pressing on with the assault on 'settler' communities throughout the country, with the long-term objective of clearing the Rift Valley of Kikuyu and returning control of the country to the 'indigenous' population (i.e., those who are not Kikuyu). The election clearly demonstrated the primacy of ethnicity over ideology. Of all the myriad sources for internal divisions within the opposition – between compromisers and purists, old and young, politicians and professionals, conservatives and radicals – it was the division between Kikuyu and Luo which eclipsed all else. Communal solidarity did not have to be enforced but was clearly voluntary in the homelands of the four major Presidential candidates. As President Moi warned, multi-party democracy has intensified ethnic rivalries and completed the isolation of the Kikuyu who, even more than the Luo in the 1960s, are totally identified with the opposition.

Thus, although single-party states are unlikely to sustain accountability – a concept which many political scientists have identified as the key to democratic government – they may create an effective 'political order' in Africa's ethnically divided societies. They provide some controls on centrifugal tendencies that threaten to fragment the still comparatively insecure and weakly institutionalised state structures. Even single-party rule may provide a more attractive alternative to multi-partyism in the form of single-party states, in which each party is all powerful in its own ethnic stronghold, but where one group controls the centre and the distribution of patronage and development.

Perhaps of greater short-term interest, however, was the virtual death of *Harambee,* which for the previous three decades had provided an important means for politicians to keep in touch with their constituents and, as Jennifer Widner has demonstrated, enabled the regime to direct funds to areas which might have felt neglected by official state expenditure. The onset of multi-party politics, however, compelled Provincial Administrators to ban all Harambee meetings as they would have provided a focus for opposition leaders' activities in the run-up to the campaign and, furthermore, might have been an uncontrollable source of funds for the opposition parties, challenging KANU's financial supremacy.

One lesson from this book is that multi-party democracy, interpreted as multiple national parties competing openly and nationally, still does not exist in Kenya, and is unlikely to do so in the foreseeable future. Kenya did not experience a true multi-party election, despite the apparent situation in Nairobi. Instead, the country underwent a set of single-party elections, a heavily biased campaign and a tilted electoral process. These still did not deliver quite the result the state required, necessitating a last-minute 'correction'. The failure to accept the legitimacy of opposition in deed, rather than word, remains a key feature of Kenyan politics and a key weakness in the move to sustainable multi-party democracy. This is a situation designed to debilitate opposition parties. The continuing vitality of patron–client relations in the electoral process does not bode well for the future of Western-style multi-party democracy in either Kenya or Africa. Kenya's political culture is now well established as one of using representatives, civil servants and others to compete for resources from the centre. Politics is fought on a local basis, and the winners at each level move on upwards, to be initiated into the next level of secrets of the state. Once there, they act as both national leaders and local representatives, simultaneously vilified and celebrated for their ability to rig the distribution of development aid, foreign money or other sources of gain to their constituents. As the Independence era throughout Africa showed, and Kenya 30 years later has demonstrated again, neo-patrimonialism almost inevitably fragments African societies along the primary fault-lines of ethnicity.[7]

The events of 1992–4 clearly demonstrated the primacy of individuals and of ethnicity over policy, ideology and class, though the ethnic identification revealed was more a rational reflection of economic self-interest than some 'traditional' pattern of political orientation. The previous 30 years of neo-patrimonial ethnic and regional clientage have created an enduring political culture of sectional competition for power, and for the goods that follow. While the actors changed, and the identities of the so-called ethnic communities altered, the fundamental principle remained – that the competition for power would be fought between ethnic coalitions built around powerful individuals. Thus, during 1992, an incorporationist trans-ethnic movement for national renewal, human rights and economic liberalisation disintegrated into three bitterly opposed, ethnically focused teams competing to seize political power for themselves, and incapable of compromise in their quest to control, rather than dismantle, the apparatus of the state. The multi-party years also revealed a deep, underlying tension within Kenya between the pastoral peoples of the arid and less-developed regions – little-educated, economically disadvantaged, outnumbered, yet controlling most of the country's land (and a disproportionate number of Parliamentary seats) – and the numerous, better-educated, land-hungry agricultural peoples of the densely populated fertile zones. It was this struggle for access to land, the key resource in a fast-growing agricultural country, which provided the dynamic for many of the events of these tempestuous years.[8]

Multi-party competition also starkly revealed the lack of political principle within the Kenyan élite. The primary objective of most political leaders seemed to be personal gain and financial advantage. Kenya proved to have few statesmen or citizens of political principle. Many were open to the highest bidder, which inevitably, given its control of the state, was KANU. Only in the ethnic homelands of the opposition Presidential candidates did the near-certainty of electoral defeat and the prospect of violence against political opportunists, if they stood for KANU, override these calculations. Although a number of new faces appeared on the political scene, a notable phenomenon was the resilience of the old political order and its personnel. Even the so-called Young Turks of FORD were in the main successful businessmen and lawyers in their late forties, hardly a revolutionary cohort. All the significant Presidential candidates were figures from the past, and two of the three opposition leaders – Oginga Odinga and Mwai Kibaki – were former Vice-Presidents. The election was fought, in many areas, by venerable warhorses of the single-party era, now decked out in new multi-party colours without having changed their policies or attitudes fundamentally. Over much of the country, pre-existing local political factions simply aligned themselves with different national parties, without any deep commitment to the ideals they represented. Although the multi-party era genuinely brought in new faces, 1992 did not mark a fundamental shift in the composition of the political élite.

The failure of the election to oust the Moi government, and the inability of the observer groups to detect the abuses that occurred, marked the end of two years during which political reform had held pride of place, and eventually left the West with no choice but to accept the legitimacy of the Moi regime. Yet, despite the failure of Kenya's 'second liberation struggle', the country by 1994 was very different from in 1989. The campaign for political pluralism transformed the political climate dramatically. Whatever its weaknesses, the democratisation process has broadened political and social freedoms in Kenya significantly, and empowered a lively and controversial press, although this has come under sustained attack. Economic freedoms have also expanded, particularly since the election, when Western pressure and the critical economic situation forced the government into limited reforms. Attempts by Kenya to go it alone economically in March 1993 swiftly foundered, compelling the government to accede to Western demands for economic liberalisation, in return for a resumption of aid and an end to inconvenient pressure over political reform. Since the election, Western governments, as in the 1980s, have concentrated primarily upon economic reform, downplaying the importance of continuing political progress.[9]

The regime's attempt to satisfy Western donors since 1992 by liberalising the economy and reducing the role played by the state has created divisions within KANU which reflect an enduring difference in the perception of the purpose of political power. Many African élites have been willing to compromise political power to achieve economic rewards. A substantial minority, however – most notably in places like Zaire and Liberia – appear to view political power for themselves and their communities as an end in itself, and are willing to destroy the state and the economy, if need be, to maintain it. In Kenya, hardliners, who would prefer a scorched-earth 'autarchic' economic policy, dismissing all pressure for change, have struggled since January 1993 for control of policy with pragmatic reformers who provide the 'acceptable face' of the regime, such as the Finance Minister Musalia Mudavadi, the Foreign Minister Stephen Musyoka and the experienced technocrat Simeon Nyachae, who took over the Agriculture Ministry. The economic problems which confronted the regime after the election, however, have proved so severe that President Moi has attempted to keep the hardliners under control. His fundamental problem remains that any attempt to revitalise peasant production by price liberalisation and privatisation would primarily benefit the Kikuyu, the largest and most developed ethnic group in Kenya, while reducing the patronage resources of the state and the flow of funds to KANU's ethnic strongholds.

The experience of the post-election period suggests that the underlying dynamics of political activity were not altered by the sudden introduction of a four-party system. The government and the Provincial Administration have continued to harass the opposition and have eroded its support. As long as President Moi remains at the helm, KANU seems set to win the next election, leaving only a rump of opposition MPs, of whom at least half will be Kikuyu. Indeed, the opposition parties will probably be reduced to 60 or 70 MPs or less after the next elections in 1997, compared with a possible 140 for KANU, giving KANU the crucial two-thirds majority it needs to effect constitutional change. The sole Kikuyu leader with some credibility as a national statesman remains former Vice-President Mwai Kibaki, but his personal failings and passivity have intensified doubts about his fitness for office.[10] In most parts of the country, apart from Central Province, the opposition exists on the sufferance of the state. If the regime took the decision to 'pay the price' in violence, economic disruption and Western disapproval of suppressing the opposition parties, they could be snuffed out and their leaders silenced.

Although KANU won, repressive legislation remained in force, the opposition remained harassed, ethnic violence was on the rise and the economy declined, the advent of multi-party politics did alter Kenyan life profoundly. Alternative centres of power emerged, creating a climate in which people felt free for the first time in nearly a decade to denounce political leaders and to criticise the regime. It would have been unthinkable before December 1991 for Kikuyu peasants, assembled on the village green at Komothai in Githunguri constituency, to shout in unison '*Kwaheri* [goodbye] Moi, *Kwaheri* Biwott, *Kwaheri* Kamotho, *Kwaheri* Magugu, *Kwaheri* Nassir', as they did at a DP rally on 27 December 1992, or openly to talk of the Kenya Commercial Bank as 'the Kalenjin Cash Box'. Multi-partyism awoke enormous political activism, creating important checks and balances within the system which did not exist before. As we have noted, the development of a relatively autonomous press was a major achievement. The 1985–90 'mature' Moi state had completely destroyed the autonomous press, but after 1991 it mushroomed despite severe repression. For the first time since 1964 centres of independent political power began to roll back the power of the state, enhancing civil society, at the same time as economic pressure from outside forced the state grudgingly to divest itself of some of its key instruments of economic control. Although it is unlikely that the opposition can seize power under the current political system, it is equally unlikely that they can be completely reincorporated and silenced. Pandora's box cannot be closed.

The West, Foreign Observers and Aid Conditionality

The intricacies of Western government and multilateral aid policy, and their influence on African governments, are a subject for a book in themselves. Nonetheless, Kenya clearly represented a setback in the use of economic assistance to promote democracy and human rights. Foreign observers were heavily influenced by their success at the Zambian election in November 1991 and tended to apply this model to Kenya. The big difference was that the elections had been 'fair' in Zambia but were heavily rigged in Kenya. President Kaunda was either more confident of victory than President Moi – which, given the result, seems unlikely – or he did not fear defeat and was willing to risk open and fair elections. Moi, by contrast, was determined to win. The external observer groups, as expected, provided little more than a minor deterrent to state manipulation, and the late arrival of most foreign observers and their limited understanding of Kenyan elections ensured that the advice of the more experienced staff who knew the country was overruled by visitors' perceptions of happy queues and orderly voting. Despite their bluster, this fact, and the disagreements within the observer groups over what they actually saw, has ensured that no group unequivocally condemned the election. Once the election was over, and the Commonwealth and other international observers had departed, and the United States was becoming ever more deeply involved in Somalia and the resumption of rapid disbursement aid was still far away, Kenyans were left to sort out their political future without outside intervention. A mood of exhaustion and anger pervaded the country during 1993–4: anger at the government for remaining in power, and with the opposition for its inability to agree upon a common Presidential candidate or political strategy. The 1992 election was seen by many as a transitional one, but whether it will lead towards a fully democratic future or a return to authoritarianism is far from clear.

The opposition's early protests in April 1992 that there was no point in going ahead with the election were probably correct. From registration onwards the opposition parties were in trouble. The choice was bleak: to heighten the conflict would have been a high-risk strategy, but might have increased their chances of defeating KANU. The evidence of the ethnic clashes in 1992, and KANU's threats throughout the campaign of the dire consequences awaiting those that failed to vote for the ruling party, intimidated many immigrant communities in KANU strongholds to abstain or to support the regime. Some, however, ignored the warnings. During 1993 these communities came under sustained and coordinated assault from the state by Kalenjin and Maasai 'warriors', and from KANU youth-wingers. The post-election attacks on Kikuyu residents in Trans-Nzoia and Narok, or on Kamba immigrants in the Shimba Hills in Kwale District, have demonstrated that the regime has little interest in anything other than complete submission and reincorporation on its own terms. The prognosis for the Kikuyu community is bleak and, given Kikuyuland's centrality to cash crop exports, the future prospects for Kenya's economic development and its peaceful political evolution are equally pessimistic.

We have also raised the issue of the value of election monitoring. Despite its obvious failings, we still feel that monitoring is an essential part of any political and human rights strategy. In Kenya, despite the errors and failings of the various observer organisations, their presence certainly contributed to the fairness of the December 1992 election. Without them, the campaign, the poll and the count would have been even less fair. Western observers were completely unprepared, however, for the sophisticated manner in which the Kenyan authorities rigged the result. In previous Third World elections, the electoral fraud has usually been so blatant or crude that it was obvious what was happening. In Kenya, they faced a clever and unscrupulous regime and were outsmarted. Election monitoring has no purpose unless rewards and penalties can be imposed. The lesson from Kenya is that even when this approach is attempted, a competent cheat can rely on time, political and financial weakness or self-interest among both voters and the international donor community, intimidation, and brinkmanship to win. A common international norm, defining what constitutes a 'free and fair' election, would be extremely useful – we have not even tried to address this task here. 'Free and fair' elections are simultaneously a key component of democratic reform and fundamentally irrelevant. The long-term existence of democratic institutions, as distinct from the short-run holding of an election, cannot be created through externally imposed and monitored elections. Only an army of occupation, a balance of terror between rival political factions (as in Columbia), or the popular will can maintain democracy. Thus, in the last analysis, holding an 'observed election' is of marginal importance to the West and, indeed, to Kenyans. Democratic values have to be internalized if they are to be sustained.

Internally agreed norms on what constitutes fairness, perhaps graded from level A to F, where A is a ideal achieved by few Western countries, and F is the tyrant's view of an election, might provide a useful starting point. If international observers were asked to rank the electoral process for fairness from A to F, rather than to decide whether it was 'fair' or 'unfair', as in Kenya, more sensible answers might have emerged from the observer groups, probably granting the December 1992 election a 'C–' grade, as the *Daily Nation* suggested. Such observations, of course, could not compel nations to behave in a more democratic fashion but they might shame certain governments into improving and encourage non-governmental organisations to strengthen civil society, laying the foundations for a more democratic political culture. Local and domestic observer teams complement one another: local organisations lack the resources, the experience, and the strength to stand up to government pressure, to monitor elections without external assistance; but international observers can only operate effectively if they are closely linked with events on the ground and in the polling and counting stations, in a collaborative alliance with local monitoring organisations.

The West in 1992 played a confusing role, acting as judges of the Kenyans' success at meeting Western standards of democracy, yet without the long-term willingness to impose such standards upon them. The donor governments, moreover, were themselves divided about what could and should be done to ensure democratic elections, and were governed primarily by short-term interests. KANU knew it could not rig the election too blatantly in front of Western observers but – and this was the key point – the government had to win. KANU, consequently, had to conceal its election malpractice just sufficiently to ensure that the election was judged satisfactory, receiving the benefit of the doubt. KANU's conversion to multi-party democracy, therefore, was a tactical move to ensure that economic assistance would be restored, and did not extend to permitting the election of a new President. In these circumstances, the events of 1992 clearly demonstrated that monitoring as a short-term process or in isolation from local observers is largely futile. Monitors were needed to report on registration, the primaries, and freedom of campaigning, as well as to view the final poll and the count. The external teams, moreover, even those of the IRI and the Commonwealth, lacked the personnel to place observers in every polling station and at every count. A joint effort with NEMU or, at the very least, greater sharing of information, would have enabled the observers to form a more accurate assessment of the election and, possibly, to prevent some of the more flagrant electoral malpractice.

The Economy, Ideology and Policy

The huge economic problems facing Kenya – massive population growth with only slowly expanding resources, huge and growing unemployment, regular crop failures and foreign exchange shortages – were in no way aided by the events of 1992. The Provincial Administration and the central civil service remain as highly politicised as under the single-party state before December 1991, while corruption remains as widespread and as blatant as ever. The country's have-nots, especially the residents of its burgeoning shanty towns, turn to crime in order to survive, while the morale and discipline of the undermanned and under-resourced police force continue to break down. As then Minister of Finance Mwai Kibaki predicted in 1978, Kenya has exhausted the easy options for economic growth; the future would be much more difficult than the first 15 years of the country's independence.

As 1994 opened, it seemed extremely doubtful that any of the opposition parties in their current form could address seriously the key questions facing Kenya economically and socially. On the other hand, it was also far from clear that the government could do so either. It appeared that 'fiddling whilst Rome burns' remained the order of the day, in part because any attempt to liberalise the economy would not only reduce the patronage available to the regime in terms of remunerative jobs and access to loans, but would also economically reward the Kikuyu areas, the bastion of the opposition. The Moi regime is as determined as ever to reduce the economic influence of the Kikuyu and to reward those areas that remained loyal to KANU during 1992.

KANU has never been a strongly ideological party, and has followed a moderate capitalist road of development, though combined with heavy state control. The *Nyayo* (literally, footsteps) 'philosophy' espoused by President Moi was one of obedience rather than an attempt to devise a coherent ideology. The opposition, despite its radical stance on some issues, did not differ fundamentally in objectives or ideology from KANU. All the parties publicly proclaimed the virtues of private enterprise and structural adjustment. The major difference was over practice and stewardship, not policy: the opposition parties were more likely to attempt actually to do what was promised in their manifestos. FORD-Kenya was probably the most left-wing; the DP leaned slightly to the right, but both were committed to economic liberalisation, unlike the ruling party.

The ruling party for the past 30 years was likely to make the fewest changes to the system; and Ford-Kenya the most, although some of its old guard were as statist in their assumptions as KANU's leadership. KANU's victory ensured that the state's economic power would, at best, be cut back rather than dismantled. Economic liberalisation, culminating in a free market, would hit the regime's political bases extremely hard and reward the Kikuyu, undoing President Moi's systematic reconstruction of Kenya's political economy since 1978 and destroying KANU's patron–client political system, which had just returned Moi and his allies to power.

The opposition parties would probably have done slightly better. Nevertheless, there was an underlying tension between those whose primary interest was in taking control of the state machine, and those whose interest was in dismantling it. If a miracle had happened and the opposition had won so huge a victory that KANU had been completely unable to disguise it, and military movements on their borders by American troops in Somalia had persuaded the Moi government that it must concede, the opposition parties would have been deeply divided internally on this fundamental issue. FORD-Kenya was probably correct to advocate the dismantling of the Provincial Administration, though its plan to assign greater powers to municipal and county councils was fraught with danger. Despite their protestations, it is likely that some of the instruments of state control would have proved too useful to dismantle, and would have been deployed to control KANU supporters and to harass ex-government figures, as has occurred after regime transitions in Malawi and Zambia. Economically, FORD-Kenya and the DP would have attempted to liberalise the economy, but the DP was more committed ideologically and its supporters would have benefited more than the Luo from such measures. A FORD-Asili victory would undoubtedly have provoked a bitter internal struggle, with Matiba stripping pro-KANU areas of development funds, transferring resources to Kikuyuland in a reverse image of the regime's development strategy.

Moi: The Man and the Leader

President Moi remains an enigma. Those who know him disagree about his understanding of the problems confronting the nation. There is no doubt, however, that despite his lack of formal education, he is a formidable political operator – in his own words, 'a Professor of Politics', indeed. Although President Moi is continually accused of relying too much on advisers, they have come and gone whilst he endures. Moi is clearly a hard man, willing to kill to defend his position, but also a populist with a deep desire to be loved. Many of the regime's problems, of course, lie in his past and the position that he was forced to adopt. Moi lived in President Kenyatta's shadow for many years, protected from the stronger Kikuyu 'political barons' around *Mzee* as a useful compromise Vice-President, who would not be tempted, like Odinga or Tom Mboya, to become over-ambitious. Knowing his proper place, Moi maintained a low profile and suffered humiliating insults from powerful Kikuyu politicians and Administrators, who underestimated his abilities, while quietly building support for his own bid for power. With Njoroge Mungai's defeat in the 1974 General Election, the Kiambaa-Gatundu family clique suddenly found themselves without a viable candidate for the succession as Kenyatta entered his closing years. Nevertheless, Moi was fortunate to survive the 'Change the Constitution' movement in 1976 and the 1977 KANU elections to take power on Kenyatta's sudden death in August 1978.[11] There is a sense in which Moi has attempted assiduously to live up to the image of the Presidency set by Kenyatta: the image of the Father of the Nation, standing above politics, with unquestioned authority to lead.[12]

If this image had been a largely accurate reflection of Kenyatta's position as President – based on his lifetime of political activity, his creation first of Kikuyu sub-nationalism and then of Kenyan nationalism, leading the country to Independence at the personal cost of 15 years in exile and nine in prison – this could never be true for his successor, whoever it was. President Moi, as Kenya's second President, faced four fundamental problems which always threatened to undermine his authority and to bring him into direct confrontation with the largest, wealthiest, and most educated regions of the country. First, and most obviously, he represented a small, little-developed community, to the north of the country, which formed only a small part of the fourth- or fifth-largest Kenyan ethnic group. In a statist society, where the distribution of rewards is based on preferential access to the centre, and where the traditional basis of distribution has been ethnicity, Moi was never going to be trusted by the Kikuyu or by the other larger communities. Indeed, the opposition to Moi's succession demonstrated that many Kikuyu were paranoid that the Kalenjin would reap disproportionate rewards, just as the Kikuyu had done under Kenyatta. Moreover, because the Kikuyu élite had run Kenya for the past 15 years, Moi had to fight to break the Kikuyu stranglehold over the economy, the political system, and the civil service. Secondly, Moi was not the father of Independence. Worse, Moi, like the Kalenjin, had been on the 'wrong side' during the nationalist struggle (having been appointed by the British to the colonial Legislative Council in 1956) and in the 'wrong party' at Independence. Moi had only entered the Cabinet in 1964 as one of the first defectors from KADU, and lacked the legitimising authority of having led the struggle for Independence or of having suffered for his people (unlike FORD-Kenya's Oginga Odinga). Thirdly (and hardly his fault), he did not have the personal charisma or education of Kenyatta. As a man of limited education, not renowned for his intellectual abilities (unlike DP leader Mwai Kibaki) or oratorical skills (like FORD-Asili's Kenneth Matiba), Moi at first was surrounded by clever people whom he could not trust. As a result, he came increasingly to rely on close friends and less-educated populists whom he found less of a threat. Finally, he inherited the country at a time when the best years of economic prosperity were already over. The 1980s were not a good time for Kenya economically, though the Moi government's policies did little to help. His years as President have been marked by continuing, probably increasing, corruption and Moi has been less able than Kenyatta to control the excesses of his colleagues, presiding over the gradual weakening of the economy. There is no excuse for his use of state power, corruption, and extortion to build a massive business empire, amass large Swiss bank accounts, and assemble all the other apparatus of a dictator. We have seen that it is possible to draw an analogy between agricultural and pastoral modes of production and Kikuyu and Kalenjin corruption. Moi's years in power have been marked by 'overgrazing' or 'slash and burn' forms of corruption, rather than the 'Mr 10 per cent' exploitation of an existing asset which characterised the Kenyatta era. Whether because of incompetence or malice, the Kalenjin and Luhya élites who have extracted surpluses from state institutions under Moi have tended to take rather more and with more serious consequences on the remaining infrastructure than the Kikuyu did in the Kenyatta era. The looting of the NSSF provides a classic example. Although the full details of what has happened to the retirement benefits of hundreds of thousands of workers are still not known, it is clear that they will never recover the full value of the money, extracted from the fund by various transactions to finance KANU's 1992 election campaign and to line the pockets of the Moi élite.

Until February 1990, despite its many abuses, it was possible to argue that Moi's regime was no more violent and repressive than Kenyatta's. Although the institutional structure and respect for civil rights had been deeply eroded since 1978, Kenyatta had begun the process. Moi had repressed the *Mwakenya* dissidents in 1986 and used this challenge to the state as an excuse to repress others, but it was Kenyatta who had established the one-party state, refused to permit the formation of new opposition parties, and detained the leaders of the KPU, banning the party in preference to facing Odinga at the polls. It had been under Kenyatta that Cabinet Minister Mboya and J. M. Kariuki had been murdered by the security forces, while no senior leader had been killed under Moi. Robert Ouko's murder in February 1990, however, shattered such claims, while the ethnic clashes of 1992 and 1993 went far beyond anything that Kenyatta had countenanced. Now, there is a danger that Moi and KANU will find that violence breeds violence, and that the more they use force to control the opposition, the more force they will need. The application of state force to maintain order or to intimidate the opposition will inevitably harm the economy, particularly as it will be directed disproportionately at the most productive and educated segment of society, the Kikuyu.

The Primacy of the Kikuyu

The events of the past 15 years have suggested that, given the current shortage of resources, Kenya cannot be a thriving, progressive African nation without Kikuyu representation at the highest levels of the government and civil service. The evidence of Kenya, and of Uganda before Yoweri Museveni seized power in 1986, is that it is far harder for a political élite, from an economically under-developed part of the country, to govern a state and retain the support of the economically developed communities than it is the other way round. Attempts to divorce the political and economic élites and divert the flow of funds to the periphery generate political tension which harm economic productivity in the long term. To solve its economic problems, Kenya must provide incentives to peasant cash crop producers who grow tea, coffee and pyrethrum, a large proportion of whom are Kikuyu. Hence economic improvement depends on rewarding the Kikuyu areas to the long-term benefit of all Kenyans. The Moi regime is unwilling to do this; indeed, it has has shown itself determined to hinder the flow of resources to opposition strongholds like Central Province. Events since the December 1992 election, moreover, suggest that in a statist society political opposition only survives if it is supported and financed by an indigenous bourgeoisie. Thus, the Kikuyu have remained implacably hostile to the government, while opposition MPs and many of their supporters in South Nyanza (FORD-Kenya) and Kakamega (FORD-Asili) have defected back to KANU. In Kenya, it seems likely in the long run that only the Kikuyu parties are capable of withstanding pressure to come to terms with the regime, supported by a well-developed peasant economy. As opposition supporters – both members of the élite and ordinary citizens – have discovered, there are no rewards, certainly no money, in being against the government. The opposition press and Kikuyu businesses continue to be squeezed financially, deprived of government advertisements, contracts and loans. If the opposition was based in Kenya's less prosperous, less developed areas, like KANU, it would have little hope of surviving or of maintaining an independent press.

An Élite Society

After 30 years of Independence, Kenya remains an élite society in orientation and leadership. Although Kenyans now have a firm grip on their own economy, and are proportionately less dependent on foreign capital than they were, internally there remain huge class and wealth differentials, which are formalising into clear class divisions. The children of the pre-Independence élites have inherited or seized extensive property through their control of the state and the economy, and continue to dominate the political world. Although the population has increased nearly fivefold since Independence and the economy has become much more complex, the Independence generation of political and business leaders retain control over the state to an extraordinary extent. Thus, of the four major Presidential candidates in December 1992, one (Odinga) had been Vice-President at Independence, another (Moi) Deputy Leader of the main opposition party, a third (Matiba) a Permanent Secretary in the civil service, and the fourth (Kibaki) a senior figure in the main nationalist party's political secretariat and a junior Minister in the first post-Independence government. Many second-rank figures in the opposition parties such as Keen, Karanja and Shikuku had been politically prominent 30 years earlier.

Kenya in the late 1980s had shown signs of becoming a semi-feudal polity. The President (the King) ruled an apathetic population through force, with the support of key military, church and political figures. Resources were extracted from the peasantry to fund disproportionate excess at the court. Individuals barons (Provincial and District Commissioners, and certain favoured KANU leaders) ruled over their District fiefdoms with an iron hand, maintaining their own private military forces (*askaris* or youth-wingers), extracting tribute from the populace, and representing their subjects in the centre. They too, however, were subject to the President's (the King's) whim. Surrounded by courtiers, the President (the King) maintained a huge personal fortune, indistinguishable from the state's exchequer, which he dispensed to buy loyalty. Almost all members of the ruling élite were related in some way to each other or to previous élite generations. Political marriages were common, and the élite closed ranks against outsiders (the peasant leaders) who occasionally made it into the central counsels. The authority of an individual in the system, derived as much from his person and his connections as from his office.

This semi-feudal system, however, could not contain the demands of powerful patrons when the economic crisis of the 1980s severely reduced the state's resources, and compelled the President to reallocate resources in order to preserve the loyalty of his own closest allies. State patronage had hitherto enabled the Independence political élite not only to entrench their position as a ruling class, but also to maintain control of the political process both in their localities and in Nairobi. The crisis of resource distribution in the 1980s, however, shattered the power of certain District bosses, made the position of others precarious, and incited widespread opposition to the regime and its local representatives in the areas hardest hit by the reconstruction. Some rose in rebellion to protect their estates (Matiba, Rubia and Wanjigi), while others attempted to appease the regime and in the process alienated their followers (Kamotho, Magugu, Mwangale and the DP leaders in Kiambu).

The Lessons of History

The events of December 1992 and subsequently suggest that the advent of multi-party politics in December 1991 did not really change anything. Kenya remains an authoritarian state. If the government had considered that it was likely to lose the election, it would simply have cheated more. President Moi and his colleagues had no intention of retiring gracefully.

The lesson of history also suggests that opposition parties do not last long in Kenyan politics. One year after losing the 1963 election, KADU, enfeebled by gradual defections, was absorbed into KANU. In 1969, after three years opposition, the Kenya People's Union of Odinga was banned and its leaders detained. There is no evidence to suggest that anything has changed. The regime still refuses to acknowledge the legitimacy of its opposition which seems unlikely to survive as a national force (rather than as regional parties). The example of previous opposition parties and the events of 1993 suggest that individual opposition politicians will be coopted one by one, and that after the 1997 elections Kenya will be on the verge of becoming a single-party state once more. The opposition parties will be forced by economic and political pressure back into their ethnic bastions. The Luo areas lack the economic wealth to sustain long-term opposition – as Oginga Odinga recognised before his death, seeking to reach an accord with President Moi. FORD-Asili is in disarray as Matiba becomes ever more irascible and unpredictable, and his health remains precarious. Without his financial support, few FORD-Asili MPs could fight another election. The DP has remained out of the political limelight, suggesting that Kibaki and his colleagues are either playing a game of masterly political inactivity (which seems improbable) or that they lack the will to confront the regime and endanger their lives and business fortunes. Meanwhile, KANU's unwillingness to share power in any way has been demonstrated repeatedly since 1992, as the Provincial Administration and the police have been used to harass those opposition politicians who cannot be bought, while continuing ethnic violence has solidified KANU's control of its heartlands. Only a few isolated politicians associated with Paul Muite and Charity Ngilu seem willing to build a coalition to challenge the regime, and extensive efforts have been made to build some trans-party national force on a new basis (in effect rebuilding the original FORD). But Muite too has attempted to re-establish Kikuyu unity before reaching out to other ethnic groups. This strategy is more likely to drive other ethnic groups, who remain as fearful as ever of renewed Kikuyu hegemony, into the arms of the government as it is to lay the foundation of a stronger and more effective opposition party. Thus, KANU is likely to win the next General Election with considerably greater ease than in 1992.

Unfortunately, events suggest that despite the veneer of democracy and economic liberalisation, the Kenyan leadership has no intention of handing over power to any other group at any point in the foreseeable future. The deep tensions created by the ethnic clashes, the government's strategy of manipulating communal rivalries and the ethnic nature of multi-party politics in the country have seriously damaged Kenya's national identity – with a reversion towards the ethnic community, not the country, as the primary focus of identity. It is likely that the intrinsic economic instability which liberalism creates will eventually bring the KANU government down, but this will take many years. As long as President Moi himself remains in sound health, his coalition is likely to remain intact, and KANU will retain power until the millennium. In Kenya at least, in the multi-party democracy crisis of the early 1990s, the *ancient regime* survived: the system triumphed.

Notes

1 Jennifer A. Widner, *The Rise of A Party-State in Kenya* (Berkeley: University of California Press, 1992), *passim.*
2 *Ibid.*, p. 224.
3 The circulation of the magazines plummeted after the election, falling from approximately 40,000 per issue at the peak of political interest to only 4,000 in 1993. As a result, many pro-opposition magazines, denied government advertising, were forced out of business during the two years after the election. This was the consequence of impending bankruptcy as much as of continuing harassment from the authorities (although this continued as well). Only the *Economic Review,* the best and most cautious, survived because of its specialist niche in the market.
4 During the next three years some established figures returned to the fold, most notably Kimani wa Nyoike, who by 1995 was operating as Matiba's leading adviser and *de facto* Secretary General of the Matiba faction.
5 J. M. Lonsdale, 'States and social processes in Africa', *African Studies Review,* Vol. 24, Nos 2–3 (1981).
6 The 1995 KAMATUSA-GEMA talks marked the beginning of an attempt by Kikuyu business leaders and politicians to reopen dialogue with the regime, outlining the terms of a post-Moi accommodation between the Kalenjin and Kikuyu élites. This potential alliance is embodied in the person of Vice-President Saitoti.
7 Various editions of the pro-opposition magazine *Society* provided graphic accounts of the ethnic clashes. See especially the issues of 9 March 1992, pp. 6–9; 4 May 1992, pp. 6–12; 11 May 1992, pp. 8–18; and 25 May 1992, pp. 9–18.
8 See above, especially Chapter 8.
9 At a meeting in the American Embassy on 30 December 1992, the day after the General Election, senior Embassy and USAID officials acknowledged that little more could be done on the political front. The government had gambled and won. In the future, leverage on the Moi regime would have to focus on economic reforms. See the *Economist* Intelligence Unit's *Quarterly Country Reports* during 1993 and 1994. Kenya's economic performance improved dramatically during 1994, but Western donors became increasingly concerned not only about the deteriorating budgetary position but also about declining human rights. This resulted in a meeting of the Paris Group to reconsider Kenya's case at the end of July 1995.
10 Kenneth Matiba remains popular among poorer Kikuyu voters in Murang'a and Nairobi (although he has lost ground in Kiambu) and might still secure 15 per cent of the Presidential vote in 1997.
11 David W. Throup, 'The construction and destruction of the Kenyatta state', in Michael G. Schatzberg (ed.), *The Political Economy of Kenya* (New York: Praeger, 1987).
12 Perhaps best exemplified by George I. Godia's short book, *Understanding* Nyayo: *Principles and Policies in Contemporary Kenya* (Nairobi: Transafrica, 1984).

Appendices

1. KANU Primary Results, 1992

DATE	DISTRICT	SEAT	CANDIDATE	RESULT	%
11/9/92	NAIROBI	STAREHE	KIRIMA GERISHON KAMAU	WON	
11/9/92	NAIROBI	STAREHE	LUBIA MUDENGANI	LOST	
	NAIROBI	EMBAKASI	MWENJE DAVID S. K.	WON	
	NAIROBI	EMBAKASI	KATUA MARGARET MARY	LOST	
	NAIROBI	EMBAKASI	WERE SIMBA	LOST	
	NAIROBI	MATHARE	MAINA ZACHARIA NGUKU	?	
11/9/92	NAIROBI	DAGORETTI	GACHANJA CLEMENT	UNOPPOSED	100
	NAIROBI	MAKADARA	OMIDO FREDERICK ESAU	?	
	NAIROBI	KAMUKUNJI	KURIA JAMES KARIUKI NJIRE	?	
	NAIROBI	KAMUKUNJI	OMBETE LIVINGSTONE MAINA	LOST	
	NAIROBI	KAMUKUNJI	KIBUE ALI MOHAMMED	LOST	
	NAIROBI	LANGATA	LEAKEY PHILIP EDWARD	WON	
	NAIROBI	LANGATA	OLINDO DR PEREZ	LOST	
	NAIROBI	WESTLANDS	MUNGAI DR NJOROGE	3,203	59
	NAIROBI	WESTLANDS	WALJI AMIN MOHAMMED SADRUDIN	2,244	41
	MURANG'A	KIHARU	MBOTE WILLIAM NJOROGE	UNOPPOSED	100
	MURANG'A	GATANGA(1)	NJOROGE FRANCIS NDUNGU	WON	
	MURANG'A	GATANGA(1)	MUKUNYA MUGO	LOST	
12/2/92	MURANG'A	GATANGA(2)	NJOROGE FRANCIS NDUNGU	571	69
12/2/92	MURANG'A	GATANGA(2)	MUKUNYA MUGO	262	31
	MURANG'A	MAKUYU	KIMANI JOHN KIBUGA	UNOPPOSED	100
	MURANG'A	KIGUMO	NG'ANG'A NORMAN NJUGUNA	UNOPPOSED	100
	MURANG'A	KANDARA	KIMANI WILFRED MBURU	UNOPPOSED	100
	MURANG'A	KANGEMA	KAMOTHO JOHN JOSEPH	UNOPPOSED	100
	KIAMBU	KIKUYU	NJOROGE SAMUEL MUIRURI	UNOPPOSED	100
	KIAMBU	KIAMBAA(1)	KIBARABARA GERISHON NGUGI	298	50
	KIAMBU	KIAMBAA(1)	KABAKI GEOFREY GAKURE	297	50
13/11/92	KIAMBU	KIAMBAA(2)	KABAKI GEOFREY GAKURE	292	88
13/11/92	KIAMBU	KIAMBAA(2)	KIBARABARA GERISHON NGUGI	40	12
12/1/92	KIAMBU	KIAMBAA(3)	KIBARABARA GERISHON NGUGI	WON ?	
	KIAMBU	GITHUNGURI	MAGUGU ARTHUR	UNOPPOSED	100
	KIAMBU	JUJA(1)	MUIGAI BEN KINYANJUI	1,137	58
	KIAMBU	JUJA(1)	KAMAU WAIRA	807	41
	KIAMBU	JUJA(1)	KIHORO SIMON	33	2
12/1/92	KIAMBU	JUJA(2)	MUIGAI BEN KINYANJUI	1,200	75
12/1/92	KIAMBU	JUJA(2)	KAMAU WAIRA	400	25
	KIAMBU	LIMURU	KANYINGI SIMON KURIA	UNOPPOSED	100
	KIAMBU	GATUNDU	KARIUKI PATRICK MUIRURI	WON	
	KIAMBU	LARI	?	?	
	NYANDARUA	KIPIPIRI	KABINGU-MUREGI JAMES	UNOPPOSED	100
	NYANDARUA	KINANGOP	KIMEMIA JOSIAH MUNYUA	WON	
	NYANDARUA	KINANGOP	KINYIRIRIA	LOST	
	NYANDARUA	NDARAGWA	MUCHIRI GEOFFREY GACHARA	?	
	NYERI	OTHAYA	WAHOME SIMON KIBERA	WON	
	NYERI	OTHAYA	MBOGA TITUS MUTURI	LOST	
	NYERI	NYERI TOWN	MUTOTHORI STEPHEN MUGO	WON	
	NYERI	NYERI TOWN	KAMARA CHARLES MWANIKI	LOST	
	NYERI	TETU	KANYI NAHASHON WAITHAKA	?	
	NYERI	KIENI	MUREITHI JOEL MURUTHI	WON	
	NYERI	MUKURUEINI	KARIUKI EDWARD KABOGO	1,277	76
	NYERI	MUKURUEINI	NJURURI NGUMBA	396	24
	NYERI	MATHIRA	KUGURU DAVIDSON NGIBUINI	?	
	KIRINYAGA	GICHUGU	NJUNO NAHASHON NJUNU	1,039	82
	KIRINYAGA	GICHUGU	NJINJO TERESIO MUCHIRA	229	18

Appendix 1: KANU Primary Results 1992

DATE	DISTRICT	SEAT	CANDIDATE	RESULT	%
	KIRINYAGA	NDIA	MUIRU JAMES MAINA	?	
	KIRINYAGA	MWEA	KATHIGI KIBUGI	?	
	EMBU	RUNYENJES(1)	KIMANI MRS LYDIA WANJIRU	WON	
	EMBU	RUNYENJES(1)	KARINGI MBARARI	LOST	
	EMBU	RUNYENJES(1)	MUNYI KAMWITHI	LOST	
12/2/92	EMBU	RUNYENJES(2)	KIMANI MRS LYDIA WANJIRU	WON	
12/2/92	EMBU	RUNYENJES(2)	MUNYI KAMWITHI	LOST	
	EMBU	SIAKAGO	MBOGO EUSTACE ROY KANTHINTHI	WON	
	EMBU	SIAKAGO	MATE SYLVESTER	LOST	
	EMBU	GACHOKA(1)	SILA JAPETH MUTISO	WON	
	EMBU	GACHOKA(1)	NYAGAH BEATRICE KANANI	LOST	
	EMBU	GACHOKA(1)	MARINGA JOEL GITHAKA	LOST	
	EMBU	GACHOKA(2)	MARINGA JOEL GITHAKA	2,296	37
	EMBU	GACHOKA(2)	SILA JAPETH MUTISO	2,222	36
	EMBU	GACHOKA(2)	NYAGAH BEATRICE KANANI	1,440	23
	EMBU	GACHOKA(2)	MBUNGU BARNABAS	287	5
	MERU	IGEMBE	KALWEO JACKSON ITIRITHIA	WON	
	MERU	IGEMBE	MALEBE JOSEPH MUENDA	LOST	
	MERU	TIGANIA	KARAURI MATHEW ADAMS	WON	
	MERU	TIGANIA	MWONGO JACOB	LOST	
	MERU	NTONYIRI	MUTURIA JOSEPH K	WON ?	
	MERU	IMENTI N.	RUTERE SILAS MURIUKI	7,216	57
	MERU	IMENTI N.	ANGAINE JACKSON HARVESTER	5,324	42
	MERU	IMENTI N.	M'MUNGANA PETER KIUNGA	10	0
	MERU	IMENTI CEN.	M'MUKINDIA KIRUGI LAIBONI	WON ?	
	MERU	IMENTI S	M'MBIJIWE GILBERT KABEERE	WON	
	MERU	IMENTI S	KAARIA BENSON	LOST	
	THARAKA-NITHI	NITHI(1)	MUREITHI PETERSON MUREITHI	6,124	55
	THARAKA-NITHI	NITHI(1)	MUTEGI ERASTUS	5,053	45
12/5/92	THARAKA-NITHI	NITHI(2)	MUREITHI PETERSON MUREITHI	?	
	THARAKA-NITHI	THARAKA	KAGWIMA FRANCIS NYAMU	UNOPPOSED	100
	MACHAKOS	MASINGA(1)	KILUTA COL RONALD JOHN	4,199	59
	MACHAKOS	MASINGA(1)	KIILU SIMON	2,928	41
12/2/92	MACHAKOS	MASINGA(2)	KILUTA COL RONALD JOHN	5,014	74
12/2/92	MACHAKOS	MASINGA(2)	KIILU SIMON	1,744	26
	MACHAKOS	YATTA	WAMBUA FRANCIS	LOST	
	MACHAKOS	YATTA	1 other	LOST	
	MACHAKOS	YATTA	MUTISO GIDEON MUNYAO	4,771	
12/5/92	MACHAKOS	YATTA(2)	?	?	
	MACHAKOS	KANGUNDO	NGUTU JOSEPH KIMEU	8,728	79
	MACHAKOS	KANGUNDO	MULI STEPHEN NDAMBUKI	2,340	21
	MACHAKOS	KATHIANI	MULINGE GEN. JACKSON KIMEU	7,723	78
	MACHAKOS	KATHIANI	KITELE LABAN MAINGI	2,123	22
	MACHAKOS	MACHAKOS TOWN	KYALO JOHN MUSEMBI	UNOPPOSED	100
	MACHAKOS	MWALA	KAVISI PETER MUTUA	WON	
	MAKUENI	MBOONI	MAKAU JOHNSTONE	7,005	70
	MAKUENI	MBOONI	MUSILA WALI	1,642	16
	MAKUENI	MBOONI	NDISYO SIMON KIOKO	1,393	14
	MAKUENI	KILOME(1)	NDILINGI ANTONY W.	5,483	54
	MAKUENI	KILOME(1)	MUSEMBI JOHN M.	2,171	21
	MAKUENI	KILOME(1)	MAINDI GERVAISE T. M.	1,748	17
	MAKUENI	KILOME(1)	MUTUNGI FAUSTINE MUTEVU	500	5
	MAKUENI	KILOME(1)	MAINGI MUSIU GABRIEL	200	2
12/4/92	MAKUENI	KILOME(2)	NDILINGI ANTONY W.	8,214	56
12/4/92	MAKUENI	KILOME(2)	MAINDI GERVAISE T. M.	6,260	43
12/4/92	MAKUENI	KILOME(2)	MAINGI MUSIU GABRIEL	123	1
12/4/92	MAKUENI	KILOME(2)	MUSEMBI JOHN M.	102	1
12/4/92	MAKUENI	KILOME(2)	MUTUNGI FAUSTINE MUTEVU	2	0
	MAKUENI	MAKUENI(1)	KYONDA STEPHEN	UNOPPOSED	100
28/11/92	MAKUENI	MAKUENI(2)	MAUNDU PETER ELIUD MUTUA	4,329	94
28/11/92	MAKUENI	MAKUENI(2)	KYONDA STEPHEN	275	6
	MAKUENI	KIBWEZI	MULWA JACKSON KASANGA	UNOPPOSED	100
	KITUI	KITUI N.	MUSYOKA STEPHEN	UNOPPOSED	100
	KITUI	KITUI W.	MWENDWA MRS WINIFRED NYIVA	WON	
	KITUI	KITUI W.	MUTHUI PAUL SAITI	LOST	
	KITUI	KITUI W.	KALAVI JOSEPH	LOST	

Appendix 1: KANU Primary Results 1992

DATE	DISTRICT	SEAT	CANDIDATE	RESULT	%
	KITUI	KITUI CENTRAL	NDOTTO GEORGE	UNOPPOSED	100
	KITUI	MUTITO	NDAMBUKI MUTINDA	WON	
	KITUI	MUTITO	MWEU EZEKIEL	LOST	
	KITUI	MUTOMO	MUOKI ISAAC MULATYA	WON	
	KITUI	MUTOMO	MBAI PHILIP NZUKI	LOST	
11/11/92	ISIOLO	ISIOLO N.	No Result	?	
12/2/92	ISIOLO	ISIOLO N. (2 or 3)	KARA ISAAK	4,967	100
12/2/92	ISIOLO	ISIOLO N. (2 or 3)	MOKKU CHARFANE GUYO	4,418	47
?	ISIOLO	ISIOLO S	?	?	
?	MARSABIT	MOYALE(1)	No election	?	
12/2/92	MARSABIT	MOYALE(2)	?	?	
11/9/92	MARSABIT	N. HORR	GODANA DR BONAYA ADHI	UNOPPOSED	100
?	MARSABIT	SAKU	?	?	
?	MARSABIT	LAISAMIS(1)	?	?	
12/4/92	MARSABIT	LAISAMIS(2)	?	?	
	WAJIR	WAJIR EAST	SHEIKH ABDI MOHAMMED	WON ?	
	WAJIR	WAJIR S	AHMED ARALE HASSAN	2,889	63
	WAJIR	WAJIR S	OGLE NOOR ABDI	1,669	37
	WAJIR	WAJIR W.	MOHAMMED AHMED KHALIF	WON	
	WAJIR	WAJIR W.	HUSSEIN HAJI IBRAHIM ALI	LOST	
	MANDERA	MANDERA W.	MAALIM ADEN ABDULLAHI	WON	
	MANDERA	MANDERA W.	AMIN SAYID MOHAMMED	LOST	
	MANDERA	MANDERA CEN..	NOOR ADAN MOHAMMED	WON	
	MANDERA	MANDERA CEN.	BARICHA ALI ABDI	LOST	
	MANDERA	MANDERA E.	ISAAK SHABAN ALI	2,849	42
	MANDERA	MANDERA E.	AMIN MOHAMMED SHEIKH	1,403	21
	MANDERA	MANDERA E.	SOMO MOHAMMED NOOR	1,328	20
	MANDERA	MANDERA E.	AHMED ABDULRAHI SHEIKH	1,224	18
12/1/92	MANDERA	MANDERA E.(2)	?	?	
11/9/92	GARISSA	DUJIS	MAALIM MOHAMMED	UNOPPOSED	100
	GARISSA	LAGDERA	SIAT HAJIR SHIDE	?	
11/9/92	GARISSA	FAFI	SALAT IBRAHIM ABDALLAH	WON	
11/9/92	GARISSA	FAFI	OSMAN IBRAHIM IRSHAD	LOST	
11/9/92	GARISSA	IJARA	ARTE NASSIR MAALIM	WON	
	TANA-RIVER	GARSEN	KOMORA YUDA	WON	
	TANA-RIVER	GARSEN	WAKOLE ABDI SHONGOLO	LOST	
	TANA-RIVER	GARSEN	DDAIDDO ISRAEL LEKWA	LOST	
	TANA-RIVER	GALOLE(1)	MUGAVA TOLA KOFA	WON	
	TANA-RIVER	GALOLE(1)	SOBA MOHAMMED OMAR SAID	LOST	
12/5/92	TANA-RIVER	GALOLE(2)	?	?	
	KILIFI	BAHARI(1)	MUMBA JOHN SAFARI	3,666	54
12/1/92	KILIFI	BAHARI(2)	MUMBA JOHN SAFARI	4,366	45
	KILIFI	BAHARI(1)	LEWA TIMOTHY MTWANA	3,156	46
12/1/92	KILIFI	BAHARI(2)	LEWA TIMOTHY MTWANA	4,366	45
12/1/92	KILIFI	BAHARI(2)	MOHAMMED KENNY S.	818	8
12/1/92	KILIFI	BAHARI(2)	MBOJA MAURICE	77	1
12/5/92	KILIFI	BAHARI(3)	MUMBA JOHN SAFARI	WON	
12/5/92	KILIFI	BAHARI(3)	LEWA TIMOTHY MTWANA	LOST	
	KILIFI	KALOLENI	KEAH MATHIAS	WON	
	KILIFI	KALOLENI	MWACHIRO LESLEY BETAWA	LOST	
	KILIFI	GANZE	NGALA NOAH KATANA	WON	
	KILIFI	GANZE	NDZARO HENRY KATANA	LOST	
	KILIFI	MALINDI(1)	BADAWY ABUBAKAR MOHAMMED AHMED	4,150	52
	KILIFI	MALINDI(1)	TUVA FRANCIS BOBI	2,511	31
	KILIFI	MALINDI(1)	MATTAZA ANDREW	935	12
	KILIFI	MALINDI(1)	KUPALIA MORRIS	462	6
12/5/92	KILIFI	MALINDI(2)	TUVA FRANCIS BOBI	4,651	94
12/5/92	KILIFI	MALINDI(2)	BADAWY ABUBAKAR MOHAMMED AHMED	274	6
	KILIFI	MAGARINI	NDZAI JONATHAN KATANA	WON	
	KWALE	MSAMBWENI	MWAMZANDI KASSIM BAKARI	WON	
	KWALE	KINANGO	RAI SAMUEL GONZI	WON	
	KWALE	KINANGO	BIDU ALI	LOST	
	KWALE	KINANGO	MATANO ROBERT STANLEY	LOST	
	KWALE	KINANGO	One other	LOST	
	KWALE	MATUGA	BOY BOY JUMA	WON	
	KWALE	MATUGA	NZAI TIMOTHY K.	LOST	
	LAMU	LAMU E.(1)	CHIAMA ABUBAKAR	3,358	68
	LAMU	LAMU E.(1)	ABUBAKAR MADHBUTI MOHAMMED	1,582	32
12/2/92	LAMU	LAMU E.(2)	?	?	
	LAMU	LAMU W.	ALI ABDULKARIM MOHAMMED	2,418	47
	LAMU	LAMU W.	CHEKA ABDULRAHMAN OMAR	1,870	37

Appendix 1: KANU Primary Results 1992

DATE	DISTRICT	SEAT	CANDIDATE	RESULT	%
	LAMU	LAMU W.	GEDARA ABDULREHMAN	466	9
	LAMU	LAMU W.	MAHRUS ABDALLAH	186	4
	LAMU	LAMU W.	BURJA ABDUL AZIZ	152	3
	MOMBASA	KISAUNI	MAITHA EMMANUEL KARISSA JAMES	4,657	59
	MOMBASA	KISAUNI	HEMED SAID-HEMED	3,201	41
	MOMBASA	KISAUNI	MBWANA ABDALLA		0
	MOMBASA	LIKONI(1)	SHAKOMBO RASHID	WON	
	MOMBASA	LIKONI(1)	MWIDAU ABDULKADIR ABDALLA	LOST	
	MOMBASA	LIKONI(2)	SHAKOMBO RASHID	LOST	
	MOMBASA	LIKONI(2)	MWIDAU ABDULKADIR ABDALLA	WON	
12/5/92	MOMBASA	LIKONI(3)	?	?	
	MOMBASA	MVITA	NASSIR SHARRIF	UNOPPOSED	100
	MOMBASA	CHANGAMWE	KAJEMBE RAMADHAN SEIF	UNOPPOSED	100
	TAITA-TAVETA	TAVETA	CRITICOS BASIL	WON	
	TAITA-TAVETA	TAVETA	MNENE OTHINIEL JOHN	LOST	
	TAITA-TAVETA	TAVETA	KUBO MWACHARO	LOST	
	TAITA-TAVETA	WUNDANYI	MBELA DARIUS MSAGHA	5,414	82
	TAITA-TAVETA	WUNDANYI	MLAMBA MATHIAS	1,192	18
	TAITA-TAVETA	VOI	MBELA DOUGLAS DANIEL	WON	
	TAITA-TAVETA	VOI	KACHILA ADIEL	LOST	
	TAITA-TAVETA	MWATATE(1)	MWANJOGI BALDWIN MWAKUGU	3,234	54
	TAITA-TAVETA	MWATATE(1)	MCHARO ELIUD MWAKIO	2,719	46
12/5/93	TAITA-TAVETA	MWATATE(2)	MCHARO ELIUD MWAKIO	3,253	54
12/5/93	TAITA-TAVETA	MWATATE(2)	MWANJOGI BALDWIN MWAKUGU	2,724	46
	LAIKIPIA	LAIKIPIA E.	KAPARO KAUSAI FRANCIS XAVIER OLE	UNOPPOSED	100
	LAIKIPIA	LAIKIPIA W.	KARIUKI GODFREY GITAHI	UNOPPOSED	100
	NAKURU	NAKURU E.	MAINA JOSEPH KURIA	WON	
	NAKURU	NAKURU E.	KINUTHIA DAVID MWANIKI	LOST	
	NAKURU	NAKURU E.	MUNYUA ISAAC MWANGI	LOST	
	NAKURU	NAKURU TOWN	ASANYO GEOFFREY MAKANA	WON	
	NAKURU	NAKURU TOWN	KORIR RAPHAEL	LOST	
13/11/92	NAKURU	MOLO	KEBENEI JOSEPH KIPKURGAT	WON	
13/11/92	NAKURU	MOLO	KIPKURGAT SAMMY	LOST	
13/11/92	NAKURU	MOLO	4 others	LOST	
	NAKURU	RONGAI	KOMEN WILLIAM ARAP	WON	
	NAKURU	RONGAI	BOMETT ERIC KIBET KORAS	LOST	
	NAKURU	NAKURU N.	?	?	
	KAJIADO	KAJIADO N.	SAITOTI GEORGE	UNOPPOSED	100
	KAJIADO	KAJIADO CEN.(1)	PARSAOTI GODFREY	UNOPPOSED	100
21/11/92	KAJIADO	KAJIADO CEN.(2)	LENTANTE DAVID OLE SANKORI	6,032	46
21/11/92	KAJIADO	KAJIADO CEN.(2)	NKASIKOI PETER	3,630	27
21/11/92	KAJIADO	KAJIADO CEN.(2)	PARSAOTI GODFREY	3,575	27
?	KAJIADO	KAJIADO S	SINGARU PHILIP LAMPAT OLE	?	
	NAROK	NAROK N.	NTIMAMA WILLIAM OLE	UNOPPOSED	100
	NAROK	NAROK W.	SUNKULI JULIUS OLE	15,824	57
	NAROK	NAROK W.	BIRIR RICHARD BWOGO ARAP	11,255	41
	NAROK	NAROK W.	SOMPISHA FRANCIS OSILO OLE	625	2
	NAROK	NAROK S	TUYA SAMSON OLE	13,711	67
	NAROK	NAROK S	NKANAE SAOLI OLE	6,809	33
	NAROK	NAROK S	KAPEEN LIVINGSTONE OLE	82	0
	KERIO	KERIO CENTRAL	CHEMITEI JOHN CHERUIYOT	LOST	
	KERIO	KERIO CENTRAL	CHEPKOK PAUL RUTO	10,157	
	KERIO	KERIO S	BIWOTT NICHOLAS KIPRONO	17,900	100
	KERIO	KERIO S	SEII MRS TABITHA	81	0
	KERIO	KERIO W.(1)	KEINO BOAZ KIPCHUMBA	8,564	100
	KERIO	KERIO W.(1)	MUTWOL FRANCIS	7,480	47
12/2/92	KERIO	KERIO W.(2)	KEINO BOAZ KIPCHUMBA	8,803	100
12/2/92	KERIO	KERIO W.(2)	MUTWOL FRANCIS	8,773	50
	KERIO	KERIO E.	TOO VINCENT ARAP	LOST	
	KERIO	KERIO E.	CHESEREK FREDERICK KISANG ARAP	5,349	
	KERIO	KERIO E.	KIPKORIR ROBERT KIPTOO	2,851	
	BARINGO	BARINGO E.	LOTODO JOSEPH DALDOSO	3,009	100
	BARINGO	BARINGO E.	KATURKANA SAMSON TWARITH	294	9
	BARINGO	BARINGO CEN.	MOI DANIEL ARAP	UNOPPOSED	100
	BARINGO	BARINGO N.	ROTICH WILLIAM YATOR KAMUREN	WON	
	BARINGO	BARINGO N.	CHEBOIWO HENRY	LOST	
	BARINGO	BARINGO S	BOMETT GERALD	LOST	
	BARINGO	BARINGO S	MOROGO WILLIAM G.	WON	
	BOMET	KONOIN	CHEBELYON NATHANIEL K. ARAP	8,736	56
	BOMET	KONOIN	KITUR RAPHAEL KIPRONO ARAP	5,187	33

Appendix 1: KANU Primary Results 1992

DATE	DISTRICT	SEAT	CANDIDATE	RESULT	%
	BOMET	KONOIN	TOO FRANCIS KAPSIELE	919	6
	BOMET	KONOIN	TERER JOHN KIPNGETICH ARAP	853	5
	BOMET	CHEPALUNGU	KOECH JOHN KIPSANG ARAP	19,611	50
	BOMET	CHEPALUNGU	KIMETO ANTHONY SOTET	13,380	34
	BOMET	CHEPALUNGU	KETTENYA WILLIAM KIPKEMBOI	5,698	14
	BOMET	CHEPALUNGU	SOI ALFRED KIMUNAI ARAP	525	1
	BOMET	CHEPALUNGU	NG'OK MRS ALICE	347	1
	BOMET	CHEPALUNGU	BETT MR	30	0
	BOMET	BOMET	KONES KIPKALYA ARAP	17,371	64
	BOMET	BOMET	SITONIK DR WILSON	8,964	33
	BOMET	BOMET	LAGAT DR WILSON	802	3
12/1/92	BOMET	BOMET(2)	KONES KIPKALYA ARAP	?	
	KERICHO	BURET	SIGEI PHILIP KIPSETE	LOST	
	KERICHO	BURET	NGENO DR JONATHAN KIMETIT	23,000	
	KERICHO	BURET	RONO JOEL KIPKORIR ARAP	23	
	KERICHO	BELGUT(1)	KIRIOR KIPTORUS ARAP	WON	
	KERICHO	BELGUT(1)	CHEPKWONY	LOST	
12/2/92	KERICHO	BELGUT(2)	KIRIOR KIPTORUS ARAP	16,227	51
12/2/92	KERICHO	BELGUT(2)	KIRUI CHARLES D. K.	15,634	49
	KERICHO	KIPKELION	TANUI DANIEL KIPKORIR ARAP	WON	
	KERICHO	KIPKELION	KIKWAI WILLIAM	LOST	
11/9/92	NANDI	MOSOP	SAMBU JOHN KIPKORIR	5,263	32
11/9/92	NANDI	MOSOP	CHOGE KIPSANG	2,966	18
11/9/92	NANDI	MOSOP	METTO STANLEY KIPTOO	2,934	18
11/9/92	NANDI	MOSOP	MAIYO AGGREY	2,926	18
11/9/92	NANDI	MOSOP	TOO MARK ARAP	2,242	13
11/9/92	NANDI	MOSOP	KOSITANY BENJAMIN	211	1
11/9/92	NANDI	MOSOP	MUREI CHRISTOPHER ARAP	67	0
11/9/92	NANDI	ALDAI	TITI JOHN PAUL	11,998	58
11/9/92	NANDI	ALDAI	CHERUIYOT JOHN	3,461	17
11/9/92	NANDI	ALDAI	CHOGE SIMEON	2,929	14
11/9/92	NANDI	ALDAI	CHOGE SAMMY	2,367	11
?	NANDI	TINDERET	KOSGEY HENRY KIPRONO ARAP	UNOPPOSED	100
	WEST_POKOT	KACHILEBA	NANG'OLE PETER LOCHAUN	?	
	WEST_POKOT	KAPENGURIA	LOTODO FRANCIS POLIS LOILE	10,400	85
	WEST_POKOT	KAPENGURIA	LOTIM EMMANUEL	1,850	15
?	WEST_POKOT	SIGOR(1)	LOMADA CHRISTOPHER MOTONYWO	WON	
12/2/92	WEST_POKOT	SIGOR(2)	RURINO PHILIP RUTO	5,807	51
12/2/92	WEST_POKOT	SIGOR(2)	LOMADA CHRISTOPHER MOTONYWO	5,690	49
	TURKANA	TURKANA NRTH	EKIDOR JAPHETH LOTUKOI	4,308	55
	TURKANA	TURKANA NRTH	EKARAN LOOLEL ANDREW	2,117	27
	TURKANA	TURKANA NRTH	AKAL JULIUS ADAPEL	1,479	19
	TURKANA	TURKANA CEN.	EJORE PATRICK MZEE	2,930	59
	TURKANA	TURKANA CEN.	EMANA EMMANUEL	1,540	31
	TURKANA	TURKANA CEN.	LOKURUKA MICHAEL NAPOO	525	11
	TURKANA	TURKANA CEN.	3 others		
	TURKANA	TURKANA STH	EWOTON FRANCIS IGWATON	3,145	56
	TURKANA	TURKANA STH	ANGELEI PETER	2,439	44
	SAMBURU	SAMBURU E.	LESHORE SAMMY PIRISA	WON	
	SAMBURU	SAMBURU E.	LALAMPAA JOB	LOST	
	SAMBURU	SAMBURU W.	LENGEES PETER STEVE	WON	
	SAMBURU	SAMBURU W.	LOTITIYO PETER LEKAIKUM	LOST	
	SAMBURU	SAMBURU W.	ROSION CHARLES L.	LOST	
	SAMBURU	SAMBURU W.	EBIOYARRE GABRIEL	LOST	
	SAMBURU	SAMBURU W.	LENAIROCHI	LOST	
	SAMBURU	SAMBURU W.	LALAIKIPIAN GEORGE	LOST	
	UASIN_GISHU	ELDORET NRTH(1)	CHESIRE REUBEN	WON	
	UASIN_GISHU	ELDORET NRTH(1)	SAINA WILLIAM MOROGE ARAP	LOST	
	UASIN_GISHU	ELDORET NRTH(1)	WANYONYI JONNEX	LOST	
22/11/92	UASIN_GISHU	ELDORET NRTH(5)	SAINA WILLIAM MOROGE ARAP	7,742	58
22/11/92	UASIN_GISHU	ELDORET NRTH(5)	CHESIRE REUBEN	4,870	36
22/11/92	UASIN_GISHU	ELDORET NRTH(5)	WANYONYI JONNEX	782	6
	UASIN_GISHU	ELDORET E.(1)	BARMASAI JOEL F. KIMURAI	8,392	48
	UASIN_GISHU	ELDORET E.(1)	TARAR FRANCIS ARAP	6,485	37
	UASIN_GISHU	ELDORET E.(1)	KIPSANAI JOSEPH	2,393	14
	UASIN_GISHU	ELDORET E.(1)	CHAMUR CHRISTINE	83	0
12/1/92	UASIN_GISHU	ELDORET E.(2)	BARMASAI JOEL F. KIMURAI	10,329	63
12/1/92	UASIN_GISHU	ELDORET E.(2)	TARAR FRANCIS ARAP	6,142	37
	UASIN_GISHU	ELDORET STH	MISOI DR JOSEPH	12,274	82
	UASIN_GISHU	ELDORET STH	KORIR WILSON	1,571	11
	UASIN_GISHU	ELDORET STH	BIRECH PAUL K. K. A.	1,083	7

Appendix 1: KANU Primary Results 1992

DATE	DISTRICT	SEAT	CANDIDATE	RESULT	%
	TRANS-NZOIA	KWANZA	WEKESA NOAH	WON	
	TRANS-NZOIA	KWANZA	MOIBEN SAMUEL	LOST	
	TRANS-NZOIA	KWANZA	NGEIYWA LOVIAN	LOST	
	TRANS-NZOIA	KWANZA	KITITIYO MICHAEL	LOST	
	TRANS-NZOIA	SABOTI	WABUGE WAFULA	WON	
	TRANS-NZOIA	SABOTI	SIYOI CHECKMAN	LOST	
	TRANS-NZOIA	SABOTI	JIPCHO BEN	LOST	
	TRANS-NZOIA	SABOTI	?	LOST	
	TRANS-NZOIA	CHERANGANI	KIRWA KIPRUTO ARAP	WON	
	TRANS-NZOIA	CHERANGANI	KITTONY MRS ZIPPORAHY	LOST	
	TRANS-NZOIA	CHERANGANI	KOSGEI MUSA	LOST	
	TRANS-NZOIA	CHERANGANI	YEGO DANIEL KIBIWOT ARAP	LOST	
	TRANS-NZOIA	CHERANGANI	YEGO JOHN	LOST	
	TRANS-NZOIA	CHERANGANI	ROTICH JOHN KIRWA ARAP	LOST	
	TRANS-NZOIA	CHERANGANI	KOREN JOHN	LOST	
	BUNGOMA	KIMILILI	MWANGALE ELIJAH WASIKE	UNOPPOSED	100
	BUNGOMA	WEBUYE	MANG'OLI JOASH WALUBENGO	UNOPPOSED	100
	BUNGOMA	SIRISIA	MULIRO JOSEPH	4,380	76
	BUNGOMA	SIRISIA	NAKITARE PAUL	596	10
	BUNGOMA	SIRISIA	KISUYA PETER JUSTUS	584	10
	BUNGOMA	SIRISIA	KOKONYA PETER	215	4
	BUNGOMA	KANDUYI	MAKHANU MAURICE S.	UNOPPOSED	100
	BUNGOMA	MOUNT ELGON(1)	KISIERO WILBERFORCE ARAP	5,039	
	BUNGOMA	MOUNT ELGON(1)	CHESEBE FRED	3,905	
	BUNGOMA	MOUNT ELGON(1)	KAPONDI ALFRED CHASADE	LOST	
	BUNGOMA	MOUNT ELGON(1)	MNERIA ANDREW	LOST	
	BUNGOMA	MOUNT ELGON(1)	CHEPKURUI PETER	LOST	
12/2/92	BUNGOMA	MOUNT ELGON(2)	KISIERO WILBERFORCE ARAP	5,689	45
12/2/92	BUNGOMA	MOUNT ELGON(2)	KAPONDI ALFRED CHASADE	4,623	37
12/2/92	BUNGOMA	MOUNT ELGON(2)	KISIWA SIMON	2,312	18
	BUSIA	AMAGORO	ODUYA GEORGE FREDERICK OPRONG	WON	
	BUSIA	AMAGORO	OTWANI PANCRAS	2,314	
	BUSIA	NAMBALE	MASINDE PHILIP JOSEPH W.	?	
	BUSIA	SAMIA	AWORI ARTHUR MOODY	5,416	93
	BUSIA	SAMIA	OJIAMBO JULIA	395	7
	BUSIA	BUNYALA	OSOGO JAMES CHARLES NAKHAWANGA	WON	
	BUSIA	BUNYALA	OKONDO PETER	LOST	
	BUSIA	BUNYALA	GUMO FRERDERICK	LOST	
	VIHIGA	SABATIA	MUDAVADI WYCLIFFE MUSALIA	UNOPPOSED	100
	VIHIGA	VIHIGA	LIGALE ANDREW	5,987	79
	VIHIGA	VIHIGA	KIFORO TOM	1,581	21
	VIHIGA	EMUHAYA(1)	MUKUNA KENNETH SANDE	7,533	46
	VIHIGA	EMUHAYA(1)	MULICHWA SHELDON	6,523	40
	VIHIGA	EMUHAYA(1)	OKANG'A RAPHAEL RICHARD	2,324	14
	VIHIGA	EMUHAYA(1)	MASINDE ABBYSAI NAMBUTE	120	1
12/1/92	VIHIGA	EMUHAYA(2)	MULICHWA SHELDON	11,416	52
12/1/92	VIHIGA	EMUHAYA(2)	MUKUNA KENNETH SANDE	10,601	48
	VIHIGA	HAMISI	M'MAITSE VINCENT SAKWA	14,046	77
	VIHIGA	HAMISI	GIMOSE CHARLES GUMINI	4,083	23
	KAKAMEGA	MALAVA	ANGATIA JOSHUA MULANDE	?	
	KAKAMEGA	LUGARI	NABWERA BURUDI	4,354	80
	KAKAMEGA	LUGARI	WANYAMA BENJAMIN	650	12
	KAKAMEGA	LUGARI	LIGALA MARK	348	6
	KAKAMEGA	LUGARI	SEPIIRA MARK	66	1
	KAKAMEGA	MUMIAS(1)	WAMEYO ELON WILLIS	LOST	
12/1/92	KAKAMEGA	MUMIAS(2)	?	?	
	KAKAMEGA	LURAMBI(1)	NDOMBI WASIKE	5,314	51
	KAKAMEGA	LURAMBI(1)	OTUTU REUBEN WILLIAM	5,080	49
12/2/92	KAKAMEGA	LURAMBI(2)	OTUTU REUBEN WILLIAM	?	
	KAKAMEGA	SHINYALU(1)	LIJOODI JAPETH	4,117	55
	KAKAMEGA	SHINYALU(1)	MULAMA DAVID AMAHWA	3,362	45
12/1/92	KAKAMEGA	SHINYALU(2)	LIJOODI JAPETH	LOST	
	KAKAMEGA	IKOLOMANI(1)	MUGALLA JOSEPH JOLLY	WON	
12/2/92	KAKAMEGA	IKOLOMANI(2)	MUGALLA JOSEPH JOLLY	WON	
12/2/92	KAKAMEGA	IKOLOMANI(2)	LIDIGU NORMAN	LOST	
	KAKAMEGA	BUTERE(1)	OKWARA JOHN	WON	
	KAKAMEGA	BUTERE(1)	MALUMBE ELIAKIM	LOST	
	KAKAMEGA	BUTERE(1)	LUMASAYI FRANCIS ATWOLI	LOST	
12/1/92	KAKAMEGA	BUTERE(2)	LUMASAYI FRANCIS ATWOLI	WON	
12/1/92	KAKAMEGA	BUTERE(2)	OKWARA JOHN	LOST	
	SIAYA	UGENYA	OLUOCH ARCHBISHOP		

Appendix 1: KANU Primary Results 1992

DATE	DISTRICT	SEAT	CANDIDATE	RESULT	%
			STEPHEN A. ONDIEK	WON	
	SIAYA	ALEGO	UMIDHA JOHN OWENJA	WON	
	SIAYA	ALEGO	JOWE DICKSON	LOST	
	SIAYA	GEM	OGOT MRS GRACE EMILY ARINYI	WON	
	SIAYA	BONDO	OMAMO WILLIAM ODONGO	WON	
	SIAYA	RARIEDA	OKENDO HENRY OUMA	WON	
	SIAYA	RARIEDA	JALANG'O ROBERT	LOST	
	KISUMU	KISUMU TOWN	OKUOGA DR CHRISTOPHER	WON	
	KISUMU	KISUMU RURAL	AYAH WILSON NDOLO	?	
	KISUMU	NYANDO	OWUOR JAMES MIRUKA	?	
	KISUMU	MUHORONI	BONYO JOHN ISAYA P.	?	
	KISUMU	NYAKACH	K'OMBUDO OJWANG	?	
10/1/192	HOMA-BAY	KASIPUL-KABONDO	KAPERE AUSTIN AUMA	WON	
10/1/192	HOMA-BAY	KASIPUL-KABONDO	MBORI JAMES EZEKIEL	LOST	
	HOMA-BAY	KARACHUONYO	AMAYO LAZARUS OMBAYI	WON	
	HOMA-BAY	KARACHUONYO	OWUOR GEORGE AGOLA	LOST	
	HOMA-BAY	NDHIWA(1)	OGINGO MATHEW KAVIN OTIENO	6,000	90
	HOMA-BAY	NDHIWA(1)	CHIENG' ELISHA AKECH	700	10
12/5/92	HOMA-BAY	NDHIWA(2)	OGINGO MATHEW KAVIN OTIENO	5,016	63
12/5/92	HOMA-BAY	NDHIWA(2)	CHIENG' ELISHA AKECH	2,999	37
	HOMA-BAY	RANGWE	OKUNDI DANIEL OJIJO	WON	
	HOMA-BAY	RANGWE	NDONG RAYMOND OLOO	LOST	
	HOMA-BAY	MBITA	NYAKIAMO PETER C. J. O.	UNOPPOSED	100
	MIGORI	RONGO	OTIENO DALMAS ANYANGO	?	
	MIGORI	MIGORI	OKWANYO JOHN HENRY	29,217	89
	MIGORI	MIGORI	INDALO REV PETER	3,488	11
	MIGORI	NYATIKE	OLANG' ZABLON OWIGO	?	
	MIGORI	KURIA(1)	MWITA WALTER ELIJAH	6,344	35
	MIGORI	KURIA(1)	MAROA MAASAI	6,145	34
	MIGORI	KURIA(1)	MANGA SHADRACH RODGER	5,540	31
12/5/92	MIGORI	KURIA(2)	MANGA SHADRACH RODGER	9,048	52
12/5/92	MIGORI	KURIA(2)	MAROA MAASAI	5,238	30
12/5/92	MIGORI	KURIA(2)	MWITA WALTER ELIJAH	3,060	18
	KISII	BONCHARI	BOSIRE MARK GICHABA	2,481	57
	KISII	BONCHARI	KEBATI DR. PROTAS MOMANYI	1,854	43
	KISII	S. MUGIRANGO(1)	KOMBO DAVID ONDIMO	16,650	100
12/7/92	KISII	S. MUGIRANGO(2)	OYONDI REUBEN ONESERIO	15,441	100
	KISII	S. MUGIRANGO(1)	OYONDI REUBEN ONESERIO	12,999	100
12/7/92	KISII	S. MUGIRANGO(2)	KOMBO DAVID ONDIMO	10,811	100
	KISII	BOMACHOGE	MAGARA ZEDEKIAH MEKENYE	LOST	
	KISII	BOMACHOGE	ANYIENE ZEPHANIAH MOGUNDE	9,133	
	KISII	BOMACHOGE	NYARANGO ZACHARIA N.	6,667	
	KISII	BOBASI	OBURE CHRISTOPHER	13,272	67
	KISII	BOBASI	MANOTI STEPHEN KENGERE	6,464	33
2/11/1992	KISII	BOBASI(2)	MANOTI STEPHEN KENGERE	WON	
12/1/92	KISII	NYARIBARI MASABA(2)	MANDAKU DR HEZRON	13,537	100
	KISII	NYARIBARI MASABA(1)	MANDAKU DR HEZRON	11,833	100
12/1/92	KISII	NYARIBARI MASABA(2)	ONGERI PROF SAM	10,094	100
	KISII	NYARIBARI MASABA(1)	ONGERI PROF SAM	6,349	100
	KISII	NYARIBARI CHACHE	NYACHAE SIMEON	UNOPPOSED	100
	KISII	KITUTU CHACHE	ONYONKA DR ZACHARY	UNOPPOSED	100
	NYAMIRA	KITUTU MASABA(1)	NYAMBATI WALTER OISEBE	4,321	36
	NYAMIRA	KITUTU MASABA(1)	MOMANYI AUGUSTUS HASTINGS OTIENO	3,615	30
	NYAMIRA	KITUTU MASABA(1)	SIMBA NELSON GICHABA	2,152	18
	NYAMIRA	KITUTU MASABA(1)	ONDIEKI FREDERICK NAFTALI	1,989	16
	NYAMIRA	KITUTU MASABA(1)	ABAKI CLEMENT OKENYE	?	0
12/1/92	NYAMIRA	KITUTU MASABA(2)	NYAMBATI WALTER OISEBE	4,889	70
12/1/92	NYAMIRA	KITUTU MASABA(2)	MOMANYI AUGUSTUS HASTINGS OTIENO	1,820	26
12/1/92	NYAMIRA	KITUTU MASABA(2)	SIMBA NELSON GICHABA	280	4
	NYAMIRA	W MUGIRANGO	SAGWE TOM MORWABE	9,903	67
	NYAMIRA	W MUGIRANGO	ONYANCHA DAVID ONASI	4,895	33
	NYAMIRA	N MUGIRANGO	MARITA LIVINGSTONE ATEBE	6,178	55
	NYAMIRA	N MUGIRANGO	MOTURI ALFAYO NYARANGI	5,106	45

2. 1992 Parliamentary Election Results

DISTRICT	CONSTITUENCY	CANDIDATES	PARTY	VOTE	%
NAIROBI	STAREHE	KIMONDO KIRUHI	FORD(A)	17,908	40.86
NAIROBI	STAREHE	KIRIMA GERISHON KAMAU	KANU	8,907	20.32
NAIROBI	STAREHE	RUBIA CHARLES WANYOIKE	KNC	6,307	14.39
NAIROBI	STAREHE	GATONDO JUSTUS NYAMO	DP	6,142	14.01
NAIROBI	STAREHE	ORIE MRS MARY ROGO MANDULI	FORD(K)	4,229	9.65
NAIROBI	STAREHE	KIRAGU PETERSON MWANGI	PICK	257	0.59
NAIROBI	STAREHE	QAMBO WAQAMBO	SDP	77	0.18
NAIROBI	STAREHE		SPOILT		0.00
NAIROBI	STAREHE		**TOTAL**	**43,827**	**100.00**
NAIROBI	EMBAKASI	ROHIU HENRY MURIAMA	FORD(A)	18,477	34.18
NAIROBI	EMBAKASI	MUCHIRI GODFREY MUHURI	DP	15,039	27.82
NAIROBI	EMBAKASI	WAIYAKI DR MUNYUA	FORD(K)	12,772	23.63
NAIROBI	EMBAKASI	MWENJE DAVID S. K.	KANU	6,590	12.19
NAIROBI	EMBAKASI	NDIRANGU DICKENS KABUA	KNC	395	0.73
NAIROBI	EMBAKASI	MWERU JIDRUPH	PICK	230	0.43
NAIROBI	EMBAKASI		SPOILT	551	1.02
NAIROBI	EMBAKASI		**TOTAL**	**54,054**	**100.00**
NAIROBI	MATHARE	MACHARIA GEOFFREY MUREYA	FORD(A)	23,836	36.18
NAIROBI	MATHARE	MASINDE DR FREDERICK SIKUKU	FORD(K)	19,579	29.72
NAIROBI	MATHARE	NGUMBA ANDREW KIMANI	DP	15,147	22.99
NAIROBI	MATHARE	MAINA ZACHARIA NGUKU	KANU	7,315	11.10
NAIROBI	MATHARE		SPOILT		0.00
NAIROBI	MATHARE		TOTAL	65,877	100.00
NAIROBI	DAGORETTI	KAMUNYU CHRISTOPHER KARIUKI	FORD(A)	29,863	63.38
NAIROBI	DAGORETTI	MUGO MRS BETH WAMBUI	DP	7,292	15.48
NAIROBI	DAGORETTI	GACHANJA CLEMENT	KANU	5,833	12.38
NAIROBI	DAGORETTI	GITONGA MAHINDI WA	FORD(K)	3,707	7.87
NAIROBI	DAGORETTI		SPOILT	419	0.89
NAIROBI	DAGORETTI		**TOTAL**	**47,114**	**100.00**
NAIROBI	MAKADARA	OMUKERE JOHN	FORD(A)	12,668	28.58
NAIROBI	MAKADARA	KHAMINWA JOHN MUGALASINGA	FORD(K)	11,009	24.83
NAIROBI	MAKADARA	MAKANGA F. MWANGI	DP	8,486	19.14
NAIROBI	MAKADARA	OMIDO FREDERICK ESAU	KANU	8,416	18.98
NAIROBI	MAKADARA	WAITHAKA KIHARA	KNC	3,238	7.30
NAIROBI	MAKADARA	WA KIMOTHO JOHN MWAKI	PICK	287	0.65
NAIROBI	MAKADARA		SPOILT	228	0.51
NAIROBI	MAKADARA		**TOTAL**	**20,655**	**100.00**
NAIROBI	KAMUKUNJI	NTHENGE GEORGE GREGORY WILSON N.	FORD(A)	16,847	41.45
NAIROBI	KAMUKUNJI	ADAMS HASSAN ALI	DP	7,338	18.05
NAIROBI	KAMUKUNJI	ANYANGO JAMES JALANGO	FORD(K)	6,233	15.34
NAIROBI	KAMUKUNJI	KURIA JAMES KARIUKI NJIRE	KANU	5,818	14.31
NAIROBI	KAMUKUNJI	WANJIGI JAMES MAINA	KNC	3,642	8.96
NAIROBI	KAMUKUNJI	MPONDA JUMA MOHAMED	PICK	766	1.88
NAIROBI	KAMUKUNJI		SPOILT		0.00
NAIROBI	KAMUKUNJI		**TOTAL**	**16,459**	**100.00**
NAIROBI	LANGATA	ODINGA RAILA	FORD(K)	24,261	43.23
NAIROBI	LANGATA	RUGENDO RICHARD KIMANI	FORD(A)	13,430	23.93
NAIROBI	LANGATA	LEAKEY PHILIP EDWARD	KANU	11,901	21.20
NAIROBI	LANGATA	MATHAI ANDREW STEPHEN MWANGI	DP	6,282	11.19

Appendix 2: 1992 Parliamentary Election Results

DISTRICT	CONSTITUENCY	CANDIDATES	PARTY	VOTE	%
NAIROBI	LANGATA	ANDOVE LEO WIJENJE	KSC	250	0.45
NAIROBI	LANGATA	Perez Olindo rejected - no Kiswahili certificate	PICK		0.00
NAIROBI	LANGATA		SPOILT		0.00
NAIROBI	LANGATA		**TOTAL**	**56,124**	**100.00**
NAIROBI	WESTLANDS	WALJI AMIN MOHAMMED SADRUDIN	KANU	8,687	32.29
NAIROBI	WESTLANDS	NG'ANG'A WANGUHU	FORD(A)	7,602	28.26
NAIROBI	WESTLANDS	TETT MRS BETTY NJERI	DP	5,609	20.85
NAIROBI	WESTLANDS	NJUGUNA SAMUEL MUCIRI WA	FORD(K)	2,545	9.46
NAIROBI	WESTLANDS	HARUN JOHN MWAI	PICK	1,902	7.07
NAIROBI	WESTLANDS	WACHIRA-WAWERU ISAAC	KNC	212	0.79
NAIROBI	WESTLANDS	MBUGUA KAMAU WA	KSC	83	0.31
NAIROBI	WESTLANDS		SPOILT	260	0.97
NAIROBI	WESTLANDS		**TOTAL**	**26,900**	**100.00**
MURANG'A	KIHARU	MATIBA KENNETH STANLEY NJINDO	FORD(A)	57,585	98.65
MURANG'A	KIHARU	MBOTE WILLIAM NJOROGE	KANU	781	1.34
MURANG'A	KIHARU	no candidate nominated	DP		0.00
MURANG'A	KIHARU	no candidate nominated	FORD(K)		0.00
MURANG'A	KIHARU		SPOILT	5	0.01
MURANG'A	KIHARU		**TOTAL**	**58,371**	**100.00**
MURANG'A	GATANGA	WANYOIKE JOSEPHAT MBURU	FORD(A)	21,315	81.01
MURANG'A	GATANGA	MWICIGI GEORGE NDUNGU	KNC	2,302	8.75
MURANG'A	GATANGA	GACHUI JOHN MWAURA	DP	2,101	7.98
MURANG'A	GATANGA	NJOROGE FRANCIS NDUNGU	KANU	301	1.14
MURANG'A	GATANGA	NG'ANG'A DAVID MUKARA	KENDA	294	1.12
MURANG'A	GATANGA	no candidate nominated	FORD(K)		0.00
MURANG'A	GATANGA		SPOILT		0.00
MURANG'A	GATANGA		**TOTAL**	**26,313**	**100.00**
MURANG'A	MAKUYU	NJOROGE JULIUS NJUGUNA	FORD(A)	13,029	71.01
MURANG'A	MAKUYU	KIRUBI STEPHEN GATU	DP	2,313	12.61
MURANG'A	MAKUYU	MANJAU PETER MWAI	KNC	1,532	8.35
MURANG'A	MAKUYU	KIMANI JOHN KIBUGA	KANU	1,258	6.86
MURANG'A	MAKUYU	Joseph Ndungu Nduati time barred	FORD(K)		0.00
MURANG'A	MAKUYU		SPOILT	217	1.18
MURANG'A	MAKUYU		**TOTAL**	**18,349**	**100.00**
MURANG'A	KIGUMO	MWAURA JOHN BAPTISTE KIRORE	FORD(A)	50,527	92.77
MURANG'A	KIGUMO	HEHO JOSEPH KARIUKI	DP	2,828	5.19
MURANG'A	KIGUMO	KIHARA ONESMUS MWANGI	PICK	543	1.00
MURANG'A	KIGUMO	NGANG'A NORMAN	KANU	346	0.64
MURANG'A	KIGUMO	no candidate nominated	FORD(K)		0.00
MURANG'A	KIGUMO		SPOILT	221	0.41
MURANG'A	KIGUMO		**TOTAL**	**54,465**	**100.00**
MURANG'A	KANDARA	KARENGE GACURU MUGO WA	FORD(A)	36,484	88.95
MURANG'A	KANDARA	MWAURA ARCHANGEL K.	DP	1,890	4.61
MURANG'A	KANDARA	NGETHE DAVID WAWERU	FORD(K)	1,119	2.73
MURANG'A	KANDARA	MUGO DR WILSON	KNC	1,033	2.52
MURANG'A	KANDARA	KIMANI WILFRED MBURU	KANU	492	1.20
MURANG'A	KANDARA		SPOILT		0.00
MURANG'A	KANDARA		**TOTAL**	**41,018**	**100.00**
MURANG'A	KANGEMA	MICHUKI JOHN NJOROGE	FORD(A)	38,620	73.16
MURANG'A	KANGEMA	KAMOTHO JOHN JOSEPH	KANU	7,436	14.09
MURANG'A	KANGEMA	NJAKWE FRANCIS MAINA	DP	5,069	9.60
MURANG'A	KANGEMA	KARIUKI ISAAC NGOTHO WA	FORD(K)	1,237	2.34
MURANG'A	KANGEMA		SPOILT	428	0.81
MURANG'A	KANGEMA		**TOTAL**	**52,790**	**100.00**
KIAMBU	KIKUYU	MUITE PAUL KIBUGE	FORD(K)	38,416	71.97
KIAMBU	KIKUYU	KENYANJUI MARTIN WAINAINA	FORD(A)	12,070	22.61
KIAMBU	KIKUYU	KINYANJUI PETER KABIBI	DP	1,936	3.63
KIAMBU	KIKUYU	NJOROGE SAMUEL MUIRURI	KANU	751	1.41
KIAMBU	KIKUYU	KINUTHIA JAMES MURIU	KENDA	207	0.39
KIAMBU	KIKUYU		SPOILT		0.00
KIAMBU	KIKUYU		**TOTAL**	**53,380**	**100.00**
KIAMBU	KIAMBAA	ICHARIA JOHN KAMAU	FORD(A)	34,208	69.89
KIAMBU	KIAMBAA	KARUME JAMES NJENGA	DP	11,912	24.34
KIAMBU	KIAMBAA	KARIUKI LAWRENCE NGINYO	FORD(K)	1,986	4.06
KIAMBU	KIAMBAA	KIBARABARA GERISHON NGUGI	KANU	836	1.71

Appendix 2: 1992 Parliamentary Election Results

DISTRICT	CONSTITUENCY	CANDIDATES	PARTY	VOTE	%
KIAMBU	KIAMBAA		SPOILT	94	0.19
KIAMBU	KIAMBAA		**TOTAL**	**49,036**	**100.19**
KIAMBU	GITHUNGURI	KARANJA DR. JOSEPHAT NJUGUNA	FORD(A)	34,019	78.06
KIAMBU	GITHUNGURI	MAGUGU ARTHUR KINYANJUI	KANU	4,498	10.32
KIAMBU	GITHUNGURI	WARUHIU MRS ROSE WAIRIMU	DP	3,451	7.92
KIAMBU	GITHUNGURI	NJUGUNA PETER KARUGA WA	PICK	693	1.59
KIAMBU	GITHUNGURI	KIBURI NEWTON KOGI	KNC	524	1.20
KIAMBU	GITHUNGURI	MWAURA NGOIMA WA	FORD(K)	210	0.48
KIAMBU	GITHUNGURI		SPOILT	184	0.42
KIAMBU	GITHUNGURI		**TOTAL**	**43,579**	**100.00**
KIAMBU	JUJA	NDICHO STEFFAN RUGENDO NDABI	FORD(A)	35,187	68.21
KIAMBU	JUJA	MUHOHO DR GEORGE KAMAU	DP	8,393	16.27
KIAMBU	JUJA	KAHENGERI GITU WA	FORD(K)	3,987	7.73
KIAMBU	JUJA	MUIGAI BEN KINYANJUI	KANU	3,126	6.06
KIAMBU	JUJA	NJOROGE PROF RAPHAEL J.	KNC	661	1.28
KIAMBU	JUJA	KANG'ETHE WILSON KIMANI	KENDA	234	0.45
KIAMBU	JUJA		SPOILT		0.00
KIAMBU	JUJA		**TOTAL**	**51,588**	**100.00**
KIAMBU	LIMURU	NYANJA GEORGE BONIFACE	FORD(A)	26,752	85.37
KIAMBU	LIMURU	KANYINGI SIMON KURIA	KANU	1,959	6.25
KIAMBU	LIMURU	MWAURA SAMUEL NGIGI	DP	1,551	4.95
KIAMBU	LIMURU	MWANIKI CHARLES	FORD(K)	665	2.12
KIAMBU	LIMURU	WAWERU J. MBUGUA	KNC	180	0.57
KIAMBU	LIMURU	KARIUKI JORAM GATHINGI	KENDA	36	0.11
KIAMBU	LIMURU		SPOILT	192	0.61
KIAMBU	LIMURU		**TOTAL**	**31,335**	**100.00**
KIAMBU	GATUNDU	GITAU ANTONY KAMUIRU	FORD(A)	34,104	56.65
KIAMBU	GATUNDU	MUIGAI NGENGI	DP	21,780	36.18
KIAMBU	GATUNDU	GAKUNJU ZACHARIAH KIMEMIA	FORD(K)	2,611	4.34
KIAMBU	GATUNDU	KARIUKI PATRICK MUIRURI	KANU	1,701	2.83
KIAMBU	GATUNDU		SPOILT		0.00
KIAMBU	GATUNDU		**TOTAL**	**60,196**	**100.00**
KIAMBU	LARI	GITONGA PHILIP	FORD(A)	24,017	84.42
KIAMBU	LARI	KARANJA BISHOP PHILIP NDUNGU	KNC	1,698	5.97
KIAMBU	LARI	MWAI PAULINE WANGU	DP	1,356	4.77
KIAMBU	LARI	KIMATHI VISCOUNT JAMES	KANU	1,004	3.53
KIAMBU	LARI	MBURU TIRUS CHEGE	FORD(K)	374	1.31
KIAMBU	LARI		SPOILT		0.00
KIAMBU	LARI		**TOTAL**	**28,449**	**100.00**
NYANDARUA	KIPIPIRI	MUCHEMI LAVAN NGATIA	FORD(A)	24,210	63.46
NYANDARUA	KIPIPIRI	GITHIOMI PAUL MWANGI	DP	12,197	31.97
NYANDARUA	KIPIPIRI	KABINGU-MUREGI JAMES	KANU	1,175	3.08
NYANDARUA	KIPIPIRI	KAGIMBI JOHN NYORO	FORD(K)	199	0.52
NYANDARUA	KIPIPIRI		SPOILT	371	0.97
NYANDARUA	KIPIPIRI		**TOTAL**	**38,152**	**100.00**
NYANDARUA	KINANGOP	WANJIRU MARY	FORD(A)	20,144	58.11
NYANDARUA	KINANGOP	KIRIKA WAITHAKA MWANGI	DP	9,814	28.31
NYANDARUA	KINANGOP	WA NYOIKE KIMANI	KNC	3,669	10.58
NYANDARUA	KINANGOP	KIMEMIA JOSIAH MUNYUA	KANU	895	2.58
NYANDARUA	KINANGOP	NJOROGE LEONARD G.	FORD(K)		0.00
NYANDARUA	KINANGOP		SPOILT	144	0.42
NYANDARUA	KINANGOP		**TOTAL**	**34,666**	**100.00**
NYANDARUA	NDARAGWA	GICHUKI WASHINGTON MWANGI	DP	22,854	72.28
NYANDARUA	NDARAGWA	MANYARA DICKSON MWANGI	FORD(A)	6,436	20.35
NYANDARUA	NDARAGWA	KIARIE THOMAS J. WAIYWAINI	PICK	1,373	4.34
NYANDARUA	NDARAGWA	MUCHIRI GEOFFREY GACHARA	KANU	956	3.02
NYANDARUA	NDARAGWA	no candidate nominated	FORD(K)		0.00
NYANDARUA	NDARAGWA		SPOILT		0.00
NYANDARUA	NDARAGWA		**TOTAL**	**31,619**	**100.00**
NYERI	OTHAYA	KIBAKI MWAI	DP	31,536	98.90
NYERI	OTHAYA	WAHOME SIMON KIBERA	KANU	276	0.87
NYERI	OTHAYA	John G. Wang'ondu stood down on nom day	FORD(K)		0.00
NYERI	OTHAYA	no candidate nominated	FORD(A)		0.00
NYERI	OTHAYA		SPOILT	74	0.23
NYERI	OTHAYA		**TOTAL**	**31,886**	**100.00**

Appendix 2: 1992 Parliamentary Election Results

DISTRICT	CONSTITUENCY	CANDIDATES	PARTY	VOTE	%
NYERI	NYERI TOWN	MATHENGE ISIAH MWAI	DP	29,844	83.49
NYERI	NYERI TOWN	NDIRANGU ISAAC WAIHENYA	KNC	2,991	8.37
NYERI	NYERI TOWN	MARINE JOHN WAGURA	FORD(A)	1,639	4.59
NYERI	NYERI TOWN	MUTOTHORI STEPHEN MUGO	KANU	1,270	3.55
NYERI	NYERI TOWN	no candidate nominated	FORD(K)		0.00
NYERI	NYERI TOWN		SPOILT		0.00
NYERI	NYERI TOWN		**TOTAL**	**35,744**	**100.00**
NYERI	TETU	GETHENJI JOSEPH AUGUSTINE	DP	28,085	94.05
NYERI	TETU	KANYI NAHASHON WAITHAKA	KANU	1,498	5.02
NYERI	TETU	RINGUI CHARLES MWANGI	FORD(A)	164	0.55
NYERI	TETU	no candidate nominated	FORD(K)		0.00
NYERI	TETU		SPOILT	114	0.38
NYERI	TETU		**TOTAL**	**29,861**	**100.00**
NYERI	KIENI	KAIRO DAVID MUNENE	DP	31,447	92.30
NYERI	KIENI	MUREITHI JOEL MURUTHI	KANU	1,186	3.48
NYERI	KIENI	MBAO JOHN	FORD(A)	976	2.86
NYERI	KIENI	KANJA WARURU	FORD(K)	258	0.76
NYERI	KIENI		SPOILT	205	0.60
NYERI	KIENI		**TOTAL**	**34,072**	**100.00**
NYERI	MUKURUEINI	MUTAHI DAVID MUHIKA	DP	20,117	69.93
NYERI	MUKURUEINI	KAMAU JOHN WAWERU	KNC	5,094	17.71
NYERI	MUKURUEINI	GITHINJI CHARCHI	FORD(A)	2,517	8.75
NYERI	MUKURUEINI	KARIUKI EDWARD KABOGO	KANU	572	1.99
NYERI	MUKURUEINI	GICHUKI BENSON BERNARD MBUCHU	PICK	117	0.41
NYERI	MUKURUEINI	MURIUKI NJUNJIRI	FORD(K)	214	0.74
NYERI	MUKURUEINI		SPOILT	138	0.48
NYERI	MUKURUEINI		**TOTAL**	**28,769**	**100.00**
NYERI	MATHIRA	WAMAE ELIUD MATU	DP	47,256	87.77
NYERI	MATHIRA	KUGURU DAVIDSON NGIBUINI	KANU	4,310	8.01
NYERI	MATHIRA	KEBUCHI CHARLES N.	KNC	1,688	3.14
NYERI	MATHIRA	NDIRANGU BERNARD M.	FORD(A)	585	1.09
NYERI	MATHIRA	no candidate nominated	FORD(K)		0.00
NYERI	MATHIRA		SPOILT		0.00
NYERI	MATHIRA		**TOTAL**	**53,839**	**100.00**
KIRINYAGA	GICHUGU	NJOKA MARTHA	DP	21,512	56.55
KIRINYAGA	GICHUGU	KARIITHI GEOFFREY KAREHIA	FORD(A)	13,908	36.56
KIRINYAGA	GICHUGU	NJUNO NAHASHON NJUNU	KANU	2,037	5.35
KIRINYAGA	GICHUGU	MAMBO CYRIL K.	FORD(K)	129	0.34
KIRINYAGA	GICHUGU		SPOILT	456	1.20
KIRINYAGA	GICHUGU		**TOTAL**	**38,042**	**100.00**
KIRINYAGA	NDIA	MBUI NICHOLAS KINYUA	DP	29,017	54.97
KIRINYAGA	NDIA	KERIRI JOHN MATERE	KNC	11,911	22.57
KIRINYAGA	NDIA	KIBICHO JAMES KAREU	FORD(A)	10,148	19.23
KIRINYAGA	NDIA	MUIRU JAMES MAINA	KANU	907	1.72
KIRINYAGA	NDIA	NJIRU JAMES NJAGI	FORD(K)	726	1.38
KIRINYAGA	NDIA	MWEA BENJAMIN	PICK	75	0.14
KIRINYAGA	NDIA		SPOILT		0.00
KIRINYAGA	NDIA		**TOTAL**	**52,784**	**100.00**
KIRINYAGA	MWEA	NJERU BISHOP ALLAN MURIGU	DP	19,395	66.51
KIRINYAGA	MWEA	KIRAGU STEPHEN KABUIYO	FORD(A)	7,619	26.13
KIRINYAGA	MWEA	MWANGI JAMES MUGO	KNC	1,380	4.73
KIRINYAGA	MWEA	KATHIGI KIBUGI	KANU	733	2.51
KIRINYAGA	MWEA	no candidate nominated	FORD(K)		0.00
KIRINYAGA	MWEA		SPOILT	36	0.12
KIRINYAGA	MWEA		**TOTAL**	**29,163**	**100.00**
EMBU	RUNYENJES	NDIGWA PETER NJERU	DP	43,894	70.38
EMBU	RUNYENJES	KATHANGU AUGUSTINE NJERU	FORD(A)	13,795	22.12
EMBU	RUNYENJES	KIMANI MRS LYDIA WANJIRU	KANU	2,990	4.79
EMBU	RUNYENJES	MUGENI MARGARET WEVETI	FORD(K)	1,691	2.71
EMBU	RUNYENJES		SPOILT		0.00
EMBU	RUNYENJES		**TOTAL**	**62,370**	**100.00**
EMBU	SIAKAGO	NDWIGA GERALD IRERI	KNC	3,926	29.03
EMBU	SIAKAGO	NJUE ELTON NJERU	DP	3,440	25.43

Appendix 2: 1992 Parliamentary Election Results

DISTRICT	CONSTITUENCY	CANDIDATES	PARTY	VOTE	%
EMBU	SIAKAGO	KAGO FRANCIS	FORD(A)	2,836	20.97
EMBU	SIAKAGO	MATE SYLVESTER	FORD(K)	1,672	12.36
EMBU	SIAKAGO	MBOGO EUSTACE ROY KANTHINTHI	KANU	1,652	12.21
EMBU	SIAKAGO		SPOILT		0.00
EMBU	SIAKAGO		**TOTAL**	**13,526**	**100.00**
EMBU	GACHOKA	NYAGAH NORMAN	DP	11,545	31.64
EMBU	GACHOKA	KAGONDU ELIKANA MURIUKI	FORD(A)	11,025	30.21
EMBU	GACHOKA	MARINGA JOEL GITHAKA	KANU	8,801	24.12
EMBU	GACHOKA	MINIGI DIONISION NDUMA	KNC	1,784	4.89
EMBU	GACHOKA	NYAGAH BEATRICE KANANI	FORD(K)	1,309	3.59
EMBU	GACHOKA		SPOILT	2,029	5.56
EMBU	GACHOKA		**TOTAL**	**36,493**	**100.00**
MERU	IGEMBE	KALWEO JACKSON ITIRITHIA	KANU	8,074	47.46
MERU	IGEMBE	MBAABU ERASTUS KIRIMANIA	DP	7,126	41.88
MERU	IGEMBE	MALEBE JOSEPH MUENDA	PICK	1,630	9.58
MERU	IGEMBE	KARUNGE ISAAC	FORD(A)	184	1.08
MERU	IGEMBE	Joseph K..Kumari papers refused	FORD(K)		0.00
MERU	IGEMBE		SPOILT		0.00
MERU	IGEMBE		**TOTAL**	**17,014**	**100.00**
MERU	NTONYIRI	MAOKA RICHARD MAORE	DP	8,239	62.85
MERU	NTONYIRI	MUTURIA JOSEPH K	KANU	4,582	34.95
MERU	NTONYIRI	MUTUURA EDWARD	KNC	75	0.57
MERU	NTONYIRI	KIGWATHI WILFRED BAKIBURU	FORD(A)	43	0.33
MERU	NTONYIRI	MURIUKI JOHN MWITHIA	FORD(K)	12	0.09
MERU	NTONYIRI		SPOILT	158	1.21
MERU	NTONYIRI		**TOTAL**	**13,109**	**100.00**
MERU	TIGANIA	NDUBAI BENJAMIN REVEL P.	DP	22,119	57.51
MERU	TIGANIA	KARAURI MATHEW ADAMS	KANU	10,553	27.44
MERU	TIGANIA	M'MWERERIA GODFREY KAIBIRIA	KNC	5,054	13.14
MERU	TIGANIA	NKURARU NTAI WA	FORD(K)	602	1.57
MERU	TIGANIA	MWONGO JACOB EBAE	PICK	131	0.34
MERU	TIGANIA	no candidate nominated	FORD(A)		
MERU	TIGANIA		SPOILT		0.00
MERU	TIGANIA		**TOTAL**	**38,459**	**100.00**
MERU	IMENTI N.	MWIRARIA DAVID	DP	35,380	72.04
MERU	IMENTI N.	RUTERE SILAS MURIUKI	KANU	12,702	25.86
MERU	IMENTI N.	MUKIRA N. MBAYA	FORD(K)	530	1.08
MERU	IMENTI N.	M'MUNGANA PETER KIUNGA	FORD(A)	502	1.02
MERU	IMENTI N.		SPOILT		0.00
MERU	IMENTI N.		**TOTAL**	**49,114**	**100.00**
MERU	IMENTI CEN.	M'MUKINDIA KIRUGI LAIBONI	KANU	12,102	31.00
MERU	IMENTI CEN.	KINYUA HENRY	KNC	10,549	27.02
MERU	IMENTI CEN.	IMANYARA GITOBU	FORD(K)	8,260	21.16
MERU	IMENTI CEN.	MUTHAMIA JULIUS	DP	7,878	20.18
MERU	IMENTI CEN.	no candidate nominated	FORD(A)		0.00
MERU	IMENTI CEN.		SPOILT	246	0.63
MERU	IMENTI CEN.		**TOTAL**	**39,035**	**100.00**
MERU	IMENTI S.	MURUNGI KIRATIU	FORD(K)	17,867	42.91
MERU	IMENTI S.	MUGAMBI DAVID PIUS	DP	16,078	38.61
MERU	IMENTI S.	M'MBIJIWE GILBERT KABEERE	KANU	6,046	14.52
MERU	IMENTI S.	IMUNDE REV. LAWFORD	KSC	684	1.64
MERU	IMENTI S.	KIOGA MURUGU	FORD(A)	492	1.18
MERU	IMENTI S.	KIOME SEBASTIAN MUTHAURA	KNC	288	0.69
MERU	IMENTI S.		SPOILT	188	0.45
MERU	IMENTI S.		**TOTAL**	**41,643**	**100.00**
THARAKA NITHI	NITHI	MUTANI BERNARD NJOKA	DP	39,584	74.34
THARAKA NITHI	NITHI	MUREITHI PETERSON MUREITHI	KANU	11,387	21.39
THARAKA NITHI	NITHI	M'MUCHAI NABEA	FORD(A)	1,520	2.85
THARAKA NITHI	NITHI	MURUNGI GERALD J.	FORD(K)	439	0.82
THARAKA NITHI	NITHI	MUTUNGA ELIJAH	KSC	317	0.60
THARAKA NITHI	NITHI		SPOILT		0.00
THARAKA NITHI	NITHI		**TOTAL**	**53,247**	**100.00**
THARAKA NITHI	THARAKA	KAGWIMA FRANCIS NYAMU	KANU	10,065	57.09
THARAKA NITHI	THARAKA	WAKIONDO SILAS JEDIEL NJAGE	DP	6,663	37.80

Appendix 2: 1992 Parliamentary Election Results

DISTRICT	CONSTITUENCY	CANDIDATES	PARTY	VOTE	%
THARAKA NITHI	THARAKA	KAUNA DANIEL R.	FORD(K)	546	3.10
THARAKA NITHI	THARAKA	MUCHEE ALEXANDER	FORD(A)	355	2.01
THARAKA NITHI	THARAKA		SPOILT		0.00
THARAKA NITHI	THARAKA		**TOTAL**	**17,629**	**100.00**
MACHAKOS	MASINGA	KILUTA COL RONALD JOHN	KANU	10,172	73.23
MACHAKOS	MASINGA	MATHUKI LAWRENCE KAMINZA	DP	2,335	16.81
MACHAKOS	MASINGA	MATHUSI SAMUEL IMARA	FORD(A)	1,228	8.84
MACHAKOS	MASINGA	no candidate nominated	FORD(K)		0.00
MACHAKOS	MASINGA		SPOILT	155	1.12
MACHAKOS	MASINGA		**TOTAL**	**13,890**	**100.00**
MACHAKOS	YATTA	MUTISO GIDEON MUNYAO	KANU	9,042	51.89
MACHAKOS	YATTA	SUVA DR FORTUNATUS J. MUTUNE	DP	4,736	27.18
MACHAKOS	YATTA	MUINDI SAMUEL NYAANGI	FORD(A)	3,222	18.49
MACHAKOS	YATTA	KIAMBA JAMES	FORD(K)	426	2.44
MACHAKOS	YATTA		SPOILT		0.00
MACHAKOS	YATTA		**TOTAL**	**17,426**	**100.00**
MACHAKOS	KANGUNDO	MULUSYA JOSEPH WAMBUA	DP	19,068	52.64
MACHAKOS	KANGUNDO	NGUTU JOSEPH KIMEU	KANU	14,996	41.40
MACHAKOS	KANGUNDO	MULI STEPHEN	FORD(A)	1,658	4.58
MACHAKOS	KANGUNDO	MUTUKU I. MUTUA	PICK	310	0.86
MACHAKOS	KANGUNDO	MBALI ONESMUS MUSYOKA	KNC	193	0.53
MACHAKOS	KANGUNDO	Daniel Keino Kituni time barred	FORD(K)		0.00
MACHAKOS	KANGUNDO		SPOILT		0.00
MACHAKOS	KANGUNDO		**TOTAL**	**36,225**	**100.00**
MACHAKOS	KATHIANI	MULINGE GEN. JACKSON KIMEU	KANU	16,633	64.45
MACHAKOS	KATHIANI	NDETI PATRICK MUKETHE	DP	5,332	20.66
MACHAKOS	KATHIANI	MUTUNGA AARON NTHENGE	FORD(A)	2,789	10.81
MACHAKOS	KATHIANI	MANG'ELE SAMUEL KIOKO	FORD(K)	1,053	4.08
MACHAKOS	KATHIANI		SPOILT		0.00
MACHAKOS	KATHIANI		**TOTAL**	**25,807**	**100.00**
MACHAKOS	MACHAKOS TOWN	KYALO JOHN MUSEMBI	KANU	13,804	54.18
MACHAKOS	"	KIKUYU JONESMUS MWANZA	DP	7,789	30.57
MACHAKOS	"	KALUNDE JOSEPH MUSAU	FORD(A)	3,256	12.78
MACHAKOS	"	MBOLE DANSON PAUL	FORD(K)	628	2.46
MACHAKOS	"		SPOILT	0	0.00
MACHAKOS	"		**TOTAL**	**25,477**	**100.00**
MACHAKOS	MWALA	KAVISI PETER MUTUA	KANU	12,080	46.03
MACHAKOS	MWALA	MUNYAO JOSEPH KONZOLO	DP	11,517	43.88
MACHAKOS	MWALA	WAMBUA ANTONY N.	FORD(K)	297	1.13
MACHAKOS	MWALA	KATIKU BERNARD	PICK	290	1.10
MACHAKOS	MWALA	WAMBUA GIDEON NZOIKA	FORD(A)	2,062	7.86
MACHAKOS	MWALA		SPOILT		0.00
MACHAKOS	MWALA		**TOTAL**	**26,246**	**100.00**
MAKUENI	MBOONI	MAKAU JOHNSTONE M.	KANU	10,390	44.23
MAKUENI	MBOONI	KALULU FREDERICK MULINGE	DP	7,739	32.94
MAKUENI	MBOONI	MUSILA STEPHEN	FORD(A)	3,170	13.49
MAKUENI	MBOONI	ILUMBE MICHAEL B. M.	FORD(K)	2,193	9.34
MAKUENI	MBOONI		SPOILT		0.00
MAKUENI	MBOONI		**TOTAL**	**23,492**	**100.00**
MAKUENI	KILOME	NDILINGI ANTONY W.	KANU	23,519	68.51
MAKUENI	KILOME	MBOLE PAUL M.	DP	4,332	12.62
MAKUENI	KILOME	KIMAU JOSEPH	FORD(K)	3,201	9.33
MAKUENI	KILOME	MUSEMBI JOHN M.	FORD(A)	1,907	5.56
MAKUENI	KILOME	MULILI JOHN M.	KNC	849	2.47
MAKUENI	KILOME		SPOILT	519	1.51
MAKUENI	KILOME		**TOTAL**	**34,327**	**100.00**
MAKUENI	MAKUENI	MAUNDU PETER ELIUD MUTUA	KANU	9,954	43.61
MAKUENI	MAKUENI	SUMBI PROF PAUL	DP	9,117	39.94
MAKUENI	MAKUENI	MUSOMBA MAURICE KIVUVA	FORD(A)	3,353	14.69
MAKUENI	MAKUENI	NGUNDO JOEL MUTUNGA	FORD(K)	401	1.76
MAKUENI	MAKUENI		SPOILT		0.00
MAKUENI	MAKUENI		**TOTAL**	**22,825**	**100.00**

DISTRICT	CONSTITUENCY	CANDIDATES	PARTY	VOTE	%
MAKUENI	KIBWEZI	NDETEI MRS AGNES M.	DP	11,710	57.30
MAKUENI	KIBWEZI	MULWA JACKSON KASANGA	KANU	6,651	32.55
MAKUENI	KIBWEZI	MBOKO ONESMUS MUTINDA	FORD(A)	1,009	4.94
MAKUENI	KIBWEZI	KIEMA JOHN	FORD(K)	714	3.49
MAKUENI	KIBWEZI		SPOILT	352	1.72
MAKUENI	KIBWEZI		**TOTAL**	**20,436**	**100.00**
KITUI	KITUI N.	MUSYOKA STEPHEN KILONZO	KANU	20,613	54.29
KITUI	KITUI N.	MULYUNGI JOSEPHAT	DP	15,487	40.79
KITUI	KITUI N.	KITEMA P. NDUE	KNC	1,275	3.36
KITUI	KITUI N.	KITONGA JUSTUS MUTHANGIA	FORD(K)	386	1.02
KITUI	KITUI N.	no candidate nominated	FORD(A)		0.00
KITUI	KITUI N.		SPOILT	209	0.55
KITUI	KITUI N.		**TOTAL**	**37,970**	**100.00**
KITUI	KITUI W.	MWENDWA MRS WINIFRED NYIVA	KANU	8,295	36.32
KITUI	KITUI W.	NYENZE FRANCIS	FORD(A)	7,730	33.84
KITUI	KITUI W.	MWENDWA KYALE	DP	5,091	22.29
KITUI	KITUI W.	KILIKU GEORGE S.	KNC	1,080	4.73
KITUI	KITUI W.	MUNYASIA PERMENAS NZILU	FORD(K)	269	1.18
KITUI	KITUI W.		SPOILT	376	1.65
KITUI	KITUI W.		**TOTAL**	**22,841**	**100.00**
KITUI	KITUI CEN.	NGULI MRS CHARITY KALUKI MWENDWA	DP	17,340	49.40
KITUI	KITUI CEN.	NDOTTO GEORGE MUTUA	KANU	16,494	46.99
KITUI	KITUI CEN.	KITHEKA DANIEL MUTHUI	FORD(K)	935	2.66
KITUI	KITUI CEN.	MUKALA G. MUMO	FORD(A)	331	0.94
KITUI	KITUI CEN.	Titus Mbathi rejected - only 6 seconders	KNC		0.00
KITUI	KITUI CEN.		SPOILT		0.00
KITUI	KITUI CEN.		**TOTAL**	**35,100**	**100.00**
KITUI	MUTITO	NDAMBUKI MUTINDA	KANU	7,406	54.13
KITUI	MUTITO	KITONGA JAMES MUTHUSI	DP	5,876	42.95
KITUI	MUTITO	NDUNDA WAMBUA	FORD(A)	179	1.31
KITUI	MUTITO	MULATYA REV. STEPHEN	FORD(K)	220	1.61
KITUI	MUTITO		SPOILT		0.00
KITUI	MUTITO		**TOTAL**	**13,681**	**100.00**
KITUI	MUTOMO	MUOKI ISAAC MULATYA	KANU	6,298	39.11
KITUI	MUTOMO	IVUTI PATRICE EZEKIEL MAUNGU	FORD(A)	4,942	30.69
KITUI	MUTOMO	MUTINDA KASINGA	DP	3,737	23.20
KITUI	MUTOMO	NGUNA BONAVENTURE M.	FORD(K)	1,128	7.00
KITUI	MUTOMO		SPOILT		0.00
KITUI	MUTOMO		**TOTAL**	**16,105**	**100.00**
ISIOLO	ISIOLO N.	MOKKU CHARFANE GUYO	KANU	6,106	45.32
ISIOLO	ISIOLO N.	GAJI TACHE WAKO	DP	5,551	41.20
ISIOLO	ISIOLO N.	NASURU ROMANO LOSIKE	FORD(K)	1,354	10.05
ISIOLO	ISIOLO N.	DABASO BORU DIKA	FORD(A)	294	2.18
ISIOLO	ISIOLO N.	M'MUKIRA JOHN MBAYA	KNC	133	0.99
ISIOLO	ISIOLO N.		SPOILT	34	0.25
ISIOLO	ISIOLO N.		**TOTAL**	**13,472**	**100.00**
ISIOLO	ISIOLO S.	WAKO ABDULLAHI HAJI	KANU	3,770	76.02
ISIOLO	ISIOLO S.	BONAYA ADAM WAKO	DP	946	19.08
ISIOLO	ISIOLO S.	GUYO HASSAN SHUYO	FORD(A)	230	4.64
ISIOLO	ISIOLO S.	IBRAHIM NASUR	FORD(K)	13	0.26
ISIOLO	ISIOLO S.		SPOILT		0.00
ISIOLO	ISIOLO S.		**TOTAL**	**4,959**	**100.00**
MARSABIT	MOYALE	GALGALO MOHAMMED MALICHA	KANU	7,650	93.19
MARSABIT	MOYALE	ARERO HUSSEIN SORA	FORD(A)	494	6.02
MARSABIT	MOYALE	ARARU OSMAN ABAJILLO	DP	65	0.79
MARSABIT	MOYALE	CHALOLE WACHU BULE	FORD(K)	0	0.00
MARSABIT	MOYALE		SPOILT		0.00
MARSABIT	MOYALE		**TOTAL**	**8,209**	**100.00**
MARSABIT	N. HORR	GODANA DR BONAYA ADHI	KANU	5,360	85.97
MARSABIT	N. HORR	BORU ABDIKADIR YAKANI	DP	859	13.78
MARSABIT	N. HORR	SHARIFF MUHESIN ABDIKADIR	FORD(A)	1	0.02
MARSABIT	N. HORR	no candidate nominated	FORD(K)		0.00
MARSABIT	N. HORR		SPOILT	15	0.24
MARSABIT	N. HORR		**TOTAL**	**6,235**	**100.00**

Appendix 2: 1992 Parliamentary Election Results

DISTRICT	CONSTITUENCY	CANDIDATES	PARTY	VOTE	%
MARSABIT	SAKU	FALANA JARSO JILO	KANU	5,726	61.42
MARSABIT	SAKU	WAQC HALAKHE DIDA	KNC	1,831	19.64
MARSABIT	SAKU	LOLTOME MATHEW LOLE	FORD(K)	1,238	13.28
MARSABIT	SAKU	WABWERA SAID DABASSO	DP	312	3.35
MARSABIT	SAKU	GURACH DENGE WARIO	FORD(A)	170	1.82
MARSABIT	SAKU		SPOILT	46	0.49
MARSABIT	SAKU		**TOTAL**	**9,323**	**100.00**
MARSABIT	LAISAMIS	KOCHALE ROBERT INTARAMATU	KANU	6,273	88.79
MARSABIT	LAISAMIS	SEYE SEKOTEY	DP	734	10.39
MARSABIT	LAISAMIS	ILO JOSEPH ARITE	FORD(A)	12	0.17
MARSABIT	LAISAMIS	no candidate nominated	FORD(K)		0.00
MARSABIT	LAISAMIS		SPOILT	46	0.65
MARSABIT	LAISAMIS		**TOTAL**	**7,065**	**100.00**
WAJIR	WAJIR E.	SHEIKH ABDI MOHAMMED	KANU	5,017	64.27
WAJIR	WAJIR E.	MOHAMMED ABDI	FORD(A)	2,610	33.44
WAJIR	WAJIR E.	HASSAN OMAR	DP	134	1.72
WAJIR	WAJIR E.	HUSSEIN MAHAD ISSAK	KNC	33	0.42
WAJIR	WAJIR E.	Sharif S. Mohammed defected to KANU	FORD(K)		0.00
WAJIR	WAJIR E.		SPOILT	12	0.15
WAJIR	WAJIR E.		**TOTAL**	**7,806**	**100.00**
WAJIR	WAJIR S.	AHMED ARALE HASSAN	KANU	4,211	65.34
WAJIR	WAJIR S.	OGLE AHMED ABDI	DP	1,910	29.64
WAJIR	WAJIR S.	WARFA DR SIRAT OSMAN	FORD(K)	320	4.97
WAJIR	WAJIR S.	HIRSI ABDI ALI	FORD(A)	2	0.03
WAJIR	WAJIR S.	ABDULLAHI MOHAMMED ALI	KNC	2	0.03
WAJIR	WAJIR S.		SPOILT		0.00
WAJIR	WAJIR S.		**TOTAL**	**6,445**	**100.00**
WAJIR	WAJIR W.	MOHAMMED AHMED KHALIF	KANU	5,675	51.24
WAJIR	WAJIR W.	HUSSEIN ABDULLAHI MAALIM ADAN	FORD(A)	5,357	48.37
WAJIR	WAJIR W.	HUSSEIN IBRAHIM ALI	KSC	43	0.39
WAJIR	WAJIR W.	Abdullahi I. Ali waylaid en route	DP		0.00
WAJIR	WAJIR W.	Abdi C. Mohammed refused nomination	FORD(K)		0.00
WAJIR	WAJIR W.		SPOILT		0.00
WAJIR	WAJIR W.		**TOTAL**	**11,075**	**100.00**
MANDERA	MANDERA W.	MAALIM ADEN ABDULLAHI	KANU	2,720	83.41
MANDERA	MANDERA W.	SHEIKH ABDIRAHMAN ALI	FORD(K)	461	14.14
MANDERA	MANDERA W.	BAROW NOOR IBRAHIM	FORD(A)	73	2.24
MANDERA	MANDERA W.	HASSAN KULOW MAALIM	DP	7	0.21
MANDERA	MANDERA W.		SPOILT		0.00
MANDERA	MANDERA W.		**TOTAL**	**14,336**	**100.00**
MANDERA	MANDERA CEN.	NOOR ADAN MOHAMMED	KANU	5,749	60.41
MANDERA	MANDERA CEN.	BARICHA ALI ABDI	FORD(K)	3,768	39.59
MANDERA	MANDERA CEN.	ADAN ENOW	DP	0	0.00
MANDERA	MANDERA CEN.	no candidate nominated	FORD(A)		0.00
MANDERA	MANDERA CEN.		SPOILT		0.00
MANDERA	MANDERA CEN.		**TOTAL**	**9,517**	**100.00**
MANDERA	MANDERA E.	AHMED ABDULLAHI SHEIKH	PICK	6,146	53.56
MANDERA	MANDERA E.	ISAIK SHABAN ALI	KANU	5,262	45.85
MANDERA	MANDERA E.	YUSUF ISMAIL ALI	FORD(K)	41	0.36
MANDERA	MANDERA E.	MAALIM MOHAMMED ALI	FORD(A)	21	0.18
MANDERA	MANDERA E.	OSMAN KHALIF ABDI	DP	6	0.05
MANDERA	MANDERA E.		SPOILT		0.00
MANDERA	MANDERA E.		**TOTAL**	**11,476**	**100.00**
GARISSA	DUJIS	MAALIM HUSSEIN MOHAMMED	KANU	9,825	79.69
GARISSA	DUJIS	HAJI ABDULLAHI MOHAMMED	DP	1,839	14.92
GARISSA	DUJIS	HASSAN ABDIKADIR YUSUF	FORD(K)	478	3.88
GARISSA	DUJIS	NOOR MOGOW ABDI	FORD(A)	174	1.41
GARISSA	DUJIS	SHURIE HASSAN OSMAN	KSC	13	0.11
GARISSA	DUJIS		SPOILT		0.00
GARISSA	DUJIS		**TOTAL**	**12,329**	**100.00**
GARISSA	LAGDERA	MOHAMMED FARAH MAALIM	FORD(K)	2,735	51.03
GARISSA	LAGDERA	SIAT HAJIR SHIDE	KANU	2,582	48.17
GARISSA	LAGDERA	MURSAL AHMED SHEIKH	FORD(A)	15	0.28

Appendix 2: 1992 Parliamentary Election Results

DISTRICT	CONSTITUENCY	CANDIDATES	PARTY	VOTE	%
GARISSA	LAGDERA	MOHAMMED YUSUF HAJI	DP	10	0.19
GARISSA	LAGDERA		SPOILT	18	0.34
GARISSA	LAGDERA		**TOTAL**	**5,360**	**100.00**
GARISSA	FAFI	SALAT IBRAHIM ABDALLAH	KANU	3,117	97.47
GARISSA	FAFI	GEDI HAJI YUSUF	DP	41	1.28
GARISSA	FAFI	HUJALE ALI DUNTOW	FORD(A)	26	0.81
GARISSA	FAFI	OLOW MOHAMMED DEGHOW	FORD(K)	14	0.44
GARISSA	FAFI		SPOILT		0.00
GARISSA	FAFI		**TOTAL**	**3,198**	**100.00**
GARISSA	IJARA	ARTE NASSIR MAALIM KORIO	KANU	2,761	96.14
GARISSA	IJARA	MAHAT ABDIRAHAMAN S.	FORD(K)	82	2.86
GARISSA	IJARA	GOH DEGOW IBRAHIM	FORD(A)	26	0.91
GARISSA	IJARA	MUHUMED HASSAN HUSSEIN	DP	3	0.10
GARISSA	IJARA		SPOILT		0.00
GARISSA	IJARA		**TOTAL**	**2,872**	**100.00**
TANA RIVER	GARSEN	KOMORA YUDA	KANU	7,168	47.56
TANA RIVER	GARSEN	SHAMBARO MOLU GALOGALO	FORD(K)	6,511	43.21
TANA RIVER	GARSEN	ROVA SAID MOHAMMED	DP	828	5.49
TANA RIVER	GARSEN	WAKOLE ABDI SHONGOLO	FORD(A)	122	0.81
TANA RIVER	GARSEN	OMARI ABAE KALASIGHA	KNC	275	1.82
TANA RIVER	GARSEN		SPOILT	166	1.10
TANA RIVER	GARSEN		**TOTAL**	**15,070**	**100.00**
TANA RIVER	GALOLE	MUGAVA TOLA KOFA	KANU	6,477	58.86
TANA-RIVER	GALOLE	GALGALO SHEIKH MOHAMMED ABDI	FORD(K)	3,967	36.05
TANA-RIVER	GALOLE	WAITHAKA ANDREW SOLOMON	FORD(A)	560	5.09
TANA-RIVER	GALOLE	Loka Madhah rejected - no statutory certificate	DP		0.00
TANA-RIVER	GALOLE		SPOILT		0.00
TANA-RIVER	GALOLE		**TOTAL**	**11,004**	**100.00**
KILIFI	BAHARI	MUMBA JOHN SAFARI	KANU	14,677	68.12
KILIFI	BAHARI	MWAKALU JEMBE	FORD(K)	5,170	24.00
KILIFI	BAHARI	MWAGANDA GILBERT ARLINGTON	FORD(A)	886	4.11
KILIFI	BAHARI	KANGWANA JAMES ROBERT	DP	812	3.77
KILIFI	BAHARI		SPOILT		0.00
KILIFI	BAHARI		**TOTAL**	**21,545**	**100.00**
KILIFI	KALOLENI	KEAH BENEDICT MATHIAS	KANU	16,126	71.05
KILIFI	KALOLENI	WA TSUMA DR ANDERSON CHIBULE	KNC	4,647	20.47
KILIFI	KALOLENI	NGALA GABRIEL KINDA	DP	967	4.26
KILIFI	KALOLENI	KATANA HAROLD RUA	FORD(A)	956	4.21
KILIFI	KALOLENI	Prof. Katama Mkangi waylaid	FORD(K)		0.00
KILIFI	KALOLENI		SPOILT		0.00
KILIFI	KALOLENI		**TOTAL**	**22,696**	**100.00**
KILIFI	GANZE	NGALA NOAH KATANA	KANU	8,500	88.27
KILIFI	GANZE	BAYA KENNETH KIRISA	DP	1,015	10.54
KILIFI	GANZE	MWARO MAURICE MURE	FORD(A)	115	1.19
KILIFI	GANZE	Moses Kitunga Jofwah ambushed	FORD(K)		0.00
KILIFI	GANZE		SPOILT		0.00
KILIFI	GANZE		**TOTAL**	**9,630**	**100.00**
KILIFI	MALINDI	BADAWY ABUBAKAR MOHAMMED AHMED	KANU	11,384	65.11
KILIFI	MALINDI	TSUMA ERASTUS CHARO	FORD(K)	2,884	16.49
KILIFI	MALINDI	YAHYA MOHAMMED	DP	1,324	7.57
KILIFI	MALINDI	JAFWAH DAVID MUKARE	KNC	1,185	6.78
KILIFI	MALINDI	ALI SWALEH ALI	FORD(A)	708	4.05
KILIFI	MALINDI		SPOILT		0.00
KILIFI	MALINDI		**TOTAL**	**17,485**	**100.00**
KILIFI	MAGARINI	NDZAI JONATHAN KATANA	KANU	8,025	86.93
KILIFI	MAGARINI	MOLLE SIMEON ALFRED	FORD(K)	856	9.27
KILIFI	MAGARINI	TOYA GIDEON BAYA	DP	163	1.77
KILIFI	MAGARINI	MALI HARRISON GARAMA KOMBE	PICK	135	1.46
KILIFI	MAGARINI	no candidate nominated	KNC		
KILIFI	MAGARINI	no candidate nominated	FORD(A)		
KILIFI	MAGARINI		SPOILT	53	0.57
KILIFI	MAGARINI		**TOTAL**	**9,232**	**100.00**
KWALE	MSAMBWENI	MWAMZANDI KASSIM BAKARI	KANU	12,921	52.25

Appendix 2: 1992 Parliamentary Election Results

DISTRICT	CONSTITUENCY	CANDIDATES	PARTY	VOTE	%
KWALE	MSAMBWENI	WAMATAI MRS MARERE M.	DP	9,839	39.79
KWALE	MSAMBWENI	KASIRANI MZEE MWAMWIRU	FORD(K)	992	4.01
KWALE	MSAMBWENI	MWALIMU KITAMBI HAMISI	FORD(A)	608	2.46
KWALE	MSAMBWENI	BARUA RASHID MOHAMMED	KNC	111	0.45
KWALE	MSAMBWENI		SPOILT	256	1.04
KWALE	MSAMBWENI		**TOTAL**	**24,727**	**100.00**
KWALE	KINANGO	RAI SAMUEL NGONZI	KANU	10,269	87.93
KWALE	KINANGO	NDEGWA PATRICK JOHO	DP	825	7.06
KWALE	KINANGO	CHIKUTA JULIUS CHIIRU	FORD(K)	459	3.93
KWALE	KINANGO	Daniel Munga detained by police	FORD(A)		0.00
KWALE	KINANGO	HASSAN SAID	KNC		0.00
KWALE	KINANGO		SPOILT	125	1.07
KWALE	KINANGO		**TOTAL**	**11,678**	**100.00**
KWALE	MATUGA	BOY BOY JUMA	KANU	13,414	66.05
KWALE	MATUGA	NZILI MUDZO KUHENDERWA	DP	5,130	25.26
KWALE	MATUGA	GAKESHO OMARI ABDALLA	FORD(A)	945	4.65
KWALE	MATUGA	WARRAKAH MBWANA ALI	FORD(K)	820	4.04
KWALE	MATUGA	KITAMBI HAMISI M.	KNC	0	0.00
KWALE	MATUGA		SPOILT		0.00
KWALE	MATUGA		**TOTAL**	**20,309**	**100.00**
LAMU	LAMU E.	MOHAMMED ABU THIABA	KANU	3,309	51.36
LAMU	LAMU E.	HASHIM MOHAMMED SALIM	FORD(K)	2,064	32.03
LAMU	LAMU E.	SOMO ABU BOA	DP	992	15.40
LAMU	LAMU E.	KUSOMA MOHAMMED BUNU	FORD(A)	32	0.50
LAMU	LAMU E.		SPOILT	46	0.71
LAMU	LAMU E.		**TOTAL**	**6,443**	**100.00**
LAMU	LAMU W.	ALI ABDULKARIM MOHAMMED	KANU	6,992	51.55
LAMU	LAMU W.	ABDALLA NASSIR BWANA MKUU	DP	2,920	21.53
LAMU	LAMU W.	GAITARA BERNARD KIARIE	FORD(A)	2,575	18.98
LAMU	LAMU W.	HILALI ABDULRAHMAN MOHAMMED	FORD(K)	922	6.80
LAMU	LAMU W.		SPOILT	155	1.14
LAMU	LAMU W.		**TOTAL**	**13,564**	**100.00**
MOMBASA	KISAUNI	MZEE PROF RASHID MOHAMMED	FORD(K)	10,627	35.61
MOMBASA	KISAUNI	MAITHA EMMANUEL KARISSA JAMES	KANU	10,557	35.38
MOMBASA	KISAUNI	SIMBA SALIM RASHID	FORD(A)	4,287	14.37
MOMBASA	KISAUNI	JAHAZI MOHAMMED MWINYI MTWANA	DP	4,108	13.77
MOMBASA	KISAUNI	BWANAMAKO MAUR A.	KNC	264	0.88
MOMBASA	KISAUNI		SPOILT		0.00
MOMBASA	KISAUNI		**TOTAL**	**29,843**	**100.00**
MOMBASA	LIKONI	MWAVUMO KHALIF SALIM	FORD(K)	7,274	45.80
MOMBASA	LIKONI	MKONJERU LABAN AMBEI	FORD(A)	3,798	23.91
MOMBASA	LIKONI	MWIDAU ABDULKADIR ABDALLA	KANU	3,738	23.53
MOMBASA	LIKONI	MWEA MRS GRACE	DP	955	6.01
MOMBASA	LIKONI	NGOMBO GEORGE STEPHENS	KNC	118	0.74
MOMBASA	LIKONI		SPOILT		0.00
MOMBASA	LIKONI		**TOTAL**	**15,883**	**100.00**
MOMBASA	MVITA	NASSIR SHARRIF TAIB	KANU	8,627	33.10
MOMBASA	MVITA	MWINYI OMAR SHIMBWA	FORD(K)	8,275	31.75
MOMBASA	MVITA	BAMAHRIZ AHMED SALIM	FORD(A)	6,016	23.08
MOMBASA	MVITA	YUNIS ISMAEL MOHAMMED	DP	2,698	10.35
MOMBASA	MVITA	SALIM MOHAMMED FATMA JENEBY	KNC	144	0.55
MOMBASA	MVITA		SPOILT	303	1.16
MOMBASA	MVITA		**TOTAL**	**26,063**	**100.00**
MOMBASA	CHANGAMWE	KILIKU JOSEPH KENNEDY	DP	9,247	34.86
MOMBASA	CHANGAMWE	FAKIL MOHAMMED MWINYIHAJI	FORD(K)	7,753	29.23
MOMBASA	CHANGAMWE	KAJEMBE RAMADHAN SEIF	KANU	5,766	21.74
MOMBASA	CHANGAMWE	KAVUI PHILIP NZOIKA	FORD(A)	3,252	12.26
MOMBASA	CHANGAMWE		SPOILT	508	1.92
MOMBASA	CHANGAMWE		**TOTAL**	**26,526**	**100.00**
TAITA-TAVETA	TAVETA	CRITICOS BASIL	KANU	5,140	59.63
TAITA TAVETA	TAVETA	LUKINDO NORMAN NTHENGE	FORD(A)	1,886	21.88
TAITA-TAVETA	TAVETA	KUBO MWACHARO	DP	891	10.34
TAITA-TAVETA	TAVETA	MSUYA CRISPUS KEAH LESHAMBA	FORD(K)	619	7.18
TAITA-TAVETA	TAVETA		SPOILT	84	0.97

Appendix 2: 1992 Parliamentary Election Results

DISTRICT	CONSTITUENCY	CANDIDATES	PARTY	VOTE	%
TAITA-TAVETA	TAVETA		**TOTAL**	**8,620**	**100.00**
TAITA-TAVETA	WUNDANYI	MBELA DARIUS MSAGHA	KANU	7,927	73.57
TAITA-TAVETA	WUNDANYI	WA MWACHOFI MBORIO MASHENGU	DP	1,612	14.96
TAITA-TAVETA	WUNDANYI	MWANGOLA PATRICK JOEL	FORD(A)	1,115	10.35
TAITA-TAVETA	WUNDANYI	no candidate	FORD(K)		0.00
TAITA-TAVETA	WUNDANYI		SPOILT	121	1.12
TAITA-TAVETA	WUNDANYI		**TOTAL**	**10,775**	**100.00**
TAITA-TAVETA	VOI	MBELA DOUGLAS DANIEL	KANU	4,293	53.60
TAITA-TAVETA	VOI	MWAMUNGA ELIUD TIMOTHY	DP	2,789	34.82
TAITA-TAVETA	VOI	KACHULA EMPHRAIM MWATABU R.	FORD(K)	647	8.08
TAITA-TAVETA	VOI	no candidate nominated	FORD(A)		0.00
TAITA-TAVETA	VOI		SPOILT	280	3.50
TAITA-TAVETA	VOI		**TOTAL**	**8,009**	**100.00**
TAITA-TAVETA	MWATATE	MCHARO ELIUD MWAKIO	KANU	5,938	57.23
TAITA TAVETA	MWATATE	MWANJOGI BALDWIN MWAKUGU	FORD(A)	2,946	28.40
TAITA TAVETA	MWATATE	MWATELA CALISTO ANDREW	DP	1,061	10.23
TAITA TAVETA	MWATATE	MBELA ALLEN MATISHO	FORD(K)	430	4.14
TAITA TAVETA	MWATATE		SPOILT		0.00
TAITA TAVETA	MWATATE		**TOTAL**	**10,375**	**100.00**
LAIKIPIA	LAIKIPIA E.	MUKORA CHARLES NDERITU	DP	21,949	72.34
LAIKIPIA	LAIKIPIA E.	KAPARO KAUSAI FRANCIS XAVIER OLE	KANU	7,920	26.10
LAIKIPIA	LAIKIPIA E.	MAILYANI PETER MUNGATHIA	FORD(A)	474	1.56
LAIKIPIA	LAIKIPIA E.	no candidate nominated	FORD(K)		0.00
LAIKIPIA	LAIKIPIA EAST		SPOILT		0.00
LAIKIPIA	LAIKIPIA EAST		**TOTAL**	**30,343**	**100.00**
LAIKIPIA	LAIKIPIA W.	KIMANI DIXON KIHIKA	DP	33,386	74.38
LAIKIPIA	LAIKIPIA W.	KARIUKI GODFREY GITAHI	KANU	7,562	16.85
LAIKIPIA	LAIKIPIA W.	NDUNGU EVANS MUNGAI	FORD(A)	3,493	7.78
LAIKIPIA	LAIKIPIA W.	MATHENGE JOSEPH GITHAE	PICK	223	0.50
LAIKIPIA	LAIKIPIA W.	no candidate nominated	FORD(K)		0.00
LAIKIPIA	LAIKIPIA W.		SPOILT	220	0.49
LAIKIPIA	LAIKIPIA W.		**TOTAL**	**44,884**	**100.00**
NAKURU	NAKURU EAST	WANYANGE FRANCIS JOHN	FORD(A)	37,684	62.12
NAKURU	NAKURU EAST	WAGARA JAMES KEFFA NJUGUNA	DP	8,941	14.74
NAKURU	NAKURU EAST	MAINA JOSEPH KURIA	KANU	6,942	11.44
NAKURU	NAKURU EAST	NJENGA S. KIMANI	FORD(K)	5,094	8.40
NAKURU	NAKURU EAST	KAIRO SIMON THUO	KNC	1,998	3.29
NAKURU	NAKURU EAST		SPOILT		0.00
NAKURU	NAKURU EAST		**TOTAL**	**105,763**	**100.00**
NAKURU	NAKURU T	OYONDI DR CHARLES LWALI	FORD(A)	28,178	45.23
NAKURU	NAKURU T	KAMANAGARA JOHN MAINA	FORD(K)	11,996	19.25
NAKURU	NAKURU T	MWITHAGA MARK WARUIRU	DP	10,812	17.35
NAKURU	NAKURU T	ASANYO GEOFFREY MAKANA	KANU	10,323	16.57
NAKURU	NAKURU T	KIMEMIA AMOS KABIRU	KNC	535	0.86
NAKURU	NAKURU T	GICHURU JOSEPH MBUTHIA	PICK	451	0.72
NAKURU	NAKURU T		SPOILT	9	0.01
NAKURU	NAKURU T		**TOTAL**	**168,067**	**100.00**
NAKURU	MOLO	MUNGAI JOHN NJENGA	FORD(A)	57,631	59.76
NAKURU	MOLO	KEBENEI JOSEPH KIPKURGAT	KANU	33,016	34.23
NAKURU	MOLO	KIHIU SAMUEL KURIA	DP	5,081	5.27
NAKURU	MOLO	Fred O. Muhando refused nomination	FORD(K)		0.00
NAKURU	MOLO		SPOILT	713	0.74
NAKURU	MOLO		**TOTAL**	**286,638**	**100.00**
NAKURU	RONGAI	KOMEN WILLIAM KIPROP ARAP	KANU	15,020	46.75
NAKURU	RONGAI	NJUGUNA PETER NJUGI	FORD(A)	11,198	34.86
NAKURU	RONGAI	NDERITU RENISON WAWERU	DP	3,698	11.51
NAKURU	RONGAI	MBUTHIA JONATHAN KAMEANAH	FORD(K)	1,908	5.94
NAKURU	RONGAI		SPOILT	303	0.94
NAKURU	RONGAI		**TOTAL**	**319,478**	**100.00**
NAKURU	NAKURU N.	KIMANI BISHOP JOSEPH	FORD(A)	19,675	61.57
NAKURU	NAKURU N.	KURIA JOSEPH MUKERA	DP	8,727	27.31
NAKURU	NAKURU N.	NJOROGE TIRUS WAINAINA	KANU	2,251	7.04
NAKURU	NAKURU N.	NDUNG'U BIDEN N.	FORD(K)	731	2.29
NAKURU	NAKURU N.	no candidate nominated	KNC		0.00

Appendix 2: 1992 Parliamentary Election Results

DISTRICT	CONSTITUENCY	CANDIDATES	PARTY	VOTE	%
NAKURU	NAKURU N.		SPOILT	572	1.79
NAKURU	NAKURU N.		**TOTAL**	**31,956**	**100.00**
KAJIADO	KAJIADO N.	SAITOTI GEORGE	KANU	18,940	51.25
KAJIADO	KAJIADO N.	KEEN JOHN	DP	8,242	22.30
KAJIADO	KAJIADO N.	ODUPOY PHILIP LEPISH	FORD(A)	8,088	21.88
KAJIADO	KAJIADO N.	OTIENO MRS VIRGINIA WAMBUI	FORD(K)	970	2.62
KAJIADO	KAJIADO N.	SEKI OLIVER	KNC	141	0.38
KAJIADO	KAJIADO N.		SPOILT	576	1.56
KAJIADO	KAJIADO N.		**TOTAL**	**36,957**	**100.00**
KAJIADO	KAJIADO CEN.	LENTANTE DAVID OLE SANKORI	KANU	11,262	55.86
KAJIADO	KAJIADO CEN.	OLOONTOSAI MOSES	DP	8,543	42.37
KAJIADO	KAJIADO CEN.	PENETI PAUL	FORD(K)	278	1.38
KAJIADO	KAJIADO CEN.	no candidate nominated	FORD(A)		0.00
KAJIADO	KAJIADO CEN.		SPOILT	78	0.39
KAJIADO	KAJIADO CEN.		**TOTAL**	**20,161**	**100.00**
KAJIADO	KAJIADO S.	SINGARU PHILIP LAMPAT OLE	KANU	12,293	53.18
KAJIADO	KAJIADO S.	PARPAI GEOFFREY	DP	9,383	40.59
KAJIADO	KAJIADO S.	GATHIRU JAMES KIMANI	FORD(A)	1,145	4.95
KAJIADO	KAJIADO S.	Leonard Partino vanished en route	FORD(K)		0.00
KAJIADO	KAJIADO S.		SPOILT	296	1.28
KAJIADO	KAJIADO S.		**TOTAL**	**23,117**	**100.00**
NAROK	NAROK N.	NTIMAMA WILLIAM OLE	KANU	24,523	62.69
NAROK	NAROK N.	LEMPAKA HARUN OLE	FORD(A)	9,489	24.26
NAROK	NAROK N.	TIAMPATTI JOHN MUSUNI OLE	DP	4,305	11.01
NAROK	NAROK N.	MPARU JACKSON ONTETIA OLE	FORD(K)	248	0.63
NAROK	NAROK N.		SPOILT	552	1.41
NAROK	NAROK N.		**TOTAL**	**39,117**	**100.00**
NAROK	NAROK W.	SUNKULI JULIUS OLE	KANU	16,694	57.41
NAROK	NAROK W.	BIRIR RICHARD BWOGO ARAP	PICK	11,200	38.52
NAROK	NAROK W.	TOMPOY PETER OLE	DP	1,185	4.08
NAROK	NAROK W.	Michael ole Sereria's papers refused	FORD(A)		0.00
NAROK	NAROK W.	Candidate (name unknown) waylaid	FORD(K)		0.00
NAROK	NAROK W.		SPOILT		0.00
NAROK	NAROK W.		**TOTAL**	**Unopposed**	**100.00**
NAROK	NAROK S.	TUYA SAMSON OLE	KANU	---	100.00
NAROK	NAROK S.	no candidate nominated	FORD(A)		0.00
NAROK	NAROK S.	Livingstone ole Kapeen time barred	DP		0.00
NAROK	NAROK S.	ole Nkanai vanished	FORD(K)		0.00
NAROK	NAROK S.		SPOILT		0.00
NAROK	NAROK S.		**TOTAL**	**Unopposed**	**100.00**
ELGEYO-MARAKWET	KERIO CEN.	CHEPKOK PAUL RUTO	KANU	---	100.00
"	KERIO CEN.	Samuel Mwaura waylaid	FORD(A)		0.00
"	KERIO CEN.	no candidate nominated	FORD(K)		0.00
"	KERIO CEN.	no candidate nominated	DP		0.00
"	KERIO CEN.		SPOILT		0.00
"	KERIO CEN.		**TOTAL**	**Unopposed**	**100.00**
"	KERIO S.	BIWOTT NICHOLAS KIPRONO	KANU	25,427	97.93
"	KERIO S.	SEII MRS TABITHA	DP	467	1.80
"	KERIO S.	no candidate nominated	FORD(K)		0.00
"	KERIO S.	no candidate nominated	FORD(A)		0.00
"	KERIO S.		SPOILT	70	0.27
"	KERIO S.		**TOTAL**	**25,964**	**100.00**
"	KERIO W.	KEINO BOAZ KIPCHUMBA	KANU	---	100.00
"	KERIO W.	no candidate nominated	DP		0.00
"	KERIO W.	John Chebeii waylaid	FORD(A)		0.00
"	KERIO W.	Francis Kadenge abducted	FORD(K)		0.00
"	KERIO W.		SPOILT		0.00
"	KERIO W.		**TOTAL**	**Unopposed**	**100.00**
"	KERIO EAST	CHESEREK FREDERICK KISANG ARAP	KANU	---	100.00
"	KERIO EAST	Francis Cheptile waylaid	FORD(A)		0.00
"	KERIO EAST	Kibor arap Talai waylaid en route	FORD(K)		0.00

Appendix 2: 1992 Parliamentary Election Results

DISTRICT	CONSTITUENCY	CANDIDATES	PARTY	VOTE	%
ELGEYO-MARAKWET	KERIO EAST	Ruto Belibeit waylaid	DP		0.00
"	KERIO EAST		SPOILT		0.00
"	KERIO EAST		**TOTAL**	**Unopposed**	**100.00**
BARINGO	BARINGO EAST	LOTODO JOSEPH DALDOSO	KANU	---	100.00
BARINGO	BARINGO EAST	John Gakuo waylaid	FORD(A)		0.00
BARINGO	BARINGO EAST	no candidate nominated	FORD(K)		0.00
BARINGO	BARINGO EAST	John K. Loikiaratum waylaid	DP		0.00
BARINGO	BARINGO EAST		SPOILT		0.00
BARINGO	BARINGO EAST		**TOTAL**	**Unopposed**	**100.00**
BARINGO	BARINGO CEN.	MOI DANIEL TOROITICH ARAP	KANU	---	100.00
BARINGO	BARINGO CEN.	Patrick Chege Njuguna kidnapped	FORD(A)		0.00
BARINGO	BARINGO CEN.	no candidate nominated	FORD(K)		0.00
BARINGO	BARINGO CEN.	Amos Kandie papers refused	DP		0.00
BARINGO	BARINGO CEN.		SPOILT		0.00
BARINGO	BARINGO CEN.		**TOTAL**	**Unopposed**	**100.00**
BARINGO	BARINGO N.	ROTICH WILLIAM YATOR KAMUREN	KANU	---	100.00
BARINGO	BARINGO N.	Joseph Theuri refused nomination	FORD(A)		0.00
BARINGO	BARINGO N.	Eric Kiptoon abducted	FORD(K)		0.00
BARINGO	BARINGO N.	Henry Cheboiwo's papers destroyed	DP		0.00
BARINGO	BARINGO N.		SPOILT		0.00
BARINGO	BARINGO N.		**TOTAL**	**Unopposed**	**100.00**
BARINGO	BARINGO S.	MOROGO WILLIAM G.	KANU	---	100.00
BARINGO	BARINGO S.	Abbas Mawboob waylaid	FORD(A)		0.00
BARINGO	BARINGO S.	no candidate nominated	FORD(K)		0.00
BARINGO	BARINGO S.	Dr. Ben Sadalla waylaid en route	DP		0.00
BARINGO	BARINGO S.		SPOILT		0.00
BARINGO	BARINGO S.		**TOTAL**	**Unopposed**	**100.00**
BOMET	KONOIN	CHEBELYON NATHANIEL K. ARAP	KANU	---	100.00
BOMET	KONOIN	Peter K. Bett did not turn up	KSC		0.00
BOMET	KONOIN	no candidate nominated	FORD(A)		0.00
BOMET	KONOIN	no candidate nominated	FORD(K)		0.00
BOMET	KONOIN	no candidate nominated	DP		0.00
BOMET	KONOIN		SPOILT		0.00
BOMET	KONOIN		**TOTAL**	**Unopposed**	**100.00**
BOMET	CHEPALUNGU	KOECH JOHN KIPSANG ARAP	KANU	---	100.00
BOMET	CHEPALUNGU	no candidate nominated	FORD(A)		0.00
BOMET	CHEPALUNGU	no candidate nominated	FORD(K)		0.00
BOMET	CHEPALUNGU	no candidate nominated	DP		0.00
BOMET	CHEPALUNGU		SPOILT		0.00
BOMET	CHEPALUNGU		**TOTAL**	**Unopposed**	**100.00**
BOMET	BOMET	KONES KIPKALYA ARAP	KANU	---	100.00
BOMET	BOMET	no candidate nominated	FORD(A)		0.00
BOMET	BOMET	no candidate nominated	FORD(K)		0.00
BOMET	BOMET	no candidate nominated	DP		0.00
BOMET	BOMET		SPOILT		0.00
BOMET	BOMET		**TOTAL**	**Unopposed**	**100.00**
KERICHO	BURET	NGENO DR JONATHAN KIMETIT	KANU	---	100.00
KERICHO	BURET	SIGEI PHILIP KIPSETE	PICK		0.00
KERICHO	BURET	RONO JOEL KIPKORIR ARAP	FORD(K)		0.00
KERICHO	BURET	no candidate nominated	FORD(A)		0.00
KERICHO	BURET	no candidate nominated	DP		0.00
KERICHO	BURET		SPOILT	227	0.00
KERICHO	BURET		**TOTAL**	**Unopposed**	**100.00**
KERICHO	BELGUT	KIRIOR KIPTORUS ARAP	KANU	---	100.00
KERICHO	BELGUT	no candidate nominated	FORD(A)		0.00
KERICHO	BELGUT	Mr. Rotich disappeared	FORD(K)		0.00
KERICHO	BELGUT	no candidate nominated	DP		0.00
KERICHO	BELGUT		SPOILT		0.00
KERICHO	BELGUT		**TOTAL**	**Unopposed**	**100.00**
KERICHO	KIPKELION	TANUI DANIEL KIPKORIR ARAP	KANU	43,334	75.82
KERICHO	KIPKELION	KEINO MOSES KIPRONO ARAP	FORD(K)	6,242	10.92
KERICHO	KIPKELION	KABUGI MANNASEH N.	FORD(A)	5,901	10.32

DISTRICT	CONSTITUENCY	CANDIDATES	PARTY	VOTE	%
KERICHO	KIPKELION	KOSKEI WILSON KIPNGETICH ARAP	PICK	199	0.35
KERICHO	KIPKELION	KENDUIYWO GEOFFREY N.	DP	1,477	2.58
KERICHO	KIPKELION		SPOILT		0.00
KERICHO	KIPKELION		**TOTAL**	**57,153**	**100.00**
NANDI	MOSOP	SAMBU JOHN KIPKORIR	KANU	---	100.00
NANDI	MOSOP	Noah Kimutai stood down 1 Dec. 92	FORD(A)		0.00
NANDI	MOSOP	no candidate nominated	FORD(K)		0.00
NANDI	MOSOP	no candidate nominated	DP		0.00
NANDI	MOSOP		SPOILT		0.00
NANDI	MOSOP		**TOTAL**	**Unopposed**	**100.00**
NANDI	ALDAI	TITI JOHN PAUL	KANU	---	100.00
NANDI	ALDAI	David M. Choge defected 1 Dec. 92	FORD(A)		0.00
NANDI	ALDAI	John Chirchir Birgen ambushed	FORD(K)		0.00
NANDI	ALDAI	no candidate nominated	DP		0.00
NANDI	ALDAI		SPOILT		0.00
NANDI	ALDAI		**TOTAL**	**Unopposed**	**100.00**
NANDI	TINDERET	KOSGEY HENRY KIPRONO ARAP	KANU	---	100.00
NANDI	TINDERET	Robert Kiptoo Korir defected 29 Nov. 92	FORD(A)		0.00
NANDI	TINDERET	no candidate nominated	FORD(K)		0.00
NANDI	TINDERET	Kimunai arap Sego waylaid	DP		0.00
NANDI	TINDERET		SPOILT		0.00
NANDI	TINDERET		**TOTAL**	**Unopposed**	**100.00**
POKOT	KACHILEBA	NANG'OLE PETER LOCHAUN	KANU	6,023	89.82
POKOT	KACHILEBA	LOCHAKAI JOHN WILLIAM	DP	432	6.44
POKOT	KACHILEBA	HUSSEIN NASSUR	FORD(K)	18	0.27
POKOT	KACHILEBA	MICHAEL LUBUINI	FORD(A)	233	3.47
POKOT	KACHILEBA		SPOILT		0.00
POKOT	KACHILEBA		**TOTAL**	**6,706**	**100.00**
POKOT	KAPENGURIA	LOTODO FRANCIS POLIS LOILE	KANU	23,152	89.07
POKOT	KAPENGURIA	LUKWOE JAMES	FORD(A)	2,490	9.58
POKOT	KAPENGURIA	KIPKURGAT PHILEMON KIRUI	DP	350	1.35
POKOT	KAPENGURIA	Gregory Pogishyo waylaid	FORD(K)		0.00
POKOT	KAPENGURIA		SPOILT		0.00
POKOT	KAPENGURIA		**TOTAL**	**25,992**	**100.00**
POKOT	SIGOR	RURINO PHILIP RUTO	KANU	13,313	66.89
POKOT	SIGOR	LOMADA CHRISTOPHER MOTONYWO	PICK	6,434	32.33
POKOT	SIGOR	LOVETAKOU WILLIAM	DP	74	0.37
POKOT	SIGOR	LOMONGAINE PHILIP	FORD(A)	63	0.32
POKOT	SIGOR	AWLY DAVID LOMOGIN	FORD(K)	18	0.09
POKOT	SIGOR		SPOILT		0.00
POKOT	SIGOR		**TOTAL**	**19,902**	**100.00**
TURKANA	TURKANA N.	EKIDOR JAPHETH LOTUKOI	KANU	7,663	96.23
TURKANA	TURKANA N.	EKARAN LOOLEL ANDREW	DP	162	2.03
TURKANA	TURKANA N.	AKAL JULIUS ADAPEL	FORD(K)	138	1.73
TURKANA	TURKANA N.	no candidate nominated	FORD(A)		0.00
TURKANA	TURKANA N.		SPOILT		0.00
TURKANA	TURKANA N.		**TOTAL**	**7,963**	**100.00**
TURKANA	TURKANA CEN.	EJORE PATRICK MZEE	KANU	8,181	75.04
TURKANA	TURKANA CEN.	LOKURUKA MICHAEL NAPOO	DP	2,388	21.90
TURKANA	TURKANA CEN.	ETHURU DAVID E.	FORD(K)	333	3.05
TURKANA	TURKANA CEN.	no candidate nominated	FORD(A)		0.00
TURKANA	TURKANA CEN.		SPOILT		0.00
TURKANA	TURKANA CEN.		**TOTAL**	**10,902**	**100.00**
TURKANA	TURKANA S.	EWOTON FRANCIS IGWATON	KANU	4,623	95.30
TURKANA	TURKANA S.	SIPAYO JAMES E.	FORD(A)	206	4.25
TURKANA	TURKANA S.	Drake Situma Kundu time-barred	FORD(K)		0.00
TURKANA	TURKANA S.	Eliud Kerio Long'acha left off ballot papers.	DP		0.00
TURKANA	TURKANA S.		SPOILT	22	0.45
TURKANA	TURKANA S.		**TOTAL**	**4,851**	**100.00**
SAMBURU	SAMBURU EAST	LESHORE SAMMY PIRISA	KANU	---	100.00
SAMBURU	SAMBURU EAST	no candidate nominated	DP		0.00
SAMBURU	SAMBURU EAST	no candidate nominated	FORD(A)		0.00

Appendix 2: 1992 Parliamentary Election Results

DISTRICT	CONSTITUENCY	CANDIDATES	PARTY	VOTE	%
SAMBURU	SAMBURU EAST	Jackson K. Lessaigor waylaid en route	FORD(K)		0.00
SAMBURU	SAMBURU EAST		SPOILT		0.00
SAMBURU	SAMBURU EAST		**TOTAL**	**Unopposed**	**100.00**
SAMBURU	SAMBURU W.	LENGEES PETER STEVE	KANU	20,950	92.24
SAMBURU	SAMBURU W.	LOTITIYO PETER LEKAIKUM	FORD(K)	773	3.40
SAMBURU	SAMBURU W.	LEPARACHAU JOSHUA SAMBIYENI	DP	771	3.39
SAMBURU	SAMBURU W.	LALAIKIPIAN GEORGE	FORD(A)	219	0.96
SAMBURU	SAMBURU W.		SPOILT		0.00
SAMBURU	SAMBURU W.		**TOTAL**	**22,713**	**100.00**
UASIN-GISHU	ELDORET N.	SAINA WILLIAM MOROGE ARAP	KANU	34,129	58.52
UASIN-GISHU	ELDORET N.	MIROYA JASON AMBE	FORD(A)	15,153	25.98
UASIN-GISHU	ELDORET N.	OMIDO DAVID A.	FORD(K)	6,109	10.47
UASIN-GISHU	ELDORET N.	TANUI DAVID	DP	2,462	4.22
UASIN-GISHU	ELDORET N.		SPOILT	472	0.81
UASIN-GISHU	ELDORET N.		**TOTAL**	**58,325**	**100.00**
UASIN-GISHU	ELDORET EAST	BARMASAI JOEL F. KIMURAI	KANU	30,735	82.84
UASIN-GISHU	ELDORET EAST	MWANGI JOSEPH NJUGUNA	FORD(A)	4,878	13.15
UASIN-GISHU	ELDORET EAST	MURGOR CHARLES CHANGUONY	DP	1,490	4.02
UASIN-GISHU	ELDORET EAST	no candidate nominated	FORD(K)		0.00
UASIN-GISHU	ELDORET EAST		SPOILT		0.00
UASIN-GISHU	ELDORET EAST		**TOTAL**	**37,103**	**100.00**
UASIN-GISHU	ELDORET S.	MISOI DR JOSEPH KIPTIONY ARAP	KANU	21,678	65.33
UASIN-GISHU	ELDORET S.	CHOMBA JULIUS KIIRU	FORD(A)	10,021	30.20
UASIN-GISHU	ELDORET S.	KIBERA NICHOLAS MWEMA	DP	1,484	4.47
UASIN-GISHU	ELDORET S.	no candidate nominated	FORD(K)		0.00
UASIN-GISHU	ELDORET S.		SPOILT		0.00
UASIN-GISHU	ELDORET S.		**TOTAL**	**33,183**	**100.00**
TRANS-NZOIA	KWANZA	KAPTEN GEORGE WELIME	FORD(K)	15,328	55.02
TRANS-NZOIA	KWANZA	WEKESA DR NOAH M.	KANU	9,610	34.50
TRANS-NZOIA	KWANZA	KINYANJUI PETER	DP	1,407	5.05
TRANS-NZOIA	KWANZA	NDAMWE SALIM WAMALWA	FORD(A)	1,360	4.88
TRANS-NZOIA	KWANZA	NYUKURI JOTHAN	KNC	154	0.55
TRANS-NZOIA	KWANZA		SPOILT		0.00
TRANS-NZOIA	KWANZA		**TOTAL**	**27,859**	**100.00**
TRANS-NZOIA	SABOTI	WAMALWA MICHAEL KIJANE	FORD(K)	22,315	55.69
TRANS-NZOIA	SABOTI	WABUGE WAFULA	KANU	10,279	25.65
TRANS-NZOIA	SABOTI	ANAMI SAMMY	FORD(A)	5,362	13.38
TRANS-NZOIA	SABOTI	MUSAMIA PETER MUKITE	DP	1,179	2.94
TRANS-NZOIA	SABOTI		SPOILT	938	2.34
TRANS-NZOIA	SABOTI		**TOTAL**	**40,073**	**100.00**
TRANS-NZOIA	CHERANGANI	KIRWA KIPRUTO RONO ARAP	KANU	12,373	51.97
TRANS-NZOIA	CHERANGANI	MULIRO MUKASA MWAMBU	FORD(K)	6,362	26.72
TRANS-NZOIA	CHERANGANI	MSANJA BEN WANJALA	FORD(A)	3,550	14.91
TRANS-NZOIA	CHERANGANI	CHEGE JOHN BARON WAIRINGU	DP	1,446	6.07
TRANS-NZOIA	CHERANGANI	KING'ASIA THOMAS M.	KNC	77	0.32
TRANS-NZOIA	CHERANGANI		SPOILT		0.00
TRANS-NZOIA	CHERANGANI		**TOTAL**	**23,808**	**100.00**
BUNGOMA	KIMILILI	KITUYI MUKHISA	FORD(K)	27,951	80.33
BUNGOMA	KIMILILI	MWANGALE ELIJAH WASIKE	KANU	4,357	12.52
BUNGOMA	KIMILILI	WELIME WANJALA	FORD(A)	1,302	3.74
BUNGOMA	KIMILILI	AMUTALA WYCLIFFE	DP	452	1.30
BUNGOMA	KIMILILI	NAMBILI JOSHUA	KNC	105	0.30
BUNGOMA	KIMILILI		SPOILT	627	1.80
BUNGOMA	KIMILILI		**TOTAL**	**34,794**	**100.00**
BUNGOMA	WEBUYE	KOMBO MUSIKARI	FORD(K)	13,580	43.19
BUNGOMA	WEBUYE	SAMBU ALFRED WEKESA	DP	12,026	38.25
BUNGOMA	WEBUYE	MALOBA JOSEPH	FORD(A)	4,479	14.25
BUNGOMA	WEBUYE	MANG'OLI JOASH WALUBENGO	KANU	1,050	3.34
BUNGOMA	WEBUYE		SPOILT	307	0.98
BUNGOMA	WEBUYE		**TOTAL**	**31,442**	**100.00**
BUNGOMA	SIRISIA	MUNYASIA JOHN BARASA	FORD(K)	22,899	72.36
BUNGOMA	SIRISIA	MULIRO JOSEPH	KANU	6,566	20.75

Appendix 2: 1992 Parliamentary Election Results

DISTRICT	CONSTITUENCY	CANDIDATES	PARTY	VOTE	%
BUNGOMA	SIRISIA	SIRENGO DR WILFRED SILAS	FORD(A)	1,342	4.24
BUNGOMA	SIRISIA	BARASA WYCLIFFE WASILWA HERBERT	DP	837	2.65
BUNGOMA	SIRISIA		SPOILT		0.00
BUNGOMA	SIRISIA		**TOTAL**	**31,644**	**100.00**
BUNGOMA	KANDUYI	SIFUNA LAWRENCE SIMIYU	FORD(A)	19,446	40.86
BUNGOMA	KANDUYI	KHAOYA JOSEPH WAFULA	FORD(K)	18,128	38.09
BUNGOMA	KANDUYI	MAKHANU MAURICE SIMON MAKOKA	KANU	8,877	18.65
BUNGOMA	KANDUYI	WANYAMA ALFRED	DP	1,146	2.41
BUNGOMA	KANDUYI		SPOILT		0.00
BUNGOMA	KANDUYI		**TOTAL**	**47,597**	**100.00**
BUNGOMA	MOUNT ELGON	KISIERO WILBERFORCE ARAP	KANU	20,022	78.76
BUNGOMA	MOUNT ELGON	KAKOI MOSES	FORD(K)	4,811	18.92
BUNGOMA	MOUNT ELGON	SIMIYU JOSEPH K. PRICHANI	FORD(A)	542	2.13
BUNGOMA	MOUNT ELGON	SHAPALI COSMAS	DP	48	0.19
BUNGOMA	MOUNT ELGON	no candidate nominated	KNC		0.00
BUNGOMA	MOUNT ELGON		SPOILT		0.00
BUNGOMA	MOUNT ELGON		**TOTAL**	**25,423**	**100.00**
BUSIA	AMAGORO	ODUYA GEORGE FREDERICK OPRONG	KANU	25,699	81.30
BUSIA	AMAGORO	ETYANG GABRIEL EMOJIRI	DP	3,684	11.65
BUSIA	AMAGORO	OMACHAR IGNATIUS BARASA	PICK	2,226	7.04
BUSIA	AMAGORO	no candidate nominated	FORD(A)		0.00
BUSIA	AMAGORO	Sospeter O. Ojaamong time-barred	FORD(K)		0.00
BUSIA	AMAGORO		SPOILT		0.00
BUSIA	AMAGORO		**TOTAL**	**31,609**	**100.00**
BUSIA	NAMBALE	MASINDE PHILIP JOSEPH W.	KANU	17,534	44.40
BUSIA	NAMBALE	OKEMO CHRISTANTUS	FORD(A)	16,773	42.47
BUSIA	NAMBALE	AKHAABI GERVASE KATWA	FORD(K)	4,470	11.32
BUSIA	NAMBALE	MASIBAYI GERALD FRANCIS KUCHIO	DP	713	1.81
BUSIA	NAMBALE		SPOILT		0.00
BUSIA	NAMBALE		**TOTAL**	**39,490**	**100.00**
BUSIA	SAMIA	AWORI ARTHUR MOODY	KANU	8,633	74.97
BUSIA	SAMIA	RABALA NICHOLAS	FORD(K)	1,794	15.58
BUSIA	SAMIA	Henry Odaba prevented from being nominated	DP		0.00
BUSIA	SAMIA	Michael Namudiero kidnapped	FORD(A)		0.00
BUSIA	SAMIA		SPOILT	1,089	9.46
BUSIA	SAMIA		**TOTAL**	**11,516**	**100.00**
BUSIA	BUNYALA	OSOGO JAMES CHARLES NAKHAWANGA	KANU	7,932	55.51
BUSIA	BUNYALA	OKONDO PETER JOSEPH HABENGA	PICK	5,154	36.07
BUSIA	BUNYALA	ONALO PETER AGWELI	FORD(K)	1,039	7.27
BUSIA	BUNYALA	OKOTCH JAMES OMBERE	DP	113	0.79
BUSIA	BUNYALA	PAMBA STEPHEN M.	FORD(A)	52	0.36
BUSIA	BUNYALA		SPOILT		0.00
BUSIA	BUNYALA		**TOTAL**	**14,290**	**100.00**
VIHIGA	SABATIA	MUDAVADI WYCLIFFE MUSALIA	KANU	20,256	80.52
VIHIGA	SABATIA	AMENDI JOHN	FORD(A)	4,149	16.49
VIHIGA	SABATIA	ILAGOSWA DAVID LIDEBE RIBEDA	FORD(K)	513	2.04
VIHIGA	SABATIA	YASENA ELLY A.	DP	237	0.94
VIHIGA	SABATIA		SPOILT		0.00
VIHIGA	SABATIA		**TOTAL**	**25,155**	**100.00**
VIHIGA	VIHIGA	LIGALE ANDREW	KANU	10,116	57.76
VIHIGA	VIHIGA	SEMO BAHATI MUSIRA	FORD(A)	6,800	38.83
VIHIGA	VIHIGA	MBAJA OYANGI	FORD(K)	424	2.42
VIHIGA	VIHIGA	no candidate nominated	DP		0.00
VIHIGA	VIHIGA		SPOILT	173	0.99
VIHIGA	VIHIGA		**TOTAL**	**17,513**	**100.00**
VIHIGA	EMUHAYA	MULICHWA SHELDON	KANU	13,607	47.00
VIHIGA	EMUHAYA	NASIBI REUBEN INDIATSI	FORD(A)	8,317	28.73
VIHIGA	EMUHAYA	OKANG'A RAPHAEL RICHARD	DP	6,304	21.77
VIHIGA	EMUHAYA	MUKARA BLASIO	FORD(K)	724	2.50
VIHIGA	EMUHAYA		SPOILT		0.00
VIHIGA	EMUHAYA		**TOTAL**	**28,952**	**100.00**
VIHIGA	HAMISI	KHANERI NICODEMUS NEWTON	FORD(A)	11,718	48.65

Appendix 2: 1992 Parliamentary Election Results

DISTRICT	CONSTITUENCY	CANDIDATES	PARTY	VOTE	%
VIHIGA	HAMISI	M'MAITSE VINCENT SAKWA	KANU	11,556	47.98
VIHIGA	HAMISI	ONAMU JAMES HARRY	DP	810	3.36
VIHIGA	HAMISI	no candidate nominated	FORD(K)		0.00
VIHIGA	HAMISI		SPOILT		0.00
VIHIGA	HAMISI		**TOTAL**	**24,084**	**100.00**
KAKAMEGA	MALAVA	ANGATIA JOSHUA MULANDE	KANU	9,854	49.02
KAKAMEGA	MALAVA	SAKWA THOMAS ALPHEW	FORD(A)	9,554	47.53
KAKAMEGA	MALAVA	NABWERA REUBEN MATANDA	DP	207	1.03
KAKAMEGA	MALAVA	Andrew Mulamba defected to KANU 4/12/92	FORD(K)		0.00
KAKAMEGA	MALAVA		SPOILT	487	2.42
KAKAMEGA	MALAVA		**TOTAL**	**20,102**	**100.00**
KAKAMEGA	LUGARI	SIFUNA APILI WAWILE	FORD(A)	20,065	69.68
KAKAMEGA	LUGARI	NABWERA BURUDI	KANU	6,359	22.08
KAKAMEGA	LUGARI	NYUKURI FRANCIS SITATI	FORD(K)	1,121	3.89
KAKAMEGA	LUGARI	LAMBA TIMOTHY BARTHOLEMEW	DP	560	1.94
KAKAMEGA	LUGARI	WANYAMA JOHN	KNC	34	0.12
KAKAMEGA	LUGARI		SPOILT	656	2.28
KAKAMEGA	LUGARI		**TOTAL**	**28,795**	**100.00**
KAKAMEGA	MUMIAS	WAMEYO DR ELON WILLIS	KANU	19,026	45.73
KAKAMEGA	MUMIAS	OBONGITA FRANCIS NAMATSI	FORD(A)	16,218	38.98
KAKAMEGA	MUMIAS	MUNYENDO DAVID	FORD(K)	3,312	7.96
KAKAMEGA	MUMIAS	LUTTA BENNA	DP	1,942	4.67
KAKAMEGA	MUMIAS	MANDU JOHN P. SHIKUNYU	PICK	220	0.53
KAKAMEGA	MUMIAS		SPOILT	887	2.13
KAKAMEGA	MUMIAS		**TOTAL**	**41,605**	**100.00**
KAKAMEGA	LURAMBI	OMMANI REV JAVAN	FORD(A)	21,395	62.54
KAKAMEGA	LURAMBI	OTUTU REUBEN WILLIAM	KANU	10,695	31.26
KAKAMEGA	LURAMBI	AMBUNDO NASHON JOSHUA	FORD(K)	1,625	4.75
KAKAMEGA	LURAMBI	WITUKA MANOA	DP	495	1.45
KAKAMEGA	LURAMBI		SPOILT		0.00
KAKAMEGA	LURAMBI		**TOTAL**	**34,210**	**100.00**
KAKAMEGA	SHINYALU	SHAMALLA JAPETH	FORD(A)	11,407	54.12
KAKAMEGA	SHINYALU	MULAMA DAVID AMAHWA	KANU	8,982	42.61
KAKAMEGA	SHINYALU	LIGABO DR MACHANGA	FORD(K)	385	1.83
KAKAMEGA	SHINYALU	ODANGA JOSHUA SHIDAMBASI	DP	111	0.53
KAKAMEGA	SHINYALU		SPOILT	194	0.92
KAKAMEGA	SHINYALU		**TOTAL**	**21,079**	**100.00**
KAKAMEGA	IKOLOMANI	ASHIONO BENJAMIN MAGWAKA	FORD(A)	8,297	55.60
KAKAMEGA	IKOLOMANI	MUGALLA JOSEPH JOLLY	KANU	5,693	38.15
KAKAMEGA	IKOLOMANI	LICHUNJU CHARLES	DP	697	4.67
KAKAMEGA	IKOLOMANI	LUGONZO SETH MWINAMO	FORD(K)	176	1.18
KAKAMEGA	IKOLOMANI	OKWANDA MATHEW M.	KNC	61	0.41
KAKAMEGA	IKOLOMANI		SPOILT		0.00
KAKAMEGA	IKOLOMANI		**TOTAL**	**14,924**	**100.00**
KAKAMEGA	BUTERE	SHIKUKU JOSEPH MARTIN	FORD(A)	22,203	69.23
KAKAMEGA	BUTERE	LUMASAYI FRANCIS ATWOLI	KANU	8,019	25.00
KAKAMEGA	BUTERE	WEBUKO DR HEZRON INYUDO	FORD(K)	1,337	4.17
KAKAMEGA	BUTERE	NDAUYA JOHN OMOMANGARE	DP	276	0.86
KAKAMEGA	BUTERE		SPOILT	235	0.73
KAKAMEGA	BUTERE		**TOTAL**	**32,070**	**100.00**
SIAYA	UGENYA	ORENGO JAMES	FORD(K)	37,236	91.15
SIAYA	UGENYA	OLUOCH ARCHBSHP STEPHEN A. ONDIEK	KANU	2,756	6.75
SIAYA	UGENYA	OMONDI JOSEPH B. OTIENO	DP	691	1.69
SIAYA	UGENYA	NYAGWALA FREDERICK	FORD(A)	168	0.41
SIAYA	UGENYA		SPOILT		0.00
SIAYA	UGENYA		**TOTAL**	**40,851**	**100.00**
SIAYA	ALEGO	MAK'ONYANGO OTIENO	FORD(K)	31,515	97.98
SIAYA	ALEGO	UMIDHA JOHN OWENJA	KANU	615	1.91
SIAYA	ALEGO	JOWE DICKSON	PICK	35	0.11
SIAYA	ALEGO	no candidate nominated	DP		0.00
SIAYA	ALEGO	no candidate nominated	FORD(A)		0.00
SIAYA	ALEGO		SPOILT		0.00
SIAYA	ALEGO		**TOTAL**	**32,165**	**100.00**

Appendix 2: 1992 Parliamentary Election Results

DISTRICT	CONSTITUENCY	CANDIDATES	PARTY	VOTE	%
SIAYA	GEM	OKOO-OMBAKA DR. OKI	FORD(K)	29,984	93.96
SIAYA	GEM	OGOT MRS GRACE EMILY ARINYI	KANU	1,605	5.03
SIAYA	GEM	no candidate nominated	DP		0.00
SIAYA	GEM	no candidate nominated	FORD(A)		0.00
SIAYA	GEM		SPOILT	323	1.01
SIAYA	GEM		**TOTAL**	**31,912**	**100.00**
SIAYA	BONDO	ODINGA JARAMOGI OGINGA	FORD(K)	22,292	94.52
SIAYA	BONDO	OMAMO WILLIAM ODONGO	KANU	1,292	5.48
SIAYA	BONDO	no candidate nominated	DP		0.00
SIAYA	BONDO	no candidate nominated	FORD(A)		0.00
SIAYA	BONDO		SPOILT		0.00
SIAYA	BONDO		**TOTAL**	**23,584**	**100.00**
SIAYA	RARIEDA	ACHIENG-ONEKO RAMOGI	FORD(K)	22,601	94.19
SIAYA	RARIEDA	OKENDO HENRY OUMA	KANU	1,394	5.81
SIAYA	RARIEDA	no candidate nominated	DP		0.00
SIAYA	RARIEDA	no candidate nominated	FORD(A)		0.00
SIAYA	RARIEDA		SPOILT		0.00
SIAYA	RARIEDA		**TOTAL**	**23,995**	**100.00**
KISUMU	KISUMU T	OMINO JOAB H. ONYANGO	FORD(K)	58,613	89.62
KISUMU	KISUMU T	AGENG'O JIM AGGREY	KANU	4,395	6.72
KISUMU	KISUMU T	ADUOGO JACOB	FORD(A)	1,893	2.89
KISUMU	KISUMU T	KAYANDA DANIEL WILSON	DP	502	0.77
KISUMU	KISUMU T		SPOILT		0.00
KISUMU	KISUMU T		**TOTAL**	**65,403**	**100.00**
KISUMU	KISUMU R*	NYONG'O PETER ANYANG'	FORD(K)	23,538	90.58
KISUMU	KISUMU R	AYAH WILSON NDOLO	KANU	2,314	8.90
KISUMU	KISUMU R	no candidate nominated	DP		0.00
KISUMU	KISUMU R	no candidate nominated	FORD(A)		0.00
KISUMU	KISUMU R		SPOILT	135	0.52
KISUMU	KISUMU R		**TOTAL**	**25,987**	**100.00**
KISUMU	NYANDO	OTIENO CLARKSON KARANI	FORD(K)	26,096	98.01
KISUMU	NYANDO	OWUOR JAMES MIRUKA	KANU	332	1.25
KISUMU	NYANDO	Joash Obongo did not turn up	DP		0.00
KISUMU	NYANDO	no candidate nominated	FORD(A)		0.00
KISUMU	NYANDO		SPOILT	199	0.75
KISUMU	NYANDO		**TOTAL**	**26,627**	**100.00**
KISUMU	MUHORONI	OGEKA JUSTUS A.	FORD(K)	29,241	95.41
KISUMU	MUHORONI	BONYO JOHN ISAYA P.	KANU	895	2.92
KISUMU	MUHORONI	OCHIENG' ALBERT HENRY	DP	212	0.69
KISUMU	MUHORONI	no candidate nominated	FORD(A)		0.00
KISUMU	MUHORONI		SPOILT	300	0.98
KISUMU	MUHORONI		**TOTAL**	**30,648**	**100.00**
KISUMU	NYAKACH	AKUMU JAMES DENIS	FORD(K)	26,514	97.63
KISUMU	NYAKACH	K'OMBUDO OJWANG	KANU	644	2.37
KISUMU	NYAKACH	OTANA EDWARD OYUGI	PICK	0	0.00
KISUMU	NYAKACH	no candidate nominated	DP		0.00
KISUMU	NYAKACH	no candidate nominated	FORD(A)		0.00
KISUMU	NYAKACH		SPOILT		0.00
KISUMU	NYAKACH		**TOTAL**	**27,158**	**100.00**
HOMA BAY	KASIPUL-KABONDO	K'OPIYO DR GERALD OTIENO	FORD(K)	30,018	94.63
HOMA BAY	"	OTULA WILLIAM OLOO	PICK	1,340	4.22
HOMA BAY	"	KAPERE AUSTIN AUMA	KANU	362	1.14
HOMA BAY	"	NYAKOE CHARLES JUMA	FORD(A)	0	0.00
HOMA BAY	"	no candidate nominated	DP		0.00
HOMA BAY	"		SPOILT		0.00
HOMA BAY	"		**TOTAL**	**31,720**	**100.00**
HOMA BAY	KARACHUONYO	ASIYO PHOEBE MUGA	FORD(K)	26,063	84.30
HOMA BAY	"	AMAYO LAZARUS OMBAYI	KANU	4,854	15.70
HOMA BAY	"	no candidate nominated	DP		0.00
HOMA BAY	"	no candidate nominated	FORD(A)		0.00
HOMA BAY	"		SPOILT		0.00
HOMA BAY	"		**TOTAL**	**30,917**	**100.00**

*** Rural**

Appendix 2: 1992 Parliamentary Election Results

DISTRICT	CONSTITUENCY	CANDIDATES	PARTY	VOTE	%
HOMA BAY	NDHIWA	OBONDO TOM	FORD(K)	24,308	97.19
HOMA BAY	NDHIWA	OGINGO MATHEW KAVIN OTIENO	KANU	635	2.54
HOMA BAY	NDHIWA	OWINO JOSEPH DEYA	DP	21	0.08
HOMA BAY	NDHIWA	no candidate nominated	FORD(A)		0.00
HOMA BAY	NDHIWA		SPOILT	47	0.19
HOMA BAY	NDHIWA		TOTAL	25,011	100.00
HOMA BAY	RANGWE	MUGA JOSEPH OUMA	FORD(K)	31,852	95.41
HOMA BAY	RANGWE	OKUNDI DANIEL OJIJO	KANU	1,531	4.59
HOMA BAY	RANGWE	no candidate nominated	DP		0.00
HOMA BAY	RANGWE	no candidate nominated	FORD(A)		0.00
HOMA BAY	RANGWE		SPOILT		0.00
HOMA BAY	RANGWE		**TOTAL**	**33,383**	**100.00**
HOMA BAY	MBITA	OPERE DR. VALENTINE OMOLO	FORD(K)	24,771	91.61
HOMA BAY	MBITA	NYAKIAMO PETER C. J. O.	KANU	2,114	7.82
HOMA BAY	MBITA	NYAMBEGA THOMAS OLANDO	DP	63	0.23
HOMA BAY	MBITA	NYAKIRA JAMES	FORD(A)	49	0.18
HOMA BAY	MBITA		SPOILT	42	0.16
HOMA BAY	MBITA		**TOTAL**	**27,039**	**100.00**
MIGORI	RONGO	ALOUCH JOHN LINUS	FORD(K)	27,038	89.57
MIGORI	RONGO	OTIENO DALMAS ANYANGO	KANU	3,013	9.98
MIGORI	RONGO	no candidate nominated	DP		0.00
MIGORI	RONGO	no candidate nominated	FORD(A)		0.00
MIGORI	RONGO		SPOILT	137	0.45
MIGORI	RONGO		**TOTAL**	**30,188**	**100.00**
MIGORI	MIGORI	OWINO CHARLES O.	FORD(K)	35,562	88.28
MIGORI	MIGORI	OKWANYO JOHN HENRY	KANU	4,660	11.57
MIGORI	MIGORI	no candidate nominated	DP		0.00
MIGORI	MIGORI	no candidate nominated	FORD(A)		0.00
MIGORI	MIGORI		SPOILT	62	0.15
MIGORI	MIGORI		**TOTAL**	**40,284**	**100.00**
MIGORI	NYATIKE	OGUR TOBIAS OCHOLA ORAO	FORD(K)	18,149	90.83
MIGORI	NYATIKE	OLANG' ZABLON OWIGO	KANU	1,833	9.17
MIGORI	NYATIKE	no candidate nominated	DP		0.00
MIGORI	NYATIKE	no candidate nominated	FORD(A)		0.00
MIGORI	NYATIKE		SPOILT		0.00
MIGORI	NYATIKE		**TOTAL**	**19,982**	**100.00**
MIGORI	KURIA	MANGA SHADRACH RODGER	KANU	13,234	82.32
MIGORI	KURIA	MANGERA JOHN	FORD(K)	1,238	7.70
MIGORI	KURIA	GIBAGIRI WEIRIA	FORD(A)	852	5.30
MIGORI	KURIA	OMARI ADEN MARWA	DP	752	4.68
MIGORI	KURIA	Samson M. Marwa refused nom - no seconder	KSC		0.00
MIGORI	KURIA		SPOILT		0.00
MIGORI	KURIA		**TOTAL**	**16,076**	**100.00**
KISII	BONCHARI	KEBATI DR. PROTAS MOMANYI	DP	6,034	52.52
KISII	BONCHARI	BOSIRE MARK GICHABA	KANU	4,288	37.32
KISII	BONCHARI	OBOTE PHILIP MOTONU	FORD(A)	850	7.40
KISII	BONCHARI	MAGARA ZEDEKIAH MEKENYE	FORD(K)	317	2.76
KISII	BONCHARI	John M. Nyakundi time-barred	KSC		0.00
KISII	BONCHARI		SPOILT		0.00
KISII	BONCHARI		**TOTAL**	**11,489**	**100.00**
KISII	S. MUGIRANGO	OYONDI REUBEN ONESERIO	KANU	9,763	53.06
KISII	S. MUGIRANGO	KOMBO DAVID ONDIMO	PICK	7,282	39.57
KISII	S. MUGIRANGO	NYAMWEYA MANSON OYONGO	FORD(K)	1,116	6.06
KISII	S. MUGIRANGO	ONYONYI KEFA	DP	175	0.95
KISII	S. MUGIRANGO	NYANGARISI JUSTUS	FORD(A)	65	0.35
KISII	S. MUGIRANGO		SPOILT		0.00
KISII	S. MUGIRANGO		**TOTAL**	**18,401**	**100.00**
KISII	BOMACHOGE	OBURE FERDINAND	FORD(K)	11,850	52.30
KISII	BOMACHOGE	ANYIENE ZEPHANIAH MOGUNDE	KANU	7,558	33.36
KISII	BOMACHOGE	NYAMWAMU FRED	DP	1,909	8.43
KISII	BOMACHOGE	MASESE OGEMBO	KNC	950	4.19
KISII	BOMACHOGE	MIGIRA ELIJAH MAOBE	FORD(A)	389	1.72
KISII	BOMACHOGE		SPOILT		0.00
KISII	BOMACHOGE		**TOTAL**	**22,656**	**100.00**

Appendix 2: 1992 Parliamentary Election Results

DISTRICT	CONSTITUENCY	CANDIDATES	PARTY	VOTE	%
KISII	BOBASI	MANOTI STEPHEN KENGERE	KANU	11,267	49.29
KISII	BOBASI	MATOKE DANIEL OGUTU	DP	7,537	32.97
KISII	BOBASI	RAINI RAPHAEL	FORD(K)	1,905	8.33
KISII	BOBASI	NYANCHIRI DANIEL OENGA	KNC	1,083	4.74
KISII	BOBASI	MORACHA DAVID NYARERU	FORD(A)	464	2.03
KISII	BOBASI		SPOILT	601	2.63
KISII	BOBASI		**TOTAL**	**22,857**	**100.00**
KISII	NYARIBARI MASABA	MANDAKU DR HEZRON	KANU	9,606	48.28
KISII	"	NYAMWEYA JAMES	DP	9,365	47.07
KISII	"	NYAMWANGE ISAAC	FORD(K)	348	1.75
KISII	"	ONGERI DANIEL NYAATA	FORD(A)	151	0.76
KISII	"		SPOILT	428	2.15
KISII	"		**TOTAL**	**19,898**	**100.00**
KISII	NYARIBARI CHACHE	NYACHAE SIMEON	KANU	15,871	63.87
KISII	"	OGEMBO DR SAMUEL BEDE	DP	6,331	25.48
KISII	"	BICHAGE CHRISTOPHER M.	FORD(K)	1,808	7.28
KISII	"	NYAMWANGE DANIEL MOMANYI	FORD(A)	177	0.71
KISII	"		SPOILT	663	2.67
KISII	"		TOTAL	24,850	100.00
KISII	KITUTU CHACHE	ONYONKA DR ZACHARY	KANU	7,197	33.35
KISII	"	NYAKUNDI JAMES THOMAS	DP	6,545	30.32
KISII	"	SIRO NICHOLAS	PICK	5,160	23.91
KISII	"	GICHANA DENIS ONGOI	FORD(K)	1,695	7.85
KISII	KITUTU CHACHE	KEBABE SAMUEL OBEGI	FORD(A)	259	1.20
KISII	"	OCHONG'A ZEPHANIA	KSC	165	0.76
KISII	"		SPOILT	562	2.60
KISII	"		**TOTAL**	**21,583**	**100.00**
NYAMIRA	KITUTU MASABA	ANYONA GEORGE MOSETTI	KSC	15,687	64.89
NYAMIRA	KITUTU MASABA	NYAMBATI WALTER OISEBE	KANU	4,805	19.88
NYAMIRA	KITUTU MASABA	MANYIBE FRANCIS OMURWA	DP	1,803	7.46
NYAMIRA	KITUTU MASABA	ABUYA ABUYA	FORD(K)	1,383	5.72
NYAMIRA	KITUTU MASABA	MOSETI ERASTUS	FORD(A)	496	2.05
NYAMIRA	KITUTU MASABA		SPOILT		0.00
NYAMIRA	KITUTU MASABA		**TOTAL**	**24,174**	**100.00**
NYAMIRA	W. MUGIRANGO	OBWOCHA HENRY ONYANCHA	FORD(K)	9,704	44.75
NYAMIRA	W. MUGIRANGO	SAGWE TOM MORWABE	KANU	7,359	33.94
NYAMIRA	W. MUGIRANGO	NYAKANG'O DAVID OSERO	DP	3,875	17.87
NYAMIRA	W. MUGIRANGO	MARWANGA JOSEPH MONGARE	FORD(A)	468	2.16
NYAMIRA	W. MUGIRANGO	NYARIBARI MATHEW ONDEYO	KSC	279	1.29
NYAMIRA	W. MUGIRANGO		SPOILT		0.00
NYAMIRA	W. MUGIRANGO		**TOTAL**	**21,685**	**100.00**
NYAMIRA	N. MUGIRANGO	MARITA LIVINGSTONE ATEBE	KANU	10,085	38.58
NYAMIRA	N. MUGIRANGO	MASANYA GODFREY OKERI	DP	9,948	38.05
NYAMIRA	N. MUGIRANGO	MOGAMBI ALEXANDER IBRAHIM	FORD(K)	4,010	15.34
NYAMIRA	N. MUGIRANGO	MOTURI ALFAYO NYARANGI	FORD(A)	1,378	5.27
NYAMIRA	N. MUGIRANGO	NYAGAWACHI JOSIAH	KSC	90	0.34
NYAMIRA	N. MUGIRANGO		SPOILT	632	2.42
NYAMIRA	N. MUGIRANGO		**TOTAL**	**26,143**	**100.00**

Indicates candidate defected to KANU after nomination

Appendix 3. Presidential election results 1992

Province	District	Constituency	Moi	Matiba	Kibaki	Odinga	Anyona	Harun	Ng'ang'a	WaTsuma	Spoilt	Tctal	Registered	%Turnout	%Spoilt
NAIROBI	NAIROBI	STAREHE	6337	23726	8649	4082	34	37	0	87		42952	84594	50.77	
NAIROBI	NAIROBI	EMBAKASI	6534	23035	13292	9996	0	37	32	87	556	53569	91688	58.43	1.04
NAIROBI	NAIROBI	MATHARE	7216	29829	9835	18200	110	45	103	122		65460	115733	56.56	
NAIROBI	NAIROBI	DAGORETTI	6038	31867	5753	2220	95	33	24	57	419	46506	70656	65.82	0.90
NAIROBI	NAIROBI	MAKADARA	8554	15941	9542	9668	65	73	34	80	272	44229	85285	51.86	0.61
NAIROBI	NAIROBI	KAMUKUNJI	6717	18135	9112	6183	56	62	43	75		40383	74258	54.38	
NAIROBI	NAIROBI	LANGATA	12305	13737	7834	22800	109	34	32	61		56912	102840	55.34	
NAIROBI	NAIROBI	WESTLANDS	8709	9271	5700	2696	47	152	18	50	408	27051	48760	55.47	1.51
CENTRAL	MURANG'A	KIHARU	687	58293	747	1108	99	14	5	215	250	61418	69282	88.64	0.41
CENTRAL	MURANG'A	GATANGA	180	29150	1580	70	118	37	57	187	470	31849	37086	85.87	1.47
CENTRAL	MURANG'A	MAKUYU	1342	16367	778	177	73	19	40	135	446	19377	28511	67.96	2.30
CENTRAL	MURANG'A	KIGUMO	171	53868	856	50	98	19	11	99		55172	63416	87.00	
CENTRAL	MURANG'A	KANDARA	272	42442	888	80	139	20	15	141		43997	51870	84.82	
CENTRAL	MURANG'A	KANGEMA	1809	48321	2088	100	110	37	10	195	467	53137	61660	86.17	0.87
CENTRAL	KIAMBU	KIKUYU	869	46277	2488	3246	44	24	44	53		53045	62106	85.41	
CENTRAL	KIAMBU	KIAMBAA	847	41798	5252	552	84	32	17	66	723	49371	59723	82.66	1.46
CENTRAL	KIAMBU	GITHUNGURI	1003	42502	1914	117	99	33	11	86		45765	52618	86.98	
CENTRAL	KIAMBU	JUJA	3358	37948	6249	3600	76	42	51	189	702	52215	76923	67.88	1.34
CENTRAL	KIAMBU	LIMURU	1578	27943	1309	752	45	14	18	29	293	31981	38943	82.12	0.92
CENTRAL	KIAMBU	GATUNDU	260	53644	6002	173	93	30	26	84		60312	70545	85.49	
CENTRAL	KIAMBU	LARI	195	27127	1130	117	46	19	1	69		28704	32683	87.82	
CENTRAL	NYANDARUA	KIPIPIRI	795	26401	11602	211	76	42	16	172	372	39687	47750	83.11	0.94
CENTRAL	NYANDARUA	KINANGOP	557	25255	7435	129	57	32	13	110		33588	39661	84.69	
CENTRAL	NYANDARUA	NDARAGWA	641	7769	23141	82	0	63	9	80		31785	37476	84.81	
CENTRAL	NYERI	OTHAYA	343	353	31576	42	8	28	5	20		32375	35281	91.76	
CENTRAL	NYERI	NYERI TOWN	1052	1868	31314	511	27	43	11	71		34897	44523	78.38	
CENTRAL	NYERI	TETU	525	292	28700	51	34	39	6	35		29682	34153	86.91	
CENTRAL	NYERI	KIENI	1176	1075	30786	83	54	62	4	108		33348	40292	82.77	
CENTRAL	NYERI	MUKURUEINI	422	1681	26501	27	47	37	7	69		28791	31979	90.03	
CENTRAL	NYERI	MATHIRA	1461	913	49691	99	71	106	14	134		52489	61165	85.82	
CENTRAL	KIRINYAGA	GICHUGU	1176	13276	24892	60	17	80	17	129		39647	44180	89.74	
CENTRAL	KIRINYAGA	NDIA	808	10463	40384	195	204	159	371	371	803	53758	66592	80.73	1.49
CENTRAL	KIRINYAGA	MWEA	366	6214	21890	51	48	47	59	533		29208	36631	79.74	
EASTERN	EMBU	RUNYENJES	3284	12981	39426	492	127	189	49	197		56745	75644	75.02	
EASTERN	EMBU	SIAKAGO	926	4099	7827	255	31	28	9	161		13336	18944	70.40	
EASTERN	EMBU	GACHOKA	7054	13791	13065	76	67	34	18	274		34379	46727	73.57	
EASTERN	MERU	IGEMBE	8127	358	8870	74	23	129	5	0		17586	32073	54.83	
EASTERN	MERU	NTONYIRI	6590	136	6406	29	9	13	30	0		13213	22945	57.58	

Appendix 3: 1992 Presidential Election Results

Province	District	Constituency	Moi	Matiba	Kibaki	Odinga	Anyona	Harun	Ng'ang'a	Wa Tsuma	Spoilt	Tctal	Registered	%Turnout	%Spoilt
EASTERN	MERU	TIGANIA	8297	1049	28529	317	204	0	13	32		38441	64961	59.18	
EASTERN	MERU	IMENTI NORTH	7952	1733	38888	803	42	62	22	145		49647	68505	72.47	
EASTERN	MERU	IMENTI CENTRAL	11487	551	23889	1159	57	43	35	255		37476	44059	85.06	
EASTERN	MERU	IMENTI SOUTH	2366	1472	35576	1578	105	64	38	65		41264	50550	81.63	
EASTERN	THARAKA-NITHI	NITHI	6730	2215	41787	2391	119	154	40	89		53525	66561	80.41	
EASTERN	"	THARAKA	4873	392	12513	84	34	29	14	31		17970	24119	74.51	
EASTERN	MACHAKOS	MASINGA	9467	2063	2196	234	50	55	19	32	308	14424	26021	55.43	2.14
EASTERN	MACHAKOS	YATTA	9143	4533	3352	223	66	30	30	51		17428	29931	58.23	
EASTERN	MACHAKOS	KANGUNDO	14905	2064	19183	193	84	141	24	81		36675	66550	55.11	
EASTERN	MACHAKOS	KATHIANI	15110	3522	5997	1101	34	37	35	87		25923	44933	57.69	
EASTERN	MACHAKOS	MACHAKOS TOWN	13832	2929	8455	500	63	43	41	24	516	26403	42814	61.66	1.95
EASTERN	MACHAKOS	MWALA	11180	1990	11774	217	108	113	40	41		25463	40496	62.88	
EASTERN	MAKUENI	MBOONI	10021	3014	9509	564	89	113	61	50		23421	42655	54.91	
EASTERN	MAKUENI	KILOME	23596	2732	6428	845	122	65	75	115	644	34622	57345	60.37	1.86
EASTERN	MAKUENI	MAKUENI	10270	2746	9071	215	90	113	41	120		22666	41766	54.27	
EASTERN	MAKUENI	KIBWEZI	7409	1405	9823	522	7	78	31	185	513	19973	37912	52.68	2.57
EASTERN	KITUI	KITUI NORTH	21047	13791	13604	376	97	34	18	274		49241	60959	80.78	
EASTERN	KITUI	KITUI WEST	8733	5271	6845	224	43	40	22	113		21291	44268	48.10	
EASTERN	KITUI	KITUI CENTRAL	16852	1900	16390	483	50	60	58	266		36059	51675	69.78	
EASTERN	KITUI	MUTITO	5964	571	6795	189	31	38	19	28	204	13839	22494	61.52	1.47
EASTERN	KITUI	MUTOMO	4813	4561	5664	279	32	39	25	53		15466	29892	51.73	
EASTERN	ISIOLO	ISIOLO NORTH	8393	484	4287	231	4	0	9	7		13415	24125	55.61	
EASTERN	ISIOLO	ISIOLO SOUTH	4413	190	372	35	2	6	0	0		5018	8703	57.66	
EASTERN	MARSABIT	MOYALE	10638	1890	88	31	0	0	0	0		12647	16843	75.09	
EASTERN	MARSABIT	NORTH HORR	5434	7	767	10	2	2	1	0		6223	11151	55.81	
EASTERN	MARSABIT	SAKU	7966	562	380	79	3	10	2	48		9050	13293	68.08	
EASTERN	MARSABIT	LAISAMIS	6963	3	11	41	1	1	0	0		7020	11406	61.55	
NORTH-EAST	WAJIR	WAJIR EAST	5600	1975	247	47	0	2	1	0	14	7886	13583	58.06	0.18
NORTH-EAST	WAJIR	WAJIR SOUTH	4730	7	1642	96	1	0	1	0		6477	12220	53.00	
NORTH-EAST	WAJIR	WAJIR WEST	6405	4277	398	30	8	2	3	3		11126	18194	61.15	
NORTH-EAST	MANDERA	MANDERA WEST	2695	341	4	248	0	1	1	0		3290	9606	34.25	
NORTH-EAST	MANDERA	MANDERA CENTRAL	6580	171	25	2788	0	0	4	0		9568	15837	60.42	
NORTH-EAST	MANDERA	MANDERA EAST	10270	252	72	124	0	2	3	0		10723	18215	58.87	
NORTH-EAST	GARISSA	DUJIS	10470	385	888	614	12	7	9	11		12396	24994	49.60	
NORTH-EAST	GARISSA	LAGDERA	4039	13	13	1249	0	0	2	0		5316	10837	49.05	
NORTH-EAST	GARISSA	FAFI	3131	55	15	6	0	1	3	1		3212	9694	33.13	
NORTH-EAST	GARISSA	IJARA	2770	14	17	40	0	0	0	0		2841	7908	35.93	
COAST	TANA RIVER	GARSEN	9006	99	623	5551	22	6	10	64	157	15538	27039	57.47	1.01

Appendix 3: 1992 Presidential Election Results

Province	District	Constituency	Moi	Matiba	Kibaki	Odinga	Anyona	Harun	Ng'ang'a	WaTsuma	Spoilt	Tctal	Registered	%Turnout	%Spoilt
COAST	TANA RIVER	GALOLE	6919	285	931	3002	41	5	25	24		11232	22035	50.97	
COAST	KILIFI	BAHARI	14590	925	683	3002	1	0	24	0		19225	42273	45.48	
COAST	KILIFI	KALOLENI	17854	963	539	2	0	0	0	3770		23128	43484	53.18	
COAST	KILIFI	GANZE	10686	100	916	14	11	15	33	22		11797	18343	64.31	
COAST	KILIFI	MALINDI	15095	1103	1409	1391	23	2	10	443		19476	38486	50.61	
COAST	KILIFI	MAGARINI	8201	53	155	399	10	12	6	19	76	8931	18733	47.68	0.85
COAST	KWALE	MSAMBWENI	17728	1122	4383	1171	51	22	23	131	256	24887	34726	71.67	1.03
COAST	KWALE	KINANGO	10038	351	758	301	19	7	30	103		11607	23982	48.40	
COAST	KWALE	MATUGA	16245	695	2636	817	43	15	14	183		20648	34728	59.46	
COAST	LAMU	LAMU EAST	4027	50	587	1593	11	3	22	7	116	6416	8539	75.14	1.81
COAST	LAMU	LAMU WEST	6992	2575	2920	922	32	20	12	30	222	13725	20410	67.23	1.62
COAST	MOMBASA	KISAUNI	12230	5914	2926	8664	36	15	57	335	1365	31542	78179	40.35	4.33
COAST	MOMBASA	LIKONI	4577	3290	1120	5661	12	7	0	124		14791	40553	36.47	
COAST	MOMBASA	MVITA	9611	5971	2714	6923	3	15	81	153	838	26309	75737	34.74	3.19
COAST	MOMBASA	CHANGAMWE	6272	7254	4619	7442	26	23	57	156	529	26378	63220	41.72	2.01
COAST	TAITA-TAVETA	TAVETA	5116	1412	1237	736	27	6	0	6		8540	12987	65.76	
COAST	TAITA-TAVETA	WUNDANYI	7575	1553	1183	111	62	15	12	27		10538	17163	61.40	
COAST	TAITA-TAVETA	VOI	7067	557	2992	526	33	22	16	22	384	11619	19523	59.51	3.30
COAST	TAITA-TAVETA	MWATATE	7705	1142	917	434	42	16	7	23		10286	17238	59.67	
RIFT VALLEY	LAIKIPIA	LAIKIPIA EAST	6742	1142	21837	456	9	40	8	23		30257	42331	71.48	
RIFT VALLEY	LAIKIPIA	LAIKIPIA WEST	7562	5578	31178	253	20	65	11	86	255	45008	60418	74.50	0.57
RIFT VALLEY	NAKURU	NAKURU EAST	8319	47778	6850	4726	114	73	41	214		68115	90469	75.29	
RIFT VALLEY	NAKURU	NAKURU TOWN	10304	28916	8592	10759	64	31	63	76		58805	100322	58.62	
RIFT VALLEY	NAKURU	MOLO	35113	55279	5236	2177	186	44	67	99	657	98858	120705	81.90	0.66
RIFT VALLEY	NAKURU	RONGAI	14951	12482	2856	1770	62	25	29	50	629	32854	43235	75.99	1.91
RIFT VALLEY	NAKURU	NAKURU NORTH	2142	24055	6453	403	43	22	0	81		33199	41883	79.27	
RIFT VALLEY	KAJIADO	KAJIADO NORTH	17478	13867	4118	1090	53	29	18	69	704	37426	52556	71.21	1.88
RIFT VALLEY	KAJIADO	KAJIADO CENTRAL	16724	624	2418	225	16	6	8	9	122	20152	26422	76.27	0.61
RIFT VALLEY	KAJIADO	KAJIADO SOUTH	13921	4375	4310	391	22	8	5	6	284	23322	30605	76.20	1.22
RIFT VALLEY	NAROK	NAROK NORTH	22675	10014	3138	407	41	16	9	31		36331	49692	73.11	
RIFT VALLEY	NAROK	NAROK WEST	28019	193	268	4085	15	60	7	4		32651	37033	88.17	
RIFT VALLEY	NAROK	NAROK SOUTH	30063	476	390	71	20	9	3	7	0	31039	38794	80.01	0.00
RIFT VALLEY	ELGEYO-MARAKWET	KERIO CENTRAL	16408	89	38	35	3	1	0	1	20	16595	19328	**85.86**	0.12
RIFT VALLEY	"	KERIO SOUTH	25704	167	81	25	9	1	4	1	29	26021	29814	87.28	0.11
RIFT VALLEY	"	KERIO WEST	19563	931	34	113	13	3	4	4		20665	22900	90.24	
RIFT VALLEY	"	KERIO EAST	18394	27	4	2	1	0	0	1		18429	21444	85.94	
RIFT VALLEY	BARINGO	BARINGO EAST	9183	2	42	1	1	0	0	0	0	9229	10958	**84.22**	0
RIFT VALLEY	BARINGO	BARINGO CENTRAL	35170	55	107	91	1	3	3	0	35	35465	39522	**89.73**	0.10

Appendix 3: 1992 Presidential Election Results

Province	District	Constituency	Moi	Matiba	Kibaki	Odinga	Anyona	Harun	Ng'ang'a	WaTsuma	Spoilt	Tctal	Registered	%Turnout	%Spoilt
RIFT VALLEY	BARINGO	BARINGO NORTH	25256	5	42	3	1	0	0	0	21	25328	27588	**91.81**	0.08
RIFT VALLEY	BARINGO	BARINGO SOUTH	32891	3813	415	219	31	16	8	33	130	37556	41467	**90.57**	0.35
RIFT VALLEY	BOMET	KONOIN	25562	331	525	1741	25	2	69	8	149	28412	37357	76.05	0.52
RIFT VALLEY	BOMET	CHEPALUNGU	50565	17	30	5	11	1	2	1	68	50700	55257	**91.75**	0.13
RIFT VALLEY	BOMET	BOMET	42841	27	25	12	14	1	1	3		42924	47123	91.09	
RIFT VALLEY	KERICHO	BURET	46625	41	67	142	17	2	5	1	293	47193	54774	86.16	0.62
RIFT VALLEY	KERICHO	BELGUT	57584	101	56	103	6	3	0	1	47	57901	64546	89.70	0.08
RIFT VALLEY	KERICHO	KIPKELION	43217	8174	3043	4979	66	10	83	56		59628	75203	79.29	
RIFT VALLEY	NANDI	MOSOP	29272	77	52	27	31	3	3	10	171	29646	34971	84.77	0.58
RIFT VALLEY	NANDI	ALDAI	47550	377	251	309	47	17	20	40	227	48838	58521	83.45	0.46
RIFT VALLEY	NANDI	TINDERET	38255	1298	250	998	34	16	30	19	234	41134	53803	76.45	0.57
RIFT VALLEY	POKOT	KACHILEBA	6580	96	39	23	3	1	1	0		6743	11585	58.20	
RIFT VALLEY	POKOT	KAPENGURIA	22668	2062	280	614	40	15	18	25		25722	35952	71.55	
RIFT VALLEY	POKOT	SIGOR	19707	91	51	28	7	15	1	0		19900	26428	75.30	
RIFT VALLEY	TURKANA	TURKANA NORTH	7856	35	42	42	4	2	10	5	0	7996	24884	32.13	0
RIFT VALLEY	TURKANA	TURKANA CENTRAL	9110	294	1408	283	2	5	7	2	0	11111	13025	85.30	0
RIFT VALLEY	TURKANA	TURKANA SOUTH	4553	118	169	25	3	10	6	5	17	4906	18533	26.47	0.34
RIFT VALLEY	SAMBURU	SAMBURU EAST	7567	14	105	13	0	0	0	1		7700	11308	68.09	
RIFT VALLEY	SAMBURU	SAMBURU WEST	23022	132	988	131	1	6	3	11		24294	32313	75.18	
RIFT VALLEY	UASIN-GISHU	ELDORET NORTH	35252	16494	1490	4384	66	11	37	28		57762	84751	68.15	
RIFT VALLEY	UASIN-GISHU	ELDORET EAST	30713	10100	10	0	0	0	0	0		40823	47910	85.21	
RIFT VALLEY	UASIN-GISHU	ELDORET SOUTH	21590	9661	835	1453	59	18	14	34	301	33965	49057	69.24	0.89
RIFT VALLEY	TRANS-NZOIA	KWANZA	9307	3476	665	14705	31	8	118	21		28331	41398	68.44	
RIFT VALLEY	TRANS-NZOIA	SABOTI	10513	8317	1059	19959	52	8	181	17		40106	60855	65.91	
RIFT VALLEY	TRANS-NZOIA	CHERANGANI	11871	4917	968	6294	51	7	85	27		24220	32243	75.12	
WESTERN	BUNGOMA	KIMILILI	4083	6115	368	24798	47	6	410	28	629	36484	47343	77.07	1.72
WESTERN	BUNGOMA	WEBUYE	3911	7052	7179	13458	103	25	195	41		31964	47426	67.40	
WESTERN	BUNGOMA	SIRISIA	4169	3492	477	21669	66	0	232	15		30120	42061	71.61	
WESTERN	BUNGOMA	KANDUYI	6714	23107	954	15935	117	4	153	36		47020	69969	67.20	
WESTERN	BUNGOMA	MOUNT ELGON	20295	665	24	4632	10	3	49	0		25678	32958	77.91	
WESTERN	BUSIA	AMAGORO	27230	2684	579	1183	48	158	124	41		32047	44756	71.60	
WESTERN	BUSIA	NAMBALE	19931	5137	536	14792	55	50	50	72		40623	63572	63.90	
WESTERN	BUSIA	SAMIA	8443	2843	61	218	12	1	5	90	289	11962	25120	47.62	2.42
WESTERN	BUSIA	BUNYALA	8828	554	154	942	1	3906	5	8		14398	18681	77.07	
WESTERN	VIHIGA	SABATIA	19889	7919	248	860	55	0	43	0		29014	38198	75.96	
WESTERN	VIHIGA	VIHIGA	10454	6354	120	373	64	10	12	19		17406	25250	68.93	
WESTERN	VIHIGA	EMUHAYA	12380	14070	1301	619	0	0	0	0		28370	48695	58.26	
WESTERN	VIHIGA	HAMISI	12781	10934	299	131	2	11	13	18	178	24367	39826	61.18	0.73
WESTERN	KAKAMEGA	MALAVA	9851	9259	104	372	34	16	16	21	437	20110	31530	63.78	2.17

Appendix 3: 1992 Presidential Election Results

Province	District	Constituency	Moi	Matiba	Kibaki	Odinga	Anyona	Harun	Ng'ang'a	WaTsuma	Spoilt	Tctal	Registered	%Turnout	%Spoilt
WESTERN	KAKAMEGA	LUGARI	5515	20002	355	1433	107	22	55	57	646	28192	46260	60.94	2.29
WESTERN	KAKAMEGA	MUMIAS	18454	18546	610	3600	66	28	52	27	889	42272	63844	66.21	2.10
WESTERN	KAKAMEGA	LURAMBI	10695	21395	198	1626	84	39	491	38		34566	56569	61.10	
WESTERN	KAKAMEGA	SHINYALU	7652	13339	120	406	52	10	232	26	322	22159	35846	61.82	1.45
WESTERN	KAKAMEGA	IKOLOMANI	5235	9091	262	104	36	10	15	15	312	15080	22083	68.29	2.07
WESTERN	KAKAMEGA	BUTERE	8118	22046	209	1665	86	14	47	33		32218	51129	63.01	
NYANZA	SIAYA	UGENYA	236	164	219	38098	19	3	82	2		38823	52467	74.00	
NYANZA	SIAYA	ALEGO	442	38	9	38015	7	0	42	3		38556	52523	73.41	
NYANZA	SIAYA	GEM	901	38	9	30268	7	0	42	3		31268	41616	75.13	
NYANZA	SIAYA	BONDO	1188	7	8	22309	3	0	59	0	62	23636	31063	76.10	0.26
NYANZA	SIAYA	RARIEDA	966	7	6	22974	12	3	38	2	52	24060	30997	77.62	0.22
NYANZA	KISUMU	KISUMU TOWN	4156	2371	590	58143	53	14	218	9	281	65835	99915	65.89	0.43
NYANZA	KISUMU	KISUMU RURAL	1660	106	15	24706	10	0	0	4		26501	35428	74.80	
NYANZA	KISUMU	NYANDO	263	19	16	29497	11	5	15	0		29826	32897	90.66	
NYANZA	KISUMU	MUHORONI	775	348	202	29171	18	10	51	2	208	30785	43895	70.13	0.68
NYANZA	KISUMU	NYAKACH	363	24	14	26932	5	1	31	3		27373	33960	80.60	
NYANZA	HOMA_BAY	KASIPUL-KABONDO	167	13	10	35037	10	3	31	0		35271	44055	80.06	
NYANZA	HOMA_BAY	KARACHUONYO	860	5	1	30197	1	0	24	0		31088	41363	75.16	
NYANZA	HOMA_BAY	NDHIWA	251	6	2	24798	3	1	13	0		25074	32798	76.45	
NYANZA	HOMA_BAY	RANGWE	877	67	50	31699	12	0	72	0		32777	47754	68.64	
NYANZA	HOMA_BAY	MBITA	572	24	29	26686	4	3	19	0		27337	37682	72.55	
NYANZA	MIGORI	RONGO	1836	9	8	27066	5	0	9	0		28933	45054	64.29	
NYANZA	MIGORI	MIGORI	4532	226	85	35452	17	20	57	57		40446	56299	71.84	
NYANZA	MIGORI	NYATIKE	1246	17	5	18956	7	1	17	1		20250	27651	73.23	
NYANZA	MIGORI	KURIA	14007	1401	465	349	29	5	10	14		16280	26682	61.01	
NYANZA	KISII	BONCHARI	4271	1003	5282	713	154	20	8	14	290	11755	20496	57.35	2.47
NYANZA	KISII	SOUTH MUGIRANGO	10232	1376	2325	4050	63	252	57	11		18366	35604	51.58	
NYANZA	KISII	BOMACHOGE	6644	250	909	13164	57	6	245	36		21311	36567	58.28	
NYANZA	KISII	BOBASI	6314	1670	3331	10182	161	30	217	114	774	22793	41869	54.43	3.39
NYANZA	KISII	NYARIBARI MASABA	8676	377	8429	1723	170	46	44	14	645	20124	38997	51.60	3.20
NYANZA	KISII	NYARIBARI CHACHE	14815	477	5660	2517	253	20	44	14	747	24547	50257	48.84	3.04
NYANZA	KISII	KITUTU CHACHE	7126	808	9310	4413	246	353	92	0	0	22348	43697	51.14	
NYANZA	NYAMIRA	KITUTU MASABA	4349	514	2530	10497	5181	33	144	30		23278	42690	54.53	
NYANZA	NYAMIRA	WEST MUGIRANGO	7752	1030	4296	7909	405	13	127	13	526	22071	36501	60.47	2.38
NYANZA	NYAMIRA	NORTH MUGIRANGO	9942	1501	7963	5897	132	40	178	19		25672	44265	58.00	
		TOTAL	1970771	1419308	1040997	959088	14000	9363	7581	14540	24003	5459651	7913090	69.00	0.44

4. *Defectors During the Campaign*

NAME	PARTY	CONSTITUENCY	DATE
Philip Kipsete Sigei	PICK	Buret	14/12/92
Mohammed Maalim Ali	FORD-Asili	Mandera East	16/12/92
Mahat Isaak Hussein	KNC	Wajir East	16/12/92
Charles Juma Nyakoe	FORD-Asili	Kasipul-Kenyaabondo	17/12/92
Degow Ibrahim Goh	FORD-Asili	Ijara	17/12/92
Abdikadir Hassan	FORD-Kenya (National Treasurer)	Dujis	18/12/92
Wachu Chachole	FORD-Kenya	Moyale	18/12/92
Philip Kipkorir Rono	PICK	Buret	18/12/92
Davidson MorachaNyareru	FORD-Asili	Bobasi	18/12/92
Daniel Momanyi Nyamwange	FORD-Asili	Nyaribari Chache	18/12/92
Wilfred Siras Sirengo	FORD-Asili	Sirisia	18/12/92
Albert Henry Ochieng'	DP	Muhoroni	18/12/92
Wilfred Kigwathi	FORD-Asili	Ntonyiri	18/12/92
John Muriuki Mwithya	FORD-Kenya	Ntonyiri	18/12/92
Lool Andrew Ekran	DP	Turkana North	18/12/92
Joseph Arite Ilo	FORD-Asili	Laisamis	18/12/92
Michael Lurkuruka	DP	Turkana Central	18/12/92
Eliud Kerio Long'acha	DP	Turkana South	18/12/92
Mwalimu Hassan	FORD-Asili	Msambweni	18/12/92
James E Sipayo	FORD-Asili	Turkana South	20/12/92
Julius Ekaral	FORD-Kenya	Turkana North	20/12/92
David Ethuru	FORD-Kenya	Turkana Central	20/12/92
Michael Napoo Lokuruka	DP	Turkana Central	20/12/92
Noor Ibrahim Barrow	FORD-Asili	Mandera West	21/12/92
Dr Khalif Osman	DP	Mandera East	21/12/92
Kulow Hassan	DP	Mandera West	21/12/92
Enow Adawa	DP	Mandera Central	21/12/92
Peter Mailanyi	FORD-Asili	Laikipia East	21/12/92
Ignatius Baraza Omachar	PICK	Amagoro	22/12/92
Jackson ole Mparu	FORD-Kenya	Narok North	23/12/92
Daniel Wilson Kayanda	DP	Kisumu Town	24/12/92
John P.S. Mandu	PICK	Mumias	24/12/92
Abdi Ali Baricha	FORD-Kenya	Mandera Central	25/12/92
John William Lokichai	DP	Kachileba	25/12/92
Nassir Hussein	FORD-Kenya	Kachileba	25/12/92
Michael Lorun	FORD-Asili	Kachileba	25/12/92
Mohammed Abdi Abdullahi	KNC	Wajir South	25/12/92
Abdirahman Ali Sheikh	FORD-Kenya	Mandera West	25/12/92
Hussein Hassan Mohammed	DP	Ijara	25/12/92
Abdirahman Mahat	FORD-Kenya	Ijara	25/12/92
Mogow Abdi Noor	FORD-Asili	Dujis	25/12/92
Yusuf Haji Gedi	DP	Fafi	25/12/92
Ali Duntow Hujale	FORD-Asili	Fafi	25/12/92
Onesmus Mboki	FORD-Asili	Kibwezi	26/12/92
Joseph Deya Owino	DP	Ndhiwa	27/12/92

5. By-Elections in Kenya, 1993–7

Seat	Date	% Turnout	KANU	FORD-K	FORD-A	DP	KNC	KSC	PICK	NDP
Bonchari	29/12/92	55.8	37.2	2.8	7.4	52.5	0	0	0	0
	22/05/93	40.2	66.8	15.5	10	7 1	0	0.6	0	0
KANU gain from DP after defection										
Migori	29/12/92	66.1	11.6	88.4	0	0	0	0	0	0
	22/05/93	44.1	17.4	82.6	0	0	0	0	0	0
Held by FORD-Kenya after defection										
Hamisi 1	29/12/92	60.2	48.1	0	48.6	3.4	0	0	0	0
	14/10/93	35.5	82.9	0	15.8	1.3	0	0	0	0
KANU gain from FORD-Asili after defection										
Makuyu	29/12/92	67.4	7.1	0	72.7	12.9	8.5	0	0	0
	14/10/93	40.9	23.5	0	76 5	0	0	0	0	0
Held by FORD-Asili after defection										
Kisauni	29/12/92	38.1	35.4	35.6	14.4	13.8	0 9	0	0	0
	24/12/93	19.5	43.4	54 1	2.5	0	0	0	0	0
Held by FORD-Kenya after election petition										
Lugari	29/12/92	70.1	21 4	8.1	67.5	1 9	1.1	0	0	0
	04/03/94	37.1	51.5	45.3	3.2	0	0	0	0	0
KANU gain from FORD-Asili after defection										
Bondo	29/12/92	75.5	5.1	94.9	0	0	0	0	0	0
	29/06/94	52.2	21.4	78.6	0	0	0	0	0	0
Held by FORD-Kenya after death										

Appendix 5: By-Elections in Kenya, 1993–7

Seat	Date	% Turnout	KANU	FORD-K	FORD-A	DP	KNC	KSC	PICK	NDP
Githunguri	29/12/92 81.6	10.5	0.5	79.7	8 1	1.2	0	0	0	
	29/06/94	53.1	15.1	0	84.9	0	0	0	0	0
Held by FORD-Asili after death										
Ikolomani	29/12/92 67.1	38.2	1.2	55.6	4 7	0.4	0	0	0	
	29/06/94	38.6	86 1	13 9	0	0	0	0	0	0
KANU gain from FORD-Asili after defection										
Lurambi	29/12/92 61.1	31.3	4.8	62.5	1.4	0	0	0	0	
	29/06/94	27.2	62.2	36.5	1.3	0	0	0	0	0
KANU gain from FORD-Asili after defection										
Mathare 1	29/12/92 56.5	11.1	29.7	36.2	23.1	0	0	0	0	
	29/06/94	14.1	21.9	41.1	37.1	0	0	0	0	0
FORD-Kenya gain from FORD-Asili after election petition										
Ndhiwa	29/12/92	86.6	2.5	97.4	0	0.1	0	0	0	0
	29/06/94	40.8	16.5	83.5	0	0	0	0	0	0
Held by FORD-Kenya after defection										
Shinyalu	29/12/92	58.2	43.1	1.8	54.6	0.5	0	0	0	0
	29/06/94	35.5	83.8	16.2	0	0	0	0	0	0
KANU gain from FORD-Asili after defection										
Starehe 1	29/12/92	47.5	14.8	10.6	42.8	15.4	15.8	0	0.6	0
	02/11/94	6.8	33.8	8.6	43.1	13.7	0	0	0.8	0.2
Held by FORD-Asili after defection										

Appendix 5: By-Elections in Kenya, 1993–7

Seat	Date	% Turnout	KANU	FORD-K	FORD-A	DP	KNC	KSC	PICK	NDP
Mathare 2	29/12/92	56.6	11.1	29.7	36.2	23.1	0	0	0	0
	29/06/94	14.1	21.9	41.1	37.1	0	0	0	0	0
	02/11/94	13.5	28.9	41.1	27.7	2.2	0	0	0	0
Held by FORD-Kenya after death										
Mandera E	29/12/92	64.7	45.9	0.4	0.2	0.1	0	0	53.6	0
	21/01/95	45.7	89.8	5.8	3.8	0.2	0.4	0	0.1	0
KANU gain from PICK after election petition										
Webuye	29/12/92	67.8	17.1	42.3	3.3	37.5	0	0	0	0
	21/01/95	42.1	32.2	65.9	1.1	0	0	0.7	0	0
Held by FORD-Kenya after election petition with a new candidate										
Changamwe	29/12/92	42.3	22.6	30.4	12.8	36.3	0	0	0	0
	13/06/95	13.3	44.8	0	0	54.5	0.7	0	0	0
Held by DP after election petition										
Machakos	29/12/92	59.7	54.2	2.5	12.8	30.6	0	0	0	0
		26.1	71.6	0	0	28.4	0	0	0	0
Held by KANU after death										
Kipipiri	29/12/92	80.1	3.1	0.5	64.1	32.3	0	0	0	0
	04/09/95	38.1	17.5	0	0	82.5	0	0	0	0
DP gain from FORD-Asili afler death										
Nyatike	29/12/92	70.8	9.2	90.8	0	0	0	0	0	0
	07/12/95	33.8	33.8	66.2	0	0	0	0	0	0
Held by FORD-Kenya after defection										

Appendix 5: By-Elections in Kenya, 1993–7

Seat	Date	% Turnout	KANU	FORD-K	FORD-A	DP	KNC	KSC	PICK	NDP
Siakago	29/12/92	72.4	12.1	12.4	20.9	25.4	29.1	0	0	0
	07/12/95	39.5	77.5	0	0	21.7	0.8	0	0	0
KANU gain from KNC after defection										
Kerio C	29/12/92	unopposed	100	0	0	0	0	0	0	0
	14/03/96	unopposed	100	0	0	0	0	0	0	0
KANU hold unopposed after death										
Kibwezi	29/12/92	53.6	33.1	3.6	5.1	58.3	0	0	0	0
	14/03/96	13.1	90.1	0	0	9.9	0	0	0	0
KANU gain from DP after defection										
Turkana C	29/12/92	42.1	75.1	3.1	0	21.9	0	0	0	0
	14/03/96	unopposed	100	0	0	0	0	0	0	0
KANU hold unopposed after death										
Starehe 2	29/12/92	47.5	14.8	10.6	42.8	15.4	15.8	0	0.6	0
	02/11/94	6.8	33.8	8.6	43.1	13.7	0	0	0.8	0.2
	10/04/96	4.1	57.1	2.7	39.9	0	0	0	0	0.3
KANU gain from FORD-Asili after resignation										
Hamisi 2	29/12/92	60.2	48.1	0	48.6	3.4	0	0	0	0
	14/10/93	35.5	82.9	0	15.8	1.3	0	0	0	0
	10/06/94	31.1	77.6	22.4	0	0	0	0	0	0
KANU hold after death										

Appendix 5: By-Elections in Kenya, 1993–7

Seat	Date	% Turnout	KANU	FORD-K	FORD-A	DP	KNC	KSC	PICK	NDP
Westlands	29/12/92	54.7	32.6	9.6	28.5	21.1	0.8	0.3	7.2	0
	10/06/96	6.3	39.7	0	3.4	34.4	0	0	22.5	0
KANU hold after death										
Kitutu-	29/12/92	43.5	38.1	0	0	27.3	0	0	34.6	0
Chache	21/01/97	23.4	73.8	19.4	0	1.7	0	0	0	5.2
KANU hold after death										
Langata	29/12/92	54.6	21.3	43.4	24.1	11.3	0	0	0	0
	11/03/97	6.8	26.8	0	4.1	0	0.4	0	0	68.7
NDP gain from FORD-Kenya after defection										

Index

Index